SOUTH CAROLINA
DEED ABSTRACTS 1719-1772

VOL. I

Abstracted by

Clara A. Langley

Southern Historical Press, Inc.
Greenville, South Carolina

Copyright 1983 by:
Southern Historical Press, Inc.

All rights reserved. No part of this publication may be reproduced, stored in a retrieval system or transmitted in any form or by any means without the prior permission of the publisher.

SOUTHERN HISTORICAL PRESS, INC.
PO BOX 1267
Greenville, SC 29601

ISBN #0-89308-271-6

Printed in the United States of America

To

AGNES LELAND BALDWIN

whose dedicated efforts have made the
sources for South Carolina History and
Genealogy widely available to persons doing
South Carolina Research

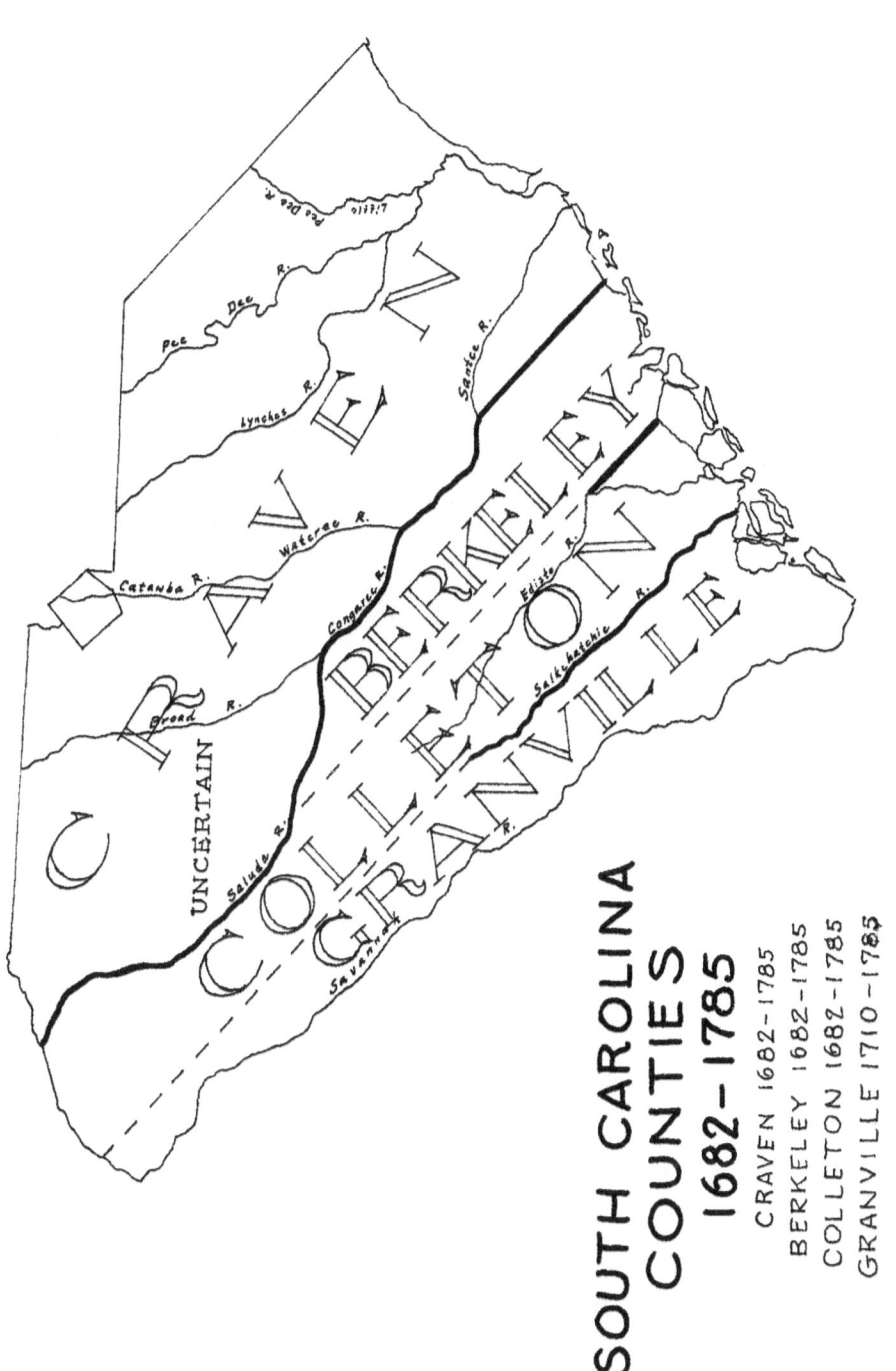

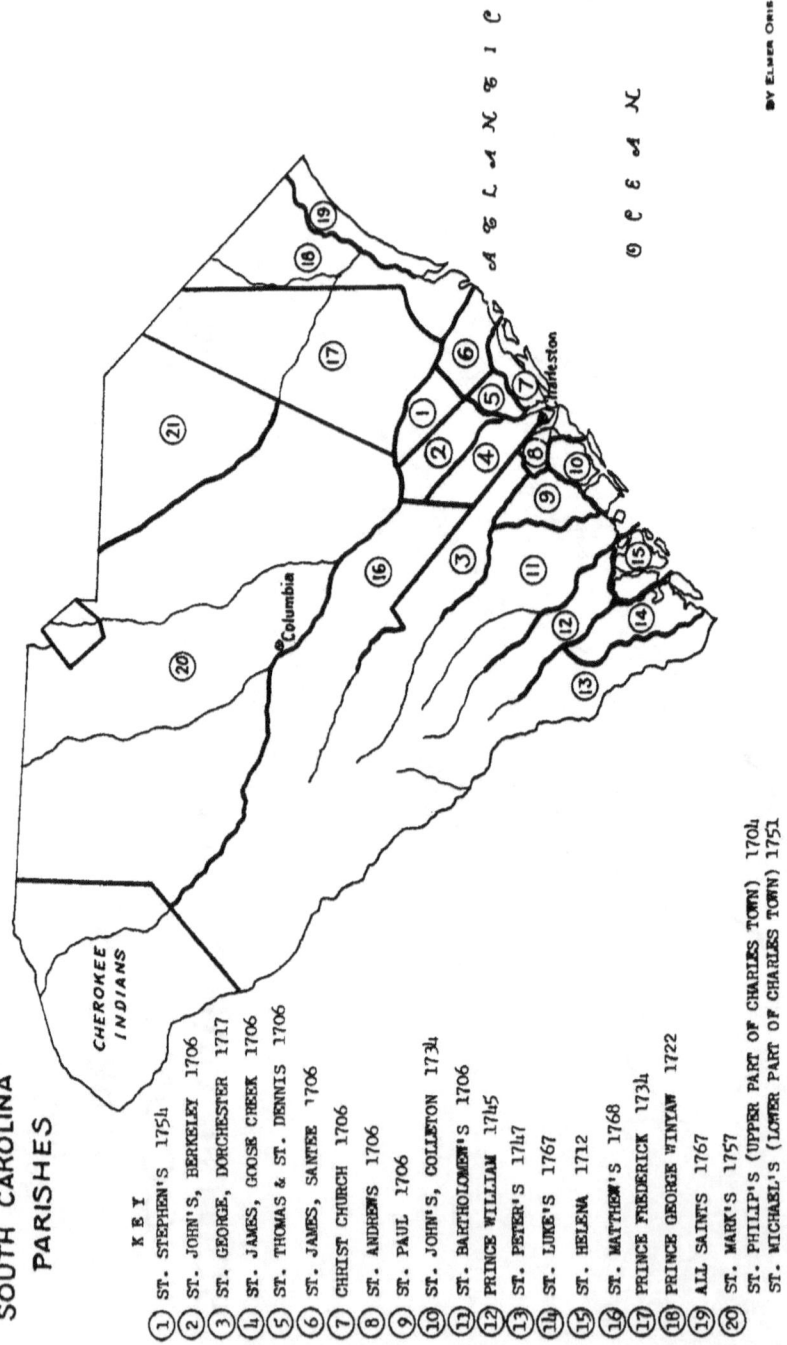

INTRODUCTION

Before 1790, land transactions for the entire State of South Carolina were recorded in Charleston. Many of these records are now in the custody of the Charleston County Register of Mesne Conveyance. Between 1936 and 1938 the Works Progress Administration employed Miss Clara A. Langley to prepare abstracts of the earliest seventy-four volumes of conveyances and miscellaneous records that remained in Charleston, and these abstracts are being published here for the first time. Proprietary land records and all Royal grants had earlier been transferred to Columbia, and were not abstracted.

These four volumes of deeds consist largely of abstracts of conveyances or transfers of title to land that had earlier been granted. Conveyances during the Royal period ususally took the form of a "lease and release." Under English law, for an unrestricted conveyance to be made, a buyer had to have possession of a piece of land as a lessor. A separate "lease" for a nominal amount gave him tenancy rights for up to a year. He became eligible to claim possession one day following execution of the lease and thus became entitled to obtain a "release" that gave him absolute and unqualified ownership. These "L. & R." documents contain essentially the same information, and each set was accordingly abstracted as though it were a single record.

Volumes of conveyances were ordinarily used to record only "mesne" or intermediate conveyances. The volumes of "miscellaneous records" that are intermixed in series with them contain any document that a colonist was willing to pay to have registered. Most commonly, these are mortgages and assignments of mortgages, bonds and counterbonds, bills of sale, powers of attorney and revocations of powers of attorney, and apprenticeship agreements. Some other types include bills of exchange, judgments, receipts, petitions, contracts, and purchases of freedom.

The abstracts of all of these records attempt to give every name, relationship, profession, and place mentioned. Only the wording common to every record type was intentionally omitted. Most of this information is accessible only through the indexes prepared for this publication. The names of lessors and lessees was published in 1977 by the Southern Historical Press in *Index to*

Deeds of the Province and State of South Carolina, 1719-1785, and Charleston District, 1785-1800, but this volume did not include the names of adjacent property owners, plantations, and creeks or other information such as professions and Indian names. All of this information has been conscientiously indexed by the indexing staff of Southern Historical Press, and it will be of great assistance in the preparation of local histories and family histories.

Each volume of the records abstracted carries a separate letter designation. The first set was lettered A through Z. The letter B was used twice and so was made B and B-2 (or Ba and Bb). Next, the double letters AA-ZZ were used, and afterwards the letters A through Z again with a 3 added (A3-Z3). The letters U and JJ appear to have been omitted.

Deeds were recorded in roughly chronological order, but some were recorded many years after they were written. For nearly all of the period covered, Charleston was the only place in the Province where deeds could be recorded, and colonists who lived elsewhere had to apply for registration there. Some deeds were never recorded, particularly during the transition from Proprietary to Royal government (1719-1731) and during the period of the American Revolution.

The great majority of conveyances were recorded, though, and they are a tremendously important source of information about most of the 18th Century residents of South Carolina. With no Pre-Revolutionary census and with nearly all early tax records missing, these deeds are the most inclusive set of records available, and they contain the only mention of many individuals in the surviving public records. Only grants and wills are of comparable importance. Very often, a place of residence can be ascertained for an individual and with this knowledge a researcher can turn to local records such as church registers for additional information.

Title searchers who need to exhaust every possibility should consult not only conveyances, grants, and wills, but also collections of plats and memorials in the State Archives. Other significant collections of land records are in the South Caroliniana Library in Columbia and in the Register of Mesne Conveyance and the South Carolina Historical Society in Charleston. For legal purposes, the earliest surviving copies of all of these records should be consulted to minimize the possibility of a transcription error. In the case of the W.P.A. abstracts, Miss Langley first made notes; these were neatly copied in longhand (the second generation copy of the names); the longhand copy was typed with a cloth ribbon and was too indistinct to be reproduced (the third generation copy). All of the information had to be retyped for this publication, which is four generations removed from the certified copies, which themselves were not originals. The typist who prepared the final typescript, Mrs. Pearl Baker, consulted Miss Langley's initial notes whenever questions arose and typed from the handwritten abstracts for the final volumes of deeds that had not previously been typed. She did everything feasible to ensure the accuracy of each entry.

Ideally, the final typescript should have been compared with the copies given to each property owner, but most of these originals have not survived, and even the ones in public collections are widely scattered. The certified copies in the Register of Mesne Conveyance would have been an adequate substitute, but many of them have deteriorated greatly in nearly a half century, and a careful comparison would have required thousands of hours and would have had to be done by a volunteer experienced in reading 18th Century handwriting and knowledgeable of South Carolina names. This too proved unfeasible. As a whole, the present publication is an amazingly accurate version that is far more useful than the official records themselves because they are much less thoroughly indexed.

Moreover, the publication of these records fills a major gap for genealogists and historians. Even individuals of the Proprietary Period were better known because of Agnes Leland Baldwin's *First Settlers of South Carolina, 1670-1680* and A.S. Sally, Jr.'s *Warrants for Land in South Carolina, 1672-1711*. Mrs. Baldwin's work has been expanded to include every known reference to every individual who settled in South Carolina before 1700, and the publication of this research will be forthcoming. After the Revolution, the Census of 1790 and subsequent national censuses have most Americans represented. It was for the period of Royal Government that we knew the least about South Carolinians, and now Mrs. Baldwin has helped to fill this gap by initiating this publication and by seeing it through.

                                        Gene Waddell,
                                        Director
                                        South Carolina Historical Society

CONTENTS

Introduction vii
Deeds Book "A," 1719-1721 1
Deeds Book "Ba," 1720-1722 14
Deeds Book "Bb," 1718-1723 27
Deeds Book "C," 1718-1723 37
Deeds Book "D," 1723-1725 44
Deeds Book "E," 1723-1728 70
Deeds Book "F," 1723-1728 87
Deeds Book "G," 1727-1729 101
Deeds Book "H," 1726-1730 114
Deeds Book "I," 1730-1731 137
Deeds Book "K," 1731-1733 166
Deeds Book "La," 1726-1728 183
Deeds Book "Lb," 1732-1733 197
Deeds Book "M," Apr. 1734-Nov. 1734 209
Deeds Book "N," 1734-1735 217
Deeds Book "O," May 1735-Dec. 1735 228
Deeds Book "P," Dec. 1735-June 1736 241
Deeds Book "Q," June 1736-Mar. 1737 255
Deeds Book "R," Apr. 1737-Dec. 1737 275
Deeds Book "S," 1737-1739 300
Deeds Book "T," 1739-1740 345

DEEDS BOOK "A"
1719-1721

Book A, p. 1
19 Jan. 1719
BENJAMIN CATTLE of Berkeley Co., planter, Executor of JOHN WHITMARSH SENIOR, to ANDREW ALLEN of Charleston, merchant, and JOHN FENWICK, for ₤ 227 current SC money, insurance policies, and money due thereon, and one fourth part of the good snow and of the cargo in her. Whereas JOHN WHITMARSH, SENIOR, was sole owner of one-fourth part of the good snow, called John Adventure, ELIAS HULIEN master, and of one-fourth her masts, etc. and cargo in her, and whereas JOHN WHITMARSH, SENIOR, insured the snow, in Bristoll, for ₤ 400 sterling, for a voyage from Barbadoes to Africa to SC, and whereas the snow was lost and the aforesaid sum became due to him and whereas BENJAMIN CATTLE agreed to make an absolute assignment and conveyance of such sums and insurance policies to ALLEN and FENWICK for ₤ 227 and for the better recovery of the sums due BENJAMIN CATTLE appointed ANDREW ALLEN and JOHN FENWICK his attorneys. BENJAMIN CATTELL. Witnesses: BENJ'A. ROMSEY, SR.; JAMES WILLSON; BENJAMIN ROMSEY, JR.; SAMUELL SYMONS. Before T. HEPWORTH.

Book A, p. 5
12 Feb. 1719
Mortgage
TOBIAS FITCH, Berkeley Co., SC, planter to WILLIAM LIVINGSTON, of Charleston, clerk. Whereas FITCH on 7 Feb. 1719 became bound to LIVINGSTON in penal sum of ₤ 2000 current SC money conditioned for delivery of 47,000 weight good and merchantable rice in barrels on bay in Charleston on 6 Feb. 1720, for securing the payment and delivery (and for five shillings paid by LIVINGSTON to FITCH), FITCH delivered to LIVINGSTON 7 Negro men, 1 Negro woman, 2 Negro girls and 2 Negro boys. Negro boy PETER delivered. Witnesses: JOHN WALLIS; ELIZABETH WALLIS; EBENEZER MOODY. Before SAM EVELEIGH.

Book A, p. 10
2 Sept. 1717
Mortgage
JOHN KINARD, of Christ Church Parish, Berkeley Co., planter, to CHARLES HILL, of Charleston, merchant. Bond in penal sum of ₤ 1320 SC money conditioned for the payment of ₤ 660; ₤ 360 to be paid 2 Sept. 1718 with interest, and ₤ 330 on 2 Sept. 1719 with interest. Witnesses: BENJAMIN DENNIS; RICHARD HILL; COL. JOHN BARNWELL. Before THOS. HEPWORTH.

Book A, p. 11
2 Sept. 1717
JOHN KINARD, of Christ Church Parish, Berkeley Co., SC, planter, to CHARLES HILL, of St. Phillips Parish, Charleston, merchant. Whereas the Lords Proprs. by several grants gave JOHN BELL two tracts of land containing 760 a., English measure, on Coppehee Sound in Christ Church Parish, bounding SE on said Sound, SW on JOHN SIMONS, NE on JOHN JEFFINS, NW on JOTHAM GIBBONS and part on said SIMONS; and whereas the two tracts by several mesne conveyances became vested in JOHN KINARD; KINARD for ₤ 660 current SC money, now sells to HILL the two tracts of 760 a., also 4 Negro men, 1 Indian, and 2 Negro women. Witnesses: BENJAMIN DENNIS, RICHARD HILL, JNO. BARNWELL. Delivery of Negro man TONY before JOHN BEE, SAM EVELEIGH, RICHARD HILL. Delivery of land and tenements before JOHN ZILSER, PHILIP GIVENS. Sworn before T. HEPWORTH.

Book A, p. 17
29 & 30 July 1719
L & R
REV. GILBERT JONES, Rector Christ Church Parish, Berkeley Co., SC, and JOHN BEE, of Charleston, merchant, sole executors of last will of BERNARD CHRISTIAN COOPER, surgeon, to RICHARD SPLATT, merchant, of Charleston. Whereas an act of assembly, ratified 20 Feb. 1718 impowered the executors to dispose of COOPER'S estate to pay his debts, the executors sold to SPLATT, for ₤ 900, 500 a. at Goose Creek (purchased by COOPER from BENJAMIN PERRYMAN), bounding N on Goose Creek; on all other sides by WILLIAM STEAD (formerly JOHN PIGHT'S) and forty a. of marsh adjoining. Witnesses: WILLIAM GUY, ROBERT HUME, T. HEPWORTH. Before T. HEPWORTH.

Book A, p. 27
2 April 1720
TOBIAS FITCH, planter, of SC, to SAMUEL DEANE, ESQ., 3 Negro men for ₤ 420 SC money. Witnesses: GER'D. MONGER; JOHN CHAMPNEYS.

1

Book A, p. 28   City of Bristol, England. ABRA ELTON, Mayor.
30 Sept. 1719   Various creditors of THOMAS FRY, merchant, of
                      Island of Jamaica, appeared before MAYOR ELTON
and made oath as follows: JOHN KING, Sheriff, said FRY was indebted to
him and WALTER KING, merchant, for merchandise. WILLIAM HART consigned
goods to THOMAS FRY and SAMUEL SHAW (FRY'S partner). ROBERT PAIGE, merchant, consigned wine. EDWARD CURTIS, sugar baker, said that ABRAHAM
HOOK, EDMUND BAUGH, WILLIAM JOHNSON, and himself, merchants, and part
owners of the ship Cambridge Galley of Bristol, sent the ship and a considerable cargo to FRY. FRANCIS STEPHENS, mariner, said FRY was indebted
to him. THOMAS CLAYTON said he and his brother SETH CLAYTON, JOHN HITCHING, JOHN MORGAN and JOHN BAKER consigned merchandise to SHAW and FRY.
REV. JOHN FRANKLIN said FRY was indebted to him for merchandise. All,
except CLAYTON, said they could not adjust the accounts without sight of
the books of account kept by FRY.

Book A, p. 32   ELIZABETH FRY, widow of THOMAS FRY, Bristol,
28 Sept. 1719   England appointed JOHN KING, Sherif, and WILLIAM HART, ESQ., of Bristol, her attorneys.
Witnesses: JAMES COKER, ALEXANDER SUMMERS. COKER and SUMMERS appeared
before THOMAS HEPWORTH, Charleston, SC, 3 Mar. 1719.

Book A, p. 34   JOHN KING, and WILLIAM HART, ESQRS., attorneys
30 Sept. 1719   for ELIZABETH FRY, appointed CAPT. BENJAMIN
                      ROMSEY, of Bristol, their attorney. Witnesses: ALEXANDER SUMMERS, JAMES COKER. SUMMERS and COKER appeared before
THOMAS HEPWORTH, Charleston, 3 Jan. 1719.

Book A, p. 35   JOHN FRANKLIN, D.D., JOHN KING, ESQ., WILLIAM
30 Sept. 1719   HART, ESQ., JOSEPH KIPPIN, shoemaker, THOMAS
                      CLAYTON, merchant, ROBERT PAIGE, merchant, EDWARD CURTIS, sugar baker, FRANCIS STEPHENS, mariner, all of Bristol, England, creditors of THOMAS FRY, merchant, of Island of Jamaica, appointed
BENJAMIN ROMSEY, of Bristol, mariner, their attorney to recover from
GEORGE FOOKES of Charleston, merchant (executor of THOMAS FRY) and others
in SC, money and merchandise due them from FRY and to enforce FOOKES to
produce the books and accounts of THOMAS FRY and make payment proportionately. Witnesses: JAMES COKER, ALEXANDER SUMMERS. SUMMERS and COKER
appeared before THOMAS HEPWORTH 3 Jan. 1719.

Book A, p. 38   TOBIAS FITCH, planter, and MARIANNE his wife,
21 & 22 Apr. 1720   of Berkeley Co., SC, to JOHN COMBES, merchant,
L & R   for ₤ 1000, SC money, 900 a. where TOBIAS
                      FITCH "now dwells", devised to TOBIAS by his
father's will; on north side Ashley River, in Berkeley Co., SW on Ashley
River, SE JOHN STOCKS, NE WIDOW SUSANNAH FITCH, NW HENRY WOOD. Witnesses: ROBERT HUME, JOHN BARTON, THOMAS WILKINSON. Before THOMAS HEPWORTH.

Book A, p. 46   RICHARD TOOKERMAN and KATHERINE, his wife, to
21 Feb. 1718/9   GEORGE FOOKES, merchant, 3 Negro men, 1 Negro
                      woman and her child, and 1 Indian girl, for
₤ 1200. Witnesses: WILLIAM BLAKEWEY, BENJAMIN WHITAKER, SAMUEL DEANE.
Sworn before THOMAS HEPWORTH.

Book A, p. 48   GEORGE FOOKES, for ₤ 1000, sold the above
3 May 1720   slaves to WILLIAM BLAKEWEY and JOSEPH WRAGG,
                      merchant. Witnesses: THOMAS HEPWORTH, RICHARD
SPLATT, ROBERT HUME. Before GEORGE CHICKEN, JP & JQ.

Book A, p. 49   EDWARD WEEKLEY, planter, Berkeley Co., SC, by
4 May 1720   bond to WILLIAM DRY, merchant, in penal sum of
                      ₤ 776.12 conditioned for payment of ₤ 388.6.0
on 4th May next ensuing, with interest. Witnesses: SAMUEL PICKERING,
WILLIAM WEEKLEY.

Book A, p. 51   EDWARD WEEKLEY, planter, Berkeley Co., SC, to
4 May 1720   WILLIAM DRY, merchant, Berkeley Co., for ₤
                      776.6.0 current SC money, 3 Negro men, 1 Indian boy; conditioned for the payment of ₤ 388.6.0 on 4th May next ensuing, with interest. Witnesses: SAMUEL PICKERING, WILLIAM WEEKLEY.

Before ARTHUR MIDDLETON, J.P.

Book A, p. 53   JOHN SAVY, of SC, planter, for valuable con-
5 Feb. 1719/20   sideration; to JACOB SATUR, merchant; 3 Negro
                            men, 1 Negro woman, 1 Negro boy, 1 Indian wo-
man. Condition for redemption, that JOHN SAVY pay JACOB SATUR, 26,000
lbs. merchantable rice on 26 Mar. 1721 in Charleston. Witnesses: WIL-
LIAM SANDERS, JOHN SIMMONS. Before WILLIAM BLAKEWEY, J.P.

Book A, p. 55   Received of Mad'm: HALL ANN, Dellamare two
                            pieces of scarlett durant containing one hun-
dred & seven yards together to be dyed black and two night gowns with a
lineing to be dyed green, for sch. doe promise to be accountable for.
JOHN DENISE & CO. Charleston Aug. 5th: 1719

Book A, p. 55   JONATHAN MILNER, carpenter, and MARY his wife,
28 June 1720   of Berkeley Co., SC, to HENRY PERONNEAU, mer-
Mortgage   chant, of Charleston, 50 a. in Berkeley Co., N
                            & S on STEPHEN BULLOCK, E THOMAS FITZGERALD, W
on creek out of Wando River; MILNER being bound to PERONNEAU in penal sum
of ₤ 204, for the payment of ₤ 102.5.0 on 28th June next ensuing with interest at rate of ₤ 10 % per annum. Witnesses: WILLIAM BILLING, JIFFORD
ATWELL. Mortgage paid in full 12 June 1725. Witness, JACOB MOTTE, Register.

Book A, p. 62   JONATHAN MILNER, carpenter, Berkeley Co., SC,
28 June 1720   under bond to HENRY PERONNEAU, merchant, of
                            Charleston, for ₤ 204 with interest at ₤ 10 %
per annum to be paid 28 June 1721.

Book A, p. 63   JOHN DELABERE, of SC, gentleman, sold to CAPT.
23 July 1720   PETER BOYNTON, of SC, for ₤ 121, 1 cask pew-
                            ter, 2 boxes soap, invoiced at ₤ 39.11.7 pro-
clamation money, shipped on board the Duck sloop, ROBERT ROATHE, COMMAND-
ER, consigned to MESSRS. BAGGS & CO. New Providence. Witnesses: DANIEL
GREENE, ANDREW ROWAN, ELIAS HANCOCK.

Book A, p. 64   JOHN DELABERE, gentleman, of SC, by bond to
23 July 1720   CAPT. PETER BOYNTON, of SC, in the penal sum
                            of ₤ 150 current SC money conditioned for pay-
ment of ₤ 121 or goods mentioned in a certain bill of sale. Witnesses:
ANDREW ROWAN; DANIEL GREENE; ELIAS HANCOCK.

Book A, p. 65   ROGER SAUNDERS, planter, of Berkeley Co., and
25 Mar. 1720   ESTER, his wife, to THOMAS DIMES, merchant, of
Mortgage   Charleston, for ₤ 1586 current SC money, 670
                            a. purchased by SAUNDERS from RICHARD EDGELL,
plot made by COL. THOMAS BROUGHTON for THOMAS JONES in 1707; also 500 a.
which SAUNDERS purchased from JOHN WARD, in Berkeley Co., butting NW on
JAMES SINGLETON, SE on THOMAS SPARKES: Also 3 Negro men, 4 Negro women,
1 Indian man. The condition for redemption was that ROGER SAUNDERS pay
THOMAS DYMES ₤ 1586 current SC money in merchantable rice at 40s. per 100
delivered upon Charleston Bay on 1st Feb. 1720 with interest at the rate
of 10% per annum. Witnesses: JOSEPH MASSEY, HUMPHREY HULL. Before THOM-
AS HEPWORTH.

Book A, p. 69   GEORGE LONG, mariner, commander of the PINK
13 Aug. 1720   ELIZABETH riding at anchor in Charleston har-
Mortgage   bor, "took up" ₤ 500 current SC money of DAN-
                            IEL GREEN, merchant, of Charleston, to pay off
and discharge the wages due several mariners and other necessities for a
voyage to Great Britain and drew several bills of exchange on JOHN LONG,
merchant, London, to pay DANIEL GREEN ₤ 125 sterling money of Great Britain, each, thirty days after date, and for security assigned the Pink
Elizabeth and appurtenances to DANIEL GREEN. Witnesses: ROBERT HUME, ED-
WARD BENNETT, JOHN (his mark) GIBBON. Before THOMAS HEPWORTH.

Book A, p. 71   GEORGE LONG, mariner, commander of the Pink
11 Aug. 1720   Elizabeth riding at anchor in Charleston har-
Mortgage   bor, "took up" of ROBERT HUME, gent., ₤ 100 to

pay wages due several mariners and for necessities for a voyage to Great Britain and drew 3 bills of exchange for ₤ 25 sterling each, on JOHN LONG, merchant, London, and for security assigned the Pink Elizabeth and appurtenances to ROBERT HUME JR. Witnesses: THOMAS CONYERS, DANIEL WALKER, JOHN (his mark) GIBBONS. Before THOS. HEPWORTH.

Book A, p. 73
3 Sept. 1708
Bond

RICHARD MARSDEN, clerk, to ALEXANDER PARRIS, merchant, both of Charleston, SC, for ₤ 260. MARSDEN received ₤ 182 current SC money from PARRIS, giving PARRIS 4 bills of exchange at 20 days, for ₤ 130 sterling English money, on THOMAS MARSDEN, merchant, in London, the condition being that if 1 bill be protested MARSDEN will pay PARRIS ₤ 130 English money with 20% for exchange and 10% more for protest charges and all other charges. Witnesses: THOMAS CUTLER, JOSEPH COLLIER, THOMAS LAMBOLL. Before THOMAS HEPWORTH.

Book A, p. 75

Copia. "So: Carolina Sept. 3d. 1708. Fond Father 20 days sight of this my second of exchange my first third nor fourth of the same tenor & date not being paid, pay to MAJ'R. ALEXR. PARRIS or order the sum of 130 pounds sterling (value here recd) make good payment & place the same to the acct. of your obedient son RID. (RIDDLEY) MARSDEN to MR. THOMAS MARSDEN, merchant, in St. Martins Lane, London, pay the contents to MR. JOHN LLOYD or his order its mine ALEXANDR. PARRIS." On 9 Dec. 1708 at request of JOHN LLOYD, merchant, London, JAMES DUNNIDGE, Notary & Tabellion Publick, London, presented the bill of exchange to MR. THOMAS MARSDEN who refused to pay. Witnesses to protest: THOMAS MOTT, JOHN TREBELL.

Book A, p. 77
24 May 1720

Before THOMAS COOKE, Notary & Tabellion Publick, in Dublin, Ireland appeared JOSEPH MARRIOTT, of Dublin, gent; MEHITABEL, alias RAYNER, alias TAYLOR, his wife, sister to EBENEZER TAYLOR of Charleston, SC: SAMUEL TAYLOR, of Dublin, weaver; and BENJAMIN TAYLOR of Dublin, merchant (brothers of EBENEZER TAYLOR): WILLIAM GREEN, gentleman, of Dublin; CATHERINE GREEN, alias RAYNER, his wife, (daughter of ANNE CARROLL, alias RAYNER, alias TAYLOR, sister to EBENEZER TAYLOR); and BRYAN CARROLL, of Dublin, merchant; in behalf of WILLIAM CARROLL, BENJAMIN CARROLL, and JOHN CARROLL, minors, children of ANNE CARROLL; and appointed PETER TAYLOR, of Dublin, merchant, son of BENJAMIN TAYLOR, their attorney to administer the estate of EBENEZER TAYLOR. CHRISTOPHER DOWNS and ROBERT CURTIS witnessed the signatures of SAMUEL TAYLOR, BENJAMIN TAYLOR and BRYAN CARROLL. CHRISTOPHER DOWNS and GEORGE MOORE witnessed the signatures of JOSEPH MARRIOTT, MEHITABEL MARRIOTT, WILLIAM GREEN and KATHERINE GREEN.

Book A, p. 81
15 & 16 Nov. 1720
L & R

JOSEPH DILL, mariner, of Berkeley Co., SC, and ELIZABETH his wife to HENRY MILLER, merchant, of Island of Jamaica, for ₤ 125 current money of Jamaica, one half of a town lot in Kingston, by will dated 6 Feb. 1706 to her granddaughter ELIZABETH CROSSKEYS (wife of the above JOSEPH DILL), daughter of JOHN CROSSKEYS and ELIZABETH his wife. Witnesses: GEORGE BARWICK, HILL CROFT, JOHN CROFT. Before SAMUEL EVELEIGH.

Book A, p. 89
21 Nov. 1720
Bond

JOSEPH WRAGG, JOB ROTHMAHLER, THOMAS DYMES, merchants, WILLIAM RHETT, ESQ., and JOHN HUTCHINSON, gentleman, all of Charleston, SC, to BENJAMIN PHIPPS, mariner, of Charleston, commander of the Raymond Galley, in penal sum of ₤ 4600 lawful money of Great Britain, conditioned for the payment of ₤ 2300 on 1st June 1721. Witnesses: ROBERT HUME, JAMES LOYDELL. Before THOMAS HEPWORTH.

Book A, p. 91
21 Nov. 1720
Bond

JOSEPH WRAGG, JOB ROTHMAHLER, THOMAS DYMES, merchants, WILLIAM RHETT, ESQ., and JOHN HUTCHINSON, gentleman, all of Charleston, SC, to BENJAMIN PHIPPS, mariner, commander of the Raymond Galley, in penal sum of ₤ 3000 lawful money of Great Britain, conditioned for payment of ₤ 1500 on 1st June 1722. Witnesses: ROBERT HUME, JAMES LOYDELL. Before THOMAS HEPWORTH.

Book A, p. 93   JOSEPH WRAGG, JOB RATHMAHLER, THOMAS DYMES,
21 Nov. 1720   merchants, WILLIAM RHETT, ESQ., and JOHN
Bond   HUTCHINSON, gentlemen, all of Charleston, SC,
           to BENJAMIN PHIPPS, mariner, of Charleston,
master of the Raymond Galley, in penal sum of L 3000, conditioned for the
payment of L 1500 in lawful money of Great Britain on 1st August 1722.
Witnesses: ROBERT HUME, JAMES LOYDELL. Before THOMAS HEPWORTH.

Book A, p. 95   SAMUEL WRAGG, merchant, of London, appointed
7 July 1720   JOSEPH WRAGG, merchant, of Charleston, SC, his
Letter of Attorney   attorney with power to sell any of the Negroes,
           stock and things belonging to his plantations
in SC. Witnesses: JOHN HEXT, GEORGE JONES, before JAMES (JACOBUS) DUN-
NIDGE, Notary & Tabellion Publick, in London, JOHN HEXT, witness, appeared before THOMAS HEPWORTH, in Carolina, on 19 Sept. 1720.

Book A, p. 97   REV. WILLIAM GUY, clerk, and REBECCA his wife,
8 Apr. 1717   JAMES MACKALL, gentleman, and SARAH his wife,
           and MARY BASDEN, spinster, all of Charleston,
SC, to JOSEPH WRAGG, gentleman, of Charleston, for L 300 2 parts of 2
town lots, Nos. 38 and 81, fronting 41 feet on a street, 144 feet deep;
JOSEPH WRAGG to pay the Lords Proprs. 1 penny per a. Whereas CHARLES
BASDEN, gentleman, of Charleston, died intestate, owning part of town lot
#38, S on Broad, W on TIMOTHY BELLAMY, E on SAMUEL WRAGG, and his estate
descended to MARY BASDEN, SARAH MACKALL and REBECCA GUY, daughters of
CHARLES BASDEN and co-heiresses; and whereas MARY BASDEN, widow of
CHARLES BASDEN, purchased on 21st Mar. 1698, from JOSEPH CROSSKEYS, mari-
ner, and MARGARET his wife, part of town lot #81, butting W part on PETER
BRUTELL, E on SAMUEL WRAGG, s on TIMOTHY BELLAMY, N on...BOLLARD; and
MARY BASDEN, by will, proved and recorded 15 July 1715, bequeathed this
piece of ground, amongst other lands, to MARY BASDEN, SARAH DOUGLAS (now
MACKALL) and REBECCA GUY, share and share alike; now they sell to WRAGG.
Witnesses: DANIEL PEROT, ROBERT TAYLOR, THOMAS HEPWORTH. Receipt wit-
nessed by DANIEL PEROT, ROBERT TAYLOR, THOS. HEPWORTH. Before THOMAS
HEPWORTH. JOHN CROFT, Register.

Book A, p. 101   JOB BURNETT, merchant, JOSEPH WALKER, gold-
17 June (British style) SMITH, and JOSEPH KANE, clothier, all of Dub-
1720   lin, deposed as follows: JOB BURNETT and JO-
Affidavit   SEPH WALKER deposed they knew the REV. MR.
           EBENEZER TAYLOR, clerk, left Ireland 30 years
before and had heard he died near Charleston, SC; that they knew him to
be brother to MRS. MEHITABEL MARRIOTT (alias RAYNER, alias TAYLOR) now
wife of JOSEPH MARRIOTT, gentleman, of Dublin; and knew them to be then
living and to be sister and brothers to EBENEZER TAYLOR; that they knew
MRS. CATHERINE GREEN (alias RAYNER) wife of WILLIAM GREEN, gentleman, of
Dublin, to be living and daughter of ANN CARROLL (alias RAYNER, alias
TAYLOR) sister to EBENEZER TAYLOR. JOB BURNETT deposed that WILLIAM
CARROLL, BENJAMIN CARROLL, and JOHN CARROLL were minors, and children of
ANN CARROLL (alias RAYNER, alias TAYLOR) and believed the minors to be
living. JOSEPH KANE deposed he knew EBENEZER TAYLOR in Ireland and had
heard he died in America and was reputed to be brother to MEHITABEL
MARRIOTT, SAMUEL TAYLOR and BENJAMIN TAYLOR, and that he believes them to
be brothers and sister to EBENEZER TAYLOR. Sworn before THOMAS QUIN,
Justice of Peace in Co. and City of Dublin, Ireland, in presence of
THOMAS COOKE, Notary & Tabellion Public, Dublin. "We the persons here-
under subscribing merchants in Dublin do hereby certify and attest that
THOMAS QUIN, ESQ....is a Justice of the Peace in this city, and that MR.
THOMAS COOKE....is a Notary & Tabellion Publick...." THOMAS WEBSTER,
THOMAS PUTLAND, DAVID LATOUCHE, JOS. NUTTALL, JOHN SHAW, WILLIAM, ALD-
RICHE, HUGH CUMING, ROBT. RAYNER, JOHN CUMING, PER. BERE, WILLIAM HEND-
RICK, JOHN AIGVINTS, JOHN FORBES, WILLIAM MORRIS, JOHN READ. JOHN CROFT,
Register.

Book A, p. 103   Before the HON. RICHARD ALLEIN, ESQ., Chief
           Justice of Court of Common Pleas in SC, Aug.
Court, 1720. "Afterwards to wit, the 10th day of this instant Aug., came
as well the aforesaid JOHN FENWICK, as the said ALEXANDER PARRIS Jun; by
their attornies...and the jurors to WITT, FRANCIS LEBRASSEUR, JOHN LAU-
RANCE, DANIEL TOWNSEND, ELIAS HANCOCK, JAMES MCCOON, JOHN PARKER, JOHN

BRITTEN, GEORGE HESCOTT, ANTHONY BONNEAU, ANDREW DEVEAUX, NICHOLAS BERN-
CHETT, and JOHN BENNET, being duely impanelled.....do say that the said
ALEXANDER doth owe to the aforesaid JOHN the...sum of 1,400 pounds....and
also the sum of 18 pounds 9 shillings and 10 pence for his costs &
charges" "Received the 3rd of Oct. Anno Dom 1720 of ROBERT HUME attorney
of the plaintiff in his cause, and execution against the goods of the defendant ALEXANDER PARRIS Jun...NATH. PARTRIDGE, Marshall." JOHN CROFT,
Register.

Book A, p. 104 RICHARD FLOYD, of St. Johns Island, to JOHN
15 Nov. 1720 FENWICK, of St. Johns Island, in penal sum of
Bond ↳ 400 conditioned for payment of ↳ 200 on 1st
Feb. 1721. To secure payment mortgaged 2 Ne-
groes. Witnesses: THOMAS PRITCHARD, JOHN (his mark) MOON, RICHARD (his
mark) FLOYD, JR. Same witnesses to delivery of 2 Negroes.

Book A, p. 105 STEPHEN RUSSELL, shoemaker, to JOHN HEARN and
29 June 1720 JOHN SANDIFORD, hat-makers, all of SC, for ↳
Mortgage 101.3.3. 255 a. on James Island. Whereas WIL-
LIAM RUSSELL, cooper, uncle to STEPHEN, was
granted 255 a. of land on James Island by the Lords Proprs. on 14th Apr.
1710; and whereas GEORGE RUSSELL (father of STEPHEN) (brother of WILLIAM)
planter, and lawful heir of WILLIAM, by will dated 15 Sept. 1710 bequeathed the 255 a. to STEPHEN; now STEPHEN mortgages the land to HEARN and
SANDIFORD. Witnesses: SAMUEL WITTER, ELIZABETH DRACHE, JAMES WITTER.
Before SAMUEL EVELEIGH.

Book A, p. 107 "Oct. ye 8th. 1720. MR. BROWN. One sloop
Dolphin now being laden and fitted for ye Sea,
and you being ships master, our orders are for you to embrace the first
fair wind and weather, and proceed for SC and there to deliver your cargo
as bills of lading specify and dispose of our cargo as you shall think to
our best advantage, and if you have any opportunity, sell the sloop as
you shall think fit and remit the net proceeds for....or Boston which you
may think best for our good, so having no more to add but we remain yr
owners. OLIVER CARPENTER, EPHRAIM ARNOLD, BENJAMIN CARPENTER, JOHN
BROWN." JOHN CROFT, Register.

Book A, p. 109 PETER DUGUE, of St. Andrews Parish, Island of
2 May 1718 Jamaica, for valuable considerations made his
Letter of Attorney well beloved friend, JOSEPH WRAGG, of SC, his
attorney. Witnesses: JOHN MARTEN, (CAPT)
MICHAEL DUROUZEAUX. Before THOMAS HEPWORTH. JOHN CROFT, Register.

Book A, p. 110 WILLIAM SMITH, vintner, and ANN his wife, of
13 May 1692 Berkeley Co., SC, to JOHN WATKINS, mariner,
for ↳ 65 lawful current money, sold 1/4 of
town lot #85, containing 1/4 a., occupied by JACOB GUERARD, bounding N on
NICHOLAS TOWNSEND; S & W on part of same lot. Whereas NOAH ROYES, cordwainer, of Charleston, SC, on 6 July 1687, for ↳ 6 sold to ROBERT SKEL-
TON, cordwainer, the above part of a town lot; and whereas SKELTON, on 28
Jan. 1687, for a consideration sold it to EDWARD LOUGHTON, carpenter; and
whereas LOUGHTON, on 5 Apr. 1688, for a certain sum sold to WILLIAM
SMITH; now SMITH sells to WATKINS. Witnesses: J. GUERARD, EDMD. BELLIN-
GER, ANTHONY DODSWORTH, JS. GUERARD.

Book A, p. 113 Before JAMES DUNNIDGE, Notary & Tabellion Pub-
20 May 1720 lick, London. CHARLES CHISWELL, late of Wil-
Power of Attorney liamsburg, Va., now in London, appointed COL.
WILLIAM RHETT, SR., and WILLIAM RHETT, JR.,
merchants, of Charleston, SC, his attorneys to sue and recover from SAM-
UEL DEANE, merchant, of Charleston. Witnesses: EDWARD SWINFEN, SAMUEL
WRAGG.

Book A, p. 115 SIR HOVENDEN WALKER, knight, of Goose Creek
12 Apr. 1720 Parish, Berkeley Co., SC, appointed CAPT.
Power of Attorney ROBERT HOWE, DR. JAMES CAVANAH, and HENRY
HOUSER, merchant, his attorneys. Witnesses:
ADAM BEAUCHAMP, JOHN BROWN, LUCY BROWN. Before THOMAS HEPWORTH. JOHN
CROFT, Register.

Book A, p. 119   JOHN EVANS, planter, Berkeley Co., SC, and
1 & 2 July 1720   PENELOPE his wife; MOSES PLUMMER and JANE his
L & R   wife; sold to RICHARD SPLATT, merchant, of
                         Charleston, for ₤300 current SC money, 110 a.
in Berkeley Co. on head of a creek out of Wando River, bounding E on
Creek, marsh, and JONATHAN RUSS; S on JONATHAN RUSS; NW on THOMAS PADGETT
and RICHARD SMITH; NE on RICHARD SMITH. Witnesses: ROBERT HUME, RICHARD
SMITH, PHILIP CHEEVERS. Before THOMAS HEPWORTH. JOHN CROFT, Register.

Book A, p. 124   EDWARD CLEMENTS, mariner, of Somersetshire Co.,
21 Dec. 1720   and JAMES DUNFORD, mariner, of Middlesex Co.
Power of Attorney   England, appointed WILLIAM ELLIOTT, bricklayer,
                         of Charleston, SC, their attorney. Witnesses:
WILLIAM HADDOCK (HAYDOCK), mariner, JOHN BRADSHAW. Before BENJAMIN WHIT-
AKER. JOHN CROFT, Register.

Book A, p. 125   JAMES BERGERON, of New York City, indebted to
15 May 1716   JOHN SAMUEL LAURAN, of NY City, for ₤20, cur-
Affidavit   rent NY money, to be paid "at the death day of
                         ESTER PELE, of Staten Island, a widow". Wit-
nesses: ANDREW LAURAN, JANE LAURAN, THOMAS BRADY. Registered in SC 15
Feb. 1720/21. JOHN CROFT, Register.

Book A, p. 126   EPHRAIM GILBERT, mariner, of Bermuda, received
23 June 1719   of THOMAS WETHERLY, SR., 1 Indian man to be
                         sold in New England or Bermuda, as GILBERT
should think proper, and in lieu of said Indian, when disposed of, to return 1 Negro man, woman, or boy by first opportunity, "the danger of the
seas and other casualtys that may happen only excepted". Witnesses: JOHN
DICKINSON, THOMAS NASH, THOMAS WEATHERLY, JR.

Book A, p. 126   JONATHAN SKRINE, merchant, of Charleston, SC,
27 & 29 May 1720   and ELIZABETH his wife, to PAUL LE ESCOT,
L & R   clerk, formerly of Charleston, now of Dover,
                         Co. Kent, Kingdom of Great Britain. Whereas
JONATHAN SKRINE became bound to PAUL LE ESCOT in the penal sum of ₤1200
current SC money, conditioned for the payment of ₤600 like money, with
interest at ₤10 per annum; to secure payment and for 10 shillings paid
by SKRINE to LE ESCOT, SKRINE sells LE ESCOT part of lot #42, fronting S
on Broad St. 31 feet; N on lots of MR. SERURIER (alias SMITH); E on WIL-
LIAM LIVINGSTON. Provided that if SKRINE pays LE ESCOT, in dwelling
house of PETER MANIGAULT, in Charleston, ₤600 current money, with interest, on 28 Apr. 1721, this bond to be void. Witnesses: WILLIAM BIL-
LING, TIFFORD ATWELL.

Book A, p. 131   JOEL POINSETT, planter, of Berkeley Co., SC,
3 & 4 Apr. 1719   and SUSANNAH his wife, sold to ISAAC PORCHER,
                         SR., planter, of SC, for ₤600 current SC
money, that 1/3 part of a 1/4 part of lot #37 in Charleston formerly belonging to PETER POINSETT, brother of JOEL, which said 1/3 part of the
1/4 part, being 1/12 of said lot, fronting westward on a street parallel
to Cooper River 38½ ft. and in depth to eastward 37 ft. 10 in. butting N
on a neighborhood lane, S on part of same lot owned by ABRAHAM LESSEUR, E
on part of same lot belonging to MRS. JANE POINSETT, sister of JOEL.
Witnesses: JOHN GENDRON, JACOB LUCE, ROBERT HUME, T. HEYWORTH, PETER
FILLIEW, J. YEOMANS, GEORGE PAWLEY. Witnesses to receipt, JOHN GENDRON,
JACOB LUCE, ROBERT HUME, T. HEPWORTH. JOHN CROFT, Register.

Book A, p. 132   THOMAS HOLTON, of Charleston, chairmaker,
21 June 1720   appointed his loving friend JOHN STONE, block-
Power of Attorney   maker, his attorney, giving him power to dis-
                         pose of his town lot #224 in Charleston, bound-
ing S on MR. LEGARE. Also his plantation of 250 a. called Long Island,
in Berkeley Co. Witnesses: NATHANIEL PARTRIDGE, WILLIAM BILLING. Before
THOMAS HEPWORTH. JOHN CROFT, Register.

Book A, p. 134   JOHN BEAN, tanner, of Charleston, SC, for the
24 Aug. 1720   love and affection he bore unto ESTER BEAN,
                         his faithful and loved wife, native of Santee,
gave her 1 Negro man about 35 years old, 1 Indian boy, his goods and

chattles, personal estate, etc., in SC. Witnesses: JOHN LAURENS, DANIEL PEROT, CORNELIUS BATTOON. Before SAMUEL PRIOLEAU. JOHN CROFT, Register.

Book A, p. 135
3 Apr. 1719
Mortgage

FRANCIS YONGE, ESQ., of SC, by bond dated 30 Mar. 1719, to RICHARD SPLATT, merchant, of Charleston, in penal sum of L 2000 current SC money, conditioned to pay, on 1st Mar. next, 27,000 weight merchantable rice in barrels; and whereas YONGE is further indebted to SPLATT in the quantity of 5,000 weight of merchantable rice, to be paid 1st Mar. next, now to secure payment and delivery of the rice and barrels, YONGE mortgages to SPLATT 8 Negroes; 5 men and 3 women. Witnesses: WILLIAM BLAKEWEY, THOMAS CONYERS. Before THOS. HEPWORTH. JOHN CROFT, Register.

Book A, p. 138
17 & 18 Nov. 1720
L & R

EDWARD CORANT, tailor, of Charleston, to RICHARD SPLATT, merchant, for L 200 current SC money, a plantation of 100 a. on Goose Creek, Berkeley Co., bounding E on BRYAN RALEY, formerly THOMAS FERGUSON; W on RICHARD SPLATT, formerly BENJ. PERRYMAN. Witnesses: ROBERT HUME, ROBERT HOW, JOSEPH WRAGG. Witness to receipt: ROBERT HUME. Before THOMAS HEPWORTH. JOHN CROFT, Register.

Book A, p. 144
16 Mar. 1720/1

ISAAC RAMACK, of Berkeley Co., planter, for L 97.15 sh. current SC money, sold to JAMES MAZYCK DUPOIDSDOR, merchant, of Charleston, 1 Negro man, unless redeemed on Mar. 16 next. Witnesses: WILLIAM STREET, ELIZABETH STREET, THOMAS WALKER. Before SAMUEL EVELEIGH. JOHN CROFT, Register.

Book A, p. 146
23 & 24 May 1718
L & R

PETER MILLER, planter, of Westmoreland Parish, Island of Jamaica, and ALICE his wife; ELIZABETH PARKER, widow; and REBECCA GUNN, spinster, all of the same place (ALICE, ELIZABETH and REBECCA being sisters, and all nieces and co-heiresses of THOMAS GUNN, cooper, their uncle, of the Parish of Port Royall, island of Jamaica); to HENRY MILLER, mariner, of St. Andrews Parish, Jamaica; for L 10 apiece, current money of Jamaica to each of them paid. Whereas the RT. HON. WILLIAM, Earl of Craven, Palatine; CHRISTOPHER, Duke of Albermarle; ANTHONY, Lord Ashley; GEORGE, Lord Carteret; SIR PETER COLLETON, Baronet; SETH SETHELL, ESQ.; THOMAS ARCHDALE, ESQ; and THOMAS AMY, ESQ.; the true and absolute Lords and Proprietors of SC by their order in writing, dated 18 Apr. 1684 directed to their Gov. of the Province, and more especially by their letters patent under the public seal dated 24 Aug. 1688, granted SAMUEL WILSON, gentleman, a plantation of 1000 a. English measure, in Berkeley Co., butting N on eastern branch of the T. of Cooper River; E on ELIZABETH WILLIS and vacant land; S on vacant land; W on Hagar Creek; and whereas SAMUEL WILSON on 28 Aug. 1690, for L 41, sold the plantation to THOMAS GUNN; and whereas THOMAS GUNN died intestate, leaving 4 nieces, ALICE, ELIZABETH, REBECCA, and 1 other, his co-heirs in fee simple. Witnesses: JOHN LONDON, JOHN ROBERTOWN. Witness to receipt: JOHN ROBERTOWN. ALICE MILLER examined privately signed voluntarily. Before WILLIAM WILLIAMS. Entered in office of enrolment 31 Jan. 1718, Liber 56. fols. 92, 93. JA. DANIELL, Secretary.

Book A. p. 156
3 Feb. 1718
Power of Attorney

HENRY MILLER, mariner, of Kingston, Jamaica. Whereas HENRY MILLER purchased from PETER MILLER and ALICE his wife; ELIZABETH PARKER; and REBECCA GUNN, (see above) a plantation of 1000 a. English measure in Berkeley Co., SC, HENRY MILLER appoints his trusty and well beloved friends CAPT. WM. RHETT, SR. and WILLIAM RHETT, JR., of SC, his attorneys to take possession of the said plantation. Witnesses: RICHARD BULLARD, JOHN RATTELL, HOPKIN BULLARD. RICHARD BULLARD and HOPKIN BULLARD appeared before NICHOLAS TROTT, Chief Justice of SC.

Book A, p. 158
12 & 21 Jan. 1720
L & R

CAPT. HENRY MILLER, merchant, of Kingston, Jamaica, and AGNES his wife, for L 343 current money of Jamaica, sold to COL. WILLIAM RHETT merchant, of Charleston, and SARAH his wife a plantation of 1000 a., in Berkeley Co. (see above). AGNES examined privately signed voluntarily. Witnesses: JOHN MARSHALL, GEORGE BARWICK. Before RICHARD MILL. Enrolled in office of enrolment 24 Jan. 1720 Libro 63, fol. 12. R. BAILLIE, Secretary. JOHN CROFT, Register.

Book, p. 166
5 Apr. 1721

Before JOHN BARKSDALE, ESQ., Justice of the Peace for Berkeley Co., appeared CAPT. JAMES BANBURY, master of the sloop Bonnetta, who deposed that he, with the sloop, was employed by the Government of the Province of SC to go under a flag of truce to transport 40 odd Spanish prisoners to St. Augustine, a Spanish garrison, to exchange for about the same number of English prisoners taken by several Spanish privateers and carried to that port; that CAPT. HILDERLY, commander of his Majesty's ship Flamborough, proposed to the government that he would man the said sloop out of the Flamborough provided the government would give them provisions for the voyage. Accordingly CAPT. HILDERLY put 50 seamen on board and one of his own officers. And it was agreed before deponent sailed that they should be under deponent's direction, but that after CAPT. HILDERLY'S sailors came on board he sent on board what goods he pleased and some contrary to deponent's (owner's) orders, who expressly forbade taking such goods on board; but the sloop's company, being the said HILDERLY'S own men, took the command from deponent and did as they pleased the whole voyage; and at deponent's arrival at St. Augustine sold the Spaniards 2 chests of arms (which were taken out of his Majesty's ship Flamborough by CAPT. HILDERLY'S order and put on board deponent's sloop) and other goods in barter for cotton, etc. And whereas it is falsely insinuated by some ill disposed persons that gun powder and great guns were put on board the sloop Bonetta on account of the owners of said sloop with design to trade and sell to the Spaniards at St. Augustine; now deponent states that there was not 1 grain of gun powder either sold or given to the Spaniards directly or indirectly and that the most part of the 2 barrels of powder was brought back again in said sloop to Charleston except about a dozen pounds of it expended in the voyage. Deponent further states that as soon as they arrived before the bar of St. Augustine that Gov. sent out 2 privateer sloops with about 140 men who anchored by them, and the Spanish captain seeing they had 8 great guns mounted, told deponent they must have 4 of those great guns and gave deponent to understand that if they refused to part with them he would take them away by force. The Spanish sloops being of greater force, and double his number of men, deponent was obliged to part with 4 of the great guns to 1 of the captains who did not pay deponent above 1/2 the value of the guns, etc. Deponent further states that the 4 guns were not disposed of voluntarily nor had deponent any order, direct or indirect, to sell or part with the guns but was constrained to let them go, rather than have any difference with the Spaniards. JOHN CROFT, Register.

Book A, p. 168
1 Sept. 1720
Power of Attorney

Before SAMUEL MARTIN (MARTYN), Notary & Tabellion Public, London. WALTER SUTTON, felt-maker, of West Smithfield, London, appointed JACOB SATUR, merchant, of Charleston, SC, at present in London, his attorney, to recover from SAMUEL PICKERING, merchant, of SC, any money goods or thing due SUTTON. Witnesses: GEORGE THOMPSON, EDWARD CROFT. EDWARD CROFT appeared before THOMAS HEPWORTH 12 Apr. 1721. JOHN CROFT, Register.

Book A, p. 172
8 & 9 Feb. 1720
L & R

JONATHAN SKRINE, merchant, of Charleston, SC, and ELIZABETH his wife to ROBERT HUME, gentleman, of Charleston, for L 800 current SC money, part of lot #42 in Charleston in possession of ROBERT JOHNSTON; S 31 feet on Broad St., N to lot formerly of MR. SERURIER (alias SMITH). E on part same lot formerly of WILLIAM LIVINGSTON, now of JAMES MAZYCK. Witnesses to lease: THOMAS HEPWORTH, ROBERT TRADD, J. HUTCHINSON. Witnesses to release and receipt: THOMAS HEPWORTH, JAB. WOOLFORD. Before THOMAS HEPWORTH. JOHN CROFT, Register.

Book A, p. 178
1 Jan. 1720
Mortgage

RICHARD BEDON, planter, Berkeley Co., SC, by bond 25 Nov. 1719 to JOSEPH WRAGG, JOB ROTHMAHLER, and THOMAS DYNES, merchant, Charleston, in penal sum of L 1600 current SC money, conditioned for payment in 36,000 weight merchantable rice in good barrels, clear of all charges, in Charleston, on 1st Jan. 1721. To secure payment,

and for ᏝЬ 5 paid BEDON by WRAGG, ROTHMAHLER and DYNES, BEDON mortgaged 4
Negro men, 1 Negro delivered. Witnesses: SAMUEL HILLES, BARTHOLOMEW (his
mark) RICHARDSON.

Book A, p. 180   RICHARD BEDON, planter, Berkeley Co., SC, to
5 Apr. 1721   JOSEPH WRAGG and JOB ROTHMAHLER, merchants, of
Mortgage   Charleston, for Ь 763:14 shillings current SC
                         money, sold 500 a. in Berkeley Co., bounding
NE on COL. THOMAS BROUGHTON and ANDREW PERCIVAL; on other sides on vacant
land. Plat dated 9 May 1711. Also 3 Negro men, 1 Negro woman. Condition: BEDON to pay WRAGG and ROTHMAHLER the above sum 18 Feb. 1721. Witnesses: SAMUEL HILLES, BARTHOLOMEW (his mark) RICHARDSON. JOHN CROFT,
Register.

Book A, p. 186   SARAH DANIEL, widow of ROBERT DANIEL, Charles-
16 Apr. 1719   ton, to MARTHA DANIEL, widow, of Berkeley Co.,
                         SC. Whereas SARAH DANIEL possessed for the
term of her natural life 2 lots, Nos. 33 & 34, in Charleston, 600 feet
front, bounding E on Cooper River; W on lands unknown; N on marsh belonging to MARTHA DANIEL; S on part of lot of FRANCIS HOLMES; and whereas the
HON. COL. ROBERT DANIEL by his will, dated 1st May 1718, duly executed,
devised the lots to MARTHA DANIEL, now, in consideration of 100-ft.
northern part of lot #34, intended to be granted by MARTHA to SARAH after
the execution of these presents, SARAH surrenders to MARTHA the 2 town
lots Nos. 33 & 34, except the 100 feet above mentioned. Witnesses: WIL-
LIAM BLAKEWEY, W. BILLING. JOHN CROFT, Register.

Book A, p. 188   SARAH RHETT, Administratrix of Estate of JONA-
16 Feb. 1708   THAN AMORY, merchant, of Charleston, SC to
                         BENTLY COOKE, planter, of Berkeley Co. JONA-
THAN AMORY owned several town lots and several large tracts of land in
SC, some with houses and tenements, and by will dated 23 Nov. 1690/1
appointed his wife MARTHA sole executrix during her lifetime, and after
her death his 2 sons THOMAS and ROBERT, authorizing her to dispose of all
or part of his real estate. MARTHA died a short time afterwards and a
few days later, ROBERT, an infant died. THOMAS, being in England, the
administration of the personal estate of JONATHAN was granted, with will
annexed, to SARAH RHETT, who was also executrix of the will of MARTHA
AMORY and afterwards legally appointed and chosen curatrix of THOMAS,
(only son and heir), and guardian of SARAH, the only living daughter of
JONATHAN. And whereas SARAH RHETT made it manifest to the General Assembly of SC that for the payment of debts and legacies and disposition of
the remainder of the estate it was necessary to sell the real estate,
SARAH obtained an act, ratified in open Assembly 1st Mar. 1700, allowing
her to sell, by and with "the advice and consent of JOB HOWE and RALPH
IZARD, ESQRS., and not otherwise".

Now, for Ь 130 current SC money, SARAH RHETT sells BENTLY COOKE: 10 a.,
English measure, in Berkeley Co., near Charleston, bounding N on ISAAC
MAZYCK; S on Charleston line; W on Broad Path; E on JONATHAN AMORY'S
land; which 10 a. were purchased from ISAAC MAZYCK, merchant.

Also: 10 a., English measure, on Charleston Neck, bounding N & W on JOHN
COMING and Cooper River; E & S on town lots; which 10 a. was purchased
from JOB HOWES, gentleman.

Also: Town lot #48, in Charleston, purchased from JOB HOWES, on a little
creek on north end of Charleston; bounding N on Creek and JOHN COMING'S
plantation; S on town lot of JOHN COMING; E on Cooper River; W on vacant
lot.

Also: 4 town lots in Charleston, Nos. 302, 303, 304, & 305 purchased from
DANIEL HUGER, merchant.

Also: 7 lots in Charleston, Nos. 121, 122, 123, 136, 137, 208 & 209
granted JONATHAN AMORY by the Lords Proprs. 13 Aug. 1695. Witnesses:
SOLOMON LEGARE, ISAAC PORCHER.

Book A, p. 194   Reciting the above, RALPH IZARD (JOB HOWES
                         being deceased) consents to, ratifies and

confirms the sale. 19 Mar. 1708. Witnesses: BENTLY COOKE, MARY PEARCE.

Book A, p. 198 BENTLY COOKE, planter, of Berkeley Co., SC,
16 Apr. 1711 sold to WILLIAM RHETT, merchant, of Charleston,
SC, and SARAH his wife, for Ł 130 current SC
money, 10 a. English measure, in Berkeley Co., near Charleston (purchased by JONATHAN AMORY from ISAAC MAZYCK, merchant), butting N on ISAAC MAZYCK; S on Charleston line; W on Broad Path; E on lands of heirs of JONATHAN AMORY.

Also: 10 a., English measure, in Berkeley Co., on Charleston Neck (purchased by JONATHAN AMORY from JOB HOWES, gentleman), butting on JOHN COMING N & W and on Cooper River; E & S on town lots.

Also: lot #48 in Charleston (formerly belonging to JOHN COMING), purchased by JONATHAN AMORY from JOB HOWES; butting E on Cooper River; W on vacant lots.

Also: 4 town lots in Charleston; Nos. 302, 303, 304, 305, purchased by JONATHAN AMORY of DANIEL HUGER, merchant.

Also: 7 lots in Charleston, Nos. 121, 122, 123, 136, 137, 208, 209 granted by the Lords Proprs. to JONATHAN AMORY by 7 grants each dated 13 Aug. 1695. Witnesses: JOHN GUERARD, BENJAMIN GODIN. Witnesses to receipt and delivery; SARAH CROOKE, MARY CRONY.

Book A, p. 202 JACOB SATUR, merchant, of Charleston, SC, to
18 & 19 Apr. 1721 WILLIAM WALLACE, merchant, of Berkeley Co.:
L & R whereas the RT. HON. ANTHONY LORD ASHLEY late
Earl of Shaftsbury, 1 of the proprietors of Carolina, by virtue of a grant from the rest of the Lords Proprs. to his grandfather ANTHONY, Earl of Shaftsbury (dated 18 Mar. 1675 and entered in the secretary's office with a plat) owned 12,000 a. called Ashley Barony & St. Giles; and whereas the RT. HON. ANTHONY LORD ASHLEY, son & heir apparent of the RT. HON. ANTHONY, Earl of Shaftsbury, on 20 July 1698, for the love & affection he had for his brother the HON. MAURICE, and in consideration of 5 shillings, ANTHONY grants MAURICE, amongst other things, proprietorship of all his lands in SC; and whereas MAURICE by L & R, 2 & 3 Aug. 1717, sold to SAMUEL WRAGG, merchant, the Barony above mentioned; and whereas by L & R, 5 & 6 Aug., 1720, SAMUEL WRAGG, for Ł 300 sterling money of Great Britain, sold JACOB SATUR part of Ashley Barony or St. Giles, containing 3000 a.; now for Ł 5900 current SC money, SATUR sells to WALLACE, 1791-1/2 a., part of the 3000 a.; butting N on SAMUEL CLARKE; S on ROBERT JOHNSON (alias BLACK ROBIN); E on ALEXANDER SKENE; W on ROBERT JOHNSON (alias BLACK ROBIN); free from all dowers and thirds which MARY the wife of SAMUEL WRAGG and MARY the wife of JACOB SATUR may claim. Witnesses: JOHN CROFT, JOHN CAWOOD, MAURICE HARVEY. Before SAMUEL EVELEIGH. JOHN CROFT, Register.

Book A, p. 212 Whereas JACOB SATUR, merchant, of Charleston,
19 Apr. 1721 by L & R, 18 & 19 Apr. 1721, sold WILLIAM WAL-
Acknowledgement of debt LACE, merchant, of Berkeley Co., 1791-1/2 a.
for Ł 5900; now for 10 shillings paid by WALLACE to SATUR, SATUR promises that he and MARY his wife shall, before the end of HILLARY term next ensuing, in due for of law, acknowledge and levy before his Majesty's Justices of the Court of Common Pleas, at Westminster, Great Britain, "1 or more fine or fines, Sur Cognizance de Droit come Ceo: & ca" to WALLACE 1791-1/2 a., part of Ashley Barony, "according to the usual course practice & method of levying of fines in the courts of Westminster aforesaid which said fine so to be had & levyed of ye said premises" shall be and inure to the use and behoof of WILLIAM WALLACE. Witnesses: JOHN CROFT, JOHN CAWOOD, MAURICE HARVEY.

Book A, p. 214 JACOB SATUR, merchant, of Charleston, SC, to
19 Apr. 1721 WILLIAM WALLACE, merchant, of Berkeley Co.,
Bond for Ł 10,000 current SC money, conditioned for
fulfilling agreements made in L & R, 18 & 19
Apr. 1721. Witnesses: JOHN CROFT, JOHN CAWOOD, MAURICE HARVEY.

Book A, p. 216 Petition to the HON. JAMES MOORE, ESQR. Gov.

of SC, from WILLIAM WALLACE, merchant, showing that WALLACE had interviewed ALEXANDER SKENE and PETER GOLDING, road commissioners, and GEORGE FLOOD, SAM CLARK, RICHARD BAKER, and JOSIAH OSGOOD through whose land the road was to be run but, a controversy arising, MR. SKENE demanded the services of a surveyor. Unknown to WALLACE and SKENE, the others applied to MR. BEDON and MR. GOLDING and proceeded to run a road through petitioner's plantation, even the middle of his Negro houses, petitioner begs order to stop proceedings and for a surveyor to join MESSRS. SKENE, BEDON and GOLDING in laying out a convenient road. Petition granted by GOV. JAMES MOORE and MAJOR HERBERT appointed surveyor, who, with the consent of ALEXANDER SKENE and RICHARD BEDON, and at the request of SAMUEL CLARKE, JOSIAH OSGOOD and RICHARD BAKER, ran a straight road through petitioner's land from Stevens Bridge to the king's high road leading to Waste Savannah, (from JACOB'S CREEK to Waste Savannah), 23 Feb. 1720/21.

Book A, p. 218
18 & 19 Apr. 1721
L & R

ROWLAND STORY, planter, of Berkeley Co., SC, and ELIZABETH his wife (1 of the daughters of JOSEPH ELLICOTT, planter) to JOHN WATKINSON, mariner, of SC, for L 520 current SC money, part of 2 lots in Charleston, Nos. 24 & 25, fronting 46 ft. westward on street running from Cooper River to New Church and 104 feet on Tradd Street (leading from Bay to house of BENJAMIN DE LA CONSEILLERS; N on part lot #25 belonging to ROWLAND STORY occupied by JOHN CAWOOD; E on part lot #24 belonging to ISAAC MAZYCK occupied by WILLIAM WATSON, GARRAT VANVELSIN and BENJAMIN MASSY; except part leased 26 May 1712 to GARRAT VANVELSIN, cordwainer, of Charleston, for 10 years (still enduring) at yearly rent of 20 shillings current SC money; and also except 1 part leased 10 May 1720 to WILLIAM WATSON, joiner, of Charleston, for 3 years (still enduring) at the yearly rent of L 74 current money payable quarterly in rice at 40 shillings per hundred. Witnesses to deed and receipt: ROBERT HUME, SAMUEL EVELEIGH, T. HEPWORTH. Before WILLIAM BULL. JOHN CORFT, Register.

Book A, p. 226
1 July 1714
Deed of Sale

THOMAS DISTON, ESQ., Berkeley Co., SC and ELIZABETH his wife to JOHN ASH, 500 a. in Berkeley Co. bounding N & W on THOMAS DISTON, S & E on vacant land, which land was granted THOMAS DISTON 3 June 1714 by THE HON. CHARLES CRAVEN, ESQ., Gov., and the Lords & Proprietors. Witnesses to Deed: ROBERT WILSON, NATHANIEL RISCO. Before GEORGE CRICHTON. Witnesses to possession and delivery: NICHOLAS BOHUN, BENJAMIN WARING. JOHN CROFT, Register.

Book A, p. 228
9 Sept. 1720
Power of Attorney

JOHN BAPTISTA ASH, gentleman of Bath Co., NC, late of SC, appointed LANDGRAVE JOSEPH MORTON of SC his attorney to dispose of 500 a. near the ponds or head of Ashley River, in Berkeley Co., SC, purchased from THOMAS DISTON, gentleman, 1 July 1714, bounding N & W on THOMAS DISTON; S & E on vacant land. Witness: CAPT. OTHNIEL BEALE. Before SAM. EVELEIGH. JOHN CROFT, Register.

Book A, p. 230
4 Mar. 1720/21
Bond

RICHARD FLOYD, planter, of Colleton Co., to ANTHONY MATTHEWS, JOHN LEROCHE & FRANCIS HOLMES, JR., merchants, of Charleston, for L 875 SC money, conditioned for payment of L 437, 7 shillings on 25 Mar. 1722. RICHARD (his mark) FLOYD. Witnesses: THOMAS BARTON, WILLIAM BILLING.

Book A, p. 231
4 Mar. 1720/21
Mortgage

RICHARD (his mark) FLOYD, planter, of Colleton Co., SC, to ANTHONY MATTHEWS, JOHN LEROCHE & FRANCIS HOLMES, JR., merchants, of Charleston, in penal sum of L 875 current SC money conditioned for payment of L 437, 7 shillings on 25 Mar. 1722, and for security conveyed 600 a. in Colleton Co. (grant dated 23 July 1711 signed by THE HON. ROBERT GIBBES, ESQ. late Gov. and the Lords Proprs): NE on Ambrose Hill; SE on vacant land; SW on MICHAEL RENOLDS; NW on marsh land. Witnesses: THOMAS BARTON; WILLIAM BILLING.

Book A, p. 234
21 Nov. 1716
Sale

DANIEL HUGER, of Berkeley Co., and ELIZABETH his wife, for L 300, to JAMES NICHOLAS MAYRANT and PAUL MAYRANT, of Berkeley Co., 1190 a.

(4 grants, 4 plots). Whereas the Lords Proprs. granted DANIEL HUGER 690 a. in 3 tracts; vlz., 1 containing 300 a. by grant dated 14 Feb. 1696 signed by JOHN ARCHDALE, JOSEPH MORTON, THOMAS CARY and JAMES MOORE; 1 containing 160 a. by grant dated 2 Feb. 1703/4 signed by NATHANIEL JOHNSON, JAMES MOORE, JOB HOWES and NICHOLAS TROTT; 1 230 a. by grant dated 14 Sept. 1705 signed by NATHANIEL JOHNSON, JAMES MOORE and NICHOLAS TROTT: and whereas DANIEL HUGER by will dated 20 Oct. 1711, recorded 28 May 1712, gave his son DANIEL HUGER the above 690 a.; and whereas the Lords Proprs. on 17 Dec. 1714 granted DANIEL HUGER, JR. 500 a. joining the above: (grant signed by CHARLES CRAVEN, RALPH IZARD, SAM. EVELEIGH, ROBERT DANIEL and CHARLES HART): now DANIEL HUGER sells as above. Witnesses: JEAN PETINEAU; PETER GUERARD. Before JOHN HARLESTON, J.P. for Berkeley Co., 3 May 1721. JOHN CROFT, Register.

Book A, p. 236
28 May 1719
Bond

GEORGE LOGAN, SR., ESQ., of Berkeley Co., SC, to WILLIAM BLAKEWEY and RICHARD HARRIS, ESQS., of Berkeley Co. and ANDREW ALLEN, merchant, of Charleston, Ł 3000 current SC money, conditioned for the payment of Ł 1500 to ANN DANIEL as follows: whereas a marriage is intended between GEORGE LOGAN, SR. and MARTHA DANIEL, SR. (widow of the HON. COL. ROBERT DANIEL, late Deputy Gov. of SC) whereby LOGAN will be entitled to a considerable number of slaves and other personal estate belonging to her, LOGAN agrees to pay ANN DANIEL (daughter of MARTHA) Ł 1500 current money within 2 months next after she shall either attain the age of 16 or be married. Witnesses: THOMAS HEPWORTH, ROBERT HUME, HANNAH WRATH. (Note: ANN will be 16 on 15 Apr. 1726.)

Book A, p. 238
11 Mar. 1720/21
Bond

GEORGE LOGAN, gentleman, of Berkeley Co., and MARTHA LOGAN (widow of GEORGE LOGAN) to ANDREW ALLEN, RICHARD HARRIS & WILLIAM BLAKEWEY (in trust for JOHN DANIEL, son of the HON. ROBERT DANIEL, ESQ.) for Ł 600 current SC money, conditioned for payment of Ł 300 with full interest at 10% for each Ł 100 per annum, in trust for JOHN DANIEL, on 11 Mar. 1721. Witnesses: WILLIAM HAMMERTON; EDWARD RAWLINGS.

Book A, p. 239
15 Aug. 1714
Apprenticeship

WILLIAM (his mark) MURRY, son of SUSANNA MURRY, voluntarily apprentices himself to COL. WILLIAM RHETT, merchant, of Charleston, SC, for 8 years, "the said apprentice his said Master shall faithfully serve, his secrets keep, his lawfull comands everywhere gladly do. He shall do no damage to his said Master nor see it to be done by others. He shall not waste his said Masters goods, nor lend them unlawfully to any at cards, dice, or at any other unlawfull game, he shall not play, but in all things behave himself, as a good & faithfull apprentice ought to do. And the said COL. WILLIAM RHETT his said Master, shall provide him the said WILLIAM MURRY with good & sufficient meats, drink, washing, lodging & apparell fit for such an apprentice during the said term. And at ye end or expiration, the said Master doth oblige himself, to give to ye said apprentice 2 new suites of apparel, the 1 for Sundays the other for working days". Witnesses: WILLIAM RHETT, JR., RICHARD ROWE. J.C. Register

Book A, p. 240

Copia. Tenore praesentium nos JOHANNES, permissione divina London Episcopus, ad quem Omnis et Omni moda Juris dictio Spiratantis et Ecclesiastica infra Diocesin London durante visitation Nostra Episcopali Spectat et pertinet. Notum facimus Universii quod primo die Mensis Octobris Anno Dom. Millimo Septingentesimo Decimo quinto Coram Venlo. Viro JOHANNE Exton Legm Dre Sue Dilecti Uri Humfridi Henchman Legm. etiam Doctoris Vriaxy nri in Spiribus Gentis, probatum approbatum et insinuatum fuit tertum JOHANNIS LEA nuper proice Hee (Stee?) MARIA ALDERMANBARY. London defuncti presentibus Annex Commissaqs (?) fuit Administratio Omnium et Singulor Conoram jurium et Creditorum dicti defuncti, et eius testamentum qualitercunqs (?) tangen et Concernen Eliza. LEA Sorone hurali et latima dicti defuncti Unica Executrice in dicto testamento Nominat' primitus de bene et fideliter Administrando eadem ae de pleno et fideli Inventaxio Omnium et Singuloram Conoi...jurium et Creditorum humet. Conficiend et illud in Registram Episcopale London Citra vel ante Ultimum diem mensis Jan.: prox future Exhibend, leq plano et vero Compo Calco Sive Racocimo inde Redond ad lta Dei Evangelia Jurat Dat. Die Mensis Anoq Dni pradictis. Ed:

ALEXANDER, Reglius.

With the Seale of ye Prerogative Court of Canterbury in red wax appending. The aforegoing Coppy agreeth verbatim with its originall, which after due examination, I attest in London this 24 day of Aug. Ann Dni: 172 O Ja/bus/D-nnidge, Not/rius/: Pub/ius/. (Seale)

Book A, p. 241 MRS. ELIZABETH GRICE (formerly LEA) widow of
24 Aug. 1720   JOHN GRICE, merchant, of London, sole executrix of the probated will of her brother JOHN LEA, late citizen and cooper of London, appointed WILLIAM RHETT, SR. of Charleston, SC, her attorney to handle property in SC. Witnesses: RICHARD SHUBRICK; CAPT. JOHN SMYTER.

DEEDS BOOK "Ba"
1720-1722

Book Ba, p. 1   JOHN HUTCHINSON, apothecary, of Charleston, SC,
20 & 21 Dec. 1720   and ANNE his wife to FRANCIS PAGETT, planter,
L & R   of Berkeley Co., for ₤ 1200 current SC money,
                       1/2 of a quarter part of a town lot #27 in Charleston on a neighborhood alley running from Bay St. by the houses of JOHN BUCKLEY, DR. JOHN THOMAS and THOMAS HEPWORTH'S corner house; bounding S 28 ft. on the alley, W on ELISHA PRIOLEAU; E 85 ft. 10 in. on THOMAS LAMBOLL; N on ELISHA PRIOLEAU's lot. Witnesses: THOMAS HEPWORTH, ROBERT HUME. Before SAM EVELEIGH. R. YONGE, Register.

Book Ba, p. 7   JONATHAN FITCH, planter, of SC, to ANNE DRAY-
21 Mar. 1720/21   TON in penal sum of ₤ 1000 conditioned for pay-
Bond   ment of ₤ 500 current SC money with interest;
                       and to secure payment delivered 5 Negro men. Witnesses: JOSEPH CLARE, THOMAS (his mark) HOLMAN. Possession given to RICHARD FULLER in behalf of ANNE DRAYTON 5 June 1721. Before FRANCIS YONGE, 1 of his Majesty's council.

Book Ba, p. 9   RICHARD BEDON, planter, Berkeley Co., SC, for
30 May 1721   ₤ 352: 10 sh. current SC money to ANNE DRAY-
Mortgage   TON, widow: 1 Indian man, 3 Negro women; unless redeemed 11 Jan. next. Witnesses: ROBERT HUME, ROBERT HOW. ROBERT YONGE, Register.

Book Ba, p. 10   FRANCIS YONGE, merchant, of SC, sole owner of
29 May 1721   good sloop the Quadrumity and her equipment,
Sale   SOLOMON MIDDLETON, master, for 500 pieces of 8, to WOODES ROGERS, ESQ., Gov. of Island of Providence, 5/8 parts of said sloop (purchased from WILLIAM WAGNER, merchant, 12 Apr. 1721), riding at anchor in Charleston Harbor. Witnesses: JAMES SMITH, PETER GOUDETT. Before JOHN BARKSDALE. ROBERT YONGE, Register.

Book Ba, p. 11   SARAH BEAMOUR, widow, of Berkeley Co., for ₤
15 Jan. 1720   1370 current money to WILLIAM HARVEY, butcher,
Sale   of SC, 2 Negro men, 3 Negro women, 4 Negro
                       boys, 1 Negro girl. Witnesses: ROBERT HUME, ROBERT HOWE. ROBERT YONGE, Register.

Book Ba, p. 12   WOODES ROGERS, ESQ., Gov. of Bahamas, for ₤
19 June 1721   2600 current SC money, to CHARLES HILL, mer-
Sale   chant, of SC, 1/2-part of 40-ton sloop Quadrimity, SOLOMON MIDDLETON, master, and half her equipment; also, 1/3 part of 50-ton sloop Sea Nymph, JOHN COCHRAN, master, and 1/3 her equipment; also such goods lately shipped on board said sloop consigned to DR. ANDREW ROWAN as listed in schedule annexed; and all profits and proceeds. ROGERS appoints CHARLES HILL his attorney to receive the 2 sloops and goods and act for him. Witnesses: BENJAMIN WHITAKER, JACOB MOTTE. Before JOHN BARKSDALE. Schedule attached including item "100 pounds sterling in bills of exchange on JOHN MULCASTER, ESQ." ROBERT YONGE, Register.

14

Book Ba, p. 14   JOHN GIBBS (GIBBES) planter, Berkeley Co., SC,
22 Feb. 1718/9   to RICHARD CAPERS, SR., tanner, of Colleton Co.
Sale   Whereas JOSEPH BLAKE, ESQ., Propr. & Gov., and
                      the other Lords Proprs. on 29 May 1704 granted
ROBERT GIBBS, ESQ. 500 a. English measure in Colleton Co. at the head of
the western branch of the north branch of Stono River, bounding E on
marsh and swamp; and whereas ROBERT GIBBS by deed of gift on 4 Oct. 1710
gave the 500 a. to his son JOHN GIBBS; now JOHN GIBBS, for Ł 1000 current
SC money, sells the 500 a. to RICHARD CAPERS, SR. Witnesses: THOMAS CA-
PERS, MARY CAPERS, JOHN WELLS. Before JOHN BARKSDALE. ROBERT YONGE,
Register.

Book Ba, p. 17   JOHN GIBBS, planter, of SC, to RICHARD CAPERS,
22 Feb. 1718/19   tanner, of Colleton Co., SC, Ł 4000 current SC
Bond   money, conditioned for fulfilling agreements
                      in bill of sale of this date. Witnesses:
THOMAS CAPERS, MARY CAPERS, JOHN WELLS. Before JOHN BARKSDALE. ROBERT
YONGE, Register.

Book Ba, p. 18   SARAH BEAMOR, widow, of Berkeley Co., for Ł
11 & 12 July 1721   200 current SC money and other considerations,
L & R   sold WILLIAM BELLINGER, planter, of Colleton
                      Co., SC, 190 a. in Berkeley Co., bounding W on
MR. MERRYES; N on MR. IZARD & MR. FOSTER (FORSTER); E on Cooper River and
a marsh. Witnesses: THOMAS BARTON, ROBERT HUME, ROBERT HOWE. ROBERT
YONGE, Register.

Book Ba, p. 21   WILLIAM BELLINGER, planter, of Colleton Co.,
12 July 1721   SC, and SARAH BEAMOUR, widow, of Berkeley Co.
Agreement   Whereas, by L & R dated 11 & 12 July 1721,
                      SARAH BEAMOUR sold to WILLIAM BELLINGER 190 a.
(page 18) now SARAH BEAMOUR and WILLIAM BELLINGER agree that JAMES BEA-
MOUR, a minor, son & heir of JACOB BEAMOUR, planter, of Colleton Co., or
the said SARAH BEAMOUR shall on 6 Jan. 1729 convey to WILLIAM BELLINGER
535 a. in Colleton Co. formerly given by MARGARET BEAMOUR to JACOB BEA-
MOUR; bounding E on land given by MARGARET BEAMOUR, widow, to her oldest
son JOHN BEAMOUR; N on JOHN WILLIAMSON. Witnesses: THOMAS BARTON, ROBERT
HUME, ROBERT HOWE. ROBERT YONGE, Register. Memo: "Search has been made
for the within mentioned tract of 190 a. of land pr me ROBERT YONGE for
MR. WILLIAM BELLINGER and not being to be found".

Book Ba, p. 23   SARAH BEAMOUR, widow, of Berkeley Co., to WIL-
12 July 1721   LIAM BELLINGER, planter, of Colleton Co., Ł
Bond   500 current SC money. Whereas JACOB BEAMOUR,
                      planter, of Colleton Co., by will dated 6 July
1710 gave his loving wife SARAH his whole estate for as long as she kept
herself a widow by his name but if she altered her condition he gave 1/3
to her and the rest to remain in her hands for his son JAMES BEAMOUR till
he reaches 21, or marries, but if the son die febore then his part should
remain with SARAH; and whereas WILLIAM BELLINGER paid SARAH BEAMOUR Ł 600
current money for certain lands; now the condition of this bond is that
SARAH and JAMES BEAMOUR convey to WILLIAM BELLINGER a certain tract of
535 a. in Colleton Co. formerly given by MARGARET BEAMOUR to JACOB BEA-
MOUR, father of JAMES; bounding E on land formerly given by MARGARET BEA-
MOUR, widow, to her oldest son JOHN BEAMOUR; N on JOHN WILLIAMSON. Lease,
release, defeasance and bond proved 14 July 1721 before JOHN BARKSDALE.
ROBERT YONGE, Register.

Book Ba, p. 25   Protested bill of exchange, dated Charleston,
15 Dec. 1708   SC, 6 July 1708, for Ł 62:10:7 sterling.
                      Drawn by RIDDLEY MARSDEN on his father THOMAS
MARSDEN, merchant, St. Martins Lane, London, to be paid "MR. JOHN LEA or
his order as the order of your friend & GEO: Logan Charles Town Aug. 7, ??
1708". Presented by Ja/bus/ (JAMES) DUNNIDGE, Not. Public. ROBERT YONGE,
Register.

Book Ba, p. 26   JAMES BROWN (BROWNE), planter, Berkeley Co.,
1 Jan. 1720   SC, to JOSEPH WRAGG & JOB ROTHMAHLER, mer-
                      chants, of Charleston, SC, for Ł 500 current
SC money a plantation called Lynch Grove containing 710 a. near head of

Wando River in Christ Church Parish with buildings, crops, cattle, horses, etc. & 25 slaves and all real and personal estate, goods and chattles in said Parish unless redeemed by payment in Charleston of Ł 500 current SC money or value in pitch tar or rice at market price on 10 Dec. 1722. Witnesses: ALEXANDER SIMPSON, THOMAS HEADINGTON. Seizin and possession taken by JOSEPH WRAGG & JOB ROTHMAHLER by delivery of 20 shillings current money 10 Jan. 1720. Witnesses: ALEXANDER SIMPSON, THOMAS HEADINGTON. ROBERT YONGE, Register. WRAGG & ROTHMAHLER, for 5 shillings, paid them by JAMES BROWNE surrender Lynch Grove Plantation mortgage 1 July 1721. Before JOHN BARKSDALE. Memo of satisfaction entered 7 Sept. 1721 by ROBERT YONGE.

Book Ba, p. 29　　　　　　JUDITH DUBOURDIEU, widow, of Berkeley Co., SC,
29 July 1720　　　　　　　in consideration of marriage contract between
Gift & Agreement　　　　　JAMES COLLETON and her daughter JUDITH DUBOURDIEU granted 1/3 part of land in her possession to JAMES COLLETON "and also the third part of the Negroes wch is already sheared and as soon as the howing time is over the said JAMES COLLETON shall be put in possession both of the land and Negroes by the provisoe; that the hand of the said JAMES COLLETON shall help to put in the crop that is now upon the ground and also to clean the rice fit for markett; because the said rice is designed to pay the debts of the plantation or in part of which the said COLLETON is to pay the third part as well as to have the third of the said cropt debts paid; and I SAMUEL DUBOURDIEU do agree and consent conjoyntly with my mother to this above gift and agreement". Witnesses: MAJOR PERCIVEL (PERCIVAL) PAWLEY, PAUL PETER LEBAS. Before BENJAMIN WHITAKER. ROBERT YONGE, Register, 19 Sept. 1720 6 Negroes delivered to JAMES COLLETON and JUDITH (daughter) as part of daughter's fortune. Witnesses: HENRY SIMMONS, PAUL TRAPIER.

Book Ba, p. 31　　　　　　Protested bill of exchange dated SC 17 Jan.
23 May 1721　　　　　　　1720/21. Ł 31 to be paid at 30 days to DANIEL
　　　　　　　　　　　　　GREEN or order "for value rec'd for the support of his majesties garrison under my command at Nassau on Providence" signed WOODES ROGERS and addressed to JOHN MULCASTER, ESQ. at his office over the horse guards near Charing Cross London. Presented at request of MR. FRANCIS GREEN of London, merchant, by THOMAS BOCKING, Not. Pub. who went to the office of JOHN MULCASTER but he was out of town. Witnesses: WILLIAM PAINE, WILLIAM FOX. ROBERT YONGE, Register.

Book Ba, p. 37　　　　　　MARTHA DANIEL, widow, Berkeley Co., to SAMUEL
15 & 16 Apr. 1719　　　　 EVELEIGH and ALEXANDER PARRIS, ESQRS. of
L & R　　　　　　　　　　Charleston. Whereas the HON. ROBERT DANIEL
　　　　　　　　　　　　　owned a plantation of 549 a. on St. Thomas's Island, Berkeley Co., bounding E on Wando River, W on JOHN CODNER, N on MARTHA DANIEL'S land, S on Cooper River, on which plantation SARAH DANIEL and ROBERT DANIEL, her son live; and whereas ROBERT DANIEL by will dated 1 May 1718 devised the plantation to MARTHA, and divers controversies and disputes arose between SARAH and MARTHA; MARTHA claiming the plantation under will of said ROBERT her husband; SARAH (in behalf of her son ROBERT, a minor) claiming the same plantation by virtue of the statute of limitation inasmuch as ROBERT DANIEL, husband of SARAH, only son of ROBERT the husband of MARTHA, had been in peaceable possession for 14 years before the making and publishing of the last will of ROBERT the grandfather; and whereas the parties wish to end the controversy, and MARTHA desires the 549 a. vested in ROBERT the grandson: in consideration of the premises and of the natural love and affection MARTHA bears ROBERT the grandson, and for the advancement of MARMADUKE DANIEL, another grandson of ROBERT her husband in case ROBERT the grandson should die without issue; and for other considerations: MARTHA sold the plantation to SAMUEL EVELEIGH and ALEXANDER PARRIS in trust for SARAH DANIEL until ROBERT should be 21; then to ROBERT for his lifetime; after his death to heirs of MARMADUKE; lacking such heirs, then to SARAH, mother of ROBERT and MARMADUKE; nothing to deprive SARAH of her right or title of dower and thirds. Several provisoes were added in case the grandfather's will should be contested by ROBERT and MARMADUKE. Witnesses: WILLIAM BLAKEWEY, WILLIAM BILLING. ROBERT YONGE, Register.

Book Ba, p. 39　　　　　　JASPER ASHWORTH, ESQ. & SUSANNA his wife, of

10 & 11 Aug. 1720　　　　　　St. George's Parish, Island of Jamaica, for
L & R　　　　　　　　　　　　₤ 1300 current money of Jamaica sold to WIL-
　　　　　　　　　　　　　　 LIAM GIBBON & ANDREW ALLEN, merchants, of St.
Philip's Parish, Charleston, 3000 a. known as Thorowgoods, in Parish of
St. James, Goose Creek, SC; also all Negro, Mulatto, Indian and other
slaves; all live stock, goods and chattles; all lands, tenements, goods
and slaves in St. Philip's Parish belonging to JASPER ASHWORTH and SUSAN-
NA his wife; also all other lands, tenements, slaves and property in St.
Philip's and St. James's Parishes intended to be granted to JASPER ASH-
WORTH by 2 indentures, 1 dated 17 Oct. 1716 by WILLIAM HAWETT, ESQ., of
Port Royall Parish, Island of Jamaica and MARY his wife; the other after
the death of WILLIAM HAWITT on 1 Mar. 1719 by MARY HAWETT widow (except
60 a. conveyed by JASPER ASHWORTH to 1 SINGLETON, and such other lands as
have been sold by GIBBON & ALLEN as attorneys for JASPER ASHWORTH. Whereas 17 Oct. 1716 WILLIAM HAWETT, ESQ., of Port Royall Parish, Jamaica,
sold ROBERT GOODWIN, gentleman, of the same place, 1/6 part of all his
real and personal estate of whatever nature, on condition that ROBERT
GOODWIN should receive no benefit from the 1/6 part until after the death
of WILLIAM HAWETT. It was further agreed that the said 1/6 part should
be liable with the other 5/6 parts of the estate to pay ₤ 1000 current
Jamaican money as follows: ₤ 500 to be paid to HAWETT ASHWORTH, a minor,
nephew-in-law to WILLIAM HAWETT on 26 Mar. 1722; also ₤ 500 to be paid
MARY LANCASTER, niece-in-law, at age of 21 or on her marriage day: and
whereas said indenture was executed in trust and for the support of MARY,
the wife of WILLIAM HAWETT after his death, ROBERT GOODWIN by deed poll
on same date declared same so to be and released to MARY HAWETT all his
claim to said 1/6 part: and whereas WILLIAM HAWETT & MARY his wife sold
JASPER ASHWORTH on 17 Oct. 1716 the remaining 5/6 part of the estate; and
whereas WILLIAM died and MARY deeded JASPER 1/6 part, as above, also her
real and personal estate of every kind in any part of the world; and
whereas WILLIAM HAWETT at this time owned other property; now, JASPER
ASHWORTH & SUSANNA his wife, convey to GIBBON and ALLEN (1/2 to GIBBON &
1/2 to ALLEN). Witnessed in Jamaica by: S. ORGILL, MICHAEL FARRILL,
RICHARD WARRINGTON, ELEAZER ALLEN, JOHN MASTERS. Before Fort/es/ Dwarris.
Enrolled in office of enrolment 18 July 1721 Lib. 66 fol. 38 & 39, RICH-
ARD BAILIE, Secy. JOHN MASTERS appeared before GEORGE CHICKEN, J.P. for
Berkeley Co., SC, 28 Aug. 1721. ROBERT YONGE, Register. SUSANNA ASH-
WORTH, being private examined, signed voluntarily.

Book Ba, p. 50　　　　　　　JAMES BROWN, planter, Berkeley Co., to WILLIAM
28 Aug. 1721　　　　　　　　SCOTT and ARCHIBALD STOBO, gentlemen, attor-
Release　　　　　　　　　　neys to ELIZABETH BERRY, widow of JAMES BERRY,
　　　　　　　　　　　　　　Boston, New England, for ₤ 1322:16 sh. current
SC money, 710 a. on Wando Neck, Berkeley Co., known as Lynch Grove with
standing crop of rice and 10 slaves conditioned upon BROWN paying SCOTT &
STOTO, her attorneys, ₤ 1302:6 sh. current SC money or deliver the value
in tar or rice at current market price at Charleston. BROWN agreed that
all the rice made in 1721 shall be at disposal of SCOTT & STOBO, also
such part of the next (1723) rice crop as will pay the amount due them on
10 Apr. 1723. Witnesses: WILLIAM BLAKEWEY, JOHN HALL. ROBERT YONGE,
Register.

Book Ba, p. 54　　　　　　　TOBIAS FITCH, of St. Andrews Parish, Berkeley
11 Sept. 1721　　　　　　　Co., SC, to JACOB BELL, merchant, of Charles-
Sale　　　　　　　　　　　　ton, for ₤ 130 current SC money, sold 1 Negro
　　　　　　　　　　　　　　boy. Witnesses: ELIAS HANCOCK, THOMAS ELLERY.
ROBERT YONGE, Register.

Book Ba, p. 56　　　　　　　TOBIAS FITCH, planter, of St. Andrews Parish,
11 Sept. 1721　　　　　　　Berkeley Co., SC, to JACOB BELL, merchant, of
Indemnity Bond　　　　　　　Charleston, for ₤ 260 current SC money to in-
　　　　　　　　　　　　　　demnify BELL against any claim in connection
with the sale of Negro boy. Witnesses: ELIAS HANCOCK, THOMAS ELLERY.
ROBERT YONGE, Register.

Book Ba, p. 57　　　　　　　JOSEPH STONE (son of JOHN STONE, JR.) tanner,
23 Aug. 1721　　　　　　　　of St. Thomas Parish, Berkeley Co., SC, for ₤
Deed of Sale　　　　　　　　50 current SC money, 80 a. to ROBERT CLYATT.
　　　　　　　　　　　　　　Whereas JOHN STONE (the father) gave his son
JOSEPH 195 a. in Thomas Parish on the east side of Cooper River bounding

N on JEREMIAH RUSSELL, S on land given by the father JOHN STONE to his son JOHN, brother of JOSEPH, by deed of gift dated 22 Apr. 1715 (the witnesses being HANNAH CLYATT, MARY MORANEY, DEBORAH STONE, and ROBERT CLYATT); now JOSEPH sells to his brother-in-law ROBERT CLYATT 80 a. on east side of Cooper River in St. Thomas Parish, beginning at easternmost part of JOSEPH'S land running W 40 chains, and from SE corner towards N 20 ch., bounding on land his brother JOHN STONE sold to his sister HANNAH CLYATT, and on land of FRANCIS PAGETT & JEREMIAH RUSSELL (RUSSEL). Witnesses: PAUL VIART, MARY BUTLER, BENJAMIN STONE. Plot surveyed by ROBERT CLYATT at request of JOSEPH STONE 23 Aug. 1721. Before JOSIAS DUPRE. ROBERT YONGE, Register.

Book Ba, p. 60
10 Mar. 1718/19
Deed of Sale

JOHN STONE, JR. & SUSANNA his wife, for ₤ 60 current SC money sold HANNAH CLYATT, their sister, 64 a. on E side Cooper River in St. Thomas Parish, beginning at easternmost part of their land and bounding on lands of FRANCIS PAGETT, JOSEPH FORD, WILLIAM POOL, JOHN MILLMAN, & JOSEPH STONE, their brother. Witnesses: JOHN ATKIN (ATTKIN), PAUL VIART, MARY CARROL. Plot surveyed by ROBERT CLYATT 9 Mar. 1718/19 at request of JOHN STONE. Before JOSIAS DUPRE. ROBERT YONGE, Register.

Book Ba, p. 62
10 Mar. 1718/19
Bond

JOHN STONE, JR., cordwainer or shoemaker, of St. Thomas Parish, Berkeley Co., SC, to HANNAH CLYATT, his sister, for ₤ 120 current SC money, conditioned for keeping the agreements in the above sale. Witnesses: JOHN AKIN, PAUL VIART, MARY CARROL. Before JOSIAS DUPRE. ROBERT YONGE, Register.

Book Ba, p. 64
23 Aug. 1721
Bond of Performance

JOSEPH STONE, of St. Thomas Parish, Berkeley Co., SC, for ₤ 100 current SC money, to ROBERT CLYATT, of same place, conditioned for keeping agreements in deed of sale of 80 a. of even date. Witnesses: PAUL VIART, MARY BUTTLER, BENJAMIN STONE. Before JOSIAS DUPRE. ROBERT YONGE, Register.

Book Ba, p. 65
16 Aug. 1721
Bargain and Sale

JONATHAN SKRINE, merchant, of Charleston, Berkeley Co., SC, for ₤ 300 current SC money, sold 3 Negro slaves (2 men, 1 girl) to the HON. ROBERT JOHNSON, ESQ.; conditioned for the payment of ₤ 315 on 17 Feb. 1722. This bargain and sale, and 1 mortgage of plantation for ₤ 100 on even date, made for payment of sum and for security. Witnesses to bargain and sale, receipt, and assignment of slaves: WILLIAM BETSON, JACOB WOOLFORD, THOMAS ELLERY.

Book Ba, p. 68
16 Aug. 1721
Bill of Sale

WILLIAM SINGLETON, planter, of St. George's Parish, Berkeley Co., SC, for "valuable sum of money" sold EDWARD ARDEN, planter, of same place, 1 Negro man. Witnesses: RICHARD BEDON, JOHN ARDEN.

Book Ba, p. 68
13 Aug. 1721
Bond

WILLIAM SINGLETON, planter, St. George's Parish, Berkeley Co., SC, to EDWARD ARDEN, planter, of same place, in penal sum of ₤ 216:10 sh. current SC money, conditioned for payment of ₤ 108 like money on 15 Jan. Witnesses: RICHARD BEDON, JOHN ARDEN. ROBERT YONGE, Register.

Book Ba, p. 69
13 Jan. 1721
Bond & Judgment

WILLIAM SINGLETON, of St. George's Parish, Berkeley Co., SC, authorized THOMAS HEPWORTH, BENJAMIN WHITAKER, & ROBERT HUME, gentlemen, to appear for him at the suit of EDWARD ARDEN, of Berkeley Co., SC, in court of common pleas, Charleston, SC, and confess a judgment "upon a declaration there to be filed against me upon a bond of the penalty of ₤ 216:10:" paid SINGLETON conditioned for payment of ₤ 108, 5 sh. on 15 Jan. 1721, or in merchantable dressed deer skins at 8 sh. 9d. per pd., delivered to him in Charleston. Witnesses: RICHARD BEDON, JOHN ARDEN. ROBERT YONGE, Register.

Book Ba, p. 70   WILLIAM MCPHERSON (MACKPHERSON), planter,

4 Sept. 1721   Colleton Co., SC, bound to THOMAS TOWNSEND,
Bill of Sale   planter, Colleton Co., SC, in penal sum of Ł
                                300 current SC money conditioned for payment
of Ł 150 at sundry times; viz. Ł 50 on Nov. next; Ł 50 in Nov. "next come
a year"; Ł 50 in Nov. "next come 2 years"; and for security delivered 1
slave, 1 horse. Witnesses: GEORGE FORD, WILLIAM HARDEN. ROBERT YONGE,
Register.

Book Ba, p. 72   EBENEZER FORD, to JEREMIAH RUSSELL (RUSSEL),
30 Sept. 1721   for good causes and Ł 681 current SC money,
Deed of Mortgage   250 a. in Berkeley Co., NE on CHARLES HAYES; E
                                on FRANCIS PAGETT (formerly DR. BRENANT); S on
JOHN STONE, SR.; W on WILLIAM POOL. Also 2 Negro men; the condition being that FORD pay Ł 681 due on a bond on which JEREMIAH RUSSELL became
security 1 Mar. next ensuing or pay the sum in a bond of even date. Witnesses: JAMES ROWLAND (ROWLINE), SAMUEL BENNETT. Before JOHN BARKSDALE.
ROBERT YONGE, Register.

Book Ba, p. 74   ROBERT (his mark) SWETMAN (SWETTMAN), planter,
6 Oct. 1721   Berkeley Co., SC, and MARGARET (her mark) his
Bond   wife, to CHARLES HILL, ESQ., of Charleston.
                                Whereas ROBERT SWETMAN by bond of even date is
bound to CHARLES HILL in penal sum of Ł 460 current SC money conditioned
for payment of Ł 230 with interest on 11 Aug. next; now for security SWET-
MAN sells HILL 400 a. English measure, in Berkeley Co., S on Simmons's
Creek; N on said creek, W on SAMUEL COMMANDER, E on RICHARD BERESFORD,
ESQ., granted SWETMAN by Lords Proprs. 10 Dec. 1711. Witnesses: BENJAMIN
WHITAKER, EDWARD EDWARDS. Before WILLIAM BLAKEWEY. ROBERT YONGE, Reg-
ister.

Book Ba, p. 77   GEORGE PETERSON, merchant, of Charleston, and
24 & 25 Sept. 1716   ELIZABETH his wife, to JOHN MOOR, planter, of
L & R   Berkeley Co., SC, part of a town lot (now let
                                to THOMAS CONIERS & DANIEL TOWNSEND), bounding
E 26-1/2 ft. on Bay Street from southernmost jamb of a stack of brick
chimneys to a neighborhood alley; W on alley 119 feet; bounding W on
THOMAS ELLIOTT from street to partition pales; S on land of BENJAMIN
SCHENCKING 16-1/2 ft. as represented in plat drawn above deed of grant of
BENJAMIN SCHENCKING and MARGARET his wife to JOHN FLAVEL. Whereas GEORGE
PETERSON on this date became bound to JOHN MOOR in 7 separate bonds, each
in the penal sum of Ł 300 current SC money, each conditioned for payment
of Ł 150 like money on 25 Dec. in the years 1717, 1718, 1719, 1720, 1721,
1722, 1723; and whereas JOHN FLAVEL, mariner, of Charleston, by will dated 11 Oct. 1710, duly proved and published, amongst other things bequeathed to his daughter ELIZABETH FLAVEL (now wife of GEORGE PETERSON) part of
a lot in Charleston which he purchased from BENJAMIN SCHENCKING, ESQ., of
Berkeley Co., and MARGARET his wife: now, to secure payment of the various bonds (Ł 1050 total) GEORGE PETERSON sells the lot to JOHN MOOR.
Witnesses: JOHN WALLIS, WILLIAM BILLING, DR. WILLIAM CROOK, RICHARD ROWE.
Before THOMAS HEPWORTH. ROBERT YONGE, Register.

Book Ba, p. 87   ELIZABETH PETERSON, wife of GEORGE PETERSON,
26 Sept. 1716   merchant, of Charleston, SC, being privately
Renunciation of Dower   examined by NICHOLAS TROTT, ESQ., Chief Jus-
                                tice of court of common pleas, declared she
voluntarily joined her husband in conveying by L & R, dated 24 & 25 Sept.
1716, to JOHN MOOR of Berkeley Co., SC, part of a town lot (as described
on page 77) and released her right to the lot. ROBERT YONGE, Register.

Book Ba, p. 89   JONATHAN EVANS, cooper, of Berkeley Co., SC,
20 June 1720   sole executor of the will of his father, to
Sale   his younger brother DANIEL EVANS, part of the
                                estate, or 1 Negro woman named MOREAH, "which
slave by her honest industry gotten a sum of money in order to purchase
her freedom"; and for improving his brother's interest JONATHAN made an
agreement with the slave MOREAH that for Ł 90 current SC money he would
set her free. Witnesses: WILLIAM HOLMES, BENJAMIN STILES. Before THOMAS
HEPWORTH. ROBERT YONGE, Register.

Book Ba, p. 91   WILLIAM TRYON, SR., merchant, of London, executor of will of ROWLAND TRYON, merchant, appointed WILLIAM RHETT SR. and WILLIAM RHETT JR. OF SC, his attorneys to sue ALEXANDER SKENE and the executors of COL. GEORGE LOGAN for all debts due him on the balance of any account either in his own right or as executor of estate of ROWLAND TRYON, or to take mortgages or securities. Witnesses: JACOB SATUR, JOHN SKENE. Before RICHARD ALLEIN ESQ. ROBERT YONGE, Register.

Book Ba, p. 94
2 & 3 July 1721
L & R

SAMUEL PRIOLEAU, jeweler, of Charleston, SC, and MARY MAGDELINE his wife to JOHN LLOYD (LOYD) ESQ. of Charleston, for ₤ 1900 current SC money, part of a town lot #36 in Charleston, bounding E on a street 25 ft; depth E & W 87 feet; butting N on another part of same lot formerly owned by WILLIAM SMITH ESQ; S on land of JOHN FRASIER, formerly of JOSEPH ELLIOTT, planter. And as there is reason to believe that the chief messuage or dwelling on the lot, built by SAMUEL PRIOLEAU, is built 2 or 3 feet into the Great Street fronting the same, now SAMUEL PRIOLEAU agrees that if the dwelling house or any part of it shall be pulled down or moved he will pay JOHN LLOYD all such damages as may be sustained, excepting the piazza or balcony adjoining the dwelling house for the removal of which he shall not be answerable in any respect whatsoever. Witnesses: RICHARD ALLEIN, WILLIAM BILLING. Before THOMAS HEPWORTH. ROBERT YONGE, Register.

Book Ba, p. 100
23 Dec. 1701
Agreement

ELIZABETH CURTIS, Colleton Co., SC, whereas WILLIAM, Earl of Craven, Palatine, & the Lords Proprs. under the hand of the RT. HON. JOSEPH BLAKE, Propr. & Gov., the HON. JOSEPH MORTON, JAMES MOORE, STEPHEN BULL, & WILLIAM HAWETT on 2 Jan. 1697 granted DANIEL CURTIS (husband of ELIZABETH) 2250 a. English measure in Colleton Co., bounding SE on Wadmelaw River; S & W & N on Toogoodoo Creek; E on CURTIS'S land; and whereas by Act of Parliament ratified at Charleston 16 Nov. 1700 ELIZABETH was given authority to sell her husband's real estate; now, ELIZABETH, for causes and considerations and especially in consideration of a marriage to be made between CHRISTOPHER WILKINSON, planter, of SC, and herself, and because CHRISTOPHER was bound on even date in sum of ₤ 250 payable to LANDGRAVE JOSEPH MORTON for performance of a certain condition; also in consideration of 1 gold guinea paid to ELIZABETH; ELIZABETH assigns to CHRISTOPHER the above 2250 a. Witnesses: JOHN BEAMOUR, JOHN WILLIAMSON, JOSEPH MORTON, JOSEPH RUSSEL. Before ABRAHAM EVE. ROBERT YONGE, Register.

Book Ba, p. 103
23 Dec. 1701
Agreement

ELIZABETH CURTIS, of Colleton Co., to CAPT. CHRISTOPHER WILKINSON, whereas WILLIAM, Earl of Craven, Palatine, & the Lords Proprs., on 10 Jan. 1695 granted ROBERT FENWICK 500 a. in Colleton Co. on N side Wadmelaw River, E on marsh & creeks; W on vacant land, S on marsh & creeks, N on COL. JOSEPH BLAKE, & marsh & creeks: and whereas ROBERT FENWICK on 25 Jan. 1695 sold the land to DANIEL CURTIS; and whereas, ELIZABETH, by Act of Parliament ratified at Charleston 16 Nov. 1700, was given authority to sell her husband's real estate: now ELIZABETH, in consideration of a proposed marriage between CHRISTOPHER WILKINSON, planter, of SC, and herself, and because CHRISTOPHER gave bond on this date to LANDGRAVE JOSEPH MORTON in the amount of ₤ 280 for the performance of a certain condition, and for 1 gold guinea paid ELIZABETH by CHRISTOPHER, ELIZABETH conveyed the 500 a. to CHRISTOPHER. Witnesses: JOHN BEAMOR, JOSEPH MORTON, JOSEPH RUSSEL, JOHN WILLIAMSON. Before ABRAHAM EVE. ROBERT YONGE, Register.

Book Ba, p. 106
20 Oct. 1719
Deed of Gift

ABRAHAM WARNOCK, Berkeley Co., SC, for love & affection gives his son ABRAHAM 500 a. and 7 Negro slaves (1 woman, 5 boys, 1 girl) & 2 horses, either on day of his marriage or day his father dies; but if ABRAHAM should die before marriage, or before his father, the property to return to the father. Signed EBZR (?) WARNOCK. Witnesses: ANDREW WARNOCK, JUDITH (her mark) WARNOCK, JO. CUMING. Before ROBERT KING. ROBERT YONGE, Register.

Book Ba, p. 108
12 Dec. 1721
Bond

JAMES WRIXHAM, planter, Colleton Co., SC, to GEORGE BASSETT, in penal sum of ₤ 190 current money conditioned for payment of ₤ 95 on 1

Mar. next; sold 1 Negro man, and if Negro should die, run away, be disabled, or lost before he come into the possession of GEORGE BASSETT, the loss or damage to be borne by WRIXHAM. Witnesses: JANE WRIXHAM, JOHN (his mark) WARNER. ROBERT YONGE. Register.

Book Ba, p. 110　　　　　JOSEPH WRAGG & JOB ROTHMAHLER, merchants,
21 Nov. 1720　　　　　　THOMAS DYMES, merchant, WILLIAM PLATT, ESQ. &
Bond　　　　　　　　　　JOHN HUTCHINSON, gentleman, all of Charleston,
　　　　　　　　　　　　Berkeley Co., SC, bound to BENJAMIN PHIPPS,
mariner, master of the RAYMOND GALLEY in penal sum of ₤ 4600 of Great Britain, conditioned for payment of ₤ 2300 like money on 1 June 1720. Witnesses: ROBERT HUME, JAMES LYDELL. Before THOMAS HEPWORTH. ROBERT YONGE, Register. Memo on back: "Pay the contents of the within to ROBERT RUDDOCK or order BENJA. PHIPPS. Rec'd. the full contents of this bond ROBT. RUDDOCK. Witness THO. HODGKIN for my mast'r JOHN MEREWETHER." Original presented by SAMUEL WRAGG, merchant, of London, to Ja/bus/ DUNNIDGE, Not. Pub. ROBERT YONGE, Register.

Book Ba, p. 114　　　　　RICHARD (his mark) BALL, planter, Craven Co.,
8 Apr. 1721　　　　　　　SC, for ₤ 300 SC money sold to THOMAS WILKIN-
Sale　　　　　　　　　　SON, planter, Berkeley Co., 500 a. "in the Co.
　　　　　　　　　　　　and Province aforesaid". Witnesses: JOHN DOSSEY, GEORGE MOORE. Before CHARLES COLLETON. ROBERT YONGE, Register.

Book Ba, p. 116　　　　　JOHN DEAR (DARE), cooper, Berkeley Co., SC, to
4 & 5 Jan. 1721　　　　　JOHN SAUNDERS, planter, Berkeley Co., *320 a.
L & R　　　　　　　　　　in Colleton Co.: NE & E & SE on impassible
　　　　　　　　　　　　swamp; W & S on Ashepoo Creek. Witnesses:
ROBERT HUME, SAM. EVELEIGH, JOHN DEAR JR. Before THOMAS HEPWORTH. ROBERT YONGE, Register. (*for ₤ 100 SC money).

Book Ba, p. 121　　　　　JOHN DEAR, cooper, of Charleston, for ₤ 200 SC
4 & 5 Jan. 1721　　　　　money, sold to JOHN SAUNDERS, planter, Berke-
L & R　　　　　　　　　　ley Co., 500 a. in Colleton Co., bounding NE &
　　　　　　　　　　　　NNW on Lalie Creek, SW & S on impassible swamp,
SE on EDWARD DREPER. Witnesses: ROBERT HUME, SAMUEL EVELEIGH, JOHN DEAR JR. Before THOMAS HEPWORTH. ROBERT YONGE, Register.

Book Ba, p. 126　　　　　JOHN SAUNDERS, planter, Berkeley Co., declares
5 Jan. 1721　　　　　　　that ₤ 100 (part of the ₤ 200 mentioned in L &
Deed of Trust　　　　　　R page 121) belonged to THOMAS MOUNTJOY, mer-
　　　　　　　　　　　　chant, of Berkeley Co., and that JOHN SAUNDERS'S name was used only in trust, that the land was bought by SAUNDERS and MOUNTJOY. Witnesses: ROBERT HUME, SAMUEL SLEIGH (?), JOHN DEAR JR.

Book Ba, p. 128　　　　　BENJAMIN GIBBES, Berkeley Co., for ₤ 444 to
18 July 1721　　　　　　 JOHN GIBBES, of same place, 148 a., part of
Deed of Sale　　　　　　 1000 a. first purchased by EDWARD MIDDLETON;
　　　　　　　　　　　　who conveyed it to ROBERT MOLLOCH; who by his attorney conveyed it to MOSES MADINA; who sold it to COL. THOMAS BROUGHTON; who sold it to BENJAMIN GIBBES, party hereto; the 148 a. bounding S & W on part said tract; N on JOHN GIBBES and THOMAS MOORE; E on CAPT. WM. DRY. Witnesses: ANNE SMITH, JOHN HERBERT, JROFF (?) BURROWS. COL. JOHN HERBERT appointed attorney to give possession of the land and possession given in presence of JROFF (?) BURROWS, JOHN MACTEER. Before JOHN BUTLER. ROBERT YONGE, Register.

Book Ba, p. 131　　　　　JONATHAN SKRINE, merchant, & ELIZABETH his
16 Aug. 1721　　　　　　 wife, to the HON. ROBERT JOHNSON ESQ., both of
Mortgage　　　　　　　　 Charleston, for ₤ 300 current SC money, 100 a.
　　　　　　　　　　　　in Berkeley Co., bounding SW on GEORGE CHICKEN; N & E on JOHANNA BAKER; W on DANIEL DEAN; SE on BARNABY BAYLEY, particularly the dwelling house built by JONATHAN SKRINE and appurtenances purchased by SKRINE from BARNABY BAYLEY & MARTHA his wife, but if SKRINE pays JOHNSON ₤ 315 current SC money with interest on 17 Feb. 1721, this agreement to be void. Witnesses: WILLIAM BETSON, JACOB WOOLFORD, THOMAS ELLERY. ROBERT YONGE, Register.

Book Ba, p. 135　　　　　RICHARD BAKER, planter, & ELIZABETH (her mark)
2 January 1720　　　　　 his wife of St. James Goosecreek, Berkeley Co.,

Release   SC, to ROGER MOORE, gentleman, of Goosecreek,
                                  for ₤ 600 current SC money, 616 a. English mea-
sure in Berkeley Co., of which 446 a. were granted 5 May 1717; the other
170 a. being part of a tract of 350 granted THOMAS BAKER on same date;
bounding S on LANDGRAVE THOMAS SMITH & JOHN MOORE; E on MEBSHOE; N on
JOHN WARE & WIDOW BAKER; W on J. SKRINE. ELIZABETH BAKER freely surrendered all her right & title to the land. Witnesses: JOHN VICARIDGE, ROW-
LAND HILDERSLEY, JOHN MOORE. Before THOMAS HEPWORTH. ROBERT YONGE, Register.

Book Ba, p. 138   JOHN LUCAS, ESQ. of Island of Antigua revokes
2 Dec. 1721   power of attorney given JOHN HOWES, gentleman,
Changing Attorneys   of SC, for that he "behaved himself greatly to
                                  my hindrance" and appoints the HON. ALEXANDER
SKENE ESQ. in his place to administer his property in SC. Witnesses:
JOSEPH FOYE, commander of the Pheasant, & AMOS WADLAND. FRANCIS YONGE,
Register.

Book Ba, p. 140   FRANCIS LESCOTT (FRANCOISE L'ESCOTT) of
21 June 1720   Charleston, wife of PAUL L'ESCOTT, clerk, form-
Letter of Attorney   erly of Charleston now of Dover, Co. Kent, Eng-
                                  land, appoints in her stead PETER MANIGAULT,
victualer, of Charleston, PAUL L'ESCOTT on Feb. 1718 appointed his wife
FRANCIS his attorney to administer & dispose of his estate in SC, & she
appoints MANIGAULT. Witnesses: WILLIAM BILLING, TIFFORD ATTWELL. Before
SAMUEL EVELEIGH. ROBERT YONGE, Register.

Book Ba, p. 142   NATHANIEL FORD (FOARD), planter, of Berkeley
5 Feb. 1721   Co., SC, to RICHARD SPLATT, merchant, of
Mortgage   Charleston, for ₤ 129:2:6 current SC money, 1
                                  Negro man, 1 Negro woman, conditioned for pay-
ment of above sum with interest on 16 Oct. 1722. Witnesses: ROBERT JOHN-
STON, ROBERT HUME. *ROBERT YONGE, Register. *Before WILLIAM BLAKEWAY.

Book Ba, p. 144   JACOB SATUR, merchant, of Berkeley Co., SC, to
28 Mar. 1721   JOSIAH OSGOOD, house carpenter, for ₤ 331:5:0
Bargain & Sale   current SC money, 132-½ a. English measure,
                                  part of Ashley Barony granted the RT. HON. AN-
THONY LORD ASHLEY Earl of Shaftsbury on 18 Mar. 1675 & afterwards granted
to the HON. MAURICE ASHLEY by his brother ANTHONY LORD ASHLEY Earl of
Shaftsbury grandson of the first ANTHONY 12 JULY 1698 & granted by MAU-
RICE to SAMUEL WRAGG, merchant of London in 1717. WRAGG conveyed 3000 a.
to JACOB SATUR 6 Aug. 1720, & now SATUR sells 132½ a. bounding NE on
MICHAEL BACON; SE on WILLIAM WALLACE; SW on SAMUEL CLERK; NW on THOMAS
BAKER; the whole lot of 920 acres having been surveyed by MAJOR JOHN HER-
BERTT 5 Jan. 1718. Witnesses: THOMAS WARING, WILLIAM WALLACE, PETER
GOLDING. Before THOMAS SATUR. ROBERT YONGE, Register.

Book Ba, p. 147   COL. ALEXANDER MACKEY, gentleman, to WILLIAM
26 Feb. 1721/2   FOSTER, both of Charleston, for ₤ 203, 1 Negro
Bill of Sale   woman & her 3 children conditioned for payment
                                  of ₤ 203 on 26 June 1722. Witnesses: JOHN
LANG, JOHN CONN, PROVIDENCE DICKS. Before JOHN BARKSDALE. ROBERT YONGE,
Register.

Book Ba, p. 149   ALEXANDER MACKEY 450 a. to DANIEL DICKS for ₤
22 Feb. 1721   450. Whereas WILLIAM, Earl of Craven, Pala-
Release   tine & the Lords Proprs. on 1 June 1709 grant-
                                  ed said ROBERT POWELL, tailor, 450 a. English
measure in Granville Co., on Port Royall Island bounding N on RICHARD
HAZARD; E on THOMAS & JOSEPH PARMENTER; S & W on marshes & creeks; POWELL
sold to ALEXANDER MACKEY for ₤ 45; now ALEXANDER MACKEY conveys to DANIEL
DICKS. Witnesses: JAMES RAWLINGS, THOMAS (his mark) STONE, JAMES BAL-
NEAVIS (?). Before JOHN BARKSDALE. ROBERT YONGE, Register.

Book Ba, p. 151   GERRARD (GEORGE ?) MONGER, gentleman, & JANE
8 & 9 Feb. 1721   his wife, of Berkeley Co., SC, to JOHN WATKIN-
L & R   SON, mariner, of London now residing in
                                  Charleston for ₤ 150 current SC money, the
northern half of lot #77 in Charleston formerly given by ROBERT GIBBES to

22

JAMES STANYARN, former husband of JANE in exchange for another lot and willed to JANE by STANYARN; bounding E on a street parallel with Cooper River; W on a marsh; N on MRS. WILLIS'S lot; S on other half of lot. Witnesses: BENJAMIN WHITAKER, JOHN LAURENCE, ROBERT HUME, ROBERT YONGE, Register.

Book Ba, p. 156
25 & 26 Jan. 1721
L & R

JOHN DUNSTON by his attorneys LANDGRAVE THOMAS SMITH & JACOB SATUR, merchants, to JOHN WATKINSON, mariner, of London, now residing in Charleston, SC, for Ł 380 current SC money, 1/2 of a lot in Charleston, bounding N on WILLIAM WEEKLEY; S on BENJAMIN GODDING; W on MRS. ELEANOR WRIGHT; E on street leading from Ashley River to the new church now building. JOHN DUNSTON, merchant, of London was eldest son & heir of JOHN DUNSTON, merchant, of Tower Hill, London (the father being only brother and heir of WILSON DUNSTON, merchant, of Charleston, SC). On 14 Sept. 1720 JOHN DUNSTON, the son, party hereto, by letter of attorney signed in London in the presence of RICHARD WISE Notary & Tabellion Public appointed LANDGRAVE THOMAS SMITH & JACOB SATUR his attorneys in SC to sell a lot in Charleston which he owned as heir of WILSON DUNSTON. Witnesses: JAMES KINLOCK, ROBERT BREWTON, ROBERT HUME, THOMAS HEPWORTH.

Book Ba, p. 161
23 & 24 Mar. 1721
L. Mortgage

PETER POITEVANT, planter, & SUSANNA (her mark), his wife of Berkeley Co., to JOHN BRETON, merchant, of Charleston, 3 tracts of land; viz. 150 a. (part of 300 a.), on SE side of Cooper River "within land" bounding SE on JONATHAN RUSS; NE, NW, & SW on DANIEL TREZEVANT; the other 150 a. having been sold by PETER POITEVINT to his brother ANTHONY POITEVINT. Also 600 a. English measure, an inland plantation in Berkeley Co., bounding S on large swamp at head of Wando River; E & N on SOLOMON BRUMMER; W on ANTHONY BONNEAU. Also 92 a. on SE side of Cooper River, inland, (part of 530 a. belonging to DANIEL TREZEVANT) bounding NW on CORNELIUS PRANPAIN; SW on PETER POITEVINT; NE on DANIEL TREZEVANT (see plat annexed to conveyance made by DANIEL TREZEVANT & SUSANNA his wife to PETER POITEVINT). Whereas the HON. JAMES MOORE, ESQ., Gov., LANDGRAVE JOSEPH MORTON, LANDGRAVE EDMUND BELLINGER & COL. ROBERT DANIEL ESQ. appointed by JOHN EARL of Bath Palatine & the Lords Proprs. on 6 Apr. 1703 granted PETER POITEVINT 300 a. in Berkeley Co. (recorded 18 Feb. 1708 in Book CF fol 79); and PETER granted 150 a. to his brother JONATHAN POITEVINT; and whereas the HON. SIR NATHANIEL JOHNSON, Knight, Gov., JAMES MOORE & NICHOLAS TROTT, commissioners appointed by his excellency JOHN LORD Granville, Palatine & the Lords Proprs. on 5 May 1704 granted PETER POITEVINT 600 a. English measure at head of Wando River (registered in C fol 300); and whereas DANIEL TREZEVANT & SUSANNA his wife on 17 June 1707 by their deed of feoffment registered in Book C. fol. 4 reciting that his excellency JOHN LORD Granville, Palatine & the Lords Proprs. on 7 Dec. 1703 had granted them 530 a. in Berkeley Co. (see above) for Ł 39 sold 92 a. (part of the 530 a.) to PETER POITEVINT; and whereas PETER POITEVINT on 15 Mar. 1721 gave JOHN BRETON 4 bonds, each in penal sum of Ł 1264:19:8 current SC money & each conditioned for payment of Ł 632:9:10 with interest at house of JOHN BRETON in Charleston on 15 Mar. of the years 1722, 1723, 1724, & 1725 respectively; now to become payment of the 4 bonds POITEVINT conveys to BRETON the 3 tracts of land and delivers to him 6 Negro men & 4 Negro women. Should POITEVINT pay the above obligations the bargain sale to be void should any payment be defaulted to sale to become effective immediately PETER POITEVINT promises that SUSANNA will release her dower before the HON. CHARLES HILL, C.J. of Court of Common Pleas within 6 months. Witnesses: RICHART ALLEIN, WILLIAM BILLING, JOHN METHERINGHAM. ROBERT YONGE, Register.

Book Ba, p. 174
2 Apr. 1722
Bond & Mortgage

JOHN BEAMOR, planter, of Colleton Co. to FRANCIS HOLMES SR. & FRANCIS HOLMES JR., whereas JOHN BEAMOR had given FRANCIS HOLMES SR. & the penal sum of Ł 1100 current money conditioned for the payment of Ł 550 on 1 Feb. 1722/3; for security delivered to FRANCIS HOLMES SR. & FRANCIS HOLMES JR. 5 Negro men. If any of the Negroes should happen to die, run away, be disabled or lost, before coming to the hands of HOLMES SR. & HOLMES JR. the loss to be borne by BEAMOR. Witnesses: WILLIAM SCOTT, JOHN ELLIS. ROBERT YONGE, Register.

Book Ba, p. 176　　　　　　JOHN BEAMOR, Colleton Co., to FRANCIS HOLMES
2 Apr. 1722　　　　　　　　SR. & FRANCIS HOLMES JR., merchants, in
Bond　　　　　　　　　　　　Charleston, in penal sum of ₤ 1100 current SC
　　　　　　　　　　　　　　money conditioned for payment of ₤ 550 like
money on 1 Feb. 1722/3. Witnesses: WILLIAM SCOTT, JOHN ELLIS. ROBERT
YONGE, Register.

Book Ba, p. 177　　　　　　NATHANIEL ADAMS, mariner, of Falmouth, England
22 Mar. 1721　　　　　　　 to RICHARD CAPERS, Berkeley Co., SC in trust
Deed of Trust　　　　　　 for 5 shillings & natural love and affection
　　　　　　　　　　　　　　which NATHANIEL bears towards ELIZABETH ADAMS,
widow of DAVID ADAMS (NATHANIEL'S brother) & for other considerations,
NATHANIEL grants RICHARD CAPERS, 3 houses; 1 being on the whart in
Charleston, New England, late belonging to 1 Lord & since recovered by
due course of law by NATHANIEL; 1 at the north end of Charleston, New
England, adjoining a house occupied by ELIAS STONE; another house near
the Fisherman's Strand in Falmouth, Co. Cornwall, England, and all the
appurtenances to the 3 houses; upon the special trust that RICHARD CAPERS
shall permit NATHANIEL ADAMS to take 1/2 the rents, issues & profits
accruing from the 3 houses during the term of his natural life; and upon
trust that RICHARD CAPERS shall permit ELIZABETH ADAMS to receive the
other half of the rents issues & profits from the 3 houses for the term
of her natural life; and also upon the special trust that at the decease
of NATHANIEL ADAMS, RICHARD CAPERS shall convey the 3 houses and all his
interest & claim to ELIZABETH ADAMS; but should ELIZABETH die before NA-
THANIEL then RICHARD CAPERS shall receive 1/2 the rents, etc., during the
life of NATHANIEL for the use of the surviving children of ELIZABETH,
share & share alike. At the death of both NATHANIEL & ELIZABETH, the
houses to be sold & the money divided equally amongst ELIZABETH'S children. For the further consideration of 5 shillings NATHANIEL gives CAPERS
all his plate, jewels, money, goods, chattles & all his personal estate
in trust; CAPERS to permit NATHANIEL to have 1/2 during his natural life;
CAPERS to have the other half delivered to ELIZABETH. Witnesses: MARTHA
LOGAN, WILLIAM BLAKEWAY. Before JOHN BARKSDALE. ROBERT YONGE, Register.

Book Ba, p. 180　　　　　　WILLIAM WALKER, for love & natural affection
7 Mar. 1721　　　　　　　　towards his daughter-in-law MARY EVANS, spin-
Deed of Trust　　　　　　 ster, & for her maintenance & education & for
　　　　　　　　　　　　　　5 shillings paid by CAPT. NATHANIEL PARTRIDGE,
gentleman, all of Charleston, & for other considerations, WALKER delivers
to PARTRIDGE 1 Indian girl, 2 feather beds, blankets, pillows, curtains,
valences, 6 rush bottomed chairs with black frames, 1 looking glass, 1
large hair trunk in trust for MARY EVANS. Witnesses: JOHN BROWN, REBECCA
CORBEN. ROBERT YONGE, Register.

Book Ba, p. 181　　　　　　WILLIAM RHETT, JR., merchant, of Charleston,
28 Mar. 1719　　　　　　　 appointed his loving father COL. WM. RHETT his
Power of Attorney　　　　 attorney to collect debts, enter suit for re-
　　　　　　　　　　　　　　covery, etc. Witnesses: ROBERT HUME, RICHARD
ROWE, GEORGE HOSE (HOW ?). ROBERT YONGE, Register.

Book Ba, p. 182　　　　　　WILLIAM ELLIOTT, planter, of Berkeley Co. &
5 May 1722　　　　　　　　 CATHERINE his wife to THOMAS KIMBERLY, chair-
Deed of Feoffment　　　　 master & ISABEL his wife, of Charleston, for ₤
　　　　　　　　　　　　　　400 current SC money part of lot #10 in
Charleston fronting 20 on Callibeufs Lane; W on WILLIAM ELLIOTT; E on
THOMAS ELLIOTT; S 87 feet for the term of their lives & afterwards to
their daughter ANNA GOOLE. Witnesses: CAPT. THOMAS FLEMING, DANIEL TOWN-
SEND. Before CHARLES HILL, C.J. ROBERT YONGE, Register.

Book Ba, p. 184　　　　　　TOBIAS FITCH, gentleman, & MARIANA his wife to
26 & 27 Mar. 1722　　　　 GEORGE SMITH ESQ. all of Berkeley Co. for ₤
L & R　　　　　　　　　　　1500 current SC money, that is to say, ₤ 1200
　　　　　　　　　　　　　　paid to BENJAMIN DELA CONSEILLERY & BENJAMIN
GODDING (GODDEN), merchants, of Charleston, attorneys for JOHN COMBES,
mariner, of London, being the principal & interest due on a mortgage made
to him by TOBIAS FITCH on the plantation & dwelling house; ₤ 300 residue
paid to FITCH, 973 a. where TOBIAS FITCH lives, on N side Ashley River,
bounding SW on Ashley River; SE on JOHN STOCKS; NE on GEORGE SMITH (formerly SUSANNA FITCH, widow); NW on HENRY WOOD; the tract being in several

plots devised to TOBIAS by his father JONATHAN FITCH. Witnesses: GARRATT VANVELSIN, THOMAS SMITH JR., JONATHAN FITCH, THOMAS ELLERY. ROBERT YONGE, Register.

Book Ba, p. 189 SUSANNA (her mark) FITCH, widow, of Charleston
26 & 27 Mar. 1722 of the 1st part; JONATHAN FITCH, planter, &
L & R, Tripartite ANNE (ANNETTE) his wife, of Berkeley Co., of
the 2nd part; & GEORGE SMITH, ESQ. of the 3rd part. SUSANNA FITCH & JONATHAN FITCH to GEORGE SMITH 93½ (33½) a. in Berkeley Co., occupied by JONATHAN FITCH for Ŀ 160 current money (that is, Ŀ 20 each to SUSANNA & JONATHAN) bounding NW on JOHN STOCKS; E on GEORGE SMITH; S on Ashley River; N on a path or roadway. Whereas JONATHAN FITCH, husband of SUSANNA, & father of this JONATHAN by will 4 Nov. 1715 gave his wife SUSANNA & son JOSEPH (after several bequest) the residue of his real & personal estate to be divided between them; and whereas JOSEPH, & his wife CONSTANT, on 11 Oct., 1721 sold to JONATHAN FITCH 16 3/4 a. (formerly belonging to EDWARD JOHNSON, now to JOSEPH FITCH being part of the real estate willed to JOSEPH by his father and being half of the 33½ a. now conveyed to GEORGE SMITH by SUSANNA & JONATHAN) bounding NW on JOHN STOCKS; E on GEORGE SMITH; S on Ashley River. Witnesses to SUSANNA FITCH'S signature: GARRATT VANVELSIN, THOMAS ELLERY. Witnesses to JONATHAN & ANNE FITCH'S signatures: GARRATT VANVELSIN, THOMAS SMITH JR., THOMAS ELLERY. Witnesses to SUSANNAS receipt: GARRATT VANVELSIN, THOMAS CAPERS, THOMAS ELLERY. ROBERT YONGE, Register.

Book Ba, p. 193 RICHARD GODFREY, planter, & SUSANNA his wife
3 Jan. 1721 of Berkeley Co., to WILLIAM HENDRICK, house
Bill of Sale carpenter, of Colleton Co. for 226 a. assign
to HENDRICK 300 a. on E side South Edisto River; bounding S & N on RICHARD GODFREY; E on vacant land; W on Ponpon. Witnesses: JAMES WRIXHAM, GEORGE HAMLIN. Before JOHN JACKSON. ROBERT YONGE, Register.

Book Ba, p. 195 RICHARD GODFREY, planter, of Berkeley Co., to
3 Jan. 1721 WILLIAM HENDRICK, house carpenter, of Colleton
Bond Co., in the full sum of Ŀ 1000 current SC money. Whereas GODFREY sold HENDRICK 300 a. on E side South Edisto River, now if the house, land, etc., are on this date free from all debts & charges, this obligation to be void. Witnesses: JAMES WRIXHAM, GEORGE HAMLIN. Before J. JACKSON. ROBERT YONGE, Register.

Book Ba, p. 196 WILLIAM LIVINGSTON, clerk, & HANNAH, his wife
(?) Mar. 1719 of Charleston to JOHN SMELIE, planter, of Col-
Release leton Co., for Ŀ 700 current SC money, 400 a.
on E side of the freshes of Edisto commonly called Drumhall, 200 a. of which LIVINGSTON purchased from RICHARD EDGELL, & the other 200 a. from WILLIAM MEGGETT; bounding part on New London, part on MEGGETTS land. HANNAH renounced all her interest & claim. Witnesses: LAWRENCE DENNIS, JOHN EDWARDS. Before JOHN BARKSDALE. ROBERT YONGE, Register.

Book Ba, p. 198 THOMAS (his mark) ELLIS, cordwainer, & JULIANA
12 Apr. 1722 his wife, to JOHN WRITTER (WITTER ?) cooper,
Bill of Sale for Ŀ 332 current SC money, 150 a. on James
Island in Berkeley Co.; bounding N part on JOHN CLAPP part on EDWARD DRAKE; S on ROBERT GOFF; E on JAMES WRITTER; W on HENRY THOMAS. JULIANA freely & willingly surrenders her right of dower. Whereas JOSEPH BLAKE, Gov., & the Lords Proprs. granted JOHN ELLIS 150 a., English measure in Berkeley Co.; & whereas JOHN ENGLISH on 6 May 1699 for Ŀ 25 currency sold the 150 a. to JOANNA, widow of ROBERT COLE; and whereas ROBERT COLE, eldest son & heir of JOANNA, for Ŀ 25 current SC money on 31 Jan. 1707/8 sold the 150 a. to THOMAS ELLIS; now ELLIS sells to WRITTER. Witnesses: JOHN SANDIFORD, SAMUEL WRITTER. Before JOHN BARKSDALE. ROBERT YONGE, Register.

Book Ba, p. 201 JOHN (his mark) KING, planter, & VIOLETTA, his
26 Jan. 1721/2 wife, of James Island, Berkeley Co., to JOHN
Deed of Sale SANDIFORD, hatmaker, for Ŀ 34:17:6 currency
15½ a. (part of 150 a.) on James Island; bounding N on part of the 150 a. sold to JOSEPH RIVERS; E on another part of

the 150 a. still owned by KING; S & W partly on marsh, partly on JOHN SAN-
DIFORD. Whereas FRANCIS MARSEAU, widow, by will dated 12 June 1708 be-
queathed to DANIEL QUINTARD 150 a. on James Island; and whereas DANIEL
QUINTARD for ₤ 50 currency sold JOHN KING the 150 a. (plat certified by
JAMES WRITTER, surveyor, 16 Feb. 1692). Now KING sells to SANDIFORD.
Witnesses: JOHN WRITTER, ELIZABETH (her mark) GANTLETT, JAMES WRITTER.
Before JOHN BARKSDALE. ROBERT YONGE, Register.

Book Ba, p. 203
11 Apr. 1722
Deed of Gift

MARIAN, (her mark) GANTLETT, widow, of James Island for natural love & affection to her daughter ELIZABETH, wife of JEREMIAH RIVERS, planter, & for other considerations 50 a. on
James Island bounding W on JOHN ELLIS; E on other half of 100 a.; S on a
marsh of the Great Sound; N on a Savanna. After death of ELIZABETH the
land to go to her son ROBERT RIVERS; should ROBERT die without heirs,
then to her 2 daughters SARAH & ELIZABETH RIVERS. Delivery by turf &
twig. Whereas JOSEPH BLAKE, Gov., LANDGRAVE JOSEPH MORTON, EDMUND BELL-
INGER, & JAMES MOORE, ESQS., on 17 Aug. 1700 for ₤ 2, granted MARIAN GANT-
LETT 100 a. on James Island, Berkeley Co.; now MARIAN GANTLETT gives
daughter ELIZABETH RIVERS the western half of the 100 a. Witnesses: JOHN
WITTER (swore by affirmation, not by book), SAMUEL WITTER. Before JOHN
BARKSDALE. ROBERT YONGE, Register.

Book Ba, p. 204
2 Mar. 1721/2
Mortgage

ROBERT WILKINSON, planter, of Granville Co.,
to WILLIAM GIBBON, ₤ 126 SC money, 700 a. in
2 tracts; 1 being 500 a., the other 200 a., on
Wimbee Island Granville Co. Whereas the HON.
WILLIAM BULL ESQ. of Berkeley Co., on 2 Mar. 1721 sold to ROBERT WILKIN-
SON 500 a. in Granville Co. on Wimbee Island, Walnut Bluff, bounding S on
a creek & on all other sides on vacant land; & whereas THOMAS DAWES, of
Granville Co. on 16 July 1711 sold to ROBERT WILKINSON 500 a. in Granville Co. on Wimbee Island, bounding NE on the land purchased from WIL-
LIAM BULL & on all other sides on vacant land; and whereas ROBERT WILKIN-
SON by L & R sold to the HON. WILLIAM GIBBON, of Charleston, 300 a, (being the westernmost part of the 500 a. purchased from THOMAS DAWES) bounding E on the other part of the 500 a. & divided from it by a line running
30° to the westward of the north 1 & 20 chain distant in a right line
from the corner of said 500 a. next the house of ROBERT WILKINSON; E on
WILLIAM GIBBON; S on a marsh & creek out of Beaufort River; and whereas
ROBERT WILKINSON on even date gave bond to WILLIAM GIBBON in the penal
sum of ₤ 250 currency conditioned for payment of ₤ 126 on 2 Mar. 1722;
now, to secure payment, WILKINSON sells GIBBON the 500 a. purchased from
WILLIAM BULL on Wimbee Island; also 200 a. on Wimbee Island (being the
remaining part of 500 a. purchased from THOMAS DAWES); upon the condition
that if WILKINSON pays GIBBON ₤ 126 with interest on 2 Mar. 1722 this
deed to be void. Witnesses: JOHN CROFT, EDWARD CROFT. Before CHARLEST
HART. ROBERT YONGE, Register.

Book Ba, p. 207
19 July 1721
Power of Attorney

GEORGE (his mark) MONTGOMERY of NC gives his
wife ELIZABETH power of attorney to handle his
land, cattle, goods, etc., in NC. Witnesses:
BOYFIELD PLUMBE, MARY PLUMBE.

Book Ba, p. 207
1 Feb. 1721
Deed of Sale, Tripartite

EDWARD WEEKLEY, planter, of Berkeley Co., of
1st part; ROBERT HUME, gentleman, of Charleston, of 2nd part; SAMUEL EVELEIGH, merchant,
of Charleston, of 3rd part. EDWARD WEEKLEY
for ₤ 100 SC money sells to ROBERT HUME lot #311 (part of the square lot
#97 taken up by JOHN ARCHDALE) free of any title of dower of WEEKLEY'S
late wife; bounding W on MR. SADLER; N on a street leading from Cooper
River by the lots of MAYBANK & PENDARVIS; E on a street going from the
market place to the church formerly called new church, now old church; S
on THOMAS CARY. In order that the estate hereby granted may be lawfully
executed WEEKLEY appoints SAMUEL EVELEIGH his attorney to take possession
& deliver to HUME. Witnesses: WILLIAM SKIPPER, ANNE SKIPPER. Possession
taken & delivery made in presence of EDWARD RAWLING. ROBERT YONGE, Register.

Book Ba, p. 210
30 June 1722

JONAS (his mark) NUTTING, joiner, of "Charles
City" & Port to ALEXANDER KINLOCK, merchant,

Bill of Sale   for ₤ 145 current money, 1 Negro man. Witness-
                                es: JOHN BARKSDALE, JOHN WALLIS, JACOB ASHTON.
ROBERT YONGE, Register.

Book Ba, p. 211   WILLIAM SCOTT releases his interest in a mort-
11 Aug. 1722   gage "as to the land". ROBERT YONGE, Register.
Memorandum

Book Ba, p. 211   EDWARD DEARSLEY, son of SUSANNA KURFORD (?) to
20 Sept. 1722   WILLIAM MORALL (MORILL) & WILLIAM LEWIS, plant-
Bill of Sale   ers, of Berkeley Co., for ₤ 100 a certain
                                tract of land about 400 a., left to DEARSLEY
by his father COL. GEORGE DEARSLEY, at head of Wando River, bodering S on
GEORGE SMITH; N on MR. SEALS; with all & singular except the lightwood.
Witnesses: JOHN HALL, JAMES FITZGERALD, JOHN STEVENSON. Before JOHN
BARKSDALE. ROBERT YONGE, Register.

DEEDS BOOK "Bb"
1718-1723

Book Bb, p. 1   PETER VILLEPONTOUX & PETER MANIGAULT, both mer-
1 Feb. 1720   chants of Charleston, (MANIGAULT becoming a
Bond   party at request of VILLEPONTOUX for his debts)
                                to ELIZABETH BURETELL, widow, of Charleston, in
penal sum of ₤ 600 currency conditioned for payment of ₤ 300 with interest on 1 May 1721. To secure MANIGAULT, VILLEPONTOUX gave MANIGAULT a
bond in penal sum of ₤ 600 for payment of ₤ 300 to ELIZABETH BURETELL
with interest at 4% on 1 May to discharge the first bond. Whereas SAMUEL
PRIOLEAU ESQ. on 2 Jan. 1720 gave PETER VILLEPONTOUX a bond in penal sum
of ₤ 2200 for payment of ₤ 1100 (₤ 500 to be paid 30 Apr. next, ₤ 300 on
30 Apr. 1722 with interest at 10%, & ₤ 300 on 30 Apr. 1723 with like interest); and whereas on 3 Jan. 1720 SAMUEL PRIOLEAU & MARY MAGDALEN his
wife, to secure payment of ₤ 1100, conveyed to VILLEPONTOUX 600 a. on W
side Medway River, bounding E on Medway River; W on MRS. DAVIS; widow; N
on a creek & on LANDGRAVE THOMAS SMITH; S on SAMUEL PRIOLEAU; and whereas VILLEPONTOUX, to secure MANIGAULT, agrees to assign to him the 600 a.
& SAMUEL PRIOLEAU'S obligation & all money due thereon, VILLEPONTOUX
appoints PETER MANIGAULT his attorney to receive money due from PRIOLEAU.
VILLEPONTOUX also delivers to MANIGAULT 3 slaves. Witnesses: ANDREW (his
mark) LEGER, ROBERT HUME. ROBERT YONGE, Register.

Book Bb, p. 7   SAMUEL PRIOLEAU ESQ. & MARY MAGDALEN his wife,
3 Jan. 1720   of Charleston to PETER VILLEPONTOUX, gentleman,
Mortgage   of Charleston, 600 a on Medway River. Whereas
                                PRIOLEAU on 2 Jan. 1720 gave VILLEPONTOUX a
bond in penal sum of ₤ 2200 for payment of ₤ 1100 (₤ 500 to be paid 30
Apr. 1721, ₤ 300 on 30 Apr. 1722, & ₤ 300 on Apr. 1723, with interest at
10%), now PRIOLEAU & his wife for security convey to VILLEPONTOUX 600 a.
on W side Medway River, bounding E on Medway River; W on MRS. DAVIS, widow; N on a large creek & LANDGRAVE THOMAS SMITH; S on SAMUEL PRIOLEAU.
PRIOLEAU agrees that within 10 days he will cause MARY MAGDALEN to release all her title of dower before the chief Justice. Witnesses: JAMES
ST. JULIEN, BENJAMIN WHITAKER. ROBERT YONGE, Register.

Book Bb, p. 11   EDWARD RAWLINGS, joiner, & MARY his wife to
7 & 8 Mar. 1721   ROBERT HUME, gentleman, all of Charleston, for
L & R   ₤ 200 current SC money, 1/3 part of 3 lots in
                                Charleston willed by MARY CROSS to WILLIAM
BAILEY, SUSANNA RAWLINGS & MARY BASDEN; fronting N on a street leading E
from Cooper River by MESSRS. GIBBON & ALLEN 2/3 parts of the whole front
of said 3 lots on said street; S on PETER MANIGAULT "as now fenct in" &
on TOBIAS FITCH; W on other parts said 3 lots; E on RICHARD BERESFORD ESQ.
(formerly MR. JACKSON). Witnesses to L & R: ALEXANDER PARRIS, SAMUEL
CREAFORD, CHILDERMUS CROFT. Witnesses to Receipt: EDWARD RAWLINGS, MARY
RAWLINGS, ALEXANDER PARRIS, SAMUEL CREAFORD, CHILDERMUS CROFT. Before
ROBERT YONGE, Register.

Book Bb, p. 15   MARY PARKER, widow, of Berkeley Co., of 1st
21 Aug. 1721   part; WILLIAM GIBBON & ANDREW ALLEN, merchants

Agreement Tripartite. of Charleston, of the 2nd part; JOSEPH MEAD, planter, of Berkeley Co., of the 3rd part. Whereas a marriage is intended between MARY PARKER & JOSEPH MEAD & it is agreed that MARY'S real & personal estate is to be conveyed to GIBBON & ALLEN in trust; now MARY (with JOSEPH'S consent) conveys to GIBBON & ALLEN all her property, also her Negro, Indian & Mulatto slaves, household goods, cattle, plate, plantation tools, etc., upon trust that they will permit MARY to hold the property during her natural life, then to permit SARAH, BENJAMIN, JOSEPH, MARTHA, & JOHN (children of MARY by her former husband) & the future children of MARY & JOSEPH to hold the property; & it agreed that it shall be lawfull for MARY to change or revoke the trust and appointment. JOSEPH MEAD agrees with GIBBON & ALLEN that MARY may make her will & he will assist GIBBON & ALLEN in executing it. Should the marriage not take place this agreement to be void. Witnesses: GEORGE BURNETT, MARY BURNETT. Before THOMAS HEPWORTH. ROBERT YONGE, Register.

Book Bb, p. 20
2 July 1722
Exchange

Agreement (in duplicate) between JOHN GODFREY, ESQ. & BENJAMIN WHITAKER ESQ. & SARAH his wife, all of Berkeley Co., JOHN GODFREY gives BENJAMIN WHITAKER 160 a. English measure, on Ashley River, bounding E on BENJAMIN GODFREY; W & S on CAPT. JOHN WOODWARD; N on marsh. In exchange, BENJAMIN & SARAH WHITAKER give JOHN GODFREY 224 a. on Stono River allotted to SARAH on the division of the lands of CAPT. JOHN GODFREY, her father. One copy signed by JOHN GODFREY, the other copy signed by SARAH WHITAKER & BENJAMIN WHITAKER. Witnesses: RICHARD GODFREY, BENJAMIN GODFREY. ROBERT YONGE, Register.

Book Bb, p. 24
14 Apr. 1722
Protest

In 7th year of the RT. HON. CHARLES of Province of Mary land & Avalon, LORD BARON of Baltimore, etc., JOHN SMITER, commander of the Carolina, galley, JOHN SWAIN, mate, & EDWARD BROWN, boatswain, testified that on Tuesday 27 Mar. last, on their way to SC the ship sprang a leak which they could not stop & they with SAMUEL GREEN, carpenter of the ship, SAMUEL FERRELL, GEORGE WILLIS & JOHN TAYLOR, sailors, MARY WALKER, MARY GRIFFIS & HOVENDEN WALKER passengers put off in the long boat & continued on board until 2 O'clock Sat. aft. Mar. 31 following when they spied the King George, CAPT. JOHN BROWN, commander, who brought them to Chesapeake Bay. Before JOHN BEALE, Dep. Not. Pub. dwelling at Annapolis, & deputed by the HON. PHILEMON LLOYD, ESQ. Dep. Sec'y. & Not. Pub. ROBERT YONGE, Register. JOHN BROWN, commander of the King George of London, & THOMAS TIVETOR, mate, declared that on Sat., Mar. 31, last, on their way to Maryland, a long boat came alongside containing JOHN SMITER, JOHN SWAIN, SAMUEL GREEN, EDWARD BROWN, SAMUEL MERRILL, GEORGE WILLIS, JOHN TAYLOR, MARY WALKER, MARY GRIFFIS & OVENDEN WALKER & they brought them to Chesapeake Bay. Before JOHN BEALE, N.P. ROBERT YONGE, Register.

Book Bb, p. 26
17 July 1722
Deed

Whereas BENJAMIN QUELCH by note dated London 22 Mar. 1702 acknowledged receipt from MRS. MARTHA ATTWOOD of ₤ 170 sterling bearing interest at 5%; & whereas MARTHA ATTWOOD married ISAAC POWELL, tobacconist of Great Marlow, Co. of Bucks, Great Britain who by deed poll 8 May 1717 assigned the note to WILLIAM QUELCH, citizen & draper of London, appointing WILLIAM QUELCH his attorney to demand & take the money & interest & whereas he obtained at Court of Common Pleas at "Charles City" from the HON. CHARLES HILL, ESQ., & his asst. judges, a judgement for ₤ 354:3:0 sterling & costs against ELIZABETH QUELCH & BENJAMIN QUELCH; & whereas ELIZABETH & BENJAMIN suggested ROBERT HUME attorney for WILLIAM certain payments (broken page); now ELIZABETH for securing payment of ₤ 500 & ₤ 400 convey to WILLIAM QUELCH 10 Negroes. Witnesses: WILLIAM BILLING, JOHN WALLIS. ROBERT YONGE, Register.

Book Bb, p. 29
23 & 24 Apr. 1722
L & R & Mortgage

ALEXANDER SKENE, ESQ., & JEMIMA, his wife, of Berkeley Co., SC, to WILLIAM TRYON, merchant, of London, 2700 a. in Berkeley Co., bounding SE on SAMUEL WRAGG, NW on WILLIAM WALLACE: SW on PETER CATTLE (CATTELL?); NE on Ashley River. Whereas SKENE this date gave 2 bonds to TRYON, 1 in penal sum of ₤ 970 sterling of Great Britain for payment of ₤ 485:9:9; with interest at 5% on 27 Apr. 1725; the other for ₤ 970 for payment of ₤ 485 on 27 Apr. 1727; now to secure payment SKENE conveys to TRYON 2700 a. as above & 20 slaves; JEMIMA to appear before the Chief Justice & relinquish her title of dower. Witnesses: JACOB SATUR, ELEASER ALLEN, BENJAMIN WHITAKER. ROBERT YONGE, Register.

Book Bb, p. 39
16 July 1722
Bill of Sale

THOMAS FARR, to ANNE DRAYTON, for ₤ 350 currency 450 a. in Colleton Co. "Whereas on 12 Sept. 1694, the Lords Proprs. for ₤ 70:10 granted MARGARET BREMOR, widow, Colleton Co., 1430 a., English measure; & whereas MARGARET BEAMOR & JACOB BEAMOR on 6 July 1710 sold JOHN BEAMOR 900 a. fronting S on N side Stono River; W on THOMAS FARR; E on JOHN BEAMOR; NW on vacant land; & whereas JOHN BEAMOR & JOHANNA, his wife, on 29 Oct. 1712, for ₤ 400, sold the 900 a. to JOHN WILLIAMSON; & whereas JOHN WILLIAMSON on 16 Feb. 1712, for ₤ 200 sold 450 a. to THOMAS FARR; now FARR conveys 450 a. to ANNE DRAYTON. Witnesses: CHRISTOPHER WILKINSON, RICHARD BUTLER. Before GEORGE SMITH, Asst. Judge of General Court. ROBERT YONGE, Register.

Book Bb, p 42
21 May 1722
Bond

EDWARD CURRENT, of Colleton Co., to JOHN FENWICKE, ESQ., in penal sum of ₤ 400 currency for payment of ₤ 100 currency & 5000 lbs. rice on 1 Jan. 1722, for security delivers 2 Negro men. Witnesses: WILLIAM GIBBES, MARY HOPKINS. Before BENJAMIN WHITAKER. ROBERT YONGE, Register.

Book Bb, p. 44
21 May 1722
Bond

EDWARD CURRENT, tailor of Colleton Co., to JOHN FENWICKE, ESQ. in sum of ₤ 400 SC money for payment of ₤ 100 SC money & 5000 lbs. rice on 1 Jan. 1722. Witnesses: WILLIAM GIBBES, MARY HOPKINS. ROBERT YONGE, Register.

Book Bb, p. 45
25 & 26 Feb. 1721
L & R & Mortgage

ROWLAND STORY, shipwright, & ELIZABETH, his wife of James Island, Berkeley Co., to ARTHUR HALL, planter, of James Island, for ₤ currency, 150 a. part of STORY'S plantation, devised to ELIZABETH by her father JOSEPH ELLIOTT, & adjoining ARTHUR HALL on north, should STORY pay HALL ₤ 500 currency on 27 Feb. 1720 this conveyance to be void. Witnesses: GARRATT VANVELSIN, STEPHEN CLIFFORD, THOMAS ELLERY. Before JOHN FENWICKE, Asst. Judge. ROBERT YONGE, Register.

Book Bb, p. 51
29 Oct. 1719
Bond

ISAAC RAMACK, planter, & MARY, his wife, to SAMUEL DEAN in penal sum of ₤ 218 for payment of ₤ 109 currency with interest; for security deliver 1 Negro man. Witnesses: GILBERT JONES, NEVIL MIDWELL, JOHN CHAMPNEYS. ROBERT YONGE, Register.

Book Bb, p. 53
4 June 1722
Agreement

ALEXANDER PARRIS & JOHN DELA BERE to clear title & ownership in Archers Island, in Port Royall Sound, containing 3020 a. (conveyed by COL. ALEXANDER PARRIS of Charleston, to said ALEXANDER PARRIS & JOHN DELA BERE) without defining exact ownership of each half. Agreed that the half part with all the contiguous broken island next the entrance to Port Royall harbor (1510 a.) should belong to PARRIS, the other half, with contiguous broken islands, to the NW next Beaufort town (1510 a.) should belong to DELA BERE. Witnesses: JOHN BARNWELL, JACOB WRIGHT. ROBERT YONGE, Register.

Book Bb, p. 54
12 Nov. 1722
Mortgage

GEORGE VINSON, planter, of Colleton Co., to WILLIAM FISHBURN, tailor, of Dorchester, Berkely Co., 200 a. on S side Ponpon River, Colleton Co., bounding S on THOMAS ELLIOTT, SR.; W on GEORGE VINSON; N on MR. WOTT (?); E on MOSES MARTIN; also 5 slaves; also all his stock of neat cattle horses & hoggs. Should VINSON pay FISHBURN ₤ 400 currency on 12 Nov. 1724 this mortgage to be void. Witnesses: JACOB GENT, THOMAS OSGOOD JR., ROBERT WILLSON. Before WILLIAM WALLACE. ROBERT YONGE, Register.

Book Bb, p. 56
10 Oct. 1722
Bill of Sale

GEORGE SMITH, planter, of Berkeley Co., to JAMES MACKEWN, of "Charles City", whereas SMITH this date gave bond to MACKEWN in penal

sum of Ł 100 currency conditioned for payment of Ł 50 on 1 Dec. 1724 with
interest at 10%, now for security, SMITH delivers to MACKEWN 1 Negro woman & 1 Negro man. Witnesses: WILLIAM LOUGHTON, SAMUEL SMITH. ROBERT
YONGE, Register.

Book Bb, p. 58   GEORGE SMITH, planter, of Berkeley Co., to
10 Oct. 1722   JAMES MACKEWN, gentleman, of "Charles City" in
Bond   penal sum of Ł 100 currency conditioned for
                        payment of Ł 50 with interest, on 1 Dec. 1724.
Witnesses: WILLIAM LOUGHTON, SAMUEL SMITH. ROBERT YONGE, Register.

Book Bb, p. 59   JOSEPH WRAGG & JOB ROTHMAHLER, merchants, THOM-
21 Nov. 1720   AS DYMES, merchant, WILLIAM RHETT, ESQ., &
Bond (copy)   JOHN HUTCHINSON, gentleman, to BENJAMIN PHIPPS
                        residing in Charleston, mariner, & commander
of the RAYMOND, galley, in penal sum of Ł 3000 of Great Britain, conditioned for payment of Ł 1500 on 1 June 1722. Witnesses: ROBERT HUME,
JAMES LEYDELL, JOHN MEREWETHER. Before THOMAS HEPWORTH. JOHN CROFT,
Register. "Pay the contents of the within to NOBLEST RUDDOCK or order.
BENJAMIN PHIPPS". "Pay the contents of the within to CAPT. JAS. DAY or
order. No: RUDDOCK". "Pay the contents to MESSRS. HERON & Company, it's
mine, JAMES DAY." On (June 1722 SAMUEL WRAGG paid Ł 1500 to in full of
bond to JOHN HERON CO. & GEORGE ARNOLD.

Book Bb, p. 60   JOSEPH WRAGG & JOB ROTHMAHLER, merchants, THOM-
21 Nov. 1720   AS DYMES, merchant, WILLIAM RHETT, ESQ., &
Bond (Copy)   JOHN HUTCHINSON, gentleman, all of Charleston,
                        to BENJAMIN PHIPPS, mariner & commander of The
Raymond, galley, now residing in Charleston, in penal sum of Ł 3000 of
Great Britain, conditioned for payment of Ł 1500 on 1 Aug. 1722. Wit-
nesses: ROBERT HUME, JAMES LEYDELL. Before THOMAS HEPWORTH. SAMUEL
WRAGG'S signature witnessed in London by THOMAS HODGKINS. ROBERT YONGE,
Register. PHIPPS assigns his interest in the Lord ("being the remainder
& in full for a cargo of slaves") to NOBLEST RUDDOCK. RUDDOCK assigns
his interest to GEORGE ARNOLD. Witnesses to both assignments: RICHARD
BUTLER, THOMAS CROGAN. ARNOLD received Ł 1500 in full. The 2 foregoing
copies produced by SAMUEL WRAGG, merchant, of London, were attested in
London 21 Sept. 1722 before JACOBUS DUNNIDGE, N.P. ROBERT YONGE, Register.

Book Bb, p. 62   MARY MEADE, widow, to WILLIAM GIBBON & ANDREW
6 Aug. 1722   ALLEN, in trust for JOSEPH MEADE, whereas by
Deed of Trust   indenture tripartite on 21 Aug. 1721 between
                        MARY MEADE (by the name of MARY PARKER, of
Berkeley Co.) widow, of the 1st. part; GIBBON & ALLEN, merchants, of
Charleston, of 2nd part; & JOSEPH MEADE of 3rd part; reciting that a marriage was intended between MARY & JOSEPH; & whereas MARY (with JOSEPH as
party thereto) conveyed to GIBBON & ALLEN, in trust all her real estate,
her Negro, Indian & Mulatto slaves, & all her personal estate, household
goods, cattle, tools, etc., for the use of MARY during her life, & afterwards to SARAH, BENJAMIN, JOSEPH, MARTHA, & JOHN (children of MARY by her
first husband) & to such children as MARY & JOSEPH may have, with the
proviso that MARY may revoke such trust; now MARY, by power of this proviso, does revoke the trust & conveys all her real & personal property to
GIBBON & ALLEN in trust for JOSEPH MEADE. Witnesses: THOMAS BULLING,
JOHN STORY, THOMAS SPARKES. Before BENJAMIN WHITAKER. ROBERT YONGE,
Register.

Book Bb, p. 67   MARY (her mark) DANFORTH, spinster, of Newbury,
26 Oct. 1722   Essex Co., Massachusetts, appointed her trusty
Power of Attorney   friend, CAPT. RICHARD THOMAS, commander of The
                        Hawk, brigantine, her attorney. Witnesses:
PHILIP MARETT, HENRY ARBURY, mariners of The Hawk. Before EDWARD HUTCHIN-
SON, J.P. of Suffolk. Before JOHN BARKSDALE of Charleston, SC. ROBERT
YONGE, Register.

Book Bb, p. 69   "Memorandum that entry was made that on Thurs-
                        day the 17 of Jan. 1722 THOMAS GREEN ye son of
DAN'LL GREEN, merchant and ELIZABETH his wife was baptized; whose sure-
ties JANE BUCKALL and ROBT. YONGE. Born the 6th Nov.". ROBERT YONGE,

Register.

Book Bb, p. 70 DANIEL GIBSON, surgeon, of Charleston, ap-
9 Jan. 1722 points his truste friend HENRY PALMER, mer-
Power of Attorney chant, of London, his attorney, to collect
from the commissioners appointed for the care
of the sick & hurt seamen the money due him for his care & maintenance of
the sick & wounded seamen of HMS The Greyhound by order of CAPT. EDWARD
SMITH, commander of The Greyhound. Witnesses in SC: RICHARD QUICK, THOM-
AS COLE, ROBERT YONGE, Register. Memo: 4 sick tickets for sick & wounded
men put ashore at Charleston for cure & quarters to MR. DANIEL GIBSON,
City Chirurgeon, listed the following: JAMES CRIGHTON, a fever. JAMES
MORRICE, left leg shot & fracture of right arm. RICHARD WOODMAN, shot
through left leg. ROBERT BRADLEY, shot through left arm. WILLIAM RICH-
ARDSON, incised wound on metacarpal. GEORGE WELCH, wounds in body & arms.
THOMAS PETTY, wound in head. THOMAS HAYNES, wounds in head & right arm.
WILLIAM TILBURN, wound in elbow. GEORGE WATTS, wound in cheek. LEWES
JOYCE blown up with gun powder. JOHN GUNSTON shot through right arm.
EDWARD JONES, bloody flux. RICHARD FRENCH, a fever.

Book Bb, p. 72 JOHN DELA BERE, merchant, to ALEXANDER PARRIS,
27 Dec. 1722 ESQ., all of Charleston, 1375 a. on Archers
Mortgage Island & 5 Negroes, & his cattle as security
on joint bonds to JOB ROTHMAHLER, merchant.
Whereas PARRIS & DELA BERE'S debts, gave 2 bonds to JOB ROTHMAHLER, merchant, of Charleston, both in penal sum of L 1200 SC money conditioned
for payment of L 600 with interest; 1 on 27 Mar. 1723, the other on 27
Sept. 1723; & whereas DELA BERE gave 2 counter bonds to PARRIS in L 2400
for payment of said L 600 each, acquitting PARRIS; now, for security,
DELA BERE leases to PARRIS 1375 a. or half part of a Barony formerly belonging to COL. ROBERT DANIEL, known as Archers Island, at mouth of Port
Royal River, Granville Co., being the greatest of the Islands of the Barony; also 1 Negro man, 2 Negro women, 2 Negro girls, & all his horses,
cattle, sheep & swine on the island. Witnesses: JOHN CROFT, ALEXANDER
NISBETT, HILL CROFT, BENJAMIN GODFREY. ROBERT YONGE, Register.

Book Bb, p. 83 JOHN DELA BERE, merchant, to ALEXANDER PARRIS,
31 Dec. 1722 ESQ., both of Charleston, 2 lots in Beaufort.
Mortgage Whereas DELA BERE gave bond this date to
PARRIS in penal sum of L 414 SC money for pay-
ment of L 207 & interest on 28 Mar. 1723, now for security DELA BERE conveys to PARRIS lot # 62 in Beaufort, Granville Co., & the lot # 62 &
premisses fronting the bay where DELA BERE dwells. Witnesses: JOHN CROFT,
ALEXANDER NISBETT, HILL CROFT, BENJAMIN GODFREY. ROBERT YONGE, Register.

Book Bb, p. 89 JOHN DELA BERE, merchant, to ALEXANDER PARRIS,
31 Dec. 1722 ESQ., both of Charleston, in penal sum of L
Bond 414 SC money for payment of L 207 with inter-
est at 10% on 28 Mar. 1723. Witnesses: JOHN
CROFT, ALEXANDER NISBETT, HILL CROFT, BENJAMIN GODFREY. ROBERT YONGE,
Register.

Book Bb, p. 90 JOHN DELA BERE, merchant, to ALEXANDER PARRIS,
26 Dec. 1722 ESQ., both of Charleston, in penal sum of L
Counter Bond 2400 SC money to secure PARRIS who was bound
jointly with DELA BERE to JOB ROTHMAHLER, mer-
chant, of Charleston in L 1200 conditioned for payment of L 600 on 27
Mar. 1723. Witnesses: JOHN CROFT, ALEXANDER NISBETT, HILL CROFT, BENJA-
MIN GODFREY. ROBERT YONGE, Register.

Book Bb, p. 91 JOHN DELA BERE, merchant, to ALEXANDER PARRIS,
27 Dec. 1722 ESQ., both of Charleston, in penal sum of L
Counter Bond 2400 SC money to secure PARRIS who was bound
jointly with DELABERE to JOB ROTHMAHLER, mer-
chant, of Charleston, in L 1200 conditioned for payment of L 600 on 27
Sept. 1723. Witnesses: JOHN CROFT, ALEXANDER NISBETT, HILL CROFT, BENJA-
MIN GODFREY. ROBERT YONGE, Register.

Book Bb, p. 93 EDMUND PORTER, of SC, appointed BENJAMIN WHIT-
19 Dec. 1722 AKER, ESQ., Attorney General of SC, his

Power of Attorney attorney with power to collect money, etc. Witnesses: THOMAS COOPER, THOMAS LAMBOLL. ROBERT YONGE, Register.

Book Bb, p. 95
20 Dec. 1722
Bill of Sale

EDMUND PORTER, gentleman of SC, to BENJAMIN WHITAKER, 1 Negro man, 1 Negro woman. Whereas EDWARD NEWMAN, gentleman, of SC, drew 3 bills of exchange on same date for ₤ 35 sterling each on EDWARD NEWMAN, leather gilder, in St. Paul's churchyard, London, payable to EDMUND PORTER; & whereas BENJAMIN WHITAKER, ESQ., of SC, endorsed the bills & became security for their payment; now PORTER, for security, conveys to WHITAKER 2 Negroes. Witness: BENJAMIN GODFREY. ROBERT YONGE, Register.

Book Bb, p. 96
30 June 1721
Mortgage

JONATHAN SKRINE, merchant, whereas SKRINE gave bond 30 Nov. 1720 to MESSRS. WRAGG & ROTHMAHLER & THOMAS DYMES for ₤ 1600 SC money conditioned for payment of 32,000 lbs. rice to WRAGG. ROTHMAHLER & DYMES in Charleston on 1 Jan. 1721; & whereas SKRINE gave bond this date to WRAGG, ROTHMAHLER & DYMES for ₤ 1300 SC money conditioned for payment of ₤ 654:10 on 1 Jan. 1722; now, to secure payment, SKRINE conveys to WRAGG, ROTHMAHLER & DYMES 6 Negro men & 1 Negro boy. Witnesses: ROBERT HUME, ROBERT HOWE. Livery & seizin witnessed by ROBERT HUME, BENJAMIN RAMSEY JR. ROBERT YONGE, Register.

Book Bb, p. 99
22 Jan. 1722/3
Mortgage

EDWARD KEATING, planter, of St. James Goosecreek, Berkeley Co., to JOHN OULDFIELD, of same Parish, for ₤ 1000 currency, 5 Negro men, 6 Negro women, 1 Indian boy, 1 Negro boy, 2 Negro girls, bought from different persons at sundry times. Whereas OULDFIELD, for KEATING'S debts, became jointly bound with KEATING on 15 Oct. 1721 to JOHN GREENLAND, planter, of Berkeley Co., in penal sum of ₤ 1600 for payment of ₤ 800, therefore if KEATING pays GREENLAND ₤ 800 & acquits OULDFIELD, this deed to be void. Witnesses: JOSEPH NORMAN, JOHN BAYLY. ROBERT YONGE, Register.

Book Bb, p. 101
15 Dec. 1722
Memo

THOMAS ELLERY, gentleman, deposed before THOMAS HEPWORTH, ESQ., J.P. that "about the date of the within deed he did see the same duely executed by the several parties thereto Vizt. SUSANNAH FITCH, widow, JONATHAN FITCH and ANNE his wife, and that he the deponent, THOMAS SMITH ESQ., CAPT. GERRARD VANVELSIN, and THOMAS CAPERS did severally subscribe their names as witnesses thereto."

Book Bb, p. 101
15 Dec. 1722
Memo

THOMAS ELLERY, gentleman, deposed before THOMAS HEPWORTH, ESQ., J.P., that "Sometime on about the date of the within written deed he did see the same duely executed by the several parties thereto Vizt. SUSANNAH FITCH, widow, JONATHAN FITCH, and ANNE his wife and that he the deponent with THOMAS SMITH, ESQ., CAPT. GARRETT VANVELSEN and THOMAS CAPERS did severally subscribe their names as witnesses thereunto." ROBERT YONGE, Register.

Book Bb, p. 102
21 Oct. 1722
Power of Attorney

THE HON. JOHN COLLETON, ESQ., of St. John's Parish, Island of Barbados, appointed his well beloved friends CHARLES HILL, JOHN HARLESTON, ROGER MOORE, & MAJOR PERCIVAL RAWLY, ESQRS., of SC, his attorneys, to collect money due from his son or sons & to handle his property in SC. Witnesses: WILLIAM ROBINSON, ROBERT HADWEN. WILLIAM ROBERTSON appeared before THOMAS HEPWORTH, ESQ., dep. recorder of Charles City, ROBERT YONGE, Register.

Book Bb, p. 105
25 May 1722
Bond

THEOPHILUS HASTINGS & JANE (her mark) his wife, of Berkeley Co., to COL. MICHAEL BREWTON, of Charleston, in penal sum of ₤ 800 currency for payment of ₤ 400 on 25 Nov. 1723, & for security convey to BREWTON 2 Negro men, 1 Negro boy, 1 Negro wench & her 2 children. Should any of the slaves happen to die, run away, be disabled, or lost before coming to the hands of BREWTON, the loss & damage to be borne by HASTINGS. Witnesses: JOHN CROFT, ESTHER CONYERS. Before THOMAS

HEPWORTH. ROBERT YONGE, Register.

Book Bb, p. 108　　　　　　　WILLIAM WALLACE, merchant, to PETER CEELY, mar-
7 Feb. 1722/3　　　　　　　　iner, now residing at "Charles City", SC, 15
Mortgage　　　　　　　　　　Negroes, 100 neat cattle, 6 horses, mares, 20
　　　　　　　　　　　　　　sheep, 1 clock, 1 pine "screwtore" (secretary?), 1 large silver tankard conditioned for payment to CEELY by WAL-
LACE, of ₤ 4365:19:4-1/2 in rice at 40 shil. per 100 on last day of Feb.
1723/4 as mentioned in a bond of this date. Witnesses: PETER CATTELL,
THOMAS LAMBOLL. Before WILLIAM WALLACE. Witnesses to delivery of 1 Negro in name of the schedule: FRANCIS JOHNSTON, MARY LOUGHTON. ROBERT
YONGE, Register.

Book Bb, p. 110　　　　　　　WILLIAM HAMMERTON, gentleman, to WILLIAM RHETT,
20 May 1718　　　　　　　　　ESQ., both of Charleston, in penal sum of ₤
Bond　　　　　　　　　　　　1300 SC money for payment of 352 ounces of
　　　　　　　　　　　　　　fine silver with interest at 10% on 20 Nov.
1718. Witnesses: RICHARD WHIGG, RICHARD ROWE. Before JOHN CROFT, sole
N.P. of SC. ROBERT YONGE, Register.

Book Bb, p. 111　　　　　　　HENRY MICHAUS deposed before GEORGE SMITH,
14 Mar. 1722/3　　　　　　　 ESQ., that he saw ANTHONY BOURAN deliver to
Memo　　　　　　　　　　　　STEPHEN FOX 316 a. bounding NW on JOHN CATTLE;
　　　　　　　　　　　　　　W on THOMAS ELLIOTT; S part on HENRY MICHAUS &
part on STEPHEN FOX; E on vacant land; that the plat annexed to the grant
is the true plat of said land, the grant being signed by JOSEPH BLAKE,
JOSEPH MORTON, JOHN MORTON, JAMES MOORE, THOMAS CARY, & WILLIAM HAWETT &
dated 14 July 1698. Witnesses to delivery of land: JONATHAN FITCH, JOHN
WILLIAMSON, JOSEPH HEAP. ROBERT YONGE, Register.

Book Bb, p. 112　　　　　　　This certifies that on 4 Jan. 1722/3 WILLIAM
11 Mar. 1722/3　　　　　　　 WALLACE sold to JOSIAH OSGOOD, planter, both
Memo　　　　　　　　　　　　of Berkeley Co., for a valuable consideration,
　　　　　　　　　　　　　　1 Negro boy. Witnesses: GENDEON FAUCHRAUD,
THOMAS SNOW. Before THOMAS SATUR. ROBERT YONGE, Register.

Book Bb, p. 113　　　　　　　ARCHIBALD COCKRAN, of Antigua, on recommenda-
(no date)　　　　　　　　　　tion of GEN. HAMILTON, write to (name omitted)
Power of Attorney　　　　　　asking him to be his attorney. ARCHIBALD'S
　　　　　　　　　　　　　　brother, ROBERT COCKRAN, had about 600 a. near
Charleston, stocked it with Negroes, cattle, etc., & put it in care of
JOHN ABRAHAM MOTTE, his attorney. MOTTE died & his brother ISAAC MOTTE
took possession. ISAAC MOTTE dying, the government took possession of
the Negroes. ARCHIBALD COCKRAN then impowerd ELEAZER ALLEN to sell the
land & Negroes, which ARCHIBALD understands he has done & taken a bond
from the buyer between ₤ 700 & ₤ 800. ARCHIBALD COCKRAN asks his attorney to ascertan the name of the purchaser, collect, & remit to him in
Barbados. "The GENERALL MR. TANKERD, MR. LUCAS and all your acquaint-
ances here are well and often drink your health". Registered 23 Mar.
1722/3 by ROBERT YONGE, Register.

Book Bb, p. 115　　　　　　　WILLIAM WALLACE, merchant, & ELIZABETH, his
12 & 13 Mar. 1722　　　　　　wife, of Berkeley Co., to THOMAS LAMBOLL, gent-
L & R　　　　　　　　　　　leman, of "Charles City", for ₤ 300 SC money 3
　　　　　　　　　　　　　　town lots & a piece of land & marsh "within
the platt of Charles City and port"; viz. 1 lot granted by Lords Proprs.
to JOHN STEPHENS, bounding S on Ashley River; W on JOHN HARTLEY; N on a
small passage way leading west from the little street between the above
lots; another lot, granted to said JOHN STEVENS bounding E on a little
street running N from Ashley River to the broad path or high road going
into the country; another lot, bounding S on the small passage way (mentioned above); to the E on the little street aforesaid; W on a marsh in
Ashley River; N on a lot granted to JOHN STEVENS; another lot bounding E
on the little street; S on last mentioned lot; W on said marsh; N on a
lot granted to JOHN JONES, gunsmith; also another plat of land & marsh,
consisting of several town lots bought from the HON. LANDGRAVE THOMAS
SMITH, ESQ., lying on the bay near the S end of the city, commonly called
White Point; measuring 260 feet front easterly on Cooper River from a lot
belonging formerly to JAMES PEARTREE, now to COL. JOHN FENWICKE & 528
feet in depth from low water mark to a white stone placed at the SW

corner of said plat of land & marsh, bounded on S by a line running from said stone to a stake set up at the front of the firm ground; W by another line running from said stone to another white stone placed on S side of a pond & marsh within the limits of said plat; bounding W & S on lots of THOMAS SMITH, ESQ., eldest son of LANDGRAVE THOMAS SMITH. Whereas the Palatine & the Lords Proprs. by 3 deeds granted JOHN STEVENS 3 lots in Charleston; & whereas STEVENS by will dated 24 Dec. 1717 ordained that all lands not thereby given should be sold if necessary & that after his wife had taken her thirds the profits should be used for the education of his children, & appointed THOMAS WARING his executor; & whereas WARING after the death of STEVENS, proved the will; & whereas the personal estate not being sufficient to maintain & educate his children & his wife being in want of her thirds, WARING on 15 June 1722 sold to WILLIAM WALLACE, 3 town lots; & whereas the Palatine & Lords Proprs. granted the HON. LANDGRAVE THOMAS SMITH, ESQ., certain lots of land & marsh in S part of Charleston; & whereas LANDGRAVE THOMAS SMITH by will dated 26 June 1692 gave the residue of his real & personal estate to his eldest son, THOMAS, making son THOMAS sole executor; & whereas son THOMAS on 30 Jan. 1722 sold to WILLIAM WALLACE a plat of land & marsh; now WALLACE sells LAMBOLL the 3 lots purchased from WARING & a plat of land & marsh. Witnesses: JOHN BURROWS, THOMAS WEEKLEY. Before THOMAS WARING. ROBERT YONGE, Register.

Book Bb, p. 129
13 Mar. 1722
Bond of Performance

WILLIAM WALLACE, merchant, & ELIZABETH, his wife, of Berkeley Co., to THOMAS LAMBOLL, gentleman, of "Charles City & Port," in penal sum of ₤ 2000 sterling of Great Britain conditioned for observing all agreements in L & R (see p. 115). Witnesses: JOHN BURROWS, THOMAS WEEKLEY. Before THOMAS WARING. ROBERT YONGE, Register.

Book Bb, p. 130
8 Mar. 1721
Deed in Trust

EDWARD RAWLINGS, joiner, of Charleston, in consideration that MARY, his wife, joined with him in conveying to ROBERT HUME, gentleman, of Charleston, a lot in which EDWARD & MARY were jointenants, for the raising of ₤ 200 currency to pay EDWARD'S debts, for ₤ 5 currency, sold to WILLIAM MILES, planter, of Berkeley Co., 1 Negro woman & 1 Negro boy, in trust for EDWARD & MARY RAWLINGS during their lives, then for their daughter MARY & any future children. Witnesses: ROBERT HUME, SAMUEL CRAFORD, CHILDERMUS CROFT. ROBERT YONGE, Register.

Book Bb, p. 132
21 & 22 Mar. 1722
L & R

WILLIAM SCOTT, merchant, to FRANCIS HOLMES, merchant, both of "Charles City," for ₤ 1000 SC money 1120 a. in Clarendon Co., bounding E on a marsh & creek out of Port Royall River; W on Port Royall River; S on another creek. Whereas the Lords Proprs. on 12 Jan. 1699 granted JOHN PINNY 1120 a. in Clarendon; & whereas on 4 June 1702 the Lords Proprs. & the HON. JAMES MOORE ESQ., Gov., for ₤ 28:8 granted the land to PINNY free of all quit rents; & whereas WILLIAM SCOTT on 27 Mar. 1719, for ₤ 500 SC money, bought the 1120 a. from PINNY; now SCOTT sells to HOLMES. Witnesses: THOMAS SMITH, JOSEPH SMITH, ROBERT JOHNSTON. ROBERT YONGE, Register.

Book Bb, p. 138
3 Oct. 1721
Release & Mortgage

ANTHONY DEBOURDEAUX, carpenter, & MARIAN, his to WILLIAM GIBBON, merchant, all of Charleston for ₤ 253 SC money, 587 a. in Berkeley Co., bounding NW on MR. AKINS; S on WILLIAM NORTH; SE on JOHN FOGARTIE; NE on DONOMAN; should DEBOURDEAUX pay GIBBON ₤ 253 on 1 May 1723 this mortgage to be void. Witnesses: THOMAS HEPWORTH, JOHN CROFT, ROBERT HUME. JAMES DEBOURDEAUX paid ₤ 480 SC money in full to R. HOW. Witness: RICHARD HARRISON.

Book Bb, p. 142
20 Feb. 1722
Mortgage

SUSANNAH FITCH, widow, of Charleston, to ANNE DRAYTON, widow, of Berkeley Co., for ₤ 250 SC money, 4 Negro women, subject to redemption by SUSANNAH on 20 Feb. 1723 on payment of ₤ 275. Witnessed: ELIZABETH STEVENS, MATHURIN BORGARD, ROBERT HUME. Before JOHN FENWICK. ROBERT YONGE, Register.

Book Bb, p. 144
11 & 12 Mar. 1722

EDMUND ROBINSON, mariner, & ANNE, his wife, only daughter & heir of JOHN BUTLER, to

L & R   WILLIAM RHETT & ELEAZER ALLEN, merchants, &
                                    JOHN CROFT, gentleman, all of Charleston, to
the use of EDMUND & ANNE ROBINSON in consideration of the marriage solem-
nized between EDMUND & ANNE & for the settling of the several plantations
& appurtenances & in consideration of ₤ 5 apiece, SC money, paid to ED-
MUND & ANNE, they sell 1 portion of land which JOHN BUTLER bought from
JOHN COMBES & ELIZABETH his wife, lying in the town of St. John's Island
of Antigua, being E & W 50 feet; N & S 80 feet; bounding E on EDWARD
CHESTER SR.; W on WILLIAM MOULES; N on High Street; S on CHRISTOPHER
STOODLEY; also 50 a. in Burmada (?) Town, Berkeley Co., bounding S on
WILLIAM VIPER; W on a creek of Wando River; N on THOMAS ALLEN; E on THOM-
AS FITZGERALD. Witnesses: THOMAS BARTON, JOHN PICK, ROBERT HUME. Before
BENJAMIN WHITAKER. ROBERT YONGE, Register.

Book Bb, p. 149   THOMAS BROUGHTON, ESQ. to FRANCIS LEJAU, plant-
21 Mar. 1722/3   er, both of Berkeley Co., for ₤ 20 SC money,
Release   640 a. English measure, part of 48,000 a.
                                    granted by the HON. CHARLES CRAVEN ESQ. & the
Lords Proprs. on 19 Aug. 1714 to LANDGRAVE ROBERT DANIEL; which 640 a.
DANIEL for ₤ 12:16 sold to THOMAS BROUGHTON. ANNE BROUGHTON, wife of
THOMAS, freely surrenders her right of dower & thirds. Witnesses: ALEX-
ANDER PARRIS, DANIEL GREEN, JOHN VICARIDGE. ROBERT YONGE, Register.

Book Bb, p. 151   WILLIAM LADSON to his loving brother SAMUEL
19 Feb. 1720   LADSON, for love, goodwill & affection, 100 a.
Deed of Gift   in Berkeley Co., bounding NW on WILLIAM LADSON;
                                    S on MRS. ANNE DRAYTON; SE on ROBERT ELLIOTT;
NE on JAMES STANYARNE. Witnesses: EDWARD PERRY, JACOB LADSON, SAMUEL BOW-
MAN, ABRAHAM LADSON. Before WILLIAM CATTELL. ROBERT YONGE, Register.

Book Bb, p. 153   RICHARD RIGBY, of Misley Hall, Essex Co.,
29 Mar. 1723   Great Britain, now of Island of Jamacia & ANNE
Power of Attorney   his wife, as executors & guardians, appoint
                                    THOMAS GADSDEN, of Charleston, their attorney.
Whereas JOHN PERRIE, merchant, formerly of Island of Antigua, lately of
St. James Parish, Westminster, Middlesex Co., appointed his daughters
ANNE & DOROTHY & his brother EDWARD joint executors of his will dated 24
June in 7th year of Queen Anne recorded in prerogative court of Canter-
bury; & whereas ANNE married RICHARD RIGBY (DOROTHY not yet attaining law-
ful age) so that RIGBY becomes sole executor; & whereas JOHN PERRIE left
2 other daughters, MARY & ELIZABETH (ELIZABETH having died) & willed to
MARY a plantation in SC.: RICHARD & ANNE being guardians of DOROTHY &
MARY appoint RICHARD'S trusty friend THOMAS GADSDEN their attorney to
handle the estate, Negroes, etc., in SC. Witnesses: SAMUEL SIMONS,
CHARLES (his mark) DALLEY. Before JOHN BARKSDALE. ROBERT YONGE, Register.

Book Bb, p. 156   ALEXANDER COLLINS, planter, & SARAH his wife,
17 Apr. 1723   to STEPHEN SEAVEY, shipwright, all of Craven
Release   Co., for ₤ 300 SC money, 376 a. on Tebwin,
                                    Craven Co., bounding according to plat. Wit-
nesses: ARTHUR HALL, JOHN GREENLAND, CHILDERMUS CROFT. Before JOHN BARKS-
DALE. ROBERT YONGE, Register. Whereas his EXCELLENCY JOHN, LORD GRAN-
VILLE, Palatine, WILLIAM LORD CRAVEN, JOHN LORD CARTERET, MAURICE ASHLEY,
ESQ., JOHN COLLETON, BARONET, & the Lords Proprs. on 18 June 1702 impow-
ered the RT. HON. SIR NATHANIEL JOHNSON, Knight, Gov. of SC & NC, JAMES
MOORE, NICHOLAS TROTT & JOB HOWES, ESQRS., to grant lands, they, on 12
Jan. 1705, for ₤ 7:10:5 granted CAPT. JOHN COLLINS 376 a. English measure,
in Craven Co. Signatures to grant: NATHANIEL JOHNSON, JAMES MOORE, NICH-
OLAS TROTT. On 10 Dec. 1705, JOB HOWES, surveyor general, laid out the
375 a. bounding S on JAMES BASFORD & on MARK SLOWMAN; W on BASFORD; N &
E on vacant land. Plat certified 1 Jan. 1705.

Book Bb, p. 163   JOHN WOODWARD, gentleman, of St. Andrews Par-
8 June 1722   ish, Berkeley Co., to RICHARD WILMOTT, mer-
Bond   chant, of London, in penal sum of ₤ 4855:8:3
                                    SC money to be paid to EDWARD BRAILSFORD, mer-
chant, of SC conditioned for payment of ₤ 2427:12:4 to BRAILSFORD with
interest at 10% on 1 Feb. 1723. Witnesses: WILLIAM ROKEBY, WILLIAM
STREET. Before ARTHUR MIDDLETON. ROBERT YONGE, Register.

Book Bb, p. 164   JOHN WOODWARD, gentleman, of St. Andrews Par-
8 June 1722   ish, Berkeley Co., to RICHARD WILMOT, merchant,
Bond   of London, in penal sum of ℒ 6000 SC money to
                       be paid to EDWARD BRAILSFORD, merchant, of SC
conditioned for payment of ℒ 3000 with interest at 10% to BRAILSFORD on 1
Feb. 1723. Witnesses: WILLIAM TOKEBY, WILLIAM STREET. Before ARTHUR
MIDDLETON. ROBERT YONGE, Register.

Book Bb, p. 165   HUGH HEXT, ESQ. of Colleton Co., to the REV.
1 May 1723   COMMISSARY (?) WILLIAM TREDWELL BULL in penal
Bond   sum of ℒ 600 sterling of Great Britain, condi-
                       tioned for payment of ℒ 315 sterling of Great
Britain on 1 May 1725 at any place in London or Westminster as appointed
by BULL. Witnesses: GEORGE CLARIDGE, THOMAS JOHN ELLIOTT, WILLIAM FLECK-
NOW. Before ALEXANDER PARRIS. ROBERT YONGE, Register.

Book Bb, p. 166   HUGH HEXT, ESQ. of Colleton Co., to the REV.
1 May 1723   COMMISSARY WILLIAM TREDWELL BULL, in penal sum
Bond   of ℒ 400 sterling of Great Britain conditioned
                       for payment of ℒ 225 sterling of Great Britain
on 1 May 1724 at such place in London & Westminster as BULL shall appoint.
Witnesses: GEORGE CLARIDGE, THOMAS JOHN ELLIOTT, WILLIAM FLECKNOW. Before ALEXANDER PARRIS. ROBERT YONGE, Register.

Book Bb, p. 167   COL. ABRAHAM EVE, ESQ. of Colleton Co., to
2 & 3 Feb. 1721   MATHURINE BOGAR, gardener, of Charleston, for
L & R   ℒ 120 current SC money 1/3 part of 3 a. which
                       EVE bought from CAPT. BENJAMIN SCHENCKINGH,
known as SCHENCKINGH'S SQUARE in Charleston, which third part bounds N on
BENJAMIN WHITAKER, ESQ.; S on ABRAHAM EVE; E on a street leading by the
old church; W on another street leading to entrance of Broad Path. Witnesses: THOMAS HEPWORTH, BENJAMIN DENNIS, JOHN BROWN. Before THOMAS HEP-
WORTH. ROBERT YONGE, Register.

Book Bb, p. 171   JOHN PELOQUIN & AUGUSTUS JAY, merchants, of
26 Jan. 1722/3   N.Y. appointed trusty & loving friend BENJAMIN
Power of Attorney   D'HARRIETTE, merchant, of N.Y. their attorney
                       to receive or sue for money due from ISAAC
EMANUEL, at SC. Witnesses: ALEXANDER PHENIX, JOHN INGLIS. Before JOHN
BARKSDALE. ROBERT YONGE, Register.

Book Bb, p. 172   WILLIAM WYE of SC to RICHARD HIGGINSON, mer-
4 Feb. 1719   chant of London, in penal sum of ℒ 40 money of
Bond   Great Britain, conditioned for payment of ℒ 20
                       like money on 24 Aug. 1719 with interest at 5%.
Witnesses: EDWARD ARDEN, JOHN CLIPPERTON, ROBERT YONGE, (ROBERT HUME?).
Before ALEXANDER PARRIS. ROBERT YONGE, Register.

Book Bb, p. 173   JOHN ASH, gentleman, formerly of SC now of
5 Apr. 1723   Bath Co. NC, appoints MRS. SARAH MORTON, widow
Power of Attorney   of LANDGRAVE JOSEPH MORTON, his attorney with
                       full power to dispose of the 500 a. near the
head of Ashley River which he purchased from THOMAS DISTON, gentleman.
Witnesses: COL. MAURICE MOORE, CAPT. EDMUND PORTER, JOHN DAVIS. Before
ALEXANDER PARRIS. ROBERT YONGE, Register.

Book Bb, p. 176   To the worthy the treasurer to the honble the
                       society for propagating the gospel in foreign
parts. Then be pleased to pay to MR. DANL. BELL, master of the ship MARY,
or order, the sum of 12 pounds, of current money of Great Britain, value
received by me which will become due to me from the society by Christmas
next after the date hereof taking his receipt therefore and placing it to
the account of your most humble servant BRIAN HUNT, missionary of St.
Johns, SC. May 27, 1723. ROBERT YONGE, Register.

DEEDS BOOK "C"
1718-1723

Book C, p. 1   REBECKAH BARKER, widow, of Parish of St. James,
28 Nov. 1718   Goose Creek, Berkeley Co., SC, for Ł 300 cur-
Sale   rent SC money, to JOHN MOORE, planter, of same
                              place; 201 a. in St. James Goose being part of
the 615 a. on which she lives. Witnesses: JOHN VICARIDGE, JOHN BAYLEY.
Land delivered 26 Feb. 1718/9. Witnesses: FRANCIS CHICKEN, JOHN BAYLEY,
NATHANIEL MOORE. Before BENJAMIN SCHENCKING 23 May 1723. ROBERT YONGE,
Register.

Book C, p. 4   JOHN COWAN & DOROTHY his wife appointed JOHN
--- 1723   FRAZIER, shop keeper of Charleston, to sell
Power of Attorney   1/2 lot #125 in Charleston, bounding N on ROB-
                              ERT HARVEY'S land (formerly JOHN FROWMAN'S).
Witnesses: ROWLAND EVANS, JOHN EMMENES, JOSEPH PARMENTER. DOROTHY COWAN
(wife of JOHN) being examined by THOS. INNS 6 June 1723 declared she signed without compulsion. ROBERT YONGE, Register.

Book C, p. 6   JOHN FRAZIER, shop keeper of Charleston, At-
26 June 1723   torney for JOHN COWAN, planter, of Granville
Sale   Co. and DOROTHY his wife, for Ł 70 current SC
                              money to EDGAR WELLS, planter, of Berkeley Co.,
1/2 town lot #125 butting on ROBERT HARVEY'S land (formerly JOHN FROW-
MAN'S). Witnesses: WILLIAM BULL, JOHN TOPAR, JOHN BALLANTINE. ROBERT
YONGE, Register.

Book C, p. 8   BENJAMIN SUMNER, planter, & PERSIS his wife,
2 Mar. 1719   of Berkeley Co., SC, for Ł 125, to MICHAEL BA-
Sale   CON, planter, of Dorchester, Berkeley Co.,
"the 5th lot on the first range of the first
division of lots within Dorchester" containing 50 a. (except 1 a. which
BENJAMIN SUMNER reserves fronting on the Broad Path 8 rods), bounding E
on MICHAL BACON, S on Ashley River, W on BENJAMIN SUMNER, N on JOSEPH
SUMNER. Witnesses: THOMAS OSGOOD, JR; EBENEZER WAY. Before THOMAS SATUR
on 24 May 1723. ROBERT YONGE, Register.

Book C, p. 11   MANLY WILLIAMSON, planter, of Berkeley Co., SC,
26 Apr. 1723   to ISAAC MAZYCK, merchant, of Charleston, in
Bill of Sale   penal sum of Ł 846 current SC money condition-
                              ed for payment of Ł 423 or value in rice at
rate of 35 shillings per 100 wt. on Bay of Charleston with interest at
10% on 1 Feb. next and for security assigned 10 Negroes (7 men, 2 women,
1 girl). Witnesses: PETER DE ST. JULIEN, JAMES ST. JULIEN. ROBERT YONGE,
Register.

Book C, p. 14   LANDGRAVE THOMAS SMITH of Goose Creek and MARY
25 Nov. 1720   his wife, for love & affection & Ł 50 current
Deed of Gift   SC money, to son-in-law JOHN MOORE, gentleman,
                              of Goose Creek, 500 a. in Berkeley Co., bound-
ing S & E on LANDGRAVE THOMAS SMITH, N on RICHARD BAKER, W on BARNABY
REALLY. MARY freely surrendered her right of dower and thirds. Witnesses: CAPT. EDWARD HYRNE, ELIZABETH WEEKLEY, BARBARA HYRNE. Before THOMAS
SMITH. ROBERT YONGE, Register.

Book C, p. 17   JACOB SATUR, formerly merchant, Berkeley Co.,
28 Mar. 1721   SC, for Ł 250 current SC money, to MICHAEL BA-
Release   CON, planter, of Berkeley Co., 100 a. English
                              measure, part of "Ashley Barony or Saint Giles"
granted 18 Mar. 1675 to the RT. HON. ANTHONY LORD ASHLEY, Earl of Shaftsbury, and afterwards his grandson ANTHONY LORD ASHLEY granted said Barony
to the HON. MAURICE ASHLEY ESQ. his brother 20 July 1698, and by MAURICE
ASHLEY granted in 1717 to SAMUEL WRAGG, merchant, of London. SAMUEL
WRAGG on 6 AUG. 1720 granted to JACOB SATUR 3000 a. of said Barony of
which the aforesaid 100 a. is part; bounding NW on Ashley River & THOMAS
BAKER; SE on JOSIAH OSGOOD, SE on WILLIAM WALLACE; surveyed by MAJOR JOHN
HERBERT 5 Jan. 1718. Witnesses: THOMAS WARING, THOMAS OSGOOD, PETER
GOULDING (GOLDING). Before THOMAS SATUR. ROBERT YONGE, Register.

Book C, p. 23   THEOPHILUS HASTINGS & JANE (her mark) his wife,
17 June 1723   of Berkeley Co., for L 650 current SC money,
Sale   to MANLY WILLIAMSON, planter, of same place, 5 Negroes (2 men, 1 woman, 1 boy, 1 girl). Witnesses: THOMAS BUTLER, JOHN CAMPNEY (CHAMPNEY). Before JOHN BARKSDALE. ROBERT YONGE, Register.

Book C, p. 26   PETER LESADE, planter, of Berkeley Co., to
16 & 17 Sept. 1723   CHARLES HILL, ESQ., of Charles City, as secur-
L & R by Mortgage   ity on bond of even date in penal sum of L 1600 for payment of L 880 currency with interest on 17 Sept. 1727, 4 tracts of land in Berkeley Co. devised to PETER LESADE by JAMES LESADE; 174 a., part of 240 a. granted by GOV. JOHN ARCHDALE on 19 Sept. 1696 to JAMES LESADE (the 66 a. now belonging to ANDREW DEVEAUX); also 119 a., part of 285 a. purchased by JAMES LESADE from GOV. JOSEPH BLAKE & the Lords Proprs. on 24 Feb. 1696 (the 166 a. now belonging to ANDREW DEVEAUX); also 65 a. purchased by JAMES LESADE from GOV. JOSEPH BLAKE & the Lords Proprs. on 24 Feb. 1696; also 100 a. granted by GOV. JOSEPH BLAKE on 8 Sept. 1797 to JAMES LESADE. Witnesses: CAPT. FAYR. HALL, ANDREW BROUGHTON. Before BENJAMIN WHITAKER, J.P. ROBERT YONGE, Register.

Book C, p. 38   PETER LESADE, planter, of Berkeley Co., to
17 Sept. 1723   CHARLES HILL, of Charles City, in penal sum of
Bond   L 1600 for payment of L 880 currency with interest on 17 Sept. 1727. Witnesses: CAPT. FAYR. HALL, ANDREW BROUGHTON. Before BENJAMIN WHITAKER, J.P. ROBERT YONGE, Register.

Book C, p. 40   (See p. 79). SUSANNAH WIGINGTON, of Charles
1 Oct. 1722   City, to MARY BASDEN, spinster; JONATHAN COL-
Gift   LINS, mariner, & SARAH his wife, of Charles City; and WILLIAM GUY, cleric, & REBECCA his wife, of St. Andrews Parish, Berkeley Co., for valuable causes & considerations, the dwelling house in which JONATHAN & SARAH COLLINS now live, with the adjoining land, as devised by will of MARY NARY; also the lot formerly belonging to CAPT. JOHN CLAPP, bounding W on DR. COOPER; N on Broad Street (which lot was devised by MARY CROSSE after the death of her son WILLIAM BAYLEY to MARY BASDEN, the mother, & to SUSANNAH WIGINGTON. Whereas MARY CROSSE, widow, of Charles City, by will dated 28 Aug. 1698 devised to her son WILLIAM BAYLEY, a lot in Charleston which formerly belonged to CAPT. JOHN CLAPP, with the houses & buildings thereon, during his lifetime & after his death equally to her 2 daughters MARY BASDEN, widow (mother of MARY BASDEN, party hereto, & of SARAH COLLINS & REBECCA GUY) & said SUSANNAH (by name of SUSANNAH RAWLINGS); & whereas MARY CROS CROSSE gave her daughter, MARY BASDEN (the mother) half of her lot in Charleston, fronting the wharf, where she then lived, that is, the half lot next to CAPT. RHETT where MR. BUCKLEY lately lived; & whereas soon after WILLIAM BAYLEY'S death SUSANNAH WIGINGTON, by deed of feoffment dated 25 Apr. 1702, conveyed to MARY BASDEN, the mother (by name of MARY NARY, wife of NICHOLAS NARY, gentleman, of Charleston) her half lot (formerly CAPT. JOHN CLAPP'S); & whereas MARY BASDEN, the mother (by name of MARY NARY, widow) bequeathed to her son NICHOLAS NARY, the dwelling house in which she lived, with the land belonging thereto, fronting the bay & adjoining WILLIAM RHETT; also her lot formerly belonging to CAPT. JOHN CLAPP, adjoining DR. COOPER'S lot; & whereas it was always the declared intention of MARY NARY that in case son NICHOLAS died before reaching 21 the lands should go to MARY BASDEN (party hereto), SARAH COLLINS & REBECCA GUY, equally; but because her will was made during her last illness & the clause omitted unintentionally; now, NICHOLAS having died recently, SUSANNAH carries out her mother's desire by transferring the 2 lots. Witnesses: HARRAL BLY, JOSUE MARINEUR, CHILDERMAS CROFT. Before JOSEPH WRAGG, J.P. JACOB MOTTE, Register.

Book C, p. 45   JOSEPH LESEUR (LESIR), cordwainer, of Berkeley
17 & 18 Jan. 1721   Co., to THOMAS DIXON, bricklayer, of Charles-
L & R   ton, for L 100 currency, 53 a. on James Island, bounding E on JOSEPH STANYARD; S on RIVERS STANYARD; W on JOHN MOORE; N on MR. BATOON. Witnesses: JOHN CROFT, EDWARD CROFT, CHILERMAS CROFT. Before CHARLES HILL, J.P. JACOB MOTTE,

Register.

Book C, p. 53 & 61　　　　SAMUEL EVELEIGH, merchant, to JOSEPH WRAGG,
6 & 7 Oct. 1723　　　　　 merchant, (agent of JOHN CROWLEY, ESQ., of Lon-
L & R by Mortgage　　　　don), both of Charleston, as security on bond
　　　　　　　　　　　　 of even date in penal sum of Ł 8000 for payment of Ł 4000 currency, with interest, on 7 Oct. 1724; part of lot #4 in
Charleston, fronting E 70 ft. on the street next to Cooper River; bound-
ing S 230 ft. on the part belonging to widow of DR. WILLIAM CROOK; W on
WILLIAM CHAPMAN, tanner; N on CAPT. GEORGE SMITH; also 550 a. in Berkeley
Co. (granted to JAMES SUTHESS on 5 Sept. 1709); also 1120 a. nigh Wacamaw
River in Winyah River, Craven Co., purchased from LANDGRAVE THOMAS SMITH;
also 2 Negro men, 4 Negro women and 1 girl. Negro boy delivered for all.
Witnesses: ROBERT HUME, WILLIAM SMITH. Before RICHARD SPLATT, J.P. JA-
COB MOTTE, Register.

Book C, p. 58 & 72　　　　JOHN HODGSON, planter, Berkeley Co., for 5
11 Sept. 1723　　　　　　 shillings and other consideration sold HENRY
Lease　　　　　　　　　　 PERONNEAU, merchant, of Charleston, 400 a. in
　　　　　　　　　　　　 Berkeley Co., bounding NE on THOMAS COOKE; SE
on JOHN BOAN; SW on vacant land. Witnesses: JOHN JEFFORDS, EDWARD CROFT,
ROBERT HUME. Before BENJAMIN WHITAKER. JACOB MOTTE, Register.

Book C, p. 61　　　　　　 SAMUEL EVELEIGH, merchant, of Charleston to
7 Oct. 1723　　　　　　　 JOSEPH WRAGG, merchant, of Charleston and fac-
Mortgage　　　　　　　　 tor or agent of JOHN CROWLEY, ESQ. of London,
　　　　　　　　　　　　 in trust for JOHN CROWLEY and subject to redemption; Whereas SAMUEL EVELEIGH stands bound to JOSEPH WRAGG as agent
of JOHN CROWLEY in the penal sum of Ł 8000 current SC money conditioned
for payment of Ł 4000 like money on 7 Oct. 1724 with interest, now for
security and other considerations EVELEIGH sells WRAGG lot #4 in Charleston, 70 ft. front, 230 ft. deep, bounding S on widow of DR. WILLIAM CROOK;
W on WILLIAM CHAPMAN, tanner; N on CAPT. GEORGE SMITH; E on street parallel with Cooper River; also 550 a. in Berkeley Co. granted 5 Sept. 1709
to JAMES SUTHESS; also 1120 a. near Waccamaw River in Winyah River, Crav-
en Co., formerly sold by LANDGRAVE THOMAS SMITH to SAMUEL EVELEIGH. EVE-
LEIGH also sells WRAGG, in trust for CROWLEY, 2 Negro men, 4 Negro women,
1 Negro girl. Witnesses: ROBERT HUME, WILLIAM SMITH. Before RICHARD
SPLATT. JACOB MOTTE, Register.

Book C, p. 72　　　　　　 JOHN HODGSON, planter, of Berkeley Co., to
12 Sept. 1723　　　　　　 HENRY PERONNEAU, merchant, of Charleston.
Mortgage　　　　　　　　 Whereas HODGSON is bound to PERONNEAU in the
　　　　　　　　　　　　 penal sum of Ł 520 current SC money conditioned for payment of Ł 260 like money on 11 Sept. next with interest, now,
for security, HODGSON sells PERONNEAU 400 a. in Berkeley Co., bounding NE
on THOMAS COOK; SE on JOHN BOEN; SW & NW on vacant land. HODGSON also
delivered to PERONNEAU 2 Negroes. Witnesses: JOHN JEFFORDS, EDWARD CROFT,
ROBERT HUME. Before BENJAMIN WHITAKER. JACOB MOTTE, Register. "Received 5 Oct. by the hands of MR. FRANCIS DECHAMP" Ł 3400:10 sh. in full payment. HENRY PERONNEAU.

Book C, p. 79　　　　　　 SUSANNAH WIGINGTON (WIGGINTON), of Charleston;
19 Sept. 1722　　　　　　 THOMAS HEPWORTH & ANNE his wife; MARY BLAMYER,
Conveyance　　　　　　　 widow; JOHN BAYLEY, planter; and ROBERT HUME,
　　　　　　　　　　　　 gentleman, & SOPHIA his wife; to MARY BASDEN,
spinster; JONATHAN COLLINS, mariner, & SARAH his wife (all of Charleston);
and WILLIAM GUY, clerk, & REBECCA his wife, of St. Andrews Parish. Whereas MARY NARY, widow (mother of MARY BASDEN, SARAH COLLINS & REBECCA GUY)
by will gave her son NICHOLAS NARY her dwelling house and land belonging
to it fronting the bay and adjoining the house of WILLIAM RHETT, also her
lot formerly belonging to CAPT. JOHN CLAPP and adjoining land of DR. COOP-
ER; and whereas during her lifetime she had always declared that in case
her son NICHOLAS died without issue and before reaching 21 the property
should be divided equally amongst her daughters; and whereas MARY NARY
died without inserting her real intention in her will; and whereas NICHO-
LAS died under 21 and without issue; and the lands ought in equity to go
to MARY, SARAH & REBECCA; and whereas SUSANNAH WIGINGTON, THOMAS HEPWORTH
& ANNE his wife, MARY BLAMYER, JOHN BAYLEY, and ROBERT HUME & SOPHIA his
wife, are minded to convey the lands to MARY BASDEN, JONATHAN COLLINS and

WILLIAM GUY the dwelling house and adjoining land and part of the lot adjoining DR. COOPER fronting N on Broad Street. Witnesses: ROWLAND STORY, EDWARD SCULL, CHILDERMUS CROFT. Before JOSEPH WRAGG. JACOT MOTTE, Register.

Book C, p. 85
27 Feb. 1720
Sale

WILLIAM PARROT & ANNE his wife, of Colleton Co., for Ł 120 current SC money, to THOMAS DIXON, bricklayer of Berkeley Co. Whereas JAMES COLLETON, ESQ., Gov., & the Lords Proprs. granted 14 Aug. 1689 to DYRECK HOOGLANT 1 town lot #115 in Charleston, bounding E on a street running from Bennson's Landing; W on SOLOMON LEGARE; N on a street running west from MR. RICHARD TRADD; S on THOMAS HOLTON; and whereas DYRECK HOOGLANT on 26 Mar. 1702 by ABRAHAM SANDFORD his attorney for Ł 10 current money sold the lot to JOHN COLLINS; and COLLINS by will dated 13 Aug. 1707 bequeathed it to his wife ELIZABETH COLLINS; and ELIZABETH on 6 Nov. 1710 by Deed of Gift (recorded in Book G. fol. 132 by ISAAC PORCHER, Dep. Secy.) conveyed it to WILLIAM PARROT her son; now PARROT sells to DIXON. Witnesses to sale: RICHARD ROWE, STEPHEN RUSSELL. Witnesses to receipt: JOHN GRIMBALL, SOLOMON LEGARE, CHARLOTTE SORTIN. Before JOHN BARKSDALE. JOHN MOTTE, Register.

Book C, p. 91
30 Oct. 1719
Power of Attorney

CHARLES FRANCHOMME, merchant, of Charleston, Berkeley Co., intending to depart for England, appointed JOHN GENDRON, merchant, and THOMAS HEPWORTH, ESQ., both of Charleston, his attorneys, to manage his affairs during his absence and in case of the death of either, nominated ELISHA PRIOLEAU, merchant, of Charleston, the successor. Witnesses: COL. MILES BREWTON, RICHARD SPLATT. Before WILLIAM BLAKEWEY. JACOB MOTTE, Register.

Book C, p. 96
1 Sept. 1720
Mortgage

JOHN KEYNARD (KINARD), planter, of Berkeley Co., bound to ROGER MOORE, planter, of same place, in penal sum of Ł 920 current SC money conditioned for payment of Ł 460 on 22 Sept. 1720 and for security delivered 6 Negro slaves. Witnesses: BENJAMIN SCHENCKINGH, HON. CHAS. HILL. Before RICHARD ALLEIN. JACOB MOTTE, Register.

Book C, p. 99
1 Sept. 1720
Mortgage

JOHN KINARD, planter, of Berkeley Co., bound to ROGER MOORE, planter, in penal sum of Ł 920 current money conditioned for payment of Ł 460 on 22 Sept. 1720. Witnesses: BENJAMIN SCHENCKINGH, HON. CHARLES HILL. Before RICHARD ALLEIN. JACOB MOTTE, Register.

Book C, p. 100
14 Aug. 1723
Lease

JOHN FOGARTIE, planter, of Berkeley Co., for 5 shillings, to WILLIAM GIBBONS, ESQ. of Charleston, 300 a., being part of 640 a. in St. Thomas's Parish, bounding NE on LEWIS DUTART; NW on land sold to ROBERT HUME by JOHN FOGARTIE; SW on STEPHEN FOGARTIE; SE on RICHARD BERESFORD'S land. Witnesses: ROBERT HUME, CHILDERMUS CROFT. Before WILLIAM BLAKEWEY. JACOB MOTTE, Register.

Book C, p. 103
15 Aug. 1723
Bond

JOHN FOGARTIE, planter, of Berkeley Co., bound to WILLIAM GIBBON, ESQ. of Charleston, in penal sum of Ł 1528 current SC money conditioned for the payment of Ł 764:10 sh. on 16 Aug. 1724. Witnesses: ROBERT HUME, CHILDERMUS CROFT. Before WILLIAM BLAKEWEY. JACOB MOTTE, Register.

Book C, p. 105
15 Aug. 1723
Mortgage

JOHN FOGARTIE, planter, of Berkeley Co., to WILLIAM GIBBON, ESQ. of Charleston. Whereas JOHN FOGARTIE became bound this date to WILLIAM GIBBON in penal sum of Ł 1528 current SC money conditioned for payment of Ł 764:10 sh. on 16 Aug. 1724 now for security FOGARTIE mortgages to GIBBON 300 a. (part of a larger tract of 640 a. in Berkeley Co. lying in Parish of St. Thomas, bounding NE on LEWIS DUTART; NW on land sold to ROBERT HUME by JOHN FOGARTIE; SW on STEPHEN FOGARTIE; SE on RICHARD BERESFORD'S land. Also 5 Negro slaves. Witnesses ROBERT HUME, CHILDERMUS CROFT. Before WILLIAM BLAKEWEY. JACOB MOTTE,

Register.

Book C, p. 113 WILLIAM SMITH, planter, of Berkeley Co., to
19 May 1722 WILLIAM GIBBON, ESQ. of Charleston, lot #156
Mortgage in Charleston and 57 oz. of plate conditioned
for payment of ₺ 143:10 sh. on 19 May 1724
with interest. Witnesses: THOMAS HEPWORTH, THOMAS COOPER, CHILDERMUS
CROFT. Before WILLIAM BLAKEWEY. JACOB MOTTE, Register.

Book C, p. 117 WILLIAM ELLIOTT, planter, of Berkeley Co., to
15 Nov. 1722 THOMAS KIMBERLY, chair maker, & IZABEL his
Release wife, of Charleston, for ₺ 100 current SC money, sold part of town lot #10 to them for the
term of their natural lives and after their death to their daughter ANNA
GOOLE; fronting 5 ft. on Callibeauf's Lane, W on other part of WILLIAM
ELLIOTT'S lot; E 87 ft. on KIMBERLY'S lot. Witnesses: GEORGE DANBRIDGE,
EDWARD CROFT. Before HON. CHARLES HILL, ESQ., Chief Justice of SC.
JACOB MOTTE, Register.

Book C, p. 120 JOHN GENDRON ESQ., of Craven Co., SC and THOM-
22 & 23 July 1723 AS HEPWORTH ESQ. of Charleston, attorneys for
L & R CHARLES FRANCHOME, merchant, late of Charleston now in England, for ₺ 1350 current SC money, to DANIEL HUGER ESQ. of Berkeley Co. Whereas FRANCHOME by Letter of
Attorney dated 30 Oct. 1719, recorded in Book C fol. 91-95, ordained
GENDRON and HEPWORTH, his attorneys, to sell his property in SC; and
whereas FRANCHOME owns part of lot #26 and buildings in Charleston purchased 8 Dec. 1712 from JOHN POSTELL and MARY ESTER POSTELL (See Book H
fol. 309); and whereas GENDRON and HEPWORTH have agreed to sell to HUGER.
Bounding north 61 ft. on Broad Street; E 63 ft. on THOMAS HOWARD; S on
SAMUEL PRIOLEAU (formerly of PETER GUERARD); W on a street leading from
the brick church southward; which premises are occupied by PETER PARIS
and HENRY VARNS (VARNER). Witnesses: WILLIAM GIBBON, H. HOUSER, PIERRE
PARIS. Before CHARLES HILL. JACOB MOTTE, Register.

Book C, p. 133 MARTHA DANIELL, wife of the HON. LANDGRAVE
20 Aug. 1714 ROBERT DANIEL, of Berkeley Co. Whereas ROBERT
Renunciation of Dower DANIEL for a "competent sum" by 4 Deeds of
Feoffment conveyed to THOMAS BROUGHTON 4
tracts of land in Berkeley Co. containing 2640 a., MARTHA quit claimed
her right and title of dower in the 4 tracts. Witness: JOHN CROFT. Before CHARLES HILL. JACOB MOTTE, Register.

Book C, p. 136 JOHN GIBBES, gentleman, of Berkeley Co., bound
19 June 1723 to THOMAS BROUGHTON ESQ. of same Co., in penal
Bond sum of ₺ 2000 current SC money. Whereas, by
indenture 2 Sept. 1716, JOHN GIBBES in consideration of a marriage to be solemnized between said JOHN GIBBES and ANN,
daughter of THOMAS BROUGHTON, and in pursuance of certain articles executed before said marriage; and also in consideration of a considerable marriage portion paid GIBBES by BROUGHTON; and also, in consideration of
love and affection for his wife ANN and for her support and maintenance
should she survive him; GIBBES conveys to BROUGHTON, in trust for ANN,
1/3 part of 400 a. mentioned in indenture; and whereas GIBBES with the
consent and approbation of both THOMAS BROUGHTON and wife ANN has sold
the 400 a. so that ANN can have no claim to her 1/3 part; now if the
heirs of JOHN GIBBES pay THOMAS BROUGHTON ₺ 1000 (for sole use of ANN)
within 9 months after death of JOHN this obligation to be void. Witnesses: JOHN CROFT, J. BONNETHEAU, CHILDERMUS CROFT. Before CHARLES HILL.
JACOB MOTTE, Register.

Book C, p. 139 JOHN GIBBES, gentleman, of Berkeley Co., to
19 June 1723 THOMAS BROUGHTON ESQ. of same Co. In consid-
Deed of Conveyance eration of a marriage between JOHN GIBBES and
ANN, daughter of THOMAS BROUGHTON, and in pursuance of articles signed before marriage; in consideration of a competent marriage portion paid GIBBES; and in consideration of the love and
affection he bears his wife ANN; GIBBES conveys to BROUGHTON 1/3 of his
slaves in trust for ANN; and 5 slaves to ANN for her sole use. Witnesses: JOHN CROFT, J. BONNETHEAU, CHILDERMUS CROFT. Before CHARLESS HILL.

JACOB MOTTE, Register.

Book C, p. 145   RICHARD GODFREY & BENJAMIN GODFREY, planters
9 Nov. 1723   of St. Andrew Parish, SC, bound to THOMAS DIX-
Bond   ON, bricklayer, in penal sum of ₤ 800 current
                     SC money conditioned for payment of ₤ 400 and
interest on 9 Nov. 1725. Witnesses: JOHN TOPER, CORNELIUS BATTOON. Before JOHN BARKSDALE. JACOB MOTTE, Register.

Book C, p. 146   BENJAMIN GODFREY & RICHARD GODFREY, planters,
9 Nov. 1723   St. Andrews Parish, bound to THOMAS DIXON,
Bond   bricklayer, in penal sum of ₤ 200 current SC
                     money conditioned for payment of ₤ 100 with
interest on 9 Nov. 1725. Witnesses: JOHN TOPER, CORNELIUS BATTOON. Before JOHN BARKSDALE. JACOB MOTTE, Register.

Book C, p. 148   RICHARD ROWE, of Charleston, to EDWARD THOMAS,
20 & 21 July 1723   planter, of Berkeley Co., for ₤ 1308 current
L & R   SC money 872 a. in Berkeley Co. which RICHARD
                     ROWE bought from JOHN MOORE; bounding S on
MOORE'S old plot; N on HENRY FARWELL. Witnesses: PETER VILLEPONTOUX, SAMUEL SMITH. Before CHARLES HILL. JACOB MOTTE, Register.

Book C, p. 155   ROBERT DANIELL, planter, of Berkeley Co., and
3 & 4 Oct. 1723   HELLEN his wife to MARMADUKE DANIELL, planter,
L & R   of Berkeley Co. for ₤ 1500 current SC money,
                     84 a. in Berkeley Co. given to HELLEN by will
of her father COL. GEORGE LOGAN; bounding N on MR. WATKINS; E on Broad
Path; S on MR. CARTWRIGHT; W on marsh of Ashley River & MR. CARTWRIGHT.
Witnesses: ISAAC LESESNE, M. NEWBOROUGH, JONATHAN SINGLETARY, MORRIS (his
mark) RIVERS. Before DANIEL HUGER. JACOB MOTTE, Register.

Book C, p. 164   JONATHAN TUBB, mariner, of Charleston, SC, ap-
2 Sept. 1720   pointed his trusty & loving friend THOMAS KEM-
Power of Attorney   BERLY of Charleston his attorney with power to
                     collect debts, etc. Witnesses: THOMAS ELLIOTT,
JOHN JEFFORDS, DANIEL TOWNSEND. Before JOHN BARKSDALE. JACOB MOTTE, Register.

Book C, p. 167   GEORGE (his mark) FLOOD, sawyer, of Berkeley
21 Dec. 1723   Co., conveyed to THOMAS CUTFIELD, planter, 2
Mortgage   adjoining tracts of land in Berkeley Co. con-
                     taining 270 a.; 100 a. being part of Ashley
Barony which FLOOD purchased from JAMES BAKER; bounding NW on ROBERT
JOHNSON alias BLACK ROBIN; the other 170 a. bounding NW on PETER GOULD-
ING; SW on RICHARD BAKER; SE on CAPT. RICHARD DEVON; NE on first mention-
ed 100 a.; GEORGE FLOOD being lawful owner by grand & indenture signed by
ISAAC MAZYCK, merchant of Charleston and grant signed by JAMES BAKER;
conditioned for payment of ₤ 376:12 sh. current SC money and 14,117 lbs.
rice delivered at Charleston on 1 Mar. 1724/25. Witnesses: JOSEPH BAKER,
JOHN BAKER. Before THOMAS WARING. JACOB MOTTE, Register.

Book C, p. 171   THOMAS AMORY, merchant, of Boston, and REBEC-
19 Nov. 1723   CA his wife to ELEAZER ALLEN, merchant, of
Sale   Charleston, SC, for ₤ 650 current Boston mon-
                     ey, 1/2 of lot #19 in Charleston SC occupied
by ALICE HOY, widow, fronting 85 ft. English measure on bay and 126 ft.
English measure deep; bounding E on bay; S on land of COL. JOHN LYNCH,
merchant, of London (formerly of RICHARD CODNER); W on lot belonging
partly to JONATHAN RUSS partly to GEORGE LEE (formerly belonging to JOHN
ASHBY ESQ.); N on GEORGE HESCOT (formerly of CAPT. JOHN GUPPEL). Also
all that part of a front lot to the east of the city wall lying before
said half lot down to low water mark. Witnesses: ISAAC HOLMES, CHARLES
BURNHAM. Payment made by 2 bonds given by ELEAZER ALLEN and BENJAMIN DE
LA CONSEILLERE of Charleston to THOMAS AMORY and delivered to his attorney FRANCIS HOLMES. THOMAS AMORY and REBECCA acknowledged their deed before J. WILLARD. ISAAC HOLMES appeared before CHARLES HILL. JACOB MOTTE,
Register.

Book C, p. 182   REBEKAH AMORY, wife of THOMAS AMORY, merchant,

19 Nov. 1723   of Boston, Mass., being privately examined,
Renunciation of Dower   declared she freely and voluntarily joined her
                           husband in the above conveyance and quit claim-
ed her right to town lot #19. Before JOSIAH WILLARD, ESQ., J.P. & Sec'y.
of Province of Mass. JACOB MOTTE, Register.

Book C, p. 185   WILLIAM RHETT the younger, of Charleston, now
17 & 18 Sept. 1722   residing in Parish of St. Michael Cornhill,
L & R   London, merchant, for ₤ 60 of Great Britain
                           money, to JACOB SATUR, merchant, of London;
part of lot or garden #113 in Charleston; also 2 wooden houses built
thereon and formerly occupied by GEORGE FRANCKLYN, now by BENJAMIN DONNIS
(DENIS) and abutting on the dwelling house of NICHOLAS TROTT. Witnesses:
THOMAS DYMES, JACOB BELL, WILLIAM EASON, THOMAS HOPKINS. Before CHARLES
HILL. JACOB MOTTE, Register.

Book C, p. 196   JOSEPH FITCH, SUSANNA (her mark) FITCH, and
10 Jan. 1723   TOBIAS FITCH, of Berkeley Co., SC, bound to
Mortgage   ISAAC MAZYCK, merchant, of Charleston, in pe-
                           nal sum of ₤ 2400 SC money, conditioned for
paymentof ₤ 1200 with interest on 10 Jan. 1724; and for security delivered 2 Negro men, 3 Negro boys, 4 Negro women, 2 Negro girls; and if any of
the Negroes should happen to die, run away, be disabled, or lost before
coming into MAZYCK'S possession, the loss or damage to be sustained by
the FITCHES. Witnesses: JOHN LAURENS, JOHN BONNIN, JOHN CROFT. Before
THOMAS HEPWORTH. JACOB MOTTE, Register.

Book C, p. 200   MARY (her mark) HARTMAN, of Christ Church Par-
26 Dec. 1721   ish, Berkeley Co., SC, to her children as fol-
Deed of Gift   lows: to son JOHN she gives 1 man, 1 boy; to
                           son WARREN she gives 2 men, 1 boy; to son WIL-
LIAM she gives 1 man, 1 woman, 1 boy; to daughter ELIZABETH she lends 1
girl; to daughter HANNAH she gives 2 boys. She gives 1 girl to be appraised after her death and "equally divided" amongst 3 sons. To each of
3 sons she gives 1/3 of all stock & cattle, household goods, tools, plantation tools, etc. She appointed PHILIP JONES, planter of same parish,
sole executor. Witnesses: ROBERT HART, JOHN GREGORY, JAMES CORNELIUS
(CORNELIOUS) DILLON. Before JOHN BARKSDALE. JACOB MOTTE, Register.

Book C, p. 203   RICHARD RIGBY of Kingston, Jamaica. Whereas
17 Oct. 1723   JOHN PERRIE formerly of Island of Antigua,
Letter of Attorney   late of Parish of St. James Westminster, Co.
                           of Middlesex, merchant, by will dated 24 June
(7th year of Q. ANNE) appointed his daughter ANNE PERRIE & DOROTHY PERRIE
& brother EDWARD PERRIE executors (will proved & recorded in Prerogative
Court of Canterbury); and whereas daughter ANNE married RICHARD RIGBY (&
is 21) & the other daughter DOROTHY is not yet 21, RICHARD RIGBY becomes
sole executor; and whereas JOHN PERRIE left 2 other daughters, ELIZABETH
& MARY, (ELIZABETH died) & JOHN PERRIE bequeathed daughter MARY a plantation in SC which he had purchased; and whereas MARY PERRIE has chosen
RICHARD RIGBY her guardian "before his Grace HENRY Duke of Portland", etc.??
RICHARD RIGBY, (executor in right of his wife & guardian of MARY) appoints trusty friends THOMAS GADSDEN & BENJAMIN WHITAKER, ESQS. of SC,
his attorneys to administer the estate in SC. Signed in Jamaica. Witnesses: JOHN STOLLARD, JOHN FOWLER. JOHN STOLLARD appeared before JOHN
BARKSDALE in Charleston 16 Dec. 1723. JACOB MOTTE, Register.

Book C, p. 207   JAMES DAVIS, glover, of Charleston, with love
26 Oct. 1723   and affection to his wife MARGARET DAVIS; 1
Deed of Gift   Negro man & all real & personal estate, books,
                           accounts, & bonds. Witnesses: WILLIAM DIXCE,
JACOB ASHTON, JOHN BROWN. Before CHARLES HILL. JACOB MOTTE, Register.

Book C, p. 209   POWELL HAYWOOD, vintner, of Charleston, to
11 July 1723   JANE MICHELL (JEAN MACHELL) wife of NICHOLAS
Deed of Gift   MICHELL; 1 Negro boy, 1 Negro girl for her
                           sole use. Witnesses: WILLIAM DIXCE (DIXCEY),
MARY SIMONS, JOHN BROWN. Before CHARLES HILL. JACOB MOTTE, Register.

Book C, p. 210   WILLIAM FLAVELL, gentleman, to JOHN MOORE,

18 Apr. 1723   gentleman (both of Charleston) for 10 sh.,
Lease   that brick tenement in Broad Street where ED-
                                MOND ROBINSON lives, being "the middlemost 3rd
part of 1/2 part" of lot #38 bounding W on other part of lot in possession of MARY BLAMYER; E on other part said lot belonging to REBECCA FLA-
VELL, widow; & piece of land adjoining the whole depth of lot. Witnesses: MILES BREWTON, ROBERT HUME. Before THOMAS HEPWORTH. JACOB MOTTE,
Register.

Book C, p. 213   WILLIAM FLAVELL, gentleman, to JOHN MOORE,
19 Apr. 1723   gentleman (both of Charleston) for L 528 cur-
Mortgage   rent SC money, same lot & description as page
                                210: on condition that if WILLIAM FLAVELL pays
JOHN MOORE L 528 on 20 Oct. 1723 the lease & this mortgage to be void.
Witnesses: MILES BREWTON (MICHAEL BRETON), ROBERT HUME. Before THOMAS
HEPWORTH. JACOB MOTTE, Register.

Book C, p. 218   The above mortgage paid June 11th 1733 at WIL-
                                LIAM FLAVELLS house. Receipt signed by JOHN
MOORE. JOSEPH FOX, Deputy Register.

Book C, p. 129   JONATHAN DRAKE, felt maker, & MARY his wife,
23 Mar. 1723/24   for love & affection quit claimed to their
Deed of Gift   brother SAMUEL DRAKE, cordwainer, 280 a. on
                                James Island, Berkeley Co., SC, bounding N on
branch of James Town Creek; E on JOSEPH ATTWELL; W on SAMUEL SCREVEN;
which 280 a. were owned by EDWARD DRAKE their father & by his will given
to SAMUEL. Witnesses: WILLIAM DRAKE JR., EBENEZER MALERY, THOMAS WESBURY.
Before GEORGE CHICKEN. JACOB MOTTE, Register.

Book C, p. 221   MARY (her mark) COLLINS & ANDREW COLLINS to
14 Mar. 1723/4   FRANCIS AVANT, 400 a. Whereas FRANCIS AVANT
Release   of Black River died possessed of 500 a. on N
                                side Black River by virtue of grant from SIR
NATHANIEL JOHNSON & Lords Proprs. & by will gave the 500 a. to his wife
MARY AVANT, now MARY (now wife of ANDREW COLLINS) for love & affection &
for L 50 gives her son FRANCIS AVANT her whole right title & interest in
400 a.; (being 4/5 of the front of the 500 a., beginning at mouth of
creek, downwards on river, thence backwards). ANDREW COLLINS having in
writing (before marrying MARY AVANT) released all right, to said land,
now confirms the quit claim. Witnesses: MEREDITH HUGHES, PETER SANDERS,
ANTHONY ATKINSON. Before GEORGE SMITH. JACOB MOTTE, Register.

Book C, p. 223   THOMAS JONES, of Colleton Co., for L 13 SC mon-
14 Jan. 1691   ey, sold to ROGER NEWINGTON 300 a. fronting on
Deed & Agreement   the west of Bohera Creek with a patent for &
                                plot of the land; provided ROGER NEWINGTON
keeps harmless the said THOMAS JONES from all rents & dues upon said land.
Witnesses: WILLIAM (his mark) WELLS. EDMUND JERVIS on 6 May 1724 ANNE
JONES (formerly wife of THOMAS JONES now wife of SOLOMON LEGARE) acknow-
ledged that she & THOMAS JONES signed & delivered the above deed, before
JOHN BARKSDALE. JACOB MOTTE, Register.

                           DEEDS BOOK "D"
                              1723-1725

Book D, p. 1   ARTHUR FOSTER, planter, of Berkeley Co., &
28 Mar. 1721   MARY his wife to WILLIAM LIVINGSTON, clerk, of
Mortgage   Charleston, for L 450 current money, 370 a.
                                called GIBBONS BLUFF, in Berkeley Co.; bound-
ing E on Cooper River (formerly Etiwan); N on Wasah Creek; S on MRS.
SARAH BEAMOR (formerly CHRISTOPHER EDWARDS); W on RALPH ISARD & WILLIAM
SKIPPER; provided that should ARTHUR FOSTER pay WILLIAM LIVINGSTON 23,000
lbs. merchantable rice in barrels on Bay of Charleston on 1 Feb. next
this agreement to be void. Witnesses: ROBERT HUME, EBENEZER MOODY. Before SAMUEL EVELEIGH. JOHN CROFT, Register. HANNAH LIVINGSTON acknowledges receipt of L 550 in satisfaction. Witness: JACOB MOTTE, Register.

Book D, p. 5   SAMUEL WRAGG, merchant, to JACOB SATUR, mer-
5 & 6 Aug. 1720   chant, both of London, for ₺ 300 English money
L & R   3000 a. being part of Ashley Barony & St. Gil-
                      es, in Berkeley Co., on south side of head of
Ashley River. Whereas the RT. HON. ANTHONY LORD ASHLEY, Earl of Shaftsbury, proprietor, by virtue of a grant from the rest of the proprietors
made to his grandfather ANTHONY, Earl of Shaftsbury dated 18 Mar. 1675 of
12,000 a. commonly called Ashley Barony and St. Giles; and whereas ANTHO-
NY LORD ASHLEY on 20 July 1698 granted to his brother the HON. MAURICE
ASHLEY all his lands in America; and whereas MAURICE ASHLEY, by L & R the
2 & 3 Aug. 1717 conveyed the 12,000 a. to SAMUEL WRAGG, merchant, of
Charleston; now WRAGG sells 3000 a. to SATUR. Witnesses: A. KYNASTON,
EDWARD CROFT, THOMAS PRESTON. Before SAMUEL EVELEIGH. JOHN CROFT, Reg-
ister.

Book D, p. 6   ROBERT (his mark) SWETMAN, planter, of Berke-
6 Mar. 1723   ley Co., and MARGARET his wife, to CHARLES
Lease   HILL, ESQ. of Charleston, for 5 sh., 400 a.
                      English measure, in Berkeley Co. granted by
Lords Proprs. 10 Dec. 1711 to ROBERT SWETMAN; bounding S & N on Simmons
Creek, a part of Cooper River; W on SAMUEL COMMANDER; E on RICHARD BERES-
FORD, ESQ. JACOB MOTTE, Register.

Book D, p. 11   JOSEPH LORD, clerk, of Chatham, Barnstable Co.,
12 Sept. 1720   Province of Mass. Bay, appointed THOMAS WARING,
Letter of Attorney   gentleman, of Berkeley Co., SC, his attorney
                      to handle his property in SC. Witnesses: THOM-
AS LORD, RICHARD KETTELL, RICHARD FOSTER, WILLIAM BARNETT. Before SAMUEL
LYNDE, Boston, Suffolk Co., SAMUEL TYLER, Notary & Tabellion Public.

Book D, p. 12   JOHN BEAMOR, gentleman, of Granville Co., for
26 Feb. 1719/20   love & affection gave his daughter FLORENCE
Deed of Gift   BEAMOR, 2 Negro men, 1 Negro woman & 2 Negro
                      girls, reserving to himself the use of the
Negroes until she reaches the age of 21 or marries; he obliges himself to
deliver to her the 2 Negro men, 2 Negro women, 1 Negro boy, 1 Negro girl
(mortality excepted); this gift in no wise to exclude her from any benefit she should receive from his will or by law. Witnesses: JOSEPH MORTON,
BRIDGET BRAILSFORD, SARAH MORTON. Before H. WILKINSON. JACOB MOTTE,
Register.

Book D, p. 13   JOHN DOUGLASS, gentleman, & SARAH his wife
4 Oct. 1714   (late SARAH BASDEN) & REBECCA BASDEN, spin-
Deed of Sale   sters & daughters & co-heiresses of CHARLES
                      BASDEN, and MARY NARY (late MARY BASDEN, wid-
ow of CHARLES BASDEN), all of Charleston, SC, for ₺ 700 current SC money
to JOSEPH HOLBEATH (HOLDBEALETT), gentleman, of Charleston, 1/2 of town
lot #9. Whereas WILLIAM, Earl of Craven, Palatine, & the Lords Proprs.
on 14 Nov. 1680 granted JOHN MITCHELL 1 town lot #9; and whereas JOHN
MITCHELL on 4 Dec. 16, conveyed it to JOHN COTTINGHAM, planter, and
whereas JOHN COTTINGHAM on 23 Dec. 1682 in his will appointed EDWARD MAYS
& JOHN LADSON his executors in trust with power to sell his land and
houses for the payment of his debts and for the use of his daughter
SARAH; and whereas EDWARD MAYS & JOHN LADSON, executors, on 3 Sept. 1683,
for ₺ 50 sold 1/2 of the lot to ANDREW PERCIVAL, gentleman, bounding E on
Cooper River; W on HENRY SWEETING'S lot; N on the other half of lot #9;
S on HENRY SYMONDS; and whereas ANDREW PERCIVAL, on 10 Oct. 1693, for ₺
80 currency sold the 1/2 lot to CHARLES BASDEN; and whereas CHARLES BAS-
DEN; died intestate & his real estate descended to his son CHARLES BAS-
DEN; and whereas CHARLES, the son, died before reaching 21 years of age,
& the estate became vested in the daughters, MARY BASDEN, SARAH BASDEN,
(now SARAH DOUGLASS), and REBECCA BASDEN as co-heiresses; now they sell
to JOSEPH HOLBEATH, the 1/2 of town lot #9 bounding E on Cooper River; W
on HENRY SWEETING; N on the other 1/2 of lot #9; S on LT. COL. ALEXANDER
PARRIS (formerly MAJOR WILLIAM SMITH). MARY NARY voluntarily releases
her claim. Witnesses: WILLIAM CALVERT, CAPT. JAMES HILL, CAPT. THOMAS
HEPWORTH. JOHN CROFT, Register.

Book D, p. 16   JOSEPH HOLBEATH, gentlemen, of Charleston, to
20 Apr. 1716   JONATHAN FITCH, gentleman, of Berkeley Co.,

Deed of Sale　　　　　　　　for ℔ 1400 current SC money, 1/2 of town lot # 9 bounding E on Cooper River; W on HENRY SWEETing; N on other half of lot #9; S on COL. ALEXANDER PARRIS; which half lot JOSEPH HOLBEATH had purchased from JOHN DOUGLASS & SARAH (BASDEN) his wife, MARY BASDEN, REBECCA BASDEN, & MARY NARY (widow of CHARLES BASDEN). Witnesses: BENJAMIN QUELCH JR., JOHN CROFT, CHARLES HART.　　On 30 Apr. 1716 CAPT. MATTHEW PORTER, attorney for JOSEPH HOLBEATH took quiet possession and delivered to JONATHAN FITCH. Witnesses: S. HEPWORTH, NATHANIEL PARTRIDGE.

Book D, p. 18　　　　　　　JOSEPH HOLBEATH, gentleman, of Charleston, ap-
20 Apr. 1716　　　　　　　pointed MATHEW PORTER his attorney to take
Power of Attorney　　　　possession of the above half lot and deliver
　　　　　　　　　　　　　to JONATHAN FITCH. Witnesses: CHARLES HART,
JOHN CROFT, BENJAMIN QUELCH, JR.

Book D, p. 18　　　　　　　ROBERT SWEETMAN, planter, and MARGARET his
7 Mar. 1723　　　　　　　　wife, of Berkeley Co., to CHARLES HILL, 400 a.
Release　　　　　　　　　　& cattle. Whereas ROBERT (his mark) SWEETMAN
　　　　　　　　　　　　　& MARGARET (her mark) his wife, on 6 Oct. 1721 gave bond to CHARLES HILL in the penal sum of ℔ 460 currency conditioned for the payment of ℔ 230 on 1 Aug. next with interest, and for security (MARGARET signing also) turned over to HILL 400 a. English measure in Berkeley Co., bounding S & N on Simmon's Creek (part of Cooper River); W on SAMUEL COMMANDER; E of RICHARD BERESFORD; which land was granted on 10 Dec. 1711 to SWEETMAN by the Lords Proprs. The mortgage not being paid at the proper time, (℔ 245:5 sh. being due) and for ℔ 222:15 sh. more, SWEETMAN releases the 400 a. and delivers 20 cows, 6 steers, 6 neat cattle 2 years old, 6 neat cattle 1 year old, 3 horses, and 1 mare. Witnesses: BENJAMIN WHITAKER, LAWRENCE COULLIETTE. Before WILLIAM GIBBON. JACOB MOTTE, Register.

Book D, p. 21　　　　　　　"Charleston, Mar. 28th: 1724. Received of
　　　　　　　　　　　　　PETER BOYNTON in behalf of WILLIAM BETTSON deceased 201 pounds 15 sh. in full of all accounts from said BOYNTON to the estate of the deceased. Recd. pr. THO. BROUGHTON. Registered this 28th day of Mar. 1724. By JACOB MOTTE, Register."

Book D, p. 22　　　　　　　The HON. ALEXANDER SKENE, & JAMIMAH, his wife,
6 & 7 June 1723　　　　　　to WILLIAM WALLACE, both of Berkeley Co., SC,
L & R　　　　　　　　　　　for ℔ 5 sh. with proviso named below.　790 a.
　　　　　　　　　　　　　formerly sold by WALLACE to SKENE part of which is known as Cow Savanna, part of Ashley Barony, on S side of Ashley River, bounding W on SAMUEL CLARKE; S ROBERT JOHNSON, alias Black Robin; E on WILLIAM WALLACE & ALEXANDER SKENE; W on ROBERT JOHNSON alias Black Robin; the plat drawn by COL. JOHN HERBERT being in the hands of ALEXANDER SKENE; provided ALEXANDER SKENE pays WILLIAM WALLACE ℔ 3555 current SC money on 20 Feb. next. Witnesses: MARK CATESBY, JOHN BORROSE, THOMAS WEEKLEY.　On 7 June 1723 the HON. ALEXANDER SKENE paid WILLIAM WALLACE ℔ 619, part of the ℔ 3555. Before BENJAMIN WHITAKER.　JACOB MOTTE, Register.

Book D, p. 27　　　　　　　WILLIAM WALLACE ESQ., merchant, of Berkeley
1 & 2 Mar. 1723　　　　　　Co., SC, to PETER CEELY, mariner, of Topsham,
Lease & Mortgage　　　　　Great Britain, now of SC, for ℔ 5114:2:9 current money, 2 tracts of land; 790 a. & 501-½ a.; subject to the condition for redemption by SKENE, (page 22). Whereas by L & R, 6 & 7 June 1723 ALEXANDER SKENE conveyed to WILLIAM WALLACE 790 a. (part of which is called Cow Savanna) in Ashley Barony on south side of Ashley River bounding W on SAMUEL CLARKE; S on ROBERT JOHNSON, alias Black Robin; E on WILLIAM WALLACE & ALEXANDER SKENE; and whereas on 7 June 1722 ALEXANDER SKENE gave WILLIAM WALLACE a bond in the penal sum of ℔ 7110 conditioned for the payment of ℔ 3555 on 20 Jan. 1723; and whereas it is mentioned by indorsement on the said bond that this is the amount of the mortgage; and whereas the release shows receipt of ℔ 619 part payment, and there is now due ℔ 2936 with interest; now WALLACE sells CEELY the above 790 a. and also 501-½ a. on which WILLIAM WALLACE lives on south side of Ashley River; bounding NW on Ashley River; SE part on above 790 a. & part on ALEXANDER SKENE; W on WILLIAM WALLACE.　WALLACE appoints CEELY his attorney in this matter to collect, sue for, etc.

46

Should WALLACE pay CEELY L 4366 currency in Charleston on 1 Feb. 1724 in good & merchantable rice at 40 sh. per 100 & casks at 10 sh. each, with interest, & also L 748:2:9 currency on 1 Feb. 1724, with interest this mortgage to be void. Witnesses: JOSEPH WRAGG, ROBERT HUME. Before WILLIAM GIBBON. JACOB MOTTE, Register.

Book D, p. 37
20 Apr. 1721
Deed of Sale

JOHN GODFREY, planter, son of RICHARD, to JOHN FENWICKE, ESQ. both of Colleton Co., for L 1400 current SC money, 500 a. on Johns Island. Whereas the HON. SIR NATHANIEL JOHNSON, Gov. & the Lords Proprs. 24 Nov. 1709 granted COL. ROBERT GIBBES, of Berkeley Co., 500 a. on St. Johns Island, Colleton Co.; bounding NE on Stono River; SE on JOHN RAVEN; (all other sides on JOHN FENWICKE (formerly COL. ROBERT GIBBES); and whereas by Deed of Feoffment 8 Apr. 1714 GIBBES conveyed the 500 a. to GODFREY, confirming the title in his will; now GODFREY conveys the 500 a. to FENWICKE. Witnesses: JOHN RAVEN, JOHN (his mark) FREEMAN, THOMAS HAY. Before ALEXANDER PARRIS. JACOB MOTTE, Register.

Book D, p. 41
21 & 22 Feb. 1721
L & R

ALEXANDER MACKAY (MCKEY), Indian trader, & HELENA, his wife, of Charleston, to JOHN FENWICKE, ESQ. of Colleton Co. for L 950 current SC money, part of lot #204 in Charleston purchased by JAMES PARETREE (PEARTRA), shipwright, from JOHN VANDERHORST; bounding E on Cooper River 98 ft.; S on LANDGRAVE THOMAS SMITH 475 ft.; W on the street leading from White Point to the old church; N on CAPT. GILL BELCHER; freely cleared of HELENA MACKAY'S right or title of dower. Witnesses: WILLIAM MARR, PROVIDENCE DICKS, ROBERT HUME. Before THOMAS HEPWORTH. JACOB MOTTE, Register.

Book D, p. 46
25 Oct. 1722
Warrant of Attorney

To THOMAS ELLERY, ROBERT HUME & WILLIAM BELLING, gentleman, attorneys to authorize them to appear for EBENEZER BECKHAM, blacksmith, of Charleston, at suit of JOHN HOGG, mariner, in Court of Common Pleas, & confess a judgement for L 176 currency due on bond conditioned for payment of L 87:10 sh. on day of demand 1722. Witnesses: THOMAS COLE, THOMAS ELLERY. Before THOMAS HEPWORTH. JACOB MOTTE, Register.

Book D, p. 47
25 Oct. 1722
Bond

EBENEZER BECKHAM, blacksmith of "Charles City" to JOHN HOGG, mariner, in penal sum of L 176 currency, conditioned for payment of L 87:10 sh. & interest in demand. Witnesses: THOMAS COLE, THOMAS ELLERY. Before THOMAS HEPWORTH. JACOB MOTTE, Register.

Book D, p. 48
25 May 1717
Bond

ISAAC MAZYCK, merchant, to BENJAMIN GODING, merchant, both of Charleston, in sum of L 3000 SC money conditioned for payment of marriage portion equal to that given other of his daughters. Whereas a marriage is to be solemnized between BENJAMIN GODING & MARIANNE, 1 of the daughters of the above ISAAC MAZYCK, if it takes place ISAAC MAZYCK will give or will to BENJAMIN GODING for a marriage portion such sums of money, lands, good, & chattles as will equal the values given any other of his daughters or to any husband of his other daughters. Witnesses: HENRY HOUSER, JACOB LUCE. On 21 Aug. 1722 HENRY HOUSER appeared before ARTHUR MIDDLETON. JACOB MOTTE, Register.

Book D, p. 49
23 & 24 Mar. 1725
L & R

STEPHEN (his mark) MONK, ESQ., of Goose Creek, Berkeley Co., son & heir of JOHN MONK, ESQ., cassique, to GEORGE PETERSON, planter, of same Co., for L 64 current SC money, 640 a. in Berkeley Co., part of 24,000 a. granted by the proprietors to JOHN MONK, having the form laid down in plat by the HON. WILLIAM BULL, ESQ., deputy surveyor general; bounding N on vacant land; W on HENRY SIMMONS; S on Watboo Barony; E on a swamp. Witnesses: JOHN BAYLEY, JOSHUA GREEN, JOHN HERBERT. Before JONATHAN SKRINE. JACOB MOTTE, Register.

Book D, p. 53
4 June 1716
Deed of Sale

CHARLES HILL, ESQ., & ELIZABETH his wife to JOSEPH WATERS (WHETTERS), planter, both of Berkeley Co. for L 150 current SC money, 500 a. on NW side of Sewee Bay, bounding SE on

Sewee Bay; SW on CAPT. HARTMAN (formerly JOHN ABRAHAM MOTTE); NE on MR. SIBLEY; ELIZABETH HILL giving free & unconstrained assent & quit claiming her dower. Whereas the Lords Proprs. on 1 Sept. 1706 granted JOHN ABRAHAM MOTTE 500 a. on the NW side of Sewee Bay in Berkeley Co.; and whereas JOHN ABRAHAM MOTTE died seized of the 500 a.; and whereas ISAAC MOTTE, administrator of the will of JOHN ABRAHAM MOTTE on 6 June 1712 for Ł 50 current money sold the 500 a. to CHARLES HILL, ESQ., to pay the debts of JOHN ABRAHAM MOTTE (Act of Assembly ratified 10 Nov. 1711); now HILL sells to WATERS. Witnesses: SAMUEL EVELEIGH, WILLIAM CAPERS, GEORGE CLARKE. Before JOHN CAWOOD. JACOB MOTTE, Register.

Book D, p. 56
18 Sept. 1723
Renunciation of Dower

ESTHER BUTLER, widow, renounces her right of dower & thirds should she marry WILLIAM ELLIOTT & survive him. Whereas a marriage is to be solemnized between WILLIAM ELLIOTT, planter, of Berkeley Co. & ESTHER BUTLER, widow; and whereas WILLIAM ELLIOTT for providing an estate in jointure to ESTHER BUTLER during her natural life should she survive him, by deed this date conveyed to RICHARD BUTLER, planter, & GEORGE SMITH, ESQ., both of Berkeley Co., in trust, part of a part of lot #10 in "Charles City" 69 ft. on N side, on S side 73 ft. "which is 4 ft. more than the north side by reason of the kitchen in breadth from N to S 43 ft. with a passage in the N side 10 ft. wide reaching to the street", together with the mansion house kitchen & other buildings. Now ESTHER agrees to accept the use of the lot & premises in full satisfaction for any right of dower & thirds. Witnesses: ALEXANDER PARRIS, JOHN BROWN, PETER TAYLOR. Before CHARLES HILL. JACOB MOTTE, Register.

Book D, p. 57
14 Apr. 1724
Mortgage

JOHN SALTON, mariner, to THOMAS PALMER & PETER HERMAN, planters, of St. John's Parish Berkeley County, for Ł 300 the sloop or small 18-ton vessel Elizabeth new in JOHN SALTON'S possession with her appurtenances, anchors, cables PATTEREROES & CANOE conditioned for the payment of Ł 300 current money with interest on 1 Apr. 1725. Witnesses: JOHN LAPIERRE, WILLIAM SMITH. Before JOHN BARKSDALE. JACOB MOTTE, Register.

Book D, p. 59
5 & 6 June 1719
Deed of Sale & Bond

JOHN MOORE, gentleman, of Berkeley Co., for 5 sh., & in consideration of the marriage between RICHARD ROWE & daughter MARTHA, JOHN MOORE conveys, to son-in-law RICHARD ROWE the southernmost third part of a half town lot #15, bounding N on other 2/3 of said half lot; E on the Bay & Cooper River; S on a house belonging to JOHN MOORES wife, MARGARET; W on a neighborhood street. MOORE gives bond to ROWE in penal sum of Ł 500 that in his will he will give ROWE the southernmost 8 ft. 4 in. of land part of the remaining part of the half part of lot #15. Witnesses: PERCIVAL PAWLEY, JOHN CROFT. Before JOHN BARKSDALE. JACOB MOTTE, Register.

Book D, p. 62
26 May 1718
Deed of Sale

PETER GUERARD to JOHN NICHOLSON, cooper, for Ł 200 current SC money, 50 a. in Berkeley Co., bounding SW on PETER STANDLEY (formerly EDWARD STANLEY); NW, NE, & SE on MARTHA WILLIAMS (formerly MRS. FRANCIS WILLIAMS). Whereas WILLIAM, Earl of Craven, Palatine & the Lords Proprs. on 8 Mar. 1706/7 impowered the RT. HON, SIR NATHANIEL JOHNSON, Knight, Gov., etc., of SC & NC, the HON. NICHOLAS TROTT, THOMAS BROUGHTON, ROBERT GIBBES, HENRY NOBLE & JOHN ASHLEY, ESQ. to grant lands; & whereas they granted FRANCIS WILLIAM 1000 a. in Berkeley Co., bounding NW on LANDGRAVE THOMAS COLLETON'S Barony; and whereas WILLIAM by will dated 20 June 1716 gave PETER GUERARD 50 a. (part of the 1000 a.); now PETER GUERARD sells to JOHN NICHOLSON. Witnesses: THOMAS WHITTEN, CHRISTOPHER ARTHUR, EDWARD (his mark) HOWARD. Livery & seizen given by turf & twig. Before DANIEL HUGER. JACOB MOTTE, Register.

Book D, p. 64
6 & 7 May 1724
L & R

CHRISTOPHER ARTHUR, planter, to JOHN NICHOLSON, planter, for Ł 500 current SC money 200 a. in Berkeley Co., part of a Barony given DOMINICK ARTHUR, bounding NW on EDWARD STANLEY. Witnesses: BENJAMIN WHITAKER, JOHN BUCKNALL. Before JOHN BARKSDALE. JACOB MOTTE, Register.

Book D, p. 67   WILLIAM LIVINGSTON, clerk, & ANN his wife, to
28 Oct. 1717   PETER ST. JULIAN, of Berkeley Co., for ₤ 380
Deed of Sale   SC money part of a lot of land within the
                gates of Charleston & 50 ft. on the Broad St.
towards the northward; W 80 ft. on PAUL L'ESCOT; E on PETER ST. JULIAN.
Witnesses: PAUL L'ESCOT, PAUL DOUXSAINT. Before THOMAS BROUGHTON. JACOB
MOTTE, Register.

Book D, p. 69   CHARLES BURNHAM, planter, to HANNAH LIVINGSTON
20 May 1724   executrix of will of WILLIAM LIVINGSTON, gen-
Mortgage   tleman, all of Berkeley Co., for ₤ 650:19:3
                current SC money, 370 a. called Gibbons Bluff,
with certain provisoes. Whereas on 28 Mar. 1721 ARTHUR FOSTER, planter,
& MARY his wife, mortgaged to WILLIAM LIVINGSTON 370 a. called Gibbons
Bluff, Berkeley Co., bounding E on Etewan River (now Cooper River); N on
Wasah Creek; S on MRS. SARAH BEAMOR (formerly CHRISTOPHER EDWARDS); W on
RALPH IZARD & WILLIAM SKIPPER; the condition to the mortgage being that
should ARTHUR or MARY FOSTER deliver to LIVINGSTON 23,000 lbs. good rice
in barrels, on Bay of Charleston, on 1 Feb. next the mortgage to be void;
& whereas FOSTER on 28 Mar. 1721 gave bond to LIVINGSTON in penal sum of
₤ 1100 SC money conditioned for payment of the 23,000 lbs. of rice on 1
Feb. next; & whereas FOSTER did not pay the rice but agreed to pay ₤ 529
in money & for security gave another bond dated 27 Aug. 1722 in penal sum
of ₤ 1100 for true payment of ₤ 529 on 21 Feb. 1723 with interest & whereas ARTHUR & MARY FOSTER by L & R, 21 & 22 Feb. 1722 sold the 370 a. to
CHARLES BURNHAM; & whereas FOSTER did not pay the ₤ 529 & interest
(amounting now to ₤ 650:19:3 & CHARLES BURNHAM has agreed to pay this sum;
now BURNHAM sells to HANNAH LIVINGSTON with the proviso that should BURN-
HAM pay her ₤ 716:19:3 on 20 May 1725 this mortgage to be void. Witnesses: THOMAS HEPWORTH, ROBERT HUME. Before JOSEPH WRAGG. JACOB MOTTE, Register. "Received Feb. 28, 1729, of MR. JOSEPH TOWNSEND & MARY his wife
the full contents of this mortgage for the use of MR. WILLIAM LIVINGSTONS
estate as executor which mortgage I sign over to them. JOHN DART. Witness: WILLIAM COLLINS, JA. GREEME". Before DANIEL GREENE. JACOB MOTTE,
Register.

Book D, p. 74   JAMES MOORE, ESQ. to THOMAS OSGOOD, SR., car-
2 Apr. 1723   penter, both of Berkeley Co. for ₤ 5 SC money,
Deed of Feoffment lot #57 in Dorchester containing 1/4 a. Wit-
                nesses: ARTHUR MIDDLETON, JAMES POSTELL, THOM-
AS WARING. Before BENJAMIN WHITAKER. JACOB MOTTE, Register.

Book D, p. 76   The HON. JOSEPH BLAKE to BENJAMIN WARING, ESQ.,
4 May 1724   both of Berkeley Co., for ₤ 10 current SC mon-
Deed of Feoffment ey, lot #49 in Dorchester containing 1/4 a.
                Witnesses: THOMAS WARING, RICHARD BEADON. Be-
fore ALEXANDER SKENE. JACOB MOTTE, Register.

Book D, p. 77   GEORGE SMITH, planter, of Berkeley Co., to
7 & June 1724 MARK OLIVER, victualler, of Charleston, for ₤
L & R Mortgage 200 current SC money, 190 a. in Berkeley Co.,
                bounding SW on eastern branch of Wando River;
NW on CAPT. JOHN DEARSLEY; SE on WILLIAM BALLAUGH; NE on GEORGE SMITH.
Whereas GEORGE SMITH gave bond this date to MARK OLIVER in penal sum of
₤ 400 for payment of ₤ 200 & interest at MARK OLIVER'S house in Charleston on 8 Dec. 1725, now for security, SMITH conveys to OLIVER the above
190 a., but should SMITH pay OLIVER ₤ 200 & interest at proper place &
time this mortgage to be void. Witnesses: WILLIAM BILLING, LEONARD DOB-
BIN, ALEXANDER CLENCH. Before JOHN BARKSDALE. JACOB MOTTE, Register.

Book D, p. 82   MOSES NORMAN, cooper, & REBEKAH his wife, to
23 Nov. 1720   FRANCIS HOLMES, SR., merchant, of Charleston,
Deed of Sale   for ₤ 300 SC money 300 a. at Beach Hill, Col-
                leton Co., bounding E on JOSEPH SMITH & JOHN
SIMMONS; N on WILLIAM GIBBONS; S on ROGER SUMMERS; W on MOSES NORMAN.
REBEKAH freely surrenders her right of dower. Witnesses: SAMUEL SUMMER,
JOSEPH SMITH, JOB CHAMBERLINE. NORMAN delivered possession to THOMAS
WARING & JOHN SIMMONS in behalf of FRANCIS HOLMES, SR. Before JOHN
BARKSDALE. JACOB MOTTE, Register.

Book D, p. 84
15 Apr. 1724
Deed of Sale

WILLIAM EVE, of Ickenham, Co. of Middlesex, England, now of SC, only son & heir of JOHN EVE, to ROBERT YOUNG, gentleman, & HANNAH his wife, (relict & sole executrix of will of ABRAHAM EVE, of St. Paul's, Colleton Co.) for ₤ 250 money of Great Britain (₤ 100 to be paid in 3 months; ₤ 100 on 10 May 1726; ₤ 50 on 10 May 1727, at London) & other considerations, sells 956 a. on head of Tooboodoo Creek, Colleton Co., bounding E on ARCHIBALD STOBO; W on JAMES GILBERTSON; W on ARCHIBALD STOBO; S on JAMES GILBERTSON & releases all claim to any personal estate of ABRAHAM EVE. Whereas ABRAHAM EVE by will dated 22 Mar. 1722 gave 1 full half of the clear profits of his whole estate, real & personal (except what was bequeathed to his dearly beloved wife HANNAH) for the use of the right heir (make) of his brother JOHN EVE of Ickenham, near Uxbridge (if any such male heir should be living at time of his decease) to be remitted to him yearly, & also willed all his real & personal estate, after the death of HANNAH, to said make heir; now WILLIAM EVE sells YOUNG 956 a. in Colleton Co. Witnesses: HON. ARTHUR MIDDLETON, CHRISTOPHER WILKINSON, JOHN SKENE. Before THOMAS FARR. JACOB MOTTE, Register.

Book D, p. 87
8 Dec. 1719
Deed of Sale

JOHN WATKINS, planter, to JUDITH LADSON, both of Charleston Neck, for ₤ 24:5 sh. current SC money, 6 1/2 a., English measure, part of a great tract formerly belonging to WILLIAM ALLEN COOPER, bounding N on the "Rat Trap" belonging to CHARLES HART, ESQ.; W & S on JOHN WATKINS; E on the High Road or Broad Path. Witnesses: JOHN LADSON, MARTHA LITTEN, THOMAS MOORE, CHARLES HART, J.Q. JACOB MOTTE, Register.

Book D, p. 89
7 July 1724
Mortgage

STEPHEN RUSSELL, cordwainer, of Berkeley Co., to MICHAEL JEANES, merchant, of Charleston, in consideration of a bond of this date wherein RUSSELL is bound to JEANES in penal sum of ₤ 545:13:6 for payment of ₤ 272:16:9 SC money on 11 Nov. 1725 for security conveys to JEANES 155 a. on James Island, Berkeley Co., (plat attached to grant signed by the HON. EDWARD TYNTE, Gov., 14 Apr. 1710) bounding S on a Great Sound; E & N on marsh & a creek; W on ALEXANDER SPENCER (formerly EDWARD WESTBERRY). Witnesses: JOHN BOYDEN, JAMES KILPATRICK. Before CHARLES HILL. JACOB MOTTE, Register.

Book D, p. 92
6 Aug. 1724
Deed of Sale

ISAAC DUGUE, shipwright, to his brother-in-law, PAUL TRAPIER, planter, for ₤ 250 SC money, 1/2 of 1/4 of a half town lot in Charleston. Whereas JAMES DUGUE, SR., father of ISAAC, by will dated 28 May 1696 gave his 5 children, ISAAC, PETER, MARY, JUDITH & ELIZABETH, & his granddaughter MARIANE DUGUE all his real & personal estate, share & share alike; and whereas the estate was duly divided on 27 Oct. 1696, among other things allowing ISAAC DUGUE & his sister ELIZABETH (in equal halves) a certain part of a lot in Charleston being 1/4 of 1/2 of 1 town lot fronting to the Broad Street, bounding S on the Broad Street, E on DR. JOHN DELEAUHE, W & N on ELIZABETH BURTELL, which part of a lot their father JAMES had purchased from JAMES DUBOURDEAUX, blacksmith, on 31 Oct. 1687; and whereas PAUL TRAPIER by marrying ELIZABETH DUGUE became heir to 1/2 of the 1/4 part of the 1/2 town lot & half the buildings; now ISAAC DUGUE sells his half to TRAPIER. Witnesses: JAMES SEARON, PETER HERMAN, ANTHONY BONNEAU, JR. Before THOMAS HEPWORTH. JACOB MOTTE, Register.

Book D, p. 95
10 Sept. 1710
Deed of Gift

ELLENER (her mark) BENTLEY, of Berkeley Co., for love & affection to her son & daughter, JOHN & ANN DASHWOOD, planter, 50 a. English measure, bounding SE on Boowat Creek; NE on ELLENER BENTLEY; NW on JOHN BOONE; SW on PETER BOUDON (BEDON?). Witnesses: THOMAS LOREY, JOTHAM (his mark) GIBENS, JOHN (his mark) MORGAN. Possession given by turf & twig. Before THOMAS BOONE. JACOB MOTTE, Register.

Book D, p. 96
13 July 1722
Power of Attorney

ROBERT TENNATT (TANNATT), commander of the Pearl Galley of Bristol, Great Britain, appointed CHARLES HILL, merchant, of "Charles

City," SC, his attorney. Witnesses: MOSES WILSON, JACOB MOTTE. Before JOHN CAWOOD. JACOB MOTTE, Register.

Book D, p. 98   JONAS BONHOSTE, planter, to HENRY PERONNEAU,
24 Aug. 1724   merchant, of Charleston, 750 a., English mea-
Lease   sure, where BONHOSTE lives, at head of Wando
                     River, part of 3 tracts formerly granted to
DANIEL MCGREGORY (see p. 100).

Book D, p. 100   JONAS BONHOSTE, planter, of 1st part; CATHER-
25 Aug. 1724   INE (her mark) LAPOSTRE, widow, of 2nd part;
Mortgage, by Release, HENRY PERONNEAU, merchant, of Charleston, of
Tripartite   3rd part. Whereas JONAS BONHOSTE & CATHERINE
                     LAPOSTRE on this date, stand bound to HENRY
PERONNEAU in penal sum of Ł 1000 for true payment of Ł 948:10 & interest
at 10% on 1 Mar. 1725, for security mortgages to PERONNEAU 750 a. at head
of Wando River; BONHOSTE also delivers to PERONNEAU 6 Negro men, 2 Negro
women, 3 Negro boys and 1 Negro girl. For better security, CATHERINE LA-
POSTRE delivers to PERONNEAU 6 Negro slaves. Should CATHERINE & JONAS
pay PERONNEAU Ł 948:10 with interest at proper time these indentures to
be void. Witnesses: ROBERT HUME, MAURICE HARVEY, CHILDERMUS CROFT. Before THOMAS HEPWORTH, Chief Justice. JACOB MOTTE, Register. "Recd. of
MR. JONAS BONHOSTE /by the hands of MR. ELIAS FOISSEN/ the 17th May 1729
the sum of 1,020 pounds in full payment & satisfaction of the within
mortgage /HENRY PERONNEAU. Witness: JACOB MOTTE, Register." Plot of 750
a. made by JOHN HERBERT 25 Aug. 1724.

Book D, p. 106   JOHN (his mark) BELL, SR., planter, & PRISCIL-
9 & 10 Dec. 1720   LA, his wife, to ELIAS HORRY, planter, all of
L & R   Craven Co., for Ł 600 SC money, 1000 a. in 2
                     tracts; 500 a. in Craven Co., bounding S on a
creek & Santee River; W on other part JOHN BELL'S land; also 500 a. in
Craven Co., bounding S on a creek; W on CAPT. GAILLARD: N on vacant land;
E on JOHN BELL. Witnesses: EDWARD WEEKLEY, MEREDITH HUGHES, ANDREW COL-
LINS. Witness to signing of receipt by PRISCILLA; THOMAS HEPWORTH. Be-
fore JAMES NICHOLAS MAYRANT. JACOB MOTTE, Register.

Book D, p. 109   JOSEPH (his mark) SPENCER, JR., & AUGUSTUS
25 Feb. 1723/4   LAURANCE to RICHARD EDGHILL, of Craven Co. for
Mortgage   divers good reasons & for 150 barrels good
                     pitch paid them by EDGHILL assign to EDGHILL
500 a. in Craven Co. bounding N on Wambaw Creek, E on MICHAEL CLINCH; S
on ELIAS HORRY; W on RICHARD EDGHILL; also all the horses, mares, black
cattle & hogs on the plantation. Should SPENCER & LAURANCE pay EDGHILL
150 barrels of pitch in Charleston on 1 Feb. 1728 with interest at end of
every 12 months beginning Feb. next, this mortgage, & also a bond of even
date, to be void. Witnesses: MORRIS MURSEE, WILLIAM BOHANAN, JOHN SPENC-
ER, SAMUEL BENNET. Before JAMES NICHOLAS MAYRANT. JACOB MOTTE, Register.
Ł 300 paid in full satisfaction of mortgage 10 Apr. 1729 to RICHARD EDG-
HILL. Witness, JACOB MOTTE, Register.

Book D, p. 111   JAMES CANTY, planter, of Ashley Ferry, to JOHN
8 Feb. 1724   HILL, carpenter, of Dorchester, in sum of Ł
Bond   1000 SC money to secure JOHN HILL against
                     suits & controversies by the heirs of JAMES
CANTY of ELIZABETH his wife on account of 100 a. conveyed to HILL by L &
R, 7 & 8 Feb. 1724. Witnesses: WILLIAM WALLACE, GEORGE CANTY, MARGARET
(her mark) ARDEN. Before THOMAS WARING. JACOB MOTTE, Register.

Book D, p. 112   JAMES BROWN (BROWNE), planter, to HENRY LIVING-
30 & 31 July 1722   STON, planter, both of Berkeley Co., for Ł
L & R   1500 SC money, 3 tracts of land; 200 a., 210
                     a., & 300 a., which he bought from JOHN LYNCH,
merchant, by Deed of Feoffment 12 Mar. 1715; which 710 a. taken as 1
tract is known as Lynch grove plantation on Wando Neck, Berkeley Co., the
1 tract bounding E & N on JOHN HOLIBUSH, S on JOHN BOWEN & JOHN BURKE, W
on WILLIAM WHITE. JAMES BROWN to cause HANNAH, his wife, to appear before CHARLES HILL, C. J. of Court of Common Pleas on 20 Aug. next & release her title of dower. Witnesses: ANTHONY WHITE, ROBERT HUME, WILLIAM
SCOTT. Before BENJAMIN WHITAKER. JACOB MOTTE, Register.

Book D, p. 118   HENRY LIVINGSTON, gentleman, of Berkeley Co.
1 July 1722   testifies that his name was used in the pur-
Declaration of Trust   chase of Lynch Grove plantation (710 a.) at
                        the appointment of JOHN LENOIR. Whereas by L
& R, 1 July 1722 JAMES BROWN for L 1500 SC money sold HENRY LIVINGSTON 3
tracts of land (see page 112); & whereas LIVINGSTON gave several bonds to
several persons to whom BROWN is indebted; and whereas LIVINGSTON purchased the 3 tracts of land in trust for the HON. JOHN LENOIR, ESQ., of
the Island of Barbadoes; now LIVINGSTON promises to convey the land to
LENOIR upon LENOIR'S paying LIVINGSTON'S several bonds. Witnesses: WIL-
LIAM SCOTT, ANTHONY WHITE, ROBERT HUME. Before BENJAMIN WHITAKER. JACOB
MOTTE, Register.

Book D, p. 120   CAPT. GERSHAM HAWKS, planter, of Berkeley Co.,
1 July 1713   to FRANCIS HOLMES, merchant, of Boston, New
Deed of Feoffment   England, for L 40 SC money 500 a. (the western-
                        most part of 1000 a.). Whereas HIS EXCELLENCY
JOHN EARL of Bath & the Lords Proprs. by grant under the hands of the HON.
JAMES MOORE, ESQ., Gov., dated 17 May 1701 gave CAPT. ROBERT FENWICKE
1000 a., English measure, in Berkeley Co.; & whereas FENWICKE on 31 Mar.
1703 for L 78:9:7 sold LADY REBECCA AXTELL the 1000 a.; & whereas REBECCA
AXTELL on 12 May 1712 for L 100 sold to CAPT. GERSHAM HAWKS the 1000 a.
and 33-3/4 a. more adjoining the 1000 a. on the N side of the head of
Ashley River, bounding S on Dorchester land; & NE & W on vacant land; now
HAWKS sells to HOLMES. Witnesses: DAVID FERGUSON, ISAAC BRUNSON, JOHN
CORFT. On 5 Oct. 1723 CAPT. HAWKS took possession & delivered to DAVID
FERGUSON on behalf of FRANCIS HOLMES. Witnesses: ISAAC BRUNSON, ROBERT
(his mark) MILLER, SR. Before SAMUEL EVELEIGH. JACOB MOTTE, Register.

Book D, p. 123   WILLIAM SANDERS, planter, of St. George's Par-
2 Sept. 1724   ish, Berkeley Co., to SAMUEL BARONS, merchant,
L & R   of London, for L 30 sterling of Great Britain,
                        1000 a. in Berkeley Co. on NE side Ashley Riv-
er within land, granted 5 Apr. 1705 by the Lords Proprs. to WILLIAM SAND-
ERS, planter, father of above WILLIAM SANDERS, plat made 28 Aug. 1704 by
the HON. JOB HOWES, ESQ. Surveyor general; bounding NW on GEORGE IZARD;
SW on GEORGE IZARD & ISAAC PORCHER: SE on THEODORE VEREDITTY; NE on va-
cant land. Witnesses: RICHARD SPLATT, ANNA SANDERS, MARGARET SANDERS,
THOMAS (his mark) SIMSON. On 9 Sept. 1724 delivery made to RICHARD
SPLATT in behalf of SAMUEL BARONS. Before WILLIAM BLAKEWEY. JACOB
MOTTE, Register.

Book D, p. 128   The HON. ARTHUR MIDDLETON, ESQ., & FRANCIS
8 & 9 Mar. 1720   HOLMES, SR., merchant, attorneys of THOMAS
L & R   AMORY, of Boston, to RICHARD SPLATT, merchant,
                        of "Charles City" for L 400 currency, part of
lot #79 in Charleston bounding S 65 ft. on a street leading from Cooper
River to Ashley River; N on THOMAS AMORY; E 205 ft. on other part of lot
called Saw Pitt formerly belonging to JOHN CROSKEYS now to executors of
MATHEW PORTER; W on ARTHUR MIDDLETON. Whereas the HON. WILLIAM EARL of
Craven, Palatine, & the Lords Proprs. by grant 17 Aug. 1783 gave JONATHAN
FITCH, SR. 1 lot in "Charles City" #79; & whereas FITCH willed the lot to
his daughters RACHEL & SARAH; & whereas JAMES STANYARNE & RACHEL, his
wife, JOHN NORTON & SARAH his wife, by bill of sale dated 28 Oct. 1691
sold the lot to JONATHAN ANORY, SR. late of SC; and whereas part of the
lot was willed to THOMAS AMORY by JONATHAN AMORY his father; and whereas
THOMAS AMORY on 15 Nov. 1722 appointed ARTHUR MIDDLETON & FRANCIS HOLMES
jointly his attorneys to handle his real estate in SC; now MIDDLETON &
HOLMES sell to SPLATT part of lot #67. Witnesses to signature of FRANCIS
HOLMES: BENJAMIN WHITAKER, ROBERT HUME, WILLIAM SCOTT. Witnesses to signature of ARTHUR MIDDLETON: BENJAMIN WHITAKER, ROBERT HUME, RALPH IZARD,
WILLIAM BULL. Before CHARLES HILL. JACOB MOTTE, Register.

Book D, p. 133   JONATHAN FITCH, gentleman, of Berkeley Co., to
15 Aug. 1716   THOMAS ELLIOTT, ESQ., of Colleton Co., for L
Deed of Sale   1600 SC money 1/2 of lot #9 in Charleston
                        bounding E on Cooper River; W on HENRY SWEET-
ING; N on part same lot; S on half a lot of COL. ALEXANDER PARRIS; which
half lot JONATHAN FITCH purchased from JOSEPH HOLBEATH, gentleman. Witnesses: DANIEL GREEN, MANLEY WILLIAMSON, LEWIS JOHN, THOMAS HEPWORTH.

Before THOMAS HEPWORTH. JACOB MOTTE, Register.

Book D, p. 135　　　　　　　JOHN LENOIR, ESQ., of town of St. Michael, Is-
11 Feb. 1723/4　　　　　　　land of Barbadoes, appointed JOHN LLOYD, ESQ.,
Power of Attorney　　　　　of Charleston, his attorney, to take posses-
　　　　　　　　　　　　　　sion of & handle his real estate & slaves in
SC. Witnesses: CAPT. OTHNIEL BEALE, JOSEPH WILLEY. Before JOSEPH WRAGG.
JACOB MOTTE, Register.

Book D, p. 136　　　　　　　LANDGRAVE THOMAS SMITH & MARY his wife to
1 Sept. 1718　　　　　　　　their son GEORGE SMITH the younger, both of
Deed of Gift　　　　　　　　Berkeley Co., for natural love & affection &
　　　　　　　　　　　　　　for ₤ 100 conveyed 1000 a. in Berkeley Co. &
2200 a. in Craven Co., also 2 town lots #117 & #146. Witnesses: EDWARD
WEEKLEY, THOMAS SMITH, JR., ELIZABETH WEEKLEY, ELIZABETH BLAKE. Before
CHARLES HILL. JACOB MOTTE, Register. Plat of 3200 a. made & certified
10 May 1718 by PERCIVALL PAWLEY, D.S.

Book D, p. 140　　　　　　　Vestry & Church Commissioners of St. Philips
17 Aug. 1724　　　　　　　　Church, Charleston, to CHARLES HILL, for ₤ 75,
Grant for Pew #11　　　　　Pew #11 in south aisle. "Whereas by an Act of
　　　　　　　　　　　　　　the General Assembly of this Province intitled
an act for carrying on the building and for finishing and compleating the
brick church in Charleston and for declaring it to be the Parish Church
of St. Philips Charleston passed the 9th day of Dec. 1720 which Act has
since been revived and confirmed it was amongst other things enacted that
the pews in the said church should be built by the direction and appointment of the commissioners therein named by and with the /advice &/ consent of the major part of the vestry; therefore, in consideration of the
generous benefaction of MR. CHARLES HILL to the said church and of his
paying" ₤ 75 they "grant unto the said CHARLES HILL and to his heirs and
assigns forever a pew in the said church distinguished in the platt of
the said pews remaining of record in the secretarys office by the number
eleven in the South Isle....<u>Provided</u> nevertheless that if the said CHARL-
ES HILL shall by /any/ manner of way or means alter the present uniformity of the said pew as it is now built by raising or lowering the same by
taking down the partition or by any other way whatsoever or if the said
CHARLES HILL shall sell or dispose of the said pew to any person or persons whatsoever except such person or persons be actually residents and
inhabitants in the said Parish than this present grant and every matter
and thing therein contained shall be void and of none effect and the said
pew No. 11 in the South Isle shall revert to the Vestry of St. Philips
Parish for the time being to be disposed of to such persons as they shall
think proper. Given under our hands and seals in the said church this
17th day of Aug. 1724. Ffr: NICHOLSON, A. GARDEN, WILLIAM GIBBON, ALEX-
ANDER PARRIS, JOS. WRAGG, WM. BLAKEWEY, ELISHA PRIOLEAU, J. HUTCHINSON,
WM. GIBBON, WM. BLAKEWEY, ALEXR. PARRIS, THOS. HEPWORTH." JACOB MOTTE,
Register.

Book D, p. 141　　　　　　　STEPHEN RUSSELL, cordwainer, to WILLIAM PAR-
12 June 1721　　　　　　　　ROTT, planter for ₤ 256 SC money 100 a. on
Release　　　　　　　　　　James Island, Berkeley Co., bounding NE on a
　　　　　　　　　　　　　　creek & marsh; S on a sound; w on dividing
line between said 100 a. & other part "said tract, the corner tree northerly is a small purismon, and outherly the orner is a small live oak at
the head of a small marsh about 14 chains a park NW 8 degrees the course
from 1 corner to the other". This land belonged to WILLIAM RUSSELL; then
to GEORGE RUSSELL (brother of WILLIAM); then to STEPHEN RUSSELL (son of
GEORGE) party hereto. JEAN RUSSELL, wife of STEPHEN, willingly surrenders her right of dowry. Witnesses: JOHN SANDIFORD, JOHN CROSKEYS, WIL-
LIAM SPENCER. Before ALEXANDER PARRIS. JACOB MOTTE, Register.

Book D, p. 143　　　　　　　JOHN (his mark) GOODBEE, (GOODBE), planter,
1 Nov. 1715　　　　　　　　 for tender love & affection to his son JAMES
Deed of Gift　　　　　　　　GOODBE the son of his wife ELIZABETH GOODBE, &
　　　　　　　　　　　　　　for other considerations, 250 a. upon the
Stoney Run between the plantation of JOHN GOODBE, SR. & that of JOHN GOOD-
BE, JR., also 1 Negro woman & 1 Negro man. In case JOHN, JR., dies with-
out issue, the land & Negroes to return to the family of the GOODBES.
Witnesses: HENRY DURANT, JOHN MCMURTRY, ANN (her mark) COOK. Before

RICHARD HARRIS.   JACOB MOTTE, Register.

Book D, p. 145   SAMUEL DAVIS, JR., planter, to EDWARD HEXT,
20 & 21 May 1724   merchant, both of Colleton Co., for ℒ 375 cur-
L & R   rent SC money, 500 a. Whereas the Lords Pro-
                       prs. on 12 Jan. 1705 for ℒ 10 granted SAMUEL
DAVIS 500 a. in Colleton Co., on NE side Ponpon River butting on lands of
JOHN BEE & WILLIAM FREEMAN; & whereas SAMUEL DAVIS by deed of gift on 20
Feb. 1713 gave the 500 a. to his son SAMUEL DVAIS; now SAMUEL DAVIS, JR.,
sells to HEXT. Witnesses: MAURICE HARVEY, JOSEPH FITCH, JOHN CROFT. Be-
fore THOMAS HEPWORTH. JACOB MOTTE, Register.

Book D, p. 150   THOMAS ELLIOTT, planter, of Colleton Co., to
5 Feb. 1714   FRANCIS HOLMES, merchant, of Charleston, for
Deed of Feoffment   ℒ 40 current SC money, part of a part of lot
                       #10, fronting 6 ft. on Callibeauf's Lane,
bounding W on said lot; E on several house of JOHN SIMMONS, FRANCIS
HOLMES, DANIEL GALE, & MR....; S 87 ft. back home to the end of other
part of THOMAS ELLIOTT'S lot, & adjoins the tenement of MR. LARUSH
(LAROCHET). Witnesses: THOMAS CATER, WILLIAM BILLING. Before JOHN BARKS-
DALE. JACOB MOTTE, Register.

Book D, p. 151   EDMOND PORTER, gentleman, to ISAAC MAZYCK, mer-
9 & 10 Nov. 1724   chant, both of Charleston, for 1 year at the
Deed of Lease   rent of ℒ 100 current SC money. A brick mes-
                       suage in the Broad Street. Whereas EDMOND POR-
TER on this date gave bond to ISAAC MAZYCK, in penal sum of ℒ 2000 for
payment of ℒ 1000 with interest on 10 Nov. 1725, now, for security, POR-
TER conveys to MAZYCK, that brick messuage, being 2 tenements, in the
Broad Street in Charleston. Witnesses: JOSEPH DE ST. JULIAN, PAUL MAZYCK,
BENJAMIN WHITAKER. Before THOMAS HEPWORTH. JACOB MOTTE, Register.

Book D, p. 157   DOMINICK SKERRETT, merchant of Island of Ma-
31 Mar. 1724   deira, appointed his trusty friend, WILLIAM
Power of Attorney   HAMERTON, ESQ., naval officer of Charleston,
                       his attorney to collect money from MESSRS. WIL-
LIAM RHETT, SR. & JR. Witnesses: WILLIAM RIDER (Consul), JAMES CLARKE.
On 1 Aug. 1724, before THOMAS HEPWORTH, C.J., appeared WILLIAM RENDELL,
master of the PINK SEA NYMPH & THOMAS BINFORD, supercargo of said ship,
who testified that SKERRETT gave them the power of attorney to hand to
HAMERTON but by misfortune being taken by a pirate 1 Spriggs Commander in
their passage from the Island of Maderas to the Port of SC were by the
said pyrates plundered and the said power of attorney of which (they believe the within to be a copy) was by them taken away and they and each
of them verily believes that DOMINICK SKERRETT the constituent within
named and the witnesses WILLIAM RIDER, Consul and JAMES CLARKE to be
their very names and their own handwriting being very conversant with
both of them." Before THOMAS HEPWORTH. JACOB MOTTE, Register.

Book D, p. 158   JOHN (his mark) ANDREWS, cordwainer, of Ponts
30 Oct. 1718   Berry, Co. of Shallop, in Shropshire, Great
Deed of Sale   Britain, now of SC, to JOHN CARNICHAEL, joiner
                       of Berkeley Co., for ℒ 80 current SC money, 2
lots in Charleston, granted by the Lords Proprs. to PETER GUERARD; by him
conveyed to CAPT. EDMOND MEDLICOAT; then came to JOHN ANDREWS as administrator of EDMOND MEDLICOTT "as by the letters of administration taken out
of Doctors Commons" June 1716; being lot #219 in Charleston, bounding E
on the great street leading from Ashley River; W on JOHN ANDREWS other
lot; S on CAPT. GEORGE RAYNER; N on DR. CHARLES BURNHAM; also lot #220
bounding E on lot #219; W on a little street running from Ashley River by
the lots of JOHN JONES & JOHN HILL; S on CAPT. GEORGE RAINER; N on DR.
CHARLES BURNHAM. Witnesses: GILBERT JONES, JOHN (his mark) FINLEY, WIL-
LIAM LAUGHTON. Before THOMAS HEPWORTH, C.J. JACOB MOTTE, Register.

Book D, p. 160   MARY BASDEN, spinster, of Charleston, the REV.
15 Apr. 1724   WILLIAM GUY, clerk of the Parish of St. An-
Release   drews, Berkeley Co., & REBECCA his wife, to
                       JOHN CARMICHAEL, carpenter, of Charleston, for
ℒ 400 current SC money, 2 lots in Charleston, Nos. 281 & 282; bounding W
on a little street running from Ashley River by MR. JONES & MR. HILL; E

54

on CORNELIUS LONGHAIR (formerly CHARLES BASDEN) & MR. TUBB; S on GEORGE CHICKEN, ESQ. (formerly BERNARD SCHERKING, ESQ.); N on ANTHONY SPENCER (formerly GEORGE RAYNOR). Whereas CHARLES BASDEN, of Charleston owned lands in Berkeley Co. & lots in Charleston; & whereas at his death the several pieces of real estate descended to MARY BASDEN, SARAH COLLINS & REBECCA GUY, sisters of CHARLES & co-heirs at law; & whereas MARY BASDEN, JONATHAN COLLINS & SARAH his wife, WILLIAM GUY & REBECCA his wife, by deed of partition tripartite 25 Jan. 1721 divided the estate amongst themselves whereby MARY BASDEN, WILLIAM GUY & REBECCA his wife be owners of 2 lots in Charleston, Nos. 281 & 282; now they sell to CARMICHAEL. Witnesses: JOHN CAWOOD, JOHN CROFT. Before THOMAS HEPWORTH, C.J. JACOB MOTTE, Register.

Book D, p. 163
9 Nov. 1722
Power of Attorney

JOHN BAYLEY, ESQ., of Ballinaclough, Co. of Tipperary, Ireland, son & heir of JOHN BAYLEY, appoints ALEXANDER TRENCH, merchant, his attorney with power to apportion & sell the land except 8000 a. as convenient. Whereas the RIGHT HON. JOHN BATH & the Lords Proprs. by Letters Patents on 16 Aug. 1698 created JOHN BAYLEY Landgrave & Cassick, granting him 43,000 a.; now BAYLEY appoints TRENCH his attorney. Witnesses: RICHARD PROST, HENRY BUCKLEY, Notary Public.

Book D, p. 165
25 Mar. 1719
Power of Attorney

CHARLES HILL, merchant, of Charleston, appointed his good friend CAPT. ROBERT SEREVEN, planter, of Berkeley Co., his attorney to take possession of a certain plantation & deliver to JOSEPH WATERS. Witnesses: SOLOMON TOZER, RICHARD HILL. Before JOHN CAWOOD. Witnesses to livery & seizin: NATHANIEL FORD, JAMES BROWN, JONATHAN WHILDEN. Before ROBERT FENWICK. Power & memorandum endorsed or deed registered in Book D, folio 53-55, omitted then & registered this 12 Jan. 1724 & 5. JACOB MOTTE, Register.

Book D, p. 166
15 & 16 Jan. 1724
L & M

The HON. ALEXANDER SKENE, ESQ., of Berkeley Co., SC to PETER CEELY, mariner, of Topsam, Great Britain, for L 2600 current SC money, 790 a., part of which is commonly known as Cow Savanna, in Ashley Baroney, on S side of head of Ashley River; bounding W on SAMUEL CLARKE; S on ROBERT JOHNSON, alias Black Robin; E on WILLIAM WALLACE, ESQ. & ALEXANDER SKENE; the marks of which are mentioned in a plat attached to release from WILLIAM WALLACE to ALEXANDER SKENE. It is agreed that if SKENE pays CEELY L 2600 current money as follows: L 1300 on 1 July 1725 & L 1300 on 1 Jan. 1725 with interest, this mortgage to be void. SKENE promises that his wife JEMIMA shall within 1 months absolutely renounce before the Chief Justice all her dower in said tract. Should SKENE fail to meet payments CEELY may sell the land at auction. To enable CEELY to dispose of the 790 a. either in the whole or in part, SKENE appoints CEELY his attorney. Witnesses: WILLIAM WALLACE, HENRY HARGRAVE. Before JOHN CAWOOD. JACOB MOTTE, Register.

Book D, p. 172

"ELIAS HORRY had a grant for 500 a. of land in Craven Co. bounding to the W on MICHAEL CLINCH to the E on DANIEL HORRY, at 1 sh. pr. 100 a., dated the 10th day of June 1718 and signed by ROBERT JOHNSON, A. SKENE, THOMAS BROUGHTON, CHARLES HART. FRANCIS YOUNG." SC. The above copy taken from great book of record #B remaining in the secretarys office of this Province page 444. Examined and attested Apr. ye 6th 1725 pr CHARLES HART, secretary. Registered the 9th of Apr. 1725. By JACOB MOTTE, Register.

Book D, p. 173
16 Sept. 1718
Bill of Sale

JOHN GODFREY, of Colleton Co., to JOHN WOODWARD, gentleman, of Colleton Co., for L 450 current SC money, 350 a. in Berkeley Co.
Whereas JOHN Earl of Bath, Palatine & the Lords Proprs by grant 11 May 1699 & under the hand of the RT. HON. JOSEPH BLAKE, ESQ., the HON. LANDGRAVE JOSEPH MORTON, ROBERT DANIEL, JAMES MOORE; EDMOND BELLINGER & JOHN ELY, ESQRS., commissions for the granting & selling of land, granted to CAPT. JOHN GODFREY 974 a. in Berkeley Co. on SW side of Ashley River, bounding NE on Ashley River; N part on Governor's Creek, part on FRANCIS BLANSHAW; W part on vacant land, part on COL. ROBERT GIBBES; SE part on Wappoe Creek, part on COL. ROBERT GIBBES; & whereas CAPT. JOHN GODFREY bequeathed to his eldest son JOHN GODFREY 500 a.

(part of the 974 a.); now JOHN GODFREY sells WOODWARD 350 a. (part of the 500 a.), the boundings of which are laid down in a general plat of all the lands of CAPT. JOHN GODFREY, the father, dated 9 Nov. 1717. Witnesses: RICHARD GODFREY, JOSEPH CLARE, JOHN PAGE. Before JOHN CAWOOD. JACOB MOTTE, Register.

Book D, p. 175
18 May 1722
Bond

REBECCA FLAVEL, widow, of Charleson gave WILLIAM GIBBON & ANDREW ALLEN, merchants, of Charleston, a bond in penal sum of ₤ 162 sterling money of Great Britain conditioned for the payment of ₤ 98-1/2 Spanish pistoles on 21 May 1723 according to a proviso in a mortgage of even date between REBECCA FLAVEL and GIBBON & ALLEN. Witnesses: GABRIEL MANIGAULT, WILLIAM FAIRCHILD, THOMAS HEPWORTH. Before CHARLES HILL. JACOB MOTTE, Register.

Book D, p. 176
17 & 18 May 1722
L & R & Mortgage

REBECCA FLAVEL (FLAVELL), widow of JOHN FLAVELL, mariner, of Charleston, to WILLIAM GIBBON & ANDREW ALLEN, merchants, of Charleston, for ₤ 81:12 sterling money of Great Britain, that messuage or tenement wherein ROBERT JOHNSON dwells fronting 16-1/2 ft. from E to W, with the ground adjoining, descending E on SAMUEL FLAVELL'S tenement; W on WILLIAM FLAVELL'S messuage where REBECCA now dwells; which messuage & ground were willed to REBECCA by JOHN FLAVELL. If REBECCA pays GIBBON & ALLEN ₤ 98-1/2 Spanish pistoles, each pistole weighing 4 penny weight 6 grains on 21 May 1723 the house & land to be re-conveyed to REBECCA. Witnesses: GABRIEL MANIGAULT, WILLIAM FAIRCHILD, THOMAS HEPWORTH. Before CHARLES HILL. JACOB MOTTE, Register.

Book D, p. 180

"DANIEL HUGER had a grant for 100 a. of land in Craven Co. on the south side of Wambah Creek bounding to /the/ west on the said DANIEL HUGER, to the east on land not laid out, to the north on the said creek and to the south on lands not laid out, paying to the Lords Proprs. on every first day of Dec. 1703, 1 sh. pr..... The said grant is dated the 16th july 1703 and signed, N. JOHNSON, JA. MOORE, NICH. TROTT". "SC. The above /copy/ taken from great book #B of records remaining in the secretary's office of this Province page 137. Examined and attested Apr. 6th, 1725 pr CHAS. HART, secretary". JACOB MOTTE, Register.

Book D, p. 181
28 Mar. 1724 in SC
Deed of Sale

JOHN PARRIS sold to his brother PETER BOYNTON, for ₤ 300 current SC money, sloop Louisa, burthen 12 tons, & her appurtenances. "Burlington May the 6th, 1724. Received of CAPT. JAMES WOMSLY 250 pounds current money of SC in full for the sloop Louisa within mentioned and all her appurtenances as she now lies at anchor in the River Delaware, PETER BOYNTON". "Sold to MR. WILLIAM YOEMANS & MR. SAMUEL PICKERING the 1/2 of the above mentioned sloop as witness my hand, July 20th, 1724. JAMES WOMESLY". JACOB MOTTE, Register.

Book D, p. 181
2 Feb. 1724
Release

BRYAN (his mark) REALY, of Berkeley Co., to JOHN CARMICHAEL, joiner, of Charleston, for ₤ 300 current SC money, 200 a. in Parish of St. James, Goose Creek, Berkeley Co., part of 400 a. granted by Lords Proprs. to WILLIAM MURRIL, & by several means conveyances became vested in BRYAN REALY; bounding SE on LANDGRAVE THOMAS SMITH; NW on RICHARD SPLATT, ESQ. (formerly EDWARD CURRENT); N on Goose Creek. Witnesses: JOHN HAMILTON, ANTHONY SPENCER, THOMAS HEPWORTH. Before THOMAS HEPWORTH, C.J. JACOB MOTTE, Register.

Book D, p. 184
22 & 23 Jan. 1724
L & R in Trust

ALEXANDER PARRIS, ESQ. & MARY his wife, of Charleston, to WILLIAM GIBBON, ESQ., of Charleston, & JONAH COLLINS, planter, of Craven Co., for the use of MARY PARRIS, 17 a. in Berkeley Co., commonly called Hogg Island, bounding as appears by a plat annexed to a grant dated 12 Sept. 1694, formerly conveyed from ELIZABETH BELLINGER to ALEXANDER PARRIS. In consideration of the fact that MARY PARRIS, at the request of her husband ALEXANDER, has renounced all her right & title of dower in 2750 a., part of a tract a mouth of Port Royall River, Granville Co., called Archers Island, lately conveyed "at twice" to ALEXANDER PARRIS, JR. & JOHN DELABERE; & for the love & affection

ALEXANDER bears his wife MARY; & for settling the lands & appurtenances; & for 20 sh. SC money; & for other good causes & considerations; & at the special instance & request, good liking & approbation of MARY, testified by her being a party hereto; ALEXANDER conveys to GIBBON & COLLINS in trust for MARY. MARY may at any time revoke this agreement. ALEXANDER PARRIS agrees to erect within 2 years a substantial house of timber according to specifications named in this indenture. Witnesses: BENJAMIN GODFREY, ROBERT NISBETT, ROBERT HUME. Before: THOMAS HEPWORTH, C.J. JACOB MOTTE, Register.

Book D, p. 188
23 Jan. 1724
Bond

DAVID SCANNELL, gentleman, late of Island of Antigua, now of SC, gave bond to WILLIAM LOUGHTON, gentleman, for ₤ 75 proclamation money, conditioned for payment upon demand of ₤ 37:10 proclamation money in silver at the rate of 6 sh. 10 pence half penny per ounce or the value thereof in rum & sugar according to the market price of those commodities in the Island of Antigua, with interest. Witnesses: JOHN WHITE, WILLIAM BILLING. Before JOHN MOORE. JACOB MOTTE, Register.

Book D, p. 189
23 Jan. 1724
Warrant of Attorney

To BENJAMIN WHITAKER, ESQ., ROBERT HUME, RICHARD ALLEN, THOMAS ELLERY & WILLIAM BILLING, gentlemen, attorneys of Court of Common Pleas authorizing them to appear for DAVID SCANNELL, gentleman, late of Island of Antigua, now of Charleston, at suit of WILLIAM LOUGHTON, gentleman, & confess a judgement against SCANNELL upon the above bond (page 186). Witnesses: JOHN WHITE, WILLIAM BILLING. Before JOHN MOORE. JACOB MOTTE, Register.

Book D, p. 190
25 Jan. 1724
Bond

DAVID SCANNELL, gentleman, late of Island of of Antigua, now of Charleston, to THOMAS FAIRCHILD, butcher of Charleston, in penal sum of ₤ 30 proclamation money for payment of ₤ 15 proclamation money in silver at the rate of 6 sh. 10 pence half penny per ounce of the value thereof in rum & sugar at the market price in Island of Antigua with interest. Witnesses: EDMUND ROBINSON, ABRAHAM LESUEUR, WILLIAM BILLING. Before JOHN MOORE. JACOB MOTTE, Register.

Book D, p. 191
25 Jan. 1724
Warrant of Attorney

To BENJAMIN WHITAKER, ESQ., ROBERT HUME, THOMAS ELLERY, RICHARD ALLIEN, & WILLIAM BILLING, gentlemen, attorneys of Court of Common Pleas authorizing them to appear for DAVID SCANNELL at the suit of THOMAS FAIRCHILD, & confess a judgment filed against SCANNELL upon the above bond (page 190). Witnesses: EDMUND ROBINSON, ABRAHAM LESUEUR, WILLIAM BILLING. Before JOHN MOORE. JACOB MOTTE, Register.

Book D, p. 192
3 Nov. 1724
Declaration of Land

Whereas in a deed of sale of a certain parcel of land on James Island to JOHN WHITTIER, cooper, it is expressed that 2 a. (the whole being 70 in all) shall be for the use of the Presbyterian church; & whereas it is said in the deed of sale that the 2 a. shall be in the NW corner of the 70 a.; & whereas JONATHAN DRAKE was the sole owner of the land; & whereas the inhabitants of the Island are not satisfied with the title; JOHN WITTER hereby declares that he has no claim whatsoever to that part where the Presbyterian church now stands & declares that the 2 a. shall be laid out where the church now stands. Witnesses: JOHN HEARNE, SAMUEL DRAKE, PETER HEARNE. Before AUTHUR HALL. JACOB MOTTE, Register.

Book D, p. 192
12 July 1722
Assignment

JOHN (his mark) ANDREWS, yeoman, of Pontsbury, Co. of Salop, Great Britain to FRANCIS GREEN, broker, of Winchester Street, London, for a "competent sum of lawfull money of Great Britain" the tenement & part of a town lot mentioned below, subject to redemption by DANIEL GREEN by his paying FRANCIS GREEN ₤ 200 with interest. Whereas DANIEL GREEN, merchant, of Charleston, & ELIZABETH his wife on 5 Dec. 1718 sold to JOHN ANDREWS, cordwainer, of Pontsbury, Co. of Salop, Great Britain but residing in SC for ₤ 300, the tenement where JOHN BROWN lately lived on part of lot #7, also part of the adjoining lot being 3 ft., part of the alley between the line formerly of GABRIEL RIBELLEAU & the line of DANIEL GREEN containing 33 ft. clear front & to run 33 ft.

57

westwardly 100 ft. from the eastern most sill of the dwelling house; the mortgage to be void if GREEN pays certain sums at certain times. Now ANDREWS sells to FRANCIS GREEN, with provision for redemption by DANIEL GREEN. Witnesses: JOSEPH HATFIELD, JOHN DANIEL. FRANCIS GREEN on 14 July 1724, in consideration of a certain competent sum of lawful money of Great Britain & for the principal money & interest due & remaining unpaid of the mortgage money acquits DANIEL GREEN & ELIZABETH his wife & surrenders to DANIEL & ELIZABETH the tenement & part of lot. Witnesses: EDMUND ROBINSON, DANIEL BELL. Before THOMAS HEPWORTH, C.J. JACOB MOTTE, Register. Receipt for ₤ 220 in full for reassignment, dated 14 July 1724, signed FRANCIS GREEN. Witness: EDMUND ROBINSON, the mortgage recited in the above deed is recorded in the secretary's office in Book K folio 227 by JOHN CROFT, D.S.

Book D, p. 196
9 July 1724
Lease

PETER LESADE, planter, to DAVID (his mark) MACQUEEN, planter, both of Berkeley Co., for yearly rent of ₤ 100 current SC money that certain piece of ground already fenced in & generally called LESADE'S Pasture containing 120 or 130 a. for term of 3 years from date. LESADE agrees to keep the fence in good repair. Witnesses: MAURICE HARVEY, JOHN CROFT. It is agreed that MACQUEEN shall have the use of 1 good room in the dwelling house on the plantation & the use of the kitchen, the liberty of planting needful provisions for himself & his servants. LESADE to have privilege of pasturing 20 head of cattle. Before THOMAS HEPWORTH, C.J. On 15 Feb. 1724 PETER LESADE assigns to CHARLES HILL, ESQ., all his interest in the above lease. Witnesses: BENJAMIN WHITAKER, JOHN BUCKNELL. Before DANIEL GREEN. JACOB MOTTE, Register.

Book D, p. 198
15 Feb. 1724
Lease

PETER LESADE, planter, to CHARLES HILL, ESQ., both of Berkeley Co. for 18 years for ₤ 50 yearly until MACQUEEN'S lease expires, & after that for ₤ 150 yearly rental, to be used for the maintenance & clothing of ANN LESADE, PETER'S child, & towards paying the sum of ₤ 880 & interest. Whereas PETER LESADE by L & R 16 & 17 Sept. 1723 for payment of ₤ 880 & interest mortgaged to CHARLES HILL 4 tracts of land containing 458 a. on S side Ashley River subject to redemption by LESADE; & whereas LESADE late rented certain pasture lands containing 130 a. to DAVID MACQUEEN for 3 years for ₤ 100 yearly with benefit of a room & use of the kitchen; now LESADE leases to HILL the 322 a., part of the 458 a., for 12 years, also the tenement & pasture; HILL to collect rent from MACQUEEN for 3 years. Witnesses: BENJAMIN WHITAKER, JOHN BUCKNALL. Before DANIEL GREEN. JACOB MOTTE, Register.

Book D, p. 200
14 Feb. 1724
Bond

The HON. CHARLES HART, ESQ., of Berkeley Co., to ELEAZER ALLEN, merchant, of Charleston, executor of will of JOANNA HAYES, of Charleston, in sum of ₤ 2126 current SC money conditioned for payment to ELEAZER ALLEN in trust for CHARLES HAYES (son of JOANNA) the sum of ₤ 1063 on 14 Feb. 1725 with interest. Witnesses: RICHARD ALLEIR, THOMAS LAMBELL, JAMES BALNEAVIS. Before ALEXANDER PARRIS. JACOB MOTTE, Register.

Book D, p. 201
23 Mar. 1712/13
Deed of Conveyance

JOHN (his mark) BELL, carpenter, who married ANN, sole executrix of 1 other JOHN BELL, bricklayer, for good causes & considerations & for 5 sh., to JOHN BELL, son & heir of deceased JOHN BELL & ANN his wife, all the real estate of the father, JOHN BELL. Witnesses: BENJAMIN RETT (?), RICHARD EDGELL, THOMAS (his mark) BLANTON. Before W. GIBBES. JACOB MOTTE, Register.

Book D, p. 202
9 Aug. 1717
Grant of Lot
#5 in Beaufort

"By virtue of a warrant under the hand and seal of the HON. ROBERT DANIEL, ESQ., Dep. Gov. dated the 12th of June 1717 I have caused to be admeasured and laid out unto COL. GEORGE CHICKEN 1 town lot in Beaufort Town in Granville Co. fronting the Bay to the S and bounden to the W by a lott #4 to the N by a lot #30, and to the east by a lot #6 and is distinctly known by the # 5 in the Grant plot of the said Town certified and returned the 27th day of July 1717. FRANCIS YOUNG Survr. Gen. On 9 Aug. 1717 the

58

HON. ROBERT DANIEL, ESQ., Dep., Gov. & the Lords Proprs. granted COL. GEORGE CHICKEN lot #5 in Beaufort, Granville Co. in free & common soccage with usual reservations in regard to hawking, hunting, base mines, etc. Names affixed to grant: SAM. EVELEIGH, FRAN. YOUNG, ROBERT (seal for grant lands) DANIELL, CHARLES HART, GEORGE CHICKEN. Recorded in secretary's office 10 Aug. 1717 folio 414. JOHN CROFT, Dep. Sec'y. On 25 Nov. 1724 GEORGE CHICKEN assigned all his right & title to plott & grant to JACOB WRIGHT. Witnesses: DAVID DURHAM, CHARLES BURLEY. Before THOMAS HEPWORTH, C.J. JACOB MOTTE, Register.

Book D, p. 202
9 Aug. 1717
Grant of Lot #30

"By virtue of a warrant under the hand and seal of the HON. ROBERT DANIEL, ESQ., Dep.Gov. dated the 12th of June 1717 I have caused to be admeasured and laid out unto COL. GEORGE CHICKEN 1 town lott in Beaufort Town in Granville Co. bounded to the S by a lott of the said COL. CHICKEN #5 to the W by a lott #29 to the NE by a street called Port Royall Street and to the E by a lott #31 and is distinctly known by/the #30/ in the grand platt of the said town, certified and returned the 27th July 1717. FRANCIS YOUNG, Survr. Gen." On 9 Aug. 1717 the HON. ROBERT DANIEL, ESQ., Dep. Gov. & the Lords Proprs. granted COL. GEORGE CHICKEN lot #30 in Beaufort, Granville Co., in free & common soccage with the usual restrictions. Names affixed to grant: SAM EVELEIGH, FRANCIS YOUNG, ROBERT (seale for grant land) DANIELL, CHARLES HART, GEORGE CHICKEN. Recorded in the secretary's office 10 Aug. 1717, folio 414 by JOHN CROFT, Dep. Survr. On 25 Nov. 1724 GEORGE CHICKEN assigned all his right & title to above lot to JACOB WRIGHT. Witnesses: DAVID DURHAM, CHARLES BURLEY. Before THOMAS HEPWORTH, C.J. JACOB MOTTE, Register.

Book D, p. 204
23 Feb. 1724
Bond

ABRAHAM SANDERS, planter, of St. Johns Parish, Berkeley Co., to JOHN VICCARIDGE, merchant, of Charleston, in sum of L 2000 current SC money conditioned for delivery of 330 barrels of good pitch on Bay of Charleston on 1 Oct. 1725. Witnesses: DANIEL HUGER, THOMAS ELLERY. Before DANIEL GREEN.

Book D, p. 206
28 Oct. 1724
Power of Attorney

WILLIAM TREDWELL BULL, clerk, of London, appointed his trusty & loving friend the REV. MR. ALEXANDER GORDEN, clerk, of Charleston, SC, his attorney to receive all money, debts, etc., due him upon the bond or bonds of CAPT. HUGH HEXT, of St. Paul's Parish, Colleton Co., SC; giving HEXT authority in his plantation in St. Paul's Parish, his Negro slaves, cattle, etc., & over the oversears. Witnesses: BENJAMIN AUSTIN, JONATHAN DANIEL, ANTHONY SEARES. Before A. SKENE.

Book D, p. 206
14 & 15 Feb. 1724
L & R & Mortgage

The HON. CHARLES HART, ESQ., of Berkeley Co., to ELEAZER ALLEN, merchant, of Charleston, executor of will of JOANNA HAYES, of Charleston, in trust for CHARLES HAYES, 120 a. known as Pat Trap Plantation. Whereas JOANNA HAYES by will dated 27 May 1724 gave ELEAZER ALLEN L 450 currency to be secured to her by CHARLES HART by a mortgage to hold to ELEAZER ALLEN in trust for the use of her son CHARLES HAYES; & gave ELEAZER ALLEN L 180 currency due her from CHARLES HART by bond dated 1 Jan. 1719 with interest in trust for her son CHARLES; & willed that ALLEN should forthwith call all the money due on the mortgage & the bond out of CHARLES HART'S hands & renew the securities as ALLEN deemed fit & apply the interest yearly to the maintenance & education of son CHARLES; & whereas the principal & interest amounted on 14 Feb. (including L 25 for renewing & recording the securities) to L 1063; & whereas CHARLES HART, renewing, gave bond to ALLEN as executor, in penal sum of L 2126 to be paid with interest 14 Feb. 1725; now to better secure payment, HART mortgages to ALLEN 120 a. known as Rat Trap Plantation on Charleston Neck, bounding on the Broad Path; N on SAMUEL WEST; S on JOHN WATKINS; W on Ashley River. Witnesses: RICHARD ALLEIN, THOMAS LAMBOLL, JAMES BALNEAVIS. "I do hereby consent to allow and deduct out of the within mortgage the sume of 38 pounds 8 shillings lent by the within named CHARLES HART to DELIA HAYES daughter of JOANNA HAYES and 12 pounds 10 shillings for a moiety of the writings. ELEAZR ALLEN". Before ALEXANDER PARRIS. JACOB MOTTE, Register.

Book D, p. 213   The HON. ARTHUR MIDDLETON, ESQ., of Berkeley

18 & 19 Mar. 1724   Co. & FRANCIS HOLMES, SR., merchant, of
L & R   Charleston, as attorney to THOMAS AMORY, mer-
                         chant of Boston, to JAMES NICHOLAS MAYRANT,
ESQ., of Craven Co., for ₤ 350 (₤ 250) current SC money, part of lot #86
in Charleston. Whereas WILLIAM, Earl of Craven, Palatine, & the Lords
Proprs. on 23 Mar. 1681 granted FRANCIS GRACIA lot #86 in Charleston in
free & common soccage; & whereas FRANCIS GRACIA on 30 Oct. 1696 sold the
lot and buildings on it to WILLIAM POPELL (POPPELL); & whereas POPPELL on
20 Jan. 1696 sold to JONATHAN AMORY part of lot #86 fronting 58 ft. on
the street & running southerly the same breadth the full depth of the lot
so that it bounded 58 ft. on the S on part of a lot occupied by JAMES
LARDAIN & NOAH ROYER, SR., bounding N on a little street leading from
Cooper River to Ashley River by the houses belonging to MAJOR ROBERT DAN-
IEL, the said AMORY, & MADAM SIMONS; W on the French church; E on other
part same lot belonging to WILLIAM POPELL; now MIDDLETON & HOLMES, SR.
(attorney with letter dated 15 Nov. 1722 for THOMAS AMORY of Boston, merchant, son & heir of JONATHAN AMORY, merchant, formerly of Charleston)
sell to MAYRANT. Witnesses: ELIAS HORRY, JOHN CROFT. Before JOHN BARKS-
DALE. JACOB MOTTE, Register.

Book D, p. 219   "DANIEL HUGER had a grant for 100 a. of land
                         in Craven Co. on the S side of Wambah Creek
bounding to the E on the said DANIEL HUGER, to the W on land not laid out,
to the N on Wambah Creek, and to the S on lands not laid out, paying to
the Lords Proprs. on every 1st day of Dec. after the 1st Day of Dec. 1703
1 sh. the said grant is dated the 16th July 1703 and signed N. JOHNSON,
JA. MOORE, NICH. TROTT. SC/the above copy taken from great book #B of
records remaining in the secretary's office of this Province page 137.
Examined and attested Apr. 6th 1725 pr CHARLES HART, Sec'y." JACOB MOTTE,
Register.

Book D, p. 220   SAMUEL EVELEIGH, merchant, of Charleston, to
21 & 22 Sept. 1724   CHRISTOPHER ARTHUR & THOMAS AKINS, planters,
L & R   of Berkeley Co., bounding N on vacant land;
                         W on MR. SOUTH CART (South East?); S on MR.
SIMONS & PETER MENIGAULT; also all his title to 510 a. in Berkeley Co.
being the tract be purchased from JAMES JENNER, bounding on lands not
then laid out. Witnesses: JOHN CROFT, RICHARD HOWE, EDWARD CROFT. Before JOHN MOORE. JACOB MOTTE, Register.

Book D, p. 224   The HON. ARTHUR MIDDLETON, ESQ. & FRANCIS
18 & 19 Mar. 1724   HOLMES, SR., merchant of Charleston (attorneys
L & R   for THOMAS AMORY, merchant, of Boston) to NOAH
                         SERRE, planter of Craven Co., for ₤ 250 cur-
rent money, 1/2 lot #86 in Charleston. Whereas WILLIAM, Earl of Craven,
Palatine, & the Lords Proprs. on 23 Mar. 1681 granted FRANCIS GRACIA lot
#85 in Charleston; & whereas GRACIA on 30 Oct. 1696 sold the lot to WIL-
LIAM POPELL; & whereas POPELL on 11 June 1696 sold 1/2 the lot known as
#86 to JONATHAN AMORY (then in possession of JONATHAN AMORY) bounding N
on a little street leading from Cooper River to Ashley River by the hous-
houses belonging to COL. ROBERT DANIELL, JONATHAN AMORY & MADAM SIMONS, S
on part of lot occupied by NOAH ROYER, SR.; W on part same lot sold by
POPELL to AMORY; E on a lot belonging to NICHOLAS TOWNSEND then in possession & right of THOMAS PINCKNEY; now MIDDLETON & HOLMES (as attorneys for
THOMAS AMORY of Boston, son & heir of JONATHAN AMORY) sell to SERRE 1/2
lot #86. Witnesses: ELIAS HORRY, JOHN CROFT. Before JOHN BARKSDALE.
JACOB MOTTE, Register.

Book D, p. 230   ARTHUR FOSTER, of Charleston, appointed WIL-
7 Apr. 1725   LIAM WATSON, joiner, of Charleston & JOHN LAD-
Power of Attorney   SON, planter, of Berkeley Co., his attorneys
                         to collect money due, etc. Witnesses: NICHO-
LAS NEWLIN, THOMAS BAKER. Before JOHN BARKSDALE. JACOB MOTTE, Register.

Book D, p. 231   EDWARD CHERNLEY (CHEARNLEY), merchant, of town
16 Dec. 1724   of St. Michaels, Island of Barbados appointed
Power of Attorney   PETER TAYLOR, merchant, of Charleston, SC, his
                         attorney, to collect, sue, settle, etc. Wit-
ness: JOSEPH DILL. Before CHARLES HILL. JACOB MOTTE, Register.

Book D, p. 232   Grant to JOHN BELL. "By virtue of a warrant
12 May 1714   under the hand and seal of the HON. COLL. ED-
                       WARD TYNTE, ESQ. Gov., bearing date the 25th
day of Dec. 1709 I have measured and laid out unto JOHN BELL, SR. 500 a.
of land in Craven Co. lying on...Creek butting and bounding to the S on
sd creek to the W on CAPT. BARTHOLOMEW GAILLARD'S land, to the N on land
not yet laid, and to the E on the said JOHN BELL'S land, and hath such
marks and trees as are specified in the above delinieted platt certified
and returned this 29th day of Apr. 1714, pr THOMAS BROUGHTON, Survr. Gen."
On 12 May 1714 the RT. HON. CHARLES CRAVEN, ESQ., Gov. & the Lords Proprs.
for ₤ 15 currency granted JOHN BELL, SR. 500 a. in Craven Co. in free &
common soccage, with the usual reservations. Names affixed: CHARLES (the
great seal) CRAVEN, AR. MIDDLETON, SAML. EVELEIGH, RICHD. BERESFORD, CHAR.
HART. Copied from book of records page 452 in secretary's office.
CHARLES HART, Sect. JACOB MOTTE, Register.

Book D, p. 233   Grant to ELIAS HORRY. By warrant under hand
1 June 1709   of the RT. HON. SIR NATHANIEL JOHNSON, Knight
                       & Gov., dated 1 Mar. 1707/8, THOMAS BROUGHTON,
Survr. Gen., laid out to ELIAS HORRY 500 a. in Craven Co. according to
plat certified 1 Mar. 1707/8. Whereas his EXCELLENCY JOHN LORD, Gren-   ???
ville, Palatine, WILLIAM LORD CRAVEN, JOHN LORD CARTERET, MAURICE ASHLEY,
ESQ., JOHN COLLETON BARONET, & the Lords proprs. by commission dated 8
Mar. 1706/7 impowered the RT. HON. SIR NATHANIEL JOHNSON, Knight, Gov.,
etc. of SC & NC, the HON. NICHOLAS TROTT, THOMAS BROUGHTON, ROBERT GIBBES,
HENRY NOBLE, JOHN ASHBY, ESQ., to grant lands, they, for ₤ 10 SC money
granted ELIAS HORRY 500 a., English measure, as above. Signatures: N.
JOHNSON (the great seal) THOS. BROUGHTON, NICHOLAS TROTT, JOHN ASHLEY,
registered 14 Mar. 1710/11 by ISAAC PORCHER. Copied from book of record
#F. in secretary's office, page 201. CHARLES HART, Sec. JACOB MOTTE,
Register.

Book D, p. 234   Grant to JOHN BELL. By warrant under hand of
12 May 1714   the HON. COL. ROBERT GIGGES, ESQ. Gov. dated
                       Oct. 1711, THOMAS BROUGHTON, Survr. Gen. laid
out to JOHN BELL, SR. 500 a. in Craven Co. on a creek, bounding S on the
creek & Santee River; W in JOHN BELL'S land. Plat certified 29 Apr. 1714.
The RT. HON. CHARLES CRAVEN, ESQ., Gov., & the Lords Proprs. for ₤ 15
granted JOHN BELL, SR. 500 a. in Craven Co. as in plat above. Signatures:
CHARLES (the great seal) CRAVEN, AR. MIDDLETON, RICHD. BERESFORD. Copied
from book of records #H, page 448 in secretary's office. CHARLES HART,
Sec'y. JACOB MOTTE, Register.

Book D, p. 235   Grant to ELIAS HORRY. By warrant under hand
23 July 1711   of the HON. ROBERT GIBBES, ESQ., Gov., dated
                       10 Sept. 1711, THOMAS BROUGHTON, Survr. Gen.,
laid out to ELIAS HORRY 55 a. in Craven Co. bounding S on Waha Creek; W
part on DANIEL HUGER, SR., part on vacant land. The HON. ROBERT GIBBES,
ESQ., Gov. & the Lords Proprs. for ₤ 1 granted 55 a., as above, to ELIAS
HORRY with the usual priviledges & reservations. Signatures: ROBERT (the
broad seal 1712/13) GIBBES, SAML. EVELEIGH, CHAR. HART, THOS. DISTON,
CHARLES BURNHAM. Copied from book H of records in secretary;s office,
page 266. CHARLES HART, Sec. JACOB MOTTE, Register.

Book D, p. 236   PETER STANLEY, planter, to JOHN NICHOLSON,
17 & 18 Mar. 1724/5   planter, for ₤ 450 current SC money 222 a. in
L & R   Berkeley Co., bounding NE on FRANCIS WILLIAMS
                       & JOHN NICHOLSON; NW on CHRISTOPHER ARTHUR &
NICHOLSON; SE on TODY HOWARD & WILLIAM WRIGHT; being a tract laid out to
EDWARD STANLEY, father of PETER. Witnesses: EDWARD COOPER, ALLEN (his
mark) BOURGAINE (BURGAINE), JOSEPH MEADE. Before DANIEL HUGER. JACOB
MOTTE, Register.

Book D, p. 239   JOHN BRAND, carpenter, to JOHN GREENLAND, vic-
29 & 30 Mar. 1725   tualler, both of Charleston, lot #164 & 1/2 of
L & R & Mortgage   lot #186. Whereas by L & R dated 16 & 17 Dec.
                       1722 JOHN BRAND sold to JOHN GREENLAND for ₤
1800 current SC money, a town lot whereon BRAND then lived, bounding E on
STEPHEN TAVERSON; W on the street running by the Quakers meeting house; N
on MARY COGSWELL; also part of a lot adjoining the above lot then in

possession of JOHN BRAND fronting 59 ft. & 223 ft. deep, bounding E on STEPHEN TAVERSON; W on the street running by the Quakers meeting house; N on MARY COGSWELL; & S on the other town lot; & whereas (by the release) JOHN BRAND promised that it should be lawful for GREENLAND to take possession free from all trouble, especially free of the dower of ELIZABETH, wife of JOHN BRAND: & whereas by covenant dated 17 Dec. 1722 JOHN BRAND agreed that he would execute before his Majesty's Court of Common Pleas at Westminster, Great Britain 1 or more fines sur cognizance de droit, etc., to JOHN GREENLAND of the lot & piece of lot & that BRAND would suffer a recovery for the better confirming the lot & piece of lot to GREENLAND; & whereas BRAND, when lately in England omitted the levying of the fine & suffering the recovery cannot now do it without prejudice to his affairs & GREENLAND is willing to accept the security hereby intended to be made for saving GREENLAND harmless from dower of ELIZABETH; now for the better securing GREENLAND, BRAND grants GREENLAND lot #164 in Charleston containing 1/2 a. bounding N on the great street leading from Cooper River to the market place; S on JOSEPH WRAGG; E on a little street leading from Ashley River by MR. JONES'S lot; W on JAMES DUGUE; also 1/2 of lot #186 bounding E on a little street leading from Ashley River to MR. JONES'S lot; N & E on MR. CRIMSTON (formerly JONAS BONHOSTE); W on part of same lot belonging to MR. DUGUE. The lot #164 and 1/2 lot #186 were granted to BRAND by L & R tripartite 1 & 2 Mar. 1723 made between MARY LAROACHES (widow & 1 of the executors of JOHN LAROACHES, merchant, of Charleston) of 1st part; JOHN BRAND of 2d part; ANTHONY MATHEWS, merchant of Charleston, of 3d part. Should BRAND keep GREENLAND indemnified from the dower of ELIZABETH this mortgage to be void. GREENLAND promises that should ELIZABETH die & should BRAND produce a certificate from the minister of the Parish where ELIZABETH may happen to die, with the oath of 2 credible persons annexed, taken before the mayor or chief magistrate or any notary public, GREENLAND will surrender this mortgage to BRAND to be cancelled. Witnesses: WILLIAM BILLING, THOMAS FAIRCHILD, JOHN LAURENS. Before CHARLES HILL. JACOB MOTTE, Register

Book D, p. 245
26 Nov. 1722
Deed of Gift

WILLIAM SHERRIFF, merchant tailor, of Charleston, for love & affection to loving & well beloved wife ISABEL 180 a. on a place called Bohicket; also a Negro man & a Negro woman. SHERRIFF appoints his trusty friend MARK OLIVER trustee to see articles of deed truly performed. Witnesses: DAVID ALLEN, DAVID ROBINSON, SAMUEL BENNETT. In memorandum WILLIAM also gives ISABEL his household goods, chattles & implements at his death. Before JOHN BARKSDALE. JACOB MOTTE, Register.

Book D, p. 246
28 Mar. 1723
Mortgage

HENRY SIMONDS of Berkeley Co., planter, & JUDITH his wife (formerly JUDITH GIRARD, daughter & heir of PETER GIRARD formerly of the city of Poitiers, Province of Poiton, France) to NATHANIEL BROUGHTON & HUGH BUTLER, planter, of Berkeley Co., "in consideration of the said BROUGHTON & BUTLER being joint securities in a bond bearing even date with these presents payable to MADAM DAMARIS DE ST. JULIEN" for ₤ 988:9:8-1/2 penny current SC money. Now HENRY SIMONS, for securing the payment, with the consent & good liking of JUDITH, his wife, testified by her signature, mortgages to BROUGHTON & BUTLER several plantations as follows: 100 a. commonly known by name of Mt. Pleasant; 200 a. of swamp adjoining; 100 a. known as Wampee; 200 a. of swamp adjoining; 500 a. of pine land; 633 a. known as Fair Spring; also 13 slaves. Should SIMONS pay BROUGHTON & BUTLER ₤ 988:9:8-1/2 on 28 Mar. next this mortgage to be void. Witnesses: ROBERT TAYLOR, ANN BUTLER. Before PETER DE ST. JULIEN. JACOB MOTTE, Register. Mortgage satisfied 10 Apr. 1726. Signed NATHANLIEL BROUGHTON. Witness: JACOB MOTTE.

Book D, p. 249
18 Feb. 1724/5
Deed of Gift

AARON WAY, SR. & WILLIAM WAY, SR., planters, of Dorchester, Berkeley Co., conveyed to NATHANIEL SUMNER, planter, of Clockister (Dorchester?) for a valuable sum of lawful money, their whole right & title & portion of inheritance in all lands belonging to the estate of WILLIAM SUMNER, of Dorchester, in New England; to wit, of lands not yet subdivided or otherwise disposed by heirs apparent; viz. their right, portion & interest in the 15th lot in the 12 divisions, & in the 50th lot in the 25 divisions, in the 36th lot in Pigeon Swamp, & in a lot in Cedar Swamp. Witnesses: AARON WAY, JR., STEPHEN DOWSE, ABIGAIL DOWSE. Before THOMAS WARING. JACOB MOTTE, Register.

Book D, p. 250
27 Apr. 1725
Deed of Gift

MOSES NORMAN of Colleton Co., SC, & BENJAMIN SUMNER & ROGER SUMNER, of Berkeley Co., planters, for a valuable sum of lawful SC money, conveyed to NATHANIEL SUMNER, planter, of Berkeley Co., their whole right & title & portion of inheritance in all lands belonging to the estate of their honored grandfather WILLIAM SUMNER of Dorchester in New England, & of his son their honored father INCREASE SUMNER; to wit, of lands not yet subdivided or disposed of by heirs apparent; viz., their portion & interest in the 15th lot in the 12 division, & in 50th lot in the 25 divisions, in the 36 lot in Pigeon Swamp, in the 10th in Puragety Swamp, & in a lot in Cedar Swamp, & in every other lot in Dorchester, New England belonging to them. Witnesses: AARON WAY, JR., THOMAS WAY, AARON WAY, SR. Before THOMAS WARING. JACOB MOTTE, Register.

Book D, p. 252
7 May 1724
Deed of Sale

JEREMIAH CLARK, planter, of Colleton Co., to TIMOTHY HENDRICKS, for 22,000-wt. of rice in barrels, 250 a., in Colleton Co., part of a tract JEREMIAH CLARK purchased from WILLIAM MAGGETT, gentleman, of Colleton Co., bounding S on a swamp on Ponpon River; N & W on JOHN SMILEY; E on JOHN PALMER. Witnesses: ALEXANDER WALKER, JOHN FERGUSON, WILLIAM BAYNARD (BANARD), WILLIAM WHIPPY. Before CHARLES HILL. JACOB MOTTE, Register.

Book D, p. 254
29 & 30 Sept. 1724
L & R

EDWARD WEEKLEY, planter, & ELIZABETH his wife, of Berkeley Co., to THOMAS ELLERY, gentleman, of Charleston, for L 1500 current SC money, 4 tracts of land laid out in 1 plantation containing at least 353 a., called WEEKLEY's Plantation, bounding E on Cooper River; W on WILLIAM DRY, RICHARD BAKER & others; N on RICHARD BAKER; S on JOSEPH HUNT & WILLIAM BAKER; S on JOSEPH HUNT & WILLIAM DRY. Whereas JOHN Earl of Bath, Palatine, GEORGE Lord Carteret, SIR JOHN COLLETON, Baronet & the Lords Proprs. on 16 Aug. 1698 impowered the HON. JOSEPH BLAKE, ESQ., JAMES MOORE, ESQ., then Gov., LANDGRAVE JOSEPH MORTON, LANDGRAVE EDMUND BELLINGER, ROBERT DANIEL & JOHN ELY, ESQ., to grant lands, whereby JAMES MOORE, LANDGRAVE JOSEPH MORTON & LANDGRAVE EDWARD (?) BELLINGER (in the absence of JOSEPH BLAKE) granted DAVID MAYBANK some land in Berkeley Co.; & whereas DAVID MAYBANK & SUSANNAH his wife by deed of feoffment 1 Dec. 1708 conveyed to EDWARD WEEKLEY 100 a.; & whereas his Excellency JOHN LORD GRANVILLE, Palatine, WILLIAM LORD CRAVEN, JOHN LORD CARTERET, MAURICE ASHLEY, ESQ., SIR JOHN COLLETON, Baronet & the Lords Proprs. impowered the RT. HON. SIR NATHANIEL JOHNSON, Knight, then Gov. of SC & NC, the HON. JAMES MOORE, ESQ., then late Gov., NICHOLAS TROTT & JOB HOWES, ESQRS., to grant lands, whereby NATHANIEL JOHNSON, Knight, JAMES MOORE, NICHOLAS TROTT & JOB HOWES, ESQRS. on 5 Oct. 1704 granted EDWARD WEEKLEY 220 a. in Berkeley Co., English measure, then in possession of WEEKLEY, except 80 a., the westernmost part of the 220 a. which WEEKLEY has since conveyed to LANDGRAVE THOMAS SMITH so that WEEKLEY possesses only 140 a. now intended to be conveyed to THOMAS ELLERY; & whereas the HON. ROBERT GIBBES, ESQ., Gov. & the Lords Proprs. granted EDWARD WEEKLEY 23 a. in Berkeley Co., plat made 5 May 1711, by the HON. THOMAS BROUGHTON, ESQ. then survyr. gen.; & whereas the HON. ROBERT DANIEL, ESQ. Dep. Gov. & the Lords Proprs. on 25 May 1717 granted EDWARD WEEKLEY 90 a. in Berkeley Co., plot made 12 Mar. 1716 by the HON. FRANCIS YOUNG, ESQ. then Survyr. Gen.; & whereas the 4 several plantations are contiguous & have been laid out in 1 distinct plantation, containing at least 353 a., on which EDWARD WEEKLEY has erected a dwelling house, Negro huts & other buildings & made various improvements; now EDWARD & ELIZABETH WEEKLEY. Witnesses: LANDGRAVE THOMAS SMITH, COL. MILES BREWTON, HENRY HARGRAVE, Dep. Sec'y. Before THOMAS HEPWORTH, C.J. JACOB MOTTE, Register.

Book D, p. 261
10 Dec. 1717
Agreement

Charleston, SC. Between MARY EVANS, widow & executrix of will of THOMAS PICKNEY, merchant of Charleson, & WILLIAM CROOK, of Charleston, Doctor in Physic. Whereas the fence of DR. WILLIAM CROOK'S land from the lower end of his lot to the front is several ft. upon the PINCKNEY line, now for preserving a good neighborly correspondence between MARY EVANS & DR. WILLIAM CROOK & for removing all

disputes that may arise, & in consideration that CROOK herein agrees to
keep the fence in repair as an annuity or acknowledgement to BRAND during
the minority of THOMAS PINCKNEY her eldest son, MARY EVANS agrees to have
a passage or cart way through the PINCKNEY land taken & included in the
fence of DR. CROOK for so long as "THOMAS PINCKNEY, her eldest son, shall
come to age agreeable to his father's will". Witnesses: JOHN SHEPPARD,
GEORGE CLARKE, ROBERT HUME. Before JOHN BARKSDALE. JACOB MOTTE, Register.

Book D, p. 262 THOMAS PINCKNEY, gentleman, of Charleston, to
23 Jan. 1724 his Excellency FRANCIS NICHOLSON, ESQ., his
L & R Majesty's Captain Gen. & Gov. in Chief of SC,
the HON. ARTHUR MIDDLETON, RALPH IZARD, BENJA-
MIN SCHENKINGH, CHARLES HART, WILLIAM GIBBONS, ESQRS., COL. ALEXANDER
PARRIS, & the REV. MR. ALEXANDER GARDEN, for L 250 current SC MONEY, the
commissioners for founding, erecting, governing, ordering & visiting a
free school for the use of the inhabitants of SC 5 a. on Charleston Neck
bequeathed him by his father, bounding SW on CAPT. JOHN HARLESTON; NE on
other 5 a. alloted to him; NW on a marsh; SE on a path leading from the
Broad Path by the parsonage to CAPT. HARLESTON'S; also that other 5 a.
alloted PINCKNEY bounding NE on HUMPHREY ROUSE; SW on marsh; SE on 1st 5
a.; SE on path leading from Broad Path to CAPT. HARLESTON'S. Whereas
AFFRA COMING, widow, late of SC, by her deed poll dated 19 Nov. 1698
granted THOMAS PINCKNEY, merchant, 10 a., part of 186 a. formerly laid
out to HENRY HUGHES; & whereas THOMAS PINCKNEY by will 12 Feb. 1703 bequeathed to his son THOMAS, party hereto, 5 a. (1/2 the 10 a.); & whereas
THOMAS PINCKNEY bequeathed the other 1/2 part of the 10 a. to be equally
divided between his wife MARY 7 his children; & whereas by Act of General
Assembly it was enacted that the HON. RALPH IZARD, ESQ., CHARLES HILL,
ESQ., ANDREW ALLEN & CAPT. ANTHONY MATHEWS make an equal division of all
the plantations, town lots, wharfs, lands, tenements, & all real estate
of THOMAS PINCKNEY, the father, amongst THOMAS PINCKNEY the eldest son,
MARY BETSON, CHARLES PINCKNEY & WILLIAM PINCKNEY, to be enjoyed by them
freed of all dowers & thirds of MARY BETSON might claim; & whereas RALPH
IZARD, CHARLES HILL, ANDREW ALLEN & ANTHONY MATHEWS by deed of partition
16 Jan. 1724 alotted to THOMAS PINCKNEY the other 5 a.; now PINCKNEY
sells the 10 a. to church sommissioners; but since PINCKNEY by his father's will has only a conditional fee at common law in the 5 a. devised to
him which condition cannot be performed until he shall have lawful issue,
PINCKNEY promises to execute all necessary conveyances to perfect the
grant. Witnesses: WILLIAM BLAKEWEY, JOSEPH BRAGG. Before ALEXANDER PAR-
RIS. JACOB MOTTE, Register.

Book D, p. 267 MOSES GRAVES, carpenter, of Berkeley Co., to
8 Sept. 1724 CHARLES DISTON, for L 140 current SC money 2
Deed of Sale tracts containing 165 a. 72 rods (approx.)
left to GRAVES by will of MARTHA GRAVES, bound-
ing "between the lands belonging to ROBERT MILLER, SR. & JOSEPH BRUNSON &
joins to a tract formerly belonging to THOMAS GRAVES". Witnesses: RICH-
ARD BEDON, WILLIAM SHIPPER, JOSEPH WHITE. Before THOMAS WARING. JACOB
MOTTE, Register.

Book D, p. 269 The HON. JOSEPH BLAKE & THOMAS WARING, ESQ.,
8 Apr. 1725 church wardens of St. George's Parish, to
Deed of Sale CHARLES DISTON, of Berkeley Co., for L 600 current SC money about 150 a. (land & house) pur-
chased from THOMAS GRAVES, bounding W & N on JOSEPH BRUNSON & lands left
by MARTHA GRAVES to her son MOSES; E & S on JOHN KITCHEN & the Dorchester
head. Whereas a law was passed 24 Mar. 1724/5 to impower the church wardens of St. George's Parish to sell the present glebe & purchase another
for the use of the rector of the Parish. Witnesses: JOSIAH WARING, JOHN
HILL. Before A. SKENE. JACOB MOTTE, Register.

Book D, p. 269 JAMES CANTEY, planter, & ELIZABETH his wife,
7 & 8 Feb. 1724 of Ashley Ferry to JOHN HILL, carpenter, of
L & R Dorchester, for L 300 current SC money, 100 a.
on Ashley River between PETER GOULDING'S land
& land formerly belonging to CHARLES TREDWELL, which was bought of DAVID
BATCHELLER & devised to ELIZABETH CANTEY by will of her father JOHN
STEPHENS of Berkeley Co. Witnesses: WILLIAM WALLACE, GEORGE CANTEY,

MARGARET (her mark) ARDEN. Receipt dated 1 Mar. 1724 for ⌊ currency &
JOHN HILL'S bond for ⌊ 200 payable 20 Mar. 1725. Before THOMAS WARING.
JACOB MOTTE, Register.

Book D, p. 273　　　　　　　　WILLIAM LIVINGSTON, gentleman, of Charleston &
30 Nov. 1714　　　　　　　　　ANNE his wife, to MARY MADELAIN FOUCHARD, sole
Release　　　　　　　　　　　　dealer, of Charleston, for ⌊ 425 current SC
　　　　　　　　　　　　　　　money part of lot #42 in Charleston, fronting
92 ft. on Broad Street (alias Cooper Street) computed from the E corner
of tenement erected on same premises where MARY MADELAINE FOUCHARD now
dwells back to MR. SERURIER'S (alias SMITH) lot. Whereas THOMAS BOLTON,
merchant, of Charleston, father of ANNE, owned lot #42 in Charleston,
bounding N 142 ft. on Broad Street, alias Cooper Street; S on MR.
SERURIER, alias SMITH; E on MR. ST. JULIEN; W on the cross street running
by the corner of MADAM BRUTELL; & whereas BOLTON by will bequeathed to
his 2 daughters REBECCA BOLTON & ANNE the residue of his real & personal
estate; & whereas REBECCA died a minor shortly after the death of her
father, whereby ANNE became absolutely seized of the premises; & whereas
ANNE married WILLIAM LIVINGSTON & ANNE sell 1/a lot #42 to MARY MADELAINE
FOUCHARD. Witnesses: PAUL LESCOT, PAUL DOUXSAINT, merchant, PETER VILLE-
PONTOUX, merchant, RICHARD ALLAIN. Before THOMAS HEPWORTH, C.J. JACOB
MOTTE, Register.

Book D, p. 276　　　　　　　　RICHARD BAKER, planter, to JOHN MOORE, gentle-
17 July 1722　　　　　　　　　man, of Berkeley Co., for 5 sh., 370 a. in
Lease　　　　　　　　　　　　　Berkeley Co., bounding NE on GEORGE FLOOD; NW
　　　　　　　　　　　　　　　on ISAAC MAZYCK (formerly belonging the HON.
CHARLES CRAVEN, ESQ., Gov.); SE on COL. WILLIAM BULL; SE ON CAPT. RICHARD
DEVON. Witnesses: WILLIAM BILLING, PETER TAYLOR, RICHARD ROWE. Before
JOHN BARKSDALE. JACOB MOTTE, Register.

Book D, p. 278　　　　　　　　JOHN CAWOOD, ESQ., of Charleston, & ELIZABETH
23 & 24 June 1725　　　　　　his wife, administrators of the goods, chat-
L & R　　　　　　　　　　　　　tles, rights & credits of the HON. WILLIAM
　　　　　　　　　　　　　　　GIBBON, ESQ., merchant, to JOB CHAMBERLINE,
planter, of Berkeley Co., for ⌊ 500 current money, 2 tracts of 640 a. ea,
in Berkeley Co. Whereas the Lords Proprs. on 23 July 1711 under hand &
seal of ROBERT GIBBES, ESQ. their Gov., granted WILLIAM GIBBON, merchant,
640 a. in Berkeley Co.; & whereas by a like grant dated 23 July 1711 the
Lords Proprs. granted WILLIAM GIBBON another 640 a. in Berkeley Co.; JOHN
& ELIZABETH CAWOOD sell to CHAMBERLINE. Witnesses: HENRY HOUSER, HENRY
HARGRAVE (Dep. Sec'y.). Before CHARLES HILL. JACOB MOTTE, Register.

Book D, p. 282　　　　　　　　JOHN GODFREY, of Parish of St. Bartholomew's,
15 Aug. 1719　　　　　　　　　Colleton Co., to well beloved sister ELIZABETH
Deed of Sale　　　　　　　　　HILL & to brother-in-law CHARLES HILL, mer-
　　　　　　　　　　　　　　　chant, of Charleston, (husband of ELIZABETH)
for natural love & affection, & for 5 sh., 224 a., known as No. 2, in
plat of CAPT. JOHN GODFREY'S land. Whereas CAPT. JOHN GODFREY by grant
under hands of JOSEPH BLAKE, ESQ., Gov., JAMES MOORE, JOSEPH MORTON &
ROBERT DANIEL, Lords Proprs., dated 11 May 1696, possessed 974 a. in
Berkeley Co.; & whereas CAPT. GODFREY by will required that the residue
of his real & personal estate, not before given, in case of the marriage
or death of his wife be equally divided to his surviving children; &
whereas by a fair division of the 974 a. ELIZABETH HILL, 1 of his daughters obtained 224 a. known as No. 2, in Parish of St. Andrews; & whereas
the right of inheritance is now rested in JOHN GODFREY, son & heir of
CAPT. JOHN GODFREY; now GODFREY grants 224 a. to sister ELIZABETH & her
husband CHARLES HILL. Witnesses: JOHN WOODWARD, THOMAS STANYARNE, BEN-
JAMIN GODFREY. Before JOHN CAWOOD. JACOT MOTTE, Register.

Book D, p. 285　　　　　　　　JOHN WOODWARD, planter, of Berkeley Co., to
3 & 4 Dec. 1722　　　　　　　CHARLES HILL, ESQ. of Charleston for ⌊ 240:15:0
L & R　　　　　　　　　　　　　currency 70-1/2 a. in Berkeley Co., bounding N
　　　　　　　　　　　　　　　on Governor's Creek; E on marsh; S on BENJAMIN
WHITAKER, ESQ.; W on CHARLES HILL. JOHN WOODWARD however gave 2 deeds of
L & R 6 & 7 Dec. 1720 to BENJAMIN GODING & BENJAMIN DELA CONSEILLERE mortgaging the premisses to secure payment of ⌊ 5893:13:8 with interest. Witnesses: JOHN GIBBES, BENJAMIN WHITAKER. Witnesses to receipt for ⌊
246-15/: BENJAMIN WHITAKER, JOHN BARNWELL. Before JOHN BARKSDALE. JACOB

MOTTE, Register.

Book D, p. 288 25 & 26 June 1725 L & R	JOHN BELL, JR., planter, to SAMUEL BLYTH, planter, both of Craven Co., for Ⱡ 635 current SC money, 2 tracts of land; 1 containing 500 a. in Craven Co., bounding W on Santee River,

E on JOHN SANEO; the other containing 400 a., being an island in Santee River, described in grant from Lords Proprs. to JOHN BELL. Witnesses: JOEL POINSETT, JONA. COLLINGS, ROBERT HUME. Before CHARLES HILL. JACOB MOTTE, Register.

Book D, p. 292 15 May 1725 Bond	RICHARD SMITH, ESQ., of Berkeley Co., to JACOB BELL, merchant, of Charleston, in penal sum of Ⱡ 1080 current money conditioned for payment of Ⱡ 538 & 1 penny on demand. Witnesses: ROB-

ERT BATEMAN, THOMAS ELLERY. Before DANIEL GREEN. JACOB MOTTE, Register.

Book D, p. 292 7 Aug. 1725 Deed of Sale	SARAH TURNER, widow of THOMAS TURNER, of St. Paul, Colleton Co., gave bond to THOMAS FLEMIN, planter, of same Parish, in penal sum of Ⱡ 2000 SC money conditioned for keeping the

agreements of a deed of sale, this date, for 275 a. on John's Island. Witnesses: THOMAS KIMBERLEY, ROBERT BOHANAN. Before JOHN BARKSDALE. JACOB MOTTE, Register. (KIMBERLEY made affirmation according to his profession). Before JOHN BARKSDALE. JACOB MOTTE, Register.

Book D, p. 293 7 Aug. 1725 Deed of Sale	SARAH TURNER, widow of THOMAS TURNER, of Parish of St. Paul, Colleton Co., to THOMAS FLEMIN, planter, for Ⱡ 550 SC money, 275 a. English measure, (part of 450 a.) on Johns Is-

land, Colleton Co.; bounding S on Bow-woc Creek (alias BROCKHAS); E on MR. WILKINS & STEPHEN FORD, JR.; N on JOHN WOODING & the creek; W on ZEKRIAH CARLILE & on SARAH TURNER. Whereas the Lords Proprs. on 17 Aug. 1700 granted CAPT. WILLIAM BROCKHAS 450 a. on Johns Island, Colleton Co. on N side Bow-woc Creek; bounding S on the creek; E on JOHN MILLEX; N on vacant land; & whereas BROCKHAS by will dated 9 Jan. 1704/5 conveyed the 450a. to ELIZABETH & SARAH WILKINSON; & whereas ELIZABETH became heir to 325 of the 450 a. by virtue of the will & married ELISHA CARLILE, planter; & whereas ELISHA CARLILE on 1 Sept. 1723 conveyed 100 of the 320 a. to STEPHEN FORD, SR.; & whereas STEPHEN FORD, SR., by deed of gift on 4 Jan. 1723 & 4 gave the 100 a. to his son THOMAS FORD; & whereas THOMAS FORD on 23 Mar. 1723/4 conveyed the 100 a. to SARAH TURNER, widow of THOMAS TURNER; & whereas ELIZABETH CARLILE died without issue, 175 of the 325 a. became the property of SARAH TURNER by virtue of will of CAPT. WILLIAM BROCKHAS (9 Jan. 1704/5); now SARAH TURNER conveys to THOMAS FLEMIN. Witnesses: THOMAS KIMBERLY, ROBERT BOHANAN. (KIMBERLY made affirmation according to his profession). Before JOHN BARKSDALE. JACOB MOTTE, Register.

Book D, p. 296 2 June 1724 Deed	JOHN MOORE, gentleman, of Charleston, to RICHARD ROWE. Whereas by deed poll 5 June 1719, JOHN MOORE for a consideration granted his son-in-law RICHARD ROWE the southernmost third

part of a 1/2 town lot #15; & whereas some part of the front of the said part of a 1/2 town lot & so down a great depth of the lot has been & remains inside his fence ever since the deed was executed; now JOHN MOORE acknowledges the fact & agrees to let RICHARD ROWE fence the 6-1/2 ft. Witnesses: MAURICE HARVEY, ROBERT HUME. Before THOMAS HEPWORTH, C.J. JACOB MOTTE, Register.

Book D, p. 297 28 & 29 Apr. 1721 L & R	JOHN KINNAIRD, planter of Berkeley Co., to CHARLES HILL, ESQ. of Charleston, for Ⱡ 500 current SC money, 2 tracts of land containing 760 a. in Christ Church Parish, granted by

Lords Proprs. to JOHN BELL & by sundry conveyances are now rested in JOHN JEFFEINS & JOTHAM GIBBONS; W on JOTHAM & JOHN SIMMS; S on JOHN SIMMS. Witnesses: ROGER MOORE, BENJAMIN WHITAKER. Before DANIEL GREEN. JACOB MOTTE, Register.

Book D, p. 300   GEORGE LOGAN, ESQ. & MARTHA his wife (late

17 & 18 June 1720 (late widw of ROBERT DANIEL, ESQ.) to CHARLES
L & R   HILL, ESQ., for L 300 current SC money, part
                   of lot #32 in Charleston, fronting 50 ft. on
Cooper River from the walls of the fortifications down to low water mark.
Whereas WILLIAM, Earl of Craven, Palatine, & the Lords Proprs. on 18 Feb.
1680 granted DAVID MAYBANK the elder lot #32 in Charleson containing 1/2
an a., English measure; & whereas DAVID MAYBANK the younger, son & heir,
by deed poll on 12 July 1692 conveyed the lot & building on it to JOSHUA
WILKS; & whereas JOSHUA WILKS on 3 Feb. 1692 sold the lot to GEORGE
DARESELY; & whereas DARESELY on 13 Dec. 1693 sold to COL. ROBERT DANIEL
the lot #32, bounding E on Cooper River; S on a street leading to Ashley
River; N on a lot of MR. FOSTER of Barbadoes; W on JONATHAN AMORY; &
whereas ROBERT DANIEL by will 1 May 1718 bequeathed to MARTHA DANIEL (his
widow, now MARTHA LOGAN) that part of lot #32 fronting 50 feet on Cooper
River, bounding N SAMUEL WRAGG; S on MRS. SUSANNA PORTER (widow of MATHEW
PORTER); now LOGAN sells to HILL & promises that MARTHA shall within 6
days appear before the Chief Justice & renounce her right of dower. Witnesses: FRANCIS LEBRASSEUR, BENJAMIN WHITAKER. Before DANIEL GREEN.
JACOB MOTTE, Register.

Book D, p. 305   SAMUEL DEAN (DEANE), merchant & MARY his wife,
10 & 11 Feb.   to CHARLES HILL, merchant, all of Charleston,
L & R   for L 500 current SC money, part of lot #11 in
                   Charleston, 86 ft. long, 27-1/2 ft. front.
Whereas WILLIAM HYDE, merchant, of Charleston, owned part of lot #11 in
Charleston, bounding S on a little neighborhood street leading to the
house of DR. JOHN HUTCHINSON & CAPT. THOMAS HEPWORTH; W on MOSES WILSON;
which property was heretofore the estate of JOSEPH CROSKEYS & conveyed by
CROSKEYS & MARGARET INGERSON, executrix of will of CROSKEYS to WILLIAM
HYDE (Act of General Assumbly 7 June 1712 to enable executor of will of
JOSEPH CROSKEYS, mariner, to sell a plantation, town lots, & real estate)
& another Act of General Assembly 18 Feb. 1714 rested the estate of WILLIAM HYDE, merchant, in trustees for payment of his debts & maintenance
of his widow ELIZABETH WIGFALL HYDE & child, (HYDE owing considerable
sums of money & his personal estate falling so short that if his real estate be not sold his creditors would lose heavily, & to remove all doubts
of the title of the real estate of HYDE, it was enacted that HYDE'S property should be rested in CAPT. ROBERT FENWICKE & BENJAMIN QUELCH as
trustees, with power to sell, & in case of their neglect or refusal to
act it would be lawful for ELIZABETH WIGFALL HYDE to dispose of the property); & whereas FENWICKE & QUELCH had neglected or refused to sell,
ELIZABETH 24 & 25 Jan. 1716 sold to SAMUEL DEAN for L 110 currency part
of lot #11; now DEAN conveys to CHARLES HILL, DEANE promises that wife
MARY will appear before NICHOLAS TROTT, ESQ., C.J. to release all her
right & title of dower. Witnesses: RICHARD ALLEIN, RICHARD HARELING.
Before JOHN CAWOOD. JACOT MOTTE, Register.

Book D, p. 311   OLIVER SPENCER, cordwainer, of Berkeley Co.,
16 Sept. 1725   grandson & heir apparent of OLIVER SPENCER,
Deed of Sale   blacksmith, to JEREMIAH MILNER, victualler,
                   son & heir apparent of JOSEPH MILNER, (in consideration of the full performance of certain agreements in deed poll
dated 5 Feb. 1694/5 between OLIVER SPENCER, the grandfather, & JOSEPH
MILNER, cordwainer, & in consideration of 5 sh.), all claim which OLIVER
SPENCER might have in the tenement & part of lot #6 in Charleston fronting 20 ft. on the street & running from the street south to THOMAS
SMITH'S lot. Witnesses: JOHN WHITE, THOMAS LAMBOLL. Before THOMAS HEPWORTH, C.J. JACOB MOTTE, Register.

Book D, p. 313   PETER MANIGAULT, vintner, & ANNE his wife to
23 & 24 July 1725 JOHN LAURENS, saddler all of Charleston, for
L & R   L 700 current SC money, 1/2 part of 3 lots
                   near the market place in Charleston which were
devised by MARY CROSS, widow, by will to her son WILLIAM BAYLEY & her
daughters MARY BASDEN (afterwards MARY NARY), & SUSANNAH RAWLINGS (afterwards SUSANNAH WIGINGTON). Witnesses: ROBERT HUME, CHILDERMUS CROFT.
Before THOMAS HEPWORTH, C.J. JACOB MOTTE, Register. Plat laid out by
CHAMPERNOON ELIOTT, survyr., 29 Mar. 1725, at request of WILLIAM GUY, for
PETER MANIGAULT out of the 3 lots formerly belonging to MRS. CROSS, bounding S on market place; W on the street per fortifications; N on remaining

part of the 3 lots now in possession of EDWARD ROLLINGS; E on lots #30 & #69 & known by #59 in model & records of Charleston.

Book D, p. 317
6 Aug. 1720
Release (Counterpart)

SAMUEL WRAGG, merchant, of London, to ALEXAN-DER SKENE, ESQ., for Ł 300 sterling of Great Britain, 3000 a., part of Ashley Barony & St. Giles. Whereas the RT. HON. ANTHONY LORD ASHLEY, Earl of Shaftsburg (by grant 18 Mar. 1675 to his grandfather) owned a great tract of 12,000 a. in Berkeley Co. called Ashley Barony & St. Giles; & whereas ANTHONY LORD ASHLEY on 20 July 1698 granted all his property in SC to his brother the HON. MAURICE ASHLEY, ESQ.; & whereas MAURICE by L & R 2 & 3 Aug. 1717 conveyed the 12,000 a. to SAMUEL WRAGG; now WRAGG sells 3000 a. to SKENE. Witnesses: BENJAMIN WHITAKER, RICHARD LAMBTON. Before WILLIAM BLAKEWEY. JACOB MOTTE, Register.

Book D, p. 322
23 Sept. 1725
Mortgage

THOMAS FARR mortgages to CHRISTOPHER WILKINSON, for Ł 1034:18:6, 2 tracts; 300 a. & 450 a., in Colleton Co., subject to redemption 23 Sept. 1727. Whereas the Lords Proprs. on 12 Sept. 1694, for Ł 70:10 sh. current money granted MARGARET BEAMER, widow, of Colleton Co., 1430 a., English measure, in Colleton Co.; & whereas MARGARET BEAMER & JACOB BEAMER by bill of sale & for Ł 10 on 6 July 1710 conveyed to JOHN BEAMER 900 a. (part of the 1430 a.) fronting S on N side Stono River; W on THOMAS FARR, E on JACOB BEAMER; NW on vacant land; & whereas JOHN BEAMER & JOHANNA his wife by bill of sale 29 Oct. 1712, for Ł 400 current SC money conveyed the 900 a. to JOHN WILLIAMSON; & whereas JOHN WILLIAMSON by bill of sale 16 Feb. 1712, for Ł 200 conveyed 450 a. (part of the 900 a.) to THOMAS FARR; & whereas the Lords Proprs. on 18 May 1694, for Ł 15, conveyed to NICHOLAS MARDEN, victualler, of Berkeley Co., 300 a. English measure, in Colleton Co.; & whereas NICHOLAS MARDEN by bill of sale 13 Sept. 1694, for Ł 19:10 sh., conveyed the 300 a. to JOHN FARR; & whereas THOMAS FARR, as heir to JOHN FARR, became owner of the 300 a.; now THOMAS FARR mortgages the tracts (450 a. & 300 a.) to CHRISTOPHER WILKINSON. Witnesses: ARCHIBALD STOBO, ELIZABETH STOBO (wife of ARCHIBALD), ROBERT YOUNG (YONGE). Before ROBERT YONGE, Asst. Judge for Will Town Precinct. JACOT MOTTE, Register.

Book D, p. 325
27 & 28 Dec. 1724
L & R & Mortgage

GEORGE SINCLAIR, Doctor in Physic, to WILLIAM GIBBON & ANDREW ALLEN, merchants, all of Charleston, for Ł 250 of Great Britain, part of 3 lots in Charleston Nos. 188, 189, & 79, fronting 190-1/2 ft. S in a street running E & W from Cooper River, running E backwards to Presbyterian meeting house; bounding E on JOHN HUTCHINSON; W on other part of the 3 lots belonging to WILLIAM GIBBON & ANDREW ALLEN, measuring from HUTCHINSON'S fence 190-1/2 ft., including the house where BENJAMIN WHITAKER, ESQ. lived; upon condition that is SINCLAIR pays GIBBON & ALLEN Ł 250 money of Great Britain as follows, Ł 125 on 27 Dec. 1725 & Ł 125 on 27 Dec. 1726. Witnesses: JOEL POINSETT, ROBERT HUME, CHILDERMUS CROFT. Before THOMAS HEPWORTH. JACOB MOTTE, Register.

Book D, p. 329
23 Nov. 1725
Mortgage

JAMES (JACQUE) ROULAIN & MAGDALEN (her mark) his wife, to JOHN LAURENS, part of lot #59 in Charleston. Whereas JAMES ROULAIN on 10 Sept. 1725 gave bond to JOHN LAURENS, saddler, both of Charleston, in penal sum of Ł 400 current SC money conditioned for payment of Ł 200 on 1 Mar. 1725; now, for security, ROULAIN & wife MARGARET convey to LAURENS part of lot #59 in Charleston fronting 20 ft. on the market place; running back 100 ft., bounding E on MRS. HANNAH ROYER; W on STEPHEN MILLER; N on JOHN LAURENS. Witnesses: JAMES LUCUSS (?), CORNELIUS BATTOON. Before JOHN BARKSDALE. JACOB MOTTE, Register.

Book D, p. 331
7 & 8 July 1725
Settlement

WILLIAM GIBBS, ESQ. & ALICE his wife, of Colleton Co., in trust to THOMAS BROUGHTON, ESQ. of Berkeley Co., 200 a. on John's Island, Colleton Co. which he purchased from COL. JOHN FENWICKE; bounding E on CAPT. JOHN RAVEN; S on land surveyed by HENRY NICHOLS for ABRAHAM WAIGHT (a minor); on all other sides on JOHN FENWICKE. In consideration of the fact that THOMAS BROUGHTON at the request & direction of WILLIAM GIBBS & ALICE his wife (pursuant to a clause contained in a deed of settlement dated 7 Aug. 1716 & made before the marriage of

WILLIAM & ALICE) conveyed to WILLIAM HARVEY of Charleston 2 tracts of 214 a. & 200 a. in Berkeley Co. at Wappoo Creek; & to settle the lands hereafter described for the purposes mentioned in these presents; & also for 10 sh. current SC money apiece paid by THOMAS BROUGHTON to WILLIAM & ALICE GIBBS; now WILLIAM & ALICE convey 200 a. to BROUGHTON for the use of WILLIAM & ALICE during their lives & then to their heirs. It is agreed that GIBBS, with the voluntary consent of ALICE, may lease, sell or dispose of all or any part of the 200 a. during their joint lives, registering such agreement in the secretary's office, the money to be used as agreed above. Should GIBBS be evicted from the land he agrees to make over to BROUGHTON, as shall be taken away. Witnesses: JOHN FENWICKE, CULCH GOLIGHTLY, WILLIAM ALLEN. Before THOMAS HEPWORTH. JACOB MOTTE, Register.

Book D, p. 335
6 & 7 Sept. 1725
L & R

WILLIAM (his mark) TAYLOR, planter, to JOSEPH STANYARNE, planter both of Berkeley Co., for ₤ 500 current SC money, 2 tracts; 1 being 150 a. in Colleton C. on N side Pollock Creek, bounding S on Pollock Creek; E on THOMAS DIDLEY & vacant land; N & W on vacant land; the other containing 100 a. in Colleton Co. bounding S on Pollock Creek; E on WILLIAM TAYLOR; W on ROBERT OLE; N on vacant land. Witnesses: ANTHONY MATHEWS, JR., THOMAS STANYARNE, JAMES STOBO. Before DANIEL GREEN. JACOT MOTTE, Register.

Book D, p. 339
5 & 6 Aug. 1720
L & R

SAMUEL WRAGG, merchant, of London, to ALEXANDER SKENE, ESQ., for ₤ 300 money of Great Britain, 3000 a. (part of the Ashley Barony and St. Giles). Whereas the RT. HON. ANTHONY LORD ASHLEY, Earl of Shaftsbury, 1 of the Lords Proprs., through grant 18 Mar. 1675 to his grandfather ANTHONY, Earl of Shaftsbury of 12,000 a., commonly called Ashley Barony and St. Giles became possessed of the Barony; & whereas on July 1698 he conveyed his property in SC to his brother the HON. MAURICE ASHLEY, ESQ.; & MAURICE by L & R 2 & 3 Aug. 1717 conveyed to SAMUEL WRAGG, merchant, of SC, the 12,000 a. with the usual reservations; now WRAGG 3000 a. (part of the 12,000 a.) to SKENE. Witnesses: JAMES FISHER, DANIEL BELL, SAMUEL DEANE, JOHN SMYTER, FRANCIS YONGE. Before CHARLES HILL. JACOB MOTTE, Register.

Book D, p. 345
25 Apr. 1723
Bill of Sale

WILLIAM NASH & PRUDENCE his wife, to JOHN FREER, planter, both of Colleton Co., for ₤ 140 current SC money, 103 a., bounding S on Bedinwah Creek; W on LANDGRAVE MORTON; N on PETER BROWN; E on WILLIAM NASH. Witnesses: JONATHAN THOMAS, JOHN DEAR, SR., JOHN DEAR, JR. Before CHRISTOPHER WILKINSON. JACOB MOTTE, Register.

Book D, p. 347
8 Aug. 1717
Agreement

GRACE BUCKLEY grants NATHANIEL WILLIAMS free liberty after her decease to dwell, plant, & cut timber upon the land which was formerly ROBERT LEWIS'S. Witness: GEORGE SMITH. Before JOHN BARKSDALE. JACOB MOTTE, Register.

Book D, p. 347
14 Mar. 1723
Power of Attorney

PETER CEELY, mariner, formerly of Topsam, Great Britain, now of SC, appointed ROBERT HUME, gentleman, of Charleston, his attorney to recover all debts & sums of money due CEELY. Witness: WILLIAM SMITH. JACOB MOTTE, Register. Before JOSEPH WRAGG. JACOB MOTTE, Register.

Book D, p. 348
10 & 11 Oct.
L & R

THOMAS HERBERT, planter, of Hobcaw, Berkeley Co., to MARTHA CROOK, widow, of Charleston, for ₤ 200 current SC money, 200 a. at Hobcaw, bounding N on Molasses Creek; W on WILLIAM WATSON; N on Molasses Creek; S on JACOB BOND; MARTHA CROOK to hold the land free of the dower & thirds of MARY, wife of THOMAS HERBERT. Should THOMAS HERBERT pay MARTHA CROOK ₤ 220 current SC money on 12 Oct. 1724 this sale to be void. Witnesses: SAMUEL PENHALLOW, THOMAS ELLERY. Before THOMAS HEPWORTH, C.J.

Book D, p. 352
5 Jan. 1725

ALBERT MULLER, merchant, for divers good causes & consideration, releases to JOHN

Release of Covenants LAURENS, saddler, both of Charleston, all benefits & advantages due MULLER in a brick tenement on Broad Street. Whereas JOHN LAURENS & ESTER his wife by L & R, 4 & 5 Jan. 1725 sold to ALBERT MULLER a brick messuage of 2 tenements, Broad Street, (it being agreed in the release that JOHN LAURENS & ESTER were, or 1 of them was, the lawful owners of the premises, etc.); now MULLER quit claims to LAURENS (as effectually as if the release had not been made). Witnesses: WILLIAM VISSER, ROBERT HUME. Before THOMAS HEPWORTH, C.J. JACOB MOTTE, Register.

Book D, p. 354
5 Jan. 1725
Release

JOHN LLOYD, ESQ., of Charleston, SC, to JOHN LENOIR, ESQ., of the Island of Barbadoes, for L 1100 SC money, 3 tracts; 200 a., 210 a., & 300 a. which HENRY LIVINGSTON purchased from JAMES BROWN, making 1 tract of 710 a., commonly called Lynch Grove Plantation, on Wando Neck, Berkeley Co.; bounding E on JOHN HOLLYBUSH; S on JOHN BURKE; W on WILLIAM WHITE. Whereas JOHN LLOYD by deed poll Feb. 2, 1724 testified that 3 tracts were conveyed to him in trust by HENRY LIVINGSTON, gentleman, of Berkeley Co., until he should be reimbursed by JOHN LENOIR L 1096:3:10:3 SC money, paid to discharge bonds entered into by LIVINGSTON in payment for 710 a., with interest, & LLOYD'S commissions, costs & charges; after such payments to the use of JOHN LENOIR; now LLOYD conveys to LENOIR the 710 a. Witnesses: MARY RUSSELL, T. AKIN, ROBERT HUME. Before BENJAMIN WHITAKER. JACOB MOTTE, Register.

Book D, p. 357
18 July 1722
Mortgage

RICHARD BAKER, planter, & ELIZABETH, his wife, to JOHN MOORE, gentleman, all of Berkeley Co., 370 a. Whereas ROGER SAUNDERS, gentleman, by deed of feoffment on 30 Jan. 1711 reciting that whereas WILLIAM Lord Craven, Palatine, under the lands of the HON. COL. ROBERT GIBBES, ESQ., Gov., & the Lords Proprs. on 16 Aug. 1710 granted WILLIAM SAUNDERS, ESQ., 640 a., English measure, in Berkeley Co. on SW side Ashley River, bounding SE on FORTESCUE TURBERVILLE, ESQ.; NE on Ashley Barony; NW on the HON. COL. EDWARD TYNTE, Gov.; SW on vacant land; & whereas SAUNDERS at his death was much in debted to sundry people; & whereas by Act of Assembly 1 Mar. 1710 ROGER SAUNDERS, administrator of estate of WILLIAM, was enabled to sell lands to pay such debts, and for L 50 sold to ISAAC MAZYCK the 640 a.; & whereas ISAAC MAZYCK & MARIAN his wife on 15 May 1722 for L 788 sold to RICHARD BAKER (370 a. part of 640 a.) bounding NE on GEORGE FLOOD; NW on ISAAC MAZYCK (formerly the HON. CHARLES CRAVEN, Gov.); SW on COL. WILLIAM BULL; SE on CAPT. RICHARD DEVON; & whereas RICHARD BAKER on 18 July 1722 gave bond to JOHN MOORE in penal sum of L 1000 for payment of 34,000 lbs. rice in barrels in Charleston on Feb. 1, next; now for security BAKER conveys to MOORE 370 a., ELIZABETH, wife of RICHARD BAKER to relinquish her right & title of dower before next Feb. conrt. BAKER paid the rice & interest Aug. 20, 1728. Witnesses: WILLIAM BILLING, PETER TAYLOR, RICHARD ROWE. Before JOHN BARKSDALE. JACOB MOTTE, Register.

DEEDS BOOK "E"
1723-1728

Book E, p. 1
1 July 1717
Release

LANDGRAVE THOMAS SMITH, ESQ., and COL. GEORGE SMITH, gentleman, both of Berkeley Co., attorneys to GEORGE SMITH, ESQ., late of SC, now of Island of Bermuda & DOROTHY his wife, to CAPT. MATHEW PORTER, gentleman of Charleston, for L 120 currency of Island of Bermuda the northern half of lot #1 in Charleston, bounding E 51 ft. on Cooper River; S on MAJOR PERCIVAL CRAWLEY (PAWLEY?); W on LANDGRAVE SMITH'S marsh; N on DR. JOHN HUTCHINSON. Whereas, WILLIAM, Earl of Craven, Palatine & the Lords Proprs. on 26 July granted MAURICE MATHEWS & JAMES MOORE, ESQS., 2 adjoyning lots in Charleston, Nos. 1 & 102; & whereas JAMES MOORE on 24 Feb. 1693 sold the northernmost half of lot #1 to PETER GIRARD, merchant, bounding S on the half belonging to ELISHA BENNET, mariner; N on MAJOR JOHN BOONE; E 51 ft. on the wharf on Cooper River; W on lot #102 sold by MAURICE MATHEWS & JAMES MOORE to ELISHA BENNETT; & whereas GIRARD & GAILLARD on 7 Dec. 1696 for L 168 SC money sold the half lot to JAMES RISBEE; & whereas JAMES RISBEE & JANE his wife in 1714 sold not only the half lot to GEORGE SMITH but also all RISBEE'S real & personal estate in SC, nothing reserved; & whereas GEORGE SMITH & DOROTHY, his wife, on 31 July 1713 appointed LANDGRAVE THOMAS SMITH, GEORGE SMITH, & ROBERT TRADD their attorneys to dispose of all such houses, lands, Negroes & cattle, etc., in SC belonging to them; now THOMAS & GEORGE SMITH, as attorneys sell to MATHEW PORTER. Witnesses: CAPT. DANIEL GREEN, MAURICE HARVEY, COL. MILES BREWTON, THOMAS SMITH, THOMAS HEPWORTH. Before SAM EVELEIGH. JACOB MOTTE, Register.

Book E, p. 10
4 & 5 Dec. 1724
L & R

JACOB MOTTE, merchant, of Charleston, to GEORGE BENISON, of Berkeley Co., for ₤ 690 SC money 462 a. in Berkeley Co., bounding SW on JOHN PERRY'S land known as Yough Hall; NW on THOMAS BARTON & MR. WOODING; E on Boowat Creek; NE on GEORGE BENTLY. Whereas PETER BOWDON owned 462 a., English measure, in Berkeley Co., & on 16 Jan. 1709 immediately before his departure from this province appointed JOHN ABRAHAM MOTTE & TANNAH BOWDON his attorneys with power to take possession & dispose his property; & whereas MOTTE & BOWDON on 26 Mar. 1711 sold the 462 a. to STEPHEN SARAZEN; & whereas SARAZEN on 26 Mar. 1711 sold the land to JOHN ABRAHAM MOTTE; & whereas MOTTE died intestate, the land descended to his son & heir JACOB MOTTE; now JACOB sells to BENISON. Witnesses: THOMAS BOONE, JOHN YOUNG, LAWRENCE COULLIETTE. Before CHARLES HILL. JACOB MOTTE, Register.

Book E, p. 19
23 & 24 July 1722
L & R

JOHN BONHOSTE, planter, & MARIANNE, his wife, to GEORGE BENISON, planter, of Berkeley Co., for ₤ 525 SC money 500 a. in Berkeley Co., bounding E on DUBOIS; W on ANTHONY BONNEAU; N on JONAS BONHOSTE; S on JOHN WITE. Whereas on 27 Apr. 1710 DANIEL MCGRIGORY, planter, & SARAH his wife sold to JACOB LAPORTE(LAPOTRE?), merchant, for ₤ 100 currency, 1000 a., English measure, in Berkeley Co., bounding NW on ANTHONY BONNEAUS; S & E on DANIEL MCGRIGORY; & whereas LAPOTRE by will 13 Oct. 1710 bequeathed to his 2 sons, JONAS BONHOSTE & JOHN BONHOSTE, 2500 a., afterward equally divided between them; now JOHN BONHOSTE sells 500 a. to BENISON, free from dower & thirds of MARIANNE BONHOSTE. JONAS insists on having the custody of the deed poll, plat & grant, but agrees to show them when necessary. Witnesses: PETER TAYLOR, WILLIAM BILLING. Before CHARLES HILL. JACOB MOTTE, Register.

Book E, p. 28
8 Mar. 1717
Release

JOHN MILNER, mariner, & ELIZABETH his wife to ANDREW ALLEN & ROBERT TRADD, merchants, all of Charleston, for ₤ 54 SC money, the tenement occupied by widow SUSANNAH PORTER & part of lot #66 in Charleston, bounding W 200 ft. on the street leading to the new brick church; S 60 ft. on the French church; N on the new church; E on part same lot belonging to MRS. MARY MULLINS. JOHN promises that ELIZABETH shall appear before NICHOLAS TROTT, ESQ., C.J., & voluntarily renounce her right or title of dower. Witnesses: ROBERT HUME, HENRY BARTON, JOHN MILNER, THOMAS HEPWORTH. Before DANIEL GREEN. JACOB MOTTE, Register.

Book E, p. 35
8 Mar. 1717
Deed

ANDREW ALLEN & ROBERT TRADD, executors of will of MATHEW PORTER, whereas by L & R, 7 & 8 Mar. 1717 (see page 28) MILNER sold to ALLEN & TRADD, merchants, a tenement & part of lot #66 in Charleston; & whereas MATHEW PORTER, sawyer, by will dated 15 Nov. 1716 bequeathed to his wife SUSANNAH all his real estate during her life & after her death the real estate to be sold & the money equally divided between his mother, MARY PORTER, his brother JOHN & JAMES, & his sister HANNAH living in Great Britain, & appointed SUSANNAH PORTER, ANDREW ALLEN, & ROBERT TRADD executors; & whereas MATHEW PORTER in his lifetime agreed to buy the premises from JOHN MILNER for ₤ 54 & paid ₤ 20 as part but died before the execution of the conveyance; now ALLEN & TRADD declared that the ₤ 54 belonged to the estate of MATHEW PORTER & that their names were used only in trust & that they will permit SUSANNAH PORTER to hold the tenement & part of lot during her life then they will sell the premises & divide the money according to PORTER'S will. Witnesses: MICHAEL BREWTON, THOMAS HEPWORTH, ROBERT HUME. Before DANIEL GREEN. JACOB MOTTE, Register.

Book E, p. 38   ROBERT HUME, gentleman, & SOPHIA, his wife, of
18 Feb. 1725   Charleston to THOMAS FLEMIN, planter, of Col-
Release   leton Co., for Ł 600 SC money, part of lot #71
                          fronting N 35 ft. English measure, on Broad
Street; bounding W on DR. CHRISTIAN COOPER'S house and lot now belonging
to his daughter; E on part same lot #71 formerly belonging to CAPT. JOHN
CLAPP & afterward willed by MARY CROSS to her 2 daughters MARY BASDEN,
widow, & SUSANNA RAWLINGS. Witnesses: MARY BLAMYER, SAMUEL PRIOLEAU.
Before JOHN CROFT, Master in Chancery. JACOB MOTTE, Register.

Book E, p. 41   MARY BASDEN, spinster, JONATHAN COLLINS, mari-
30 Nov. 1722   ner, & SARAH his wife, of Charleston, the REV.
Release   MR. WILLIAM GUY, clerk, & REBECCA, his wife,
                          of St. Andrew's Parish, Berkeley Co., to ROB-
ERT HUME, gentleman, of Charleston, for Ł 200 SC money, part of lot #71
in Charleston, fronting N on Broad Street 35 ft., English measure; W on a
house & lot formerly belonging to DR. CHRISTIAN COOPER but now to his
daughter; E on another part of lot #71 formerly belonging to CAPT. JOHN
CLAPP, afterward willed by MRS. MARY CROSS to her 2 daughters, MARY BAS-
DEN, widow, & SUSANNAH RAWLINGS. Witnesses: HARRAL BLY, JOSUE MARINEURE.
Before JOHN CROFT, Master in Chancery. JACOB MOTTE, Register.

Book E, p. 44   SAMUEL EVELEIGH, merchant, to JOSEPH WRAGG,
6 & 7 Jan. 1725   merchant, both of Charleston, for Ł 4537:10 SC
L & R & Mortgage   money, part of lot #4 in Charleston, 75 ft. in
                          front, 230 ft. deep, bounding S on part of
said lot belonging to CAPT. BENJAMIN ROMSEY; W on WILLIAM CHAPMAN, tanner;
N on CAPT. GEORGE SMITH; E ON street next to & parallel with Cooper River;
also 550 a. in Berkeley Co., granted 5 Sept. 1709 to JAMES SUTHERS; also
1120 a. nigh Wacamaw River in Winyah River, Craven Co., sold by LANDGRAVE
THOMAS SMITH to SAMUEL EVELEIGH. Should EVELEIGH pay WRAGG Ł 4537:10 in
rice at 40 sh. per cwt. & casks at 7 sh. 6d apiece delivered in Charleston on 7 Feb. 1725 also pay all his debts to WRAGG this mortgage to be
void. Witnesses: ROBERT HUME, CHILDERMUS CROFT. Before JOHN CROFT,
Master in Chancery. JACOB MOTTE, Register. RICHARD LAMBTON, surviving
partner of WRAGG & LAMBTON, declared mortgage paid in full & that MRS.
JUDITH WRAGG, executrix, desired him to enter the satisfaction 22 Aug.
1752. Witness: WILLIAM HOPTON.

Book E, p. 53   GEORGE SMITH, of Berkeley Co., to MARK OLIVER,
15 Feb. 1725   victualler, of Charleston, 190 a. Whereas by
Deed   L & R, 7 & 8 June 1724 SMITH mortgaged to
                          OLIVER 190 a. in Berkeley Co., bounding SW on
Wando River; NW on CAPT. GEORGE DEARSLY; SE ON WILLIAM BALLAUGH; NE on
GEORGE SMITH; for Ł 200 & interest at 10% payable 8 Dec. 1725; & whereas
no payment has been made by SMITH; now SMITH conveys the 190 a. to OLIVER
without benefit of redemption. Witnesses: ROBERT HUME, CHILDERMUS CROFT.
Before JOHN CROFT, M.C. JACOB MOTTE, Register.

Book E, p. 56   GEORGE SMITH, planter, of Berkeley Co., to
14 & 15 Feb. 1725   MARK OLIVER, vintner (?) of Charleston, for
L & R   Ł 192 SC money; 192 a. in Berkeley Co., bound-
                          ing N & E on THOMAS RICHARDSON; S on WILLIAM
BALLOUGH; W on DEARSLY. Witnesses: ROBERT HUME, CHILDERMUS CROFT. Before JOHN CROFT, M.C. JACOB MOTTE, Register.

Book E, p. 62   MARTHA CROOK, widow, of the first part; ANDREW
10 & 11 May 1725   ALLEN & JOHN CAWOOD, merchants, of the second
L & R, Tripartite   part; & BENJAMIN ROMSEY, merchant, of the
                          third part; all of Charleston. MARTHA CROOK
to ALLEN & CAWOOD, in trust, several lots of land in Charleston. Whereas
a marriage is intended between MARTHA CROOK & BENJAMIN ROMSEY they agree
that several lots be conveyed to ALLEN & CAWOOD in trust; now, to settle
the real estate & slaves, MARTHA with the advice & agreement of BENJAMIN
conveys to ALLEN & CAWOOD, lot #77 & lot #4, fronting 27 ft. on the wharf
from EVELEIGH'S house to the PINCKNEY line; by S side of wharf line by S
line of EVELEIGH'S house to easternmost part of the brick chimney of said
house 16-1/2 ft.; by S side of chimney 8 ft.; then from SW corner of
chimney to PINCKNEY'S line 27 ft.; from thence a long square 27 ft. broad
to westernmost line of lot; bounding E on Charleston Wharf or Bay; W on a

marsh; N on EVELEIGH'S house; S on PINCKNEY; also that slip of land which MARTHA bought from PINCKNEY, bounding N on part of lot #4; fronting the Bay 5 ft.; going W whole depth of lot; to hold lot #77 to the use of BENJAMIN ROMSEY; to hold lot #4 & slip of land to the use of BENJAMIN & MARTHA during their natural lives, then to their issue; in default of issue, then to BENJAMIN'S heirs. MARTHA delivers to ALLEN & CAWOOD 1 Negro man, 1 Negro boy & 1 Negro girl, in trust for MARTHA & BENJAMIN. Witnesses: PETER CEELY, ROBERT HUME. Before THOMAS HEPWORTH. JACOB MOTTE, Register.

Book E, p. 69
21 Jan. 1724
Mortgage

EDWARD KEATING, planter, of Goose Creek, Berkeley Co., to JOHN MOORE, gentleman, of Charleston. Whereas on 20 Jan. 1724 JOHN MOORE & RACHEL, his wife, conveyed to EDWARD KEATING 2 plantations containing 870 a. & 500 a.; & whereas they agreed that KEATING should deliver 137,000 lbs. of rice on Bay of Charleston the purchase price & that KEATING should give 2 bonds, each in the penal sum of ₤ 3000 current money, each conditioned for the delivery of 68,500 lbs. rice at certain times; KEATING also to give MOORE a mortgage on the 2 plantations as security; now KEATING gives MOORE the mortgage as agreed. The 500 a. bounds N on MR. ALSTON; S on JOHN MOORE; W on MOORE & JONATHAN PALMER. Witnesses: PETER VILLEPONTOUX, THOMAS ELLERY. Before THOMAS HEPWORTH, C. J. JACOB MOTTE, Register. On 20 Oct. 1726 KEATING paid JOHN MOORE ₤ 4000 in full satisfaction of mortgage. Witness: JACOB MOTTE, Register.

Book E, p. 73
4 & 5 Nov. 1725
L & R

JOHN VICARIDGE, gentleman, to JOHN LLOYD, gentleman, both of Charleston, for ₤ 220 current money of Great Britain 620 a., English measure, in St. James Parish, Goose Creek, bounding S on JAMES MOORE, ESQ., NW on ANDREW ALLEN (formerly WILLIAM THOROWGOOD); SW on WILLIAM DRY; NE on ROGER MOORE, ESQ.; except 28 a. leased 15 Oct. 1720 by BICARIDGE to RICHARD WALKER, tailor, & CATHERINE his wife, for the rent of 1 large fat turkey cock on every 24 Dec. during the term of their natural lives. Whereas ROBERT STEVENS, ESQ., of St. James, Goose Creek, owned 2 tracts, 1 containing 170 a., the other 450 a., making 1 tract of 620 a., English measure, bounding S on JAMES MOORE; NW on ANDREW ALLEN (formerly WILLIAM THOROWGOOD); all other sides on vacant land; & by will 8 Sept. 1720 devised the land to his kinsman JOHN VICARIDGE; now VICARIDGE conveys to LLOYD. Witnesses: RICHARD ROWE, T. AKIN, RICHARD ALLEIN. Before BENJAMIN WHITAKER. JACOB MOTTE, Register.

Book E, p. 80
10 Nov. 1725
Mortgage

WILLIAM STREET, victualler & ELIZABETH his wife, of Ferry Town, to ANN DRAYTON, widow, all of Berkeley Co., for ₤ 250 SC money, 1 lot #3 in Ferry Town, formerly called Butters Town, 105-1/2 ft. square, fronting 2 broad streets, bounding SE & SW on the broad streets; NE on lot #2, as by plat attached to B/S 20 Aug. 1722 from SHEM BUTLER, gentleman, & ESTHER his wife; lot #3 being occupied by CAPT. EDMUND BELLINGER. Should STREET pay ANN DRAYTON ₤ 25 SC money on 10 Nov. 1726 & ₤ 275 on 10 Nov. 1727 this mortgage to be void. Witnesses: WILLIAM (ISAAC) EMANUEL, JOHN MASON. Before THOMAS DYMES. JACOB MOTTE, Register.

Book E, p. 84
Oct. 17, 1723

Received of MR. ELIAS HANCOCKE 1 tankard, 1 punch bole, 1 cuppe & 1 spoon all of silver, which I promise to be accountable for on demand as witness my hand 45 ounces 14 penny weight. EDWD. SWINFEN, recorded 19 Mar. 1725 by JACOB MOTTE, Register.

Book E, p. 85
28 Mar. 1725
Agreement

RICHARD FULLER, planter, & MARY his wife (daughter of THOMAS DRAYTON, planter), of 1 part and ANN DRAYTON, widow & executrix of will of THOMAS DRAYTON, of the other part. Whereas THOMAS DRAYTON by will dated 5 June 1715 gave his daughter the above MARY, ₤ 1000 SC money & her choice of 1 Negro woman; & whereas disputes & lawsuits have occurred between RICHARD FULLER & ANN DRAYTON regarding ownership of some horses & cattle which FULLER claimed were given to his wife by her father in his lifetime, & RICHARD & ANN have agreed to end such differences, ANN agreeing to pay RICHARD ₤ 500 currency in full of all demands, RICHARD agreeing to assign to ANN all his interest in the stock; now RICHARD & MARY FULLER acknowledge receipt of ₤ 1000 & 1 Negro woman from ANN DRAYTON; ANN gives them ₺ 500 for the horses & cattle usually ranging about Spoon Savanna Cowpen. Witnesses: FRANCIS LADSON, ROBERT LADSON. Before THOMAS DYMES. JACOB MOTTE, Register.

Book E, p. 87　　　　　　　RICHARD FULLER, planter, of Berkeley Co., to
28 Mar. 1726　　　　　　　the HON. WILLIAM BULL & GEORGE SMITH, ESQ., in
Bond　　　　　　　　　　　penal sum of ₺ 1000 SC money, conditioned for
　　　　　　　　　　　　　the payment to BULL & SMITH, by his heirs or
executors within 6 months after the death of RICHARD FULLER, ₺ 500 in rice at 40 sh. cwt. or in silver at 40 sh. per oz., in trust for MARY, wife of RICHARD, or in case of her death, in trust for ANN BOOTH FULLER, daughter of RICHARD & MARY; & in case of death of ANN BOOTH, then in trust for RICHARD FULLER, their son. Witnesses: FRANCIS LADSON, ROBERT LADSON. Before THOMAS DYMES. JACOB MOTTE, Register.

Book E, p. 89　　　　　　　ELEAZER ALLEN, merchant, & SARAH his wife, of
4 Apr. 1726　　　　　　　　Charleston, to SAMUEL SCRIVEN, shipwright, of
Release　　　　　　　　　　James Island, for ₺ 400 SC money part of lot
　　　　　　　　　　　　　#64 in Charleston fronting N & S 33 ft. on the
street leading from the new church to Ashley River; bounding N on part same lot belonging ELIZABETH ADAMS, widow, S on RICHARD CAPERS; & 1 side on SAMUEL EVELEIGH. ALLEN promises that SARAH, his wife, will relinquish her title of dower & thirds. Witnesses: ANDREW ALLEN, RICHARD ALLEIN, PETER TAYLOR. Before THOMAS HEPWORTH, C.J. JACOB MOTTE, Register.

Book E, p. 94　　　　　　　JOHN GALE, carpenter, & SARAH, his wife, of
10 Oct. 1712　　　　　　　 Port Royall, Island of Jamaica, to JOHN CROS-
Deed of Sale　　　　　　　KEYS, merchant, formerly of Jamaica now of
　　　　　　　　　　　　　Berkeley Co., for ₺ 500 currency of Island of
Jamaica, 3360 a. in Berkeley Co., commonly called Coatbaw between Medway & Cooper River. Whereas his excellency WILLIAM EARL OF CRAVEN, Palatin, & the Lords Proprs. under the hand of the HON. JOHN ARCHDALE, ESQ., late Gov. of Carolina, on 9 Oct. 1696 granted JONATHAN AMORY 3360 a., English measures, in Berkeley Co., (formerly belonging to DR. JOHN HARDY but forfeited for non-payment of rent); & whereas AMORY on 9 Aug. 1697 sold JOHN GALE (father of above JOHN) the 3360 a.; & whereas JOHN, the father, & the land became the property of JOHN, the son, now GALE, with SARAH'S consent, conveys Coatbaw to CROSKEYS. Witnesses: CAPT. JOHN MARSHALL, RICHARD CAMPLIN, mate; RICHARD LODGE. Before WILLIAM PUCKLE. SARAH being privately examined declared she signed willingly. MARSHALL & CAMPLIN appeared before H. WIGINGTON. On 13 Jan. 1712/13 CAPT. JONATHAN DRAKE, attorney to JOHN GALE, took possession & delivered to JOHN CROSKEYS. Witnesses: MARY DRAKE, CATHERINE (her mark) WATIES, HUMPHREY AXALL, JR. Before H. WIGINGTON. JACOB MOTTE, Register.

Book E, p. 101　　　　　　 JOSEPH CROSKEYS, planter, of Berkeley Co., to
30 July 1725　　　　　　　 NATHANIEL SNOW, SR., for ₺ 2200 SC money, 2500
Deed of Sale　　　　　　　a., English measure, in Berkeley Co. Witness-
　　　　　　　　　　　　　es: THOMAS WESBURY, JOHN (his mark) ROOE, ALEX-
ANDER KINLOCK, merchant. Delivery by turf & twig. Before BENJAMIN WARING. JACOB MOTTE, Register.

Book E, p. 104　　　　　　 NATHANIEL SNOW, SR., practitioner, in physic,
8 & 9 Sept. 1725　　　　　& ANN his wife, Berkeley Co., to ALEXANDER NIS-
L & R　　　　　　　　　　 BETT, merchant, of Charleston, for ₺ 2500 SC
　　　　　　　　　　　　　money 2500 a., commonly called Cutt-baw (Coat-
baw) purchased by SNOW from JOSEPH CROSKEYS, part of 2800 a. granted by Lords Proprs. to JOSEPH CROSKEYS, father of JOSEPH CROSKEYS, on 6 Jan. 1714. Witnesses: JAMES PAINE, ROBERT HALEBURTON, JAMES BULLOCK. Before JAMES KINLOCH. JACOB MOTTE, Register.

BOOK E, p. 110　　　　　　 JOHN ELDERS, planter, & MARY his wife, of
8 Apr. 1726　　　　　　　　Berkeley Co., to ALEXANDER NISBETT, merchant,
Mortgage　　　　　　　　　 of Charleston, for ₺ 701 SC money, 3 tracts of
　　　　　　　　　　　　　land, 1 of 340 a. on NW side of Cooper River;
bounding E & S on Medway or Back River & Forster's Creek; N on JOHN BONEE; W on WILLIAM WATIES; except a lease of 300 a. to JOHN BLAKE, planter, of Berkeley Co., for the term of his natural life. Also 45 a., an island, bounding E on Medway River; S on Appeboo or Foster's Creek; W & N on marsh. Also 305 a. bounding E on Medway River; S on ROBERT SKELTON;

should ELDERS pay NISBETT ₤ 701:15 SC money on 8 July 1726 this mortgage to be void. Witnesses: JAMES WATT, ROBERT NISBETT, ROBERT HUME. Before ALEXANDER PARRIS. JACOB MOTTE, Register.

Book E, p. 116   JAMES FITZGERALD, joiner, of Christ Church Par-
1 Nov. 1725   ish, appointed his good friend JOHN HALE, gen-
Power of Attorney   tleman, of same Parish, his attorney, to dis-
                     pose of his lands, Negroes, goods & chattles,
& to divide amongst his brothers & sisters, or their substitutes, all money due him & all the estate left by his father, THOMAS FITZGERALD. Witnesses: ROBERT CRAWFORD, JOHN STEVENSON. Before DANIEL GREEN. JACOB
MOTTE, Register.

Book E, p. 118   JAMES FITZGARLD(?), joiner, to JOHN HALE, gen-
31 Oct. & 1 Nov. 1725 tleman, both of Berkeley Co., for ₤ 150 SC mon-
L & Mortgage   ey, his third part of 185 a., in Berkeley Co.,
                      left to him & his brothers by his father THOM-
AS FITZGARLD, bounding S on ANTHONY WHITE & JOHN CLEMONS; W on WILLIAM
VISSER; E on JOHN WHITE. Should FITZGARLD pay HALE ₤ 150 on 1 Nov. 1726
this mortgage to be void. Witnesses: ROBERT CRAWFORD, JOHN STEVENSON.
Before DANIEL GREEN. JACOB MOTTE, Register.

Book E, p. 123   JOSEPH CROSKEYS, cooper, & JOHN WITTER, cooper,
26 Nov. 1723   to THOMAS CROSKEYS (brother of JOSEPH) for
Deed of Sale   ₤ 400 SC money, 300 a. on W & S side Cooper
                      River, part of Courtbaw bounding E on Cooper
River; N & S & W on Westow Armes, a part of the Courtbaw tract. Whereas
JOHN CROSKEYS, merchant, by will 18 Feb. 1718/9 bequeathed to his son
JOSEPH CROSKEYS, his place called Courtbaw (Coatbaw?) except 300 a. which
he bequeathed JOHN WITTER provided he settled on it in 6 years after his
death otherwise to belong to son JOSEPH CROSKEYS; & whereas because the
term limited by will for settlement of the 300 a. by WITTER has not expired & WITTER cannot give a title to the land, JOSEPH being willing that
his brother THOMAS CROSKEYS may posses the land rather than some one else,
joins WITTER in making a title by a deed of sale; therefore CROSKEYS &
WITTER sell THOMAS CROSKEYS 300 a. & WITTER'S stock of cattle with the
proviso that THOMAS shall not sell to any one but JOSEPH. MARY WITTER
also signs. Witnesses: ELIZABETH DILL, JOHN CROSKEYS. On 20 Apr. 1726
JOSEPH DILL appeared before ALEXANDER PARRIS & testified he saw JOSEPH
CROSKEYS, JOHN WITTER & MARY WITTER deliver to THOMAS SNOW. JACOB MOTTE,
Register.

Book E, p. 127   JOSEPH CROSKEYS, cooper, & THOMAS CROSKEYS,
25 Aug. 1724   planter, to THOMAS SNOW, carpenter, for ₤ 440
Deed of Sale   SC money, 300 a. on Cooper River, called West-
                      ow Arms, a part of the Courtbaw tract. Where-
as their father, JOHN CROSKEYS, merchant, by will 18 Feb. 1718/9 all his
tract called Courtbaw to his son JOSEPH, except 300 a. which he bequeathed to JOHN WITTER, cooper, provided he settled on it within 6 years after
JOHN'S death, otherwise to go to JOSEPH; & whereas the time not having
expired, JOSEPH joined JOHN WITTER, in the sale, 26 Nov. 1723, of the 300
a. to brother THOMAS CROSKEYS with the proviso that THOMAS not sell to
any one but JOSEPH; & whereas THOMAS has not yet power to dispose of the
land, JOSEPH joins THOMAS in selling the 300 a. to THOMAS SNOW. ELIZA-
BETH (her mark) wife of THOMAS CROSKEYS, also signed. Witnesses: JOHN
CROSKEYS, SAMUEL RIVERS, WILLIAM PARROTT. Before ARTHUR HALL. JACOB
MOTTE, Register.

Book E, p. 130   THOMAS SNOW, carpenter, of Berkeley Co., to
8 & 9 Sept. 1725   ALEXANDER NISBETT, merchant, of Charleston,
L & R   for ₤ 300 SC money, 300 A. lately purchased
                      from THOMAS CROSKEYS, planter, commonly call-
ed Cuttbaw (Courtbaw, Coatbaw?) part of 2800 a. granted 6 Jan. 1714 by
the Lords Proprs. to JOSEPH CROSKEYS, father of THOMAS. Witnesses: ROB-
ERT HALEBURTON, JAMES PAINE, JAMES BULLOCK. Before JAMES KINLOCH. JACOB
MOTTE, Register.

Book E, p. 136   TOBIAS FITCH, planter, & MARIANNE, his wife,
11 & 12 July 1720   daughter of JAMES DUGUE, JR. & of Dame MARIAN
L & R   HENRY his wife & granddaughter of JAMES DUGUE,

Sr., to ANDREW DUPUY, merchant, of Charleston, for Ł 200 SC money, the northern half of lot #70 in Charleston, divided in middle of E & W lines, bounding N on BARNARD SCHENCKINGH; S on other half; E on west side of a street parallel with Cooper River. Whereas JAMES DUGUE, SR., possessing a good estate & half of lot #70 in Charleston, by will dated 28 May 1696 gave his granddaughter MARIANNE 1/6 of his real & personal estate ordaining, that should any of his children, under age, should want a division made to obtain his part, the same should proceed by the advice of the majority, the others not to appeal, appointing his son PETER DUGUE sole executor; & whereas on 27 Oct. 1696, PETER DUGUE, executor, agreed with SAMUEL DUBONDIEU(?), ESQ., & JUDITH his wife, JAMES DUBOSE & MARY his wife, & MARIANNE, widow of JAMES DUGUE, JR., on behalf of her daughters MARIANNE, wife of TOBIAS FITCH, that MARIANNE (wife of JAMES DUGUE, JR.) for her daughter MARIANNE should take & keep as her share at the expiration of 2-1/2 years, town lot #70; now FITCH sells DUPUY half of lot #70. Witnesses: ROBERT HUME, WILLIAM HARVEY, JOHN ROYER. Before JOHN CROFT, M.C. JACOB MOTTE, Register.

Book E, p. 143
17 Mar. 1725
Release

JAMES LARDAN (LARDANT?), carpenter, of Colleton Co., son & heir of JAMES LARDAN, to PAUL DOUXSAINT, merchant, of Charleston, for Ł 300 SC money, half of lot #43, in Charleston, bounding N on French church; S on JOHN BRETON, merchant, (formerly NOAH ROYER); E on a swamp; W on a street leading from Ashley River to new brick church. Witnesses: SAMUEL PRIOLEAU, JAMES ST. JULIEN, HENRY GIGMILLIAT. Before THOMAS HEPWORTH, C.J. JACOB MOTTE, Register.

Book E, p. 148
28 Mar. 1722
Tripartite

THOMAS SATUR, merchant, of Dorchester, SC, of the first part; JACOB SATUR, merchant, formerly of London, now of SC of second part; ELEAZER ALLEN, merchant, of Charleston, of the third part; WILLIAM RHETT, JR., merchant, of Charleston, of fourth part. These have agreed to become co-partners in a store at Dorchester, on land owned by THOMAS SATUR, (details of agreement given in full. Inventory of stock given). Witnesses: RICHARD ALLEIN, WILLIAM BILLING, GEORGE HOKE. Names appearing in inventory are: ROBERT WILSON, PETER CATTLE, ROBERT WINN, THOMAS BAKER, MALACHI GLAZE(?), WILLIAM WAY, JR., JOHN BUGGS, JOB CHAMBERLINE, JAMES BOSWOOD, JOSIAH OSGOOD, JOHN SIMMONS, PHILEMON HOSIER, BENJAMIN SUMNER, JOHN COSENS, THOMAS WAY, MOSES NORMAN, ROGER SUMNER, JAMES POSTELL, DANIEL STEWART. JACOB MOTTE, Register.

Book E, p. 166
18 & 19 Dec. 1724
L & R

In trust. JOHN HUTCHINSON, practitioner in physic, of Charleston, to the HON. ARTHUR MIDDLETON, ESQ., & the HON. RALPH IZARD, ESQ., both of Berkeley Co., for 5 sh. & for natural love & affection which HUTCHINSON bears for daughter ANNE & son THOMAS & for settling the N part of the S part of lot #2 with the brick mansion, & for other considerations, HUTCHINSON conveys to MIDDLETON & IZARD in trust the N part of lot #2, bounding E on the Bay; N on JOSEPH BOON; W on a marsh of LANDGRAVE THOMAS SMITH; S on the S part of the lot belonging to JOHN HUTCHINSON & extending to the line dividing the 2 tenements of the brick house, going W by a line as the fence stands to W boundary of the N part of the lot; also the brick mansion on the N half occupied by PAUL JENNYS; in trust for JOHN HUTCHINSON during his life; then for daughter ANN; in default of ANN; then to son THOMAS; in default of both then to the heirs of JOHN. JOHN HUTCHINSON owns the southern part of lot #2 in Charleston fronting 51 ft. on Cooper River, bounding S 212 ft. on CAPT. MATHEW PORTER (formerly CAPT. GEORGE SMITH); W on a marsh of LANDGRAVE THOMAS SMITH; N on JOSEPH BOON; with a large brick house of 2 tenements, the S tenement occupied by JOHN HUTCHINSON, the N by PAUL JENNYS. Witnesses: NICHOLAS TROTT, LAWRENCE COULLIETTE, PETER TAYLOR. Before ALEXANDER PARRIS. JACOB MOTTE, Register.

Book E, p. 180
31 May 1726
Bond

NATHANIEL MOORE & ROGER MOORE, gentlemen, of St. James, Goose Creek, Berkeley Co., to ISAAC MAZYCK, merchant, of Charleston, in penal sum of Ł 500 SC money, conditioned for keeping agreements made in L & R, 30 & 31 May 1726 between NATHANIEL MOORE & SARAH his wife & ISAAC MAZYCK. Witnesses: RALPH IZARD, JAMES ST. JULIEN, RICHARD ALLEIN. Before ARTHUR MIDDLETON. JACOB MOTTE, Register.

Book E, p. 181
10 June 1726
Mortgage

THOMAS SATUR, gentleman, to BENJAMIN GODING & ABRAHAM SATUR, merchants, all of Berkeley Co., for Ł 2327:19 SC money mortgages 550 a. commonly known as MOSES MARTIN'S land, in Berkeley Co., bounding N on GRESHAM HOWE; E on Dorchester land; S & W on REBECCA AXTELL; also lot #17 in Dorchester containing 50 a. bounding E on THOMAS WAY; S on Ashley River; W on JOHN HILL; N by line between 1st & 2nd range of lots; also lot #19 in Dorchester containing 50 a., bounding S on Ashley River; W on THOMAS WAY; E on SAMUEL WAY, JR.; N by a line between 1st & 2nd range of lots; also lot #20 bounding S on Ashley River; W on THOMAS SATUR; E on AARON WAY, SR.; N by a line between 1st & 2nd range of lots; also a swamp of 20 a. adjoining the small lots on S & W of Dorchester; also 4 small lots, Nos. 55, 78, 80, & 81; also 11 lots of 2 a. each near Dorchester, Nos. 3, 4, 7, 9, 10, 12, 15, 20, 21, 22, & 25, commonly called The Common; conditioned for payment of Ł 2327:19:7 currency on 1st Jan. 1727. Witnesses: JOHN BUGG, JAMES CORBIN, THOMAS KIMBERLY. Before JOSEPH BLAKE. JACOB MOTTE, Register.

Book E, p. 186
16 July 1723
Release

ALEXANDER COLLINS, planter, of Berkeley Co., to JONAH COLLINS, ESQ., of Craven Co., quit claims all actions, suits, bills, bonds, money, judgements, etc., etc. Witnesses: THOMAS BARKSDALE, RICHARD SMITH, THOMAS HEPWORTH. Before DANIEL GREEN. JACOB MOTTE, Register.

Book E, p. 187
2 & 3 Sept. 1725
L & R

GEORGE PAWLEY, planter, (son & heir of ANN PAWLEY who was sister & heir of ANTHONY SHOREY, JR., a minor, son & heir of ANTHONY SHOREY, planter, & MARY, his wife), to JOHN BRETON, merchant, of Charleston, for Ł 1359:11:6 SC money, his part of lot #26 fronting 51 ft. on S side Broad St., Charleston; bounding W 97 ft. on part same lot belonging JOHN BRETON; E on FRANCIS HOLMES; S on CHARLES HILL. Witnesses: ELISHA PRIOLEAU, JR., CAMUEL PRIOLEAU, ROBERT HUME. Before JOHN BARKSDALE. JACOB MOTTE, Register.

Book E, p. 194
3 Sept. 1725
Bond

GEORGE PAWLEY, planter, of Berkeley Co., to JOHN BRETON, merchant, of Charleston, in penal sum of Ł 2000 SC money, for true observance of the articles contained in L & R, page 187. Witnesses: ELISHA PRIOLEAU, JR., SAMUEL PRIOLEAU, ROBERT HUME. Before JOHN BARKSDALE. JACOB MOTTE, Register.

Book E, p. 197
15 June 1726
Power of Attorney

JOHN JONES, of Dorchester, Berkeley Co., appoints THOMAS CUTFIELD, of Dorchester, his attorney, to transact all matters. Witnesses: MAURICE HARVEY, JOHN NESS. Before CHARLES HILL. JACOB MOTTE, Register.

Book E, p. 198
25 Mar. 1726
Mortgage

THOMAS ELLERY, gentleman, to ROBERT HUME, gentleman, both of Charleston, for Ł 600 SC money, 353 a. in Berkeley Co., bounding E on Cooper River; W on WILLIAM DRY & RICHARD BAKER & others; N on RICHARD BAKER; S on WILLIAM DRY & JOSEPH ? Whereas his Excellency JOHN, Earl of Bath, Palatine, & the Lords Proprs. on 16 Aug. 1698 impowered the HON. JAMES MOORE, ESQ., their deputies to grant land & JAMES MOORE & deputies granted to DAVID MAYBANK 100 a., English measure, in Berkeley Co., & whereas his Excellency JOHN, Lord Granville, Palatine, & the Lords Proprs. impowered the RT. HON. Sir NATHANIEL JOHNSON, Knight, then Gov. of NC & SC & others to grant lands & they on 5 Oct. 1704 granted to EDWARD WEEKLY 220 a., English measures, in Berkeley Co., & whereas WEEKLY conveyed 80 of the westernmost to LANDGRAVE THOMAS SMITH; & whereas the HON. ROBERT GIBBES, ESQ., Gov. & the Lords Proprs. granted EDWARD WEEKLY 23 a. in Berkeley Co., & whereas the HON. ROBERT DANIEL, ESQ., Dep. Gov. & the Lords Proprs. on 25 May 1717 granted EDWARD WEEKLY 90 a. in Berkeley Co., & whereas the 4 tracts are contiguous & laid out in 1 tract containing about 353 a. (exclusive of the 80) which by various conveyances have descended to THOMAS ELLERY; now, ELLERY mortgages to HUME to assure payment by ELLERY of Ł 600 currency; Ł 300 on 25 Dec. next & Ł 300 on 26 Dec. 1727. Witnesses: JOHN CROFT, CHILDERMUS CROFT. Before ---- WHITAKER. JACOB MOTTE, Register. Mortgage satisfied 7 June 1726 by payment to ROBERT HUME. Witnesses: CHARLES HILL, JACOB MOTTE.

Book E, p. 204   Charleston. JOHN, Lord Berkeley, Palatine, &
3 Oct. 1679   the Lords Proprs., to ANTHONY SHOREY, town lot
Grant   #26 at Oyster Point. Signatures: JOSEPH WEST;
                        WILLIAM FULLER; RICHARD CONANT; WILLIAM OWEN.
By warrant from the HON. COL. JOSEPH WEST, Gov., dated 18 May 1678 THOMAS
MATHEW, Survy. or Gen., laid out to ANTHONY SHOREY on 25 May 1678 lot #26
on Oyster Point, bounding S on MRS. ELIZABETH E--VE: N on great street
leading from Cooper River to the market; E on THEOPHILUS -----?; W on
street parallel with Cooper River. JACOB MOTTE, Register.

Book E, p. 205   EDWARD WEEKLY, of Berkeley Co., to THOMAS CA-
25 Feb. 1725/6   TOR (CATERS) (in consideration of CATOR paying
Mortgage   Ł 125 currency on 6 Dec. 1726 for WEEKLY)
                        mortgages to CATOR 20 a. on N side Gourdin's
Creek & the remainder of land on the other side of old broad path adjoin-
ing CAPT. JOHN WATS, being part of LANDGRAVE SMITH'S & GOURDIN'S plats,
to assure payment by WEEKLY of Ł 175 6 Dec. 1726. Witnesses: LANDGRAVE
THOMAS SMITH, SARAH SMITH, MARY (her mark) GREY. Before LANDGRAVE THOMAS
SMITH. JACOB MOTTE, Register.

Book E, p. 209   EDWARD EDWARDS, planter, & MARY his wife,
9 & 10 May 1726   (late MARY SEARES daughter of ROBERT & ANNE
L & R   SEARES, ANNE SEARES being only daughter of
                        GRACE BUCKLEY, widow), to ROBERT HUME, gentle-
man, of Charleston, for Ł 250 SC money; the northernmost third part of
lot #51 in Charleston, bounding E 33 ft. 4 in. on Bay; S 260 ft. on middle part of lot #51 belonging CHRISTOPHER ARTHUR; W on Sir PETER COLLE-
TON'S Square; N on lot #50 belonging LANDGRAVE COLLETON; which part of
lot was purchased 23 Feb. 1719 by GRACE BUCKLEY from ISAAC MAZYCK & MARI-
ANNE his wife & bequeathed by GRACE BUCKLEY to MARY, wife of EDWARD ED-
WARDS. Witnesses: MARY BLAMYER, CHILDERMUS CROFT, THOMAS HEPWORTH. Before BENJAMIN WITAKER. JACOB MOTTE, Register.

Book E, p. 216   WILLIAM LIVINGSTON, Minister of the Gospel, &
28 Feb. 1711   MARY his wife, to MOSES WILSON, butcher, of
Deed of Sale   Charleston, for Ł 20 currency; part of 3 lots
                        Nos. 171, 172, & 173, bounding E on street
that runs to Benson's Point; N & S on other parts said lots still belonging to LIVINGSTON. The lots sold front 97 ft. on the street, run 200 ft.
parallel with the broad street to the W boundary of lot #101. WILLIAM
LIVINGSTON originally owned 4-1/2 lots (2-1/4 a.) Nos. 160, 162, 171,
172, 173 (formerly belonging to JAMES DUBOURDIEU (DEBORDIEU); bounding S
on a great street leading from Cooper River to the market place; E on a
little street leading from Ashley River to house of WILLIAM LIVINGSTON; N
on a little street running from Cooper River parallel with the 4-1/2 lots;
W on PETER CHEVALIER'S lots. MARY LIVINGSTON renounces her right & title
of dower. Witnesses: JOHN POLLOCK, DANIEL FIDLING; H. WIGINGTON, JOSEPH
BURRIDGE. Witnesses to receipt: ARCHIBALD EVERARD, H. WIGINGTON, DANIEL
FIDLING. Before JOHN BARKSDALE. JACOB MOTTE, Register.

Book E, p. 220   JOHN DUBRUIL, joiner, to MOSES WILSON, butcher,
4 July 1713   both of Charleston, for Ł 30 currency, the
Deed of Feoffment   full half quarter part of lot #11 which was
                        purchased in fee by JOHN DUBRUIL from REBECCA
FLAREL, widow & executrix of the will of CAPT. JOHN FLAREL, marine, (being vested in JOHN FLAREL by 2 Acts of Assembly made & ratified at
Charleston); which part of a lot 28-1/2 ft. by 86 ft.; bounds S on an
alley running from the Bay by the house of FRANCIS LEBRASSEUR, DR. JOHN
HUTCHINSON & CAPT. THOMAS HEPWORTH; E on the other part of lot formerly
belonging to JOSEPH CROSKEYS, merchant, now to WILLIAM HYDE, merchant; N
on FRANCIS HOLMES of Boston; W on --?-- CLIFFORD. Witnesses: HENRY WIG-
INGTON, JOHN HUTCHINSON, ABRAHAM LESUEUR, DANIEL FIDLING. Witnesses to
possession & seizin: JOHN HUTCHINSON, DANIEL FIDLING, PAUL FIDLING, HENRY
WIGINGTON. Before JOHN BARKSDALE. JACOB MOTTE, Register.

Book E, p. 225   JACOB SATUR, merchant, of London, appointed
17 Nov. 1725   BENJAMIN GODING & ABRAHAM SATUR, merchant, of
Power of Attorney   Charleston, SC, his attorneys, to collect

money, dispose of his real estate, Negroes & possessions in SC. Before
JAMES TILSON, Not. & Tabellion Pub., London. Witnesses: ROBERT CLARKE,
JOHN THOMPSON. Both witnesses appeared before BENJAMIN DELACONSEILLERS.
JACOB MOTTE, Register.

Book E, p. 227 JOHN CROFT, merchant, to ROBERT HUME, gentle-
11 Feb. 1724   man, both of Charleston, for ₤ 200 SC money,
Mortgage   300 a. in Granville Co., on N side Coosa River,
                bounding E on CAPT. SEAMORE BURROWS; N on MAU-
RICE HARVEY; W on HILL CROFT; also 3 lots in Beaufort Nos. 20, 34 & 204,
bounding as follows: #20 to W on #9; N on #60; E on #2; & fronting the
Bay on S; lot #34 bounded S on #36; W on #33; N on Port Royall St.; E on
#35; lot #204 bounded S by #203; W by Charles St.; N by northern bounds
of town; E by #205. Should CROFT pay HUME ₤ 220 SC money on 10 Feb. 1725
this to be void. Witnesses: JOHN GARNER, HENRY GIGMILLIAT. Before JO-
SEPH WRAGG. JACOB MOTTE, Register. On 23 Oct. 1732 CAPT. JOHN CROFT
paid ROBERT HUME ₤ 371:3:9 in full of principal & interest. Witness:
JACOB MOTTE.

Book E, p. 231 JOHN BAYLEY, cordwainer, of Berkeley Co., son
25 Jan. 1721   & heir of WILLIAM BAYLEY, mariner, to ISAAC
Release   HOLMES, mariner, of Charleston, for ₤ 420 SC
                money, part of lot #31 in Charleston, from N
to S 40 ft., English measure; fronting to a street leading from Ashley
River to the new church now building; bounding N on part same lot; S on
WILLIAM WEEKLEY, gentleman, W on NICHOLAS NARY. Witnesses: MOSES WILSON,
ANDREW MARSCHALCK(?), ROBERT HUME, ABRAHAM LESUEUR, THOMAS HEPWORTH. Be-
fore JOHN BARKSDALE. JACOB MOTTE, Register.

Book E, p. 237 JOHN BAYLEY, cordwainer, of Berkeley Co., son
1 May 1722   heir of WILLIAM BAYLEY, mariner, to ISAAC
Release   HOLMES, mariner, of Charleston, for ₤ 160 SC
                money, part of lot #31(?), containing in front
to a certain street leading from Ashley River to the new church now building, N to S, 22 ft. English measure; bounding N on part of same lot; S on
part same lot sold by BAYLEY to HOLMES; W on NICHOLAS NARY. Witnesses:
MOSES WILSON, DANIEL FIDLING, JOHN WILSON, EDWARD CROFT. Before JOHN
CROFT, M.C. JACOB MOTTE, Register.

Book E, p. 242 JOHN BAYLEY, cordwainer, of Berkeley Co., son
31 May 1722   & heir of WILLIAM BAYLEY, mariner, of Charles-
Release   ton, to MOSES WILSON, of Charleston, for ₤ 150
                SC money, that part of lot #31 in Charleston,
20 ft. English measure in front from N to S to a street leading from Ashley River to the new church now building; bounding N on part same lot
sold by BAYLEY to ISAAC HOLMES; W on NICHOLAS NARY. Witnesses: JOEL POIN-
SETT, JOHN SMITH, SAMUEL GRASSETT, EDWARD CROFT. Before JOHN CROFT, M.C.

Book E, p. 246 WILLIAM LAUGHTON & MARY, his wife, of Charles-
16 Nov. 1725   ton, to MOSES WILSON, gentleman, all of
Release   Charleston, for ₤ 150 SC money, part of lot
                #31 in Charleston, fronting 5 ft. (?) to a
street leading from Ashley River to the new church; bounding N on part
same lot belonging to LOUGHTON; S on part same lot belonging to WILSON; W
on JONATHAN COLLINS. Witnesses: THOMAS FAIRCHILD, WILLIAM FAIRCHILD, DAN-
IEL FIDLING, EDWARD CROFT. Before JOHN BARKSDALE. JACOB MOTTE, Register.

Book E, p. 249 JOHN MOORE, planter, to MARY BASDEN, spinster,
18 Sept. 1725   of Charleston, for ₤ 800 SC money, half of lot
Mortgage   #16 in Charleston fronting E 50 ft. on the Bay;
                which half lot was willed by MARY CROSSE to
her daughter MARY BASDEN (widow); bounding S on WILLIAM RHETT; N on part
same lot belonging MAJOR THOMAS HEPWORTH; W on an alley leading from the
broad street. Should MOORE pay MARY ₤ 880 SC money on 18 Sept. next
(1725) this mortgage to be void. Witnesses: ROBERT HUME, CHILDERMUS
CROFT. Before JOHN CROFT, M.C. JACOB MOTTE, Register.

Book E, p. 254 ROBERT BISHOP, & MARY his wife, of St. Phil-
16 Jan. 1709   ip's Parish, to CAPT. JOHN GIBBES, of St. Jo-
Deed of Sale   seph's Parish, for ₤ 700 SC money & valuable

considerations all their estate & interest in SC which estate was willed
1 Nov. 1703 to MARY by her brother JOHN BERRINGER. Witnesses: STEPHEN
GIBBES, BENJAMIN GIBBES, BEN ---TERMAN. MARY signed voluntarily before
THOMAS MAZYCK 28 Jan. 1709. Before ALEXANDER SKENE. JACOB MOTTE, Register.

Book E, p. 255   LANDGRAVE THOMAS SMITH, son & heir of LAND-
21 Mar. 1723   GRAVE THOMAS SMITH, & MARY his wife, to ELIAS
Deed of Sale   HORRY, for L 60 SC money, 1000 a. in Craven
                       Co., part of the 48,000 a. granted the father
by his Excellency WILLIAM, Earl of Craven, Palatine, & the Lords Proprs.
in 1691. MARY willingly releases her claim. Witnesses: SARAH SMITH,
FARMER BULL, MARY (her mark) GREY. Plat given on 13 May 1691 by warrant
of ROBERT DANIEL, ESQ., GOV., ISAAC LEGRAND, D.S. surveyed part of THOMAS
SMITH'S patent. On 20 Sept. 1716 ROBERT DANIEL, Gov. HAD ISAAC LEGRAND,
D.S., survey 500 a. belonging THOMAS SMITH, planter, on 25 Mar. 17--
THOMAS SMITH appointed ISAAC LEGRAND his attorney to take possession &
deliver to ISAAC HORRY of Santee. Before GEORGE SMITH. JACOB MOTTE,
Register.

Book E, p. 258   LANDGRAVE THOMAS SMITH, son & heir of LAND-
21 Mar. 1723   GRAVE THOMAS SMITH, & MARY his wife, to ELIAS
Deed of Sale   HORRY of Santee, for L 60 SC money, 1000 a. in
                       Craven Co., part of the 48,000 a. granted the
father by WILLIAM, Earl of Craven, Palatine, & the Lords Proprs. in 1691.
MARY willingly releases her claim. Witnesses: SARAH SMITH, FARMER BULL,
MARY (her mark) GREY. On 20 Sept. 1716 ISAAC LEGRAND, D.S. by warrant
from the HON. ROBERT DANIEL, Gov., surveyed 500 a. of THOMAS SMITH'S
land; & also another 500 a. Plats given. Before GEORGE SMITH. JACOB
MOTTE, Register.

Book E, p. 261   LANDGRAVE THOMAS SMITH, son & heir of LAND-
10 May 1726   GRAVE THOMAS SMITH, & MARY his wife, to ISAAC
Deed of Sale   LEGRAND, for L 30 SC money, 500 a. in Craven
                       Co., part of the 48,000 a. granted THOMAS
SMITH by his Excellency WILLIAM, Earl of Craven, & the Lords Proprs., in
1691. MARY willingly releases her claim. Plat given. Witnesses: SARAH
SMITH, FARMER BULL, MARY (her mark) GREY. 500 a. surveyed by ISAAC LE-
GRAND, S.D., by warrant of the HON. ROBERT DANIEL, Gov. Before GEORGE
SMITH. JACOB MOTTE, Register.

Book E, p. 264   JOHN ASHBEY, ESQ., grandson & heir of JOHN
16 Nov. 1724   ASHBEY, Cassique, to RICHARD SMITH, for L 100
Deed of Sale   SC money, 700 a. in Craven Co. Witnesses:
                       T. AKIN, EBENEZER FORD (FOORD), JAMES MAXWELL,
FRANCIS PADGITT, JR. Witness to receipt: M. NERBOROUGH, JAMES MAXWELL.
Before RICHARD HARRIS. JACOB MOTTE, Register.

Book E, p. 266   RICHARD SMITH, of Craven Co., to JOHN PETER
30 Sept. 1725   SOMERHOEFF, for L 500 SC money, 700 a. in Crav-
Deed of Sale   en Co. Witnesses: GEORGE LOGAN, JOHN NICHOL-
                       SON, THOMAS STORY. Before JOHN BARKSDALE.
JACOB MOTTE, Register.

Book E, p. 269   JAMES FITZGERALD (FITZGARLD), joiner, of Berke-
19 & 20 July 1726   ley Co., to MAURICE HARVEY, ESQ., of Charles-
L & R   ton, for L 192:10 SC money, 70 a. on Hobcaw
                       Neck, commonly called Bermudoes Town, part of
210 a. in Berkeley Co., bounding S on Cornbow (?) Creek; E on JOHN WHITE;
N on part of the 210 a.; W on WILLIAM FISHER; W & S on JOHN CLEMONS &
ANTHONY WHITE. Witnesses: JOHN NESS, LAURENCE COULLIETTE. Before BENJA-
MIN WHITAKER. JACOB MOTTE. Register.

Book E, p. 273   By the HON. ARTHUR MIDDLETON, ESQ., President,
22 Apr. 1726   , Comm.-in-Chief, & Ordinary of SC to the HON.
Warrant   RALPH IZARD, ESQ., WILLIAM DRY, ESQ., BENJAMIN
                       WARING, ROGER MOORE, authorizing them to ap-
praise the personal estate & effects of ROBERT HOW, gentleman, of St.
Anne's Parish, Goose Creek, Berkeley Co., who died intestate leaving MARY,
his widow, & 1 child JOB HOW. MARY HOW later married THOMAS CLIFFORD,

gentleman, of St. James, Goose Creek, & asks distribution of ROBERT HOW'S
estate. After appraisement 1/3 of the money to go to THOMAS CLIFFORD
(MARY'S share); 2/3 for JOB HOW, minor. Certified by CHARLES HART, Sec.
Recorded in Book E, page 64, in Secretary's office by HENRY HARGRAVE,
Dep. Sec. to JOB HOW, 43 slaves, to CLIFFORD, 29 slaves. CLIFFORD to
take household goods, tools, horses, cattle, giving bond to MIDDLETON for
their value in proclamation, payable without interest when JOB comes of
age. Before THOMAS HEPWORTH. JACOB MOTTE, Register.

Book E, p. 276　　　　　JOHN GIBBES, gentleman, & THOMAS BROUGHTON,
12 July 1722　　　　　　ESQ., of St. Johns, both of Berkeley Co., to
Bond　　　　　　　　　　ARTHUR MIDDLETON, ESQ., of St. James, Goose
　　　　　　　　　　　　Creek, in penal sum of L 10,000 SC money, con-
ditioned for keeping agreement in L & R, 11 & 12 July, 1726. Witnesses:
EDWARD SMITH, gentleman, NATHANIEL BROUGHTON, gentleman. Before THOMAS
HEPWORTH, C.J. JACOB MOTTE, Register.

Book E, p. 277　　　　　JOHN GIBBES, gentleman, & ANNE, his wife, to
11 & 12 July 1722　　　 ARTHUR MIDDLETON, ESQ., all of Berkeley Co.,
L & R　　　　　　　　　 for L 4,000 SC money, 1440 a. in Goose Creek
　　　　　　　　　　　　bounding N & NW on MATHEW BAIRD & ANDREW ALLEN;
S on BENJAMIN MARION; W on ABRAHAM DELAPLAINE; E & SE on THOMAS MOORE &
BENJAMIN GIBBES. JOHN GIBBES to cause ANNE to release her dower before
last day of Sept. next. Witnesses: HENRY HOUSER, EDWARD SMITH, ANDREW
BROUGHTON. Before THOMAS HEPWORTH, C.J. JACOB MOTTE, Register.

Book E, p. 286　　　　　Before CHARLES HILL, C.J. of Ct. of C.P. ap-
10 Apr. 1722　　　　　　peared ANNE, wife of JOHN GIBBES, gentleman,
Renunciation of Dower　 of Berkeley Co., & voluntarily joined with her
　　　　　　　　　　　　husband in conveying 1440 a. to ARTHUR MIDDLE-
TON (see page 277). Recorded in Book of R. of D. pp. 140 & 141 by JOHN
WALLIS. JACOB MOTTE, Register.

Book E, p. 288　　　　　ISAAC LEGRAND, planter, of Craven Co., to AL-
28 Feb. 1726　　　　　　BERT MULLER, merchant, of Charleston, for
Mortgage　　　　　　　　L 1263 SC money, 4 tracts; namely, 200 a.
　　　　　　　　　　　　granted 24 Mar. 1701 by Lords Proprs. to HENRY
BRUNEAU; also 100 a. granted NICHOLAS SNEED on 9 Apr. 1702; also 500 a.
granted ISAAC LEGRAND on 9 May 1709; also 400 a. granted ISAAC LEGRAND on
9 May 1709; all in Craven Co., ANNE FRANCIS, wife of ISAAC LEGRAND TO
make absolute renunciation of her dower within 12 months. Should LEGRAND
pay MULLER L 1263 SC money on 28 Feb. next. Witnesses: JAMES WOOLFORD,
ROBERT HUME. Before JOHN CROFT, M.C. JACOB MOTTE, Register. Mortgage
satisfied 10 Apr. 1731 by payment of L 1400 by ISAAC LEGRAND to ANDREW
ALLEN, admr. to ALBERT MULLER. Witness: JACOB MOTTE.

Book E, p. 296　　　　　PETER VILLEPONTOUX, cooper, & FRANCES, his
8 & 9 July 1776　　　　 wife, of Berkeley Co., to HENRY PERONNEAU,
L & Mortgage　　　　　　merchant, of Charleston, for 100 a. granted to
　　　　　　　　　　　　JOHN BOONE & by him conveyed to WILLIAM WELSBY,
who conveyed to JONATHAN DRAKE, who conveyed to JOHN MOORE, who conveyed
to PETER VILLEPONTOUX; on S side Ashley River & N side James Island;
bounding N on river; S on SAMUEL THRIFT & marsh; W on part same land belonging PETER VILLEPONTOUX; also 16 a. E of above land on Kuskewaw Creek,
omitted from original plot & grant but set down in plot of these 100 a.;
also 7 slaves. Whereas PETER VILLEPONTOUX this date gave bond to HENRY
PERONNEAU in penal sum of L 2000 SC money conditioned for payment of
L 1000 on 8 July next with interest at 10%; now, for security, & for
other considerations, PETER & FRANCES convey to PERONNEAU 2 tracts of
land; also 7 slaves (1 man, 3 boys, 1 woman, 1 girl, 1 Indian woman).
Witnesses: JOSEPH WARMINGHAM, ISAAC HOLMES, HENRY PERONNEAU, JR. Before
JOHN BARKSDALE. JACOB MOTTE, Register. Mortgage satisfied 16 June 1732
by payment of L 1368:10 by PETER VILLEPONTOUX to HENRY PERONNEAU. Witness: JACOB MOTTE, Register.

Book E, p. 304　　　　　The HON. CHARLES HART, ESQ., of Berkeley Co.,
11 & 12 June 1726　　　 to THOMAS COOPER, gentleman, & ELEANA, his
L & R　　　　　　　　　 wife, of Charleston, for L 1750 SC money, 140
　　　　　　　　　　　　a. on the neck in Berkeley Co., commonly called the Rat Trap, in the Broad Path leading from Charleston; bounding E on

the Broad Path; W on Ashley River; N on SAMUEL WEST; S on JOHN WATKINS. Witnesses: HENRY HARGRAVE, JOHN HAMILTON. Before WILLIAM BLAKEWEY. JACOB MOTTE, Register.

Book E, p. 311 JOHN (his mark) SUMMERS, planter, & SUSANNA
12 & 13 Aug. 1726 his wife, of Berkeley Co., to JOHN WATKINSON,
L & R mariner, of Charleston, for L 1500 SC money,
the southernmost 1/4 part lot #18 in Charleston, on which 5 tenements stand, 1 possessed by JOHN SUMMERS, 1 occupied by ELIZABETH WILLIAMS, 1 occupied by SAMUEL SMITH, 1 occupied by THOMAS FITZGAROLD, 1 occupied by a Negro woman; also an empty building. Whereas the HON. JAMES MOORE, ESQ., Gov. & the Lords Proprs. on 28 Aug. 1701 granted JOHN ASHBY lot #18 in Charleston; & whereas JOHN ASHBY by will appointed CONSTANTIA ASHBY & THOMAS BROUGHTON his executors to sell the lot & apply the money towards paying his debts; & whereas by deed of feoffment on 25 June 1719 recorded 8 Sept. 1719 in Book K, fol. 367 CONSTANTIA ASHBY & THOMAS BROUGHTON sold this lot to GEORGE LEA & JAMES SADLER, carpenters, of Charleston; bounding N on a little street running W from house of JONATHAN AMORY, by MR. SIMMONS'S house to the old burying place; W on a little neighborhood street running N from MR. LOUGHTON'S house to AMORY'S house; S on lot #17 called CODNER'S lot; E on lot #19 called MR. AMORY'S, DR. BURNHAM & JOHN GUPPEL'S lot; & whereas on 12 Mar. 1719 by indenture reciting that GEORGE LEA & JAMES SADLER had sold to JOSEPH LEA & MOSES PLUMER the northern half of lot #18 & had agreed to divide the remaining half between them, it was agreed that JAMES SADLER should have the south half of the half lot fronting 46 ft. on the street running W from LOUGHTON'S to AMORY'S house; S on GODNER'S lot; N on other part lot #18; & whereas the south part being 1/4 of lot #18 by several conveyances has become vested in JOHN SUMMERS; now SUMMERS sells to WATKINSON. Witnesses: WILLIAM WATSON, ROBERT HUME. Before JOHN CROFT, M.C. JACOB MOTTE, Register.

Book E, p. 319 NATHANIEL MOORE, gentleman, & SARAH his wife,
31 May 1726 of St. James, Goose Creek, Berkeley Co., to
Release ISAAC MAZYCK, merchant, of Charleston, for
L 3500 SC money 900 a. in St. James, Goose Creek, bounding SW on Forsters Creek; SE on NICHOLAS BENNETT; N & NW on JOHN DAVIS; E on ANNE DAVIS. NATHANIEL will cause SARAH to renounce her dower by 1 Sept. next. Witnesses: RALPH IZARD, JAMES ST. JULIEN, RICHARD ALLEIN. Before ARTHUR MIDDLETON. JACOB MOTTE, Register.

Book E, p. 324 JOSEPH (his mark) DANDFORD, fisherman, of
11 Dec. 1725 Charleston, to WILLIAM GRAY, carpenter, of
Lease in Trust Berkeley Co., & JAMES BANBURY, mariner, of
Charleston, for 5 sh. & other considerations, 50 a., lately purchased from JONATHAN EVANS & ELIZABETH his wife, on James Island, bounding N on SAMUEL THRIFT; E on JOSEPH STANYARNE; S on ALBERT DETMAR; W on JOHN CROSKEYS; also the house & part of lot on W side Charleston, where JOSEPH DANFORD lives & lately purchased from THOMAS HOLTON. A release tripartite is intended to be made next day between JOSEPH DANFORD of 1st part; WILLIAM GRAY & JAMES BANBURY of 2nd part; MARGARET GRAY, daughter of WILLIAM, of 3rd part. Witnesses: JOHN BEE, JAMES BAMBURG, JUDITH BANBURY. Before JOHN BARKSDALE. JACOB MOTTE, Register.

Book E, p. 326 Partition of estate of THOMAS PINCKNEY. RALPH
16 Jan. 1724 IZARD, CHARLES HILL, ANTHONY MATHEWS & ANDREW
Partition ALLEN being appointed by an Act of Assembly to
divide the estate of THOMAS PINCKNEY, merchant, of Charleston, amongst his widow & children, appraised the real estate at L 8380 SC money & allotted to MRS. MARY BETSON (formerly widow of THOMAS PINCKNEY) part of 2 lots Nos. 20 & 73 value L 1000 & the sum of L 190 currency to be paid by her eldest son THOMAS PINCKNEY; also L 905 currency to be paid by her youngest son WILLIAM in full of her share of real estate. They allotted to THOMAS PINCKNEY, the eldest son, 451 a. (9 a. less than in the grant), on E side Ashley River, value L 2255 currency also 5 a. behind the parsonage value L 170 currency bounding NE on HUMPHRY -----; NW on marsh; SW on 5 a. willed THOMAS by his father; SE on a path leading from broad path by the parsonage to CAPT. HARLESTON, for which he shall pay his mother L 190 & to his brother CHARLES PINCKNEY

Ł 145. They allotted to CHARLES, the 2nd son part of lot #3 on Bay in
Charleston with the buildings & the shoal water before the lot, value
Ł 1950 currency & sum of Ł 145 to be paid him by THOMAS; they allotted to
WILLIAM PINCKNEY, youngest son, part of lot #5 & buildings thereon & the
bridge of wharf & the shoal water before the house of WILLIAM GIBBON,
ESQ., value Ł 3000, he to pay his mother Ł 905. Before DANIEL GREENE.
JACOB MOTTE, Register.

Book E, p. 329   WILLIAM SMITH, planter, son & heir of WILLIAM
12 Jan. 1721   SMITH, planter, of Berkeley Co., to NATHANIEL
Deed of Sale   PARTRIDGE, gentleman, of Charleston, for Ł 800
                       SC money, 81 a. on Charleston Neck, bounding N
on JOHN PENDARVIS; S on JAMES MCLOUGHLIN; W on a marsh. Witnesses: WIL-
LIAM BILLING, ALEXANDER CLENCH, REBECCA CORBIN. Witnesses to livery &
seizin: THOMAS LOCKYEAR, REBECCA CORBIN (later REBECCA CROFTS), ALEXANDER
CLENCH, SARAH CLIFFORD. Before JOHN BARKSDALE. JACOB MOTTE, Register.

Book E, p. 332   CHARLES PINCKNEY, of London, appoints his
15 April 1726   mother, MRS. MARY BETSON, widow, his attorney
Power of Attorney   to sell part of lot #3 in Charleston, fronting
                       30 ft.; also the land before the 30 ft. to low
water mark. Whereas by Act of General Assembly ratified at Charleston 15
Feb. 1725 the HON. RALPH IZARD, ESQ., CHARLES HILL, ESQ., ANDREW ALLEN,
CAPT. ANTHONY MATHEWS, merchant, were appointed to make partitions of
lands & tenements of THOMAS PINCKNEY, merchant, between his widow & child-
ren; & whereas they on 16 Jan. 1723 allotted CHARLES PINCKNEY, gentleman,
2nd son, now residing in London, part of lot #3 bounding 67 ft. on
Charleston Bay; S on part same lot; N on BENJAMIN RUMSEY (formerly DR.
WM. CROOK); & whereas several ft. of land so assigned from the front of
the lot to the lower end within the fence of BENJAMIN RUMSEY which RUM-
SEYS unjustly holds & occupies; now CHARLES PINCKNEY appoints his mother,
MRS. MARY BETSON, widow, his attorney to take posession of his property,
eject RUMSEY, & sell his part of lot #3, & the land in front down to low
water mark. Witnesses: BENJAMIN AUSTIN, RICHARD SPLATT, STEPHEN BULL.
Before DANIEL GREENE. JACOB MOTTE, Register.

Book E, p. 335   NATHANIEL (his mark) WILLIAMS (alias BLACK
1 Mar. 1705   NATT) carpenter, & planter, to GRACE BUCKLEY,
Bill of Sale   widow, for Ł 28 SC money, 100 a. English meas-
                       ure where WILLIAMS lives, on Itchancanboo
Creek on Cooper River bounding on GRACE BUCKLEY on 1 side & on WILLIAMS
on the other, which he purchased from JEANE CLIFT, widow. Delivery by
turf & twig. Witnesses: GEORGE SMITH, ANN SYER, ROBER SYER. Before DAN-
IEL GREENE. JACOB MOTTE, Register.

Book E, p. 337   JONATHAN STOCKS, cordwainer, & ELLINOR his
11 July 1726   wife, of Christ Church Parish, Berkeley Co.,
Bond of Performance   to JOHN BENNETT, carpenter, of same place, in
                       penal sum of Ł 1000 SC money, conditioned for
keeping BENNETT in peaceable possession of 1000 a. sold him this date.
Witnesses: GEORGE BENISON, JOHN YOUNG. Before JOHN BARKSDALE. JACOB
MOTTE, Register.

Book E, p. 338   JONATHAN STOCKS, cordwainer, & ELLINOR his
11 July 1726   wife, to JOHN BENNETT, carpenter, all of
L & R   Christ Church Parish, Berkeley Co., for Ł 200
                       SC money, 100 a. in Berkeley Co., bounding NE
on EPHRAIM WINGOOD; NW on ISHAMAR WOODIN; SE on Boowat Creek; SW on said
BENTLY (BENNETT?). Witnesses: GEORGE DENISON, JOHN YOUNG. Before THOMAS
BARKSDALE. JACOB MOTTE, Register.

Book E, p. 344   MARY BETSON, widow, in behalf of her son
1 & 2 Sept. 1726   CHARLES PINCKNEY, gentleman, of London, form-
L & R Tripartite   erly of Charleston, SC, of the 1st part; the
                       HON. JOHN FENWICK, ESQ., of Charleston, of the
1nd part; & THOMAS PINCKNEY & WILLIAM PINCKNEY (sons of MARY BETSON, THOM-
AS PINCKNEY & MARY (now BETSON) of the 3rd part. Whereas THOMAS PINCKNEY,
the father, owned lot #3 (1/2 a. English measure), in Charleston fronting
the Bay; bounding W on marsh; S on WILLIAM NOWELL; N on WILLIAM WILLIAMS;
& whereas he also owned 1 front lot (#327) or shole, fronting W on the

wharf line laid out by the commissioners, opposite lot #3, bounding N on land opposite WILLIAM WILLIAMS lot #4; S on a front lot opposite WILLIAM NOWELL'S lot #2; E on Cooper River; down to low water mark, excepting 35 ft. which THOMAS PINCKNEY, the father, sold to GEORGE SMITH but now occupied by THOMAS LLOYD; & whereas THOMAS PINCKNEY by will dated 12 Feb. 1703 gave his real estate to his wife MARY & sons THOMAS & WILLIAM to be equally divided; & whereas the HON. RALPH IZARD, CHARLES HILL, ESQ., ANDREW ALLEN & CAPT. ANTHONY MATHEWS were appointed to make partition, which they did (see p. 326 for details); & whereas CHARLES PINCKNEY on 15 Apr. 1726 appointed his mother, MARY BETSON, his attorney, with power to dispose of part of his lots Nos. 3 & 327, i.e., fronting 30 ft. & whole depth of lot, also the land lying before the 30 ft. down to low water mark; & whereas he later authorized her to sell 2 ft. more; now MARY BETSON sells 32 ft. of lot #3 to FENWICK for Ł 2560 SC money; bounding E on the Bay; S on THOMAS LLOYD; N on CHARLES PINCKNEY; W on MR. CHAPMAN; the full breadth of 32 ft. to run from the E part of the lot on the Bay to the W end that runs into the marsh & adjoins CHAPMAN'S; also 32 ft. of the land shole or lot #327 lying before the above 32 ft. lot, running from N side of LLOYD'S bridge from the Bay down to low water mark. THOMAS & WILLIAM PINCKNEY confirm FENWICK in his possession. Witnesses: PAUL JENYS, HENRY GIGMILLIAT, MOSES BENNET. Before THOMAS HEPWORTH, C.J. JACOB MOTTE, Register. Plat of 1000 a., part of 2500 a. formerly belonging LADY REBEKAH AXTELS, Berkeley Co., NE side Ashley River, within land, bounding N on REBEKAH AXTEL & MOSES MARTIN; E on Dorchester; W on REBEKAH AXTEL; laid out for MADAM ANN BOONE, which 1000 a. is known as Newington or the Hill G., & measured at request of LADY AXTEL to LADY ELIZABETH BLAKE on 15 Apr. 1711. Certified by WILLIAM BULL, D.S. 6 Oct. 1726. Before GEORGE SMITH. JACOB MOTTE, Register.

Book E, p. 358
13 July 1721
Deed of Sale

ROBERT HARVEY, butcher, & ELIZABETH (her mark) his wife, to ELIAS HANCOCK, victualler, all of Charleston, for Ł 130 SC money, part of lot #92, in Charleston, 100 ft. front, 123 ft. deep; bounding N on CORNELIUS BATTOON; E on MRS. ELIZABETH TOOMER; S on Tradd St.; W on Benson St. Whereas on 17 July 1715 by deed of feoffment between ELIZABETH HARVEY, widow, & ROBERT HARVEY, both of Charleston, reciting that ELIZABETH owned a part of a town lot formerly belonging to EDWARD BERRY which BERRY bequeathed to his wife JULIAN, & reciting further that JULIAN BERRY by letter of attorney authorized ELIZABETH HARVEY to dispose of the lot, & ELIZABETH sold for Ł 15 currency to ROBERT HARVEY the part of the lot in Charleston bounding N on JOHN TOOMER & adjoining a lot belonging to ISAAC CORD; now ROBERT HARVEY sells to HANCOCK & agrees to procure ELIZABETH'S renunciation of dower. Witnesses: WILLIAM BILLING, JOHN TOPER. Before JOHN MOORE. JACOB MOTTE, Register.

Book E, p. 364
1 & 2 Feb. 1725
L & R

RICHARD SHUBRICK, merchant, of London, now of Charleston, to THOMAS COOPER, gentleman, & ELEANA his wife, for Ł 1800 SC money; a tenement & part of lot #17 on the Bay, now occupied by ELEAZER ALLEN, merchant, bounding E 25 ft. on Cooper River; S 70 ft. on RICHARD CODNER; W on RICHARD CODNER; N on the 5 ft. left for an alley with other 5 ft. from MR. AMORY (now ELEAZER ALLEN). JANE, wife of RICHARD SHUBRICK to have no right of dower in lot. Witnesses: JOHN SHEPPARD, RICHARD BEDON, RICHARD ALLEIN. Before JOHN BARKSDALE. JACOB MOTTE, Register.

Book E, p. 371
15 & 17 Sept. 1726
L & R

The HON. LANDGRAVE THOMAS SMITH, & MARY his wife, of Berkeley Co., to PETER ROBERT of St. James, Santee, Craven Co., for Ł 100 SC money, 1000 a. in Craven Co., bounding NE on NICHOLAS LEMUD & PETER ROBERT. Whereas his Excellency WILLIAM LORD CRAVEN, Palatine & the Lords Proprs. on 13 May 1691 granted LANDGRAVE THOMAS SMITH 48,000 a.; & whereas ISAAC LEGRAND by warrant under hand & seal of the HON. ROBERT DANIEL, ESQ., Dep. Gov., dated 27 Sept. 1716 laid out 1000 a. in 2 tracts of 500 a. each; now SMITH sells the 1000 a. to ROBERT. Witnesses: WILLIAM WATIES, ANTHONY ATKINSON. Before WILLIAM DRAKE. JACOB MOTTE, Register.

Book E, p. 379
13 July 1703

CLEMENT BROWN, planter, of Berkeley Co., to WILLIAM RHETT, mariner, & SARAH his wife, of

Charleston, for Ŀ 15 SC money, lot #53 in Charleston, bounding E on ALEXANDER PARRIS (formerly HENRY SIMONS); W on the great street parallel with Cooper River & leading to the market place; S on FINLEY MARTIN (formerly MR. SEALE); N on JONATHAN AMORY. Witnesses: NICHOLAS TROTT, ALEXANDER PARRIS, GEORGE EVANS. Witnesses to possession & seizin: GEORGE EVANS, JOHN TOOMER. Before THOMAS HEPWORTH, C.J. JACOB MOTTE, Register.

Book E, p. 383
9 Oct. 1723
Deed of Sale

DANIEL DONOVAN, planter, of St. John Parish, Berkeley Co., to ELIAS HANCOCK, merchant, of Charleston, for Ŀ 60 SC money, town lot #225. Whereas the HON. LANDGRAVE THOMAS SMITH, Gov., with PAUL GRIMBALL, JOSEPH BLAKE & RICHARD CONANT (elected trustees to see the Gov. sign grants) granted 1 CLEWER lot #225 in Charleston, which grant has been so abused that the plat of the lot has been torn from it & the boundaries cannot be described; & whereas EDMOND ELLIS, Doctor in Physic, & ELIZABETH CLEWER, widow, gave bond 3 Mar. 1702 in penal sum of Ŀ 100 & executed a bill of sale to DANIEL DONOVAN, which bond DONOVAN enjoyed for 7 yrs. until his death & his son DANIEL DONOVAN has since held the bond undisturbed, now DONOVAN sells to HANCOCK. Witnesses: TOBIAS FITCH, RICHARD FULLER, THOMAS ELLERY. Before JOHN MOORE. JACOB MOTTE, Register.

Book E, p. 386
26 Aug. 1726
Agreement

JOHN FITZGARLD, joiner, to JOHN HALE, planter, for Ŀ 40 as part of the yearly rent of 70 a. (part of estate left by THOMAS FITZGARLD) on Berkeley Co., bounding E on GARRARD FITZGARLD; W on WILLIAM VISHER & CAPT. EDMUND ROBINSON; N on JOSHUA WILKS & the rice house plantation; with privilege of cutting wood, building, clearing, planting, etc., for 4 years, at the rent of Ŀ 15 yearly. Witnesses: JOHN STEVENSON, ELIZABETH HALE. Before DANIEL GREEN. JACOB MOTTE, Register.

Book E, p. 388
11 & 12 Nov. 1726
L & R & Mortgage

JOHN STANYARNE, planter, & ANNE his wife, of Colleton Co., to JOHN WRIGHT, merchant, of Charleston, for Ŀ 508:16:8 SC money, 100 a. in Colleton Co., on SE side Stono River, willed to JOHN by his father THOMAS STANYARNE, bounding NW on marsh; SW on JOHN STANYARNE; SE on MR. WAIGHT; NE on WILLIAM STANYARNE; conditioned for payment by STANYARNE to WRIGHT of the above sum on 1 Jan. 1726. Witnesses: THOMAS MONTJOY, ROBERT HUME. Before THOMAS HEPWORTH, C.J. JACOB MOTTE, Register.

Book E, p. 397
13 & 14 Sept. 1726
L & R

CHARLES HILL, merchant, & ELIZABETH his wife, of Berkeley Co., to THOMAS BOONE, ESQ., for Ŀ 1140 SC money, 1 tracts (of 760 a.) in Christ Church Parish, Berkeley Co., originally granted to JOHN BELL, bounding E on Copahee Sound; N on JOHN JEFFINS (GEVINS) & JOTHAM GIBBONS; W on JOTHAM GIBBONS & JOHN SIMMS (SIMONS); S on JOHN SIMMS. ELIZABETH is to renounce her dower. Witnesses: JACOB MOTTE, THOMAS LAROCHES, WILLIAM CATTELL, JR. Before GEORGE SMITH, Asst. Justice. JACOB MOTTE, Register.

Book E, p. 403
28 & 29 Oct. 1726
L & R

JACOB MOTTE, merchant, & ELIZABETH his wife, to FRANCIS BRITTON, planter, both of Berkeley Co., for Ŀ 500 SC money, 500 a. in Craven Co., on N side Santee River. ELIZABETH freely renounces her dower. Witnesses: ROBERT TRADD, ESTER (her mark) HAWKINS. Before GEORGE SMITH. JACOB MOTTE, Register.

Book E, p. 407
13 & 14 May 1725
L & R

JOHN (JEAN) GARNIER, barber, & MAGDALEN his wife, of Charleston, & JOHN POSTEL, JR., planter, & MARGARET his wife, of Berkeley Co., & ANTHONY POITEVIN, barber, of Charleston, to DAVID RUSS, planter, of Berkeley Co., for Ŀ 500 SC money 400 a. in Berkeley Co., as described in the grant from the Lords Proprs. to ANTHONY POITEVIN, planter, of Berkeley Co. Witnesses: A. DEVEAUX, MARKE OLIVER, ROBERT HUME, CHILDERMUS CROFT. Before BENJAMIN WHITAKER. JACOB MOTTE, Register.

Book E, p. 414
22 & 23 Aug. 1726

DAVID RUSS, planter, of Berkeley Co., to ALEXANDER NISBETT, merchant, of Charleston, for

Ł 420:11:1 SC money, 400 a. English measure in Berkeley Co., bounding as described in plat annexed to grant from Lords Proprs. to ANTHONY POITEVIN, planter, of Berkeley Co., conditioned for payment of above sum by RUSS to NISBETT on 1 Jan. next. Witnesses: WALTER DALLAS, HUGH CAMPBELL, WALTER NISBETT. Before ALEXANDER PARRIS. JACOB MOTTE, Register.

Book E, p. 420
20 Oct. 1726
Deed of Sale

JOHN ASHBY, gentleman, of Berkeley Co., to PAUL DOUXSAINT, merchant, of Charleston, for Ł 100 SC money, 1000 a. in Wambaw Swamp, Craven Co., bounding N on BARTHOLOMEW GAILLARD; W on ISAAC LEGRAND; S on PHILIP GENDRON, ESQ.; E on vacant land. Whereas the RT. HON. WILLIAM LORD CRAVEN, Palatine, & the Lords Proprs., by letters patent on 25 Oct. 1682 granted JOHN ASHBY, ESQ., 24,000 a. surveyed by WILLIAM BULL, S.G., now JOHN ASHBY, son & heir, sells 1000 a. to DOUXSAINT. Witnesses: JAMES ST. JULIEN, merchant, ISAAC CHARDON, merchant, JOHN CROFT. Before THOMAS HEPWORTH, C.J. JACOB MOTTE, Register.

Book E, p. 425
28 & 29 Nov. 1726
L & R

JOHN CROSKEYS, planter, & ELIZABETH (her mark) his wife, of James Island, to JOHN MCKAY, merchant, of Charleston, for Ł 160 SC money, 50 a. on James Island, bounding N on SAMUEL FRITH (formerly AMBROSE DENISON); E on JOHN NICHOLS; W on ALEXANDER SPENCER; S on ALEXANDER SPENCER; being part of 400 a. granted EDWARD WESTBURY & JOAN PULFORD, later owned by THOMAS, son of EDWARD WESTBURY, & after several conveyances became the property of CROSKEYS. Witnesses: SAMUEL PRIOLEAU, THOMAS CROSKEYS, RICHARD ALLEIN. Before DANIEL GREENE. JACOB MOTTE, Register.

Book E, p. 430
28 & 29 Nov. 1726
L & R & Mortgage

THOMAS CROSKEYS, planter, of James Island, to JOHN MCKAY, merchant, of Charleston, 105 a. called JOHN ELLIS'S Island, about 200 yds. S of James Island, as security on bond given this date by CROSKEYS to MCKAY in penal sum of Ł 520 SC money conditioned for payment of Ł 260 on 29 Aug. next; also 1 Negro man & 1 Negro woman. Witnesses: RICHARD ALLEIN, SAMUEL PRIOLEAU, H. PERONNEAU, JR. Before DANIEL GREENE. JACOB MOTTE, Register.

Book E, p. 437
1 Jan. 1725/6
Agreement

BARNABY (his mark) RILEY, JOHN CARMICHAEL, THOMAS KIMBERLY & CORNELIUS LONGHARE agree to leave 10 ft. on either side of their lot for a perpetual street 25 ft. wide. Witnesses: FRANCIS GRACIA, NATHANIEL FARR. Before DANIEL GREENE. JACOB MOTTE, Register.

Book E, p. 438
11 July 1726
Mortgage

HENRY SIMONS, planter, to THOMAS CUTFIELD, merchant, both of Berkeley Co., for divers considerations, 635 a. bounding N on PAUL TRAPIER; E on PETER DE ST. JULIEN; S on PETER HARMAN; W on a great swamp; conditioned for the payment of Ł 460 SC money by SIMONS to CUTFIELD on 1 Jan. next. Witnesses: JOHN MARION, BENJAMIN MARION, JOHN (his mark) DINGLE. Before ALEXANDER SKENE. JACOB MOTTE, Register.

Book E, p. 440
12 & 13 July 1726
L & R & Mortgage

SAMUEL RESCOE, planter, of Berkeley Co., to JOSEPH WRAGG, merchant, of Charleston, 500 a. in Berkeley Co., bounding N on ARTHUR MIDDLETON; E on JOHN JONES; as security on bond dated 14 July 1726 in penal sum of Ł 2000 SC money conditioned for payment of Ł 1000 on 1 Jan. 1726. Witnesses: RICHARD LAMBTON, JOHN COLCOCK. Before JOHN BARKSDALE. JACOB MOTTE, Register.

Book E, p. 448
24 Oct. 1726
Mortgage

WILLIAM HATTON, Indian trader, & MARGARET his wife, of Berkeley Co., to JONATHAN SKRINE, planter, of Craven Co., for Ł 600 SC money, 80 a. in St. James Parish, Goose Creek, commonly called Sociable Hill (lately purchased by HATTON from SKRINE), bounding NE on ROGER MOORE; NW on JOB ROTHMAHLER; SE on BARNABY RAYLES; SW on COL. GEORGE CHICKEN; conditioned for the payment of Ł 600 currency by HATTON to SKRINE on 31 Oct. next. Witnesses: THOMAS CLIFFORD, JOHN BAYLEY (BAGLE). Before BENJAMIN WARING. JACOT MOTTE, Register.

Book E, p. 452

JOHN WILLIAMSON, yeoman, of Stono, Colleton

Deed of Sale   Co., to PHEBE PETER, of Stono, his mother-in-
                                law, for ₤ 125 SC money, a certain tract in
Stono, near the bridge, part of 450 a. belonging to the house called the
Fort, being a legacy to JOHN WILLIAMSON from JOB COBUS. Witnesses: RICH-
ARD CAPERS, THOMAS CAPERS, ROYALL SPRY. Before DANIEL GREENE. JACOB
MOTTE, Register.

DEEDS BOOK "F"
1723-1728

Book F, p. 1   JOSEPH (his mark) GRIFFIN, planter, & JOYCE
11 & 12 Sept. 1726   (her mark) GRIFFIN, to BENJAMIN CHILD, planter
L & R   both of Berkeley Co., for ₤ 423:10 SC money,
                                77 a., part of 177 a., in St. George's Parish,
Berkeley Co., bounding S on BENJAMIN CHILDS; E on land conveyed by JOSEPH
GRIFFIN to RALPH IZARD & WILLIAM BULL for the use of JOSEPH CHILDS, a
minor; N on PETER GUERON & CHARLES BARKER; W on JOSEPH GRIFFIN. Witness-
es: JAMES CANTEY, ANGELLE COONE, CHARLES BARKER. Before DANIEL GREENE.
JACOB MOTTE, Register.

Book F, p. 6   JOHN GODFREY, planter, & MARY his wife to ED-
25 Aug. 1712   WARD CLIFT, planter, all of Colleton Co., for
Deed of Sale   ₤ 30 SC money, 200 a. in Colleton Co. on W
                                side Edisto River; bounding E on the River; W
on Mr. ____; S on MR. BOONE; N on JOHN GODFREY, which land was granted by
the RT. HON. SIR NATHANIEL JOHNSON, Knight, Gov. of NC & SC, & the Lords
Proprs. on 1 Dec. 1710 to JOHN GODFREY. Witnesses: JOSEPH HEAPE, RICHARD
GODFREY, JOSEPH (his mark) FARLEY. Before JOHN WOODWARD, JOSEPH HEAPE,
planter, of Wappoo, Parish of St. Andrews, appeared as witness before
THOMAS HEPWORTH, C.J. JACOB MOTTE, Register.

Book F, p. 10   JOHN BAYLEY, of Ballinaclough, Co. of Tipper-
14 Dec. 1726   ary, Ireland, son & heir of JOHN BAYLEY, ESQ.,
L & R   of same place, & ALEXANDER TRENCH, merchant,
                                of Charleston & attorney of JOHN BAYLEY the
son, to JAMES BROWN, planter, of Craven Co., for ₤ 500 SC money, 2000 a.
in Craven Co., bounding NE on the N branch of Black River & running NWW
175½ ch. beginning at an Indian old field formerly claimed by MR. MILLER,
at a beech tree, to NW on vacant land claimed by JOHN NEWMITH & DUGEE
MCKEGGAN; SW 124-½ ch; to SW on vacant land 168 ch; SE, S & SE on vacant
land 124=½ ch; NNE to said Indian old field whereas the RT. HON. JOHN,
Earl of Bath & the Lords Proprs. on 16 Aug. 1698 by letters patents created JOHN BAYLEY, the father, Landgrave & Casseck, granting him 48,000 a.
in SC; & whereas JOHN BAYLEY the son, on 19 Nov. 1722 appointed ALEXANDER
TRANCH his attorney; with power to reserve 8000 a. for use of JOHN BAYLEY
& dispose of the rest of the land as seemed most convenient; now TRENCH
sells to BROWN. Witnesses: JOEL POINSETT; THOMAS CONYBEAR; ROBERT NIS-
BETT. Witnesses & receipt: JOEL HOLMES (?), THOMAS CONYBEAR, ROBERT NIS-
BETT. Before JOHN BARKSDALE. JACOB MOTTE, Register.

Book F, p. 17   THOMAS HEPWORTH, ESQ. & ANN his wife, to HENRY
9 & 10 Dec. 1726   ST. JULIEN, gentlemen, both of Charleston, for
L & R   ₤ 415 SC money, 660 a., in Berkeley Co., with-
                                in land; bounding W on LAMBERT SANDERS; N on
THOMAS PALMER; S & E on vacant land. Witnesses: JOHN FENWICKE, PETER DE
ST. JULIEN, JOSEPH DE ST. JULIEN. JACOB MOTTE, Register.

Book F, p. 23   JOHN BAYLEY, ESQ., of Ballanclough, Co. of
28 & 29 Nov. 1726   Tipperary, Ireland, by his attorney ALEXANDER
L & R   TRENCH, merchant, of Charleston, SC, to JOHN
                                ALLSTON, planter, of Berkeley Co., for ₤ 150
SC money, 643 a. in Berkeley Co., bounding NE on SAMUEL WIGFALL; E on
JOHN HUGGINS; S on PETER COUILLANDANDAU; W on ANTHONY BONNEAU; SW on LEW-
IS MOUSON; NW on JOHN ALLSTON. Whereas the RT. HON. JOHN, Earl of Bath,
& the Lords Proprs. by letters patents created JOHN BAILY the father a
Landgrave & Cassick granting him 48,000 a.; & whereas JOHN BAYLY, the son
& heir, on 9 Nov. 1722 appointed ALEXANDER TRENCH his attorney with power
to reserve 8000 a. for JOHN BAYLY & dispose of the rest of the land; now

Trench conveys 643 a. to ALLSTON. Witnesses: ISAAC MAZYCK, JR., PAUL
CHARRON, JAMES DE ST.JULIEN, ISAAC MAZYCK, JR., PAUL CHARRON, JAMES DE ST.
JULIEN. Before PETER DE ST.JULIAN. JACOB MOTTE, Register.

Book F, p. 29
21 Mar. 1719
Deed in Trust

WILLIAM LIVINGSTON, clerk, of Charleston, in
trust to THOMAS SMITH, JR., gentleman of Berkeley Co., for 5 sh. confirms SMITH in 2000 a.
(except 250 a.); i.e., 1750 a. the southern-
most of the 4000 a., on E side of freshes of Edisto River; lying nearest
JAMES RIXAM (BIXHAM?), running from Ponpon or Edisto River back directly
to the E by a straight line; for the sole use of THOMAS SMITH, JR. & the
children of JOHN ASH, ESQ.; viz. JOHN RICHARD, ALGERNON, SAMUEL, ISABELLA
(wife of BENJAMIN BERRY, shipwright), THEADORE (wife of JOSEPH LAWS,
planter). Whereas some time before the death of MARY wife of WILLIAM
LIVINGSTON, (executrix of JOHN ASH, ESQ. of Baho) Ł 50 currency was paid
out of ASH'S estate to WILLIAM LIVINGSTON for 2000 a. (part of 4000 a.)
which LIVINGSTON had purchased from LANDGRAVE ROBERT DANIEL, in which
2000 a. all the legatees of ASH were equally interested, & MARY dying before conveyance was formally made, now LIVINGSTON conveys 1750 a. to
SMITH & the children of JOHN ASH. Witnesses "according to their profession":, ELIZABETH SMILIE. Before CHRISTOPHER WILKINSON. JACOB MOTTE,
Register.

Book F, p. 33
2 & 3 Jan. 1726
L & R

THOMAS ELLERY, gentleman, & ANNE his wife, to
ELIZABETH CAWOOD, widow, both of Charleston,
for Ł 2500 SC money, 4 tracts in 1 plantation
of 353 a. in Berkeley Co., bounding E on Coop-
er River; W on WILLIAM DRY, RICHARD BAKER & others; N on RICHARD BAKER; S
on JOSEPH HURST & WILLIAM DRY. Whereas his Excellency JOHN, Earl of Bath,
Palatine, & the Lords Proprs. on 16 Aug. 1698 impowered the HON. JOSEPH
BLAKE, ESQ., JAMES MOORE, ESQ., Gov., LANDGRAVE JOSEPH MORTON, LANDGRAVE
EDMOND BELLINGER, ROBERT DANIEL, JOHN ELY, ESQ., to grant lands & they
granted 100 a. English measure in Berkeley Co., to DAVID MAYBANK; whereas
DAVID MAYBANK & SUSANNAH his wife, by deed of feoffment, on 1 Dec. 1708
conveyed the 100 a. to EDWARD WEEKLEY, gentleman; & whereas his Excellen-
cy JOHN LORD GRANVILLE, Palatine, & the Lords Proprs. impowered the RT.
HON. SIR NATHANIEL JOHNSON, Knight, Gov. of NC & SC & their deputies to
grant lands & they on 5 Oct. 1704 granted EDWARD WEEKLEY 220 a., English
measure in Berkeley Co., the westernmost 80 a. of which WEEKLEY sold to
LANDGRAVE THOMAS SMITH, the balance of which, 140 a. he sold to THOMAS
ELLERY; & whereas the HON. ROBERT GIBBS, ESQ., Gov., & the Lords Proprs.
granted EDWARD WEEKLEY the 23 a. in Berkeley Co. (the plot dated 5 May
1711 laid down on same parchment on which grant is written); & whereas
the HON. ROBERT DANIEL, ESQ., Dep. Gov., & the Lords Proprs. on 25 May
1717 granted EDWARD WEEKLEY 90 a. in Berkeley Co. (plat 12 Mar. 1716); &
whereas the 4 tracts have been laid out in 1 tract of 353 a. on which ED-
WARD WEEKLEY & THOMAS ELLERY have built houses & improvements; & whereas
EDWARD WEEKLEY & ELIZABETH his wife by L & R, 29 & 30 Sept. 1724 sold the
tracts to ELLERY; now ELLERY & wife sell to ELIZABETH CAWOOD, free of
dower of ANNE. Witnesses: CHARLES HILL, WILLIAM VISSER, THOMAS LAMBOLL.
Before BENJAMIN WHITAKER. JACOB MOTTE, Register.

Book F, p. 44
11 & 12 Mar. 1725
Bill of Sale & Release

GEORGE ATCHISON (ACHESON), merchant of Charleston, (son of DAVID ATCHISON of the Parish of
Gumberhees & Stewarty of Anandate, North Britain, & nephew of JAMES GILBERTSON, alias ATCHI-
SON, planter of Colleton Co., SC) to ELIZABETH HYRNE, widow & HENRY HYRNE,
merchant, of Charleston, for Ł 110 money of Great Britain 500 a. in Colleton Co. bounding SE on a branch of Tupedoo (Tugedoo) Creek; SW on Proprietor BLAKE. Whereas his Excellency JOHN LORD GRANVILLE, Palatine, &
the Lords Proprs. by grant under the RT. HON. SIR NATHANIEL JOHNSON,
Knight, Gov., etc., on 15 Sept. 1705, granted JAMES GILBERTSON 500 a.,
English measure, in Colleton Co., & whereas GILBERTSON, alias ATCHISON,
by will dated 16 Aug. 1720 gave the 500 a. to "his" brother DAVID'S son
now in England; 2 now GEORGE sells to ELIZABETH HYRNE & HENRY HYRNE. Witnesses: BURRELL MASSINGBERD HYRNE, ROBERT HUME. Before DANIEL GREENE.
JACOB MOTTE, Register.

Book F, p. 52
30 Apr. 1724

JAMES NICHOLAS MAYRANT, ESQ. & SUSANNAH (SUS-
ANNE) his wife, of Craven Co., to DANIEL HUGER,

L & R   Esq. of Berkeley Co., for ₤ 500 SC money,
                                   1500 a. in 3 tracts; being 2 tracts of 500 a.
each in Berkeley Co., bounding NW & SE on each other; SE on CAPT. ELIAS
BALL; SW on WILLIAM WATIES; NE & NW & SW on vacant land; also 500 a. in
Berkeley Co., bounding NE & SE on vacant land; SW on the above land.
Whereas the Lords Proprs. by 2 deeds dated 19 Mar. 1718, granted FRANCIS
HARRIS 2 tracts of 500 a. each in Berkeley Co.; & whereas FRANCIS HARRIS
& SARAH his wife on 26 Mar. 1719 conveyed the 1000 a. to NICHOLAS MAYRANT,
gentleman, of Berkeley Co.; & whereas NICHOLAS MAYRANT on 28 Apr. 1724
gave the 2 tracts to his son JAMES NICHOLAS MAYRANT; & whereas the Lords
Proprs. on 21 Mar. 1715 granted ANDREW DUPEY 500 a. in Berkeley Co.; &
whereas DUPEY on 12 Jan. 1716 sold the 500 a. to JAMES NICHOLAS MAYRANT &
his brother PAUL MAYRANT; & whereas PAUL MAYRANT died & JAMES NICHOLAS
MAYRANT became sole owner; now MAYRANT sells to HUGER. Witnesses: JOHN
GENDRON, PAUL MAZYCK, ISAAC CHARDON. Before DANIEL GREENE. JACOB MOTTE,
Register & ELLIONER (her mark) his wife.

Book F, p. 61   RICHARD GRIMSTON, gentleman, to ELIAS HANCOCK,
27 & 28 Feb. 1726   vintner, both of Charleston, for ₤ 700 SC mon-
L & R   ey, lot #229 in Charleston containing 1/2 a.
                                   English measure, purchased by GRIMSTON from
THOMAS DIXON, of James Island, bricklayer & MARY his wife on Nov. 1722,
bounding S on the little street leading from Cooper River by RICHARD
TRADD to GEORGE KEELING; N on MR. DUGEE; E on JOHN HILL; W on THOMAS ROSE.
Witnesses: EDWARD CROFT, ROBERT RANDALL, THOMAS BARTRAM, JOHN CROFT. Be-
fore THOMAS HEPWORTH, C.J. JACOB MOTTE, Register.

Book F, p. 67   JONATHAN COLLINGS, mariner, agrees with STEPH-
1 Mar. 1726   EN WILLIAMS, butcher, both of Charleston, that
Agreement   in case COLLINGS does not become a co-partner
                                   in butchering with JAMES ROWSE on 1 Sept. 1728
he will immediately pay WILLIAMS ₤ 100 sterling of Great Britain: WIL-
LIAMS agrees with COLLINGS that in case COLLINGS & ROWSE are co-partners
in butchering on that date WILLIAMS will serve COLLINGS as his servant
for 7 years beginning 1 Sept. 1728; each binding himself to the other in
penalty of ₤ 200 sterling of Great Britain. Witness: RICHARD GILES. Before DANIEL GREEN. JACOB MOTTE, Register.

Book F, p. 68   THOMAS GADSDEN, gentleman, of Berkeley Co., to
29 July 1726   FRANCIS LEBRASSEUR, merchant, of Charleston,
Bill of Sale   for 5 sh. currency, a piece of land bounding S
                                   104 ft. on MRS. SARAH RHETT'S pasture; W 240
ft. on his own pasture; N on his own pasture; E on marsh next Cooper River. Witnesses: JAMES PAINE, AUGUSTUS DELABASTIE. Before JOHN BARKSDALE.
JACOB MOTTE, Register.

Book F, p. 71   SAMUEL LOWLE, cooper, of Willtown Precinct,
11 June 1726   Colleton Co., to TIMOTHY HENDRICKS, planter,
Bond   of same place, in penal sum of ₤ 2000 SC money,
                                   conditioned for keeping the agreements of a
deed of conveyance this date conveying to HENDRICKS 150 a., (part of 2
tracts surveyed by THOMAS BROUGHTON under 2 warrants under the HON. ROB-
ERT GIBBES, ESQ., Gov., 1 dated 19 Feb. 1708, the other 8 Aug. 1711);
stating that MORGERY, wife of SAMUEL LOWLE, shall not evict HENDRICKS
should SAMUEL die nor recover any dower or thirds. Witnesses: WILLIAM
WHIPPY, JAMES COCHRAN, JAMES SMYTH. Before CHRISTOPHER WILKINSON. JACOB
MOTTE, Register.

Book F, p. 73   SAMUEL LOWLE, cooper, of Ponpon, Colleton Co.,
11 June 1726   to TIMOTHY HENDRICKS, planter, of same place,
Release   for ₤ 2000 SC money, 150 a. on N side Edisto
                                   River freshes in Colleton Co., bounding N on
JAMES FULTON & LANDGRAVE JOSEPH MORTON; E & S on SAMUEL LOWLE; W on MOSES
MARTIN; which land shall be divided thus; beginning N corner joining
JAMES FULTON. S halfway the line joining to MOSES MARTIN, E till the
150 a. is measured. MORGERY (her mark) wife of SAMUEL LOWLE renounces
her claim of dower. Witnesses: WILLIAM WHIPPY, JAMES COCHRAN, JAMES
SMYTH. Before CHRISTOPHER WILKINSON. JACOB MOTTE, Register.

Book F, p. 77   MARY LAROACH (LAROCHE) (LAROACHES), widow &

27 & 28 Nov. 1724 & executrix of will of JOHN LAROACH, merchant
L & R of Charleston, to PETER DE ST.JULIEN, ESQ., of
 Berkeley Co., for Ⱡ 1150 SC money 2 tracts,
550 & 528 a., 1078 a. total, in Berkeley Co., bounding E on PETER DE ST.
JULIEN & DANIEL RAVENEL; W on WILLIAM BALL; N on PETER DE ST.JULIEN &
JAMES DE ST.JULIEN; S on DANIEL RAVENEL. Whereas JOHN LAROACHES by will
dated 9 Aug. 1723 authorized MARY LAROACHES during the minority of his
son DANIEL to dispose of said lands, now MARY sells to DE ST.JULIEN. Witnesses: JOHN HUTCHINSON, ANTHONY MATHEWS, JOB ROTHMAHLER. Before WILLIAM
BLAKEWEY. JACOB MOTTE, Register.

Book F, p. 85 ROYALL SPRY, planter, of Ponpon, Colleton Co.,
4 June 1723 to DANIEL HENDRICK, cordwinder, of same place,
Release for Ⱡ 200 SC money, 100 a. on N side Edisto
 River freshes, in Colleton Co., bounding N on
DANIEL HENDRICK; E & S on ROYALL SPRY; W on Bees Creek, divided thus, begin at joining of DANIEL HENDRICK & run E & W joining ROYALL SPRY, run S
till 100 a. are measured. Witnesses: JOHN PETERS, THOMAS SACHEVERILL,
MARY SACHEVERILL. Before CHRISTOPHER WILKINSON, Asst. Judge. JACOB
MOTTE, Register.

Book F, p. 87 ROYALL SPRY, planter, of Ponpon, Colleton Co.,
4 June 1723 to DANIEL HENDRICK, of same place, in penal
Bond sum of Ⱡ 1000 SC money, conditioned for performing the covenants in deed of sale of 100 a.
on this date. Witnesses: JOHN PETERS, THOMAS SACHEVERILL, MARY SACHEVERILL. Before CHRISTOPHER WILKINSON. JACOB MOTTE, Register.

Book F, p. 88 ALEXANDER TRENCH binds himself to JOHN BENSTON
19 Sept. 1726 & WILLIAM WATIES in sum of Ⱡ 1000 SC money, to
Obligation confirm their title to 4000 a., part of the
 land granted JOHN BAYLEY, of Ireland, as soon
as survey is made. Witnesses: CH. SOUTHACK, ELIAS HANCOCK. Before DANIEL GREENE. JACOB MOTTE, Register.

Book F, p. 90 THOMAS GADSDEN, ESQ., of Berkeley Co., to CAPT.
23 & 24 Mar. 1726 GEORGE ANSON, ESQ., Commander HMS The Scarbo-
L & R rough at anchor in Charleston Harbor, for
 Ⱡ 300 sterl. of Great Britain 63 or 64 a. in
Berkeley Co., where THOMAS GADSDEN liver & bought from ISAAC MAZYCK; &
marsh land to the E; bounding E on Cooper River; W on Broad Path; N on
marsh belonging ISAAC MAZYCK & COL. GRANY; S on MRS. SARAH RHETT; reserving a path & the use of the wells to ISAAC MAZYCK. Whereas the HON. JOHN
ARCHDALE, Gov. of SC, & the Lords Proprs. on 14 Oct. 1690 granted ISAAC
MAZYCK 90 a. English measure in Berkeley Co.; & whereas the HON. SIR NATHANIEL JOHNSON, Knight, Gov. of SC, & the Lords Proprs. on 1 Feb. 1706
granted ISAAC MAZYCK 71 a. English measure in Berkeley Co.; & whereas
ISAAC MAZYCK on 9 Apr. 1710 with the consent of MARIANA, his wife, conveyed to COL. EDWARD TYNTE, Gov. of NC & SC about 63 or 64 a. & the marsh
land fronting on Cooper River running as far north as the marsh on the
backside of the garden; & whereas by several conveyances cancelling the
1 above the land & marsh became again the property of ISAAC MAZYCK; &
whereas ISAAC & MARIANA MAZYCK on 29 Oct. 1720 conveyed the property to
THOMAS GADSDEN, reserving to MAZYCK a way through the plantation from the
Broad Path to the bridge across the marsh & the use of the wells; & whereas on 29 July 1726 THOMAS GADSDEN conveyed part of the land to FRANCIS
LEBRASSEUR, merchant, of Charleston, bounding S 244 ft. on MRS. SARAH
RHETT'S pasture; W & N on THOMAS GADSDEN, fronting E on Cooper River 104
ft.; now GADSDEN conveys to ANSON. Witnesses: WILLIAM SAXBY, ROBERT HUME.
Before DANIEL GREEN. JACOB MOTTE, Register.

Book F, p. 100 LAURENCE DENNIS, ESQ. & PROVIDENCE, his wife,
31 Dec. 1726 of Charleston, to son-in-law BENJAMIN D'HARR-
Deed of Gift IETTE, JR., merchant, & ANN his wife (their
 daughter), for natural love & affection, lot
(part of ?) #35 in Charleston. Whereas WILLIAM, Earl of Craven, Palatine,
ANTHONY LORD ASHLEY, GEORGE LORD CARTERET, Sir PETER COLLETON, Baronet,
SETH SOUTHELL, THOMAS ARCHDALE & THOMAS AMY, ESQ. by grant under the hand
of the HON. LANDGRAVE THOMAS SMITH, Gov., dated 15 May 1694 gave JOHN
BELL an a. lot #35 in Charleston, English measure; & whereas BELL on 29

Sept. 1716 conveyed the lot to the HON. WILLIAM GIBBON, ESQ., of Charleston; bounding E on MR. CROSSE; W on NOAH ROYER, JR.; S on WILLIAM BOLLOUGH; N on NOAH ROYER; & whereas GIBBON by L & R, 11 & 12 Oct. 1723 sold part of the lot to LAURENCE DENNIS for L 500 SC money, 51-1/2 ft. front, bounding E on MAJ. THOMAS HEPWORTH (formerly CROSSE); W on JOHN BRETTON (formerly NOAH ROYER, JR.); S on WILLIAM BOLLOUGH; N on LAURENCE DENNIS (formerly NOAH ROYER, SR.); now LAURENCE & PROVIDENCE DENNIS give the lot to their daughter ANNE, wife of BENJAMIN D'HARRIETTE, JR. Witnesses: THOMAS WESLYD, HENRY HARGRAVE. Before DANIEL GREEN. JACOB MOTTE, Register.

Book F, p. 104
22 & 23 Nov. 1726
L & R

JOHN BAYLY, ESQ., son & heir of JOHN BAYLEY, ESQ. of Ballinaclough, Co. of Tipperary, Ireland, & ALEXANDER TRENCH, merchant, of Charleston & attorney for JOHN BAYLEY, to JOSEPH DE ST. JULIEN of Berkeley Co., for L 25 SC money, 93 a. in Berkeley Co., bounding N on JOSEPH DE ST. JULIEN; E on JAMES & PAUL DE ST. JULIEN; S on WILLIAM BALL; W on DANIEL DONOVANE. Whereas the RT. HON. JOHN, Earl of Bath & the Lords Proprs. on 16 Aug. 1698 created JOHN BAYLEY, the father, a Landgrave, giving him 48,000 a.; & whereas JOHN BAYLEY, the son, on 9 Nov. 1722 appointed ALEXANDER TRENCH his attorney with power to reserve 8000 a. for JOHN BAYLY & sell the rest of the land; now TRENCH, as attorney, sells 93 a. to DE ST. JULIEN. Witnesses: HENRY GIGNILLIAT, JEAN GARNIER, ANTHONY PORTOVINE (POITEVIN). Before PETER DE ST. JULIEN. JACOB MOTTE, Register.

Book F, p. 110
5 & 6 Apr. 1727
L & R

ALEXANDER TRENCH, merchant, of Charleston & attorney for JOHN BAYLEY (son & heir of JOHN BAYLEY, ESQ. of Ballinaclough, Co. of Tipperary, Ireland) to BENJAMIN GODIN, merchant, of Charleston, for L 700 SC money, 3000 a. in Craven Co., bounding NE on PAUL DOUXSAINT & ISAAC LEGRAND; on all other sides on vacant land. (See p. 104 how JOHN BAYLEY inherited 48,000 a. from his father & appointed ALEXANDER TRENCH his attorney to dispose of all the land except 8000 a.). Witnesses: PETER DE ST. JULIEN, JAMES DE ST. JULIEN, JOHN GUERARD. Before BENJAMIN DE LACONSEILLERE. 3000 a. laid out in Wambah Swamp, Craven Co., on 4 Apr. 1727 by WILLIAM BULL, D.S.G. JACOB MOTTE, Register.

Book F, p. 117
7 Aug. 1711
Deed of Gift

WILLOUGBY GIBBES, widow, to JOHN HERBERT, planter, & SARAH his wife, all of Berkeley Co., for 5 sh., 200 a., English measure, with the marsh before it; bounding W on Goose Creek & marsh; all other sides by tract on which WILLOUGHBY GIBBES lives. Witnesses: COL. JAMES MOORE, THOMAS BARKER, JOHN MUSGROVE. Before NICHOLAS TROTT, C.J. JACOB MOTTE, Register.

Book F, p. 120
13 & 14 May 1727
L & R

JAMES BEAMOR, planter, of Berkeley Co., son & heir of JACOB BEAMOR, planter, to THOMAS HEPWORTH, ESQ. & ANN his wife, of Charleston, for L 1200 SC money, 70 a. on which SARAH BEAMOR, mother of JAMES, lives, on Charleston Neck; being 2 tracts, 1 of 55 a. granted JOHN BIRD, the other 15 a. bought by SIMON VALLENTINE from JOHN KING & JUDAH HOLLY bush & afterwards became vested in JACOB BEAMOR. Witnesses: DANIEL GREENE, THOMAS ELLERY, ROBERT HUME. Before WILLIAM BLAKEWEY. JACOB MOTTE, Register.

Book F, p. 126
27 & 28 Apr. 1727
L & R & Mortgage

HENRY SIMONS, planter, & JUDITH his wife, late JUDITH GUERARD, daughter of PETER GUERARD, to SOLOMON LEGARE, merchant, of Charleston, for L 367:7:6 SC money, 3 lots Nos. 201, 203, & 206 in Charleston; bounding E on a marsh at head of COL. DANIELL'S Creek; W on the great street leading from Oyster Point to the market place by CAPT. SIMOND'S lot; lot #201 bounding N on PETER GUERARD; lot #203 bounding N & S on PETER GUERARD; lot #206 bounding S on PETER GUERARD; N on DANIELL'S Creek. Should SIMONS pay LEGARE the purchase money on 25 May 1728 this mortgage to be void. Witnesses: JOHN JONES, SAMUEL ROSCO, ROBERT TAYLOR. Before JOHN BARKSDALE. JACOT MOTTE, Register. Mortgage satisfied in full 14 Feb. 1731.

Book F, p. 135

HENRY SIMONS, planter, of Berkeley Co., to

28 Apr. 1727   SOLOMON LEGARE, merchant, of Charleston, in
Bond   penal sum of ₤ 730 SC money, conditioned for
                  payment of ₤ 367:7:6 SC money on 25 May 1728,
for keeping the agreements in the above mortgage. Witnesses: JOHN JONES,
ROBERT TAYLOR. Before JOHN BARKSDALE. JACOB MOTTE, Register.

Book F, p. 137   ALEXANDER TRENCH, merchant, to ABRAHAM SATUR,
2 & 3 May 1727   merchant, for ₤ 150 SC money, 1362 a. in Cra-
L & R   ven Co., bounding N on ABRAHAM SATUR & on all
                  other sides on vacant land. Whereas the RT.
HON. JOHN, Earl of Bath, Palatine, & the Lords Proprs. on 16 Aug. 1698
create JOHN BAYLEY, of Ballinaclough, Co. of Tipperary, Ireland, a Landgrave, granting him 48,000 a.; & whereas JOHN BAYLEY, son & heir, on 19
Nov: appointed ALEXANDER TRENCH, of Charleston, his attorney, with authority to reserve 8000 a. for BAYLEY'S use & sell the rest; now TRENCH sells
1362 a. to SATUR. Witnesses: GREG HAINES, JOHN LEWIS. Before DANIEL
GREENE. JACOB MOTTE, Register.

Book F, p. 146   NATHANIEL MOORE, gentleman, & SARAH his wife,
20 & 21 Dec. 1725 of St. James, Goose Creek, Berkeley Co., to
L & R   JOHN SUMMERS, planter, of Berkeley Co., for
                  ₤ 480 SC money, 18 a., about 2 miles up the
Broad Path from Charleston. Witnesses: JOHN MOORE, JOHN DAVIS, JOHN CHES-
TER. Before ALEXANDER PARRIS, Asst. Judge. JACOB MOTTE, Register.

Book F, p. 152   THOMAS HEPWORTH, ESQ. & ANN his wife, to JOHN
18 & 19 May 1727 WATKINSON, mariner, for ₤ 761 SC money, 1/4
L & R & Mortgage lot #16 in Charleston, fronting 25 ft. on the
                  Bay, bounding N on MRS. MARY BLAMYER; S on
JOHN MOORE (formerly MRS. NARY); W on an alley; conditioned for the pay-
ment of above sum with interest, by HEPWORTH to WATKINSON on 1 Jan. 1727.
Witnesses: JAMES KILPATRICK, ROBERT HUME. Before DANIEL GREENE. JACOB
MOTTE, Register. Mortgage paid in full 7 Oct. 1729, to ROBERT HUME, at-
torney for WATKINSON.

Book F, p. 158   GEORGE LEA, shipwright, & LYDIA his wife, &
3 Feb. 1719   JAMES (his mark) SADLER, carpenter, & ELLINER
Release   (her mark) his wife, to JOSEPH LEA, shipwright,
                  all of Charleston, for ₤ 100 SC money, 1/4 lot
#18 in Charleston, bounding N on 1/4 same lot belonging JAMES SADLER; S
on other half of lot; W on little street running N from MR. LAUGHTON'S
house; E on part lot #19 called MARTHA LITTEN'S. Witnesses: GILLSON
CLAPP, JOHN JEFFORDS, GEORGE HESKET, THOMAS WILLARD. Before JOHN BARKS-
DALE. JACOB MOTTE, Register.

Book F, p. 162   JOHN WILLIAMSON, planter, & MARY, his wife, of
16 Nov. 1721   St. Paul's Parish, Colleton Co., to MRS. PHEBE
Bill of Sale   PETRE (PETER) for ₤ 300 SC money, 150 a.
                  Whereas THOMAS SMITH, Gov., & the Lords Proprs.
on 24 July 1694 granted JOHN WILLIAMSON 150 a., known as Stono; & whereas
WILLIAMSON bequeathed the land to his eldest son JOHN; now JOHN, with his
wife MARY'S consent, conveys to MRS. PETER. Witnesses: THOMAS PETER, WIL-
LIAM BOWER, WILLIAM WILLIAMSON, MARGARET WILLIAMSON. Before DANIEL
GREEN. JACOB MOTTE, Register.

Book F, p. 165   JOHN (his mark) SUMMERS, planter, & SUSANNAH
16 & 18 Aug. 1726 (her mark) his wife, of Berkeley Co., to MARK
L & R   OLIVER, victualer, of Charleston, for ₤ 470
                  SC money, 18 a. about 2 miles up the Broad
Path from Charleston, according to plott dated 11 May 1694. Witnesses:
SAMUEL MORRIS, MICHAEL JEANES, MATHEW NEWBOROUGH. Before JOHN BARKSDALE.
JACOB MOTTE, Register.

Book F, p. 170   JOHN (his mark) SUMMERS, planter, of Berkeley
18 Aug. 1726   Co., to MARK OLIVER, victualer, of St. Phil-
Bond   ip's Parish, Charleston, in penal sum of
                  ₤ 1418 SC money, conditioned for keeping agree-
ments in sale of this date. Witnesses: WILLIAM MCECHEM, RICHARD ASH,
MATHEW NEWBOROUGH. Before JOHN BARKSDALE. JACOB MOTTE, Register.

Book F, p. 172   ALEXANDER TRENCH, merchant, as attorney for
18 & 19 Apr. 1729   JOHN BAYLEY, to MEREDITH HUGHES, planter, of
L & R   Prince George Parish, Craven Co., for (unknown
                        sum), 200 a. English measure, bounding S on
Black River; NW on JOHN HOOPER; SE on a creek; which land was surveyed by
a Deputy of Surveyor General for JOHN BAYLEY as part of 48,000 granted
his father by letters patents (see p. 10 for details). Witnesses: WIL-
LIAM SMITH, WILLIAM LOUGHTON, THOMAS MORRITT. Before DANIEL GREENE. JA-
COB MOTTE, Register.

Book F, p. 182   SARAH BEAMOR, widow, to JOHN BARTON, gentleman,
21 Jan. 1723   both of Berkeley Co., for L 100 SC money,
Release   whereas his Excellency JOHN LORD GRANVILLE,
                        Palatine, & the Lords Proprs. under the hands
of JOSEPH MORTON, ESQ., Gov., ARTHUR MIDDLETON, ANDREW PERCIVAL, MAURICE
MATTHEWS, & JOHN GODFREY, on Mar. 1683, granted to PAUL GRIMBOLD (GRIM-
BALL?) that point of 30 a. on Cooper River, bounding SW on PAUL GRIMBOLD;
NE on a marsh; SE & NW on 2 marshes; & whereas SARAH BEAMOR, widow, pur-
chased the tract; now she sells to BARTON. Witnesses: DANIEL MCKELLVEY,
JOHN (his mark) PERRYMAN, BENJAMIN DENNIS. Witnesses to livery & seizin:
MARY (her mark) PERRIMAY, JOHN (his mark) PERRIMAN, BENJAMIN DENNIS. Be-
fore JOHN BARKSDALE. JACOB MOTTE, Register.

Book F, p. 186   JOHN DELIESSLINNE, planter, & MAGDELANE, his
13 & 14 Dec. 1726   wife, of French Santee, Craven Co., to ABRAHAM
L & R   SATUR, merchant of Charleston, for L 500 SC
                        money, 500 a. at head of & on S side of Int-
chaw (Itchaw) Creek; bounding E on CHARLES CHAMPIGNON; W on EBENEZER FORD:
N on ISAAC LEGRAND; S on NICHOLAS LANGLOIS. Whereas the HON. ROBERT GIB-
BES, ESQ., Gov., SAMUEL EVELEIGH, STEPHEN GIBBES, CHARLES BURNHAM, & the
Lords Proprs. on 28 June 1711 granted JOHN HARTMAN 500 a. in Craven Co.,
bounding NE on JAMES SERON, & on all sides on vacant land; & whereas JOHN
HARTMAN & MARY his wife on 15 Dec. 1712 sold the land to HENRY BRUNEAU,
ESQ.; & whereas HENRY BRUNEAU & MARY ANNE his wife on 2 Feb. 1713 sold to
PETER LEGER, planter, of Craven Co., & whereas LEGER by will dated 22 Oct.
1722 willed that his wife MARY should dispose of the plantation & use the
money as mentioned therein, appointing her executrix; & whereas by L & R,
30 & 31 Sept. 1723 MARY LEGER sold to JOHN DELIESSELINNE; now he sells to
SATUR; MAGDELANE to renounce her dower before the HON. THOMAS HEPWORTH,
C.J. Witnesses to JOHN'S signature: JAMES KINLOCH, RICHARD ALLEIN, SAM-
UEL PRIOLEAU. Witnesses to MAGDELANE'S signature: JAMES KINLOCH, ETIENNE
DUMAY, JACOB JEANNERETT. Before WILLIAM BULL. JACOB MOTTE, Register.

Book F, p. 194   SARAH BEAMOR, widow, of Berkeley Co., to THOM-
9 & 10 June 1727   AS ELLERY, gentleman, of Charleston, as secur-
L & Mortgage   ity on bond given by SARAH to ELLERY on 8 June
                        1727 in penal sum of L 535 with interest on 11
June 1728; 190 a. on Charleston Neck, bounding W on RALPH IZARD, ESQ.; S
on the Quarter House & THOMAS HEPWORTH (formerly JAMES BEAMOR); E on
Cooper River. Witnesses: MATHEW NEWBOROUGH, DANIEL GREENE. Before ALEX-
ANDER PARRIS. JACOB MOTTE, Register.

Book F, p. 200   SARAH BEAMOR, widow, of Berkeley Co., to THOM-
8 June 1727   AS ELLERY, gentleman, of Charleston, in penal
Bond   sum of L 1070 conditioned for payment of
                        L 588:10 currency on 11 June 1728. Witnesses:
MATHEW NEWBOROUGH, DANIEL GREENE. Before ALEXANDER PARRIS. JACOB MOTTE,
Register.

Book F, p. 201   SARAH BEAMOR, widow, of Berkeley Co., to DAN-
13 June 1727   IEL GREENE, merchant, of Charleston, in penal
Bond   sum of L 1200 conditioned for payment of 936
                        lbs. weight of heavy dressed merchantable deer
skins on Bay of Charleston on 1 Dec. next, or their value in currency,
with interest, on 13 June 1728, & also L 176 paid by DANIEL GREENE for
SARAH BEAMOR to JOHN CARMICHAEL (being SARAH'S proper debt). Witnesses:
MATHEW NEWBOROUGH, THOMAS ELLERY. Before ALEXANDER PARRIS. JACOB MOTTE,
Register.

Book F, p. 203   SARAH BEAMOR, widow, of Berkeley Co., to

13 & 14 June 1727 L & Mortgage	secure payment of above bond to (page 201) DANIEL GREENE, mortgages with certain provisos 190 a. on Charleston Neck bounding W on

RALPH IZARD, ESQ.; S on the Quarter House & THOMAS HEPWORTH (formerly JAMES BEAMOR; E on Cooper River. Witnesses: MATHEW NEWBOROUGH, THOMAS ELLERY. Before ALEXANDER PARRIS. JACOB MOTTE, Register. Mortgage paid 22 May 1728 by COL. JOHN FENWICKE & JOSEPH WRAGG. Witness: DANIEL GREENE.

Book F, p. 211 13 June 1727 Mortgage	THOMAS PADGETT (PAGITT), planter, & ANNE his wife of Berkeley Co., to ALEXANDER NISBETT, merchant, of Charleston, for ₤ 1652 SC money, 2 tracts, 300 a. & 170 a., 470 a. in all, in

Berkeley Co., bounding according to plat & grant by the HON. ROBERT GIBBES dated 23 July 1711; & another plat & grant by the HON. SIR NATHANIEL JOHNSON dated 18 Sept. 1703 to PATRICK SCOTT, & bill of sale from SCOTT TO PADGETT; as security for the payment of the above sum by PADGETT to NISBETT on 1 Jan. 1727/8. Witnesses: JAMES (his mark) MALLETT, MARY (her mark) MALLETT, HUGH CAMPBELL. Before ALEXANDER PARRIS. JACOB MOTTE, Register. Mortgage satisfied 2 May 1732. Witness: JACOB MOTTE, Register.

Book F, p. 215 3 & 4 Feb. 1725 L & Mortgage	BENJAMIN SCHENCKING, ESQ. & MARGARET, his wife, of Berkeley Co., to RICHARD MILES, merchant, of Island of Maderas, to secure 2 bonds in penal sum of ₤ 3000 SC each conditioned for

payment of ₤ 1500 at the dwelling house of BENJAMIN DELACONSEILLERE, ESQ. in Charleston, 1 payable on 3 Feb. 1726, the other payable 3 Feb. 1727, mortgages 2 plantations, 1 200 a. the other 500 a., making 1 tract of 700 a., in Goose Creek; the 200 a. tract bounding N on Red Bank; E on the Cooper River; S on BENJAMIN SCHINCKING; W on the 500 a. tract; the 500 a. tract bounding SW on Goose Creek; SE on Cooper River; NE on the 200 a. tract & on BENJAMIN SCHINCKING; NW on ROBERT HOWES (?). BENJAMIN promises to procure MARGARET'S renunciation of dower. Witnesses to BENJAMIN'S signature: BENJAMIN DELA CONSEILLERE, RICHARD ALLEIN, WILLIAM BILLING. Witnesses to MARGARET'S signature: RICHARD ALLEIN, JOHN BASSETT. Before DANIEL GREENE. JACOB MOTTE, Register. Mortgage paid in full 18 July 1731 to BENJAMIN DELA CONSEILLERE as attorney for executors of RICHARD MILES.

Book F, p. 228 22 & 23 June 1727 L & R	ELIZABETH QUELCH, widow of BENJAMIN QUELCH, to ROBERT FLADGER, planter, both of Berkeley Co., for ₤ 300 SC money & a bond for payment of ₤ 400 on 1 Mar. next; a cypress swamp of 300 a.

English measure, in Berkeley Co., at head of Wepetaw Creek, a branch of Wando River, bounding S on the creek & marsh & on WILLIAM RUBERY, & on vacant land; all other sides on vacant land plat dated 10 Sept. 1705. Witnesses: JOHN WALLIS, JOHN ROPER, WILLIAM SMITH. Before JOHN BARKSDALE. JACOB MOTTE, Register.

Book F, p. 235 27 Feb. 1726/7 Deed of Sale	SAMUEL JOHNS, & DOROTHY (her mark) his wife, of St. Andrews Parish, Berkeley Co., to WILLIAM BULL & WILLIAM CATTELL, of same parish, for ₤ 600 SC money, 2 tracts, 50 a. & 7 a., to

be added to the Parish Clebe. Whereas the Lords Proprs. under the hands of RT. HON. SIR NATHANIEL JOHNSON, Gov. etc. on 14 April 1709 granted SAMUEL JONES 50 a. in Berkeley Co. on SE side of Cuppein Creek; & on 14 May 1707 granted ISAAC STUART 20 a. on SE side same creek bounding SW on the above 50 a.; SE oN WILLIAM FULLER, SR.; NW on marsh & said creek; & whereas 7 a. (part of the 20 a.) now belongs to SAMUEL JONES; now SAMUEL & DOROTHY sell the 50 a. & the 7 a. to BULL & CATTELL for the use of St. Andrews Parish; the 57 a. bounding NW on marsh & Cuppein Creek; NE on the broad road leading by St. Andrews church; SE on WILLIAM FULLER, Sr.; SW on the parsonage or clebe of St. Andrews church. Witnesses: STEPHEN BULL, BURRELL MASSINGBERD HYRNE, MARY BULL, WILLIAM GUY. Witnesses to possession, livery & seizin by HYRNE: WILLIAM GUY, WILLIAM MILES, STEPHEN BULL, MARY BULL. Before CHARLES HILL. JACOB MOTTE, Register.

Book F, p. 239 4 & 5 July 1727	SAMUEL BLYTH, planter, of Craven Co., to JOHN HUGGINS, planter, of Berkeley Co., for ₤ 520

L & R   SAMUEL BLYTH, planter, of Craven Co., to JOHN
                                  HUGGINS, planter, of Berkeley Co., for Ł 520
SC money, 500 a. in Craven Co., bounding S & W on Santee River; E on JOHN
SANSON; also an island of 400 a. in Santee River described in grant from
Lords Proprs. to JOHN BELL. Witnesses: JOHN WALLIS, CATHERINE RAPER,
LAWRENCE COULLIETTE. Before JOHN WALLIS. JACOB MOTTE, Register.

Book F, p. 245   RICHARD (his mark) FLOYD, cordwainer & JEMIMS
18 & 19 July 1727   (her mark) his wife, of Colleton Co., to AN-
L & R   THONEY MATHEWS, SR., merchant, of Charleston,
                                  for Ł 600 SC money, 300 a. on Johns Island, in
Colleton Co., bounding S on JOHN POYST (?) & WILLIAM WILKINS; W on MI-
CHAEL REYNOLDS; N on RICHARD FLOYD; E on AMBROSE HILL; SE on WILLIAM AR-
NOLD. Witnesses: SAMUEL MORRIS, CHILDERMUS CROFT, ABRAHAM CROFT. Before
RICHARD ALLEIN. JACOB MOTTE, Register.

Book F, p. 251   Landgrave ROBERT DANIELL, ESQ., & HELEN his
1 & 2 Sept. 1726   wife, of Berkeley Co., to ROBERT HUME, gentle-
L & R   man, of Charleston, for Ł 1500 SC money, 84 a.
                                  on Charleston Neck, willed to HELEN by her
father COL. GEORGE LOGAN; bounding N on JONATHAN COLLINS (formerly JOHN
WATKINS); E on the Broad Path leading to CHARLESTON; S on CARTWRIGHT land;
W on CARTWRIGHT & on marsh. Witnesses: THOMAS HEPWORTH, JAMES ROWS. Before JACOB WRAGG. JACOB MOTTE, Register.

Book F, p. 259   JOHN GIBBES, gentleman son & heir of JOHN
4 & 5 Apr. 1720   GIBBES formerly of Barbadoes later of SC, &
L & R   ANNE his wife, of Berkeley Co., to PETER BACOT,
                                  planter, of Charleston, for Ł 130 SC money,
132 a., part of 1800 a. formerly belonging to JOHN BERRINGER, at head of
Goose Creek; bounding N on MR. DELAPLAN; NE & SE on JOHN GIBBES; S on
FRANCIS GUERING. Witnesses: THOMAS CORDES, JOHN NUTKINS, BENJAMIN MARION.
Before ARTHUR MIDDLETON. JACOB MOTTE, Register.

Book F, p. 266   PETER BACOT, planter, & MARY his wife, to the
6 & 7 July 1727   Hon. ARTHUR MIDDLETON, ESQ.; for Ł 500 SC mon-
L & R   ey, 103 a., part of 132 a. purchased by BACOT
                                  from JOHN GIBBES on 4 & 5 Apr. 1720, at head
of Goose Creek, Berkeley Co., bounding NW on MR. DELAPLAN; NE & SE on
JOHN GIBBES; S on FRANCIS GUERIN. Witnesses: CHARLES HART, ALEXANDER
PARRIS, HENRY HARGRAVE, JOHN (his mark) DINGLE, MARY DINGLE. Before DAN-
IEL GREENE. JACOB MOTTE, Register.

Book F, p. 274   GILLSON CLAPP, merchant, & MARGARET his wife,
1 & 2 Sept. 1726   of Berkeley Co., to ROBERT HUME, gentleman, of
L & R   Charleston, for Ł 3500 SC money; 4 tracts of
                                  112 a., 13 a., 39-1/2 a., & 10 a.; total 174-
1/2 a.; bounding N on COL. ROBERT JOHNSON; S on CHARLES HART, ESQ., W on
the highway from Charleston; E on marsh of Cooper River. Whereas the
Lords Proprs. under Sir NATHANIEL JOHNSON, Knight, Gov., Capt., Gen. &
Admiral of SC had formerly granted JOSEPH PENDARVIS 137 a. & that 1/2 a.
(part of the 137 a.) had become vested in ELIZABETH SINDRY, widow, late
ELIZABETH CLAPP, & granted ELIZABETH SINDRY 13 a. (part of land granted
to HENRY SIMMONS); & whereas ELIZABETH CLAPP (SINDRY) on 24 Apr. 1705
purchased from RICHARD CARTWRIGHT 39-1/2 a. adjoining her land; & whereas
ELIZABETH SINDRY bequeathed the several tracts to her son GILLSON CLAPP;
& whereas GILLSON CLAPP on 14 June 1720 purchased from EDWARD WEEKLEY 10
a., formerly COCKFIELD, adjoining his land; now CLAPP sells the 4 tracts
to HUME. MARGARET is to renounce her dower. Witnesses: THOMAS HEPWORTH,
THOMAS BARNES. Before JOSEPH WRAGG. JACOB MOTTE, Register.

Book F, p. 284   JOHN CASWELL, gentleman, & MARTHA his wife, of
3 Aug. 1727   Colleton Co., to THOMAS SACHEVERILL, planter,
Release   & MARY his wife, 2 tracts, total 813 a., in
                                  Colleton Co. Whereas MATTHEW BEE, planter, of
Colleton Co., owned 2313 a. & died intestate leaving a widow, 1 son JO-
SEPH, & 3 daughters MARY, SARAH & MARTHA; & whereas son JOSEPH died under
age & the 3 daughters became entitled to the land; & whereas DOROTHY, the
widow of MATTHEW, married WILLIAM STEVENSON & they had 1 daughter ANNI-
BALL; & whereas at DOROTHY'S request the 3 daughters agreed to give 300 a.

(part of the 2313 a.) to ANNIBAL STEVENSON; which deed was also executed by THOMAS SACHEVERILL husband of MARY the eldest daughter & by JOHN CASWELL husband of SARAH the second daughter; & whereas at the request of the 3 daughters a division of the remainder was made by CAPT. JOHN JACKSON, DANIEL HENDRICKS & JOHN SMILIE to every one including JOHN ARNOTT (ARNOLD?) now husband of MARTHA, the youngest; THOMAS & MARY SACHEVERILL getting 513 a. on SE side of S. Colleton River, bounding W on other lands of MATTHEW BEE & on vacant land; N on MOSES PINGREE; E & S on vacant land; plat dated 23 July 1711; also 300 a. of back land in Colleton Co., bounding SE on MATHEW BEE; SW on JAMES BASFORD; NW & NE on vacant land; plat dated 23 July 1711; their share being 813 a. Now for 10 sh. paid to each of them, JOHN & SARAH CASWELL, JOHN & MARTHA ARNOTT confirm the 2 tracts to THOMAS & MARY SACHEVERILL. Witnesses: CHRISTOPHER SMITH, SAMUEL SMITH, JOHN CROFT. Before JOHN BARKSDALE. JACOB MOTTE, Register.

Book F, p. 289
7 & 8 Aug. 1727
L & R

THOMAS CROSKEYS, planter, & ELIZABETH his wife, of James Island to JOHN MCKAY, merchant, of Charleston, for ₤ 130 SC money, JOHN ELLIS Island containing 105 a. about 200 yds. S of James Island. Witnesses: WILLIAM BILLING, JOSEPH RIVERS. Before JOHN BARKSDALE. JACOB MOTTE, Register.

Book F, p. 294
5 Apr. 1726
Release

JOHN (his mark) KITCHEN, planter, to JOHN HILL, joiner, & MARY his wife, all of Berkeley Co., for ₤ 40 SC money, 2 lots in Dorchester, Nos. 102 & 103, bounding NE & NW by THOMAS WAIES (?) or streets; SE by WILLIAM WAY, SR.; SW by JOHN STEVENS. Witnesses: ANN BRUNSON, JANE PELLET, ELIZABETH (her mark) KINDALL. Before THOMAS WARING. JACOB MOTTE, Register.

Book F, p. 297
15 Oct. 1717
Deed of Gift

THOMAS (his mark) ELLIS, planter, of James Island, to his children ELIZABETH & MARY, for love & affection, the land & houses formerly belonging to ZACHARIAH EAVER (?) their grandfather with an inventory this date. Witnesses: JOHN WITTER, WILLIAM CHAPMAN. Before CHARLES HILL. JACOB MOTTE, Register.

Book F, p. 298
21 June 1727
Mortgage

EDWARD THOMAS, of St. Johns Parish, Berkeley Co., to JOHN OULDFIELD, of St. James, Goose Creek, for ₤ 1200 SC money, 872 a. in 2 tracts, 1 372 a., the other 500 a. in Berkeley Co., formerly belonging to JOHN MOORE. Whereas JOHN OULDFIELD at the request of EDWARD THOMAS on 14 Mar. 1725 became bound with THOMAS to the Hon. ARTHUR MIDDLETON, ESQ., president in the penal sum of ₤ 2400 conditioned for the payment of ₤ 1200 currency at a certain time, if THOMAS pays MIDDLETON the ₤ 1200 then OULDFIELD will return the deeds & writings to THOMAS as received. Witnesses: WILLIAM WATIES, THOMAS COOPER. Before HUGH BUTLER, J.P. JACOB MOTTE, Register. EDWARD THOMAS, by hand of THOMAS ELLERY paid the mortgage & interest in full to OULDFIELD.

Book F, p. 302
19 Apr. 1725
Agreement re Survivorship

ROBERT GILCREST, merchant, of Charleston & MATHEW SMALLWOOD, planter, of St. Andrews Parish, purchased 17 & 18 Apr. 1725 from JOSEPH BLAKE, ESQ., planter, 640 a. in Colleton Co., whose boundings are 1 island & part of another island on the W side Wad-Wadmelah River, N on broken islands, S on marsh, E on DANIEL GARTICE; for which the paid ₤ 800 (i.e. ₤ 400 each). Now they agree that GILCREST keep the L & R & other writings but SMALLWOOD may demand them & a just division to be made so each may know their own portion, each being entitled to sell; etc. Witnesses: WILLIAM WINDERAS, ROGER (his mark) NEWINGTON, THOMAS GOBLE. Before DANIEL GREENE. JACOB MOTTE, Register.

Book F, p. 305
25 Jan. 1726
Bill of Sale

VINCENT GUERIN, planter, of Berkeley Co., to his son ISAAC GUERIN, for ₤ 6000 SC money, 500 a. where the father lives, bounding E on MICHAEL DARBY; W on MADAM MCMORTHY; N on ANTHONY BOURDEAUX; also 625 a. in Berkeley Co., known as Bullhead, bounding S on ANTHONY BOURDEAUX; E on JOSEPH SINGLETARY; also the houses, horses, mares, cattle, hogs, household goods on the 2 tracts. Witnesses: ISAAC FAIRAND, ROBERT HOW. Before GEORGE LOGAN, ESQ., J.P. JACOB MOTTE,

Register.

Book F, p. 307　　　　　THOMAS SACHEVERILL, planter, & MARY his wife,
3 Aug. 1727　　　　　　of Colleton Co., & JOHN ARNOLL, gentleman &
Release　　　　　　　　MARTHA his wife, of Charleston, to JOHN CAS-
　　　　　　　　　　　　WELL, planter, & SARAH his wife, of Colleton
Co., in 2 tracts. Whereas (see page 284) MATHEW BEE, planter, of Colleton Co., owned 2313 a.; died intestate, leaving widow DOROTHY, son JOSEPH
who died under age, & 3 daughters, MARY the eldest married THOMAS SACHE-
VERILL, SARAH the second married JOHN CASWELL, & MARTHA the youngest married JOHN ARNOLL; & whereas widow DOROTHY married WILLIAM STEVENSON &
they had 1 daughter ANNIBALL; & whereas it was agreed that 300 a. be giv-
en ANNIBALL & the rest apportioned to the 3 daughters, which division was
made by CAPT. JOHN JACKSON, DANIEL HENDRICK & JOHN SMILIE to the satisfaction of all; & whereas they allotted JOHN & SARAH CASWELL 200 a. in
Colleton Co., on E side of Bees Creek, a fresh water creek out of Edisto
River, bounding N on JONATHAN HAYNS & vacant land; S on JAMES ROGERS; E
on vacant land; also 300 a. on E side Bees Creek bounding N & W on the
creek; S on MATHEW BEE; E on vacant land; now to confirm the partition, &
for 10 sh. paid to THOMAS & MARY SACHEVERILL, & JOHN & MARTHA ARNOLL,
THOMAS & MARY confirm the 2 tracts to JOHN & SARAH CASWELL. Witnesses:
CHRISTOPHER SMITH, SAMUEL SMITH, JOHN CROFT. Before JOHN BARKSDALE.
JACOB MOTTE, Register.

Book F, p. 312　　　　　PETER JOHNSON, JR., planter, & DEBORAH his
14 Oct. 1727　　　　　　wife, of Berkeley Co., to ALEXANDER NISBETT,
Mortgage　　　　　　　　merchant, of Charleston, for ₤ 771:7 SC money,
　　　　　　　　　　　　400 a. in Berkeley Co., granted to RICHARD
GRIFFIN on 11 Jan. 1700, & sold by ELIN GRIFFIN 7 Feb. 1725; conditioned
for the payment by JOHNSON to NISBETT of said sum on 1 Oct. 1730. Witnesses: WALTER NISBETT, JAMES MENZIES, HUGH CAMPBELL. Before ALEXANDER
PARRIS. JACOB MOTTE, Register. Mortgage paid in full on 9 Sept. 1731 to
HUGH CAMPBELL, attorney for estate of ALEXANDER NISBETT.

Book F, p. 317　　　　　HENRY SIMONS, & JUDITH his wife, of Berkeley
5 Oct. 1727　　　　　　 Co., to ALEXANDER NISBETT, merchant, of
Mortgage　　　　　　　　Charleston, for ₤ 889:15 SC money, 500 a. in
　　　　　　　　　　　　Berkeley Co. called Wapta; conditioned for the
payment by SIMONS to NISBETT of the above sum with interest on 1 Jan.
1728/9. Witnesses: JOHN WILLIAMS, WILLIAM SIMONS, HUGH CAMPBELL. Before
ALEXANDER PARRIS. JACOB MOTTE, Register.

Book F, p. 322　　　　　THOMAS SACHEVERILL, planter & MARY his wife,
3 Aug. 1727　　　　　　& JOHN CASWELL, planter, & SARAH his wife, all
Release　　　　　　　　of Colleton Co., to JOHN ARNOLL (ARNOLD), gen-
　　　　　　　　　　　　tleman & MARTHA his wife, of Charleston, 3
tracts, 400 a., 200 a. & 100 a. (700 a.). Whereas (see page 284) MATHEW
BEE, planter, of Colleton Co., owned 2313 a., died intestate leaving widow DOROTHY, 1 son JOSEPH who died under age, & 3 daughters, MARY the eldest married THOMAS SACHEVERILL, SARAH the second married JOHN CASWELL,
& MARTHA the youngest married JOHN ARNOLL; & whereas widow DOROTHY married WILLIAM STEVENSON & they had 1 daughter ANNIBALL; & whereas it was
agreed that 300 a. be given to ANNIBALL & the rest apportioned to the 3
daughters, which division was made by CAPT. JOHN JACKSON, DANIEL HENDRICK
& JOHN SMILIE to the satisfaction of all; & whereas they allotted to
MARTHA later wife of JOHN ARNOLL 400 a. bounding W on JOHN PECUM & on all
other sides by vacant land; also 200 a. on NE side of S Colleton River,
bounding W on EBENEZER WALCOAT; S on MATHEW BEE; N & E on vacant land;
also 100 a. on E side Ponpon River bounding S on MATHEW BEE & other sides
on vacant land; now THOMAS & MARY SACHEVERILL & JOHN CASWELL & his wife
confirm JOHN & MARTHA ARNOLD in the above tracts. Witnesses: CHRISTOPHER
SMITH, SAMUEL SMITH, JOHN CROFT. Before JOHN BARKSDALE. JACOB MOTTE,
Register.

Book F, p. 327　　　　　JOHN ARNOLL (ARNOLD), innholder, & MARTHA his
5 & 6 Dec. 1727　　　　wife (late MARTHA BEE 1 of 3 sisters & co-
L & R　　　　　　　　　heirs of JOSEPH BEE, only son & heir of MATHEW
　　　　　　　　　　　　BEE, (see p. 284) planter, of Colleton Co.) to
JAMES BULLOCK, merchant, of Charleston, for ₤ 1000 SC money, 400 a. in
Colleton Co., bounding W on JOHN PECUM & on all other sides on vacant

land; also 200 a. on NE side Colleton River bounding W on EBENEZER WAL-
COTE; S on MATHEW BEE; also 100 a. on E side Ponpon River, bounding S on
MATHEW BEE & all other sides on vacant land. Witnesses: DANIEL GREENE,
ROBERT HUME, JAMES PAINE. Before DANIEL GREENE. JACOB MOTTE, Register.

Book F, p. 337   WILLIAM FULLER, & ELIZABETH his wife, of Berke-
2 Oct. 1707   ley Co. on Ashley River, to JOHN JACKSON, of
Deed of Sale   same Co., for Ł 80 silver SC money secured to
                        be paid to FULLER by bill under hand & seal of
JOHN JACKSON, 1 tract of 650 a. English measure in 2 plotts, lying at a
place called the Harlowing Place, on Combahee River, Colleton Co. Witnesses: NATHANIEL NICHOLLS, SAMUEL NICHOLLS, EDWARD (his mark) CLEIFT.
Before JOHN BARNWELL, J.P. for Granville Co. JACOB MOTTE, Register.

Book F, p. 339   FRANCIS GODDARD, planter, of Berkeley Co., of
17 & 18 Nov. 1727   Berkeley Co. of 1st. part; THOMAS HASELL, Rec-
L & R. Tripartite   tor of Parish of St. Thomas, JAMES MAYRANT,
                        THOMAS PAGET, JOHN MOORE, JAMES AKIN, JAMES
MAXWELL, THOMAS ASHBY, & SAMUEL SIMMONS, planters, vestrymen of St. Thomas, Parish, of 2nd part; THOMAS BROUGHTON, ESQ. of Berkeley Co., executor
of will of RICHARD BERESFORD, planter, of Berkeley Co., of 3rd part.
Whereas RICHARD BERESFORD bequeathed to THOMAS BROUGHTON the yearly profits & produce of his real & personal estate not before devised until his
son JOHN BERESFORD should reach 21 yrs., upon trust that BROUGHTON should
pay the same into the hands of the said vestry to be disposed of as follows: 1/3 to the schoolmaster; 2/3 for the support & education of the
children of the parish poor, (see Bk   P.); in case of no schoolmaster teaching in the parish, a school to be built, or the profits put
out at interest; the vestry to choose the school master & that BROUGHTON
should have a vote in naming the schoolmaster & in the disposition of the
profits; & whereas no schoolmaster has been in the parish since death of
RICHARD BERESFORD, the vestry & BROUGHTON decided to purchase land for a
free school; & whereas the Lords Proprs. on 13 July 1696 granted MATHEW
TULLADA 320 a. which he on 16 Jan. 1713 sold to FRANCIS GODDARD; & whereas the Lords Proprs. on 15 Sept. 1705 granted MATHEW TULLADA another 300
a. which on 6 Aug. 1714 he sold to ANN DANIELL, daughter of ROBERT DAN-
IELL, ESQ. giving ROBERT DANIELL the power to dispose of; & whereas ROB-
ERT DANIELL sold the 300 a. for ANN to FRANCIS GODDARD for Ł 300 but ROB-
ERT died before he could execute a deed, wherefore MARTHA DANIELL, widow
of ROBERT & mother of ANN, as executor on 16 June 1718 confirmed the 300
a. to GODDARD; now GODDARD for Ł 1200 SC money, sells to the rector, vestrymen & their successors, 2 tracts of 320 a. & 300 a., as above recited,
except 20 a. (part of the 300 a.) adjoining SWEATMANS Bridge, for a free
school in accordance with BERESFORD'S will. Witnesses: RICHARD HARRIS,
JOHN LAPIERRE, HUGH CAMPBELL, MATTHEW QUASH, JACOB WOOLFORD, ROBERT HOW.
Before DANIEL GREENE. JACOB MOTTE, Register.

Book F, p. 351   WILLIAM AXSON & SAMUEL AXSON, shoemakers, of
26 Dec. 1724   Charleston, gave SAMUEL PICKERING, merchant,
Deed of Feoffment & Bond   of Charleston, a bond in the penal sum of
                            Ł 500 SC money, to confirm sale on this date,
to PICKERING, for Ł 80, of half of lot #143 in Charleston, bounding N on
DANIEL TOWNSEND; S on WILLIAM AXTON; W on a little street; E on COL. WIL-
LIAM BULL. Witnesses: JOEL POINSETT, WILLIAM YEOMANS, ROBERT HUME. Before CHARLES HILL. JACOB MOTTE, Register.

Book F, p. 357   ALEXANDER TRENCH, merchant, attorney for JOHN
1 & 2 Sept. 1727   BAYLEY of Ireland, to THOMAS FARR, JR., plant-
L & R   er, of Colleton Co., for Ł 95 SC money, 352 a.
                        of vacant land in Colleton Co., bounding S & E
on WILLIAMSON'S tract called Spoones: W on MANLY WILLIAMSON; N on a great
swamp joining Spoone Saranna which is the swamp called Cawcaw. Whereas
the Rt. Hon. JOHN EARL OF BATH & the Lords Proprs. by letters patents on
16 Aug. 1698 created JOHN BAILEY, of Ballinaclough Co. of Tipparary, Ireland, a Landgrave son & heir, on 9 Nov. 1722 appointed ALEXANDER TRENCH,
of Charleston his attorney, with authority to reserve 8000 a. to JOHN
BAYLEY & dispose of the remainder; now TRENCH sells 382 a. to FARR. Witnesses: WILLIAM TUNLY, M.C.; JOHN LEWIS. Before CHARLES HILL. JACOB
MOTTE, Register.

Book F, p. 363　　　　　　　CHARLES PINCKNEY, gentleman, formerly of
2 Jan. 1727　　　　　　　　Charleston, now of London, ratifies to the Hon.
Confirmation of Title　　　JOHN FENWICK, ESQ. of Charleston, his title to
　　　　　　　　　　　　　lots Nos. 3 & 329 on Bay in Charleston. Whereas by L & R tripartite 2 & 3 Sept. 1726 MARY BETSON, widow, of Charleston
in behalf of her son CHARLES PINCKNEY of 1st part; JOHN FENWICK of the
2nd part; & THOMAS & WILLIAM PINCKNEY, brothers of CHARLES, of 3rd part;
MARY BETSON for ₺ 2560 currency sold FENWICK part of lot #3 fronting 32
ft. E on Bay in Charleston; bounding S 276 ft. in THOMAS LLOYD; N on
CHARLES PINCKNEY; W on MR. CHAPMAN; also 32 ft. of shole or lot #3, running from N side LLOYD'S lot or shole #327 from Bay to low water mark;
now CHARLES PINCKNEY confirms FENWICK'S title to the 2 lots, but because
CHARLES still owns parts of the lots he keeps the original grants. Witnesses: ROBERT HUME, JOHN CROFT. Before BENJAMIN WHITAKER. JACOB MOTTE,
Register.

Book F, p. 368　　　　　　　JOHN (his mark) BELL, SR., planter, of Craven
17 June 1727　　　　　　　　Co., to WILLIAM SWINTON, merchant, of Prince
Mortgage　　　　　　　　　 George Parish, Craven Co., for ₺ 400 SC money,
　　　　　　　　　　　　　1000 a. on head of Sampit Creek, with the appurtenances, excepting crops; also 58 head of cattle; conditioned for the
payment of above sum with interest by BELL to SWINTON on 1 Mar. 1727/8.
Witnesses: PRISCILLA BELL, FRANCIS BRITTEN. Delivery by turf & twig.
Before EDWARD HYRNE. JACOB MOTTE, Register.

Book F, p. 372　　　　　　　ARTHUR FOSTER & JOHN FOSTER, gentlemen, both
5 May 1726 (Brit. style)　 of Drumgoon, Co. of Fermanah, & brothers of
Power of Attorney　　　　　ANDREW FOSTER, merchant, of Charleston, SC,
　　　　　　　　　　　　　appeared before MICHAEL COLE, ESQ., Provost of
the town of Iniskellen, Fermanah, & appointed ALEXANDER TRENCH, gentleman,
of Charleston their attorney with authority to handle whatever real or
personal estate was bequeathed them by will of ANDREW 7 represent them
generally. JAMES JOHNSON, ESQ. of Little Mount before MICHAEL COLE deposed that ARTHUR & JOHN were lawful brothers of ANDREW & all the sons of
ANDREW FOSTER, gentleman, of Drumgoone. JACOB MOTTE, Register.

Book F, p. 374　　　　　　　ROGER MOORE, ESQ., & CATHERINE his wife, of
3 & 4 Oct. 1727　　　　　　Berkeley Co., to ROBERT HUME, gentleman, of
L & R　　　　　　　　　　　Charleston, for ₺ 4000 SC money, 800 a. where
　　　　　　　　　　　　　MOORE now lives in Parish of St. James Goose
Creek, bounding SW on land called Thorogoods belonging to ANDREW ALLEN; E
on DAVID WEBSTER; N on COL. GEORGE CHICKEN; SE on ROGER MOORE (formerly
COL. JAMES MOORE); which 800 a. was granted by Lords Proprs. to JAMES WIL-
LIAMS, surgeon, on 2 July 1683; also 90 a. in same parish which MOORE re-
cently purchased from COL. JAMES MOORE; bounding SW on JOHN LLOYD (form-
erly ROBERT STEVENS); N on the above 800 a.; E on COL. JAMES MOORE. CATH-
ERINE to renounce her dower within 3 months. Witnesses: JOHN CHESTER,
RICHARD (his mark) WALKER, JOSEPH WRAGG, RICHARD LAMBTON. Before JOSEPH
WRAGG. JACOB MOTTE, Register.

Book F, p. 383　　　　　　　ROGER MOORE, ESQ., & CATHERINE his wife, of
17 & 18 Jan. 1727　　　　　Berkeley Co., to JOSEPH WRAGG, merchant, of
L & R　　　　　　　　　　　Charleston, for ₺ 4000 SC money, 1346 a. in St.
　　　　　　　　　　　　　James Goose Creek & St. Johns, bounding according to plat. CATHERINE to renounce her dower within 3 months. Witnesses: RICHARD LAMBTON, ROBERT HUME. Before BENJAMIN WHITAKER. JACOB MOTTE,
Register.

Book F, p. 391　　　　　　　JOSEPH LEA, surrenders to EDWARD EDWARDS &
9 Jan. 1727　　　　　　　　MARY his wife for ₺ 400 SC money, right of
Quit Claim　　　　　　　　 possession to the half part of a plantation,
　　　　　　　　　　　　　etc., owned by his wife CATHERINE. Whereas
JOSEPH LEA married CATHERINE SYER, spinster, who owned half a plantation
of 365 a. in Parish of St. Thomas, Berkeley Co., on NE side Cooper River,
bounding SE on Ittewan Creek; SW on NATHANIEL WILLIAMS; NW part on branch
of Clouters Creek & part on RICHARD HARRIS; NE on RICHARD HARRIS; also a
proportion of the dwelling house, & half the other buildings; & whereas
JOSEPH & CATHERINE had 2 sons, JOSEPH & ROBERT SYER; & whereas CATHERINE
died & both sons died soon afterwards & the right of inheritance came to
MARY SYER, CATHERINE'S only sister, who had married EDWARD EDWARDS,

planter of Berkeley Co.; but JOSEPH, through the children, became entitled to CATHERINE'S half share during his natural life as tenant & by the "Curtesie of England" is in possession; now LEA surrenders his claim. Witnesses: MARK OLIVER, JOHN WARMINGHAM, WILLIAM SMITH. Before DANIEL GREENE. JACOB MOTTE, Register.

Book F, p. 396
10 Jan. 1727
Quit Claim

JOSEPH LEA, shipwright, surrenders to EDWARD EDWARDS, & MARY his wife, possession of part of a lot in Charleston, for L 300 SC money. Whereas JOSEPH LEA married CATHERINE SYER, spinster, of Berkeley Co., & she owned part of a lot in Charleston formerly belonging to CHRISTOPHER GERARD, bounding N 40 ft. on the street leading to the Bay; W 103 ft. on the street running by lands formerly belonging to WILLIAM CHAPMAN; S on RICHARD CAPERS; E on CHARLES BASDEN; & whereas JOSEPH had 2 sons, JOSEPH & ROBERT SYER, by CATHERINE, & whereas CATHERINE died & the 2 children died soon afterwards so that her estate descended to her only sister MARY SYER, wife of EDWARD EDWARDS, planter of Berkeley Co.; but because of the children JOSEPH had the right to hold the property as tenant during his natural life by "Curtisie of England". Now LEA surrenders possession to EDWARD & MARY EDWARDS. Witnesses: MARK OLIVER, JOHN WARMINGHAM, WILLIAM SMITH. Before DANIEL GREENE. JACOB MOTTE, Register.

Book F, p. 400
12 & 13 Jan. 1727
L & R

EDWARD EDWARDS, planter, & MARY his wife, to JOSEPH LEA, shipwright, all of Berkeley Co., for L 1300 SC money, part of a lot in Charleston bounding N 40 ft. on the street leading to the Bay; W 103 ft. on the street running by WILLIAM CHAPMAN; S on RICHARD CAPERS; E on CHARLES BADSEN. Witnesses: MARK OLIVER, JOHN WARMINGHAM, WILLIAM SMITH. Before DANIEL GREENE. JACOB MOTTE, Register.

Book F, p. 409
1 & 2 May 1727
L & R

ALEXANDER TRENCH, attorney for JOHN BAYLY, of Ireland, to WILLIAM WILLIAMSON, planter, of Colleton Co., for L 62:10 currency, 250 a. in Colleton Co., bounding SW on WILLIAM WILLIAMSON; W on JOSEPH PECKHAM; NE on WILLIAM WILLIAMSON; NW on BRYAN RELEY. Whereas the Rt. Hon. JOHN EARL OF BATH & Lords Proprs. by letters patents on 16 Aug. 1698 created JOHN BAYLY of Ballinaclough, Co. of Tipperary, Ireland, the father, Landgrave & Cassick, granting him 48,000 a.; & whereas JOHN BAYLY, son & heir, on 9 Nov. 1722 appointed ALEXANDER TRENCH, merchant of Charleston, his attorney with authority to set aside 8,000 a. for JOHN BAYLY & dispose of the rest; now TRENCH sells 250 a. to WILLIAMSON. Witnesses: HENRY GIGNILLIATT, JOHN CROFT. Before DANIEL GREENE. JACOB MOTTE, Register.

Book F, p. 417
18 Nov. 1727
L & R

EPHRAIM MIKELL, JR., planter, & MARY (her mark) his wife, to THOMAS GRIMBALL, planter, all of Colleton Co., for L 480 SC money, 200 a. on Edisto Island, bounding S on NATHEW CREAST; W on ICHABOD FRYE; N on a creek on N. Edisto River. Witnesses: ALEXANDER WALKER, PAUL GRIMBALL, CHARLES (his mark) ELLIOTT. Before DANIEL GREENE. JACOB MOTTE, Register.

Book F, p. 420
15 & 16 Feb. 1727
L & R

ALEXANDER TRENCH, merchant, of Charleston, as attorney, for JOHN BAYLY, of Ireland, to JOHN LLOYD, ESQ., of Berkeley Co., for L 40 SC money, 162 a. in Berkeley Co., bounding N on ANDREW ALLEN; E on ROGER MOORE; S on RALPH IZARD & JOHN LLOYD; W on Round Savanna. Whereas the Rt. Hon. JOHN EARL OF BATH & the Lords Proprs. by letters patents on 16 Aug. 1698 created JOHN BAYLY, the father, Landgrave & Cassick, granting him 49,000 a.; & whereas JOHN BAYLY, son & heir, on 9 Nov. 1722 appointed ALEXANDER TRENCH, merchant, of Charleston, his attorneywith power to reserve 8000 a. for JOHN BAYLY & sell the rest; now TRENCH sells 162 a. to LLOYD. Witnesses: JAMES BALLINTINE, JOHN MILLNER. Before ALEXANDER PARRIS. JACOB MOTTE, Register.

Book F, p. 427
17 Apr. 1727
Mortgage

HEZEKIAH RUSS, planter, of Berkeley Co., to ALEXANDER NISBETT, merchant, of Charleston, for L 244:18:6:3 SC money, 200 a. according to plat & grant to JOHN CARRIER dated 10 Apr.

1714, who sold to WILLIAM BROCKINGTON in 1717; who sold to HEZEKIAH RUSS on 23 May 1727; conditioned for payment of above sum by Russ to NISBETT on 1 Jan. 1727/8. Witnesses: WALTER NISBETT, JOHN BECKITT, HUGH CAMPBELL. Before ALEXANDER PARRIS. JACOB MOTTE, Register. Mortgage paid in full 9 Apr. 1729.

Book F, p. 431　　　　　　　JOHN SULLIVAN, cordwinder, of Berkeley Co., to
8 & 9 May 1727　　　　　　 THOMAS DIXON, bricklayer, of Charleston, for
L & R　　　　　　　　　　　Ł 700 SC money, 100 a. on NE side of Ashley
　　　　　　　　　　　　　　River. Whereas SULLIVAN owned 100 a., part of
2 tracts, in Berkeley Co., on NE side of Ashley River, bounding S on WIL-
LIAM ELLIOTT; W on Ashley River; N on JOHN COCKFIELD; E on the 2 tracts,
as by 2 plats both dated 22 Jan. 1672/3; now SULLIVAN sells to DIXSON.
MARGARET (her mark) MELLS (MELL), party hereto, freely & without compul-
sion, for 10 sh. sells her right & title. Witnesses: JOHN MELL, WILLIAM
STOCKS. Before DANIEL GREENE. JACOB MOTTE, Register.

Book F, p. 444　　　　　　　MANLY WILLIAMSON, planter, to ROGER SAUNDERS,
2 Mar. 1727/8　　　　　　　planter, both of Berkeley Co., for Ł 700 SC
Mortgage　　　　　　　　　 money, 640 a. in St. Paul's Parish, condition-
　　　　　　　　　　　　　　ed for payment of above sum by WILLIAMSON to
SAUNDERS on 1 Mar. next. Witnesses: JOEL POINSETT, RICHARD MILLER. Before DANIEL GREENE. JACOB MOTTE, Register.

Book F, p. 446　　　　　　　JOHN BEAMOR, planter, to JONATHAN NORTON,
31 May 1726　　　　　　　　planter, both of Granville Co., for Ł 50 SC
Deed of Sale　　　　　　　 money, lot #12 in Beaufort. Witnesses: JAMES
　　　　　　　　　　　　　　DUNLOP, JAMES LYDELL. Before JOHN DELEBERE.
JACOB MOTTE, Register.

Book F, p. 448　　　　　　　JONATHAN NORTON of Granville Co., to ALEXANDER
27 Apr. 1726　　　　　　　 NISBETT, merchant, of Charleston, for Ł 80 SC
Release　　　　　　　　　　money, 1 lot #12 in Beaufort fronting S on the
　　　　　　　　　　　　　　Bay; bounding W on lot #11; N on lot #39; E on
lot #13 of CAPT. WILLIAM SCOTT. Witnesses: JAMES LYDELL, AQUILA ROSS,
ALEXANDER PARRIS, JR. Before JOHN DELEBERE. JACOB MOTTE, Register.

```
                       DEEDS BOOK "G"
                         1727-1729
```

Book G, p. 1　　　　　　　　JOSEPH FITCH, planter, & CONSTANTINE his wife,
1 & 2 Mar.　　　　　　　　　only daughter of MANLY WILLIAMSON, planter, to
L & Mortgage　　　　　　　 THOMAS DYMES, merchant, all of Berkeley Co.,
　　　　　　　　　　　　　　whereas MANLY WILLIAMSON gave bond 14 Feb.
1726 to THOMAS DYMES in penal sum of Ł 3600 SC money conditioned for payment of Ł 1800 like money with interest on 1 Mar. next on which he defaulted; & whereas DYMES, at the request of WILLIAMSON & JOSEPH FITCH ex-
tended the time to 1 Mar. 1728 when Ł 2167:4 will be due; now for security, FITCH & his wife mortgage to DYMES 300 a. where FITCH lives, bequeathed to CONSTANTINE by her father, on NE side Ashley River, consisting of
76 a. granted JOHN FIELD; 210 a. granted WILLIAM WILLIAMSON; & 14 a.,
part of a large tract belonging to MANLY WILLIAMSON, son of MANLY WILLIAM-
SON; the 300 a. bounding NE & SE on MANLY WILLIAMSON the son, NW on CAT-
TELL (formerly THOMAS PINCKNEY); W on marsh; E on RALPH IZARD. Witnesses: JOHN HOGG, ROBERT HUME. Before THOMAS COOPER. JACOB MOTTE, Register.

Book G, p. 11　　　　　　　 SAMUEL FLARELL, mariner, by ANDREW ALLEN, mer-
12 & 13 Dec. 1727　　　　　chant, his attorney, both of Charleston, to
L & R　　　　　　　　　　　the Hon. ARTHUR MIDDLETON, ESQ., of Berkeley
　　　　　　　　　　　　　　Co., for Ł 1300 SC money, the brick house
where MRS. MARY BLAMYER lives, fronting S 16-1/2 ft. on Broad Street,
bounding N on COL. JOHN LYNCH; W on JOSEPH WRAGG'S brick house (formerly
SAMUEL WRAGG); E on houses belonging to WILLIAM FLARELL & occupied by
WILLIAM TILLY & built on part of the lot. Witnesses: CHARLES HART, RICH-
ARD HARRIS, ROBERT HUME. Before JOHN WRIGHT. JACOB MOTTE, Register.

Book G, p. 19　　　　　　　 REBECCA FLARELL, widow, to THOMAS DIXSON,
23 & 24 Feb. 1720　　　　　bricklayer, both of Charleston, for Ł 950 SC

L & R money, part of lot #38 in Charleston, fronting 29 ft. S on the Broad Street; bounding E 67 ft. on SAMUEL FLARELL; W & N on the other part of REBECCA FLARELL'S lot. Witnesses: WILLIAM FLARELL, ROBERT HUME. Before JOHN WRIGHT. JACOB MOTTE, Register.

Book G, p. 28　　　　　　SARAH BEAMOR (BEAMER), widow, of Berkeley Co.,
1 & 2 Mar. 1727　　　　　to DANIEL GREENE, ESQ., of Charleston. Where-
L. BOND & Mortgage　　　as SARAH BEAMOR on 1 Mar. 1727 gave a bond to
　　　　　　　　　　　　DANIEL GREENE in the penal sum of ₤ 1243 currency conditioned for payment of ₤ 621:16:1-1/2 on 15 May 1728, now, to secure payment, SARAH mortgages to GREEN 190 a. on Charleston Neck; bounding W on RALPH IZARD, ESQ.; S on the Quarter House & THOMAS HEPWORTH (formerly JAMES BEAMER); E on Cooper River; subject to proviso (?) made by WILLIAM BELLINGER; & another mortgage from SARAH BEAMER to THOMAS ELLERY, gentlemen, of Charleston, on 9 & 10 June 1727 to secure payment of ₤ 588:10 currency; & another mortgage to DANIEL GREENE for ₤ 588:10 currency. Witnesses: WALTER COX, ROBERT RANDALL. Before JOHN WRIGHT. JACOB MOTTE, Register. Mortgage discharged 22 May 1728 by JOHN FENWICKE & JOSEPH WRAGG.

Book G, p. 38　　　　　　JOHN BAYLY, of Ireland, by his attorney ALEX-
22 & 23 Jan. 1726　　　　ANDER TRENCH, merchant of Charleston, to DUGAT
L & R　　　　　　　　　　MAKEKEN, of Craven Co., for ₤ 125 SC money,
　　　　　　　　　　　　500 a. in Craven Co., bounding according to plat. Whereas the Rt. Hon. JOHN EARL OF BATH, Palatine, & the Lords Proprs. by letters patents on 16 Aug. 1698, granted JOHN BAYLY, ESQ. the father, of Co. Tipperary 48,000 a. in SC; & whereas JOHN BAYLY, son & heir, on 9 Nov. 1722 appointed ALEXANDER TRENCH, his attorney, with authority to reserve 8,000 a. for JOHN BAYLY & sell the rest, now TRENCH sells 500 a. to MAKEKEN. Witnesses: HENRY GIBBES, THOMAS LOCKYER, JOHN BRAND. Before WILLIAM RHETT. JACOB MOTTE, Register.

Book G, p. 45　　　　　　PATRICK (his mark) STEWART, planter, of Berke-
24 July 1694　　　　　　ley Co., to WILLIAM BALLAUGH, gentleman, of
Deed of Sale　　　　　　Charleston, for ₤ 10 sterling, lot #443 in
　　　　　　　　　　　　Charleston bounding N on the street leading from Cooper River by GEORGE KEELING; S on JOHN FROWMAN; E on JAMES FLOWERS; W on the street leading from Ashley River by MR. JONES. Witnesses: FINDLA MARTIN, JOHN (his mark) FROWMAN, JOHN ALSTON, JOHN HILL, THOMAS BERTINSHAW. Before PAUL GRIMBALL. JACOB MOTTE, Register.

Book G, p. 48　　　　　　By warrant from the Hon. ROBERT JOHNSON, ESQ.
25 Mar. 1719　　　　　　Gov. of SC, FRANCIS YONGE, Survey or General,
　　　　　　　　　　　　measured & laid out to COL. JOHN BARNWELL, lot #300 in Beaufort, bounding S on the Bay of Beaufort; W on EDWARD ELLIS; N on MORGAN ELLIS; E on CHARLES STREET. JACOB MOTTE, Register.

Book G, p. 49　　　　　　JOHN BAYLY, of Ireland, by his attorney ALEX-
1 & 2 Feb. 1727　　　　　ANDER TRENCH, of Charleston, to THOMAS FARR,
L & R　　　　　　　　　　JR., planter, of Colleton Co., for ₤ 150 SC
　　　　　　　　　　　　money, 2 tracts in Colleton Co.; 1 of 100 a. bounding N on CHRISTOPHER WILKINSON; E on THOMAS FARR, SR.; S on JOHN TUCKER & THOMAS FARR, JR.; W on vacant land; the other 500 a. bounding N on THOMAS FARR, E on WILLIAM FULLER; S on COL. BLAKE & THOMAS FARR, JR.; W on THOMAS FARR, SR. Whereas the Rt. Hon. JOHN EARL OF BATH & the Lords Proprs. on 16 Aug. 1698 created JOHN BAYLY, of Ballinaclough, Co. of Tipperary, Ireland, a Landgrave, granting him 48,000 a.; & whereas JOHN BAYLY, son & heir, on 9 Nov. 1722 appointed ALEXANDER TRENCH, merchant of Charleston, his attorney, with authority to reserve 8,000 a. for JOHN BAYLY & sell the rest; now TRENCH sells Farr 600 a. in 2 tracts. Witnesses: JOSEPH SKINNER; WILLIAM CHAPMAN; JOHN CROFT. Before DANIEL GREENE. JACOB MOTTE, Register.

Book G, p. 58　　　　　　EBENEZER DICKS, joiner, to JOHN JOHNSTON, cord-
16 Mar. 1726　　　　　　winder, both of Granville Co., for ₤ 580 SC
L & R　　　　　　　　　　money, 600 a. granted DICKS by the Lords
　　　　　　　　　　　　Proprs. on 8 Nov. 1710, on Port Royall River, bounding according to plat. Witnesses: THOMAS INNS, THOMAS STONE, WILLIAM MITCHELL. Before JOHN DELA BERE. JACOB MOTTE, Register.

Book G, p. 66   EBENEZER DICKS, joiner, to JOHN JOHNSTON, cord-
16 Mar. 1726   winder, both of Granville Co., for ₤ 580 SC
Bill of Sale   money, 600 a. which ARTHUR DICKS, father of
                        EBENEZER, purchased from the Lords Proprs. on
8 Nov. 1710, on Port Royall River, bounding according to plat. Witnesses:
WILLIAM HAZZARD, JOSEPH BRYAN, JAMES FISHER. Before DANIEL GREENE. JA-
COB MOTTE, Register.

Book G, p. 69   JOHN LAURENS, saddler, & ESTHER his wife to
15 & 16 Sept. 1725   STEPHEN MILLER, shopkeeper, both of Charleston,
L & R   for ₤ 475 SC money, part of lot #56 in Charles-
                        ton, fronting 50 ft. on the market place;
bounding E 100 ft. on part of same lot sold by LAURENS to JAMES ROWLAIN;
W on part same lot sold by LAURENS to JACOB BONNEAU; N on part of same
lot in possession of LAURENS. Witnesses: WILLEM VIPER, MATHURINE BOIGARD,
PAUL CHARRON. Before DANIEL GREENE. JACOB MOTTE, Register.

Book G, p. 78   STEPHEN FORD, SR., to his eldest son GEORGE
29 Apr. 1717   FORD, weaver, for affection & goodwill, 400 a.
Deed of Gift   reserving 1/2 the cypress timber for himself.
                        Whereas his Excellency JOHN EARL OF BATH, Pala-
tine, & the Lords Proprs. on 26 Sept. 1702 granted STEPHEN FORD, SR., 360
a. in Colleton Co., bounding SW on RALPH EMMS; NE on THOMAS ELIOT; & on
all other sides on vacant land; now STEPHEN gives his eldest son GEORGE
the 360 a. & also 40 a. adjoining upon the S or SE of the 360 a. Witnesses: THOMAS TOWNSEND, JOHN BOYDEN. Before DANIEL GREENE. JACOB MOTTE,
Register.

Book G, p. 81   HENRY SIMONS of Berkeley Co., appoints his
16 Apr. 1728   well beloved wife JUDITH & his well beloved
Power of Attorney   friend DANIEL DONOVAN, of Berkeley Co., his
                        attorneys with full power to collect debts &
sell his real estate. Witnesses: SAMUEL TWINE, DANIEL (his mark) WIL-
LIAMS. Before PETER DE ST.JULIEN. JACOB MOTTE, Register.

Book G, p. 83   ALEXANDER TRENCH, attorney for JOHN BAYLY, of
1 Apr. 1728   Ballinaclough, Co. of Tipperary, Ireland, to
L   CAPT. HUGH HEXT, gentleman, of Colleton Co.,
                        SC, for 10 sh. currency; 310 a. bounding N on
HUGH HEXT; E on JOHN TUCKER & THOMAS ELLIOTT; S on MR. FARR; W on CAPT.
WILKENSON. Witnesses: JOHN STUART, SARAH STEWART.

Book G, p. 86   THOMAS DIXSON, bricklayer, & MARY his wife, to
17 & 18 Nov. 1727   STEPHEN MILLER, mariner, all of Charleston,
L & R   for ₤ 156 SC money, part of lot #115 in
                        Charleston, fronting N 26 ft. on Tradd St.,
bounding W 100 ft. on NICHOLAS HAYNES; S on THOMAS HOLTON; E on THOMAS
DIXSON. Witnesses: JOHN MELLENS, WILLIAM ELLIS. Before DANIEL GREENE,
ESQ. JACOB MOTTE, Register.

Book G, p. 95   JOHN BARTON, gentleman, to THOMAS ELLERY, gen-
20 & 21 Mar. 1727   tleman, & DANIEL GREEN, merchant, all of
L & R   Charleston, for ₤ 380 SC money, 30 a. on Coop-
                        er River, conditioned for the payment by BAR-
TON to ELLERY & GREENE of ₤ 380 currency, with interest, on 21 June 1728.
Whereas JOHN, Lord Granville, Palatine, & the Lords Proprs. under the
hands of JOSEPH MORTON, Gov., ARTHUR MIDDLETON, ANDREW PERCIVALL, MAURICE
MATHEWS & JOHN GODFREY on 30 Mar. 1783 granted PAUL GRIMBALL 30 a. on
Cooper River bounding SW on PAUL GRIMBALL; NE on a great marsh SE & NW on
2 marshes; & whereas PAUL GRIMBALL conveyed the 30 a. to SARAH BEAMOR,
widow; & whereas SARAH BEAMOR for ₤ 100 currency by deed of feoffment on
21 Jan. 1723 conveyed the land to JOHN BARTON; now JOHN BARTON mortgages
the land to ELLERY & GREEN. Witnesses: WILLIAM TUNLEY, GEORGE BAMPFIELD.
Before JOHN WRIGHT. JACOB MOTTE, Register.

Book G, p. 106   CHARLES HART, ESQ., of Berkeley Co., to ROBERT
21 & 22 May 1728   HUME, Gentleman, of Charleston, for ₤ 150 SC
L & R   money, 10 a. on Charleston neck on E side of
                        the Broad Path, bounding on all other sides on
ROBERT HUME; which 10 a. JOHN WATKINS, planter, of Berkeley Co., by deed

of feoffment dated 2 Jan. 1726 conveyed to CHARLES HART. Witnesses: THOMAS CHAMBERS, HENRY HARGRAVE. Before ALEXANDER PARRIS, J.P. JACOB MOTTE, Register.

Book G, p. 113
9 & 10 May 1728
L & R

EDMUND PORTER, ESQ. & ELIZABETH, his wife, of Albermarle Co., NC, to JOHN STANYARNE, planter, of Colleton Co., for ₤ 1300 SC money, 1/2 of Caywah Island, SC containing 1350 a. bounding E on other half of island; W on Stono Creek; N on Caywah River; S on the sea. Whereas JOHN PETERSON (ELIZABETH'S nephew) owned 1/2 of Cayway Island, SC & died in Sept. 1727 before coming of age & the land became the property of EDMUND & ELIZABETH PORTER, she being heir-at-law, being sister to JOHN PETERSON'S father; & whereas EDMUND PORTER on 16 Jan. 1727 appointed ELIZABETH his attorney; now EDMUND & ELIZABETH sell to STANYARNE. Witnesses: ROBERT HUME, GILES COOKE. Before DANIEL GREENE, J.P. JACOB MOTTE, Register.

Book G, p. 125
16 Jan. 1727/8
Letter of Attorney

EDMUND PORTER, gentleman, of NC appoints his wife ELIZABETH his attorney. ELIZABETH was a sister of JOHN PETERSON'S father & elder daughter of RICHARD PETERSON, JOHN'S grandfather. By the death of ELIZABETH'S mother & of JOHN PETERSON her nephew, EDMUND & ELIZABETH PORTER became heirs to sundry lands, Negroes, good & chattels. Now EDMUND appoints ELIZABETH his attorney to take out of the hands of JONATHAN DRAKE all his property either in SC on near the town of Nassau, New Providence, & dispose of it. Witnesses: THOMAS BELL, WILLIAM WILLIAMS. Recorded 3 May 1728 in secretary's office in Book F P. 80. HENRY HARGRAVE, Dep. Sec. JACOB MOTTE, Register. EDMUND PORTER appeared & signed before Sir RICHARD EVERARD, Baronet, Gov. of NC at Edenton, NC 16 Jan. 1727/8. R. FORSTER, Dep. Sec.

Book G, p. 128
22 & 23 May 1728
L & R

EDMUND PORTER, ESQ. & ELIZABETH his wife & attorney, of Albermarle Co., NC, to LAURENCE DENNIS, planter, of Charleston, for ₤ 220 SC money, 54 a. on James Island & 1 a. on the creek & lands of HESTER KING. Whereas JOHN PETERSON of Berkeley Co. (netpher to ELIZABETH) owned 54 a. on James Island, SC, bounding EW & S on LAURENCE DENNIS; & N on HESTER KING; also 1 a. on the creek & lands of HESTER KING, widow; & whereas JOHN PETERSON died Sept. 1727 under 21 years of age, whereby the lands came to EDMUND & ELIZABETH PORTER through ELIZABETH (JOHN'S father's sister); & whereas EDMUND PORTER on 16 Jan. 1727 appointed ELIZABETH his attorney; now they convey to DENNIS. Witnesses: CHARLES ODINGSELLS, GILES COOKE. Before DANIEL GREENE, J.P. JACOB MOTTE, Register.

Book G, p. 139
20 & 21 May 1728
L & R by Mortgage

SARAH BEAMOR, widow, of Berkeley Co., to JOHN FENWICKE & JOSEPH WRAGG, merchants, of Charleston, as security on bond this date, mortgage 190 a. on Charleston Neck, bounding W on RALPH IZARD, ESQ., S on the Quarter House on THOMAS HEPWORTH; E on Cooper River. Whereas SARAH BEAMOR with JAMES BEAMOR, Indian Trader, gave bond this date to FENWICKE & WRAGG for ₤ 7800 SC money conditioned for payment of ₤ 3932:10 on 21 May 1730; now, to secure payment for all money, goods & produce they owe FENWICKE & WRAGG they convey the 190 a. to FENWICKE & WRAGG. Witnesses: JOHN CROFT, ROBERT HUME. Before DANIEL GREENE, J.P. JACOB MOTTE, Register.

Book G, p. 148
16 Aug. 1725
Power of Attorney

WILLIAM TREDWELL BULL, clerk, Rector of Greensted, Essex Co., appointed his loving friends the Rev. MR. ALEXANDER GARDEN, Rector of St. Philips, Charleston, SC, & EDWARD BRAILSFORD, merchant, his attorneys, to receive money & debts & 5 orders to his overseers on his plantations, & do all things needful. Witnesses: WILLIAM GUY, LEWIS JONES. Before ALEXANDER PARRIS, J.P. JACOB MOTTE, Register.

Book G, p. 150
27 & 28 Dec. 1723
L & R

JOHN BAILY (BAYLEY), cordwinder, to MATHEW BEARD, planter, all of Berkeley Co., for ₤ 625 SC money, 560 a. in 2 tracts, 300 a. on Johns Island, Colleton Co., as described in a plat granted by Sir NATHANIEL JOHNSON, Knight, on 15 Dec. 1705; also 260 a.

adjoining the 300 a., as described in a plat granted by Sir NATHANIEL
JOHNSON on 1 Dec. (Sept ?) 1706. Witnesses: JOSEPH DILL, JOSEPH CROSKEYS,
ROBERT HUME. Before DANIEL GREENE, J.P. JACOB MOTTE, Register.

Book G, p. 157　　　　　　　JOHN BAILY (BAYLEY) cordwinder, & JOHN CROS-
28 Dec. 1723　　　　　　　　KEYS, planter, to MATHEW BEARD, planter, all
Bond　　　　　　　　　　　　of Berkeley Co., in penal sum of ₤ 1250 SC mon-
　　　　　　　　　　　　　　ey. Whereas by L & R, 15 & 16 Oct. 1723 JOHN
CROSKEYS & ELIZABETH his wife conveyed to JOHN BAILY 300 a. adjoining; &
whereas JOHN BAILY by L & R, 27 & 28 Dec. 1723 conveyed the 2 tracts to
MATHEW BEARD; now if JOHN & ELIZABETH CROSKEYS & JOHN BAILEY keep their
agreements & MATHEW BEARD quietly & peaceably holds the 2 tracts this
bond to become void. Witnesses: JOSEPH CROSKEYS, JOSEPH DILL, ROBERT
HUME. Before DANIEL GREENE, J.P. JACOB MOTTE, Register.

Book G, p. 160　　　　　　　JOHN FOGARTY, planter, of St. Thomas & St.
3 Nov. 1721　　　　　　　　 Dennis Parish, Berkeley Co., to his son
Deed of Gift　　　　　　　　STEPHEN FOGARTY, for love & affection, 100 a.,
　　　　　　　　　　　　　　bounding NE on JOHN FOGARTY; SW on EDGAR WELLS;
NW on THOMAS HOWARD; also 1 Negro girl. Witnesses: VINCENT GUERIN, JO-
SEPH ROPER, EDGAR WELLS, MICHAEL DARBY. Before ROBERT DANIELL, J.P. JA-
COB MOTTE, Register.

Book G, p. 161　　　　　　　JOHN FOGARTY, of Berkeley Co., to his son
5 Mar. 1725/6　　　　　　　 STEPHEN FOGARTY, for love & affection & other
Deed of Gift　　　　　　　　considerations, 40 a. bounding NE on JOHN FOG-
　　　　　　　　　　　　　　ARTY; SW on STEPHEN FOGARTY; NW on ROBERT HUME;
SE on RICHARD BERESFORD. Witnesses: EDGAR WELLS, JOHN DUTARQUE, MICHAEL
DARBY. Before ROBERT DANIELL, J.P. JACOB MOTTE, Register.

Book G, p. 163　　　　　　　CHARLES HILL, ESQ. of Charleston to ROBERT
7 Mar. 1723　　　　　　　　 SWETMAN, planter, & MARGARET his wife, of
Lease　　　　　　　　　　　 Berkeley Co. for good will & 5 sh. during
　　　　　　　　　　　　　　their natural lives, 400 a. in Berkeley Co.,
(sold this date by SWETMAN to HILL); also 20 cows, 6 steers, 6 head neat
cattle 2 years old, & 6 head 1 year old, 3 horses & 1 mare provided ROB-
ERT & MARGARET do not waste, sell, or alien any of the animals. Witnesses: BENJAMIN WHITAKER, LAURENCE COULLIETTE. HILL also promises within 1
year to let them have a slave. Before DANIEL GREENE, J.P. JACOB MOTTE,
Register.

Book G, p. 165　　　　　　　MANLY WILLIAMSON, planter, of Berkeley Co.,
30 May 1728　　　　　　　　 gave bond to ROGER SAUNDERS, of same place, in
Bond & Mortgage　　　　　　 penal sum of ₤ 2166 SC money conditioned for
　　　　　　　　　　　　　　payment of ₤ 1083 & interest at 10% on 1 Mar.
1728/9 & conveys to SAUNDERS 640 a. in Colleton Co. Granted 23 July 1711
to MANLY WILLIAMSON, his father. Witnesses: JOHN MELL, ABRAHAM BURNLEY,
THOMAS SMITH, JR. Before DANIEL GREENE, J.P. JACOB MOTTE, Register.

Book G, p. 170　　　　　　　ALEXANDER TRENCH, as attorney for JOHN BAILEY,
25 & 26 Nov. 1726　　　　　 of Ballinaclough, Tipperary Co., Ireland to
L & R　　　　　　　　　　　 JONATHAN RUSS, planter, of Berkeley Co., for
　　　　　　　　　　　　　　₤ 75 SC money, 300 a. known as Hartyes Island
in Wando River. Whereas the Rt. Hon. JOHN, EARL OF BATH & the Lords
Proprs. on 16 Aug. 1698 by letters patents created JOHN BAYLEY (the
father) Landgrave & Cassique, granting him 48,000 a. in SC; & whereas
JOHN BAYLEY, son & heir, on 9 Nov. 1722 appointed ALEXANDER TRENCH of
Charleston his attorney, with authority to set aside 8000 a., for JOHN
BAYLEY'S use & sell the rest; now TRENCH sells RUSS 300 a. Witnesses:
JOHN BRAND, WILLIAM HARVEY, WILLIAM HALES. Before CHARLES HILL, J.P.
JACOB MOTTE, Register.

Book G, p. 177　　　　　　　JONATHAN RUSS & ABIJAH RUSS, planters, sons &
24 June 1728　　　　　　　　executors of will of JONATHAN RUSS, carpenter,
Deed of Sale　　　　　　　　to FRANCIS GODDARD, planter, all of Berkeley
　　　　　　　　　　　　　　Co., for ₤ 610 SC money 300 a. in Berkeley Co.,
known as Heartys Island in Wando River. Whereas JONATHAN RUSS, the father, owned 300 a. known as Heartys Island in Wando River; & whereas he,
on 29 Jan. 1726, made his will & ordered the plantation sold, appointing
his 2 sons his executors; now they sell to GODDARD. Witnesses: DANIEL

GREENE, WILLIAM WEEKLEY, DAVID ANDERSON, CHALRES PINCKNEY. Before JOHN WRIGHT, J.P. JACOB MOTTE, Register.

Book G, p. 183　　　　　　　CHARLES HART, ESQ. to JOHN BENSTON, merchant,
29 June 1728　　　　　　　　for ₤ 110 SC money, 2 lots, Nos. 3 & 38, in
Deed of Sale　　　　　　　　Beaufort; lot #3 bounding S on the bay; W on
　　　　　　　　　　　　　　lot #2; N on lot #29; E on lot #4; lot #38
bounding S on lot #39; W on Scotts Street; N on lot #37; E on lot #41. Whereas the Hon. ROBERT DANIELL, Dep. Gov., & the Lords Proprs. on 13 Aug. 1717 granted CHARLES HART lot #3 in Beaufort Town, Granville Co.; & whereas on same date they also granted CHARLES HART lot #38 in Beaufort; now HART sells both lots to BENSTON. Witnesses: JOEL POINSETT, HENRY HARGRAVE. Before THOMAS BARTON, J.P. JACOB MOTTE, Register.

Book G, p. 187　　　　　　　JOHN DAVIS, planter, & ANN his wife, to LEVI
20 & 23 Jan. 1727　　　　　　GUICHARD, gentleman, all of Berkeley Co., for
L & R　　　　　　　　　　　　₤ 1200 SC money, 350 a. on Forsters Creek,
　　　　　　　　　　　　　　Berkeley Co., granted by Lords Proprs. on 25
Sept. 1696 to WILLIAM WAITIES & by deed of feoffment conveyed on 13 Oct. 1703 by WATIES to HENRY PERONNEAU; & by PERONNEAU conveyed on 16 July 1714 to MORDECAI NATHAN; by NATHAN on 6 Jan. 1715 conveyed to JOHN HODGSON; by HODGSON on 3 Mar. 1717 conveyed to ROGER MOORE; & by MOORE on 20 Oct. 1718 conveyed to ANN DAVIS, mother of JOHN DAVIS; and at her death was inherited by JOHN; bounding E on JOHN ELDROSE; NW on NICHOLAS BENNET; SW on Forsters Creek. ANN DAVIS to renounce her dower with 3 months. Witnesses JOHN'S signature: ISAAC MAZYCK, JR., ROBERT HUME. Witnesses to ANN'S signature: ALEXANDER NISBETT, ALEXANDER PERONNEAU. Before DANIEL GREENE, J.P. JACOB MOTTE, Register.

Book G, p. 197　　　　　　　ALEXANDER TRENCH, as attorney for JOHN BAYLY,
8 & 9 Mar. 1724　　　　　　　of Ballinaclough, Co. of Tipperary, Ireland,
L & R　　　　　　　　　　　　to ANTHONY WHITE, planter, of Bermudas Town,
　　　　　　　　　　　　　　Berkeley Co., SC, for ₤ 125 SC money, 500 a.,
English measure, in Craven Co., in Winyah on north branch of Black River, bounding S & W on THOMAS HEALY; N on EDWARD CLARK & THOMAS HENLY; E on N branch of Black River. Whereas the Rt. Hon. JOHN, EARL OF BATH, Palatine, & the Lords Proprs. by letters patents on 16 Aug. 1698 created JOHN BAYLY, the father, Landgrave & Cassique, granting him 48,000 a. in SC; & whereas JOHN BAYLY, son & heir, on 9 Nov. 1722 appointed ALEXANDER TRENCH, merchant of Charleston, his attorney with authority to reserve 8000 a. for JOHN BAYLY & sell the rest; now TRENCH sells 500 a. to WHITE. Witnesses: THOMAS SMITH, PETER VILLEPONTOUX, WILLIAM SMITH. Before DANIEL HUGER, J.P. JACOB MOTTE, Register.

Book G, p. 209　　　　　　　ALEXANDER TRENCH, as attorney for JOHN BAYLY,
7 & 8 June 1728　　　　　　　of Ballinaclough, Co. of Tipperary, Ireland
L & R　　　　　　　　　　　　(see page 197) to JOHN GREEN, planter, of Win-
　　　　　　　　　　　　　　yaw, Prince George Parish, Craven Co., for
₤ 75 SC money, 300 a., English measure, in Winyaw, Craven Co., bounding N & S on vacant land; W on Wackamaw Creek. Witnesses: JOHN SHEPPARD, JOHN DART. Before DANIEL HUGER, J.P. JACOB MOTTE, Register.

Book G, p. 220　　　　　　　ALEXANDER TRENCH, merchant, of Charleston, as
3 & 4 Dec. 1727　　　　　　　attorney for JOHN BAYLY, of Ballinaclough,
L & R　　　　　　　　　　　　Ireland, (see page 197) to ANTHONY WHITE,
　　　　　　　　　　　　　　planter, of Prince George Parish, Craven Co.,
for ₤ 125 SC money, 500 a., English measure, in Winyaw, on N side Black River, bounding E on MORRIS MURFEE; S on the Great Swamp; W on WILLIAM SWINTON; N on vacant land. Witnesses: ABRAHAM SATUR, SAMUEL HENDERSON. Before DANIEL HUGER, J.P. JACOB MOTTE, Register.

Book G, p. 230　　　　　　　RACHEL (her mark) BRAGGAINS, for love & affec-
13 Mar. 1727　　　　　　　　tion, to her husband, WILLIAM BRAGGAINS, plant-
Deed of Gift　　　　　　　　er, 150 a. in Colleton Co., on N side Camba-
　　　　　　　　　　　　　　chee River, bounding S & W on a marsh & a
swamp; NW on vacant land; plat dated 4 Apr. 1703; also 500 a., in Colleton Co., on N side Cambachee River, bounding N on vacant land; E on a swamp; S on WILLIAM FULLER; W on a swamp & marsh, plat dated 7 Feb. 1705/6. Witnesses: EDWARD BRAILSFORD, THOMAS HILL, EDWARD (his mark) MEREDITH. Before ARTHUR MIDDLETON, J.P. JACOB MOTTE, Register.

Book G, p. 232   ALEXANDER TRENCH, merchant, of Charleston, as
3 & 4 Dec. 1727   attorney for JOHN BAYLY of Ballinaclough, Co.
L & R   of Tipperary, Ireland (see page 197) to AN-
                           THONY WHITE, planter, of Prince George Parish,
Craven Co., for ₤ 75 SC money, 300 a., English measure, in Winyaw on N
side Black River, commonly called Mount Hope; bounding SE on JOHN HAYES;
SW on N. branch Black River; NW on MORRIS MURFEE. Witnesses: ABRAHAM
SATUR, SAMUEL HENDERSON. Before DANIEL HUGER, J.P. JACOB MOTTE, Register.

Book G, p. 241   ALEXANDER TRENCH, merchant, of Charleston, as
15 & 16 July 1728   attorney for JOHN BAYLY, of Ballinaclough, Co.
L & R   of Tipperary, Ireland, (see page 197) to HUGH
                           BRYAN, of Colleton Co., for ₤ 150 SC money,
600 a. of vacant land in Colleton Co., bounding N on JOHN SONCLIES & HUGH
BRYAN; S & SW on JAMES COCHRAN & S Edisto River. Witnesses: JOHN DORSEY,
JOHN GREENLAND. Before DANIEL HUGER, J.P. JACOB MOTTE, Register.

Book G, p. 247   ARTHUR HALL, planter, of Berkeley Co., to ROB-
16 Apr. 1720   ERT SEABROOK, planter, of Colleton Co., for
Deed of Sale   ₤ 600 & other considerations, 370 a. on Wadma-
                           law Island, adjoining SAMUEL UNDERWOOD (form-
erly RICHARD UNDERWOOD), being part of 1800 a. surveyed to CAPT. ROBERT
SEABROOK (father-in-law to ARTHUR HALL) as surveyed by RICHARD BERESFORD,
Dep. Surv. in Apr. 1699, plat certified by Landgrave EDMUND BELLINGER,
Surv. Gen., on 1 Oct. 1701; which 372 a. was conveyed by deed of gift 21
Aug. 1710 to ARTHUR HALL by CAPT. ROBERT SEABROOK (his father-in-law)
bearing W.B.S.°, from the major part of the 1800 a., being part thereof
running between the major part & SAMUEL UNDERWOOD. Witnesses: THOMAS
SEABROOK, WILLIAM PARROTT, LUD. GRANT. Possession, livery & seizin delivered to ROBERT SEABROOK by ARTHUR HALL & MARY HALL. Before DANIEL
GREENE, J.P. JACOB MOTTE, Register.

Book G, p. 251   JOHN FOGARTY, platner, to JOHN COLLWELL, butch-
3 & 4 June 1728   er, both of Berkeley Co., for ₤ 800 SC money,
L & R   300 a., part of 640 a. in St. Thomas Parish,
                           Berkeley Co., bounding NE on LOUIS DUTART; NW
on land sold by FOGARTY to ROBERT HUME; SW on STEVEN FOGARTY; SE on RICHARD BERESFORD. Witnesses: ARCHIBALD YOUNG (YONGE), VICTOR BARRY, JOHN
CROFT. Before DANIEL GREENE, J.P. JACOB MOTTE, Register.

Book G, p. 357   TWEEDIE SOMERVILLE, merchant, & ELIZABETH his
5 June 1728   wife (late ELIZABETH CAWOOD surviving adminis-
Quit claim   tratix of the goods, rights & credits of WIL-
                           LIAM GIBBON, ESQ. of Charleston & sister &
heir at law of said WILLIAM GIBBON) to JOHN COLWELL, butcher, of Berkeley
Co., for ₤ 719:4:10 SC money, the 300 a. mentioned below. Whereas by L &
R, 14 & 15 Aug. 1723 JOHN FOGARTY, planter, of Berkeley Co., conveyed to
WILLIAM GIBBON, ESQ. of Charleston, 300 a., part of 640 a. in St. Thomas
Parish, Berkeley Co., bounding NE on LUIS DUTART; NW on ROBERT HUME; SW
on STEPHEN FOGARTY; SE on RICHARD BERESFORD; with the proviso that if FOGARTY paid GIBBON ₤ 764:10: SC money on 16 Aug. 1724 the transfer would be
void; & whereas FOGARTY later sold JOHN COLWELL the 300 a. sucject to the
above mortgage; & whereas there is now ₤ 719:4:10 principal & itnerest
due; now TWEEDIE & ELIZABETH (GIBBON) SOMERVILLE release their claim to
COLWELL. Witnesses: ROBERT FLADGER, ROBERT HUME. Before DANIEL GREENE,
J.P. JACOB MOTTE, Register.

Book G, p. 260   JOHN COLWELL, butcher, of Berkeley Co., to
9 & 10 July 1728   TWEEDIE SOMERVILLE, merchant, of Charleston,
L & R by Mortgage   for ₤ 773:3:4 SC money, 300 a., part of 640 a.
                           in Berkeley Co., in Parish of St. Thomas,
bounding NE on LUIS DUTART; NW on land sold by JOHN FOGARTY to ROBERT
HUME; SW on STEPHEN FOGARTY; SE on RICHARD BERESFORD; should COLWELL pay
SOMERVILLE the above amount on 1 Mar. 1728 this mortgage to be void.
Witnesses: ROBERT FLADGER, ROBERT HUME. Before JOHN WRIGHT, J.P. JACOB
MOTTE, Register.

Book G, p. 266   ROBERT WRIGHT, gentleman, to ANDREW ALLEN,
6 & 7 June 1728   CHARLES HILL, & TWEEDIE SOMERVILLE, all of

L & R in Trust   Berkeley Co., in consideration of the marriage
                                   already solemnized between ROBERT WRIGHT & GIB-
BON CAWOOD (only daughter of JOHN CAWOOD); & for love & affection ROBERT
bears for his wife GIBBON; & for 2/3 the real & personal estate of JOHN
CAWOOD which ROBERT WRIGHT has already received; & for 10 sh.; WRIGHT conveys to ALLEN, HILL & SOMERVILLE (trustees) 500 a. on S side of head of
Ashley River, bounding E & S on ALEXANDER SKENE; NW on JOSIAH OSGOOD; NE
on ROBERT WRIGHT, SR. (formerly WILLIAM WALLACE); to hold to the use of
ROBERT WRIGHT during his lifetime; then to ALLEN, HILL & SOMERVILLE in
trust for GIBBON, his wife, during her life. Should ROBERT WRIGHT convey
to the trustees any other land of same value then this instrument may be
voided; but should GIBBON die without issue this agreement ceases. Witnesses: BENJAMIN WHITAKER, THOMAS LAMBOLL, ROBERT HUME. Before JOHN
WRIGHT, J.P.   JACOB MOTTE, Register.

Book G, p. 272   THOMAS (his mark) BURTON, planter, of Craven
13 Aug. 1728   Co., to HENRY PERONNEAU, SR., merchant, of
Mortgage   Charleston, for ₤ 330:8:2 SC money, 300 a. in
                                   Berkeley Co., St. Thomas Parish on E side Coop-
er River; bounding W & N on Simmons Creek; E on SAMUEL COMMANDER; S on
RICHARD BERESFORD; conditioned for the payment of the above sum, with interest, by BURTON to PERONNEAU on 13 Aug. 1730. Witnesses: ROBERT STEELE,
JOHN CROFT.   JACOB MOTTE, Register.

Book G, p. 276   JOHN WATKINS, planter, to CHARLES HART, ESQ.,
2 Jan. 1726   both of Berkeley Co., for ₤ 50, 10 a. on
Conveyance   Charleston Neck. Whereas in 1720 WATKINS sold
                                   HART 10 a. on Charleston Neck on E side of the
broad path & bounding on all other sides on GILSON CLAPP; & whereas WAT-
KINS received from HART ₤ 50 in full & no conveyance has yet been made,
now WATKINS confirms to HART 10 a. on Charleston Neck on E side of the
broad path & bounding on all other sides by ROBERT HUME. Witnesses: WIL-
LIAM BLAKEWEY, LAWRENCE COULLIETTE, JOHN CONYERS. Before DANIEL GREENE,
J.P.   JACOB MOTTE, Register.

Book G, p. 279   JOHN DANIEL, gentleman, of Thomas's Island,
22 & 23 July 1728   Parish of St. Thomas, Berkeley Co., to THOMAS
L & R by Mortgage   HASELL, Rector of St. Thomas Parish, the Hon.
                                   THOMAS BROUGHTON (executor of will of RICHARD
BERESFORD), RICHARD HARRIS, JOHN MOORE, FRANCIS GODDARD, JOHN STEWART,
JOHN ASHBY, & ROBERT DANIEL, vestrymen, for ₤ 500 currency, mortgages
700 a. on St. Thomas Island, bounding S & W on ROBERT DANIEL & estate of
RICHARD CODNER; N on ISAAC LESESNE & a creek; E on Wando River. Whereas
RICHARD BERESFORD by will dated May 1715 bequeathed to THOMAS BROUGHTON &
his executors, in trust the residue of the yearly profits of his real &
personal estate not previously devised until his son JOHN should come of
age, the profits to paid to the vestry & dispose of by them as follows:
1/3 to the schoolmaster & 2/3 towards the support & education of such of
the poor children of the Parish as should be sent there to school, or put
the money out at interest; & whereas BROUGHTON has on hand ₤ 3500 currency which he & the vestry have agreed to put out at interest; now for
₤ 500 they take a mortgage on 700 a. on St. Thomas Island devised by will
of ROBERT DANIELL to his widow MARTHA DANIELL the mother of JOHN party
hereto; which 700 a. MARTHA, when she married GEORGE LOGAN, settled in
trust for her son JOHN DANIELL. Witnesses: JACOB WOOLFORD, THOMAS ELLERY.
Before TWEEDIE SOMERVILLE, J.P.   JACOB MOTTE, Register.

Book G, p. 287   ROBERT DANIELL, of Thomas Island, St. Thomas
22 & 23 July 1728   Parish, Berkeley Co., to THOMAS HASELL, rector,
L & R by Mortgage   the Hon. THOMAS BROUGHTON (executor of will of
                                   RICHARD BERESFORD) & RICHARD HARRIS, JOHN
MOORE, FRANCIS GODDARD, JOHN STEWARD & JOHN ASHBY, vestrymen (see page
279 for particulars of BERESFORD'S will) for ₤ 500, mortgages 549 a. on
St. Thomas Island where ROBERT DANIEL lives, bounding E on Wando River; W
on estate of RICHARD CODNER; N on JOHN DANIEL; S on Cooper River; except
300 a. granted MARMADUKE DANIELL for life by ROBERT DANIEL; which 549 a.
was settled on ROBERT by his mother MARTHA (later MARTHA LOGAN). Witnesses: JACOB WOOLFORD, THOMAS ELLERY. Before TWEEDIE SOMERVILLE, J.P. JA-
COB MOTTE, Register

Book G, p. 296   FRANCIS GODDARD, planter, of St. Thomas Parish,
22 & 23 July 1728   Berkeley Co., to THOMAS HASELL, rector of St.
Mortgage   Thomas Parish, the Hon. THOMAS BROUGHTON (ex-
                          ecutor of will of RICHARD BERESFORD), RICHARD
HARRIS, JOHN MOORE, JOHN STEWARD, JOHN ASHBY, & ROBERT DANIELL, vestrymen,
(see page 279 for particulars of BERESFORD'S will) for L 300 SC money,
mortgages 300 a. known as Hearty's Island, on Wando River. Witnesses:
JACOB WOOLFORD, THOMAS ELLERY. Before TWEEDIE SOMERVILLE, J.P. JACOB
MOTTE, Register.

Book G, p. 303   JOHN ASHBY, (eldest son & heir of JOHN ASHBY)
22 & 23 July 1728   of St. Thomas Parish, Berkeley Co., to THOMAS
Mortgage   HASELL, rector, the Hon. THOMAS BROUGHTON (ex-
                          ecutor of will of RICHARD BERESFORD), RICHARD
HARRIS, JOHN MOORE, FRANCIS GODDARD, JOHN STEWARD, & ROBERT DANIELL, vestrymen of St. Thomas Parish (see page 279 for particulars of BERESFORD'S
will), for L 500 currency, mortgages 250 a. on E side of the eastern
branch of the T of Cooper River, bounding NE on Ashby's Creek; NW on E
branch of Cooper River; SW on HENRY HARRIS & vacant land; SE on vacant
land; according to plat annexed to grant to JOHN ASHBY (the father) dated
9 Sept. 1696. Witnesses: JACOB WOOLFORD, THOMAS ELLERY. Before TWEEDIE
SOMERVILLE, J.P. JACOB MOTTE, Register. Mortgage satisfied 16 Feb. 1737
by MRS. ELIZABETH VICARIDGE. Signatures: R. HOW, ROBERT AUSTIN.

Book G, p. 311   JOHN MOORE, gentleman, of St. Thomas Parish,
2 Sept. 1728   Berkeley Co., to JOHN OLDFIELD, gentleman, of
Deed of Sale   Goose Creek, 414 a. in 2 tracts. Whereas
                          ISAAC LEWIS (LUIS), planter, & SARAH his wife,
of Charleston, by release dated 1 May 1725, conveyed to JOHN MOORE 276 a.
in the Parish of St. James & St. Johns, Berkeley, bounding N on COL. THOM-
AS BROUGHTON; S on DR. TOMAN; E on ISAAC LEWIS & JOHN OLDFIELD; W on JOHN
OLDFIELD; also 138 a. described in deed of feoffment to ISAAC LEWIS to
pay JOHN MOORE L 3510 SC money at times agreed upon. Now MOORE, for
L 2000, (principal & interest due on the mortgage) transfers to OLDFIELD
the 2 tracts & the bond given by LEWIS to MOORE. Witnesses: GEORGE BAMP-
FIELD, RICHARD ROWE, THOMAS ELLERY. Before WILLIAM RHETT, J.P. JACOB
MOTTE, Register.

Book G, p. 314   EDWARD EDWARDS, planter, to THOMAS HASELL, rec-
22 & 23 July 1728   tor; the Hon. THOMAS BROUGHTON (executor of
Mortgage   will of RICHARD BERESFORD); RICHARD HARRIS,
                          JOHN MOORE, FRANCIS GODDARD, JOHN STEWARD,
JOHN ASHBY & ROBERT DANIEL, vestrymen, all of St. Thomas Parish, Berkeley
Co., (see page 279 for details of BERESFORD'S will), for L 300 currency
mortgages 365 a. on NE side Cooper River, bounding SE on Itawan Creek; SW
on NATHANIEL WILLIAMS; NW on a branch of Clowters Creek & RICHARD HARRIS;
NE on RICHARD HARRIS; as specified in plat annexed to grant 23 July 1711
by Lords Proprs. to GRACE BUCKLEY, widow. Witnesses: JACOB WOOLFORD,
THOMAS ELLERY. Before TWEEDIE SOMERVILLE, J.P. JACOB MOTTE, Register.

Book G, p. 323   EDMUND PORTER, ESQ. of NC by ELIZABETH (his
23 May 1728   wife & attorney) agrees with LAURENCE DENNIS
Agreement   that DENNIS shall retain L 110 (1/2 the pur-
                          chase price) until EDMUND shall procure from 1
ELEANOR WHITE, or her heirs, a good conveyance of a parcel of land.
Whereas EDMUND PORTER & ELIZABETH his wife for L 220 SC money sold LAU-
RENCE DENNIS 54 a. on James Island which by the death of JOHN PETERSON
(ELIZABETH'S nephew) descended to EDMUND & ELIZABETH through ELIZABETH; &
whereas DENNIS this date gave EDMUND & ELIZABETH a bond in penal sum of
L 220 to secure payment of L 110 on 1 Feb. next; & whereas there leved in
the Island of Jamaica 1 ELEANOR WHITE, widow, who if living is co-heir
with ELIZABETH, being ELIZABETH'S sister, now EDMUND agrees that DENNIS
will keep half the money until a proper conveyance can be obtained from
ELEANOR or her heirs. Witnesses: CHARLES ODINGSELLS, GILES COOKE. Before DANIEL GREENE, J.P. JACOB MOTTE, Register.

Book G, p. 325   THOMAS PAGITT, (eldest son & heir of JOHN
22 & 23 July 1728   PAGITT) planter, to THOMAS HASELL, rector; the
Mortgage   Hon. THOMAS BROUGHTON (executor of will of
                          RICHARD BERESFORD); RICHARD HARRIS, JOHN MOORE

FRANCIS GODDARD, JOHN STEWARD, JOHN ASHBY & ROBERT DANIELL, vestrymen, all of St. Thomas Parish, Berkeley Co. (see page 279 for details of BERESFORD'S will) for L 300 currency, mortgages 280 a., on N side of Watcooe Creek; bounding S on PATRICK SCOTT; W on Watcooe Creek & vacant land; N on vacant land; E on PHINEAS ROGERS; as specified in grant from Lords Proprs. to JOHN PAGITT (THOMAS'S father) on 26 Feb. 1696. Witnesses: JACOB WOOLFORD, THOMAS ELLERY. Before TWEEDIE SOMERVILLE, J.P. JACOB MOTTE, Register.

Book G, p. 333
3 July 1728
Mortgage

PETER HERMAN, planter, of Berkeley Co., to JOHN BENSTONE & GABRIEL MANIGAULT, merchants, of Charleston, for L 1742:10 currency, 980 a. in 2 tracts in Berkeley Co., bounding N & E on HENRY SIMMONS; S on JAMES COLLETON; W on WILLIAM GREENLAND. Witnesses: WILLIAM WATIES, FRANCIS MURILL. Before DANIEL GREENE, J.P. JACOB MOTTE, Register.

Book G, p. 336
22 & 23 July 1728
L & R by Mortgage

WILLIAM POOLE, carpenter, son & heir of WILLIAM POOLE, planter, to THOMAS HASELL, rector, the Hon. THOMAS BROUGHTON (executor of will of RICHARD BERESFORD), RICHARD HARRIS, JOHN MOORE, FRANCIS GODDARD, JOHN STEWARD, JOHN ASHBY & ROBERT DANIEL, vestrymen, all of St. Thomas Parish, Berkeley Co., (see page 279 for details of BERESFORD'S will), for L 400 currency, mortgaged 2 tracts; 1 of 150 a. on the E side Cooper River on Wisboo Creek, bounding NE on Wisboo Creek; SE on DENNIS HAYES & HUMPHREY TURQUET; S on WILLIAM POOLE (formerly THOMAS MONCK) as specified in grant dated 5 May 1704 from Lords Proprs. to WILLIAM POOLE (the father); the other containing 120 a. bounding N on RICHARD DARNY & WILLIAM POOLE; E on HUMPHREY TURQUET; S & W on vacant land; as specified in grant from Lords Proprs. to THOMAS MONCK on 5 May 1704 & conveyed by MONCK 1 June 1705 to WILLIAM POOLE, the father. Witnesses: JACOB WOOLFORD, THOMAS ELLERY. Before TWEEDIE SOMERVILLE. JACOB MOTTE, Register. Mortgage satisfied 23 July 1728. Certified by ALEXANDER GARDEN, JR., treasurer of vestry to WILLIAM HOPTON, Pub. Reg.

Book G, p. 347
3 Sept. 1728
Conveyance

JOSEPH SUMNER, WILLIAM WAY SUMNER, & SAMUEL SUMNER, planters, of St. Paul's Parish, Colleton Co., to NATHANIEL SUMNER, planter, of Dorchester, Berkeley Co., for a valuable sum all their claim to all lands or lots of land belonging to them in Dorchester, Suffolk Co., New England, particularly in lots #10, #15, #36, #50, & 1 in a Cedar Swamp even 3/7 part of the right & interest belonging to their honoured father INCREASE SUMNER in each of the aforesaid lots. Witnesses: RICHARD WARING, MOSES WAY, BARAK NORMAN. Before ROBERT WRIGHT, J.P. JACOB MOTTE, Register.

Book G, p. 348
13 & 14 Sept. 1728
L & R by Mortgage

ABRAHAM SANDERS, planter, of St. Johns Parish, Berkeley Co., to JOHN VICKARIDGE, merchant, of Charleston, for L 736 SC money, 576 a. in St. John's Parish, bounding E on HENRY RUSSELL & on all other sides on vacant land. Mortgage to be paid 13 Jan. 1729. Witnesses: HUGH BUTLER, JOHN LEWIS. Before JOHN WRIGHT, J.P. JACOB MOTTE, Register.

Book G, p. 353
30 & 31 July 1728
L & R

THOMAS ELLERY, gentleman, & ANN his wife, to ARCHIBALD YONGE, joiner, all of Charleston, for L 400 currency, the westernmost corner piece of lot #223, 100 ft. from N to S; 50 ft. English measure from E to W; bounding E on part of same lot lately sold by THOMAS & ANN ELLERY to STEPHEN LAYCROFT; W on street running from Ashley River to the broad path; S on THOMAS LOYD or WILLIAM CATTELL; N on street running from ANDREW ALLEN to MR. DELA CONSEILLERE. Whereas on 26 Mar. 1694 the Hon. THOMAS SMITH, Gov. & Landgrave, directed the Surv. Gen. to lay out for PATRICK STEWARD a town lot #223 bounding N on the street leading from Cooper River by GEORGE KEATINGS; S on JOHN FREEMAN'S lot (or FROWMAN'S); E on JAMES FLOWERS; W on the street leading from Ashley River by MR. JONES; & whereas PATRICK STEWARD on 24 July 1694 sold the lot to WILLIAM BALLAUGH; & whereas BALLAUGH died intestate & the lot descended to his son & heir JOHN BALLOUGH who also died intestate & the lot descended to his 2 daughters ELIZABETH & MARTHA BALLOUGH. ELIZABETH, the elder, married SAMUEL BULLOCK, planter, of Christ Church Parish, & whereas SAMUEL & ELIZABETH BULLOCK by L & R, 11 & 12 Jan. 1727 sold to THOMAS ELLERY the western half of lot #223 lying opposite the new house & lot of ELIAS HANCOCK & fronting the street leading from ANDREW ALLEN to MR. DELA CONSEILLERE on the N (which is the same street mentioned in the ancient deeds to run from Cooper River by GEORGE KEATINGS to another street running from Ashley River to the broad path on the W, which is the same street mentioned in the old grants to run from Ashley River to MR. JONES); to the other half lot on the E, JOHN FREEMAN'S lot on the W; now ELLERY sells part of lot #223 to YONGE. Witnesses: RICHARD ALLEIN, RICHARD ROWE. Before DANIEL GREENE, J.P. JACOB MOTTE, Register.

Book G, p. 362
22 & 23 July 1728
L & R by Mortgage

JOHN STEWARD, planter, to THOMAS HASELL, rector, the Hon. THOMAS BROUGHTON (executor of will of RICHARD BERESFORD, see page 279 for details), RICHARD HARRIS, JOHN MOORE, FRANCIS GODDARD, JOHN ASHBY & ROBERT DANIEL, vestrymen, all of the Parish of St. Thomas, Berkeley Co., for Ŀ 500 currency, mortgages 230 a. English measure on NW side of Wateree Creek out of Wando River, bounding SE on the creek; SW on CAPT. RICHARD HARRIS (formerly THOMAS LAKE); NW on JOHN ANNANT; NE on PATRICK STEWARD; which 230 a. JOHN ANNANT & MARY his wife sold on 12 Oct. 1709 to MRS. FRANCES STEWARD, widow, mother of JOHN STEWARD (party hereto) & which she by deed of gift on 4 Oct. 1710 settled on her son JOHN STEWARD. Witnesses: JACOB WOOLFORD, THOMAS ELLERY. Before TWEEDIE SOMERVILLE. JACOB MOTTE, Register.

Book G, p. 371
30 Nov. 1727

EBENEZER DICKS, planter, of Colleton Co., to CAPT. JOHN BENSTON, of Charleston, for Ŀ 275, 450 a. (part of 1000 odd a.) on St. Helena's Island, bounding W on a branch of Port Royall River; N on Cowcus Creek; E & SE on marshes & a small creek between it & St. Helena; being an Island joining St. Helena's Island; also the horses, hogs, cows, & wild cattle, & all such tame cattle on the island bearing his father's brand. Whereas ARTHUR DICKS (EBENEZER'S father) by will dated 26 Aug. 1720 gave his beloved son EBENEZER a plantation on St. Helena's Island containing 1000 odd a., with all the horses, cattle & stock on the plantation; & whereas the plantation was in ARTHUR DICK'S life time, laid out & 2 grants made from the Lords Proprs., vizt., 1 of about 600 a., the other of about 450 a., now sold by EBENEZER to JOHN BENSTON; now EBENEZER DICKS sells 450 a. to BENSTON. Witnesses: EDWARD SCOTT, NATHANIEL BARNWELL, WILLIAM MITCHELL. Before TWEEDIE SOMERVILLE, J.P. JACOB MOTTE, Register.

Book G, p. 375
2 July 1728
Agreement

SAMUEL WRAGG, merchant, of London, & ROBERT JOHNSON, ESQ., formerly of SC but now of Westminster, sign articles of agreement as follows: SAMUEL WRAGG agrees to sell to ROBERT JOHNSON for Ŀ 105 money of Great Britain, a lot of land on NE end of the bay in Charleston, SC, which he purchased from COL. DANIELL & adjoining ARTHUR LANGHORNE'S lot; 50 ft. front & 180 ft. deep. SAMUEL WRAGG appoints JOSEPH WRAGG, merchant, of Charleston, his attorney to deliver possession to ROBERT JOHNSON, binding himself to JOHNSON in the penal sum of Ŀ 210 money of Great Britain. Witnesses: F. SWAIN, THOMAS PEARSON, JR. Witnesses to receipt: F. SWAIN, CHARLES MOLLOY. THOMAS PEARSON (mariner) appeared before TWEEDIE SOMERVILLE, J.P. JACOB MOTTE, Register.

Book G, p. 376
3 & 4 Oct. 1728
L & R by Mortgage

WILLIAM PINCKNEY, gentleman, (1 of the sons of THOMAS PINCKNEY, merchant) & RUTH his wife, to BENJAMIN DELA CONSEILLERE, merchant, all of Charleston, for Ŀ 800 SC money, mortgages that messuage or tenement where SOLOMON TOZER lives on the bay of Charleston, bounding N on CAPT. ANTHONY MATTHEWS; S on a neightborhool alley between WILLIAM PINCKNEY & TWEEDIE SOMERVILLE (owner of a large brick messuage formerly belonging to WILLIAM GIBBON); also the messuage or tenement where WILLIAM PINCKNEY lives, at the lower end of said alley; which 2 tenements are on the northernmost part of lot #5 formerly sold by Landgrave THOMAS SMITH to THOMAS PINCKNEY; also the part of lot #5 with the several warehouses, stores & other buildings & improvements thereon; also the yard & backside belonging, adjoining, & usually held with the same. Witnesses: JACOB MOTTE, ROBERT HUME. Before JOHN WRIGHT, J.P. JACOB MOTTE, Register.

Book G, p. 384 3 Nov. 1728 Deed of Gift	SARAH BARKER, widow, for love & affection, to her son CHARLES BARKER, planter, of Berkeley Co., 2 adjoining tracts of pine land; 1 containing 640 a., the other 605 a., partly in

Goose Creek Parish & partly in St. Georges Parish; NW of her son JOHN BARKER'S plantation, & bounding on WILLIAM BURNLEY, GEORGE BURNETT, JOHN STONE, THOMAS BULLINE, PETER GARON; also 500 a. on Santee River adjoining JOHN HEIRN. Witnesses: ANN CAUTEY, MARY BARTON, JOHN PARKER. Before JAMES FERGUSON, J.P. JACOB MOTTE, Register.

Book G, p. 385 23 Oct. 1728 Revocation of Letter of Attorney	JONATHAN TUBB, mariner, had appointed THOMAS KEMBERLY, of Charleston, his attorney. Now he revokes the letter of attorney & all authority. Witnesses: SAMUEL WATTS, JOHN GREENE. Before DANIEL GREENE, J.P. JACOB MOTTE, Register.

Book G, p. 286 27 Apr. 1721	JONATHAN COLLINS (COLLINGS), SARAH COLLINS, WILLIAM GUY, REBECKAH GUY, & MARY BASDEN to JONATHAN TUBB, mariner, all of SC for L 125 SC

money, lot #279 in Charleston which WILLIAM EARL OF CRAVEN, Palatine, & the Lords Proprs. on 13 June 1794 granted CAPT. CHARLES BASDEN, bounding E on the great street leading from the market place; W on a lot belonging to CHARLES BASDEN; N on another lot belonging to CAPT. CHARLES BASDEN; S on BERNARD SCHENCKINGH. Witnesses: PIERRE MANIGAULT, ROBERT HUME. Before JOSEPH WRAGG. JACOB MOTTE, Register.

Book G, p. 389 18 & 19 July 1728 L & R by Mortgage	NATHANIEL SNOW, planter, of Berkeley Co., to ALEXANDER NISBETT, merchant, of Charleston, for L 1024:15:1-1/2 SC money, 800 a. in Berkeley Co., known as Red Bank plantation. Wit-

nesses: THOMAS SNOW, WILLIAM SNOW, HUGH CAMPBELL. Before DANIEL GREENE, J.P. JACOB MOTTE, Register.

Book G, p. 395 30 Jan. 1723 Deed of Gift	DENNIS (his mark) MORAINE, planter, of Berkeley Co., to his brother EDMUND MORAINE, for love & affection, 44 a. bounding SE on JOHN MORAINE; NE on WILLIAM COUK; NW on MARY CRUS-

TOE; SW on JAMES EDEN. Should EDMUND MORAINE & his children all die before the children come of age the land to return to brother JOHN MORAINE & his children. Witnesses: JAMES EDEN, JOHN HENDRICK, JOSEPH JOLLY. Before THOMAS BOONE, J.P. JACOB MOTTE, Register.

Book G, p. 396 21 Mar. 1725/6 Deed of Gift	SUSANNAH (her mark) FITCH, widow, to her grandson STEPHEN FITCH (son of JONATHAN FITCH) all of Berkeley Co., for love & affection, her plantation on or near Spoons Savanna, being

1/6 of a tract of 2300 a. given by her husband JONATHAN FITCH to be divided equally between herself & her son JOSEPH. Should STEPHEN FITCH die before coming of age the land to go to his brother THOMAS FITCH. STEPHEN to have no right to the land until after her death unless she thinks proper. Witnesses: TOBIAS FITCH, ROGER SAUNDERS, RACHEL EDGELL. Before DANIEL GREENE, J.P. JACOB MOTTE, Register.

Book G, p. 397 21 Mar. 1725/6 Deed of Gift	SUSANNAH (her mark) FITCH, widow to her grandson JONATHAN FITCH (son of JONATHAN FITCH) of Berkeley Co., for love & affection, her plantation of 250 a. where she lives, known as

Andrews, given her by her husband, bounding SW on Ashley River; NW on her grandson JONATHAN FITCH; SE on her grandson THOMAS FITCH, minor. Witnesses: TOBIAS FITCH, ROGER SAUNDERS, RACHEL EDGELL. Before DANIEL GREEN, J.P. JACOB MOTTE, Register.

Book G, p. 398 22 Feb. 1726 Release	JOSEPH (his mark) PARMETER (PARMENTER), ESQ., of Granville Co., to ALEXANDER NISBETT, merchant, of Charleston, for L 200 SC money, 200 a., on Port Royall, Granville Co., granted JO-

SEPH PARMETER by the Lords Proprs. in 1714, bounding W on THOMAS PARMETER; N on JOSEPH PARMETER; E on marsh & creeks; S on SAMUEL WATTSON. Witnesses: THOMAS INNS, THOMAS STONE, WILLIAM HAYNES. Before JOHN DELABERE, J.P. JACOB MOTTE, Register.

Book G, p. 402   JOHN (his mark) KITCHIN, planter, of Berkeley
21 Nov. 1728   Co., to ANN BROUNSON, wife of JOSEPH BROUNSON,
Deed of Sale   for Ł 350 currency, 2 parcels of land in Berke-
                        ley Co., about 250 a. in all; 150 a. bounding
SE on JOSEPH BROUNSON, SR., W & SW on THOMAS GRAVES; N on JOSEPH BROUNSON;
all other parts on JOHN STEVENS; 100 a. bounding S on JOSEPH BROUNSON; W
on land known as Mill Land; N on MOSES WAY; E on JOSEPH BROUNSON. Witnesses: THOMAS OSGOOD, CHARLES DISTON, ROBERT MILLER, JR. Before A.
SKENE. JACOB MOTTE, Register.

Book G, p. 404   WILLIAM WAY, JR., planter, & THANKFULL (her
15 Mar. 1722/3   mark) his wife of Beach Hill, Colleton Co., to
Deed of Sale   JOSEPH BRUNSON, SR., planter, for a valuable
                        sum, 45 a. within Dorchester lands in Berkeley
Co., numbered 22, bounding E on a highway; S on JOHN STEVENS; W on JOSEPH
BROUNSON; N on JOHN HAWKS. Witnesses: MOSES WAY, EBENEZER WAY, SARAH WAY.
Before THOMAS SATUR. JACOB MOTTE, Register.

Book G, p. 406   PETER (his mark) MONIER, planter, & MOSES MON-
25 Dec. 1728   IER, mariner, both of Berkeley Co., agrees as
Agreement   follows: whereas PETER MONIER owns 70 a. on SE
                        side of eastern branch of the T of Cooper Riv-
er, bounding SW on Lynch's Creek; SE on PETER DUTARTE; NE on JOHNSON
LYNCH; NW on NICHOLAS BOCHET; & he also owns 2 Negro women about 11 head
of cattle, & some household stuff; now, for the love he bears MOSES MON-
IER, he conveys the land, slaves, & cattle to MOSES during the natural
life of PETER; MOSES agreeing to keep & well maintain PETER during his
natural life, etc. Witnesses: FRANCIS DESCHAMPS, CATHERINE PEYRE, PHILIP
(his mark) COMBE. Before ANTHONY BONNEAU, J.P. JACOB MOTTE, Register.

Book G, p. 409   JOHN BRETON, merchant, of the 1st part; THOMAS
20 & 21 Dec. 1728   COOPER & MARGARET MAGDALENE COOPER his wife
L & R   (grand daughter of JOHN BRETON) of the 2nd
                        part; & MAGDALENE JENEAN (JUNEAU), widow, of
the 3rd part; all of Charleston. JOHN BRETON, for natural love & affection for his granddaughter MARGARET MAGDALENE COOPER & in consideration
of a marriage lately solemnized between THOMAS COOPER & MARGARET MAGDA-
LENE COOPER, conveys to MAGDALENE JENEAN in trust, the messuage or tenement & the land on which it is erected, now in the tenue of JOHN BRETON,
being part of lot #26 fronting 31 ft. on Broad Street, & 97 ft. deep;
bounding E on THOMAS FLEMING; S on CHARLES HILL; W on JOHN ARNOLL; in
trust for JOHN BRETON for his life then for THOMAS COOPER & his wife &
their heirs. Witnesses: JOHN METHRINGHAM, JOHN SAXBURY, CHARLES PINCKNEY.
Before DANIEL GREENE, J.P. JACOB MOTTE, Register.

Book G, p. 416   JOHN BRETON, merchant, to THOMAS COOPER & MAR-
23 & 24 Dec. 1728   GARET MAGDALENE his wife (granddaughter of
L & R   JOHN BEATON) for love & affection & in consid-
                        eration of the marriage between THOMAS & MAR-
GARET MAGDALENE, & for 10 sh., part of lot #26 the messuage or tenement
fronting 20 ft. on Broad Street with the land on which it stands, 97 ft.
deep, lately occupied by CAPT. THOMAS FLEMING; bounding N on Broad Street;
E on ISAAC HOLMES; S on CHARLES HILL; W on JOHN BRETON. Witnesses: JOHN
METHRINGHAM, JOHN SAXBURY, CHARLES PINCKNEY. Before DANIEL GREENE, J.P.
JACOB MOTTE, Register.

Book G, p. 421   JOHN LENOIR, ESQ., of the town of St. Michael,
15 May 1727   Island of Barbados, bequeaths 1/2 his wordly
Will   estate to his dearly beloved wife MARTHA in
                        lieu of dower; the other half to his son ROB-
ERT. Should ROBERT die without issue before coming of age his share to
go to wife MARTHA. Believing MARTHA now pregnant, the child, if male, to
receive Ł 500 cut of estate devised MARTHA & ROBERT when 21; if female,
when she is 18. Wife MARTHA appointed sole executrix. Witnesses: ARTHUR
UPTON, HENRY WARREN, ROBERT WARREN. His Excellency, ARTHUR UPTON, appeared before HENRY WORSLEY, at Pilgrim, on 2 June 1727. Will proved at Barbadoes, 7 June 1727.

Book G, p. 423   GILES COOKE, of St. Michael, Barbadoes, to
19 Mar. 1725   JOHN LENOIR, gentlemen, of the same place, for

113

Mortgage   L 350 currency of Barbadoes, & interest, 710 a.
                            commonly called Lynch Grove Plantation, on
Wando Neck, Berkeley Co., SC, bounding S on JOHN BROWN & JOHN BURKE; W on
WILLIAM WHITE; N on JOHN HOLLYBUSH. Witnesses: JOSEPH COBB, ROBERT LYDON.
Recorded 16 Aug. 1727 WILLIAM WEBSTER, Dep. Sec., appeared before his Ex-
cellency HENRY WORSLEY, Capt. Gen. & Gov. in Chief of the Charribbee Is-
lands, etc., etc., at Pilgrim 9 Dec. 1728. JACOB MOTTE, Register.

Book G, p. 426   JOHN HAWKS, planter, to WILLIAM BRANFORD, SR.,
30 Jan. 1728/9   planter of St. Andrews Parish, for L 405 cur-
Deed of Sale   rency, 90 a. in Dorchester, being 2 adjoining
                            lots #23 & 24 which HAWKS purchased, with
other lands, from JOSEPH LORD, Minister of the Gospel, through LORD'S
attorney THOMAS WARING; the 90 a. bounding W on JOHN KITCHEN; NE on SAM-
UEL WAY; SE on a highway; SW on JOSEPH BRUNSON, SR. Witnesses: WILLIAM
GLAZE, PETER GIRARDEAU, MARY BRANFORD. Before WILLIAM BULL, J.P. JACOB
MOTTE, Register.

Book G, p. 429   JOHN (his mark) KITCHEN, planter, to JOSEPH
27 Oct. 1720   BRUNSON, planter, both of Berkeley Co., for a
Deed of Sale   valuable sum, 50 a. in Berkeley Co., bounding
                            NE on WILLIAM WAY; SW on MARTHA GRAVES; NW on
JOHN KITCHEN. Witnesses: THOMAS WAY, JOSIAH OSGOOD, SAMUEL WAY, JR. OS-
GOOD & WAY made oath according to their profession. Before A. SKENE.
JACOB MOTTE, Register.

BOOK G, p. 431   ABRAHAM NEAL, planter, of Berkeley Co., to
27 June 1723   JOHN BROWN, for L 250 currency, 91 a. Whereas
Deed of Sale   the Rt. Hon. WILLIAM, EARL OF CRAVEN, Palatine,
                            & the Lords Proprs. by grant dated 8 July 1612
under the hands of the Rt. Hon. JOHN ARCHDALE, Gov., the Hon. JOSEPH
BLAKE & the Hon. THOMAS CARY conveyed to THOMAS CLARKE 100 a., English
measure, on S side Ashley River; & whereas CLARKE on 12 Oct. 1695 conveyed the 100 a. to JACOB NEAL; & the land came to ABRAHAM NEAL; now ABRAHAM
sells 91 a. to BROWN. Witnesses: WILLIAM HOLMAN, SAMUEL TURNER, HEZEKIAH
WOOD, DAVID (his mark) MCQUEEN. JOHN BROWN on 27 June 1723 assigns all
his right & his wife's right in the 91 a. to WILLIAM BRANFORD, planter,
of Berkeley Co. for L 260 currency. Signed JOHN BROWN, FRANCIS (his
mark) BROWN. Witnesses: WILLIAM HOLMAN, JAMES SAMWAYS, SAMUEL TURNER,
HEZEKIAH WOOD, ABRAHAM NEAL. Before WILLIAM BULL, J.P. JACOB MOTTE,
Register.

Book G, p. 434   JOHN BAYLEY, son & heir of Landgrave JOHN
22 & 23 Jan. 1726   BAYLY, of Ballinaclough, Co. of Tipperary,
L & R   Ireland (see page 197 for details), by his
                            attorney ALEXANDER TRENCH, merchant, of
Charleston, to JOHN MESMITH, of Craven Co., for L 125 SC money, 500 a. in
Craven Co., bounding according to plat. Witnesses: HENRY GIBBES, THOMAS
LOCKYER, JOHN BRAND. Before JOHN WALLIS, J.P. JACOB MOTTE, Register.

                        DEEDS BOOK "H"
                          1726-1730

Book H, p. 1   THOMAS CUTTFIELD, merchant, of Berkeley Co.,
16 Feb. 1726/7   SC, to EDWARD PERRY for L 450 current SC money,
Release   288 a. in Berkeley Co. bounding NW on SUSANAH
                            BAKER; SE on COL. WILLIAM BULL; SW on COL.
BULL; NW on land called Cittlesbees land. Witnesses: THOMAS MILES, THOM-
AS (his mark) TURNER, JEREMIAH MILES. Possession given in presence of
THOMAS MILES, JOSEPH BAKER, SAMUEL SUMNER. Before WILLIAM BULL. JACOB
MOTTE, Register.

Book H, p. 2   SUSANNAH WIGINGTON, daughter of MARY CROSS &
3 Oct. 1719   widow of EDWARD RAWLINGS, of Charleston, quit
Deed   claimed to THOMAS HEPWORTH & ANNE his wife,
                            all her title in the tenement occupied by MARK
OLIVER on bay of Charleston; also 1/4 part of lot #16 fronting 25 ft., on
which the tenement is built; bounding N on MARY BLAMYER; S on NICHOLAS

NARY. Before JOHN CROFT, M.C. JACOB MOTTE, Register.

Book H, p. 2　　　　　　　STEPHEN (his mark) MONCK, ESQ., of Goose Creek,
8 & 9 Jan. 1728　　　　　Berkeley Co., SC, son & heir of JOHN MONCK,
Release　　　　　　　　　ESQ., 1 of the Cassiques of SC, to WILLIAM
　　　　　　　　　　　　　GLASE, planter, of St. George's Parish, Berke-
ley Co., SC, for L 30 current SC money, 100 a. in St. George's Parish;
part of 24,000 a. granted JOHN MONCK by the Lords Proprs & surveyed by
the Hon. WILLIAM BULL, ESQ., Dept. Surv. Gen.; bounding NE partly on MOLS-
CHI GLAZE, partly on COL. CHARLESWORTH GLOVER; SE on MR. DUNNING; SW on
GEORGE CHICKEN; NW on Dorchester Line. Witnesses: JOHN BAYLEY, JOHN DAV-
IS. Before T. CLIFFORD. JACOB MOTTE, Register.

Book H, p. 5　　　　　　　THOMAS OSGOOD, SR., wheelwright, of Berkeley
19 Jan. 1714/15　　　　　Co., SC, for natural love & affection, to well
Deed　　　　　　　　　　beloved son JOSIAH OSGOOD; 4 a. in Dorchester
　　　　　　　　　　　　　bounding E on GEORGE CHICKEN; N on the broad
path or highway; S on Boasoo Creek; W on THOMAS OSGOOD, SR., also 2 small
lots in Dorchester on S side of Boasoo Creek #80 & #81 containing 1/4 a.
each. Witnesses: CHARLES TREADWELL, SAMUEL CLARK, JONATHAN CLARK. Before A. SKENE. JACOB MOTTE, Register.

Book H, p. 6　　　　　　　WILLIAM LIVINGSTON, gentleman, of Charleston,
26 Nov. 1715　　　　　　& ANN his wife, to WILLIAM HARVEY, JR., butch-
Deed of Feoffment　　　er, of Charleston, for L 110, a corner town
　　　　　　　　　　　　　lot lying without the gates of Charleston,
fronting 239 ft. on Broad Street & 94 ft. backwards to WILLIAM LIVING-
STON'S lot; bounding W on STEPHEN TAVERCON; E on another street with the
tenement thereon formerly in possession of DAVID BALANTINE now WILLIAM
HARVEY'S. Witnesses: JOSEPH BLAKE, WILLIAM BILLING. Before ALEXANDER
PARRIS. JACOB MOTTE, Register.

Book H, p. 7　　　　　　　WILLIAM HARVEY, butcher & SARAH his wife, to
4 & 5 Mar. 1728　　　　CHARLES HILL, merchant, & ELIZABETH his wife,
L & R　　　　　　　　　　all of Charleston. Whereas on 26 Nov. 1715
　　　　　　　　　　　　　WM. LIVINGSTON sold WILLIAM HARVEY, JR. (see
above) a corner lot on Broad Street outside the gates of Charleston, now
for 10 slaves delivered & 10 slaves to be delivered & for 10 sh. lot
(part of lot #160) fronting 92-1/2 ft. on Broad Street (& fronting JOHN
BRAND'S house in Broad Street) bounding westerly on a brick chimney & an
oven; & in depth 95-1/2 ft. fron S end of HARVEY'S house N to MRS. DRAY-
TON'S fence, also the large house thereon now in WM. HARVEY'S possession;
also a kitchen & out houses on the lot now in possession of MR. FOUNT-
AINEA, shoemaker. Witnesses: JOHN BRAND, HENRY HARGRAVE. Before ALEXAN-
DER PARRIS. JACOB MOTTE, Register.

Book H, p. 11　　　　　　BENJAMIN SCHENCKINGH, ESQ. & MARGARET his wife,
30 & 31 Dec. 1728　　　of Berkrley Co., SC, to BENJAMIN GODIN (GODDIN)
L & R Mortgage　　　　　& BENJAMIN DELA CONSEILLERE, merchants, of
　　　　　　　　　　　　　Charleston for L 510 SC money. 800 a., part
of a large tract called Boohawe (BOOCHAWE) alias Bonds Bank, in Berkeley
Co., bounding SW on ARTHUR MIDDLETON, ESQ.; NE on JOB HOWE; NE on PAUL
MAZYCK (formerly JOHN DAVISO; NW on COL. SMITH; W on WILLIAM DRY, ESQ.
Witnesses: ROBERT HUME, JOHN CROFT. Before JOHN WRIGHT. JACOB MOTTE,
Register.

Book H, p. 14　　　　　　BENJAMIN SCHENCKINGH, ESQ., of Berkeley Co.,
1 & 2 Jan. 1728　　　　SC, & MARGARET his wife, to RICHARD MILES, mer-
L & R & Mortgage　　　　chant, of the Island of Madera; whereas on 3
　　　　　　　　　　　　　Feb. 1725, BENJAMIN SCHENCKINGH became bound
to RICHARD MILES in the penal sum of L 3000 SC money for the payment of
L 1500 on 3 Feb. 1726; & whereas L 1500 remains due; & whereas SCHENCKIN-
GH by another obligation on 3 Feb. 1727 became bound to MILES in another
penal sum of L 3000 for payment of L 1500 on 3 Feb. 1727 of which L 1500
is still due; & whereas SCHENCKING this date by another obligation became
bound to MILES in the penal sum of L 720 for payment of L 360:17:6 on 1
Jan. 1726; now for securing payment of these sums & interest SCHENCKINGH
releases to MILES 800 a., being part of a larger tract called Boochwe,
alias Bonds Bank, in Berkeley Co., bounding SW on ARTHUR MIDDLETON, ESQ.;
NE on JOB HOWE; NE on PAUL MAZYCK (formerly JOHN DAVIS); NW on COL. SMITH;

Won WILLIAM DRY, ESQ. SCHENCKINGH declares the land free & clear except for L & R, 30 & 31 Dec. 1727 mortgaging the premises in full to BENJAMIN GODIN & BENJAMIN DELA CONSEILLERE, merchants, of Charleston, for L 510. Witnesses: ROBERT HUME, JOHN CROFT. Before JOHN WRIGHT. JACOB MOTTE, Register.

Book H, p. 17
15 Mar. 1728
Release

GEORGE CLAYPOOLE, joiner, late of Philadelphia, now of Charleston, SC, to THOMAS KIMBERLY, chairmaker, for L 400 SC money; whereas HUMPHREY ROUSE, gentleman, of Berkeley Co., SC, bought 6 a. English measure, near Charleston from ISAAC MAZYCK, merchant, & by will dated 20 May 1706 bequeathed them to his wife REBECCA; & whereas REBECCA afterwards married RICHARD WEEKLY, gentleman, of Berkeley Co., & by L & R, 10 & 11 Oct. 1712 RICHARD & REBECCA WEEKLY sold to WILLIAM RHETT, ESQ. of Charleston the 6 a. of land in trust with the proviso that RHETT would permit RICHARD & REBECCA WEEKLY to enjoy the premises during their lifetime without rendering an account, & after their death the land to go to REBECCA'S heirs; & whereas REBECCA died intestate leaving 1 daughter REBECCA (wife of JOSEPH CLAYPOOLE; joiner, of Philadelphia); & whereas daughter REBECCA CLAYPOOLE died, leaving the above GEORGE CLAYPOOLE her eldest son & heir at law; & whereas GEORGE CLAYPOOLE by the solemn affirmation of his uncle GEORGE CLAYPOOLE, merchant, of Philadelphia & by the oath of ANN POUND, spinster, of Philadelphia, taken before THOMAS LAURENCE, ESQ. mayor of Philadelphia on 27 Nov. last, now CLAYPOOLE sells to KIMBERLY the 6 a., bounding E on the Broad Path; S on ISAAC MAZYCK; W on AFRA COMING, widow. Witnesses: RICHARD EDGELL, W. MCKENZIE, JOHN CROFT. Before JOHN WRIGHT. JACOB MOTTE, Register.

Book H, p. 20
27 Nov. 1728
Testimony

Before THOMAS LAWRENCE, ESQ., mayor of Philadelphia, Penna., appeared GEORGE CLAYPOOLE, merchant, aged 53, who declared that his nephew GEORGE, also present, was the eldest son & heir at law of REBECCA CLAYPOOLE, widow of JOSEPH CLAYPOOLE, joiner, of Philadelphia & that he & JOSEPH were brothers. Seal of the City of Philadelphia 1701. JACOB MOTTE, Register.

Book H, p. 20
27 Nov. 1728
Testimony

Before THOMAS LAWRENCE, ESQ., mayor of Philadelphia, appeared ANN (her mark) POUND, spinster, aged 65 years & declared that GEORGE CLAYPOOLE (present) was son & heir at law to REBECCA widow of JOSEPH CLAYPOOLE; that she was present at his birth as the mothers nurse. JACOB MOTTE, Register.

Book H, p. 21
19 & 20 Mar. 1728/9
L & R

THOMAS HEYWARD, hatmaker, of Berkeley Co., & HESTER his wife to JOHN RAVEN, planter, of Colleton Co., for L 1694 current SC money 1/4 of town lot #26 on Broad Street in Charleston, bounding W 94 ft. on DANIEL HUGER & ELISHA PRIOLEAU; S on THOMAS HEPWORTH, ESQ. & COL. ARTHUR HALL; E on JOHN RAVEN'S land; N 60 ft. on Broad Street. Whereas THOMAS HEYWARD owned the above part of town lot & by will dated 28 Sept. 1699 bequeathed it to MARGARET his wife; & whereas MARGARET by deed of gift 18 Nov. 1700 gave the 1/4 of town lot #26 to her son THOMAS HEYWARD (party hereto); now HEYWARD sells to RAVEN. Witnesses: THOMAS MOUNJOY, HENRY BEDON. Before JOHN WRIGHT. JACOB MOTTE, Register.

Book H, p. 23
31 Mar. 1714
Deed of Feoffment

COL. ROBERT DANIEL, SR., gentleman, of Berkeley Co., SC, & MARTHA his wife to SAMUEL WRAGG, merchant, of Charleston for L 125 SC money, part of town lot #32 measuring 50 ft. front next Cooper River; bounding N on ARTHUR LANGHARNE; W on land of heirs of JOHN CROSKEYS, mariner; S on COL. ROBERT DANIEL'S land. Witnesses: ARTHUR LANGHARNE, JOSEPH WRAGG, JOB ROTHMAHLER. JOSEPH WRAGG appeared before RICHARD ALLEIN, C.J. OF SC on 14 Mar. 1728. JACOB MOTTE, Register.

Book H, p. 25
13 & 14 Mar. 1728
L & R

JOSEPH WRAGG, merchant of Charleston, attorney for SAMUEL WRAGG of London, merchant, to ROBERT JOHNSON, ESQ., of SC (now in Great Britain) for L 105 sterling part of town lot #32 measuring 50 ft. front next Cooper River; bounding N on ARTHUR LANGHARNE; W on land of heirs of JOHN CROSKEYS, mariner; S on COL. ROBERT DANIEL.

Whereas COL. ROBERT DANIEL, JR., gentleman, of Berkeley Co., SC, & MARTHA his wife by deed of feoffment 31 Mar. 1714 sold SAMUEL WRAGG, then of Charleston, part of town lot #32. Witnesses: RICHARD LAMBTON, THOMAS ELLERY. Before RICHARD ALLEIN, C.J. JACOB MOTTE, Register.

Book H, p. 27
15 Apr. 1697
Deed of Gift

HENRY SALTUS, mariner, of Charleston, for love & affection, gave his children PROVIDENCE & JOHN his goods, chattles, debts, ready money, plate, rings, household stuff, apparel, utensils, brass, pewter, bedding, etc. Witnesses: SAMUEL WILLIAMSON, HENRY WIGINGTON, ALEXANDER PARRIS appeared before TWEEDIE SOMERVILLE 4 Apr. 1729 to testify to the handwriting of the above witnesses & stated he heard about 16 years before that HENRY SALTUS was drowned in Jamaica & believed him dead. JACOB MOTTE, Register.

Book H, p. 28
13 Feb. 1728
Articles of Agreement

Between ABIJAH RUSS, planter, Berkeley Co., SC, & JOHN BRUCE, merchant, of Charleston. Whereas HEZEKIAH RUSS, brother of ABIJAH, owns 200 a. on Cooper River which on 29 Mar. 1715 was granted by Gov. CHARLES CRAVEN & the Lords Proprs. to JOHN CAREER, & by several conveyances became vested in HEZEKIAH; now ABIJAH promises that on 1 Apr. next he will get HEZEKIAH to sell to JOHN BRUCE, in fee simple, the 200 a., freed of the jointure dower & thirds of CATHERINE, wife of HEZEKIAH; & JOHN BRUCE promises ABIJAH, that upon the conveyance being made as aforesaid by HEZEKIAH, he will pay to HEZEKIAH or his order ₤ 183 SC money; each being bond to the other in penal sum of ₤ 300 current money. Witnesses: CHARLES PINCKNEY, E. PINCKNEY. JACOB MOTTE, Register.

Book H, p. 29
12 & 13 Mar. 1728
L & R

HEZEKIAH RUSS, planter, of Berkeley Co., SC to JOHN BRUCE, merchant, of Charleston, for ₤ 183 SC money 200 a. in Berkeley Co., purchased by HEZEKIAH RUSS from WILLIAM BROCKINTON, bounding N on PETER CONLIES; E on ANN COOK, widow; S on PETER JOHNSON, JR.; W on Morriles Creek running into Cooper River. Witnesses: JOHN FOGARTIE, JOHN ST. MARTIN, JEREMIAH VAREEN. "Apr. the 9th, 1729. Then rec'd. of JOHN BRUCE" the sum of ₤ 183:10 "for land y^t. I sold to the s^d. BRUCE as witness my hand. ABIJAH RUSS." Before JOHN WRIGHT. JACOB MOTTE, Register.

Book H, p. 31
11 Apr. 1729
Mortgage

ROBERT REYNOLDS, of North Kingstown, in Colony of Rhode Island to SAMUEL SHEIFFIELD & BONONI GARDENER, of Newport, R.I., for ₤ 125 current money of New England, sold 200 a. in R.I. willed to ROBERT RENOLDS by his father ROBERT RENOLDS (the farm now being occupied by JOHN EARLE); bounding E on JOSEPH RENOLDS; N on SAMUEL ANTHONY; S on GEORGE HAZARD; W on JOSEPH RENOLDS. Conditioned that RENOLDS pay SHEFFIELD & GARDENER ₤ 125 current R.I. money on 12 May next. Witnesses: JOHN MCNAIRE, WILLIAM MAY. Before DANIEL GREENE. JACOB MOTTE, Register.

Book H, p. 32
11 & 12 Apr. 1729
L & R

JOHN ELDER (ELDERS), carpenter, of Berkeley Co., & SARAH his wife to LEVY GUICHARD, gentleman, for ₤ 180 SC money 183 a. in Parish of St. James, Goose Creek, part of tract of 340 a. granted NICHOLAS BENNETT 12 May 1703 (1723 ?) by Proprs. Dep. which 340 a. was inherited by, & divided equally between, the 2 daughters of NICHOLAS, namely, SARAH (party hereto) & MARY; bounding SW on remainder of tract; NW on MR. MAZYCK; NE on ZACHARIAH VILLEPONTOUX; SE on LEVY GUICHARD; SARAH (her mark) wife of JOHN ELDER, to renounce her title of dower within 3 months. Witnesses: FELIX PELLETT, RALPH IZARD. Before RICHARD ALLEIN. JACOB MOTTE, Register.

Book H, p. 35
7 Aug. 1725
Deed of Sale

JOHN PETER, JR., planter, of PonPon on E side of Edisto River freshes, Colleton Co., SC, to CHRISTOPHER SMITH, planter, of same place for ₤ 250 SC money, 1/2 of a tract containing 500 a. formerly belonging to DR. ALEXANDER CURSIN, bounding N on THOMAS BRANFORD (formerly JAMES WRIXHAM); E on WILLIAM MCPHERSIN; S on WILLIAM FREEMAN; W on Edisto River; which tract of land shall be divided across the middle by a N & S line; that adjoining the river to be CHRISTOPHER

SMITH'S. Witnesses: JOHN BULL, WILLIAM HENDRICK, WILLIAM PETER. Memo: 4 Nov. 1725 CHRISTOPHER SMITH signed this deed of sale over to JOHN SPLATT. Before THOMAS FARR. JACOB MOTTE, Register.

Book H, p. 36
7 Aug. 1725
Bond

JOHN PETER, JR., planter, of PonPon on E side of Edisto River, freshes, Colleton Co., SC, bound to CHRISTOPHER SMITH, planter, of same place, in sum of ₤ 3000 current SC money conditioned for keeping conditions comprised in deed of sale of 250 a. this date. Witnesses: JOHN BULL, WILLIAM HENDRICK, WILLIAM PETER. On 1 Nov. 1725 CHRISTOPHER SMITH signed this bond over to JOHN SPLATT. Before THOMAS FARR. JACOB MOTTE, Register.

Book H, p. 37
1 Nov. 1725
Deed of Sale

CHRISTOPHER SMITH, planter, of Willtown precinct, Colleton Co., SC, & SUSANNAH his wife to JOHN SPLATT, planter, of same place for ₤ 400 SC money sold 1/2 of a tract of 500 a. on E side Edisto freshes formerly belonging to DR. ALEXANDER CURSIN, bounding N on THOMAS BRANFORD (formerly JAMES WRIXHAM); E on WILLIAM MCPHERSIN; S on WILLIAM FREEMAN; W on Edisto River; which tract shall be divided across the middle by a N & S line, the 1/2, adjoining the river to be JOHN SPLATT'S. SUSANNAH, wife of CHRISTOPHER SMITH, for 5 sh., agrees to renounce her dower. Witnesses: HUGH BRYAN, GEORGE HAMLIN, JOHN (his mark) GIVEN. Before CHRISTOPHER WILKINSON. JACOB MOTTE, Register.

Book H, p. 38
1 Nov. 1725
Bond

CHRISTOPHER SMITH, planter, of Willtown precinct, Colleton Co., SC, bound to JOHN SPLATT, planter, of same place, in sum of ₤ 800 SC money conditioned for observing terms of deed of sale of 250 a. this date. Witnesses: HUGH BRYAN, GEORGE HAMLIN, JOHN (his mark) GIVEN. Before CHRISTOPHER WILKINSON. JACOB MOTTE, Register.

Book H, p. 39
7 & 8 Apr. 1729
L & R

AUGUSTUS LAURNES, planter, of Parish of St. James Santee, SC, to SOLOMON LEGARE, JR., currier, of Charleston, for ₤ 250 SC money 500 a. in Craven Co. bounding N on Wambaw Creek; E on MICHAEL CLINCH; S on ELIAS HORRY; W on RICHARD EDGELL; according to 2 plots & grants dated 9 Aug. 1717 each containing 250 a. Witnesses: THOMAS BARKSDALE, JOHN LAURENS. JACOB MOTTE, Register.

Book H, p. 41
23 Mar. 1728
Quit Claim

THOMAS CLIFFORD, planter, of Berkeley Co., SC, son of ELIAS CLIFFORD & SARAH his wife, daughter of THOMAS BARKER, SR., by his first wife & sister to THOMAS BARKER, JR., son of THOMAS BARKER, SR. by his first wife; which said THOMAS BARKER, JR. married REBECCA MORE, now wife of WILLIAM DRY & had issue by her only 1 son named JOHN who died before reaching 21) for divers considerations released to WILLIAM DRY, ESQ. of St. James Goose Creek, his claim to 750 a. in Parish of St. James Goose Creek, where WILLIAM DRY lives bounding N on vacant land taken up by WILLIAM DRY; E on COL. JAMES MOORE & BENJAMIN SCHENCKING, ESQ.; S & W on the Hon. ARTHUR MIDDLETON, ESQ., Pres., & BENJAMIN GIBBES. Witnesses: JOHN STORY, PHILIP REILY, GEORGE CRICHTON. Before RALPH IZARD. JACOB MOTTE, Register.

Book H, p. 42
12 Mar. 1723
Bond

DAVID GUERARD, eldest son & heir of JOHN GUERARD, to BENJAMIN GODIN surviving executor of will of JOHN GUERARD, in trust, several brick buildings in Charleston. Whereas JOHN GUERARD owned a brick dwelling house fronting E on bay of Charleston where he lived & brick storehouses adjoining, & by will dated 21 June 1714 gave them to DAVID GUERARD, chargeable nevertheless with the payment of ₤ 1500 current money at age of 21, which he willed to be equally divided amongst his wife MARTHA & his children, BENJAMIN, DAVID, JOHN & MARTHA & should any child die before 21 or marrying that part to be divided amongst the survivors; & whereas 1 child, BENJAMIN died in infancy, & the shares of the 3 children amounted to ₤ 400 each & the mothers share ₤ 300, which ₤ 300 was paid by BENJAMIN GODIN to THOMAS CLIFFORD in right of his wife; & whereas DAVID GUERARD has paid JOHN his brother ₤ 200; & whereas DAVID GUERARD, to secure payment of ₤ 200 & interest to JOHN, gave bond to BENJAMIN GODIN in penal sum of ₤ 400 for payment of ₤ 200 to GODIN (in trust for JOHN) on 12 Mar. 1724; & to secure payment of ₤ 400 to MARTHA gave GODIN another bond payable 12 Mar. 1724; now to secure payment of the 2 bonds DAVID GUERARD releases to BENJAMIN GODIN the houses (mentioned above, the storehouses being occupied by THOMAS CONIERS, victualer). Witnesses: ROBERT HUME, RICHARD ALLEIN, JOHN GUERARD, W. MCKENZIE. Before TWEEDIE SOMERVILLE. JACOB MOTTE, Register. On 10 Apr. 1754 ALEXANDER GARDEN (who married MARTHA GUERARD) & JOHN GUERARD acknowledged payment in full. Witnesses: PETER JOHN MONCLAR.

Book H, p. 44
30 Aug. 1728
L & R

JOHN (his mark) PORTER, flax dresser, of Reading, Berks Co., (brother & heir of MATTHEW PORTER, sawyer, of Charleston) to SAMUEL WATLINGTON citizen & linen draper of London & JAMES MEFFANT, mariner, of Stephney, Co. of Middlesex, for ₤ 50 English money paid & ₤ 50 to be paid before delivery all real estate in SC owned by MATTHEW PORTER at time of his death & to which JOHN PORTER is entitled as heir at law of MATTHEW PORTER, or of MARY PORTER, JAMES PORTER, & HANNAH PORTER. Whereas MATTHEW PORTER by will dated 15 Nov. 1717 devised his estate to his mother MARY PORTER & his brothers JOHN PORTER & JAMES PORTER & his sister HANNAH PORTER, subject to an estate for life to his wife SUSANNAH PORTER; whereas MARY & JAMES died without issue; & whereas HANNAH died leaving 1 child; now WATLINGTON & MIFFANT have agreed to purchase from JOHN PORTER. Witnesses: AARON KEMP, JOSEPH BISCOE. JACOB MOTTE, Register.

Book H, p. 46
12 Sept. 1728
Deposition

Before Sir EDWARD BECKER, Knight, Lord & Mayor of London, in King's Court held in Chamber of GUILD HALL, London appeared JOSEPH BISCOE, gentleman, of the Inner Temple, London, & testified he saw JOHN PORTER, sawyer, of Reading, Berks Co., brother & heir of MATHEW PORTER of Charleston, SC, deliver L & R, dated 30 & 31 Aug. last, made between JOHN PORTER & SAMUEL WATLINGTON citizen & linen draper of London & JAMES MIFFANT, mariner of Stepney, Middlesex Co., & that JOHN PORTER signed a receipt of 2 sums of money. Signed "JACKSON". JACOB MOTTE, Register.

Book H, p. 47
20 Apr. 1729
L & R

CAPT. EDWARD SCOTT, planter, & MARY his wife, of Beaufort Town, Port Royall, Granville Co., SC, to ANTHONY MATHEWS, JR., of Charleston, for ₤ 960:19:3 SC money, 200 a. on Wambee Island, Granville Co. granted to WILLIAM LESSLEY & surveyed 6 Jan. 1704, & sold Aug. 24, 1728 by CATHERINE DUVALL LESSLEY'S daughter to CAPT. EDWARD SCOTT 24 Aug. 1728; bounding W on WILLIAM BULL; N on a tract laid out for LESSLEY; S on Bulls Creek; E on marshes & creeks; subject to redemption on 20 Apr. 1731. Witnesses: Rev. MR. LEWIS JONES, THOMAS WIGG. Before JOHN DELABERE. JACOB MOTTE, Register.

Book H, p. 50
27 & 28 Mar. 1729
L & R

HANNAH GUERARD, widow, & ANDREW BROUGHTON, gentleman, & HANNAH his wife, all of St. John's Parish, to JOHN GUERARD, merchant, of Charleston, for 10 sh. & other considerations 500 a. in Berkeley Co. on N side of eastern branch of the T of Cooper River; bounding S on said branch; E on JOHN GUERARD (formerly COL. THOMAS BROUGHTON); W on ANTHONY BONNEAU, SR. (formerly MR. MARRANT) N on   ; also 281 a. on N side of eastern branch of the T of Cooper River, bounding S on said branch; W on said 500 a.; E on ANDREW BROUGHTON (formerly PETER JACOB GUERARD); N on ANTHONY BONNEAU (formerly MR. MARRANT). Witnesses: NATHANIEL BROUGHTON, JAMES LEBAS, MARTHA GARDEN. Before JOHN GIBBES. JACOB MOTTE, Register.

Book H. p. 53
1 & 2 Feb. 1727
L & R

SARAH BEAMOR, widow & JAMES BEAMOR, Indian trader, only son & heir at law of JACOB BEAMOR, planter, all of Berkeley Co., SC, to WILLIAM BELLINGER, gentleman, of Colleton Co., 535 a. in Colleton Co., bounding W on land formerly given by MARGARET BEAMOR, widow, (grandmother, to said JAMES BEAMOR) to her eldest son JOHN BEAMOR; N on JOHN WILLIAMSON; E & S on Stono River; which said 535 a. were given by MARGARET BEAMOR to her son JACOB BEAMOR who willed it as above. Whereas JACOB BEAMOR, husband of SARAH & father of JAMES, by will dated 6 July 1710 gave his loving wife SARAH all his real & personal estate as long as she kept herself his wife, but on her marriage he gave her heirs 1/3 only, the residue to reamin in her hands for his son JAMES; & whereas SARAH has remained a widow & JAMES has reached the age of 21, the 535 a. becomes vested in SARAH & JAMES; now in consideration of WILLIAM BELLINGER'S cancelling a L & R, dated 11 & 12 July 1721 by which SARAH had released 190 a. in Berkeley Co. to BELLINGER; & also in consideration of ₤ 600 paid by BELLINGER on 12 July 1721; & for 10 sh. paid this date, SARAH & JAMES sell to BELLINGER. Witnesses to SARAH'S signature: THOMAS FAIRCHILD, CHILDERMUS CROFT. Witnesses to JAMES'S signature: JOHN HERBERT, WILLIAM HATTON, CHARLES BURLEY. Before CHARLES HILL.

Book H, p. 57
6 & 7 June 1727
L & R

The Hon. Landgrave THOMAS SMITH, ESQ. of Berkeley Co., to ISAAC PORCHER, planter for ₤ 387 SC money 1290 a. English measure in Berkeley Co. on SE side of Wasensaw Swamp; part of 48,000 a. granted by Lords Proprs., to Landgrave THOMAS SMITH, bounding N on ISAAC PORCHER, & PETER & MARIANNE PORCHER; E on WILLIAM ADAMS & vacant land; S partly on WILLIAM ADAMS; W on WILLIAM ADAMS, FRANCIS CORDES, & CORNELIUS DUPRE. Witnesses: NATHAN BASSETT, FARMER BULL. Before DANIEL GREENE. JACOB MOTTE, Register.

Book H, p. 60
18 Oct. 1697
Deed of Gift

HENRY SALTUS, mariner, of Charleston for love & affection to well beloved son & daughter, JOHN & PROVIDENCE, & other considerations, part of town lot in Charleston opposite lot on which JOHN ALEXANDER, merchant dwells; also 1 Indian boy. Witnesses: ANTHONY SHORY, JOHN BUCKLEY, HENRY WIGINGTON.

Book H, p. 61
30 May 1729
Testimony

ALEXANDER PARRIS, ESQ. appeared before CHARLES HILL, ESQ. & deposed be believed HENRY SALTUS, mariner, dead, having heard, 16 years before, that SALTUS was drowned during a hurricane at Jamaica; & testified to hand writing of SALTUS, COOPER, BUCKLEY & WIGINGTON in above deed. Witnesses: CHARLES STILL. JACOB MOTTE, Register.

Book H, p. 63
18 & 19 May 1728
L & R

JOHN ASHBY the younger of SC, gentleman, eldest son & heir of JOHN ASHBY the elder (JOHN ASHBY the elder of SC was eldest son & heir of JOHN ASHBY, merchant, of London) to THEODESIA ASHBY & JEMIMA ASHBY, spinsters, 2 daughters of JOHN ASHBY, merchant, of London; for ₤ 400 English, "1 full fourth part in 4 parts to be equally divided" of 3 tenements & appurtenances on Fryday Street, Parish of St. Margaret Moses, London, which ELIZABETH ASHBY, widow, grandmother of JOHN ASHBY the younger holds during her life. Witnesses: THOMAS HASELL, WALTER DALLAS, ARCHIBALD HAMILTON. Before DANIEL HUGER. JACOB MOTTE, Register.

Book H, p. 65
26 & 27 May 1729
L & R

WILLIAM SNOW, planter, of Berkeley Co., SC to ALEXANDER NISBETT, merchant, of Charleston for ₤ 2000 SC money 725 a. in Berkeley Co., called Red Bank, being the plantation mortgaged to NISBETT; & being part of 800 a. granted by the Lords Proprs. to NATHANIEL SNOW, father of WILLIAM by 2 grants dated 30 (20 ?) Jan. 1710. Witnesses: ALEXANDER KINLOCH, NATHANIEL DEAN, JOHN SNOW, HUGH CAMPBELL. Before ANTHONY BONNEAU. JACOB MOTTE, Register.

Book H, p. 68
27 Dec. 1711
Deed of Sale

JOSIAS DUPRE (DUPREE) SR., planter, & MARTHA his wife, of Berkeley Co., to the Rev. MR. THOMAS HASELL, Minister of the Gospel, for ₤ 50 SC money, 140 a. in Berkeley Co. Whereas EDWARD HOWARD, plat-er, sold JOSIAS DUPRE 140 a. in Berkeley Co., bounding NW on eastern branch of T of Cooper River; SW on PETER FOURE; SE & NE on vacant land (plat made by MAURICE MATHEWS, Surv. Gen. 9 May 1684); & whereas JOHN GRANVILLE, ESQ., Palatine & the Lords Proprs. by grant 18 Dec. 1703 granted JOSIA'S DUPRE the above land; now DUPRE sell to THOMAS HASELL; wife MARTHA quit claiming all her right. Witnesses: JOHN LAPIERRE, PIERRE AUNAN, SAMUEL BURCHAM, NICHOLAS DELONGUEMARE. Before NICHOLAS TROTT, C.J. JACOB MOTTE, Register.

Book H, p. 71

CORNELIUS DUPRE, planter, & JANE his wife to

THOMAS HASELL, Minister of the Gospel, for L 260 SC money 200 a. in Berkeley Co. bounding NW on eastern branch of T of Cooper River; SW on THOMAS HASELL; SE & NE on vacant land. Whereas JOHN GRANVILLE, ESQ., Palatine & the Lords Proprs. in 18 Sept. 1703 granted JOSIAS DUPRE, SR. 200 a. on S side of eastern branch of Cooper River; & whereas the said tract was on 27 June sold to JOSIAS DUPRE, JR.; & whereas on 20 July 1706 JOSIAS DUPRE, JR. sold to EDGAR WELLS, shipwright; & EDGAR WELLS on 9 May 1909 sold to CORNELIUS DUPRE; now CORNELIUS DUPRE sells to THOMAS HASELL; wife JANE gave full assent. Witnesses: JAMES MAXWELL, MARY MAXWELL, MARY ASHBY. Before DANIEL HUGER at Pompion Hill. JACOB MOTTE, Register.

Book H, p. 73
16 Aug. 1723
Deed of Sale

JOHN (his mark) STRAHAN, planter, & ELIZABETH (her mark) his wife, of Berkeley Co., to THOMAS HASELL, Rector of Parish of St. Thomas for L 200 SC money 200 a. Whereas JOHN GRANVILLE, ESQ., Palatine & the Lords Proprs. & under the hands of the Hon. Sir NATHANIEL JOHNSON & Commissioners granted on 2 Aug. 1707 to JOHN STRAHAN 200 a. in Berkeley Co., bounding NW on eastern branch of T of Cooper River; SW on THOMAS HASELL; NE on JOHN ASHBY; SE on said ASHBY, (plat dated 8 Mar. 1704/5 by JOB HOWS (?) Surv. Gen.). Wife ELIZABETH voluntarily released her claim. Witnesses: JOSIAS DUPRE, PETER SIMONS, THOMAS ASHBY. Before DANIEL HUGER, at Pompion Hill. JACOB MOTTE, Register.

Book H, p. 76
29 & 30 July 1728
L & R

JOHN NICHOLSON, planter, of Berkeley Co., to THOMAS HASELL, rector of Parish of St. Thomas, for L 1000 SC money, 403 a., in 2 tracts, 1 containing 200 a. in Berkeley Co. bounding NW on JOHN NICHOLSON (formerly EDWARD STANLEY) being part of a barony purchased by DOMINICK ARTHUR from PETER COLLETON of the Island of Barbados, since purchased by JOHN NICHOLSON from CHRISTOPHER ARTHUR, heir & successor to DOMINICK ARTHUR by L & R, 6 & 7 May 1724; the other containing 203 a. in Berkeley Co., bounding SE on WILLIAM WRIGHT & BRYAN HENLEY; NE partly on said NICHOLSON (formerly FRANCIS WILLIAMS) partly on EDWARD HOWARD; SW on above Barony & 200 a.; NW on said NICHOLSON; this 203 a. being part of 228 a. purchased by EDWARD HANLEY from Lords Proprs., grant & plat dated 23 Sept. 1710 & since purchased by JOHN NICHOLSON from PETER HANLEY (STANLEY?) son & heir of EDWARD HANLEY by L & R, 17 & 18 Mar. 1724/5. Witnesses: MATTHEW QUASH, WILLIAM ELLIOTT (ELLDOTT), SUSANNA STANLEY (HANLEY ?). Before DANIEL HUGER. JACOB MOTTE, Register.

Book H, p. 80
20 & 21 Apr. 1727
L & R

The Hon. JOSEPH BLAKE, ESQ. to GEORGE SMITH, ESQ., both of Berkleye Co., SC, for L 100 SC money 2 tracts of 500 a. each. Whereas the Lords Proprs. by grant 29 Oct. 1707 underhand of the Hon. Sir NATHANIEL JOHNSON, Knight, Gov., granted JOHN BAKER 500 a. English measure in Granville Co., being part of Combe Island, bounding NW & S in Combe Island, & all other sides by creeks & marshes of Port Royall River; & whereas JOHN BAKER & SARAH his wife on 21 July 1711 sold the 500 a. to MADAM ELIZABETH BLAKE; & whereas on 17 June 1714 Hon. CHARLES CRAVEN Gov., & the Lords Proprs. granted LADY ELIZABETH BLAKE 500 a. in Granville Co. in S side of Coosow River on Combe Island, bounding N on said River; E part on WILLIAM HOLMES & part on ROBERT COCHRAN; S & W on ELIZABETH BLAKE'S land; & whereas LADY ELIZABETH BLAKE by will dated 30 Sept. 1725 after several bequests devised the remainder of her estate, real & personal to her son JOSEPH BLAKE; now COL. JOSEPH BLAKE sells to GEORGE SMITH. Witnesses: CAPT. WALTER IZARD, GILLSON CLAPP, FRANCIS FOSTER. Before ALEXANDER PARRIS. JACOB MOTTE, Register.

Book H, p. 84
17 May 1729
Letter of Attorney

JOHN BURKE (RURK), merchant, of Island of Antigua appointed JAMES COWLES, merchant, of SC, his attorney to demand & sue for 20 hogshead of musovada sugar shipped on board the ship Dave, RICHARD SIMCOS, commander, the sugar being the property of JOSEPH TRENCH of Barbadoes, consigned to GEORGE LASCELL & JOHN HANBURY, merchants, of London. Witnesses: THOMAS HOB, THOMAS WILLIAMS. Before DANIEL GREENE. JACOB MOTTE, Register.

Book H, p. 85
22 & 23 Jan. 1727
L & R

ALEXANDER PARRIS, ESQ. to TWEEDIE SOMERVILLE, ESQ. & ELIZABETH his wife, only sister & administrator of WILLIAM GIBBON, ESQ. all of

Charleston, SC for 1/2 of lot #8 containing 1/4 a. purchased by ALEXANDER PARRIS from WILLIAM SMITH, vintner; bounding N on WILLIAM ELLIOTT (formerly ANDREW PERCIVALL, ESQ.); W on HENRY BEDON (formerly JOSEPH ELLIOTT); S on other half of the lot belonging to JOHN WRIGHT (formerly JOSEPH KEY); E on Bay Street; with large dwelling house thereon where ALEXANDER PARRIS lives; also 4 tracts in Christ Church Parish, Berkeley Co., making 1 plantation of 1024 a. called Islington Plantation; 540 a. purchased by PARRIS from JOHN & RICHARD WOODWARD; 484 a. being 3 grants to PARRIS; bounding W & SW on Shem (Shemhe) Creek to JOSEPH LAW on E; to ELIZABETH QUELCH on N. Whereas the Hon. WILLIAM GIBBON, ESQ., Council Member, on 22 Sept. 1721 at the special request of ALEXANDER PARRIS enter into 2 bonds to KING GEORGE in penal sum of L 5000 SC money each with the condition that PARRIS render to the Assembly a true account of all sums handled by him as Treasurer of the Province; now, as security, PARRIS sells SOMERVILLE his half of lot #8. Witnesses: JAMES MCNABNEY, THOMAS ELLERY. Before CHARLES HILL. JACOB MOTTE, Register.

Book H, p. 92
2 May 1729
L & R

JOHN BAYLEY, of Ballinaclough, Co. of Tipperary, Ireland, son & heir of JOHN BAYLEY of same place & ALEXANDER TRENCH, merchant, of Charleston, SC, attorney for JOHN BAYLEY, to JOSEPH RUSS, planter, of Berkeley Co., for L 125 SC money 500 a. in Berkeley Co. bounding N on FRANCIS SIMMONS; W on SAMUEL SIMMONS; S on JOHN RUSS; E on HANNAH DUNHAM. Whereas the Rt. Hon. JOHN EARL OF BATH by letters patent dated 16 Aug. 1698 created JOHN BAYLEY, the father, Landgrave & Cassique of SC, & granted him 48,000 a.; & whereas JOHN BAYLEY, the son, by letter of attorney on 9 Nov. 1722 made ALEXANDER TRENCH his attorney with power to take 8000 a. out of the 48,000 a. for JOHN BAYLEY'S use & sell the rest; now TRENCH sells to RUSS. Witnesses: ALEXANDER NISBETT, WILLIAM KNIGHT. Before ALEXANDER PARRIS. JACOB MOTTE, Register.

Book H, p. 95
18 June 1729
Mortgage

JOSEPH RUSS, planter, to ALEXANDER NISBETT, merchant, both of Berkeley Co., SC, for L 422:12 sh. SC money 500 a. in Berkeley Co., bounding N on FRANCIS SIMMONS; W on SAMUEL SIMMONS; S on JOHN RUSS; E on JOHN DUNHAM (see L & R, 1 & 2 May 1729, ALEXANDER TRENCH to JOSEPH RUSS) conditioned for payment of L 422:12 sh. by RUSS to NISBETT on 1 Jan. 1729 for redemption. Witnesses: WALTER NISBETT, DAVID RUSS, HUGH CAMPBELL. Before ALEXANDER PARRIS. JACOB MOTTE, Register.

Book H, p. 97
12 Sept. 1723
Partition

PETER LESADE, planter, to ANDREW DEVEAUX. Whereas PETER LESADE, father of PETER LESADE party hereto, planter, by will dated 9 Aug. 1716 gave his daughter ANNE (sister of PETER, wife of JOHN GERARDEAU) 250 a., part of the Old Town plantation, to be laid out as convenient & taken out of that part adjoining FRANCIS BLANSHAWE beginning at W Penny Creek, running in direct line to son JOHN GUERARDEAU'S plantation. After the death of JOHN GERARDEAU ANNE married ANDREW DEVEAUX, planter, of Berkeley Co. on 21 Aug. 1723 PETER LESADE at request of ANDREW & ANNE DEVEAUX asked CHAMPERNOWN ELLIOTT to lay out the 250 a. bounding E on Westpenny Creek; N on LESADE; S on CAPT. RICHARD GODFREY; S on lands of ANDREW DEVEAUX called Westpenny. Witnesses: JOHN CHAMPNEYS, JOSEPH BALEY (BAYLY). Before DANIEL GREENE. JACOB MOTTE, Register.

Book H, p. 99
4 & 5 July 1729
L & R

The Hon. ALEXANDER SKENE, ESQ. & JEMIMA his wife of Berkeley Co., SC, to CAPT. WILLIAM DOUGHLASS (DOUGLAS) commander of <u>HMS The Happy</u> for L 5045 SC money (ie L 1400 current money) & for further sum of L 3640 secured to be paid to SKENE 1009 a. in Parish of St. George, Berkeley Co. part of Ashley Barony called Wampee Savanah Plantation bounding NE on CAPT. THOMAS GADSDEN; SW on PETER CATTELL (purchased from ALEXANDER SKENE); SE on SAMUEL WRAGG, merchant of London; NW on JACOB SATUR; also a lot fronting 100 ft. on S side of Ashley River beginning 20 ft. below the new bridge lately built over the Ashley at Dorchester & 60 ft. back from river. JEMIMA to renounce her inheritance within 3 months. Witnesses: WILLIAM WOOD, JOHN SKENE. Before DANIEL GREENE. JACOB MOTTE, Register.

Book H, p. 104 CATHERINE DUVALL, widow, of Granville Co., SC,
Deed of Sale to EDWARD SCOTT, of same place for L 150 lawful money 100 a. in Granville Co. on Port Royall Island granted CATHERINE DUVAL by Lords Proprs. Witnesses: WILLIAM HAZZARD, JACOB WRIGHT. Before JOHN DELABERE 15 June 1729. JACOB MOTTE, Register.

Book H, p. 105 CATHERINE DUVALL, widow, of Granville Co., SC
21 Aug. 1729 (8 ?) to EDWARD SCOTT of same place for L 750 lawful
Deed of Sale money 500 a. in Granville Co. on Port Royall Island granted CATHERINE DUVALL by the Lords Proprs. also all stock of neat cattle & hogs as appraised by WILLIAM HAZARD, JACOB WRIGHT, & EDWARD ELLIS. Witnesses: WILLIAM HAZZARD (HAZARD), JACOB WRIGHT. Before JOHN DELABERE. JACOB MOTTE, Register.

Book H, p. 106 ELIZABETH WHETHERICK, widow, of Berkeley Co.,
2 July 1729 SC, for love & good will, to her loving sister
Deed of Gift ANN, wife of THOMAS ELLIOTT, SR., 100 a. in Berkeley Co., bounding S on MR. SUMMER; E on MR. SANDERS & MR. CHINNER; W on ELIZABETH WHETHERICK. Witnesses: MARY BURNHAM, MARTHA DANDRIDGE, CHARLES BURNHAM. Before TWEEDIE SOMERVILLE. JACOB MOTTE, Register.

Book H. p. 107 ROBERT DANIEL, ESQ. (Landgrave by right of
13 Mar. 1728 succession) to ISAAC LESESNE of Berkeley Co.
Deed of Sale for L 25 current SC money 500 a. in Craven Co. bounding S on ROBERT DANIEL; E on ISAAC LESESNE; other sides on vacant land. JOHN EARL OF BATH, Palatine, & the Lords Proprs. by letters patent created COL. ROBERT DANIEL, grandfather of above ROBERT DANIEL, a Landgrave, granting him 48,000 a. Witnesses: JOHN STEWART, HENRY BOSSARD, STEPHEN LEE. Before THOMAS COOPER. JACOB MOTTE, Register.

Book H, p. 109 ROBERT DANIEL, ESQ. (Landgrave by right of
13 Mar. 1728 succession) to ISAAC LESEANE of Berkeley Co.,
Deed of Sale for L 25 current SC money, 500 a. in Craven Co. bounding S on RICHARD SMITH; N on ROBERT DANIEL; E & W on vacant land. JOHN EARL OF BATH, Palatine, & the Lords Proprs. by letters patent created COL. ROBERT DANIEL, grandfather of above ROBERT DANIEL, a Landgrave, granting him 48,000 a. Witnesses: JOHN STEWART, HENRY BOSSARD, STEPHEN LEE. Before THOMAS COOPER. JACOB MOTTE, Register.

Book H, p. 111 DANIEL HUGER, planter, & ELIZABETH his wife,
16 Sept. 1726 of Berkeley Co., to JAMES SAVINEAU, planter,
Deed of Sale of same county, for L 1000 current SC money, 1000 a. Whereas the Lords Proprs. on 9 Mar. 1716/17 granted DANIEL HUGER 1000 a. in Craven Co. bounding N on Wambas Creek; SW on LEWIS GUARDIN; NE on PETER PERDRIAU; now HUGER sells to SAVINEAU. Witnesses: ANDREW BROUGHTON, THOMAS CORDES. Witnesses to livery & seizin: LOUIS GOURDIN, PETER PERDRIAU. Before DANIEL GREENE. JACOB MOTTE, Register.

Book H. p. 113 THOMAS BROUGHTON, ESQ., & ANNE his wife of
19 June 1722 (1723 ?) Berkeley Co., SC, to JOHN GIBBES, gentleman
L & R for L 1350 current SC money, 927 a. in Berkeley Co., bounding E on CAPT. NATHANIEL BROUGHTON; S on THOMAS BROUGHTON; W & N on Sir JOHN COLLETON. Witnesses: JOHN CROFT, J. BONNETHEAU, CHILDERMUS CROFT. Before ALEXANDER PARRIS. JACOB MOTTE, Register.

Book H, p. 117 THOMAS HEPWORTH, ESQ. & ANN his wife to ROBERT
18 & 19 May 1727 HUME, gentleman, all of Charleston, for L 488
L & R lawful money, 70 a. on Charleston Neck on which SARAH BEAMOR lived, lately purchased from her son JAMES, being 2 tracts; 1 of 55 a. granted to JOHN BIRD; the other 15 a. purchased from JOHN KING & JUDAH HOLLYBUSH by SIMON VALENTINE; provided that if HEPWORTH pays HUME L 488 on 19 May 1728 with interest this L & R to be void. Witnesses: DANIEL GREENE, JAMES KILPATRICK. Before JOHN WRIGHT. JACOB MOTTE, Register. 7 Oct. 1729 MRS. ANNE HEPWORRH,

executor of will of THOMAS HEPWORTH paid ROBERT HUME ₺ 603:16:0 current money. Witness, JACOB MOTTE, Register.

Book H, p. 121 Landgrave THOMAS SMITH, ESQ. of Berkeley Co.,
26 Aug. 1729 to JOSIAH CANTEY, planter, of Craven Co., for
Mortgage ₺ 5 current SC money, 360 a. Whereas WILLIAM
CANTEY, planter, of Craven Co., father of JOSIAH, on 2 Apr. 1713 mortgaged to the above THOMAS SMITH all his plantation of 360 a. in Berkeley Co. granted him by his father GEORGE CANTEY; & whereas there was a proviso in the mortgage for the redemption upon payment of ₺ 612:17:3 & interest on 2 Apr. 1714 in merchantable pitch by delivery of 200 barrels yearly to THOMAS SMITH; & whereas the land was forfeited; now SMITH conveys the 360 a. JOSIAH CANTEY; & MARY, wife of Landgrave SMITH, freely & willingly surrenders her dowry. Witnesses: JOHN BAYLY, JA. BOSWOOD. Before DANIEL GREENE. JACOB MOTTE, Register.

Book H, p. 123 JOHN FOGARTIE (FOGARTY), planter, of Berkeley
1 & 2 Aug. 1723 Co., SC, to ROBERT HUME, gentleman of Charles-
L & R ton for ₺ 100 current SC money, 360 a. in
Berkeley Co., bounding SE on LEWIS DUTART & JOHN FOGARTY; SW on MARY WARNOCK; NW on JASPER BASKERFIELD. Witnesses: WILLIAM GIBBON, CHILDERMAS CROFT. Before JOHN WRIGHT. JACOB MOTTE, Register.

Book H, p. 127 JOHN FILBIN, planter, Berkeley Co., to JOHN
8 & 9 Sept. 1729 LAURENS (LAWRENS), saddler, Charleston, for
L & R ₺ 1000 current SC money, 340 a. called Mavericks on NW side Goosecreek granted by Lords Proprs. on 14 July 1677 to JOHN MAVERICK bounding S on creek & marsh; W on MADAM WILLOUGHBY GIBBES; N & E on HUGH GRANGE, THOMAS GRANGE & MADAM EMPEROR; also 260 a. marsh, granted 13 Jan. 1710 by Lords Proprs. to MADAM AMERANTO EMPEROR adjoining above 340 a. & MADAM EMPEROR on 1 side & Goosecreek on other; which 2 tracts, making 1 plantation of 600 a. by several mesne conveyances have become legally vested in JOHN FILBIN. Witnesses: CHARLES PINCKNEY, JEAN GARNIER, HENRY GIGNILLIATT. Before DANIEL HUGER. JACOB MOTTE, Register.

Book H, p. 131 THOMAS BARKER, planter, son & heir of THOMAS
20 May 1712 BARKER, joiner, to Landgrave THOMAS SMITH, ESQ.
Quit claim all of Berkeley Co., for 5 sh. & in performance of certain agreements of this date wherein SARAH BAKER (administratrix of THOMAS BARKER) for valuable considerations agreed with THOMAS SMITH that THOMAS BARKER should claim 1170 a. in Berkeley Co. formerly mortgaged by BARKER to SMITH for a very large sum now BARKER (the son) quit claims all title his right & conveys to THOMAS SMITH the 1170 a. on N side Ashley River between the lands of JONATHAN FITCH & MR. WELLS (formerly JOSEPH HOLDRIDGE). Witnesses: ARTHUR MIDDLETON, R. WIGINGTON, FRANCIS LEBRASSEUR, JOHN CROFT. Before ALEXANDER PARRIS. JACOB MOTTE, Register.

Book H, p. 133 HENRY LEWIS, planter, to SUSANNAH DUBOSE, wid-
18 June 1726 ow, both of Berkeley Co. for 350 current SC
Release money, 500 a. in Berkeley Co., bounding E on
FRANCIS BRITTON; N on ELIAS FOIGIN; NW & SW on MR. CAPERS & CHARLES LEWIS; NE on JONAS BONHOST. Witnesses: BIERRE CHABAR, JONATHAN WHILDEN (WEILDING), ROBERT HOW. Before JACOB BOND. JACOB MOTTE, Register.

Book H, p. 135 JOHN BAYLY, ESQ. of Ballinaclough, Co. of Tip-
1 & 2 June 1729 erary, Ireland, son & heir of JOHN BAYLY &
L & R ALEXANDER TRENCH, merchant, of Charleston, SC
& attorney for JOHN BAYLY, the son, to CAPT. JOHN GASCOIGNE, of HMS The Alborough for ₺ 5 current SC money, 500 a. on Trench Island, Granville Co., SC, bounding S on ROGER MOORE; W on Dawfuskie River; N on ALEXANDER TRENCH; E on New River. Whereas the Rt. Hon. JOHN EARL OF BATH & the Lords Proprs. by letters patent on 16 Aug. 1698 created JOHN BAYLY, the father, Landgrave & Cassique, GRANTINGHAM 48,000 a.; & whereas JOHN BAYLY the son, by deed poll 9 Nov. 1722 appointed ALEXANDER TRENCH his attorney in SC; & whereas certain parts of the 48,000 a. have been laid out to be sold; now TRENCH, as attorney, sells 1 part to

GASCRIGNE. Witnesses: JOHN HUTCHINSON, ROBERT WRIGHT. Before TWEEDIE SOMERVILLE. JACOB MOTTE, Register.

Book H, p. 138
29 Mar. 1726
Deed of Sale

PETER POITEVINT & SUSANNAH (her mark) his wife to son ANTHONY POITEVINT, for L 500 current SC money, 420 a. in Berkeley Co., bounding E on MR. MAYRANT & CAPT. ANTHONY BONNEAU; S on MAJOR LYNCH; W on LEWIS DUTARAUE; N on JOHN FOGARTIE. Whereas the Rt. Hon. CHARLES CRAVEN & the Lords Proprs. granted SOLOMON BUMARD 420 a. in Berkeley Co., which he willed to his daughter MARTHA (wife of THEODORE TRESVANT), who conveyed the tract to PETER POITEVINT. Witnesses: THEODORE TRESVANT, JOHN SNOWS, NICHOLAS BESKETT. Before ANTHONY BONNEAU. JACOB MOTTE, Register.

Book H, p. 140
8 & 9 Mar. 1727
L & R

THOMAS AMORY, merchant, & REBECCA, his wife, of Boston, by their attorney FRANCIS HOLMES, merchant, of Charleston, SC (appointed 16 Jan. 1727) to ISAAC HOLMES, merchant, of Charleston, for L 105 current SC money, part of town lot in Charleston 50 ft. N to S bounding E on ISAAC HOLMES & EBENEZER HOLMES; W on the Hon. ARTHUR MIDDLETON, ESQ.; N & S on JOHN SIMONS (SIMMONS). Witnesses: JOHN SIMMONS, JOHN LEWIS. Before ELEAZER ALLEN. JACOB MOTTE, Register.

Book H, p. 144
15 Aug. 1711
Deed of Sale

PAUL TORQUET, shipwright, & JANE, his wife to ANTHONY BONNEAU, cooper, both of Berkeley Co., for L 25 current SC money, 450 a. English on E side Cooper River granted by JOHN LORD GRANVILLE, Palatine & the Lords Proprs. on 5 May 1704 to PAUL TORQUET, bounding N & W of Cooper River; E on MR. GUN; S on THOMAS AKIN, now TORQUET sells to BONNEAU. JANE quit claimed her dower. PAUL TORQUET appointed JOHN PETTINEAU, planter, his attorney to give possession & seizin. Witnesses to deed poll: JOHN LAROCHES, BENJAMIN MORTIMORE, MARYANN MORTIMORE. Witnesses to delivery: JOHN LAROCHES, JOHN HENRY BONNEAU. Before H. WIGINGTON. JACOB MOTTE, Register.

Book H, p. 147
8 Sept. 1729
Conveyance

JOSEPH BEECH, mechanic, youngest & only surviving son of CHRISTOPHER BEECH to JOHN CUMING for L 40 (L 50) current SC money 10 a. being part of 270 a. bounding W on eastern branch of Cooper River; N on creek that goes by & nearest to the front door of the mansion house; eastward on a qually to the Broad Path; S "on land belonging to sd JOHN CUMING & the sd land belonging to sd JOHN CUMING & the sd land contains by estemation 10 a....that...ly's on the W & S side of the creek that is the landing & nearest to the mansion houseof the sd CHRISTOPHER BEECH, SENR. & from the sd river & along the sd creek where the common path is between the mansion house of the sd CUMING & the mansion house now of JOHN STRAHAN". Whereas CHRISTOPHER BEECH of the Parish of St. Thomas, Berkeley Co., SC willed to each of his 3 eldest sons a certain tract of land upon certain conditions; viz. that each of the 3 eldest sons should pay to JOSEPH the youngest son certain sums of money, & should any of the 3 eldest sons die without issue then JOSEPH should possess the first vacant land; & whereas the tract of land containing CHRISTOPHER'S mansion house (270 a.) was bequeathed to RICHARD the eldest & he died without marriage, & JOSEPH being "sole surviving son & brother" so that JOSEPH becomes indisputable heir; now JOSEPH sells to COMING 10 a. Witnesses: SAMUEL GREY, MICHAEL MAC NEMARA, GEORGE (his mark) BROWN, PETER TAMPLETT, WILLIAM AUGUSTINE. Witnesses to possesion: ISAAC CHILD, MICHAL MACNAMARA, WILLIAM (WALTER) AUGUSTINE, SAMUEL GREY. Before ANTHONY BONNEAU. JACOB MOTTE, Register.

Book H, p. 149
21 July 1711
Bargain & Sale

PAUL TURQUET, (TORQUET) shipwright, & JANE his wife to ANTHONY BONNEAU, cooper for L 150 current money, 890 a. in 2 tracts of land in Berkeley Co., bounding E on DENNIS HAYS, MR. MAYRANT, & Cooper River; W on JOHN PETTINEAU & JAMES CHILD; S on PETTINEAU & JOHN HARLESTON; N on MAYRANT & JAMES CHILD (formerly PERCIVAL PAWLEY). Whereas the Palatine & Lords Proprs. & by the public seal of the Province under the hands of the Hon. Sir NATHANIEL JOHNSON, Knight, Gov., (& for L 9) granted 5 May 1704 PAUL TORQUET 450 a. (formerly granted JOSIAH WALLIS) in Berkeley Co.; & whereas his Excellency JOHN LORD

GRANVILLE Palatine & the Lords Proprs. by another deed (& for ⌊ 9:16) on
14 Mar. 1704 granted PAUL TORQUET 490 a. in same county. Now TORQUET
(JANE giving her full assent) by signing & sealing) sells BONNEAU 2
tracts containing 940 a. except 50 a. sold JOHN PETTINEAU. Witnesses:
BENJAMIN MORTIMORE, JOHN CROFT. Witnesses to possession & seizin: JEAN
PETTINEAU, P. ROBERT, JR., JOHN HENRY BONNEAU, JACOB BONNEAU. Before
HENRY WIGINGTON. JACOB MOTTE, Register.

Book H, p. 151 JOHN LYNCH, merchant, of London, appoints JO-
? Nov. 1724   SEPH WRAGG, merchant of Charleston, SC, his
Letter of Attorney attorney to handle his holdings in SC particu-
               larly part of lot #81 in Charleston purchased
by JOHN LYNCH from BERNARD CHRISTIAN COOPER, chyrurgeon. Witnesses:
CHARLES ODINGSELLS, CAPT. PETER BROCK. PETER BROCK appeared before WIL-
LIAM BLAKEWEY 21 Apr. 1725. JOSEPH WRAGG appearing before BENJAMIN DELA
CONSEILLERS made oath that the words "I shall abide by the agreement (if
any you have made) about the sale of my house but hope it is for ⌊ 120
Jamaica money or ⌊ 90 money of London..." are a true copy of a paragraph
of a letter dated Kingston, Jamaica, 29 May 1729 signed by the above
named JOHN LYNCH. JACOB MOTTE, Register.

Book H, p. 153 JOHN LYNCH, merchant, of Island of Jamaica
10 & 11 Oct. 1729 (formerly of London) of the 1st part; MARY
L & R   DIXON, Sole trader, of Charleston, SC, of the
               2nd part, & THOMAS BOWLIN & SUSANNAH his wife,
SAMUEL PUGSON (son of SUSANNAH), CHARLES DIXON, & ANNA MEHITABEL WALKER-
LY (SUSANNAHS BOWLIN'S grandchildren) of the 3rd part for ⌊ 60 current
money paid by THOMAS & SUSANNAH BOWLIN sold to MARY DIXON in trust for
the sue of THOMAS & SUSANNAH BOWLIN during their lives, then for the
benefit of SAMUEL PUGSON; & for want of heirs to SAMUEL PUGSON then to
CHARLES DIXON & ANNA MEHITABEL WALKERLY. Delivered by JOSEPH WRAGG as
attorney for JOHN LYNCH, lot #81 in Charleston granted to JOHN LYNCH by
BERNHARD CHRISTIAN COOPER, 104 ft. E to W; 19 ft. N to S; on FLAVELL; S
on DAVID LAUGHTON JOMER; W on JAMES INGERSON. Witnesses: PETER HORRY,
CHARLES PINCKNEY. Before THOMAS BURTON. JACOB MOTTE, Register.

Book H, p. 157 MARGARET (her mark) SWETMAN, widow, for ⌊ 50
15 Oct. 1729   current SC money secured to be paid by CHARLES
Quit Claim   HILL, ESQ. to her annually for the rest of her
               natural life assigns all her claim in 400 a.
in Berkeley Co. sold by MARGARET & her husband ROBERT SWETMAN to CHARLES
HILL; also 20 cows, 6 steers, 6 neat cattle 2 years old, 6 neat cattle 1
year old, 3 horses. Witnesses: THOMAS LAROCHE, MICHAEL MILLURE. Before
ALEXANDER PARRIS. JACOB MOTTE, Register.

Book H, p. 158 JOSEPH BEECH, wheelwright, to PETER TAMPLET,
9 Sept. 1729   cordwainer, both of Berkeley Co., SC, for
Conveyance   ⌊ 200 SC currency, 200 a., bounding S on WIL-
               LIAM NICHOLE; E on JOHN ASHBY, ESQ.; N on JO-
SEPH BEECH; W on JOHN CUMING. Whereas CHRISTOPHER BEECH, shipwright, of
Parish of St. Thomas, Berkeley Co., bequeathed certain tracts of land to
his 3 eldest sons, RICHARD, CHRISTOPHER & JOHN; & whereas CHRISTOPHER the
father bequeathed JOHN 300 a.; & whereas RICHARD, CHRISTOPHER & JOHN died,
JOSEPH the youngest & only surviving son becoming undoubted heir of broth-
er JOHN; now JOSEPH sells 2/3 of JOHN'S land to TAMPLET. Witnesses: JOHN
CUMING, JOHN (his mark) STRAHAN. Before ANTHONY BONNEAU. JACOB MOTTE,
Register.

Book H, p. 160 JOHN BAYLY, ESQ. of Ballinaclough, Co. of Tip-
16 & 17 Oct. 1729 perary Ireland (son of JOHN BAYLY) & ALEXANDER
L & R   TRENCH, merchant, of Charleston, SC & attorney
               to JOHN BAYLY the son, to MOSES WILLSON, plant-
er of Berkeley Co., for ⌊ 37 current SC money, 150 a. in Colleton Co.,
bounding N onLeadingway Creek; S on SAMUEL DAVIS; E on SAMUEL DAVIS; W on
JOHN JARVIS; NE on BENJAMIN DENNIS. Whereas the Rt. Hon. JOHN EARL OF
BATH & the Lords Proprs. by letters patent 16 Aug. 1698 created JOHN BAY-
LY, the father, Landgrave & Cassique of SC granting him 48,000 a.; &
whereas JOHN BAYLY, the son, 9 Nov. 1722 appointed ALEXANDER TRENCH his
attorney with power to apportion & sell the land (except 8000 a.). Witnesses: CHARLESWORTH GLOVER, DANIEL FIDLING, RICHARD WIGG. Before DANIEL

126

GREENE.   JACOB MOTTE, Register.

Book H, p. 163   JOHN BONHOSTE, planter, & MAREANN his wife to
6 & 7 June 1726   HENRY LEWIS, planter, all of Berkeley Co., SC
L & R   for ₤ 750 current SC money, 400 a. Whereas by
                         deed of feoffment 27 Apr. 1710 between DANIEL
MCGREGORY, planter, & SARAH his wife of 1 part & JACOB LAPORTE, merchant
of the other, MCGREGORY for ₤ 100 current money sold LAPORTE 1000 a. English measure in Berkeley Co., bounding NW in ANTHONY BONNEAU; S & E on
said DANIEL MCGREGORY; & whereas JACOB LAPORTE by will 13 Oct. 1710 bequeathed his 2 sons THOMAS & JOHN 2500 a. in SC; now JOHN BONHOSTE sells
400 a. to HENRY LEWIS & will cause MAREANN his wife to relinquish her
claim of dower in the 400 a. Witnesses: PIERRE CHABER, JONATHAN WHILDEN,
ROBERT HOW. Before JACOB BOND. JACOB MOTTE, Register.

Book H, p. 166   ABRAHAM SANDERS, planter, to HUGH BUTLER, ESQ.
16 June 1729   of Fairlawn, St. John's Parish, Berkeley Co.,
Mortgage   DANIEL RAVENEL & ROBERT TAYLOR, gentlemen, for
                         ₤ 750 current money, 760 a. in Berkeley Co.,
bounding N on THOMAS CHINNERS; E on ELIZABETH CHINNERS; all other sides
on vacant land; conditioned for redemption on 16 June 1730. Witnesses:
PAUL RAVENEL, CHARLES RICHEBOURG. Before PETER DE ST. JULIEN. JACOB
MOTTE, Register.

Book H, p. 169   JACOB WOOLFORD, gentleman, of Charleston, to
24 & 25 Apr. 1729   the Rev. MR. THOMAS HASELL, rector of the Par-
L & Mortgage   ish of St. Thomas, the Hon. THOMAS BROUGHTON,
                         ESQ. (executor of will of RICHARD BERESFORD),
RICHARD HARRIS, SAMUEL SIMMONS, WILLIAM POOLE, ISAAC LESESNE, THOMAS ASH-
BY, THOMAS PAGITT & ROBERT STEWARD, vestrymen, for ₤ 800 mortgages 245 a.
in 2 tracts; 1 105 a. on St. Thomas's Island, Berkeley Co., bounding NW
on Watcoe Creek; SW on JOHN DUNHAM; SE & NE on RICHARD CODNER'S heirs;
the other 140 a. English measure on St. Thomas's Island, bounding S on
Wando River; N on JOHN DUNHAM; W on MR. LESESNE; E on RICHARD CODNER'S
heirs; whereas RICHARD BERESFORD by will dated May 1715 bequeathed to
THOMAS BROUGHTON in special trust the yearly profits of his real & personal estate not before devised by will until his son JOHN BERESFORD
should come of age, THOMAS BROUGHTON to pay same to the vestry for certain purposed (see previous books for full recitation); & whereas THOMAS
BROUGHTON has in his hands ₤ 2000 & upwards current SC money, part of the
profits, which he & the major part of the vestrymen (named above) have
agreed shall be placed at interest, now JACOB WOOLFORD mortgages 245 a.
to be redeemed by payment of ₤ 800 with interest on 25 Mar. 1730. Witnesses: ROBERT HOW, THOMAS ELLERY. Before ALEXANDER PARRIS. JACOB MOTTE,
Register.

Book H, p. 174   ROBERT DANIEL, ESQ. of Thomas Island, Parish
3 & 4 July 1729   of St. Thomas, Berkeley Co., SC, to the Rev.
L & Mortgage   MR. THOMAS HASELL, rector, the Hon. THOMAS
                         BROUGHTON, ESQ. (executor of will of RICHARD
BERESFORD, ESQ. the details of which are given in previous books) RICHARD
HARRIS, SAMUEL SIMMONS, WILLIAM POOLE, ISAAC LESESNE, THOMAS ASHBY, vestrymen, of St. Thomas Parish, for ₤ 500, 549 a. settled a ROBERT DANIEL
by MARTHA DANIEL (later MARTHA LOGAN) widow by release 16 Apr. 1719,
bounding E on Wando River; W on RICHARD CODNER'S heirs; N on JOHN DANIEL,
gentleman; S on Cooper River, except 30 a. granted to MARMADUKE DANIEL
for life by ROBERT DANIEL. The 549 a. were mortgaged on 23 July 1728 by
ROBERT DANIEL to the vestrymen to secure payment of ₤ 500 & interest.
Witnesses: JACOB WOOLFORD, THOMAS ELLERY. Before ALEXANDER PARRIS. JA-
COB MOTTE, Register.

Book H, p. 180   VINCENT GUERING (GUERRIN), planter, & JUDITH
3 & 4 July 1729   his wife of the Parish of St. Thomas & St. Den-
L & Mortgage   nis to the Rev. MR. THOMAS HASELL, rector, the
                         Hon. THOMAS BROUGHTON, ESQ., executor of will
of RICHARD BERESFORD, the details of whose will are published elsewhere,
RICHARD HARRIS, SAMUEL SIMONS, WILLIAM POOLE, ISAAC LESESNE, THOMAS ASH-
BY, THOMAS PAGITT, & ROBERT STEWART, vestrymen for ₤ 1200 current money,
mortgaged 500 a. in 2 tracts of land; 1 400 a. on N side of NE branch
of Wandoe River; W on JOHN WESTCOAT (formerly WILLIAM NORTH); E on MARY

WARNOCK; S on a creek; N on JOHN ROBBERY (ROOBERY); the other 100 a. on N side of NE branch of Wandoe River; W on WILLIAM DANFORTH (formerly WILLIAM NORTH); E on THOMAS BARKFIELD (?) (formerly THOMAS BOZIER), S on THOMAS BOISIER; N on JOHN ROOBERY. Witnesses: JACOB WOOLFORD, THOMAS ELLERY. Before ALEXANDER PARRIS. JACOB MOTTE, Register. Mortgage paid in full 31 January 1734 to ROBERT HOW, clerk of vestry. Witness: NATHANIEL JOHNSON, Pub. Reg.

Book H, p. 186　　　　　　ISAAC GUERRIN, planter, of Parish of St. Thom-
16 & 17 June 1729　　　　as & St. Dennis, to VINCENT GUERRIN, planter
L & R　　　　　　　　　　of same place, for ₤ 4000 current money 2
　　　　　　　　　　　　　tracts; 1 of 500 a. whereon ISAAC GUERRIN
lives, in Berkeley Co., bounding E on MICHAEL DARBY; W on MADAM MCMORTRAY; N on ANDREW BORDEAUX; the other of 625 a. in Berkeley Co. called Bullhead, bounding S on ANDREW BORDEAUX; E on JOSEPH SINGLETARY. Witnesses: WILLIAM BILLING, THOMAS ELLERY. Before ALEXANDER PARRIS. JACOB MOTTE, Register.

Book H, p. 189　　　　　　THOMAS DIXSON, bricklayer, & MARY his wife, to
11 & 12 July 1727　　　　NICHOLAS HAYNES, vintner, all of Charleston,
L & R　　　　　　　　　　SC, for ₤ 208 current SC money part of town
　　　　　　　　　　　　　lot #115 fronting 40 ft. on Tradd Street; running 100 ft. back; S on THOMAS HOLTON; W on JOHN SMITH; E on part of same lot. Witnesses: WILLIAM DIXCE, JOHN CROFT. Before DANIEL GREENE. JACOB MOTTE, Register.

Book H, p. 192　　　　　　NICHOLAS HAYNES, vintner, & MARTHA his wife to
9 & 10 Apr. 1729　　　　　STEPHEN MILLER, mariner, all of Charleston, SC
L & R　　　　　　　　　　for ₤ 260 current SC money part of town lot
　　　　　　　　　　　　　#115 fronting 40 ft. on Tradd Street, running backwards 100 ft., bounding S on THOMAS HOLTON; E on part of same lot; W on JOHN SMITH, pilot. Witnesses: JOHN CROFT, EDWARD CROFT. Before DANIEL GREENE. JACOB MOTTE, Register.

Book H, p. 195　　　　　　BENJAMIN WARING, of Berkeley Co., SC, to
18 & 19 July 1727　　　　GEORGE SMITH, for ₤ 125, 500 a. English mea-
L & R　　　　　　　　　　sure. Whereas the Lords Proprs. of SC granted
　　　　　　　　　　　　　ROBERT DANIEL a Landgrave's patent with 48,000 a.; & whereas ROBERT DANIEL sold several parcels of land to Landgrave THOMAS SMITH including 1 tract of 500 a. on W side Wincaw River bounding NE on Wincaw River; SE on GEORGE SMITH; NW on EDWARD HYRNE; & whereas Landgrave THOMAS SMITH on 20 Feb. 1718/9 sold the 500 a. to BENJAMIN WARING; now WARING sells to GEORGE SMITH. Witnesses: GEORGE SMITH, THOMAS SMITH, JR., HUGH WENTWORTH. Before TWEEDIE SOMERVILLE. JACOB MOTTE, Register.

Book H, p. 197　　　　　　JACOB TAYLOR, yeoman, of Concord, Co. of Mid-
16 Oct. 1729　　　　　　　dlesex, Province of Massachusetts Bay, New
Letter of Attorney　　　 England, only surviving brother of ISAAC TAY-
　　　　　　　　　　　　　LOR, planter, of Ponpon, St. Paul's Parish, SC
appointed his trusty friend ROBERT LEWIS, mariner, of Charleston, SC, his attorney, to handle the estate in SC left by ISAAC TAYLOR. Witnesses: RICHARD HOLMES, EDWARD BARBOUR, WILLIAM FARR. Before DANIEL GREENE. JACOB MOTTE, Register.

Book H, p. 198　　　　　　JOHN RAVEN, JR., planter, for love & affection
6 June 1729　　　　　　　 to THOMAS LADSON & SARAH his wife 350 a. in SC
Deed of Gift　　　　　　 adjoining lands of MAJOR WILLIAM ALLEN & ABRA-
　　　　　　　　　　　　　HAM WAIGHT, JR. Delivery by turf & twig.
Witnesses: HUGH HEXT, GEORGE HEXT, FRANCIS HEXT, JOHN STANYORNE. Before JOHN FENWICKE. JACOB MOTTE, Register.

Book H, p. 198　　　　　　WILLIAM FLECKNOWE, planter, & MARY (her mark)
25 & 26 Mar. 1728　　　　his wife, to SAMUEL UNDERWOOD, all of St.
L & R　　　　　　　　　　Paul's Parish, Colleton Co., SC, for ₤ 300;
　　　　　　　　　　　　　100 a. on Wadmalaw Island, Colleton Co., bounding S on THOMAS GABLE; N on JAMES YONGE from whom WILLIAM FLECKNOWE purchased the land; E on SAMUEL JONES; W on HENRY WALKER (formerly WILLIAM FLECKNOWE). Witnesses: JOHN ROPER, THOMAS ELLERY. Before ALEXANDER PARRIS. JACOB MOTTE, Register.

Book H, p. 202　　　　　　　THOMAS CARTER, heir & administrator to estate
3 Sept. 1729　　　　　　　　of ANN LUDLAM widow, (mother of THOMAS CARTER)
R & Power of Attorney　　　of SC, to CAPT. JAMES OMER, of London, for
　　　　　　　　　　　　　　good causes & considerations to all the real &
personal estate, (lands, tenements, slaves, etc.) left him by his mother,
ANN LUDLAM; THOMAS CARTER appointing JAMES OMER his attorney. Witnesses:
FRANCIS BRAMHAM, HENRY MAY. On 17 Dec. 1729 FRANCIS BRAMHAM, Chief Mate,
& HENRY MAY, mariner, belonging to the ship True Love riding at SC appeared before CHARLES HART. JACOB MOTTE, Register.

Book H, p. 204　　　　　　　WILLIAM WHIPPY, planter, of Colleton Co., SC,
29 Apr. 1728　　　　　　　　for love & affection of his brother JOSEPH, of
Deed of Gift　　　　　　　　same place, 200 a. (part of tract of 430 a.)
　　　　　　　　　　　　　　with the proviso that the land shall be sold
to no one but said WILLIAM WHIPPY; should JOSEPH die without issue, the
land to go to a brother, ROBERT WHIPPY. Witnesses: TIMOTHY HENDRICK,
THOMAS SACHEVERELL, JAMES COCHRAN. Before DANIEL GREENE. JACOB MOTTE,
Register.

Book H, p. 205　　　　　　　WILLIAM WHIPPY, planter, of Colleton Co., to
29 Apr. 1728　　　　　　　　his brother ROBERT WHIPPY of same parish, for
Deed of Gift　　　　　　　　love & affection 230 a. on a neck of land on
　　　　　　　　　　　　　　Edisto Island provided ROBERT sells to no one
but WILLIAM. Witnesses: TIMOTHY HENDRECK, THOMAS SACHEVERILL, JAMES
COCHARN. Before DANIEL GREENE. JACOB MOTTE, Register.

Book H, p. 206　　　　　　　ROBERT TAYLOR & WILLIAM GREENLAND, gentlemen,
7 Nov. 1729　　　　　　　　 of Berkeley Co., SC, to RENE MARCHAND for ₺ 36,
Deed of Sale　　　　　　　　current SC money, 210 a. called White Hall,
　　　　　　　　　　　　　　bounding N on JAMES TELLERS; E on HENRY RUS-
SELL; S on Fairlawn Barony; W on MARY VERDITY. Whereas JOHN MILLES,
planter, owned several tracts of land in Berkeley Co., & by will dated
17 Jan. 1728/9 recorded in the secretary's office appointed ROBERT TAYLOR
& WILLIAM GREENLAND his executors with power to sell all or any part of
his lands, now TAYLOR & GREENLAND sell to MARCHAND. Witnesses: ALEXANDER
KINLOCH, CATHERINE BETTESON. Before DANIEL GREENE. JACOB MOTTE, Register.

Book H, p. 209　　　　　　　SARAH BEAMOR, widow, attorney for BENJAMIN
20 Jan. 1723　　　　　　　　PERRIMAN, Indian trader, to ROBERT MCKELVIN,
Deed of Sale　　　　　　　　planter, all of Berkeley Co., SC, for ₺ 200 SC
　　　　　　　　　　　　　　money, 180 a. bounding NE on Landgrave THOMAS
SMITH; SE on JOHN PERRIMAN; SW on CHARLES GRADY; NW on MR. STEAD. (Livery & seizin by turf & twig). Witnesses: JOHN BARTON, BENJAMIN DENNIS.
Before THOMAS BARTON. JACOB MOTTE, Register.

Book H. p. 211　　　　　　　MARY BANKS, to CHARLES BURNHAM, executor of
24 Dec. 1720　　　　　　　　the will of CHARLES BURNHAM, his father, all
Deed of Sale　　　　　　　　of St. Philip's Parish, Charleston, for ₺ 30
　　　　　　　　　　　　　　currency 2 a. bounding S on part of the tract
on which CHARLES BURNHAM the son lives; E on JAMES MCLOUGHLIN; N on MRS.
PARTRIDGE; W on the Broad Path leading from Charleston to the Quarter
House. Witnesses: MARTHA HUNT, THOMAS BENNETT. Before TWEEDIE SOMER-
VILLE. JACOB MOTTE, Register.

Book H, p. 212　　　　　　　JOSEPH BOONE, ESQ. of Charleston to his only
5 June 1729　　　　　　　　 son THOMAS BOONE, for natural love & affection
Deed of Gift　　　　　　　　& other causes, 500 a. in Colleton Co. on W
　　　　　　　　　　　　　　side S Edisto River; bounding NW on JOSEPH
BOONE; NE on WILLIAM BULL; SE on vacant land; SW on MOSES MARTIN & WIL-
LIAM BULL. Witnesses: ANTHONY MATHEWS, PAUL JENYS, THOMAS BEDON. Before
DANIEL GREENE. JACOB MOTTE, Register.

Book H, p. 213　　　　　　　THOMAS BOONE, to CHARLESWORTH GLOVER, gentle-
7 Nov. 1729　　　　　　　　 man of St. George's Parish, for ₺ 1000 current
Deed of Sale　　　　　　　　SC money, 500 a. in Colleton Co., granted to
　　　　　　　　　　　　　　JOSEPH BOONE & given by him to his son THOMAS,
on W side S Edisto River bounding NW on JOSEPH BOONE; NE on WILLIAM BULL;
SE on vacant land; W on MOSES MARTIN & WILLIAM BULL. Witnesses: LAWRENCE
BUTTERWORTH, WILSON SANDERS, MARY FOSTER. Before DANIEL GREENE. JACOB

MOTTE, Register.

Book H, p. 215 JOSEPH BOONE, ESQ. of Berkeley Co. to CHARLES-
15 Dec. 1729   WORTH GLOVER, gentleman, of St. George's Par-
Deed of Sale   ish, for ₤ 1000 current money, 500 a. in Col-
                leton Co. on W side S Edisto River, bounding N
on COL. WILLIAM BULL; NW on THOMAS JONES; W on BRYAN KELLY; SW on JOHN
GODFREY; SW on MOSES MARTIN; SE on land sold CHARLESWORTH GLOVER by THOM-
AS BOONE (formerly JOSEPH BOONE'S). Witnesses: ANTHONY MATHEWS, SR.,
JAMES MATHEWS. Before DANIEL GREENE. JACOB MOTTE, Register.

Book H, p. 216 DAVID DURHAM, gentleman, to his God daughter
21 June 1719   CATHERINE CHICKEN, daughter of COL. GEORGE
Deed of Gift   CHICKEN, ESQ. all of Berkeley Co., for good
                will & affection & other considerations, 270 a.
surveyed in the time of the Hon. CHARLES CRAVEN, ESQ., Gov. of SC; DAVID
DURHAM to have the use of the land during his life; after his death to
his heirs; afterwards to CATHERINE CHICKEN. Witnesses: JOHN OULDFIELD,
SR., DANIEL HUNT. Before JAMES KINLOCK. JACOB MOTTE, Register.

Book H, p. 218 JOHN HALE, son of JOHN HALE, planter, to THOM-
23 Sept. 1729   AS BOONE, planter, all of Berkeley Co., 500 a.
Mortgage   & 6 Negroes. Whereas THOMAS BOONE & JOHN HALE,
                JR. gave bond to DANIEL GREENE on 14 Aug. 1729
in penal sum of ₤ 2000 currency for JOHN HALE'S keeping certain articles
of an agreement dated 14 Aug. (made between DANIEL GREENE, administrator
for JOHN HALE, SR. of the 1 part & JOHN HALE, JR. & ANDREW QUELCH who had
married ELIZABETH the daughter of JOHN HALE, SR., of the other part); &
whereas THOMAS BOONE, with JOHN HALE, JR., became bound on 14 Aug. 1729
to DANIEL GREENE in certain arbitration bonds of ₤ 2000 penalty for JOHN
HALE'S abiding by an award to be made by CHARLES HILL & CAPT. OTHNIELE
BEALE, indifferently named, elected & chosen for JOHN HALE & ANDREW
QUELCH as well as for DANIEL GREENE; now JOHN HALE, in consideration of
THOMAS BOONE'S becoming bound with JOHN HALE, & to secure BOONE from suit,
& for 10 sh. paid HALE by BOONE, confirms BOONE in his possession (sale
dated 22 Sept. 1728 of 500 a.) & HALE delivers to BOONE 6 Negroes. Wit-
nesses: JOHN BRUCE, CHARLES PINCKNEY. Before DANIEL GREENE. JACOB MOTTE,
Register. This mortgage satisfied 17 Apr. 1739; signed by THOMAS BOONE.
Witness: ROBERT AUSTIN.

Book H, p. 221 ALEXANDER TRENCH, of Charleston, merchant, at-
4 & 5 Dec. 1729 torney for JOHN BAYLY of Ballinaclough, Co. of
L & R   Tipperary, Ireland, son & heir of JOHN BAYLY,
                to ANTHONY WHITE, planter, of Prince George's
Parish for ₤ 103 current SC money, 412 a. in Craven Co. part of 48,000 a.
granted JOHN BAYLY, SR. by letters patent bounding NW on JOHN LANE (LANCE);
S on JOHN THOMSON; NE on ANTHONY WHITE. Whereas the Rt. Hon. JOHN EARL
OF BATH, Palatine, & the Lords Proprs. by letters patent on 16 Aug. 1698
created JOHN BAYLY, the father, a Landgrave, giving him 48,000 a. of land;
& whereas JOHN BAYLY, the son & heir, on 9 Nov. 1722, appointed ALEXANDER
TRENCH his attorney with power to sell all or part of the 48,000 a. (re-
serving 8,000 a.); now TRENCH sells 412 a. to WHITE. Witnesses: JOHN WAT-
SON, JOHN ARNOLL, JA. DICKSONS. Before TWEEDIE SOMERVILLE. JACOB MOTTE,
Register.

Book H, p. 227 WILLIAM RUSSELL, felt maker, & ABIGAIL, his
15 Oct. 1729   wife, to JOHN SANDIFORD, felt maker, for ₤ 123
Deed of Sale   current SC money 25 a. on James Island which
                RUSSELL purchased 10 June 1729 from JOHN
HEARNE for ₤ 4 current SC money; bounding N on JOHN HYRNE (HEARNE); S on
THOMAS ROSES CHILD (formerly JAMES WITTER); E on JOHN SANDIFORD. Witnesses: JOHN WITTER, JOSEPH ATWELL, BENJAMIN ATWELL, JAMES SCREVEN. Before DANIEL GREENE. JACOB MOTTE, Register.

Book H, p. 229 JOSEPH DANFORD, fisherman & MARGARET his wife
4 Apr. 1727   to SOLOMON MIDDLETON, mariner, for ₤ 400 cur-
Deed of Sale   rent SC money, part of lot #222 of Charleston,
                on W side of Charleston, fronting 28 ft. to
the E, where SOLOMON MIDDLETON now lives, being part of the lot which JO-
SEPH DANFORD purchased from THOMAS HOLTON. MARGARET DANFORD voluntarily

released all her claim. Witnesses: JAMES LAURENS, MARY CARTWRIGHT, WIL-
LIAM SMITH, Register. Before CHARLES HILL. JACOB MOTTE, Register.

Book H, p. 231   NICHOLAS MAYRANT, gentleman, to SAMUEL PRIO-
20 & 21 July 1720   LEAU, ESQ., both of Berkeley Co., for Ł 200
L & R   current SC money lot #26 in Charleston, 30 ft.
                              & 62 ft., bounding W on a cross street; S on
MAJ. THOMAS HEPWORTH; N on CHARLES FRANCHOOME, ESQ.; E on THOMAS HOWARD.
Witness: HENRY GRGNILLIATT. Before JOHN WRIGHT. JACOB MOTTE, Register.

Book H, p. 234   JOHN BAYLY, ESQ., of Ballinaclough, Co. of Tip-
1 & 2 Dec. 1727   perary, Ireland, son & heir of JOHN BAYLY, &
L & R   ALEXANDER TRENCH, merchant, of Charleston, SC,
                              attorney for JOHN BAYLY, JR., to NOAH SERRE,
planter, of Craven Co., for Ł 125 current SC money 500 a. in Craven Co.
on N side of Santee River bounding N on JAMES NICHOLAS MAYRANT; E on JOHN
BELL; S & W on vacant land; whereas the Rt. Hon. JOHN, EARL OF BATH, &
the Lords Proprs. by letters patent on 16 Aug. 1698, created JOHN BAYLY,
SR., Landgrave & granted him 48,000 a. of land; & whereas JOHN BAYLY, son
& heir, on 9 Nov. 1722 appointed ALEXANDER TRENCH his attorney with power
to sell any part thereof (reserving 8000 a. for BAYLY); now TRENCH sells
500 a. to NOAH SERRE. Witnesses: HENRY GIGNILLIATT, GABRIEL MARION, JOHN
CROFT. Before DANIEL GREENE. JACOB MOTTE, Register.

Book H, p. 238   SAMUEL PRIOLEAU, jeweller & MARY MAGDALENE his
22 & 23 Oct. 1729   wife, of Charleston, to DANIEL HUGER, of St.
L & R   John's Parish, Berkeley Co., for Ł 700 current
                              SC money, part of lot #26 fronting westwardly
on cross street 30 ft.; S 62 ft. on JAMES KILPATRICK, formerly MAJ. THOM-
AS HEPWORTH; N on part of same lot; E on JOHN RAVEN. Witnesses: ROBERT
HUME, JOHN HORRY, ANDREW DEVEAUX, JR. Before JACOB BOND. JACOB MOTTE,
Register.

Book H, p. 242   SAMUEL PRIOLEAU, jeweler, & MARY MAGDALEN of
23 Oct. 1729   Charleston, being under bond to DANIEL HUGER,
Mortgage   ESQ. of St. John's Parish, Berkeley Co., in
                              the sum of Ł 700 SC money, confirm HUGER in
his possession of the premises by L & R 22 & 23 Oct. 1729 (see p. 238).
Witnesses: ROBERT HUME, JOHN HORRY, ANDRES DEVEAUX, JR.

Book H, p. 243   MARY MAGDALEN DUPOIDSDOR, widow, to CHARLES
22 & 23 Jan. 1729   BEE, gentleman, both of Charleston, for Ł 3500
L & R   current SC money lot #42 in Charleston bound-
                              ing E, on a cross street that leads up to the
church; W on ROBERT HUME; N on JOHN GARNIER; S on the broad street. Witnesses: JOHN SMITH, FRANCIS SUREAU, HENRY HARGRAVE. Before ALEXANDER
PARRIS. JACOB MOTTE, Register.

Book H, p. 247   JOHN LENOIR, ESQ. of St. Michael, Barbados, to
17 & 18 Mar. 1725   GILES COOK (COOKE) gentleman, of the same town
L & R   for Ł 350 current Barbados money 710 a. called
                              Lynch Grove Plantation, on Wando Neck, Berke-
ley Co., SC., bounding E on JOHN HOLLYBUSH; S on JOHN BROWN & JOHN BURK;
W on WILLIAM WHITE; N on JOHN HOLLYBUSH. Witnesses: JOSEPH COBB, ROBERT
LYDON, GILES COOKE, JR. Before JOHN WRIGHT. JACOB MOTTE, Register.

Book H, p. 252   ANNE HEPWORTH, widow, to STEPHEN MONEIR, shop-
7 & 8 Oct. 1729   keeper, both of Charleston, for Ł 2000 current
L & R   SC money 1/4 part of lot #16 in Charleston;
                              fronting 25 ft. on the bay; W on an alley;
also part of a low water lot 25 ft. wide bounding N on MRS. MARY BLAMYER;
S on part of same lot belonging to JOHN MOORE, ESQ. (formerly MRS. MARY
NARY). Witnesses: JOHN BONNIN, JOHN CROFT. Before DANIEL GREENE. JACOB
MOTTE, Register.

Book H, p. 256   The Hon. ALEXANDER SKENE, ESQ., & JEMIMA, his
15 & 16 Jan. 1729   wife, to CHARLES HILL, ESQ., both of Charles-
L & R   ton for Ł 308 current SC money; 44 a., part of
                              a larger tract purchased by SKENE from SAMUEL
WRAGG, merchant, of London, being part of Ashley Barony & St. Giles

bounding NE on Ashley River; NW on the broad path leading to Dorchester new bridge; SE on SAMUEL WRAGG.

See previous pages how Ashley Barony & St. Giles (12,000 a.) was conveyed by the Rt. Hon. LORD ASHLEY, Earl of Shaftsbury conveyed to his grandson ANTHONY by him to his brother MAURICE; by him to SAMUEL WRAGG; 3000 a. by WRAGG to ALEXANDER SKENE; now 44 a. by SKENE to HILL. SKENE promises that his wife, JEMIMA, shall on 16 Apr. next appear before the Chief Justice & quit claim all her dower. Witnesses: HENRY HARGRAVE, BENJAMIN WHITAKER. Witnesses to receipt: BENJAMIN WHITAKER, THOMAS LAROCHE. Before JOHN WRIGHT. JACOB MOTTE, Register.

Book H, p. 261
17 Feb. 1729/30
Mortgage

JOHN KITCHEN, planter, & ELIZABETH his wife bound to MATHEW BEARD, planter, all of Berkeley Co., SC, in penal sum of Ł 200 current SC money conditioned for the payment of Ł 200 with interest on 1 Mar. 1731/2 & for security assign to BEARD 56 a. bounding N on JOSEPH BRUNSON; S on MATHEW BEARD; W on CHARLES DISTANCE; also several slaves. Before A. SKENE. JACOB MOTTE, Register.

Book H, p. 262
20 & 21 Sept. 1723
L & R

ANDREW DEVEAUX, planter, & ANNE, his wife, of Berkeley Co. to JOHN GARNIER, barber, of Charleston, for Ł 1500 current SC money, 2 tracts of land; 1 being 200 a., English measure, called Westpenny on W side of Old Town Creek, now occupied by ANDREW DEVEAUX; bounding E & SE on Old Town Creek; S part on CHARLES HILL (formerly CAPT. JOHN CODFREY) & part on vacant land; W on vacant land; N on ANDREW DEVEAUX (formerly JAMES LESADE); the other being 250 a., English measure, occupied by ANDREW & ANNE DEVEAUX, part of Old Town plantation which formerly belonged to JAMES LESADE & given by him by will to his daughter ANNE, then wife of JOHN GIRRARDEAU now wife of ANDREW DEVEAUX; bounding E on Westpenny Creek; N on PETER LESADE; SW on CAPT. RICHARD GODFREY; S on ANDREW & ANNE DEVEAUX. Witnesses: JOHN BROWN, JOHN CORBETT, PETER TAYLOR. Before JOHN WRIGHT. JACOB MOTTE, Register.

Book H, p. 268
7 & 8 Oct. 1723
L & R

JOHN GARNIER, barber, & MAGDALEINE his wife, of Charleston, to ANDREW DEVEAUX, planter, & ANNE his wife, of Berkeley Co., for Ł 1500 current SC money, the same 2 tracts of land (200 a. & 250 a.) which he had purchased from ANDREW DEVEAUX on 21 Sept. 1723. Witnesses: JOHN BRETON, PETER TAYLOR. Before JOHN WRIGHT. JACOB MOTTE, Register.

Book H, p. 275
24 & 25 Feb. 1729
L & R

RICHARD ROWE, gentleman, of Charleston, to JOHN HERRING, ESQ., of Middlesex Co., England, for Ł 100 English money sterling, the southernmost third part of the half part of lot #15 in Charleston. Whereas JOHN MOORE, gentleman, of Berkeley Co., SC, by deed of feoffment 5 June 1719, sold to RICHARD ROWE the southern part of lot #12 in Charleston, bounding N on the other 2/3 of same lot; E on the bay & Cooper River; S on a "house belonging to his then wife but now to RICHARD ROWE"; W on a neighborhood alley; & whereas RICHARD ROWE on this date became bound to JOHN HERRING in penal sum of Ł 200 English money sterling conditioned for the payment of Ł 100 like sterling, with interest, on 25 Feb. 1730; now, to secure payment, ROWE releases to HERRING 1/3 of a 1/2 town lot #15 in Charleston. Witnesses: ANTHONY HUGGETT, BENJAMIN WHITAKER. Before DANIEL GREENE. JACOB MOTTE, Register.

Book H, p. 280
19 & 20 Jan. 1729
L & R

JOHN GODFREY, planter, & MARY his wife, of Colleton Co., to SARAH WOODWARD, widow, of Berkeley Co., for Ł 1850 current SC money; 700 a. in Colleton Co., being part of 1055 a. laid out by FRANCIS YONGE, ESQ., Survyr. Gen. & granted by the Lords Proprs. to JOHN BAYLY, of the Kingdom of Ireland; devised by him to his son JOHN BAYLY; sold by ALEXANDER TRENCH, attorney & agent of JOHN BAYLY, the son, to JOHN GODFREY; bounding N on RALPH EMMA; S part on MANLEY WILLIAMSON, part on RICHARD GODFREY, part on WILLIAM TREDWELL BULL; E on part of same land; W on JONATHAN FITCH. Witnesses: THOMAS STANYARNE, SAMUEL SCREVEN, JOHN BURENS. Witnesses to receipt: THOMAS STANYARNE, ELIZABETH WRIGHT. Before JOHN WRIGHT. JACOB MOTTE, Register.

Book H, p. 284   JOHN GODFREY, planter, of Colleton Co., to
20 Jan. 1729   SARAH WOODWARD, widow of Berkeley Co., in the
Bond   penal sum of L 1850 current SC money. Whereas
                         by L & R, 19 & 20 Jan. 1729 JOHN GODFREY &
MARY his wife sold SARAH WOODWARD, widow, for L 1850 current SC money,
700 a. of land (see above); JOHN & MARY GODFREY give bond for the true
performance of the conditions of the release. Witnesses: THOMAS STAN-
YARNE, SAMUEL SCREVEN, JOHN BURENS. Before JOHN WRIGHT. JACOB MOTTE,
Register.

Book H, p. 285   TIMOTHY HENDRICK, planter, to HUGH BRYAN, car-
26 & 27 Jan. 1725   penter, both of Colleton Co., for L 151 cur-
L & R   rent SC money, 250 a., (part of a tract of
                         land purchased by CAPT. WILLIAM MAGOTT from
JOHN ASH, part of which tract CAPT. MAGOTT sold to JEREMIAH CLARKE on 7
June 1720; & JEREMIAH CLARK conveyed the 250 a. to TIMOTHY HENDRICK on 6
May 1724); bounding S & W on a swamp on Ponpon River; N on JOHN SMELIE; E
on COL. JOHN PALMER. Witnesses: JOHN SMELIE, JAMES SMITH, ELIZABETH
SMELIE. Before CHRISTOPHER WILKINSON. By JACOB MOTTE, Register.

Book H, p. 288   SUSANNAH WIGINGTON, widow, formerly wife of
16 Mar. 1721   EDWARD RAWLINGS & daughter of MARY CROSS, to
Exchange of Real Estate ROBERT HUME, gentleman, both of Charleston; &
                         HUME to SUSANNAH. Whereas SUSANNAH WIGINGTON
owns the westernmost third part of the northernmost half part of 3 town
lots (formerly devised by MARY CROSS to her daughters MARY BASDEN & SUS-
ANNAH RAWLINGS; & whereas ROBERT HUME owns the other 2/3 of the northermost half part of the said 3 town lots; & whereas it is agreed between
SUSANNAH WIGINGTON & ROBERT HUME that the westermost half part of the 3
town lots shall be conveyed to ROBERT HUME & the easterrmost half part of
the said 2/3 parts of the northermost half part of the half of the 3 town
lots shall be conveyed to SUSANNAH WIGINGTON; now, in pursuance of this
agreement, & for L 5 currency paid to SUSANNAH by ROBERT HUME, SUSANNAH
WIGINGTON gives ROBERT HUME the westermost 1/3 of the northermost 1/2
part of the 3 lots, bounding E on other part of the 3 lots; S on MRS.
MANIGAULT; N on a street running E from Cooper River; on a street running
N & S; & ROBERT HUME, in pursuance of the agreement, & for L 5 paid him
by SUSANNAH, gives SUSANNAH the easterrmost half part of his 2/3 parts of
the northermost 1/2 part of the 3 town lots; bounding W on other part of
the northermost half part of the 3 lots; E on MR. JACKSON; N on a street
running W from Cooper River; S on MR. MANIGAULT. Witnesses: MARY BLAMYER,
CHILDERMUS CROFT. Before TWEEDIE SOMERVILLE. JACOB MOTTE, Register.

Book H, p. 290   JOHN CATTELL, planter, & SARAH, his wife
28 & 29 Nov. 1729   (daughter of ARTHUR HALL, ESQ. of Berkeley Co.)
L & R   to COL. ARTHUR HALL & WILLIAM CATTELL, ESQ. of
                         Berkeley Co. on S side of
Ashley River; bounding N on Ashley River; on all other parts on WILLIAM
FULLER, FRANCIS LADSON, STEPHEN FOX & JOHN CATTELL. In consideration of
the marriage of JOHN & SARAH CATTELL, & to settle the plantation, & for
L 5 apiece paid to JOHN & SARAH by HALL WILLIAM CATTELL, JOHN & SARAH release to ARTHUR HALL & WILLIAM CATTELL, the 300 a., to the use of SARAH
during the term of her natural life & afterwards to her eldest son or
heirs. Witnesses: THOMAS SEABROOK, WILLIAM FERGUSON, NICHOLAS SMITH of
James Island. Before ALEXANDER PARRIS. JACOB MOTTE, Register.

Book H, p. 294   JAMES BULLOCK, merchant, & JANE his wife, late
13 Mar. 1709   of Willtown, now of Charleston, SC, to JOHN
Bond & Mortgage   HERRING, ESQ. of Gov. Street near New Bond
                         Street, London, for L 500 Mexico & Peru silver
coin; 3 tracts of land. Whereas JAMES BULLOCK gave bond this date to
JOHN HERRING for L 500 English money conditioned for payment of 937 oz.
tenpeny weight of Mexico & Peru silver coin with interest on 13 Mar. 1730,
now JAMES & JANE BULLOCK for the L 500 & to secure payment sold HERRING 3
tracts of land; 400 a. in Colleton Co.; bounding W on JOHN PEACOM; on all
other sides on vacant land; having such shape as specified in the plat
annexed to the grant of the Lords Proprs. dated 6 May 1704; also 200 a.
in Colleton Co. on NE side of S Colleton River; bounding W on EBENEZER
WALCUT; S on MATHEW BEE; N & E on land vacant when surveyed; having such
shape as specified in the plat attached to grant from Lords Proprs. dated

23 July 1711; also 100 a. in Colleton Co. on E side Ponpon River, bounding S on MATHEW BEE; on all other sides by land vacant when surveyed; having such shape as specified in plat attached to grant from Lords Proprs. dated 23 July 1711. BULLOCK also sells HERRING 12 Negro slaves. Witnesses: MEECHEN, WILLIAM LIVINGSTON. Before DANIEL GREENE. JACOB MOTTE, Register.

Book H, p. 298　　　　URIAH EDWARDS, blacksmith, & REBECCA his wife,
9 & 10 Feb. 1727　　　of Berkeley Co., to DANIEL STEWART, carpenter,
L & R　　　　　　　　of Dorchester, Berkeley Co., for L 230 current
　　　　　　　　　　　SC money the 14th lot in the 1st range of the
1st division of lots in Dorchester, containing 50 a., bounding E on JOHN STEVEN'S heirs; S on Ashley River; W on JOHN GORTON & on the broad path; in width 4 rods, running along by GORTON'S line about 60 rods then crossing the 14th lot with a gradual descent & to the N on the line between the 1st & 2nd range. REBECCA signed voluntarily. Witnesses: THOMAS SNOW, HANNAH SNOW, JOHN CONNYER. Before ALEXANDER SKENE. JACOB MOTTE, Register.

Book H, p. 301　　　　JOSEPH BLAKE, planter, to THOMAS GADSDEN, both
9 Feb. 1729　　　　　of Berkeley Co., for L 80 current SC money 2 a.
Bill of Sale　　　　　bounding W on CAPT. GADSDEN; on all other
　　　　　　　　　　　sides on JOSEPH BLAKE; being part of 210 a.
granted by the Lords Proprs. to COL. GEORGE LOGAN on 19 Jan. 1699. Witnesses: MARY WALKER, WALTER BURN. Before DANIEL GREENE. JACOB MOTTE, Register.

Book H, p. 302　　　　JOSEPH BLAKE, planter, to THOMAS GADSDEN, gen-
26 June 1729　　　　　tleman, both of Berkeley Co., for L 1300 cur-
Bill of Sale　　　　　rent SC money, 65 a. on Charleston Neck, bound-
　　　　　　　　　　　ing N on ROBERT CARTWRIGHT; E on COL. JOSEPH
BLAKE; S on WILLIAM SMITH; W on Ashley River marsh; being part of 190 a. granted by the Lords Proprs. on 2 Mar. 1701 to PATRICK SCOTT, planter. Witnesses: EDWARD WEEKLY, WILLIAM WEEKLY, DANIEL CARTWRIGHT, JOHN BAYLY. Before DANIEL GREENE. JACOB MOTTE, Register.

Book H, p. 304　　　　JOHN BAYLY, ESQ., son & heir of JOHN BAYLY of
5 & 6 Nov. 1729　　　Ballinaclough, Co. of Tipperary, Ireland, by
L & R　　　　　　　　his attorney ALEXANDER TRENCH, merchant, of
　　　　　　　　　　　Charleston, to THOMAS GADSDEN, gentleman, of
Berkeley Co., for L 1500 current SC money, 30 a. of marsh land. Whereas the Rt. Hon. JOHN EARL OF BATH & the Proprs. by letters patents on 16 Aug. 1798 made JOHN BAYLY, the father, Landgrave & Cassique, granting him 48,000 a. of land; & whereas, JOHN BAYLY, son & heir, on 9 Nov. 1722 appointed ALEXANDER TRENCH his attorney with power to sell the land after reserving 8,000 a. for BAYLY'S use; & whereas the lands were laid out; now TRENCH sells GADSDEN 30 a. of marsh, part inclosed in the land of THOMAS GADSDEN the other part fronting on a creek from Ashley River; bounding SW on MR. SMITH'S land as by a marked tree live oak 3x; & to the N on ROBERT CARTWRIGHT as by a marked tree live oak 3x. Witnesses: JAMES NEALE, WALTER BURN. Before DANIEL GREENE. JACOB MOTTE, Register.

Book H, p. 306　　　　JONATHAN DRAKE, hatmaker, & MARY his wife, to
3 Nov. 1724　　　　　JOHN WITTER, cooper, 68 a. for L 280 current
Bill of Sale　　　　　SC money. Whereas the Hon. JAMES MOORE, ESQ.,
　　　　　　　　　　　Gov., EDMUND BELLINGER, & JOSEPH MORTON, ESQ.,
by commission dated 16 Aug. 1698 authorized to sell & grant lands, for L 1:8 sh. current SC money granted JONATHAN DRAKE 70 a., English measure, in Berkeley Co.; on James Island, Berkeley, bounding NE on EDWARD DRAKE; SW on JOHN WITTER (formerly JOHN ELLIS) & partly on CAPT. DENNIS (formerly JOHN CLOP); NW on said DENNIN (formerly said CLOP); SE on land laid out to PETER HEARNE, now possessed by JAMES WITTER (see plat by JAMES WITTER, surveyor, dated 20 Apr. 1699). Now JONATHAN & MARY DRAKE sell the 70 a. (excepting 2 a. on the NW corner of the tract which has been appointed for a Meeting house for the Presbyterian Society to worship God). Witnesses to JONATHAN'S signature: JOHN HEARNE, SAMUEL DRAKE, PETER HEARNE. Witnesses to MARY'S signature: THOMAS WESBORY, WILLIAM DRAKE. Before DANIEL GREENE. JACOB MOTTE, Register.

Book H, p. 309　　　　REBECCA FLAVEL, widow to JOHN NEWFUILLE

27 & 28 Apr. 1730		(NEUFVILLE?), wine cooper, both of Charleston,
L & R		Berkeley Co., for Ł 500 current SC money part

27 & 28 Apr. 1730   (NEUFVILLE?), wine cooper, both of Charleston,
L & R   Berkeley Co., for Ł 500 current SC money part of town lot #38 fronting 24 on a public alley that joins Broad Street, running 52 ft. W; bounding E on the alley; S on a part of the lot belonging to MRS. REBECCA FLAVELL, now occupied by ANNE MORGAN; N on part of a lot belonging to MR. THOMAS BOWLING & occupied by MR. ROBERT JOHNSTON; W on land belonging to REBECCA FLAVEL. Witnesses: ISAAC MAZYCK, JR., ABRAHAM CROFT, JOHN CROFT. Before DANIEL GREENE. JACOB MOTTE, Register.

Book H, p. 312   SAMUEL FLAVEL to REBECCA FLAVEL, widow, for
24 Feb. 1721   Ł 1000 current SC money part of a half lot #28,
Release   in Charleston. Whereas JOHN FLAVEL, mariner, of Charleston, by will dated 11 Oct. 1710 gave his son, the above SAMUEL, part of a half lot #38 which he had purchased from THOMAS WYCH, citizen & apothecary of London, that is to say, his part to contain 25 ft. fronting the great street leading from Cooper River to the market place & going N on a straight line 25 ft. wide to the end of the said half part of the lot, which part was bounding S on the great street; E on CAPT. EDWARD LOUGHTON between whom & the half part of the lot is a public alley; N on COL. LYNCH (formerly THOMAS SUMMERS & previously MAJOR GEORGE EVANS), occupied by NATHANIEL WILLIAMSON, merchant; W on another part of the half lot; together with a messuage or tenement on the lot occupied by a MRS. CARTER, widow (formerly by ZEBULON CARTER, mariner). Witnesses: SAMUEL SMITH, WILLIAM FLAVELL. Before BENJAMIN WHITAKER. JACOB MOTTE, Register.

Book H, p. 315   COL. ROBERT DANIEL, SR. & MARTHA his wife to
28 Mar. 1715   RICHARD CODNER, both of Berkeley Co., for
Deed of Sale   Ł 250 current SC money, & other considerations, 172 a. on THOMAS'S Island in 2 tracts; 1 part being 62 a. known as Brady's Island, alias St. Iagoes Island; the other part being 110 a. bounding N on Watcoe Creek; E on JOHN DUNCAN; S on ISAAC LESESNE; W on Watcoe Creek. Whereas the said ROBERT DANIEL purchased from the Lords Proprs. 172 a. in 2 plats annexed to 2 grants, 1 under the hand of the Hon. ROBERT GIBBES, ESQ., Gov., the other under the hands of JOHN ARCHDALE, ESQ., Gov., situated on Thomas's Island. MARTHA DANIEL freely yields to CODNER all her title of dower. Witnesses: ISAAC LESESNE, CHARLES BURNHAM, JUDITH (her mark) DANIEL, ELIZABETH (her mark) LESESNE. 28 Dec. 1717, DANIEL appoints ISAAC LESESNE, planter, his attorney to deliver possession & seizin. Witnesses: W. BLAKEWEY, FRANCIS YONGE. Witnesses to delivery: RICHARD SINGLETARY, THOMAS VALLEY, SOLOMON GUMBERS. Before THOMAS COOPER 5 May 1730. JACOB MOTTE, Register.

Book H, p. 317   RICHARD CODNER, gentleman, & SABINA his wife
17 July 1717   for various cause & considerations especially
Deed of Gift   for the love he bears his 2 Godsons, WILLIAM & BENJAMIN STEWART (alias) BURNHAM, sons of MRS. ELIZABETH STEWART) & for 5 sh. gives BRADY'S or St. Lagoes Island (62 a.) to BENJAMIN STEWART, but if he should die without issue then to CHARLES STEWART, his brother (son of ELIZABETH); & gives the 110 a. to WILLIAM, but should WILLIAM die without issue then to BENJAMIN, & in case of failure of BENJAMIN then to his brother CHARLES. RICHARD CODNER had purchased this land from the Hon. COL. ROBERT DANIEL. Should MRS. ELIZABETH STEWART, now absent from SC, return unmarried she shall enjoy BRADY'S or St. Iagoes Island only during the time she remains single. SABINA CODNER wife of RICHARD, freely yields all her title of dower. Witnesses: ISAAC LESESNE, JOHN (his mark) ST. MARTIN, ELIZABETH ROSE. On 5 May 1730 ISAAC LESESNE declared he saw RICHARD & SABINA CODNER deliver this deed to RICHARD SINGLETARY (?). Before THOMAS COOPER. JACOB MOTTE, Register.

Book H, p. 319   THOMAS BACON, of St. George's Parish, to WIL-
2 Dec. 1729   LIAM BULL, ROBERT LADSON, EDWARD PERRY, WIL-
Deed of Sale   LIAM ELLIOTT (son of JOHN ELLIOTTO, RICHARD BAKER, JOSEPH BACON, JOHN BAKER, THOMAS BAKER, SAMUEL STEVENS, & BENJAMIN PERRY, 2 a. in Berkeley Co. on S side Ashley River, in St. George's Parish; bounding NE on Ashley River; SE on a road leading to the bridge called Stevens or Bacons bridge; SW & NW on THOMAS BACON. Witnesses: PETER PERRY, WILLIAM STEVENS. Before WILLIAM CATTELL. JACOB MOTTE, Register.

Book H, p. 320   JOHN RIDLEY, planter & UNITY, his wife, of
13 Aug. 1729   Craven Co., to the Rev. MR. THOMAS MERRITT,
Lease   Rector of Prince George Parish, Craven Co.,
                        for ₤ 200 currency, 500 a., part of 1,000 a.
sold to JOHN RIDLEY by the Hon. Landgrave THOMAS SMITH, ESQ.; bounding S
on Sampeate (Sampit ?) or Town River; E on Canaan Creek; N & W on part of
the 1,000 a. now in possession of NATHANIEL FORD, shipwright. Witnesses:
ANTHONY ATKINSON, DANIEL MCGINNE, MATHEW QUASH. Before MEREDITH HUGHES.
JACOB MOTTE, Register.

Book H, p. 324   JOHN RIDLEY, planter, & UNITY his wife, of
13 Aug. 1729   Craven Co., to the Rev. MR. THOMAS MORRITT,
Lease   Rector of Prince George's Parish, Winyah, Cra-
                        ven Co., for ₤ 245 current SC money, 250 a.,
bounding N on Black River; E on the parsonage land of Prince George's
Parish; S on vacant land; also 100 a. W of the 250 a., laid out to RIDLEY
by the Dep. of the Surveyor General, but not yet purchased. Witnesses:
ANTHONY ATKINSON, DANIEL MCGINNE, MATHEW QUASH. Before MEREDITH HUGHES.
JACOB MOTTE, Register.

Book H, p. 327   THOMAS JONES, planter, & ELIZABETH (her mark)
10 & 11 Sept. 1728   his wife, to JOHN MACTEER, planter, all of
L & R   Colleton Co., for ₤ 425 current SC money, 300
                        a. on SW side of PonPon River, Colleton Co.,
bounding N on WILSON SANDERS (SAUNDERS); W on vacant land; all other
sides on THOMAS JONES; being part of 738 a. purchased by JONES from STE-
PHEN MON, ESQ., Cassique, by deeds 10 & 11 Aug. 1723. Witnesses: JOHN
PUNNETT, JAMES MARTIN, JOHN JONES. Before J. FERGUSON. JACOB MOTTE,
Register.

Book H, p. 330   THOMAS JONES, planter, to JOHN MACTEER, both
11 May 1730   Colleton Co., in penal sum of ₤ 2000 current
Bond   SC money. Whereas THOMAS JONES by L & R dated
                        10 & 11 Sept. 1728 sold JOHN MACTEER, for
₤ 450 current SC money, 300 a. on Ponpon, Colleton Co., adjoining the
land where THOMAS JONES lives, JONES now gives bond to secure the land to
MACTEER against all claims. Witnesses: JAMES FERGUSON, JOSHUA SANDERS,
WILLIAM SANDERS. Before WILLIAM CATTELL. JACOB MOTTE, Register.

Book H, p. 331   Between ALEXANDER SKENE, ESQ. & MRS. ISABEL
6 May 1728   PALMER, widow, both of Berkeley Co. Whereas a
Agreement   marriage is intended to be solemnized between
                        JOHN SKENE, ESQ., son of ALEXANDER SKENE, &
MRS. HANNAH PALMER, granddaughter of ISABEL PALMER; & whereas ROBERT PAL-
MER, mariner, of Charleston, by will dated 19 Feb. 1724 directed that all
his estate should be equally divided & distributed between his mother
ISABEL PALMER, & his 4 children, HANNAH, ROBERT, JOHN & JOSEPH PALMER,
share & share alike, & that should any of his children die before reaching 21 that part should be distributed equally among the survivors; &
whereas 2 of the children, ROBERT & JOSEPH died; & whereas the estate of
ROBERT PALMER at the time of his death consisted chiefly of outstanding
debts, goods, merchandises, & effects in foreign parts so that no certain
estimate can be made, but to the intent that a sufficient settlement may
be made for HANNAH, it is mutually agreed between ALEXANDER SKENE & ISA-
BEL PALMER that so soon as HANNAH'S portion of her father's estate is
paid to JOHN SKENE, ALEXANDER SKENE shall settle so much land or so many
Negroes & other slaves as shall equal in value her share which JOHN SKENE
shall receive in right of his intended wife in trust to ISABEL PALMER.
Witnesses: JAMES MACALPIN, BENJAMIN WHITAKER. "Rec'd. the full contents
of the within articles except 105 pounds 11 sh. & 3 pence sterling.
Stepe'd. by Mr. SAML. WRAGG, merchant, in London & yet unsettled rec'd.
pr. me J. SKENE". Before DANIEL GREENE. JACOB MOTTE, Register.

Book H, p. 332   JOSEPH BOONE, gentleman, JOSEPH MACKEY, car-
21 May 1730   penter, both of Berkeley Co., for ₤ 500 cur-
Deed of Sale   rent SC money, 250 a. in Colleton Co., on the
                        W side of S Edisto River; bounding N on JOSEPH
DIDCOTT; W on THOMAS ELLIOTT; S on EDWARD RIPPEN; E on JOSEPH BOONE. Wit-
nesses: SAMUEL EVELEIGH, JAMES MATHEWES. Before DANIEL GREENE. JACOB
MOTTE, Register.

Book H, p. 334   ANTHONY BONNEAU, cooper for natural love &
19 June 1697   affection to his daughter MARY BONNEAU & for
Deed of Gift   other motives 1 ful third part of town lot #39
                            in Charleston, granted ANTHONY BONNEAU by WIL-
LIAM EARL OF CRAVEN, Palatine & the Lords Proprs. 11 June 1694, 19 ft.
front, 104 ft. deep; bounding N on WILLIAM CAPERS (formerly WILLIAM POP-
PELL); E & W on another part of same lot; N on WILLIAM MARSHALL (formerly
THOMAS NOBEL). Witnesses: NO ROYER, DANIEL BONALLE, PETER LASALL. Be- ??
fore JAMES MOORE. JACOB MOTTE, Register.

Book H, p. 335   CHRISTOPHER JARRARD (JANARD) (JARAND), butcher,
24 Nov. 1698   to JOHN BURKLEY, merchant, both of Berkeley Co.
Bill of Sale   for Ł 85: 15 sh. sterling, part of a lot of
                            land formerly belonging to CAPT. CHARLES BAS-
DEN & purchased by CHRISTOPHER JARAND from CAPT. JOHN EMPEROR, containing
40 ft.; on the street running from the wharf on bank to JOSEPH HODGES;
bounding W on the street running by WILLIAM CHAPMAN; S on the lot of RICH-
ARD CAPERS; E on CAPT. CHARLES BASDEN; also 3 Negro men; conditioned for
the payment by JARRAND on 24 May 1698 to BUCKLEY, at Charleston, the sum
of Ł 85:15 sh. according to his bond of even date. Witnesses: CHARLES
BASDEN, PHILIPS BUCKLEY, WILLIAM BULL. Livery seizen given by turf &
twig. Before ROBERT DANIEL on 29 Nov. 1699. Registered 29 May 1730 by
JACOB MOTTE.

Book H, p. 337   ALEXANDER DELONGUEMARE, of Berkeley Co., to
2 & 3 Dec. 1725   JOHN FRAZIER, merchant, of Charleston, for
L & R   Ł 700 current SC money, part of lot #39 in
                            Charleston 22 ft. by 104 ft, fronting E on a
street, S & W on JOHN BULLOCK; N on WILLIAM CAPERS. Witnesses: JOHN
LAURENS, JOHN CROFT. Before JOSEPH WRAGG. JACOB MOTTE, Register.

Book H, p. 339   JOHN MOORE, gentleman, to HENRY PERONNEAU, mer-
18 & 19 May 1730   chant, both of Charleston, for Ł 1349:15 sh.
Mortgage   current SC money, 1/2 part of lot #16 in
                            Charleston formerly devised by MARY CROSS in
her will to her daughter MARY BASDEN, widow, fronting 50 ft. on the bay;
S on WILLIAM RHETT; N on other part same lot belonging STEPHEN MILLER; W
on an alley leading from the broad street. It is agreed that if MOORE
pays PERONNEAU Ł 1349:15 sh. on 19 May 1731 this mortgage to be void.
Witnesses: JOHN BROWN, CHARLES PERONNEAU. Before DANIEL GREENE. JACOB
MOTTE, Register.

DEEDS BOOK "I"
1730-1731

Book I, p. 1   MARK (his mark) SLOMAN, planter, formerly of
22 & 23 May 1730   St. Christopher's Island, now of Berkeley Co.,
L & R   SC, & JOHN SLOMAN (son of said MARK) to JOHN
                            WILLETT, of St. Christopher's Island, for
Ł 200 money of Great Britain, 20 a. in Christ Church Parish (alias Nicho-
las Town Parish) on St. Christopher's Island, bounding E on GEORGE TAYLOR;
W on a gut & EDMUND AKERS; S on the upper common path; lately occupied by
JOHN VANDERPOOLE. Witnesses: JOHN BRYAN, WILLIAM MACKEY, DANIEL MCGRIG-
OR. Before CHARLES HILL. JACOB MOTTE, Register.

Book I, p. 5   JOSEPH LEA, shipwright, & ISABELL (her mark)
8 & 9 Oct. 1729   his wife, to JOHN FRAIZER, merchant, of
L & R   Charleston, for Ł 1300 SC money, part of lot
                            #73 in Charleston, bounding N 40 ft. on the
street leading to the bay; W 103 ft. on the street running by WILLIAM
CHAPMAN; S on RICHARD CAPERS; E on the widow PARTRIDGE (formerly CHARLES
BASDEN). Witnesses: MARK OLIVER, ALEXANDER STEWART, HENRY HARGRAVE. Before CHARLES HILL, J.P. JACOB MOTTE, Register.

Book I, p. 11   ISAAC TAYLOR, of Colleton Co., to loving son-
13 June 1715   in-law EBENEZER WALCUTT, for good will & af-
Deed of Gift   fection, 200 a., bounding N on ISAAC TAYLOR;
                            E on vacant land; SW on a creek of Edisto

River. Witnesses: ALEXANDER GARRAN, JAMES FULTON. Before JOHN PALMER. JACOB MOTTE, Register.

Book I, p. 12 ROBERT BREWTON, merchant, & MELICENT his wife,
4 & 5 Jan. 1722 to JOHN FRAZIER, merchant, both of Charleston,
L & R for ₤ 500 SC money, that messuage or tenement
where ROBERT BREWTON lives, & the little piece of ground behind it, being part of lot #39, bounding N 16 ft. on a street parallel with Cooper River; W on MARY BULLOCK, widow of JOHN BULLOCK; E 33 ft. on New Church Street. Witnesses: JOHN BALLANTINE, JAMES BALLANTINE, THOMAS HEPWORTH. Before CHARLES HILL, J.P. JACOB MOTTE, Register.

Book I, p. 16 THOMAS BENNETT, tailor, of Christ Church Par-
25 Apr. 1730 ish as attorney for JOHN GIVENS, to CHARLES
Deed of Sale HILL, merchant, of Charleston, for ₤ 400 cur-
rency, 100 a. in Berkeley Co. on the head of Wackendaw, bounding E on PETER FRY; N on schoolhouse grounds; S on PHILIP JONES. Whereas JOHN GIVENS, at the Two Brothers Cabbage Inlet, on N side Cape Fear River, NC, on 14 Mar. 1729 appointed THOMAS BENNETT his attorney to sell his lands in SC, now BENNETT sells to HILL. Witnesses: HENRY HARGRAVE, THOMAS LAROCHE. Before TWEEDIE SOMERVILLE, J.P. JACOB MOTTE, Register.

Book I, p. 20 THOMAS BENNETT, tailor, of Christ Church Par-
25 Apr. 1730 ish, attorney for JOHN GIVENS, to CHARLES HILL,
Deed of Sale merchant, of Charleston, for ₤ 200 currency
part of lot #250 in Charleston, bounding W on THOMAS BOONE; E 50 ft. on JOHN EALIS; N on MADAM SARAH FENWICK; S on a little street leading to the new arch made over the creek by MILES BREWTON'S saw house. Whereas JOHN GIVENS, at the Two Brothers Cabbage Inlet, on N side Cape Fear River, NC, on 14 Mar. 1729 appointed THOMAS BENNETT his attorney to sell his lands in SC, now BENNETT sells to HILL. Witnesses: HENRY HARGRAVE, THOMAS LAROCHE. Before TWEEDIE SOMERVILLE, J.P. JACOB MOTTE, Register.

Book I, p. 23 ANNE HEPWORTH, widow, to ROBERT HUME, both of
10 & 11 June 1730 Charleston, for ₤ 645 currency, 70 a. in 2
L & R by Mortgage tracts on Charleston Neck where MRS. SARAH
BEAMOR lived; 1 tract of 55 a. formerly granted to JOHN BIRD; the other 15 a. purchased by SIMON BALLANTINE from JOHN KING & JUDAH HOLLYBUSH. Whereas ROBERT HUME, for ANNE HEPWORTH'S debts, gave bond this date to JOHN FENWICK, JOSEPH WRAGG, PAUL JENYS, OTHNIELE BEALE, & THOMAS LAMBOLL, merchants of Charleston, in the penal sum of ₤ 1290 SC money conditioned for the payment of ₤ 645 currency on 11 Mar. 1730, now ANNE conveys to HUME 70 a. to secure payment. Witnesses: ED. RAWLINGS, STEPHEN DRAYTON. Before JOSEPH WRAGG. JACOB MOTTE, Register. Mortgage satisfied 23 Mar. 1731. Signed ROBERT HUME. JACOB MOTTE.

Book I, p. 29 DUNKIN (his mark) MCGREGORY, JOHN (his mark)
6 Jan. 1726/9 JUNE, & MARY (her mark) MCGREGORY convey to
Conveyance THOMAS WITTEN, of Berkeley Co., the plat &
grant for 500 a. in Berkeley Co., which belonged to HUGH CARRON, husband of MARTHA WILLIAMS, also the purchase recepit & all their claim to the land. Witnesses: EDWARD HOWE, ANN JUNE. Before DANIEL HUGER, J.P. JACOB MOTTE, Register.

Book I, p. 30 CHARLES HILL, merchant, & ELIZABETH his wife,
20 & 21 May 1730 to JAMES FOWLER, vintner, & MARTHA his wife,
L & R all of Charleston, for ₤ 3000 SC money, part
of lot #11 86 ft. by 22-1/2 ft., bounding S on a little nieghborhood street leading to DR. JOHN HUTCHINSON & CAPT. THOMAS HEPWORTH; N on FRANCIS HOLMES; E on LEWIS LAUSAE: W on MOSES WILSON; free from ELIZABETH'S dower. Witnesses: THOMAS FAIRCHILD, HENRY HARGRAVE. Before TWEEDIE SOMERVILLE, J.P. JACOB MOTTE, Register.

Book I, p. 36 JAMES FOWLER, vintner, & MARTHA his wife, to
22 May 1730 CHARLES HILL, merchant, all of Charleston, to
Mortgage secure payment of ₤ 2150 convey to HILL part
of lot #11, 86 ft. by 27-1/2 ft., bounding S on a little neighborhood street leading to DR. JOHN HUTCHINSON & CAPT.

THOMAS HEPWORTH; N on FRANCIS HOLMES; E on LEWIS LAUSAC; W on MOSES WILSON. Whereas JAMES FOWLER this date gave 2 bonds to CHARLES HILL, 1 in the penal sum of ₤ 2100 currency conditioned for the payment of ₤ 1050 like money on 22 Nov. next, the other for ₤ 2200 payable 22 May 1731, now FOWLER gives part of lot #11 as security. Witnesses: JAMES FOWLER, MARTHA FOWLER, CHARLES HILL. Before TWEEDIE SOMERVILLE, J.P. JACOB MOTTE, Register. Mortgage satisfied Apr. 1732.

Book I, 38
21 Sept. 1727
Deed of Sale

JOHN DUBOSE, planter, & SUSANNAH his wife, of Craven Co., to JAMES BREMAR, planter of Berkeley Co., for ₤ 800 SC money, 305 a., English measure in Berkeley Co., bounding N & E on JAMES BREMAR; N on JACOB BONNEAU (formerly PETER VIDEAU; W on EDWARD DANERLY (formerly JOHN CARTOE); SW on FRANCIS PAGITT; SE on PETER BREMAR. Whereas his Excellency JOHN, Lord Granville, Palatine, & the Lords Proprs. on 5 May 1724 granted PETER POITEVINT 400 a., English measure on the E branch of Cooper River, bounding NW on JOHN CARTOE & on DR. DANIEL BREBANT (formerly JAMES BOURDEAUX) & on SOLOMON BREMAR; NE on PETER POITEVINT & on DANIEL FRIZEDON & on SOLOMON BREMAR & on vacant land; SE on FREIZERAN (FRIZEDON), POITEVINT & vacant land; SW on FREIZEREN, FRANCIS PAGET, & PETER JOHNSON, SR., according to plat in possession of JAMES BREMAR; & whereas PETER POITEVINT in 1709 conveyed 305 a. to JAMES LEMONIER, carpenter, of Berkeley Co., bounding NW on JOHN CARTOE; & whereas LEMONIER bequeathed the 305 a. to his son & daughter SUSANNAH; & whereas JAMES LEMONIER, the heir, died & JOHN DUBOSE became sole heir by right of his wife SUSANNAH; now they sell to BREMAR, free from the dowry of SUSANAH. Witnesses: ROBERT HOW, JAMES ROBERT, ABRAHAM THOMAS. Witnesses to possession & delivery: FRANCIS MORINA, LOUIS PALMAVIN, ROBERT HOW. Before THOMAS LYNCH, J.P. JACOB MOTTE, Register.

Book I, p. 43
18 Dec. 1722
Agreement

JAMES BREMAR & PETER BREMAR, sons of SOLOMON BREMAR, of St. Thomas Parish, Berkeley Co., agree upon a plan to divide the property left them by their father as follows: whereas their father, SOLOMON BREMOR, bequeathed JAMES & PETER 3 parcels of land in St. Thomas Parish near the lands of MR. VIDEAU & MR. BEASEAU, 1 being 390 a. on which their father first settled & purchased from the Lords Proprs. in 1704 in the time of Gov. JOHNSTON; 1 being 365 a. which he purchased from the Lords Proprs. in 1706, also in the time of Gov. JOHNSTON; & 1 of 640 a. which he purchased from the Lords Proprs. 1710 & called Bull Head; & whereas SOLOMON willed that his sons should cast lots to determine who should have the first settled plantation & who should have Bull Head, & willed that they should share equally the plantation between Bull Head & the 1 purchased in 1706; now JAMES & PETER agree that whoever happens to get Bull Head shall also have the plantation lying between Bull Head & the 1 first settled (i.e. the 1 purchased in 1706); & whereas SOLOMON willed that the owner of Bull Head should have 1 Negro man more than the son who received the first settled place (if he lives thereon; if not, the Negro to be sold & the money divided among JAMES, PETER & their sister MARTHA); now JAMES & PETER give up their share of the Negra man to the 1 who gets Bull Head; they also agree to cast lots to decide who should have Bull Head & who should have the plantation purchased in 1704. Witnesses: D. TRESEVANT, NICHOLAS BOCHET, ISAAC TREZVANT, ROBERT CLYATT. Before ANTHONY BONNEAU, J.P. JACOB MOTTE, Register.

Book I, p. 46
18 Dec. 1722
Memorandum

NICHOLAS BOCHETT, ISAAC TREZEVANT & ROBERT CLYATT bear witness that on this date JAMES BREMAR & PETER BREMAR, sons of SOLOMON BREMAR, of St. Thomas Parish, drew lots to determine who should have Bull Head Plantation & who should have the plantation their father purchased in 1710, according to their father's will dated 13 Sept. 1720, & the lot fell to PETER to have Bullhead & PETER was content to let JAMES have the first settled plantation (i.e. the 1 purchased in 1704). JAMES gave PETER full & quite possession of both Bullhead & the interlying plantation, (i.e. the 1 purchased in 1706). Possession given each other by delivery of dirt & twig. Before ANTHONY BONNEAU, J.P. JACOB MOTTE, Register.

Book I, p. 48
18 Dec. 1722

PETER BREMAR, planter, to his brother JAMES BREMAR, both of St. Thomas Parish, in the sum

Bond of ℒ 2000 SC money, conditioned for keeping the above agreement (p. 46). Witnesses: D. TRESEVANT, NICHOLAS BOCHET, ISAAC TRESEVANT, ROBERT CLYATT. Before ANTHONY BONNEAU, J.P. JACOB MOTTE, Register.

Book I, p. 49
24 & 25 June 1729
L & R

THOMAS AKIN, planter (by his attorney ARCHIBALD HAMILTON, gentleman) & MARGARET his wife, to JAMES AKIN, gentleman, all of Berkeley Co., for ℒ 1000 currency, that 1/2 undivided part of several plantations containing 200 a.; 150 a.; & 320 a; (i.e. 670 a.) granted THOMAS AKIN, the father, & bequeathed by him to son THOMAS; also his interest in 55 a. granted JOHN AKIN & bounding N on PAUL TURQUET; S on Cooper River; S on THOMAS AKIN; W on Cooper River. Whereas WILLIAM, Earl of Craven, Palatine, & the Lords Proprs. under the hand of the Hon. THOMAS SMITH Landgrave, Gov. & Principal Trustee, PAUL GRIMBALL, JOSEPH BLAKE & RICHARD CONANT, Trustees for conveying land in SC, on 12 Sept. 1694. JONATHAN AMORY, gentleman, of Berkeley Co., 200 a, English measure, in Berkeley Co.; & whereas AMORY on 30 May 1695 by deed of feoffment conveyed the 200 a. to THOMAS AKIN, the elder, planter; & whereas, WILLIAM, Earl of Craven, Palatine, & the Lords Proprs. under the hand of the Hon. JOSEPH BLAKE, Gov., THOMAS CARY, JOSEPH MORTON, JAMES MORE, & WILLIAM HAWETT on 1 Sept. 1697 granted THOMAS AKIN, the elder, 150 a., English measure, in Berkeley Co.; & whereas his Excellency JOHN GRANVILLE & the Lords Proprs. under the hand of the Hon. NATHANIEL JOHNSON, Gov., NICHOLAS TROTT, JAMES MOORE, & JOB HOW on 18 Sept. 1703 granted THOMAS AKIN, the elder, 320 a., English measure, in Berkeley Co.; & whereas THOMAS AKIN the elder, on 7 June 1705 by will bequeathed to his son JOHN AKIN 1/3 part of his real estate & bequeathed to his other 2 sons, THOMAS & JAMES, the other 2/3; & whereas the Hon. COL. ROBERT DANIEL, Dep. Gov., & the Lords Proprs. on 25 May 1717 granted JOHN AKIN (son of THOMAS the elder) 55 a. in Berkeley Co., bounding N on PAUL TORQUET; S on Cooper River; E on THOMAS AKIN; W on Cooper River; & whereas JOHN AKIN on 17 Jan. 1721 by will bequeathed all his real & personal estate to his mother ELIZABETH AKIN for her lifetime then to be divided amongst his brothers & sisters as his mother saw fit; now THOMAS sells to JAMES AKIN. Witnesses: STEPHEN LEE, THOMAS VALLEY, GEORGE SMITH. Before ROBERT DANIELL, J.P. JACOB MOTTE, Register.

Book I, p. 59
22 May 1706
Deed of Sale

JOHN WILLIAMSON, cordwinder, of Colleton Co., to RALPH EMMS, SR., planter, 360 a., part of 1000 a., English measure, which JOHN, Lord Granville, Palatine, under the hand of NATHANIEL JOHNSON, Knight, Gov., Chief Trustee, & the rest of the Trustees, on 8 Feb. 1704 granted to JOHN WILLIAMSON. Witnesses: JACOB BEAMOUR, CALEB TOOMER, THOMAS ELLIOTT. Before DANIEL GREENE, J.P. JACOB MOTTE, Register.

Book I, p. 62
20 Apr. 1727
Deed of Sale

PETER STANLEY, son, heir & successor to EDWARD STANLEY, to JOHN NICHOLSON, planter, for good causes & valuable considerations & for 1 gold guinea, 62 a. in Berkeley Co. Whereas his Excellency WILLIAM, Earl of Craven, Palatine, & the Lords Proprs. on 8 Mar. 1706/7 impowered the Rt. Hon. Sir NATHANIEL JOHNSON, Knight, Gov., et., the Hon. NICHOLAS TROTT, THOMAS BROUGHTON, ROBERT GIBBS, HENRY NOBLE & JOHN ASHBY, or any 3 of them, to grant lands; & whereas the Rt. Hon. Sir NATHANIEL JOHNSON, Gov., & the Hon. COL. THOMAS BROUGHTON & ROBERT GIVVS granted FRANCIS WILLIAMS 1000 a. in Berkeley Co., bounding NW on Landgrave THOMAS COLLETON'S Barony; & whereas FRANCIS WILLIAMS sold to EDWARD STANLEY 62 a. (part of the 1000 a.); now PETER STANLEY conveys to JOHN NICHOLSON. Witnesses: DUNCAN (his mark) MCGREGORY, AMY STANLEY, MATT QUASH. Livery & seizin by turf & twig. Before ANTHONY BONNEAU, J.P. JACOB MOTTE, Register.

Book I, p. 64
18 & 19 July 1729
L & R

ELIZABETH (her mark) AKIN, widow, to JAMES AKIN, gentleman, both of Berkeley Co., for ℒ 400 currency, 2 tracts of 50 a. & 70 a. (120 a.) bounding as follows: the 50 a. bounding S on THOMAS LYNE; E on vacant land; N on HUGH FLING; W on Cooper River; the 70 a. bounding W on Cooper River; N on THOMAS AKIN & vacant land; E & S on vacant land. Whereas WILLIAM, Earl of Craven, Palatine & the

Lords Proprs. under the hands of the Hon. JOSEPH BLAKE, Gov., JAMES MOORE, JOSEPH MORTON, STEPHEN BULL & WILLIAM HAWETT on 2 Jan. 1697/8 granted HUGH FLING 50 a., English measure, in Berkeley Co.; & whereas his Excellency WILLIAM, Earl of Craven, Palatine, & the Lords Proprs. under the hand of the Hon. JOSEPH BLAKE, Gov., JAMES MOORE, JOSEPH MORTON, STEPHEN BULL, & WILLIAM HAWETT on 2 Jan. 1697/8 granted HUGH FLING 70 a., English measure, in Berkeley Co.; & by an Act of the Assembly ratified 25 Feb. 1714/15 his Excellency JOHN, Lord Carteret, Palatine, & the Lords Proprs., etc., vested the 2 tracts in ELIZABETH AKIN, widow (no conveyance having been made before his death by HUGH FLING to ELIZABETH); & whereas the Hon. COL. ROBERT DANIELL & the Lords Proprs. on 25 May 1717 granted JOHN AKIN, son of ELIZABETH AKIN, 55 a. in Berkeley Co.; & whereas JOHN AKIN by will dated 17 Jan. 1720/1 bequeathed all his real & personal estate to his mother ELIZABETH AKIN for her lifetime then to be divided among his brothers & sisters as his mother should think fit; now ELIZABETH sells the 2 tracts to JAMES AKIN. Witnesses: ARCHIBALD HAMILTON, GEORGE THREDCRAFT, JONATHAN SINGLETARY. Before ANTHONY BONNEAU, J.P. JACOB MOTTE, Register.

Book I, p. 74
17 May 1728
Deed of Sale

WILLIAM FISHBURN, tailor, to WILLIAM WELLS weaver, both of Berkeley Co., for L 100 currency, 13-1/4 a., 8 rods, lying on a 3 square at the upper end of Dorchester land, bounding S on JOHN STEVENS; NW on JOSEPH BLAKE (formerly Lady REBECCA ANTEL); E on NATHAN WHITE. Witnesses: JAMES BOGGS, JOHN (his mark) ELDERS. Before A. SKENE. JACOB MOTTE, Register.

Book I, p. 76
1 & 2 Sept. 1729
L & R

JOHN LLOYD, ESQ., & SARAH his wife, of Goosecreek; JEREMIAH RUSSELL, planter, & MARY his wife, of the Parish of St. Thomas; MARTHA MCGREGOR, widow; & ELIZABETH AKIN, spinster; all of Berkeley Co., (SARAH LLOYD, MARY RUSSELL, MARTHA MCGREGOR, & ELIZABETH AKIN being daughters of THOMAS AKIN, planter, & sisters of JOHN AKIN, son of THOMAS AKIN) to JAMES AKIN, planter, of the Parish of St. Thomas, for L 400 currency (i.e. L 100 paid to JOHN & SARAH LLOYD; L 100 paid to JEREMIAH & MARY RUSSELL; L 100 paid to MARTHA MCGREGOR; L 100 paid to ELIZABETH AKIN) all their interest in 1/2 part of the freehold estate of THOMAS AKIN the elder, bequeathed by him to JOHN AKIN, & by JOHN'S will bequeathed to them; also their interest in 55 a. purchased by JOHN from the Lords Proprs. Whereas WILLIAM, Earl of Craven, Palatine, & the Lords Proprs. under the hand of the Hon. THOMAS SMITH Landgrave, Gov. & Principal Trustee, PAUL GRIMBALL, JOSEPH BLAKE & RICHARD CONANT, Trustees for conveying land in SC, on 12 Sept. 1694 granted JONATHAN AMORY 200 a., English measure, in Berkeley Co.; & whereas AMORY by deed of feoffment on 13 Aug. 1695 conveyed the 200 a. to THOMAS AKIN the elder; & whereas WILLIAM, Earl of Craven, Palatine, & the Lords Proprs. under the hand of the Hon. JOSEPH BLAKE, Gov., THOMAS GARY, JOSEPH MORTON, JAMES MOORE, & WILLIAM HAWETT on 1 Sept. 1697 granted to THOMAS AKIN the elder 150 a., English measure; & whereas his Excellency JOHN, Lord Granville, Palatine, & the Lords Proprs. under the hand of the Hon. NATHANIEL JOHNSON, Gov., NICHOLAS TROTT, JAMES MOORE & JOB HOW on 18 Sept. 1703 granted THOMAS AKIN the elder 320 a., English measure; & whereas THOMAS AKIN the elder on 7 June 1705 by will bequeathed to his son JOHN 1/3 part of his real estate, giving his other 2 sons, THOMAS & JAMES, the other 2/3; & whereas the Hon. COL. ROBERT DANIELL, Dep. Gov. & the Lords Proprs. on 25 May 1717 granted JOHN AKIN (the son) 55 a. in Berkeley Co., bounding N on PAUL TORQUET; S on Cooper River; E on THOMAS AKIN; W on Cooper River; & whereas JOHN AKIN by will dated 17 Jan. 1720/21 bequeathed all his real & personal estate to his mother, ELIZABETH AKIN, for her lifetime, then to be divided among his brothers & sisters as she thought fit; & whereas ELIZABETH AKIN, widow, with the knowledge & consent of JOHN & SARAH LLOYD, JEREMIAH & MARY RUSSELL, MARTHA MCGREGOR, widow & ELIZABETH AKIN, spinster, on 19 July 1729 conveyed all her interest in son JOHN'S property to JAMES AKIN; now they convey to JAMES AKIN all their interest in JOHN AKIN'S third & their interest in the 55 a. Witnesses: ELIZABETH RUSSELL, JOSEPH RUSSELL, ABRAHAM GANGUME. Before ANTHONY BONNEAU, J.P. JACOB MOTTE, Register.

Book I, p. 88
8 June 1727
Release

JOHN METHRINGHAM, joiner, & MARY, his wife, to THOMAS BOONE, gentleman, all of Christ Church Parish, for L 300 SC money, lot #250 in

Charleston, bounding E on JOHN GEVINS; W 100 ft. English measure on a little street; N on MADAM SARAH FENWICKE; S 100 ft. on a little street leading to the new arch made over the creek by MILES BREWTON'S saw house. Witnesses: ARCHIBALD MACDOWELL, THOMAS GOREING, EBENEZER MALLERY. Before JACOB BOND, J.P. JACOB MOTTE, Register.

Book I, p. 92
11 & 12 Aug. 1730
L & R

JOHN BAYLY, of Ballinaclough, Co. of Tipperary, Ireland, by his attorney, ALEXANDER TRENCH of Charleston, to EDWARD THOMAS, planter, of St. John's Parish, Berkeley Co., for ₤ 65 currency, 270 a. in St. James Parish Goosecreek, bounding S on Landgrave THOMAS SMITH; N on MRS. DURHAM, widow. Whereas the Rt. JOHN, EARL OF BATH, & the Lords Proprs. by letters patents on 16 Aug. 1698 created JOHN BAYLY, the father, Landgrave & Cassique, granting him 48,000 a.; & whereas JOHN BAYLY, son & heir, on 9 Nov. 1722, appointed ALEXANDER TRENCH, merchant of Charleston, his attorney with authority to reserve 8000 a. for JOHN BAYLY'S use & dispose of the rest of the land; now TRENCH sells 270 a. to EDWARD THOMAS. Witnesses: JAMES NEALE, THOMAS ELLERY. Before ALEXANDER PARRIS, J.P. JACOB MOTTE, Register.

Book I, p. 97
6 & 7 Aug. 1730
L & R

DANIEL LAROCHE & THOMAS LAROCHE, planters, of Berkeley Co., to CATHERINE IOORE, of Charleston, for ₤ 1350 currency, a piece of land in Charleston 25 ft. front, 112 ft. deep, bounding E on LYDIA DURHAM; N on THOMAS ELLIOTT, SR., W on a neighborhood alley parallel with Cooper River. Witnesses: GUER. VANVELSEN, HENRY BEDON. Before CHARLES HILL, J.P. JACOB MOTTE, Register.

Book I, p. 103
8 & 9 Sept. 1730
L & R by Mortgage

THOMAS BARTON, of Charleston to JOHN VANDERHORST, planter, of Christ Church Parish, for ₤ 600 SC money, 450 a. English measure in Berkeley Co., on E side Dawtaw Creek, bounding W on Dawtaw Creek, marsh, & THEOPHILUS PATEY; E on 50 a. (part of 500 a. granted JOHN BOONE & by him sold to ITHAMAR WOODIN, planter); N on ROBERT FENWICK, merchant, & vacant land; S on vacant land. Whereas the Hon. JAMES MOORE, Gov., & the Lords Proprs., on 18 July 1701 granted JOHN BOONE 500 a. on E side Dawtaw Creek bounding W on Dawtaw Creek & marsh & on THEOPHILUS PATEY; E S & N on vacant land, as surveyed by JAMES WITTER; & whereas JOHN BOONE by deed of feofment on 11 Apr. 1702 conveyed all the land (450 a. English measure) then in his possession to THOMAS BARTON, merchant of Charleston, bounding W on Dawtaw Creek, marsh, & THEOPHILUS PATEY; E on ITHAMAR WOODIN, planter, N on ROBERT FENWICK, merchant, & vacant land; S on vacant land; now BARTON mortgages the land to VANDERHORST. Witnesses: WILLIAM SCOTT, JAMES FISHER. Before CHARLES HILL, J.P. JACOB MOTTE, Register.

Book I, p. 110
9 & 10 June 1730
L & R

JOHN GOUGH, gentleman, & MARY his wife, to GEORGE LEA, shipwright, of Charleston, for ₤ 500 currency, 2/3 of lot #51 in Charleston, bounding E 66 ft. 8 in. on Cooper River; W on Sir PETER COLLETON's Square; N 224 ft. on the other third part; S on lot #80; also, that piece of land before the 2/3 part of lot #51 extending down to low water mark. Witnesses: DOMINICK ROCHE, JACOB SATUR. Before DANIEL HUGER, J.P. JACOB MOTTE, Register.

Book I, p. 115
12 Aug. 1718
Deed of Sale

DR. DANIEL BREBANT, & MAGDALENE his wife, to FRANCIS PAGITT, planter, all of Berkeley Co., for ₤ 400 SC money, 2 plantations, 1 of 500 a., purchased from MARGARET POITEVINT, JUDITH D'BORDEAUX & ANTHONY D'BORDEAUX on 24 Feb. 1708/9 on S side Lynch's Creek & SE side of eastern branch of T of Cooper River, bounding NW on the creek, HENRY BIDEAU & DENNIS HAYES; SE on PETER POITEVINT; the other tract containing 26 a. bounding NE on Wisbow Creek; SW on the 500 a. in Berkeley Co., which their father JAMES D'BORDEAUX bequeathed them by will dated 19 Sept. 1699 & granted to DANIEL BREBANT on 24 Nov. 1709 by the Hon. Sir NATHANIEL JOHNSON, Knight, Gob., etc., THOMAS BROUGHTON & JOHN ASHBY; & whereas DANIEL BREBANT was on 14 Apr. 1710 granted 26 a., bounding NE on Wisbow Creek; SW on the 500 a.; NW on CHARLES HAYES; grant signed by EDWARD HUNT, THOMAS TURBEVILLE, ROBERT GIVVES, THOMAS BROUGHTON & ROBERT DANIELL (folio 295). MAGDELINE BREBANT voluntarily releases her claim. Witnesses: NICHOLAS LANGLAIS, PETER (PIERRE) NORMAND, FRANCIS (his mark) NEVEAU, JOSIAS JUNE, HENRY COFFARD, ROBERT CLYATT. Before DANIELL HUGER, J.P. JACOB MOTTE, Register.

Book I, p. 120
29 & 30 Jan. 1725
L & R

JOHN BAYLY, of Ballinaclough, Co. of Tipperary, Ireland (see page 92) by his attorney ALEXANDER TRENCH, merchant, of Charleston, to WILLIAM MARTIN, planter, of Colleton Co., for ₤ 260:5 SC money, 500 a. in Colleton Co., bounding N on JOHN NEWTON; E on MR. MOLLETION & JOSEPH BOONE; S on JOHN MARTIN; W on MR. HOWARD. Witnesses: THOMAS PINCKNEY, WILLIAM PINCKNEY, JOHN BROWN. Before JOHN WRIGHT, J.P. JACOB MOTTE, Register.

Book I, p. 125
21 & 22 Oct. 1730
L & R Tripartite

The Hon. NICHOLAS TROTT, ESQ., OF St. Philip's Parish, Charleston, & SARAH his wife (late SARAH RHETT, widow of WILLIAM RHETT) of the 1st part; the Rev. MR. ALEXANDER GARDEN, rector of the Parish, JOHN FENWICK & ELEAZER ALLEN (3 of the commissioners for finishing the New Brick Church in Charleston) of the 2nd part; & ROBERT BREWTON & JACOB MOTTE, (church wardens of St. Philip's Parish) of the 3rd part. The 3 commissioners (GARDEN, FENWICK & TROTT) for ₤ 400 SC money (& for 10 sh. paid by ROBERT BREWTON & JACOB MOTTE, purchased from NICHOLAS & SARAH TROTT, 1/3 of lot #192 in Charleston, being the middle 1/3 of the lot running from the street in front back to CAPT. HENRY SIMONDS; bounding S on 1/3 part & N on the other 1/3; E on the New Brick Church; W on HENRY SIMONDS; fronting 41-1/2 ft. English measure on the Brick Church & being 222 ft. from E to W. Whereas by Act of General Assembly ratified 17 Apr. 1725 impowering the commissioners of the New Brick Church in Charleston to purchase a lot (or lots) in Charleston for a churchyard (reciting that the church was nearing completion & it was absolutely necessary to purchase land for a burying place, & there was no land adjoining the church appropriated or purchased for a church yard); & whereas ALEXANDER GARDEN, JOHN FENWICK & ELEAZER ALLEN agreed with NICHOLAS TROTT & SARAH his wife for the purchase of 1/3 of a lot for ₤ 400 currency, now the purchase is completed. Witnesses: RICHARD ROWE, THOMAS BAKER, PETER HORRY, WILLIAM ROMSEY. Before ALEXANDER PARRIS, J.P. JACOB MOTTE, Register.

Book I, p. 133
31 Oct. 1730
Deed of Sale

JOHN DAVIS, planter, of Colleton Co., to WILLIAM PERRIMAN, of Berkeley Co., for ₤ 225 currency, 200 a. English measure in Colleton Co. Witnesses: THOMAS BOONE, ROBERT HIETT, JOHN JONES. Before TWEEDIE SOMERVILLE, J.P. JACOB MOTTE, Register.

Book I, p. 134
27 & 28 Oct. 1730
L & R by Mortgage

WILLIAM SCOTT, merchant, & SUSANAH his wife, of Charleston, to JAMES BERRIE, merchant, of Boston, for ₤ 500 SC money, 9 lots in Colleton Co. & 2 lots in Beaufort, 1 lot #43 in New London, bounding S on CAPT. THOMAS BRUCE'S lot #44; E on Fleet Street: N on CAPT. BRUCE'S lot #42; W on S Edisto River; 2 lot #68 in New London, being part of Kingston Square; bounding S on Chesly Road; E on lot #84; N on lot #67; W on Fleet Street; 3. lot #44 in New London, bounding S on land outside the town; E on Fleet Street; N on lot #43; W on S Edisto River; which 3 lots were separately granted on 17 May 1717 to CAPT. THOMAS BRUCE then a partner of WILLIAM SCOTT; 4. lot #81 in New London, on Marlborough Square, bounding N on Newport Street; E on Queen Street; S on WILLIAM SCOTT'S lot #82; W on lot #65; 5. lot #83 in New London in Kingston Square, New London, bounding N on Hatton St.; E on Queen St.; S on WILLIAM SCOTT'S lot #84; W on lot #67; 6. lot #84 in New London on Kingston Square, New London; bounding N on WILLIAM SCOTT'S lot #83; E on Queen St.; S on Chesly Road; W on lot #68; 7. lot #65 in New London, bounding N on Newport St.; E on lot #81; S on WILLIAM SCOTT'S lot #66; W on Fleet St.; S lot #66 in New London bounding N on lot #65; E on lot #82; S on Hatton St.; W on Fleet St.; 9. lot #67, in New London bounding N on Hatton St.; E on lot #83; S on lot #68; W on Fleet St.; all of which lots were granted to WILLIAM SCOTT by several warrants dated 5 June 1717; 10. also lot #13 in Beaufort, Granville Co., granted SCOTT on 23 July 1717, fronting S on the bay; W on lot #12; N on lot #43; E on lot #14; 11. & lot #114 in Beaufort granted SCOTT on 7 July 1717, bounding S on Port Royall St.; W on lot #113; N on lot #109; E on Johns St.; granted to SCOTT on 7 July

1717, bounding S on Port Royall St.; W on lot #113; N on lot #109; E on
Johns St.; granted to SCOTT on 7 1717; SUSANNAH to renounce her thirds &
dower before RICHARD ALLEN, C.J. Witnesses: JOHN MOULTRIE, ROWLAND
VAUGHN. Before TWEEDIE SOMERVILLE, J.P. JACOB MOTTE, Register.

Book I, p. 145   ROBERT SINCKLARE, planter, to PETER SAUNDERS,
30 June 1719   planter, both of Craven Co., for a competent
Deed of Sale   sum, 400 a. where SINCLARE lived. Witnesses:
                 MEREDITH HUGHES, JOHN NE SMITH. Before JOHN
WALLIS, J.P. JACOB MOTTE, Register.

Book I, p. 146   WILLIAM STEADS, gentleman, to SAMUEL MORRIS,
25 Mar. 1730   for rents & covenants agreed upon, leases or
Lease   farmlets for 5 years, for ₤ 50 currency yearly,
                 a piece of land bounding SE on RICHARD SPLATT;
& from an old Negro house or corn house to a large oak in the pasture;
thence N to a path by the woodside along the 2, 3, or 4 hickories on the
bank of Goosecreek; & to SW on WILLIAM STEAD & the broad path. Witnesses:
THOMAS HONAHAN, ELIZABETH (her mark) PEMBERTON. Before TWEEDIE SOMER-
VILLE, J.P. JACOB MOTTE, Register.

Book I, p. 148   JAMES AKIN, planter, to THOMAS HASELL, rector,
16 & 17 Nov. 1730 the Hon. THOMAS BROUGHTON (executor of will of
L & R by Mortgage RICHARD BERESFORD), RICHARD HARRIS, THOMAS PAG-
                  ITT, ROBERT STEWART, JOHN MOORE, JOHN DANIEL &
THOMAS BONNY, vestrymen, all of St. Thomas Parish, Berkeley Co., for
₤ 1200, & interest, several tracts making 845 a. Whereas RICHARD BERES-
FORD by will dated May 1715 bequeathed to his executor THOMAS BROUGHTON
until his son JOHN BERESFORD should come of age the residue of the yearly
profits of his real & personal estate in trust to be paid to the vestry
of St. Thomas Parish; 1/3 to the schoolmaster & 2/3 to support & educate
such poor children as should be sent there to school, etc.; or the money
to be placed out at interest; & whereas BROUGHTON has ₤ 1200 currency on
hand which he & the vestry have agreed to invest; & whereas JAMES AKIN
(see page 76 for full details) owns several tracts of land totaling 845
a.; now AKIN mortgages this land to the vestry. Witnesses: WILLIAM HODG-
KINSON, THOMAS ELLERY. Before ALEXANDER PARRIS, J.P. JACOB MOTTE, Register.   ALEXANDER GARDEN, Rector, declared mortgage fully paid 17 July
1754. Witness: WILLIAM HOPTON.

Book I, p. 160   WILLIAM WILKINS & SARAH his wife, to ZEBULON
27 Jan. 1729/30   GUY, 60 a. on S side of James Island, on Baths
Deed of Sale   Point, bounding W on MARIAN GONTELETT; S on a
                  marsh; N on a   ; the 60 a. to be run from
a N & S line, the western end joining on MRS. GANTLITT. Witnesses: WIL-
LIAM SPENCER, BENJAMIN STILES, WILLIAM ALLIN. Before TWEEDIE SOMERVILLE,
J.P. JACOB MOTTE, Register.

Book I, p. 162   THOMAS ELLIOTT, planter, to his son WILLIAM
5 Jan. 1720   ELLIOTT, for love & good will, 650 a. English
Deed of Gift   measure, at Winners, Colleton Co., an inland
                 plantation bounding S on RALPH EMMS; also 8
Negroes. Delivery by turf & twig. Should WILLIAM die without issue, the
land to return to THOMAS'S children. Witnesses: JOHN CHAPLIN, PHOEBE
CHAPLIN. JOHN CHAPLIN testified according to his profession. Before
JOHN PALMER, J.P. JACOB MOTTE, Register.

Book I, p. 163   JOHN RAPER, vintner, & CATHERINE his wife, to
11 & 12 Feb. 1727 THOMAS COOPER, gentleman, & ELEANA his wife,
L & R by Mortgage all of Charleston, for ₤ 1800 SC money, part
                  of lot #17 in Charleston occupied by COOPER,
fronting E 25 ft. on Cooper River & bounding S 70 ft. on RICHARD CODNER;
W on RICHARD CODNER; N on the 10 ft. neighborhood alley 5 ft. of which
belonged to ELEAZER ALLEN (formerly JONATHAN AMORY). Witnesses: BENJAMIN
WHITAKER, GEORGE BAMPFIELD. Before DANIEL GREENE, J.P. JACOB MOTTE,
Register.

Book I, p. 169   JOHN RAPER, vintner, gave bond to THOMAS COOP-
10 Feb. 1727   ER, gentleman both of Charleston, in the penal
Bond   sum of ₤ 1300 like money with interest on 1

Feb. 1730. Witnesses: BENJAMIN WHITAKER, GEORGE BAMPFIELD. Before DANIEL GREENE, J.P. JACOB MOTTE, Register.

Book I, p. 170 List of Bills of Exchange in various amounts
Jan. & Feb. 1729/30 drawn by Sir ALEXANDER CUMING (COMINGS), Baronet. To JAMES CROHATT on GEORGE MIDDLETON; to DAVID CROHATT on ALEXANDER IRVIN; to JOSEPH WRAGG on JOHN HERRING, ESQ.; to JAMES CROHATT on GEORGE MIDDLETON; to JOHN RAPER on HENRY TURNER; to MUNGO WELSH on JOHN PATTERSON; to JOHN RAPER on JOHN WHITE; to DAVID CROHATT on ALEXANDER IRVIN; to JAMES CROHATT on GEORGE MIDDLETON; ditto; to JOHN HERRING, ESQ.; to MR. GADSDEN on GEORGE MIDDLETON; to DAVID CROHATT on JOHN HERRING; to JOSEPH WYATT on JOHN HERRING; to JOHN RAPER, ditto; ditto; to JAMES CROHATT on GEORGE MIDDLETON.

Book I, p. 171 Credit balance DAVID CROHATT'S account due to
List of "Debts" Sir ALEXANDER COMINGE; RICHARD ROWE to JOHN HERRING; JAMES BULLOCK to ditto; BENJAMIN SCHENCKINGH to ditto; JOHN MAGGOTT to ditto; JACOB BOND to ditto; JAMES RIPAULT to ditto; WILLIAM ADDAMS to ditto; WILLIAM PINCKNEY to ditto; HENRY GIGNILLIATT to ditto; ELEAZER ALLEN to HELEN & CATHERINE SWINTON; JAMES KILPATRICK to Sir ALEXANDER CUMING; JAMES CROHATT & JAMES PAIN to ditto; MR. WEAVER to Sir ALEXANDER CUMING; MR. WRIGHT, etc. to MRS. SWINTON; STEPHEN LEYCRAFT to JOHN HERRING; JOHN ATCHINSON, etc. to ditto; ALEXANDER TRENCH to JAMES BRUCE; MR. WRIGHT to MRS. SWINTON; JOHN FIELD to Sir ALEXANDER CUMING; MR. MASSEY to Sir ALEXANDER CUMING; MR. CROFT to JOHN HERRING; JOHN LEWIS to Sir ALEXANDER CUMING; THOMAS HOLTON to JOHN HERRING; MR. MORTIMER to ditto; MR. LLOYD to JOHN HERRING; MARGARET GRANT to Sir ALEXANDER CUMING; WILSON SAUNDERS to MR. SWINTON; JOSEPH MACKEY to MRS. SWINTON; CAPT. FITCH bond to MRS. SWINTON, returned; town lot bought of some man; 5 slaves bought from CAPT. ARNOLD; 1 slave from CAPT. DOUGHLAS; 1 from JAMES CROHATT; island bought from MR. HILL; 19 Negroes from RAPER & THOMSON; a deduction for CAPT. FITCH; ALEXANDER SKENE'S bond to Sir ALEXANDER CUMING; JAMES GRAME, ditto; GEORGE BAMPFIELD, ditto; WILLIAM YEOMAN'S note; CAPT. GADSDEN; DANIEL HUNT, Indian trader's bond; JOHN RAPER'S note; HILL CROFT'S silver in the hands of JAMES CROHATT; DR. COOPER'S bond; MR. RAPER'S bond.

Book I, p. 172 Charleston, SC. ALEXANDER CUMING declares
Apr. 25, 1730 that the above bills amounting to ₤ 4355 sterling were drawn by him to be applied to the use of the persons mentioned & used the money loaned to several persons on different securities (bonds, judgments, mortgages, etc.) & bought lands, houses, Negroes, horses, etc., for their use, therefore these effects should be first liable; & thirdly he agrees that his half pay as captain on the Irish Establishment shall be liable; he also agrees that his coat works in Gloucestershire shall be liable. Witness: ALEXANDER STEWART. Before DANIEL GREEN, J.P. JACOB MOTTE, Register.

Book I, p. 174 WILLIAM FLAVEL, executor of will of GEORGE
27 June 1727 PETERSON, to JAMES GAY, planter, of Berkeley
Deed of Sale Co., for ₤ 100 SC money, a wooden house lately occupied by GEORGE PETERSON, now by MRS. ELIZABETH PETERSON, widow of GEORGE, which house stands on land belonging to JOHN PAMOR. Delivery of a key of the house in the name of the whole. Witnesses: WILLIAM DANIEL, CATHERINE DANIEL.

Book I, p. 175 JAMES GRAY, of St. John's Parish, Berkeley Co.,
25 Dec. 1730 to ALEXANDER MCBRIDE, for ₤ 100 currency, the
Deed of Sale above house (p. 174). Witnesses: ROBERT TAYLOR, WILLIAM SANDERS, JAMES TILLY. Before PETER DE ST. JULIEN, J.P. JACOB MOTTE, Register.

Book I, p. 176 FRANCIS LEBRASSEUR, merchant, & CATHERINE, his
29 July 1726 wife, of Berkeley Co., to THOMAS GADSDEN, gen-
Deed of Gift tleman, in trust for his daughter ELIZABETH GADSDEN (God-daughter of FRANCIS LEBRASSEUR) for love & esteem, effective after their death), a piece of land described below. Whereas CAPT. THOMAS GADSDEN this date conveyed to FRANCIS LEBRASSEUR a piece of land bounding S 240 ft. on MRS. SARAH RHETT'S pasture, W 104 ft. on his pasture N on his pasture; E on marsh of Cooper River.

Witnesses: JAMES PAINE, A. DELABASTIE. Before THOMAS BARTON, J.P. JACOB MOTTE, Register.

Book I, p. 179   The Hon. ALEXANDER SKENE, ESQ., to THOMAS GAD-
29 Apr. 1727   SDEN, ESQ., both of Berkeley Co., for ₤ 1400
Release   SC money, 300 a., part of Ashley Barony, bound-
ing NE & SW on ALEXANDER SKENE; NW on ROBERT WRIGHT; SW on ? GADSDEN to have convenient passage for themselves, their slaves & cattle through the back avenue which goes from Wampee Savanna to the high road on S side of Ashley River. Whereas the Lords Proprs. on 18 Mar. 1675 granted ANTHONY, Earl of Shaftsbury 12,000 a. commonly called Ashley Barony & St. Giles, which descended to his grandson the Rt. Hon. ANTHONY, Lord Ashley, Earl of Shaftsbury, also a Lords Proprs.; & whereas on 20 July 1698 for natural love & affection he gave his brother the Hon. MAURICE ASHLEY all his proprietorship, lands, & tenements in SC; & whereas MAURICE ASHLEY on 2 & 3 Aug. 1717 conveyed the Barony to SAMUEL on 5 & 6 Aug. 1720 sold 3000 a. (part of the 12,000 a.) to ALEXANDER SKENE; now SKENE sells 300 a. (part of 3,000 a.) to GADSDEN. Witnesses: PAUL VIART, BENJAMIN WHITAKER. Before DANIEL GREENE, J.P. JACOB MOTTE, Register.

Book I, p. 184   JAMES BOSWOOD, planter, & SINDINAH, his wife,
28 Sept. 1720   to well beloved son-in-law THOMAS MELL, cord-
Deed of Gift   winder, & MARY, his wife, all of Berkeley Co.,
for parental love & affection 117 a., part of 550 a. formerly belonging to the Rev. MR. WILLIAM LIVINGSTON; bounding E on CAPT. GRANT; S on JAMES BOSWOOD & JOHN STOCK; W & N on the remainder of the 550 a., plat dated 4 Dec. 1719. Witnesses: CHARLES LESLIE; ELIZABETH BOSWOOD, TOBIAS FITCH. Before RALPH IZARD, J.P. JACOB MOTTE, Register.

Book I, p. 187   JOSEPH BEECH, wheelwright, to WILLIAM NICHOL,
9 Sept. 1729   both of Berkeley Co., for certain value receiv-
Deed of Sale   ed & a certain sum of currency, 100 a. (1/3
part of 300 a.) boundins A on JOHN CUMINGS; E on JAMES BOISSO; N on PETER TAMPLETT (the remaining 200 a.); W on JOSEPH BEECH. Whereas CHRISTOPHER BEECH, SR., shipwright, of St. Thomas Parish, Berkeley Co., bequeathed certain tracts of land to his 3 eldest sons, RICHARD, CHRISTOPHER, & JOHN BEECH; & whereas he bequeathed to his third son, JOHN, 300 a.; & whereas RICHARD, CHRISTOPHER & JOHN died & JOSEPH BEECH (the youngest & only surviving son of CHRISTOPHER BEECH, SR., & heir of his brother JOHN); now JOSEPH sells 1/3 the 300 a. tract to NICHOL. Witnesses: JOHN CUMING, PETER TAMPLETT. Before ANTHONY BONNEAU, J.P. JACOB MOTTE, Register.

Book I, p. 190   PETER TAMPLETT, cordwinder, of St. Thomas Par-
11 Sept. 1729   ish, Berkeley Co., to JOHN CUMING, for ₤ 70
Deed of Sale   currency, 135 a., bounding S on JOHN CUMING; E
on JOHN BEECH; N on JOSEPH BEECH; W on Cooper River. Whereas MARY BEECH, widow of CHRISTOPHER BEECH, shipwright, during her widowhood purchased from JOSEPH BLAKE, her brother, 270 a. (deed of sale & plat being in possession of JOHN CUMING) & by will bequeathed the land to her 2 eldest daughters GRACE & CHRISTINA, to be equally divided between them; & whereas GRACE, the elder, married JOHN CUMING, & CHRISTINA (the 2nd daughter) married PETER TAMPLETT: & therefore CUMING & TAMPLETT became co-heirs; now TAMPLETT sells his half to CUMING. Witnesses: JOSEPH BEECH, JOHN (his mark) STRACHAN, ROBERT THOMSON, ELIZABETH (her mark) STRACHAN. Before ANTHONY BONNEAU, J.P. JACOB MOTTE, Register.

Book I, p. 193   RICHARD BAKER, to JOHN TENDEN, planter, both
21 Aug. 1730   of Colleton Co., in penal sum of ₤ 600 curren-
Bond & Mortgage   cy conditioned for the payment of ₤ 300 with
interest on 6 Jan. 1731/2 & for security conveys to TENDEN 100 a. (purchased from JOHN TENDEN & pricked off upon the plat of ISAAC WAIGHT). Witnesses: HENRY HODGKINS, THOMAS TATTNELL. Before DANIEL GREENE, J.P. JACOB MOTTE, Register.

Book I, p. 195   JOHN CATTELL (CATTLE), planter to ARTHUR HALL,
26 & 26 July 1730   both of Berkeley Co., for ₤ 853:6:8 SC money,
L & R by Mortgage   400 a., on inland plantation on SW side of Ashley River bounding NW on JOHN CATTELL; SE & S

on Mrs. ANN DRAYTON. Witnesses: THOMAS LAMBOLL, JOHN CROFT. Witnesses to receipt: JOHN CROFT, JOHN DART. Before DANIEL HUGER, J.P. JACOB MOTTE, Register.

Book I, p. 202 JOHN CATTELL (CATTLE), to ARTHUR HALL, ESQ.,
24 July 1730   both of Berkeley Co., in the penal sum of
Bond   ₤ 1706:13:4 currency conditioned for the pay-
               ment of ₤ 853:6:8 on 24 Mar. 1730 to JOHN FEN-
WICK, JOSEPH WRAGG, PAUL JENYS, OTHNIEL BEALE & THOMAS LAMBOLL; HALL (at the special request & for the proper debt of CATTELL) being found with CATTELL. Witnesses: THOMAS LAMBOLL, JOHN CROFT. Before DANIEL HUGER, J.P. JACOB MOTTE, Register.

Book I, p. 204   THOMAS AKIN, gentleman, of St. Thomas & St.
18 June 1729   Dennis Parish, Berkeley Co., appointed his
Letter of Attorney friend ARCHIBALD HAMILTON, gentleman, of the
                   same parish, his attorney with authority to
sell his plantation where he formerly dwelt, containing 335 a. on Cooper River & with the money so obtained to pay AKIN'S debts, etc.; THOMAS AKIN being on a journey to Cape Fear; the land to be free from the right of dower of wife MARGARET. Witnesses: DANIEL (his mark) MCDANIEL, AMEY STANLEY. Before DANIEL HUGER, J.P.

Book I, p. 206   MICHAEL BLACKWELL, blacksmith, of the Parish
15 June 1723   of St. Thomas & St. Dennis, Berkeley Co., to
Deed of Sale   PETER JOHNSON, SR., planter, for ₤ 2 SC money,
                 100 a. purchased from JOHN LAPIER, the French
minister, bounding on GEORGE JUNE & PETER DUTARTRE, lying in Parish of St. Thomas & St. Dennis on E side of Cooper River, within land; also 1 Negro woman & 1 Negro boy, both purchased from PETER POITEVINT, SR.; 1 Indian girl; & all his cattle, horses, working tools, household goods & all his substance of what kind, nature, or quality soever. Possession given by delivery of 1 oak twig with the dirt thereunto annexed & 1 Indian girl. Witnesses: JEREMIAH RUSSELL, PETER JOHNSON, JR., ROBERT CLYATT. Before ANTHONY BONNEAU, J.P. JACOB MOTTE, Register.

Book I, p. 208   EDWARD JASPER, ESQ. of Tower Hill, London, ap-
18 Dec. 1730   pointed MATHEW MORRIS, ESQ., Commander of HMS
Letter of Attorney the <u>Lowestoff</u> & JOHN GASCOIGNE, ESQ., Comman-
                   der of HMS the <u>Aldborough</u> his attorneys with
authority to buy & sell land & tenements in SC or elsewhere. Before THOMAS BOCKING, N.P. in London. Witnesses: BENJAMIN AUSTINE, JOHN GASCOIGNE. Witnesses to BOCKING'S authority in London: THOMAS BROWN, N.P., ARTHUR LONE BOWMAN, N.P. JACOB MOTTE, Register.

Book I, p. 211 The Rt. Hon. Sir NATHANIEL JOHNSON, Knight,
14 May 1707   Gov., Capt., Gen. & Admiral of S & NC & the
Conveyance   Lords Proprs. (NICHOLAS TROTT, THOMAS BROUGH-
                TON, & HENRY NOBLE) for ₤ 4 granted MATHEW BEE
200 a., English measure, in Colleton Co. in free & common soccage. On 29 Aug. 1709 MATHEW BEE sold the 200 a. for ₤ 12 to JOHN BEE. Witnesses: JOHN HAYES, SAMUEL LOWLE, JAMES FULTON. Before JAMES COCHRAN. JACOB MOTTE, Register.

Book I, p. 213   ALEXANDER PARRIS, ESQ. & MARY his wife, of
3 & 4 Mar. 1730   Charleston of the 1st part; JONAH COLLINS,
L & R Tripartite   planter, of Colleton Co., of the 2nd part; &
                     JOHN GASCOIGNE, ESQ. Captain of HMS of war the
<u>Aldborough</u> now in Charleston harbor, of the 3rd part. ALEXANDER PARRIS & MARY, his wife, & JONAH COLLINS (appointed by MARY COLLINS) for ₤ 480 SC money convey to JOHN GASCOIGNE 17 a. known as Hog Island. Whereas WILLIAM, Earl of Craven & the Lords Proprs. on 12 Sept. 1694 granted EDMUND BELLINGER, Landgrave, of Berkeley Co., 17 a., English measure, commonly called Hog Island, bounding N on Hog Island Creek; S on Sullivant's Creek; E & W on a marsh; & whereas on 23 Mar. 1708 ELIZABETH BELLINGER, widow of EDMUND, sold the 17 a. to ALEXANDER PARRIS; & whereas on 22 & 23 Jan. 1724 ALEXANDER PARRIS & MARY, his wife, conveyed the 17 a. to WILLIAM GIBBON & JONAH COLLINS in trust for MARY PARRIS with the agreement that MARY might revoke the trust at any time; & whereas JOHN GASCOIGNE has agreed to purchase the 17 a. for ₤ 480 SC money; now, to enable JONAH

COLLINS to convey the land to GASCOIGNE, MARY PARRIS revokes the trust agreement & the conveyance is completed. Witnesses: JACOB WOOLFORD, JOHN CHAMPNEYS, ROBERT HUME. Before JOSEPH WRAGG, J.P. JACOB MOTTE, Register.

Book I, p. 222
2 & 3 Mar. 1730
L & R

REBECCA FLAVELL, widow, to JOHN NEWFUILLE (NEUFVILLE), wine cooper, both of Charleston, for L 245 SC money, part of lot #38 in Charleston, fronting E 11 ft. 9 in. on a public alley joining Broad Street & running W 52 ft.; bounding S on a part of the lot formerly occupied by REBECCA FLAVELL, now by DAVID ALLEN; N on part of same lot purchased by JOHN NEUFVILLE from REBECCA FLAVELL; W on other land owned by REBECCA FLAVELL. Witnesses: HENRY GIGNILLIATT, JOHN REYNOLDS, JOHN CROFTS. Before TWEEDIE SOMERVILLE, J.P. JACOB MOTTE, Register.

Book I, p. 228
2 & 3 Jan. 1730
L & R by Mortgage

HEZEKIAH EMMS, planter of Colleton Co., to RICHARD WRIGHT, planter of Berkeley Co., for L 600 currency with interest, 2 tracts in Colleton Co. granted by Lords Proprs. 20 Jan. 1703/4; 1 containing 100 a. bound W on RALPH EMMS & vacant land; the other, 220 a. bounding E on THOMAS ELLIOTT & vacant lands. Date of redemption 2 Jan. next. Witnesses: RICHARD GODFREY, JOSEPH FULLER. Before JOHN WRIGHT, J.P. JACOB MOTTE, Register.

Book I, p. 234
23 & 24 Oct. 1730
Deed of Gift

JOHN MOORE, ESQ., & RACHEL, his wife, of Charleston, to their eldest son WILLIAM MOORE, gentleman, of Goosecreek, for natural love & affection, 3 plantations; 1 containing 600 a. in Berkeley Co., granted by Lords Proprs. to JOHN GUPPELL & now the property of JOHN MOORE who married MARY, the widow of JOHN GUPPELL on N side of W branch of T of Cooper River, bounding SW on branch of Cooper River; E & SE on MR. PALMER & land formerly belonging to THOMAS HUBBARD but now to JOHN MOORE; N & NW on JOHN ALSTON & ROBERT QUARTERMAN; NE on ELIAS BELL; another containing 140 a. bounding NW & N on the foregoing plantation; SE on the glebe land of St. John's Parish (formerly THOMAS HUBBARD'S); SW on Cooper River; which 140 a. JOHN MOORE purchased from SAMUEL MASTERS & ANNA his wife on 17 & 18 Dec. 1722; & another containing 500 a. bounding N on THOMAS FARWELL; S on CHARLES CRAIGIE & GEORGE PAWLEY; E on STEPHEN ALSTON; SW on EDWARD THOMAS; which 500 a. was granted 2 June 1718 to JOHN MOORE; the 3 tracts making 1240 a. Witnesses: JOHN CROFT, JACOB WOOLFORD, THOMAS ELLERY. Witnesses to RACHEL MOORE'S signature: ELIZABETH FLAY, J. Q. JONES, THOMAS ELLERY. Before JOHN WALLIS. JACOB MOTTE, Register.

Book I, p. 241
16 & 17 Apr. 1730
L & R

JOHN CATTELL, planter (son & heir of JOHN CATTELL, planter) to STEPHEN DRAYTON, gentleman, both of Berkeley Co., for L 1800 SC money, 400 a. (part of 1030 a. alloted to JOHN, the son, when the father's land was divided in accordance with an Act of the General Assembly) which 400 a., an inland plantation of SW side of Ashley River had been previously mortgaged to COL. ARTHUR HALL; bounding NW on JOHN CATTELL; NE & S on STEPHEN DRAYTON; defendes from any claim of dower by SARAH CATTELL, wife of JOHN CATTELL. Witnesses: JOHN RIGG, J. BADENHOP, ROBERT HUME. Before JOSEPH WRAGG. JACOB MOTTE, Register.

Book I, p. 249
3 May 1729
Deed of Sale

JAMES BLAIR, victualler, of Charleston, to DANIEL GREENE, merchant, of Charleston, for L 50 SC money, 100 a. on St. Helena, Colleton Co. lately in possession of JOSEPH WRIGHT, between the land of COL. WILLIAM BULL & that of ARCHIBALD CALDER. Witnesses: JOHN GREENE, SAMUEL WATTS. Before JOHN WRIGHT, J.P. JACOB MOTTE, Register.

Book I, p. 250
29 & 30 Mar. 1731
L & R

THOMAS ELLERY, gentleman, & ANNE, his wife, to THOMAS COOPER, merchant, & MARY MAGDELINE, his wife, all of Charleston, for L 500 SC money, part of lots #188, #189, & #79 in Charleston (being the easternmost part of land described below), being 42 ft. from E to W & 200 ft. from N to S bounding E on CAPT. WILLIAM WARDEN; W on THOMAS ELLERY; N on THOMAS ELLERY; S on Dock Street; free from the dower of ANNA, wife of THOMAS ELLERY. Whereas on 2 Dec. 1730 ANDREW ALLEN, merchant, for ₤ 1700 SC money paid bona fide, sold THOMAS ELLERY part of lots #188, #189 & #79 in Charleston, bounding W on other parts of said lots in possession of TWEEDIE SOMERVILLE, ESQ., & to the little house & lands belonging to the dissenting congregation; N on the dissenting burying place; E 237 ft. on the part of the lot in possession of CAPT. WILLIAM WARDEN (which he purchased from ANDREW ALLEN); S 127 ft. 4 in. on Dock Street; from the W side of CAPT. WARDEN'S NW post at the N end, to the E part of the Meeting Houses pales being 103 ft. 6 in.; from the corner post of the vault to MR. SOMERVILLE'S fence 23 ft. 10 in.; & 229 ft. 3 in. from N to S on the W side, according to the deed by which ALLEN claimed the land; & all appurtenances to the dwelling house as used by JOHN BROWN, gentleman, his under tenants, or assigns; now ELLERY'S conveys the eastern part to COOPER. Witnesses: WALTER COX, JONATHAN COLLINGS. Before ALEXANDER PARRIS, J.P. JACOB MOTTE, Register.

Book I, p. 258
12 & 13 Apr. 1731
L & R

CAPT. EDWARD SCOTT & MARY, his wife of Beaufort, Port Royall, Granville Co., to ALEXANDER VANDERDUSSEN, gentleman, of Charleston, for ₤ 960:19:3 SC money, 500 a. on Wambee Island, Granville Co., bounding W on WILLIAM BULL; N on WILLIAM LESSLY; S on Bulls Creek; E on marshes & creeks of Little Port Royall River; which by patent under the Rt. Hon. Sir NATHANIEL JOHNSON, Gov. of SC & NC, JAMES MOORE & NICHOLAS TROTT on 20 Mar. 1705 was granted in fee simple to WILLIAM LESSLY, & was interited by his only daughter CATHERINE DUVALL, widow; who conveyed it on 21 Aug. 1728 conveyed it to EDWARD SCOTT; now SCOTT conveys to VANDERDUSSEN. Witnesses: ROBERT WRIGHT, JAMES GREENE. Before TWEEDIE SOMERVILLE, J.P. JACOB MOTTE, Register.

Book I, p. 265
19 Sept. 1726
Deed of Gift

JOHN (his mark) GIVENS, planter, of Christ Church Parish, Berkeley Co., to well beloved son THOMAS BENNETT, for natural love & affection, & good causes & considerations, 50 a., bounding W & S on JOHN GIVENS. Delivery by turf & twig. Witnesses: MARY (her mark) GIVENS, JOSEPH FREEMAN. Before THOMAS BOONE, J.P. JACOB MOTTE, Register.

Book I, p. 267
6 Dec. 1729
Deed of Sale

FRANCIS GODDARD, planter, to THOMAS FAIRLASS, planter, both of Berkeley Co., for ₤ 300 SC money, 20 a. known as Goddard's Reserve, having been reserved by GODDARD in a release of 600 a. on which he lived to the vestry of the Parish of St. Thomas. ELIZABETH HOW, ROBERT HOW. Before DANIEL GREENE, J.P. JACOB MOTTE, Register.

Book I, p. 268
15 & 16 Apr. 1730
L & R

THOMAS STANYARNE, planter, & DOROTHY (her mark) his wife, to ROBERT SAMMS, planter, all of Colleton Co., for ₤ 300 SC money, 150 a. commonly known as the THOMAS STANYARNE Plantation, on Wadmalaw Island, bounding S on BENJAMIN DENNIS & WILLIAM AVILLE; E on THOMAS STANYARNE; N on WILLIAM SAMMS; W on ROBERT SAMMS. Witnesses: WILLIAM SAMMS, RICHARD FREEMAN. Before DANIEL GREENE, J.P. JACOB MOTTE, Register.

Book I, p. 274
16 Apr. 1730
Bond

THOMAS STANYARNE, planter, of Colleton Co., gives bond to ROBERT SAMMS for ₤ 1000 SC money, as security on the above conveyance (page 268). Witnesses: WILLIAM SAMMS, RICHARD FREMAN. Before DANIEL GREENE, J.P. JACOB MOTTE, Register.

Book I, p. 276
25 July 1730
Deed of Sale

THOMAS PARMENTER, JR., to BARNABAS GILBERT, gentleman, both of Granville Co., for ₤ 300 SC money, 300 SC money, 300 A. in Granville Co. Whereas the Hon. ROBERT GIBBES, ESQ., Gov. of SC & the Lords Proprs. on 27 June 1711 under the hand of the Hon. ROBERT DANIELL, SAMUEL EVELEIGH, THOMAS SMITH, THOMAS DISTON, commissioners for granting & selling land, granted THOMAS PARMENTER 300 a. on Port Royall Island, Granville Co., bounding N on MARK MATTHEWS; W on RICHARD HAZARD; S on THOMAS PARMENTER; E on PETER PARMENTER & PARMENTER's Creek; now PARMENTER sells to GILBERT. Witnesses: JAMES SEARLS, GREGORY SISON, WILLIAM HAYNES. Before JOHN DELABERA, J.P. JACOB MOTTE, Register.

Book I, p. 279   EDWARD KEATING, planter, of Berkeley Co., to
5 & 6 Apr. 1731   JOSEPH WRAGG, merchant, of Charleston, for
L & R   L 375 SC money, 1/2 of 20 a. near Charleston,
                        free of claim of dower by MARY KEATING; bound-
ing SE on ISAAC MAZYCK, merchant; SW on the Broad Path; NW on the other
half of the 20 a.; which half KEATING purchased from WILLIAM SKINNER; &
which had been conveyed to WILLIAM SKINNER brocklayer, & ANNE, his wife
(formerly ANNE BARLYCORN), by deed of gift or feofment by RICHARD BARLY-
CORN, mariner, son & heir of NICHOLAS BARLYCORN. Witnesses: JOB ROTHMAH-
LER, ISAAC CHILD, ISAAC NORMAN. Before JOB ROTHMAHLER, J.P. JACOB MOTTE,
Register.

Book I, p. 286   EDWARD KEATING, planter, of Berkeley Co., to
6 Apr. 1731   JOSEPH WRAGG, merchant, of Charleston, for
Bond   L 400 SC money as security on above conveyance
                        (page 279). Witnesses: JOB ROTHMAHLER, ISAAC
CHILD, ISAAC NORMAN. Before JOB ROTHMAHLER, J.P. JACOB MOTTE, Register.

Book I, p. 288   STEPHEN DRAYTON paid ARTHUR HALL L 863:12:6
6 May 1731   currency, principal & interest on mortgage,
Satisfaction of Mortgage also L 5:5 which HALL paid JACOB MOTTE for
                        registering the mortgage. Witnesses: THOMAS
LLOYD, THOMAS LAMBOLL. Before ALEXANDER PARRIS, J.P. JACOB MOTTE, Register.

Book I, p. 288   ARTHUR FOSTER, planter, & MARY, his wife, to
22 Feb. 1722   CHARLES BURNHAM, all of Berkeley Co., for
Release   L 2000 SC money, 370 a. known as Gibbons Bluff,
                        in Berkeley Co., bounding E on Itawan River
(Cooper River); N on Wosah Creek; S on MRS. SARAH BEAMOR (formerly CHRIST-
OPHER EDWARDS); W on RALPH IZARD & WILLIAM SKIPPER; free except for 1
mortgage dated 28 Mar. 1721 given WILLIAM LIVINGSTON, clerk, in Charles-
ton, for 1000 years for payment of 3000 lbs. rice in a certain manner.
Witnesses: ROBERT HUME, THOMAS FLEMING, CHILDERMUS CROFT. Before DANIEL
GREENE, J.P. JACOB MOTTE, Register.

Book I, p. 294   FRANCIS SIMONS, planter, & ANNE his wife, to
19 Dec. 1730   THOMAS HASELL, rector, the Hon. THOMAS BROUGH-
L & R by Mortgage   TON (executor of will of RICHARD BERESFORD,
                        see page 148 for details), JOHN MOORE, THOMAS
BONNY, JOHN DANIEL, ROBERT STEWART, & THOMAS PAGISS, vestrymen of the
Parish of St. Thomas, for L 500 currency, 2 plantations, or 1000 a. in
all. Whereas the Rt. Hon. CHARLES CRAVEN, Gov., & the Lords Proprs. by
grant under the hand of the Gov. & of RALPH IZARD, CHARLES HART, SAMUEL
EVELEIGH & NICHOLAS TROTT, Dated 3 Apr. 1713 granted BENJAMIN SIMONS 500
a. in Berkeley Co.; & whereas the Hon. ROBERT DANIEL, ESQ., Dep. Gov., &
the Lords Proprs. by grant under the hand to the Gov., & of CHARLES HART,
FRANCIS YONGE, SAMUEL EVELEIGH, GEORGE CHICKEN & NICHOLAS TROTT, dated
25 July 1717, gave BENJAMIN SIMONS another 500 a.; & whereas BENJAMIN
SIMONS by will dated 14 June 1717 bequeathed the 1000 a. to his son FRAN-
CIS SIMONS; now FRANCIS mortgages the land to the vestry of St. Thomas
Parish. Witnesses: WALTER COX, THOMAS ELLERY, ARCHIBALD YONGE, JAMES
MAXWELL. Before DANIEL GREENE, J.P. JACOB MOTTE, Register. On 4 May
1753 ALEXANDER GARDEN, JR., rector, declared the principal & interest due
fully paid by FRANCIS SIMONS, son of the mortgager. Witness: WILLIAM
HOPTON.

Book I, p. 302   PETER JOHNSON, SR., planter, to NICHOLAS BO-
17 & 18 Nov. 1730   CHET, planter, both of Berkeley Co., for L 127
L & R   SC money, 100 a. on SE side of E branch of T
                        of Cooper River, bounding SW on Lynch's Creek;
SE on NICHOLAS BOCHET; NE on JOHNSON LYNCH; NW on NICHOLAS BOCHET. Whereas his Excellency JOHN, EARL OF BATH, Palatine, & the Lords Proprs. by
grant under the hands of the Hon. JAMES MOORE, ESQ., etc., dated 4 June
1701 gave JOSEPH MARBEUF L00 a. on the S side of E branch of the T of
Cooper River; & whereas MARBEUF sold the 100 a. to GIDEON & GABRIEL FER-
RON; & whereas GAVRIEL FERRON & CATHERINE his wife (heirs of GIDEON) for
L 44 currency sold the 100 a. to ANDREW DUPUY on 17 Jan. 1711/12; & whereas ANDREW DUPUY & JANE his wife on 8 Nov. 1716 sold the land to the Rev.
MR. JOHN LAPIERE; & whereas MR. LAPIERE & SUSANAH his wife, on 28 Nov.

1717, sold the 100 a. to MICHAEL BLACKWELL; & whereas BLACKWELL, on 15
June 1723 sold the land to PETER JOHNSON, SR.; now JOHNSON conveys to BO-
CHET. Witnesses: PETER JOHNSON, JR.; HENRY VIDEAU. Before ANTHONY BON-
NEAU, J.P. JACOB MOTTE, Register.

Book I, p. 308 PETER JOHNSON, SR. to NICHOLAS BOCHET, for
18 Nov. 1730 Ł 1000 currency, as security in above trans-
Bond action (p. 302). Witnesses: PETER JOHNSON,
  JR., HENRY VIDEAU. Before ANTHONY BONNEAU,
J.P. JACOB MOTTE, Register.

Book I, p. 311 NICHOLAS BOCHET, planter, & MARY his wife, of
1 May 1731 Berkeley Co., for the love & affection they
Deed of Gift bear unto the Evangelist of Our blessed Lord &
  Saviour Jesus Christ, & unto the Church of the
same belonging to the French Protestants whereof they profess themselves
members; with certain conditions; 100 a. purchased from PETER JOHNSON,
SR. for Ł 127 currency on 18 Nov, 1730 on SE side of of E branch of T of
Cooper River; bounding SW on Lynch Creek; SE on NICHOLAS BOCHET; NE on
JOHNSON LYNCH; NW on NICHOLAS BOCHET; to be used for a parsonage & glebe
land for the French Parish called St. Dennis for so long as the Divine
service be in the French language used by the congregation of the Parish;
should the service be performed in the English language, or should it
cease to be a Parish, the 100 acres to return to NICHOLAS BOCHET to be
disposed of as follows: whereas most of the French inhabitants & others
of St. Dennis Parish contributed liberally towards the building of a parsonage & made it convenient for a minister to liver there, should the 100
a. be returned to BOCHET or his heirs the land should be sold & the money
apportioned amongst those contributors. Witnesses: FRANCIS PAGITT, DAN-
IEL JAUDON, THEODORE TREZEVANT, DAVID BALDY, HENRY VIDEAU, ISAAC TREZE-
VANT. Before ANTHONY BONNEAU, J.P. JACOB MOTTE, Register.

Book I, p. 313 WILLIAM MCPHERSON, planter, of Colleton Co.,
25 Feb. 1720/21 to JOHN BEE, planter, for Ł 100 currency, 500
Deed of Sale a. on S side Cusahatchee, Granville Co.,
  bounding NW to SW on vacant land; SE on WIL-
LIAM DOWNS. Witnesses: WILLIAM MELVEN, JACOB DORROM, JAMES FULTON. Before CHARLES HILL, J.P. JACOB MOTTE, Register.

Book I, p. 315 HENRY CHIDLEY, carpenter, & ANNE, his wife, to
23 & 25 Sept. 1729 THOMAS DIXON, bricklayer, both of Charleston,
L & R for Ł 300 SC money, 1/2 of lot #125 containing
  1/4 a., English measure, on E side of the
street leading from Ashley River to the Broad Path, bounding N on the
other half; S & E on a swamp; free of the dower & thirds of ANNE. Witnesses: RICHARD COLLWALL, JOHN ARNOLT, SAMUEL SMITH. Before THOMAS BAR-
TON, J.P. JACOB MOTTE, Register.

Book I, p. 319 JOSEPH WRAGG, SR., merchant, of Dorchester,
27 & 28 June 1728 Berkeley Co., to JOSEPH WRAGG, JR., merchant,
L & R by Mortgage of Charleston, for Ł 300 SC money, 50 a. in
  Berkeley Co., near Dorchester, bounding S on
Ashley River; W on AARON WAY, SR.; N on undivided land; E on AARON WAY,
JR. Should WRAGG, SR. pay WRAGG, JR. Ł 3000 SC on 1 Aug. 1728 according
to a certain obligation of this date this release to be void. Witnesses:
RICHARD LAMBTON, ROBERT HUME. Before TWEEDIE SOMERVILLE, J.P. JACOB
MOTTE, Register.

Book I, p. 325 BENJAMIN GODFREY, planter, of Berkeley Co., to
27 Feb. 1730 BENJAMIN WHITAKER, ESQ., of Charleston, as se-
L & R by Mortgage curity (on bond given this date by GODFREY to
  WHITAKER in the penal sum of Ł 10,500 currency
conditioned for the payment of Ł 5250 currency on 27 Feb. 1731 with in-
terest at 10%), 160 a., English measure on Ashley River, bounding E on
BENJAMIN GODFREY; W & S on land BENJAMIN WHITAKER purchased from CAPT.
JOHN WOODWARD; N on marsh; which land by deed of exchange was conveyed to
BENJAMIN WHITAKER by JOHN GODFREY, gentleman; also 86 a. which BENJAMIN
WHITAKER purchased from JOHN WOODWARD, bounding NW on BENJAMIN GODFREY;
SE on JOHN WOODWARD; also the vacant land lying between which was pur-
chased by BENJAMIN WHITAKER from ALEXANDER TRENCH; also 424 a. bounding

151

N on CHARLES HILL, ESQ.; S on MR. LUCAS; E on BENJAMIN GODFREY (bought from WHITAKER); W on JOHN GODFREY, JR.; which tract was allotted to BENJAMIN GODFREY when CAPT. JOHN GODFREY lands were divided amongst his children; also 200 a. which had been settled on ELIZABETH GIBBES by ROBERT GIBBES, ESQ., & by her bequeathed to BENJAMIN GODFREY, which tract runs from Ashley River to Wappoo, bounding E & S on WILLIAM HARVEY; N & W on BENJAMIN WHITAKER & JOHN WOODWARD. BENJAMIN GODFREY also delivers to BENJAMIN WHITAKER 4 Negro men, 1 Negro woman & her child. MARGARET GODFREY TO renounce her dower within 2 months. Witnesses: ANDREW DEVEAUX, JAMES DEVEAUX. Because the sum to be paid in present currency equals Ł 750 sterling money of Great Britain, it is agreed that the sums due shall be valued in sterling money at above rate & paid in SC currency according to the usual exchange as if Ł 750 sterling were to be paid. Before DANIEL GREENE, J.P. JACOB MOTTE, Register.

Book I, p. 331
20 & 21 May 1731
L & R

OBADIAH ALLEN, planter, & BRIDGET his wife, of Berkeley Co., to JOHN LAURENS, saddler, of Charleston, for Ł 600 SC money, lot #315 in Charleston, bounding S on the Market Place; E on JOSEPH BLAKE, ESQ.; W on WILLIAM BRADLY; N on COL. THOMAS CARY. Witnesses: JOHN COLCOCK, RICHARD WIGG, WILLIAM CATTELL, JR., BENJAMIN ADDISON, JOHN CARION, JAMES LESESNE. Before DANIEL GREENE, J.P. JACOB MOTTE, Register.

Book I, p. 336
22 May 1731
Bond

OBADIAH ALLEN, planter, of Berkeley Co., gives bond to JOHN LAURENS, saddler, of Charleston, in the sum of Ł 1000 SC money, as security that BRIDGET ALLEN, wife of OBADIAH, shall within 3 months renounce all her claim to lot #315 (p. 331). Witnesses: BENJAMIN ADDISON, JOHN CARION, JAMES LESESNE. Before DANIEL GREENE, J.P. JACOB MOTTE, Register.

Book I, p. 337
18 Oct. 1709
Deed of Sale

JOHNSON LYNCH, to JOHN BLAKE, planter, both of Berkeley Co., for Ł 40 currency, 100 a. butting on the land of CHRISTOPHER BEECH, having for breadth "13 chains & 15 links the chaine 66 ft.", the length from NW to SE; the breadth SW & NE. Witnesses: CHRISTOPHER BEECH, ROBERT CLYATT, JOSEPH ROPER. MARGARET LYNCH, wife of JOHNSON, renounced her claim. JOHNSON LYNCH writes that whereas the breadth is said to be 13 chain & 15 links it must be 14 ch. & 13 links. Memo on 15 June 1729 JOHN BLAKE for a certain sum conveys the above land to JOHN CUMING. Witnesses: JOHN FOGARTIE, SAMUEL GREY, ROBERT TOMSON. ROBERT CLYATT appeared before MEREDITH HUGHES. JACOB MOTTE, Register.

Book I, p. 346
1 & 2 May 1731
L & R

JOHN BAYLY, son & heir of JOHN BAYLY of Ballinaclough, Co. of Tipperary, Ireland, by his attorney ALEXANDER TRENCH, merchant, of Charleston (see page 92 for details) to HUGH BRYAN, planter, of Colleton Co., for Ł 30 SC money, 111 a. in Colleton Co., bounding N on ISRAEL ANDREWS; E on JOHN HENNEWAY; S & SW on JOHN BULL; W on WILLIAM ORWILL. Witnesses: WILLIAM SMITH, THOMAS BEDON. Before DANIEL GREENE, J.P. JACOB MOTTE, Register.

Book I, p. 351
10 & 11 Sept. 1730
Deed of Gift

ELIAS HORRY, planter, of St. James Santee, to his son DANIEL HORRY, for love & affection, 555 a. in Craven Co., bounding N & E on Wambaw Creek; S on Murphey's Creek; N & NW on ELIAS HORRY & MICHAEL CLINCH; which 555 a. was formerly laid out in 2 tracts of 500 a. & 55 a. Witnesses: ELIZABETH HUGER, JOHN HORRY. Before DANIEL HUGER, J.P. JACOB MOTTE, Register.

Book I, p. 357
10 & 11 Sept. 1730
Deed of Gift

DANIEL HUGER, planter, of St. John's Parish, to DANIEL HORRY, planter, for natural love & affection, 200 a. in Craven Co., bounding N on Wambaw Creek; S on MICHAEL CLINCH'S creek; which 200 a. was laid out in 2 tracts, each of 100 a. each. Witnesses: DANIEL HANLEY, JOHN HORRY, JOHN (his mark) JUNE. Before ANTHONY BONNEAU, J.P. JACOB MOTTE, Register.

Book I, p. 363

JOSEPH BEECH to JOHN CUMING, both of Berkeley

5 Jan. 1729/30   Co., for ₤ 500 currency (by prompt payment of
Deed of Sale   ₤ 200 & bond for ₤ 300), 270 a. in St. Thomas
                       Parish, bounding S on JOHN CUMMING; E on land
which CUMING purchased from RICHARD HEATLY S on E branch of Cooper River;
W on JOHN CUMING. Whereas CHRISTOPHER BEECH, shipwright, bequeathed 3
different tracts of land to his 3 eldest sons, RICHARD, CHRISTOPHER &
JOHN, & in case of their death without issue the first vacant land should
go to JOSEPH BEECH, & whereas RICHARD died without marriage or issue &
JOSEPH inherited the 270 a. with the mansion & dwelling house that belong-
ed to his father CHRISTOPHER; now JOSEPH sells to CUMING. Witnesses:
JOHN (his mark) STRAHAN, ROBERT THOMASON, RICHARD BLAKE, ALEXANDER MCKAY
(MCKOY). Before ANTHONY BONNEAU, J.P.   JACOB MOTTE, Register.

Book I, p. 366   RICHARD DEVON, merchant & rope-maker, of Par-
18 July 1726   ish of St. Mary Magdelin, Bermondsey, Surrey
Will   Co., England, by his last will commits his
                       body to interred at Rhy gate, Surry Co., near
his deceased relations; appoints his friends ROBERT WILLIMOTT & LAMBER
LUDLOW, merchants of London, his executors until his son CHARLES DEVON
shall return to London from New England & bequeaths them ₤ 20 sterling
apiece for their pains; Item: gave son RICHARD DEVON ₤ 500 money of
Great Britain; Item: gave son-in-law POTTER HASKINES ₤ 700 money of
Great Britain; Item: gave his mother, ANNA BROOK, ₤ 10 for mourning;
gave his brother JOHN ₤ 10 for mourning; gave his brother ROBERT BROOK &
his wife ₤ 10 each for mourning; gave his sister, JOYCE LONG, ₤ 50 also
for mourning; gave his sister CATHRINE BROOK ₤ 50 also ₤ 10 for mourning;
gave his friends CAPT. GEORGE MORRIS & CAPT. SAMUEL ELIOT ₤ 10 each for
mourning; gave his foreman in the rope ground, STEPHEN CHANDLER, ₤ 20;
directed his executors to sell both his rope grounds, 1 in Bormondsey &
the other at or near Blackwall, & the utensils & appurtenances; after all
debts & expenses are paid the residue of all real & personal estate to
his son CHARLES DEVON; appointed son CHARLES sole executor so soon as he
returns to London. Witnesses: THOMAS SHARPE, ABSALOM BURT. WILLIAM HALL-
AWAY, M.P. in Shad Thames.

(Paragraphs in Latin not translated)

Book I, p. 369   CHARLES DEVON, mariner, of the Parish of St.
22 Feb. 1730   Mary Magdeline, Bermondsey, Surrey Co., (son,
Letter of Attorney   heir & executor of the will of RICHARD DEVON,
                       his father), appointed ANDREW ALLEN, merchant,
of Charleston, SC his attorney, to convey to RALPH IZARD, ESQ., of
Charleston, for ₤ 3000 SC money, 1000 a. in SC which formerly belonged to
RICHARD DEVON, now the property of CHARLES DEVON. Before WILLIAM HOLLO-
WAY, N.P., dwelling in Shad Thames, Southwark, near London. Witnesses:
SAMUEL ELLIOTT, STEPHEN CHANDLER. JACOB MOTTE, Register.

Book I, p. 371   CHARLES DEVON, mariner, of the Parish of St.
1 & 2 June 1731   Mary Magdeline, Bermondsey, Surrey Co., Great
L & R   Britain (son, heir, & executor of last will of
                       his father RICHARD DEVON, rope-maker & mer-
chant), by ANDREW ALLEN, merchant, of Charleston, SC, his attorney, (p.
369) to RALPH IZARD, ESQ., of Berkeley Co., SC, for ₤ 3000 SC money, 2
tracts; 1 containing 640 a. in Berkeley Co. on SW side Ashley River,
bounding NW on WILLIAM SANDERS; NE & SE on the Earl of Shaftsbury's (Ashley) Barony; the other containing 400 a. on SW side of Ashley River,
bounding NW on MAJ. THOMAS HEPWORTH & WILLIAM BULL; NE on LORD SHAFTS-
BURY'S (Ashley) Barony; SE on JOHN RAVEN & ROBERT LADSON; SW on FRANCIS
LADSON. Whereas RICHARD DEVON owned 2 tracts, or 1040 a., in Berkeley
Co., & whereas he, on 12 Oct. 1729 appointed ANDREW ALLEN his attorney
with authority to sell the land; & whereas on 1 Aug. 1730 RALPH IZARD
contracted with ALLEN for the purchase of the 640 a. granted THOMAS HEP-
WORTH on 24 Sept. 1710 & the 400 a. granted HEPWORTH 28 July 1711; IZARD
agreeing to give ALLEN bond in the penal sum of ₤ 6000 assuring the payment of ₤ 3000; & whereas RICHARD DEVON died & his son CHARLES inherited
the land before the conveyance was made; & whereas CHARLES DEVON appointed ALLEN his attorney, with authority to convey to IZARD; now the conveyance is completed. Witnesses: JOHN BUCHANAN, JOHN BLAMYER, ROBERT HUME.
Before JOHN DELABERE, J.P.   JACOB MOTTE, Register.

Book I, p. 381 THOMAS ELLIOTT, SR., & ANNE his wife, of Long
23 Dec. 1728 Point, Berkeley Co., for love & affection &
Deed of Gift other valuable considerations, to well beloved
son JOSEPH ELLIOTT, 500 a. on N side Stono
River; bounding S on Stono River; on all other sides on WILLIAM ELLIOTT,
JR. Witnesses: MARTHA DANDRIDGE, MARY DANDRIDGE, JOHN WELLS. Before WILLIAM CATTELL, J.P. JACOB MOTTE, Register.

Book I, p. 388 WILLIAM SCOTT, merchant, & SUSANNAH, his wife,
13 & 14 July 1731 of Charleston, to JAMES SMYTH, planter, of
L & R Colleton Co., for Ł 110 SC money, 10 lots in
New London, Colleton Co., lot #43, bounding S
on lot #44 belonging to CAPT. THOMAS BRUCE; E on FLEET, SR.; N on lot #7,
belonging to CAPT. THOMAS BRUCE; W by S Edisto River; lot #68, part of
Kingston Square, bounding S on Chelsey Road; E on lot #84; N on lot #67;
W on Fleet St.; lot #44 bounding S by land outside the town; E on Fleet
St.; N on lot #43; W on S Edisto River; which 3 lots by 3 several warrants dated 17 May 1717 were granted to CAPT. THOMAS BRUCE then partner
of WILLIAM SCOTT; lot #81 in Marlboro Square, bounding N on Newport St.;
E on Queen St.; S on lot #82 belonging to WILLIAM SCOTT; W on lot #65;
lot #82 in Marlboro Square, bounding N on lot #81; E on Queen St.; S on
Hatton St.; W on lot #66; lot #83 in Kingston Square, bounding N on Hatton St.; E on Queen St.; S on lot #84 belonging to WILLIAM SCOTT; W on
lot #67; lot #84 on Kingston Square, bounding N on lot #83 belonging to
WILLIAM SCOTT; E on Queen St.; S by Chelsey Road; W on lot #68; lot #65
bounding N on Newport St.; E on lot #81; S on lot #66 belonging to WILLIAM SCOTT; W on Fleet St.; lot #66 bounding N on lot #65; E on lot #82;
S on Hatton St.; W on Fleet St.; lot #67 bounding N on Hatton St.; E on
lot #83; S on lot #68; W on Fleet St. All of which were by several warrants dated 5 June 1717 granted to WILLIAM SCOTT; SUSANAH to renounce all
her claim at any time when required. Witnesses: WILLIAM ROPER, WILLIAM
TENNANT. Before CHARLES HILL, J.P.

Book I, p. 392 JOSEPH LAW & BENJAMIN LAW, sons of NATHANIEL
10 July 1731 LAW, planter of Christ Church Parish, Berkeley
Partition & Gift Co., to their brother NATHANIEL LAW, for natural love & affection & 10 sh. apiece, his portion of their father's estate. Whereas NATHANIEL LAW, the father bequeathed 1055 a. on the beach to be divided amongst his 6 children, JOSEPH, BENJAMIN, HEPZIBA, ANNE, BULA & NATHANIEL; bounding W on RICHARD
HALL; S on land known as Umprey Primates; the oldest first to make his
choice & when equally shared to be enjoyed by all & for want of issue, to
be equally divided amongst the survivors; & whereas the land was divided
& NATHANIEL entitled to his 1/6 part bounding W on JAMES BAIN; E & SE on
JOSEPH LAW; S & E on The Sound; & whereas HEPZIBA, ANNE, & BULA died; now
JOSEPH & BENJAMIN divide the land & give NATHANIEL his share. Witnesses:
ISAAC COUSIERAT, ROWLAND VAUGHAN. Before TWEEDIE SOMERVILLE, J.P. JACOB
MOTTE, Register.

Book I, p. 395 NATHANIEL LAW, son of NATHANIEL LAW, planter,
12 & 13 July 1731 & JAMES ACKENE, mariner, of Charleston, to
L & R JAMES BERRIE, merchant, of Charleston, for
Ł 130 currency paid to NATHANIEL LAW & Ł 265:5
paid to JAMES ACKENE (Ł 395:5 in all) 1/6 part of 1055 a., lately belonging to NATHANIEL LAW, SR., on the beach in Christ Church Parish; bounding
W on JAMES PAINE; E & SE on JOSEPH LAW; S & E on The Sound. Witnesses:
ISAAC COUSSIERAT, ROWLAND VAUGHAN. Before TWEEDIE SOMERVILLE, J.P. JACOB MOTTE, Register.

Book I, p. 403 JAMES TAGGART, gentleman, to DAVID HEARTY,
13 & 15 July 1731 cordwainer, both of Berkeley Co., for Ł 180 SC
L & R money, 100 a., English measure, in Berkeley
Co., bounding NW on the Glebe land of the Parish; NE & SE on COL. ROBERT DANIEL. Witnesses: ABIJAH RUSS, ROBERT HOW.
Before DANIEL GREENE, J.P. JACOB MOTTE, Register.

Book I, p. 408 BENJAMIN DELACONSEILLERE, ESQ., to ALEXANDER
13 July 1731 VANDERDUSSEN, ESQ., both of Charleston, in the
Bond & Mortgage sum of Ł 1000 money of Great Britain. Whereas
VANDERDUSSEN, by L & R, 8 & 9 July 1731

purchased from BENJAMIN SCHINCKINGH & MARGARET his wife, for L 4000 currency, 700 a. in Berkeley Co. in 2 tracts; & whereas BENJAMIN & MARGARET SCHENCKINGH by L & R, 3 & 4 Feb. 1725 had mortgaged the 2 tracts to RICHARD MILES, merchant, of the Island of Madera for L 3000 currency; & whereas the L 3000 & interest is still due; & whereas RICHARD MILES died the 7 July 1730 & by will appointed JOHN MILES, JOSEPH PACE, JR., RICHARD RIDER, & JOHN BROWNING his executors & they have not appointed any attorney to receive the money & record the mortgage; & whereas VANDERDUSSEN is ready to purchase the incumbrance & satisfy the same so far as the L 4000 amounts; & whereas BENJAMIN DELACONSEILLERE by virtue of a letter dated 12 Jan. last part directed to him from JOSEPH PACE, JR. (only acting executor of the will of RICHARD MILES) which authorized him to receive the principal & interest due on the mortgage but has not sufficient power to release & discharge the mortgage upon record in due form of law; & whereas VANDERDUSSEN has paid DELA CONSEILLERE L 4000 SC money & has received the original mortgage deeds; now DELA CONSEILLERE gives bond that a proper discharge of the mortgage shall be entered within 2 years. Witnesses: DANIEL WELSHHUYSEN, JAMES GREEME. Before TWEEDIE SOMERVILLE, J.P. JACOB MOTTE, Register. Memo. ALEXANDER VANDERDUSSEN declares that BENJAMIN DELA CONSEILLERE has complied with the conditions of this obligation & the obligation is discharged. JACOB MOTTE, Register.

Book I, p. 412
5 & 6 May 1731
L & R by Mortgage

JOHN SKENE, ESQ. & HANNAH his wife, of Berkeley Co., to ALEXANDER VANDERDUSSEN, ESQ. of Charleston, for L 114:5:8-1/2 money of Great Britain, 500 a. on S side Ashley River, part of Ashley Barony, bounding SE on SAMUEL WRAGG, merchant, of London; SW on THOMAS GADSDEN; NW on ROBERT WRIGHT; N on ALEXANDER SKENE; which 500 a. by L & R dated 6 & 7 Jan. 1728/9 were conveyed by ALEXANDER SKENE & JEMIMA his wife to JOHN SKENE & HANNAH his wife; conditioned for the payment of the above amount with interest at 10% on 6 May 1732; the land to be free from HANNAH'S claim of dower. Witnesses: JAMES GREEME, JERMYN WRIGHT. Before TWEEDIE SOMERVILLE, J.P. JACOB MOTTE, Register.

Book I, p. 419
29 & 30 June 1731
L & R

MILES BREWTON & THOMAS LAMBOLL, gentlemen, of Charleston, executors of the will of ROBERT TRADD, gentleman, to JACOB MOTTE, merchant, of Charleston, for L 586:10 SC money, part of lot #60 belonging to ROBERT TRADD on the S side of Tradd Street adjoining & bounding E on part of a town lot owned by GEORGE CHICKEN; W on part of lot #60 formerly belonging to ROBERT TRADD & sold by MILES BREWTON & THOMAS LAMBOLL to JOHN DART; N on Tradd St.; S by MILES BREWTON; containing so many ft. from N to S as is described in the town plott; & is separated from JOHN DART by a dividing line run S between them from a stake in the ground at the NE corner of JOHN DART'S lot; being 187 ft. 4 in. distant easterly from the NW corner of the said lot to another stake in the SE corner of JOHN DART'S part at the like distance E from the SW corner of said lot; together with the brick chimney & other appurtenances. Whereas ROBERT TRADD owned the above land & by will dated 21 July 1730 appointed MILES BREWTON & THOMAS LAMBOLL his executors with authority to sell his corner lot on S side of Tradd Street; W on the great street leading from   to the old churchyard & Market Place (page broken); now the executors sell part to JACOB MOTT. Witnesses: ROBERT BREWTON, JOHN DART, DANIEL TOWNSEND. Before TWEEDIE SOMERVILLE, J.P. JACOB MOTTE, Register.

Book I, p. 426
2 Aug. 1731
Lease

JAMES MURRILLE, of Church Parish, for good considerations, farm lets for 20 years to THOMAS HAMLIN, brick layer, of same Parish, 80 a. bounding SW on JONATHAN MURRILLE; NE on JAMES MARRILLE where he now lives; SE on a marsh; NW on JOHN HUGGINS; at the yearly rent of 20 sh. if demanded. Witnesses: HENRY BENNETT, THOMAS JONES, THOMAS JONES. Before THOMAS BARTON, J.P. JACOB MOTTE, Register.

Book I, p. 427
25 July 1731
Mortgage

GEORGE CHICKEN, planter, of Berkeley Co., to ROBERT AUSTIN, merchant, of Charleston, for L 1700 currency with interest, 500 a. in Berkeley Co., bounding S & E on Landgrave THOMAS SMITH; N on RICHARD BAKER; W on BARNABY REALLY. Witnesses: JOHN KING, CHARLES BURLEY. Before NATHANIEL BROUGHTON, J.P. JACOB MOTTE, Register.

Book I, p. 430　　　　　　　JOHN BAYLY, son & heir of JOHN BAYLY, of Bal-
9 & 10 July 1731　　　　　　linaclough, Co. of Tipperary, Ireland, by his
L & R　　　　　　　　　　　attorney ALEXANDER TRENCH, merchant of Charles-
　　　　　　　　　　　　　　ton (see page 92) to JACOB MOTTE, merchant, of
Charleston, for L 90 SC money, a lot of vacant land containing 1/4 of an
a. & 60 sq. ft., 36 ft. broad & 300 ft. long, on the shoal water before
the bay of Charleston, bounding N on JOSEPH DEYS, E on Cooper River; S on
land of JACOB MOTTE bequeathed to him by ROBERT TRADD; W on the front
line or brick wall of Charleston Bay; & lies opposite part of lot #7 before the dwelling house of DANIEL GREENE, & an alley between the houses
of DANIEL GREENE & JACOB MOTTE. Witnesses: WILLIAM GEOMANS, GABRIEL ES-
COTT. Before TWEEDIE SOMERVILLE, J.P. JACOB MOTTE, Register.

Book I, p. 435　　　　　　　ROBERT NISBETT, merchant, & MARY his wife to
3 & 4 Aug. 1731　　　　　　 ALEXANDER VANDERDUSSEN, all of Charleston, for
L & R by Mortgage　　　　　L 1000 SC money & interest, payable Feb. 4
　　　　　　　　　　　　　　next, part of a lot in Charleston on Poin-
sett's Alley running from Cooper River W by DR. JOHN THOMAS, MOSES WIL-
SON, butcher, & DR. JOHN HUTCHINSON, bounding S 29 ft. on the alley; E on
SHEM BUTLER; N on ?; W on DR. JAMES KILPATRICK (formerly THOMAS HEPWORTH).
Witnesses: JAMES GREEME, VICKERS BURGES. Before ROBERT WRIGHT. JACOB
MOTTE, Register.

Book I, p. 443　　　　　　　EDWARD NORTH, planter, of Colleton Co., to AN-
13 July 1731　　　　　　　　DREW ALLEN & GABRIEL MANIGAULT, merchants, of
Mortgage　　　　　　　　　　Charleston, for L 1500 currency, payable with
　　　　　　　　　　　　　　interest on 13 July 1735, 500 a. in 2 tracts;
1 of 300 a.; the other of 200 a. in the N part of 450 a. joining the 300
a.; all contained in a plat of 4000 a. granted to COL. ROBERT DANIEL.
Witnesses: JOSHUA SANDERS, JOSEPH JONES, WILLIAM SANDERS. Before J. FER-
GUSON, J.P. JACOB MOTTE, Register. Mortgage satisfied by payment by ED-
WARD NORTH to GABRIEL MANIGAULT, discharged. Witness: JOHN PENNYMAN for
NATHANIEL JOHNSON, ESQ., Pub. Reg.

Book I, p. 443　　　　　　　ABRAHAM WARNOCK, planter, of Berkeley Co., to
3 Mar. 1716　　　　　　　　 his well beloved granddaughter, MARY KING, for
Deed of Gift　　　　　　　　natural love & affection & other considera-
　　　　　　　　　　　　　　tions, 200 a., 1 part of 400 a. formerly called
RICHARD BERESFORD'S Cowpen or Great Savannah which is to be equally divided between ABRAHAM WARNOCK & MARY KING. Witnesses: JOHN MOSER, HUGH FISH-
ER, NATHANIEL FORD. Before THOMAS WARING, J.P. JACOB MOTTE, Register.

Book I, p. 447　　　　　　　HUGH HEXT, ESQ., & SARAH his wife, & GEORGE
3 & 4 Sept. 1731　　　　　　HADRELL, planter, & SUSANNAH his wife, all of
L & R. Tripartite　　　　　Christ Church Parish, of the 1st part: ALEX-
　　　　　　　　　　　　　　ANDER GARDEN, rector of the Parish of St.
Philip's Charleston, JOHN FENWICK & ELEAZER ALLEN, 3 of the commissioners
appointed for the carrying on & finishing the New Brick Church in Charleston, of the 2nd part; & JACOB MOTTE & ROBERT AUSTIN, merchants, churchwardens of the Parish of St. Philip's Church of the 3rd part. Whereas an
Act of Assembly ratified 17 Apr. 1725 impowered the commissioners of the
New Brick Church to purchase convenient lots for a churchyard; the church
nearing completion & there being an absolute necessity for a churchyard
or burying place & no land adjoining the church having been appropriated;
& to prevent the owners of lots from refusing to sell or charging exorbi-
tant prices to appoint 3 freeholders to appraise the lots, giving the
owners 20 days in which to appoint 3 other freeholders to join the 1st 3
in making, the appraisals, the appraisals to be returned to the secretary's office within 40 days, & the owner required to make conveyance
within 10 days after appraisement; & whereas ALEXANDER GARDEN, JOHN FEN-
WICK & ELEAZER ALLEN wished to purchase from HUGH & SARAH HEXT & GEORGE
& SUSANNAH HADRELL part of lot #67 adjoining the church & appointed BEN-
JAMIN D'HARRIETTE, WILLIAM YEOMANS, & GABRIEL MANIGAULT their appraisers
& HUGH HEXT & GEORGE HADRELL appointed JOHN MOORE, JOHN SIMONS & GEORGE
DUCATT, their appraisers, & they valued the land at L 3 some sh. per ft.
front; now HUGH & SARAH HEXT & GEORGE & SUSANNAH HADRELL for L 194:17:2
currency (& for 10 sh. ea. paid by MOTTE & AUSTIN to the HEXTS & HADRELLS)
convey to the commissioners & church wardens part of lot #67 adjoining
the church, being 58 ft. 2 in. square at the lower end of the lot; formerly belonging to MARY MILLINS, widow, & devised to her 2 nieces SARAH

HEXT & SUSANNAH HADRELL. Witnesses: ROBERT HUME, GABRIEL MANIGAULT, DANIEL GREENE. Before TWEEDIE SOMERVILLE, J.P. JACOB MOTTE, Register.

Book I, p. 458 ROBERT HUME, gentleman, & SOPHIA his wife, of
17 & 18 Dec. 1730 Berkeley Co., to JAMES OMER, mariner, formerly
L & R of London, now of SC, for ₤ 307:10 SC money,
the northernmost third part of lot #51 in
Charleston, bounding E 33 ft. 4 in. on the Bay or Front Street on Cooper River; S 206 ft. on the middle part of the lot formerly belonging to CHRISTOPHER ARTHUR but now to JOHN GOUGH; W on Sir PETER COLLETON's square; N on lot #50 belonging to Landgrave COLLETON; which third part HUME purchased from EDWARD EDWARDS & MARY his wife, planter, of Berkeley Co., on 10 May 1726. Witnesses: WILLIAM DRY, WILLIAM YEOMANS. Before DANIEL GREENE, J.P. JACOB MOTTE, Register.

Book I, p. 463 HUMPHREY JOHNSON, mariner, to JOSEPH WRAGG,
8 & 9 Sept. 1729 merchant, both of Charleston, for ₤ 520 SC
L & R by Mortgage money, payable 1 Jan. 1729, 2 tracts; 1 of
1000 a. on NE branch of Cape Fair River about 1-1/2 miles above Smith's Creek, beginning at a cypress at the mouth of a creek & running N 15 wtts. 102 poles along the river to a cypress at a creek's mouth; thence along the courses of the creek to a cypress 422 poles distant in a straight line; thence NE 82° 313 poles; thence S 15 E 311 poles; thence S 68 W 310 poles to a cypress; thence S 77° E 461 poles along a creek to 1 st. station; the other of 640 a. on the NE branch of Cape Fair River, about 1-1/2 miles above Smith's Creek; beginning at a gum at a creek's mouth, running thence S 15°. E 160 poles along the river to a state; thence S 81 E 620 poles to a pine; thence N 15° W 300 poles to a pine; thence S 54° W 160 poles thence along the courses of the creek to the 1st station. Witnesses: PETER HORRY, WILLIAM ROMSEY. Before DANIEL GREENE, J.P. JACOB MOTTE, Register.

Book I, p. 469 MANASSEH COURAGE, of Prince George Parish,
8 Sept. 1730 Winyaw, Craven Co., to his sister MAGDELINE
Deed of Gift LENUD, wife of NICHOLAS LENUD, of the same
Parish, for natural love & affection & other considerations, during her life, 400 a. where NICHOLAS LENUD now lives on N side Santee River, being part of the land inherited by MANASSEH COURAGE from FRANCIS COURAGE, bounding S & E on part of MANASSEH COURAGE'S land; N on vacant land; W on JONATHAN SKRINE; after her death to ALBERT & NICHOLAS, JR., sons of NICHOLAS & MAGDELINE LENUD. Signed by MANASSEH COURAGE & MAGDALINE (her mark) COURAGE. Witnesses: ABRAHAM MICHAU, THOMAS HOWARD, RENE (his mark) LENUD, JAMES ROBERT. Possession given by turf & twig according to custom. Before PETER ROBERT. JACOB MOTTE, Register.

Book I, p. 472 MATHURIN GUERIN, planter, of Goosecreek, to
1 & 2 Oct. 1731 JOHN LAURENS, saddler, of Charleston, for
L & R ₤ 1300 SC money, that piece of his town lots
in Charleston fronting E 100 ft. on the corner of a broad street that goes from White Point to the Presbyterian Meeting & 235 ft. deep; bounding N 132 ft. on the Market Place & 103 ft. on part of GUERIN'S land; W 100 ft. bounding on MRS. ELIZABETH STEVENS & part on land belonging to the French Church; S 235 ft. on part of GUERIN'S land. Witnesses: EDWIN STEADS, THOMAS CORBETT, BENJAMIN ADDISON. Before DANIEL GREENE, J.P. JACOB MOTTE, Register.

Book I, p. 476 ROWLAND STORY, planter, & ELIZABETH his wife,
9 & 10 Oct. 1724 to JOHN BEE, planter, all of Berkeley Co., for
L & R ₤ 450 SC money, 2 lots #24 & #25 in Charleston,
bounding W on a street running from Ashley River towards the New Brick Church; S on other part of the lots belonging to CAPT. ANTHONY MATHEWS; N on JOHN CHAPMAN; STORY being rightfully seized of the 2 lots except for a unexpired lease dated 9 Apr. 1717 to JOHN CAWOOD for 15 years at a yearly rent of ₤ 7 which shall hereafter be payable to BEE. Witnesses: GEORGE DUCATT, HENRY HARGRAVE, ROBERT HUME. Memo. Whereas the land is said to be 61 ft. to the W & 104 ft. from W to E, the true measure is from N to S on the front 67 ft. & from W to E 127 ft. 4 in. deep, according to certificate signed by COL. JOHN HERBERT, Dep. Surv. Witnesses: JAMES MASSEY, JOHN MILNER, ROBERT HUME. Before TWEEDIE SOMERVILLE, J.P. JACOB MOTTE, Register.

Book I, p. 482　　　　　　　JOHN HUTCHINSON, gentleman, to JOHN BEE, both
23 & 24 Aug. 1731　　　　　of Charleston, for ℔ 500 currency, & ℔ 3400
L & R　　　　　　　　　　security, the southern part of lot #2 with the
　　　　　　　　　　　　　brick messuage or tenement thereon, fronting
51 ft. toward Cooper River & 212 ft. deep (formerly conveyed to JOHN
HUTCHINSON, the father, & ANNE his wife); bounding E on the Bay; W on a
marsh belonging to Landgrave THOMAS SMITH; N on another brick messuage &
other part of the town lot settled in trust for the use of ANNE HUTCHIN-
SON, the daughter; & to the S inclosed by a brick wall bounding on land
belonging to CAPT. GEORGE SMITH, which tenement & parcel of land were devised to HUTCHINSON by his father & now occupied by JOHN BAKER, merchant;
also all houses, out houses, kitchens, storehouses, warehouses, still
houses & other buildings on the lot; except the devise of 1/3 of the lot
granted CHARLOTTE HUTCHINSON, widow of JOHN HUTCHINSON, during her natural life. Whereas the Rt. Hon. WILLIAM, Earl of Craven, Palatine, & the
Lords Proprs. on 7 Sept. 1681 granted THEOPHILUS PATEY lot #2 in Charleston; & whereas EDWARD PATEY, eldest son & heir of THEOPHILUS, on 4 Dec.
1688 assigned 1/2 the lot to JOHN BOONE, gentleman, of Charleston; &
whereas JOHN BOONE for ℔ 20 sterling on 19 Jan. 1694 sold the half-lot to
JAMES RISBEE, merchant, of the Island of Jamaica, which half lot adjoined
the land of WILLIAM NOWELL, mariner, of SC; & whereas JAMES RISBEE & JANE
his wife in 1714, for a valuable consideration, sold to GEORGE SMITH, ESQ.
of the Island of Bermuda, not only that half of lot #2 but also all his
(RISBEE'S) real & personal estate in SC, nothing excepted or reserved; &
whereas GEORGE SMITH & DOROTHY his wife on 31 July 1713 appointed Landgrave THOMAS SMITH, GEORGE SMITH & ROBERT TRADD their attorneys to dispose of the houses, lands, Negroes, cattle, etc. belonging to them in SC;
& whereas Landgrave THOMAS SMITH & GEORGE SMITH, 2 of the attorneys for
GEORGE SMITH of Bermuda, by deed of feofment 2 July 1717, for ℔ 80 currency of Island of Bermuda, conveyed to JOHN HUTCHINSON, apothecary, &
ANNE his then wife, of Charleston, the southernmost part of lot #2, fronting E 51 ft. on the Bay towards Cooper River, bounding S 212 ft. on CAPT.
GEORGE SMITH; W on Landgrave THOMAS SMITH'S marsh; N on JOSEPH BOONE, per
plat attached to deed; & whereas JOHN HUTCHINSON survived his wife ANNE &
became sole owner by will dated Oct. 1729 amongst other things devised to
his loving wife CHARLOTTE during her natural life 1/3 part of the brick
messuage or tenement in which he then dwelt, the buildings behind it &
the backyard, bounding N on another brick tenement conveyed by him to
trustees for the use of his loving daughter ANNE & devised to his son
JOHN (party hereto) the aforesaid brick tenement & other buildings & backyard belonging to it, except that his wife should have her third part during her life; now JOHN HUTCHINSON conveys to JOHN BEE. Witnesses: JAMES
GREEME, BENJAMIN WHITAKER. Before CHARLES HILL, J.P. JACOB MOTTE, Register.

Book I, p. 505　　　　　　　HENRY SHERIFFE, cooper, & MARTHA his wife, of
18 Jan. 1720/1　　　　　　Colleton Co., to BENJAMIN DENNIS, schoolmaster,
Deed of Sale　　　　　　　of Charleston, for ℔ 380 currency, 386 a.
　　　　　　　　　　　　　(Part of 500 a.) on the SW side of the creek
dividing the clear land from the other. Whereas his Excellency JOHN,
Lord Granville, Palatine, & the Lords Proprs. under the hand of Sir NA-
THANIEL JOHNSON, Knight, Gov., etc., on 14 Mar. 1704/5 granted WILLIAM
GREENE 500 a., English measure, in Colleton Co., bounding E on Bohicket
Creek & other ways; & whereas WILLIAM GREENE on 12 Jan. 1712/13 for ℔ 10
sold the 500 a. to JAMES LEROCHE, SR. & he on 7 May 1719, conveyed the
land to JANES LEROCHE, JR., who conveyed it on 14 Dec. 1719 to HENRY
SHERIFFE; now SHERIFFE conveys part (386 a.) to DENNIS. Witnesses: ADAM
BEAUCHAMP, JOHN BORWN, SAMUEL SHARTOCK. Witnesses to delivery by turf &
twig: MARY BASNETT, KATHRINE (her mark) GOFF, JOSEPH (his mark) WRIGHT.
Before JOHN BARKSDALE, J.P. Before THOMAS HEPWORTH, J.P. JACOB MOTTE,
Register.

Book I, p. 505　　　　　　　HENRY SHERIFFE, cooper, of Colleton Co., to
18 Jan. 1720　　　　　　　BEJNAMIN DENNIS, schoolmaster, of Charleston,
Bond　　　　　　　　　　　in sum of ℔ 600 SC money as security for the
　　　　　　　　　　　　　delivery of the plantation mentioned above (p.
500). Witnesses: ADAM BEAUCHAMP, JOHN BROWN, SAMUEL SHARTOCK. Before
THOMAS HEPWORTH, J.P. JACOB MOTTE, Register.

Book I, p. 506　　　　　　　DANIEL BOURGET, brewer, to ELISHA PRIOLEAU,

26 & 27 Oct. 1731   merchant, both of Charleston, for ₤ 700 cur-
L & R by Mortgage   rency, with interest, payable as agreed, part
                           of town lots Nos. 87, 88, & 89, bounding E
104 ft. on Old Church Street; & in depth on the S side for the breadth of
61 ft., 145 ft. 2 ins; & in depth on the N side for the breadth of 98 ft.,
235 ft. 2 in.; bounding W on JAMES MATHEWS; S on other part of the 3 lots
belonging to ANDREW ALLEN, JOSEPH MASSEY, BENJAMIN MASSEY, & JAMES
MATHEWS. Witnesses: JOSEPH RAPER, EDWARD WIGG, CHARLES PINCKNEY. Before
TWEEDIE SOMERVILLE, J.P. JACOB MOTTE, Register. Mortgage satisfied 10
June 1734. Witness: NATHANIEL JOHNSON.

Book I, p. 512   TWEEDIE SOMERVILLE, ESQ., to DANIEL BOURGETT,
2 & 3 Sept. 1730   shopkeeper, both of Charleston, for ₤ 1040 SC
L & R   money, part of 3 town lots Nos. 87, 88, & 89,
                           bounding E on Old Church Street leading from
Ashley River towards the Presbyterian Meeting House fronting 104 ft. from
N to S; & in depth on S side for the breadth of 61 ft., 145 ft. 2 in.; &
depth on N side for the breadth of 98 ft., 235 ft. 2 in.; bounding W on
JAMES MATHEWS; S on the part of the 3 lots belonging to ANDREW ALLEN,
JOSEPH MASSEY, BENJAMIN MASSEY & JAMES MATHEWS; free from all claim of
dower that may be brought by ELIZABETH, wife of TWEEDIE SOMERVILLE. Wit-
nesses: EDWARD WIGG, ROBERT HUME. Before FRANCIS YONGE. JACOB MOTTE,
Register.

Book I, p. 518   WILLIAM LIVINGSTON, merchant of Willtown, SC,
29 Oct. 1731   & HENRY LIVINGSTON, goldsmith, of Charleston.
Mutual Deed of Partition   Whereas the Rev. MR. WILLIAM LIVINGSTON, of
                           Ashley River, father of WILLIAM & HENRY, by
will dated 17 July 1723 bequeathed to WILLIAM, his eldest son, his choice
half of the 3 tracts he had purchased from JOHN KENNEWAY, near Ponpon River, Colleton Co., 1096 a. in all, giving the other half to his second son
HENRY; now WILLIAM & HENRY divide the land as follows, WILLIAM paying
HENRY ₤ 96 currency WILLIAM to have all the land (500 a.) in 1 plott, to
the W of the freshes of Edisto River, within land, bounding N & E on a
swamp, vacant land, JOHN JACKSON'S land, WALTER MELVIN'S land, & JOSEPH
DIDCOTT'S land; S & W on vacant land & swamp land; also a tract of 96 a.,
to the W of the freshes of Edisto River, within land, bounding S & N on
lands patented to JOHN KENNEWAY; E on JOSEPH DIDCOTT; W on vacant land;
HENRY to have 500 a. to the W of the freshes of Edisto River, within land,
bounding S on JOSEPH HOLY (HALEY) & JOSEPH DIDCOTT; W on an impassable
swamp; N on a swamp & vacant land; E on JOSEPH DIDCOTT. Witnesses: RICH-
ARD DAWKINS, SAMUEL EVELEIGH. Before TWEEDIE SOMERVILLE, J.P. JACOB
MOTTE, Register.

Book I, p. 522   JOHN KENNEWAY, planter, of Colleton Co., to
24 & 25 Mar. 1715   WILLIAM LIVINGSTON, gentleman, of Charleston,
L & R   for ₤ 200 currency, 1000 a. in 2 plats annexed
                           to 2 grants, on W side of freshes of Edisto
within land, & his interest in 96 a. between the 2 plats above mentioned,
that is in the middle of the 1000 a. bounding N on swamp land not laid
out & the lands of WALTER MELVIN; E on JOSEPH DIDCOTT; S on JOSEPH HALEY
& JAMES COCHRAN; W on swamp land not laid out; which 1000 a. were granted
to JOHN KENNEWAY by the Rt. Hon. ROBERT GIBBES, Gov. & the Lords Proprs.,
1 grant dated 13 Jan. 1710, the other 28 June 1711. Witnesses: HENRY
FRENCHAM, JOHN SMILIES, DENNIS GIBBES. Witnesses to receipt: JAMES COCH-
RAN, HENRY FRENCHAM. Before JAMES COCHRAN. JACOB MOTTE, Register.

Book I, p. 526   WILLIAM TREADWELL BULL, clerk, rector of Green-
1 July 1731   sted, Essex Co., appointed the Rev. Commissary,
Letter of Attorney   ALEXANDER GARDEN, clerk, rector of St. Phil-
                           ip's, Charleston, his attorney, to sell his
Negro or Indian slaves, cattle, hogs, implements, lands, etc., in SC,
etc., etc. Witnesses: WILLIAM MANNING, RICHARD SHUBRICK, JR., EDWARD
HEXT. Before CHARLES HILL, J.P. JACOB MOTTE, Register.

Book I, p. 528   The Rev. Mr. WILLIAM GUY, clerk, & REBECCA
15 July 1716   his wife; JAMES MCCALL & SARAH his wife; &
Deed of Sale   MARY BASDEN, spinster to GARRETT VANVELSIN,
                           shoemaker all of Charleston, for ₤ 83:15 SC
money, part of lot #73 in Charleston fronting N 38 ft. on Tradd Street

& 99 ft. deep; bounding S on WILLIAM CHAPMAN (formerly THOMAS ROSE); E on part of same lot; W on NATHANIEL PARTRIDGE. Whereas the Rt. Hon. WILLIAM, Earl of Craven, Palatine, & the Lords Proprs. on 16 Mar. 1693 granted CAPT. CHARLES BASDEN, gentleman, lot #73 bounding E on OLIVER SPENCER; W on a street running by CAPT. HENRY SIMONS & others; S on THOMAS ROSE; N on a street leading from Cooper River between the lots of RICHARD TRADD & OLIVER SPENCER: 7 whereas CHARLES BASDEN died & his estate descended to MARY BASDEN, SARAH MCCALL (formerly SARAH BASDEN) & REBECCA GUY (formerly REBECCA BASDEN) daughters & co-heiresses of CHARLES BASDEN; now they sell part of the lot to VANVELSIN. Witnesses: GILBERT JONES, CHARLES FRENCH-OMME (merchant) THOMAS HEPWORTH. Before FRANCIS YONGE, J.P. JACOB MOTTE, Register.

Book I, p. 532
9 Nov. 1731
Letter of Attorney

LAWRENCE BUTTERWORTH, mariner, of Dorchester, Parish of St. George, Berkeley Co., appointed his well beloved son GEORGE BUTTERWORTH, wheelwright, his attorney to administer his estate in the middle of the Market Place, White Haven, Co. of Cumberland, in Old England, formerly in the possession of a Mr. HAMILTON, now occupied by a Mr. STEPHENSON, BUTTERWORTH being sole owner by will of DAVID HAMILTON; also to handle his property in Arteburry, in Oxfordshire Old England. Witnesses: JOHN MASON, JAMES MENZIES, JOHN HILL. Before ALEXANDER SKENE, J.P. JACOB MOTTE, Register.

Book I, p. 534
9 Nov. 1731
Deed of Gift

LAURENCE BUTTERWORTH, mariner, of Dorchester, Parish of St. George, Berkeley Co., to his son GEORGE BUTTERWORTH, wheelwright, for good will & special affection & other considerations, all his property in White Haven, about the middle of the Market Place, Co. of Cumberland, Old England, formerly in the possession of Mr. HAMILTON, now occupied by Mr. STEVENSON; also all his property in Artiburry, Oxfordshire, Old England. Witnesses: JAMES MANZIES, JOHN HILL, JOHN MASON. Before ALEXANDER SKENE, J.P. JACOB MOTTE, Register.

Book I, p. 535
19 Nov. 1731
Deed of Gift

THOMAS RIMBERLY, gentleman, of Charleston, with the consent & approbation of his wife ISABEL, effective after their death, to daughter-in-law ANNA SHUTE, wife of JOSEPH SHUTE, for good will & affection & other considerations, 6 a., English measure, in Berkeley Co., near Charleston, which he purchased from GEORGE CLAYPOOLE on 14 & 15 Mar. 1723; & whereas THOMAS KIMBERLY & JOSEPH SHUTE have agreed to erect some buildings on the 6 a. at their joint cost, it is also agreed that the rents shall be shared equally. Witnesses: WILLIAM MCKENZIE, THOMAS FLEMING, JOHN CROFT. Before DANIEL GREENE, J.P. JACOB MOTTE, Register.

Book I, p. 537
28 & 29 Jan. 1730
Agreement Tripartite

FRANCIS LEBRASSEUR, merchant, of the 1st part; THOMAS GADSDEN, ESQ. & JOHN KING, merchant, of the 2nd part; ANNE SPLATT, widow of RICHARD SPLATT, merchant, of the 3rd part: all of Charleston. Whereas a marriage is intended between FRANCIS LEBRASSEUR & ANNE SPLATT they agree that certain property shall be conveyed to THOMAS GADSDEN & JOHN KING in trust for certain purposes. FRANCIS LEBRASSEUR therefore conveys to GADSDEN & KING that piece of land fronting 56 ft. on the Bay of Charleston formerly conveyed by BENJAMIN SCHENSKINGH & MARGARET his wife to JOHN BUCKLEY, merchant; being 116 ft. long from E to W next a neighborhood alley; on the W adjoining the land of Mr. WRAGG (formerly DR. JOHN THOMAS); also the messuage or tenement standing on the ground wherein JACOB SATUR & ISAAC DUMONS live; also several tenements & storehouses in the alley occupied by EBENEZER LYON, WILLIAM HAMERTON, CHARLES STARNE & JOHN WRIGHT; to hold the property in trust for FRANCIS LEBRASSEUR & ANNE, his intended wife. Witnesses: JOHN VICARIDGE, ROBERT HUME. Before J. BOND, J.P. JACOB MOTTE, Register.

Book I, p. 542
20 Apr. 1731
Deed of Sale

FRANCIS SIMONS, & ANNE his wife, of Berkeley Co., to his Excellency ROBERT JOHNSON, ESQ., Gov., for ₺ 750 currency, 300 a. in Berkeley Co., bounding NW, SW & SE on JOHN ASHBY; NE on ROBERT JOHNSON (formerly of the Hon. NATHANIEL JOHNSON). Witnesses: JOHN BLAKE, EDWARD HARSDWOOD. Before DANIEL GREENE, J.P. JACOB MOTTE, Reg.

Book I, p. 545
2 Nov. 1726
Deed of Sale

STEPHEN (ETIENNE) TAURON (RAUVERON), gentleman, to RICHARD GRIMSTON, gentleman, both of Charleston, for ₤ 300 SC money, part of lot #113 in Charleston, fronting 14 ft. 4 in. on Church St. & running W on which there is a small tenement 12 ft. 4 in. fronting Church St., the other 2 ft. adjoining STEPHEN TAURON, there being an old tenement thereon so that GRIMSTON cannot have immediate possession of the 2 ft. nor is he to possess the same until the old tenement is blown down or destroyed; but he is to have immediate possession of the 14 ft. 4 in. which was formerly purchased by TAURON from WILLIAM WHITE, planter, on 25 Apr. 1688, bounding E on Church St.; W on JAMES SERRURIER (alias SMITH); N on JANE DUPEY; S on part of lot owned by TAURON; GRIMSTON to hold the land free of dower of CATHERINE, wife of STEPHEN TAURON. Witnesses: HENRY GIGNIALLIATT, JOHN CROFT, JEAN GARNIER. Before DANIEL GREENE, J.P. JACOB MOTTE, Register.

Book I, p. 550
10 Feb. 1726
Deed of Sale

STEPHEN (ETIENNE) TAURON, gentleman, to ELIAS HANCOCK, vintner, both of Charleston, for ₤ 550 SC money, part of a lot in Charleston, fronting E 36 ft. on Church St., running W 90 ft.; bounding W & S on Mrs. CATHERINE NOBLE (formerly JAMES SERRURIER, alias SMITH); N on RICHARD GRIMSTON; which part of a lot had been purchased from WILLIAM WHITE, planter, 1 25 Apr. 1688. Witnesses: THOMAS FAIRCHILD, THOMAS BARTRAM, JOHN CROFT. Before DANIEL GREENE, J.P. JACOB MOTTE, Register.

Book I, p. 553
27 Dec. 1727
Deed of Sale

ELIAS HANCOCK, vintner, & MARY his wife, to RICHARD GRIMSTON, gentleman, all of Charleston, for ₤ 600 SC money, part of lot #113 in Charleston, fronting E 36 ft. on Church St., running W 90 ft., bounding W & S on Mrs. CATHERINE NOBLE (formerly JAMES SERRURIER, alias SMITH); N on RICHARD GRIMSTON; which part of a lot STEPHEN TAUURON purchased from WILLIAM WHITE & sold to ELIAS HANCOCK on 10 Jan. 1726. Witnesses: ESTIENNE TAUURON (STEPHEN TAURON); JOHN CROFT. Before DANIEL GREENE, J.P. JACOB MOTTE, Register.

Book I, p. 556
10 Mar. 1729
Deed of Sale

RICHARD GRIMSTON, gentleman, & ELINOR (her mark) his wife, to ELISHA PRIOLEAU; all of Charleston, for ₤ 1000 SC money, part of lot #113 in Charleston, fronting E on Church St. & running W 90 ft. the whole breadth except a small matter wanting to the southward bounding W & S on Mrs. CATHERINE NOBLE (formerly JAMES SERRURIER, alias SMITH); N on Mrs. JAMES DUPEY. Witnesses: FRANCIS SURREAU, COL. SAMUEL PRIOLEAU, JOHN CROFT. Before DANIEL GREENE, J.P. JACOB MOTTE, Register.

Book I, p. 560
30 Mar. 1719
Deed of Sale

ROGER (his mark) GOFF, & DOBORAH his wife, to ROGER MOORE, for ₤ 1000 SC money, 800 a., English measure in Berkeley Co., granted to JAMES WILLIAMS, surgeon, on 2 July 1633 by him conveyed to ROBERT QUARRYON 3 Dec. 1684, by him conveyed to ROGER GOFF on 13 June 1692; bounding SW on WILLIAM HAWETT; E on DAVID WEBSTER; N on COL. GEORGE CHICKEN; SE on COL. JAMES MOORE. Witnesses: JOHN HODGSON, JOHN ELDERS. Before ROBERT STEVENS. JACOB MOTTE, Register.

Book I, p. 562
15 & 16 Oct. 1731
L & R

MARY SALTUS, & ANNE SALTUS, spinsters of the Island of Bermuda (alias Somers Islands) only daughters & co-heirs of BARTHOLEMEW SALTUS who was eldest brother & heir of MARTHA JONES (formerly MARTHA SALTUS) widow of JOHN JONES, gunsmith, of SC, to THOMAS BINDORD, merchant, of Charleston, for ₤ 230 SC money, 3 lots in Charleston, Nos. 148, 149, & 150 which were granted by the Lords Proprs. by 3 grants dated 20 June 1694 to JOHN JONES. Witnesses: THOMAS WOOD, RICHARD STAMMERS, WILLIAM DUNSCOMB. ₤ 230 paid to M. BREWTON as attorney for MARY & ANNE SALTUS. Witnesses: ALEXANDER PARRIS, CHARLES BURLEY. Before DANIEL GREEN, J.P. JACOB MOTTE, Register.

Book I, p. 568
22 Jan. 1722
Deed of Sale

THOMAS HOLTON & ANNE CATHERINE (her mark) his wife, to JOSEPH DANFORD, for ₤ 70 currency & other considerations, & with ANNE CATHRINE'S free & unconstrained assent, part of lot #222 on W side of Charleston, fronting E 28 ft. Witnesses: JOHN TIPOR, SAMUEL BENNETT. Before JOHN BARKSDALE, J.P. JACOB MOTTE, Register.

Book I, p. 571
20 Mar. 1731
Deed of Sale

CHARLES KING, to ROBERT HOW, for Ł 16 SC money, 2 a. in Berkeley Co., on E the plantation of CHARLES KING commonly called Caintin on Wando River & within the breadth of 1 a. of the land belonging to Mrs. MARY POLLOCK. Witnesses: THOMAS FARLESS, JAMES TAGGART. Delivery by turf & twig. Before ROBERT DANIEL, J.P. JACOB MOTTE, Register.

Book I, p. 572
2 Feb. 1729
Mortgage

WILLIAM FISHBURN, tailor, to BENJAMIN WARING & JOSHUA GREEN, planters, all of Berkeley Co., for good considerations, conveys 2 tracts; 1 of 76 a. in Dorchester, Berkeley Co., where he lives, bought at several times by FISHBURN; the other containing 255 a. in Colleton Co., at a place known as Beach Hill where JOHN SHUT lives; also 4 Negroes (2 men, 2 women). Should FISHBURN pay WARING & GREEN Ł 700 currency with interest before the end of 4 years this deed to be void. Witnesses: JOHN LUPTON, ANN WARING, SABINA SMITH. Memo. This deed is for the use of the children of JOHN GREENE, deceased, named SUSANNAH & ELIZABETH GREENE. Signed, BENJAMIN WARING, JOSHUA GREENE. Before JOB ROTHMAHLER. JACOB MOTTE, Register.

Book I, p. 575
2 Feb. 1729
Bond

WILLIAM FISHBURN, tailor, of Berkeley Co., to BENJAMIN WARING & JOSHUA GREEN, planters, executors of JOHN GREENE, in the penal sum of Ł 1400 SC money, conditioned for redeeming the above mortgage (p. 572). Witnesses: JOHN LUPTON, SABINA SMITH. Before JOB ROTHMAHLER. JACOB MOTTE, Register.

Book I, p. 576
2 Oct. 1728
Deed of Gift

SAMUEL (his mark) FRITH to JOHN WOODSON & PHILLIS his wife, for respect, 2 a. on James Island adjoining JOHN CROSKEYS & Mr. SKINNER, for their natural lives but not to be disposed of. Witness: JOSEPH CROSKEYS. Before DANIEL GREENE, J.P. JACOB MOTTE, Register.

Book I, p. 577
22 Sept. 1731
Letter of Attorney

JOSEPH PAICE, JR., merchant, of London, executor of will of RICHARD MILES, late of Madeira, since of London, appointed BENJAMIN DELA CONSEILLERS & JOHN WRIGHT, merchants, of Charleston, his attorneys with power to receive from BENJAMIN SCHENCKINGH & OBADIAH ALLEN, merchants, of Charleston, all money due the estate of RICHARD MILES, either in his own name or as the partner of Mr. RICHBELL of Madeira & with authority to dispose of any estate belonging to RICHARD MILES. Before JOHN RUCK, M.P. of London. Witnesses: RICHARD SHUBRICK, JR., EDMUND SMYTER. SHUBRICK appeared before DANIEL GREENE, J.P. JACOB MOTTE, Register.

Book I, p. 579
11 July 1728
Agreement

JOHN ARNETT, surgeon, & RICHARD EDGELL, gentleman, both of Charleston, enter into an agreement as follows: whereas WILLIAM ELLIOTT, planter, & CATHERINE his wife, of Berkeley Co., by deed of feofment dated 5 May 1722, for Ł 400 currency, conveyed to THOMAS KIMBERLY, chairmaker, & ISABEL, his wife, of Charleston, part of lot #10 in Charleston, that is, 20 ft. fronting the lane which runs to the bay, commonly called Callibeuf's Lane, bounding W on the part of lot belonging to WILLIAM ELLIOTT; E on the part belonging to THOMAS ELLIOTT; S home to the end of WILLIAM ELLIOTT's part, being 87 ft. deep, for the term of their natural lives & afterwards to their daughter ANNE GOOL; & whereas by deed of feofment, dated 15 Nov. 1722, WILLIAM ELIOTT for Ł 100 currency conveyed to THOMAS KIMBERLY & ISABEL his wife, part of lot #10, that is, 5 ft. fronting Callibeuf's Lane, bounding W on WILLIAM ELLIOTT; E on KIMBERLY; being 87 ft. deep; for their natural lives & afterwards to ANNE GOOL, their daughter; & whereas a marriage is intended between JOHN ARNETT & ANNE GOOL, it is agreed as follows: ARNETT agrees that should the marriage occur & ANNE attains 21 years he & ANNE they will settle ANNE'S (above-named) property to the use of JOHN ARNETT for his natural life, then to the use of RICHARD EDGELL & in trust for ANNE during ANNE'S natural life, & after her decease to the heirs of children of JOHN & ANNE, if any; if none, then to ANNE'S heirs. Witnesses: C. BOULLEE, JAMES STANWAY, RICHARD EDGELL. Before DANIEL GREENE, J.P. JACOB MOTTE, Register.

Book I, p. 581
15 & 16 Dec. 1731
L & R

JOHN ALURENS, saddler, to WILLIAM MCKENZIE, merchant, both of Charleston, for ₤ 650 SC money, part of a lot in Charleston, being part of the lots JOHN LAURENS purchased from MATHURIN GUERRIN, fronting E 50 ft. on a street that runs from White Point through the Market Place to the Presbyterian Meeting House; bounding S 235 ft. on MARY GUERIN; W on the lot belonging to the trustees or elders of the French Church; N on other parts belonging to JOHN LAURENS. Witnesses: BENJAMIN ADDISON, JOHN CARRION, CHARLES PINCKNEY. Before DANIEL GREENE, J.P.

Book I, p. 588
30 Nov. & 5 Dec. 1731
L & R by Mortgage

ALEXANDER GOODBE, planter, to JOHN DANIEL, planter, both of the Parish of St. Thomas Berkeley Co., for ₤ 500 currency, 250 a., English measure, in Berkeley Co., bounding NW on ROBERT HOW; SW on BENJAMIN GODIN & the Hon. ARTHUR MIDDLETON, ESQ.; W on COL. JOHN HERBERT. Should GOODBE pay DANIEL ₤ 500 on 1 Jan. 1732 this mortgage & a bond for ₤ 1000 shall be void. Whereas the Hon. CHARLES CRAVEN, ESQ., Gov. & the Lords Proprs. by grants dated 17 Dec. 1714 & 2 plats dated 20 Sept. 1696 & another plat dated 24 Dec. 1701 granted JOHN GOODEBE, SR. 250 a. in St. James, Goosecreek,; now GOODBE mortgages the land to DANIEL. Witnesses: GEORGE LOGAN, ANTHONY WHITE, ANDREW SHAPLEY. Before THOMAS BARTON, J.P. JACOB MOTTE, Register.

Book I, p. 595
19 & 20 Nov. 1731
L & R

EDWARD THOMAS, planter, of St. John's Parish, Berkeley Co., to NOAH SERRE, planter, of St. James Santee, Craven Co., for ₤ 300 SC money; 270 a. in Berkeley Co., bounding S on Landgrave THOMAS SMITH; N on Mrs. LYDIA DURHAM. Witnesses: ISAAC MAZYCK, JR., JOHN LEWIS. Before DANIEL GREENE, J.P. JACOB MOTTE, Register.

Book I, p. 600
17 & 16 Dec. 1731
L & R

SUSANNAH WIGINGTON (formerly SUSANNAH RAWLINGS, widow of EDWARD RAWLINGS, vintner) to ROBERT HUME, gentleman, both of Charleston, for ₤ 240 SC money, 1/6 part of 3 lots in Charleston, given by MARY CORSS, widow, by her will to WILLIAM BAYLY, since deceased, to the said SUSANNAH (then RAWLINGS), & to MARY BASDEN, since deceased; fronting N 50 ft. on a street leading from Cooper River by lots formerly belonging to MESSRS. GIBBON & ALLEN, now to MESSRS. TONNERVILLE (SOVERINILLE?), ELLERY, COOPER, & CAPT. WARDEN; bounding S on land formerly belonging to PETER MANIGAULT, now to LAURENS or BONNEAU & on DUPEY (formerly TOBIAS FITCH). Witnesses: MARY BLAMYER, STEPHEN DRAYTON. Before JOSEPH WRAGG. JACOB MOTTE, Register.

Book I, p. 605
28 May 1716
Deed of Sale

CAPT. BENJAMIN QUELCH, gentleman, to JOHN SIMES, planter, both of Christ Church Parish, Berkeley Co., for ₤ 100 currency, 200 a. in Berkeley Co.; bounding NE on EDMUND MORRAIN; SW on JOHN HENDRICK. Witnesses: HENRY GILL, EDWARD OARD, BENJAMIN QUELCH, JR. Before THOMAS COOPER, J.P. JACOB MOTTE, Register.

Book I, p. 608
11 Nov. 1731
Deed of Sale

THOMAS TOWNSEND, planter, of Colleton Co., to BENJAMIN D'HARRIETTE, merchant, of Charleston, for ₤ 1200 SC money, 304 a. on Johns Island, Colleton Co. Whereas the Lords Proprs. under the hand of the Rt. Hon. Sir NATHANIEL JOHNSON, Gov., on 29 Oct. 1709 granted MILES BREWTON 400 a. in John Island, on GEORGE FROST'S Creek, bounding S & E on JOHN FROST; N on SAMUEL EVELEIGH; W on JOHN WILSON; & whereas MILES BREWTON & JEHOIDA, his wife, on 10 Nov. 1712 conveyed the 400 a. to STEPHEN FORD, SR., weaver, of Colleton Co.; & whereas STEPHEN FORD & JANE his wife on 28 July 1713 conveyed the land to their son STEPHEN FORD, JR.; & whereas STEPHEN FORD, JR. & MARY his wife on 10 Oct. 1717 sold the 400 a. to EMANUEL MARQUEZ? (MARQUIS) planter, of Colleton Co.; & whereas on 18 Jan. 1717/8 EMANUEL MARQUEZ & ELIZABETH his wife sold to THOMAS DIXON 200 a. (part of the 400) bounding on CAPT. GEORGE

FROST'S Creek & joining JOHN WILSON'S land on the W; & whereas THOMAS DIXON & MARY his wife on 31 Jan. 1718/9 sold JOHN HENRY BONNEAU, joiner, 100 a. (part of 200), bounding of GEORGE FROST'S Creek & W on JOHN WILSON; & whereas JOHN HENRY BONNEAU & ANNE his wife on 9 Mar. 1719/20 sold the 100 a. to THOMAS TOWNSEND, planter, of Colleton Co.; & whereas THOMAS DIXON & MARY his wife on 16 Mar. 1718/19 sold THOMAS TOWNSEND the other 100 a. (part of the 200 a.); & whereas EMANUEL & ELIZABETH MARQUIS on 9 Aug. 1718 sold to JOHN HILL, mariner, of Charleston, 200 a. (the remaining part of 400 a.) bounding formerly S & E on THOMAS DIXON; N on ROGER MOORE; W on JOHN WILSON; & whereas JOHN HILL & ELIZABETH his wife on 18 Jan. 1721 sold the 200 a. to THOMAS TOWNSEND; & whereas NATHANIEL NICHOLS, planter, & SARAH his wife, of Colleton Co., on 18 Aug. 1727 sold THOMAS TOWNSEND 100 a. (part of GEORGE FROST'S tract) on Johns Island, bounding S on FROST'S Creek, E on NATHANIEL NICHOLS; W on THOMAS TOWNSEND (formerly MILES BREWTON); NW on ROGER MOORE, gentleman; & whereas notwithstanding the several conveyances to THOMAS TOWNSEND of the 400 a. granted to MILES BREWTON by the Lords Proprs. according to the plat affexed to the grant, by a resurvey only 204 a. are to be found, which with the 100 a. which TOWNSEND bought from NICHOLS makes 304 a; now TOWNSEND conveys to D"HARRIETTE the 304 a. Witnesses: ELIZABETH ELLIS, JOHN SMITH, JOHN CROFT. Before GABRIEL MANIGAULT, J.P. JACOB MOTTE, Register.

Book I, p. 617
19 & 20 Mar. 1727
L & R

DENNIS (his mark) MORRAIN, planter, & ELIZABETH (her mark) his wife, to JAMES EDEN, planter, all of Berkeley Co., for ₺ 264 currency, 132 a., English measure, in Berkeley Co., bounding NE on EDMUND MORRAIN & JOHN MORRAIN; SE on EDMUND MORRAIN; NE on JOHN SEASEAU; NW on JOHN SEASEAU; SW on THOMAS BOONE (formerly BENJAMIN QUELCH). Witnesses: JOSEPH JULLY, THOMAS BOONE, J.P. JACOB MOTTE, Register.

Book I, p. 622
1 Oct. 1711
Deed of Sale

Landgrave THOMAS SMITH to JOHN SIMONS, of Charleston, for ₺ 30 currency, 990 a. (part of 24,000 a.) in Craven Co. Whereas on 18 June 1711 the Lords Proprs. under the hand of the Hon. ROBERT GIBBS, ESQ., Gov., granted ROBERT DANIEL, ESQ. several tracts in Craven Co. containing 24,000 a. (part of 48,000 given ROBERT DANIEL with his Landgrave's patent; & whereas ROBERT DANIEL on 19 June 1711 sold Landgrave THOMAS SMITH the 24,000 a.; now SMITH sells 990 a. (part of the 24,000) to SIMONS. Witnesses: WILLIAM SCREVEN, JAMES ELLIS, FRANCIS GRECIA, WILLIAM KITCHEN. On 13 Nov. 1711 JAMES CHILD, attorney to Landgrave SMITH, took possession & delivered the premises to CAPT. PERCIVAL PAWLEY, attorney for JOHN SIMONS. Witnesses: JOHN ASPENELL, JACOB BURDELL. Before HENRY WIGINGTON. Memo. On 22 Nov. 1712 the Rev. Mr. WILLIAM SCREVEN & JAMES ELLIS declared they saw Landgrave THOMAS SMITH sign, seal & deliver the deed to JOHN SIMONS. Before GEORGE SMITH, J.P. JACOB MOTTE, Register.

Book I, p. 625
22 Dec. 1712
Deed of Sale

ANNE (her mark) BLUNDELL, executrix & attorney for SAMUEL BLUNDELL, her husband, to JOHN PRIMATE, for ₺ 100, conveyed 100 a., part of 400 a. granted SAMUEL BLUNDELL. ANNE, knowing that her husband had bargained with PRIMATE for the sale of 100 a. & her husband being "gone privateering these 3 years", she gives this bill of sale until his return. Signed by JOHN BLUNDELL the son of SAMUEL & ANNE. Witnesses: BENTLY COOKE, JOHN (his mark) DRIVER, REBECCA COOKE, EASTER BLUNDELL by order of her mother who was sick delivered by turf & twig. Witnesses: BENTLY COOKE, JOHN (his mark) DRIVER, REBECCA COOKE, THOMAS PAGITT, JOHN CRISTOFELL (CHRISTOPHER) DEHEE, JAMES (his mark) MALLETT. Before ROBERT DANIEL, J.P. JACOB MOTTE, Register.

Book I, p. 627
8 Apr. 1726
Deed of Sale

HENRY SIMONS, planter of St. Johns to THOMAS SUMMERS, gentleman, of St. John's for ₺ 900 currency, 400 a., known as Mount Pleasant, in Berkeley Co., bounding S on Watboo Barony; N on Mr. DUBOURDIEU; W on Mr. BETTESON; E on RENE RAVENEL. JUDITH, the wife of HENRY SIMONS, willingly surrenders her dower. Witnesses: NATHANIEL BROUGHTON, H. BUTLER, PETER DE ST. JULIEN. Witnesses: to delivery & seizin: PAUL TRAPIER, SAMUEL DUBOURDIEU, WILLIAM (his mark) PRICE. Before THOMAS BROUGHTON, J.P. Before PETER DE ST. JULIEN, J.P. JACOB

MOTTE, Register.

Book I, p. 629　　　　　　　WILLIAM GREENLAND, planter & ANNE DONOVAN (wid-
3 & 4 Apr. 1730　　　　　　ow of DANIEL DONOVAN, planter) executors of
L & R　　　　　　　　　　　 the will of DANIEL DONOVAN dated 14 Feb. 1728,
　　　　　　　　　　　　　　 to THOMAS SUMMERS, planter, all of Berkeley
Co., for ₺ 2000 currency, 407 a. in Berkeley Co., within land, on a swamp
on the W branch of Cooper River, bounding S on WILLIAM BALL; W on SAMUEL
RUSCO & ARTHUR MIDDLETON, ESQ.; N on JOSEPH GOODBEY; E on JOSEPH DE ST.
JULIEN. Witnesses: ROBERT TAYLOR, JOHN BAYLY, SAMUEL SUMMERS. Before
THEODORE GREGORY, J.P. JACOB MOTTE, Register.

Book I, p. 635　　　　　　　ABRAHAM SANDERS, planter, to WILLIAM GREENLAND,
1 &.2 Apr. 1730　　　　　　 planter, & ANNE DONOVAN, widow of DANIEL DONO-
L & R　　　　　　　　　　　 VAN, planter, executors of the will of DANIEL
　　　　　　　　　　　　　　 DONOVAN, all of Berkeley Co., for ₺ 400 cur-
rency, paid by DANIEL DONOVAN in his life time, 407 a. in Berkeley Co.,
within land, on a swamp on the W branch of Cooper River; bounding S on
WILLIAM BALL; W on SAMUEL RUSCO & ARTHUR MIDDLETON; N on JOSEPH GOODBEY,
E on JOSEPH ST. JULIEN. Signatures: ABRAHAM SANDERS, MARGARET SANDERS
(his wife). Witnesses: JOHN BAYLY, JOHN SUMMERS, ALICE RIGGS. Before
ISAAC PORCHER, J.P. JACOB MOTTE, Register.

Book I, p. 640　　　　　　　ANNE HEPWORTH, widow of THOMAS HEPWORTH, to
25 & 26 Feb. 1731　　　　　 JAMES CROKATT, merchant, & ESTHER his wife,
L & R　　　　　　　　　　　 all of Charleston, for ₺ 1200 currency, 70 a.
　　　　　　　　　　　　　　 on Charleston Neck in 2 tracts; 1 of 55 a.
granted to JOHN BIRD, bounding E on the head of a creek of Cooper River &
CAPT. WILLIAM HAWETT; S on WILLIAM HAWETT; SW on CHRISTOPHER SMITH; NW on
THOMAS PERRIMAN, WILLIAM EDWARD, & MR. RUBURRY; the other 15 a. purchased
by SIMON VALLENTINE from JOHN KING & JUDAH HOLYBUSH & afterwards conveyed
to JACOB BEAMOR & inherited by his son JAMES BEAMOR; bounding on JOHN
BIRD'S land, S on WILLIAM HAWETT & a marsh belonging to WILLIAM EDWARDS &
on JOHN ATKINSON, schoolmaster; which 55 a. by JOHN BIRD'S will dated 3
Oct. 1711 was bequeathed in fee simple to JAMES BEAMOR who on 14 May 1727
sold the 55 a. & the 15 a. to THOMAS & ANNE HEPWORTH. Witnesses: JAMES
KILPATRICK, JAMES GREEME. Before ROBERT WRIGHT, C.J. JACOB MOTTE, Register.

Book I, p. 648　　　　　　　JOHN BAYLY, son & heir of JOHN BAYLY of Bal-
4 & 5 Mar. 1729　　　　　　 linaclough, Co. of Tipperary, Ireland, by his
L & R　　　　　　　　　　　 attorney, ALEXANDER TRENCH, merchant, of
　　　　　　　　　　　　　　 Charleston (see p. 92) to WILLIAM DANDRIDGE,
planter of Colleton Co., for ₺ 61:5 currency, 245 a. in Colleton Co.,
bounding N on WILLIAM WESTBURY; SE on JOHN NEWTON; W on THOMAS ELLIOTT,
JR. Witnesses: RICHARD GILES, ROBERT RAPER, RICHARD WIGG. Before THEO-
DORE GREGORY, J.P. JACOB MOTTE, Register.

Book I, p. 652　　　　　　　ANTHONY MATHEWS, merchant, & LOIS (her mark)
23 & 24 Feb. 1731　　　　　 his wife of Charleston, with the free consent
L & R　　　　　　　　　　　 of LOIS, to JOHN MORRALL, (MURRILL), planter,
　　　　　　　　　　　　　　 of Craven Co., for ₺ 300 currency 610 a. in
Craven Co., part of 2340 a.; also 1 a. more on N side of & part of 2340
a. 1/4 mill, English measure from the Bluff. Whereas the Hon. Landgrave
THOMAS SMITH, ESQ. on 10 Sept. 1711 sold ANTHONY MATHEWS 2340 a. in Cra-
ven Co., part of the 24,000 a. he purchased from the Hon. Landgrave ROB-
ERT DANIEL, ESQ., now MATHEWS sells 611 a. Witnesses: JAMES MATHEWS,
JOHN MATHEWS, JOHN CROFT. Before GABRIEL MANIGAULT, J.P. JACOB MOTTE,
Register.

Book I, p. 658　　　　　　　THOMAS ROSE, son & heir of THOMAS ROSE, gen-
8 Aug. 1710　　　　　　　　 tlemen, cordwinder, to HENRY SAMWEYS, planter,
Deed of Sale　　　　　　　　both of Berkeley Co., for ₺ 9 currency, lot
　　　　　　　　　　　　　　 #228 in Charleston, granted to THOMAS ROSE,
SR. by the Rt. Hon. WILLIAM, Earl of Craven, Palatine, & the Lords Proprs. under the hand of the Rt. Hon. THOMAS SMITH, Landgrave, etc. on 12
June 1694. Witnesses: WILLIAM BULL, MARY BULL. Witnesses to livery &
seizin: JOHN (his mark) BULLOCK, JOHN STEWART, NICHOLAS STEVENS. Before
DANIEL GREENE, J.P. JACOB MOTTE, Register.

Book I, p. 661　　　　　　　THOMAS KIMBERLY, merchant, to JOHN WHITTA,
16 & 17 Feb. 1731　　　　　(WHITTER), JOSEPH SHUTE, & THOMAS FLEMING,
L & R　　　　　　　　　　　merchants, all of Charleston, for L 100 cur-
　　　　　　　　　　　　　　rency, a tract of land in Charleston containing 1 rood, 29 perches, commonly called the Quakers lot, which lot THOMAS
KIMBERLY obtained by grant from his Majesty King GEORGE the Second signed
by his Excellency, ROBERT JOHNSON, ESQ., Gov., dated 3 Mar. 1731, in
trust for the use of the Quakers on which to erect a Meeting House & for
no other use. Witnesses: HENRY GIGNILLIATT, GEORGE ROLFE. It is also
agreed that THOMAS KIMBERLY be appointed 1 of the trustees. Signatures:
JOHN WHITTER, THOMAS FLEMING, JOSEPH SHUTE, THOMAS KIMBERLY. Before
JAMES ABERCROMBY, J.P. JACOB MOTTE, Register.

　　　　　　　　　　　　　　DEEDS BOOK "K"
　　　　　　　　　　　　　　　1731-1733

Book K, p. 1　　　　　　　　ARCHIBALD STOBO, clerk, of Colleton Co., to
3 Mar. 1731/2　　　　　　　his son WILLIAM STOBO, planter, of same place,
Deed of Gift　　　　　　　　for natural love & affection, 540 a. commonly
　　　　　　　　　　　　　　called Archwood, in Colleton Co., bounding E
on son JAMES STOBO; N on COL. JOSEPH BLAKE; W on ARCHIBALD STOBO; S on
ROBERT YONGE; also 250 a., being 1/2 of a tract of 500 a. joining to the
E on above 540 a.; S on ROBERT YONGE; W on land not laid out; N on JAMES
STOBO (the other 1/2 of 500 a.). ELIZABETH, wife of ARCHIBALD STOBO vol-
untarily surrenders her right of dower, & signs deed. Witnesses: JOHN
ATCHISON, WILLIAM MCECHEN, JAMES COCHRAN. Before WILLIAM LIVINGSTON, J.P.
JACOB MOTTE, Pub. Reg.

Book K, p. 4　　　　　　　　SUSANNAH WIGINTON, widow, (formerly wife of
11 Jan. 1723　　　　　　　　EDWARD RAWLINGS & 1 of the daughters of MARY
Deed of Sale　　　　　　　　CROSS, widow), to ROBERT HUME, all of Charles-
　　　　　　　　　　　　　　ton, for L 5 & other considerations, part of 3
lots in Charleston (devised by will of MARY CROSS to her son WILLIAM BAY-
LY & 2 daughters, MARY BASDEN, widow, & SUSANNAH WIGINGTON by name of SU-
SANNAH RAWLINGS), fronting N 100 ft. on a street running from Cooper Riv-
er by the lots of GIBBON & ALLEN; the depts back from N to S the whole
depth of the 3 lots from N to S except 201 feet fenced in by PETER MANI-
GAULT; bounding E on other part of the 3 lots belonging to SUSANNAH WIG-
INGTON; W on a street parallel with Cooper River toward the Presbyterian
Meeting house. Witnesses: JOB ROTHMAHLER, MARY BLAMYER, CHILDERMAS CROFT.
Before JOSEPH WRAGG, J.P. JACOB MOTTE, Pub. Reg.

Book K, p. 6　　　　　　　　CATHERINE BETTESON, widow of JOHN BETTESON,
22 Jan. 1731　　　　　　　　gentleman, to MARY BETTESON, spinster, daugh-
Deed of Sale　　　　　　　　ter of WILLIAM BETTESON, all of Berkeley Co.,
　　　　　　　　　　　　　　for L 900 SC money, all her right & title of
dower & thirds in 500 a. in St. John's Parish, Berkeley Co., bounding N
on JAMES LEBAS; S on ROBERT TAYLOR; E on Mr. DUBOURDIEU; & her claim to
any of JOHN BETTESON'S property. Witnesses: WILLIAM FRASER, WILLIAM
BRISBANE. Before THOMAS COOPER, J.P. JACOB MOTTE, Pub. Reg.

Book K, p. 8　　　　　　　　ROBERT CLEMONS (CLEMMENTS), planter, to CAPT.
14 Mar. 1731/2　　　　　　　GEORGE BENNISON, both of Christ Church Parish,
Mortgage　　　　　　　　　　Berkeley Co., for L 176:15 SC money, 148 a.
　　　　　　　　　　　　　　English measure, in Christ Church Parish, formerly purchased by JOHN BIRK, who sold to THOMAS HAMLIN, SR.; "which said
land formerly belonged to GEORGE HAMLIN & formerly to THOMAS HAMLIN, JR.
& formerly to THOMAS JONES, SR."; bounding SE on Copshee Sound; NE on
THOMAS HAMLIN, JR.; NW on CAPT. THOMAS BOONE; SW on THOMAS QUEENS land;
but a deed made by THOMAS JONES, JR. to above ROBERT CLEMENT dated 17
Nov. 1731 specifies thus: S W on land formerly belonging to JOHN GIVENS
but now in the possession of THOMAS BENNETT; NW on CAPT. THOMAS BOONE;
SE on THOMAS HAMLIN & fronting to the sea & fronting the seashore. Date
of redemption 1 Mar. 1732/3. Witnesses: THOMAS HAMLIN, SAMUEL TORSHELL,
JOHN (his mark) BENNETT. Before THOMAS BARTON, J.P. JACOB MOTTE, Pub.
Reg.

Book K, p. 10　　　　　　　　MILES BREWTON & THOMAS LAMBOLL, gentlemen, as

29 & 30 Sept. 1731　　　　　　executors of will of ROBERT TRADD, to JACOB
L & R　　　　　　　　　　　　MOTTE, merchant, of Charleston, the highest
　　　　　　　　　　　　　　　bidder, for ₤ 720 SC money, the westernmost
part of lot #60 in Charleston, bounding E on part of same lot sold by
BREWTON & LAMBOLL to DANIEL TOWNSEND, cordwainer, & separated from it by
a line to be run S between the 2 parts from a stake in the ground at NW
corner of TOWNSEND'S part to another stake at SW corner of TOWNSEND'S lot;
W on the great street running N from White Point to the Old Church Yard &
other public land allotted for a Market Place; N 100 ft. 8 in. on Tradd
St.　Whereas ROBERT TRADD by will dated 21 July 1730 appointed BREWTON &
LAMBOLL his attorneys, impowering them to sell his corner lot on S side
of Tradd St. (opposite GEORGE DUCALL, DANIEL BELL & JAMES MCNABNEY), now
they sell part to JACOB MOTTE. Witnesses: RICHARD EAGLES, EDWARD CROFT.
Before GABRIEL MANIGAULT, J.P.　JACOB MOTTE, Pub. Reg.

Book K, p. 16　　　　　　　　AQUILA ROSE, planter, to DANIEL GREENE, mer-
3 & 4 Sept. 1731　　　　　　 chant, for ₤ 30 SC money, 100 a. in Granville
L & R　　　　　　　　　　　　Co., on St. Helena Island, formerly belonging
　　　　　　　　　　　　　　　to JOHN NORTON who surveyed & sold 150 a. to
JAMES LOYADELL; bounding E on marsh; N on COL. WILLIAM BULL; W on WILLIAM
CHAPMAN; S on DANIEL GREENE (formerly JAMES LOYADELL). Witnesses: JONA-
THAN TUBB, JOSEPH PENDARVIS, JOHN GREENE. Before ALEXANDER PARRIS, J.P.
JACOB MOTTE, Pub. Reg.

Book K, p. 21　　　　　　　　THOMAS ELLERY, gentleman, & ANNE his wife, of
24 & 25 Mar. 1732　　　　　　Charleston, to EDWARD LIGHTWOOD, mariner, of
L & R by Mortgage　　　　　　the Island of New Providence, for ₤ 1000 cur-
　　　　　　　　　　　　　　　rency part of lots #188, 189, & 79, with the
dwelling house, etc., bounding E 225 ft. English measure on WILLIAM HAM-
ERTON & CAPT. WILLIAM WARDEN; W on TWEEDIE SOMERVILLE; S on Dock Street;
N on THOMAS ELLERY; adjoining the Presbyterian Burial ground; & runs be-
veling northward for the first 200 ft. where it is 58 ft. English measure
from E to W continuing N 25 ft. & for that whole 25 ft. from CAPT. WARD-
EN'S fence on the E to MR. SOMERVILLE'S fence on the W 130 ft. wide as
now fenced in & enjoyed by THOMAS ELLERY & lately purchased by him from
ANDREW ALLEN, merchant. Should ELLERY pay LIGHTWOOD ₤ 1100 currency on
26 Mar. 1733 this deed to be void. Witnesses: WILLIAM LEANDER, CHARLES
PINCKNEY. Before OTHNIEL BEALE, J.P.　JACOB MOTTE, Pub. Reg.

Book K, p. 29　　　　　　　　CHARLES CODNER, planter, to JOHN DANIELL,
14 Mar. 1731　　　　　　　　 planter, both of Berkeley Co., for ₤ 700 SC
Mortgage　　　　　　　　　　 money, 350 a. on Ittawan Island, bounding N on
　　　　　　　　　　　　　　　Beresford Creek; NE & SE on Montsom Creek; S
on Wando River; SW on JOHN MORGAN; NW on CHRISTOPHER SMITH. Date of redemption 25 Feb. 1732. Witnesses: MRS. HELEN DANIELL, ISAAC LESESNE,
HENRY BOSSARD. Before ROBERT DANIELL, J.P.　JACOB MOTTE, Pub. Reg. Mortgage satisfied 13 Dec. 1732.

Book K, p. 31　　　　　　　　JOSEPH BUTLER, planter, & MARY his wife, of
3 & 4 Apr. 1732　　　　　　　Berkeley Co., to CHARLES CRUBIN, planter, of
L & R　　　　　　　　　　　　Ashley Ferry, for ₤ 100 SC money, lot #86, be-
　　　　　　　　　　　　　　　ing 1/4 a., in Ashley River ferry town, called
Butler's Town, Berkeley Co., bounding NE on lot #85; SW on lot #87; both
belonging to JOSEPH BUTLER; NW on lot #95; SE on a street leading to Ashley River. Witnesses: STEPHEN BIGGS, JOHN (his mark) COOKFIELD. Before
WILLIAM CATTELL, J.P.　JACOB MOTTE, Register.

Book K, p. 35　　　　　　　　CAPT. JONATHAN DRAKE to JOHN WILKINS, WILLIAM
9 May 1713　　　　　　　　　 WILKINS, JOHN HEARN, & GEORGE RIVERS, trustees,
Deed of Sale　　　　　　　　 all of Berkeley Co., for ₤ 150 currency, 100 a.
　　　　　　　　　　　　　　　on James Island (part of 276 a. purchased by
DRAKE on 18 Aug. 1703 from JAMES DICKSON for ₤ 120 currency bounding N &
E on Jamestown Creek); & S on JONATHAN DRAKE. JOHN WILKINS, WILLIAM WIL-
KINS, JOHN HEARN & GEORGE RIVERS declared the purchase money belonged to
several communing members of the Presbyterian Church on James Island &
the land purchased to be for the sole use of every Presbyterian minister
hereafter chosen to be their Pastor in perpetual succession. An agreement is reached regarding the successors of the trustees, & it may not be
lawful for the trustees to convey the land for any other purpose. Signed
by JONATHAN DRAKE & MARY DRAKE, ROWLAND STORY, ANTHONY LAMBRIGHT, WILLIAM

BEST, ALEXANDER SPENCER, JOHN WITTER, ELINER HAIGE. Delivery by turf & twig. Before DANIEL GREENE, J.P. JACOB MOTTE, Register.

Book K, p. 39
25 & 26 Mar. 1732
L & R

JOHN ELDERS, planter, of Berkeley Co., to JACOB SATUR, merchant, of Charleston, for ₤ 600 SC money, an island of 45 a. on Back or Medway River, Berkeley Co.; also 261 a. where JOHN ELDERS lives, on Back or Medway River, bounding according to their plats. Witnesses: ABRAHAM SATUR, GEORGE ROLFE. Before JAMES ABERCROMBY, J.P. JACOB MOTTE, Register.

Book K, p. 45
5 & 6 Apr. 1732
L & R

JOSEPH BUTLER, planter, & MARY his wife, of Berkeley Co., to STEPHEN BIGGS, blacksmith, of Ashley Ferry Town, called Butler's Town, bounding NE on lot #88; SW on lot #90; NW on lot #98; SE on a street leading to Ashley River. Witnesses: CHARLES CRUBIN, JOHN (his mark) COCKFIELD. Before WILLIAM CATTELL, J.P. JACOB MOTTE, Register.

Book K, p. 49
16 Feb. 1731
Deed of Gift

JAMES SMYTH, (SMITH), planter, of Willtown, to WILLIAM LIVINGSTON & JAMES COCHRAN, planters of Colleton Co., in trust for MARY SMYTH, (formerly MARY COCHRAN, daughter of HUGH COCHRAN) now wife of said JAMES SMYTH, in consideration of their marriage, & for love & affection, the island 160 a. opposite Willtown which SMYTH purchased from ROBERT YONGE. SMYTH also grants LIVINGSTON & COCHRAN all the lots in Willtown which he purchased from CAPT. WILLIAM SCOTT, of Charleston; also 16 slaves; also the household goods & furniture belonging to his dwelling house. Witnesses: RICHARD WILKINS, RICHARD (his mark) STICKLEN, JOHN (his mark) BROWN. Before ROBERT YONGE, J.P. JACOB MOTTE, Register.

Book K, p. 53
18 & 19 May 1725
L & R

STEPHEN (his mark) MONK, ESQ., of Berkeley Co., son & heir of JOHN MONK, ESQ., Cassique, to WILLIAM HOLMES, joiner, of St. Paul's Parish, Colleton Co., for ₤ 38 currency, 180 a. in Colleton Co., bounding NE on MRS. BURT & THOMAS HOLMAN; NW on MR. ENDENBOROUGH; SW on CAPT. ANTHONY MATHEWS, JR.; SE on WILLIAM HOLMES; which 180 a. is part of 24,000 a. granted by the Lords Proprs. to JOHN MONK, father of STEPHEN. Witnesses: WILSON SANDERS, WILLIAM SANDERS, JOHN BAYLY. Before JOHN HERBERT, J.P. JACOB MOTTE, Register.

Book K, p. 59
24 & 25 May 1732
L & R by Mortgage

CHARLES CODNER, planter, of Berkeley Co., to JOHN TURNER, surgeon, of Charleston, for ₤ 500 SC money, part of lot #17 in Charleston, fronting E 25 ft. on the Bay; S 200 ft. part same lot owned by CODNER; W on Union St.; N on part same lot owned by JAMES NEILL & ROBERT RAPER. Should CODNER pay TURNER ₤ 500 SC money, with interest, on 26 May 1733, (being the condition of a bond of the penalty of ₤ 1000 securing payment) this mortgage to be void. CODNER delcares the lot free from dower or thirds of SABINAH ROWSE, widow of RICHARD CODNER, the father of CHARLES CODNER, & from that of ANNE, the wife of CHARLES. Witnesses: ANNE BERCHES, CHARLES PINCKNEY. Before OTHNIEL BEALE, J.P. JACOB MOTTE, Reg. Mortgage satisfied 15 Jan. 1734. Witness: NATHANIEL JOHNSON, Pub. Reg.

Book K, p. 66
13 & 14 Feb. 1728/9
L & R

PETER BENOIST, planter, & JANE, his wife, of Craven Co., to PHILIP COMBE, planter, of Berkeley Co., for ₤ 100 SC money, 130 a. in Berkeley Co. on E side of E branch of the T of Cooper River, bounding SW on Lynch's Creek; SE on GEORGE JUNE; NE & NW on JOHNSON LYNCH. Witnesses: FRANCIS DESCHAMPS, MOSES MONIER. Before ANTHONY BONNEAU, J.P. JACOB MOTTE, Register.

Book K, p. 72
19 & 20 Mar. 1732
L & R

MARY BETSON, widow, to CHARLES PINCKNEY, gentleman, both of Charleston, for ₤ 1200 SC money, part of 2 town lots #20 & 73, fronting E 65 ft. on Union St.; S 141 ft. on parts of same lots belonging to ADAM BEAUCHAMP; W & N on parts same lots belonging to MARY BETSON. Witnesses: THOMAS FAIRCHILD, ROWLAND VAUGHAN. Before

ALEXANDER PARRIS, J.P.   JACOB MOTTE, Register.

Book K, p. 78   JOSEPH GRIFFIN, Indian trader, to JACOB MOTTE,
1 & 2 June 1732   iron monger, of Charleston, for ₤ 300 currency,
L & R by Mortgage   20 a. in the Goosecreek Parish, Berkeley Co.,
                             part of a 100 a. estate of JOSEPH GRIFFIN, fa-
ther of JOSEPH, party hereto: bounding N on part of the 100 a. & adjoining the lands of BENJAMIN CHILDS & JOHN PARKER; also 1 horse, 2 mares.
Should GRIFFIN pay MOTTE ₤ 60 yearly until the whole is paid with interest, this mortgage to be void. Witnesses: JAMES FULTON, ROWLAND VAUGHAN.
Before GABRIEL MANIGAULT, J.P.   JACOB MOTTE, Register.

Book K, p. 83   ISAAC LEWIS, wheelwright, to JOHN OLDFIELD,
4 Aug. 1709   planter, both of Berkeley Co., for ₤ 50 SC mon-
Deed of Sale   ey, 590 a. on NW side Cooper River, in Berke-
                             ley Co., bounding E on JOB HOWS & lands not
laid out; N on the Rt. Hon. Sir JOHN COLLETON; S & W on land not laid out;
which land GIDEON LEWIS, brother of ISAAC, purchased from the Lords Proprs. on 15 Sept. 1705. Witnesses: JOHN BALL, EDWARD HYRNE, THOMAS GUER-
RIN, ISAAC PORCHER. Before HENRY NOBLE, J.P. JACOB MOTTE, Register.

Book K, p. 86   RALPH IZARD, ESQ., of Berkeley Co., to AARON
9 Nov. 1708   WAY, JR., weaver, of Dorchester, Berkeley Co.,
Deed of Sale   for ₤ 23 currency, the 24th lot in 1st range
                             of 1st division of lots in Dorchester contain-
ing 50 a., bounding E on SAMUEL SUMNER, SR.; S on Ashley River; W on WIL-
LIAM PRATT; N on land not divided amongst the inhabitants of Dorchester.
RALPH IZARD owned the land by deed of sale from JOHN STEVENS to whom a
great tract was granted. Witnesses: AARON WAY, SR., ROGER SUMNER. Before THOMAS BROUGHTON, J.P.   JACOB MOTTE, Register.

Book K, p. 88   SAMUEL PRIOLEAU, jeweler, & MAGDALINE his wife,
24 Sept. 1731   to ELISHA PRIOLEAU, merchant, all of Charles-
Mortgage   ton, as security on bond dated 22 Sept. 1731
                             in penal sum of ₤ 10,000 SC money conditioned
for payment of ₤ 5,000, with interest on demand, by SAMUEL to ELISHA,
700 a. on Port Royall Island, Granville Co., bounding N & E on Coosaw River; S on a creek & marsh; W on JAMES COCHRAN; & as further security conveys 51 Negro, Indian & Mustee slaves. Witnesses: JAMES RICHARD, HENRY
GIGNILLIAT. Before GABRIEL MANIGAULT, J.P.   JACOB MOTTE, Register.

Book K, p. 93   DANIEL LAROCHE, merchant, of Winyaw, son of
21 & 22 Mar. 1731   JOHN LAROCHE, merchant, of Charleston, & MARY
L & R   LAROCHE, widow of said JOHN LAROCHE, to
                             CHARLES HILL & RICHARD HILL, merchants, of
Charleston, for ₤ 3300 SC money paid to DANIEL & ₤ 700 SC money paid to
MARY, part of 2 several parts of a half town lot #9 in Charleston, fronting E 25 ft. 4 in. on the Bay; depth 217 ft.; being 16 ft. 6 in. in
breadth at W end as set out with cedar posts; bounding S on another part
of the 2 parts of the half lot #9; N on DANIEL GALE, blacksmith; W on
DANIEL LAROCHE (formerly CHARLES BASDEN); also part of adjoining lot 24
ft. 1 in. broad & 28 ft. 9 in. deep, bounding E on above land; W on WIL-
LIAM ELLIOTT; N on WILLIAM ELLIOTT; S on CATHARINE IOOR; which 2 pieces
of land are occupied by ISAAC CHARDON. Whereas JOHN LAROCHE, by will
dated 9 Aug. 1723 bequeathed to son DANIEL his dwelling on the Bay of
"Charleston" & part of a lot adjoining as far back as the fence which
"divided the land held with 2 tenements then in the possession of WILLIAM
WALKER & WILLIAM OESSER from the land enjoyed with the said messuage"; &
whereas JOHN LAROCHE by will gave his wife MARY the use of 2 rooms in
the house as long as she remained his widow; now DANIEL & MARY sell to
CHARLES & RICHARD HILL. Witnesses for DANIEL LAROCHE: DOMINICK ROCHE,
PETER SHEPHERD. Witnesses for MARY LAROCHE: THOMAS FAIRCHILD, JOHN LEWIS.
Before DANIEL GREENE, J.P.   JACOB MOTTE, Register.

Book K, p. 102   SAMUEL FLAVELL, mariner, formerly of Charles-
15 & 16 May 1728   ton, now of Providence, The Bahamas, & REBEC-
L & R   CA FLAVELL, widow, attorney for said SAMUEL
                             FLAVELL, to MOSES BENNETT, victualler, of
Charleston, for ₤ 750 SC money, part of lot #81 in Charleston, devized by
JOHN FLAVELL, mariner, of Charleston, to his son ROBERT FLAVELL who died

under the age & SAMUEL inherited; fronting E 19 ft. on a neighborhood alley; N 104 ft. on part same lot owned by WILLIAM BOLLOUGH; W on SAMUEL WRAGG, merchant, of London (formerly JOSEPH CROSKEYS); S on COL. JOHN LYNCH, (formerly MAJOR GEORGE EVANS). Witnesses: ELIZABETH PETERSON, MICHAEL JEANS, ROBERT HUME. Before THEOPHILUS GREGORY, J.P. JACOB MOTTE, Register.

Book K, p. 107　　　　　　SAMUEL FLAVELL, mariner, formerly of Charles-
17 Mar. 1727/8　　　　　　ton, now of Providence, The Bahamas, appointed
Letter of Attorney　　　　MRS. REBECCA FLAVELL of Charleston, with power
　　　　　　　　　　　　to sell his part of lot #81 in Charleston,
fronting E 19 ft. E on a neighborhood street or alley; N 104 ft. on WILLIAM BOLLOUGH; W on SAMUEL WRAGG, merchant, of London (formerly JOSEPH CORSKEYS); S on COL. JOHN LYNCH (formerly MAJ. GEORGE EVANS). Witnesses: ROGER READING, EDWARD LIGHTWOOD (mariner). LIGHTWOOD appeared before JOHN WRIGHT, J.P. JACOB MOTTE, Reigster.

Book K, p. 108　　　　　　JOHN BRAND, innholder, to JOHN LEWIS, gentle-
5 & 6 July 1732　　　　　　men, both of Charleston, for Ł 950 SC money,
L & R　　　　　　　　　　　part of 2 lots #184 & #186 in Charleston,
　　　　　　　　　　　　bounding E on a street leading up to the broad road out of town heretofore described as a little street leading from Ashley River by the lot of MR. JONES; W on estate of ELIAS HANCOCK; S on part of lot #186 sold by JOHN BRAND to MR. WITHERS; N on part of lot #184 owned by JOHN BRAND; measuring 50 ft. on the street, 200 ft. deep, & runs the whole breadth of 50 ft. as far as land belonging to JOHN REYNOLDS, then runs behind REYNOLD'S land & WILLIAM HAMERTON'S land; which land has a messuage built thereon & occupied by LAWRENCE GOULLIETTE. Witnesses: ALICE SMITH, THOMAS BECKETT. Before OTHNIEL BEALE, J.P. JACOB MOTTE, Register.

Book K, p. 116　　　　　　THOMAS AKIN, gentleman, of Parish of St. Thom-
18 June 1729　　　　　　　as & St. Dennis, Berkeley Co., on journeying
Letter of Attorney　　　　to Cape Fare appoints his friend ARCHIBALD HAM-
　　　　　　　　　　　　ILTON, gentleman, of same Parish, his attorney to handle his property & dispose of his former home of 335 a. on Cooper River, & use the money to his wife, MARGARET'S dower. Witnesses: DANIEL (his mark) MACDANIEL, AMEY STANLEY. Before DANIEL HUGER, J.P. JACOB MOTTE, Register.

Book K, p. 118　　　　　　The Hon. ROBERT FENWICK, ESQ. & SARAH his wife,
16 & 17 June 1726　　　　　of Berkeley Co., to JOSEPH MOODY, merchant, of
L & R　　　　　　　　　　　Charleston, for Ł 180 SC money, 2 half lots in
　　　　　　　　　　　　Charleston, bounding E on a little street leading from Ashley River by MR. JONES & MR. HILL; W on a street now laid out; N on lots of CAPT. HENRY SIMONDS; S on 2 half lots given by ROBERT FENWICK for the use of the Presbyterian minister. Witnesses: SAMUEL EVELEIGH, MICHAEL DARBY, JAMES FISHER. Before TWEEDIE SOMERVILLE, J.P. JACOB MOTTE, Register.

Book K, p. 124　　　　　　JOHN HAWKES (HAWKS) planter, to BARNSBY BRAN-
20 July 1731　　　　　　　FORD, planter, both of Berkeley Co., for
Deed of Sale　　　　　　　Ł 672:10 currency, 120 a. within Dorchester,
　　　　　　　　　　　　bounding E on the estate of Sir HOVENDEN WALKER (formerly JOHN BOISSEAU); N on GEORGE HAMLIN; W on JOHN HAWKS; S partly on land allowed for a highway; which tract lies partly in the land commonly called the New Granted, partly in that called Boasoo; & conveyed to HAWKS by 2 deeds of sale, 1 signed by JOSEPH LORD, Minister, on 4 Mar. 1716, the other by THOMAS WARING, atty. for JOSEPH LORD, dated 15 Aug. 1721. Witnesses: GEORGE HAMLIM, JOSIAH OSGOOD, ANNE HAMLIN. Before JOSEPH BLAKE, J.P. JACOB MOTTE, Register.

Book K, p. 127　　　　　　CHARLES LOWNDES, ESQ., of Berkeley Co., to
7 & 8 Mar. 1731　　　　　　BENJAMIN GODIN, merchant, of Charleston, as
L & R by Mortgage　　　　　security because GODIN indorsed certain bills
　　　　　　　　　　　　of exchange & for 10 sh., 500 a. in Berkeley Co., bounding S on STROUDS; E on JONES; N on JOHN WARD; also 500 a. in Berkeley Co., bounding S & E on Landgrave THOMAS SMITH; N on RICHARD BAKER; W on BARNABY REALLY; & delivered to GODIN 10 Negro slaves. CHARLES LOWNDES, according to the custom of merchants, drew 4 bills of

exchange dated 18 Feb. 1731 on PAPILLION BALL, merchant of London, 3 being for ₤ 100 sterling each, the 4th for ₤ 50 sterling, payable to BENJAMIN GODIN or order at 30 days sight; & whereas GODIN at the request of LOWNDES on 18 Feb. 1731 indorsed, according to the custom of merchants, to JAMES CROKATT, merchant, of Charleston, 4 bills of exchange whereby GODIN is become liable for the ₤ 350 sterling, & all interest, costs, etc., in case of protest; now LOWNDES gives GODIN as security 2 tracts of 500 a. each & 10 slaves. Witnesses: JOHN GUERARD, JOHN LEWIS. Before OTHNEIL BEALE, J.P. JACOB MOTTE, Register.

Book K, p. 135　　　　　　JAMES BULLOCK, planter, & JANE his wife, of
12 & 13 June 1732　　　　Willtown, Colleton Co., to JOHN HAY, merchant,
L & R by Mortgage　　　　of Charleston, for ₤ 4000 SC money that messuage or tenement being lot #13 in Wiltown; also 400 a. in Colleton Co., bounding W on JOHN PEACUM, originally granted by the Lords Proprs. to JOHN BEE & conveyed to BULLOCK; also 100 a. formerly granted to MATHEW BEE, on E side Ponpon River; also 200 a. granted to MATHEW BEE, bounding N on EBENEZER WALCOOT; E on MATHEW BEE; also 12 Negroes. Should the BULLOCKS pay HAY ₤ 4000 currency with interest or such other sums as may be awarded HAY by JAMES CROKATT & JOHN RIGG, arbitrators by virtue of bonds of award & submission dated 10 June executed by BULLOCK & HAY, or awarded to HAY by the umpire nominated by the arbitrators. Date of redemption, 25 Mar. 1734. Witnesses: The Rev. Mr. JOHN WITHERSPOON (by the form of his profession), JOSIAH STANYARD. Before TWEEDIE SOMERVILLE, J.P. JACOB MOTTE, Register.

Book K, p. 140　　　　　　RICHARD MURPHY, planter, to DANIEL MCEUEN,
11 & 12 Aug. 1731　　　　planter, both of Colleton Co., for ₤ 190 SC
L & R　　　　　　　　　　money, 121 a. in Colleton Co., purchased by
　　　　　　　　　　　　　MURPHY on 1 & 2 June last from ALEXANDER
TRENCH, merchant, bounding N on JAMES MARTIN; W on DAVID ALLEN, vintner, formerly of Colleton Co., now of Charleston; S on WILLIAM OSWILL, planter; E on CAPT. JOHN WHITMARSH, planter. Witnesses: JAMES MARTIN, ALEXANDER MCKOY. Before JOSHUA SANDERS, J.P. JACOB MOTTE, Register.

Book K, p. 146　　　　　　JANE (her mark) BASSETT (BISSETT), alias PACK-
23 & 24 Aug. 1732　　　　QUENETT, widow of ELIAS BASSETT, chamois dress-
L & R　　　　　　　　　　er, to WILLIAM CARWITHEN, cabinet maker, &
　　　　　　　　　　　　　MARY his wife, daughter of JANE & ELIAS BASSETT, all of Charleston, by authority of will of ELIAS & for natural love & affection, in consideration of the marriage of MARY & WILLIAM, & for ₤ 500 currency, part of lot #37 in Charleston, fronting N 62 ft. on the Middle St.; leading from WILLIAM ELLICOTT'S wharf to New Church St.; bounding W 80 ft. on WILLIAM YEOMANS; E on part same lot lately in possession of her son-in-law FRANCIS GRACIA; S 54 ft. on STEPHEN BEDON. Witnesses: SAMUEL FLEY, ETIENNE DUVAL, CHARLES PINCKNEY. Before DANIEL GREENE, J.P. JACOB MOTTE, Register.

Book K, p. 151　　　　　　JANE (her mark) BISSETT (BASSETT), alias PAC-
24 Aug. 1732　　　　　　　QUENET, widow, of Charleston, to her grand-
Deed of Gift　　　　　　 daughter, JANE DALTON, daughter of her eldest
　　　　　　　　　　　　　daughter CATHRINE, wife of JAMES DALTON, for
love & affection for her maintenance & her advancement in marriage, etc., part of lot in Middle St. that leads from WILLIAM ELLIOTT'S wharf to the New Church St., fronting N 22 ft. on Middle St.; 80 ft. deep; & "between" Mr. STEPHEN BEDON'S land 16-1/2 ft.; bounding E on DANIEL FIDLING; S on STEPHEN BEDON; W on land where JANE BISSETT lives. Witnesses: SAMUEL FLEY, ETIENNE DUVAL, CHARLES PINCKNEY. Before DANIEL GREENE, J.P. JACOB MOTTE, Register.

Book K, p. 153　　　　　　　　　　　 JANE (her mark) BISSETT (BASSETT), alias PAC-
23 & 24 Aug. 1732　　　　　　　　　 QUENET, widow of ELIAS BISSETT, chamois dress-
Deed of Gift with Proviso　　　　 er, of Charleston, to JAMES DALTON, shop keeper, & CATHRINE his wife, daughter of JANE &
ELIAS BISSETT, for love & affection for daughter CATHRINE & in consideration of her marriage, & for ₤ 500 currency, part of a lot in Charleston, fronting N 36 ft. 10 in. on Middle St. leading from WILLIAM ELLIOTT'S wharf to New Church St.; 42 ft. deep; bounding E & S on ABRAHAM LESOEUR (LESSUR), vintner; W on PETER FILLEUX; providing JAMES & CATHRINE DALTON, with 6 mos. after the death of JANE BISSETT, execute to her son &

daughter, WILLIAM & MARY CARWITHEN, a release & confirmation of their rights to the part town lot #37 where JANE BISSETT lives fronting N 62 ft. on Middle St.; S 54 ft. on back "between" STEPHEN BEDON'S land; 84 ft. on W on WILLIAM YEOMANS, merchant, E on part lot #37 in possession of FRANCIS GRACIA. In case of their neglect or refusal, the part lot first mentioned to go to JAMES & CATHRINE DALTON for use of WILLIAM & MARY CARWITHEN. Witnesses: ETIENNE DUVAL, CHARLES PINCKNEY. Before DANIEL GREENE, J.P. JACOB MOTTE, Register.

Book K, p. 158
6 & 7 June 1732
L & R by Mortgage

JOHN LAURENS, saddler, & ESTHER his wife, to JOHN TURNER, surgeon, all of Charleston, for ₤ 800 SC money, lot #315, bounding S 67 ft. on the Market Place; E 360 ft. on JOSEPH BLAKE, ESQ.; W on JOHN HOLLYBUSH, planter (formerly WILLIAM BRADLY); N on ROBERT HUME (formerly COL. THOMAS CAREY) & STEPHEN BEDON. Date of redemption 7 June 1733. Witnesses: CHARLES PINCKNEY. Before OTHNIEL BEALE, J.P. JACOB MOTTE, Register. On 16 Jan. 1737 ROBERT WOOD acknowledges receipt of ₤ 439:6 the full balance of the above mortgage. Witness: ROBERT AUSTIN, then Pub. Reg.

Book K, p. 166
11 & 12 July 1732
L & R by Mortgage

JOHN LAURENS, saddler, & ESTHER his wife, to JOHN TURNER, surgeon, all of Charleston, for ₤ 707 SC money, part of lot #59 bounding S 62 ft. on the Market Place, fronting W 92 ft. on the street leading from White Point through the Market Place by the Presbyterian Meeting House; bounding E on STEPHEN MILLER; N on JOHN LAURENS. Date of redemption, 16 June 1733. The premises free of ESTHER'S claim of dower. Witnesses: ISAAC HOLMES, CHARLES PINCKNEY. Before OTHNIEL BEALE, J.P. JACOB MOTTE, Register. Mortgage satisfied 6 June 1738 to HENRY WOOD, exec. Witness: ROBERT AUSTIN, Pub. Reg.

Book K, p. 173
2 & 3 Oct. 1732
L & R

THOMAS FAIRCHILD, butcher, to CATHRINE BETTISON, widow, both of Charleston, for ₤ 450 SC money, a lot fronting E 45 ft. on Friend St.; bounding N 140 ft. on JAMES MACKEWEN; S on THOMAS FAIRCHILD; W on RICHARD MASON. Witnesses: JAMES MICHIE, JOHN SHEPPARD, MARY BAKER. Before DANIEL GREENE, J.P. JACOB MOTTE, Register.

Book K, p. 177
7 Aug. 1732
Letter of Attorney

WILLIAM AXSON, of Island of Curacoa, West Indies, appointed his father, WILLIAM AXSON, of Charleston, his attorney to sell his lot in Charleston which he, as eldest son & heir, inherited from his mother MARY AXSON, wife of said WILLIAM AXSON. Witnesses: JOHN CRUGER, JR., MICHAEL MICKALLS. Before JACOB D'PETERSEN, Secry. JACOB MOTTE, Register.

Book K, p. 178
2 & 3 Oct. 1732
L & R

JACOB WOOLFORD, gentleman, & ELIZABETH, his wife, to THOMAS WALKER, mariner, of Charleston & JOHN WALKER, planter, for ₤ 1700 currency, 105 a. on Thomas Island, Berkeley Co., part of 210 a. granted COL. ROBERT DANIELL, bounding NW on Watcoe Creek; SW on JOHN DURHAM; SE & NE on RICHARD COGNER, the remainder of the 210 a.; also 140 a. English measure on Thomas Island, bounding S on Wando River; N on JOHN DUNHAM; W on ISAAC LESESNE; E on RICHARD CODNER; both tracts free from ELIZABETH WOOLFORD'S claim of dower & all mortgages except 1 dated 25 Apr. 1729 to COL. THOMAS BROUGHTON, the Rev. Mr. THOMAS HASWELL, RICHARD HARRIS, SAMUEL SIMONS, WILLIAM POOL, ISAAC LESESNE, THOMAS ASHBY, THOMAS PAGETT, & ROBERT STEWARD, for ₤ 800. Witnesses: CATHRINE WOODMON, THOMAS COOPER, JOHN ATKIN. Before DANIEL GREENE, J.P. JACOB MOTTE, Register.

Book K, p. 185
31 Oct. 1732
Deed of Sale

THOMAS BROUGHTON, ESQ., of St. John's Parish, Berkeley Co., to CAPT. THOMAS JOHNSON, commander of Fort Moore, SC, for ₤ 3000 currency, 1000 a. in Berkeley Co., granted to Landgrave ROBERT DANIELL by the Hon. CHARLES CRAVEN, Gov., & Lords Proprs. on 19 Aug. 1714 & sold by him to BROUGHTON on 20 Aug. 1714; bounding SE on ANDREW PERCIVAL; SW on RICHARD BEDON; NE on a cypress swamp; NW on lands not laid out & on THOMAS STEER. Witnesses: CHARLOTTE LATOUR, ISAAC AMYAND, THOMAS ATKINSON. ANNE BROUGHTON, wife of THOMAS freely surrendered her dower & thirds. Before NATHANIEL BROUGHTON, J.P. JACOB MOTTE, Register.

Book K, p. 188 RICHARD BAKER, chirurgeon, to GEORGE MORELAND,
1 June 1732   innholder, both of Colleton Co., as security
Mortgage   on a bond in penal sum of ℔ 151:10:4 currency
              conditioned for payment of ℔ 75:15:2 on 1 Dec.
next, & by turf & twig delivers to MORELAND, 100 a. on John's Island, bounding E on THOMAS WEVERLY; NW on ISAAC WAIGHT; S on Wadmalaw (Wad-madmelaw) River; which tract was purchased by BAKER from JOHN FENDIN. Witnesses: THOMAS LAW, ANN (her mark) LAW. Before DANIEL GREENE, J.P. JACOB MOTTE, Register.

Book K, p. 190 RICHARD BAKER, chirurgeon, to GEORGE MORELAND,
1 June 1732   innholder, both of Colleton Co., in penal sum
Bond   of ℔ 151:10:4 conditioned for payment of
              ℔ 75:15:2 on 1 Dec. next. Witnesses: THOMAS
LAS, ANN (her mark) LAW. Before DANIEL GREENE, ESQ. JACOB MOTTE, Register.

Book K, p. 191 WILLIAM WATSON, joiner, & MARY his wife, to
2 & 3 Oct. 1732 JOHN DANIEL, ship carpenter, all of Charleston,
L & R   for ℔ 520 SC money, part of lot #115 in
                Charleston, fronting E 32 ft. on the street
leading to Ashley River, & 100 ft. deep, bounding S on a house & lot belonging THOMAS HOLTON; N on EDWARD VANVELZIN; W on part same lot; MARY WATSON to renounce her dower before Nov. court. Whereas the said part of lot was conveyed to WILLIAM WATSON by JOHN ARNOLD, shop keeper of Charleston, & MARY his wife, by L & R, dated 20 & 21 Mar. 1729 together with another part of 2 lots #236 & #237, now WATSON agrees to show his papers when necessary to manifest DANIEL'S title. Witnesses: RICHARD ALLEIN, JOHN FRASER. Witnesses: GEORGE HESKETT, ROWLAND VAUGHAN. Before THEOPHILUS GREGORY, J.P. JACOB MOTTE, Reg.

Book K, p. 198 EDWARD JASPER, of Tower Hill, London, appoint-
1 June 1731   ed CAPT. JOHN GASCOIGNE, of H.M.S. The Albor-
Letter of Attorney ough, now at Carolina, his attorney, to mark,
                set out, take up & manage his Barony, or tract
of 12,000 a. English measure in SC, purchased by him 12 Dec. 1730 from WILLIAM WIGHT, ESQ., & MARY PENELOPE WATTS his wife, of Blakesly, Northampton Co., & THOMAS LOWNDES, gentleman, of the Parish of John the Evangelist, City of Westminster. Witnesses: DANIEL MACARTHY, JAMES ALLEN. JAMES ALLEN, gentleman, of London, testified before FRANCIS CHILD, ESQ., Lord Mayor & the Aldermen, of London in the King's Majesty Court, in the Chamber of the Guild Hall. Signed JACKSON. JACOB MOTTE, Register.

Book K, p. 200 JOHN ROBERTS of Dean's Court, Co. of Middlesex,
1 Aug. 1731   appointed CAPT. JOHN GASCOIGNE, of H.M.S. the
Letter of Attorney Alborough, now at Carolina, his attorney, to
                mark, set out, take up & manage his estate in
SC consisting of 2 several Baronies in SC each containing 12,000 a. English measure, on the 2 rivers May & Wackamaw, granted ROBERTS by the Rt. Hon. JOHN, Lord Carteret by 2 deeds of L & R on 18 & 19 Feb. 1730; also 6 Baronies in SC, each containing 12,000 a. English measure, 2 of which are Yamassee lands, 4 not Yamassee lands, granted ROBERTS by the Rt. Hon. JOHN, Lord Carteret, by 6 several deeds of L & R, all dated 4 & 5 June 1731. Witnesses: EDWARD LEE, JAMES ALLEN, JAMES ALLEN, gentleman, of London, testified before FRANCIS CHILD, ESQ., Lord Mayor, & the aldermen of London in the King's Majesty Court in the Chamber of the Guild Hall. Signed JACKSON. JACOB MOTTE, Register.

Book K, p. 205   JOHN ARNOLD, shop keeper, & MARY his wife, to
20 & 21 Mar. 1729 WILLIAM WATSON, joiner, all of Charleston, for
L & R   ℔ 600 SC money, part of 2 lots #236 & #237,
                 fronting E 23 ft. on a street leading from
White Point to the High Road, bounding N on land bequeathed by JAMES ELLIS to his son JOHN ELLIS; S on lot #236 or on a cross street leading to the bay; also part of lot #115 fronting E 32 ft. on the street leading to Ashley River; bounding S 100 ft. on THOMAS HOLTON'S house & lot; N on EDWARD VANVELZIN; W on part same lot. Witnesses: JOHN (his mark) TRICKER,

HENRY HARGRAVE.   Before THEOPHILUS GREGORY, J.P.   JACOB MOTTE, Register.

Book K, p. 208   MICHAEL BACON, planter, of Berkeley Co., to
18 Aug. 1718   ROGER SUMNER, planter, of same place, for an
Deed of Sale   equivalent compensation, 50 a., about 50 ch.
                           long & 10 ch. broad, bounding NE & NW on MI-
CHAEL BACON; SE on THOMAS SNOW; SW on his own land. Witnesses: THOMAS
OSGOOD, JOSIAH OSGOOD, BENJAMIN SUMNER. Before ALEXANDER SKENE, J.P.
JACOB MOTTE, Register.

Book K, p. 210   WILLIAM DONNING, ESQ. & GEORGE NICHOLAS, ESQ.
11 July 1732   agree as follows: Whereas DONNING has actually
Agreement   sold to NICHOLAS, & put him in possession of,
                           1200 a. on N side Ashley River, in St.
George's Parish, commonly called Woodsbury, for which NICHOLAS agreed to
pay DONNING 20 sh. sterling per a. as follows: L 1500 currency on sealing
this deed; the balance to continue at 5% for 1 yr., & in case of default
at end of year the unpaid balance to carry 10% until fully paid; & for
security NICHOLAS promises to give DONNING his mortgage & bond on the
whole land for the unpaid sum: DONNING promises that as soon as the land
is surveyed & ascertained he will execute the deeds: NICHOLAS agrees to
pay 20 sh. sterling per a. for every a. over the 1200 a. Witnesses: ROB-
ERT WRIGHT, ALEXANDER SKENE. Before ROBERT WRIGHT, C.J. JACOB MOTTE,
Register.

Book K, p. 211   DAVID (his mark) BATCHELOR, planter, to MOSES
2 Dec. 1717   MARTIN, planter, both of Berkeley Co., for
Deed of Sale   L 1 currency, the 21st lot designed for a
                           place of trade in Dorchester, Berkeley Co.,
being 1/4 a. bounding E on a highway; S on a highway; W on a highway; N
on JOHN GORTON; which lot BATCHELOR purchased from JOHN STEVENS, planter,
of Berkeley Co.; deed acknowledged before the Hon. COL. THOMAS BROUGHTON
1 day in 1717. Witnesses: AEILLS DEMINE, CHARLES TREDWELL, ROBERT (his
mark) MILLER. Before THOMAS BROUGHTON 2 Dec. 1717. JACOB MOTTE, Reg.

Book K, p. 213   EBENEZER WALCUTT, (WALCOTT), planter, & ELIZA-
7 Feb. 1721   BETH (her mark) his wife, to MOSES MARTIN,
Deed of Sale   planter, all of Colleton Co., for L 4:14 cur-
                           rency, 156-1/2 a. in Colleton Co., bounding N
on JAMES FULTON; E on SAMUEL LOWELL; S on JAMES COCHRAN; W on EBENEZER
WALCUTT, PETER FOSTER, & JOHN PENNY; which tract was granted to WALCUTT
by the Lords Proprs. & the Hon. ROBERT GIBBS, ESQ., Gov. in 1711. Witnesses: JAMES DUNLEP, ABRAHAM GRAHAM. Before JOHN JACKSON, J.P. Delivery by turf & twig. JACOB MOTTE, Register.

Book K, p. 215   ELEAZER ALLEN, merchant, & SARAH his wife, to
6 & 7 Dec. 1732   JAMES CROKATT, merchant, all of Charleston,
L & R   for L 4000 SC money, half of lot #19 now occu-
                           pied by BASTIAN HUGO, fronting E 93-1/2 ft.
English measure on the Bay; JOHN RAPER (formerly RICHARD CODNER); W on a
lot belonging to JONATHAN RUSS & GEORGE LEA (formerly to JOHN ASHBY); N
on GEORGE HASCOTT (formerly CAPT. JOHN GUPPELL); also that part of a
front lot E of the Town Wall lying before the full half lot down to low
water mark. Witnesses: CATHRINE MOORE, THOMAS CLIFFORD, CHARLES PINCKNEY.
Before THEOPHILUS GREGORY, J.P. JACOB MOTTE, Register.

Book K, p. 224   DANIEL CARTWRIGHT, planter, & SARAH his wife,
11 & 12 July 1732   of Berkeley Co., to JAMES CROKATT, merchant, &
L & R   ESTHER his wife of Charleston, for L 1380 SC
                           money, 46 a. inherited by DANIEL from his
brother ROBERT CARTWRIGHT, in St. Philips's Parish, bounding E on JOSEPH
BLAKE, ESQ.; S on THOMAS GADSDEN; W & N on RICHARD CARTWRIGHT. Witnesses:
ISAAC HOLMES, BENJAMIN SMITH, CHARLES PINCKNEY, WILLIAM MCCLEUR. Before
JAMES KINLOCK, J.P. JACOB MOTTE, Reg.

Book K, p. 229   JOHN PENNY, & HANNAH (her mark) his wife, to
18 Dec. 1718   MOSES MARTIN, all of Colleton Co., for L 200
Deed of Sale   SC money, 100 a. on N side Pompon River, with-
                           in land, granted PENNY by the Lords Proprs.
under the Hon. ROBERT JOHNSON, Gov., on 18 Dec. 1718; bounding N on

WILLIAM PETER. HANNAH renounces her dower. Witnesses: ARCHIBALD STOBO, HENRY JACKSON, ROBERT PENNY. Before JOSHUA SANDERS, J.P. JACOB MOTTE, Register.

Book K, p. 233　　　　　　　WILLIAM SANDERS, planter, to LAWRENS SANDERS,
14 Oct. 1720　　　　　　　　planter, both of St. George Parish, Berkeley
Deed of Sale　　　　　　　　Co., for L 300 SC money, 300 a. in Berkeley
　　　　　　　　　　　　　　Co., bounding N on BENJAMIN IZARD; E & S on
WILLIAM STEED; W on CAPT. WILLIAM SANDERS. Witnesses: JEHU STANYARNE, MARGARET SANDERS (spinster). Before THEOPHILUS GREGORY, J.P. JACOB MOTTE, Register.

Book K, p. 235　　　　　　　JOHN VICARIDGE, merchant, of Charleston, to
14 & 15 July 1732　　　　　　RICHARD SHUBRICK, merchant, of London, as se-
L & R by Mortgage　　　　　 curity on a bond dated 14 July 1732 in penal
　　　　　　　　　　　　　　sum of L 1900 SC money conditioned for the
payment of L 934:6 SC money on 25 Mar. next, 400 a. in St. John's Parish, on W side of W branch of Cooper River, bounding E on Watboo Barony; S on Sir JOHN COLLETON; on other sides on JAMES LEBAS; which 400 a. was purchased from JAMES LEBAS. Witnesses: JOHN GUERARD, JOHN LEWIS. Before JOHN HAMMERTON, J.P. JACOB WHITE, Register.

Book K, p. 242　　　　　　　THOMAS TOWNSEND, to WILLIAM TOWNSEND, both of
10 June 1729　　　　　　　　Colleton Co., for L 10, 213 a. on Combe Neck,
Deed of Sale　　　　　　　　bounding N on said TOWNSEND & JOHN FELL; E on
　　　　　　　　　　　　　　JOHN HELLEWARD; S on lands not laid out; W on
JOHN FELLE & SNARD; also 300 a. on N side Cumbee River; also 8 Negro slaves. Witnesses: HENRY COPEN, JAMES WILKINS. Before THOMAS LADSON, J.P. JACOB MOTTE, Register.

Book K, p. 244　　　　　　　JOSEPH LORD, minister, to JOHN HAWKS, planter,
4 Mar. 1716/17　　　　　　　both of Dorchester, Berkeley Co., for L 50
Deed of Sale　　　　　　　　currency 100 a. in that part of Dorchester,
　　　　　　　　　　　　　　commonly called New Grant & partly in that
part formerly called Boascoo; bounding E on Sir HOVENDEN WALKER (formerly JOHN BOISSEAU); S on JOSEPH LORD; W on JOSEPH BROWNSON; N on MOSES WAY. Witnesses: JOSEPH SMITH, SAMUEL WAY, SUSANNAH SMITH. Before CHARLES HILL, J.P. JACOB MOTTE, Register.

Book K, p. 246　　　　　　　Dame (Madam) REBECCA AXTELL, widow to CAPT.
12 May 1712　　　　　　　　 GERSHOM HAWKS, planter, both of Berkeley Co.,
Deed of Sale　　　　　　　　for L 100 currency, 1033-3/4 a. on N side Ash-
　　　　　　　　　　　　　　ley River, within land, bounding S on Dorchest-
er land; NE & W on land laid out according to plat dated 17 May 1701. Witnesses: THOMAS DISTON, ROBERT (his mark) MILLER, JOHN HAWK. Before GEORGE CHRICHTEN, J.P. JACOB MOTTE, Register.

Book K, p. 249　　　　　　　JOHN CARMICHAEL, gentleman, of Colleton Co.,
15 & 16 June 1732　　　　　　to MICHAEL JEANS, glazier, of Charleston, for
L & R　　　　　　　　　　　 L 180 SC money, that part of lot #282 fronting
　　　　　　　　　　　　　　N 30 ft. on a small street leading from the
new prison to the new church, which street by mutual agreement was left out of the lands of JOHN CORMICHAEL & BRYAN RAYLY; 90 ft. deep; bounding W on JOHN CARMICHAEL; S on GEORGE CHICKEN; E on EDWARD WEEKLEY. Witnesses: EDWARD WEEKLY, THOMAS MELL, RICHARD IRISH. Before DANIEL GREENE, J.P. JACOB MOTTE, Register.

Book K, p. 253　　　　　　　JAMES STEWARD (STEWART) & ROBERT STEWARD,
13 July 1728　　　　　　　　planters, sons of FRANCES STEWARD, widow, all
Deed of Gift　　　　　　　　of St. Thomas Parish, Berkeley, to their broth-
　　　　　　　　　　　　　　er, JOHN STEWARD, for natural love & affection,
all their claim to 230 a. English measure on NW side of Watcoe Creek (out of Wando River), purchased by their mother FRANCES STEWARD on 12 Oct. 1709 from JOHN ANNANT & MARY his wife; bounding SW on CAPT. RICHARD HARRIS (then of CAPT. LAKE); N on JOHN ANNANT; NE on PATRICK STEWARD. Whereas on 4 Oct. 1710, in consideration of his natural love & affection & "dutifulness," FRANCIS gave her eldest son JOHN STEWARD the 230 a. with the proviso that in case he died without heirs the land should be divided between her 2 youngest sons, JAMES & ROBERT, now they quitclaim to JOHN. Witnesses: DAVID ANDERSON, THOMAS BARTRAM, JACOB WOOLFORD. Before

THEOPHILUS GREGORY, J.P.   JACOB MOTTE, Register.

Book K, p. 255   JONATHAN DRAKE to JOHN HEARN, GEORGE RIVERS,
7 May 1732   JOHN SANDIFORD, & PETER HEARN, trustees, 2 a.
Confirmation of Deed   English measure on James Island where the
                             Presbyterian church now stands including the
clear ground & remainder contiguous, with all buildings erected or to be
erected. Whereas COL. JONATHAN DRAKE, father of JONATHAN the party hereto, on 11 Jan. 1700 purchased from Gov. JAMES MOORE & the Lords Proprs.
70 a. of land (measured by JAMES WITTER, surveyor), & on 3 Nov. 1724 sold
the tract to JOHN WITTER except 2 a. on which to erect a church for the
Presbyterians, but the boundings were not set forth clearly in the deed,
wherefore the father (COL. JONATHAN DRAKE) drew up a short memorial showing where the 2 a. should be taken out, i.e. where the old church once
stood & the remainder contiguous taking in the cleared land where the new
church now stands, to which instrument JOHN WITTER not only consented but
also signed (dated the same day as the deed & recorded 13 Feb. 1724 in
the Register's Book D folio 192), now the son clears the title. The 70 a.
tract bounded NW on SAMUEL DRAKE (formerly EDWARD DRAKE); W on JOHN
WITTER (formerly JOHN ELLIS) & CAPT. DENNIS (formerly JOHN CLAPP); NW on
DENNIS (formerly JOHN CLAPP); SE on JAMES WITTER (formerly PETER HEARN).
DRAKE outlines method of electing trustees, etc. Witnesses: MARY DRAKE,
THOMAS WESTBURRY, WILLIAM GOODILL, SAMUEL DRAKE. Before DANIEL GREEN,
J.P.   JACOB MOTTE, Register.

Book K, p. 259   FRANCIS MORINNA, chirurgeon, of Craven Co., to
26 Nov. 1725   ISAAC PORCHER, SR., chirurgeon, of Berkeley
Mortgage   Co., as security on a bond of even date in pen-
                             al sum of L 405:17:3 SC money conditioned for
payment of L 202:18:7 on 26 Nov. 1731, 300 a. English measure in Craven
Co., on S side Santee River, bounding S on vacant land; E on FRANCIS MO-
RINNA; W on the Parsonage of St. James Santee. FRANCIS MORINNA by marrying ANNA D'RICHBOURG, widow of Claudius D'Richbourg, clerk, of Craven Co.,
became possessed of D'RICHBOURGH estate; & ISAAC PORCHER, SR. by a Court
of Orphans was nominated guardian of the 3 D'RICHBOURG children, JAMES,
CLAUDIUS & ELIZABETH; MERINNA gives PORCHER a bond to secure payment of
the several sums due the children & conveys 300 a. Witnesses: ARCHIBALD
YOUNG, WILLIAM (his mark) SKINNER. Before THOMAS BROUGHTON, J.P.   JACOB
MOTTE, Register.

Book K, p. 263   PATRICK SCOTT, planter, & SARAH (her mark) his
26 Sept. 1706   wife, of Berkeley Co., to ABRAHAM WARNOCK,
Deed of Sale   CAPT. JONSON LYNCH, & THOMAS LYNCH, elders of
                             the Presbyterian congregation in Charleston,
for L 10 currency, for the support of a Presbyterian minister at Wando
River, 100 a. English measure bounding E on Wando River; N on lands laid
out to King CHARLES; which 100 a. was granted to SCOTT on 17 Sept. 1703
by JOHN GRANVILLE, Palatine, & the Lords Proprs. by deed signed by the
Rt. Hon. Sir NATHANIEL JOHNSON, Knight, Gov. of SC & NC, etc. Witnesses:
JAMOIN JOEL POINSETT, ROBERT TRADD, PATRICK MARTIN. Before ALEXANDER
PARRIS, J.P.   JACOB MOTTE, Register.

Book K, p. 266   JOHN (his mark) ST. MARTIN, carpenter, to Land-
19 & 20 Feb. 1730   grave ROBERT DANIELL, both of Berkeley Co.,
L & R   for L 400 currency, 140 a. in Berkeley Co.,
                             where JOHN ST. MARTIN lives, bounding N on
JONATHAN RUSS; S on a creek of Wando River; E on marshes of Wando; W on
RICHARD BERESFORD & JONATHAN RUSS. Witnesses: WILLIAM WEEKLEY, HENRY
BOSSARD. Before JOHN DANIEL, J.P.   JACOB MOTTE, Register.

Book K, p. 270   THOMAS RUSS, planter, & MARY his wife, to Land-
19 Feb. 1730   grave ROBERT DANIEL, both of Berkeley Co., for
Lease   5 sh. currency, 590 a. in Berkeley Co., bound-
                             ing NE on Mr. SECAR; S on RICHARD BERESFORD
SW on DAVID RUSS. Witnesses: ISAAC LESESNE, JAMES STEWART, ROBERT HOW.

Book K, p. 272   CHARLES LOWNDES, ESQ., of Berkeley Co., to
1 & 2 Feb. 1732   JOHN COLLETON of Fairlawn Barony, as security
L & R by Mortgage   to COLLETON for endorsing a bond given by
                             LOWNDES to JAMES CROKATT, merchant, of

Charleston, in the penal sum of ₺ 5200 currency, conditioned for payment of ₺ 2600 currency, with interest, on 2 Feb. 1733, 500 a. in Berkeley Co., bounding S on STROUD; E on JONES; N on JOHN WARD; also 500 a. bounding S & E on Landgrave THOMAS SMITH; N on RICHARD BAKER; W on BARNABY REALLY, planter. LOWNDES also delivered to COLLETON 12 Negro slaves. Witnesses: MARY SAUREAU, THOMAS ELLERY. Before WILLIAM LIVINGSTON, J.P. JACOB MOTTE, Register.

Book K, p. 280
1 Jan. 1732
Quitclaim

PETER LESADE (3d), planter (only son of PETER LESADE 2nd & his wife ANN GABRIEL LESADE) to PETER LESADE (2d), planter, both of St. Andrew's Parish, Berkeley Co., for ₺ 2500 currency, 960 a. commonly called Old Town plantation (except 250 a.) for resting the absolute fee simple & inheritance in PETER LESADE (2d). Whereas JAMES LESADE, brother of PETER LESADE (1st) owned 960 a. called Old Town plantation bounding on lands belonging to PETER LESADE (1st); NW on HENRY SAMWAYS; & whereas JAMES LESADE by will dated 3 Nov. 1703 bequeathed all his real & personal estate to his wife ELIZABETH LESADE for the term of her natural life so long as she remained a widow, then half to PETER LESADE (1st) & the other half to MARY NEAL, sister of JAMES LESADE, or to her children DANIEL, MARY, PETER, SUSANNAH, & JANE NEAL, with the proviso that if MARY or any of her children, then living in Europe, did not claim their half share, or make themselves known within 3 years after the death of JAMES LESADE, their half should descend to PETER LESADE (1st) his brother; & whereas neither MARY NEAL nor any of her children, claimed their share in that period, the plantation descended to PETER LESADE (1st); & whereas PETER LESADE (1st) owned another plantation of 200 a. (Westpenny) on W side of head of Old Town Creek, bounding S on CAPT. JOHN GODFREY & lands not laid out; N on JAMES LESADE; & being so seized PETER LESADE (1st) bequeathed to his wife ANN LESADE all his real & personal estate for her natural life, & afterwards to his son PETER LESADE (2nd); & to his daughter ANN GIRARDEAU, wife of JOHN GIRARDEAU he bequeathed the 250 a. (part of Old Town joining a part formerly belonging to FRANCIS BLACHARD, being at West Penny Creek & running in a direct line to his son JOHN GIRARDEAU'S, to be laid out as his executors should think fit) & the 200 a. formerly belonging to FRANCIS BLANCHARD (the 200 a. & 250 a. making 450 a.) with the proviso that PETER LESADE (2nd) be allowed to enjoy the plantation of 200 a. (Westpenny) until he should be in possession of Old Town plantation; & whereas ANN LESADE (wife of PETER 1st) dies 5 Oct. 1716 & Old Town plantation (except 250 a.) "were expectant to" PETER LESADE (2nd) after the death of ELIZABETH (widow of JAMES LESADE); & whereas in consideration of the marriage already solemnized between PETER LESADE (2nd) & ANN GABRIEL, & for the settling of a complete jointure, provision & maintenance on ANN should she survive PETER (2nd), & in full satisfaction of all dower which ANN GABRIEL might have after PETER'S (2nd) death, & towards the maintenance of ANN LESADE the younger (party hereto), & the children & future children of PETER, (2nd). On 2 Mar. 1716 PETER LESADE (2nd) & ANN GABRIEL his wife executed a deed of trust, conveying to PETER POITEVINT & JACOB CAILLEAU, trustees, planters of Berkeley Co., all the reversion & remainder of the 960 a. (except 250 a.) to the use of PETER LESADE (2nd) during his lifetime, then to the heirs of PETER LESADE (2nd) & ANN GABRIEL; & whereas at that time they had only 1 son, PETER (3rd); & whereas ELIZABETH (widow of JAMESO died 1 Jan. 1724 & PETER (2nd) immediately took 200 a. English measure being 1/2 of 400 a. surveyed by WILLIAM WINDRES, which 400 a. was granted 15 Dec. 1705 to HENRY WALKER by the Lords Proprs. under the Rt. Hon. Sir NATHANIEL JOHNSON, Knight, Gov., etc., & lying between the head of Wadwadmelaw River & Bohicket Creek bridge; the 200 a. bounding N on Wadmelaw River; E on SAMUEL JONES; S on Bohicket Creek; W on Mr. GOBLE & JAMES YOUNG. Witnesses: JONATHAN STOCK, DANIEL MCFARLAND. Delivery by turf & twig. Before JOHN FENWICKE, J.P. JACOB MOTTE, Register.

Book K, p. 300
12 Mar. 1723/4
Deed of Sale

JAMES (his mark) YOUNG, planter, & ANN (her mark) his wife, to SAMUEL JONES, planter, all of Colleton Co., for ₺ 225 currency, 150 a. English measure, part of 400 a. measured by WILLIAM WINDRES, surveyor, which 400 a. was granted by Gov. NATHANIEL JOHNSON & the Lords Proprs., on 5 Jan. 1704/5 to JAMES YOUNG, & lying between the head of Wad-wadmelaw River & Bohicket Creek; the 150 a. being pricked off on the grant & bounding N on JAMES YOUNG; E on SAMUEL JONES;

Son GOBLE; W on HENRY WALKER. Witnesses: THOMAS PRENTICE, JONATHAN THOMAS. Delivery by turf & twig. Before DANIEL GREENE, J.P. JACOB MOTTE, Register.

Book K, p. 304　　　　　　　PETER LESADE (2nd), planter, of St. Andrew's
4 & 5 Jan. 1732　　　　　　Parish, to DANIEL CARTWRIGHT, planter, of St.
L & R　　　　　　　　　　　Philip's Parish, Berkeley Co., for ₤ 3144 SC
　　　　　　　　　　　　　　money, 960 a. (except 250 a.), commonly called
Old Town Plantation. Se p. 280 for details of LESADE'S title. Witnesses: EDWARD WEEKLY, BENJAMIN WHITAKER. Before DANIEL GREENE, J.P. JACOB MOTTE, Register.

Book K, p. 317　　　　　　　WILLIAM WAY, SR., planter of Beach Hill, Col-
10 Apr. 1728　　　　　　　　leton Co., to SAMUEL WAY, SR., carpenter of
Deed of Sale　　　　　　　　Dorchester, Berkeley Co., for a valuable sum,
　　　　　　　　　　　　　　45 a. (#25) in Dorchester, bounding E & N on a
highway; S & W on JOHN HAWKES. Witnesses: RICHARD CUTFIELD, MOSES WAY, ABIGAIL DOWSE. Before RICHARD WARING, J.P. JACOB MOTTE, Register.

Book K, p. 319　　　　　　　THOMAS CLIFFORD, ESQ., & MARY his wife, with
22 Feb. 1732　　　　　　　　her free assent, to the Hon. ARTHUR MIDDLETON,
Deed of Sale　　　　　　　　ESQ., both of Berkeley Co., for ₤ 1200 SC mon-
　　　　　　　　　　　　　　ey, 500 a. granted by the Lords Proprs. to
RICHARD BUTLER & by him conveyed to JOHN GLOVER, planter, & by him to THOMAS CLIFFORD; bounding SSE & SW on ARTHUR MIDDLETON; N & NE on ABRAHAM DUPONT. Witnesses: JOHN BARKER, MARY WATSON, JOHN CROFT. Before DANIEL GREENE, J.P. JACOB MOTTE, Register.

Book K, p. 324　　　　　　　GEORGE CHICKEN, planter, to NOAH SERRE, for
20 Feb. 1732　　　　　　　　₤ 424 currency, 2 tracts of land. Whereas COL.
Deed of Sale　　　　　　　　JOHN GENDRON & Mrs. JUDITH ROBERT, executors
　　　　　　　　　　　　　　of the will of PETER ROBERT, ESQ., with author-
ity to dispose of his lands & released to GEORGE CHICKEN 2 tracts of land, 1 of 500 a. in Prince George's Parish, on N side Santee River, the other of 200 a. in St. James Santee, now CHICKEN conveys the 2 tracts to SERRE. Witnesses: JAMES KINLOCH, JOHN HENTIE. Before DANIEL GREENE, J.P. JACOB MOTTE, Register.

Book K, p. 327　　　　　　　JOHN BROWN, planter, & FRANCES (her mark) his
26 & 27 Jan. 1732　　　　　wife, of Berkeley Co., to WILLIAM BRANFORD,
L & R　　　　　　　　　　　for ₤ 260 SC money, 91 a., part of 100 a.
　　　　　　　　　　　　　　granted to THOMAS CLARK, which 91 a. bounds N
on Ashley River; S on PETER LESADE; E on THOMAS ROSE; W on WILLIAM BRANFORD. Witnesses: ANDREW DEVEAUX, PETER GIRRARDEAU, ANDREW DEVEAUX, JR., SAMUEL STOCK. Before DANIEL GREENE, J.P. JACOB MOTTE, Register.

Book K, p. 331　　　　　　　DANIEL CARTWRIGHT, planter, & SARAH his wife,
15 & 16 Mar. 1732　　　　　of St. Philip's Parish, Berkeley Co., to WIL-
L & R by Mortgage　　　　　LIAM BRANFORD, planter, of St. Andrew's Parish,
　　　　　　　　　　　　　　Berkeley, for ₤ 1500 SC money, 960 a. (except
250 a.) known as Old Town plantation purchased by CARTWRIGHT from PETER LESADE the elder (2nd) on 12 Jan. 1732; see p. 280 for full details; the condition for redemption being that CARTWRIGHT pay BRANFORD the full sum of ₤ 1950 currency (the principal with int. for 3 yrs.) in certain sums on certain dates. Witnesses: PETER GIRRARDEAU, CHILDERMAS CROFT. Before DANIEL GREENE, J.P. JACOB MOTTE, Register.

Book K, p. 342　　　　　　　RICHARD BAKER, of Berkeley Co., & ELIZABETH
5 Mar. 1722　　　　　　　　 (her mark) his wife, to MALACHI GLAZE, planter,
Deed of Sale　　　　　　　　for ₤ 250 currency, 500 a. in Berkeley Co.,
　　　　　　　　　　　　　　conveyed by SAMUEL SUMNER & SARAH his wife on
1 Feb. 1714/15; bounding S on ROBERT MILLER (formerly called the Sawmill land); E on WILLIAM WALLACE (formerly MOSES WAY). Witnesses: SAMUEL CLARK, JONATHAN CLARK, THOMAS (his mark) SMITH; CLARK being sworn according to his profession. Before ROBERT WRIGHT, C.J. JACOB MOTTE, Register.

Book K, p. 344　　　　　　　JOSEPH LORD, Minister of the Gospel, formerly
15 Aug. 1721　　　　　　　　of Dorchester, now in New England, by his at-
Deed of Sale　　　　　　　　torney THOMAS WARING, planter, to JOHN HAWKES,
　　　　　　　　　　　　　　planter, all of Berkeley Co., for ₤ 300

currency, 150 a. in Dorchester, bounding W on JOSEPH BRUNSON; S on JOHN KITCHEN; SE on Mr. BOSOE & a highway & lot #25 belonging to WILLIAM WAY, JR.; NE on JOHN HAWKES (formerly JOSEPH LORD) & on WILLIAM WAY; the grant signed by JOHN STEVENS, ISAAC PROCHER, JR., ROBERT MILLER & MOSES WAY being recorded in the secretary's office in Charleston. Letter of attorney registered in Berkeley Co., fol. 11 on 17 May 1721. Witnesses: THOMAS OSGOOD, JR., URIAH EDWARDS, MICHAEL BACON. BACON & OSGOOD made oath according to their profession. Before ALEXANDER SKENE, J.P. JACOB MOTTE, Register.

Book K, p. 348
9 & 10 July 1731
L & R

JAMES GREENE, planter, & SUSANNAH (her mark) his wife, to GEORGE SIMONA, cooper, all of Colleton Co., for ₤ 200 SC money, 50 a. in Colleton Co., bounding E & S on DR. WILLIAM MCGILIVRAY; W on a creek; N on JAMES GREEN. Witnesses: MARE TRUCKET, PETER GENES, WILLIAM GREEN. Before ROBERT WRIGHT, C.J. JACOB MOTTE, Register.

Book, p. 354
10 May 1728
Bond

FRANCIS YONGE, of St. James Parish, Westminister, to SAMUEL WRAGG, merchant, of London in penal sum of ₤ 1040 money of Great Britain conditioned for the payment of ₤ 520 with interest on 19 May 1729. Witnesses: WILLIAM WARDEN, JAMES FISHER. On Mar. 22, 1732, RICHARD LAMBTON, as attorney for WRAGG acknowledged receipt of ₤ 519:10 sterling in part payment of bond. Before ROBERT WRIGHT, J.P. JACOB MOTTE, Register.

Book K, p. 355
27 Nov. 1732
Deed of Sale

BENJAMIN TURNER, blacksmith, to WILLIAM HOLMAN, planter, of Berkeley Co., for ₤ 270 SC money & other considerations, 270 a. in Colleton Co., granted 23 July 1711 by Gov. ROBERT GIBBES & the Lords Proprs. bounding E on JOHN PALMER; W on SAMUEL SHEPPARD & ELIAS FISHER; N on Chehaw River. Witnesses: HENRY YONGE, THOMAS BUTLER, KEN. BRIAN, JOHN GREENE, DANIEL GREENE, JR. Before DANIEL GREENE, J.P. JACOB MOTTE, Register.

Book K, p. 358
6 Mar. 1732
Mortgage

JOHN RUSS, planter, to ALEXANDER NISBETT, merchant, of Charleston, for ₤ 449:12 SC money, 266 a. in Berkeley Co., now occupied by JOHN RUSS, on the condition that RUSS pays NISBETT ₤ 449:12 SC money on 1 Jan. 1734 with interest on 1 Jan. 1734. Witnesses: JONATHAN DRAKE, MATHEW DRAKE, JOSEPH RUSS, WALTER NISBETT. Before ALEXANDER PARRIS, J.P. JACOB MOTTE, Register.

Book K, p. 361
8 & 9 Oct. 1731
L & R

SAMUEL WRAGG, merchant, of London, to JAMES CROKATT, merchant, of Charleston, for ₤ 630 money of Great Britain, that brick messuage on N side Broad St. in Charleston, purchased by WRAGG from MARGARET INGERSON, widow; bounding W on JOSEPH WRAGG, merchant; E on a lot & brick house of JAMES CROKATT (formerly of REBECCA FLAVELL, widow). WRAGG agrees that he & his wife MARY shall appear before the Court of Common Pleas at Westminster to acknowledge CROKATT'S title. Witnesses: EDWARD NEALE, JOHN HARWOOD. JACOB MOTTE, Register.

Book K, p. 368
25 Oct. 1732
Affidavit

JOHN HARWOOD, getnleman, of the Parish of St. Mildred, Poultney, London, appeared before Sir FRANCIS CHILD, Knight, Lord Mayor of London & the Aldermen, & testified that on 9 Oct. 1731 he saw SAMUEL WRAGG, merchant, sign the L & R, 8 & 9 Oct. 1731 to the use of JAMES CROKATT, of Charleston, SC & that WRAGG signed a receipt for ₤ 630, & that EDWARD NEALE, merchant, of Lombard St., London signed as witness. Signed, SMITH. JACOB MOTTE, Register.

Book K, p. 369
16 Apr. 1728
Deed of Sale

ROBERT COLE, to EDWARD CORUNT, planter, both of Colleton Co., for ₤ 200, sold 200 a. as measured by the Lords Proprs. on Wadwadmelaw Island, Colleton Co., bounding E on JOHN ELLIS; S on THOMAS UPHAM; W on WILLIAM WILLIAMS; N on Wadwadmelaw River & marsh. Signed by ROBERT COLE & MARY COLE. Witnesses: WILLIAM FLECKNOW, ABIGAIL PETERSON, MARY (her mark) FLECKNOW. Before THOMAS LADSON, J.P. JACOB MOTTE, Register.

Book K, p. 372   RALPH JERMAN, planter, & MARGARET his wife, to
12 & 13 Apr. 1733   WILLIAM SWINTON, planter, all of Craven Co.,
L & R   for L 500 SC money, 625 a. in Craven Co.,
                        bounding SW on N branch of Black River; SE on
JOHN BROWN; NW on JOHN THOMPSON; as shown in 2 plats. Witnesses: THOMAS
LAROCHE, MARY SPENCER. Before CHALRES HILL, J.P. JACOB MOTTE, Register.

Book K, p. 377   ZACHARIAN CARLILE, planter, to JOSEPH STANYARN,
27 & 28 Oct. 1731   planter, both of Colleton Co., for L 150 SC
L & R   money, 50 a. on John"s Island, Colleton Co.,
                        bounding N on WILLIAM DAVIS Creek; SW on WIL-
LIAM WILKINS; S on ZACHARIAH CARLILE; E on JOHN MARSHALL. Witnesses:
WILLIAM WALSBE, THOMAS INNS, JOHN (his mark) TENDIN. Before DANIEL
GREENE, J.P. JACOB MOTTE, Register.

Book K, p. 382   MOSES MARTIN, planter, of St. Paul's Parish,
27 Apr. 1731   Colleton Co., to his son MOSES MARTIN, cooper,
Deed of Gift   of same place, for love & affection, & with
                        the consent of his wife GRACE MARTIN, his 2
plantations on E side Ponpon River where he lives; 1 of 100 a. bounding E
on WILLIAM MCECHEN; S of JOHN PETER; the other of 156 a., bounding N on
JAMES FULTON; S on WILLIAM MCECHEN; also 30 slaves; except that MOSES MAR-
TIN, SR. & his wife GRACE to have the use of land & slaves during their
lifetime. Witnesses: JOHN ANDREW, ALEXANDER (his mark) MELVEN, THOMAS
MELVEN. Before WILLIAM LIVINGSTON. JACOB MOTTE, Register.

Book K, p. 383   JOHN PETER, planter, to his brother CHRIST-
1 Mar. 1730   OPHER PETER, planter, both of Colleton Co.,
Deed of Gift   for love & affection, 250 a., English measure
                        in Colleton Co., being the eastern half of
500 a. granted by the Lords Proprs. to DR. ALEXANDER CURSON; bounding N
on WILLIAM BRANFORD; E on JOHN HAYNES; S on WILLIAM FREEMAN & EDWARD &
JOSEPH HAYNES; W on other half owned by JOHN SPLATT. Witnesses: JOHN
FISHER, ANTHONY SAXBY. Before ROBERT YONGE, J.P. JACOB MOTTE, Register.

Book K, p. 384   CHARLES HAYES, planter, of Berkeley Co., to
9 Mar. 1732   his brother GEORGE HAYES, for love & affection
Deed of Gift   & 20 sh. currency, 255 a. on which his father
                        CHARLES HAYES lived, being half of 510 a.,
with the dwelling house, etc. Witnesses: HENRY DURANT, JOSEPH WARNOCK,
REBECCA FLAVELL. Witnesses: to possession & seizin: REBEKAH GOODBE, HEN-
RY DURANT, JOSEPH WARNOCK. Before MICHAEL DARBY, J.P. JACOB MOTTE, Reg.

Book K, p. 386   RIVERS STANYARN, planter, to JOSEPH STANYARN,
6 & 7 July 1730   planter, both of Colleton Co., for L 325 SC
L & R   money, 350 a., called Folly Island, in Berke-
                        ley Co., bounding E on the sea; NW of marsh &
a creek of the Sound on S side James Island; NE on a creek out of S channel of Ashley River. Witnesses: JOHN FIDLING, JOHN CROFT. Before GAB-
RIEL MANIGAULT, J.P. JACOB MOTTE, Register.

Book K, p. 392   JOSEPH (his mark) HARLEY, planter, of Colleton
18 Apr. 1733   Co., to ROYALL SPRY, as security for endorsing
Mortgage   2 bonds made by HARLEY to BENJAMIN GODIN &
                        JOHN GUERRARD, merchants, of Charleston, in
the penal sum of L 1000: 2d currency, conditioned for the payment of
L 241 on 1 Jan. 1733; L 263:10:1 on 1 Jan. 1734; 410 a. in Colleton Co.,
bounding N on JOHN KENEWAY; E on JOSEPH DIDCOTT; S on JOHN ANDREW & lands
not laid out; W on lands not laid out. One fine hat delivered in lieu of
land. Witnesses: CHRISTOPHER SMITH, HENRY GIBBES. Before CHARLES PINCK-
NEY, J.P. JACOB MOTTE, Register. Mortgage declared satisfied by ROYALL
SPRY. Witness: NATHANIEL JOHNSON, Pub. Reg.

Book K, p. 395   JOHN STANYARN, planter, & MAGDALEN his wife,
6 & 7 July 1732   with free consent of MAGDALEN, to JOSEPH STAN-
L & R   YARN, planter, both of Colleton Co., for L 160
                        SC money, 100 a. in Colleton Co., bounding W
on CAPT. ANTHONY MATHEWS; N on JOHN MARSHALL; S on a creek or marsh.
Witnesses: JOHN MCKAY, JOHN CROFT. Before GABRIEL MANIGAULT, J.P. JACOB
MOTTE, Register.

Book K, p. 401	JOHN STANYARN, planter, & MAGDALEN his wife,
6 & 7 July 1732	with the free consent of MAGDALEN, to JOSEPH
L & R	STANYARN, planter, both of Colleton Co., for

Ł 50 SC money, all the half part of the real estate of WILLIAM RIVERS which WILLIAM RIVERS gave to WILLIAM STANYARN. Whereas WILLIAM RIVERS, carpenter, of Berkeley Co., by will dated 3 Oct. 1717, bequeathed to his 2 grandsons WILLIAM & RIVERS STANYARN all his real estate as follows: to WILLIAM, his mansion & half his lands; to RIVERS, the other half; should either wish to sell he shall sell only to his brother; should WILLIAM OR RIVERS die before inheriting then his share to go to grandson JOSEPH STANYARN, observing the last paragraph of the will; & whereas WILLIAM STANYARN, died before taking possession & his portion went to JOSEPH; now JOHN to prevent any lawsuit against his brother JOSEPH, conveys WILLIAM STANYARN'S half to his brother JOSEPH STANYARN. Witnesses: JOHN MACKAY, JOHN CROFT. Before GABRIEL MANIGAULT, J.P. JACOB MOTTE, Register.

Book K, p. 407　　　JAMES HASELL, gentleman, & SUSANNAH his wife,
15 & 16 Nov. 1732　　of Charleston, to ABRAHAM SATUR, gentleman, of
L & R by Mortgage　　St. James Goosecreek, as security for the payment of Ł 2000 currency at the times & in the amounts agreed upon, convey 700 a. in St. James Goosecreek Parish, Berkeley Co., bounding E on Beck River, or Medway River; W on BENJAMIN WARING & SABINA SMITH; N on Landgrave THOMAS SMITH; S on a creek 7 SAMUEL PRIOLEAU. Witnesses: JAMES KINLOCH, JOHN LEWIS, ABRAHAM SATUR releases any claim for suit. Before BENJAMIN GODIN, J.P. JACOB MOTTE, Register.

Book K, p. 414　　　JOHN WILSON, cordwianer, of Berkeley Co., to
5 July 1731　　　　 STEPHEN FORD, planter, of Colleton Co., bond
Bond　　　　　　　　in penal sum of Ł 1600 SC money, as security on the sale of 200 a. for 3 head of cattle. Whereas JOHN WILSON, father of said JOHN WILSON, owned 200 a. in Colleton Co., at the head of Frost's Creek, adjoining 400 a. belonging to MICHAEL BRUINGTON, which 200 a. are now occupied by THOMAS FLEMING & STEPHEN FORD, now JOHN WILSON conveys the 200 a. to FORD for 3 head of cattle valued at Ł 12 SC money & gives FORD a bond as security. Witnesses: GEORGE MORELAND, LOUIS LAFONTAINE, STEPHEN FORD. Before JOHN PALMER, J.P. JACOB MOTTE, Register.

Book K, p. 416　　　JOHN BAYLEY, cordwainer, only son & heir of
2 Feb. 1731　　　　 WILLIAM BAYLEY & HANNAH his wife, to WILLIAM
Deed of Sale　　　　VISSER, planter, all of Berkeley Co., for Ł 30 currency, 25 a. in Christ Church Parish, being half of 50 a. which belonged to WILLIAM BAYLEY; which 25 a. are bounding E on the other half, or 25 a., sold by JOHN BAYLEY to JOHN EVANS, shipwright, & now in the possession of JONATHAN STOCKS; N & W on JOHN HALE; S on Quelch's Creek. Witnesses: GARET VANVELZIN, THOMAS LAMBOLL. Before CHARLES HILL, J.P. JACOB MOTTE, Register.

Book K, p. 418　　　His Excellency ROBERT JOHNSON, ESQ., by com-
Memorandum　　　　　mission dated the 2d May 1733 appointed NATHANIEL JOHNSON, ESQ. to be Public Register who appointed the same day JOSEPH FOX, ESQ., Deputy who received 11 books from Mr. JACOB MOTTE the 5th day of May 1733.

Book K, p. 419　　　THOMAS (his mark) MANNING, planter, of Colle-
12 Mar. 1720　　　　ton Co., to JOHN HICKS, planter, of same place,
Deed of Sale　　　　for Ł 40 SC money, 127 a. as measured by the Lords Proprs., on Wadmalaw Island, Colleton Co., bounding S on Bohicket Creek; E on WILLIAM WEST; N on WILLIAM ADAMS. Witnesses: HESTER (her mark) NEWINGTON, WILLIAM (his mark) ELKYNS, SAMUEL SHODDOCK. Before THEOPHILUS GREGORY, J.P. JOSEPH FOX, Dep. Reg.

Book K, p. 421　　　JAMES GREEN, planter, & SUSANNAH (her mark)
4 Apr. 1723　　　　 his wife, of Wadmalaw Island, Colleton Co., to
Deed of Gift　　　　JONATHAN THOMAS & ANN his wife, daughter of JAMES & SUSANNAH GREEN, for ANN'S use, 75 a., bounding on JOHN SAM on 1 side & on JOSEPH ALIEN (?) (formerly JOSEPH PAWLEY). Witnesses: JOHN SAM, JOSEPH GIBINS. Before ROBERT YONGE, J.P. JOSEPH FOX, Dep. Reg.

Book K, p. 422   THOMAS ELLERY, gentleman, & ANN his wife, to
5 & 6 May 1731   WILLIAM HAMMERTON, ESQ., all of Charleston,
L & R   for ₤ 360 currency, the eastermost part of
                   lots #188, #189, & #79 in Charleston which
THOMAS ELLERY lately purchased from ANDREW ALLEN, bounding E 200 ft. on
THOMAS COOPER (purchased from ELLERY); W on THOMAS ELLERY; N 30 ft. on
THOMAS ELLERY; S 30 ft. on Dock St. Witnesses: CHARLES BESWICKE, JOSEPH
FIDLER. Before ALEXANDER PARRIS, J.P. Witnesses to receipt: JOHN BALLAN-
TINE, JOHN CHAMPNEYS. JOSEPH FOX, Dep. Reg.

Book K, p. 428   JOHN BAGEN, to JOHN PAYCOM, both of Colleton
7 May 1733   Co., all his claim in 500 a. Whereas OWEN BA-
Quit Claim   GEN for a certain consideration sold to JOHN
                   PAYCOM on 9 Nov. 1710 a tract of 500 a. in
Colleton Co., within land, in Horse Shoe Savannah, bounding N on JOHN
CATTLE & on all other sides on land not then laid out; & whereas the deed
of sale has been accidentally defaced, obliterated & torn so that JOHN
PAYCOM may be in danger of losing the land, now JOHN BAGEN, only son &
heir of OWEN BAGEN, for 10 sh. assigns all right he may have to PAYCOM.
Witnesses: JAMES FULTON, THOMAS CLIFFORD, THOMAS SACHEVERELL. Before
DANIEL GREENE, J.P. JOSEPH FOX, Dep. Reg.

Book K, p. 430   JONATHAN BETTISON, planter, to JOHN PAYCOMB,
10 & 11 Jan. 1732/3 both of Colleton Co., for ₤ 315 SC money, 126
L & R   a. at Horseshoe, Colleton Co., bounding S on
                   PEYCOMB; being part of 250 a. sold by JOHN
PEYCOMB to JONATHAN BETTISON, the 250 a. being part of 500 a. granted to
PAYCOMB (PEYCOMB). HESTER, wife of JONATHAN BETTISON, freely resigns her
right of dower. Witnesses: THOMAS CLIFFORD, MATHEW GUERIN, THOMAS MALL-
DEN. Before DANIEL GREENE, J.P. JOSEPH FOX, Dep. Reg.

Book K, p. 434   ISAAC MAZYCK, of Charleston, to BARTHOLOMEW
11 Nov. 1717   GAILLARD, of Craven Co., for ₤ 375 currency,
Deed of Sale   10 a. on the W side of the Broad Path, Charles-
                   ton, bounding S on Charleston lots; N on Wick-
ley; W on Glebe or Parsonage; which 10 a. is part of 90 a. granted to
ISAAC MAZYCK by the Lords Proprs. on 24 Oct. 1696 on N side of Charleston
& W of Cooper River. Witnesses: PETER DE ST. JULIEN, BENJAMIN GODIN, PAUL
DOUXSAINT. Witnesses to possession & delivery: BENJAMIN GODIN, SAMUEL
PRIOLEAU, THOMAS SATUR, PETER DE ST. JULIEN. Before DANIEL GREENE, J.P.
JOSEPH FOX, Dep. Reg.

Book K, p. 437   WILLIAM NASH, SR., planter, & SUSANNAH his
29 Apr. 1731   wife, to JONATHAN THOMAS, planter, all of Col-
L & R   leton Co., for ₤ 280 SC money, 140 a. on Wad-
                   wadmelaw Island, Colleton Co., bounding E on
JOHN NASH; W on Wad-wadmalaw River; N on WILLIAM MCGILLIVRAY; S on JOSEPH
MORTON. Witnesses: EPHRAIM MIKELL, ROBERT WINN, JOHN (his mark) HAMILTON.
Before ROBERT YONGE, J.P. JOSEPH FOX, Dep. Reg.

Book K, p. 443   WILLIAM NASH, planter, to JONATHAN THOMAS,
29 June 1731   planter, both of Colleton Co., in penal sum of
Bond   ₤ 800 conditioned for fulfilling the above cov-
                   enants. Witnesses: EPHRAIM MIKELL, ROBERT
WINN, JOHN (his mark) HAMILTON. Before ROBERT YONGE, M.P. JOSEPH FOX,
Dep. Reg.

Book K, p. 444   THOMAS WARING, ESQ., of Berkeley Co., as at-
26 Mar. 1724   torney for JOSEPH LORD, of Chatham, New Eng-
Deed of Sale   land, to JOSEPH BRUNSON, planter, of Berkeley
                   Co., for ₤ 22:10 currency, the 10th lot in the
2nd division containing 45 a.; bounding E on JOHN STEVENS; S on JOHN
WHITE; W on ROBERT MILLER; N on a rangeway. Letter of attorney, dated 13
Sept. 1720, proved in Boston, recorded in Registers Office, SC, Book C,
fol. 11, on 17 May 1721. Witnesses: AARON WAY, JR., JOSEPH SMITH, NATH-
ANIEL SUMNER. SUMNER made oath according to his profession. Before ALEX-
ANDER SKENE, J.P. JOSEPH FOX, Dep. Reg.

Book K, p. 446   SAMUEL WAY, JR., to JOSEPH BRUNSON, SR., both
4 Dec. 1732   of Berkeley Co., for value received, 100 a. in

Deed of Sale | St. George Parish, Berkeley Co., bounding E on JOHN HAWKS; S on JOSEPH BRUNSON; W & N on ROBERT MILLER, SR. Witnesses: ROGER SUMNER, NATHANIEL WAY. Before JOSEPH BLAKE, J.P. JOSEPH FOX, Dep. Reg.

Book K, p. 448
21 Sept. 1702
Deed of Gift

JOHN STEVENS, planter, of Berkeley Co., to the inhabitants of Dorchester, particularly WILLIAM PRATT, INCREASE SUMNER, & THOMAS OSGOOD, SR., as feoffees instructed by the inhabitants of Dorchester, for the Minister of the Congregational Church now settled in Dorchester, the 9th lot in the 1st range of the 1st division in Dorchester (which was formerly 2 tracts, 1 called Boasoo, the other Rose's land), containing 50 a., bounding E on JOSEPH LORD; S on Ashley River; W on WILLIAM WAY, JR., N on line dividing 1st & 2nd ranges; & the 1st lot in 2nd division containing 45 a.; bounding E by a division way; S on a highway between 1st & 2nd division; W on Dame REBECCA AXTELL; N on WILLIAM WAY, SR.; also 4 small lots #13, #33, & #112, in a place designed for a place of trade; and 1/26 part of all undivided land in Dorchester. The above lands were granted to JOHN STEVENS by 2 trants signed by Gov. JOSEPH BLAKE & the Lords Proprs. on 1st. Feb. 1699/1700, which have reference to 2 former grants, 1 dated 7 July 1696, the other dated 9 Sept. 1696, in which all the above tract now called Dorchester is granted to JOHN STEVENS in free & common soccage. Witnesses: JOSEPH LORD, MOSES WAY, NATHANIEL SUMNER. Before B. WARING, J.P. JOSEPH FOX, Dep. Reg.

DEEDS BOOK "La"
1726-1728

Book La, p. 1
11 & 12 Sept. 1726
L & R

JOSEPH (his mark) GRIFFIN, planter, to BENJAMIN CHILDS, planter, both of Berkeley Co., for Ł 423:10 SC money, 77 a., part of 177 a., in St. George's Parish, Berkeley Co., bounding S on BENJAMIN CHILDS; E on land conveyed by JOSEPH GRIFFEN to RALPH IZARD & WILLIAM BULL for the use of JOSEPH CHILDS, a minor; N on PETER GENRON & CHARLES BARKER; W on JOSEPH GRIFFIN. Signed by JOSEPH (his mark) GRIFFIN, JOYCE (her mark) GRIFFEN. Witnesses: JAMES CANTEY, ANGELLE COONE, CHARLES BARKER. Before DANIEL GREENE, J.P. JACOB MOTTE, Reg.

Book La, p. 6
Aug. 1712
Deed of Sale

JOHN GODFREY, with the consent of MARY, his wife, of Berkeley Co., to EDWARD CLIFT, planter, of Colleton Co., for Ł 30 currency, 200 a. on W side Edisto River, bounding S on Mr. BOONE; N on JOHN GODFREY; granted to GODFREY by Gov. NATHANIEL JOHNSON & the Lords Proprs. on 1 Dec. 1710. Witnesses: JOSEPH HEAPE, RICHARD GODFREY, JOSEPH (his mark) FARLEY. Before JOHN WOODWARD. HEAP, planter, of Wappo, St. Andrew's Parish, appeared before THOMAS HEPWORTH, C.J., 6 Dec. 1726 & acknowledged signatures. JACOB MOTTE, Reg.

Book La, p. 11
14 Dec. 1726
L & R

ALEXANDER TRENCH, merchant, of Charleston, as attorney for JOHN BAYLY of Ballinaclough, Ireland, to JAMES BROWN, planter, of Craven Co., for Ł 500 SC money, 2000 a. in Craven Co., bounding NE on N Branch of Black River & running a NW W course 175-1/2 ch., beginning at an Indian Old Field formerly claimed by Mr. MILLER, at a beech tree; NW on vacant land claimed by JOHN NISMITH & DUGALD MCKEGGAN, running SW 124-1/2 ch.; SW on vacant land 168 ch. SE & by S.; & SE on vacant land running 124-1/2 ch. N NE to the Indian Old Field. Whereas the Rt. Hon. JOHN, EARL OF BATH, & the Lords Proprs. by letters patents dated 16 Aug. 1698 created JOHN BAYLY, of Ballinaclough, Co. of Tipperary, Ireland, a Landgrave & Cassique of SC, granting him 48,000 a. in SC; & whereas JOHN BAYLY, son & heir of said JOHN BAYLY, on 19 Nov. 1722 appointed ALEXANDER TRENCH, merchant, of Charleston, his attorney, giving him authority to set aside 8,000 a. for the use of JOHN BAYLY & sell the rest; now TRENCH sells 2,000 a. to JAMES BROWN. Witnesses: JOEL POINSETT, THOMAS CONYBEAR, ROBERT NISBETT. Before JOHN BARKSDALE, J.P. JACOB MOTTE, Reg.

Book La, p. 17 | THOMAS HEPWORTH, ESQ. & ANNE his wife, of

9 & 10 Dec. 1726   Charleston, to HENRY DE ST.JULIEN, gentleman,
L & R   of Berkeley Co., for L 415 SC money, 660 a. in
                          Berkeley Co., within land, bounding W on LAM-
BERT SANDERS; N on THOMAS PALMER; S & E on land not laid out. Witnesses:
JOHN FENWICK, PETER DE ST.JULIEN, JOSEPH DE ST.JULIEN. JACOB MOTTE, Reg-
ister.

Book La, p. 23   JOHN BAYLY, of Ballinaclough, Co. of Tipperary,
28 & 29 Nov. 1726   (see p. 11) by his attorney ALEXANDER TRENCH,
L & R   merchant, of Charleston, to JOHN ALSTON, plant-
                          er, of Berkeley Co., for L 150 SC money, 643 a.
in Berkeley Co., bounding NE on SAMUEL WIGFALL; E on JOHN HUGGINS; S on
PETER COUILLANDAU; W on ANTHONY BONNEAU; SW on LEWIS MOUSON; NW on JOHN
ALSTON. Witnesses: ISAAC MAZYCK, JR., PAUL CHARRON, JAMES DE. ST.JULIEN.
PETER DE ST.JULIEN, J.P. JACOB MOTTE, Register.

Book La, p. 29   WILLIAM LIVINGSTON, clerk, of Charleston, to
21 Mar. 1719   THOMAS SMITH, JR., gentleman, of Berkeley Co.
Deed in Trust   Whereas sometime before the death of MARY LIV-
                          INGSTON (wife of WILLIAM) executrix of JOHN
ASH; of Daho, L 50 currency out of ASH'S estate had been paid to WILLIAM
LIVINGSTON for 2000 a. (part of 4000 a. which LIVINGSTON had purchased
from Landgrave ROBERT DANIELL) in which 2000 a. all the legatees of JOHN
ASH were to have equal share & benefit, but MARY dying before a formal
conveyance of the sum could be made, now LIVINGSTON conveys to THOMAS
SMITH, JR., 2000 a. (except 250 a.) LIVINGSTON'S own share, ie, 1750 a.
(the S part of the 4000 a. purchased from DANIELL) on E side of freshes
of Edisto River nearest to JAMES RIXAM'S land, to be run from Ponpon or
Edisto River directly E by a straight line; in trust for the use of THOM-
AS SMITH, JR. & the children of JOHN ASH, vizt: JOHN, RICHARD, ALGERNON,
SAMUEL, ISABELLA, wife of BENJAMIN BERRY, shipwright, & THEADORE, wife of
JOSEPH LAWS, planter, to be equally between THOMAS SMITH & the children.
Witnesses: JOHN SMILIE & ELIZABETH SMILIE, sworn according to their pro-
fession. Before CHRISTOPHER WILKINSON, J.P. JACOB MOTTE, Register.

Book La, p. 33   THOMAS ELLERY, gentleman, & ANNE his wife, to
2 & 3 Jan. 1726   ELIZABETH CAWOOD, widow, all of Charleston,
L & R   for L 2500 money, 4 adjoining tracts laid into
                          1 plantation of 350 a. on Cooper River, bound-
ing W on WILLIAM DRY, RICHARD BAKER & others; N on RICHARD BAKER; S on
JOSEPH HURST & WILLIAM DRY. Whereas his Excellency JOHN, EARL OF BATH,
Palatine, & the Lords Proprs. on 16 Aug. 1698 impowered the Hon. JOSEPH
BLAKE, JAMES MOORE, Landgrave JOSEPH MORTON, Landgrave EDMUND BELLINGER,
ROBERT DANIELL & JOHN ELY to sell lands, they granted DAVID MAYBANK 100 a.
English measure, in Berkeley Co.; & whereas DAVID MAYBANK & SUSANNAH his
wife by deed of feofment on 1 Dec. 1708 conveyed the land to EDWARD WEEK-
LEY, gentleman; & whereas his Excellency, JOHN LORD GRANVILLE, Palatine,
& the Lords Proprs. impowered the Rt. Hon. Sir NATHANIEL JOHNSON, Knight,
Gov. of NC & SC & others to sell lands & they on 5 Oct. 1704 granted ED-
WARD WEEKLEY 220 a., English measure, except 80 a. which WEEKLEY sold to
Landgrave THOMAS SMITH, leaving 140 a. in WEEKLEY'S possession which he
conveyed to THOMAS ELLERY; & whereas the Hon. ROBERT GIBBES, Gov., & the
Lords Proprs. granted WEEKLEY 23 a. (plat on grant dated 5 May 1711); &
whereas the Hon. ROBERT DANIELL, Dep. Gov., & the Lords Proprs. on 25
May 1717 granted WEEKLEY 90 a. (plat attached to grant dated 12 Mar.
1716); & whereas the 4 tracts are contiguous & have been laid out in 1
plantation & a dwelling house has been erected & other improvements made;
& whereas EDWARD WEEKLEY & ELIZABETH his wife by L & R, 29 & 30 Sept.
1724 sold the 4 tracts of 350 a. to THOMAS ELLERY; now ELLERY sells to
MRS. ELIZABETH CAWOOD free of ANNE'S dower. Witnesses: CHARLES HILL,
WILLIAM VISSER, THOMAS LAMBOLL. Before BENJAMIN WHITAKER, J.P. JACOB
MOTTE, Register.

Book La, p. 44   GEORGE ATCHISON (ACHISON), merchant, now of
11 & 12 Mar. 1725   Charleston (son of DAVID ATCHISON, late of the
L & R   Parish of Cumberhees & Stewarty of Anadate,
                          North Britain, & nephew of JAMES GILBERTSON,
alias ACHISON, late planter of Colleton Co., SC) to ELIZABETH HYRNE, widow, & HENRY HYRNE, merchant, for L 110 money of Great Britain, 500 a. in
Colleton Co., bounding SE on a branch of Tugedoo Creek; SW on Propr.

BLAKE. Whereas JOHN, Lord Granville, Palatine, & the Lords Proprs. by grant under the Rt. Hon. Sir NATHANIEL JOHNSON, Knight, Gov., etc. on 15 Sept. 1705 gave JAMES GILBERTSON 500 a., English measure in Colleton Co., bounding as above; & whereas JAMES GILBERTSON, alias ATCHISON, by will dated 16 Aug. 1720 bequeathed the 500 a. to GEORGE ATCHISON (his brother DAVID'S son, now in England); now ATCHISON sells to the HYRNES. Witnesses: BURRELL MASSINGBERD HYRNE, ROBERT HUME. Before DANIEL GREENE, J.P. JACOB MOTTE, Register.

Book La, p. 51
30 Apr. 1724
L & R

JAMES NICHOLAS MAYRANT, ESQ., & SUSANNAH his wife, of Craven Co., to DANIEL HUGER, ESQ., of Berkeley Co., for ₤ 500 SC money, 2 tracts in Berkeley Co., of 500 a. each, bounding NW & SE on each other, SE on CAPT. ELIAS BALL; SW on WILLIAM WATIES; NE, SW, & NW on land not laid out; also 500 a. (formerly ANDREW DUPEY'S) in Berkeley Co., bounding NE & SE on land not laid out; SW on above said land formerly belonging FRANCIS HARRIS. Whereas the Lords Proprs. by 2 grants dated 19 Mar. 1718 gave FRANCIS HARRIS 2 tracts of 500 a. each in Berkeley Co.; & whereas FRANCIS HARRIS & SARAH his wife on 26 Mar. 1719 sold the 1000 a. to NICHOLAS MYRANT, & whereas the Lords Proprs. on 21 Mar. 1715 granted ANDREW DUPEY 500 a. in Berkeley Co., which he on 12 Jan. 1716 sold to JAMES NISHOLAS MYRANT & PAUL MAYRANT (his brother); & whereas PAUL MAYRAND died & JAMES NICHOLAS MAYRANT became sole owner of the 500 a.; now he sells the 3 tracts to DANIEL HUGER. Witnesses: JOHN GENDRON, PAUL MAZYCK, ISAAC CHARDON. Before DANIEL GREENE, J.P. JACOB MOTTE, Register.

Book La, p. 60
27 & 28 Feb. 1726
L & R

RICHARD GRIMSTON, gentleman, & ELLINOR (her mark) his wife, to ELIAS HANCOCK, vintner, all of Charleston, for ₤ 700 SC money, lot #229 in Charleston, containing 1/2 a. English measure, bounding S on a little street leading from Cooper River by RICHARD TRADD'S to GEORGE KEELING'S; N on MR. DUGUE; E on JOHN HILL; W on THOMAS ROSE; which lot #229 was purchased by GRIMSTON on 20 Dec. 1722 from THOMAS DIXON, bricklayer, & MARY his wife, of James Island. Witnesses: EDWARD CROFT, ROBERT RANDALL, THOMAS BARTRAU, JOHN CROFT. Before THOMAS HEPWORTH, C.J. JACOB MOTTE, Register.

Book La, p. 66
1 Mar. 1726
Memorandum

JONATHAN COLLINGS, mariner, & STEPHEN WILLIAMS, butcher, both of Charleston, made this agreement. Should COLLINGS not become a co-partner in butchering with 1 JAMES ROUSE by 1 Sept. 1728 he will pay WILLIAMS ₤ 100 sterling of Great Britain. WILLIAMS promises COLLINGS that should COLLINGS & ROUSE become co-partners by that date he will serve COLLINGS (COLLINS) as his servant for 7 years beginning that date. Each binds himself to the other in the penalty of ₤ 200 sterling of Great Britain. Witness: RICHARD GILES. Before DANIEL GREENE, J.P. JACOB MOTTE, Register.

Book La, p. 67
29 July 1726
Deed of Sale

THOMAS GADSDEN, gentleman, of Berkeley Co., to FRANCIS LEBRASSEUR, merchant, of Charleston, for 5 sh., a piece of land bounding S 240 ft. on MRS. SARAH RHETT'S pasture; W 104 ft. on his (GADSDEN'S) pasture; N on his pasture; E on marsh; as enclosed with cedar posts, rails & palings at LEBRASSERUR'S charge. Witnesses: JAMES PAINE, AUGUSTUS DELABASTIE. Before JOHN BARKSDALE, J.P. JACOB MOTTE, Register.

Book La, p. 70
11 June 1726
Bond

SAMUEL TOWLE (LOWLE), cooper, of Willtown Colleton Co., to TIMOTHY HENDRICK, planter, of same place, bond for ₤ 2000 SC money, to secure to HENDRICK a deed of conveyance this date, of 150 a., (part of 2 tracts laid out by THOMAS BROUGHTON, Sur. Gen., in accordance with 2 warrants under the Hon. ROBERT GIBBS, ESQ., Gov. of SC, 1 dated 19 Feb. 1708 the other 8 Aug. 1711) & to assure HENDRICK that MARGERY, wife of SAMUEL TOWLE shall not evict him or recover her dower. Witnesses: WILLIAM WHIPPY, JAMES COCKRAN, JAMES SMYTH (sworn according to their profession). Before CHRISTOPHER WILKINSON, J.P. JACOB MOTTE, Register.

Book La, p. 72   SAMUELTOWLE, cooper, of Ponpon, Colleton Co.,
11 June 1726   to TIMOTHY HENDRICK, planter, of Colleton Co.,
Deed of Sale   for ₤ 2000 SC money, 150 a. on N side Edisto
                       River freshes in Colleton Co., bounding N on
JAMES FULTON & Landgrave JOSEPH MORTON; E & S on SAMUEL TOWLES; W on
MOSES MARTIN; the tract divided thus: begin at N corner joining JAMES
FULTON, run S halfway the line joining to MOSES MARTIN, then E till 150 a.
is measured. MARGERY (her mark) renounces her dower. Witnesses: WILLIAM
WHIPPY, JAMES COCKRAN, JAMES SMYTH, sowrn according to their profession.
Before CHRISTOPHER WILKINSON, J.P. JACOB MOTTE, Register.

Book La, p. 76   MARY LAROCHE, widow & executrix of JOHN LA-
27 & 28 Nov. 1724   ROCHE, merchant, of Charleston, to PETER DE ST.
L & R   JULIEN, ESQ., of Berkeley Co., for ₤ 1150 SC
                       money, 2 tracts of 550 & 528 a., making 1
tract of 1078 a., in Berkeley Co., which JOHN LAROCHE by will dated 9 Aug.
1723 authorized his executrix (during the minority of his son DANIEL) to
sell; bounding E on PETER DE ST.JULIEN & DANIEL RAVENEL; W on WILLIAM
BALL; N on PETER DE ST.JULIEN & JAMES DE ST.JULIEN; S on DANIEL RAVENEL.
Witnesses: JOHN HUTCHINSON, ANTHONY MATHEWS, JOB ROTHMAHLER. Before WIL-
LIAM BLAKEWAY, J.P. JACOB MOTTE, Register.

Book La, p. 84   ROYALL SPRY, planter, to DANIEL HENDRICK, cord-
4 June 1723   winder, both of Ponpon, Colleton Co., for
Deed of Sale   ₤ 200 SC money 100 a. on N side Edisto River
                       freshes, bounding N on DANIEL HENDRICK; E & S
on ROYALL SPRY; W on Bee's Creek; to be divided thus: begin at joining of
DANIEL HENDRICK, to run E & W joining to ROYALL SPRY, then S until 100 a.
are measured. Witnesses: JOHN PETERS, THOMAS SACHEVERILL, MARY SACHEVE-
RILL. Before CHRISTOPHER WILKINSON, ASST. Judge for Willtown. JACOB
MOTTE, Register.

Book La, p. 86   ROYALL SPRY, planter, to DANIEL HENDRICK, both
4 June 1723   of Ponpon, Colleton Co., in ₤ 1000 SC money,
Bond   conditioned for keeping agreements in above
                       bill of sale. Witnesses: JOHN PETERS, THOMAS
SACHEVERILL, MARY SACHEVERILL. Before CHRISTOPHER WILKINSON, J.P. JACOB
MOTTE, Register.

Book La, p. 87   ALEXANDER TRENCH, as attorney for JOHN BAYLY
9 Sept. 1726   Ireland (see p. 11) to JOHN BENSTON & WILLIAM
Bond   WATIES, (in consideration of BENSTON & WATIES
                       owing him ₤ 620 & having paid him ₤ 20 SC mon-
ey, (₤ 640 total) for 4000 a., part of the grant to JOHN BAYLY) bond in
the sum of ₤ 1000 to confirm their title free of all charges except the
fees due the Surv. Gen. Witnesses: G. SOUTHACK, ELIAS HANCOCK. Before
DANIEL GREENE, J.P. JACOB MOTTE, Register.

Book La, p. 89   THOMAS GADSDEN, ESQ., of Berkeley Co., to CAPT.
23 & 24 Mar. 1726   GEORGE ANSON, commander of H.M.S. the <u>Scar-</u>
L & R   <u>borough</u>, in Charleston Harbor, for ₤ 300 ster-
                       ling of Great Britain 63 or 64 a., part of
90 a., whereon THOMAS GADSDEN lives & which he bought from ISAAC MAZYCK,
except a piece sold to FRANCIS LEBRASSEUR, & marsh land. Whereas the Hon.
JOHN ARCHDALE, Gov. of SC & the Lords Proprs. on 14 Oct. 1696 for ₤ 1:16
SC money, granted ISAAC MAZYCK 90 a. English measure, in Berkeley Co..; &
whereas the Hon. Sir NATHANIEL JOHNSON, Knight, Gov. of SC, & the Lords
Proprs. on 1 Feb. 1706 for ₤ 1:8 granted ISAAC MAZYCK 71 a. in Berkeley
Co.; & whereas ISAAC MAZYCK, with the consent of his wife MARIANA, by
deed poll on 9 Apr. 1710 conveyed to COL. EDWARD TYNTE, Gov. of S & NC,
63 or 64 a. & all the marsh land E of the plantation fronting on Cooper
River, running as far N as the marsh on the backside of the garden; &
whereas the 63 or 64 a. & the marsh land, by the canceling of the deed
poll & by sundry conveyances became re-invested in ISAAC MAZYCK; & whereas ISAAC MAXYCK & MARIANA his wife on 29 Oct. 1720 sold the 63 or 64 a.
to THOMAS GADSDEN, reserving to MAZYCK a way through the plantation from
the Broad Path to the bridge which runs across the marsh to a plantation
owned by ISAAC MAZYCK, also liberty to carry away water out of the well
or spring sufficient for their use; & whereas by deed pool dated 29 July
1726 THOMAS GADSDEN sold to FRANCIS LEBRASSEUR, merchant, of Charleston,

part of the 63 or 64 a., bounding S 244 ft. on Mrs. SARAH RHETT'S pasture, W & N on THOMAS GADSDEN, E 104 ft. on the marsh of Cooper River, all enclosed with cedar posts & rails; now GADSDEN sells to ANSON the 63 or 64 a. (part of 90 a.) in Berkeley Co., (except that part sold to LEBRASSEUR) bounding E on Cooper River; W on the Broad Path; N on a marsh belonging to ISAAC MAZYCK and land of COL. GRANGE; S on Mrs. SARAH RHETT; always reserving the above rights to MAZYCK & reserving the right of ingress & egress to LEBRASSEUR. Witnesses: WILLIAM SAXBY, ROBERT HUME. Before DANIEL GREENE, J.P. JACOB MOTTE, Register.

Book La, p. 100　　LAWRENCE DENNIS, ESQ., & PROVIDENCE his wife,
31 Dec. 1726　　　of Charleston, to their son-in-law BENJAMIN
Deed of Gift　　　D'HARRIETTE, JR., merchant, & ANNE his wife,
　　　　　　　　　their daughter, for natural love & affection,
lot #35 in Charleston containing 1 a. English measure, granted by WILLIAM, Earl of Craven, Palatine, ANTHONY, Lord Ashley, GEORGE Lord Carteret, Sir PETER COLLETON, Baronet, SETH SOUTHELL, THOMAS ARCHDALE & THOMAS AMY, ESQ., Lords Proprs., & signed by the Hon. Landgrave THOMAS SMITH, on 15 May 1694 to JOHN BELL & conveyed by BELL by deed of feofment dated 29 Sept. 1716 to the Hon. WILLIAM GIBBON, who by L & R, 11 & 12 Oct. 1723, for Ł 500 currency, sold the lot to LAWRENCE DENNIS; fronting 51-1/2 ft., & bounding E on MAJ. THOMAS HEPWROTH (formerly Mr. CROSSE); W on JOHN BRETTON (formerly NOAH ROYER, JR.); S on WILLIAM BALLOUGH; N on LAWRENCE DENNIS (formerly NOAH ROYER, SR.). Witnesses: THOMAS WESTLYD, HENRY HARGRAVE. Before DANIEL GREENE, J P. JACOB MOTTE, Register.

Book La, p. 103　　ALEXANDER TRENCH, merchant, of Charleston, as
22 & 23 Nov. 1726　attorney for JOHN BAYLY, of Ballinaclough,
L & R　　　　　　　Ireland (see p. 11), to JOSEPH DE ST.JULIEN.
　　　　　　　　　gentleman, of Berkeley Co., for Ł 25 SC money,
93 a. in Berkeley Co., bounding N on JOSEPH DE ST.JULIEN; E on JAMES & PAUL DE ST.JULIEN; S on WILLIAM BALL; W on DANIEL DONOVANE. Witnesses: HENRY GIGNILLIAT, JEAN GARNIER, ANTHONY PORTEVINE. Before PETER DE ST. JULIEN, J.P. JACOB MOTTE, Register.

Book La, p. 109　　ALEXANDER TRENCH, merchant, of Charleston, as
5 & 6 Apr. 1727　　attorney for JOHN BAYLY, of Ballinaclough,
L & R　　　　　　　Ireland (see p. 11), to BENJAMIN GODIN, mer-
　　　　　　　　　chant, of Charleston, for Ł 700 SC money, 5000
a. in Craven Co., bounding NE on PAUL DOUXSAINT & ISAAC LEGRAND; all other sides on land not laid out. Witnesses: PETER DE ST.JULIEN, JAMES DE ST.JULIEN, JOHN GUERARD. Before BENJAMIN DELACONSEILLERE. The 3000 a. in Wambah Swamp, Craven Co., part of 48,000 a., surveyed & certified 4 Apr. 1727 by WILLIAM BULL, B.S.G. JACOB MOTTE, Register.

Book La, p. 116　　WILLOUGHBY GIBBES, widow, of Berkeley Co., to
7 Aug. 1711　　　　JOHN HERBERT, planter, & SARAH his wife, for
Deed of Sale　　　5 sh., 200 a., English measure, part of the
　　　　　　　　　plantation on which she lives, with the marsh
before it, bounding W on Goosecreek & its marshes & on all other sides on her plantation. Witnesses: COL. JAMES MOORE, THOMAS BARKER, JON. MUSGROVE. Before NICHOLAS TROTT, C.J. JACOB MOTTE, Register.

Book La, p. 119　　JAMES BEAMOR, planter, son & heir of JACOB
13 & 14 May 1727　BEAMOR, planter, of Berkeley Co., to THOMAS
L & R　　　　　　　HEPWORTH, ESQ., & ANNE his wife, of Charleston,
　　　　　　　　　for Ł 1200 SC money, 70 a. on which SARAH BEA-
MOR, mother of JAMES, lives, on Charleston Neck, being 2 tracts, 1 of 55 a. granted JOHN BIRD, the other 15 a. bought by SIMON VALLENTINE from JOHN KING & JUDAH HOLLYBUSH & later acquired by JACOB BEAMOR. Witnesses: DANIEL GREENE, THOMAS ELLERY, ROBERT HUME. Before WILLIAM BLAKEWAY, J.P. JACOB MOTTE, Register.

Book La, p. 125　　HENRY SIMONS, planter, & JUDITH his wife,
27 & 28 Apr. 1727　(daughter of PETER GUERARD, planter) to SOLO-
L & R by Mortgage　MON LEGARE, merchant, of Charleston, for
　　　　　　　　　Ł 367:7:6 SC money 3 lots in Charleston lot
#201, bounding E on a marsh at the head of COL. DANIELL'S Creek; W on the great street leading from Oyster Point to the Market Place by CAPT. SIMONDS lot; N on PETER GUERARD; also lot #203 bounding E on same marsh; W

on said great street; N & S on PETER GUERARD; also lot #206, bounding E on same marsh; W on the great street; S on PETER GUERARD; N on said creek; conditioned for the payment of said sum on 25 May 1728. Witnesses: JOHN JONES, SAMUEL RUSCO, ROBERT TAYLOR. Before JOHN BARKSDALE, J.P. JACOB MOTTE, Register. SOLOMON LEGARE received from WILLIAM WATIES L 500 in full satisfaction on 14 Feb. 1732. Witness: JACOB MOTTE, Register.

Book La, p. 134
28 Apr. 1727
Bond

HENRY SIMONS, planter, of Berkeley Co., to SOLOMON LEGARE, merchant, of Charleston, in sum of L 730 SC money conditioned for keeping the above agreement. Witnesses: JOHN JONES, ROBERT TAYLOR. Before JONN BARKSDALE, J.P. JACOB MOTTE, Register.

Book La, p. 136
2 & 3 May 1727
L & R

ALEXANDER TRENCH, merchant, of Charleston as attorney for JOHN BAYLY, of Ballinaclough, Ireland (see p. 11) to ABRAHAM SATUR, merchant, of Charleston, for L 150 SC money, 1362 a. in Craven Co., bounding E & W & S on lands not laid out; N on ABRAHAM SATUR. Witnesses: GREG. HAINES, JOHN LEWIS. Before DANIEL GREENE, J.P. JACOB MOTTE, Register.

Book La, p. 145
20 & 21 Dec. 1725
L & R

NATHANIEL MOORE, gentleman, & SARAH his wife, of St. James Goosecreek, Berkeley Co., to JOHN SUMNERS, planter, of Berkeley Co., for L 480 SC money, 18 a. about 2 miles up the Broad Path from Charleston. Witnesses: JOHN MOORE, JOHN DAVIS, JOHN CHESTER. Before the Hon. ALEXANDER PARRIS, Asst. Judge. JACOB MOTTE, Register.

Book La, p. 151
18 & 19 May 1727
L & R by Mortgage

THOMAS HEPWROTH, ESQ., & ANNE his wife, of Charleston, to JOHN WATKINSON, mariner, for L 761 SC money, 1/4 of lot 16 in Charleston, fronting 25 ft. on the Bay, bounding W on an alley; N on Mrs. MARY BLAMYER; S on JOHN MOORE (formerly Mrs. MARY NARY); conditioned for the payment of said sum on 1 Jan. 1727 with interest. Witnesses: JAMES KILPATRICK, ROBERT HUME. Before DANIEL GREENE, J.P. JACOB MOTTE, Register. ROBERT JAMES, attorney for WATKINSON, acknowledged receipt of L 941:14:9 in full payment of 7 Oct. 1729. Witnesses: JACOB MOTTE, Register.

Book La, p. 158
3 Feb. 1719
Deed of Sale

GEORGE LEA, shipwright, & LYDIA his wife, & JAMES (his mark) SADLER, carpenter, & ELLINOR (her mark) his wife, to JOSEPH LEA, shipwright, all of Charleston, for L 100 currency, 1/4 of lot #18, bounding N on JAMES SADLER; S on 1/2 lot #18; W on a little street running N from Mr. LOUGHTON'S house; E on part lot #19 called MARTHA LITTENS. Witnesses: GILSON CLAPP, JOHN JEFFERDS, GEORGE HESKET, THOMAS WILLARD. Before JOHN BARKSDALE, J.P. JACOB MOTTE, Register.

Book La, p. 161
16 Nov. 1721
Deed of Sale

JOHN WILLIAMSON, planter, of St. Paul's Parish, Colleton Co., with the free consent of his MARY to Mrs. PHEBE PETRE (PETER), for L 300 currency, 150 a. known as Stono, granted by Gov. THOMAS SMITH & the Lords Proprs. on 24 July 1694 to JOHN WILLIAMSON & bequeathed by him to his eldest son JOHN, party hereto. Witnesses: THOMAS PETER, WILLIAM BOWER, WILLIAM WILLIAMSON, MARGARET WILLIAMSON. Before DANIEL GREENE, J.P. JACOB MOTTE, Register.

Book La, p. 164
17 & 18 Aug. 1726
L & R

JOHN (his mark) SUMERS (SUMNERS), planter, & SUSANNAH (her mark) his wife, of Berkeley Co., to MARK OLIVER, victualer, of Charleston, for L 470 currency, 18 a. about 2 miles up the Broad Path from Charleston (see p. 145), plat dated 11 May 1694. Witnesses: SAMUEL MORRIS, MICHAEL JEANES, MATHEW NEWBOROUGH. Before JOHN BARKSDALE, J.P. JACOB MOTTE, Register.

Book La, p. 170
18 Aug. 1726
Bond

JOHN (his mark) SUMMERS, planter, of Berkeley, to MARK OLIVER, victualer, of St. Philip's Parish, Charleston, in sum of L 1418 currency, conditioned for keeping the agreements in the above sale. Witnesses: WILLIAM MCECHEN, RICHARD ASH, MATHEW NEWBOROUGH.

Before JOHN BARKSDALE, J.P. JACOB MOTTE, Register.

Book La, p. 171　　　　　　　ALEXANDER TRENCH, merchant, of Charleston, as
18 & 19 Apr. 1727　　　　　　attorney for JOHN BAYLY, of Ballinaclough,
L & R　　　　　　　　　　　　Ireland (see p. 11), to MEREDITH HUGHES, plant-
　　　　　　　　　　　　　　er of Prince George Parish, Craven Co., for
Ł　SC money, 200 a. English measure in Craven Co., bounding S on Black
River; NW on JOHN HOOVER; SE on a branch of Black River. Witnesses: WIL-
LIAM SMITH, WILLIAM LOUGHTON, THOMAS MERRITT. Before DANIEL GREENE, J.P.
JACOB MOTTE, Register.

Book La, p. 181　　　　　　　SARAH (her mark) BEAMOR, widow, to JOHN BARTON,
21 Jan. 1723　　　　　　　　gentleman, both of Berkeley Co., for Ł 100 cur-
Deed of Sale　　　　　　　　rency, 30 a. on Cooper River granted by JOHN,
　　　　　　　　　　　　　　Lord Granville, Palatine, & the Lords Proprs.,
signed by JOSEPH MORTON, Gov., ARTHUR MIDDLETON, ANDREW PERCIVAL, MAURICE
MATHEWS, & JOHN GODFREY, on 30 Mar. 1683 to PAUL GRIMBALL, who sold the
land to Mrs. SARAH BEAMOR; bounding SW on PAUL GRIMBALL; NE on marsh; SE
& NW on 2 marshes. Witnesses: DANIEL MCKELVEY, JOHN (his mark) PERRIMAN,
BENJAMIN DENNIS. Witnesses to possession & seizin: MARY (her mark) PERRI-
MAN, JOHN (his mark) PERRIMAN, BENJAMIN DENNIS. Before JOHN BARKSDALE,
J.P. JACOB MOTTE, Register.

Book La, p. 185　　　　　　　JOHN DELIESSELINE, planter, of French Santee,
13 & 14 Dec. 1726　　　　　 Craven Co., & MAGDELANE his wife, to ABRAHAM
L & R　　　　　　　　　　　　SATUR, merchant, of Charleston, for Ł 500 SC
　　　　　　　　　　　　　　money, 500 a. on S side Itchaw Creek, Craven
Co., bounding NE on JAMES SEROU, all other sides on vacant land; which
land was granted by the Hon. ROBERT GIBBES, Gov., SAMUEL EVELEIGH, STEPH-
EN GIBBES, CHARLES BURHAM & the Lords Proprs. on 28 June 1711 to JOHN
HARTMAN, & sold by JOHN HARTMAN & MARY his wife by deed of feoffment dated 15 Dec. 1712 to HENRY BRUNEAU; & conveyed by HENRY BRUNEAU & MARY ANNE
his wife by deed of feoffment dated 2 Feb. 1713 to PETER LEGER, planter
of Craven Co.; who by will dated 22 Oct. 1722 commanded his wife MARY to
sell the land, appointing her executrix; & she by L & R on 30 & 31 Sept.
1723 sold to JOHN DELIESSELINE: bounding E on CHARLES CHAMPIGNION; W on
EBENEZER FORD; N on ISAAC LEGRAND; S on NICHOLAS LANGLOIS. MAGDELAINE,
when requested, to appear before the Hon. THOMAS HEPWORTH, C.J. & renounce her dower. Witnesses to JOHN'S signature: JAMES KINLOCH, RICHARD
ALLEIN, SAMUEL PRIOLEAU. Witnesses to MAGDELENE'S signature: JAMES KIN-
LOCH, ETIENNE DUMAY, JACOB JEANNERET. Before WILLIAM BULL. JACOB MOTTE,
Register.

Book La, p. 193　　　　　　　SARAH BEAMOR, widow, of Berkeley Co., to THOM-
9 & 10 June 1727　　　　　　AS ELLERY, gentleman, of Charleston, as secu-
L & R by Mortgage　　　　　 rity on bond dated 8 June, in penal sum of
　　　　　　　　　　　　　　Ł 1070 currency conditioned for the payment of
Ł 535 currency, payable with interest on 11 June 1728, 190 a. on Charleston Neck, bounding W on RALPH IZARD & the Quarter House; S on THOMAS HEP-
WORTH (formerly JAMES BEAMOR); E on Cooper River; free of all claim except a conveyance from SARAH BEAMOR to WILLIAM BELLINGER for the purposes
set forth in a defeasance made by WILLIAM BELLINGER to SARAH BEAMOR. Wit-
nesses: MATHEW NEWBOROUGH, CAPT. DANIEL GREENE. Before ALEXANDER PARRIS,
J.P. JACOB MOTTE, Register.

Book La, p. 200　　　　　　　SARAH BEAMOR, widow of Berkeley Co., to THOMAS
8 June 1727　　　　　　　　　ELLERY, gentleman, of Charleston, in penal sum
Bond　　　　　　　　　　　　 of Ł 1070 conditioned for the payment of
　　　　　　　　　　　　　　Ł 588:10 on 11 June 1728. Witnesses: MATHEW
NEWBOROUGH, CAPT. DANIEL GREENE. Before ALEXANDER PARRIS, J.P. JACOB
MOTTE, Register.

Book La, p. 200　　　　　　　SARAH BEAMOR, widow of Berkeley Co., to DANIEL
12 June 1727　　　　　　　　 GREENE, merchant, of Charleston, in the sum of
Bond　　　　　　　　　　　　 Ł 1200 conditioned for the payment of 936 lbs.
　　　　　　　　　　　　　　of heavy dressed merchantable deer skins on
the Bay on 1 Dec. next, or their value in currency with legal interest on
13 June 1728; also Ł 176 currency paid by DANIEL GREEN for SARAH BEAMOR
to JOHN CARMICHAEL (for her debt). Witnesses: MATHEW NEWBOROUGH, THOMAS
ELLERY. Before ALEXANDER PARRIS, J.P. JACOB MOTTE, Register.

Book La, p. 202
13 & 14 June 1727
L & R by Mortgage

SARAH BEAMOR, widow of Berkeley Co., to DANIEL GREENE, gentleman, of Charleston, as security on the above bond (p. 200), 190 a. on Charleston Neck (see p. 193) free of all claim except 1 conveyance by SARAH BEAMOR to WILLIAM BELLINGER for the purposes mentioned in an instrument purporting to be a defeasance by WILLIAM BELLINGER to SARAH BEAMOR; also except another deed 10 June 1727 to THOMAS ELLERY. Witnesses: MATHEW NEWBOROUGH, THOMAS ELLERY. Before ALEXANDER PARRIS, J.P. JACOB MCTTE, Register.

Book La, p. 209
22 May 1728

This mortgage paid & discharged by COL. JOHN FENWICKE & JOSEPH WRAGG. Signed DANIEL GREEN. Witness JACOB MOTTE, Register.

Book La, p. 210
13 June 1727
Mortgage

THOMAS PADGETT, planter, & ANNE his wife, of Berkeley Co., to ALEXANDER NISBETT, merchant, of Charleston, for Ł 1652 SC money, 470 a. (300 & 170) in Berkeley Co., bounding according to plat & grant dated 23 July 1711 by the Hon. ROBERT GIBBES & another plat & grant by the Hon. Sir NATHANIEL JOHNSON dated 18 Sept. 1703 to PATRICK SCOTT & SCOTT'S bill of sale to PADGETT; conditioned for the payment of said sum on 1 Jan. 1727/8. Witnesses: JAMES (his mark) MALLETT, MARY (her mark) MALLETT, HUGH CAMPBELL. Before ALEXANDER PARRIS, J.P. JACOB MOTTE, Register. Mortgage satisfied 2 May 1732. Signed: ALEXANDER NISBETT. Witness: JACOB MOTTE, Register.

Book La, p. 214
3 & 4 Feb. 1725
L & R by Mortgage

BENJAMIN SCHENCKINGH, ESQ., & MARGARET his wife, of Berkeley Co., to RICHARD MILES, merchant, of the Island of Maderas, as security on 2 bonds of 3 Feb. 1725 in penal sum of Ł 3000 SC money each, conditioned for the payment of Ł 1500 like money each to MILES at the dwelling house of BENJAMIN DELA CONSEILLERE, ESQ. in Charleston 1 on 3 Feb. 1726, the other on 3 Feb. 1727; 2 tracts of 200 a. & 500 a., making 1 tract of 700 a., in Goosecreek; the 200 a. bounding N on Red Bank; E on Cooper River; S on BENJAMIN SCHENCKINGH; W on the 500 a.; the 500 a. bounding SW on Goosecreek; SE on Cooper River; NE on the 200 a. & BENJAMIN SCHENCKINGH; NW on ROBERT HOWE. MARGARET, wife of BENJAMIN SCHENCKINGH, to relinquish her dower when requested. Witnesses to BENJAMIN'S signature: BENJAMIN DELA CONSEILLERE, RICHARD ALLEIN, WILLIAM BILLING. Witnesses to MARGARET'S signature: RICHARD ALLEIN, JOHN BASSETT. Before DANIEL GREENE, J.P. JACOB MOTTE, Register. Mortgage satisfied 18 July 1731; signed BENJAMIN DELA CONSEILLERE, attorney to the executor of RICHARD MILES. Witness: JACOB MOTTE, Register.

Book La, p. 227
22 & 23 June 1727
L & R

ELIZABETH QUELCH, widow, to ROBERT FLADGER, planter, both of Berkeley Co., for Ł 300 SC money, & for a bond from FLADGER, this date, in penal sum of Ł 1600 SC money conditioned for the payment of Ł 400 on 13 Sept. next & Ł 400 on 1 Mar. next; a cypress swamp of 300 a. English measure on Wapetau, a branch at head of Wando River, bounding S on creek & marsh & WILLIAM RUBERY; & on all other sides on lands not laid out according to plat dated 10 Sept. 1705. Witnesses: JOHN WALLIS, JOHN RAPER, WILLIAM SMITH. Before JOHN BARKSDALE, J.P. JACOB MOTTE, Register.

Book La, p. 234
27 Feb. 1726/7
L & R

SAMUEL JONES & DOROTHY (her mark) his wife, of St. Andrews Parish, Berkeley Co., to WILLIAM BULL & WILLIAM CATTELL, of same Parish, for Ł 600 SC money, 50 a. & 7 a. making 57 a., in Berkeley Co., to be added to the Parish Glebe. Whereas the Rt. Hon. Sir NATHANIEL JOHNSON, Gov. & the Lords Proprs. on 14 Apr. 1709 granted SAMUEL JONES 50 a. in Berkeley Co., on SE side of Cuppein Creek & on 14 May 1707 granted ISAAC STUART 20 a. on SE side Cuppein Creek, bounding SW on the 50 a.; SE on WILLIAM FULLER, SR.; & NW on marsh & the creek; & whereas 7 a. (part of the 20 a.) now belong to SAMUEL JONES; now JONES & his wife sell 57 a.; bounding NW on marsh & creek; NE on broad road leading by St. Andrews Church; SE on WILLIAM FULLER, SR.; SW on the parsonage or Glebe. Witnesses: WILLIAM GUY, BURRELL MASSINGBERD HYRNE, MARY BULL, STEPHEN BULL. HYRNE on behalf of JONES took peaceable possession & seizin & delivered to BULL & CATTELL. Witnesses: WILLIAM GUY, WILLIAM MILES,

STEPHEN BULL, MARY BULL.   Before CHARLES HILL, J.P.   JACOB MOTTE, Register.

Book La, p. 238   SAMUEL BLYTH, planter, of Craven Co., to JOHN
4 & 5 July 1727   HUGGINS, planter, of Berkeley Co., for L 520
L & R   SC money 2 tracts, 1 of 500 a. in Craven Co.,
                          bounding S & W on Santee River; E on JOHN SAN-
SON; also, an island of 400 a. in Santee River as described in a plat annexed to the grant from the Lords Proprs. to JOHN BELL. Witnesses: JOHN WALLIS, CATHERINE RAPER, LAWRENCE COULLIETTE. Before JOHN WALLIS, J.P. JACOB MOTTE, Register.

Book La, p. 244   RICHARD (his mark) FLOYD, cordwainer, & JEMIMA
18 & 19 July 1727   (her mark) his wife, of Colleton Co., to AN-
                          THONY MATHEWS, SR., merchant, of Charleston,
for L 600 SC money, 300 a. on Johns Island, bounding S on JOHN PRESCOTT & WILLIAM WILKINS; W on MICHAEL RENOLDS; N on RICHARD FLOYD; E on AMBROSE HILL; SE on WILLIAM ARNOLD. Witnesses: SAMUEL MORRIS, CHILDERMAS CROFT, ABRAHAM CROFT. Before RICHARD ALLEIN, C.J. JACOB MOTTE, Register.

Book La, p. 250   Landgrave ROBERT DANIELL, & HELEN his wife
1 & 2 Sept. 1726   (daughter of COL. GEORGE LOGAN) of Berkeley
L & R   Co., to ROBERT HUME, gentleman, of Charleston,
                          for L 1500 SC money, 84 a. on Charleston Neck,
bounding N on JONATHAN COLLINS (formerly JOHN WATKINS); E on the Broad Path leading to Charleston; S on CARTWRIGHT'S land; W on Ashley River marsh & CARTWRIGHT; which 84 a. were given to HELEN by her father's will. Witnesses: THOMAS HEPWORTH, JAMES ROWS. Before JOSEPH WRAGG, J.P. JACOB MOTTE, Register.

Book La, p. 258   JOHN GIBBES, gentleman, (son & heir of JOHN
4 & 5 Apr. 1720   GIBBES, ESQ. formerly of the Island of Barba-
L & R   dos, late of SC) & ANNE his wife, to PETER BA-
                          COT, planter, of Charleston, for L 130 SC money, 132 a. at head of Goose Creek, part of 1800 a. formerly belonging to JOHN BERRINGER, bounding NW on MR. DELA PLAIN; NE & SE on JOHN GIBBES; S on FRANCIS GUERIN. Witnesses: THOMAS CORDES, JOHN NUTKINS, BENJAMIN MARION. Before ARTHUR MIDDLETON, J.P. JACOB MOTTE, Register.

Book La, p. 265   PETER BACOT, planter, & MARY his wife, to the
6 & 7 July 1727   Hon. ARTHUR MIDDLETON, ESQ., for L 500 curren-
L & R   cy, 103 a. part of 132 a. purchased from JOHN
                          GIBBES, (see p. 258). Witnesses: CHARLES HART, ALEXANDER PARRIS, HENRY HARGRAVE, JOHN (his mark) DINGLEE, MARY DINGLEE. Before DANIEL GREENE, J.P. JACOB MOTTE, Register.

Book La, p. 273   GILSON CLAPP, merchant, & MARGARET his wife,
1 & 2 Sept. 1726   of Berkeley Co., to ROBERT HUME, gentleman, of
L & R   Charleston, for L 3500 SC money, 4 tracts of
                          112 a., 13 a., 39-1/2 a. & 10a., making 1 plantation of 174-1/2 a. on Charleston Neck, bounding N on COL. ROBERT JOHNSON; S on CHARLES HART; W on the highway leading from Charleston; E on Cooper River marsh. MARGARET to renounce her dower within 3 months. Whereas the Lords Proprs. under Sir NATHANIEL JOHNSON, Knight, Gob., etc., by grant reciting that they had previously granted JOSEPH PENDARVIS 137 a. & that 112 a. (part of the 137) were then invested in ELIZABETH SINDRY, widow (ELIZABETH CLAPP), together with 13 a. (part of a larger tract granted by HENRY SIMMONS & after several conveyances became vested in ELIZABETH SINDRY; the plat of the 13 a. annexed to plat of 112 a.); & whereas the said ELIZABETH CLAPP purchased from RICHARD CARTWRIGHT 39-1/2 a. adjoining her tract as by a plat attached to the deed of feoffment dated 24 Apr. 1705; & whereas ELIZABETH SINDRY bequeathed the several tracts to her son GILSON CLAPP; & whereas GILSON CLAPP on 14 June 1720 purchased from EDWARD WEEKLEY 10 a. (formerly COCKFIELD) adjoining his land; now CLAPP sells the land to HUME. Witnesses: THOMAS HEPWORTH, THOMAS BARNES. Before JOSEPH WRAGG, J.P. JACOB MOTTE, Register.

Book La, p. 283   JOHN CASWELL, gentleman, & MARTHA his wife, to
3 Aug. 1727   THOMAS SACHEVERILL, planter, & MARY his wife,
Confirmation of   all of Colleton Co., 2 tracts of 513 A. & 300

Apportionment, (cont)   a., (813 a.). Whereas MATHEW BEE, planter, of Colleton Co., owned several tracts of about 2313 a. & died intestate, leaving a widow, 1 son, JOSEPH; & 3 daughters, MARY, SAWAH, & MARTHA; & whereas JOSEPH the son, died a minor whereby the 3 daughters became co-heirs; & whereas DOROTHY (the widow) married WILLIAM STEVENSON & they had 1 daughter ANNIBALL; & whereas, at DOROTHY'S request, the 3 daughters agreed that 1 tract of 300 should be given to ANNIBAL, which deed was executed by the 3 daughters & by THOMAS SACHEVERILL (the husband of MARY the eldest) & by JOHN COSWELL (husband of SARAH, the second); & whereas at the request of the 3 daughters & with the consent of their husbands, (including JOHN ARNOLD who married MARTHA the youngest) the remaining 2013 a. were satisfactorily divided & apportioned by CAPT. JOHN JACKSON, DANIEL HENDRICKS & JOHN SMILIE; so that THOMAS & MARY SACHEVERILL received 513 a. on SE side Colleton River, bounding W on other land of MATHEW BEE & lands not laid out; N on MOSES PINGREE; E & S on lands not laid out when the grant was made by the Lords Proprs. on 23 July 1711; also 300 a. of back land bounding SE on other lands of MATHEW BEE; SW on JAMES BASFORD; NW & NE on land not laid out when another grant was made dated 23 July 1711; now for 10 shillings paid to JOHN & SARAH CASWELL & to JOHN & MARTHA ARNOLD, they confirm THOMAS & MARY SACHEVERILL in their portion. Witnesses: SAMUEL SMITH, JOHN CROFT. Before JOHN BARKSDALE, J.P. JACOB MOTTE, Register.

Book La, p. 288   THOMAS CROSKEYS, planter, & ELIZABETH (her
7 & 8 Aug. 1727   mark) his wife, of James Island, to JOHN MCKAY,
L & R   merchant, of Charleston, for L 130 currency,
                  105 a. commonly called John Ellis Island,
about 200 yards S of James Island; free from ELIZABETH'S dower. Forasmuch as the title deeds to the island cannot be readily produced, CROSKEYS promises to produce them within 10 days. Witnesses: WILLIAM BILLING, JOSEPH RIVERS. Before JOHN BARKSDALE, J.P. JACOB MOTTE, Register.

Book La, p. 293   JOHN (his mark) KITCHIN, planter, to JOHN HILL,
5 Apr. 1726   joiner, & MARY his wife, all of Berkeley Co.,
Deed of Sale   for L 40 SC money, lots #102 & 103 in Dor-
                  chester, bounding NE-NW by "THOMAS WAIES or
STREETS"; SE by WILLIAM WAY, SR.; SW on JOHN STEVENS. Witnesses: ANN BRUNSON, JANE PELLET, ELIZABETH (her mark) KINDALL. Before THOMAS WARING, J.P. JACOB MOTTE, Register.

Book La, p. 296   THOMAS (his mark) ELLIS, planter, of James Is-
15 Oct. 1717   land, to his children ELIZABETH & MARY, for
Deed of Gift   love & affection, the land & houses formerly
                  belonging to their grandfather, ZACHARIAH
EAVES, with an inventory of even date signed by THOMAS ELLIS. Witnesses: JOHN WITTER, WILLIAM CHAPMAN. Before CHARLES HILL, J.P. JACOB MOTTE, Register.

Book La, p. 297   EDWARD THOMAS, of St. John's Parish, Berkeley
21 June 1727   Co., to JAMES OULDFIELD, of St. James Goose-
Mortgage   creek, for L 1200 currency, 2 tracts of 372 a.
                  & 500 a., formerly owned by JOHN MOORE. Whereas JOHN OULDFIELD at THOMAS'S request on 14 Mar. 1725 joined THOMAS in giving a bond to the Hon. ARTHUR MIDDLETON in penal sum of L 2400 conditioned for payment of L 1200 currency, THOMAS gives OULDFIELD a mortgage on 872 a. Witnesses: WILLIAM WATIES, THOMAS COOPER. Before HUGH BUTLER, J.P. JACOB MOTTE, Register. Mortgage satisfied with interest by THOMAS (by the hand of THOMAS ELLERY). Witness: JACOB MOTTE, Register.

Book La, p. 301   ROBERT GILCREST, merchant, of Charleston &
19 Apr. 1725   MATHEW SMALLWOOD, planter, of St. Andrews Par-
Agreement   ish, make an agreement concerning the land
                  they purchased jointly from JOSEPH BLAKE.
Whereas GILCREST & SMALLWOOD purchased from JOSEPH BLAKE, planter, 640 a. in Colleton Co. whose boundings are 1 island & part of another island on W side Wad-wadmelah River; N on Broken Islands; S on marsh; E on DANIEL CARTICE'S land; each paying L 400 (L 800 total) SC money (see L & R, 17 & 18 Apr. 1725), each paying an equal right in the land, now GILCREST & SMALLWOOD, for peaceable considerations, agree that GILCREST hold the papers in safe-keeping but that SMALLWOOD may have then on demand when

necessary, etc. Witnesses: WILLIAM WINDERAS, ROGER (his mark) NEWINGTON, THOMAS GOBLE (GEBLE). Before DANIEL GREENE, J.P. JACOB MOTTE, Register.

Book La, p. 304　　　　VINCENT GUERIN, planter, of Berkeley Co., to
25 Jan. 1726　　　　　his son ISAAC GUERIN, for ₤ 6000 SC money, 500
Deed of Sale　　　　　a. on which VINCENT lives, bounding E on MICH-
　　　　　　　　　　　AEL DARBY; W on MADAM MCMORTRY; N on ANTHONY
BORDEAUX; also 625 a. in Berkeley Co., commonly called Bullhead, bounding S on ANTHONY BORDEAUX; E on JOSEPH SINGLETARY; also all horses, cattle, hogs, household goods, etc., etc. Witnesses: ISAAC FAIRAND, ROBERT HOW. Possession & seizin by delivery of 1 mare. Before GEORGE LOGAN, J.P. JACOB MOTTE, Register.

Book La, p. 306　　　　THOMAS SACHEVERILL, planter, & MARY his wife;
3 Aug. 1727　　　　　& JOHN ARNOLL, gentleman, & MARTHA his wife,
Confirmation of　　　of Charleston, to JOHN CASWELL, planter, &
Apportionment　　　　SARAH his wife, of Colleton Co., 2 tracts of
　　　　　　　　　　　200 a. & 300 a. (500 a. total); the 200 a.
tract bounding W on Bee's Creek; N on JONATHAN HAYNE & land not laid out; S on JAMES ROGERS; E on land not laid out; as specified in plat attached to grant dated 5 Nov. 1701: the 300 a. tract bounding N & W on Bee's Creek; S on MATHEW BEE; E on land not laid out; as by plat & grant dated 23 July 1711. (See p. 283 for division of MATHEW BEE'S estate). Witnesses: CHRISTOPHER SMITH, SAMUEL SMITH, JOHN CROFT. Before JOHN BARKSDALE, J.P. JACOB MOTTE, Register.

Book La, p. 311　　　　PETER JOHNSON, JR., planter, & DEBORAH his
14 Oct. 1727　　　　　wife, of Berkeley Co., to ALEXANDER NISBETT,
Mortgage　　　　　　　merchant, of Charleston, for ₤ 771:7 SC money,
　　　　　　　　　　　400 a. in Berkeley Co., as granted 11 Jan.
1700 to RICHARD GRIFFIN & sold by GRIFFIN on 9 Feb. 1725; conditioned for the re-payment of the above sum by 1 Oct. 1730. Witnesses: WALTER NISBETT, JAMES MENZIES, HUGH CAMPBELL. Before ALEXANDER PARRIS, J.P. JACOB MOTTE, Register. Mortgage declared satisfied 9 Sept. 1731 by HUGH CAMPBELL, attorney for estate of ALEXANDER NISBETT. Witness: JACOB MOTTE, Register.

Book La, p. 316　　　　HENRY SIMONS, & JUDITH his wife, of Berkeley
5 Oct. 1727　　　　　Co., to ALEXANDER NISBETT, merchant, of
Mortgage　　　　　　　Charleston, for ₤ 889:15 SC money, 500 a. call-
　　　　　　　　　　　ed Wapta, in Berkeley Co., conditioned for the
re-payment of the above sum, with interest, by 1 Jan. 1728/9. Witnesses: JOHN WILLIAMS, WILLIAM SIMONS, HUGH CAMPBELL. Before ALEXANDER PARRIS, J.P. JACOB MOTTE, Register.

Book La, p. 321　　　　THOMAS SACHEVERILL, planter, & MARY his wife;
3 Aug. 1727　　　　　JOHN CASWELL, planter, & SARAH his wife, all
Confirmation of　　　of Colleton Co., to JOHN ARNOLD, gentleman, &
Apportionment　　　　MARTHA his wife, of Charleston, 3 tracts of
　　　　　　　　　　　400 a. & 200 a. & 100 A. (700 total); the 400
a. bounding W on JOHN PECUM & on all other sides on land not laid out, according to plat attached to grant dated 6 May 1704; the 200 a. on NE side S Colleton River, bounding W on EBENEZER WALCOAT; S on MATHEW BEE; N & E on land not laid out; according to plat attached to grant dated 20 July 1711; the 100 a. on E side PonPon River bounding S on MATHEW BEE & all other sides on land not laid out, according to plat attached to grant dated 23 July 1711. (See p. 283 for details of MATHEW BEE'S estate). Witnesses: CHRISTOPHER SMITH, SAMUEL SMITH, JOHN CROFT. Before JOHN BARKSDALE, J.P. JACOB MOTTE, Register.

Book La, p. 326　　　　JOHN ARNOLL (ARNOLD), innholder, & MARTHA his
5 & 6 Dec. 1727　　　wife (late MARTHA BEE, 1 of the 3 sisters &
L & R　　　　　　　　co-heirs with JOSEPH BEE, only son of MATHEW
　　　　　　　　　　　BEE, planter of Colleton Co., see p. 283), to
JAMES BULLOCK, merchant, of Charleston, for ₤ 1000 SC money the 700 a. in Colleton Co., allotted to JOHN & MARTHA ARNOLD as their portion of MATHEW BEE'S estate. See p. 283 & 321. Witnesses: DANIEL GREENE, ROBERT HUME, JAMES PAINE. Before DANIEL GREENE, J.P. JACOB MOTTE, Register.

Book La, p. 336　　　　WILLIAM FULLER, & ELIZABETH his wife, to JOHN

2 Oct. 1707   JACKSON, all of Berkeley Co., for ₤ 80 silver
Deed of Sale   currency secured by bill, "1 tract of 650 a.
                        Enclish measure, in 2 plats, at the "Horlowing
Place". Witnesses: NATHANIEL NICHOLS, SAMUEL NICHOLS, EDWARD (his mark)
CLEIFT. Before JOHN BARNWELL, J.P. JACOB MOTTE, Register.

Book La, p. 338   FRANCIS GODDARD, planter, of Berkeley Co., of
17 & 18 Nov. 1727   the 1st. part; THOMAS HASELL, rector of Parish
L & R, Tripartite   of St. Thomas, JAMES MYRANT, THOMAS PAGET,
                        JOHN MOORE, JAMES AKIN, JAMES MAXWELL, THOMAS
ASHBY, & SAMUEL SIMMONS, vestrymen of St. Thomas, of 2nd part; THOMAS
BROUGHTON, ESQ., executor of will of RICHARD BERESFORD, planter, of 3rd
part. Whereas RICHARD BERESFORD (after other legacies) bequeathed the
rest of the yearly profits & produce of his real & personal estate (until
his son JOHN should come of age) to his executors upon special trust for
several uses; that is, THOMAS BROUGHTON to pay the profits yearly to the
vestry of St. Thomas to use 1/3 to the schoolmaster, 2/3 towards the education of the children of the poor, etc., or put the money out at interest. There having been no schoolmaster since BERESFORD'S death, BROUGH-
TON & the vestry decide to purchase land for a free school. Whereas the
Lords Proprs. on 13 July 1696 granted MATHEW TULLADA 320 a. in Berkeley
Co., which TULLADA on 16 Jan. 1713 conveyed to FRANCIS GODDARD; & whereas
the Lords Proprs. on 15 Sept. 1705 granted TULLADA another tract of 300 a.
which TULLADA on 6 Aug. 1714 conveyed to ANN DANIELL (daughter of ROBERT
DANIELLO with the condition that ROBERT DANIELL should have power to dispose of the land for ANN'S benefit; & whereas ROBERT DANIELL sold the 300
a. for ₤ 300 to FRANCIS GODDARD, but DANIELL died before he could execute
a conveyance & MARTHA DANIELL, mother of ANN, & widow & executrix & devisee of ROBERT DANIELL, by deed of feoffment dated 16 June 1718 confirmed to GODDARD the 300 a.; now GODDARD, for ₤ 1200 SC money, conveys to
the Rector & Vestry of St. Thomas Parish, the 2 tracts of 320 a. & 300 a.
as described in the 2 plats, except 20 a., part of the 300 a., adjoining
Sweatman's Bridge. Witnesses: RICHARD HARRIS, JOHN LAPIERRE, HUGH CAMP-
BELL, MATTHEW QUASH, JACOB WOOLFORD, ROBERT HOW. Before DANIEL GREENE,
J.P. JACOB MOTTE, Register.

Book La, p. 350   WILLIAM AXSON & SAMUEL AXSON, shoemakers, to
26 Dec. 1724   SAMUEL PICKERING, merchant, all of Charleston,
Deed of Feoffment   for ₤ 80 SC money, half of lot #143, bounding
                        N on DANIEL TOWNSEND; S on WILLIAM AXSON; W on
a little street; E on COL. WILLIAM BULL. Witnesses: JOEL POINSETT, WIL-
LIAM YEOMANS, ROBERT HUME. Before CHARLES HILL, J.P. JACOB MOTTE, Register.

Book La, p. 353   WILLIAM & SAMUEL AXSON, shoemakers, to SAMUEL
26 Dec. 1724   PICKERING, merchant, all of Charleston, bond
Bond   for ₤ 500 SC money, to secure PICKERING'S
                        title to half lot #143 (see p. 350). Witness-
es: JOEL POINSETT, WILLIAM YEOMANS, ROBERT HUME. Before CHARLES HILL,
J.P. JACOB MOTTE, Register.

Book La, p. 355   ALEXAND TRENCH, merchant, of Charleston, as
1 & 2 Sept. 1727   attorney for JOHN BAYLY, of Ballinaclough,
L & R   Ireland (see p. 11 for details) to THOMAS
                        FARR, JR., planter, of Colleton Co., for ₤ 95
SC money, 382 a. in Colleton Co., bounding S & E on WILLIAMSON'S tract
called Spoones; W on MANLY WILLIAMSON; N on Cawcaw Swamp, a great swamp
adjoining Spoone Savanna. Witnesses: WILLIAM TUNLY, M.C.; JOHN LEWIS.
Before CHARLES HILL, J.P. JACOB MOTTE, Register.

Book La, p. 361   CHARLES PINCKNEY, gentleman, late of Charles-
2 Jan. 1727   ton now of London, to the Hon. JOHN FENWICKE,
Confirmation of Title   ESQ. of Charleston. Whereas by L & R Tripar-
                        tite dated 2 & 3 Sept. 1726 made by MARY BET-
SON, widow, on behalf of CHARLES PINCKNEY, her son, of 1st. part; JOHN
FENWICKE of 2nd. part; THOMAS PINCKNEY & WILLIAM PINCKNEY, gentlemen, of
the 3rd. part; MARY BETSON for ₤ 2560 SC money, sold JOHN FENWICKE part
of lot #3 fronting E 32 ft. on the Bay; S on THOMAS LLOYD; N on CHARLES
PINCKNEY; W on MR. CHAPMAN; the full breadth of 32 ft. to run from the E
part on the Bay to the W end that runs into the marsh & adjoins CHAPMAN'S

lot; depth 276 ft.; also 32 ft. of the shole or lot #327 lying before lot #3 the whole breadth of the 32 ft. of shole #327 to continue & run from N side LLOYD'S lot #327 from Bay down to low water mark; now for the better strengthening of FENWICKE'S title to lot #3 (32 ft. by 276 ft.) & to the part of lot #327 (32 ft. down to low water), & also for ₤ 2560 paid or secured to be paid, CHARLES PINCKNEY confirms the 2 parts of the 2 lots to FENWICKE. Forasmuch as the other parts of the 2 lots are still in the possession of CHARLES PINCKNEY, undisposed of, PINCKNEY retains the original grants but will produce them when desired. Witnesses: ROBERT HUME, JOHN CROFT. Before BENJAMIN WHITAKER, J.P. JACOB MOTTE, Register.

Book La, p. 366
17 June 1727
Mortgage

JOHN (his mark) BELL, SR., planter, of Craven Co., to WILLIAM SWINTON, merchant, of Prince George Parish, Craven Co., for ₤ 400 SC money 1000 a. at head of Sampit Creek, bounding according to plat (except the crops), also 38 head of neat cattle, conditioned for the repayment of ₤ 400 SC with interest, according to bond of this date, on 1 Mar. 1727/8. Witnesses: PRISCILLA BELL, FRANCIS BRITTEN. Delivery by turf & twig & 1 cow. Before EDWARD HYRNE, J.P. JACOB MOTTE, Register.

Book La, p. 370
5 May 1726
British Style
Letter of Attorney

ARTHUR FORSTER & JOHN FORSTER, gentlemen, of Drumboon, Fermanagh Co., Ireland, brothers of ANDREW FORSTER, merchant, of Charleston, SC (all sons of ANDREW FORSTER, gentleman of Drumgoone) appointed ALEXANDER TRENCH, merchant, of Charleston, their attorney. Before MICHAEL COLE, N.P., Provost of Inniskiller, Fermanagh. Witnesses: JAMES JOHNSON, ESQ., of Little Mount, MICHAEL COLE. JACOB MOTTE, Register.

Book La, p. 372
3 & 4 Oct. 1727
L & R

ROGER MOORE, ESQ., & CATHERINE his wife, of Berkeley Co., to ROBERT HUME, gentleman, of Charleston, for ₤ 4000 SC money, 800 a., where MOORE now lives, in St. James Goosecreek, Berkeley Co., bounding SW on ANDREW ALLEN'S land called Thorogoods; E on DAVID WEBSTER; N on COL. GEORGE CHICKEN; SE on ROGER MOORE (formerly COL. JAMES MOORE); which 800 a. was granted on 2 July 1683 to JAMES WILLIAMS, surgeon, & after several conveyances came to ROGER MOORE; also 90 a. in St. James Goosecreek, purchased from COL. JAMES MOORE, part of the plantation where JAMES lived, bounding SW on JOHN LLOYD (formerly ROBERT STEVENS); N on the 800 a.; E on COL. JAMES MOORE. CATHERINE MOORE to make absolute renunciation of her dower within 3 months. Witnesses: JON. CHESTER, RICHARD (his mark) WALKER, JOSEPH WRAGG, RICHARD LAMBTON. Before JOSEPH WRAGG, J.P. JACOB MOTTE, Register.

Book La, p. 381
17 & 18 Jan. 1727
L & R

ROGER MOORE, ESQ., & CATHERINE his wife, of Berkeley Co., to JOSEPH WRAGG, merchant, of Charleston for ₤ 400 SC money, 1346 a. in St. James Goosecreek & St. John's Parishes. Witnesses: RICHARD LAMBTON, ROBERT HUME, BENJAMIN WHITAKER, J.P. JACOB MOTTE, Register.

Book La, p. 389
9 Jan. 1727
Deed of Sale

JOSEPH LEA, shipwright, of Berkeley Co., to EDWARD EDWARDS planter, & MARY his wife, of Berkeley Co. for ₤ 400 SC money, surrenders his claim & possession of his deceased wife's property which he was holding as tenant for the term of his natural life by the courtesy of England. JOSEPH LEA married CATHERINE SYER who, besides owning other real estate, was the owner of half a tract of 365 a. in St. Thomas Parish, Berkeley Co., on NE side Cooper River; bounding SE on Ittewan Creek; SW on NATHANIEL WILLIAMS; NW on a branch of Clowters Creek; & RICHARD HARRIS; NE on RICHARD HARRIS. She also owned her allotment out of the dwelling house & all other buildings. They had 2 children, JOSEPH & ROBERT SYER. CATHERINE died & the children died soon afterwards, whereby her property of right belonged to her only sister MARY SYER, sole heir. MARY had married EDWARD EDWARDS. But because of the birth of the children JOSEPH LEA was entitled to hold the land during his lifetime. Now he sells his interest to EDWARD & MARY EDWARDS. Witnesses: MARK OLIVER, JOHN WARMINGHAM, WILLIAM SMITH. Before DANIEL GREENE, J.P. JACOB MOTTE, Register.

Book La, p. 394   JOSEPH LEA, shipwright, to EDWARD EDWARDS,
10 Jan. 1727   planter, & MARY his wife, all of Berkeley Co.,
Deed of Sale   for L 300 SC money, surrenders his claim to &
                            possession of his deceased wife's property
which he was holding as tenant for the term of his natural life by the
courtesy of England. JOSEPH LEA married CATHERINE SYER who, besides owning other real estate, owned part of a lot in Charleston formerly belonging to CHRISTOPHER GERARD, bounding N 40 ft. on the street leading to the
Bay; W 103 ft. on the street running by WILLIAM CHAPMAN; S on RICHARD
CAPERS; E on CHARLES BASDEN. JOSEPH & CATHERINE LEA had 2 children, JO-
SEPH & ROBERT SYER. CATHERINE died & the children died soon after, whereby her property of right belonged to her only sister & heir, MARY SYER,
who had married EDWARD EDWARDS. But because of the birth of the children
JOSEPH LEA was entitled to hold the lot during his lifetime. Now he
sells his interest to EDWARD & MARY EDWARDS. Witnesses: MARK OLIVER,
JOHN WARMINGHAM, WILLIAM SMITH. Before DANIEL GREENE, J.P. JACOB MOTTE,
Register.

Book La, p. 398   EDWARD EDWARDS, planter, & MARY his wife, to
12 & 13 Jan. 1727   JOSEPH LEA, shipwright, all of Berkeley Co.,
L & R   for L 1300 SC money, part of a lot in Charles-
                            ton bounding N 40 ft. on the street leading to
the Bay; W 103 ft. on the street running by WILLIAM CHAPMAN; S on RICHARD
CAPERS; E on CHARLES BASDEN. Witnesses: MARK OLIVER, JOHN WARMINGHAM,
WILLIAM SMITH. Before DANIEL GREENE, J.P. JACOB MOTTE, Register.

Book La, p. 407   JOHN BAYLY, of Ballinaclough, Ireland, by his
1 & 2 May 1727   attorney, ALEXANDER TRENCH, merchant, of
L & R   Charleston (see p. 11 for details) to WILLIAM
                            WILLIAMSON, planter, of Colleton Co., for
L 62:10 currency, 250 a. in Colleton Co., bounding SW on WILLIAM WILLIAM-
SON; W on JOSEPH PEEKHAM; NE on WILLIAM WILLIAMSON; NW on BRYAN RELY.
Witnesses: HENRY GIGNILLIATT, JOHN CROFT. Before DANIEL GREENE, J.P.
JACOB MOTTE, Register.

Book La, p. 413   EPHRAIM MIKELL, JR., planter, & MARY (her
18 Nov. 1727   mark) his wife, to THOMAS GRIMBALL, planter,
L & R   all of Colleton Co., for L 480 currency, 200 a.
                            on Edisto Island, (part attached to grant).
Witnesses: ALEXANDER WALKER, PAUL GRIMBALL, CHARLES (his mark) ELLIOTT.
Before DANIEL GREENE, J.P. JACOB MOTTE, Register.

Book La, p. 418   JOHN BAYLY, of Ballinaclough, Ireland, by his
15 & 16 Feb. 1727   attorney ALEXANDER TRENCH, merchant, of
                            Charleston (see p. 11 for details), to JOHN
LLOYD, ESQ., of Berkeley Co., for L 40 SC money, 162 a. in Berkeley Co.,
bounding N on ANDREW ALLEN; E on ROGER MOORE; S on RALPH IZARD & JOHN
LLOYD; W on ROUND SAVANNA. Witnesses: JAMES BALLINTINE, JOHN MILLNER.
Before ALEXANDER PARRIS, J.P. JACOB MOTTE, Register.

Book La, p. 425   HEZEKIAH RUSS, planter of Berkeley Co., to
17 Apr. 1727   ALEXANDER NISBETT, merchant, of Charleston,
Mortgage   for L 240:18:6:3 SC money, 200 a. (according
                            to plat & grant to JOHN CARRIER dated 29 Mar.
1715, & bill of sale to JOHN JEFFERS dated 10 Apr. 1714; & deed to WIL-
LIAM BROCKINGTON dated 19 Dec. 1717, & bill of sale to HEZEKIAH RUSS dated 23 May 1727), conditioned for the repayment of the above sum to NIS-
BETT on 1 Jan. 1, 1727/8. Witnesses: WALTER NISBETT, JOHN BECKITT, HUGH
CAMPBELL. Before ALEXANDER PARRIS, J.P. JACOB MOTTE, Register. Mortgage satisfied 9 Apr. 1729.

Book La, p. 429   JOHN SULLIVAN, cordwinder, of Berkeley Co., to
8 & 9 May 1727   THOMAS DIXSON, bricklayer, of Charleston, for
L & R   L 700 SC money, 100 a. (part of 2 tracts) on
                            NE side Ashley River, bounding S on MRS. WIL-
LIAM ELLIOT; N on JOHN COCKFIELD; E on other part of the 2 tracts accord-
ing to 2 plats dated 22 Jan. 1672/3. MARGARET (her mark) MELLS, (MELL)
party hereto, for 10 shillings renounces all her title. Witnesses: JOHN
LUPTON, JOHN MELL, WILLIAM STOCKS. Before DANIEL GREENE, J.P. JACOB
MOTTE, Register.

Book La, p. 437　　　　　MANLY WILLIAMSON, planter, of Berkeley Co., to
31 Mar. 1727　　　　　　ISAAC MAZYCK, merchant, of Charleston, as se-
Mortgage　　　　　　　　curity on bond of this date in penal sum of
　　　　　　　　　　　　Ł 1092:10 SC money, conditioned for the pay-
ment of Ł 546:5 on 1 Feb. 1727, 500 a. on N side Ashley River called
Stono Point, bounding N on CHRISTOPHER SMITH; E on JOHN MELL; W on
CHARLES FIELD; also 6 Negro slaves. Witnesses: ISAAC MAZYCK, JR., JOHN
CROFT. Before DANIEL HUGER, J.P. JACOB MOTTE, Register.

Book La, p. 442　　　　　MANLEY WILLIAMSON, planter, to ROGER SAUNDERS,
2 Mar. 1727/8　　　　　　planter, both of Berkeley Co., for Ł 700 cur-
Mortgage　　　　　　　　rency, 640 (?) a. in St. Paul's Parish, con-
　　　　　　　　　　　　ditioned for the repayment of the Ł 700 to
SAUNDERS on 1 Mar. next. Witnesses: JOEL POINSETT, RICHARD MILLER. Before DANIEL GREENE, J.P. JACOB MOTTE, Register.

Book La, p. 444　　　　　JOHN BEAMOR, planter, to JONATHAN NORTON,
31 May 1726　　　　　　　planter, both of Granville Co., for Ł 50 cur-
Deed of Sale　　　　　　rency, lot #12 in Beaufort. Witnesses: JAMES
　　　　　　　　　　　　DUNLEP, JAMES LOYDELL. Before JOHN DELABERE,
J.P. JACOB MOTTE, Register.

Book La, p. 446　　　　　JONATHAN NORTON, of Granville Co., to ALEXAN-
27 Apr. 1726　　　　　　DER NISBETT, merchant, of Charleston, for Ł 80
Deed of Sale　　　　　　SC money, lot #12 in Beaufort, bounding S on
　　　　　　　　　　　　the Bay; W on lot #11; N on lot #39; E on
CAPT. WILLIAM SCOTT'S lot #13. Witnesses: JAMES LOYDELL, AQUILA ROSE,
ALEXANDER PARRIS, JR. Before JOHN DELEBERE. JACOB MOTTE, Register.

DEEDS BOOK "Lb"
1732-1733

Book Lb, p. 1　　　　　　EBENEZER WAY, to THOMAS OSGOOD & STEPHEN DOWSE,
6 June 1720　　　　　　　representing the Society of Dorchester, for 27
Deed of Sale　　　　　　barrels of merchantable pitch, or the value of
　　　　　　　　　　　　2700 lbs. of merchantable rice, 50 a. in Berke-
ley or Colleton Co., part of the tranct purchased by WAY from THOMAS OS-
GOOD; bounding E on WILLIAM BURNLEY; S on COL. WILLIAM BULL; W on EBENEZ-
ER WAY; N on JOSEPH SUMNER; the 50 a. to be used as a "a ministry lot."
Witnesses: JO. CUMYNG, THOMAS HOWSON, HENRY WAY, SAMUEL SUMNER. Before
RICHARD WARING, J.P. JOSEPH FOX, Dep. Reg.

Book Lb, p. 4　　　　　　THOMAS WARING, planter, of Berkeley Co., as
15 Aug. 1721　　　　　　attorney for the Rev. MR. JOSEPH LORD, Minis-
Deed of Sale　　　　　　ter of the Gospel, late of Dorchester, Berke-
　　　　　　　　　　　　ley Co., now of New England, to THOMAS OSGOOD,
JR., for 75 barrels of merchantable pitch, 100 a. in 2 adjoining lots of
50 a. each in Dorchester, bounding SE on JOHN GORTON; SW on Ashley River;
NW on JOSEPH LORD; NE on a dividing line between the ranges of lots.
Letter of attorney dated 13 Sept. 1720 & registered in SC on 17 May 1721
in Bk. C fol. 11. Of the 2 deeds, 1 was signed by JOHN STEVENS No. 11,
registered 29 Dec. 1701 by THOMAS ROSE fol. 216; the other signed by
ISAAC PORCHER, JR. impowered by Act of Parliament past 12 Dec. 1712, then
belonged to DANIEL CHASTAIGNERS CHILD No. 12, recorded in secretary's Bk.
I fol 514, 17 Apr. 1717. Witnesses: URIAH EDWARDS, JOHN HAWKES, MICHAEL
BACON; BACON & HAWKS according to the form of their profession. Before
ALEXANDER SKENE, J.P. JOSEPH FOX, Dep. Reg.

Book Lb, p. 8　　　　　　THOMAS WARING, planter, of Berkeley Co., as
15 Aug. 1721　　　　　　attorney for the Rev. MR. JOSEPH LORD, Minis-
Deed of Sale　　　　　　ter of the Gospel, formerly of Dorchester,
　　　　　　　　　　　　Berkeley Co., now of New England, to MICHAEL
BACON, NATHANIEL SUMNER, THOMAS OSGOOD, JR., & the Society of Inhabit-
ants of Dorchester under the ministry of the Rev. MR. HUGH FISHER, for
Ł 150 currency, 1 lot of 50 a. in Dorchester, free from claim of dower by
ABIGAIL, the wife of JOSEPH LORD; bounding SE on THOMAS OSGOOD, JR.
(formerly JOSEPH LORD); S on Ashley River; NW on the ministry lot; NE on
a dividing line. The deed to the 50 a. signed by JOHN STEVENS 20 Dec.

1707 (?). Letter of attorney dated 13 Sept. 1720 & registered in SC 17 May 1721 in Bk C. fol. 11. Witnesses: URIAH EDWARDS, JOHN HAWKES, JOHN GORTON; HAWKS & GORTON according to the form of their profession. Before ALEXANDER SKENE, J.P. JOSEPH FOX, Dep. Reg.

Book Lb, p. 13 THOMAS (his mark) OSGOOD, SR., of Berkeley Co.,
12 Oct. 1726 to his son JOSIAH OSGOOD, wheelwright, for
Deed of Gift love & affection, lot #7 the 7th lot, contain-
ing 4-3/4 a., in Dorchester, part of a tract formerly called Mill Land, lately divided into lots by the inhabitants of Dorchester; also a small lot of 1/4 a., #86, on S side Boasoo Creek. Witnesses: THOMAS OSGOOD, JR., WILLIAM FISHBURN, JOHN DOW. Before ROBERT WRIGHT, J.P. JOSEPH FOX, Dep. Reg.

Book Lb, p. 15 THOMAS OSGOOD, SR., wheelwright, of Dorchester,
10 Mar. 1725/6 Berkeley Co., to his son, THOMAS OSGOOD, JR.,
Deed of Gift house carpenter, for love & affection, the 6th
lot in Dorchester, containing 2 a., on S side of Broad Path; also 1 lot #57 in Dorchester containing 1/4 a. Witnesses: WILLIAM WELLS, CHARLES STARNES, GABRIEL PEACOCK. Witnesses to possession & delivery: STEPHEN DOWSE, WILLIAM BRUCE.. Before DANIEL GREENE, J.P. JOSEPH FOX, Dep. Reg.

Book Lb, p. 18 MOSES NORMAN, planter, of Colleton Co., to
7 May 1733 THOMAS SNOW, tanner, of Berkeley Co., for ₤ 53
Deed of Sale currency, 26 a. in Berkeley Co., at the head
of Ashley River, bounding N on the County Road or Broad Path, & all other sides on MOSES NORMAN. Witnesses: THOMAS OSGOOD, URIAH EDWARDS, JONATHAN CLARK. Before THOMAS WARING, J.P. JOSEPH FOX, Dep. Reg.

Book Lb, p. 20 JOSIAH OSGOOD, SAMUEL CLARK, JONATHAN CLARK,
17 May 1733 THOMAS (his mark) SNOW & HANNAH his wife, &
Quit Claim SAMUEL WAY, planters of Berkeley Co., for div-
ers good causes, quit claimed to THOMAS OSGOOD, wheelwright of Dorchester, all their right, by will of THOMAS OSGOOD, SR. in lot #13, the 13th lot in 2nd vidision, containing 45 a. Witnesses: URIAH EDWARDS, BARAK NORMAN, JOHN GORTON, SAMSON LALO. Before THOMAS WARING, J.P. JOSEPH FOX, Dep. Reg.

Book Lb, p. 22 ELIZABETH HAMMERTON, widow of WILLIAM HAMMER-
27 & 28 Mar. 1733 TON, ESQ., to THOMAS COOPER, merchant, & MAR-
L & R GARET MAGDALENE, his wife, all of Charleston,
for ₤ 500 SC money, part of lots 188, 189, & 79 in Charleston, bounding E on THOMAS COOPER (formerly THOMAS ELLERY); W & N on THOMAS ELLERY; S on Dock Street; being 30 ft. from E to W & 200 ft. from N to S. Whereas THOMAS ELLERY, gentleman & ANNA his wife, of Charleston, by L & R, 5 & 6 May 1731, for ₤ 360 currency sold to WILLIAM HAMMERTON the E part of the remainder of the land which ELLERY had purchased from ANDREW ALLEN, 30 ft. by 200 ft., bounding as above, part of lots 188, 189, & 79; & whereas WILLIAM HAMMERTON by will dated 21 Apr. 1732 bequeathed to his wife, ELIZABETH, all his real & personal estate, whether land, money, slaves, debts, or bonds, etc.; now she sells the above land to COOPER. Witnesses: JOHN HAMMERTON, WILLIAM POWELL. Before ALEXANDER PARRIS, J.P. JOSEPH FOX, Dep. Reg.

Book Lb, p. 31 COL. ROBERT DANIELL, SR., gentleman & MARTHA
31 Mar. 1714 his wife, of Berkeley Co., to ARTHUR LAUGHARNS,
Deed of Sale merchant, of Charleston, for ₤ 125 SC money,
part of lot #32 fronting 50 ft. on Cooper River; bounding N on FRANCIS HOLMES & JOHN SIMMONS; W on heirs of JOSEPH CROSKEYS, mariner; S on COL. ROBERT DANIELL. Witnesses: SAMUEL WRAGG, JOSEPH WRAGG, JOB ROTHMAHLER. Before JOSEPH FOX, J.P. JOSEPH FOX, Dep. Reg.

Book Lb, p. 36 (See p. 41) BENJAMIN DENNIS, gentleman, of
1 May 1733 Berkeley Co., to JOSEPH WRAGG, ESQ., of
Lease Charleston, for 10 shillings SC money, 46 a.
on Charleston Neck, bounding N on heirs of HILL (HILDERSON) CROFT (formerly MR. BERESFORD); E on marsh; S on JAMES

CROKATT (formerly JOHN BURD); W on the Broad Path leading to Charleston. Witnesses: THOMAS ELLERY, JOHN LEWIS. Before JOSEPH FOX, J.P. & Dep. Reg.

Book Lb, p. 39
19 May 1733
Mortgage

(See p. 39) JOHN PAGE, planter, to WILLIAM PETERS, both of Colleton Co., a security on bond this date in penal sum of ₤ 2000 conditioned for the payment of ₤ 1100 with interest to commence 1 Jan. 1734, conveys to PETER 432 a. on S side Tooboodoo Creek, bounding E on the creek; W & N on WILLIAM EDDINGS; S on Dedcots Creek; & as security on an additional ₤ 1100 payable 1 Jan. 1735. (₤ 330 (₤ 2200 total) delivered several slaves. Witnesses: ROBERT YONGE, GEORGE NORELAND, WILLIAM BOWER. Before ALEXANDER PARRIS, J.P. JOSEPH FOX, Dep. Reg.

Book Lb, p. 41
2 May 1733
Mortgage

(See p. 36) BENJAMIN DENNIS, gentleman, of Berkeley Co., to JOSEPH WRAGG, ESQ., of Charleston, as security on bond this date in penal sum of ₤ 2860 SC money, conditioned for the payment of ₤ 1430 on 2 May 1734, 46 a. on Charleston Neck, bounding N on heirs of HILL CROFT (formerly MR. BERESFORD); E on marsh; S on JAMES CROKATT (formerly JOHN BURD); W on the Broad Path leading to Charleston. If payment is made in full at the proper time then this mortgage & the bill of sale of even date for 6 Negro slaves, made as further security, shall be void. Witnesses: THOMAS ELLERY, JOHN LEWIS. Before JOSEPH FOX, J.P. & Dep. Reg.

Book Lb, p. 46
29 May 1733
Mortgage

(See p. 39) JOHN PAGE, planter, to WILLIAM PETERS, planter, both of Colleton Co., as security on bond dated 19 May 1733 in penal sum of ₤ 2000 conditioned for the payment of ₤ 1100 with interest to begin 1 Jan. 1734, 432 a. on S side Tooboodoo Creek, bounding E on the creek; W & N on WILLIAM EDDINGS; S on Didcots Creek; & for security on another sum of ₤ 1100 (total ₤ 2200) assigns several slaves, also 4 feather beds, 4 iron pots, 4 horses, 40 cattle, 40 hogs, & 17 sheep. Witnesses: JOHN PETER, ROBERT (his mark) OSWELL, ALGERNON ASH. A Negro wench delivered. Before WILLIAM LIVINGSTON, J.P. JOSEPH FOX, Dep. Reg.

Book Lb, p. 49
10 & 11 May 1733
L & R

THOMAS LYNCH, ESQ., & SABINA his wife, of Berkeley Co., to WILLIAM SWINTON, ESQ., of Craven Co., for ₤ 500 SC money, 2100 a. in Craven Co., granted 28 Apr. 1733 by Gov. ROBERT JOHNSON to THOMAS LYNCH; bounding S on JOHN PRITCHARD; W on MATHEW BELL; E on JOHN BRUNSON. Witnesses: JAMES FISHER, CORNELIUS DARGON. Before DANIEL GREENE, J.P. FISHER affirmed according to his profession. JOSEPH FOX, Dep. Reg.

Book Lb, p. 55
21 May 1733
Deed of Gift

ANN CATTELL, to her son JOHN CATELL, for love & affection, 420 a. on Edisto Island, Colleton Co., granted to her grandfather THOMAS BOWER & by him willed to ANN. Witnesses: MRS. JANE CATTELL, JONATHAN JAMES. Before WILLIAM CATTELL, J.P. JOSEPH FOX, Dep. Reg.

Book Lb, p. 56
30 Mar. 1733
Mortgage

JAMES ROUSHAM, carpenter, of Dorchester, to JOHN POSTELL, SR., planter near Dorchester, for ₤ 1000 currency payable with interest on 4 Apr. next, lot #78 in Dorchester with the dwelling house & garden; also lot #18 in Willtown; also all his household goods, working tools, his horses, mares & colts, according to schedule. Witnesses: JOHN LEPPOR, JOHN MASON. Before JOHN WALTER, J.P. The schedule listed 2 feather beds performed (?), 1 desk with drawer, 1/2 doz. cane chairs, a couch, 2 tables, 2 chests of tools, 1 mare, 2 colts. JOHN FOX, Dep. Reg.

Book Lb, p. 58
20 Apr. 1733
Mortgage

THOMAS JONES, cordwainer, of Colleton Co., to CHARLES HILL, ESQ., of Charleston, as security on bond on even date in penal sum of ₤ 1637:15 SC money conditioned for the payment of ₤ 818:17:6 currency with interest on 20 Apr. 1737, 438 a. (part of

738 a.) in Colleton Co., bounding E on Edisto River Swamp; W on part of the 738 a. belonging to MR. MACTEER; N on MR. GODFREY; S on ANTHONY DODSWORTH; & for further security delivers 4 Negro slaves to HILL. Witnesses: WILLIAM FRYER, MICHAEL MILLURE. Before ALEXANDER PARRIS, J.P. JOSEPH FOX, Dep. Reg.

Book Lb, p. 63
17 & 18 May 1733
L & R by Mortgage

VINCENT GUERIN, planter, of St. Thomas Parish, Berkeley Co., to PAUL JENYS & JOHN BAKER, merchants, of Charleston, as security on bond dated 16 Nov. 1732 in penal sum of L 2700 currency conditioned for the payment of L 1349:13:5 with interest on 16 Nov. 1733; & as security for L 289:8:3 currency advanced by JENYS & BAKER to several of GUERIN'S creditors; 400 a. on N side of NE branch of Wando River; bounding W on JOHN WASTCOAT; E on MARY WARNOCK; S on a creek; N on JOHN RUBERRY; also 100 a. on same side of Wando, bounding W on WILLIAM DANFORD; E on THOMAS BASKERFIELD; S on THOMAS BOSHER; N on JOHN RUBERRY. Witnesses: CHARLES PINCKNEY, GEORGE AUSTIN, ROBERT HOW. Before CHARLES PINCKNEY, J.P. JOSEPH FOX, Dep. Reg.

Book Lb, p. 72
23 June 1733
Deed of Gift

EDMUND (his mark) JERVES, of St. Paul's Parish, Colleton Co., to ARTHUR BULL, for good causes & considerations, all his lands, goods, chattles, household stuff, etc. One Negro boy delivered in name of the whole. Witnesses: JAMES SWINHOE, JOHN WHITE. Before ROBERT YONGE, J.P. JOSEPH FOX, Dep. Reg.

Book Lb, p. 73
16 June 1733
Deed of Gift

LEWIS (his mark) DUTARQUE, planter, of the Parish of St. Thomas & St. Dennis, Berkeley Co., to his son JOHN DUTARQUE, planter, for love & affection, 350 a., part of the 600 a. on which LEWIS DUTARQUE lives; bounding S & W on RICHARD BERESFORD; N & W on LEWIS DUTARQUE; E on SOLOMON BREMAR; SE on COL. THOMAS LYNCH. Witnesses: STEPHEN FOGARTIE, JAMES FOGARTIE. Before MICHAEL DARBY, J.P. Three Negro men delivered. JOSEPH FOX, Dep. Reg.

Book Lb, p. 75
3 Mar. 1732
Deed of Sale

ANTHONY PAWLEY, planter, of Prince George Parish, to JOHN CAHUSAC, planter, of Berkeley Co., for L 230 currency, 500 a. in St. Johns Parish, Berkeley Co. Witnesses: SAMUEL DYPRE, JOHN SELLERY. JOSEPH FOX, Dep. Reg.

Book Lb, p. 76
24 & 25 July 1733
L & R

JAMES PAINE, merchant, & MARY his wife, of Charleston, to WILLIAM SWINTON, ESQ., of Craven Co., for L 400 SC money, 900 a. in Craven Co., granted by Gov. ROBERT JOHNSON on 6 Apr. 1733 to JAMES PAINE, bounding SE on Peedee River; NW on JOHN GREEN; NE on STEPHEN PROCTOR. Witnesses: ANTHONY WHITE, JOHN BESWICKE. Before TWEEDIE SOMERVILLE, J.P. JOSEPH FOX, Dep. Reg.

Book Lb, p. 82
28 Feb. 1731
Quit Claim

REBECCA COLLIER, of the Parish of St. Mary, Islington, Middlesex Co., Great Britain, widow & administrix of JOSEPH COLLIER, merchant, of London; also administrix of HANNAH SUSSEX of Islington (widow & administrix of WILLIAM SUSSEX, merchant, of London); also administrix of the estate of WILLIAM SUSSEX unadministered by HANNAH SUSSEX in her lifetime; to ALEXANDER PARRIS, ESQ., of SC; all sums of money, debts, etc., due & owing from PARRIS to JOSEPH COLLIER, THOMAS COLLIER, & WILLIAM SUSSEX. Witnesses: HUGH PERCY, EDWARD LEE, PETER GOUDET. Before DANIEL GREENE, J.P. JOSEPH FOX, Dep. Reg.

Book Lb, p. 83
12 & 13 Oct. 1730
L & R

JOHN BRAND, gentleman, to THOMAS BARTRAM, vintner, both of Charleston, for L 50 SC money, that part of lot #187 lying between the part sold to JOHN LEA (on the N) & a lot belonging to ELIAS HANCOCK & MR. GORING (on the S); bounding E on a street leading from Ashley River N to the Broad Path; W on THOMAS BARTRAM; lot #187 having been granted on 21 Nov. 1693 by the Lords Proprs. to JONAS BENHOST. Signed by JOHN BRAND & MARY (her mark) BRAND. Witness: ALICE SMITH. Before JOSEPH FOX, J.P. & Dep. Reg.

Book Lb, p. 89
1 & 2 Feb. 1731
L & R

WILLIAM STERLING (STARLAND), cordwainer, & HANNAH (her mark) his wife, of Berkeley Co., to CHARLES RUSSEL, planter, of Craven Co., for ₺ 50 SC money, 570 a. in Craven Co., granted 14 Mar. 1704 by the Lords Proprs., signed by the Hon. Sir NATHANIEL JOHNSON, Knight, Gov., etc., to GEORGE STARLING, father, of the above WILLIAM. Whereas GEORGE STERLING by will dated 8 Jan. 1706/7 bequeathed all his real & personal estate to his 3 sons, GEORGE, WILLIAM, & JOHN; & whereas GEORGE & JOHN died & the estate descended to WILLIAM; now WILLIAM STERLING sells to CHARLES RUSSEL the 570 a. bounding according to plat attached to grant. Witnesses: THOMAS OWENS, DAVID BALL, JOHN HENTIE. Before JOSEPH FOX, J.P. & Dep. Reg.

Book Lb, p. 98
26 June 1729
L & R

JONATHAN DRAKE, planter, & MARY his wife, of Berkeley Co., to ELIAS HANCOCK, vintner, of Charleston, for ₺ 60 SC, free from MARY'S title of dower, part of lot #194 in Charleston, 80 ft. front 100 ft. deep, bounding E on the street leading to MR. STEVENS; S on JOHN HILL; W & N on MR. BENHOSTE. Witnesses: JOSEPH MASSEY, THOMAS HOLTON. Before JOSEPH FOX, J.P. & Dep. Reg.

Book Lb, p. 105
9 & 10 Feb. 1727
L & R

SARAH BARKSDALE, widow & sole executrix of the will of JOHN BARKSDALE, ESQ., of Charleston, & THOMAS BARKSDALE, planter, of Berkeley Co., to ELIAS HANCOCK, victualler, of Charleston, for ₺ 800 SC money, 300 a. on NE of Ashley River, bounding SW on Hog Island Creek; NW on Capers Creek; NE on THOMAS BARKSDALE; SE on DANIEL GREENE (formerly JAMES BASFORD); being part of a larger tract granted to FLORENTIA O'SULLIVAN by the Lords Proprs. on 6 July 1680. Witnesses: SOLOMON TOZER, NICHOLAS HAYNES, NATHANIEL NEWBOROUGH. A memorial entered in auditor's office 24 May 1733. Before JOSEPH FOX, J.P. & Dep. Reg.

Book Lb, p. 112
11 July 1733
Bond

BENJAMIN DENNIS, planter, to THOMAS ELLERY, gentleman, of Charleston, in penal sum of ₺ 600 currency conditioned for the payment of ₺ 300 with interest on 30 Apr. 1734. Witnesses: PHILIP AYTON, JOHN BROWN. Before ALEXANDER PARRIS, J.P. JOSEPH FOX, Dep. Reg.

Book Lb, p. 113
10 & 11 July 1733
L & R by Mortgage

BENJAMIN DENNIS, planter, now of Charleston, to THOMAS ELLERY, gentleman, of Charleston. Whereas on this date ELLERY at the request of DENNIS entered into a bond in penal sum of ₺ 392 currency conditioned for the payment of ₺ 196 with interest to THOMAS ELLIOTT of Stono, planter, on 30 Apr., 1734; & whereas DENNIS this date gave bond to ELLERY in sum of ₺ 300 currency with interest payable 30 Apr. 1734; now DENNIS, as security on the 2 bonds, conveys to ELLERY 386 a. at Bohicket on Wadmalaw Island, St. Pauls Parish, Colleton Co., bounding E on a creek; W on Lettinwah Creek; N on ROBERT SAMS; S on JOHN DAVIS. Witnesses: JOHN BROWN, PHILIP AYTON. Before ALEXANDER PARRIS, J. P. JOSEPH FOX, Dep. Reg.

Book Lb, p. 122
25 & 27 Aug. 1733
L & R

ISAAC HOLMES, merchant, of Charleston, to his Excellency, ROBERT JOHNSON, ESQ., Capt. Gen.; Gov.; etc., for the use of his majesty King George II, for ₺ 500 currency, 100 a. on Port Royall Island, Granville Co., known as Scotts Point or Smith's Point, bounding N & W on FRANCIS HOLMES; E on Beaufort River; S on a marsh. Witnesses: JAMES WEDDERBURN, WALTER COX, JAMES ABERCROMBY. Before JOSEPH FOX, J.P. & Dep. Reg.

Book Lb, p. 129
19 Feb. 1731
Mortgage

DANIEL JAUDON, planter, of Berkeley Co., to STEPHEN MILLER, shopkeeper, of Charleston, for ₺ 700 SC money, 500 a. in Berkeley Co., bounding W on Cooper River; E & N on FRANCIS PADGET (PAGITT), S on Murrell's Creek; conditioned for the payment to MILLER of ₺ 70 SC interest money on 19 Feb. 1732, 1733, 1734, & ₺ 770 on 19 Feb. 1735. Witnesses: SOLOMON TOZER, JOHN CROFT. Before ALEXANDER PARRIS, J.P. JOSEPH FOX, Dep. Reg. Memo (p. 350) received of PETER PAGITT full contents of mortgage: STEPHEN MILLER. Witness: NATHANIEL JOHNSON.

Book Lb, p. 135   SAMUEL MASTERS, planter, of Craven Co., to
2 Mar. 1732   ISAAC CHARDON, DANIEL LAROCHE, & THOMAS LA-
Bond   ROCHE, merchants, in penal sum of ₤ 1558:14:6
                      currency conditioned for the payment of
₤ 779:14:6 with interest at 10% on 1 Mar. 1733. Witnesses: ROBERT INNES,
ISAAC SECARE, JAMES CRADDOCK. JOSEPH FOX, Dep. Reg.

Book Lb, p. 136   SAMUEL MASTERS, planter, of Craven Co., to
1 & 2 Mar. 1732   ISAAC CHARDON, DANIEL LAROCHE & THOMAS LAROCHE,
L & R by Mortgage   merchants, as security on above bond, 200 a.
                      on which MASTERS lives, in Craven Co., bound-
ing W on Winyaw River; NE & S on a Barony; & as further security delivers
2 Negro slaves, 45 milch cows with their calves, 10 steers, & all his
stock of neat cattle; also all tar kilns, lightwood gathered or ungather-
ed, barrels & barrelstaves. Witnesses: ROBERT INNES, ISAAC SECARE, JAMES
CARDDOCK. Before JOHN WELLIS, J.P. JOSEPH FOX, Dep. Reg.

Book Lb, p. 145   FRANCIS DESCHAMPS, planter, of Berkeley Co.,
23 Dec. 1732   to STEPHEN MILLER, shopkeeper, of Charleston
Mortgage   as security on bond of even date in penal sum
                      of ₤ 1200 SC money, conditioned for the pay-
ment of ₤ 600 with interest on 23 Dec. 1735, the interest money to be
paid yearly for 3 yrs., delivers 4 Negro men, 2 Negro women; also 400 a.
in Berkeley Co., bounding E on JOHN SNOW; S on JAMES BALIR & SAMUEL DUPRE;
W & N on land not laid out. Witnesses: PAUL TRAPIER, JOHN CROFT. Before
ALEXANDER PARRIS, J.P. JOSEPH FOX, Dep. Reg. Mortgage delcared satisfied 18 Aug. 1741. Witnesses: ROBERT AUSTIN, Pub. Reg.

Book Lb, p. 151   HENRY LEWIS, planter, of Craven Co., to DANIEL
7 Aug. 1733   LAROCHE, THOMAS LAROCHE & ISAAC CHARDON, mer-
Bond   chants, in penal sum of ₤ 600 currency, condi-
                      tioned for the payment of ₤ 300 on 1 Mar. 1733.
Wintesses: HUGH SWINTON, ISAAC SECARE. JOSEPH FOX, Dep. Reg.

Book Lb, p. 152   HENRY LEWIS, planter, of Craven Co., to DANIEL
7 Aug. 1733   LAROCHE, THOMAS LAROCHE, & ISAAC CHARDON, as
Mortgage   security on the above bond, delivers 7 Negro
                      slaves. Witnesses: HUGH SWINTON, ISAAC SECARE.
Before WILLIAM WHITESIDE, J.P. JOSEPH FOX, Dep. Reg.

Book Lb, p. 155   SUSANNA WIGINGTON, of Charleston, widow, form-
8 May 1724   erly the wife of EDWARD RAWLINGS & daughter of
Quit Claim   MARY PROSS, widow, to MARY BLAMYER, widow, for
                      good causes & considerations, that messuage or
tenement on the Bay of Charleston wherein JOHN WHITE now lives; also 1/4
part of lot #16, fronting 25 ft., whereon said messuage is erected; bounding N on RICHARD CODNER; S on part of lot #16 belonging to THOMAS HEP-
WORTH. Witnesses: RICHARD SPLATT, ROBERT HUME, CHILDERMAS CROFT. Before
ALEXANDER PARRIS, J.P. JOSEPH FOX, Dep. Reg.

Book Lb, p. 158   MARY BLAMYER, widow, to STEPHEN MILLER, shop-
29 June 1733   keeper, both of Charleston, for ₤ 2200 SC mon-
Deed of Sale   ey, that messuage or tenement wherein JOSHUA
                      LANCASTER lives, fronting E 25 ft. on the Bay
of Charleston, & that 1/4 part of lot #16 on which the tenement stands,
bounding N on RICHARD CODNER; S on the part owned by STEPHEN MILLER. Witnesses: JAMES CROKATT, EDWARD WIGG, JOHN CROFT. Before ALEXANDER PARRIS,
J.P. JOSEPH FOX, Dep. Reg.

Book Lb, p. 163   JONATHAN CHRISTMAS, cooper, of Craven Co., to
1 July 1733   ISAAC CHARDON, DANIEL LAROCHE & THOMAS LAROCHE
Bond   merchants, in penal sum of ₤ 374:3:10 currency,
                      conditioned for the payment of ₤ 187:1:11 with
interest on 1 Mar. 1733. Witnesses: ISAAC SECARE, JAMES CRODDACK. JO-
SEPH FOX, Dep. Reg.

Book Lb, p. 164   JONATHAN CHRISTMAS, cooper, of Craven Co., to
1 July 1733   ISAAC CHARDON, DANIEL LAROCHE, & THOMAS LA-
Mortgage   ROCHE, merchants, as security on the above
                      bond, delivers 7 cows & calves, 3 yearlings,

2 horses, 3 mares, 20 hogs. Witnesses: ISAAC SECARE, JAMES CRADDOCK. Before JOHN WALLIS, J.P. JOSEPH FOX, Dep. Reg.

Book Lb, p. 167　　　　　　　THOMAS JENKINS, planter, of Winyaw, to DANIEL
1 June 1733　　　　　　　　　LAROCHE, THOMAS LAROCHE & ISAAC CHARDON, mer-
Bond　　　　　　　　　　　　chants, in penal sum of Ł 573 currency, conditioned for the payment of Ł 286:13:6 with interest on 1 Oct. 1733. Witnesses: JOHN SELLERY, ISAAC SECARE, JAMES CRADDOCK. JOSEPH FOX, Dep. Reg.

Book Lb, p. 168　　　　　　　THOMAS JENKINS, planter, of Winyaw, to DANIEL
1 June 1733　　　　　　　　　LAROCHE, THOMAS LAROCHE, & ISAAC CHARDON, as
Mortgage　　　　　　　　　　security on the above bond, delivers 2 Negro slaves. Witnesses: JOHN SELLERY, ISAAC SECARE, JAMES CRADDOCK. Before WILLIAM WHITESIDE, J.P. JOSEPH FOX, Dep. Reg.

Book Lb, p. 171　　　　　　　WILLIAM WHITESIDE, gentleman, of Craven Co.,
8 Mar. 1732　　　　　　　　　to ISAAC CHARDON, of Berkeley Co., DANIEL LA-
Bond　　　　　　　　　　　　ROCHE & THOMAS LAROCHE, of Craven Co., merchants, in the penal sum of Ł 3083:9:3 SC money, conditioned for the payment of Ł 1541:14:7 with interest on 1 Mar. 1733. Witnesses: WILLIAM FARMER, JAMES CRADDOCK. JOSEPH FOX, Dep. Reg.

Book Lb, p. 173　　　　　　　WILLIAM WHITESIDE, gentleman, of Craven Co.,
8 Mar. 1732　　　　　　　　　to ISAAC CHARDON, of Berkeley Co., DANIEL LA-
Mortgage　　　　　　　　　　ROCHE, & THOMAS LAROCHE, of Craven Co., merchants, as security on the above bond, delivered 12 Negro slaves. Witnesses: WILLIAM FARMER, JAMES CRADDOCK. Before JOHN WALLIS, J.P. JOSEPH FOX, Dep. Reg.

Book Lb, p. 176　　　　　　　THOMAS BOSHER, planter, of Prince George Par-
1 Mar. 1732/3　　　　　　　　ish, Winyaw, to ISAAC CHARDON, of Charleston,
Bond　　　　　　　　　　　　DANIEL LAROCHE & THOMAS LAROCHE, of Georgetown, merchants, in penal sum of Ł 1150:10:3 SC money, conditioned for the payment of Ł 575:5:3 with interest on 1 Mar. 1733. Witnesses: WILLIAM FARMER, JAMES CRADDOCK. JOSEPH FOX, Dep. Reg.

Book Lb, p. 177　　　　　　　THOMAS BOSHER, planter, of Prince George Par-
1 Mar. 1732　　　　　　　　　ish, Winyah, to ISAAC CHARDON, of Charleston,
Mortgage　　　　　　　　　　DANIEL LAROCHE & THOMAS LAROCHE, of Georgetown, merchants, as security on above bond, delivered 4 Negro slaves, & all his stock, consisting of 30 cows & calves, 10 horses & mares. Witnesses: WILLIAM FARMER, JAMES CRADDOCK. Before WILLIAM WHITESIDE, J.P. JOSEPH FOX, Dep. Reg.

Book Lb, p. 181　　　　　　　SOLOMON HEWS, planter, of Prince George Parish,
14 Mar. 1732　　　　　　　　 Winyaw, to ISSAC CHARDON, of Charleston, DAN-
Bond　　　　　　　　　　　　IEL LAROCHE & THOMAS LAROCHE, of Georgetown, merchants, in penal sum of Ł 1083:3:4 SC money, conditioned for the payment of Ł 541:11:8 with interest, on 14 Mar. 1733. Witnesses: JOSIAS DUPRE, WILLIAM FARMER. JOSEPH FOX, Dep. Reg.

Book Lb, p. 182　　　　　　　SOLOMON HEWS, planter, of Prince George Parish,
14 Mar. 1732　　　　　　　　 to ISAAC CHARDON of Charleston, DANIEL LAROCHE
Mortgage　　　　　　　　　　& THOMAS LAROCHE, of Georgetown, merchants, as security on above bond, 2 Negro men, 1 black horse, 7 cows & calves, 1 tar kiln erected on land of JOSIAS DUPRE, JR. Witnesses: JOSIAS DUPRE, WILLIAM FARMER. JOSEPH FOX, Dep. Reg.

Book Lb, p. 186　　　　　　　SAMUEL EVELEIGH, ESQ., & ELIZABETH his wife,
1 & 2 Nov. 1721　　　　　　　to JOHN LLOYD, ESQ., all of Charleston, for
L & R　　　　　　　　　　　 Ł 100 currency, 640 a. in Craven Co. Whereas Gov. GIBBS granted the Hon. ROBERT DANIELL several tracts of 24,000 a. (part of 48,000 a. given said DANIELL by the Lords Proprs.) in Craven Co.; & whereas Landgrave ROBERT DANIELL on 19 June 1711 sold the 24,000 a. to THOMAS SMITH, ESQ.; & he by deed poll on 10 Sept. 1711 sold 640 a. (part of the 24,000) to SAMUEL EVELEIGH, bounding E on a salt marsh; W on Waccamaw River; N on lands not laid out; S on PERCIVAL PAWLEY; now EVELEIGH sells to LLOYD. Witnesses: SOLOMON TOZER, DUNCAN CAMPBELL. Before JOSEPH FOX, J.P. & Dep. Reg.

Book Lb, p. 192　　　　　　　ELIZABETH, wife of SAMUEL EVELEIGH, merchant,
2 Nov. 1721　　　　　　　　　of Charleston, appeared before FRANCIS YONGE,
Renunciation of Dower　　　 C.J. of Court of Common Pleas & delcared she
　　　　　　　　　　　　　　voluntarily joined with her husband in conveying by L & R on 1 & 2 Nov. 1721 to JOHN LLOYD, of Charleston, 640 a. in Craven Co., bounding E on a salt marsh; W on Waccamaw River; N on lands not laid out; S on PERCIVAL PAWLEY. JOSEPH FOX, Dep. Reg.

Book Lb, p. 194　　　　　　　JAMES COCHRAN, gentleman, of Colleton Co., son
20 Sept. 1733　　　　　　　　& heir of JAMES COCHRAN, ESQ., to ROBERT STEEL,
Confirmation of Title　　　 tanner, of Charleston. Whereas JAMES COCHRAN,
　　　　　　　　　　　　　　the father, owned 100 a. in Granville Co., now bounding N & E on marsh & Cumbee River; W on ROBERT STEEL; S on COL. JOHN PALMER; which 100 a. he sold to ROBERT STEEL, but the deeds were accidentally destroyed during the Indian War; & whereas STEEL has been in possession of the 100 a. for 27 years or more; now JAMES COCHRAN, the son, confirms STEEL'S title. Witnesses: RICHARD ALLEIN, FREDERICK MEYER. Before JOSEPH FOX, J.P. & Dep. Reg.

Book Lb, p. 198　　　　　　　ROBERT STEEL, (STEELE) tanner, of Charleston,
21 & 22 Sept. 1733　　　　　 to the Hon. WILLIAM BULL, ESQ., of Berkeley
L & R　　　　　　　　　　　　Co., for Ł 600 SC money, 265 a. in Granville
　　　　　　　　　　　　　　Co., & 100 a. Whereas by letters patent dated 28 Apr. 1733 Gov. ROBERT JOHNSON granted SAMUEL CLERK 265 a. in Granville Co., bounding E on ROBERT STEEL; S on COL. JOHN PALMER; SW on COL. WILLIAM BULL; N on a creek & COL. JOSEPH BLAKE; & whereas by L & R, 11 & 12 Dec. 1732 SAMUEL CLERK sold the 265 a. to ROBERT STEEL (bounderies given in lease & here as: N on ROBERT STEEL; W on COL. JOSEPH BLAKE; E on COL. JOHN PALMER; S on COL. WILLIAM BULL) & whereas ROBERT STEEL owned another 100 a. in Granville Co., bounding N & E on marsh & Cumbee River; W on ROBERT STEEL; S on COL. JOHN PALMER; which land was purchased from JAMES COCHRAN (the father) of Colleton Co., & the papers being destroyed in the Indian War the title was confirmed to STEEL (p. 194) by JAMES COCHRAN, the son, on 20 Sept. 1733; now STEEL sells BULL 265 a. "as first before mentioned" & 100 a. Witnesses: JOSEPH BRYAN, FREDERICK MEYER. Before JOSEPH FOX, J.P. & Dep. Reg.

Book Lb, p. 207　　　　　　　By virtue of a clause in ye Reviving Act ratified the 22d Sept. 1733, all fees mentioned in an Act "Intituled an Act for ascertaining publick officers fees" are from henceforward to be taken & received at the rate of 5 for 1; anything in ye said Act or any other Act of ye General Assembly of this province relating to fees to the contrary notwithstanding. Copy examined this 24 Sept. 1733. JAMES MICKIE, Dep. Secry.

Book Lb, p. 208　　　　　　　MARTHA ROMSEY, of Charleston, widow of BENJA-
4 & 5 Sept. 1732　　　　　　 MIN ROMSEY, mariner, of the City of Bristol,
L & R　　　　　　　　　　　　to RICHARD HILL, merchant, of Charleston, for
　　　　　　　　　　　　　　Ł 200 currency (cash) & 600 secured to be paid, part of lot #77 in Charleston bounding E on Church Street leading from Ashley River to the New Brick Church); N 135 ft. on a part of the lot 35 ft. English measure wide which MARTHA ROMSEY reserved for herself; S on Vanderhorst's Creek; W on MARTHA ROMSEY. Whereas by indenture tripartite dated 11 May 1725 between MARTHA ROMSEY (by the name of MARTHA CROOKE then widow of WILLIAM CROOKE, gentleman) of the 1st part; ANDREW ALLEN & JOHN CAWOOD, merchants, of 2nd part; & BENJAMIN ROMSEY of 3rd part; MARTHA (CROOKE) in consideration of her intended marriage to ROMSEY, & for other considerations, conveyed to ALLEN & CAWOOD to the use of ROMSEY, lot #77 in Charleston; & whereas ROMSEY by will dated 22 Mar. 1726 bequeathed his real & personal estate to his wife, including lot #77; now she sells to HILL. Witnesses: CHARLES PINCKNEY, CHILDERMAS CROFT. Witnesses: CHARLES PINCKNEY, CHILDERMAS CROFT. Witnesses to receipt of Ł 600 JOHN RIGG, JACOB MOTTE. Before ALEXANDER PARRIS, J.P. JOSEPH FOX, Dep. Reg.

Book Lb, p. 218　　　　　　　JONATHAN FITCH agrees to furnish RALPH IZARD
13 Sept. 1733　　　　　　　　by 1 Oct. next with a legal title to 160 a.
Agreement　　　　　　　　　　known as JEOFERD land adjoining THOMAS SMITH'S
　　　　　　　　　　　　　　land & to lands in IZARD'S possession which were purchased from HENROYDAH ENGLISH & to lands purchased from THOMAS

PINCKNEY. IZARD is to give FITCH 4 Negro men (part of 12 bought from MR.
JENYS) now at his plantation at the halfway House Swamp; also L 500 currency. Further agreed that FITCH will pay for surveying & conveying the
land. IZARD to run the risk of the Negroes until delivered & to deliver
them in good health. Witnesses: ALEXANDER CRAMAKE, THOMAS RASBERRY (RU-
BERRY?). Before PETER TAYLOR, J.P. JOSEPH FOX, Dep. Reg.

Book Lb, p. 219   The Hon. FRANCIS YONGE, ESQ., to ABRAHAM SATUR,
5 Apr. 1733   ESQ., of Berkeley Co., & JANE OLLIER, widow of
Mortgage   Charleston, for L 1000 currency, 296 a., bound-
                        ing E on Ashley River; S on BENJAMIN STANYARN;
W on JORDON ROCHE; N on THOMAS DRAYTON, ESQ., conditioned for the repay-
ment of L 1000 & interest on 1 Feb. next. Witnesses: ANDREW RUTLEDGE,
SARAH CARLOW. Before THEOPHILUS GREGORY, J.P. JOSEPH FOX, Dep. Reg.

Book Lb, p. 223   The Rt. Hon. JOHN, Lord Carteret, Baron of
18 & 19 Feb. 1730   Hawnes & Lord Proprs. to JOHN ROBERTS, ESQ.,
L & R   of Deans Court, Co. of Middlesex, for L 400 of
                        Great Britain, the Barony of 12,000 a., Eng-
lish measure, on the river May & adjoining the Barony of JOHN DAWSON,
ESQ., set forth & bounded by the Gov. or Surveyor General of SC. Whereas
KING CHARLES II by letters patent under the Great Seal of England granted
JOHN, Lord Carteret, & 7 others, a tract of land in America now called
Carolina, the inheritance of which was vested in the Lords Proprs.; &
whereas they agreed that a Barony of 12,000 a., English measure, on the
river May, adjoining the Barony of JOHN DAWSON, ESQ., should be granted
to JOHN, Lord Carteret, & the conveyance was made 5 Dec. 1718, & whereas
7 of the Lords Proprs. about 1729 surrendered their title to 7 parts (the
whole divided into 8) to KING GEORGE II, & to secure said surrender an
Act of Parliament was passed, entitled "An Act for Establishing an Agreement with 7 of the Lords Proprs. of Carolina for ye surrender of their
title & interest in that Province to his Majesty" in which Act was a
clause for reserving to Lord Carteret his 8th share; now he sells to ROB-
ERTS. Witnesses: RICHARD SHELTON (of London, gentleman, late Sec'y. to
Lords Proprs. in Carolina); GEORGE SHELTON. Before JOHN BARGER, ESQ.,
Lord Mayor & the Aldermen of London. Signed; JACKSON. JOSEPH FOX, Dep.
Reg.

Book Lb, p. 230   The Rt. Hon. JOHN, Lord Carteret, Baron of
18 & 19 Feb. 1730   Hawnes, & 1 of the Lords Proprs., to JOHN ROB-
L & R   ERTS, ESQ., of Deans Court, Middlesex Co., for
                        L 500 of Great Britain, the Barony of 12,000 a.
English measure, on Wackamaw River, commonly called Hobcaw Point, in Car-
olina. Whereas KING CHARLES II by letters patent granted JOHN, Lord
Carteret, & 7 others, a tract in America called Carolina, etc., etc.,
(see p. 223) now Carteret sells 12,000 a. to ROBERTS. Witness: RICHARD
SHELTON (of London, gentleman, late Sec'y. to Lords Proprs. in Carolina).
Before JOHN BARBER, Lord Mayor, & the Aldermen of London. Signed: JACK-
SON. JOSEPH FOX, Dep. Reg.

Book Lb, p. 237   DANIEL GIBSON, surgeon, of Charleston, to JOHN
22 & 23 Feb. 1732   CARRUTHERS, Master of the ship Molly, galley,
L & R by Mortgage   now at anchor in Charleston harbor, for L 400
                        British money, 1/6 part of Schenckinghs Square,
in Charleston, bounding N on part same lot; S on MATHURIN BOGARD; also
another 1/6 part of same lot, bounding N on COL. GEORGE CHICKEN; S on the
above lot; conditioned for the payment of L 440 British money in current
SC bills at the usual exchange on 23 Feb. 1733. Witnesses: ROBERT AUSTIN,
JOHN LEWIS. Before THOMAS COOPER, J.P. JOSEPH FOX, Dep. Reg.

Book Lb, p. 244   DANIEL CARTWRIGHT, planter, & SARAH his wife,
31 Oct. & 1 Nov. 1733   of Berkeley Co., to JOHN GASCOIGNE, ESQ.,
L & R by mortgage   Commander of H.M.S. Alborough, for L 130 Bri-
                        tish money, 91 a. 23 perches of land on
Charleston Neck, Berkeley Co., bounding SW on marshes of Ashley River;
SE on RICHARD CARTWRIGHT & COL. JOSEPH BLAKE; NE on the public road; conditioned for redemption by 1 Nov. next. Whereas by deed of feoffment
dated 31 Mar. 1709 ELIZABETH BEDON, widow of RICHARD CARTWRIGHT, father
of said DANIEL of Charleston, conveyed to RICHARD CARTWRIGHT, (CARTERET?),
planter, of Berkeley Co., 36-3/4 a.; & whereas by deed of feoffment dated

25 May, 1711 JOHN RAVEN, gentleman, of Colleton Co. & ELIZABETH his wife, (late ELIZABETH BEADEN, widow & executor of will of GEORGE BEADEN (BEDON), cooper of Charleston) conveyed to RICHARD CARTWRIGHT 69 a. both of which tracts were originally granted to said GEORGE BEDON, & directed by his will to be disposed of for the payment of several legacies; & whereas RICHARD CARTWRIGHT by will dated 5 Mar. 1715 bequeathed to his son DANIEL (after several legacies) the part of his tract obtained from GEORGE BEDON; now DANIEL mortgages his land to GASCOIGNE. Witnesses: SABINA ROWES, JOHN MARTINI. Before CHARLES PINCKNEY, J.P. JOSEPH FOX, Dep. Reg.

Book Lb, p. 255
25 Sept. 1733
Deed of Gift

JOHN PETER, planter, of Colleton Co., to his nephew WILLIAM PETER (son of his brother WILLIAM PETER, planter, of Colleton Co.), for love & affection, 200 a. in Colleton Co. on W side Ponpon River; bounding S & W on JOHN JACKSON; E on a swamp; N on JOHN PETER. Witnesses: MOSES MARTIN, TABITHA PETER, WILLIAM PETER. Before WILLIAM LIVINGSTON, J.P. JOSEPH FOX, Dep. Reg.

Book Lb, p. 256

"Mem'd. ALEX'R. CRAMAKE has began the office of Dep'ty. Public Register. Nov. 14th 1733."

Book Lb, p. 257
6 Oct. 1732
Deed of Gift

GEORGE SMITH, gentleman, & DOROTHY his wife (with the free consent & desire of DOROTHY) to his well beloved son-in-law, the Rev. MR. NATHAN BASSETT, clerk, & MARY his wife (well beloved daughter of GEORGE & DOROTHY SMITH) all of Charleston, for fatherly love & affection & other considerations, part of lot #5 whereon BASSETT has begun to erect certain buildings being the W part of N side of SMITH'S lot; the E end of which begins at the W part of a brick well built on SMITH'S part, & extends W to the W bounds of the lot; being 19 ft. from N to S (from an alley between GEORGE SMITH & TWEEDIE SOMERVILLE running W from the Bay), running from the well 83 ft. 8 in. W, thence W 13 ft. 6 in. in breadth from N to S (from the alley), by the whole length of the rest of SMITH'S part to the westernmost line; bounding N on the alley; E & S on part of SMITH'S lot; W on part of a lot granted THOMAS ROSELATE & conveyed to RICHARD CAPERS. Witnesses: JOHN BALLANTINE, JOHN FRANKLYN, JOHN RIVERS. Before ALEXANDER PARRIS, J.P. NATHANIEL JOHNSON, Pub. Reg.

Book Lb, p. 262
3 May 1731
Deed of Gift

GEORGE SMITH, gentleman, & DOROTHY his wife (with her free consent & desire) to his well beloved daughter MARY (wife of the Rev. MR. NATHAN BASSETT, clerk), all of Charleston, for fatherly love & affection, & to make provision for the support of MARY & her future children, & for other considerations, 172 a. in Berkeley Co., part of a larger tract at Goosecreek; with details in regard to inheritance. Witnesses: THOMAS SMITH, MARY SMITH, SR., MARY SMITH, JR. Before THEOPHILUS GREGOY, J.P. NATHANIEL JOHNSON, Pub. Reg.

Book Lb, p. 267
17 Sept. 1733
Deed of Gift

ISAAC LESESNE, SR., planter, to THOMAS VALLEY, planter, both of Berkeley Co., for good esteem, well liking, & other considerations, & ₤ 5 currency, 500 a. Whereas JOHN, EARL OF BATH, Palatine, & the Lords Proprs. by letters patent created COL. ROBERT DANIELL a Landgrave, granting him 48,000 a.; & whereas ROBERT DANIELL, ESQ., grandson & heir of COL. ROBERT DANIELL, on 13 Mar. 1728, conveyed to ISAAC LESESNE 500 a. in Craven Co., bounding S on ROBERT DANIELL, the grandson; E on ISAAC LESESNE; on other sides on vacant land; now LESESNE conveys to VALLEY. Witnesses: JOHN WALKER, SAMUEL FLEY, THOMAS THRADCRAFT. Before JOHN DANIEL, J.P. NATHANIEL JOHNSON, Pub. Reg.

Book Lb, p. 270
22 & 23 Nov. 1733
L & R

MARTHA LOGAN, widow, to Gov. ROBERT JOHNSON, for ₤ 100 currency, part of a low water lot in Charleston fronting 50 ft. on lot #32 & 50 ft. on Cooper River, bounding on all sides on land belonging to MARTHA LOGAN; which lot is in the possession of ROBERT JOHNSON by virtue of a title from JOSEPH WRAGG, merchant, of Charleston, as attorney for SAMUEL WRAGG, merchant, of London; the shape of the lot being represented on plat B attached to release. Witnesses: JOHN KING, JOHN BRAILSFORD. Before JAMES ABERCROMBY, J.P. NATHANIEL JOHNSON, P.R

Book Lb, p. 276 JOHN CHAPMAN, of Colleton Co., to JOSEPH
6 Dec. 1733 ELLIOT, son of WILLIAM ELLIOT, of Berkeley Co.,
Deed of Sale for L 2000, part of lot #25, granted to JOSEPH
ELLIOTT, grandfather of JOHN CHAPMAN, on 9 May
1694 by the Hon. THOMAS SMITH, Gov. & Trustee (recorded in Grant Book AA,
fol. 15); fronting 69 ft. on Church Street, & running back 229 ft. to
BEADON'S Street, butting 64 ft. on that street; S on JOHN BEE & WILLIAM
HARVEY; N on JOHN LLOYD & ANN SMITH. (Note: a later statement says "same
quantity of ft. front upon each street). Witnesses: EDWARD WEBB, THOMAS
ELLIOTT, JOHN MILNER. Before THOMAS DALE, J.P. NATHANIEL JOHNSON, Pub.
Reg.

Book Lb, p. 278 EPHRAIM MIKELL, planter, of Berkeley Co., to
22 Dec. 1729 CHARLES ODINGSELLS & PAUL GRIMBALL, executors
L & R by Mortgage of will of EPHRAIM MIKELL the elder, as security for the payment of several sums of money
(see below), 400 a. on Edisto Island, Berkeley Co., bounding N on ICHABOD
WINBOURN; E on THOMAS RAKE; S on the marsh of Governour's Creek; W on
marsh 7 JOSEPH PALMENTER. Whereas EPHRAIM MIKELL (party hereto) gave
bond this date to ODINGSELLS & GRIMBALL in the penal sum of L 4000 currency conditioned for the payment of several sums (L 275 each) with interest on 18 Feb. 1739, 18 Dec. 1744, 19 Apr. 1747, 24 Sept. 1749, for
the use of his sons, JOHN, the eldest; JOSEPH, the second; MIKELL (MIKELL)
the third; & BENJAMIN, the fourth; respectively; he secures the various
payments with the above mortgage. Witnesses: JAMES PARMENTER, JOSHUA
GRIMBALL, JOHN WELLS. Before THEOPHILUS GREGORY, J.P. NATHANIEL JOHNSON,
Pub. Reg.

Book Lb, p. 287 EPHRAIM MIKELL, planter, of Berkeley Co., to
22 Nov. 1729 CHARLES ODINGSELLS & PAUL GRIMBALL, planters,
Bond executors of will of EPHRAIM MIKELL, the elder,
in the penal sum of L 4000 currency condition-
ed for the payment of several sums (L 275 each) with interest on 18 Feb.
1739 for JOHN EPHRAIM'S eldest son (see p. 278) 18 Dec. 1744 for JOSEPH,
2nd son; 19 Apr. 1747 for MIKELL, 3rd son; 24 Sept. 1749, for BENJAMIN,
4th son. Witnesses: JAMES PARMENTER, JOSHUA GRIMBALL, JOHN WELLS. Before THEOPHILUS GREGORY, J.P. NATHANIEL JOHNSON, Pub. Reg.

Book Lb, p. 289 FRANCIS YONGE, ESQ., of St. Andrews Parish
10 Mar. 1732 appointed his beloved wife LYDIA & his cousin
Letter of Attorney ROBERT YONGE, ESQ., of St. Paul's Parish, his
attorneys, to handle his money, lands, Negroes,
etc. Witnesses: ANDREW RUTLEDGE, SARAH CARLOW. Before ELIAS FOISSIN,
JR., J.P. NATHANIEL JOHNSON, Pub. Reg.

Book Lb, p. 291 THOMAS BLYTHE, joiner, of Winyaw, to ISAAC
23 & 24 Jan. 1733 CHARDON, DANIEL LAROCHE & THOMAS LAROCHE, mer-
L & R by Mortgage chants, of Charleston, as security on his bond
to them dated 24 Jan. 1733 in penal sum of
L 438:13 SC money, conditioned for the payment of L 219:6 on 1 Oct. 1734,
conveys lot #116 in Georgetown containing 1/2 a., 100 ft. front & 217.9
ft. deep, bounding NE on Cross Broad Street; SE on an unnamed street; SW
on lot #115; also all his household furniture, kitchen utensils & tools
& timber (all listed); subject to redemption on 1 Oct. 1734. Witnesses:
WILLIAM COLT, ISAAC SECARE. Before WILLIAM WHITESIDE, J.P. NATHANIEL
JOHNSON, Pub. Reg.

Book Lb, p. 299 THOMAS BLYTHE, joiner, of Winyaw, to ISAAC
24 Jan. 1733 CHARDON, DANIEL LAROCHE, & THOMAS LAROCHE, mer-
Bond chants, in penal sum of L 438:13 currency conditioned for the payment of L 219:6 on 1 Oct.
1734. Witnesses: WILLIAM COLT, ISAAC SECARE. NATHANIEL JOHNSON, Pub.
Reg.

Book Lb, p. 301 CAPT. RICHARD SMITH, planter, & MARY his wife,
23 & 24 Jan. 1733 of Wineau, Craven Co., to ISAAC CHARDON, mer-
L & R chant, of Charleston, & DANIEL LAROCHE & THOM-
AS LAROCHE, merchants, of Georgetown, & ELIAS
FOISSIN, JR., gentleman, of Berkeley Co., for L 2450 currency, (to be
equally divided between them as tenants in common & not as joint tenants)

1800 a. on Cat Island at the mouth of Santee River, Craven Co., bounding NW on Landgrave THOMAS SMITH'S Barony; NE on said CAPT. SMITH; all other sides on marsh; also all the cattle & hogs (not less than 100) on Cat Island (except the working oxen). Whereas KING GEORGE II by letters patent dated 28 Apr. 1733, witnesses by Gov. ROBERT JOHNSON, granted CAPT. RICHARD SMITH 1800 a. in Craven Co. (as above), with the usual priviledges & reservations; now SMITH sells to the 4 men named above. Witnesses: JOSEPH WRAGG, NICHOLAS MAETLEYSENE (MAETEYSON), FREDERICK MEYER. Before WILLIAM SWINTON, J.P. NATHANIEL JOHNSON, Pub. Reg.

Book Lb, p. 311　　　　JONAS BONHOSTE, planter, of Seawee, Christ
29 Jan. 1733/4　　　　Church Parish, Berkeley Co., to WILLIAM PORTER,
Mortgage　　　　　　　nonconformist pastor & teacher, of Seawee, for
　　　　　　　　　　　divers good causes, 225 a. "on the front in
Seawee", between the lands of JOHN WELDON & SAMUEL SIBLEY, conditioned for the payment of ₺ 356 currency by BONHOSTE to PORTER within 4 years. Witnesses: JOHN (his mark) HUGGINS, JOHN BONHOSTE, JOHN (his mark) MURREL. Before ELIAS FOISSIN, JR., J.P. NATHANIEL JOHNSON, Pub. Reg.

Book Lb, p. 314　　　　SOLOMON LEGARE, goldsmith, & JOHN BOUNETHEAU,
9 & 10 Sept. 1731　　　cutler, to JOHN BRETON, merchant, all of
L & R　　　　　　　　　Charleston, for ₺ 300 currency paid to LEGARE
　　　　　　　　　　　by BRETON & ₺ 250 currency paid by LEGARE to
BOUNETHEAU, part of lot #163 in Charleston fronting S 48 ft. on Broad Street, & running back same breadth to S part lot #170; bounding W on WILLIAM GIBBON & ANDREW ALLEN; E on JOHN LEWIS (formerly STEPHEN TAUVRON); also part of lot #170, 48 ft. wide, bounding S on lot #163; & of such depth northerly as shall remain after 150 ft. are taken off the depth (said 150 ft. belonging to HENRY CHIDLY); W on WILLIAM GIBBON & ANDREW ALLEN; E on JOHN LEWIS (formerly STEPHEN TAUVRON). Whereas by L & R dated 28 & 29 Jan. 1730 JOHN BOUNETHEAU mortgaged to SOLOMON LEGARE, for ₺ 300 SC money, parts of lot 163 & 170 in Charleston; now LEGARE & BOUNETHEAU sell to BRETON for that amount. Witnesses: STEPHEN BEAUCHAMP, JOHN LEWIS. Before ANTHONY BONNEAU, J.P. NATHANIEL JOHNSON, Pub. Reg.

Book Lb, p. 323　　　　JONATHAN FITCH, planter, to ROGER SAUNDERS,
11 Oct. 1733　　　　　planter, both of St. Andrews Parish, N side
Lease　　　　　　　　Ashley River, for the yearly rent & other
　　　　　　　　　　agreements for the cleared land, houses, fences, etc. (except as excepted), part of 2 tracts given JONATHAN FITCH by his father JONATHAN FITCH & by his grandmother SUSANNA FITCH, containing 452-1/2 a., about 252-1/2 a. being cleared except 160 a. of wood land now in dispute between JONATHAN FITCH & RALPH IZARD, it being part of the 2 tracts. SAUNDERS to pay FITCH ₺ 10 proclamation money or its value in currency; & not to be wasteful. Should there be an Indian War & FITCH be forced to fly from the plantation he is now settling on (S of Stono) then FITCH to have the 50 a. joining the head of 70 a. SAUNDERS now lives on as long as necessary; the 50 a. of same breadth as the 70 a. & down to PINCKNEYS line. Further agreed, that should SAUNDERS die before end of term, FITCH to repossess. Witnesses: EDWARD DOYELL, JOHN MASON. Before ALEXANDER PARRIS, J.P. NATHANIEL JOHNSON, Pub. Reg.

Book Lb, p. 327　　　　JOSEPH ELLIOTT, planter, & EDITH his wife, of
6 Mar. 1733/4　　　　　Berkeley Co., to SAMUEL & WILLIAM JACKSON,
Deed of Sale　　　　　planters, of Colleton Co., for 10 shillings
　　　　　　　　　　　currency, 100 a. on E side Ashepoo River,
bounding E on WILLIAM OSWILL; S on SAMUEL & WILLIAM JACKSON; W on HENRY JACKSON; N on DAVID ALLIEN. Witnesses: JOHN COOK, JOSEPH JACKSON. Before WILLIAM LIVINGSTON, J.P. NATHANIEL JOHNSON, Pub. Reg.

Book Lb, p. 330　　　　JOSEPH BUTLER, planter of Berkeley Co., & MARY
12 & 13 Feb. 1733　　　his wife (late MARY LAROCHE, daughter & devi-
L & R　　　　　　　　　see of JAMES LAROCHE, planter of Charleston),
　　　　　　　　　　　to ROBERT STEELE, tanner, of Charleston, for
₺ 1000 currency, lot #195 in Charleston, bounding E on the great street leading from Ashley River to & through the Market Place; W on ISAAC WOODWARD (PEEDWOOD); S on WILLIAM YEOMANS (formerly JOHN HILL); N on a marsh. Whereas the Lords Proprs. granted JOHN HILL lot #195 in Charleston; & whereas JOHN HILL, son & heir of said JOHN, by deed of feoffment dated 20 Feb. 1718 sold the lot to JAMES LAROCHE, who, by will dated 14 Dec. 1719

bequeathed the lot to his daughter MARY; now MARY & her husband sell to STEELE. Witnesses: ALBERT DETMAR, SARAH HALL, CHRISTIAN (her mark) DETMER, NICHOLAS BURNHAM, CHARLEST PINCKNEY. NATHANIEL JOHNSON, Pub. Reg.

Book Lb, p. 338
2 Mar. 1733/4
Mortgage

THOMAS RIVERS, planter, of St. Andrews Parish, to WILLIAM CATTELL, as security on bond dated 24 Apr. 1733, in penal sum of ₤ 357:10:11-1/2, conditioned for the payment of ₤ 178:15:5:3 also as security on another bond of this date in penal sum of ₤ 485:6:6 conditioned for the payment of ₤ 242:13:3 conveys 175 a. (purchased by THOMAS RIVERS the elder, the purchase receipt dated 15 Sept. 1705 & other papers being held be CATTELL); bounding N on Cuppain Creek by WILLIAM CLAY'S land; S on WILLIAM ELLIOTT; E on THOMAS HOLMAN; W on SAMUEL JONES; conditioned that RIVERS pay CATTELL ₤ 421:9:2:3 currency with interest by 3 Mar. 1734/5. Witnesses: WILLIAM GEORGE FREEMAN, WILLIAM MEYRICK. Before THOMAS DALE, J.P. NATHANIEL JOHNSON, Pub. Reg.

Book Lb, p. 342
12 Jan. 1733/4
Mortgage

EDWARD (his mark) HUSSEY, inn-keeper, of St. Andrews Parish, on N side Ashley River, to JOHN MASON, schoolmaster & CHRISTIAN his wife, of same place, for ₤ 68 currency 13 a. on N side Ashley River, bounding on WILLIAM FULLER, on the Broad Path, & on JOHN HEIVSON. Whereas RICHARD RANDALL, planter, of St. Pauls Parish, Stono, & HANNAH his wife on the 2nd of this inst. sold the above 13 a. to HUSSEY, to hold during the natural life of HANNAH RANDALL; (see p. 345) now HUSSEY sells to MASON. Witnesses: THOMAS HAMILTON, THOMAS ARCHBALD. NATHANIEL JOHNSON, Pub. Reg.

Book Lb, p. 345
2 Jan. 1733/4
Mortgage

(See p. 342). RICHARD RANDAL (GLANDAL?) planter, & HANNAH his wife, to EDWARD HUSSEY, inn-keeper, all of St. Paul's Parish, Berkeley Co., for ₤ 65 currency, 13 a. on N side Ashley River, bounding on WILLIAM FULLER on the Broad Path, & on JOHN HEWSON; for the term of HANNAH'S natural life. Witnesses: JOSEPH WILLIAMS, THOMAS HAMILTON. NATHANIEL JOHNSON, Pub. Reg.

Book Lb, p. 348
12 Jan. 1733/4
Deed of Sale

EDWARD (his mark) HUSSEY (see pages 342 & 345) to JOHN MASON & CHRISTIAN his wife, for ₤ 68 currency, all his claim to the above land & to 1 bond of even date signed by RICHARD RANDALL & HANNAH his wife. Witnesses: THOMAS HAMILTON, THOMAS ARCHBALD. Before THEOPHILUS GREGORY, J.P. NATHANIEL JOHNSON, Pub. Reg.

DEEDS BOOK "M"
Apr. 1734 - Nov. 1734

Book M, p. 1
24 Feb. 1715
Deed of Sale

SAMUEL WAY, SR., planter, of Dorchester, Berkeley Co., to THOMAS WAY, house carpenter, for a valuable sum, 50 a. (except 1/2 a.) between the old landing path & HENRY WAY, in Dorchester, bounding E on HENRY WAY; S on Ashley River; W on PETER SAVEY; N on THOMAS OSGOOD & WILLIAM PRATT; which 50 a. was conveyed by HENRY WAY on 5 Sept. 1711 to SAMUEL WAY. Signed by SAMUEL WAY & RACHEL (her mark) WAY. Witnesses: AARON WAY, HENRY WAY, NATHANIEL SUMNER (according to their profession). Before THOMAS SATUR, J.P. NATHANIEL JOHNSON, Register.

Book M, p. 4
11 & 12 Mar. 1733
L & R

CAPT. JAMES LLOYD, commander of H.M. sloop (scow) The Happy, to RICHARD LAKE, ESQ., of Island of Barbadoes, for ₤ 300 SC money & other considerations, 1266 a. in Colleton Co., granted by Gov. ROBERT JOHNSON to LLOYD. Witnesses: JAMES WEDDERBURN, JOHN BRAILSFORD. Before JAMES ABERCROMBY, J.P. NATHANIEL JOHNSON, Register.

Book M, p. 10
11 July 1733
Grant

Gov. ROBERT JOHNSON, to JAMES LLOYD, commander of H.M. sloop Happy, 1266 a. in Colleton Co., with the usual provisoes & conditions. J.

BADENHOP, C.C. Land surveyed 8 Mar. 1731; certified 14 Mar. 1732, by JAMES ST. JOHN, Sur. Gen. NATHANIEL JOHNSON, Register.

Book M, p. 12　　　　　　　SAMUEL (his mark) WHELDON, of St. James Santee,
3 June 1731　　　　　　　　Craven Co., to his loving cousins, SARAH WHEL-
Deed of Gift　　　　　　　 DON & ANN WHELDON, for love & affection (un-
　　　　　　　　　　　　　less he marries), all his interest, tenements,
fields, etc. Witnesses: JOHN SLOMAN, SEARAH SOLOMAN. Before NOAH SERRE.
NATHANIEL JOHNSON, Register.

Book M, p. 14　　　　　　　DANIEL CARTWRIGHT, gentleman, & SARAH his wife,
28 Feb. & 1 Mar. 1733/4　 to CHARLES CRUBIN, planter, all of Berkeley
L & R　　　　　　　　　　　Co., for ₤ 100 SC money, lot #95 containing
　　　　　　　　　　　　　1/4 a. in Ashley River Ferry Town, called Butler's Town, bounding NE on lot #94, SW on lot #96; SE on lot #86; NW on a
street leading to Ashley River. Witnesses: WILLIAM SAXBY, JR., THOMAS
GOREING. Before THEOPHILUS GREGORY, J.P. NATHANIEL JOHNSON, Register.

Book M, p. 20　　　　　　　JAMES SEARLES, victualer, & CHRISTINA his wife,
26 & 27 Mar. 1734　　　　 of Christ Church Parish, to JOHN GASCOIGNE,
L & R by Mortgage　　　　 Captain of H.M.S. The Alborough, now in
　　　　　　　　　　　　　Charleston harbor, for ₤ 1000 (?) SC money,
17 a. known as Hog Island, also as Mount Edgecombe. Whereas WILLIAM,
Earl of Craven & the Lords Proprs. on 12 Sept. 1694 granted Landgrave
EDMUND BELLINGER of Berkeley Co. 17 a., English measure, called Hog Island, bounding N on Hog Island Creek; S on Sullivants Creek; E & W on
marsh (grant recorded in old Grant Book #1, fol. 401 & 402); & whereas on
23 Mar. 1708 ELIZABETH BELLINGER, widow of EDMUND, sold the 17 a. to ALEX-
ANDER PARRIS, ESQ., of Charleston; & whereas by L & R tripartite dated 3
& 4 Mar. 1730 between ALEXANDER PARRIS & MARY his wife of 1st part; JONAH
COLLINS, planter, of Craven Co., of 2nd part; & JOHN GASCOIGNE, Captain
of the Alborough of 3rd part; PARRIS & COLLINS conveyed Hog Island (now
called Mount Edge Combe) to GASCOIGNE (see Bk I, fol. 213, & 221 & a
memorial in auditor's office in old Grant Bk. #1, fol. 398 & 399); whereas on 26 & 27 Mar. 1734 said GASCOIGNE conveyed the land to JAMES SEARLES;
now SEARLES conveys to GASCOIGNE on the condition that should SEARLES pay
GASCOIGNE ₤ 142:17:1:3 British money in certain portions at certain times,
& keep all his agreements this mortgage to be void. Witnesses: JOHN WAT-
SON, SOLOMON MIDDLETON. Before THEOPHILUS GREGORY, J.P. NATHANIAL JOHN-
SON, Register.

Book M, p. 32　　　　　　　THOMAS RIVERS, of Berkeley Co., to CHARLES
14 Mar. 1733/4　　　　　　JONES, for ₤ 220 currency, 1 Negro man. Wit-
Deed of Sale　　　　　　　nesses: ROBERT EDGELL, RICHARD CLAY. Before
　　　　　　　　　　　　　THOMAS DRAYTON, J.P. NATHANIEL JOHNSON, Register.

Book M, p. 33　　　　　　　SAMUEL WEST, planter, of Berkeley Co., to his
8 Apr. 1734　　　　　　　　beloved brother WILLOBE WEST, for natural love
Deed of Gift　　　　　　　& affection & other considerations, 100 a.,
　　　　　　　　　　　　　part of 250 a. purchased 27 Mar. 1734 by his
father, SAMUEL WEST, from FRANCIS LADSON; the 100 a. bounding N on FRAN-
CIS LADSON; E on CHARLES WEST; S & W on STEPHEN DRAYTON. Delivery by
turf & twig. Witnesses: JOSHUA TOOMER, THOMAS BUTLER, ELISHA BUTLER.
Before WILLIAM CATTELL, J.P. NATHANIEL JOHNSON, Pub. Reg.

Book M, p. 35　　　　　　　SAMUEL WEST, planter, of Berkeley Co., to his
8 Apr. 1734　　　　　　　　beloved brother CHARLES WEST, for natural love
Deed of Gift　　　　　　　& affection & other considerations, 100 a.,
　　　　　　　　　　　　　part of 250 a. purchased 27 Mar. 1724 by SAM-
UEL WEST his father, from FRANCIS LADSON; the 100 a. bounding E on RICH-
ARD BUTLER; W & S on WILLOBE WEST; N on FRANCIS LADSON. Delivery by turf
& twig. Witnesses: JOSHUA TOOMER, THOMAS BUTLER, ELISHA BUTLER. Before
WILLIAM CATTELL, J.P. NATHANIEL JOHNSON, Register.

Book M, p. 37　　　　　　　JAMES SEARLES, victualer & periagua man, of
27 Mar. 1734　　　　　　　 Christ Church Parish, Berkeley Co., to CAPT.
Bond　　　　　　　　　　　 JOHN GASCOIGNE, commander of H.M.S. The Al-
　　　　　　　　　　　　　borough (see p. 20) now in Charleston harbor,
in penal sum of ₤ 285:14:3-1/2 British money, conditioned for the payment

of ₺ 142:17:1:3 like money, or its value, in certain portions on certain dates & also conditioned on keeping certain agreements. Witnesses: JOHN WATSON, SOLOMON MIDDLETON. NATHANIEL JOHNSON, Register.

Book M, p. 41
8 & 9 Apr. 1734
L & R

The Hon. THOMAS BROUGHTON, ESQ., of Berkeley Co., to Gov. ROBERT JOHNSON, for ₺ 3000 currency, a tract of 920 a. & a tract of 210 a. Whereas JOHN, Lord Granville, Palatine; WILLIAM, Lord Craven; JOHN, Lord Carteret; MAURICE ASHLEY, SIR JOHN COLLETON, Baronet, & the Lords Proprs. by grant dated 20 Mar. 1705, & signed by NATHANIEL JOHNSON, JAMES MOORE & NICHOLAS TROTT, conveyed to THOMAS BROUGHTON 920 a., English measure, in Berkeley Co., & by grant dated 12 June 1709 & witnessed by NATHANIEL JOHNSON, THOMAS BROUGHTON, JOHN ASHBEY, & HENRY NOBLE, the Lords Proprs., gave THOMAS BROUGHTON another tract of 210 a. in Berkeley Co.; now BROUGHTON sells the 2 tracts to JOHNSON; the 920 a. bounding SW on "Wal-hu-wa" owned by ROBERT JOHNSON (formerly SIR NATHANIEL JOHNSON); other sides on vacant land; the 210 a. bounding SE on SAMUEL KING; NW on THOMAS BROUGHTON; NE on vacant land. Witnesses: THOMAS MONCK, GABRIEL MANIGAULT, CHARLES PINCKNEY. Before THEOPHILUS GREGORY, J.P. NATHANIEL JOHNSON, Register.

Book M, p. 50
20 Mar. 1705
Grant

Whereas his Excellency JOHN, Lord Granville, Palatine; WILLIAM, Lord Craven; JOHN, Lord Carteret; MAURICE ASHLEY, ESQ., SIR JOHN COLLETON, Baronet, & the Lords Proprs. by their commission dated 18 June 1702 impowered the Rt. Hon. SIR NATHANIEL JOHNSON, Knight, Gov. of SC & NC, JAMES MOORE, NICHOLAS TROTT & JOB HOWES, ESQ., or any 3 of them to grant land; therefore, NATHANIEL JOHNSON, JAMES MOORE & NICHOLAS TROTT, for ₺ 18:8 granted the Hon. THOMAS BROUGHTON 920 a., English measure, in Berkeley Co., with the usual provisoes. NATHANIEL JOHNSON, Pub. Reg.

Book M, p. 51
12 June 1709
Grant

Whereas his Excellency JOHN, Lord Granville, Palatine; WILLIAM, Lord Craven; JOHN, Lord Carteret; MAURICE ASHLEY, ESQ., SIR JOHN COLLETON, Baronet, & the Lords Proprs. by their commission dated 8 Mar. 1706/7, impowered the Rt. Hon. SIR NATHANIEL JOHNSON, Knight, Gov., etc., the Hon. NICHOLAS TROTT, THOMAS BROUGHTON, ROBERT GIBBS, HENRY NOBLE, & JOHN ASHBY, ESQRS., or any 3 of them to grant land; therefore, THOMAS BROUGHTON, JOHN ASHBY & HENRY NOBLE, for ₺ 4:4 granted THOMAS BROUGHTON 210 a., English measure, in Berkeley Co., with the usual provisoes. NATHANIEL JOHNSON, Pub. Reg.

Book M, p. 52
16 & 17 Apr. 1734
L & R

GIDEON FAUCHERAUD, planter, & MARY his wife, with MARY'S consent, to his nephew, ABRAHAM DUPONT, planter, all of Berkeley Co., for natural love & affection, & 5 shillings proclamation money, 500 a., English measure, in Berkeley Co., on Wilkinsons Swamp, bounding SW on DANIEL DEAN; all other sides on vacant land. MARY voluntarily relinquished all her claim. Witnesses: THEODORE CHATAIGNER, MARY FITCH, TOBIAS FITCH. Before ISAAC PORCHER, J.P. NATHANIEL JOHNSON, Register.

Book M, p. 60
24 Apr. 1734
Letter of Attorney

JOHN GASCOIGNE, captain of H.M.S The Alborough now in Charleston Harbor, appoints his friend THOMAS GADSDEN, ESQ., of Charleston, his attorney, with full power. Witnesses: JOHN REYNOLDS, SAMUEL BROWNE. Before THOMAS DALE, J.P. NATHANIEL JOHNSON, Pub. Reg.

Book M, p. 61
17 & 18 Apr. 1734
L & R

JONATHAN FITCH, planter, to RALPH IZARD, ESQ., both of Berkeley Co., for ₺ 1100 SC money, 160 a. (part of 250 a.), bounding N on "Jeffords Land" owned by Landgrave THOMAS SMITH, according to line run by ARTHUR MIDDLETON; E on IZARD (formerly HINROYDA ENGLISH); S on IZARD (formerly THOMAS PINCKNEY); W on JONATHAN FITCH. Whereas the Hon. SIR NATHANIEL JOHNSON, Knight, Gov., etc., THOMAS BROUGHTON & NICHOLAS TROTT, commanders, on 1 May 1708, granted WILLIAM WILLIAMS 250 a., English measure, bounding N on Landgrave THOMAS SMITH; E on RALPH IZARD (formerly CHRISTOPHER SMITH); S on RALPH IZARD (formerly THOMAS

PINCKNEY); W on THOMAS FITCH (formerly MR. CHAPMAN) & JONATHAN FITCH (formerly ANDREW RUSS); & whereas WILLIAM WILLIAMS by will dated 2 Nov. 1710 bequeathed his real estate to HINROYDA ENGLISH, gentleman, who, by deed of feoffment dated 17 Sept. 1712 conveyed the 250 a. to EBENEZER TAYLOR, gentleman; & whereas TAYLOR, by deed of feoffment dated 12 Oct. 1714 conveyed the land to JONATHAN FITCH (grandfather of JONATHAN, party hereto), who by will dated 4 Nov. 1715, after several legacies, bequeathed the residue of his real & personal estate to be equally divided between his wife SUSANNAH FITCH & his son JOSEPH FITCH; & whereas JOSEPH FITCH & his wife CONSTANT, by deed poll dated 16 Oct. 1724, conveyed to his brother JONATHAN (father of JONATHAN, party hereto) his half of the 250 a., & whereas JONATHAN, the father by will dated 24 Oct. 1723, bequeathed to his son JONATHAN all the tract he bought from his brother JOSEPH (1/2 the 250 a.) which joins the tract belonging to his mother SUSANNAH FITCH (part of same tract devised to her by her husband); & whereas SUSANNAH (grandmother of this JONATHAN) by deed of gift dated 21 Mar. 1725 gave her grandson (JONATHAN) the plantation on which she lived, left her by her husband; & whereas JONATHAN (by his father's will & grandmother's gift) became owner of all the 250 a., now he sells 160 a. (a part) to RALPH IZARD. Should a re-survey show that the present platt appears to fall short FITCH agrees to pay IZARD L 8 currency per a. for every a. short. Witnesses: LUKE STOUTENBURGH, RICHARD ALLEIN, RALPH IZARD. Before THOMAS DALE, J.P. NATHANIEL JOHNSON, Pub. Reg.

Book M, p. 72　　　　　　　JOHN NEWTON, of Colleton Co., to EDWARD ROL-
2 Feb. 1733/4　　　　　　　INGS, 200 a. on N side of plot called Long
Deed of Gift　　　　　　　 Pine Barren. One pepper corn delivered. Witnesses: JOHN EGLEN, ANDREW (his mark) MILLER.
Before JAMES FERGUSON, J.P.　NATHANIEL JOHNSON, REgister.

Book M, p. 73　　　　　　　WILLIAM (his mark) CARLILE, tanner, of Colle-
3 Aug. 1720　　　　　　　　 ton Co., with the unconstrained consent of his
Deed of Sale　　　　　　　 wife ANN, to CAPT. HENRY NICHOLAS, for L 80 currency, 200 a. in Colleton Co., bounding N on JOHN CATTLE; other parts on CAPT. HENRY NICHOLAS. Whereas JOHN, Lord Granville, & the Lords Proprs. by 2 grants dated 2 Oct. 1704 granted WILLIAM CARLILE 2 adjoining tracts of 500 a. & 200 a.; now CARLILE & his wife sells 2 adjoining tracts (100 a. from each of the above tracts) to NICHOLAS. Witnesses: ROBERT STEVENS, MORRICE (his mark) WILLIAMS, J. WELLS; STEPHEN (his mark) FORD, JR., STEPHEN FORD, ST. Delivery by turf & twig. Before ROBERT YONGE, J.P. NATHANIEL JOHNSON, Register.

Book M, p. 76　　　　　　　HENRY GIGNILLIAT, vintner, & HESTER his wife,
14 & 15 Apr. 1734　　　　　to JOSEPH WRAGG, merchant, all of Charleston,
L & R by Mortgage　　　　　for L 4011:16:4 SC money, 1/4 lot #43 in Charleston, fronting E 25 ft. on Church Street; bounding W on PETER DE ST. JULIEN; N 142 ft. on ELIZABETH DEMARIS DE ST. JULIEN, widow; S on ISAAC MAZYCK, SR., merchant; also 50 a. in Berkeley Co., bounding N & S on STEPHEN BULLOCK; E on THOMAS FITZGERALD; W on a creek of Wando River; also 50 a. in Bermuda Town, Berkeley Co., bounding S on WILLIAM FISHER; W on a creek of Wando River; N on THOMAS ALLEN; E on THOMAS FITZGERALD; conditioned for the repayment of above sum, with interest, on 1 Jan. next. HESTER to renounce her title within 6 months. Witnesses: ROWLAND VAUGHAN, WILLIAM ROMSEY. Before THEOPHILUS GREGORY, J.P. NATHANIEL JOHNSON, Register.

Book M, p. 85　　　　　　　CHARLES WALKER, mariner, formerly of Island of
26 & 27 Apr. 1734　　　　　Jamaica, now of Charleston, & ANNA his wife,
L & R　　　　　　　　　　　to JOHN ATKIN, merchant, of Charleston, for L 500 sterling of Great Britain, all his real estate in Jamaica or elsewhere, which CHARLES or ANNA own by settlement made by JAMES CALLENDER in his lifetime or by his will. Whereas JAMES CALLENDER, of Parish of St. Elizabeth, Island of Jamaica, father of said ANNA WALKER, by will dated 5 Oct. 1727, after other bequests, gave the residue of his real & personal estate to daughter ANNA, now they sell to ATKIN. Witnesses: THOMAS WALKER, MATHEW NEUISON (?), BENJAMIN APPELBEY. Before ALEXANDER PARRIS, J.P. Before THOMAS WALKER, J.P. NATHANIEL JOHNSON, Register.

Book M, p. 91　　　　　　　ROGER SUMNER, planter, of Berkeley Co., to

2 July 1733   RICHARD BAKER, cooper, of same county, for
Deed of Sale   Ł 350 SC money, 2 tracts of land. Whereas Gov.
                            ROBERT GIBBES & the Lords Proprs. on 23 July
1711 granted ROGER SUMNER 250 a. in Berkeley Co., bounding NE on MICHAEL
BACON; other sides on vacant land; & whereas MICHAEL BACON, planter, of
Berkeley Co., on 18 Aug. 1718 conveyed to ROGER SUMNER 50 a., (50 ch. l.,
10 ch. w.) in Berkeley Co., bounding NE & NW on MICHAEL BACON; SE on THOM-
AS SNOW; SW on the above 250 a.; & whereas the 2 tracts are really in Col-
leton Co. & not in Berkeley Co.; now SUMNER sells the 2 tracts to RICHARD
BAKER. Witnesses: NATHANIEL WAY, THOMAS WAY. Before THOMAS WARING, J.P.
NATHANIEL JOHNSON, Register.

Book M, p. 96   JOHN ATKIN, merchant, of Charleston, to
9 & 10 May 1734   CHARLES WALKER, mariner, formerly of Island of
L & R   Jamaica, now of Charleston, for Ł 500 sterling
                            of Great Britain, all the lands (see p. 85)
which JAMES CALLENDER bequeathed to his daughter ANNA, wife of CHARLES
WALKER, which lands CHARLES & ANNA WALKER had conveyed to JOHN ATKIN by L
& R dated 26 & 27 Apr. 1734. Witnesses: JOHN RINIERE, ARTHUR GREEN. Before ALEXANDER PARRIS, J.P. NATHANIEL JOHNSON, Pub. Reg.

Book M, p. 103   SARAH HALL, widow, to CRAFTON KARWON, planter,
23 Feb. 1733   both of John's Island, Colleton Co., for
Release   Ł 2000 SC money, 325 a. on N side A B Poolaw
                            Creek, St. Paul's Parish, John's Island, bound-
ing E on CAPT. THOMAS FLEMING. Witnesses: THOMAS WISE, ANN FLACK. Before THEOPHILUS GREGORY, J.P. NATHANIEL JOHNSON, Register.

Book M, p. 108   CRAFTON KARWON, planter, of Johns Island, Col-
31 Mar. 1734   leton Co., to JOHN WHITFIELD, merchant, of St.
Mortgage   Philip's Parish, Charleston, as security for
                            the payment of several sums, 325 a. on N side
of A B Poolaw Creek, Johns Island, St. Paul's Parish, bounding E on CAPT.
THOMAS FLEMING. Whereas the Lords Proprs. on 11 Jan. 1700, for Ł 4 currency, granted WILLIAM BROCK 200 a., English measure, in Colleton Co., &
on 17 Aug. 1700 for Ł 9 they granted him 450 a., English measure; & whereas BROCK died intestate & his only daughter, SARAH, interited the 650 a.
& afterwards married JOHN WILKINS, planter; & whereas after SARAH WIL-
KINS'S death her 2 daughters, SARAH & ELIZABETH became co-heirs; & whereas ELIZABETH died & SARAH became sole owner, & later married MR. HALL; &
whereas by L & R dated 22 & 23 Feb. 1733 (p. 103) SARAH HALL sold 325 a.
to CRAFTON KARWON for Ł 2000 currency; & whereas KARWON, gave bond this
date to JOHN WHITFIELD in the penal sum of Ł 2000 conditioned for the
payment of Ł 600 on 31 Mar. 1735 & Ł 550 on 31 Mar. 1736; now, as security, KARWON conveys the 325 a. to WHITFIELD; the other 325 a. having been
conveyed by SARAH HALL to THOMAS FLEMMING. Witnesses: BENJAMIN WHITAKER,
WILLIAM G. FREEMAN. Before THOMAS DALE, J.P. NATHANIEL JOHNSON, Register. Mortgage satisfied 6 May 1736. Witness: JOHN PONNYMEAN. NATHANIEL
JOHNSON, Register.

Book M, p. 120   SAMUEL DRAKE, to WILLIAM SCREVEN, planter, in
25 July 1733   penal sum of Ł 5000 currency conditioned for
Bond   keeping all agreements in a Bill of Sale of
                            this date. Witnesses: JOHN WITTER, JOSEPH ATT-
WELL, BENJAMIN ATTWELL, HENRY SAMWAYS. Before THOMAS DALE, J.P. NATHAN-
IEL JOHNSON, Register.

Book M, p. 121   SAMUEL DRAKE, planter, & MARY (her mark) his
25 July 1733   wife, to WILLIAM SCREVEN, planter, all of
L & R   Berkeley Co., for Ł 2500 SC money, 170 a. on
                            James Island, bounding N on a branch of New
Town Creek; W on SAMUEL SCREVEN; S on JOHN WITTER; E on JOHN WITTER &
JOSEPH ATWELL. Witnesses: JOHN WITTER, JOSEPH ATTWELL, BENJAMIN ATTWELL,
HENRY SAMWAYS. Before THOMAS DALE, J.P. NATHANIEL JOHNSON, Pub. Reg.

Book M, p. 123   DANIEL CARTWRIGHT, gentleman, & SARAH his wife,
26 Feb. & 1 Mar. 1733/4   to JOHN WOOD, planter, all of Berkeley Co.,
L & R   for Ł 100 SC money, lot #96 in Ashley River
                            Ferry Town, called Butler's Town, containing
1/4 a., bounding NE on lot #95; SW on a street leading to the Ferry Path;

SE on lot #87; NW on a street leading to Ashley River. Witnesses: WILLIAM SAXBY, JR., CHARLES CRUBIN. Before THEOPHILUS GREGORY, J.P. NATHANIEL JOHNSON, Register.

Book M, p. 136
4 Dec. 1733
Deed of Gift

WILLIAM PARROTT, planter, & ANN his wife, of James Island, to their daughter ANN, wife of ROBERT RIVERS, JR. (son of ROBERT RIVERS, master mariner), for love & affection, 50 a., part of 100 a. where WILLIAM PARROTT lives, bounding S on the Sound; W on a small creek & adjoining 6 chains on CAPT. ROBERT RIVERS; E on marsh & creek; N on the remaining 50 a. (to go a straight course between E & S). Witnesses: JOSEPH RIVERS, STEPHEN RUSSELL, ALEXANDER SPENCER. Before THEOPHILUS GREGORY, J.P. NATHANIEL JOHNSON, Register.

Book M, p. 139
30 & 31 May 1734
L & R by Mortgage

DANIEL PEPPER, gentleman, to MARTHA MURRAY, widow, both of Berkeley Co., as security on a bond of even date in penal sum of ₺ 1660 currency, conditioned for the payment of ₺ 880 currency on L7 Jan. next, 50 a. in Berkeley Co., bounding E on SAMUEL WAY (formerly RALPH IZARD); S on Ashley River; W on JOHN STEVENS; N by a line between 1st & 2nd range. MARY PEPPER voluntarily releases her title of dower. Witnesses: JOSEPH BLAKE, THOMAS BURNLEY. Before THOMAS WARING, J.P. NATHANIEL JOHNSON, Register.

Book M, p. 147
11 & 12 June 1734
L & R

JOB HOWES, planter, of St. James Goosecreek, to BENJAMIN COACHMAN, planter, of Berkeley Co., for ₺ 500 SC money, 500 a. on N side Four Hole Swamp, bounding on all sides on vacant land. Witnesses: JOHN MOORE, CHARLES PINCKNEY. Before CHARLES PINCKNEY, J.P. NATHANIEL JOHNSON, Register.

Book M, p. 153
24 Aug. 1734
Deed of Sale

JAMES PAINE, to SOLOMON LEGARE, SR., for ₺ 10 SC money, 100 a. according to plat. Witnesses: BENJAMIN CATTLE, (CATTELL), JAMES TANNER, THOMAS SMITH. Before HENRY GIBBES, J.P. NATHANIEL JOHNSON, Register.

Book M, p. 155
21 & 22 June 1734
L & R

WILLIAM HOLMAN, planter, to WILLIAM MILES, planter, both of Berkeley Co., for ₺ 1100 currency, 103 a. (part of 215 a.) in St. Andrews Parish, Berkeley Co., on S side Copain Creek, bounding SW on THOMAS RIVERS; S on WALTER HOLMAN; E & N on WILLIAM MILES. Whereas the Lords Proprs. on 28 Aug. 1704 granted THOMAS HOLMAN, planter of Berkeley Co., father of WILLIAM, 215 a., bounding W on THOMAS RIVERS; E on Great Tupelaw Swamp; N on marshes of Copain Creek; & whereas by will dated 26 Sept. 1730 THOMAS HOLMAN bequeathed the land to his 3 sons, WILLIAM, THOMAS, & WALTER, to be equally divided, & the above 103 a. was allotted to WILLIAM; now WILLIAM sells to MILES. Witnesses: RICHARD PARRY, ROBERT BREWTON, JR., CHARLES PINCKNEY. Before HENRY GIBBES, J.P. WILLIAM HOLMAN'S confirmation of plat witnesses by JOHN MAN, LEWIS LA FONTAINE. NATHANIEL JOHNSON, Register.

Book M, p. 163
6 & 7 Mar. 1733
L & R

JOSEPH WRAGG, JAMES CROKATT, CHARLES HILL & ISAAC CHARDON, merchants, of Charleston, to JOHN RIGG, merchant, of Charleston, for ₺ 1535 SC money, part of lot #32 in Charleston, with all the front of the lot from the walls of the fortifications down to low water mark, fronting E 50 ft. on Cooper River, bounding N on Gov. ROBERT JOHNSON (formerly SAMUEL WRAGG); S on execrs. of MATHEW PORTER; W on widow of MATHEW PORTER. Witnesses: FRANCIS HOLMES, BENJAMIN SMITH, JOHN LLOYD. Before HENRY GIBBES, J.P. NATHANIEL JOHNSON, Register.

Book M, p. 170
26 & 27 Aug. 1734
L & R

JOHN RIGG, merchant, to JAMES CROKATT, merchant, both of Charleston, for ₺ 1535 currency, part of lot #32 in Charleston with all the front from the walls of the fortifications to low water mark, fronting E 50 ft. on Cooper River, bounding N on Gov. ROBERT JOHNSON (formerly SAMUEL WRAGG); S & W on MILES BREWTON (formerly MATHEW PORTER). Witnesses: JOHN LINING, JOHN LLOYD, CHARLES PINCKNEY. Before HENRY GIBBES, J.P. NATHANIEL JOHNSON, Register.

Book M, p. 175　　　　　　　JAMES CROCKATT, merchant, & ESTHER his wife,
27 & 28 Aug. 1734　　　　　 to Gov. ROBERT JOHNSON, all of Charleston, for
L & R　　　　　　　　　　　 Ł 1750 currency, part of lot #32 in Charleston,
　　　　　　　　　　　　　　with all the front part from the walls of the
fortifications to low water mark, fronting E 50 ft. on Cooper River &
bounding N on Gov. ROBERT JOHNSON (formerly SAMUEL WRAGG); S & W on MILES
BREWTON (formerly MATHEW PORTER); cleared of the dower of ESTHER CROKATT.
Witnesses: JOHN RIGG, JOHN LINING, JOHN LLOYD, CHARLES PINCKNEY. Before
HENRY GIBBES, J.P. NATHANIEL JOHNSON, Register.

Book M, p. 181　　　　　　　DANIEL GIBSON, chirurgeon, of Charleston, to
4 & 5 Sept. 1734　　　　　　BENJAMIN DELA CONSEILLERE, ESQ., as security
L & R by Mortgage　　　　　 on bond of even date in penal sum of Ł 4624
　　　　　　　　　　　　　　currency, conditioned for the payment of
Ł 2312 on 10 Nov. next, 2 sixth parts of Schenckingh's Square in Charleston, bounding E on a street on which the Presbyterian Meeting-house is
built; W on another street from Ashley River; S on MATHURINE BOIGARD; N
on COL. GEORGE CHICKEN; all of which Square was conveyed by BENJAMIN
SCHENCKINGH, ESQ. to COL. ABRAHAM EVE; & 1 of the sixth parts was conveyed by ABRAHAM EVE to DANIEL GIBSON; another sixth part to BENJAMIN WHIT-
AKER who conveyed it to DANIEL GIBSON; also the 2 dwelling houses, etc.;
the premises being free & clear except for 1 mortgage in fee CAPT. JOHN
CARUTHERS. ANNE, wife of DANIEL GIBSON, to renounce her dower within 1
month. Witnesses: JOHN WHITFIELD, WILLIAM GEORGE FREEMAN. Before ALEX-
ANDER PARRIS, J.P. NATHANIEL JOHNSON, Pub. Reg.

Book M, p. 187　　　　　　　DANIEL GIBSON, surgeon, of Charleston (after
5 Sept. 1734　　　　　　　　his death) to his loving wife ANN, for affec-
Deed of Gift　　　　　　　　tion & love & in "regard to her great industry
　　　　　　　　　　　　　　in my worldly affairs," & other causes, 2 Negro girls. Witnesses: WILLIAM HORNBY, ROBERT SHAW. NATHANIEL JOHNSON,
Register.

Book M, p. 188　　　　　　　DANIEL GIBSON, surgeon, of Charleston (after
5 Sept. 1734　　　　　　　　his death) to his loving wife ANN, for affec-
Deed of Gift　　　　　　　　tion & love & in "regard to her great industry
　　　　　　　　　　　　　　in my worldly affairs," & other causes, 18 a.
in Berkeley Co. about 2 miles up the Broad Path from Charleston, plat dated 11 May 1794 (?). Witnesses: WILLIAM HORNBY, ROBERT SHAW. NATHANIEL
JOHNSON, Register.

Book M, p. 190　　　　　　　THOMAS RIVERS, planter, to JOHN RIVERS, plant-
15 Mar. 1733　　　　　　　　er, both of Berkeley Co., for Ł 900 currency,
Deed of Sale　　　　　　　　120 a. in Berkeley Co., bounding E on THOMAS
　　　　　　　　　　　　　　HOLMAN; N on Cuppaine Creek; S on THOMAS
ELLIOTT. Witnesses: WILLIAM HOLMAN, SILAS WELLS, THOMAS STOCK. Before
WILLIAM CATTELL, J.P. Delivery by turf & twig. NATHANIEL JOHNSON, Reg-
ister.

Book M, p. 193　　　　　　　Then Rec'ed of MR. JOHN RIVERS the sum of
March ye 24^d 1733/4　　　452 pound 10 shills & 9 pence being in full
　　　　　　　　　　　　　　for the money mentioned in the within mortgage
wch was security for 2 bond from THOS. RIVERS to me under written which
sd bond I have deli'd his this day with this mortgage & I do hereby assign my righ title claim interest & demand to the same witness my hand
24^d Mar. 1733/4. W. CATTELL. Witness: DAVID RAMSAY. Registered this
30th day of Sept. 1734 pr me N. JOHNSON, Pub. Reg.

Book M, p. 193　　　　　　　DANIEL GIBSON, chirurgeon to (after his death)
17 July 1734　　　　　　　　to MARY HOWARD, spinster, both of Charleston,
Deed of Sale　　　　　　　　for Ł 200 currency, & other valuable consider-
　　　　　　　　　　　　　　tions, that house & land fronting 25 ft. on
the Broad Path as now erected & fenced in, bounding E & S on DANIEL GIB-
SON; N on COL. CHICKEN; also 1 Negro boy. Witnesses: JOHN FOWLER, ROBERT
SHAW. NATHANIEL JOHNSON, Register.

Book M, p. 196　　　　　　　EDWARD (his mark) BURNET, vintner, of Winyaw,
16 & 17 Sept. 1734　　　　　to RICHARD HILL & CO., merchants, of Charles-
L & R by Mortgage　　　　　 ton, as security on bond in penal sum of Ł 350
　　　　　　　　　　　　　　SC money conditioned for the payment of Ł 90

on 24 Dec. 1733, & ₤ 85 on 24 Dec. 1734, lot #59 in Georgetown, Prince George Parish, Winyaw, containing 1/2 a., 100 ft. front, 217.9 ft. deep, bounding NE on an unnamed street; NW on lot #58; SW on lots 21 & 22; SE on lot #60. Witnesses: ISAAC SECARE, JAMES CRADDOCK. Before THOMAS LAROCHE. NATHANIEL JOHNSON, Register.

Book M, p. 202
2 Aug. 1734
Bond

WILLIAM GRAY, planter, to TIMOTHY HENDRICK, planter, both of Colleton Co., in penal sum of ₤ 1400 SC money, conditioned for keeping the terms of a bill of sale of even date. Witnesses: JOSEPH ANDREW, JAMES MARTIN, JOHN ANDREW, JR. Before ROBERT YONGE, J.P. NATHANIEL JOHNSON, Register.

Book M, p. 203
2 Aug. 1734
Bill of Sale

WILLIAM GRAY, planter, to TIMOTHY HENDRICK, planter, both of Colleton Co., for ₤ 700, sells 200 a. in Colleton Co., bounding S on JOHN ANDREWS; W on WILLIAM GRAY; N on JOSEPH MACKEY; E on JOSEPH BOON'S Barony; granted by the Lords Proprs. to JOSEPH FARLEY & signed over to EDWARD RIPIN, who conveyed to GRAY. HANNAH, wife of WILLIAM, freely surrenders her dower. Witnesses: JOSEPH ANDREW, JAMES MARTIN, JOHN ANDREW, JR. Before ROBERT YONGE, J.P. NATHANIEL JOHNSON, Register.

Book M, p. 205
11 Jan. 1728
Deed of Sale

EDWARD (his mark) RIPPON, JR., (see p. 207) planter, to WILLIAM GRAY, SR., planter, both of Colleton Co., for ₤ 200 SC money, 200 a. bounding S on JOHN ANDREWS; N on JOHN GWIN. Witnesses: JOHN MITCHELL, JOHN ANDREW, JAMES PARMENTER. Before JOSHUA SANDERS, J.P. NATHANIEL JOHNSON, Register.

Book M, p. 207
10 Nov. 1713
Deed of Sale

(See p. 205) JOSEPH (his mark) FARLEY, carpenter, to EDWARD REAPEING, (RIPPON?) planter, both of Colleton Co., for ₤ 26 lawful money, 200 a. bounding S on MR. ANDRAS; N on JOHN GWIN. Witnesses: WILLIAM FISHBURN, ROWLAND EVANS, JOHN (his mark) WALLIS. On 11 Jan. 1728/9 (p. 209) EDWARD (his mark) RIPPIN assigned to WILLIAM GRAY all his title to this deed. Witnesses: HONEY BAYLEY, JOHN WOOD, WILLIAM GRAY. GRAY appeared before JOSHUA SANDERS, J.P. EVANS appeared before DANIEL GREENE, J.P. NATHANIEL JOHNSON, Register.

Book M, p. 209
14 & 15 June 1734
L & R

MARGARET SCHENCKINGH, widow, of St. James Goosecreek, to THOMAS CHEESMAN, merchant, late of Island of Barbados but now of Berkeley Co., SC, for ₤ 380 currency, 305 a. in Parish of St. James Goosecreek, late in possession of BENJAMIN SCHENCKINGH, husband of MARGARET, but now occupied by THOMAS CLIFFORD, ESQ., being part of 500 a. formerly known as JOHN BONER'S & purchased from THOMAS SMITH by BENJAMIN SCHENCKINGH; formerly bounding SE & SW on MRS. ANN DAVIS; all other sides on MAJ. THOMAS SMITH; but now bounding SE on ALEXANDER PARRIS, ESQ.; SW on PAUL MAZYCK, ESQ.; all other sides on land occupied by THOMAS TAYLOR; the land being free from the title or dower & thirds of SABINA, wife of THOMAS TAYLOR. Witnesses: PETER TAYLOR, WILLIAM TREWIN. Before THOMAS DALE, J.P. NATHANIEL JOHNSON, Register.

Book M, p. 218
14 & 15 June 1734
L & R

JOB HOWES, ESQ., & MARTHA his wife, of Cape Fear, NC, & THOMAS CLIFFORD, ESQ., & MARY his wife, of Berkeley Co., to THOMAS CHESSMAN, merchant, late of Island of Barbados now of Berkeley Co., SC, for ₤ 3220 SC money paid to HOWES & 10 shillings paid to CLIFFORD, 2 tracts, total 340 a., in St. James Goosecreek Parish, now occupied by THOMAS CLIFFORD; 1 tract of 290 a. granted by the Lords Proprs. to ROBERT HOWES, father of JOB, lying at head of Forsters Creek, formerly bounding N on JAMES MOOR, ESQ.; NE on CAPT. DAVID DAVIES; E on EDWARD MIDDLETON & SARAH his wife; S on NICHOLAS MAHUM & vacant land; but now bounding N & E on ARTHUR MIDDLETON, ESQ.; NE on PAUL MAZYCK; S on JOB HOWES (formerly NICHOLAS MAHUM); the other tract, 50 a., lying on N side Forsters Creek formerly granted by the Lords Proprs. to NICHOLAS MAHUM & then bounding E on creek; N on WILLIAM WAITIS; S on JOHN GOODBY & vacant land; W on vacant land; now bounding N on said tract of 290 a.; S on CHARLES PINCKNEY, ESQ. & ARTHUR MIDDLETON; W on ARTHUR MIDDLETON;

also 1 pew in the Parish Church of St. James Goosecreek wherein BENJAMIN GODIN, ESQ. now sits, formerly allotted to ROBERT HOWES, father of JOB; all free from titles of dower of MARTHA HOWES & MARY CLIFFORD. Witnesses: MARY GODDARD, WILLIAM TREWIN. Before THOMAS DALE, J.P. NATHANIEL JOHNSON, Register.

Book M, p. 230
20 & 21 Sept. 1734
L & R

ALGERNOON ASH, gentleman, to WILLIAM LIVINGSTON, ESQ., both of Colleton Co., for Ł 3000 currency, 1109 a. in Colleton Co., bounding W on land not laid out; N on an impassable Bay Swamp; S & SE on Chehaw River & marsh; & 480 a. at head of Chehaw marsh, bounding W on marsh at head of Chehaw River; N on JOHN SHEPPARD; E on SAMUEL SMALL; S on land not laid out; also 250 a. on Cuckolds Creek running into Combe River, being half a tract of 500 a.; also an island on the freshes of Edisto or Ponpon River, opposite New London alias Willtown, commonly called Eve's Island, containing 160 a.; also 9 lots in Willtown, 43, 44, 65, 66, 67, 81, 82, 83, & 84. Witnesses: JAMES GRAY, ELIZABETH GRAY, JOHN HARRIS. Before ROBERT YONGE, J.P. NATHANIEL JOHNSON, Register.

Book M, p. 238
20 & 21 Sept. 1734
L & R

WILLIAM LIVINGSTON, ESQ. & MARY his wife (daughter & devisee of HUGH COCHRAN, yeoman, of Chehoe River) to ALGERNOON ASH, gentleman, all of Colleton Co., for Ł 3000 currency, 1109 a.; 480 a.; 250 a.; Eve's Island; & 9 lots in Willtown. Whereas the Lords Proprs. on 17 May 1701 granted HUGH COCHRAN 1173 a., English measure, in Colleton Co., bounding W on vacant land; N on an impassable Bay Swamp; S & SE on Chehaw River; & whereas HUGH COCHRAN also owned 480 a. in Colleton Co., at head of Chehaw marsh, bounding W on marsh; N on JOHN SHEPPARD; E on SAMUEL SMALL; S on vacant land; & whereas HUGH COCHRAN by will bequeathed to his daughter MARY (party hereto) the tract of 1109 a. first mentioned on which he lived & the 480 a.; now WILLIAM & MARY LIVINGSTON convey to ASH the 1109 a. & 480 a.; also 250 a. on Cuckolds Creek (1/2 of a tract of 500 a. formerly belonging to WILLIAM EDWARDS); also 160 a. called Eve's Island on the freshes of Edisto (or Ponpon) River opposite New London alias Willtown; also 9 lots in Willtown, Nos. 43, 44, 65, 66, 67, 81, 82, 83, & 84. Witnesses: JAMES GRAY, ELIZABETH GRAY, JOHN HARRIS. Before ROBERT YONGE, J.P. NATHANIEL JOHNSON, Register.

Book M, p. 249
14 May 1734
Deed of Sale

SAMUEL WEST to MRS. SARAH WEST, both of Berkeley Co., for Ł 1000 currency, 50 a., part of 250 a. purchased from FRANCIS LADSON by SAMUEL WEST, SR.; bounding W on JOHN CATTELL; S on STEPHEN FOX; E on RALPH ELMES; N on FRANCIS LADSON. Witnesses: JOSHUA TOOMER, JOHN COOK. Delivery by turf & twig. Before THOMAS DRAYTON, J.P. NATHANIEL JOHNSON, Register.

DEEDS BOOK "N"
1734-1735

Book N, p. 1
20 Mar. 1731
Confirmation of Title

JOSEPH CANTEY, planter, son & heir of WILLIAM CANTEY, planter, to WILLIAM ALLEN, cooper, all of Berkeley Co. Whereas WILLIAM CANTEY on 23 Mar. 1716 sold WILLIAM ALLEN 20 a. on N side Ashley River, bounding N on JOSEPH CHILDS; E on WILLIAM CANTEY, SR., & whereas doubts have arisen touching the validity of ALLEN'S title to the 20 a., in order to remove such doubts JOSIAH CANTEY, for 10 shillings, & other considerations, forever quit claims to ALLEN all title & claim. Witness: THOMAS MILL, SAMUEL ELMES, THOMAS ELMES. Before MALACHI GLAZE, J.P. NATHANIEL JOHNSON, Register.

Book N, p. 4
29 & 30 Nov. 1734
L & R by Mortgage

JOHN BENSTONE, planter, of Christ Church Parish, Berkeley Co., to PAUL JENYS, merchant, of Charleston, for Ł 1200 SC money, 200 a. on which BENSTONE lives in Christ Church Parish, bounding S on MR. LEGARE; N on MR. STOCKS; E on THOMAS PLAYER; W on CAPT. VANDERHORST & THOMAS WHITE conditioned on the repayment of Ł 1200 on 1 Jan. next. Witnesses: ROBERT HALL, ANDREW RUTLEDGE. Before Gov. ROBERT

JOHNSON. NATHANIEL JOHNSON, Register.

Book N, p. 10
7 May 1730
Allotment of land

SARAH WOODWARD, widow of RICHARD WOODWARD; WILLIAM WILKINS & THOMAS STANYARNE, planters, all of Berkeley Co., extrix & extors of will of RICHARD WOODWARD, divide his real estate & allot to SARAH WOODWARD, widow, ELIZABETH WRIGHT (late ELIZABETH WOODWARD, daughter & co-heir) wife of RICHARD WRIGHT, merchant, of Charleston; & MARY WOODWARD (another daughter & co-heir) as follows: to SARAH WOODWARD 600 a. called Maggotts Islands, also 500 a. called Chehaw Islands, total 1100 a. for her third part for her natural life, then to such of her children as she directs: to MRS. ELIZABETH WRIGHT 467 a. on James Island on which SARAH WOODWARD now lives & is to have the use of during her natural life & widowhood at the end of which time the land shall be delivered to ELIZABETH or RICHARD WRIGHT, he to pay to MRS. WOODWARD at that time ₤ 1500 currency or ₤ 214:5:8 sterling; to ELIZABETH WRIGHT also, 60 a. on James Island, also 1050 a. called Lachleys; also 120 a. on Johns Island, total 1697; to MRS. MARY WOODWARD 196-1/2 a. called Wappoo; also 3 tracts called Saltketcher on Combey River; also 20 lots in Beaufort Port Royall; total 1676-1/2 a.; all according to plat. NATHANIEL JOHNSON, Register.

Book N, p. 13
7 May 1730
Allotment of Personal Estate

SARAH WOODWARD, widow of RICHARD WOODWARD; THOMAS STANYARNE & WILLIAM WILKINS, planters, all of Berkeley Co., executors & executrix of will of RICHARD WOODWARD; upon request of RICHARD WRIGHT, husband of ELIZABETH (daughter of co-heir of RICHARD WOODWARD); divided & allotted the Negroes, stock, tools, furniture, etc., left by RICHARD WOODWARD amongst SARAH WOODWARD, widow; ELIZABETH WRIGHT & MARY WOODWARD (another daughter & co-heir) as follows: to MRS. SARAH WOODWARD 14 slaves; to MRS. ELIZABETH WRIGHT 15 slaves; to MARY WOODWARD 15 slaves; to MRS. SARAH WOODWARD 94 cattle, 44 sheep, 7 horses; to MRS. ELIZABETH WRIGHT 94 cattle, 44 sheep, 7 horses; to MRS. MARY WOODWARD 94 cattle, 44 sheep, 7 horses; the household goods & plantation tools, as drawn, each to have the value of ₤ 405:5 shillings. NATHANIEL JOHNSON, Register.

Book N, p. 15
2 & 3 Dec. 1734
L & R by Mortgage

NATHANIEL GITTENS, planter, of Berkeley Co., to JAMES TOWNSEND, gentleman, of Charleston, for ₤ 200 currency, 30 a. in St. James Goosecreek Parish, on W side Goosecreek, bounding S on marsh, W on MR. SCHENKING; N on vacant land. Witnesses: WILLIAM RISBEY, LAWRENCE COULLIETTE. Before HENRY GIBBES, J.P. NATHANIEL JOHNSON, Pub. Reg. On p. 18 JAMES TOWNSEND declares this mortgage satisfied.

Book N, p. 23
11 & 12 Jan. 1732
L & R by Mortgage

DR. THOMAS COOPER, physician of Charleston, to ROBERT HUME, ESQ. of St. Phillip's Parish, Charleston, as security on bond of even date in penal sum of ₤ 1600 SC money conditioned for payment of ₤ 800 on 12 Jan. next, conveys the NE quarter part of lot #97 in Charleston, bounding E on a street leading from the Old Church yard to the Presbyterian Meeting House; S on STEPHEN BEDON; W on ROBERT HUME; N on a street leading to Cooper River. Witnesses: RICHARD LAMBTON, WILLIAM TREWIN. NATHANIEL JOHNSON, Register.

Book N, p. 32
21 & 22 Oct. 1734
L & R

THOMAS RIVERS, planter, of St. Andrews Parish, Berkeley Co., to THOMAS ELLERY, gentleman, of Charleston, for ₤ 200 currency that piece of land in St. Andrews Parish "nigh Ashley River Ferry," bounding E on marsh of JOHN RIVERS; W on JOHN RIVERS; N on WILLIAM CLAY; S on THOMAS ELLIOTT. Witnesses: WILLIAM HATTON, JOSEPH FIDLER, ROBERT SHAW. Before ALEXANDER PARRIS, J.P. NATHANIEL JOHNSON, Register.

Book N, p. 39
23 & 24 Dec. 1734
L & R by Mortgage

CHARLES HART, ESQ. of Berkeley Co., to JOHN WHITFIELD, merchant, of Charleston, for ₤ 1100 currency, 60 a. in Berkeley Co., bounding S on DANIEL GALE; W on GILSON CLAPP; E on marsh of Cooper River, & lately held by CHARLES HART; conditioned for the payment of ₤ 1210 on 24 Dec. 1735 by HART to WHITFIELD. Witnesses: JAMES MACAGOINE (MACKAGOINE), ROBERT VAUGHAN. Before BENJAMIN DELA CONSEILLERER,

J.P. NATHANIEL JOHNSON, Register. (See p. 155 for an addition to this mortgage).

Book N, p. 49   THOMAS BARTON, WILLIAM BARTON, JOHN BARTON &
30 & 31 Dec. 1734   ANNE BARTON to SAMUEL WRAGG, for ₺ 800 of
L & R   Great Britain, those several messuages, houses
                     or tenements in MOORE MEAD, in Parish of St.
Leonard, Shoreditch, Co. of Middlesex, lately occupied by CATHERINE BROWN,
HENRY VICKERS, WILLIAM CLENCH, ROBERT BURGESS, SAMUEL CRABTREE, GEORGE
JENKINS, WILLIAM LANE, WILLIAM JAMES, their undertenenants & assigns;
also 2 a. of garden in the Parish of Stepney alias Stebonheath, Co. of
Middlesex, lately occupied by CATHERINE HURLEY, widow, also the several
messuages, shops & sheds built upon the garden ground lately occupied by
CATHARINE HURLEY; all formerly the estate of ROBERT HUDSON & purchased
from him by JOHN BARTON abour 1714 under a decree in the High Court of
Chancery. THOMAS, WILLIAM, JOHN & ANNE BARTON also convey to WRAGG all
their respective shares in the real & personal estate of JOHN BARTON or
which they may claim under the decree touching the real & personal estate
of JOHN BARTON or of their father THOMAS BARTON. They also appoint WRAGG
their attorney, WRAGG agrees to protect them. Whereas in Trinity Term in
3rd year of KING GEORGE II's reign a suit was begun in the High & Hon.
Court of Ch. in England between THOMAS BARTON (as brother & heir of JOHN
BARTON, late citizen & freeman of London) & others against REBECCA BARTON
widow of JOHN BARTON & others to discover the real & personal estate of
JOHN BARTON (who died intestate) & to have a just distribution amongst
those entitled thereto; & whereas on 27 Oct. & 9 Nov. in 5th year of
GEORGE II's reign it was decreed that it be referred to MASTER TOTHILL,
M.C., to take an account against MENOSHAM & NICHOLAS, 2 of the dependents
who were mortgagees of part of the real estate of what is due them & to
inquire about rents, etc.; also to ascertain what REBECCA had received;
also that a receiver be appointed; (a MR. HARTOP also being a defendant);
etc., etc., & whereas THOMAS BARTON, the father, died in July 1732 having
first published his will dated 29 Jan. 1731 & bequeathed all his estate
in England (or which came to him by death of brother JOHN) equally to his
4 children (will proved under Gov. ROBERT JOHNSON) & therefore they are
entitled to a share in JOHN'S real & personal estate; & whereas on 23 May
1733 they appointed SAMUEL WRAGG, merchant, of London, their attorney; &
whereas the suit may extend over a long period at a great expense; &
whereas the 4 BARTON children have agreed to sell their interest to WRAGG;
now WRAGG purchases their interest. Witnesses: ROBERT POLLIXSON, JOHN
PAYNE, TIMOTHY MCDANIEL, ROWLAND VAUGHAN. Before BENJAMIN DELA CONSEIL-
LERE, J.P. NATHANIEL JOHNSON, Register.

Book N, p. 65   WILLIAM OSBORNE, mariner of Charleston, & HEL-
6 & 7 Sept. 1734   ENA his wife (heretofore called ELLINOR DICKS
L & R   otherwise called ELLINOR MACKEY, widow of COL.
                     ALEXANDER MACKEY, Indian trader of Granville
Co.) to CHARLES PINCKNEY, ESQ. of Charleston, for ₺ 1600 currency, 960 a.
formerly called Lookout Island, now MACKEYS Island, on W side Port Royall
River or Sound, St. Helena Parish, Granville Co., bounding S, SE & E on
Scull Point Creek; W on Lookout Island Creek. Whereas the Lords Proprs.
on 14 Apr. 1710 granted ALEXANDER MACKEY 630 a. on Lookout Island, Gran-
ville Co., bounding S on part of MACKEY'S land; E & NE on Scull Point
Creek & Port Royall Sound; W on Lookout Island Creek & marshes; & on same
date also granted MACKEY 330 a. on Lookout Island, bounding S, SE & E on
Scull Point Creek; SE on MACKEY'S land; W on Lookout Island Creek; &
whereas ALEXANDER MACKEY by will dated 29 Nov. 1711 bequeathed all his
real & personal estate to his wife ELEANOR; & whereas after his death
(Oct. 1722) ELEANOR MACKEY married WILLIAM OSBORNE; now they sell to
CHARLES PINCKNEY. Witnesses: BENJAMIN DELA CONSEILLERE, STEPHEN PROCTOR,
ROBERT BREWTON, JR. Before THOMAS DALE, J. of C.P. NATHANIEL JOHNSON,
Register.

Book N, p. 76   GILES COOKE, doctor, of Christ Church Parish,
16 Aug. 1733   to SAMUEL & ELIZA BULLOCK, for their lifetime,
Deed of Sale   110 a. fronting the river, butting on JOHN
                     HOLLYBUSH'S line; the land to return to DR.
COOKE at their death; COOKE or his heirs to pay for all improvements according to judgment of 2 men. COOKE binds himself in sum of ₺ 2000 currency to secure the BULLOCKS in their possession. Witnesses: PHANUELL

COOKE, MARY PERNELL. Before ELIAS FOISSIN, JR., J.P. NATHANIEL JOHNSON, Register.

Book N, p. 78　　　　　　　LADY ELIZABETH BLAKE of Colleton Co., widow of,
6 Sept. 1709　　　　　　　 & executrix of will of, the Hon. JOSEPH BLAKE,
Discharge of Mortgage　　 having been paid the mortgage money, ₤ 80
& Quit Claim　　　　　　　 sterling, & all interest, costs & damages, by
　　　　　　　　　　　　　　GEORGE DUCKETT, shipwright, & MARGARET his
wife, of Charleston (late MARGARET MARSHALL), quit claims & confirms to
them all her title to part of a town lot & 4 town lots. Whereas BEULAH
MARSHALL of Charleston & MARGARET his wife (who later married GEORGE DUCK-
ETT, shipwright), through MARGARET owned part of a moiety of a lot in
Charleston 54 ft. front, 97 ft. long, 1/2 formerly purchased by FINDLA
MARTIN, bounding E on ANTHONY BONNEAU, cooper; S on a street running E &
W from Cooper River to Ashley River; W on the other moiety owned by FIND-
LA MARTIN; N on JOSEPH ELLICOT; & whereas said BEULAH (through MARGARET)
owned 4 adjoining lots in Charleston, bounding W on a small creek & marsh
& CAPT. COMINGS'S line; E on ground reserved for a common burial place; S
on Ashley River; N on vacant land; & whereas BEULAH MARSHALL on 22 May
1696 mortgaged the part of lot & 4 lots for ₤ 80 SC money to the Hon. JO-
SEPH BLAKE upon the condition that DR. CHARLES MARSHALL, father of BEULAH,
should pay JOSEPH BLAKE the ₤ 80 sterling in 3 bills of exchange, or in
case of default then FINDLA MARTIN to pay; now MARGARET MARSHALL'S 2nd
husband satisfies the mortgage. Witnesses: JOSEPH BOONE (according to
his profession), HENRY WIGINGTON. Before THOMAS LAMBOLL, J.P. Page 83
gives the 4 lots as 94, 100, 114, 129. "Register in folio 169 Hobsons
grant MR. CUNE 2 lotts No. 119, 120. August ye 14 1675 (?) lade out."
NATHANIEL JOHNSON, Register.

Book N, p. 83　　　　　　　HUGH EVANS, tailor of Charleston & ELEANOR
11 & 12 Jan. 1733　　　　　(her mark) his wife, to GEORGE HAIG & FREDER-
L & R　　　　　　　　　　　ICK MEYER, gentlemen, for ₤ 400 SC money, 800
　　　　　　　　　　　　　　a. on Defaskee Island, Granville Co., granted
6 Apr. 1733 under Gov. ROBERT JOHNSON to HUGH EVANS; bounding N on ANDREW
ALLEN & vacant land; S on the Sound; SE on JAMES COCKRAN; W on JOHN
WRIGHT. Witnesses: JOSHUA MORGAN, THOMAS COLSON. Before THOMAS LAMBOLL,
J.P. NATHANIEL JOHNSON, Register.

Book N, p. 90　　　　　　　THOMAS JONES, planter, of Christ Church Parish,
27 & 28 Aug. 1734　　　　　& MARY his wife with her free consent, to JOHN
L & R　　　　　　　　　　　BAKER, planter, of same Parish, for ₤ 200 cur-
　　　　　　　　　　　　　　rency, 400 a. in Craven Co., bounding SE on
marsh & sea; NE on THOMAS THRIDCROFT (THREADCRAFT); SW on COL. THOMAS
LYNCH; other sides on vacant land. Witnesses: JOHN SAVERANCE, JOSEPH
SAVERANCE. Before ANDREW RUTLEDGE, J.P. NATHANIEL JOHNSON, Register.

Book N, p. 94　　　　　　　THOMAS FARR, planter, of St. Paul's Parish,
10 & 11 May 1734　　　　　 Colleton Co., (son & heir of ELIZABETH FARR
L & R　　　　　　　　　　　who was sister & heri of JOHN EMPEROUR), &
　　　　　　　　　　　　　　AMARINTIA his wife, to NATHANIEL GITTENS,
planter, of Berkeley Co., for ₤ 280 currency, 130 a. in St. James Goose-
creek Parish, Berkeley Co., on W side Goosecreek, bounding S on marsh; W
on MRS. SCHENCKINGH; N on vacant land; which 130 a. was granted by the
Lords Proprs. 9 Sept. 1696 to JOHN EMPEROUR, & was inherited by his sis-
ter & heir, ELIZABETH FARR; who died 15 Nov. 1725 & the land descended to
THOMAS FARR, her eldest son & heir; now he sells to CITTENS. Witnesses:
JOHN LAURENS, WILLIAM LEANDER. Before THOMAS DALE, J.P. NATHANIEL JOHN-
SON, Register.

Book N, p. 101　　　　　　 NATHANIEL GITTENS, planter, of St. James Goose-
14 & 15 Jan. 1734　　　　　creek, to THOMAS BOLTON, shopkeeper, of
L & R　　　　　　　　　　　Charleston, for ₤ 200 currency, 730 a. in St.
　　　　　　　　　　　　　　James Goosecreek Parish, Berkeley Co., bound-
ing E & S on the Creek; W on MRS. WILLEBY GIBBES, N on JOHN HARBERT.
Witnesses: WILLIAM SMITH, (gentleman), JAMES TOWNSEND. Before THOMAS
DALE, J.P. NATHANIEL JOHNSON, Register.

Book N, p. 107　　　　　　 THOMAS BOLTON, shopkeeper, of St. Philip's
16 & 17 Jan.　　　　　　　 Parish, Charleston, to JOHN LAURENS, saddler,
L & R　　　　　　　　　　　of Charleston, for ₤ 200 currency, 730 a. in

St. James Goosecreek, Berkeley Co., bounding E & S on the creek; W on MRS. WILLEBY GIBBES; N on JOHN HARBERT. Witnesses: FRANCIS YANAM, BENJAMIN ADDISON (saddler). Before THOMAS DALE, J.P. NATHANIEL JOHNSON, Register.

Book N, p. 113
12 July 1708
Deed of Feoffment

WILLIAM WILKINS, planter, of Berkeley Co., & ELIZABETH his wife, heirs & executors of will of CAPT. WILLIAM DAVIS, to RICHARD PETERSON, JR., mariner, of Berkeley Co., for ₤ 90 currency, 1/2 of a tract of 2700 a.; also half the neat cattle & hogs, etc., on the land & 1/2 their increase. Whereas JOHN, EARL OF BATH, Palatine, & the Lords Proprs. under the hands of Gov. JOSEPH BLAKE, JAMES MOORE & EDMUND BELLINGER, on 29 Mar. 1700 granted CAPT. GEORGE REYNOR 2700 a. in Colleton Co., on W side Stono River, bounding E on marsh; S on the ocean; W on Stono Creek; N on Kiawah Creek; & whereas CAPT. REYNOR on 1 Nov. 1701 sold to CAPT. WILLIAM DAVIS of Colleton Co., 1/2 of the 2700 a., now in possession of WILLIAM WILKINS; also half the neat cattle & hogs on the 2700 a.; now WILLIAM & ELIZABETH WILKINS convey to PETERSON. Deed signed by WILLIAM WILKINS, ELIZABETH WILKINS, MARY DAVIS. ELIZABETH declares she signed voluntarily, "Multa obliterato desunt." Witnesses to ELIZABETH'S signature: JOHN HEARNE (hat-maker), MARY DAVIS. Witnesses to deed of sale: ROBERT COLE, ELIZABETH GODFREY, JOHN WARD memo of delivery by turf & twig signed JOHN WITTER. Before ROBERT YONGE, J.P. JOHN HEARNE made oath according to his profession before DANIEL GREENE, J.P. NATHANIEL JOHNSON, Register.

Book N, p. 119
30 Oct. 1717
Deed of Sale

ROGER MOORE, planter, of Berkeley Co., to JOHN STANYARNE of Colleton Co., for ₤ 1000 currency, 1350 a., or 1/2 of Kiawah Island, Colleton Co. Witnesses: GEORGE HADDRELL, of Christ Church Parish, MARY HADDRELL, wife of GEORGE. Before JOHN BARKSDALE, J.P. NATHANIEL JOHNSON, Register.

Book N, p. 122
23 Jan. 1734
Lease

EDMOND PORTER, of NC & ELIZABETH his wife; & ELEANOR WHITE, widow, of Island of Jamaica (ELEANOR & ELIZABETH being aunts & co-heirs of JOHN PETERSON, planter, of Berkeley Co., who was son & heir of RICHARD PETERSON, JR., see p. 113, mariner), to JOHN STANYARNE, planter, of Colleton Co., for 10 shillings, 1/2 of Kaiway Island, containing 2700 a. on W side Stono River, bounding E on marsh; S on the ocean; W on Stono Creek; N on Kaiway Creek. Sealed & delivered by DANIEL GREENE, ESQ., as attorney for ELEANOR WHITE "& the others by virtue of the powers to the release annexed" (see p. 127). Witnesses: EDWARD CROFT, JOHN DART, CHARLES PINCKNEY. Before JACOB BOND, J.P. NATHANIEL JOHNSON, Register.

Book N, p. 124
18 Sept. 1728
Jamaica Letter of Attorney

ELEANOR (her mark) WHITE, widow, 1 of the daughters, by his wife MARY, of RICHARD PETERSON, merchant, of SC appointed her brother-in-law EDMOND PORTER, ESQ., of NC & ELIZABETH PORTER, his wife (sister of ELEANOR) her attorney to handle her estate in North America. Witnesses: JOHN STOLLARD, EDWARD CLEMENTS, JOHN STEWART. Recorded 6 Feb. 1729 in secretary's office. Bk. H. fol. 7 by HENRY HARGRAVE, Dep. Sec. STOLLARD appeared before ALEXANDER PARRIS, J.P. NATHANIEL JOHNSON, Register.

Book N, p. 127
24 Mar. 1733
Letter of Attorney

EDMOND PORTER, ESQ., of NC & ELIZABETH his wife (daughter of RICHARD PETERSON, merchant of SC & aunt of RICHARD PETERSON, planter) appoint their loving friend DANIEL GREENE, ESQ., of Charleston their attorney. Whereas JOHN PETERSON owned real estate in SC & being unmarried, at his death in Sept. 1727, his land was inherited by the sisters ELIZABETH PORTER & ELEANOR WHITE, widow, of Island of Jamaica, as aunts & co-heirs of JOHN PETERSON; & whereas ELEANOR, by deed poll dated 18 Sept. 1728, appointed EDMOND & ELIZABETH PORTER her attorneys to dispose of the lands to which she was entitled; now EDMOND & ELIZABETH appoint DANIEL GREENE their attorney. Witnesses: ANN MONTGOMERY, JOHN HAMMERTON, ELIXABETH HOOPER. Recorded 1 Jan. 1734 in Bk. B. B. fol. 331, by JOHN HAMMERTON. Before ALEXANDER PARRIS, J.P. NATHANIEL JOHNSON, Register.

Book N, p. 129 24 Jan. 1734 Release

EDMOND PORTER, ESQ. of NC, of ELIZABETH his wife, & ELEANOR WHITE, widow, of Island of Jamaica (ELEANOR & ELIZABETH being sisters, & aunts & co-heirs of JOHN PETERSON, planter of Berkeley Co.; JOHN having been son & heir of RICHARD PETERSON, JR., mariner, of Berkeley Co.), to JOHN STANYARNE, planter, of Colleton Co., for ₤ 650 currency, 1/2 of Kaiway Island, which island contains 2700 a. Whereas RICHARD PETERSON owned 1/2 of Kiaway Island (1/2 of 2700 a.), which island was granted 29 Mar. 1700 by the Lords Proprs. to GEORGE REYNOR & by several mesne conveyances became the property of RICHARD PETERSON; & whereas PETERSON willed the land to his son JOHN, who, dying unmarried & under age, in Sept. 1727, the land descended to ELIZABETH PORTER & ELEANOR WHITE (sisters) aunts & co-heirs of JOHN; now they by their attorney, sell to STANYARNE. Witnesses: EDWARD CROFT, JOHN DART, CHARLES PINCKNEY. Before JACOB BOND, J.P.

Book N, p. 136 8 & 9 Nov. 1734 L & R

COL. WILLIAM HAZZARD, SR., planter of Wambee Island (known as Port Royall Island), Granville Co., to AMBROSE REEVES (REEVE), surgeon, of Beaufort Town, for ₤ 625 currency, 147 a., English measure, on Port Royall Island, bounding E on Stewart River; N on Beaufort Town & part on JOHN WOODWARD; W & NW on Parmenters Creek; S on COL. WILLIAM BULL, plat dated 2 Mar. 1705/6. Whereas the Rt. Hon. WILLIAM, Lord Craven, Palatine, & the Lords Proprs. on 4 Jan. 1704, witnessed by Gov. NATHANIEL JOHNSON, NICHOLAS TROTT & JAMES MOORE, granted COL. WILLIAM HAZZARD, SR., the above named 147 a., now HAZZARD sells to REEVES. Witnesses: CHARLES REEVES, THOMAS BOSWICK. Before THOMAS WIGG, J.P. NATHANIEL JOHNSON, Register.

Book N, p. 143 31 Oct. 1734 Deed of Sale

JOHN STEVENS, gentleman, of St. George's Parish, Berkeley Co., to STEPHEN BULL, gentleman, of St. Paul's Parish, Colleton Co., for ₤ 30, lot #40 (1/4 a.) in Dorchester Town. ELIZABETH, wife of JOHN STEVENS signs in token of her consent. Witnesses: J. VARNOD, PHILIP AYTON. NATHANIEL JOHNSON, Register.

Book N, p. 145 9 & 10 Jan. 1733 L & R

WILLIAM BULL, of Berkeley Co., to STEPHEN BULL, of Cane Acres, Colleton Co., for ₤ 1000 currency, 2 tracts; 1 of 222 a. in Colleton Co.; the other of 520 a. in Berkeley Co. Whereas by grant dated 28 Apr. last, signed by Gov. ROBERT JOHNSON, WILLIAM BULL was given 222 a. in Colleton Co., bounding N on WILLIAM LEVINGSTON; W on Ponpon River; S on CAPT. RICHARD SHUBRICK (formerly MR. BUTOLPH'S); E on SILAS WELLS (then vacant land); & whereas the Lords Proprs. by grant, signed by Gov. ROBERT GIBBES, dated 27 June 1710, gave WILLIAM BULL 620 a. in Berkeley (?) Co., near Cane Acres in Colleton Co., bounding NE on STEPHEN BULL (formerly WILLIAM BULL); SE on WILLIAM ELLIOT; SW on PETER TAYLOR (then vacant); NW on WILLIAM BULL (then vacant); grant recorded in auditor's office in Old Grant Book #1, fols. 342, 343 on 3 Jan. 1732/3; now WILLIAM BULL sells the 222 a. & 520 a. (part of the 620 a.) Witnesses: THOMAS DRAYTON, ELIZABETH DRAYTON. NATHANIEL JOHNSON, Register.

Book N, p. 155 12 Feb. 1734 Mortgage

See P. 49, CHARLES HART, for the further sum of ₤ 350 currency, paid by JOHN WHITFIELD, declares the 60 a. to be a security to WHITFIELD for the repayment of ₤ 1210 & this ₤ 350, & interest. Witnesses: MICHAEL MILLURE, WILLIAM LEA. Before THOMAS DALE, J.P. NATHANIEL JOHNSON, Register.

Book N, p. 156 5 & 6 Jan. 1730 L & R

JONAS BONHOSTE, planter, & ELIZABETH is wife, of Christ Church Parish, to ELIAS FOISSIN, JR., planter, of the same place, for ₤ 970 SC money 1125 a. in Christ Church Parish, bounding N on ALEXANDER TROZELL & ANTHONY BONNEAU; SW on GEORGE BENSON & MRS. SUSANNAH DUBOSE; SE on JOHN HUGYAN. ELIZABETH, when requested, to sign deed & renounce her dower before the Hon. RICHARD ALLEIN, C.J. Witnesses: SAMUEL WIGFALL, DANIEL LAROCHE, ROBERT COLLES, JOHN BONHOSTE, JONATHAN (his mark) MURRILL. Before MICHAEL DARBY, J.P. NATHANIEL JOHNSON, Pub. Reg.

Book N, p. 162

WILLIAM HENDRICK, planter, of Colleton Co., to

10 Feb. 1734/5 his loving son-in-law JAMES BARRIE (BERRIE),
Deed of Gift storekeeper, & his beloved daughter PURCHASE
BARRIE, wife of JAMES, for love & affection,
200 a. as granted by Lords Proprs. to JOHN TOBYE & conveyed by him to
WILLIAM HENDRICK; also 4 Negro men, a boy, 3 Negro women, his stock of
horses, cattle, & hogs, his utensils & appurtenances, from the day of
HDNRRICK'S death & departure from this life. Witnesses: JOSHUA SANDERS,
ELIZABETH CLARK SANDERS, GEORGE HAMLIN. Before THOMAS DALE, J.P. NA-
THANIEL JOHNSON, Register.

Book N, p. 163 WILLIAM HENDRICK, planter, of Colleton Co., to
8 Feb. 1734/5 his son-in-law JAMES BERRIE (BARRIE), store-
Deed of Gift keeper, & his daughter PURCHASE (wife of JAMES
BERRIE), for love & affection, 381 a. in Col-
leton Co., bounding S on ZEKIEL BRANFORD; W on Ponpon River; N on BRYAN
REALLY; E on MR. ELLIOT & said BRANFORD; also his dwelling house on the
plantation, kitchen, etc., also 4 Negro men. Witnesses: GEORGE HAIG,
GEORGE HAMLIN, PURCHAS HENDRICK. Before THOMAS DALE, J.P. NATHANIEL
JOHNSON, Register.

Book N, p. 164 THOMAS ELLERY, gentleman, & ANNE his wife, to
1 & 2 Nov. 1734 ROWLAND VAUGHAN, gentleman, all of Charleston,
L & R for L 200 currency, & free from ANNE'S claim
of dower, that plantation or piece of land in
St. Andrews Parish, Berkeley Co., "nigh Ashley River Fetty," bounding E
on marsh of JOHN RIVERS; W on JOHN RIVERS; N on WILLIAM CLAY; S on THOMAS
ELLIOTT. Witnesses: ALEXANDER PARRIS, GEORGE HALL. Before JAMES WEDDER-
BURN. NATHANIEL JOHNSON, Register.

Book N, p. 171 BANJAMIN DENNIS, planter, of Berkeley Co., to
11 Oct. 1734 ROBERT SAMS, planter, of Colleton Co., in the
Bond sum of L 1850 SC money. Whereas DENNIS on
this date, for L 925 currency, sold SAM'S 370
a. in Colleton Co., bounding N on ROBERT SAMS; NE on a branch of Bohicket
Creek; S on JOHN DAVIS & COL. MOSES WILSON; W on MOSES WILSON & land at
head of Leadenwaw Creek; now DENNIS gives bond that he will keep the
agreements of sale. Witnesses: EDWARD WIGG, WILLIAM WITHERS. NATHANIEL
JOHNSON, Register.

Book N, p. 173 BENJAMIN DENNIS, planter, of Berkeley Co., to
10 & 11 Oct. 1734 ROBERT SAMS, planter of Colleton Co., for
L & R L 925 SC money, 370 a. in Colleton Co., part
of 500 a. granted by the Lords Proprs. (signed
by Gov. NATHANIEL JOHNSON) on 14 Mar. 1704/5 to WILLIAM GREEN; bounding N
on ROBERT SAMS; NE on a branch of Bohicket Creek; S on JOHN DAVIS & COL.
MOSES WILSON; W on MOSES WILSON & land at head of Leadenwaw Creek. Witnesses: EDWARD WIGG, WILLIAM WITHERS. Before HENRY GIBBES, J.P. NATHAN-
IEL JOHNSON, Register.

Book N, p. 179 BENJAMIN CLIFFORD, shopkeeper, & SARAH his
5 & 6 Sept. 1734 wife, to OTHNIEL BEALE & THOMAS COOPER, mer-
L & R by Mortgage chants, of Charleston, for L 1250:10:4 currency, 800 a. on Combee River, Colleton Co.
bounding N on SAMUEL NICHOLS & vacant land; W on Combee River; S on a
creek & an impassible swamp running between the 800 a. & WILLIAM PAGE'S
land; E on a swamp at head of creek; conditioned for the repayment of the
full sum with interest on 25 Mar. 1735. Witnesses: ROBERT PRINGLE,
PHILIP PRIOLEAU. Before ALEXANDER PARRIS, J.P. NATHANIEL JOHNSON, Register.

Book N, p. 186 JOSEPH BELCHER, gentleman, of Milton, Suffolk
3 June 1734 Co., Mass., to RICHARD MORTIMER, merchant, of
Deed of Sale Boston, for L 50 lawful money, all his title &
estate in Berkeley Co., SC commonly known by
name of White Point, formerly the property of GILL BELCHER, mariner, of
Charleston. ELIZABETH BELCHER, wife of JOSEPH, freely quit claims her
third part. Witnesses: AMAVIAH WINCHESTER, JR., AMAVIAH WINCHESTER. Before ROBERT SPUT (?) J.P. On 18 Feb. 1734/5 RICHARD MORTIMER (p. 187)
merchant, for L 50 SC money, sold to NATHANIEL FORD, of Charleston, SC.
his title to 1/2 the tract bought from JOSEPH BELCHER. NATHANIEL JOHNSON,

Register.

Book N, p. 187　　　　　　DANIEL CARTWRIGHT, planter, to JOHN BERESFORD,
14 & 15 Feb. 1734　　　　ESQ., both of Berkeley Co., for ₺ 4800, Old
L & R　　　　　　　　　　Town Plantation containing 710 a., on Old Town
　　　　　　　　　　　　　Creek, St. Andrews Parish, lately owned by
PETER LESADE, planter, bounding E on the Creek; W on WILLIAM BRANFORD; N
on creeks & marshes; S on ANDREW DEVEAUX. Witnesses: MALACHI GLAZE, ROW-
LAND VAUGHAN. It is agreed that CARTWRIGHT does not covenant that BERES-
FORD shall have quiet possession of 42 a. (part of the tract) now in pos-
session of the executors of THOMAS ROSE who are entitled to the same dur-
ing the life of PETER LESADE & then to revert to DANIEL CARTWRIGHT but
that BERESFORD shall enjoy the estate to which CARTWRIGHT is entitled.
Witnesses: MALACHI GLAZE, ROWLAND VAUGHAN. Before ROBERT WRIGHT, C.T.
NATHANIEL JOHNSON, Register.

Book N, p. 194　　　　　　BENJAMIN (his mark) WEBB, SR., & SARAH (her
4 Jan. 1710　　　　　　　 mark) his wife, of Berkeley Co., to his broth-
Deed of Sale　　　　　　　er THOMAS WEBB, bachelor, for ₺ 15 SC money,
　　　　　　　　　　　　　150 a. on which his father lived & which was
granted by the Lords Porprs. & JOHN, Earl of Bath, Palatine, on 16 Aug.
1698 to BENJAMIN WEBB. Witnesses: DOCTRINA THOMPSON, JOSEPH WEBB, JOHN
(his mark) STARKEY. Before ELIAS FOISSIN, JR., J.P. NATHANIEL JOHNSON,
Register.

Book N, p. 197　　　　　　JOHN PAINTER, carpenter of St. Johns Parish,
11 Dec. 1734　　　　　　　Berkeley Co., appoints his friend JOHN CUMING,
Letter of Attorney　　　　of St. Thomas Parish, Berkeley Co., his attorn-
　　　　　　　　　　　　　ey with authority to hire necessary laborers &
round up all the horses, cattle, hogs, & all stock given to JOHN PAINTER
(deed of gift dated 1 Jan. 1733/4) by JOHN STRACHANY stepfather & NAOMI
his wife, mother of JOHN PAINTER, for his use after their death: the ear
mark being a hole in the left ear & the right ear half cut off by the
length; viz, the upper half; the brand being TS. Witnesses: ISAAC DUMONS,
WILLIAM (his mark) BALDOCK. Before ANTHONY BONNEAU, J.P. NATHANIEL JOHN-
SON, Register.

Book N, p. 200　　　　　　BENJAMIN LAW, planter, & SARAH his wife, to
23 & 24 Mar. 1733　　　　DAVID ARNETT, all of Christ Church Parish,
L & R　　　　　　　　　　Berkeley Co., for ₺ 1600 SC money, 400 a. on
　　　　　　　　　　　　　the sea beach in Christ Church Parish part of
1055 a. granted to NATHANIEL LAW, father of BENJAMIN, bounding E on BEN-
JAMIN LAW; SE on sea coast; S on THOMAS BARKSDALE; W on RICHARD FOWLER;
which 400 a. was surveyed by THOMAS WHITTER. SARAH to renounce her dower
within 6 months. Witnesses: JAMES MICHIE, ROWLAND VAUGHAN. Before JAMES
WEDDERBURNE, J.P. NATHANIEL JOHNSON, Register.

Book N, p. 207　　　　　　DAVID ARNETT, planter, of Christ Church Parish,
4 & 5 Mar. 1734　　　　　Berkeley Co., to JOHN WHITFIELD, merchant, of
L & R by Mortgage　　　　Charleston, for ₺ 700 SC money, 400 a. on the
　　　　　　　　　　　　　beach in Christ Church Parish, part of 1055 a.
granted to NATHANIEL LAW, & surveyed by THOMAS WHITTER, bounding E on BEN-
JAMIN LAW; SE on sea coast; S on THOMAS BARKSDALE; W on RICHARD FOWLER;
conditioned for the payment to WHITFIELD of ₺ 770 SC money on 5 Mar. 1735.
Witnesses: BENJAMIN LAW, ROWLAND VAUGHAN. Before JAMES WEDDERBURN, J.P.
NATHANIEL JOHNSON, Register. WILLIAM CATTELL, JR. as executor of WHIT-
FIELD'S estate declared this mortgage satisfied. Witness: ROBERT AUSTIN,
Register.

Book N, p. 214　　　　　　THOMAS FORD, planter, & PATIENCE, his wife, of
7 & 8 Aug. 1734　　　　　Colleton Co., with her full consent, to WIL-
L & R　　　　　　　　　　LIAM SHACKLEFORD, planter, of Craven Co., for
　　　　　　　　　　　　　₺ 200 SC money, 650 a. in Craven Co., which
land by grant signed by Gov. ROBERT JOHNSON & dated 23 May 1734 was given
to THOMAS FORD; bounding S on WILLIAM SHACKLEFORD; W on THOMAS BOSHER;
all other sides on vacant land. Witnesses: JACOB GENT, JOHN GODFREY.
Before HENRY GIBBES, J.P. NATHANIEL JOHNSON, Register

Book N, p. 221　　　　　　ISAAC MAZYCK, JR., merchant of Charleston, to
23 Sept. 1734　　　　　　 WILLIAM SHACKLEFORD, planter, of Craven Co.,

for ⅃ 50, 50 a. in Craven Co., bounding E & S on WILLIAM SHACKLEFORD; W on THOMAS BOSHER; N on ISAAC MAZYCK; appointing DANIEL LAROCHE & THOMAS LAROCHE to give livery & seizing. Witnesses: ELIZABETH SERRE, ELIZABETH (her mark) CURBISH, JOHN BENNET. Before DAN LAROCHE, J.P. NATHANIEL JOHNSON, Register.

Book N, p. 223　　　　　WILLIAM SHACKLEFORD, planter & ESTER his wife,
20 & 24 Sept. 1734　　　of Craven Co., to ISAAC MAZYCK, JR., merchant,
L & R　　　　　　　　　　of Charleston, for ⅃ 400 currency, 650 a. in
　　　　　　　　　　　　　Craven Co., bounding S on WILLIAM SHACKLEFORD;
W on THOMAS BOSHER; all other sides on vacant land; which 650 a. on 23 May 1734 was granted (grant signed by Gov. ROBERT JOHNSON) to THOMAS FORD & sold by him on 8 Aug. 1734 to WILLIAM SHACKLEFORD. Witnesses: ELIZABETH SERRE, ELIZABETH (her mark) CURBISH, JOHN BENNET. Before THOMAS LAROCHE, J.P. NATHANIEL JOHNSON, Register.

Book N, p. 230　　　　　DANIEL GIBSON, surgeon, promises THOMAS MONCK,
6 Mar. 1734　　　　　　　merchant, both of Charleston, that he (GIBSON),
Agreement　　　　　　　　for ⅃ 56 an a. for every a., to be paid by
　　　　　　　　　　　　　MONCK within a month, will execute a good
title in law of a piece of land in St. Philip's Parish near the mile post on the E side of the High Road leading to Charleston, bounding S & E on PHILIP DAWS; N or NW on JOSEPH BLAKE; the land to be surveyed. MONCK agrees to pay GIBSON ⅃ 56 currency for every a. contained. Witnesses: LAWRENCE NEILL, JOHN GWYN. Before CHARLES PINCKNEY, J.P. NATHANIEL JOHNSON, Register.

Book N, p. 232　　　　　JOSEPH MACKEY, carpenter, & CATHERINE his wife,
13 & 14 Nov. 1734　　　　of Charleston, to JAMES ST. JOHN, Surv. Gen.,
L & R　　　　　　　　　　for ⅃ 750 SC money, 250 a., in Colleton Co.,
　　　　　　　　　　　　　on W side S Edisto River, bounding N on JOSEPH
DEDCOT; W on THOMAS ELLIOTT; S on EDWARD RIPPON; E on JOSEPH BOONE. Whereas Gov. CHARLES CRAVEN & the Lords Proprs. on 14 May 1714 granted JOSEPH BOONE the above 250 a., & he, by deed of feoffment dated 21 May 1730 conveyed the land to JOSEPH MACKEY, now MACKEY sells to ST. JOHN. Witnesses: EDWARD SHREWBURY, WILLIAM SMITH. NATHANIEL JOHNSON, Register.

Book N, p. 238　　　　　MILES BREWTON, ESQ. of Charleston, to his
24 Dec. 1733　　　　　　daughter MARY, wife of THOMAS DALE, M.D., of
Deed of Gift　　　　　　Charleston, for natural love & affection &
　　　　　　　　　　　　　other considerations, that part of a town lot
now occupied by THOMAS DALE formerly belonging to JOHN CROSKEY, merchant, fronting E 30 ft. on New Church Street, bounding N 80 ft. on MILES BREWTON; S on an alley between this lot the house & lot wherein ROBERT BREWTON, son of MILES BREWTON, lives; the lot to be free from claim of dower by SUSANNAH, wife of MILES BREWTON. Witnesses: JOHN BAKER, REBECCA BREWTON, CHARLES PINCKNEY. Before HENRY GIBBES, J.P. NATHANIEL JOHNSON, Register.

Book N, p. 242　　　　　DANIEL GIBSON, chirurgeon, & RICHARD THOMPSON,
14 June 1734　　　　　　carpenter, both of Charleston, make this agree-
Agreement　　　　　　　　ment; THOMPSON agrees to build a house for GIB-
　　　　　　　　　　　　　SON up the Broad Path where the Crown Tavern
was lately kept, GIBSON providing the timber, nails, etc., instructions given as to how the house shall be built; GIBSON to allow THOMPSON 9 months work of 2 Negro carpenters, 1 of his own & 1 belonging to DR. THOMAS BARKER; stipulations in regard to Negroes, their work, apparel, victuals, room, etc. GIBSON agrees to give THOMPSON a title to a lot on the Broad Path facing the Crown Tavern, from the cedar tree to the corner of the fence "took square" from the high road at the broad end & in depth as fenced in; to furnish the timber, etc. Each put up a ⅃ 500 bond. Witnesses: THOMAS BARKER, CHARLES ARMSTRONG. Before HENRY GIBBES, J.P. NATHANIEL JOHNSON, Register.

Book N, p. 244　　　　　CHARLES HART, ESQ. of St. Philip's Parish,
2 & 3 Apr. 1735　　　　　Charleston, to JOHN WHITFIELD, merchant, of
L & R　　　　　　　　　　Charleston, for ⅃ 250 currency, 500 a. in Col-
　　　　　　　　　　　　　leton Co., on E side S Edisto River, bounding
N on JOHN BRANDFORD & RICHARD BUTLER; E on ROGER SUMMERS; S on JOHN JACKSON; granted to CHARLES HART by the Lords Proprs. on 21 Apr. 1718, the

grant being signed by Gov. CHARLES CRAVEN, RALPH IZARD, ROBERT DANIELL, NICHOLAS TROTT, SAMUEL EVELEIGH & CHARLES HART. Witnesses: JAMES HEARN, ROWLAND VAUGHAN. Before JAMES WEDDERBURN, J.P. NATHANIEL JOHNSON, Register.

Book N, p. 250
22 & 23 Apr. 1735
L & R by Mortgage

TOBIAS FITCH, planter, of Berkeley Co., to BENJAMIN SAVAGE, merchant, & THOMAS LAMBOLL, gentleman, both of Charleston, administrators of the goods, chattels, rights & credits of GEORGE SMITH which were unadministered by ELIZABETH the widow, as security for the payment of various sums, conveys 2 tracts of land, 1783 a. & 1540 a., total 3323 a. Whereas by letters patents dated 22 Apr. 1735, signed by Gov. ROBERT JOHNSON, TOBIAS FITCH was granted 1783 a. in Berkeley Co., bounding W on a cypress swamp made by Four Hole Creek, a branch of Edisto River, also on same date another piece of 1540 a. bounding W by a cypress swamp at head of Ashley River; & whereas GEORGE SMITH at the request of FITCH, on 9 June 1730 became bound with FITCH to JOHN FENWICKE, JOSEPH WRAGG, PAUL JENYS, OTHNIEL BEALE & THOMAS LAMBOLL, merchants, of Charleston, in penal sum of ₤ 2150 currency conditioned for the payment of ₤ 1075 on 9 Mar. 1730; & whereas FITCH, at SMITH'S request, gave SMITH, a bond dated 12 June 1730 for ₤ 2300 currency with the condition that FITCH pay FENWICKE, WRAGG, JENYS, BEALE & LAMBOLL ₤ 1075 on 9 Mar. next & cancel the above bond; & whereas ₤ 1000 of the first bond; remains unpaid & whereas FITCH by bond dated this 22 Apr. for moneys paid for him by BENJAMIN SAVAGE & THOMAS LAMBOLL out of the estate of GEORGE SMITH, as administrators, stands bound for ₤ 140; now FITCH conveys 2 tracts as security. Witnesses: ROGER SAUNDERS, JAMES PAINE. Before JAMES WEDDERBURNE, J.P. NATHANIEL JOHNSON, Register.

Book N, p. 265
22 & 23 Apr. 1735
L & R by Mortgage

TOBIAS FITCH, planter, of Berkeley Co., to ROGER SAUNDERS, THOMAS ELLIOT, THOMAS BULLENE, & JAMES PAINE, gentlemen, for ₤ 1000 currency, 2 tracts of 1783 a. & 1540 a. (3323 a.) conditioned for the repayment of ₤ 1000 with interest on 23 Apr. 1736. Whereas by letters patents dated 22 Apr. 1735 Gov. ROBERT JOHNSON granted TOBIAS FITCH 1783 a. in Berkeley Co., bounding on W side on a cypress swamp made by Four Hole Creek, a branch of Edisto River, & on same date granted FITCH another tract of 1540 a. bounding on W side of a cypress swamp at head of Ashley River, now FITCH mortgages to SAUNDERS et al. Witnesses: THOMAS LAMBOLL, BNEJAMIN SAVAGE. Before JAMES WEDDERBURNE, J.P. NATHANIEL JOHNSON, Pub. Reg.

Book N, p. 276
29 Sept. 1730
Deed of Sale

ROBERT WRIGHT, the younger, of Berkeley Co., & RICHARD LAMBTON, merchant, of Charleston, to GEORGE ANSON, ESQ., of the Middle Temple, London, late commander of HMS The Garland, for ₤ 280 money of Great Britain, paid WRIGHT by ANSON & 5 shillings paid LAMBTON by ANSON, WRIGHT & LAMBTON (at WRIGHT'S request) sold ANSON half of the Barony of 12,000 a. & half the timber, etc., sold by THOMAS LOUNDES & JOHN BERESFORD to WRIGHT & LAMBTON on 21 Aug. last. Whereas ROBERT WRIGHT & RICHARD LAMBTON (in trust for WRIGHT) own a certain Barony in SC conveyed to them 21 Aug. last by THOMAS LOWNDES, gentleman, of the Parish of SD. John the evangelist in the Liberty of Westminister, Co. of Middlesex, & JOHN BERESFORD, gentleman, of Smithfield, Co. of Middlesex; & whereas GEORGE ANSON agreed with WRIGHT & LAMBTON for the purchase of half the tract for ₤ 280, now the sale is made. Witnesses: JOHN COTTON, WILLIAM BROWN. Receipt given for ₤ 45:15 shillings part payment. NATHANIEL JOHNSON, Register.

Book N, p. 280
5 & 6 May 1735
L & R

ROBERT WRIGHT, JR., of SC to GEORGE ANSON, ESQ., commander H.M.S. "Squirrel" 1/2 a Barony of 12,000 a. for ₤ 280 Britian money. See P. 276. Whereas on 29 Sept. 1730 WRIGHT & LAMBTON were entitled to a Barony to be set out in SC, conveyed to them 21 Aug. last & inrolled in the High Court of Chancery by THOMAS LOWNDES & JOHN BERESFORD; & whereas ANSON had agreed to buy 1/2 the tract for ₤ 280 & the conveyance was made, & whereas WRIGHT agreed to make any further conveyances necessary; & whereas in pursuance of a precept signed by JAMES ST. JOHN, H.M., Surv. Gen., dated 17 Dec. 1731 issued by virtue of a clause in the original grant form the Lords Proprs. of SC to JOHN

BERESFORD in trust for THOMAS LOWNDES, the 12,000 a. tract has been laid out & measured to ROBERT WRIGHT as assignee to BERESFORD; & is situated in Granville Co., bounding NW on WILLIAM HODSON; SE on May River; SW on Day's Creek; now WRIGHT absolutely confirms to ANSON 1/2 the Barony. Witnesses: ROBERT PRINGLE, BENJAMIN WHITAKER. NATHANIEL JOHNSON, Register.

Book N, p. 287　　　　　　BENJAMIN GODIN, merchant, of St. Philip's Par-
5 & 6 May 1735　　　　　　ish, Charleston, & MARYANNE his wife, to
L & R　　　　　　　　　　　CHARLES PINCKNEY, gentleman, for Ŀ 1326 SC
　　　　　　　　　　　　　money, 548 a. on E side Goose Creek in St.
James Goose Creek Parish, Berkeley Co., bounding SW on the Glebe land & 2 a. containing the Parish Church & churchyard; S on COL. JOHN HERBERT; N on ARTHUR MIDDLETON, ESQ., E on JAMES GOODBEE & CHARLES PINCKNEY. Witnesses: JOHN GUERARD, ROBERT BREWTON. Before THOMAS DALE, J.P. at the request of BENJAMIN GODIN, GEORGE HUNTER resurveyed the tract of 550 a. in St. James Parish Goose Creek. Certified 7 Mar. 1734/5. NATHANIEL JOHNSON, Register.

Book N, p. 294　　　　　　DANIEL GIBSON, surgeon, of St. Philip's Parish,
9 & 10 May 1735　　　　　 Charleston, & ANNE his wife, to THOMAS MONCK,
L & R　　　　　　　　　　　ESQ., of Charleston, for Ŀ 420 SC money, 7-1/2
　　　　　　　　　　　　　a. on Charleston Neck, bounding SE on MRS.
DAWES; SW on the high road leading to Charleston; NW on COL. JOSEPH BLAKE; NE on marsh. Witnesses: THOMAS DALE, CHARLES PINCKNEY, ROBERT BREWTON, JR. Before THOMAS DALE, J.P. Plat surveyed at request of THOMAS MONCK on 28 Mar. 1735 by JOHN OULDFIELD, Dep. Surv. NATHANIEL JOHNSON, Register.

Book N, p. 300　　　　　　JAMES LEBAS, planter, of St. Johns Paris,
21 & 22 Apr. 1735　　　　 Berkeley Co., (son & heir of PAUL PETER LEBAS,
L & R　　　　　　　　　　　planter, who was son & heir of JAMES LEBAS,
　　　　　　　　　　　　　merchant, of Charleston) & ANN his wife, to
THOMAS MONCK, ESQ., of St. Philips Parish, Charleston, for Ŀ 7112 SC money, 1000 a., part of 1500 a., on W side Biggin Creek, St. Johns Parish, bounding E on JOHN COLLETON, ESQ. of London & JAMES LEBAS & PETER COLLETON; S on JOHN COLLETON; W on MRS. COLLETON & MR. RENE, merchant, N on MAJOR HUGH BUTLER. Whereas the Lords Proprs. on 15 Nov. 1680 granted the Hon. Landgrave JOSEPH WEST 1500 a. on W side of W branch of Cooper River, & whereas W on 7 Dec. 1686 sold the 1500 a. to JAMES LEBAS the elder & at his death the land was inherited by PAUL PETER LEBAS, father of JAMES (party hereto); & whereas PAUL PETER died 8 Feb. 1724, the land descended to JAMES as eldest son & heir; now he sells part (1000 a.) to MONCK. Witnesses: NATHANIEL BROUGHTON, ANDREW BROUGHTON, THOMAS SABB. Before CHARLES PINCKNEY, J.P. Plat certified 21 Mar. 1734 by JOHN OULDFIELD, Dep. Surv. NATHANIEL JOHNSON, Register.

Book N, p. 307　　　　　　DANIEL GIBSON, surgeon, to THOMAS BOLTON, mer-
5 & 6 May 1735　　　　　　chant, of Charleston, 18 a. 1 mile from
L & R　　　　　　　　　　　Charleston. GIBSON, for natural love & affec-
　　　　　　　　　　　　　tion for his wife ANN, & to settle a separate
maintenance upon her, to be at her own disposal, conveys to BOLTON for 5 shillings 18 a. in Berkeley Co. about 1 mile up the Broad Path from Charleston, according to plat dated 11 May 1694, for the use of ANN during her natural life, then to such person as she shall name. Should she wish to dispose of the land, BOLTON shall join her in such deed. BOLTON to permit ANN to manage the tract as she thinks fit; all income to be paid ANN alone. Witnesses: RICHARD BODDICOTT, LAWRENCE NEILL, WILLIAM SMITH. Before HENRY GIBBES, J.P. NATHANIEL JOHNSON, Register.

Book N, p. 317　　　　　　ISABELL HEIDLERBERG (HEIDELBERG) (late ISABEL
10 May 1735　　　　　　　 OLIVER, widow of MARK OLIVER, & ROBERT FLADGER
Deed of Sale　　　　　　　as executrix & executor of will of MARK OLIVER)
　　　　　　　　　　　　　to THOMAS MONCK, merchant, all of Charleston,
for Ŀ 206 currency, 18 a. containing 7-1/2 a. on Charleston Neck, bounding SE on MRS. DAWES; SW on the high road leading to Charleston; NW on COL. JOSEPH BLAKE; NE on marsh. Whereas MARK OLIVER owned 18 a. on Charleston Neck in St. Philips Parish & by will dated 25 Nov. 1730 requested his executors to sell the 18 a. & put the money out at interest for the benefit of his daughter MARY to whom he had bequeathed the land

in his will; & whereas ISABELL & ROBERT FLADGER proved the will & by L & R dated 29 & 30 Oct. 1731 sold the 18 a. to DANIEL GIBSON, which papers at present are not to be found; & whereas L 206, part of the purchase money is still unpaid by GIBSON & whereas GIBSON has agreed to sell part of the land (7-1/2 a.) to MONCK for L 420 currency, & GIBSON has agreed that MONCK shall pay the executors the L 208 due; now MONCK pays that sum to the executors & gets 7-1/2 a. Witnesses: THOMAS DALE, CHARLES PINCKNEY, ROBERT BREWTON, JR. Before THOMAS DALE, J.P. NATHANIEL JOHNSON, Register.

Book N, p. 321
29 Mar. 1735
Deed of Sale

ANDREW QUELCH, of Hobcow, SC, to DR. GEORGE NOBLE, for L 500 currency, 1/2 a sloop in Quelch's Creek, with 1/2 her masts, etc., etc. Witnesses: MILES SWEENY, HENRY LEURN. On 9 May 1735 GEORGE NOBLE, sold his half share to some CAPTAIN (name blank). Witnesses: MILES SWEENEY, JOHN HAWCKES. LEURN appeared before HENRY GIBBES, J.P. as witness for QUELCH. NATHANIEL JOHNSON, Register.

Book N, p. 322
22 & 23 Apr. 1735
L & R by Mortgage

ISAAC LEWIS, planter, of St. James Goose Creek, Berkeley Co., to PAUL JENYS & JOHN BAKER, merchants, of Charleston, as security, on bond dated 3 Apr. 1735 in penal sum of L 3221:4 shillings conditioned for the payment of L 1610:12:4 & interest on 23 Apr. 1736; 2 contiguous tracts of 276 a. & 138 a. (414 a.) in St. James Goose Creek & St. Johns Parishes, bounding N on COL. THOMAS BROUGHTON & DR. TOMAN. Witnesses: ANDREW ALLEN, ROBERT BREWTON, JR. Before CHARLES PINCKNEY, J.P. NATHANIEL JOHNSON, Register. ELIAS GIBBES, executor of PAUL JENYS, the survivor of JENYS & BAKER, on 4 Apr. 1753, declared that SEDGWICK LEWIS, by agreement, had paid him L 658 in full satisfaction of his father's bond & mortgage & asked WILLIAM HOPTON to put in on record. Witness: JOHN BASSNELL.

Book N, p. 329
30 June 1729
Deed of Gift

JAMES HERNE (HEARN) carpenter, of Berkeley Co., to MRS. MARY ADAMS of Berkeley Co., for love & affection & other considerations, 2 mares, 1 gelding, 2 cows, 1 yearling, 2 feather beds & furniture, 12 chairs, 12 plates, every thing except his wearing apparel & working tools. Witnesses: MOSEAU SARRAZIN, ABRAHAM CROFT. Before DANIEL GREENE, J.P. NATHANIEL JOHNSON, Register.

Book N, p. 331
4 Mar. 1734/5
Deed of Sale

THOMAS ELLIOTT & SUSANNAH his wife, of Colleton Co., to WILLIAM FAIRCHILD, for L 5, 250 a. in Colleton Co., granted to JOHN WILLIAMSON in 1710; also 650 a. granted to ANN ELLIOTT in 1733, bounding W on Horseshoe Savanna where he now lives. Witnesses: WILLIAM CLAY, JULIAN MARONEY. Before JAMES ABERCROMBY, J.P. NATHANIEL JOHNSON, Register.

DEEDS BOOK "O"
MAY 1735 - DEC. 1735

Book O, p. 1
17 & 18 Dec. 1734
L & R by Mortgage

JOHN ABBOTT, housewright, of Prince George Parish, Craven Co., to OTHNIEL BEALE & THOMAS COOPER, merchants, of Charleston, for L 500 currency, conditioned for repayment of L 500 on 17 May 1735; 500 a., part of 1000 a. laid out & sold by Landgrave THOMAS SMITH & MARY his wife to JOHN RIDLEY; bounding S on Sanpit or Town River; E on the Rev. Mr. THOMAS MORRITT; W & N on CAPT. GEORGE SMITH. Witnesses: HANNAH GALE, PHILIP PRIOLEAU. Before ALEXANDER PARRIS, J.P. NATHANIEL JOHNSON, Register. Mortgage satisfied in full 10 Feb. 1735. Witness: NATHANIEL JOHNSON, Register.

Book O, p. 6
3 Apr. 1735
Mortgage

BENJAMIN CLIFFORD, planter, & SARAH his wife, of Colleton Co., to THOMAS BINFORD & JAMES OSMOND, merchants, of Charleston, for L 460 currency, lot #306 at upper end of Broad Street, Charleston, bounding N on Broad Street, S & W on marsh, E on REBECCA PARTRIDGE; subject to redemption for same sum with interest on 1 Mar. next.

Witnesses: NICHOLAS SMITH, EDMOND COSSINS, SAMUEL PRIOLEAU, JR. Before THOMAS DALE, J.P. NATHANIEL JOHNSON, Register.

Book O, p. 11
10 & 11 Apr. 1735
L & R

CHARLES CODNER, planter, & ANNE his wife, of Berkeley Co., to GEORGE ANSON, for ₤ 500 currency, free from ANNE'S title of dower, part of lot #17 in Charleston, bounding E 25 ft. on JOHN ROPER (formerly DR. THOMAS COOPER); W on street or lane leading from COL. MILES BREWTON'S sawpit to Broad Street; N on neighborhood alley from the Bay to Union Street; S 125 ft. on CHARLES CODNER; which part of a lot descended lineally from RICHARD CODNER, planter, of Daniell's Island, to CHARLES CODNER, part hereto, son & heir of said RICHARD. Witnesses: SD. ROWES, JAMES GROOME. NATHANIEL JOHNSON, Register.

Book O, p. 18
14 & 15 Apr. 1735
L & R by Mortgage

CHARLES CODNER, planter, & ANNE his wife, of Berkeley Co., to GEORGE ANSON, for ₤ 500 currency, 350 a. on Itowan Island, Berkeley Co., free from ANNE'S title of dower; bounding N on Beresford Creek; NE & SE on Monhom Creek; S on Wando River; SW on JOHN MORGAN; NW on CHRISTOPHER SMITH; which tract was granted by the Lords Proprs. to PHEBE CODNER, widow, & descended to her son & heir RICHARD CODNER, planter, of Daniel's Island, & then to his son & heir CHARLES, party hereto; subject to redemption by paying ₤ 500 & interest on 14 Apr. 1737. Witnesses: JAMES GROOME, JOHN STEWART. NATHANIEL JOHNSON, Register.

Book O, p. 25
19 May 1726
Deed of Sale

THOMAS SMITH, planter, to SAMUEL ASH, planter, both of Berkeley Co., for ₤ 150 SC money, 250 a., part of 4000 a. in Colleton Co., which 4000 a., English measure, was granted by Gov. ROBERT GIBBES & the Lords Proprs., to COL. ROBERT DANIELL; bounding NE on lands belonging to the Cursaw Indians; W on a river; all other sides on vacant land. Witnesses: WILLIAM SANDERS, JOHN BROWN. On 15 May 1735 HENRY LIVINGSTON appeared before THOMAS DALE, J.P. & testified to signatures of SAMUEL ASH & E. PLOMER (below). On 14 June 1728 SAMUEL ASH, for 5 shillings, signed over to BENJAMIN PERRY all his title. Witnesses: E. PLOMER, HENRY LEVINGSTON. NATHANIEL JOHNSON, Register.

Book O, p. 29
2 Jan. 1733/4
Deed of Gift

JOHN (his mark) STRACHAN, & NAOMI (her mark) his wife of St. Thomas Parish, Berkeley Co., to their son JOHN PAINTER, for love & affection & other considerations, their stock of cattle, horses & hogs, after death of JOHN & NAOMI STRACHAN. Gift & delivery of 1 pig. "N.B. reference being had to a deed of gift to NAOMI of a prior date." Witnesses: JOHN CUMING, NAOMI (her mark) PAINTER. Memo: JOHN APINTER is to give his sister PRUDENCE DEARINGTON a share of the premises. Before ANTHONY BONNEAU, J.P. NATHANIEL JOHNSON, Register.

Book O, p. 31
1 Jan. 1733/4
Deed of Gift

JOHN (his mark) STRACHAN, & NAOMI (her mark) his wife, of St. Thomas Parish, Berkeley Co., to their daughter, or step-daughter NAOMI PAINTER, for love & affection & other considerations, (after the death of JOHN & NAOMI STRACHAN), all their household furniture & everything in their house, except a chest, also plantation tools, etc. Gift & delivery of 1 feather bed. Witnesses: JOHN CUMING, JOHN PAINTER. Memo: NAOMI PAINTER is to give her sister PRUDENCE DEARINGTON "what share she thinks fit & proper." Before ANTHONY BONNEAU, J.P. NATHANIEL JOHNSON, Register.

Book O, p. 32
13 & 14 Dec. 1733
L & R

BENJAMIN LAW, planter, of Christ Church Parish, Berkeley Co., to ARTHUR FOSTER, planter, of Winyaw, Prince George Parish, Craven Co., for ₤ 10 currency, & in consideration that FOSTER has paid the expenses of surveying, etc., 500 a. in Craven Co., part of 1150 a. granted LAW as vacant land, the remaining part of which belongs to ANTHONY WHITE; which 500 a. bounds N on part of the land granted to LAW; S on JOHN PETER SOMERHOOSE; E on MR. FURBUSH. Witnesses: HENRY GIGNILLIAT, ROWLAND VAUGHAN. NATHANIEL JOHNSON, Register.

Book O, p. 37
15 & 16 Apr. 1735

JOHN SIMMONS, of Charleston, to the Rev. MR. DANIEL DWIGHT, of St. John's Parish, for

L & R	₤ 1000 currency, 990 a. in Craven Co., between Waccamaw River & the sea bounding S on CAPT.

ANTHONY MATHEWS; which land is part of 48,000 a. was granted by the Lords Proprs. in 1711 to ROBERT DANIELL. ROBERT DANIELL on 19 June 1711 sold the 990 a. to THOMAS SMITH & he sold the land to JOHN SIMMONS for ₤ 30 currency. Witnesses: WILLIAM SCOTT, OTHNIEL BEALE, ANDREW BROUGHTON. Before ALEXANDER PARRIS, J.P. NATHANIEL JOHNSON, Register.

Book O, p. 42 15 Apr. 1735 Ren. of Dower	ANN FERGUSON, wife of JAMES FERGUSON, planter, of Colleton Co., appeared before ROBERT WRIGHT, C.T., & acknowledged she voluntarily joined her husband in a release (see p. 45) dated 15

Apr. 1735, to ARTHUR MIDDLETON, ESQ., & SARAH his wife of St. James Goose Creek, of 600 a., English measure, in Colleton Co., on W side of freshes of Edisto River, bounding N on THOMAS STEERS & THOMAS JONES; also 300 a. on W side Edisto River, bounding S on JOSEPH COOPER & JOSHUA GREENE; W & N on MR. MIDDLETON & JAMES FERGUSON. NATHANIEL JOHNSON, Register.

Book O, p. 45 15 Apr. 1735 Mortgage	JAMES FERGUSON, planter, & ANN his wife, to ARTHUR MIDDLETON, ESQ., & SARAH his wife, of St. James Goose Creek, Berkeley Co., as securi-

ty on bond signed by JAMES FERGUSON & THOMAS FERGUSON, his brother, planter of Berkeley Co., dated 12 Apr. 1735, in the penal sum of ₤ 6415:11 SC money, conditioned for payment of ₤ 3207:15:6 on 12 Apr. 1736, 600 a., English measure, on W side freshes of Edisto River, bounding N on THOMAS STEER & THOMAS JONES; W & N on MR. MIDDLETON; also 300 a., English measure, in Colleton Co. on W side fresh- es of Edisto River, bounding S on JOSEPH COOPER & JOSHUA GREENE; W & N on MR. MIDDLETON & FERGUSON. Witnesses: ROBERT WRIGHT, TIMOTHY MILLECHAMPP, JANE MILLECHAMP. Before RALPH IZARD, J.P. NATHANIEL JOHNSON, Register.

Book O, p. 51 8 & 9 Feb. 1730 L & R	MOSES WILSON, planter, & MARGARET his wife, to OTHNIEL BEALE, merchant, all of Charleston, for ₤ 900 SC money part of 3 lots Nos. 171, 172, 173 in Charleston, which WILSON purchased

from WILLIAM LIVINGSTON & MARY his wife by deed of foeffment dated 28 Feb. 1711; the parts of 3 adjoining lots bounding E 97 ft. on the street run- ning to Benson's Point; the same breadth to run parallel with the Broad Street; N 200 ft. on JOHN MOORE; S on MRS. ANNE DRAYTON. Witnesses: WIL- LIAM WATSON, JOHN BONNIN, JOHN CROFT. Before ALEXANDER PARRIS, J.P.

Book O, p. 58 18 Apr. 1735 Bond	RICHARD EAGLES, planter, of St. George Parish, Berkeley Co., to JOHN WHITFIELD, merchant, of Charleston, in sum of ₤ 5000 currency to se- cure WHITFIELD in his possession of 526 a.,

sold to WHITFIELD by PHILIP AYTON, physician, of St. George Parish, by L & R, 17 & 18 this inst. Apr. Witnesses: WILLIAM PINCKNEY, JOHN WOODWARD. NATHANIEL JOHNSON, Register.

Book O, p. 59 17 & 18 Apr. 1735 L & R	PHILIP AYTON, physician, of St. George Parish, Berkeley Co., to JOHN WHITFIELD, merchant, of Charleston, for ₤ 2630 SC money, 526 a. on E side E Edisto River, Berkeley Co., bounding N

E on JOHN SIMONS & INCREASE SUMNER; NW on JOB CHAMBERLAIN; SW on JOHN BRANDFORD; SE on vacant land. Witnesses: RICHARD TODMARSH, RICHARD BAKER. Before NATHANIEL WICKHAM, J.P. NATHANIEL JOHNSON, Register.

Book O, p. 65 9 & 10 Mar. 1724 L & R	JOHN BRAND, carpenter, to JOHN LEAY, joiner, & MARY his wife, all of Charleston, for ₤ 165 currency, half of lot #187 in Charleston, fronting E 42 ft. on a little street leading

from Ashley River; W on MR. GRIMSTON; N 200 ft. on MARTIN HOLT; S on ELIAS HANCOCK; which lot #187 was granted to BRAND by L & R tripertite dated 1 & 2 Mar. 1723 made between MARY LAROCHE, widow & executor of JOHN LAROCHE, merchant, of Charleston, of 1st part; JOHN BRAND of 2nd part; ANTHONY MATHEWS, merchant, of Charleston, of 3rd part. The lot to be free from claim of dower by ELIZABETH, wife of JOHN BRAND. Whereas the title deed to lot #187 also contains a release of another lot & a half (164 & 186) to BRAND he will hold the papers & show them when necessary. Witnesses: WILLIAM BILLING, MARTIN HOLT. NATHANIEL JOHNSON, Register.

Book O, p. 72   RICHARD (his mark) FLOYD, cordwainer, of Colle-
13 July 1730   ton Co., to ANTHONY MATTHEW, SR., merchant, of
Bond   Charleston, in penal sum of Ł 1000 SC money
                  conditioned for the payment of Ł 500 SC money
with interest on 9 Mar. 1730. Witnesses: JAMES PAINE, JOHN MATHEWES,
JOHN CROFT. Before JAMES ABERCROMBY, J.P. NATHANIEL JOHNSON, Register.

Book O, p. 73   RICHARD (his mark) FLOYD, cordwainer, of Colle-
12 & 13 July 1730   ton Co., to CAPT. ANTHONY MATTHEWS, SR., mer-
L & R by Mortgage   chant, of Charleston, for Ł 1000 SC money, 274
                      a. in Colleton Co., on S side Bohicket Creek,
bounding NE on AMBROSE HILL; SW on MICHAEL RENOLDS; SE on ANTHONY MAT-
THEWS; conditioned for payment of Ł 533:6:6 SC money with interest on 9
Mar. 1730, according to bond of even date. See p. 72. Witnesses: JAMES
PAINE, JOHN MATHEWS, JOHN CROFT. Before JAMES ABERCROMBY, J.P. NATHAN-
IEL JOHNSON, Register. "Mar. 25, 1945, I do hereby acknowledge to have
received full satisfaction for the within mortgage & do fully & absolutely assign & set over all my right & title therein to MR. JOHN JURETINE as
witness my hand. ANTHONY MATTHEWS. Witness: RICHARD HARRISON."

Book O, p. 80   DANIEL GIBSON, surgeon, & ANNE his wife, to
25 & 26 Apr. 1735   JACOB MARTIN, gentleman, all of Charleston,
L & R   for Ł 7000 SC money, 2 adjoining sixth parts
                        of Schenckingh Square in Charleston, fronting
W 98-1/4 ft. on the Main Street, leading out of Charleston into the Broad
Path or High Road; bounding E 100-1/4 ft. on Old Church Street; N 471 ft.
on MRS. CATHARINE CHICKEN; S 468 ft. on MATHURIN BOGARD. Whereas by L &
R, 20 & 21 June 1722 ABRAHAM EVE, ESQ., of Colleton Co. sold to BENJAMIN
WHITAKER, ESQ., of Berkeley Co., 1/6 part of Schenckingh Square, bounding
N on DANIEL GIBSON; S on MATHURIN BOGARD (late MRS. SUSANNAH BOGARD) &
whereas by L & R, 8 & 9 Jan. 1730 BENJAMIN WHITAKER sold DANIEL GIBSON
the same sixth part; & whereas by L & R, 20 & 21 June 1722 ABRAHAM EVE
sold DANIEL GIBSON another 1/6 part of Schenckinghs Square, bounding N on
COL. GEORGE CHICKEN; S by BENJAMIN WHITAKER; now GIBSON sells 2 parts to
MARTIN. Witnesses: Plat certified 15 Apr. 1735 by GEORGE HUNTER, Sur.
Witnesses: RICHARD ALLEIN, LAURENCE COULLIETTE, FREDERICK MEYER. Before
THOMAS LAMBOLL, J.P. NATHANIEL JOHNSON, Register.

Book O, p. 89   JAMES FERGUSON, planter, of Colleton Co., to
14 Apr. 1735   ARTHUR MIDDLETON, ESQ. & SARAH his wife, of
Lease   St. James Goose Creek, Berkeley Co., for 5
                   shillings, 600 a., English measure, in Colle-
ton Co., on W side freshes of Edisto River, bounding N on THOMAS STEERS &
THOMAS JONES; W & N on MRS. SARAH MIDDLETON; also 300 a., English measure,
in Colleton Co., on W side freshes of Edisto River; bounding S on JOSEPH
GREENE; W & N on MR. MIDDLETON & MR. FERGUSON (see p. 45). Witnesses:
ROBERT WRIGHT, TIM MILLECHAMP, JANE MILLECHAMP. NATHANIEL JOHNSON, Reg-
ister.

Book O, p. 91   ALEXANDER PARRIS, ESQ., of Charleston, late
3 June 1735   Public Treasurer & Public Receiver of SC hum-
Proposal   bly proposes that in order to secure & make
                   good all moneys, etc., in his hands, or in
arrears for, he will execute when required a mortgage in fee to the Hon.
THOMAS BROUGHTON, Lt. Gov., all his house & lot on the Bay, his low water
lot, also Archers Island in Granville Co. with the stock on it; & 40
slaves. Witnesses: JOHN FENWICKE, CHARLES PINCKNEY, OTHNIEL BEALE. Before JAMES KINLOCH. NATHANIEL JOHNSON, Register.

Book O, p. 93   JOSEPH (his mark) SPENCER & JOHN (his mark)
29 & 30 May 1735   SPENCER, planters, of St. James Santee, to
L & R by Mortgage   THOMAS LYNCH, planter, of Berkeley Co., for
                       Ł 605 currency, 500 a., English measure, on
Santee River, Craven Co., conditioned for payment of Ł 605 on 30 May 1736.
Whereas the Lords Proprs. on 5 May 1703 granted PATRICK STEWART 500 a. in
Craven Co., & STEWART by will dated 29 June 1707 bequeathed to his sons
JOHN, JAMES, ROBERT & CHARLES, all his real & personal estate; & whereas
CHARLES died a minor & the other 3 inherited; & whereas JOHN, JAMES, &
ROBERT by L & R, 14 & 15 Dec. 1730 sold the 500 a. to JOSEPH & JOHN SPEN-
CER; now they mortgage to LYNCH. Witnesses: CHARLES PINCKNEY, GILLSON

CLAPP, ROBERT BREWTON, JR. Before HENRY GIBBES, J.P. NATHANIEL JOHNSON, Register. "Whereas my late father did receive the full contents of the foregoing mortgage of JOHN & JOSEPH SPENCER to him, I THOMAS LYNCH as heir & son of my said father do certifie that I am satisfied that he my said father did receive the same by the hands of MR. ISAAC MAZYCK, in consideration whereof I discharge the same." 20 Dec. 1749 THOMAS LYNCH. Witness: JOHN LOGAN.

Book O, p. 102
26 July 1728
Deed of Sale

ABRAHAM DEDCOTT, planter, of Colleton Co., & REBECCA (her mark) his wife, to THOMAS CROLL, planter, for ₤ 400 currency, 215 a. Whereas JOHN, Earl of Bath, Palatine & the Lords Proprs.; by grant signed by the Rt. Hon. JOSEPH BLAKE, dated 11 May 1699 gave JOHN DEDCOTT 430 a. in Colleton Co., being an entire island on W side Edisto River, bounding E on marsh; S & W on a creek; N on Tubedue Creek; & whereas JOHN DECOTT bequeathed to his son, ABRAHAM, half the island, containing 215 a., bounding E on marsh; S & W on a creek; N on JOHN DEDCOTT'S other half; now ABRAHAM sells his half to CROLL. Witnesses: JOHN (his mark) ROBESON, MARTHA (her mark) ROBESON, RACHEL (her mark) JEFFREY, JOHN COCHRAN. Before WILLIAM LIVINGSTON, enrolled in auditor's office by memorial in Old Grant Book 5 July 1732 fol. 163 by DANIEL GIBSON for JAMES ST. JOHN, Auditor. NATHANIEL JOHNSON, Register.

Book O, p. 106
5 June 1735
Mortgage

RICHARD MURPHEY, vintner, to WILLIAM HARDEN, planter, both of Colleton Co., for good causes & considerations, 50 a. in Colleton Co., bounding S on GEORGE FARLEY; W on JOHN MITCHELL; E & N on HUGH CAMPBELL; conditioned for payment to HARDEN of ₤ 268:5 with interest on 1 May next. Witnesses: WILLIAM (his mark) WONSLOW, JOHN MITCHELL, ALGERNOON ASH. Before JAMES BULLOCK, J.P. NATHANIEL JOHNSON, Register.

Book O, p. 109
10 & 11 June 1734
L & R

ALEXANDER GOODBEE, planter, (son of JOHN GOODBEE, planter), & ANNE his wife, of St. James Goose Creek, Berkeley Co., & JOHN DANIEL, ESQ., of Berkeley Co., to CHARLES PINCKNEY, ESQ., of Charleston, for ₤ 530 currency, 240 a. in St. James Goose Creek, bounding E on Forsters Creek; SE on JAMES GOODBEE; W on BENJAMIN GODIN, & ARTHUR MIDDLETON; N on THOMAS CLIFFORD (formerly JOB HOWES). Whereas the Lords Proprs. on 8 Sept. 1696 granted JOHN GOODBEE 50 a. on Forsters Creek; & whereas on 24 Dec. 1701 they granted the Hon. JAMES MOORE 50 a. near GOODBEE'S tract & JAMES MOORE on 2 Jan. 1711 sold his 50 a. to GOODBEE for ₤ 18 currency; & whereas the Lords Proprs. on 17 Dec. 1714 granted GOODBEE 100 a. adjoining MOORE'S 50 a. & whereas by another grant at a later date the Lords Proprs. granted GOODBEE 290 a. adjoining all 3 above named tracts, making 1 tract of 490 a.; & whereas JOHN GOODBEE granted his son JAMES the SE part, or 250 a. & kept the NW o4 240 a. till his death, & by will dated 18 Oct. 1720 bequeathed the 240 a. to his son ALEXANDER; now the GOODBEES & DANIELL sell the 240 a. to PINCKNEY. Witnesses: MRS. SARAH BLAKEWAY, ROBERT BREWTON, JR. Before THOMAS DALE, J.P. NATHANIEL JOHNSON, Register.

Book O, p. 120
29 & 30 June 1735
L & R

HUGH BRYAN, ESQ., of St. Helena Parish, Granville Co., SC to PETER FLOWER, merchant, of Fenchurch Street, London, for ₤ 2000 SC money, 1000 a. in Granville Co., granted HUGH BRYAN 23 Apr. 1735; bounding SW on JOHN POSTELL; SE on COL. WILLIAM BULL; NE on CAPT. JOHN BULL; NW on THOMAS LOWNDES. Witnesses: MAURICE LEWIS, RICHARD HALL, JR. ₤ 2000 paid by PETER FLOWER by hands of JOSEPH EDWARD FLOWER. Before HENRY GIBBES, J.P. NATHANIEL JOHNSON, Register.

Book O, p. 126
5 & 6 May 1735
L & R

WILLIAM CATTELL, ESQ., to JOHN HAYDON, cordwainer, of St. Andrews Parish, Berkeley Co., for ₤ 250 SC money, lot #30 in St. Andrews Town, containing 1/4 a., English measure, & the tenement on the lot. Whereas JOHN, Earl of Bath, Palatine, & the Lords Proprs. on 12 Oct. 1701 granted FRANCIS FIDLING 38 a., English measure, in Berkeley Co., on S side Ashley River, bounding E on marsh & creek; S on other lands of FRANCIS FIDLING; W on EDMUND BELLINGER (formerly THOMAS BUTLER); & whereas FRANCIS FIDLING & MARY his wife by deed of feoffment dated 24 Feb. 1701 conveyed the 38 a. to THOMAS ROSE, planter, of Berkeley Co., & whereas by several mesne conveyances to 38 a. came to THOMAS DYMES, merchant, of SC; & whereas at the time of his death DYNES owned a tenement at Ashley River Ferry, commonly known as Ashley Ferry Store, part of or adjoining the 38 a. which THOMAS DYMES purchased from SAMUEL DEANE, ESQ., together with the 38 a. formerly, belonging to THOMAS ROSE, & also 2 or 3 a. of marsh near the Store, & by will dated 27 Dec. 1729 appointed JOSEPH WRAGG & ROBERT HUME his executors with authority to sell the plantation; & whereas WRAGG & HUME by L & R, 21 & 22 May 1734, for L 2000 currency sold the 38 a. to WILLIAM CATTELL, also the Ashley Ferry Store & the 2 or 3 a. of marsh land; & whereas CATTELL laid out part of the 38 a. for a town called St. Andrews Town, dividing it into lots; now CATTELL sells 1 lot to HAYDON. Witnesses: JAMES SCARLETT, WILLIAM LEA, THOMAS STOCK. Before THOMAS DRAYTON, J.P. NATHANIEL JOHNSON, Register.

Book O, p. 134
18 May 1734
Deed of Gift

JEREMIAH VEREEN, of Prince George Parish, Craen Co., to his well beloved children, WILLIAM & ELIZABETH, for natural love & affeftion, as follows; to WILLIAM 2 Negroes; to ELIZABETH 2 Negro girls. Witnesses: WILLIAM POOLE, ANN CHEEVERS, JAMES ADAMS. Before ELIAS HORRY, J.P. NATHANIEL JOHNSON, Register.

Book O, p. 136
30 Mar. 1731
Deed of Sale

ELIZABETH ELLIOTT to WILLIAM FAIRCHILD, for 5 shillings, 34 a. on S part of a plat of 600 a. adjoining FAIRCHILD'S land. Witnesses: THOMAS ELLIOTT, JR., WILLIAM WILLIAMSON. Before JAMES ABERCROMBY, V.J.Q. NATHANIEL JOHNSON, Register.

Book O, p. 137
4 Mar. 1734/5
Deed of Sale

WILLIAM FAIRCHILD & MARTHA his wife to THOMAS ELLIOTT, for L 5, the 200 a. granted STEPEHN FORD in 1706; also 247 a. brought by FAIRCHILD from EDMOND BELLINGER (part of his patent), also 50 a. granted to HENRY NICHOLS in 1712; also 34 a., part of a tract granted RALPH EMONS (EMMS?) & sold by ELIZABETH ELLIOTT; also 300 a., part of 1000 a. granted THOMAS ELLIOTT, SR. Witnesses: WILLIAM CLAY, JULIEN MARENSY. Before JAMES ABERCROMBY, J.J.Q. NATHANIEL JOHNSON, Register.

Book O, p. 140
28 Sept. 1734
Mortgage

BENJAMIN HEAPE, planter, of St. Bartholomews Parish, Colleton Co., to ANDREW ALLEN & GABRIEL MANIGAULT, merchants, of Charleston, for L 700 currency, 120 a., bounding S on JOSEPH BOONE'S Barony; E on JOSHUA SANDERS; N on JOSEPH WRAGG; also 2 slaves; conditioned for redemption of same with interest on 1 Sept. next. Witnesses: JOSHUA SAUNDERS, JOSHUA GREEN. Before HENRY GIBBES, J.P. NATHANIEL JOHNSON, Register.

Book O, p. 143
5 & 6 Aug. 1733
L & R by Mortgage

JONATHAN SINGLETARY, planter, of Berkeley Co., to the rector & vestrymen of St. Thomas Parish, for L 150 currency, 115 a. on E side Cooper River bounding N on CAPT. THOMAS BONNY (formerly JOHN MILNIAN); S on JOSEPH STONE; E on THOMAS BONNY (formerly ROBERT CLYATT); being part of a tract of 390 a. granted by the Lords Proprs. to JOHN STONE (grant in possession of JOSEPH STONE, son of JOHN STONE) on 27 June 1711; redeemable with interest on 25 Mar. 1734 at the vestry room. Whereas RICHARD BERESFORD by will dated May 1715 bequeathed to THOMAS BROUGHTON, his executors & administrators, all the residue of the yearly profits of his real & personal estate, until his son JOHN BERESFORD should reach 21 years of age, upon trust that BROUGHTON should pay such profits to the vestry of St. Thomas Parish to be used in certain ways; 1/3 to the schoolmaster, 2/3 for the support & education of the children of the poor of the Parish; or to the building of a school; or be put out at interest; & whereas THOMAS HASELL, rector, & JAMES AKIN, THOMAS ASHBY, THOMAS BONNY, THOMAS PAGITT, SAMUEL SIMMONS, ALEXANDER GOODBE & ISAAC LESESNE, JR., vestrymen, let JONATHAN SINGLETARY have L 150 at interest, SINGLETARY gives them 115 a. as security. Witnesses: JACOB WOOLFORD, PETER HOW, HERCULES COYTE. Before MICHAEL DARBY, J.P. NATHANIEL JOHNSON, Register.

Book O, p. 154　　　　　　　　THOMAS WALKER, mariner, & JOHN WALKER, planter,
1 & 2 May 1734　　　　　　　 to the rector & vestrymen of St. Thomas Parish,
L & R by Mortgage　　　　　　Berkeley Co., for ℒ 800, 105 a. on Thomas's
　　　　　　　　　　　　　　　Island, bounding NW on Watcoe Creek; SW on
JOHN DUNHAM; SE & NE on RICHARD CODNER; also 140 a., English measure, on
Thomas's Island. bounding S on Wandoe River; N on JOHN DUNHAM; W on ISAAC
LESESNE; E on RICHARD CODNER; redeemable with interest on 24 Mar. 1735 at
the vestry room. Accordingly to the terms of the will of RICHARD BERES-
FORD (see p. 143) THOMAS BROUGHTON, executor, THOMAS HASELL, rector, &
JAMES AKIN, THOMAS BONNY, THOMAS ASHBY, ISAAC LESESNE, SAMUEL SIMONS, &
THOMAS PAGITT, vestrymen, let THOMAS & JOHN WALKER, have ℒ 800 at inter-
est & THOMAS & JOHN WALKER give them, as security, 2 tracts of land. Wit-
nesses: MICHAEL DARBY, ROBERT HOW. NATHANIEL JOHNSON, Register.

Book O, p. 164　　　　　　　　MOSES MARTIN, JR., planter, to ELIZABETH HILL,
25 & 26 July 1735　　　　　　 widow & executrix of the will of CHARLES HILL,
L & R by Mortgage　　　　　　of Charleston, as security on bond of this
　　　　　　　　　　　　　　　date given by MARTIN to ELIZABETH HILL in penal sum of ℒ 1672:10:8 conditioned for the payment of ℒ 836:5:4 with interest on 1 Mar. 1736, conveys 100 a. in Colleton Co., on N side Ponpon
River, bounding N on WILLIAM PETERS, which 100 a. was conveyed to MARTIN
by JOHN PINNEY & HANNAH his wife, also 156-1/2 a. in Colleton Co., bounding N on JAMES FULTON; E on SAMUEL LOYELL; S on JAMES COCHRAN; W on EBENE-
ZER WALLCOT, PETER FOSTER, & JOHN PINNEY, which tract was conveyed to
MARTIN by EBENEZER WALLCUT & ELIZABETH his wife. Witnesses: WILLIAM
GEORGE FREEMAN, BENJAMIN WHITAKER. Before THOMAS DALE, J.P. NATHANIEL
JOHNSON, Register.

Book O, p. 170　　　　　　　　THOMAS PAGITT, planter, to the rector & vestry
1 & 2 May 1733　　　　　　　 of St. Thomas Parish, Berkeley Co., for ℒ 500
L & R by Mortgage　　　　　　currency, 300 a. in St. Thomas Parish, bound-
　　　　　　　　　　　　　　　ing NE & NW on RICHARD BERESFORD; SE on JOHN
EVANS; SW on THOMAS PAGITT, BENTLY COOK & SAMUEL BLUNDELL; which 300 a.
was granted by the Lords Proprs. on 23 July 1711 to THOMAS PAGITT; also
170 a. in said Parish, bounding W & S on Watcoe Creek; N on THOMAS PAGITT;
E on PHINEAS ROGERS; SW on Habshau Creek; which 170 a. was granted by the
Lords Proprs. to PATRICK SCOTT on 18 Sept. 1703; redeemable with interest
on 25 Mar. 1734 at the vestry room. According to the terms of RICHARD
BERESFORD'S will (see p. 143) THOMAS BROUGHTON, executor, THOMAS HASELL,
rector, & JAMES AKIN, THOMAS BONNY, SAMUEL SIMONS, & ISAAC LESESNE, JR.
advanced THOMAS PAGITT ℒ 500 at interest & as security PAGITT conveyed 2
tracts of land. Witnesses: MICHAEL DARBY, ROBERT HOW. Before MICHAEL
DARBY, J.P. NATHANIEL JOHNSON, Register.

Book O, p. 180　　　　　　　　JOHN JORDAN, carpenter, of Prince George Par-
2 July 1735　　　　　　　　　 ish, Craven Co., to NATHANIEL FORD, of Berke-
Bill of Sale　　　　　　　　　ley Co., for ℒ 140 currency, 1 Negro woman &
　　　　　　　　　　　　　　　2 Negro men. Witnesses: GEORGE DICK, SAMUEL
JENNINGS. NATHANIEL JOHNSON, Register.

Book O, p. 181　　　　　　　　WILLIAM ELLIOTT to his beloved son BERNARD
6 June 1735　　　　　　　　　 ELLIOTT, planter, of St. Andrews Parish, Berke-
Deed of Gift　　　　　　　　　ley Co., for love & affection, all his 340 a.
　　　　　　　　　　　　　　　tract on N side Stono River, bounding N on
THOMAS DRAYTON; E on JOSEPH ELLIOTT; W on JOHN BANOE; S on HENRY TURNER.
Witnesses: RICHARD BUTLER, JAMES FOWLER, FRANCIS DANDRIDGE. Before THOM-
AS DALE, J.P. NATHANIEL JOHNSON, Register.

Book O, p. 182　　　　　　　　JOSEPH (his mark) BAILEY (BAILY), of Berkeley
3 Nov. 1727　　　　　　　　　 Co., to his loving & lawful wife ANN, for love
Deed of Gift　　　　　　　　　& affection, all his good, chattels, & person-
　　　　　　　　　　　　　　　al estate, etc. Delivery of 1 spoon. Witnesses: JOHN CUMING, CHRISTOPHER BEECH. Before ANTHONY BONNEAU, J.P.
NATHANIEL JOHNSON, Register.

Book O, p. 183　　　　　　　　JOHN HAMILTON, of St. Johns Parish, Berkeley
17 July 1735　　　　　　　　　Co., to WILLIAM FLOOD, of same Parish, in pe-
Bond & Mortgage　　　　　　　nal sum of ℒ 906:15 SC money, conditioned for
　　　　　　　　　　　　　　　the payment of ℒ 453:7:6 on 1 Jan. 1735/6, &
for security conveys 4 Negroes. Witnesses: LEWIS TIMOTHY, JAMES MCKELVEY.

NATHANIEL JOHNSON, Register. Mortgage satisfied 4 Feb. 1736/7. NATHAN-
IEL JOHNSON, Register.

Book O, p. 185   GEORGE LUCAS, ESQ., of Island of Antigua, West
30 June & 1 July 1735   Indies, to GEORGE STARRAT, planter, of Craven
L & R   Co., SC, for ₤ 1725:10 SC money, 1150 in Cra-
                             ven Co., bounding NW on Wackamaw River; SE on
ADAM STEWART; other sides on vacant land. Signed: GEORGE LUCAS by OTH-
NIEL BEALE, his attorney. Witnesses: CHARLES PINCKNEY, ROBERT BREWTON,
JR. Before THOMAS DALE, J.P. NATHANIEL JOHNSON, Register.

Book O, p. 187   Antigua. GEORGE LUCAS, of Island of Antigua,
15 May 1735   West Indies, appoints OTHNIEL BEALE & THOMAS
Letter of Attorney   COOPER, merchants, of Charleston, SC, his at-
                             torneys to sell his lands, crops, slaves, etc.,
in SC & remit to him in Antigua. Witnesses: JOHN JONES, GEORGE STARRAT.
JONES appeared before ANDREW RUTLEDGE, J.P. of Berkeley Co. NATHANIEL
JOHNSON, Register.

Book O, p. 188   ROBERT LISTON, shipwright, to NATHANIEL FORD,
14 May 1735   shipwright, both of Charleston, for ₤ 161
Deed of Sale   Carolina money, 1 Negro boy about 15 yrs. old.
                             Witnesses: NATHANIEL BURT, JOHN COIT. NATHAN-
IEL JOHNSON, Register.

Book O, p. 193   HENRY PERONNEAU, JR., merchant, of Charleston,
2 Nov. 1733   to JOHN WILSON & RICHARD PURCELL, planters, of
Deed of Sale   Colleton Co., for ₤ 2400 SC money, 11 Negro
                             men; 1 Negro woman; all the stock, plantation
tools, corn & peas (excepting rice & sassafras). Witnesses: JOHN LAURENS,
WILLIAM WATSON, CHARLES PINCKNEY. Before CHARLES PINCKNEY, J.P. NATHAN-
IEL JOHNSON, Register.

Book O, p. 195   HENRY PERONNEAU, JR., merchant of Charleston,
1 & 2 Nov. 1733   to JOHN WILSON & RICHARD PURCELL, planters, of
L & R   Colleton Co., for ₤ 1600 SC money, 664 a.,
                             part of 1800 a., in St. Paul's Parish, Colle-
ton Co., bounding E on COL. ARTHUR HALL; W on JOHN STANYARNE; N on Wadmalaw River; S on RICHARD FREEMAN. Witnesses: JOHN LAURENS, WILLIAM WAT-
SON, CHARLES PINCKNEY. Before CHARLES PINCKNEY, J.P. NATHANIEL JOHNSON,
Register.

Book O, p. 201   THOMAS JONES, of St. Andrews Parish, Berkeley
30 July 1735   Co., to THOMAS ELLIOTT, 197 a. in Berkeley Co.,
Mortgage   bounding E on THOMAS ELLIOTT; W on SAMUEL
                             JONES; redeemable by payment of ₤ 600 currency
by JONES to ELLIOTT on 15 Oct. next. Witnesses: ROBERT HALL, SAMUEL
JONES, THOMAS GALLWAY. Before HENRY GIBBES, J.P. NATHANIEL JOHNSON,
Register.

Book O, p. 203   RICHARD (his mark) FLOYD, SR., vintner, of St.
29 Mar. 1735   Philips Parish, Charleston, to ANN HOWARD,
Jointure   spinster, in consideration of their indended
                             marriage, for a competent jointure for ANN, &
to settle & secure to her, his intended wife, 300 a. in St. Pauls Parish,
Colleton Co., bounding W on CAPT. ANTHONY MATHEWS.; N on MICHAEL REN-
OLDS; W on Bohicket Creek & marsh; NE on MATHEW BEARD; with all goods &
chattles & stock on the plantation; also 3 Negroes; provided RICHARD
FLOYD shall have them in trust during his lifetime; & after their death
to the use of JOSEPH FLOYD & JEMIMA FLOYD, children of RICHARD FLOYD by
JEMIMA FLOYD, his deceased wife, & to SUSANNA HOWARD, daughter of said
ANN HOWARD by WILLIAM HOWARD, her deceased husband; share & share alike,
or their survivors equally. Memo: It is agreed that after 2 years, RICH-
ARD FLOYD shall dispose of the plantation if ANN insists on it. Caveated
by ANTHONY MATTHEWS till his mortgage registered. Witnesses: JOHN PENNY-
MAN, EXPERIENCE HOWARD. NATHANIEL JOHNSON, Register. A caveat entered
against this by ANTHONY MATHEWS. Vid FLOYD to MATHEWS, T.Q.

Book O, p. 206   BARTHOMEW ARTHUR, planter, of Berkeley Co.,
21 July 1735   promises ROBERT BROWN, surgeon, of same place,

Agreement to execute to BROWN a good legal title to 1300 a. in St. Thomas Parish Berkeley Co., bounding W on DANIEL HUGER & MR. ROACHE; S on Gov. ROBERT JOHNSON'S land called Silkhope; N on ROBERT SALLEY; E on JOHN HARLESTON, JR.; with the crop of rice, corn & potatoes. BROWN agrees to pay ARTHUR ¼ 3500 SC money for the tract on 20 Feb. 1737. Each binds himself to the other in penal sum of ₤ 6000 currency. Witnesses: RACHEL THOMAS, ANDREW BROWN, FRANCIS ROCHE (ROACHE). Before CHARLES PINCKNEY, J.P. NATHANIEL JOHNSON, Register.

Book O, p. 208
3 & 4 Nov. 1732
L & R

RICHARD MASON, tanner, & SUSANNA his wife, to ALEXANDER SMITH, tailor, all of Charleston, for ₤ 570 currency, part of lot #190 in Charleston, 60 ft. x 170 ft., bounding N & W on RICHARD MASON; S on Tradd Street, E on WILLIAM FAIRCHILD, son of RICHARD FAIRCHILD; SUSANNA to renounce her dower. Witnesses: JAMES KERR, JAMES HUTCHINSON, JAMES NICHIE. NATHANIEL JOHNSON, Register.

Book O, p. 213
4 Sept. 1735
Memo

JAMES KERR appeared before THOMAS LAMBOLL, J.P. & testified in regard to above deed (p. 208). NATHANIEL JOHNSON, Register.

Book O, p. 214
4 Sept. 1735
Memo

JAMES KERR appeared before THOMAS LAMBOLL, J.P. & testitied in regard to release (p. 208). NATHANIEL JOHNSON, Register.

Book O, p. 214
21 May 1726
Deed of Sale

THOMAS FORD, planter, of St. Bartholmews Parish, Colleton Co., to the Parish of St. Bartholomew, for 1 pepper corn paid by the commissioner appointed for building a church, 2 a., to be taken out of the most convenient part of his land pn PonPon for the building of a church or chapel. Witnesses: EMANUEL SMITH, THOMAS JOHNSON. NATHANIEL JOHNSON, Register.

Book O, p. 215
1 May 1703
Grant

The Lords Proprs. to SAMUEL FARLEY (FARLEE) for ₤ 4, 200 a., English measure, in Colleton Co., bounding on all sides on vacant land. Whereas JOHN, Earl of Bath, Palatine; GEORGE, Lord Carteret; SIR JOHN COLLETON; Baronet THOMAS AMY, & WILLIAM THORNBURGH, ESQRS., Lords Proprs., on 16 Aug. 1698 impowered past Gov. JOSEPH BLAKE, JAMES MOORE, present Gov., Landgrave JOSEPH MARTON & EDMUND BELLINGER, COL. ROBERT DANIEL & JOHN ELY, or any 3 of them in the absence of BLAKE, to grant lands, now BELLINGER, MOORE & DANIEL grant FARLEY 200 a. Plat certified by EDMOND BELLINGER, Sur. Gen. NATHANIEL JOHNSON, Register.

Book O, p. 217
14 & 15 July 1726
L & R

GEORGE (his mark) FARLEY, carpenter, & ELIZABETH his wife, to JOHN NEWTON, JOHN MARTIN, & the parishioners, all of St. Bartholomew's Parish, for ₤ 180 currency, 154 a. in Colleton Co., on W side PonPon River, for a parsonage; bounding N on FARLEY; E & W on vacant land; S on GEORGE TUCKER. Witnesses: JOSEPH HUNT, LEWIS MORGAN, THOMAS JOHNSON. NATHANIEL JOHNSON, Register.

Book O, p. 222
Memo

By virtue of a warrant signed by Gov. JOHN ARCHDALE, dated 10 Oct. 1696, JOHN BERESFORD, Surv., laid out for OWEN DAVIS an inland plantation of 100 a. English measure on Ischbou Creek, bounding NE on SOLOMON BRUMER & PETER VIDEAU; SE on PETER VIDEAU, (PITTER VIDOS), SW on CAPT. JOHNSON LYNCH, NW on vacant land; plat certified 10 Feb. 1696. A copy of the plat & certificate belonging to LOTTS (?) OWEN DAVIS made by ISAAC LEGRAND, Dep. Surv. on 5 June 1716. NATHANIEL JOHNSON, Register. The grant to DAVIS recorded in Secretary's office 4 Aug. 1716 fol. 392.

Book O, p. 223
7 Aug. 1716
Deed of Sale

ISAAC DAVIS, showmaker, of Berkeley Co., only son & heir of OWEN DAVIS, to ANDREW REMBERT, shoemaker, of Berkeley Co., for ₤ 105 currency, 100 a. English measure in Berkeley Co., granted by ROBERT DANIELL, Dep. Gov. & the Lords Proprs. on 4 Aug. 1716 to OWEN DAVIS, father of ISAAC; on E side Cooper River, bounding NE on JOHNSON LYNCH; NE on PETER VIDEAU; SW on PETER VIDEAU & SOLOMON BREMAR; SE on

DR. NATHANIEL SNOW. Witnesses: PIERRE VIDEAU, ANTHONY BONNEAU, ANDRE DEVEAUX. Delivery by turf & twig. Before DANIEL BREBANT, J.P. NATHANIEL JOHNSON, Register.

Book O, p. 226
29 May 1717
Deed of Sale

ANTHONY BONNEAU, cooper, & JANE (JEANNE) ELIZABETH, his wife, with her free consent, to ANDREW REMBERT, JR., shoemaker, all of Berkeley Co., for ₺ 120 currency, 100 a. (part of 800 a.), bounding SW on ANDREW REMBERT; NW on MADAM LYNCH, (widow of CAPT. JOHNSON LYNCH); NE & SE on other part of 800 a. Whereas JOHN, Lord Granville, Palatine, & the Lords Proprs. on 5 May 1704 granted ALEXANDER DELAMOTTE 800 a., English measure in Berkeley Co., on E side Cooper River, bounding SW on SOLOMON BREMAR & ANDREW REMBERT, JR. (then THOMAS BOSIER); NW on CAPT. JOHNSON LYNCH; NE & SE on vacant land; & whereas on 28 Aug. 1705 DELAMOTTE sold the 800 a. to the Hon. JAMES MOORE for ₺ 22 Carolina money; & whereas the Hon. THOMAS BROUGHTON, trustee for selling land, by virtue of an act ratified in open Assembly 5 Nov. 1709 entitled an act for making good the last will of JAMES MOORE & vesting his lands in trustees to be sold; & whereas LEWIS PASQUEREAU & JOHN GUERARD, like trustees died & the authority devolved on THOMAS BROUGHTON; & he on 10 May 1715 sold the 800 a. to DR. NATHANIEL SNOW for ₺ 50 (paid to JAMES MOORE, executor of will); & whereas DR. SNOW on 15 Feb. 1716/17 sold the land to ANTHONY BONNEAU for ₺ 800; now BONNEAU sells part (100 2.) to REMBERT. Witnesses: PIERRE STOUPAN, PIERRE VIDEAU, JEAN REMBERT. Before DANIEL HUGER; J.P. NATHANIEL JOHNSON, Register.

Book O, p. 230
29 May 1717
Bill of Sale

PETER (PIERRE) VIDEAU, planter, & JANE ELIZABETH his wife, (& with her free consent), to ANDREW REMBERT, shoemaker, of Berkeley Co., for ₺ 25 currency, 30 a. (part of 100 a.), bounding NW on ANDREW DEVEAUX (formerly PHILYMON PARMETER), NE on JOHNSON LYNCH; SE on ANDREW REMBERT; SW on other part of 100 a.; provided ANDREW REMBERT & JUDITH his wife, or any of their children possess it; but not to dispose of the 30 a. to any one but PETER VIDEAU or his son, HENRY JOSEPH, he or they paying as much as anyone else would. JANE ELIZABETH renounces her dower. Whereas WILLIAM, Earl of Craven, Palatine, & the Lords Proprs. on 9 Sept. 1696 granted PETER VIDEAU 100 a., English measure, in Berkeley Co., on E side Cooper River, now VIDEAU sells 30 a. to REMBERT with a proviso. Witnesses: LOUIS MOUZON, ANTHONY BONNEAU, JEAN REMBERT. Delivery by turf & twig. Before DANIEL HUGER, J.P. NATHANIEL JOHNSON, Register.

Book O, p. 234
4 & 5 July 1735
L & R

ANDREW REMBERT, planter, of St. James Santee Parish, Craven Co., to JAMES BREMAR, planter, of St. Thomas & St. Dennis Parish, Berkeley Co., for ₺ 600 SC money, 3 tracts; 30 a. English measure, near Ishboo Creek, in St. Thomas & St. Dennis Parish, part of 100 a. granted by the Lords Proprs. to PETER VIDEAU, bounding NW on DR. WLATER DALLAS; NE on ANTHONY BONNEAU; SE on ANDREW REMBERT; SW on HENRY VIDEAU; also 100 a. English measure in same Parish, near Ishboo Creek, which ANDREW REMBERT (father of ANDREW, party hereto) bought on 29 May 1717 from CAPT. ANTHONY BONNEAU & JANE ELIZABETH his wife, being part of 800 a. formerly granted to ALEXANDER DELAMOTTE, the 100 a. bounding SW on above 100 a.; NW on ANTHONY BONNEAU; NE & SE on remainder of the 800 a., also 100 a. English measure, on E branch Wishboo Creek, bounding NE on JAMES BREMAR & HENRY DIVEAU; SE on HENRY VIDEAU; SW on ANTHONY BONNEAU (plat & grant in possession of JAMES BREMAR). Witnesses: EDWARD HASELWOOD, ELIZABETH HASELWOOD, ROBERT HOW. Before PETER PAGETT, J.P. NATHANIEL JOHNSON, Register.

Book O, p. 241
24 & 25 Aug. 1735
L & R

WILLIAM MAGILLIVRAY, gentleman, & ELIZABETH his wife, of Colleton Co., to ZEBALON GUY, planter, of James Island, for ₺ 500 SC money, 120 a., commonly called Pawleys Point, in Colleton Co., on Wad-Wadmalaw Island, bounding NW on a creek; SW on JONATHAN THOMAS (formerly PETER BROWN); S on WILLIAM MAGILLIVRAY; N ON GEORGE SIMMONS (formerly WILLIAM WINTER). Witnesses: JONATHAN THOMAS, WILLIAM ALLIN. Before HENRY GIBBES, J.P. NATHANIEL JOHNSON, Register.

Book O, p. 247   WILLIAM LIVINGSTON, ESQ. & MARY his wife, of

22 & 23 Sept. 1735 L & R	St. Pauls Parish, Colleton Co., to JOSEPH BOWREY, gentleman, of Charleston, for Ł 3000 SC money, 1109 a., also an island of 64 a., in

Colleton Co., bounding W on vacant land; N on an impossable Bay Swamp; S & SE on Chehaw River & marsh. Witnesses: THOMAS LIVINGSTON, ANTHONY LAMBRIGHT, JOHN PACKER. Before THOMAS DALE, J.P. NATHANIEL JOHNSON, Register.

Book O, p. 253 Note	JOHN HAMMERTON begins.

Book O, p. 253 7 & 8 June 1734 L & R	JOHN TIPPER (TIPOR), sailmaker, & MARY his wife, to WILLIAM RANDALL, blacksmith, & MARY his wife, all of Charleston, for Ł 465 currency, that moiety or part of lot #210 in Charles-

ton, bounding S 207 ft. on part same lot owned by JOHN TIPPER; N on CAPT. WILLIAM PAVIT; E 50 ft. on a street leading from ASHLEY RIVER to the Broad Path; W on WILLIAM LIVINGSTON. Witnesses: JOHN PANTON, WILLIAM SMITH, THOMAS WEAVER. Witnesses to receipt: NICHOLAS ROUCH, THOMAS WEAVER, NATHANIEL JOHNSON. The probate of this release recorded in this office in Bk. Y. p. 196, 15 Apr. 1743.

Book O, p. 258 14 Oct. 1734 Renunciation of Dower	MARY TIPPER, wife of JOHN TIPPER, sailmaker, of Charleston, appeared before ROBERT WRIGHT, C.T., & acknowledged she voluntarily joined her husband in the above (p. 253) sale. NA-

THANIEL JOHNSON, Register.

Book O, p. 260 Memo	By virtue of a warrant signed by Gov. NATHANIEL JOHNSON dated ---, THOMAS BROUGHTON, Sur. Gen. caused to be surveyed for ALEXANDER MAC-

KEY 491 a. on S side Port Royall River, Granville Co., bounding E on large marshes between it & Port Royall River; S on Hog Island Creek, a branch of Port Royall River; W on a creek; N on ALEXANDER MACKEY. Plat certified 22 Sept. 1708. NATHANIEL JOHNSON, Register.

Book O, p. 260 12 & 13 June 1730 L & R	WILLIAM OSBORNE, gentleman, & ELEANOR (HELENAH) his wife, to GEORGE BAMPFIELD, ESQ., all of Charleston, for Ł 368:5 currency, 491 a. on S

side Port Royall River, Granville Co., bounding E on large marshes; S on Hog Island Creek; W on a creek; N on ALEXANDER MACKEY. The name ELEANOR changed to HELENAH & deed so signed. Witnesses: JOSEPH FIDLER, LAWRENCE COULLIETTE. Before CHARLES PINCKNEY, J.P. NATHANIEL JOHNSON, Register.

Book O, p. 266 5 May 1735 Deed of Sale	JOHN PAINTER, carpenter, of St. Johns Parish, Berkeley Co., to JOHN CUMING, planter, of St. Thomas Parish, Berkeley Co., for Ł 55 currency,

all the cattle, horses, hogs, etc., which JOHN STRACHAN & NOAMI his wife (father & mother of JOHN PAINTER) gave him by deed of gift dated 1 Jan. 1733/4, possession to be had after the death of JOHN STRACHAN & not before; the memo on the back to reckoned part of the true meaning of the above. Memo. It is intended that all of JOHN PAINTER'S real & personal estate is hereby conveyed to CUMING, goods, chattels, debts, money, horses, branded cattle, except such as have been legally disposed of; except the gift of JOHN & NOAMI STRACHAN which is to be possessed only at the death of STRACHAN. Witnesses: CUILLAUME GALLATIN, JOHN COMBE, ROBERT MORAN. Before ANTHONY BONNEAU, J.P. NATHANIEL JOHNSON, Register.

Book O, p. 268 14 & 15 Oct. 1735 L & R	The Hon. JOHN HAMMERTON, ESQ., Sec'y. of SC, to THOMAS THOMPSON, Clerk of SC for Ł 500 SC money, 1000 a. in Colleton Co., bounding part on E side, part on W side of Fish Pond Creek,

commonly called N branch of Ashepoo River; W on JAMES ST. JOHN; S on JOHN WOODWARD & lands laid out to THOMAS & ELIZABETH WOODWARD'S children & ELIZABETH, SR., other sides on vacant land, according to plat certified by JAMES ST. JOHN, Sur. Gen., annexed to grant, dated 10 Feb. 1732, & signed by Gov. ROBERT JOHNSON. Witnesses: JAMES ABERCROMBY, JAMES MICHIE. Before THOMAS DALE, J.P. NATHANIEL JOHNSON, Register.

Book O, p. 276　　　　　　　THOMAS JONES, planter, to THOMAS ELLIOTT,
15 & 16 Oct. 1735　　　　　planter, both of St. Andrews Parish, Berkeley
L & R by Mortgage　　　　　Co., for ₤ 145 SC money, 197 a. in St. Andrews
　　　　　　　　　　　　　　Parish, bounding E on THOMAS ELLIOTT; W on SAM-
UEL JONES; conditioned for redemption on 26 Mar. 1736. Witnesses: JOHN
CHAMPNEYS, THOMAS ELLERY. Before ALEXANDER FARRIS, J.P. NATHANIEL JOHN-
SON, Register.

Book O, p. 281　　　　　　　ANDREW ALLEN, merchant, to THOMAS WEAVER, car-
18 & 19 Aug. 1735　　　　　penter, both of Charleston, for ₤ 450 SC money,
L & R　　　　　　　　　　　lot #275 in Charleston, bounding N 92 ft. on
　　　　　　　　　　　　　　Queen Street, W 240-1/2 ft on ISAAC MAZYCK; S
on lot #274 owned by ANDREW ALLEN & to be sold by him to DANIEL HEXT; E
on another lot owned by ALLEN; being a long square originally granted on
12 June 1694 to WILLIAM HAWETT. Witnesses: JOHN ALLEN, THOMAS LAMBOLL.
Before THOMAS DALE, J.P. NATHANIEL JOHNSON, Register.

Book O, p. 287　　　　　　　JAMES CHILD, yeoman, of Childbury Town, St.
25 Sept. 1714　　　　　　　Johns Parish, to STEPHEN SARRAZIN, merchant,
Deed of Sale　　　　　　　　of same Parish, for ₤ 30, 7 lots in Strawberry
　　　　　　　　　　　　　　as follows: 3 front lots, 1/2 a. each, English
measure, 5 ch. 1 one ch. w., or 330 ft. 1 by 66 ft. w., being lots 8, 9 &
10, bounding NW on Craven Street; NE on Mulberry Street; SE on JOHN MOORE;
SW on SARRAZIN BAY; also 4 lots #20, 21, 28, & 29, bounding SW on Mulberry Street; NW on HESTER CHILD; NE on Church Street; SE on MARK HOLMES;
to be held in free & common soccage; a house with brick chimneys to be
built on 2 of the lots, within 1 year or else the lots to be returned to
CHILD. SARRAZIN to have privilege of river landing. Witnesses: MATHEW
NICHOLAS, WILLIAM (his mark) SKINNER. Delivery by turf & twig. NATHAN-
IEL JOHNSON, Register.

Book O, p. 289　　　　　　　EDWARD WEEKLEY & THOMAS WEEKLEY, of Charleston,
5 Nov. 1735　　　　　　　　to THOMAS BAKER, (tailor), for ₤ 250 SC money,
Deed of Sale　　　　　　　　a lot in Charleston, 30' x 100'; bounding on
　　　　　　　　　　　　　　MICHAEL JEANE & JONATHAN TUB (TUBB) & DR. GIB-
SON. Witnesses: MICHAEL MOOR, JOHN HOOK. Witnesses to receipt: JOHN LEA.
Before HENRY GIBBES, J.P. NATHANIEL JOHNSON, Register.

Book O, p. 290　　　　　　　WILLIAM MELLICHAMP, gentleman, to PAUL GRIM-
13 & 14 Sept. 1734　　　　BALL, planter, both of Colleton Co., for ₤ 300
L & R　　　　　　　　　　　SC money, 500 a. in Colleton Co., a part of
　　　　　　　　　　　　　　Watch Island; bounding N on Edisto River; S on
JOHN FRAMPTON; W on Watch Island Creek; & fronting the open sea. Witness-
es: EBENEZER PECKHAM, LYDIA PECKHAM, JANE (her mark) CASHWELL. Before
THOMAS DALE, J.P. NATHANIEL JOHNSON, Register.

Book O, p. 294　　　　　　　GERARD (his mark) FITZGERALD, planter, & MAR-
13 & 14 Nov. 1735　　　　　THA (her mark) his wife, & JOHN FITZGERALD,
L & R　　　　　　　　　　　planter, of Berkeley Co., to JOHN VAUGHAN,
　　　　　　　　　　　　　　bricklayer, of Charleston, for ₤ 440 SC money,
75 a. on Wando Neck, Christ Church Parish, Berkeley Co., on which 75 a.
GERARD FITZGERALD lately lived, bounding SW & NW on WILLIAM VISSER; E &
NE on MAJ. ROBERT BREWTON; S on MAURICE HARVEY; N on JOHN HALE. Whereas
THOMAS FITZGERALD, father of GERARD & JOHN, owned 225 a. on Wando Neck &
by will dated 12 Mar. 1718 devised to his eldest son JAMES the tract on
which he (the father) lived, on the condition that JAMES pay his brothers
JOHN & GERARD within 4 years 2/3 the value of the plantation, but in case
of JAMES'S refusal or neglect, the plantation to be divided into 3 equal
parts, 1 part to each son; & whereas JAMES did not pay his brothers but
consented to divide the plantation, & surveyed & alloted to GERARD 1/3
& GERARD took possession; & whereas JAMES died intestate; now GERALD &
JOHN sell 1/3 to VAUGHAN. Witnesses: THOMAS DALE, ROBERT BREWTON, JR.,
CHARLES PINCKNEY. Before THOMAS DALE, J.P. NATHANIEL JOHNSON, Register.

Book O, p. 301　　　　　　　ALEXANDER NISBETT, merchant, to HUGH CAMPBELL,
11 Jan. 1732　　　　　　　　for ₤ 1000 SC money, 1240 a. in Berkeley Co.,
Release　　　　　　　　　　Viz: 400 a. on Simons Creek lately owned by
　　　　　　　　　　　　　　PETER JOHNSON, JR.; 200 a. lately owned by
PETER TOMPLETT; also 640 a. lately owned by JOHN SKINNER. Witnesses: WIL-
LIAM GRAY, HENRY SIMONS, JOHN DAVENPORT. A memorial entered in Auditors

office 14 May 1733. Before ALEXANDER PARRIS, J.P. NATHANIEL JOHNSON, Register.

Book O, p. 304
4 Sept. 1735
Mortgage

WILLIAM SNOW, plat-er, of Craven Co., to ALEXANDER NISBETT, as security for several sums amounting to L 1950 SC money, 1800 a. in Craven Co., bounding SW on JAMES MOORE; NW on MRS. HILL, widow; SE on vacant land; NE on ALEXANDER NISBETT & vacant land. Whereas SNOW gave NISBETT a bond dated 10 Dec. 1734 in penal sum of L 1920 for payment of L 960 on 1 Nov. next, & another bond dated 29 Jan. 1734 in penal sum of L 1400 for payment of L 700 on 1 Mar. next; now he conveys 1800 a. as security. Witnesses: HEZEKIAH RUSS, WALTER NISBETT. Before ANTHONY BONNEAU, J.P. NATHANIEL JOHNSON, Register.

Book O, p. 308
30 & 31 July 1731
L & R

JOHN CARMICHAEL, gentleman, of Colleton Co., to EDWARD WEEKLEY, gentleman, of Berkeley Co., for L 150 currency, part of lot #282 in Charleston fronting 40 ft. on a small street leading from the new prison to the new church (which street by mutual agreement was left out of the lots of JOHN CARMICHAEL & BRIAN BAYLY) & runs 90 ft. back; bounding N on the small street; W on JOHN CARMICHAEL; S on GEORGE CHICKEN; E on JONATHAN TUBB. Witnesses: HENRY HODGKIN, ANTHONY HUGGETT, JOHN BAYLY. Before THOMAS DALE, J.P. NATHANIEL JOHNSON, Register.

Book O, p. 314
31 Aug. & 1 Sept. 1735
L & R

SAMUEL UNDERWOOD, planter, of Colleton Co., to CHARLES PERONNEAU & Co., merchants, of Colleton Co., for L 500 currency, 100 a. in Colleton Co., on Wadmalaw Island, bounding S on THOMAS GOBLE; N on JAMES YOUNG; E on SAMUEL JONES; W on WILLIAM FLECKNOW (formerly HENRY WALKER); also 530 a. on S side Wadmalaw River, bounding E on JOHN STANYARNE (formerly WILLIAM DENHAMP); W on RICHARD FREEMAN (formerly BONUM SAMS); also 250 a. on N side Cumbahee River, Colleton Co., bounding SW on ISAAC SMALLWOOD a minor (formerly JOHN SEABROOK); NW on OLIVER EBETTS; NW on HENRY FENDEN; SE on THOMAS AYRES. Witnesses: JAMES GREEN, JOSEPH GIBBONS. Before JEMMOT COBLEY, J.P. NATHANIEL JOHNSON, Register.

Book O, p. 321
1 Nov. 1735
Deed Tripartite

JAMES (his mark) STEWART, mariner, of Berkeley Co., of 1st part; SAMUEL HOLMES, bricklayer, & ELIZABETH his wife, of Charleston, of 2nd part; JOSEPH WRAGG, merchant, of Charleston, of 3rd part. Whereas by L & R, 15 & 16 Oct. 1735 SAMUEL & ELIZABETH HOLMES conveyed to JAMES STEWART in trust part of lot #115 fronting N 30 ft. on Tradd Street, bounding S on THOMAS HOLTON; E 100 ft. on part same lot; W on SOLOMON LEGARE; during their natural lives then to heirs of ELIZABETH; but STEWART should mortgage the lot to WRAGG to secure L 620 due WRAGG from HOLMES; & whereas on 20 Oct. 1735 SAMUEL & ELIZABETH HOLMES renounced their title to JAMES STEWART; & whereas WRAGG & HOLMES have this date settled their accounts & there appears to be L 538:12:6 currency due WRAGG from HOLMES for principal & interest because of (bond dated 6 June 1732) whereby WILLIAM MORGAN, brewer, of Charleston, then husband of ELIZABETH (now wife of HOLMES) became bound to JOSEPH WRAGG & ROBERT HUME, gentlemen, in penal sum of L 1116 for payment of L 550 on 1 Nov. next; & whereas the money due WRAGG & not to HUME; now STEWART, at the request of SAMUEL & ELIZABETH HOLMES, as security for payment of L 538:12:6 & interest, conveys & farm lets to WRAGG the part of lot #115 mentioned above. Should HOLMES pay WRAGG by 1st Nov. next, then WRAGG shall reconvey to STEWART. Witnesses: ROWLAND VAUGHAN, SAMUEL FISHER. Before JAMES WEDDERBURNE, J.P. NATHANIEL JOHNSON, Register.

Book O, p. 328
2 Dec. 1735
L & R

RICHARD BUTLER, planter, of St. Andrews Parish, Berkeley Co., to ROBERT COOPER, planter, of Berkeley Co., for L 300 SC money, 2000 a. in Granville Co., granted by letters patent dated 2 Dec. 1735, signed by the Hon. THOMAS BROUGHTON, Lt. Gov., to RICHARD BUTLER; lying at the head of a swamp out of Combahee River, bounding W on BELLINGER'S Barony; SE on JOSEPH ELLIOTT; NE on JOHN BULL. Witnesses: JAMES FOWLER, EDWARD FOWLER, ELISHA BUTLER. Before THOMAS DALE, J.P. NATHANIEL JOHNSON, Register.

Book O, p. 333 BENJAMIN WHITAKER, ESQ., to THOMAS MONCK, ESQ.,
5 & 6 Dec. 1735 for Ł 2000 SC money, the S part of lot #113 in
L & R Charleston, fronting 57 ft. 3 in. on Church
Street, bounding N 113 ft. 4-3/4 in. on part
same lot; 54 ft. on JOHN BERESFORD; S 108 ft. on NICHOLAS TROTT. Witnesses: CHARLES PINCKNEY, ROBERT NEWTON, JR. Before THOMAS DALE, J.P. NATHANIEL JOHNSON, Register.

DEEDS BOOK "P"
DEC. 1735 - JUNE 1736

Book P, p. 1 BARTHOLMEW ARTHUR, planter, to ROBERT QUASH,
3 & 4 Sept. 1735 planter, both of Berkeley Co., for Ł 1700 cur-
L & R rency, 500 a. in Berkeley Co., part of 1800 a.
devised to ARTHUR by will of CHRISTOPHER ARTHUR of Cypress Barony dated 24 Oct. 1724; bounding SW on DANIEL HUGER; N W on FRANCIS ROCHE; NE & SE on BARTHOMEW ARTHUR; laid off by JOHN HENTIE, Surv., 2 Sept. 1735. Witnesses: JOHN HENTIE, MATTHEW QUASH, JOAN (her mark) DYER. Before FRANCIS LEJAU, J.P. NATHANIEL JOHNSON, Register.

Book P. p. 3 Certification of plat of above 500 a. by JOHN
2 Sept. 1735 HENTIE, Surv.

Book P. p. 6 JOSIAS GAR DUPRE, planter, & ANN his wife, of
7 & 8 Nov. 1735 Craven Co., to ALEXANDER NISBETT, merchant, of
L & R Charleston, for Ł 300 SC money, 600 a. in Craven Co., on S side Peedee River granted DUPRE by the Hon. THOMAS BROUGHTON, Lt. Gov., 7 Aug. 1735; bounding W on MRS. MARY FORD; S & E on vacant land. Witnesses: JOHN THOMPSON, SR., MARY SKINNER. Before WILLIAM SWINTON, J.P. NATHANIEL JOHNSON, Register.

Book P. p. 12 Agreement MARTIN HOLT & JOHN PHELPS promise to
25 Aug. 1732 pay ROGER MOORE Ł 80 currency on 25 Feb. next
North Carolina for 2 white servants belonging to DANIEL CARTWRIGHT & THOMAS WEAVER, of Charleston. If CARTWRIGHT & WHEELER do not agree to the sale HOLT & PHELPS promise to deliver the servants (namely, JOHN EDMONDS & WILLIAM WELCH) to ROGER MOORE; MOORE to pay Ł 62 currency, due HOLT & PHELPS for taking them up & bringing them 10 miles. NATHANIEL JOHNSON, Register.

Book P, p. 12 MARTHA BEE, wife of JOHN BEE, gentleman, of
15 Feb. 1734 Charleston, appeared before ROBERT WRIGHT, C.T.
Ren. of Dower & declared she voluntarily joined her husband
on 14 Feb. 1734 in conveying to THOMAS DRAYTON, ESQ., of Berkeley Co., 2 tracts; 300 a. & 500 a., both on S side Cusahatchee, Granville Co. NATHANIEL JOHNSON, Register.

Book P, p. 14 JOHN (his mark) BEE, gentleman, & MARTHA his
13 & 14 Feb. 1734 wife, of Charleston, to THOMAS DRAYTON, ESQ.,
L & R of Berkeley Co., for Ł 2400 SC money, 2 tracts
of 300 a. & 500 a., English measure, on S side of Cusahatchee, Granville Co. Whereas SIR NATHANIEL JOHNSON, Knight, Gov., JAMES MOORE & JOB HOWES, Lords Proprs., on 1 Sept. 1706 granted to WILLIAM DOWNES 300 a., on S side Cusahatchee, bounding NW on WILLIAM MCPHERSON; SE on a creek; other sides on vacant land & whereas DOWNES died intestate leaving only 2 daughters, SARAH (who afterwards married JOHN WOOD) & ELIZABETH; & whereas JOHN WOOD, SARAH WOOD, & ELIZABETH DOWNES by deed pool 14 Jan. 1723 sold the 300 a. to JOHN BEE; & whereas Gov. NATHANIEL JOHNSON, JAMES MOORE & JOB HOWES, Lords Proprs., on 1 Sept. 1706 granted WILLIAM MCPHERSON 500 a. on S side Cusahatchee, Granville Co., bounding NW & SW on vacant land; SE on WILLIAM DOWNES; & whereas by deed pool 25 Feb. 1720 MCPHERSON sold the 500 a. to JOHN BEE; now BEE sells both tracts to DRAYTON. Witnesses: RICHARD ALLEIN, WILLIAM BULL, FREDERICK MEYER. Before ROBERT YONGE, J.P. NATHANIEL JOHNSON, Register.

Book P, p. 21 DANIEL CARTWRIGHT, planter, & SARAH his wife,
11 & 12 Dec. 1735 to BENJAMIN WHITAKER, ESQ., & SARAH his wife,
L & R for Ł 650 currency, 70 a. in St. Andrews

Parish, bounding W & S on the high road leading from Charleston to Dorchester; E on WILLIAM ELLIOTT, JR., N on JOHN COCKFIELD (formerly STEPHEN CLIFFORD & EPHRAIM PAYNE; which 70 a. is part of THOMAS BUTLER'S land now allotted to SARAH CARTWRIGHT (lately SARAH BUTLER, daughter of THOM BUTLER) by the executors of BUTLER'S will which authorized them to divide the land amongst his wife & children. Witnesses: MAURICE LEWIS, WILLIAM GEORGE FREEMAN. Before JOHN HAMMERTON, J.P. NATHANIEL JOHNSON, Register.

Book P, p. 27
17 & 18 Nov. 1735
L & R

MARGARET GODFREY & JANE MONGER, widows, acting executors of will of BENJAMIN GODFREY, planter, to THOMAS LAKE, merchant, formerly of Barbados, now of SC, for L 2832 SC money, secured to be paid by LAKE, 2 tracts; 150 a. Whereas BENJAMIN WHITAKER (by deed of exchange with JOHN GODFREY) owned 150 a., English measure, on Ashley River, bounding E on WILLIAM HARVEY (formerly BENJAMIN GODFREY; formerly (?) COL. ROBERT GIBBES; W & S on BENJAMIN WHITAKER (formerly JOHN WOODWARD); N on marsh; also 86 a. in Berkeley Co., bought from JOHN WOODWARD, bounding NE on CHARLES HILL (formerly JOHN WOODWARD); NW on ELIZABETH HILL, widow (formerly BENJAMIN GODFREY); SW on JOHN WOODWARD; SE on the 150 a.; the 2 tracts of 150 & 86 a. being part of 974 a. granted by the Lords Proprs. to CAPT. JOHN GODFREY & divided by JOHN GODFREY (eldest son & heir of CAPT. JOHN GODFREY) amongst CAPT. JOHN GODFREY'S several children; & whereas BENJAMIN WHITAKER on 24 & 25 Feb. 1730 sold the 2 tracts to BENJAMIN GODFREY, planter, of Berkeley Co., for L 5000 SC money; & whereas BENJAMIN GODFREY by will appointed his brother WILLIAM CATTELL, his wife MARGARET GODFREY, & his sisters JANE MONGER & ELIZABETH HILL his executors to dispose of the rest of his real estate; & whereas WILLIAM CATTELL & ELIZABETH HILL refused the office before the Governor & Ordinary of the Province but MARGARET MONGER & JANE MONGER accepted; now they sell the 2 tracts to LAKE. Witnesses: JOHN VANDERHORST, JAMES AMALLWOOD, JAMES SCARLETT. Before CHARLES PINCKNEY, J.P. NATHANIEL JOHNSON, Register.

Book P, p. 35
16 & 17 July 1733
L & R

DANIEL CARTWRIGHT, planter, & SARAH his wife, of Berkeley Co., to RICHARD BRICKLES, joiner, of Charleston for L 350 SC money, the S half of lot #136 in Charleston, bounding S on JOHN BRUCE; E on the Broad Path; N on JOHN MOORE (the other half). Witnesses: JAMES WITHERS, THOMAS BAKER. Before CHARLES PINCKNEY, J.P. NATHANIEL JOHNSON, Register.

Book P, p. 40
15 & 16 Dec. 1735
L & R

THOMAS LIVINGSTON (only son & heir of ANN LIVINGSTON, widow of WILLIAM LIVINGSTON, the elder, gentleman, & devisee of her former husband, JOHN ASH, ESQ.), to WILLIAM LIVINGSTON, ESQ., for L 1700 SC money, several tracts total 1535 a., in Colleton Co., bounding E on ELIZABETH GRAY, widow, & JOHN PETERS, W on Edisto on PonPon River; N on Penny's Creek; S on JAMES COCHRAN. Whereas the Lords Proprs. on 11 Mar. 1696/7 & on 15 July 1697, granted ELIZABETH SCHENCKINGH 2 tracts of 100 a. each, in Colleton Co., on a river then called Edisto or Colleton River, & a creek, which land by several conveyances came to JOHN ASH; & whereas the Lords Proprs. on 18 Sept. 1703 granted GEORGE KNATCHBULL 200 a. in Colleton Co. on E side Edisto River; & whereas KNATCHBULL by deed poll on back of grant sold the 200 a. to JOHN ASH for L 10:10:9 & whereas the Lords Proprs. on 15 Nov. 1701 granted JOHN ASH 200 a. in Colleton Co., on a creek of Edisto River; & on 1 Feb. 1667 granted him another 200 a. on E side Edisto Rover; & whereas JOHN ASH by will dated 31 Mar. 1711 appointed his wife ANN (daughter of THOMAS BOULTON) his sole executrix & bequeathed to her all his real & personal estate; & whereas she married WILLIAM LIVINGSTON, the elder, had 1 son, THOMAS LIVINGSTON (party hereto), & died intestate; & whereas Gov. ROBERT GIBBES & the Lords Proprs. on 23 July 1711 granted MOSES PINGREY 200 a. on E side Edisto River, near New London bounding W N & S on vacant swamp land; which he by deed of feoffment dated 22 Dec. 1714, for L 122 currency, sold the land to WILLIAM LIVINGSTON; & whereas the Lords Proprs. granted WILLIAM LIVINGSTON, the elder, 125 a. on N side S. Colleton River; & by another grant gave him 435 a. on E side PonPon River; & whereas he by will dated July 1723 gave his son THOMAS the plantation called Westfield which was his mother's, & all the adjacent lands which the father had bought, (total 1535 a.); now THOMAS LIVINGSTON sells to WILLIAM LIVINGSTON. Witnesses: BISHOP ROBERTS, WILLIAM GEORGE FREEMAN. Before

BENJAMIN WHITAKER, J.P. NATHANIEL JOHNSON, Register.

Book P, p. 49   RICHARD PURCELL, planter, to JOHN WILLSON,
10 Jan. 1736   planter, both of Colleton Co., for L 800 SC
Deed of Sale   money, 332 a. in Colleton Co. (half the 664 a.
                         purchased from HENRY PERONNEAU, JR.). Witness-
es: J. GILLESPIE, JAMES DUNWOODS. NATHANIEL JOHNSON, Register.

Book P, p. 49   JOHN ABBOTT, storekeeper, of Georgetown, Win-
26 July 1735   yaw, to JOSEPH SHUTE. Whereas by Article of
Mortgage   Co-partnership dated 18 June 1735 between JO-
                         SEPH SHUTE, merchant, of Charleston, of 1st
part; JOHN ABBOTT, of 2nd part; & STEPHEN BEAUCHAMP, of 3rd part; each
put in L 3000 (or its value in goods) for a store at Georgetown; & whereas SHUTE made himself liable for ABBOTTS share of L 3000; now ABBOTT, as
security, conveys to SHUTE 430 a. in Craven Co., on Little River, bounding E on the Sea; W on NICHOLAS TRUCK (?); 40 cattle; his 2 lots in
Charleston at the corner of Scriven Street, the other on Broad Street.
Witnesses: THOMAS CHARNOCK, THOMAS BURGESS. Before JOHN HAMMERTON, J.P.
NATHANIEL JOHNSON, Register.

Book P, p. 52   WILLIAM TRYON, merchant, of London, by BENJA-
30 & 31 Dec. 1736   MIN GODIN, merchant, of SC his attorney of 1st
L & R. Tripartite   part; ALEXANDER SKENE, ESQ., of 1 Berkeley Co.,
                         SC of 2nd part; JOHN CARRUTHERS, master of the
Molley, galley now of SC, of 3rd part. Whereas ALEXANDER SKENE & JEMIMA
his wife by L & R, 23 & 24 Apr. 1722, as security on SKENE'S 2 bonds to
WILLIAM TRYON, dated 24 Apr. 1722, in penal sum of L 970 sterling of
Great Britain conditioned for payment of L 485:9:9: with interest at 5%
1 on 27 Apr. 1725; 1 for payment of 485 on 7 Apr. 1727; convey to TRYON
2700 a. in Berkeley Co., bounding SE on SAMUEL WRAGG; NW on WILLIAM WAL-
LACE; SW on PETER CATTELL; NE on Ashley River; & delivered 20 slaves; &
whereas WILLIAM TRYON on 9 Nov. 1727 (as sole executor of will of _____
TRYON, merchant of London) appointed BENJAMIN GODIN of SC his attorney to
represent him in SC; & whereas the 2 bonds have not been fully paid,
L 622:12:4 being still due, which JOHN CARRUTHERS (at SKENE'S request)
has paid GODIN; & whereas CARRUTHERS also paid SKENE L 77:7:8 British money; & whereas SKENE (as security for the 2 sums) gave CARRUTHERS his bond;
payable with interest on 31 Dec. 1736; now as further security SKENE
(with TRYON'S consent) conveys to CARRUTHERS 2700 a., except 1000 a.
(part of the 2700) conveyed by SKENE to CAPT. WILLIAM DOUGLAS (now in
possession of JOHN WALTER, ESQ.) also 300 a. conveyed by SKENE to THOMAS
GADSDEN, ESQ., & delivered 20 slaves to CARRUTHERS. Witnesses: BENJAMIN
WHITAKER, WILLIAM GEORGE FREEMAN. Before BENJAMIN DELA CONSEILLERE, J.P.
NATHANIEL JOHNSON, Register.

Book P, p. 64   ISAAC PORCHER, planter, & RACHEL his wife, of
3 Jan. 1735/6   Berkeley Co., to JOHN FAIRCHILD, butcher, for
Bill of Sale   5 shillings proclamation money & other consid-
                         erations, 300 a. on Wassamasaw Swamp, Berkeley
Co., bounding SE on PETER PORCHER & heirs of CAPT. CHARLES COLLETON, SW
on CHARLES COLLETON & vacant land: NW on vacant land, NE on PETER PORCHER.
RACHEL renounces her dower. Witnesses: SUSANNA BENOIST, ELIZABETH MARI-
ANNE PORCHER, PETER PORCHER, JOHN (his mark) BIRGIS. Before JAMES ST.
JOHN, J.P. NATHANIEL JOHNSON, Register.

Book P, p. 67   CHARLES HART, ESQ., of Berkeley Co., to JOHN
9 & 10 July 1735   WHITFIELD, merchant, of Dorchester, Berkeley
L & R   Co., for L 1600 SC money, 77 a. 3 roads in St.
                         Philips Parish, Berkeley Co., bounding N by
fence of ROBERT HUME, ESQ., & marsh, S on MRS. HANNAH GALE & marsh; W on
the Broad Path; E on marsh of Cooper River. Witnesses: WILLIAM PARTRIDGE,
ROWLAND VAUGHAN. NATHANIEL JOHNSON, Register.

Book P, p. 68   Plat of above land certified by G. HUNTER,
                         surveyor.

Book P, p. 72   JOHN DANIELL, planter, of St. Thomas Parish,
9 Jan. 1735   Berkeley Co., to his nephew, ALEXANDER GOODBEE,
Deed of Gift   for love & affection, 500 a. in Craven Co.,

bounding N on CAPT. RICHARD SMITH; other sides on vacant land. Witnesses: GEORGE THREADCROFT, THOMAS THREADCROFT. NATHANIEL JOHNSON, Register.

Book P, p. 73　　　　　　　DANIEL LAROCHE & THOMAS LAROCHE, merchants of
26 Nov. 1734　　　　　　　Georgetown, Craven Co., to JAMES WITHERS, ma-
Release　　　　　　　　　son, of Charleston, for ₤ 1512 currency, 630 a.
　　　　　　　　　　　　　in Craven Co., obunding W on WILLIAM WHITESIDE;
NE on DANIEL BRITTAIN; E on a creek; S on Georgetown River. Whereas Lt. Gov. THOMAS BROUGHTON on 12 May 1735 granted JOHN OULDFIELD 630 a. in Craven Co. which OULDFIELD on 8 Aug. 1735 conveyed to DANIEL & THOMAS LAROCHE; now they sell to WITHERS. Witnesses: JAMES CRICKLOW, GEORGE DICK, JOHN OULDFIELD, JR. Before HENRY GIBBES, J.P. NATHANIEL JOHNSON, Register.

Book P, p. 77　　　　　　　JOHN CUMING (CUMMING), planter, of Berkeley
14 & 15 Jan. 1735　　　　　Co., to JONATHAN SCOTT, merchant, of Charles-
L & R by Mortgage　　　　 ton, for ₤ 200 currency, 270 a. in St. Thomas
　　　　　　　　　　　　　Parish, bounding S on JOHN CUMMING; E on JOHN
CUMMING (formerly RICHARD HEATLEY); N on E branch of Cooper River; W on JOHN CUMMING; conditioned on payment of full sum with interest by CUMMING to SCOTT on 15 Aug. next. Witnesses: THOMAS GOULD, MAURICE LEWIS. Before HENRY GIBBES, J.P. NATHANIEL JOHNSON, Register.

Book P, p. 83　　　　　　　EDWARD (his mark) BARRY, of Bay of Honduras,
14 Dec. 1727　　　　　　　 formerly of Charleston, SC to EBENEZER WYATT,
Bill of Sale　　　　　　　mariner, of Charleston, for ₤ 35 Jamaican cur-
　　　　　　　　　　　　　rency, a corner lot on N side Tradd Street,
bounding W on HANCOCK; E by the cross street. Dated at the Old River in Bay of Honduras. Witnesses: JOHN BARKER, EDWARD DICKS, JAMES ELSINOR appeared before HENRY GIBBES, J.P. NATHANIEL JOHNSON, Register.

Book P, p. 83　　　　　　　ALEXANDER NISBETT, merchant, of Charleston, to
7 & 8 Mar. 1733/4　　　　　FRANCIS PAGITT, planter, of the Parish of St.
L & R　　　　　　　　　　　Thomas & St. Dennis, for ₤ 500 currency, 400 a.
　　　　　　　　　　　　　on E side Cooper River, bounding S on Simmons
Creek; E on JOHN WALBANK; N on JOHN CORREAR. Whereas the Lords Proprs., on 11 Jan. 1700 granted RICHARD GRIFFEN 400 a. English measure in Berkeley Co., & he bequeathed the land to his wife HELEN; who on 9 Feb. 17__ sold it to PETER JOHNSON; & whereas PETER JOHNSON & DEBORAH his wife on 25 Dec. 1731 sold to HUGH CAMPBELL, who on 11 Jan. 1732 sold to ALEXANDER NISBETT; now he sells to POGITT. Witnesses: WILLIAM CLEILAND, JOHN LINING, JOHN RIGG. Before THOMAS DALE, J.P. NATHANIEL JOHNSON, Register.

Book P, p. 89　　　　　　　WILLIAM DALTON, planter, of St. Bartholmews
14 Nov. 1735　　　　　　　 Parish, Colleton Co., to RICHARD WRIGHT, ESQ.,
Bill of Sale　　　　　　　of Charleston, for ₤ 415:18:9 SC money due
　　　　　　　　　　　　　WRIGHT by DALTON, & ₤ 280 paid to DALTON by
WRIGHT, (total ₤ 695:18:9) 6 Negro slaves. Should DALTON pay WRIGHT the total sum with interest on 1 Dec. next this sale to be void. Witnesses: THOMAS (his mark) WHALEY, SR., THOMAS WHALEY, JR., 1 slave delivered.

Book P, p. 91　　　　　　　WILLIAM ELLIOTT & SHEM BUTLER, of Berkeley Co.,
20 Mar. 17??　　　　　　　 to JOHN COCKFIELD, for ₤ 200 currency, 70 a.
Deed of Sale　　　　　　　bounding E on WILLIAM DRY; SW on BARNABY BULL.
　　　　　　　　　　　　　Whereas JOHN, Earl of Bath, & the Lords Proprs.
on 17 May 1701 granted BARNABY BULL 500 a. in Berkeley Co., on N side Ashley River; & he by will dated 20 Mar. 1715 authorized WILLIAM ELLIOTT & SHEM BUTLER, his executors, to sell a part if required; now they sell 70 a. to COCKFIELD. Signed by WILLIAM ELLIOTT & ESTHER BUTLER. Witnesses: EDWARD (his mark) PERRY, JOSEPH CLARE. NATHANIEL JOHNSON, Register.

Book P, p. 94　　　　　　　JOHN COCKFIELD & RACHEL COCKFIELD of Berkeley
28 Dec. 1717　　　　　　　 Co., to EDMUND BELLINGER, for ₤ 300 currency;
Bill of Sale　　　　　　　70 a., part of 500 a. granted CAPT. BARNABY
　　　　　　　　　　　　　BULL 7 sold by his executors in trust, WILLIAM
ELLIOT & SHEM BUTLER, to COCKFIELD. Witnesses: THOMAS BONNY, MOSES (his mark) COCKFIELD, SHEM BUTLER. NATHANIEL JOHNSON, Register.

Book P, p. 96　　　　　　　EDMUND BELLINGER to his father-in-law SHEM
Date ? 1718　　　　　　　　BUTLER, 70 a. (see p. 94), for ₤ 350.

Bill of Sale   Witnesses: STANLEY WILLIAMSON (?), MOSES (his
                            mark) COCKFIELD. NATHANIEL JOHNSON, Register.

Book P, p. 96   JOHN COWEN, planter, of Granville Co., to
29 & 30 Nov. 1725   ISAAC WEIGHT, planter, of Colleton Co., for
L & R   ₤ 700 SC money, 290 a. on Johns Island, Colle-
ton Co., bounding NW on Stono River; NE on JA-
COB WEIGHT; SE on vacant land; SW on ABRAHAM WEIGHT. Witnesses: WILLIAM
STANYARNE, JOHN STANYARNE, THOMAS PARMENTER. Before JOHN FENWICKE, J.P.
NATHANIEL JOHNSON, Register.

Book P, p. 99   JOHN COWEN, planter, & SARAH (her mark) his
5 June 1729   wife, to his brother, BENJAMIN COWEN, joiner,
Deed of Sale   both of St. Pauls Parish, Colleton Co., for
                            love & affection, 2 tracts of land & half of
lot #125 in Charleston; 1 tract being 1018 a.; the other 250 a., bounding
NE on DR. CALDER, NW on RICHARD CAPERS; being part of 650 a. Witnesses:
ISAAC WEIGHT, RICHARD BAKER, WILLIAM NICHOLS. Before THOMAS LADSON, J.P.
NATHANIEL JOHNSON, Register.

Book P, p. 100   BENJAMIN COWEN, & MARIAN (her mark) his wife,
29 & 30 June 1730   to ISAAC WAIGHT (WEIGHT), all of St. Pauls
L & R   Parish, Colleton Co., for ₤ 1100 SC money,
                            1018 a. on St. Helens, Granville Co., bounding
ENE & SE on GEORGE NORTON; other sides on marsh & creeks. Witnesses: NA-
THANIEL NICHOLLS, WILLIAM NICHOLS, HENRY HODGKIN. Before ROBERT YONGE,
J.P. NATHANIEL JOHNSON, Register.

Book P, p. 104   SAMUEL (his mark) NICHOLAS, & JOAN (her mark)
30 Dec. 1731   his wife, to NATHANIEL NICHOLAS, all of Colle-
L & R   ton Co., for 10 shillings currency, 400 a.
                            Enclish measure in Colleton Co., granted by
JOHN ARCHDALE & the Lords Proprs. on 27 June 1711 to NATHANIEL NICHOLAS;
bounding SW on Goose Marsh between it & Cumbee River; SE on THOMAS LEAVY;
NE on SAMUEL NICHOLAS; NW on EDMUND DUNDON. Witnesses: JOHN TOOMER, WIL-
LIAM CHAPLIN, ANDREW LETCHY (LEICHE). Before ROBERT YONGE, J.P. NATHAN-
IEL JOHNSON, Register.

Book P, p. 107   JOHN PRITCHARD, planter, to WILLIAM SWINTON,
26 Sept. 1732   planter, both of Craven Co., for ₤ 1000 cur-
Bond   rency, as security for sale of 500 a. on which
                            he lives by 1 Nov. next. Witnesses: JAMES
FUTHEY, DAVID FULTON. Before JOHN WALLIS, J.P. NATHANIEL JOHNSON, Register.

Book P, p. 108   HENRY YONGE, of Willtown, to JAMES BULLOCK, of
4 Nov. 1734   Colleton Co., as security on bond of even date
Mortgage   in penal sum of ₤ 2000 for payment of ₤ 1000
                            with interest on 3 Nov. 1737, conveys 134 a.
in Colleton Co., bounding on New London Town (or Willtown); E on JOHN
SMELLIE; S on JAMES STOBO; W on S Edisto River; (grant dated 4 May 1734
signed by Gov. ROBERT JOHNSON); also lot #45 in New London (Willtown)
granted 25 July 1717 to JOHN BROWN; bounding N on Newport Street; E on
lot #41; S on lot #42; W on S Edisto River; also lot #41 in New London
granted 27 June 1717 to JOHN BROWN; bounding N on Newport Street, E on
Fleet Street, S on lot #42; W on lot #45; also 4 Negro slaves. Witnesses: WILLIAM STOBO, WALTER WELS (?). Before HENRY YONGE, J.P. NATHANIEL
JOHNSON, Register. See Book R for probate.

Book P, p. 111   ELIZABETH (her mark) FAIRCHILD, widow; JOHN
5 June 1735   FAIRCHILD, planter, & WILLIAM FAIRCHILD, but-
Mortgage   cher (sons of ELIZABETH FAIRCHILD), to WILLIAM
                            HARVEY, SR., all of Charleston, as security,
on their bond in sum of ₤ 834 SC money & interest, convey part of a lot
on Charleston Green (purchased from RICHARD FAIRCHILD) bounding N on the
house & land of THOMAS FAIRCHILD; W on WILLIAM HARVEY; S on Tradd Street;
E on Friend Street, containing about 13,870 sq. ft. Witnesses: RICHARD
MASON, WILLIAM SMITH. Before JAMES GREENE, J.P. NATHANIEL JOHNSON, Register.

Book P, p. 115   JOHN COLLETON, ESQ., of 1st part; CHARLES
10 & 11 Feb. 1735   LOWNDES, ESQ., of 2nd part; ROBERT HUME, ESQ.;
L & R Tripartite   of St. Philip's Parish of 3rd part; all of
                        Berkeley Co., COLLETON & LOWNDES convey to RO-
BERT HUME, for ₤ 2580 SC money paid to COLLETON 7 5 shillings paid to
LWONDES, 500 a. where LOWNDES lived, in St. James Goose Creek Parish;
bounding S & E on Landgrave THOMAS SMITH; N on JOSEPH WRAGG (formerly
RICHARD BAKER); W on EDWARD KEATING (formerly BRYAN, alias BARNABY RILEY).
Witnesses: CHARLES SHEPHEARD, THOMAS ELLERY. Before JAMES GREENE, J.P.
NATHANIEL JOHNSON, Register.

Book P, p. 120   JOHN (his mark) LAURENS, saddler, of Charles-
25 & 26 Dec. 1735   ton, to DAVID SKINNER, bricklayer, of Berkeley
L & R   Co., for ₤ 1850 SC money, 730 a. in St. James
                        Goose Creek Parish, Berkeley Co., bounding E &
S on the creek & HUGH GRANGE; W on PHILIP GIBBES; N on COL. HERBERT'S
avenue; adding marsh land to complete 730 a. HESTER LAURENS, wife of
JOHN, upon request, to renounce her dower. Witnesses: BENJAMIN ADDISON,
JOHN CARIEN. Before THOMAS DALE, J.P. NATHANIEL JOHNSON, Register.

Book P, p. 121   Memo, at JOHN LAURENS'S request G. HUNTER, sur-
                        veyor, resurveyed 585 a. in St. James Goose
Creek, bounding NE on HUGH GRANGE & CAPT. MORRIS; SE on the creek & marshes; W on PHILIP GIBBES. Certified 26 Mar. 1735.

Book P, p. 125   DAVID SKINNER, bricklayer, of Berkeley Co., to
5 & 6 Feb. 1735   JOHN LAWRENS, saddler, of Charleston, as se-
L & R by Mortgage   curity on bond dated 28 Dec. 1735 in penal sum
                        of for payment ₤ 1850 SC money on 26 Dec. 1737;
730 a. in St. James Goose Creek Parish, bounding E & S on the creek &
HUGH GRANGE; W on PHILIP GIBBES; N on COL. HERBERT'S avenue. Witnesses:
BENJAMIN ADDISON, JOHN CARION. Before THOMAS DALE, J.P. NATHANIEL JOHN-
SON, Register.

Book P, p. 131   JOHN HAMMERTON, ESQ., of St. Philips Parish,
23 & 24 Feb. 1735   Charleston, to JOHN GLENN, planter, of Winyaw,
L & R   Craven Co., for ₤ ____ currency, 400 a. in
                        Prince George Parish, Craven Co., granted by
Lt. Gov. THOMAS BROUGHTON Dec. 1737 to JOHN HAMMERTON, bounding SE on Pee-
dee River; NW on Black River; SW on WILLIAM SWINTON; NE on ELIAS FOISSIN,
JR. (formerly JOHN THOMPSON). Witnesses: CHARLES PINCKNEY, ROBERT BREW-
TON, JR. Before THOMAS DALE, J.P. NATHANIEL JOHNSON, Register.

Book P, p. 135   JOHN TOOMER, planter, & ELIZABETH his wife, to
13 & 14 Jan. 1735   JOHN TUCKER, planter, all of Colleton Co., in
L & R in Trust   trust for TUCKER TOOMER (son of JOHN) & ELIZA-
                        BETH TOOMER, his wife, for love & affection
for TUCKER TOOMER & other considerations. JOHN & ELIZABETH TOOMER convey
to JOHN TUCKER 3 adjoining tracts of land total 560 a. in Colleton Co.,
bounding W on THOMAS WALLACE & JOHN JACKSON, all other sides on Stono River, which 3 tracts were devised to JOHN TOOMER by will of his father
CALEB. Witnesses: JAMES FOWLER, THOMAS CHARNOCK. Before THOMAS DALE,
J.P. NATHANIEL JOHNSON, Register.

Book P, p. 138   Note: The page numbering in the original
                        ships from 138 to 149. C.A.L.

Book P, p. 150   ROBERT WRIGHT, ESQ., to WILLIAM ELLIOTT, plant-
30 & 31 Jan. 1735   er, both of Berkeley Co., for ₤ 200 currency
L & R   10 a. in St. George Parish, near Stevens
                        Bridge; bounding NE on a river; all other
sides on ROBERT WRIGHT. Witnesses: JOHN FRASERS, JAMES WRIGHT. Before
THOMAS DALE, J.P. NATHANIEL JOHNSON, Register.

Book P, p. 157   ALEXANDER PARRIS, ESQ., to Lt. Gov. THOMAS
13 & 14 May 1735   BROUGHTON. Whereas PARRIS for several years
L & R by Mortgage   past has been Public Treasurer & Receiver of
                        the Province & has become answerable for vari-
ous considerable sums: & whereas PARRIS on 3 July 1735 agreed to execute
a mortgage of his real & personal estate; now PARRIS releases his

dwelling house & lot on the Bay, with the low water lot; also a plantation of 1100 a. in Christ Church Parish; also Archers Island in Granville Co., also delivers 40 Negro, Indians, & Mustee slaves; all his horses; mules & neat cattle. Witnesses: ANDREW RUTLEDGE, GABRIEL MANIGAULT, ROGER SAUNDERS, JR. Before ANDREW RUTLEDGE. NATHANIEL JOHNSON, Register.

Book P, p. 164
11 & 12 Feb. 1735
L & R

GEORGE SUMMERS (SOMMERS) storekeeper, of Savannah Town, SC & HENRIETTA his wife to JOHN HEARNE, hatmaker of James Island, St. Andrews Parish, Berkeley Co., for ₤ ???, 100 a. on James Island, bounding N on JOHN SANDIFORD (formerly GEORGE RUSSAT) & JOHN HEARNE; S & SE on JOHN SANDIFORD (formerly EDWARD MEDLICOTT); W on JOHN WITTER; being part of a tract of 325 a. granted Aug. 1701 (?) the plat of which stated the 325 a. was the S part of 650 a. granted PETER HEARNE. The 325 a. were purchased by JAMES WITTER from Landgrave BELLINGER, Receiver, on 13 Mar. 1700 (?), & conveyed to DR. HENRY BOULT; who by will dated 1707 bequeathed to THOMAS ROSE 100 a.; & THOMAS ROSE the younger leaving 1 daughter (HENRIETTA, an orphan) & apparently no will, she inherited the 100 a. She married GEORGE SUMMERS formerly an Indian trader, now a storekeeper. Witnesses: NICHOLAS HAYNES, (vintner) PETER HEARNE, NICHOLAS SMITH, JOHN HENRY, ALBERT DEDMIER. Before DANIEL GREENE, J.P. NATHANIEL JOHNSON, Register.

Book P, p. 171
12 Feb. 1735
Bond

JAMES MARSH to ELIZABETH HAMMERTON in penal sum of ₤ 150 for payment of ₤ 75 with interest. Witnesses: RICHARD J. HAMMERTON. NATHANIEL JOHNSON, Register.

Book P, p. 171
11 & 12 Feb. 1735
L & R by Mortgage

JAMES MARSH, planter, to ELIZABETH HAMMERTON, widow, as security on above bond for ₤ 75, 150 a. in Kingston Township, upon Waccamaw, & 1 town lot #7 bounding SE on Waccamaw River, all other sides on vacant land, which 150 a. & lot #7 were granted by Lt. Gov. THOMAS BROUGHTON on 4 Feb. 1737 to JAMES MARSH. Witnesses: RICHARD LAKE, J. HAMMERTON. NATHANIEL JOHNSON, Register.

Book P, p. 176
21 & 22 Aug. 1735
L & R

ISAAC LEWIS, getnleman, to THOMAS CHARNACK, merchant, both of Charleston, for ₤ 110 currency, 1350 a. in Craven Co., on Long Bay. Witnesses: JOHN CHARNOCK, HUGH EVANS, SAMUEL BALDWIN, ANDREW LAURENS. Before THOMAS DALE, J.P. NATHANIEL JOHNSON, Register.

Book P, p. 179
10 & 11 Oct. 1735
L & R

BARTHOLOMEW ARTHUR, planter, to ROBERT BROWN, surgeon, both of St. Johns Parish, Berkeley Co., for ₤ 5000 SC money, 1330 a. (pages broken). Witnesses: RACHEL THOMAS, ARTHUR HAMILTON, ELIZABETH YEATS. Before HENRY GIBBES, J.P. NATHANIEL JOHNSON, Register.

Book P, p. 184
1 Mar. 1735
Deed of Gift

JOHN BRETON, merchant, to his granddaughter-in-law ELIZABETH WITHERS, wife of LAWRENCE WITHERS, peruke maker, all of Charleston, for natural love & affection, & for ₤ 100 paid by ELIZABETH WITHERS to JOHN BRETON, a lot #49 in Charleston on which are 2 tenements, 1 occupied by ____ EDDLESTON, the other by ____ CAMPBELL; bounding W on Church Street, E on the lot occupied by THOMAS BAKER; N on another lot; S on an alley leading to Union Street. Witnesses: CHARLES CRAVEN, SAMUEL SMITH. Before DANIEL GREENE, J.P. NATHANIEL JOHNSON, Register.

Book P, p. 186
Date ?
Bond

GEORGE NICHOLAS to WILLIAM DONNING in penal sum of ₤ 3044 money of Great Britain for payment of ₤ 1522 with interest at DONNING'S plantation in Berkeley Co., called The Ponds, on 11 Mar. 1730. Witnesses: RICHARD ALLEIN, WILLIAM BOWNE. Before THOMAS DALE, J.P. NATHANIEL JOHNSON, Register.

Book P, p. 187
23 Dec. 1732

SAMUEL (his mark) WOODEN, house carpenter, of Salena Essex Co., Mass. to LAWRENCE DENNIS, of

Deed of Sale   Charleston, SC, for L 46, a tract of land on
                        Johns Island, St. Pauls Parish, Colleton Co.,
bounding N on MR. LATSON; S on MR. WILKINS & MR. FLEMEN, or otherwise.
Witnesses: EBWER COLLINS, JOSEPH STEVENSON. Before BENJAMIN LYNDE, JR.,
J.P., of Salem, Mass. "True Copy" attested by JOHN CROFT, N.P. of SC.
JOSEPH MARION, N.P. of Boston, on 5 Sept. 1735 attested that BENJAMIN
LYNDE, JR., of Salem, Essex Co., Mass. was legally a J.P. NATHANIEL JOHN-
SON, Register.

Book P, p. 190   JOHN CROSKEYS & ELIZABETH his wife, to ELIZA-
28 Oct. 1725   BETH TAMKERD, for L 20 SC money, 20 a., part
Deed of Sale   of a tract given to JOHN CROSKEYS by his
                        father (JOHN CROSKEYS) on James Island; bound-
ing N on marsh; E on same tract: SW on WILLIAM CHAPMAN. Witnesses: JOHN
WITTER, NICHOLAS SPENCER. Before HENRY GIBBES, J.P. NATHANIEL JOHNSON,
Register.

Book P, p. 192   NATHANIEL WICKHAM, ESQ., to the Society for
4 & 5 Feb. 1735   the Propagation of the Gospel In Foreign Parts,
L & R by Mortgage   as security on his bond for L 416 for payment
                        of L 208 British money with interest at 10% on
5 Feb. nect, 790 a. (part known as Cow Savanna) in Ashley Barony, on S
side Ashley River, bounding W on SAMUEL CLARK; S on ROBERT JOHNSON (alias
BLACK ROBIN); E on WILLIAM WALLACE & ALEXANDER SKENE, MARY (?) wife of
NATHANIEL WICKHAM to renounce her dower. Witnesses: BENJAMIN WHITAKER,
WILLIAM GEORGE FREEMAN. Before JAMES (?) ST. JOHN, J.P. NATHANIEL JOHN-
SON, Register.

Book P, p. 198   SAMUEL DRAKE, planter, of Berkeley Co., to
Feb. 1735   LUKE STOUTENBURG, silversmith, of Charleston,
Mortgage   as security on his bond of even date in penal
                        sum of L 1000 for payment of L 500 currency,
with interest @ 10%, on 3 Feb. 1736, 400 a. on N side Wando River, bounding W on JOSEPH WARNOCK (?); N on THOMAS RUSS; E (?) on SAMUEL WARNOCK;
also delivered 4 Negro men. Witnesses: PETER GUERIN, LUKE STOUTENBURG,
JR., JOHN CROFT. Before THOMAS LAMBOLL, J.P. NATHANIEL JOHNSON, Register. Mortgage satisfied by ANTHONY BONNEAU 20 Feb. 1734 (L 777).

Book P, p. 201   CHARLES LOWNDES, of St. James Goose Creek, to
Date 1733   JOHN COLLETON. Whereas on 2 Feb. 1732 (?)
Deed of Sale   COLLETON (at request of LOWNDES & for
                        LOWNDES'S debt) joined LOWNDES in giving a
bond to JAMES CROCKET, merchant, of Charleston, in penal sum of L 5200
currency for payment of L 2600 & interest on 2 Feb. 1733, LOWNDES conveyed to COLLETON, as security, 500 a. in Berkeley Co., bounding S on
SHAND'S; N on JOHN WARD (WOOD), also 500 a. bounding S & E on Landgrave
THOMAS SMITH; N on RICHARD BAKER; W on BARNABY REALLY: & whereas CHARLES
LOWNDES is on a voyage to the Island of St. Christopher, Antigua, & will
not be able to keep his agreements but has persuaded COLLETON to sign
another bond of L 100 sterling, etc., etc., now LOWNDES, in consideration
of the above, & for L 60 currency, conveys to COLLETON the 2 tracts of
500 a. each. Witnesses: RICHARD ALLEIN, ROBERT PRINGLE, FREDERICK MEYER.
Before THOMAS LAMBOLL, J.P. NATHANIEL JOHNSON, Register.

Book P, p. 206   JOHN BASSNETT, bookkeeper, of Charleston, to
24 & 25 Mar. 1735   ELIZABETH HILL, widow & executor of will of
L & R by Mortgage   CHARLES HILL, as security on bond of even date
                        in penal sum of L 1100 (?) for payment of
L 550 currency on 26 Mar. 1737, 400 a. in Williamsburg Township, Craven
Co., bounding SW on Black River; SE on RICHARD HALL, NE & NW on vacant
land; also 2 Negro men, 2 Negro boys & 2 Negro women - 1 gold ring delivered. Witnesses: FRANCIS HOLMES, WILLIAM HOPTON. Before BENJAMIN
WHITAKER, J.P. NATHANIEL JOHNSON, Register. Mortgage satisfied 19 Nov.
1739. Witness: ROBERT AUSTIN, Register.

Book P, p. 211   GEORGE NICHOLAS, ESQ., & ELIZABETH his wife to
Date ?   WILLIAM DONNING, gentleman, as security on
L & R by Mortgage   bond in penal sum of L 3044 British money for
                        payment on 11 Mar. 1736 of L 1522 at DONNING'S
plantation called The Ponds, Berkeley Co., (formerly called Parkers

Plantation, later Percival's Lower Plantation, now Donning's Plantation, 1238 a. bounding SW on Ashley River; NE on GEORGE NICHOLAS; SE on FRANCIS TURGIS (other names mentioned being GEORGE BARNETT, ANDREW PERCIVAL, VERLINE? MALACHI GLAZE. (Paper badly torn). Witnesses: RICHARD ALLEIN, WILLIAM BROWNE. Before THOMAS DALE, J.P. NATHANIEL JOHNSON, Register.

Book P, p. 218　　　　　　　　PETER BONOIST & ABIGAIL his wife, cooper, of
13 & 14 Apr. 1736　　　　　　Berkeley Co., to JAMES GORDON, ESQ., of Craven
L & R　　　　　　　　　　　　Co., for ₤ 500 currency, 2 tracts, or 300 a.;
　　　　　　　　　　　　　　　the 1st bounding N on WILLIAM SWINTON; Waccamaw River & GORDON'S Thorofare; the 2nd bounding NE on Peedee River, GORDON's Thorofare; SW GLEN'S thorofare; SE on GEORGE PAWLEY; NW on PAWLEY'S creek. Witnesses: JOHN BROWN, RACHEL ROBERTSON, ROBERT WRIGHT, JAMES MICHIE. Before ROBERT WRIGHT, J.P. NATHANIEL JOHNSON, Register.

Book P, p. 222　　　　　　　　JOHN GOUGH, planter, of St. John's, Berkeley,
18 & 19 Aug. 1735 (?)　　　　& MARY his wife, to RICHARD MALONE, of Charles-
L & R　　　　　　　　　　　　ton, for ₤ 500, an inland tract of 500 a., in
　　　　　　　　　　　　　　　Craven Co., surveyed by JOHN COUGH, JR., Dep.
Surv. for JOHN GOUGH, SR., bounding W on JOHN SHACKELFORD; S on JOHN LANE; E on vacant land. Witnesses: RICHARD GOUGH, FRANCIS ROCHE, JAMES MCKYE. Before HENRY GIBBES, J.P. NATHANIEL JOHNSON, Register.

Book P, p. 227　　　　　　　　JOHN BERESFORD, ESQ. of Berkeley Co., of 1st
29 & 30 Mar. 1736　　　　　　part; JOSEPH WRAGG, ESQ., of Charleston of 2nd
L & R Septipartite　　　　　part; JAMES ST. JOHN, ESQ., of Charleston of
　　　　　　　　　　　　　　　3rd part; ROBERT HUME, ESQ., of Charleston of
4th part; JOB ROTHMAHLER, ESQ., of Berkeley Co., of 5th part; CHARLES RUSSELL, planter, of 6th part; THOMAS BROWN, planter, of 7th part.

Whereas Lt. Gov. THOMAS BROUGHTON by 8 separate grants dated 14 Feb. last past granted JOHN BERESFORD 8 separate tracts in Berkeley Co., viz. 227 a., 250 a., 360 a., 360 a., 327 a., 500 a., 250 a., & 792 a., situated as follows: 227 a. bounding NW on EDWARD KEATING; NE on JOHN HAMMERTON, ESQ.; SE on EDWARD KEATING; 150 a. on Twelve Mile Creek, bounding S on THOMAS BROWN; 360 a. on SE side Beaver Creek, bounding NE on JOHN BERESFORD; 360 a. on SE side Beaver Creek, bounding all sides on vacant land; 327 a. bounding NE on JOHN HAMMERTON; SE on JOHN HAMMERTON & vacant land; NW on JOHN BERESFORD; 500 a. bounding all sides on vacant land; 250 a. bounding S on JOHN BERESFORD & all other sides on vacant land; 792 a. bounding N on Santee River; E on WILLIAM YORK; S on THOMAS BROWN; W on vacant land; now for ₤ 1000 SC money JOHN BERESFORD sells the 8 tracts to the other 6 men as tenants in common & not as jointenants in trust (the whole being divided into 80 parts); 14/80 for JOHN BERESFORD; 14/80 to JOSEPH WRAGG; 14/80 to JAMES ST. JOHN; 14/80 to ROBERT HUME; 14/80 to JOB ROTHMAHTER; 5/80 to CHARLES RUSSELL; 5/80 to THOMAS BROWN. Witnesses: STEPHEN PROCTOR, THOMAS HEPWORTH. Before JAMES GRAEME, J.P. NATHANIEL JOHNSON, Register.

Book P, p. 238　　　　　　　　JOHN DUBOSE, planter, of Craven Co., to ISAAC
24 Mar. 1735　　　　　　　　　MAZYCK, merchant, of Charleston, for ₤ 1486 SC
Mortgage　　　　　　　　　　　money; 2 tracts, total 908 a.; 500 a. where
　　　　　　　　　　　　　　　DUBOSE lives, being on N side of Santee River,
bounding on the glebe land of Parish of St. James Santee; E on ANDREW REMBERT; S on ISAAC LEGRAND; the other on N side Santee River, bounding S on above tract ANDREW REMBERT; N on ____ PALMERIN & JOHN DUBOSE; E on ISAAC DUBOSE; as security for bond dated 18 Mar. 1735 in penal sum of ₤ 1486 for payment of ₤ 743 with interest on 18 Mar. 1736. Witnesses: ANDREW DELAVILLETTE, ANTHONY BOURDEAUX, ARCHIBALD HAMILTON. Before ELIAS HORRY, J.P. NATHANIEL JOHNSON, Register.

Book P, p. 241　　　　　　　　JOHN (his mark) MACCOY & RICHARD DAWSON,
24 & 25 Mar. 1736　　　　　　planters, of Colleton Co., to RICHARD HILL,
L & R by Mortgage　　　　　　merchant, as security on bond of this date
　　　　　　　　　　　　　　　given by MACCOY to HILL in sum of ₤ 834:8:10
for payment of ₤ 417:4:5 with interest on 15 Mar. next; 500 a. in Colleton Co., bounding E S & W on ABRAHAM MESHEW; N on WILLIAM EMERSON; which tract was granted by the Lords Proprs. to HENRY MESHEW & conveyed to MACCOY & DAWSON by ABRAHAM MESHEW; son & heir of HENRY MESHEW. Witnesses: WILLIAM FREEMAN, BENJAMIN WHITAKER. RICHARD HILL quit claims to

RICHARD DAWSON title to 250 a. (½ the 500). Before JAMES ST. JOHN, J.P. NATHANIEL JOHNSON, Register.

Book P, p. 246
9 & 10 Apr. 1736
L & R by Mortgage

JOSHUA WILKS (WILKES), planter, of Christ Church Parish, to ELIZABETH HILL, widow & sole executrix of will of CHARLES HILL, ESQ., as security on bond in penal sum of ₤ 2077:14 for payment of ₤ 1038:7:1:½ on 25 Mar. next; 600 a. in Christ Church Parish, Berkeley Co., bounding E on MATTHEW SMALLWOOD & MARY MACMARVILL (?); S on MATTHEW SMALLWOOD (?); W on CLEMENT WILKINSON (?) (WILLIAMSON ?); N on marsh in Wando River. Witnesses: BENJAMIN WHITAKEN, WILLIAM FREEMAN. Before JAMES ST. JOHN, J.P. NATHANIEL JOHNSON, Register. Mortgage satisfied (broken page)

Book P, p. 250
10 Jan. 1736 (?)
Deed of Gift

The Rev. MR. WILLIAM GUY to his wife REBECCA GUY, for love & affection & other considerations, lot #8 (containing ½ a., English measure), in Ashley River Ferry Town, St. Andrews Parish, Berkeley Co.; also the brick tenement on the ground. Witnesses: MRS. JANE MONGE (?), WILLIAM LEA, NICHOLAS LYNCH. Before WILLIAM CATTELL, J.P. NATHANIEL JOHNSON, Register.

Book P, p. 250
20 & 21 Dec. 1732
L & R

JOB HOWES, gentleman, late of Berkeley Co., now of Cape Fear, NC, only son & heir of ROBERT HOWES, planter, of Berkeley Co., by his attorney THOMAS CLIFFORD, ESQ., of Berkeley Co. (appointed 22 Feb. 1731), to ROBERT HUME, ESQ., of St. Philips Parish, Charleston, for ₤ 1600 SC money, 800 a. in St. James Goose Creek Parish, Berkeley Co., bounding SW on Yeoman's or Goose Creek; SE on ALEXANDER VANDERDUSSEN (formerly LEWIS PASQUEREAU); NE on ALEXANDER NISBETT (formerly NATHANIEL SNOW & JOHN GILL); NW on JAMES GRANGE (formerly JOHN EMPEROR); which 800 a. was granted by Gov. NATHANIEL JOHNSON & the Lords Proprs. on 15 Dec. 1706 to ROBERT HOWES. Witnesses: ROWLAND VAUGHAN, HENRY GIGNILLIAT. Before BENJAMIN WHITAKER, J.P. NATHANIEL JOHNSON, Register.

Book P, p. 252
22 Feb. 1731
Letter of Attorney

JOB HOWES, gentleman, appointed THOMAS CLIFFORD, of Goose Creek, his attorney, to sell his tract of 800 a., between ALEXANDER VANDERDUSSEN'S & JAMES GRANGE'S plantations, the money to be used to pay several debts of his father ROBERT HOWES to BENJAMIN GODIN & BENJAMIN DELA CONSEILLERE & of his grandmother MRS. SARAH HOWES, notwithstanding any agreement made between ARTHUR MIDDLETON, ESQ., (JOB'S guardian) & THOMAS CLIFFORD in regard to the payment of the debts. Witnesses: WILLOUGHBY HERBERT, (a woman), JOHN BRIGGS. Before JOHN HERBERT, J.P. NATHANIEL JOHNSON, Register.

Book P, p. 257
22 & 23 Apr. 1736
L & R by Mortgage

JAMES WITHERS, bricklayer, to ROBERT HUME, ESQ., both of Charleston, as security on bond of even date in penal sum of ₤ 760 money of Great Britain for payment of ₤ 380 like money (₤ 80 on 1 May 1737; ₤ 300 on 1 May 1738); 630 a. in Craven Co., bounding W on WILLIAM WHITESIDE, ESQ.; NE on DANIEL BRITTAIN; E on a creek; S on Georgetown River; also 800 a. in St. James Goose Creek Parish, on NE side Goose Creek, bounding SE on ALEXANDER VANDERDUSSEN (formerly LEWIS PASQUEREAU); NE on ALEXANDER NESBITT (formerly NATHANIEL SNOW & JOHN GILL); NW on JAMES GRANGE (formerly JOHN EMPEROR). Witnesses: JOHN THOMAS, THOMAS HEPWORTH. Before ANDREW RUTLEDGE, J.P. NATHANIEL JOHNSON, Register.

Book P, p. 262
27 Feb. 1734/5
Mortgage

JOSEPH LYONS, tanner, of Berkeley Co., being under bond to SUSANNAH COLLETON, now wife of JAMES SINGLETON, planter, of Berkeley Co., the bond dated 14 Nov. 1734 being in penal sum of ₤ 500 currency for payment of ₤ 247:10 on 1 Jan. next; now LYONS gives JAMES SINGLETON, as security, 1 white gelding branded 12; 100 neat cattle branded E & E^2. Witnesses: ISAAC PORCHER, ELIZABETH RICHEBOURG. Before THOMAS FERGUSON, J.P. NATHANIEL JOHNSON, Register.

Book P, p. 264

SAMUEL MILLER, planter, of Berkeley Co., to

1 Jan. 1735/6   JAMES SINGLETON, planter, as security on debt
Mortgage   of ℔ 394:15:5:3 currency, payable 1 May next
                             with interest conveys 2 Negro men, 1 Negro wo-
man. Witnesses: ISAAC PORCHER, SR., ISAAC PORCHER, JR. Before THOMAS
FERGUSON, J.P. NATHANIEL JOHNSON, Register.

Book P, p. 265   JAMES KELLY, planter, & JOAN (JEANE) his wife,
25 Feb. 1735   to THOMAS SULLAVANT, planter, both of Colleton
L & R   Co., for 5 shillings currency, 437 a. in Col-
                             leton Co., bounding N on THOMAS JONES; W on
THOMAS DRAYTON; S on 1 Pike; E on vacant land. Witnesses: JOHN SPENCER,
JAMES SKIRVING, RICHARD SINGLETON. NATHANIEL JOHNSON, Register.

Book P, p. 268   BENTLY COKE, planter, of Berkeley Co., to
20 & 21 Jan. 1735   ELISHA SCREVEN, planter, of Winyaw, Craven Co.,
L & R   for ℔ 100 currency, 500 a. in Craven Co.,
                             bounding E on JAMES BREMAR & JOHN GARDNER; SW
on vacant land; N on vacant land & JAMES BREMAR; which 500 a. was granted
on 7 Aug. 1735, by letters patent signed by Lt. Gov. THOMAS BROUGHTON, to
BENTLEY COKE. Witnesses: JOSEPH COKE, FREDERICK MEYER (gentleman). Before DANIEL GREENE, J.P. NATHANIEL JOHNSON, Register.

Book P, p. 273   JOHN BERESFORD, ESQ., to WILLIAM BRANDFORD,
19 & 20 Feb. 1734   planter, both of Berkeley Co., for ℔ 6000 cur-
L & R   rency; 710 a. known as Old Town Plantation; on
                             Old Town Creek, Ashley River, St. Andrews Par-
ish, lately owned by PETER LESADE, planter; bounding E on the creek; W on
WILLIAM BRANDFORD; N on creeks & marsh; S on ANDREW DEVEAUX. Witnesses:
MALACHI GLAZE, ROWLAND VAUGHAN. It is agreed that BERESFORD does not
guarantee that BRANDFORD shall have quiet possession of 42 a. now in possession of executors of THOMAS ROSE who are entitled to the same during
the lifetime of PETER LESADE than to revert to JOHN BERESFORD. Before
ROBERT WRIGHT, C.J. NATHANIEL JOHNSON, Register.

Book P, p. 277   WILLIAM OSBORNE, vintner, & HELENA his wife,
7 & 8 May 1736   to CHARLES PINCKNEY, ESQ. all of Charleston,
L & R   for ℔ 600 SC money, 500 a., being an island on
                             S side Port Royall River, bounding E on Look-
out Island Creek running from the river to Callibogee Creek; S & W on
another creek. Witnesses: ALEXANDER OSBORNE, ROBERT BREWTON, JR. Before
HENRY GIBBES, J.P. NATHANIEL JOHNSON, Register.

Book P, p. 281   WILLIAM WHITESIDE, ESQ., to DANIEL BRITTON,
20 Dec. 1735   planter, both of Craven Co., for ℔ 50 currency,
L & R   493 a. in Craven Co., granted to WILLIAM WHITE-
                             SIDE & commonly called Town Hill, on Peedee
River, bounding E on the Rev. MR. THOMAS MORRELL; N on THOMAS BESHER; NE
on MR. MOORE; S on vacant land. Witnesses: JAMES CRICHLOW, WILLIAM COLT.
Before THOMAS LAROCHE, J.P. NATHANIEL JOHNSON, Register.

Book P, p. 284   DAVID ARNOTT to JOHN WHITFIELD, as security on
5 Jan. 1735   the further sum of ℔ 273:6 currency as well as
Mortgage   ℔ 706 & interest conveys 400 a. Witnesses:
                             THOMAS BARNES, STEPHEN DYER. Before JOHN
SKENE, J.P. NATHANIEL JOHNSON, Register.

Book P, p. 285   PETER SECARE, planter, & ELIAS FOISSIN, ESQ. &
18 June 1735   MARY his wife (lately MARY LAROCHE) to BENJA-
L & R   MIN WHITAKER, ESQ., for ℔ 750, paid or secured
                             to be paid to SECARE, & ℔ 750 paid or secured
to be paid to FOISSIN & his wife, all their 2 undivided third parts (the
whole divided in 3 equal parts) of 2 lots in Charleston. Whereas STEPHEN
TAVERON, cooper, of SC by will dated 19 July 1729 bequeathed to his grandsons PETER SECARE & ISAAC SECARE & to his grand-daughter MARY LAROCHE
(now wife of ELIAS FOISSIN) a lot in Charleston fronting S 41 ft. on
Broad Street, bounding E on the lot willed to DANIEL LAROCHE & THOMAS LA-
ROCHE; W on another of his lots; N on a street; to be equally divided between them; & also bequeathed them (PETER, ISAAC, & MARY) his lot fronting S 42 ft. on Broad Street, bounding E on the last mentioned lot; W on
another of his lots; N on a street: to be equally divided between them.

MARY FOISSIN to renounce her dower within 9 months. Witnesses to PETER'S signature: GEORGE PAWLEY, PERCIVAL PAWLEY, JOHN OULDFIELD, JR. Witnesses to ELIAS & MARY'S signature: LYDIA LEA, WILLIAM GEORGE FREEMAN. Before DANIEL LAROCHE, J.P. & JACOB BOND, J.P. NATHANIEL JOHNSON, Register.

Book P, p. 291　　　　　　　EDWARD HORN (HORNE) FORREST, gentleman, late
29 & 30 Dec. 1735　　　　　of Island of Antigua, now of SC, to NICHOLAS
L & R　　　　　　　　　　　MATTEYSON, blacksmith, of Charleston, for
　　　　　　　　　　　　　　L 1000 sterling of Great Britain, 180 a. in
St. Johns Parish, Antigua, bounding on lands of CAPT. WILLIAM HORN, SAMUEL MARTIN, ESQ., HENRY MARTIN & THOMAS WILLIAMS. Witnesses: JOSEPH FIDLER, THOMAS GALLWAY FIDLER appeared before CHARLES PINCKNEY, J.P. NATHANIEL JOHNSON, Register.

Book P, p. 296　　　　　　　ROBERT BROWN, planter, of Berkeley Co., &
29 & 30 Dec. 1735　　　　　SARAH his wife, to ALEXANDER NISBETT, gentle-
L & R　　　　　　　　　　　man, of Charleston, for L 2000 currency, 640 a.
　　　　　　　　　　　　　　in Craven Co. bequeathed to him by JOHN ___ yd
of St. James Goose Creek, bounding W on Waccamaw River (Page broken). Witnesses: JAMES AKIN, RACHEL THOMAS, SOLOMON JUNE. Before BENJAMIN DELA CONSEILLERE, J.P. NATHANIEL JOHNSON, Register.

Book P, p. 299　　　　　　　ALEXANDER NISBETT, gentleman to ROBERT BROWN,
16 & 17 Apr. 1736　　　　　both of Berkeley Co., for L 2000 SC money,
L & R　　　　　　　　　　　640 a. in Craven Co., bounding E on salt marsh;
　　　　　　　　　　　　　　W on Waccamaw River; N & S on WILLIAM ALSTON;
which land NISBETT lately purchased from BROWN (p. 296). Witnesses: JOHN DEAS, JOHN NINIAN, ROBERT NINEAN. Before JAMES WEDDERBURN, J.P. NATHANIEL JOHNSON, Register.

Book P, p. 303　　　　　　　DAVID CARTWRIGHT, planter, & SARAH his wife,
11 & 12 May 1736　　　　　to EDMUND BELLINGER & ROGER SAUNDERS, ESQRS.,
L & R in Trust　　　　　　all of Berkeley Co., in trust for sole benefit
　　　　　　　　　　　　　　of SARAH CARTWRIGHT, 2 tracts of 216 & 27 a.,
11 town lots in Ashley River Ferry Town, Nos. 90, 91, 92, 93, 94, 95, 96, 97, 98, 99 & 102; 7 Negro slaves, & other goods & chattels. Whereas SHEM BUTLER, planter, owned several tracts of land, divers Negro & other slaves, & goods & chattels, & by will dated 9 Oct. 1718 bequeathed all his real & personal estate to be equally divided amongst his wife & children & appointed, as his executors, his brother RICHARD BUTLER, his brother-in-law SAMUEL WEST, & his son-in-law EDMUND BELLINGER; & whereas WEST refused the office & the others proved the will, divided & allotted the estate; & they allotted to SARAH (then unmarried) 216 a. on S side Ashley River, bounding NE on marsh & Ashley River Ferry Town; SE on EDMUND BELLINGER; SW on MRS. REBECCA BUTLER (another daughter of SHEM); NW on THOMAS BUTLER (son of SHEM); also 27 a. on N side Ashley River, bounding NE on JOHN COCKFIELD; SE on JOSEPH BUTLER (son of SHEM); SW on JOHN MILLS; W on WILLIAM BULL; also 70 a. on N side Ashley River, part of grant to BARNABY BULL; bounding NE on CAPT. WILLIAM _____ now (?) ROBERT ELLIOT, 1 side on JOHN COCKFIELD; & also allotted to SARAH 13 lots in Ashley River Ferry Town, Nos. 90, 91, 92, 93, 94, 95, 96, 97, 98, 99, 100, 101 & 102; also 7 Negro slaves; horses, neat cattle, plate, household goods, etc.; & whereas SARAH afterwards married DANIEL CARTWRIGHT & he possessed himself of the 3 plantations & the other goods & chattels by right of his wife; & whereas SARAH, in order to pay off some of DANIEL'S indebtedness, consented to the sale of the 70 a. for which DANIEL received L 700 but made no arrangement for recompensing SARAH for her marriage portion; now in consideration of the above facts, DANIEL & SARAH CARTWRIGHT convey to BELLINGER & SAUNDERS, in trust for the sole use of SARAH the 2 tracts of 216 & 27 a., 11 town lots, 7 Negro slaves, they to manage the estate for SARAH & her heirs. Witnesses: CHARLES PINCKNEY, ROBERT BREWTON, JR. Before HENRY GIBBES, J.P. NATHANIEL JOHNSON, Register.

Book P, p. 312　　　　　　　THOMAS BARTON, planter, to ELIZABETH HILL,
4 & 5 May 1736　　　　　　widow & executrix of will of CHARLES HILL,
L & R by Mortgage　　　　ESQ., as security on bond of even date in pe-
　　　　　　　　　　　　　　nal sum of L 1733:18:10 for payment of
L 866:19:5 on 5 May next; conveys 2 tracts in Christ Church Parish; 210 a. granted to JOSEPH BOONE & later became the property of GILES COOKE, practitioner in physic, who conveyed to THOMAS BARTON; bounding E on

DANIEL BULLOCK (formerly GILES COOKE); W on WILLIAM WHITE; S on JOHN EVANS; & 145 a., part of 200 a. granted WILLIAM WHITE, planter, later the property of GILES COOKE who conveyed to THOMAS BARTON, bounding E on SAMUEL BULLOCK (formerly GILES COOKE); N on Wando River; W on WILLIAM WHITE; S on JOHN EVANS. Witnesses: DANIEL CARTWRIGHT, WILLIAM FREEMAN. Before BENJAMIN WHITAKER, J.P. NATHANIEL JOHNSON, Register.

Book P, p. 316
30 & 31 Jan. 1734
L & R by Mortgage

RICHARD LAKE, ESQ., of St. Philips Parish, to THOMAS CHEESMAN, merchant, of Charleston, for ₤ 1300 currency, 1200 a. at Ashepoo, Colleton Co., bounding S on JOHN AMBROSE; on condition that LAKE pay Parish ₤ 1300 with interest on 1 Feb. 1738. Witnesses: CHARLES SHEPHEARD, CHARLES PINCKNEY. Before HENRY GIBBES, J.P. NATHANIEL JOHNSON, Register. (Mortgage evidently satisfied & acknowledged by GABRIEL MANIGAULT & witnessed by ROBERT AUSTIN, Pub. Reg.).

Book P, p. 321
6 Sept. 1732
Deed of Gift

ISAAC PORCHER, planter, to PETER PORCHER & FRANCES CORDES, planters, all of Berkeley Co., in trust for RACHEL PORCHER his eldest daughter, part of a lot in Charleston now occupied by PETER FILLEAUX (number broken out of page), bounding N on Middle Street; W on Church Street; S on part of same lot belonging to ABRAHAM LE SUEUR; E on FRANCIS GRACIA. Witnesses: JOHN BONNIN, FRANCIS VARNOD. Before THOMAS DALE, J.P. NATHANIEL JOHNSON, Register.

Book P, p. 323
22 (?) June (?) 1735 (?)
Deed of Gift in Trust

JOHN FAIRCHILD, butcher, of Berkeley Co., love & affection for his wife RACHEL & other considerations, conveys to FRANCIS CORDES, planter, of St. James Goose Creek, in trust for RACHEL FAIRCHILD, 2 Negro men & 1 Negro woman. Witnesses: MARY WESTON, ISAAC PORCHER, JR. Delivery of 1 Negro witnessed by JAMES RICHEBOURG, ISAAC PORCHER, JR., CLAUDIUS RICHBOURG. Before ISAAC PORCHER, J.P. NATHANIEL JOHNSON, Register.

Book P, p. 324
24 Jan. 1711/12
Deed of Gift

ROGER PLAYER, planter of Berkeley Co., for love & affection, to his daughter SUSANNAH on the day of her marriage, 1 Negro boy, 1 doz. pewter plates, 2 B-dishes, 1 feather bed & furniture belonging, 1 mare, 1 cedar table, 1 (dre ?) ssing box, 1 looking glass, half of a lot in (Charles ?) town bounding as in Grant, 1 great iron pot, 1 brass kettle, 1 chest drawers, 1 great Spanish chest, 1 diaper tablecloth, 5 napkins, 2 towels, 2 "pillaburs" (?) 1 set white curtains & valance, now in his dwelling house in the Co. Witnesses: THOMAS LOREY, WILLIAM WHITE. Before THOMAS HEPWORTH, J.P. NATHANIEL JOHNSON, Register.

Book P, p. 325
1 Feb. 1735 (?)
Deed of Gift

JOHN GOUGH, SR., planter, & MARY his wife, of Berkeley Co., to their beloved son, RICHARD, for love & affection, 670, part of 3500 a. in Berkeley Co. granted by Gov. NATHANIEL JOHNSON & the Lords Proprs. on 12 Oct. 1709 to JOHN GOUGH; being part of a Barony of 12,000 a. formerly belonging to PETER COLLETON, gentleman, of Barbados; the 670 a. being on the E branch of the T of Cooper River, bounding SW on NICHOLAS EARLESTON; NW & E on JOHN GOUGH, SR. Witnesses: NICHOLAS HARLESTON, ISAAC CHILD. NATHANIEL JOHNSON, Register.

Book P, p. 326
24 & 25 May 1736
L & R

MALACHI GLAZE, planter, of Berkeley Co., to ROBERT HUME, ESQ., of Charleston, for ₤ 195 SC money, 1950 a. in Craven Co., granted by letters patent, dated 22 May 1736 & signed by Lt. Gov. THOMAS BROUGHTON, to MALACHI GLAZE; bounding NW on WILLIAM HARVEY, all other sides on vacant land. Witnesses: JOHN BLAMYER, THOMAS HEPWORTH. Before JOSEPH WRAGG, J.P. NATHANIEL JOHNSON, Register.

Book P, p. 329
10 & 11 Jan. 1735
L & R

AMBROSE REEVE (REEVES), chirurgeon, to LEWIS JONES, clerk & MARGARET his wife, all of Beaufort, Granville Co., in consideration of ₤ 5 & the trust reposed in him, releases to JONES 500 a. English measure on Port Royall Island, Granville Co., bounding E on Dicks Back Creek; N on ALEXANDER MACKEY; W on vacant land; S on

KNATCHBULLS land (ROSATCHBULL). Whereas by L & R, 27 & 28 Oct. 1735 LEWIS JONES & MARGARET his wife conveyed to AMBROSE REEVE the above named 500 a. in trust to the use of LEWIS & MARGARET JONES during their lives & REEVE agreed that he would, at any time, convey the plantation to JONES; & whereas JONES & his wife on 28 Oct. last renounced all title to the land & joined in a precipe concord or fine for that purpose, MARGARET voluntarily consenting, & quit claimed to REEVE; now REEVE releases the land to them. Witnesses: RICHARD WOODWARD, JOSEPH EDWARD FLOWER. Before THOMAS WIGG, J.P. NATHANIEL JOHNSON, Register.

Book P, p. 334
25 & 26 May 1736
L & R

WILLIAM HARVEY, gentleman, of Charleston, to ROBERT HUME, ESQ., for L 265 SC money, 2650 a., in Craven Co., granted to WILLIAM HARVEY by letters patent dated 22 May 1736, signed by Lt. Gov. THOMAS BROUGHTON; bounding SE on MALACHI GLAZE; other sides on vacant land. Witnesses: JOHN BLAMYER, THOMAS HEPWORTH. Before JOSEPH WRAGG, J.P. NATHANIEL JOHNSON, Register.

Book P, p. 337
13 & 14 June 1735
L & R by Mortgage

JOHN MULLRYNE, gentleman, formerly of Island of Mounserrat but now of Granville Co., SC, to BENJAMIN GODIN, merchant, of Charleston, as security for payment of L 1214:12:2 SC money, on 1 Jan. next, 1/2 part of 1497 a. in Granville Co., bounding N on Combahee River; S on ROBERT STEEL, the Hon. WILLIAM BULL & THOMAS LOWNDES, ESQ.; & "lying round" a tract of JOSEPH BRYAN'S land; also 1/2 part of 550 a. in Granville Co., on Combahee River, bounding on all sides in above tract of 1497 a.; the 2 tracts making 1 plantation of 2047 a. Whereas by letters patent dated 22 Sept. 1734 & signed by Gov. ROBERT JOHNSON, COL. JOSEPH BLAKE was granted 1497 a. in Granville Co. with the usual provisoes; & whereas by L & R, 9 & 10 Oct. 1733 (?) JOSEPH BLAKE & SARAH his wife sold the 1497 a. to JOSEPH BRYAN; & whereas SIR NATHANIEL JOHNSON, JAMES MOORE, & JOB HOWES, Lords Proprs. on 12 Jan. 17__ (?) granted to JOSEPH BRYAN (father of JOSEPH, party hereto) 550 a., English measure, on Combahee River, bounding on all sides by a large cypress swamp; which 550 a. was in the middle of the 1497 a.; & whereas JOSEPH BRYAN, eldest son & heir, sold the 550 a. & the 1497 a. for L 1800 to BENJAMIN GODIN, who, by L & R, 9 & 10 June 1735 sold the 2 tracts to JOHN MULLRYNE; & whereas MULLRYNE gave a bond to GODIN in the penal sum of L 2429 for payment of L 1214:12:2 on 1 Jan. next; now MULLRYNE conveys half the 2 tracts to GODIN as security. Witnesses: RICHARD ALLEIN, DAVID GODIN, PETER SHAW. Before BENJAMIN DELA CONSEILLERE, J.P. NATHANIEL JOHNSON, Register. Mortgage declared satisfied 27 Jan. 1737 by FRANCIS BARBOT for BENJAMIN GODIN. ROBERT AUSTIN, Pub. Reg.

Book P, p. 344
3 & 4 June 1736
L & R by Mortgage

JOHN FAIRCHILD, butcher, & RACHEL his wife, of Berkeley Co., to BENJAMIN GODIN, merchant, of Charleston, as security for payment bond for L 3500, 5 tracts of land; 300 a., 415 a., 1000 a., 700 a., 449 a., all in Berkeley Co.; also 11 Negro men & 1 Negro woman. Whereas ISAAC PORCHER, planter, & RACHEL his wife, by deed of feoffment dated 3 Jan. 1735 conveyed to JOHN FAIRCHILD 300 a. on Wassamsaw Swamp, bounding SE on PETER PORCHER & the heirs of CAPT. CHARLES COLLETON; SW on CHARLES COLLETON & vacant land; NW on vacant land; NE on PETER PORCHER; & whereas by letters patent dated 4 Dec. 1735, signed by Lt. Gov. THOMAS BROUGHTON, JOHN FAIRCHILD was granted 415 a., bounding NW & SW on DANIEL DEAN, EDWARD KEATING, MR. FIDLER, & vacant land; S on CAPT. PORCHER; NE on ABRAHAM DUPONT; & whereas by letters patent dated 11 Dec. 1735, signed by Lt. Gov. THOMAS BROUGHTON, JOHN FAIRCHILD was granted 1000 a., bounding W on JAMES COACHMAN & JOHN OULDFIELD; N & E & S on ABRAHAM DUPONT & JOHN OULDFIELD; & whereas on 16 Apr. 1736, by letters patent signed by Lt. Gov. THOMAS BROUGHTON, JOHN NEUFVILLE, cooper, was granted 700 a., bounding S on THOMAS FAIRCHILD; all other sides on vacant land; & he, by L & R, 31 May & 1 June 1736, with ELIZABETH his wife, sold the 700 a. to JOHN FAIRCHILD; & whereas by letters patent signed by Lt. Gov. THOMAS BROUGHTON, dated (broken), JOHN FAIRCHILD was granted 449 a., bounding NE on JOHN BETTERSON; SE on ELIZABETH VERDITTY; SW on CAPT. PORCHER & vacant land; & whereas JOHN FAIRCHILD on 2 June 1736 gave bond to BENJAMIN GODIN in the penal sum of L 7000 SC money for payment of L 3500 on 2 Apr. 1737; now FAIRCHILD conveys the 5 tracts to GODIN to secure the payment. Witnesses: DAVID GODIN, JOHN HEWSON. Whereas on 5 June 1736

JOHN FAIRCHILD gave BENJAMIN GODIN another bond in the penal sum of Ł 46 for payment of Ł 23:5:6 on 2 Apr. 1737 he agrees that the above mortgaged property shall stand as of further security for the payment of this bond. Before BENJAMIN DELA CONSEILLERE. NATHANIEL JOHNSON, Register.

Book P, p. 353　　　　　THOMAS OWEN, planter, formerly of London, now
11 & 12 June 1736　　　of Granville Co., SC, to JOSEPH WRAGG & RICH-
L & R in Trust　　　　 ARD LAMBTON, merchants, of Charleston, as well
　　　　　　　　　　　　for the great love & affection he bears for
his brother, JEREMIAH OWEN, "oyleman," of London, & to NATHANIEL OWEN & FRANCES OWEN, son & daughter of JEREMIAH, as for conveying certain lands for certain purposes, & for Ł 5 paid by WRAGG & LAMBTON; THOMAS OWEN conveys to WRAGG & LAMBTON 820 a. in Granville Co. in trust for JEREMIAH OWEN during his natural life, then to his heirs or to NATHANIEL (?) & FRANCIS; which 820 a. was granted by letters patent dated 9 Apr. last past, signed by Lt. Gov. THOMAS BROUGHTON, to THOMAS OWEN; bounding E & S by JOSEPH WRAGG; N on JAMES ST. JOHN, ESQ.; W on vacant land. Witnesses: FRANCIS BAKER, JOHN HOUGHTON, THOMAS HEPWORTH. Before JAMES GREENE, J.P. NATHANIEL JOHNSON, Register.

Book P, p. 357　　　　　EDWARD (his mark) VANVELSIN, cordwainer, &
17 & 18 June 1736　　　CATHERINE his wife, of St. Philip's, Berkeley
L & R　　　　　　　　　Co., to GEORGE DICK, gentleman, of Winyaw,
　　　　　　　　　　　　Craven Co., for Ł 100 currency, 1000 a. in
Craven Co., bounding NW on Black River; SE on DANIEL & THOMAS LAROCHE; SW on ARTHUR FOSTER; NE on GEORGE DICK & DANIEL & THOMAS LAROCHE; which 1000 a. were granted (grant signed by Lt. Gov. THOMAS BROUGHTON) on 4 June 1735 to EDWARD VANVELSIN. Witnesses: JOHN BERRY, WILLIAM FLEMING. NATHANIEL JOHNSON, Register.

Book P, p. 360　　　　　THOMAS ELLERY, gentleman, & ANNE his wife, to
2 & 3 May 1736　　　　 THOMAS COOPER, merchant, & MARGARET MAGDELEN
L & R　　　　　　　　　his wife, all of Charleston, for Ł 100 SC mon-
　　　　　　　　　　　　ey, that piece of garden ground in Charleston
now occupied by THOMAS COOPER & his wife; bounding E 26 ft. on CAPT. WILLIAM WARDEN; W on THOMAS ELLERY; S 72 ft. on THOMAS COOPER; N on the Meeting Burial ground; the land being free from ANNE'S title of dower. Witnesses: ANN ROWE, PHILIP PRIOLEAU. Before HENRY GIBBES, J.P. NATHANIEL JOHNSON, Register.

Book P, p. 364　　　　　THOMAS BARSKERFIELD (BARSKERFELD), of St.
9 Aug. 1712　　　　　　Thomas Parish, Berkeley Co., to VINSON GUERIN,
Ren. of Dower &　　　　for Ł 212 SC money, 400 a. English measure, on
Deed of Sale　　　　　 N side NE branch of Wando River, granted BAR-
　　　　　　　　　　　　KERFIELD 1 June 1709 by Gov. NATHANIEL JOHNSON
& the Lords Proprs. NICHOLAS TROTT & HENRY NOBLE; bounding W on JOHN WESCOAT (formerly WILLIAM NORTH; E on MARY WARNOCK; S on a creek; N on JOHN ROOBERRY. SARAH (her mark) BARKERSFIELD, wife of THOMAS, renounces her title of dower. Witnesses: RICHARD CODNER, DANIEL JAUDON, LEWIS MOUZON, ROBERT CLYATT, JOHN BOWEN. Before MICHAEL DARBY, J.P. NATHANIEL JOHNSON, Register.

Book P, p. 368　　　　　VINCENT GUERIN, planter, & JUDITH his wife, of
19 Apr. 1734　　　　　 St. Thomas Parish, Berkeley Co., to STEPHEN
Release　　　　　　　　MILLER, merchant, of Charleston, for Ł 3000
　　　　　　　　　　　　currency, 400 a. in St. Thomas Parish on N
side NE branch of Wando River, bounding W on JOHN WESTCOAT; E on MARY WARNOCK; S on a creek; N on JOHN RUBERRY (ROOBERRY); which 400 a. was granted on 1 June 1709 by WILLIAM, Lord Craven, Palatine, & the Lords Proprs. to THOMAS BASKERFIELD; & by him sold, 9 Aug. 1712, to VINCENT GUERIN, who now sells it, free of JUDITH'S claim of dower. Witnesses: DANIEL JAUDON, MOSES MILLER, ABRAHAM MASON. Before MICHAEL DARBY, J.P. NATHANIEL JOHNSON, Register.

DEEDS BOOK "Q"
JUNE 1736 - MAR. 1737

Book Q, p. 1　　　　　　CRANSTON KARWON, planter, of St. Pauls Parish

4 June 1736　　　　　　　　　John's Island, Colleton Co., to THOMAS COOPER,
Release　　　　　　　　　　　merchant, & MARGARET MAGDALENE, his wife, of
　　　　　　　　　　　　　　　Charleston, for ₤ 1950 SC money, 325 a. on N
side A.B. Poolaw Creek, bounding E on CAPT. THOMAS FLEMING. Witnesses:
BENJAMIN D'HARRIETTE, JR., EDWARD BULLARD. Before HENRY GIBBES, J.P.
NATHANIEL JOHNSON, Register.

Book Q, p. 3　　　　　　　　ELIZABETH (her mark) FAIRCHILD, widow & execu-
15 June 1736　　　　　　　　tor of THOMAS FAIRCHILD, & WILLIAM FAIRCHILD,
Mortgage　　　　　　　　　　son & executor of will of THOMAS FAIRCHILD,
　　　　　　　　　　　　　　　dated 26 June 1733, to ELISHA PRIOLEAU, gentleman, all of Charleston: Whereas ELIZABETH FAIRCHILD & WILLIAM FAIRCHILD
in order to pay the debts of FAIRCHILD, SR., this date gave bond to PRIO-
LEAU in penal sum of ₤ 1920 SC money for payment of ₤ 960 & interest at
10% on 16 June 1737, now, to secure payment, they convey to PRIOLEAU lot
#191 in Charleston, fronting 90 ft. on Friend Street & running back 130
ft.; also all manner of household goods, etc., belonging the house &
houses wherein they now live, as beds, bedsteads, curtains, vallins, bolsters, pillows, pillow cases, sheets, blankets, rugs, quilts, tables,
table cloths, napkins, towels, chests, trunks, chest of drawers, looking
glasses, brass kettles & skillets, iron pots, pewter dishes, pewter
plates, all manner of silver plate as spoons, porringers, tankards & cups,
& all other utensils used in the house or any of the houses; also 2 Negro
women, & 1 Negro boy. Witnesses: ISRAEL DEVEAUX, JOHN CROFT. Before
HENRY GIBBES, J.P. NATHANIEL JOHNSON, Register.

Book Q, p. 7　　　　　　　　JOHN SKENE, ESQ., of Dorchester, Berkeley Co.,
17 May 1736　　　　　　　　 to RICHARD WRIGHT, ESQ., of Charleston, for
Mortgage　　　　　　　　　　₤ 311:18 currency, convey 3 Negro slaves, con-
　　　　　　　　　　　　　　　ditioned upon payment of above sum with interest on 10 July next. Witness: WILLIAM WALTER, ESQ. Before WILLIAM WAL-
LACE, J.P. NATHANIEL JOHNSON, Register.

Book Q, p. 8　　　　　　　　WILLIAM CARLILE, tanner, & ANN (her mark) his
25 Aug. 1697　　　　　　　　wife, daughter of JOSEPH PENDARVIS, all of
Release　　　　　　　　　　　Berkeley Co., to JONATHAN AMORY, merchant, of
　　　　　　　　　　　　　　　Charleston, for ₤ 7:10 sterling, lot #218 in
Charleston, bounding W on the little street that runs by MR. BOLTON'S
door; E on JONATHAN AMORY; S on GILES TITTMARSH (formerly JOSEPH PENDAR-
VIS); N on MR. IEBOTT. Whereas WILLIAM, Earl of Craven, Palatine, & the
Lords Proprs. by several grants signed by Landgrave THOMAS SMITH, dated
28 Mar. 1694, granted JOSEPH PENDARVIS 2 lots in Charleston, #217 & #218;
& whereas PENDARVIS by will dated 19 Nov. 1694 bequeathed to his 2 daughters MARY & ANN PENDARVIS the 2 lots to be equally divided between them;
& whereas GILES TITMARSH, shoemaker, & MARY his wife, daughter of JOSEPH
PENDARVIS, & WILLIAM CARLILE & ANN his wife, by deeds dated 27 July 1697
mutually agreed that TITMARSH & his wife should take the S lot #217 as
their part & CARLILE & his wife should take the N lot #218 as their part;
now CARLILE & his wife sell their lot to AMORY. Witnesses: CAPT. CHRIS-
TOPHER JARRARD, GYLES TYDMARSH, PRICILLAH (her mark) ROSE. NATHANIEL
JOHNSON, Register.

Book Q, p. 10　　　　　　　 SARAH RHETT, administratrix of will of person-
30 Mar. 1709　　　　　　　　al estate of JONATHAN AMORY, to THOMAS STUART,
Release　　　　　　　　　　　joiner, of Berkeley Co., for ₤ 30 SC money,
　　　　　　　　　　　　　　　lot #218 in Charleston containing 1/2 a. bounding S on GYLES TITMARSH; W on a street leading to MR. BURTELL'S house; N
on GEORGE BARNETT. Whereas JONATHAN AMORY owned several town lots in SC
& tenements upon them & several large tracts of land, some with houses &
tenements upon them, & by will dated 23 Nov. 1697 appointed his wife
MARTHA sole executrix & after her death his 2 sons THOMAS & ROBERT, &
authorized her to sell any part of his real estate; & whereas MARTHA died
shortly after JONATHAN & in a few days ROBERT, an infant son of JONATHAN
died, & THOMAS AMORY, son of JONATHAN, being in England, the administration of JONATHAN'S personal estate was granted to SARAH RHETT, executrix
of will of MARTHA AMORY, & afterwards curatrix of THOMAS AMORY only son &
heir & guardian of SARAH AMORY only living daughter of JONATHAN; & whereas SARAH RHETT convinced the General Assembly that in order to pay debts,
etc., the estate should be sold, otherwise the estate would run to decay
& become a great charge to hold till the heirs came of age & on 1 Mar.

1700 she was appointed administratrix with power to sell with the advice & consent of JOB HOWES & RALPH IZARD; now she sells lot #218 to STUART. Witnesses: ISAAC PORCHER, GEORGE BARNETT, THOMAS (his mark) ROE. NATHANIEL JOHNSON, Register.

Book Q, p. 15　　　　　　　JAMES HOPKINS, planter, to THOMAS BROWN, Indi-
10 & 11 Dec. 1735　　　　　an trader, both of Craven Co., for ₤ 100 cur-
L & R　　　　　　　　　　　rency, 300 a. in Craven Co., bounding NW & NE
　　　　　　　　　　　　　　on vacant land; SE on vacant land & THOMAS
BROWN; SW on Congaree River; which 300 a. were granted to HOPKINS by letters patent dated 4 Dec. 1735 & signed by Lt. Gov. THOMAS BROUGHTON. Witnesses: ALEXANDER KILPATRICK, THOMAS FLOOD. Before CHARLES RUSSELL, J.P. NATHANIEL JOHNSON, Register.

Book Q, p. 19　　　　　　　By virtue of a warrant dated 10 Aug. 1711 sign-
Warrant for Land　　　　　ed by Gov. ROBERT GIBBES, 200 a. in Colleton
　　　　　　　　　　　　　　Co. were laid out for BRYAN KELLY; to the W of
the freshes of Edisto River, within land, near the Round O Savannah; bounding all sides on vacant land. Plat certified 30 Aug. 1711 by THOMAS BROUGHTON, Sur. Gen. NATHANIEL JOHNSON, Register.

Book Q, p. 19　　　　　　　JAMES KELLY, planter, & JEAN his wife, to JOHN
21 May 1736　　　　　　　　OTTERSON, both of Colleton Co., for 5 shill-
L & R　　　　　　　　　　　ings, 200 a. in Colleton Co., bounding on va-
　　　　　　　　　　　　　　cant land. Witnesses: JAMES CRAIGIE, JOHN
LAVIS, SAMUEL RIGGS. NATHANIEL JOHNSON, Register.

Book Q, p. 22　　　　　　　WILLIAM MCGILLEVERY, gentleman, of Wadmalaw
22 June 1734　　　　　　　 Island, St. John's Parish, Colleton Co., to
Deed of Gift　　　　　　　 his loving wife ELIZABETH for love & affection,
　　　　　　　　　　　　　　100 a. purchased from JOHN FIDLING. Witnesses:
JOHN THOMAS, ROBERT SAMS. Before THOMAS DALE, J.P. NATHANIEL JOHNSON, Register.

Book Q, p. 23　　　　　　　WILLIAM MCGILLEVARY, gentleman, of Wadmalaw
22 June 1734　　　　　　　 Island, St. John's Parish, Colleton Co., to
Deed of Gift　　　　　　　 his daughter MARY MCGILLEVRAY, for love & af-
　　　　　　　　　　　　　　fection, 1 Negro man. Witnesses: JONATHAN
THOMAS, ROBERT SAMS. Before THOMAS DALE, J.P. NATHANIEL JOHNSON, Register.

Book Q, p. 24　　　　　　　WILLIAM MCGILLEVRAY, gentleman, of Wadmalaw
22 June 1734　　　　　　　 Island, St. John's Parish, Colleton Co., to
Deed of Gift　　　　　　　 his daughter ELIZABETH MCGILLEVRAY, for love &
　　　　　　　　　　　　　　affection, 1 Negro man. Witnesses: JONATHAN
THOMAS, ROBERT SAMS. Before THOMAS DALE, J.P. NATHANIEL JOHNSON, Register.

Book Q, p. 25　　　　　　　WILLIAM MCGILLEVRAY, gentleman, of Wadmalaw
22 June 1734　　　　　　　 Island, St. John's Parish, Colleton Co., to
Deed of Gift　　　　　　　 his son ROBERT, for love & affection, 1 Negro
　　　　　　　　　　　　　　man. Witnesses: JONATHAN THOMAS, ROBERT SAMS.
Before THOMAS DALE, J.P. NATHANIEL JOHNSON, Register.

Book Q, p. 25　　　　　　　WILLIAM MCGILLEVRAY, gentleman, of Wadmalaw
22 June 1734　　　　　　　 Island, St. John's Parish, Colleton Co., to
Deed of Gift　　　　　　　 his son ALEXANDER, for love & affection, 1 Ne-
　　　　　　　　　　　　　　gro man. Witnesses: JONATHAN THOMAS, ROBERT
SAMS. Before THOMAS DALE, J.P. NATHANIEL JOHNSON, Register.

Book Q, p. 26　　　　　　　WILLIAM MCGILLEVRAY, practitioner of physic,
21 Oct. 1734　　　　　　　 of Wadmalaw Island, St. John's Parish, Colle-
Bill of Sale in Trust　　 ton Co., to ROBERT SAMS, planter, of same
　　　　　　　　　　　　　　place, in trust for ELIZABETH, wife of WILLIAM
MCGILLEVRAY, 1 Negro man, 1 Negro woman, & her young child a girl about 7 months old. Witnesses: JOHN SAMS, PATRICK NORRIS. Before THOMAS DALE, J.P. NATHANIEL JOHNSON, Register.

Book Q, p. 27　　　　　　　ELISHA POINSETT (POINTSETT), mariner, formerly
19 & 20 Feb. 1734　　　　　of SC, now of Philadelphia, to WILLIAM CATTELL,

L & R by Mortgage   merchant, of Charleston, for L 90 American mon-
                              ey, according to Act of Parliament, all those
messuages or tenements & lots of ground in Charleston lately in possession of ELISHA PRIOLEAU, merchant, also all other messuages, lots, tenements & hereditaments of ELISHA POINTSETT in SC, as security on note,
bill or account taken in the name of JOHN COLCOCK for the use of WILLIAM
CATTELL from ELISHA POINTSETT, which sum & all other just debts are to be
paid CATTELL within 2 years. Witness: PETER BOYNTON, attorney for WIL-
LIAM CATTELL. On 17 July 1733, at Phildaelphia, PETER EVANS, ESQ., &
JOHN ROSS, gentleman, both of Philadelphia, appeared before THOMAS LAU-
RENCE, ESQ., mayor of Philadelphia & declared they witnessed POINSETT'S
signature to the above mortgage. RALPH ASSHETON, N.P. & Tabellion of
Pennsylvania certified their depositions. NATHANIEL JOHNSON, Register.
Mortgage declared satisfied 22 July 1736 by WILLIAM CATTELL, JR. Wit-
ness: JOHN PENNYMAN for NATHANIEL JOHNSON, Register.

Book Q, p. 30   JOSHUA SNOWDEN, & ELIZABETH SNOWDEN, of James
3 July 1736   Island, to NICHOLAS MATTHISON, blacksmith, of
Mortgage   Charleston, as security for payment of bond in
                              penal sum of L 300 SC conditioned for payment
of L 150 & interest to MATTHISON on 3 July 1737; 1 Negro woman. Witnesses: HENRY GIBBES, AARON BARTHOLOMEW TRUEHART. One gold ring delivered in
lieu of Negro woman. Before HENRY GIBBES, J.P. NATHANIEL JOHNSON, Register.

Book Q, p. 32   LAURENCE SANDERS, planter, of Colleton Co., to
30 June 1736   WILLIAM SLUDDER (SLUDDERS), LEWIS BYNON, &
Bill of Sale   JEREMIAH KNOTT, for L 60 currency, 80 a. in
                              Colleton Co., bounding on all sides on vacant
land commonly called Salt-Catchers Cowpen, which 80 a. formerly belonged
to WILSON SAUNDERS (SANDERS) & was granted, by letters patent dated 25
June 1736, signed by Lt. Gov. THOMAS BROUGHTON, to LAURENCE SANDERS. Witnesses: LUDWICK GRANT, DANIEL BUTLER, NICHOLAS HAYNES. Before DANIEL
GREENE, J.P. NATHANIEL JOHNSON, Register.

Book Q, p. 34   SAMUEL COMMANDER the younger, ELIZABETH COM-
1 & 2 June 1736   MANDER, ELISHA SCREVEN & JOHN COMMANDER, to
L & R   JOSIAH SMITH, for L 1540 currency for the use
                              of ABIGAIL, DOROTHY, FRANCES & RACHEL, daugh-
ters of SAMUEL COMMANDER the elder; 2 plantations, total 770 a., in St.
Thomas's Parish, Berkeley Co. Whereas Gov. ROBERT GIBBES & the Lords
Proprs. on 28 June 1711 granted SAMUEL COMMANDER the elder 270 a. in St.
Thomas Parish, Berkeley Co., on S side Simmons's Creek out of Cooper River, bounding E on ROBERT SWETMAN; S on RICHARD BERESFORD; W on SAMUEL
COMMANDER; & on same date granted him 500 a. in same section, bounding N
on Simmons's Creek; E on SAMUEL COMMANDER; S & W on RICHARD BERESFORD; &
whereas SAMUEL COMMANDER the elder, by will dated 17 Sept. 1733, ordered
the 2 tracts sold & the money divided equally amongst his 4 daughters; &
should any die before coming of age or before marriage that share to be
divided amongst the survivors; & appointed his wife ELIZABETH COMMANDER,
ELISHA SCREVEN, & his sons SAMUEL & JOHN COMMANDER his executors; now
they sell the 2 tracts to SMITH. Witnesses: JOSEPH COMMANDER, JOHN MC-
CANTS. Before JOHN WALLIS, J.P. NATHANIEL JOHNSON, Register.

Book Q, p. 40   FREDERICK GAILLARD, planter, to JOHN BARNETT,
8 July 1736   both of Craven Co., for L 280 currency, 500 a.
Mortgage   in Prince George Parish, granted him by WIL-
                              LIAM LEWIS, planter; bounding N on WILLIAM
LEWIS & NOAH SERRE; E on WILLIAM LEWIS & ELIAS HORRY; S on FREDERICK GAIL-
LARD; W on FREDERICK GAILLARD & NOAH SERRE; also an adjoining tract of
400 a. purchased by CAPT. BARTHOLOMEW GAILLARD; bounding S on RALPH IZARD,
ESQ.; W on ANDREW DE LAVILLETTE or RALPH IZARD; N on FREDERICK GAILLARD
(the 1st mentioned tract); E on ALCIMUS GAILLARD; total 900 a.; as secur-
ity on bond of even date in penal sum of L 560 SC money for payment of
L 280 with interest on 1 Jan. 1736. Witnesses: ELIZABETH GAILLARD, DAN-
IEL DUTARTRE, ANDREW REMBERT, JR. Before PETER ROBERT, J.P. NATHANIEL
JOHNSON, Register.

Book Q, p. 41   ROBERT WRIGHT, ESQ., of Colleton Co., to RICH-
16 & 17 June 1736   ARD LAMBTON, merchant, of Charleston, for

L & R   ℔ 200 SC money, 2000 a. in Granville Co.,
                                granted by letters patent dated 16 Apr. last,
signed by Lt. Gov. THOMAS BROUGHTON, to ROBERT WRIGHT, bounding E on
JAMES ST. JOHN & vacant land; S on MR. DU3ORDEAUX & vacant land; W & N on
vacant land. Witnesses: JOHN HUTCHINSON, WILLIAM WALTER. Before WILLIAM
WALLACE, J.P. NATHANIEL JOHNSON, Register.

Book Q, p. 45   ROBERT WRIGHT, ESQ., of Colleton Co., to THOM-
16 & 17 June 1736   AS OWEN, gentleman, of Granville Co., for
L & R   ℔ 180 SC money, 1800 a. in Granville Co.,
                                granted by letters patent, dated 9 Apr. last,
signed by Lt. Gov. THOMAS BROUGHTON, to ROBERT WRIGHT bounding N on JAMES
ST. JOHN; E on vacant land & the Hon. JOSEPH WRAGG, ESQ.; S & W on JOSEPH
WRAGG. Witnesses: JOHN HUTCHINSON, WILLIAM WALTER (WALTERS). Before
WILLIAM WALLACE, J.P. NATHANIEL JOHNSON, Register.

Book Q, p. 48   CHRISTOPHER SMITH, storekeeper, of Charleston,
26 & 27 May 1736   to THOMAS SACHEVERILL, planter, of Pon Pon,
L & R   Berkeley Co., for ℔ 475 currency, 2 tracts of
                                land; 1 of 85 a. in Colleton Co., bounding E
on MIDDLETON; S on TIMOTHY HENDRICKS; W on JAMES FELTON; N on CHRISTOPHER
SMITH; which land was granted to SMITH on 12 May 1735 by letters patent
signed by Lt. Gov. THOMAS BROUGHTON; the other tract being 1/3 the plan-
tation of 314 a. in St. Paul's Parish, Colleton Co., on E side S Colleton
River; bounding N on Old Taylor & vacant land; E on vacant land; S on
JAMES FOLKEN & vacant land; which third part was purchased 20 June 1729
by SMITH from JOHN ARNOLD, shopkeeper, of Charleston. Witnesses: SAMUEL
PRIOLEAU, THOMAS ELLERY. Before J. COLLETON, J.P. NATHANIEL JOHNSON,
Register.

Book Q, p. 54   JOB ROTHMAHLER, gentleman, of St. James Goose
6 & 7 June 1734   Creek, to DAVID CHRISTINAZ, carpenter, of
L & R   Charleston, for ℔ 450 currency, part of lot
                                #105 in Charleston, bounding N on part still
owned by ROTHMAHLER; S on WILLIAM LINTHWAITE & on ROTHMAHLER; E on JAMES
PAINE; W on 30 ft. on a street leading from White Point to the Quakers
Meeting. Witnesses: JOHN LAURENS, BENJAMIN ADDISON. Before ANTHONY
BONNEAU, J.P. NATHANIEL JOHNSON, Register.

Book Q, p. 58   JOB ROTHMAHLER, gentleman, of St. James Goose
7 June 1734   Creek, gives bond to DAVID CHRISTINAZ, carpen-
Bond of Performance   ter, of Charleston, in penal sum of ℔ 9000 cur-
                                rency, conditioned for the performance of
agreements in above L & R (p. 54) especially that ANN, wife of JOB ROTH-
MAHLER shall not claim title of dower. Witnesses: JOHN LAURENS, BENJAMIN
ADDISON. Before ANTHONY BONNEAU, J.P. NATHANIEL JOHNSON, Register.

Book Q, p. 59   DANIEL CARTWRIGHT, planter, to BENJAMIN WHIT-
19 & 20 July 1736   AKER, ESQ., as security on bond of even date
L & R by Mortgage   in penal sum of ℔ 109 sterling of Great Brit-
                                ain for payment of ℔ 54:1:9:½ with interest on
25 Mar. next; 74 a. in St. Philip's Parish, Berkeley Co., bounding E on
JOSEPH BLAKE, ESQ.; W on marsh of Ashley River; N on DANIEL CARTWRIGHT; S
on JOHN HAMMERTON, ESQ.; which land was devised to RICHARD CARTWRIGHT by
his father & by him conveyed to DANIEL CARTWRIGHT. Witnesses: THOMAS
BURRELL, WILLIAM FREEMAN. Before JAMES ST. JOHN, J.P. NATHANIEL JOHNSON,
Register. (See a subsequent mortgage page 299).

Book Q, p. 63   ELISHA POINTSETT, mariner, of Charleston, eld-
19 July 1736   est son & heir of JOEL POINTSETT, SR., vintner,
Deed of Sale   & SUSANNAH his (JOEL'S) wife, lately deceased,
                                formerly SUSANNAH VARIN, daughter of JAMES
VARIN, to the said JOEL POINTSETT, for ℔ 1300 SC money, all his interest
in the houses formerly occupied by ANNE LESADE & now owned by JOEL POIN-
SETT, & part of lot #27, on which the house stands on the back part of
the lot; fronting S 47 ft. on the neighborhood alley leading down to
ELLIOTTS wharf; E 88 ft. on FRANCIS PAGETT; W on ATKYNS; N on other part
same lot.   Whereas on 28 Dec. 1710 JOEL POINTSETT, weaver, of Berkeley
Co., & SUSANNAH his wife, sole daughter & heir of JAMES VARIN, "farm let"
to ELISHA PRIOLEAU, merchant, of Charleston, & SUSANNAH his wife, during

their lifetimes, that messuage or tenement then newly repaired & the new messuage or tenement erected on part of lot #27, both houses fronting N on Broad Street; also a tenement erected on the back part of the lot & fronting S on a neighborhood alley & occupied by ANNE LESADE, widow. Witnesses: WILLIAM WATSON, N. MAC HEYSON, PETER BENOIST, JOHN IOOR, THOMAS HEPWORTH. Before THOMAS DALE, J.P. NATHANIEL JOHNSON, Register.

Book Q, p. 65
19 July 1736
Deed of Sale

ELISHA POINTSETT, mariner, of Charleston, eldest son & heir of JOEL POINTSETT, SR., vintner, of Charleston, & SUSANNAH his wife, lately deceased, formerly SUSANNAH VARIN, daughter of JAMES VARIN, to ISAAC HOLMES, gentleman, of Charleston, for L 1000 SC money, the reversions & remainders & all the title of ELISHA POINTSETT in that messuage, part of a part of lot #27 now occupied by ISAAC HOLMES, fronting N 31 on Broad Street; bounding W 92 ft. on estate of CAPT. JOHN RAVEN; S on part same lot occupied by JOEL POINTSETT; E on part same lot in possession of SAMUEL FLEY, carpenter; which messuage is 1 of the messuages & part of lot #27 demised to ELISHA PRIOLEAU & SUSANNAH his wife. Witnesses: WILLIAM WATSON, N. MAC HEYSON, PETER BENOIST, JOHN IOOR, THOMAS HEPWORTH. Before THOMAS DALE, J.P. NATHANIEL JOHNSON, Register.

Book Q, p. 67
19 July 1736
Deed of Sale

ELISHA POINSETT (POINTSETT), mariner, of Charleston, eldest son & heir of JOEL POINTSETT, SR., vintner, & SUSANNAH his wife, lately deceased, formerly SUSANNAH VARIN, daughter of JAMES VARIN, to SAMUEL FLEY, carpenter, of Charleston, for L 700 SC money, his reversions & remainders out of that messuage or tenement, being part of lot #27, fronting N 25 on Broad Street; bounding W 92 ft. on part of same lot occupied by ISAAC HOLMES; S on MR. PAGETT; E on JOHN BRITON; which messuage is 1 of the messuages & part of lot #27 demised to ELISHA PRIOLEAU & SUSANNAH his wife, & now occupied by SAMUEL FLEY. Whereas on 28 Dec. 1710 JOEL POINTSETT, weaver, of Berkeley Co., & SUSANNAH, his wife, sole daughter & heiress of JAMES VARIN formerly of SC, demised to ELISHA PRIOLEAU, merchant, & SUSANNAH his wife, for their lifetimes that tenement then newly repaired & the new tenement standing on part of lot #27, both fronting N on Broad Street; also 1 other tenement on the back part of said lot & fronting S on a neighborhood alley & occupied by ANNE LESADE, widow; now ELISHA POINTSETT sells his title to the above houses to FLEY. Witnesses: WILLIAM WATSON, N. MAC HEYSON, PETER BENOIST, JOHN IOOR, THOMAS HEPWORTH. Before THOMAS DALE, J.P. NATHANIEL JOHNSON, Register.

Book Q, p. 69
28 & 29 July 1736
L & R

REBECCA FLAVELL, widow, to JOHN NEUFVILLE, cooper, both of Charleston, for L 2100 currency, the E part of lot #38 fronting 25 ft. on N side Broad Street; bounding E 72-1/2 ft. on Union Street; N on other part same lot in possession of JOHN NEUFVILLE; W on the part owned by REBECCA FLAVELL; & running out at the NW corner into a small nook or slip of land containing over & above the 25 ft. & 72-1/2 ft., 13-1/2 ft. from E to W & 4 ft. 4 in. from N to S. Witnesses: HENRY GIBBES, JOHN LAURENS. Before HENRY GIBBES, J.P. NATHANIEL JOHNSON, Register.

Book Q, p. 75
2 & 3 Aug. 1736
L & R

THOMAS FERGUSON, planter, & ANN his wife, of Craven Co., to WILLIAM WATSON, joiner, of Charleston, for L 700 currency, lot #249 in Charleston, bounding N on DR. CHARLES BURNHAM; S on PETER GIRRARD, merchant; E on lot #248; W on a little street that leadeth by the house of MR. JONES & MR. HILLS to the White Point. Witnesses: JOHN LEAY, MARY LEAY. Before HENRY GIBBES, J.P. NATHANIEL JOHNSON, Register.

Book Q, p. 79
7 June 1736
Bill of Sale & Mortgage

JAMES GORDON, ESQ., of Craven Co., to WILLIAM SWINTON, ESQ., as security on 2 bonds signed by SWINTON at GORDON'S request; that is, 1 bond dated 10 Jan. last to GEORGE MACKENZIE in penal sum of L 628:11:5 money of Great Britain for payment of L 314:5:8:1/2 on 10 Jan. next; also 1 dated 6 Apr. last to JOSEPH WRAGG & RICHARD LAMBTON in penal sum of L 748:3 Britain for payment of L 374:1:6 on 1 Jan. then next; conveys 26 Negro men; 6 Negro women; 4 Negro children; 150 head neat cattle with different ear marks but all branded 45; 6 horses; 4 mares. Witnesses:

HUGH SWINTON, ALEXANDER ROBERTSON. Before DANIEL LAROCHE. NATHANIEL JOHNSON, Register.

Book Q, p. 82　　　　　　　　JAMES GORDON, ESQ., to WILLIAM SWINTON, ESQ.,
7 & 8 June 1735　　　　　　both of Craven Co., as security on 2 bonds
L & R & Mortgage　　　　　signed by SWINTON at GORDON'S request; 1 to
　　　　　　　　　　　　　　　　　WILLIAM WATIES dated 6 Feb. 1735 in penal sum of ₤ 2128 currency for payment of ₤ 1064:16 on 20 Dec. 1737; 1 dated 7 Feb. 1735 to ALEXANDER NISBETT in penal sum of ₤ 1567 for payment of ₤ 783:18 on 31 Dec. 1738; several tracts of land; in Craven Co., 1 being 1050 a. bounding S on PETER SMITH; E on WILLIAM WHITESIDES; W & N on vacant land; NE on EDWARD BULLARD; which land was granted to JAMES GORDON; the other 2 tracts containing total of 650 a., bounding E on Peedee River, granted to WILLIAM KITCHEN & HUGH SWINTON & after several conveyances came to JAMES GORDON; also 300 a. granted to PETER BENOIST & conveyed by him to JAMES GORDON, bounding NW on Swinton's Creek; NE on Peedee River & Gordon's Thorofare; SW on Glen's Thorofare; SE on MAJOR GEORGE PAWLEY; also 200 a. granted to PETER BENOIST & conveyed by him to GORDON, bounding E on WILLIAM ALLSTON & PAWLEY'S Creek; N on WILLIAM SWINTON; SE on Waccamaw River; SW on Peedee River & Gordon's Thoroughfare. Witnesses: HUGH SWINTON, ALEXANDER ROBERTSON. Before DANIEL LAROCHE, J.P. NATHANIEL JOHNSON, Register.

Book Q, p. 87　　　　　　　　JOHN STUART, planter, of St. Helena Port Roy-
17 May 1736　　　　　　　　al Parish, Granville Co., to his friend & son-
Deed of Gift　　　　　　　　in-law JAMES MEGET, planter, of same Parish,
　　　　　　　　　　　　　　　　　for love & affection, 350 a. on St. Helena Island bounding NW & SW on RICHARD REYNOLDS; NE on MR. STUART; SE on marsh between said land & the hunting island. Witnesses: JOSEPH WRIGHT, JOHN FRIP, JAMES REYNOLDS (RUNNELLS). Before THOMAS WIGG, J.P. NATHANIEL JOHNSON, Register.

Book Q, p. 88　　　　　　　　THOMAS CORDES, gentleman, & CATHERINE his wife
2 & 3 Oct. 1733　　　　　　of Berkeley Co., to ISAAC CHARDON, merchant,
L & R　　　　　　　　　　　　for ₤ 100 SC money 650 a. in Colleton Co.,
　　　　　　　　　　　　　　　　　granted to THOMAS CORDES by letters patent dated 21 Apr. 1733 & signed by ROBERT JOHNSON, bounding N on ELIZABETH WOODWARD, SR.; S on JOHN GIBBES; W on said WOODWARD; E on vacant land. Witnesses: GABRIEL MARION, ANN SKINNER, DAVID DALBIAC. Before DANIEL GREENE, J.P. NATHANIEL JOHNSON, Register.

Book Q, p. 92　　　　　　　　DANIEL HUGER, ESQ. & ELIZABETH his wife, of
7 & 8 Oct. 1734　　　　　　Berkeley Co., to ISAAC CHARDON, merchant, of
L & R　　　　　　　　　　　　Charleston, for love & affection & ₤ 5 curren-
　　　　　　　　　　　　　　　　　cy, 2000 a. in Granville Co., bounding N on BENJAMIN SCHENCKINGH, ESQ.; E on WALTER EZARD, ESQ.; other sides on vacant land; which land was granted to HUGER by letters patent dated 17 May 1734, signed by Gov. ROBERT JOHNSON. Witnesses: THOMAS HENNING, EDWARD SIMPSON, JOHN STEVENSON. Before DANIEL GREENE, J.P. NATHANIEL JOHNSON, Register.

Book Q, p. 96　　　　　　　　JOHN ALLSTON, planter, of Berkeley Co., to
8 & 9 Jan. 1735　　　　　　ISAAC CHARDON, merchant, of Charleston, for
L & R　　　　　　　　　　　　₤ 1134 SC money, 643 a. in Berkeley Co., bound-
　　　　　　　　　　　　　　　　　ing NE on SAMUEL WIGFALL; E on JOHN HUGGINS; S on PETER COUILLANDEAU; W on ANTHONY BONNEAU; SW on LEWIS MOUSON; NW on JOHN ALLSTON. DEBORAH ALLSTON, wife of JOHN, to renounce her dower within 6 months. Whereas the Hon. JOHN; Earl of Bath, & the Lords Proprs. by letters patent dated 16 Aug. 1698 created JOHN BAYLEY, of Ballinaclough, Co. of Tipperary, Ireland, a Landgrave & Cassique, granting him 48,000 a.; & whereas JOHN BAYLY, son & heir, by deed poll dated 9 Nov. 1722 appointed ALEXANDER TRENCH, merchant of Charleston, his attorney with authority to set aside 8000 a. for JOHN BAYLY'S use & sell the rest; & whereas on 29 Nov. 1726 TRENCH, as attorney for BAYLY, sold JOHN ALLSTON, for ₤ 150 SC money, 643 a. in Berkeley Co.; now ALLSTON sells to CHARDON. Witnesses: JOSIAS GAR. DUPRE, SAMUEL DUPRE, JOHN ALLSTON, JR. Before THOMAS LAROCHE, J.P. NATHANIEL JOHNSON, Register.

Book Q, p. 102　　　　　　　JOHN HAMMERTON, ESQ., of St. Philip's Parish,
16 Sept. 1735　　　　　　　Charleston, to JAMES CROKATT, merchant, of

Mortgage   Charleston, for L 2000 SC money, 46 a. in St.
                            Philip's Parish, bounding E on JOSEPH BLAKE,
ESQ.; S on THOMAS GADSDEN, ESQ.; W & N on RICHARD CARTWRIGHT; conditioned
for payment of above sum to CROKATT with interest; i.e., L 1000 on 16
Sept. 1736; L 1000 on 16 Sept. 1737. Witnesses: ISAAC HOLMES, JOHN LLOYD,
CHARLES PINCKNEY. Before ROBERT WRIGHT, J.P. NATHANIEL JOHNSON, Regis-
ter.

In Bk. R page 276 CROKATT acknowledges mortgage satisfied by receiving
from HAMMERTON a bond of COL. WILLIAM WAITIE for L 1200 due 25 Mar. next
& an order on JAMES MICHIE for L 243; L 600 having been paid 7 Feb. last.
NATHANIEL JOHNSON, Register.

Book Q, p. 106   ALEXANDER VANDERDUSSEN, ESQ., of Berkeley Co.,
27 & 28 Jan. 1735   to ISAAC CHARDON, merchant, of Charleston, for
L & R   L 220 SC money, 2200 a. in Craven Co. on N
                            side Black River, bounding W N & S on vacant
land; E on MR. _____ which land was granted to VANDERDUSSEN by letters
patent dated 12 Dec. 1735 & signed by Lt. Gov. THOMAS BROUGHTON. Witnesses: GILES HOLLIDAY, PETER PRIOLEAU, JAMES CRADDOCK. Before DANIEL GREENE,
J.P. NATHANIEL JOHNSON, Register.

Book Q, p. 109   WILLIAM WEEKLEY, gentleman, eldest son & heir
27 Feb. 1735   of EDWARD WEEKLEY, eldest son & heir of EDWARD
Agreement   WEEKLEY, gentleman, of the 1st part; THOMAS
                            WEEKLEY, gentleman, 2nd son of EDWARD WEEKLEY,
of 2nd part; EDWARD WEEKLEY, gentleman, youngest son of EDWARD WEEKLEY,
of 3rd part. Whereas EDWARD WEEKLEY, the father, by will dated 3 Nov.
1731 willed that his 2000 a. at head of Sampit Creek, Winyaw, & his 500 a.
on N side of said creek be sold, as also his 500 a. on Santee River adjoining COL. THOMAS LYNCH of Canehoy be sold, & gave his son EDWARD WEEK-
LEY all his land at the Halfway House, or failing that (or value thereof ?) he gave him the land bought from JOHN CARMICHAEL in Charleston, or
either of them, the remainder to be sold, & the overplus to be divided
equally amoung his 3 sons; & appointed his sons WILLIAM & THOMAS his executors; & whereas the 500 a. on Santee was sold by EDWARD WEEKLEY the
father in his lifetime, & EDWARD the son, after his father's death, accepted the lands in Charleston purchased from JOHN CARMICAHEL instead of
the land at the Halfway House & has since sold the lands in Charleston
for his son's benefit; now, to avoid any & all disputes & controversies
touching the validity of said will of the father, & for L 50 currency
paid by WILLIAM, THOMAS & EDWARD, each to the other, they agree that the
tracts of 2000 a. at head of Sampit Creek & 500 a. on N side Sampit
Creek, & the lands near the Halfway House in Berkeley Co. on the Broad
Path about 10 miles from Charleston, whether the same be part of the Old
Halfway or the New Halfway House lands or adjoining thereto, & all the
houses & lands belonging to EDWARD WEEKLEY the father at the time of his
death (except the 500 a. sold to LYNCH & the lands in Charleston bought
from CARMICHAEL & sold by EDWARD WEEKLEY the son) shall be enjoyed by the
3 of them (WILLIAM, THOMAS & EDWARD) as tenants in common; but it is
agreed that WILLIAM & THOMAS, with EDWARD'S consent, to sell the land.
Further agreed that all money received from a sale of the lands be divided equally among the 3 of them. Should the father's personal estate fall
short of paying his debts, the balance due & all expenses to be borne by
the sons, share & share alike. Witnesses to WILLIAMS signature: RICHARD
ALLEIN, JOHN GREENE. Witnesses to THOMAS'S signature: JOS'A LOCKWOOD,
SARAH LOCKWOOD. Witnesses to EDWARD'S signature: JOS. LOCKWOOD, SARAH
LOCKWOOD, JOHN DURANT (DURAND). Before CHARLES RUSSELL, J.P. NATHANIEL
JOHNSON, Register. Probate on p. 139. JOHN GREENE testified before DAN-
IEL GREENE in regard to WILLIAM WEEKLEY'S signature.

Book Q, p. 112   WILLIAM WEEKLEY, planter, of Berkeley Co., eld-
7 & 8 Sept. 1736   est son & heir of EDWARD WEEKLEY; & MARTHA
L & R   (her mark) his wife, to WILLIAM ANDERSON, vint-
                            ner, of Craven Co., for L 927:10 currency,
600 a. on N side Sampit River, Winyaw, Craven Co., bounding E on the Rev.
MR. JOSIAH SMITH, clerk; W on WILLIAM WEEKLEY; N on vacant land; which
600 a. is part of 2000 a. granted 20 July 1718 by the Lords Proprs. to
Landgrave THOMAS SMITH & conveyed by him on 28 Aug. 1718 to EDWARD WEEK-
LEY, father of WILLIAM. Witnesses: CHARLES PINCKNEY, ROBERT BREWTON, JR.

Before THOMAS DALE, J.P. NATHANIEL JOHNSON, Register.

Book Q, p. 117 THOMAS GRAVES, planter, of Berkeley Co., to
12 Dec. 1727 MOSES GRAVES, planter, for ₤ 20 currency, 2
Deed of Sale lots, #43 & #58, in Dorchester, in a place designed for a place of trade, each containing 1/4 a., & sold by JOHN STEVENS to THOMAS GRAVES for ₤ 12; lot #43 bounding NE on AARON WAY; SE on the lot used by the ministry of the Congregational Church; SW by a street; NW on DAVID BATCHELOR; lot #58 bounding NE on BAFFORD (formerly PURCHAS SPRY); SE on a street; NW on the Hon. JAMES MOORE, ESQ.; SW on the designed market place. Witnesses: JOHN PALMER, JOSEPH PHIPPS. Before RICHARD WARING, J.P. NATHANIEL JOHNSON, Register.

Book Q, p. 119 ANTHONY POINTEVINT (POITEVINE), planter, &
19 Aug. 1736 MARY his wife, of Berkeley Co., to STEPHEN
Mortgage MILLER, merchant, of Charleston, for
₤ 347:16:8 SC money, 420 a. English measure, in St. Thomas Parish, Berkeley Co., bounding E on NICHOLAS MAYRANT & MR. BONNEAU; S on COL. THOMAS LYNCH; W on LEWIS DUTARQUE; S on JOHN FOGARTIE; conditioned for the payment of the above sum with interest on 19 Aug. 1738. Witnesses: FRANCIS DECHAMPS, ABRAHAM ROULAIN. Before MICHAEL DARBY, J.P. NATHANIEL JOHNSON, Register. Mortgage satisfied 11 Sept. 1741. Witness: ROBERT AUSTIN, Register.

Book Q, p. 122 ISAAC WAIGHT & DOROTHY (her mark) JONES, ex-
9 Sept. 1727 ecutors of will (17 Jan. 1726/7) of SAMUEL
L & R JONES, planter, of Berkeley Co., to JOHN RIVERS & WILLIAM WEBB, of Berkeley Co., for
₤ 1100 SC money, 200 a. within land, on W side Ashley River, bounding W & N on SHEM BUTLER; E on WILLIAM CLAY & vacant land; S on WILLIAM ELIOTT. Witnesses: SILAS WELLS, THOMAS STOCK. NATHANIEL JOHNSON, Register.

Book Q, p. 126 CHARLES WARHAM, joiner, of St. Philip's Parish,
7 Dec. 1734 to SOLOMON LEGARÉ, goldsmith, as security on
Mortgage bond dated 7 Dec. 1734 for ₤ 150 SC money & interest, delivered 1 Negro boy valued at
₤ 200. Date of redemption 6 Dec. 1735. Witnesses: JOSEPH MOODY, JAMES BALLANTINE. Before HENRY GIBBES, J.P. NATHANIEL JOHNSON, Register. Mortgage satisfied 14 July 1739. Witness: ROBERT AUSTIN, Register.

Book Q, p. 127 JOHN WATKINS (WATKINGS), planter, MARY (her
11 & 12 Sept. 1723 mark) his wife, of Berkeley Co., to JONATHAN
L & R COLLINGS, mariner, & SARAH, his wife, of Charleston, for ₤ 200 SC money, 143-1/2 a. in Berkeley Co., bounding W on the Broad Path; E on Ashley River; NW on ROBERT DANIELL; S on the Rat Trap belonging to CHARLES HART. Whereas JONATHAN & SARAH COLLINGS own 175 a. in Berkeley Co.; JOHN WATKINS owns 143-1/2 a. in Berkeley Co.; they agree to exchange their holdings; therefore, JONATHAN & SARAH COLLINGS convey to WATKINS 175 a. commonly called Hobcaw, Berkeley Co., bounding NW on WILLIAM WATSON; NE on CARTER COLLIS; other sides on marsh of Cooper River; & WATKINS conveys 143-1/2 a. to COLLINGS, as above. Witnesses: WILLIAM WATSON, RICHARD SPLATT, ROBERT HUME. Before JOSEPH WRAGG, J.P. NATHANIEL JOHNSON, Register.

Book Q, p. 133 JOHN LAURENS (LAURENCE) saddler, & ESTHER his
10 & 11 Sept. 1730 wife, to PETER PICOT (PICOT), shop keeper, all
L & R by Mortgage of Charleston, for ₤ 71:8:7 sterling of Great Britain, part of a town lot on which JOHN & ESTHER LAURENS live, near the market place in Charleston, fronting W 34 ft. on the great street running through the Market Place; bounding N 132 ft. on ANTHONY BONNEAU; E on JANE DUPUY & JAMES ROULIN; S on JAMES ROULIN, STEPHEN MILLER, JACOB BONNEAU & JOHN LAURENS; conditioned for the repayment of the above sum with interest on 11 Sept. 1734. Witnesses: WILLIAM LINTHWAITE, CHARLES PINCKNEY. Before THOMAS BARTON, J.P. NATHANIEL JOHNSON, Register. DANIEL BOURGET, administrator of PETER PICOT on 5 July 1742 declared mortgage satisfied. Witness: JAMES MICHIE, Dep. Reg.

Book Q, p. 138 ABRAHAM CROUCH, of St. James Santee, Craven
3 Sept. 1734 (?) Co., to JONATHAN DRAKE, of St. John's Parish,

Mortgage   Berkeley Co., as security on bond dated 18 Feb. 1734 in penal sum of L 625 conditioned for payment of L 312:10 currency, & interest on 18 Jan. next; 500 a. in St. James Santee, where CROUCH lives. JOHN COACHMAN, SARAH DANZEY, WILLIAM DRAKE.

Book Q, p. 139
21 June 1734
Bill of Sale

WILLIAM WALES, of St. James Santee, Craven Co., & DOROTHY his wife, to JONATHAN COLKINS, of Georgetown, Prince George Parish, for L 1000 SC money, 1150 a. on a neck between Little River & the sea, Prince George Parish; as sold by the Hon. THOMAS SMITH & MARY his wife to WILLIAM WATIES on 16 Sept. 1726; DOROTHY to renounce her dower when requested. SAMUEL MASTERS, WAITSTILL AVERY. Delivery witnessed by PETER LAW, WILLIAM (his mark) PRICE. NATHANIEL JOHNSON, Register.

Book Q, p. 141
13 Mar. 1734/5
Bill of Sale

WILLIAM (his mark) PRICE, planter, & ANN his wife, of Prince George Parish, Craven Co., to JONATHAN COLKINS, of Georgetown, resident at Little River, Prince George Parish, for L 300 SC money, 330 a. in Prince George Parish, bounding NE on WILLIAM WATIES; N & NW on vacant land; ANN to renounce her dower when requested. Witnesses: PETER LANE, PHILIP BAKER. NATHANIEL JOHNSON, Register.

Book Q, p. 142
24 & 25 Aug. 1736
L & R by Mortgage

JONATHAN COLKINS, planter, of Winyaw, to RICHARD HILL, merchant, of Charleston, as security on bond of even date in penal sum of L 471 SC money conditioned for payment of L 235:12 with interest on 1 Mar. next; lot #11 in Georgetown adjoining CAPT. OTHNIEL BEALE'S lot. Witnesses: BENJAMIN WHITAKER, WILLIAM FREEMAN. Before JAMES GREEME, J.P. NATHANIEL JOHNSON, Register.

Book Q, p. 146
22 & 23 Mar. 1735
L & R

RALPH IZARD, ESQ. of St. James Goose Creek & MAGDALAINE ELIZABETH his wife, 1 of the grand daughters & devisees of PETER BURTELL, merchant, of Charleston; NATHANIEL BROUGHTON, ESQ. of St. John's Parish, & CHARLOTTA HENRIETTA his wife, another granddaughter & devisee of PETER BURTELL; PAUL MAZYCK, ESQ. of St. James Goose Creek & CATHARINA his wife, great granddaughter of PETER BURTELL & only daughter & heir at law of ALEXANDER CHASTAIGNE, grandson of 1 of the devisees of PETER BURTELL; of the 1 part; & PAUL JENYS, ESQ. of Charleston, the other. IZARD, BROUGHTON, & MAZYCK & their respective wives, for L 1500 British money, sold to JENYS 1/2 of lot #28 & all of lot #29 in Charleston. Whereas the Lords Proprs. on 22 Mar. 1682 granted the Hon. Landgrave JOSEPH WEST lot #28 on N side Broad Street, bounding E on JOHN COTTINGHAM; W on New Church Street; S on Broad Street that runneth from Cooper River to the Market Place; N on lot #29; & whereas JOSEPH WEST by deed poll dated 6 July 1687 indorsed on back of said grant sold PETER BURTELL the W half of lot #28 on which a house was erected; & whereas the Lords Proprs. (date omitted) granted PETER BURTELL lot #29, bounding S on lot #28; E on HENRY SHERIFF; N on GABRIEL MANIGAULT; W on New Church Street; & whereas PETER BURTELL by will dated 29 Jan. 1762 bequeathed all his real & personal estate (after the death of his wife ELIZABETH) to be divided equally among his 3 grandchildren, ALEXANDER CHASTAIGNER (father of CATHARINE, wife of PAUL MAZYCK), MAGDALAIN ELIZABETH CHASTAIGNER (wife of RALPH IZARD), & CHARLOTTA HENRIETTA CHASTAIGNER (wife of NATHANIEL BROUGHTON); & whereas on the death of ALEXANDER CHASTAIGNER the third share descended to his only daughter CATHARINA; now the heirs sell to JENYS. Witnesses: (The Rev. Mr.) TIMOTHY MELLICHAMP, WILLIAM MIDDLETON, PETER MARION, ALEXANDER CRAMACHE. Before CHARLES PINCKNEY, J.P. NATHANIEL JOHNSON, Register.

Book Q, p. 153
29 & 30 Sept. 1736
L & R

JOHN BUCKLAND, surgeon, of Dorchester, Co. of DORSET, & SARAH his wife, 1 of the daughters of JOHN SHIPPEY, smith, of Port Royall, Granville Co., SC, & MARY SHIPPEY, spinster, of Parish of St. Mary Abchurch, London; to CHARLES PINCKNEY, ESQ., of Charleston, for L 100 SC currency, paid to JOHN SHEPPARD, merchant, of Charleston, their attorney specially appointed for the use of SARAH & MARY & 5 shillings for the use of JOHN BUCKLAND; an island of 82 a. on SW side Port Royall River bounding SE on the Sound; SW on Alatamaha River;

NW on marsh; which land was granted by the Lords Proprs. on 6 Mar. 1717 to JOHN SHIPPEY & at his death descended to SARAH BUCKLAND & MARY SHIPPEY, his only daughters & heirs at law. Witnesses: GEORGE HUNTER, JOHN TOMKINS, ROBERT BREWTON, JR. Before THOMAS DALE, J.P. NATHANIEL JOHNSON, Register.

Book Q, p. 158
15 Sept. 1735
Letter of Attorney

JOHN BUCKLAND, surgeon, of Dorchester, Co. of Dorset, & SARAH his wife, & MARY SHIPPEY, spinster, of the Parish of St. Mary Abchurch, London, appointed JOHN SHEPPARD, merchant, of Charleston, or in case of his death FRANCIS BAKER, mariner, of Charleston, their attorney. Whereas JOHN SHIPPEY, father of MARY & SARAH, died some years ago at Port Royall Island, SC, & at that time owned several parcels or grants of land in SC; viz. 300 a. at Winyaw; an island of 82 a. near Port Royall; a town lot at Port Royall; & other parcels; & whereas his widow, SARAH, is also dead, leaving only MARY & SARAH; & whereas they wish to dispose of the various tracts; now they appoint SHEPPARD their attorney, with authority to sell any or all of them. Witnesses to signatures of JOHN & SARAH: THOMAS MILLER, NICHOLAS COSSENS, WILLIAM (his mark) SMITH. Witnesses to MARY'S signature: WILLIAM (his mark) SMITH, ANN GEBSON; GEORGE SCHULTZ, N.P. SIR EDWARD BELLAMY, Knight Lord Mayor of London, certified that WILLIAM SMITH OF Hooke In Hampshire, a wagoner, appeared before him & testified to the truth of the affidavit annexed referring to signatures, etc. NATHANIEL JOHNSON, Register.

Book Q, p. 161
28 & 29 Sept. 1736
L & R by Mortgage

JOHN VAUGHAN, bricklayer, to GABRIEL MANIGAULT, merchant, both of Charleston, for L 836 currency, part of lot #121 in Charleston, fronting N 25 ft. on Broad Street; bounding E 104 ft. on RALPH RODOTA (RODDA); S on an alley; W on a street leading from the Broad Path by the Quakers Meeting House; also the brick messuage thereon; conditioned for the repayment of the above sum, with interest, on 1 Mar. next. Witnesses: THOMAS HEPWORTH, JOHN ROYER. Before JAMES ABERCROMBY, J.P. NATHANIEL JOHNSON, Register.

Book Q, p. 166
31 Dec. 1723
Release in Trust

PHILIP DAWES, ESQ., to JOHN HARLESTON, gentleman, & ROGER MOORE, gentleman, all of Berkeley Co., for 5 shillings & for the natural love & affection which PHILIP DAWES bears for his wife ANN, & to provide for her in case of his death; 102 a. English measure near Charleston, now occupied by ROBERT FLADGER; bounding E on ELIZABETH SCHENCKINGH, widow; W on PETER DE ST. JULIEN; S on WILLIAM SMITH, ESQ.; N on Cooper River; also the mansion house; in trust for the use of PHILIP & ANN DAWES. Witnesses: JOSEPH BARRY, NICHOLAS TROTT, PETER TAYLOR. Before CHARLES PINCKNEY, J.P. NATHANIEL JOHNSON, Register.

Book Q, p. 170
7 & 8 Apr. 1736
L & R by Mortgage

HALLAN (HALLANN) DELAMERE & ELIZABETH BAMFIELD, widow, to JOHN BRAND, gentleman, all of Charleston, as security on their bond of even date in penal sum of L 2000 SC money conditioned for payment of L 1000 on 8 Apr. 1739 with interest, all that lot bounding N 130 ft. on Queen Street, alias Dock Street; E 41 ft. on a street leading from Ashley River to the Broad Path; W on LYDIA WARE; S on JOHN BRAND. Witnesses: JAMES GRAEME, THOMAS BECKETT. NATHANIEL JOHNSON, Register. MARY EYCOTT (formerly MARY JOYES, widow & executrix of PETER JOYES; carpenter, of Charleston) & daughter of JOHN BRAND, declared mortgage satisfied 10 Oct. 1743. Witness: JAMES MICHIE, D.P.R.

Book Q, p. 175
3 & 4 May 1736
L & R by Mortgage

WILLIAM BRISBANE, surgeon, to JOHN BRAND, gentleman, both of Charleston, as security on bond of even date, in penal sum of L 2200 SC money for payment of L 1100 with interest on 4 May 1739; that lot in Charleston bounding E 43 ft. on the street leading from Ashley River into the Broad Path; N 130 ft. on HALLANN DELAMERE & ELIZABETH BAMPFIELD; S on JOHN BRAND; W on LYDIA WARE. Witnesses: JAMES GRAEME, THOMAS BECKITT. Agreed that 1 brick chimney standing on the S side & belonging to a house owned by BRAND shall remain to decay or be thrown by accident. Before JAMES GRAEME, J.P. NATHANIEL JOHNSON, Register. Mortgage satisfied 5 Oct. 1739. Before ROBERT AUSTIN, Register.

Book Q, p. 179   SHUBAEL TAYLOR, yeoman, of Yarmouth, Barstable
26 May 1735   Co., Massachusetts Bay, New England, appointed
Letter of Attorney   THOMAS WARING, gentleman, of Berkeley Co., SC,
                      his attorney, with authority to handle his
property in SC. Signed by SHUBAEL TAYLOR & MERCY TAYLOR, his wife. Witnesses: HEZEKIAH TAYLOR, PATIENCE CUMPPUS. Before PETER THATCHER, J.P. Registered in records of Public Notary for the port of Plymouth, New England, 27 May 1735 by JOHN WINSLOW, N.P. & Tabellion. NATHANIEL JOHNSON, Register.

Book Q, p. 180   FREDERICK GAILLARD, planter, of St. James San-
1 Apr. 1734   tee, Craven Co., to JONAH COLLINS, planter, of
Mortgage   same parish, for ₤ 110 currency, 1 Negro man &
                      1 Negro woman, as security on a bond of even
date. Witnesses: ROBERT JEFFREYS, JOHN HALE. NATHANIEL JOHNSON, Register.

Book Q, p. 181   BENJAMIN TURNER, blacksmith, of Berkeley Co.,
13 Oct. 1736   to WILLIAM HOLMAN, planter, of Colleton Co.,
Bill of Sale   for ₤ 270 currency; 270 a. in Colleton Co.,
                      bounding E on Chehaw River; W on SILAS WELLS;
N on SAMUEL STOCK; S on WILLIAM HARVEY. Witnesses: JACOB AXSON, JAMES FULTON. Before HENRY GIBBES, J.P. NATHANIEL JOHNSON, Register.

Book Q, p. 182   WILLIAM HOLMAN, planter, of St. Bartholomew's
20 Sept. 1736   Parish, Colleton Co., to his beloved wife RA-
Deed of Gift   CHEL HOLMAN, for love & affection & other con-
                      siderations, 1 Negro boy. Witnesses: SAMUEL
STOCK, ELIZABETH STOCK, HANNAH COLLINS. NATHANIEL JOHNSON, Register.

Book Q, p. 183   SOLOMON MIDDLETON, mariner, & ANNA his wife,
20 & 21 Oct. 1736   to NICHOLAS OXFORD, gentleman, all of Charles-
L & R by Mortgage   ton, for ₤ 700 SC money, part of lot #297,
                      fronting W 27 ft. on a street leading from the
Old Church Yard to the White Point; S 113-1/2 ft. on JOHN & JAMES BALLANTINE; E on JOHN VANDERHORST; N on EDMOND HOLLAND; conditioned for the repayment of said sum with interest on 21 Oct. 1737. Signed by SOLOMON MIDDLETON & ANNA MIDDLETON, his wife. Witnesses: CHARLES PINCKNEY, ROBERT BREWTON, JR. Before THOMAS DALE, J.P. NATHANIEL JOHNSON, Register. Mortgage satisfied 9 May 1737. Paid by JOHN ALLEN. Witness: JOHN PENNYMAN for NATHANIEL JOHNSON, Register.

Book Q, p. 188   ISAAC TREZVANT, planter, & SUSANNAH his wife,
22 July 1736   to DANIEL HUGER, planter, all of Berkeley Co.,
Mortgage   for ₤ 2022:6:4:1 SC money, 472 a. in Berkeley
                      Co., bounding SW on ISAAC GUERIN; NW on SOLO-
MON BREMAR; NE on ROBERT JOHNSON; SE on JOHN RUBERRY; as security on bond dated 9 July & a mortgage of Negroes of even date; conditioned for repayment of above sum on 1 Sept. next. Witnesses: ROBERT JOHNSON, ANTHONY POITVINT, MARIANE BOURDEAUX. Before PETER PAGETT, J.P. NATHANIEL JOHNSON, Register. DANIEL HUGER transferred mortgage to MARTHA HORRY & in case of death of DANIEL HORRY & ELIAS HORRY. Witness: RICHARD HARRISON.

Book Q, p. 192   Plat of 2 lots on Charles Town Green, #228 &
                      #198, equally divided into 4 half lots each
fronting 60' 6" on Tradd Street & 412 ft. deep. HENRY BEDON'S half lot, part of #228, bounding E on JAMES KERR (formerly ELIAS HANCOCK); S on Tradd Street; W on ISAAC HOLMES; N on CAPT. EDWARD CROFT. ISAAC HOLMES'S half lot, part of #228, bounding E on HENRY BEDON; W on CATHERINE SMITH; N on CAPT. EDWARD CROFT; S on Tradd Street. CATHERINE SMITH'S half lot, part of #198, bounding N on JOSEPH ELLIOTT & COL. SAMUEL PRIOLEAU; S on Tradd Street; E on ISAAC HOLMES; W on COL. PRIOLEAU'S half lot. COL. SAMUEL PRIOLEAU'S half lot, part of #198, bounding S on Tradd Street; W on Friend Street; N on another of COL. PRIOLEAU'S lots; E on CATHERINE SMITH. MRS. FAIRCHILD'S lot on opposite corner of Friend & Tradd Streets.

Book Q, p. 193   SAMUEL PRIOLEAU, ESQ., of 1st part; HENRY BE-
23 Mar. 1735   DON, carpenter, of 2nd part; ISAAC HOLMES,
Articles of Agreement butcher, of 3rd part; CATHERINE SMITH, spin-
                      ster, of 4th part; ELIZABETH FAIRCHILD, widow,

& WILLIAM FAIRCHILD, JR. of 5th part; RICHARD HILL, merchant, of 6th part, all of Charleston; MARY MACKEWN, widow, of Berkeley Co., of 7th part. Whereas SAMUEL PRIOLEAU owns lot #181 & half of lot #198 on Tradd Street, bounding S on Tradd Street; W on a little street called Friend Street laid out by mutual consent of all the above parties; N on lot #181; E on other half of #198 belonging CATHERINE SMITH; & whereas HENRY BEDON & ISAAC HOLMES own lot #228; & whereas CATHERINE SMITH is seized in fee of other half #198; & whereas ELIZABETH FAIRCHILD & WILLIAM FAIRCHILD in trust for some other person, & RICHARD HILL & MARY MACKEWN own #191 bounding S on Tradd & E on Friend Street, being part of #191; & whereas it has been agreed that for their mutual benefit & convenience Friend Street should be 20 ft. broad English measure, & remain a common streetway for his majesty's subjects & all manner of beasts, carriages, etc., from Tradd Street through lots 191, 198, 181 by a course NW $7°$ 30' to the Broad Street; & whereas various controversies have arisen concerning the boundaries of lands to which they are entitled; & whereas SAMUEL PRIOLEAU, CATHERINE SMITH, HENRY BEDON, & ISAAC HOLMES have agreed to make an equal division between them of lots #228 & 198 (each to have 60 ft. 6 in. on Tradd Street & an equal breadth & depth backwards; now to settle their differences & prevent law suits they agree; that Friend Street shall be a common street from Tradd to Broad through lots #191, 198, & 181; that it shall be 20 ft. wide, English measure; that its course shall be NW $7°$ 30 min.; that SAMUEL PRIOLEAU shall hold his share of lot #198 as follows; 60 ft. 6 in. in breadth, fronting S on Tradd; W on Friend; N on his part of lot #181; E on part #198 belonging CATHERINE SMITH; that CATHERINE SMITH shall hold her share lot #198 as follows: S 60 ft. 6 in. on Tradd; N on JOSEPH ELLIOTT & SAMUEL PRIOLEAU; E on part lot #228 belonging ISAAC HOLMES; W on part #198 belonging to PRIOLEAU; that ISAAC HOLMES shall hold his share of #228 as follows; S 60 ft. 6 in. on Tradd; E on part lot #228 belonging HENRY BEDON; W on part #198 belonging CATHERINE SMITH; N on EDWARD CROFT; that HENRY BEDON shall hold his part lot #228 as follows: S 60 ft. 6 in. on Tradd; E on JAMES KERR (formerly ELIAS HANCOCK); W on part lot #228 belonging ISAAC HOLMES; N on EDWARD CROFT. Witnesses: JOSHUA SANDERS, WILLIAM CROFT, THOMAS HOLLINS. Before HENRY GIBBES, J.P. NATHANIEL JOHNSON, Register.

Book Q, p. 197　　　　RICHARD FAIRCHILD, to MARY PARHAM, both of
1 Nov. 1715　　　　　Charleston, for Ł 10 SC money, 1/3 of a lot
Bill of Sale　　　　　#191 containing 1/2 a., English measure, granted by him to RICHARD FAIRCHILD on 19 Jan. 1709/10; bounding S on THOMAS FAIRCHILD (formerly RICHARD FAIRCHILD); N on MR. POSTELL; E on WILLIAM (?); W on THOMAS FAIRCHILD (formerly NOAH SERRE). Witnesses: RICHARD MASON, WILLIAM LOUGHTON. NATHANIEL JOHNSON, Register.

Book Q, p. 199　　　　THOMAS FAIRCHILD, to MARY PARHAM, both of
2 Nov. 1715　　　　　Charleston, for Ł 10 SC money, 1/3 of lot #190,
Bill of Sale　　　　　containing 1/2 a. English measure, conveyed by NOAH SERRE to THOMAS FAIRCHILD on 8 June 1714; bounding S on part belonging THOMAS FAIRCHILD; N on MR. POSTELL; W on GEORGE KEELING; E on part belonging to MARY PARHAM. Witnesses: JOHN BEE, RICHARD MASON, WILLIAM LOUGHTON. NATHANIEL JOHNSON, Register.

Book Q, p. 201　　　　WILLIAM GREENLAND & MARTHA his wife, of Berke-
6 Nov. 1736　　　　　ley Co., to GEORGE NEILSON, of Craven Co., for
Release　　　　　　Ł 70 SC money, 135 a. in Craven Co., on a branch of Black River, bounding NE & S on vacant land; which 135 a. was granted by Lord Carteret to WILLIAM GREENLAND. Witnesses: JOHN WILLIAMS, DAVID LAFORS, MARGARET (her mark) WINTER. Before THOMAS FERGUSON, J.P. NATHANIEL JOHNSON, Register.

Book Q, p. 204　　　　FREDERICK GAILLARD, planter, & ELIZABETH his
19 July 1736　　　　 wife, to ALCIMUS GAILLARD, planter, both of
L & R　　　　　　　Craven Co., for Ł 100 SC money, 2 plantations containing 600 a., in Craven Co., 300 a. being on N side Santee River, bounding SE on CAPT. BARTHOLOMEW GAILLARD; other sides on vacant land; the other 300 a. on S side Winyaw River's mouth; NE on Winyaw River; SE on MASKETA side; other sides on vacant land. Witnesses: JAMES BELIN, DANIEL HORRY, ALLARD BELIN. Before PETER ROBERT, J.P.

Book Q, p. 208 On 28 May 1736, at the request of BENJAMIN
Plat Certified SIMONS 125 a., part of 1000 a., in St. Thom-
as's Parish, Berkeley Co., was laid out by
ROBERT MORAN, Dep. Surv., for JACOB BONNEAU; bounding NW & NE on BENJAMIN
SIMONS; SW on CHRISTOPHER BEECHE; SE on JOHN ASHBY. NATHANIEL JOHNSON,
Register.

Book Q, p. 208 BENJAMIN SIMONS, planter, to JACOB BONNEAU,
8 & 9 June 1736 planter, both of Berkeley Co., for Ł 250 cur-
L & R rency, 125 a. in Berkeley Co., bounding NW &
NE on BENJAMIN SIMONS; SW on CHRISTOPHER BEE-
CHE; SE on JOHN ASHBY; being part of 1000 a. granted by the Lords Proprs.
to BENJAMIN SIMONS on 15 Dec. 1705 & bequeathed to his youngest son BEN-
JAMIN by will dated 17 June 1717. Witnesses: The Rev. MR. THOMAS HASELL,
rector of St. Thomas Parish JOSIAH DUPRE, ELIZABETH HASELL, ELIZABETH ASH-
BY. Before ANTHONY BONNEAU, J.P. NATHANIEL JOHNSON, Register.

Book Q, p. 211 ICHABOD FRY, planter, to CHARLES PERONNEAU &
24 & 25 Oct. 1736 Co., merchants, both of Colleton Co., for
L & R by Mortgage Ł 363:2:10 SC money, 300 a. in Colleton Co.,
on SW side of a large creek out of Edisto Riv-
er; bounding NW on WILLIAM BOWER; SW on WILLIAM BOWER & parsonage land;
SE on WILLIAM TILLY, SR. (formerly MR. TUCKER); conditioned for the re-
payment of the above sum with interest on 1 Mar. 1736. Witnesses: JOSEPH
GIBBONS, JEREMIAH CLARK. Before the Hon. ARTHUR MIDDLETON. NATHANIEL
JOHNSON, Register. Mortgage satisfied 23 Mar. 1738. Witness: ROBERT
AUSTIN, Register.

Book Q, p. 216 JOHN HAMMERTON, ESQ. of Charleston, to ALEXAN-
26 & 27 Nov. 1736 DER BENNET, ESQ., of London, Great Britain;
L & R by Mortgage for Ł 650 British money, 46 a. in St. Philip's
Parish, Charleston, Berkeley Co., bounding E
on JOSEPH BLAKE, ESQ.; S on THOMAS GADSDEN, ESQ.; W & N on RICHARD CART-
WRIGHT; also 1000 a. in Craven Co., bounding S on Peedee River; NW on MR.
LEJAU; other sides on vacant land; also 1000 a. on Peedee River in Craven
Co., bounding N on THOMAS CORDES; S on HENRY LEWIS; E on EDWARD WEEKLEY;
W on JAMES LESESNE; also 685 a. in Colleton Co., bounding NE on Pon Pon
River; SE on MR. CHAMPNEY & WILLIAM BROWN; S on MR. PARKER & JAMES FER-
GUSON; NW on WILLISON SANDERS; conditioned for the repayment of above
sum with interest on 27 Feb. next. Witnesses: MAURICE LEWIS, JOHN RAT-
TRAY. Before BENJAMIN WHITAKER, J.P. NATHANIEL JOHNSON, Register.

Book Q, p. 222 JOHN BRETON, merchant, of Charleston to his
1 Mar. 1735 daughter-in-law, MAGDALEN JUNE, widow, of
Deed of Sale Charleston, for great love & affection, & for
Ł 100 SC money, & other considerations, part
of lot #163 in Charleston, fronting S 48 ft. on Broad Street; bounding W
on JAMES GRAEME, ESQ. (formerly GIBBON & ALLEN); E on JOHN LEWIS; N on
SAMUEL SMITH, butcher (lot #170); also part of lot #11 fronting N 27 ft.
on Broad Street; running S 90 ft. deep; now occupied by SARAH & LUCY
WEAVER; also 2 Negro women, 2 Negro boys, & 1 Negro girl; JOHN BRETON to
hold them all during his natural life. Witnesses: CHARLES CRAVEN, SAMUEL
SMITH. Before DANIEL GREENE, J.P. NATHANIEL JOHNSON, Register.

Book Q, p. 224 BENJAMIN ROBERT, planter, & ABIGAIL (her mark)
9 & 10 May 1729 his wife, 1 of the daughters of JAMES HULBERT,
Deed of Sale planter; JOHN BRUNSON, planter, & ANN his wife,
another daughter of JAMES HULBERT; & WILLIAM
(his mark) ROW, cordwainer, & RACHEL (her mark) his wife, another daughter of JAMES HULBERT; of the 1 part; & NOAH SERRE, planter, of the other
part; all of Craven Co. Whereas JOHN, Lord Granville, Palatine, & the
Lords Proprs. by grant dated 15 Sept. 1705, signed by SIR NATHANIEL JOHN-
SON & others, gave PETER ROGER 300 a. English measure in Craven Co.,
bounding N on Ichaw Creek; W on ABRAHAM MICHAW; S on vacant land; E on
CHRISTOPHER MAY; & whereas PETER ROGER & ANN his wife on 7 Apr. 1718 sold
the 300 a. to CHARLES LAURENCE, cooper, of Charleston, & whereas CHARLES
LAWRENCE & MARY ANN his wife on 23 Nov. 1719 sold the land to JOHN BAR-
NET, SR., cordwainer, of Craven Co.; & whereas JOHN BARNET & HANNAH his
wife on 10 June 1720 sold to JAMES HULBERT; & on his death the 300 a. became the property of ABIGAIL, ANNE & RACHEL, as co-heirs & only surviving

children; now they & their respective husbands sell to NOAH SERRE, for
Ł 150 currency, the 300 a., bounding according to plat. Witnesses: WIL-
LIAM NEWMAN, JOHN (his mark) GODBOLD, JOHN GASQUE, JOSEPH HUGGINS, WIL-
LIAM SINGELTON (SHINGLETON). Before ELIAS HORRY, J.P., in St. James San-
tee, Craven Co.

Book Q, p. 231   THEODORE GAILLARD, planter, of Craven Co., to
4 Mar. 1735   NOAH SERRE for Ł 1800 & 10 slaves, all debts,
General Release   etc., against SERRE. Witnesses: ALEXANDER
                             CHOVIN, ISAAC CHOVIN, ESTER HEARD. Before
PETER ROBERTS, J.P. NATHANIEL JOHNSON, Register.

Book Q, p. 231   GEORGE CHICKEN, planter, & LYDIA his wife, to
21 & 22 May 1735   NOAH SERRE, ESQ., all of Craven Co., for
L & R   Ł 1400 SC money, 3 tracts of land in Craven
                             Co., 200 a. (all but 7 a. formerly sold to
ISAAC LEGRAND) bounding originally N on JOHN BOYD & PETER ROBERT; E on
NICHOLAS LETTUD (LENUD ?); W on MOSES CARION; formerly granted to PETER
COULIANDAU on 15 Sept. 1705; 200 a. on S side Santee River, bounding orig-
inally E on PAUL BRUFFEAU; S on vacant land; W on JAMES BOYD & vacant
land; granted 12 Mar. 1698/9 to HENRY AUGUSTUS CHASTAIGNER & ALEXANDER
THEREE CHASTAIGNER; 500 a. on N side Santee River, bounding originally W
on JOHN GAILLARD; E on PETER ROBERT; NW on vacant land; granted to PETER
ROBERTS 9 June 1714. Witnesses: PETER GUERRY, ROBERT CLEMMONS, JEAN MC-
CLELAN. Before ELIAS HORRY, J.P. NATHANIEL JOHNSON, Register.

Book Q, p. 235   JOHN DUTARQUE, of St. Thomas Parish, for 5
5 May 1736   shillings, releases NOAH SERRE, of St. James
General Release   Santee, all debts, etc., against SERRE. Wit-
                             nesses: ROBERT JOHNSTON, SAMUEL WELLS, JOHN
FITCH. Before PETER ROBERTS, J.P. NATHANIEL JOHNSON, Register.

Book Q, p. 236   JOHN VAUGHAN, bricklayer, to MILES BREWTON,
6 & 7 Dec. 1736   gentleman, both of Charleston, for Ł 400 SC
L & R   money, 75 a. on Wando Neck, Christ Church Par-
                             ish, Berkeley Co., bounding SW & NW on WILLIAM
VISSER; E & NE on MAJOR ROBERR BREWTON; S on MAURICE HARVEY; N on JOHN
HALES. Witnesses: JOEL POINTSETT, ROBERT BREWTON, JR. Before THOMAS
DALE, J.P. NATHANIEL JOHNSON, Register.

Book Q, p. 241   STEPHEN MILLER, merchant, of Charleston, to
20 Jan. 1730   his brother MOSES MILLER of Berkeley Co., &
Deed of Gift   his children, for natural affection & brother-
                             ly love, & other considerations, a Negro man
about 18 years old; in trust until his nephew MOSES MILLER, son of brother MOSES, shall be married or reach 21 years of age; in case of default
then to brother MOSES in trust for his daughter MAGDALENE MILLER until
she marries or comes of age; in case of default, then to brother MOSES.
Witnesses: FRANCIS DECHAMPS, ANTHONY POINTVINT. NATHANIEL JOHNSON, Register.

Book Q, p. 242   THOMAS SULLIVANT (SILLAVANT, SULLAVANT), plant-
13 & 14 Aug. 1736   er, & MARTHA his wife, to DUNKEN. MCQUEEN,
L & R   Indian trader, both of Colleton Co., for
                             Ł 2500 currency, 437 a. in Colleton Co., bound-
ing N on THOMAS JONES; E on vacant land; S on PIKE'S land; W on THOMAS
DRAYTON. Witnesses: SARAH SINGELLTON, JOHN (his mark) REED. Before HEN-
RY GIBBES, J.P. NATHANIEL JOHNSON, Register.

Book Q, p. 245   WILLIAM (his mark) JOY, SR., house carpenter,
11 Aug. 1736   of Christ Church Parish, for divers considera-
Deed of Gift   tions, to WILLIAM JOY, JR., cordwainer, half
                             an a., English measure, at head of Mackey's
Creek, Charleston, formerly belonging to NATHANIEL PULMAN; bounding W on
JOSEPH NEVES; NE on JEFFRY FLOWERS. Witnesses: WILLIAM EHNDRICK, RICHARD
FOWLER, STEPHEN HARTLEY. Before ANDREW RUTLEDGE, J.P. NATHANIEL JOHN-
SON, Register.

Book Q, p. 246   ROBERT FLADGER, planter, to COL. THOMAS LYNCH,
19 June 1735   both of Berkeley Co., as security on bond of

Mortgage   even date in penal sum of ⌊ 2000 SC money for
                                        payment of ⌊ 1000 with interest to LYNCH at
his house on Wando Neck, Christ Church Parish, on 1 Mar. 1740; 300 a. in
Berkeley Co., bounding S on DAVID BATCHLER; W on JOHN BERESFORD; N on
COL. THOMAS LYNCH; E on RICHARD CAPERS & E branch Wando River. Witnesses:
GEORGE OLIVER, JOHN BARTON, ARCHIBALD GILCHRIST. Before GEORGE LOGAN.
NATHANIEL JOHNSON, Register.

Book Q, p. 249   JAMES & MARY STEWART, of St. John's Parish,
21 June 1736   Berkeley Co., to their friend ABRAHAM SANDERS,
Deed of Gift   yeoman, of same Parish, for respect & affec-
                                        tion, 150 a. commonly called Wampee; recorded
in Auditor's Office 23 May 1733 & in Secretary's Office in Book N folio
89, 4 Dec. 1719. Witnesses: SAMUEL EDGAR, WILLIAM (his mark) HART. Before PETER DE ST. JULIEN. NATHANIEL JOHNSON, Register.

Book Q, p. 250   THOMAS HENNING, merchant, & ANNE his wife, of
21 & 22 Oct. 1736   Charleston, to JOHN BLYDESTEYN, merchant, of
L & R   London, Great Britain, for (a blank sum), 1
                                        full half part (the whole divided into 2 equal
parts) of 3 tracts of land in Craven Co.. Whereas by letters patent dated
9 Mar. 1733, signed by Gov. ROBERT JOHNSON, EDWARD SIMPSON was granted
500 a. in Craven Co., on S side Black River, bounding S on BURTONHEAD
BOUTWELL; E on vacant land; NW & NE on DANIEL JORDAN, JR.; which he sold
on 12 Mar. 1733 to THOMAS HENNING, gentleman; & whereas by letters patent
dated 13 May 1735, signed by Lt. Gov. THOMAS BROUGHTON, JOHN SUMMERS was
granted 800 a. in Craven Co., bounding on JOHN BONNELL; S on EDWARD HO-
WARD; E on Black River; N on WILLIAM BOCKINGTON; which he sold on 22 Nov.
1735 to THOMAS HENNING, merchant, of Charleston; & whereas by letters
patent, dated 14 Feb. last, THOMAS HENNING was granted 281 a. in Craven
Co., bounding S & W on THOMAS HENNING; NE on Black River; SE on _____;
now HENNING sells BLYDESTEYN 1/2 the 3 several tracts. Witnesses: THOMAS
WAY, THOMAS HEPWORTH. Before THOMAS DALE, J.P. NATHANIEL JOHNSON, Register.

Book Q, p. 259   WILLIAM DRY, ESQ., of Berkeley Co., to ROBERT
4 & 5 Oct. 1736   HUME, ESQ., of Charleston; for ⌊ 170 SC money,
L & R   1700 a. in Craven Co., on NE side Black River;
                                        bounding NW on ROBERT HUME & MR. SIMONS; other
sides on vacant land; granted by letters patent, dated 30 Sept. & signed
by Lt. Gov. THOMAS BROUGHTON to WILLIAM DRY. Witnesses: ROBERT WRIGHT,
THOMAS HEPWORTH. Before BENJAMIN WHITAKER, J.P. NATHANIEL JOHNSON, Register.

Book Q, p. 263   ROBERT HUME, ESQ., & SOPHIA his wife, of
22 & 23 Nov. 1736   Charleston, to WALTER IZARD, ESQ., of Berkeley
L & R   Co., for ⌊ 1200 SC money, 746 a. in Granville
                                        Co., bounding NW on CHARLES BARKER; NE on Com-
bee River; S on JOHN PARKER; which 746 a. was granted to DR. THOMAS COOP-
ER by letters patent dated 9 Feb. 1733. Witnesses: JAMES KILLPATRICK,
THOMAS HEPWORTH. Before JOHN CLELAND, J.P. NATHANIEL JOHNSON, Register.

Book Q, p. 268   JAMES ROBERTS, planter, & SARA his wife, of
3 & 4 Jan. 1736   Craven Co., to JOHN WHITE, planter, of Berke-
L & R   ley Co., for ⌊ 550 SC money, 400 a., part of
                                        1050 a. in Craven Co., bounding SE on JAMES
ROBERT (formerly RALPH IZARD); NE on WILLIAM BOHANON; N on JOHN DUBOSE; S
on Wadbucan Creek; all other sides on JOHN DUBOSE. Witnesses: DAVID BAL-
DY, ALCIMUS GAILLARD, WILLIAM WHITE. Before ANDREW RUTLEDGE, J.P. NA-
THANIEL JOHNSON, Register.

Book Q, p. 272   ANNE DAWES, widow of PHILIP DAWES, ESQ., of
15 & 16 Nov. 1736   Berkeley Co., to JOHN VICARIDGE, ESQ. & ELIZA-
L & R   BETH his wife, sister of ANNE DAWES, & ANNE
                                        VICARIDGE, daughter of JOHN & ELIZABETH; for
natural love & affection for her brother-in-law, sister, & niece, & for
5 shillings, & other considerations, 8 a. on W side High Road, St.
Philip's Parish, leading into Charleston; bounding S on WILLIAM ELLIOTT;
W on WILLIAM SMITH; N on DANIEL GIBSON, surgeon. Witnesses: ELIAS BALL,
JOHN COMING BALL. NATHANIEL JOHNSON, Register.

Book Q, p. 277   SYLVANUS (his mark) RICH, planter, of Colleton
___ Feb. 1734/5   Co., to RUTH WETHERSPOON (WITHERSPOON), for
Mortgage   ₤ 1176, 225 a. in Colleton Co., bounding SW on
                        MR. MIDDLETON'S land called Jupiters; N on
RICHARD GODFREY; NE on MR. SPRY; conditioned for the payment by RICH to
RUTH WITHERSPOON, of ₤ 588 currency on 1 Feb. 1737/8. Witnesses: JOHN
BEE, JR., JOHN TIREER. NATHANIEL JOHNSON, Register. Mortgage satisfied
30 Mar. 1739. Witness: CAPT. JOHN BEE. ROBERT AUSTIN, Register.

Book Q, p. 278   SARAH BARKSDALE to ALEXANDER NISBETT, merchant,
21 May 1736   for ₤ 500 currency, 600 a. in Craven Co.,
Release   bounding N & E on SAMUEL BULLOCK; other sides
                        on vacant land; which land was granted SARAH
BARKSDALE by Lt. Gov. THOMAS BROUGHTON on 9 Apr. 1736. Witnesses: JAMES
MCCLELLAN, ARCHIBALD MCGILLIVRAY. Before JOHN CLELAND, J.P. NATHANIEL
JOHNSON, Register.

Book Q, p. 281   Received 18 Feb. 1728/9 of JOHN & THOMAS RIV-
Receipt   ERS, executors of MILES RIVERS'S estate, in
                        full of all debts, (signed) JOHN WILLIAMS.
Witnesses: EDMUND BELLINGER, JAMES WALFORD. Before WILLIAM CATTELL. NA-
THANIEL JOHNSON, Register.

Book Q, p. 282   JOHN SNOW, planter, & SUSANNA, his wife, to
14 Sept. 1736   ALEXANDER NISBETT, all of Berkeley Co., for
Release   ₤ 500 currency, 500 a. in Craven Co., bounding
                        SW on the Rivers; SE on JOHN COIT; NW on HUGH
SWINTON; NE on vacant land; which land was granted to JOHN SNOW by Lt.
Gov. THOMAS BROUGHTON 26 June 1736. Witnesses: CATHERINE RUSS, HEZEKIAH
RUSS. Before JAMES WEDDERBURN, J.P. NATHANIEL JOHNSON, Register.

Book Q, p. 285   FREDERICK GAILLARD, planter, to THEODORE
26 & 27 Feb. 1734   GAILLARD, planter, both of Craven Co., for
L & R   ₤ 100 currency, 5 tracts of land in Craven Co.,
                        & 3 a. in Berkeley Co., total 1403 a.; 3 a.
bounding Charleston Plot on 1 side, the Broad Path on the other; 500 a.
on Wambaw Sawmp bounding on all sides on vacant land; 500 a. bounding SE
& E on PHILIP GENDRON; N on vacant land; W & S on BARTH GAILLARD; 250 a.,
part of Gaillard"s Island; 150 a. on N side of N branch of Santee River
bounding on Menion Creek known as Indian Land. Witnesses: GEORGE CHICKEN,
JOHN DELIESSELINNE, ISAAC LEGRAND. Before PETER ROBERT, J.P. NATHANIEL
JOHNSON, Register.

Book Q, p. 289   ARCHYBALD HAMILTON, attorney-at-law, & MAGDA-
31 Jan. & 1 Feb. 1736/7 LEN his wife, to ABRAHAM MICHAW, planter, all
L & R   of Craven Co., for ₤ 3000 SC money, 4 tracts
                        of land, in Craven Co., on N side Santee Riv-
er total 2150 a.; 500 a. bounding W on ARCHIBALD HAMILTON; SE on JAMES
ROBERT; N on vacant land; 300 a. bounding E on the above 500 a.; S on the
above tract & on vacant land; other sides on ARCHIBALD HAMILTON; 200 a.
bounding W on NICHOLAS LENUD; SE on above 300 a.; other sides on ARCHI-
BALD HAMILTON; 1150 a. bounding S & SW on last 2 tracts; NE on vacant
land. Witnesses: DAVID BALDY, JOHN CARION. Before NOAH SERRE, J.P.
NATHANIEL JOHNSON, Register.

Book Q, p. 293   JAMES ROBERT, planter, to ABRAHAM MICHAW, both
7 Feb. 1736   of Craven Co., for ₤ 3220 SC money, 25 slaves,
Mortgage   all his cattle, horses, sheep, household goods,
                        & plantation tools. Whereas JAMES ROBERT &
ARCHIBALD HAMILTON on 2 Sept. 1735 gave bond dated 2 Sept. to MAGDALEN
LENUD, widow & administratrix of NICHOLAS LENUD, planter, in penal sum of
₤ 11,200 SC money for payment of ₤ 5600 on 1 Sept. 1745; & whereas ABRA-
HAM MICHAW, assignee of MAGDALEN LENUD has been paid 1/2 the sum & interest, if, therefore, JAMES ROBERT shall pay MICHAW ₤ 830 on 1 Mar. 1737
with ₤ 2 & the sume of ₤ 1270 on 1 Mar. 1739 & ₤ 1458 in 1745, with interest, the mortgage to be void. Witnesses: JOHN DELAVELLETTE, JOHN CAR-
ION. Before BENJAMIN WHITAKER, J.P. NATHANIEL JOHNSON, Register.

Book Q, p. 295   JAMES ROBERT, planter, to ABRAHAM MICHAU,
7 Feb. 1736   planter, both of Craven Co., for ₤ 5000 SC

Mortgage NW on ABRAHAM MICH	money, 900 a. bounding S & W on JAMES KINLOCK; NW on ABRAHAM MICHAU; N on vacant land; E on

DAVID BALDY. Whereas JAMES ROBERT & ARCHIBALD HAMILTON on 2 Sept. 1735 gave bond to MAGDALEN LENUD, widow & administratrix of NICHOLAS LENUD, planter, in penal sum of ⅊ 11,200 SC money, for payment of ⅊ 5600, & interest on 1 Sept.; therefore, if JAMES ROBERTS pay ABRAHAM MICHAU, assignee of MAGDALEN LENUD, ⅊ 2800 (his part of the money) with interest on 1 Mar. 1745 this mortgage to be void. Witnesses: JOHN DELAVILLETTE, JOHN CARION. Before BENJAMIN WHITAKER, J.P. NATHANIEL JOHNSON, Register.

Book Q, p. 297 12 Feb. 1736 Memo of Mortgage	CHARLES CODNER, planter, of Berkeley Co., to THOMAS BOLTON, shopkeeper, of Charleston, for ⅊ 2158 SC money, obliges himself to execute a sufficient mortgage of his house & land now

occupied by JAMES WITHERS, bricklayer, in Charleston, on the Bay, & the low water land fronting the same, bounding E on the Bay; W on Union Street; with a proviso annexed that if CODNER pay BOLTON ⅊ 2158 with interest within 1 year from date the mortgage to be void. Signed: CHARLES CODNER, ANN CODNER. Witnesses: GEORGE DENNISTON, WILLIAM SMITH. Before HENRY GIBBES, J.P. NATHANIEL JOHNSON, Register.

Book Q, p. 297 12 Feb. 1736/7 (?) Bill of Sale	CHARLES RUSSELL, planter, of Berkeley Co., to ELIZABETH LLOYD, for 5 shillings, 300 a. in Granville Co., on N side Coosa River, commonly called Abonages, bounding W on MEREDITH HUGHES;

other sides on vacant land; plat certified & returned 9 July 1717. Witnesses: THOMAS LLOYD, CHARLES SMITH. Before ANDREW RUTLEDGE, J.P. NATHANIEL JOHNSON, Register.

Book Q, p. 299 14 Feb. 1736/7 Obligation	DANIEL CARTWRIGHT promises to pay BENJAMIN WHITAKER, ESQ., or order, ⅊ 35:15 British money, with interest on demand, & as security gives certain land (see p. 60). NATHANIEL

JOHNSON, Register.

Book Q, p. 299 15 July 1736 Deed of Gift	JOHN SUMNER, of Colleton Co., to his brother DANIEL SUMNER, for love & good will, 100 a. in Colleton Co., part of 400 a. on which his father, JOSEPH SUMNER, lived; to be measured as

follows: bounding E on THOMAS SUMNER (part of the 400 a.); S on MOSES GRAVES; W on aforesaid tract; N on SAMUEL SUMNER'S land now in possession of MOSES GRAVES. ELIZABETH, wife of JOHN SUMNER, renounces her dower. Witnesses: SAMUEL STILES, WILLIAM BURNLEY, JR. NATHANIEL JOHNSON, Register.

Book Q, p. 300 15 July 1736 Deed of Gift	JOHN SUMNER, of Colleton Co., to his brother THOMAS SUMNER, for love & good will, 100 a. in Colleton Co., part of 400 a. on which his father, JOSEPH SUMNER, lived; to be measured

from the E line of the 400 a. tract & bounding E on JOSEPH SMITH; S on THOMAS OSGOOD; W on aforesaid tract; N on SAMUEL STILES. ELIZABETH, wife of JOHN SUMNER, renounces her dower. Witnesses: SAMUEL STILES, WILLIAM BURNLEY, JR. NATHANIEL JOHNSON, Register.

Book Q, p. 301 7 & 8 July 1736 L & R	HUGH BRYAN, planter, of St. Helena, Granville Co., & CATHERINE his wife, to JONATHAN BRYAN, planter, of same place, for ⅊ 1400 currency, 700 a. in Granville Co., part of 3140 a. grant-

ed to JOSEPH BRYAN & HUGH BRYAN in jointenancy (but HUGH survived JOSEPH); bounding N on Stono Creek out of Pocotaligo River & on CAPT. EDMUND BELLINGER'S Barony; SE on other part of said 3140 a. now belonging to HUGH BRYAN; W on Pocotaligo River. Whereas by grant dated 24 Nov. 1732, JOSEPH BRIAN & HUGH BRIAN were given 3140 a. on E side of Pocotaligo River, bounding N on CAPT. EDMUND BELLINGER, E on Hoospa Creek; S on HILL CROFT & MR. PAWLEY; & whereas on 9 Feb. 1735 JOSEPH died intestate & HUGH inherited the whole; now HUGH & his wife CATHERINE sell to JONATHAN. Witnesses: JOHN BARNWELL, ROBERT PAULLING. Before THOMAS WIGG, J.P. NATHANIEL JOHNSON, Register.

Book Q, p. 306	JAMES ROBERT, planter, to ABRAHAM MICHAU,

18 Feb. 1736　　　　　　　　　planter, both of Craven Co. Whereas JAMES ROB-
L & R by Mortgage　　　　　　 ERT & ARCHIBALD HAMILTON, planters of Craven
　　　　　　　　　　　　　　　 Co., gave bond dated 2 Sept. 1735 to MAGDALEN
LENUD, widow & administratrix of NICHOLAS LENUD, planter, in penal sum of
Ł 11,200 SC money, for payment of Ł 5600 & interest; & whereas MAGDALEN
LENUD assigned the obligation to ABRAHAM MICHAU; now JAMES ROBERT gives
MICHAU, as security on the debt, 900 a., bounding S & W on JAMES KINLOCK;
NW on ABRAHAM MICHAU; N on vacant land; E on DAVID BALDY. Should ROBERT
pay his share, Ł 2800, with interest, on 1 Mar. 1745, bond to be void.
Witnesses: ANTHONY ATKINSON, JOHN ALRAN, FRANCIS (his mark) PERIET. Be-
fore NOAH SERRE, Register. NATHANIEL JOHNSON, Register.

Book Q, p. 310　　　　　　　　 HANNAH (her mark) LAURENS, widow, of Charles-
25 & 26 Feb. 1736　　　　　　　ton, to ANTHONY ATKINSON, ESQ., of Winyaw,
L & R　　　　　　　　　　　　　Craven Co., for Ł 50 SC money, 500 a. in Cra-
　　　　　　　　　　　　　　　 ven Co., on S side Black River, bounding E on
ANTHONY ATKINSON; N & W on Bohicket Creek; S on vacant land; plat dated
17 Feb. 1736/7. Witnesses: JOHN LAURENS, JOHN RATTRAY. Before THOMAS
LAMBOLL, J.P. NATHANIEL JOHNSON, Register.

Book Q, p. 315　　　　　　　　 Before the Hon. ROBERT WRIGHT, C.J., SARAH,
24 Jan. 1736　　　　　　　　　 wife of THOMAS DISTON, of Berkeley Co., ap-
Renunciation of Dower　　　　 peared & freely & voluntarily renounced her
　　　　　　　　　　　　　　　 title of dower in 1000 a. on E side Edisto River, sold by her husband to GEORGE SOMMERS. NATHANIEL JOHNSON, Register.

Book Q, p. 316　　　　　　　　 THOMAS DISTON, of Berkeley Co., to GEORGE
11 Nov. 1736　　　　　　　　　 SOMMERS, for Ł 1800 currency, 1000 a. on E
Release　　　　　　　　　　　　side Edisto River, Berkeley Co., part of a
　　　　　　　　　　　　　　　 tract surveyed for THOMAS DISTON, SR., father
of above THOMAS; plat dated 4 Nov. 1736. Witnesses: JOHN DORSEY, JAMES
DALTON. Before THOMAS DALE, J.P. NATHANIEL JOHNSON, Register.

Book Q, p. 319　　　　　　　　 DAVID CHRISTINAZ, carpenter, & FRANCOISE his
28 & 29 July 1736　　　　　　　wife, to REBECCA FLAVELL, widow, all of
L & R　　　　　　　　　　　　　Charleston, for Ł 1400 currency, part of lot
　　　　　　　　　　　　　　　 #105 fronting W 16-1/2 ft. on the E side of a
street leading from the Broad Path to Charleston by the Quaker Meeting
House; bounding N 100 ft. on the part belonging to DAVID CHRISTINAZ; E on
JOHN LEAY, joiner; S on WILLIAM LINTHWAITE & JOB ROTHMAHLER. Witnesses:
HENRY GIBBES, JOHN LAURENS, JOHN NEUFVILLE. Before HENRY GIBBES, J.P.
NATHANIEL JOHNSON, Register.

Book Q, p. 324　　　　　　　　 DAVID CHRISTINAZ, carpenter; JOHN LAURENS, sad-
29 July 1736　　　　　　　　　 dler; & JOHN NEUFVILLE, cooper; to REBECCA FLA-
Bond　　　　　　　　　　　　　 VEL, widow, all of Charleston; in penal sum of
　　　　　　　　　　　　　　　 Ł 3000 currency for keeping the agreements in
the release of even date (p. 319) made between DAVID CHRISTINAZ & FRAN-
COISE his wife of 1 part & REBECCA FLAVEL of the other. Witnesses: HENRY
GIBBES, ROBERT BREWTON, JR. Before HENRY GIBBES, J.P. NATHANIEL JOHNSON,
Register.

Book Q, p. 325　　　　　　　　 JAMES MAXWELL, planter of Berkeley Co., to
23 & 24 Feb. 1736　　　　　　　ROBERT HUME, ESQ., of Charleston, for Ł 100 SC
L & R　　　　　　　　　　　　　money, 1050 a. in Craven Co., granted to JAMES
　　　　　　　　　　　　　　　 MAXWELL by letters patent, dated 9 Feb. last &
signed by Lt. Gov. THOMAS BROUGHTON; bounding W on Peedee River; S on WAL-
TER IZARD, ESQ.; other sides on vacant land. Witnesses: CHARLES SHEP-
HEARD, THOMAS HEPWORTH. Before BENJAMIN WHITAKER, J.P. NATHANIEL JOHN-
SON, Register.

Book Q, p. 329　　　　　　　　 WALTER IZARD, ESQ., of Berkeley Co., to ROBERT
1 & 2 Mar. 1736　　　　　　　　HUME, ESQ., of Charleston, for Ł 400 SC money,
L & R　　　　　　　　　　　　　4000 a. in Craven Co., granted to WALTER IZARD
　　　　　　　　　　　　　　　 by letters patent dated 9 Feb. last & signed
by Lt. Gov. THOMAS BROUGHTON; bounding W on Peedee River; S on MR. CHICK-
EN; other sides on vacant land. Witnesses: ROBERT AUSTIN, THOMAS HEP-
WORTH. Before BENJAMIN WHITAKER, J.P. NATHANIEL JOHNSON, Register.

Book Q, p. 332　　　　　　　　 BRIAN (his mark) RAILEY, planter, of Colleton

12 & 13 Mar. 1735   Co., to MICHAEL JEANS, glazier, of Charleston,
L & R   for £ 212:10 currency, half of 2 lots, #281 &
                     282, in Charleston, fronting N 60 ft. on an
alley in which JEANES lives; S 60 ft. on CHILDERMAS CROFT; E on MICHAEL
JEANES; W on BRIAN BAILEY & CHILDERMAS CROFT; the 2 lots being the E part
of land purchased by BAILEY from the executors of JOHN CARMICHAEL pursuant to CARMICHAEL'S will & free from MARTHA RAILEY'S (wife of BRIAN)
title of dower. Witnesses: FLEET STANBROUGH, JONAH STANBROUGH, CHILDER-
MAS CROFT. Before HENRY GIBBES, J.P. NATHANIEL JOHNSON, Register.

Book Q, p. 335   STEPHEN PROCTOR, merchant, of Charleston &
12 & 13 Apr. 1733   HANNAH his wife, to HUGH SWINTON, surgeon, of
L & R   St. John's Parish, Berkeley Co., for £ 500 SC
                     money, 700 a. English measure, in Craven Co.,
bounding SE on Peedee River; N on WILLIAM WATIES; S on WILLIAM SWINTON.
Witnesses: WILLIAM SWINTON, ALEXANDER STEWART. Before JAMES WRIGHT, J.P.
NATHANIEL JOHNSON, Register.

Book Q, p. 340   JOHN SUMNER of Colleton Co., to his brother
15 July 1736   DAVID SUMNER, for love & good will, 100 a. in
Deed of Gift   Colleton Co., part of 400 a. on which his fa-
                     ther JOSEPH SUMNER lived; bounding E on DANIEL
SUMNER; S on MOSES GRAVES & the ministry land; W on JOHN SUMNER; N on
BENJAMIN SUMNER (formerly SAMUEL SUMNER). ELIZABETH SUMNER, wife of JOHN
renounces her title of dower. Witnesses: SAMUEL STILES, WILLIAM BURNLEY,
JR. NATHANIEL JOHNSON, Register.

Book Q, p. 341   WILLIAM SWINTON, ESQ., to JAMES GORDON, ESQ.
9 Jan. 1736   Whereas WILLIAM SWINTON & JAMES GORDON on 6
Cancellation of L & R   Dec. 1735 gave bond to WILLIAM WATIES in penal
                         sum of £ 2128 for payment of £ 1054:16 SC mon-
ey on 20 Dec. 1737; & on 7 Feb. 1735 they gave bond to ALEXANDER NESBITT
in penal sum of £ 1567 for payment of £ 783:18 SC money on 1 Dec. 1738; &
on 10 Jan. 1735 they gave bond to GEORGE MACKENZIE in penal sum of
£ 628:11:5 British money for payment of £ 314:5:8:1/2 like money on 10
Jan. last; & on 6 Apr. 1736 they gave bond to JOSEPH WRAGG, ESQ. in penal
sum of £ 748:3 for payment of £ 374:1:6 on 1 Jan. last; & whereas the
bonds were given for the debts of JAMES GORDON only; & whereas JAMES GOR-
DON to counter-secure SWINTON against the obligations of WATIES & NISBETT
on 7 & 8 June 1736 conveyed to SWINTON 150 a. in Craven Co., bounding S
on PETER SMITH; E on WILLIAM WHITESIDE; W & N on vacant land; NE on ED-
WARD BULLARD; also 2 tracts, total 650 a. in Craven Co., bounding E on
Peedee River, granted to WILLIAM KITCHEN & HUGH SWINTON & by sundry mesne
conveyances came to JAMES GORDON; also 300 a. in Craven Co. granted to
PETER BENOIST & conveyed to JAMES GORDON, bounding NW on Swinton's Creek;
NE on Peedee River & Gordon's Thoroughfare; W on Glen's Thoroughfare; SE
on MAJOR GEORGE PAWLEY; also 100 a., part of 200 a., in Craven Co., granted to PETER BENOIST & conveyed to GORDON, bounding E on WILLIAM ALSTON &
Pawley's Creek; N on WILLIAM SWINTON; SE on WILLIAM POOLE; SW on Peedee
River & Gordon's Thoroughfare; & whereas JAMES GORDON, to further counter-
secure SWINTON against the above obligations to MACKENZIE & WRAGG by deed
poll dated 7 June 1736 conveyed to SWINTON 26 Negro men slaves, 6 Negro
women, 4 Negro children, 150 head neat cattle branded 45, 6 horses, & 4
mares; whereas SWINTON & GORDON have agreed to cancel the several deeds &
deed poll in consideration of GORDON'S entering into satisfactory securities for paying the various obligations; now SWINTON agrees to such can-
cellations & releases GORDON from the bonds & renounces all title to the
slaves, cattle, etc. Witnesses: WILLIAM GEORGE FREEMAN, BENJAMIN WHIT-
AKER. Before THOMAS LAMBOLL, J.P. NATHANIEL JOHNSON, Register.

Book Q, p. 344   JAMES GORDON, ESQ., to WILLIAM SWINTON, ESQ.
10 & 11 Jan. 1736   Whereas GORDON this date gave SWINTON a bond
L & R by Mortgage   in penal sum of £ 628:11:5 British money on
                        this condition: SWINTON (for GORDON'S debt)
gave bond with GORDON to GEORGE MACKENZIE, merchant, of City of Bristol,
in penal sum of £ 628:11:5 sterling of Great Britain for payment of
£ 314:5:8:1/2 like money on 1 Jan. 1739; also for payment of interest at
10%; partial payments to be made on certain dates; now GORDON, as security, conveys to SWINTON, 1050 a. in Craven Co., bounding S on PETER SMITH;
E on WILLIAM WHITESIDE; W & N on vacant land; NE on EDWARD BULLARD; also

2 tracts, total 650 a. in Craven Co., bounding E on Peedee River, granted to HUGH KITCHEN & WILLIAM SWINTON & by several conveyances came to GORDON; also 300 a. in Craven Co., granted to PETER BENOIST who conveyed it to GORDON, bounding NW on Swinton's Creek; NE on Peedee River & Gordon's Thoroughfare; SW on Glen's Thoroughfare; SE on MAJOR GEORGE PAWLEY; also 100 a., part of 200 a., in Craven Co., granted to PETER BENOIST & conveyed to GORDON, bounding E on WILLIAM ALLSTON & Pawley's Creek; N on WILLIAM SWINTON; SE on WILLIAM POOLE; SW on Peedee River & Gordon's Thoroughfare; also 1550 a. on Sampit Creek, Winyaw, granted to PETER SMITH & bounding N on the above 1050 a. granted to GORDON. Witnesses: WILLIAM GEORGE FREEMAN, BENJAMIN WHITAKER. Before THOMAS LAMBOLL, J.P. NATHANIEL JOHNSON, Register.

Book Q, p. 351
12 & 13 Jan. 1736
L & R Tripartite

WILLIAM SWINTON, ESQ., of Craven Co. of 1st part; JAMES GORDON, ESQ., of Craven Co. of 2nd part; GEORGE MACKENZIE, merchant, formerly of Bristol, Great Britain, now residing in SC, of 3rd part. Whereas by L & R, 10 & 11 this Jan. JAMES GORDON conveyed to WILLIAM SWINTON, as security on a bond of this date in penal sum of ₤ 628:11:5 with the condition that whereas SWINTON (for GORDON'S debt) on this date joined GORDON in a bond to MACKENZIE in penal sum of ₤ 628:11:5 British money (see p. 344), etc., etc., now to secure payment of the ₤ 314:5:8-1/2 & interest to MACKENZIE, SWINTON & GORDON convey to MACKENZIE 1050 a., 650 a., 300 a., 100 a., & 1550 a. Witnesses: WILLIAM GEORGE FREEMAN, BENJAMIN WHITAKER. Before THOMAS LAMBOLL, J.P. NATHANIEL JOHNSON, Register.

Book Q, p. 361
20 & 21 Apr. 1736
L & R by Mortgage

ROBERT WRIGHT, JR., of Berkeley Co., to JAMES CROKATT, merchant, of Charleston, as security of bond dated 23 Mar. 1735 in penal sum of ₤ 1540 currency for payment of ₤ 770 currency or ratifying 1 order drawn by WRIGHT payable to THOMAS CLIFFORD, ESQ., for same sum with interest; & another bond dated 20 Apr. 1736 for payment of ₤ 187:6 on 1 Oct. next; 1200 a., in Granville Co., bounding W on JERMYN WRIGHT; NE on JAMES GRAEME, ESQ.; E on Day's Creek; S on a large marsh. Witnesses: BENJAMIN SMITH, JOHN LLOYD. Before HENRY GIBBES, J.P. NATHANIEL JOHNSON, Register.

DEEDS BOOK "R"
APRIL 1737 - DECEMBER 1737

Book R, p. 1
1 & 2 Nov. 1736
L & R

THOMAS ELLERY, gentleman, & ANNE his wife, to RICHARD BRICKLES, house carpenter, & SARAH his wife, all of Charleston, for ₤ 900 SC money, part of 3 lots, #188, 189, & 79, in Charleston, bounding E 30 ft. on the garden fence of THOMAS COOPER; W 50 ft. on the great street leading from Ashley River by the Market Place & Presbyterian Meeting House; S 130 ft. 9 in. on THOMAS ELLERY; N on DAVID MONFIN; free of ANNE'S claim of dower. Witnesses: J. COLLETON, N. MATTHEYSON. NATHANIEL JOHNSON, Register.

Book R, p. 2
30 Sept., & 1 Oct. 1736
L & R by Mortgage

JONATHAN COLKINS of Georgetown, Prince George ? Parish, to JOSEPH WRAGG & RICHARD LAMBTON, merchants, of Charleston, for ₤ 1000 SC money, 1150 a. in Prince George Parish, on a neck between Little River & the sea, sold to COLKINS on 21 June 1734 by WILLIAM WAITIES, & DOROTHY his wife, of St. James Santee, Craven Co., conditioned for the repayment of the ₤ 1000 currency on 30 Mar. 1738. SARAH to renounce her dower when requested. Witnesses: HENRY WILLIAMS, C. SACKVILLE. Before ROBERT AUSTIN, J.P. NATHANIEL JOHNSON, Register. RICHARD LAMBTON, surviving partner of WRAGG & LAMBTON declared mortgage satisfied 27 Apr. 1754. Witness: WILLIAM HOPTON.

Book R, p. 10
25 & 26 Feb. 1736
L & R by Mortgage

EDWARD BULLARD, merchant, & ELIZABETH his wife, to JOHN CROKAT, merchant, all of Charleston, as security on bond of even date in penal sum of ₤ 302 British money for payment of ₤ 151 British & interest on 28 Dec. next; 1700 a. in Craven Co., on Black River,

bounding NW on RICHARD WALKER, & WILLIAM BROCKINGTON; SE on ARTHUR FOR-
STER. Witnesses: ALEXANDER ROBERTSON, JOHN RATTRAY. Agreed that term of
payment shall not be 28 Feb. 1737 & that interest shall not commence until 28 Feb. 1737. Before MAURICE LEWIS, J.P. NATHANIEL JOHNSON, Register.

Book R, p. 14 JOHN RIDLEY, ship carpenter, & UNITY his wife,
23 & 24 Mar. 1736 of Charleston, to JOHN ASKINS, house carpenter,
L & R of Craven Co., for L 200 currency, 350 a. in
Craven Co., free from UNITY'S claim of dower,
bounding NE on PETER TAMPLET, other sides on vacant land; which 350 a.
was granted 9 Apr. 1736 by Lt. Gov. THOMAS BROUGHTON to RIDLEY. Witnesses: HENRY PERONNEAU, JR., ALEXANDER PERONNEAU. Before HENRY GIBBES, J.P.
NATHANIEL JOHNSON, Register.

Book R, p. 19 FREDERIC GAILLARD, planter, & ELIZABETH his
5 & 6 Aug. 1736 wife, to TACITUS GAILLARD, all of Craven Co.,
L & R for L 600 SC money, 3 tracts; 1100 a., in Cra-
ven Co., bounding E on PHILIP GENDRON; N on
BARTHOLOMEW GAILLARD; W & S on vacant land; 300 a., bounding SE on BAR-
THOLOMEW GAILLARD; other sides on vacant land; 300 a., bounding S on San-
tee River; NW on BARTHOLOMEW GAILLARD; NE on vacant land; E on JOHN BOLL.
Witnesses: PAUL BRUNEAU, ALEXANDER CHOVIN, JOHN WOOD. Before PETER ROB-
ERT, J.P. NATHANIEL JOHNSON, Register.

Book R, p. 23 JAMES ROBERT, gentleman, to DANIEL JAUDON, SR.,
1 & 6 Aug. 1734 gentleman, both of Craven Co., for L 500 SC
L & R money, 500 a. in Craven Co.; granted by Lords
Proprs. & Gov. ROBERT JOHNSON on 10 Dec. 1717
to RALPH IZARD, ESQ. & bounding SW on Wadbaccan Creek, on N branch of San-
tee River; SE on ANDREW DE LETTERS (granted RALPH IZARD); NW on JAMES ROB-
ERT; other sides on vacant lands. RALPH IZARD & ELIZABETH his wife, for
L 300 SC money, sold the land to JAMES ROBERT; on 17 Jan. 1732. Witness-
es: HENRY DURANT, JOSEPH MITCHELL, JASPER (his mark) DUBOIS. Before NOAH
SERRE, J.P. NATHANIEL JOHNSON, Register.

Book R, p. 29 GEORGE COLLETON, planter, to JAMES LE BAS,
25 Mar. 1737 ESQ., both of St. Johns, Berkeley Co., in pen-
Bond al sum of L 920 currency, for payment of
L 460:12:6 & interest on 25 Mar. 1738. Wit-
nesses: EDWARD CARPETNER, GEORGE MOORS. Before HENRY GIBBES, J.P. NA-
THANIEL JOHNSON, Register.

Book R, p. 29 GEORGE COLLETON, planter, of St. Johns, Berke-
25 Mar. 1737 ley Co., authorizes THOMAS ELLERY, MAURICE
Letter of Attorney LEWIS, & CHARLES PINCKNEY, attorneys, to appear for him at the suit of JAMES LEBAS, ESQ.
& give bond in penal sum of L 920 conditioned for payment of L 460:12:6
with interest on 25 Mar. 1738. Witnesses: EDWARD CARPENTER, GEORGE MOORS.
Before HENRY GIBBES, J.P. NATHANIEL JOHNSON, Register.

Book R, p. 30 GEORGE COLLETON, planter, of St. Johns, Berke-
25 Mar. 1737 ley Co., to JAMES LEBAS, ESQ., as security for
Mortgage payment of L 460:13:6 & interest on 25 Mar.
1738; 445 a. in Berkeley Co., commonly called
Charlesville, bounding N on vacant land; W on HENRY SIMMONS; S on Watoo
Barony; E on a swamp; & delivers to LEBAS all his stock of cattle, horses,
hogs, sheep, household, goods & every other thing belonging to him. Possession given by delivery of a mare. Witnesses: EDWARD CARPENTER, GEORGE
MOORS. Before HENRY GIBBES, J.P. NATHANIEL JOHNSON, Register.

Book R, p. 32 JOSEPH BOURY, gentleman, of Charleston, to
24 & 25 Sept. 1735 WILLIAM LIVINGSTON, ESQ., of St. Paul's Parish,
L & R by Mortgage Colleton Co., for L 2000 SC money, 1109 a. &
an island of 64 a. in Colleton Co., bounding W
on vacant land; N on an impassable Bay Swamp; S & SE on Chehaw River &
marsh; conditioned for repayment of L 2000 on 1 Aug. next. Witnesses:
THOMAS LIVINGSTON, ANTHONY LAMBRIGHT, JOHN PACKER. Before JAMES BULLOCK,
J.P. NATHANIEL JOHNSON, Register.

Book R, p. 36 ROBERT WRIGHT, JR., ESQ., of Berkeley Co.
6 Mar. 1733 agrees to convey to DOMINICK MORPHY, gentleman,
Deed of Sale on 1 Dec. 1734 for L 50 British money paid before delivery & L 550 British money to be paid
at execution of deed; 1/2 of Barony, or tract of 12,000 a. lately belonging to THOMAS LOWNDES of London but now to WRIGHT, in Granville Co.,
bounding NW on WILLIAM HODGSON; SE on the River May; SW on Day's Creek.
Witnesses: JAMES GRAME, ROBERT HALL. NATHANIEL JOHNSON, Register.

Book R, p. 37 JOHN CUMING (CUMMING) student in Divinity,
15 Feb. 1736/7 Berkeley Co., to ALEXANDER NESBITT, as securi-
Mortgage ty 60 a. in Berkeley Co., inland, bounding NE
on MARY AURANT (?); SW on THOMAS LYND; SE on
BENJAMIN SIMMONS; NW on MARY ARA AMANT (?). Date of redemption 14 Feb.
1737/8. Witnesses: JONATHON DRAKE, JEREMIAH (his mark) DOWNES. Before
JAMES WEDDERBURN, J.P. NATHANIEL JOHNSON, Register.

Book R, p. 40 JONATHAN SKRINE, gentleman, of Berkeley Co.,
5 & 6 May 1736 to JOSEPH WRAGG, ESQ., of Charleston, as se-
L & R by Mortgage curity on bond of even date in penal sum of
L 2000 SC money for payment of L 1100 on 6 May
1738; 700 a. in Craven Co., bounding N on land owned by JONATHAN SKRINE
in right of his wife; S on vacant land; E on JAMES KINLOCK, ESQ. in right
of his wife; W on ARCHIBALD HAMILTON & BARTHOLOMEW GAILLARD; which tract
was granted to GEORGE CHICKEN on 22 May last; also 450 a. in Craven Co.,
bounding N on BARTHOLOMEW GAILLARD; other sides on vacant land; which
tract was granted on 22 May last to ARCHIBALD HAMILTON. Witnesses: ED-
WARD WIGG, ROBERT HUME, WILLIAM WITHERS. Before ROBERT AUSTIN, J.P. NA-
THANIEL JOHNSON, Register.

Book R, p. 45 JOHN BENATONE, planter, to WILLIAM GASCOIGNE,
1 & 2 Apr. 1736 carpenter, of Charleston, for L 137 SC money,
L & R lot #38 in Beaufort, Granville Co., bounding
according to certificate annexed to grant.
Witnesses: THOMAS HAMILTON SCOTT, JOHN RATTRAY. Before FRANCIS LEWIS,
J.P. NATHANIEL JOHNSON, Register.

Book R, p. 49 JAMES SMALLWOOD, merchant, of Charleston, to
9 May 1737 ELIAS FOISSIN, JR., of Christ Church Parish,
Bill of Sale for L 740 currency, 6 Negroes. Witnesses: LY-
DIA LEE, WILLIAM LEE. Before HENRY GIBBES,
J.P. NATHANIEL JOHNSON, Register.

Book R, p. 50 ISAAC AMYAND, ESQ., of Berkeley Co., to DANIEL
3 & 4 May 1737 LAROCHE, merchants, of Craven Co., equally as
L & R tenants in common & not as joint tenants for
L 50 SC money, 500 a. in Queensborough Town-
ship, Craven Co., granted by Lt. Gov. THOMAS BROUGHTON on 5 July 1736 to
ISAAC AMYAND, ESQ.; bounding SE on JAMES GORDON; NW on DANIEL & THOMAS
LAROCHE; NE on Peedee River; SW on vacant land. Witnesses: PETER HORRY,
GILES HOLLIDAY. Before MAURICE LEWIS, J.P. NATHANIEL JOHNSON, Register.

Book R, p. 54 DAVID BALDY, planter, of Craven Co., to DANIEL
10 & 11 Feb. 1736 LAROCHE, merchant, of Georgetown, as security
L & R by Mortgage on bond of even days in penal sum of L 1467
currency in payment of L 360:15 on 15 Jan.
next; & L 366:15 on 15 Jan. 1738; 500 a. in Winyaw, Craven Co., bounding
S on JAMES KINLOCK; W on JAMES KINLOCK; W on JAMES ROBERT; E on LEWIS
PALMER; N on vacant land. Witnesses: LEWIS PALMARIN, MARY PALMARIN. Before WILLIAM WHITESIDES, J.P. NATHANIEL JOHNSON, Register.

Book R, p. 57 WILLIAM WESTBERY, planter, & JOAN (her mark)
12 & 13 Nov. 1736 his wife, to SAMUEL SLEIGH, planter, all of
L & R Colleton Co., for L 577:10 currency, 330 a. in
Colleton Co., bounding N on RICHARD SMITH; W
on THOMAS JONES; SW on HUGH CAMPBELL; SE on WILLIAM WESTBERY. Witnesses:
LAWRENCE SANDERS, MOSES MARTIN, ISAAC MARTIN. Before MALACHI GLAZE, J.P.
NATHANIEL JOHNSON, Register.

Book R, p. 60 (See p. 224) RICHARD GODFREY, planter, & JANE

6 July 1736   his wife, of Colleton Co., to WILLIAM CATTELL,
Release   ESQ., of Berkeley Co., for ℔ 55 currency, half
                        a tract of 1100 a. in Colleton Co., which 1100
a. was granted by Lt. Gov. THOMAS BROUGHTON on 7 Aug. 1735 to RICHARD
GODFREY; bounding N on land formerly belonging to JOHN SEABROOK; S & W on
JOHN SEABROOK'S tract commonly called MORRIS'S land; & running from a
"stake per stump" to E part of the MORRIS tract & from said stake SE 73
until it intersects the line of JOHN SEABROOK'S land, commonly called
SEABROOK'S Islands. Witnesses: ANDREW LETCH, JAMES SCARLETT. Before
WILLIAM BULL, JR., J.P. NATHANIEL JOHNSON, Register.

Book R, p. 63   RIVERS STANYARNE, gentleman, to JOSEPH STAN-
14 Apr. 1737   YARNE, gentleman, both of Colleton Co. Where-
Deed of Partition   as WILLIAM RIVERS, planter, of James Island,
                        owned 300 a. on S side Ashley River, Berkeley
Co., near the Mill Point on James Island, bounding S on marsh on the
Sound; E on marsh & WILLIAM RUSSELL; W on DANIEL LACEY & WILLIAM COOK &
marsh of Witpeneno Creek; also 70 a.; & a small adjoining island of 5 a.;
making 75 a. bounding N on EDWARD PATTERY, JAMES LESUR & marsh; S on SAM-
UEL STENT & BENJAMIN LAMBALL & marsh; W on WILLIAM WESTBERY & SAMUEL
STENT; also 170 a. on James Island, on S side Ashley River, bounding S on
WILLIAM COOK; E on a creek, marsh, & vacant land; W on Huskewah Creek,
marsh & part on 240 a. formerly belonging to DANIEL LACEY; which tract of
170 a. was granted to MARTHA PATTEY (alias TUTWELL), & purchased by WIL-
LIAM RIVERS from MARTHA & JOSEPH TUTWELL, then her husband; also Folly
Island, containing 700 a.; & whereas by will dated 3 Oct. 1717 he bequeathed to his 2 grandsons, WILLIAM & RIVERS STANYARNE all his real estate; viz. to grandson WILLIAM STANYARNE his mansion house & half his
lands; to RIVERS the other half of his land; & should either grandson die
before inheriting, willed that his grandson JOSEPH STANYARNE should inherit the share of the 1 so dying; & whereas WILLIAM STANYARNE died under
age & his moiety became vested in JOSEPH; & whereas RIVERS & JOSEPH desire to avoid all contraoversies in regard to the division of WILLIAM'S
estate; now they agree that JOSEPH shall have, as his share, all the 300
a. & Folly Island (700 a.); JOSEPH to pay RIVERS STANYARNE ℔ 412 SC money,
his part being that much more in value than that belonging to RIVERS:
RIVERS to have, as his share, the 170 a. & the 75 a., including the island of 5 a. Witnesses: RICHARD ALLEIN, WILLIAM BOWER, SARAH BOWER, JA-
COB MOTTE, J.P. NATHANIEL JOHNSON, Register.

Book R, p. 66   RIVERS STANYARNE, gentleman, to JOSEPH STAN-
14 Apr. 1737   YARNE, gentleman, both of Colleton Co. Where-
Deed of Partition   as WILLIAM RIVERS, planter, of James Island,
                        owned 300 a. near the Mill Point, James Island,
(see p. 63) 70 a.; an island of 5 a.; & Folly Island (700 a.) & whereas
by will dated 3 Oct. 1717 he bequeathed all his real estate to his 2
grandsons, WILLIAM & RIVERS STANYARNE, via. his mansion house & half the
land to WILLIAM; the other half the land to RIVERS; & should either die
before inheriting, his share to be taken by grandson JOSEPH STANYARNE; &
whereas WILLIAM died under age & JOSEPH inherited his moiety; & whereas
RIVERS & JOSEPH wish to avoid all controversies in regard to the inheritance; now they agree to an equal partition; JOSEPH to have the 300 a.,
Folly Island (700 a.); JOSEPH to pay RIVERS ℔ 412 SC money, because his
share is valued at more than the share allotted to RIVERS; RIVERS STAN-
YARNE to have as his share the 170 a. & the 70 & 5 a. Witnesses: RICHARD
ALLEIN, WILLIAM BOWER, SARAH BOWER, SARAH BOWER. Before JACOB MOTTE, J.P.
NATHANIEL JOHNSON, Register.

Book R, p. 69   RIVERS STANYARNE, gentleman, of Colleton Co.,
17 & 18 Apr. 1737   to JOHN BEE, gentleman, of Charleston, for
L & R   ℔ 3350 SC money, 170 a. on James Island on S
                        side Ashley River, bounding S on lands former-
ly belonging to WILLIAM COOK, now on the 70 a.; E on a creek, marsh, &
WILLIAM SCREVEN; W on HUSKEWAH CREEK & marsh & remainder of 240 a. formerly belonging to DANIEL LASEY, now to JOHN MCCOY; (MCKAY) also 70 a.
bounding N on JOHN MCCOY & WILLIAM SCREVEN (formerly EDWARD PATEY & JAMES
LE SUR) & the said 170 a. & marsh; S on SAMUEL RIVERS & JOHN MCCOY (formerly SAMUEL STENT & BENJAMIN LAMBELL) & marsh; E on JOSEPH STANYARNE
(formerly WILLIAM RIVERS, his grandfather) & marsh; W on JOHN MCCOY
(formerly WILLIAM WESTBERRY & SAMUEL STENT); E on JOSEPH STANYARNE

(formerly WILLIAM RIVERS). Whereas Gov. NATHANIEL JOHNSON, THOMAS BROUGHTON, NICHOLAS TROTT & ROBERT GIBBES, Lords Proprs., 54 Feb. 1706, granted ??? to MARTHA PATTEY 170 a. (part of 240 a. formerly taken up by DANIEL LACEY) on S side Ashley River, bounding S on WILLIAM COOKE; E on a creek & marsh & vacant land; W on Huskewah Creek, marsh, & the part of the 240 a. tract; & whereas JOSEPH TATNELL, planter, of Colleton Co. & MARTHA his wife (late PATTEY) by deed of feoffment dated 10 Oct. 1700 conveyed the 170 a. to WILLIAM RIVERS (grandfather of RIVERS STANYARNE); & whereas Gov. NATHANIEL JOHNSON, THOMAS BROUGHTON, HENRY NOBLE & ROBERT GIBBES, Lords Proprs. on 3 Sept. 1709 granted WILLIAM RIVERS 75 a., English measure, on James Island bounding S on SAMUEL STENT & BENJAMIN LAMBALL & marsh; N on EDWARD PATTEY, & JAMES LESUR; & marsh; E on WILLIAM RIVERS & marsh; W on WESTBERRY & SAMUEL STENT; & whereas WILLIAM RIVERS, by will dated 3 Oct. 1717, bequeathed his real estate to his 2 grandsons WILLIAM & RIVERS STANYARNE (p. 63); & whereas grandson WILLIAM died & grandson JOSEPH STANYARNE inherited WILLIAM'S portion; & whereas JOSEPH & RIVERS STANYARNE made a staisfactory division of the land (p. 63 & 66); & whereas RIVERS STANYARNE had issued & therefore became absolute owner of the 170 a. & the 75 a.; & whereas RIVERS STANYARNE sold the 5 a. island to DANIEL STENT, planter, of James Island; now RIVERS STANYARNE sells the 170 a. tract & the 70 a. tract to BEE. Witnesses: RICHARD ALLEIN, WILLIAM BOWER (BOWERS), SARAH BOWER. Before JACOB MOTTE, J.P. NATHANIEL JOHNSON, Register.

Book R, p. 77
3 & 4 May 1737
L & R Quadripartite

GEORGE NICHOLAS, ESQ., & ELIZABETH his wife, of Berkeley Co., of 1st part; JOSEPH WRAGG, ESQ. of Charleston, of 2nd part; ROBERT AUSTIN, merchant, of Charleston, of 3rd part; WILLIAM CATTELL, ESQ., of Berkeley Co., of 4th part. Whereas by letters patent dated 14 Feb. 1735, signed by Lt. Gov. THOMAS BROUGHTON, GEORGE NICHOLAS was granted 240 a. in Berkeley Co., bounding SW on said NICHOLAS; NW on MALACHI GLAZE, ESQ.; NE on CHARLES BARKER & WILLIAM BURNLEY; SE on THOMAS DISTON; & whereas GEORGE NICHOLAS gave several bonds; 1 dated 3 May inst. to JOSEPH WRAGG in penal sum of L 1274 SC money for payment of L 637:1:17 on 6 May 1738; 1 dated 3 May last to ROBERT AUSTIN in penal sum of L 4440 SC money for payment of L 2220 on 6 May 1738; 1 dated 3 May inst. to WILLIAM CATTELL in penal sum of L 2256 SC money for payment of L 1128:15:10 on 6 May 1738; now, to secure payment of the various sums on the days appointed, & for 15 shillings paid to GEORGE & ELIZABETH NICHOLAS by WRAGG, AUSTIN & CATTELL, GEORGE & ELIZABETH NICHOLAS release to WRAGG, AUSTIN, & CATTELL, the 240 a. Witnesses: ROBERT HUME, THOMAS HEPWORTH. It is agreed that 38 a. of the 240 a. belong to WILLIAM DONNING. Before JAMES MICHIE, J.P. NATHANIEL JOHNSON, Register.

Book R, p. 84
3 & 4 Jan. 1736
L & R

THOMAS ELLERY, gentleman & ANNE his wife, to JAMES OSMOND, merchant, all of Charleston, for L 4825 SC money, free from ANNE'S claim of dower, the dwelling house & other building built by ELLERY on 2 lots purchased from ANDREW ALLEN, JOHN SOMMERVILLE & SARAH SOMMERVILLE, being part of 3 lots, #188, #189, & #79, fronting S 128 ft. English measure on Queen Street from THOMAS COOPER'S house to the corner of Queen Street; bounding E 150 ft. on the garden & premises of MR. COOPER (part of same 3 lots, #188, #189 & #79 formerly sold by THOMAS ELLERY); W 150 ft. from SW corner of Queen Street on a certain great street leading from Ashley River N by the Market Place & Presbyterian Meeting House; N 130 ft. on RICHARD BRICKLOS (part of same 3 lots & lately conveyed to him by THOMAS ELLERY). Witnesses: JOHN COLLETON, J.P. NATHANIEL JOHNSON, Register. JAMES DE ST. JULIAN, CAPT. ROBERT TAYLOR. Before JACOB MOTTE, J.P.

Book R, p. 100
3 & 4 Sept. 1730
L & R by Mortgage

JOHN VICARIDGE, merchant, to ROBERT AUSTIN, merchant, both of Charleston, as security for endorsing a bond dated 23 July 1730 given by VICARIDGE to JOHN FENWICKE, JOSEPH WRAGG, PAUL JENYS, OTHNIEL BEALE & THOMAS LAMBOLL, merchants, of Charleston, in penal sum of L 1706:13:4 currency for payment of L 853:6:8 on 23 Mar. 1730; part of the lot #82 lately occupied by JOHN HOGG, fronting W 60 ft. on the street leading from Ashley River by the Quakers Meeting House; N 225 ft. on another part of same lot; S on MR. WELLS. Witnesses: PAUL TRAPIER, JOHN LEWIS. Before JOSEPH WRAGG, J.P. NATHANIEL JOHNSON, Register.

Book R, p. 104 JOHN VICARIDGE, gentleman, of Queenby (?) Hall,
21 & 22 Jan. 1736 Berkeley Co., to GEORGE SCOTT, WILLIAM POSTON,
L & R by Mortgage & TOBIAS EYSAM, merchants, of the City of London, for L 800 sterling, 1900 a. in Craven Co.,
granted by letters patent, dated 23 May 1734, signed by Gov. ROBERT JOHNSON, bounding E, on SAMUEL CLAGUE; other sides on vacant land. Should VICARIDGE pay SCOTT, POSTON & EYSAM L 800 sterling with interest at 5% on 25 Mar. 1738, this mortgage, & another mortgage of 20 slaves & a bond given this date shall be void. Witnesses: JAMES CROKATT, THOMAS ELLERY. Before HENRY GIBBES, J.P. NATHANIEL JOHNSON, Register.

Book R, p. 111 JOHN THORPE, owner of 2000 a. in Granville Co.
16 Oct. 1736 & intending to leave SC shortly, appoints his
Letter of Attorney brother, ROBERT THORPE, his attorney, with authority to sell his land. Witnesses: JAMES
ST. JOHN, JAMES WOOD. Before WILLIAM BULL, J.P. NATHANIEL JOHNSON, Register.

Book R, p. 112 HENRY GIGMILLIAT, vintner, & HESTER (ESTER)
28 & 29 Nov. 1734 his wife, to ANN KING, widow, for L 600 SC mon-
L & R by Mortgage ey, 1/4 of lot #43 in Charleston, fronting E 25 ft. on Church Street; W on PETER DE ST. JULIEN; N 142 ft. on ELIZABETH DAMARIS DE ST. JULIEN widow; S on ISAAC MAZYCK, SR., merchant; also 50 a. in Berkeley Co., bounding N & S on STEPHEN BULLOCK; E on THOMAS FITZGERALD; W on a creek out of Wando River; also 50 a. in Bermuda Town, Berkeley Co., bounding S on WILLIAM FISHER; W on a creek on Wando River; N on THOMAS ALLEN; E on THOMAS FITZGERALD. Date of redemption, 1 Jan. next. HESTER to renounce her dower within 6 months. Witnesses: ROBERT BROWN, ISAAC DUMONT. Before FRANCIS LEJAU, J.P. NATHANIEL JOHNSON, Register.

Book R, p. 118 SAMUEL BULLOCK, planter, of Berkeley Co., to
10 & 11 May 1737 JOSEPH WRAGG & RICHARD LAMBTON, merchants, of
L & R by Mortgage Charleston, as security for the repayment of L 327:5 British money, or L 2385:6 SC money on 30 Dec. 1737; 300 a. in Christ Church Parish, Berkeley Co., bounding E on JOHN HOLYBUSH; N on Wando River; which tract was granted to JOSEPH HATCHMAN on 12 Nov. 1698; also 55 a. (part of 200 a.) bounding E on the above 300 a.; N on Wando River; W on GILES COOK; which 2 tracts (300 & 55 a.) were purchased from GILES COOK by BULLOCK. Witnesses: THOMAS HEPWORTH, EDWARD WIGG. Before ROBERT AUSTIN, J.P. NATHANIEL JOHNSON, Register. RICHARD J. LAMBTON declared mortgage paid 17 Sept. 1742. Witness: JAMES MICHIE.

Book R, p. 124 MARTHA WILLIAMSON, (widow of WILLIAM WILLIAM-
8 Apr. 1737 SON) of Colleton Co., & daughter & devisee of
Deed of Sale RALPH EMONS (EMMET?), ESQ. of Colleton Co., to RICHARD WRIGHT, ESQ., of Berkeley Co., for
L 725 currency, 100 a. on NW branch of Stono River, Colleton Co., (part of 250 a. granted to RALPH EMONS); bounding S on RICHARD WRIGHT, ESQ.; E on a 276 a. tract (part of 470 a.); N on said WILLIAMSON; W on WILLIAMSON & RICHARD WRIGHT; also 276 a. granted to RALPH EMMET, bounding N on WILLIAMSON; S on RICHARD WRIGHT; W on a 100 a. tract; & is described in the plot by a tract of 238 a. & of 38 a., called MR. WRIGHT'S land, being the intermediate space between the 238 a. & the 100 a.; & on which RICHARD WRIGHT built a dwelling house. Witnesses: SUSANNA ELLIOTT, THOMAS ELLIOTT, THOMAS ELLIOTT. NATHANIEL JOHNSON, Register.

Book R, p. 128 JAMES ROBERT, planter, & SARAH his wife, to
1 & 2 Feb. 1736 HENRY DURANT, planter, all of Craven Co., for
L & R L 500 currency, 600 a. (part of 1050 a.) in Craven Co., bounding S on DANIEL JAUDON (formerly RALPH IZARD, then JAMES ROBERT); NE on JOSEPH BUGNION (formerly BOHANNON'S); N on JOHN DUBOSE; S on Wadbaccan Creek. Whereas Lt. Gob. THOMAS BROUGHTON on 7 Aug. 1735 granted JAMES ROBERT 1050 a. in Craven Co., bounding S on JAMES ROBERT (formerly RALPH IZARD); NE on BOHANNON'S; SW on Wadbaccan Creek; other sides on JOHN DUBOSE. Witnesses: JOHN DUBOSE, JOSEPH BUGNION, JAMES ADAMS. Before NOAH SERRÉ. NATHANIEL JOHNSON, Register.

Book R, p. 133   JAMES ROBERT, planter, to JAMES DURANT, plant-
3 Feb. 1736   er, both of Craven Co., in sum of Ł 1000 SC
Bond   money, as security that ROBERT will procure
                        SARAH'S renuncation of dower (before ROBERT
WRIGHT, C.J.) in the above 600 a. Witnesses: JOHN DUBOSE, JOSEPH BUGNION,
JAMES ADAMS. Before NOAH SERRE, J.P. NATHANIEL JOHNSON, Register.

Book R, p. 135   HENRY DURANT, planter, & ANN his wife, to JO-
9 & 10 Feb. 1736   SEPH BUGNION, clerk, all of Craven Co., for
L & R   Ł 1500 currency, 600 a. & 250 a. Whereas Lt.
                        Gov. THOMAS BROUGHTON on 7 Aug. 1735 granted
JAMES ROBERT, planter of Craven Co., 150 a., bounding SE on JAMES ROBERT
(formerly RALPH IZARD); NE on BOHANNON'S; SE on Wadbaccan Creek; other
sides on JOHN DUBOSE; & whereas on 2 Feb. 1736 JAMES ROBERT & SARAH his
wife sold to HENRY DURANT 600 a. (part of the 1050 a.), bounding S on
DANIEL JAUDON (formerly RALPH IZARD, then JAMES ROBERT); NE on JOSEPH
BUGNION (formerly BOHANNON'S); N on JOHN DUBOSE; S on Wadbaccan Creek; NW
on SAMUEL ROBERT; & whereas on 15 Dec. 1736 Lt. Gov. THOMAS BROUGHTON
granted HENRY DURANT 250 a. in Craven Co., bounding SW on DURANT; SE on
DANIEL JAUDON; other sides on vacant land; now DURANT sells 2 tracts to
BUGNION. Witnesses: DANIEL JAUDON, PIERE RAMBERT, PETER,DUMAY, PETER DU-
MAY, WILLIAM SHACKELFORD, THOMAS WISE. Before NOAH SERRE, J.P. NATHAN-
IEL JOHNSON, Register.

Book R, p. 140   HENRY DURANT, planter, gives bond to JOSEPH
11 Feb. 1736   BUGNION, clerk, both of Craven Co., in the sum
Bond   of Ł 1000 SC money, that he will procure his
                        wife's (ANN'S) renunciation of dower, (before
ROBERT WRIGHT, C.J.) to above tracts. Witnesses: DANIEL JAUDON, PIERRE
RAMBERT, PETER DUMAY. Before NOAH SERRE, J.P. NATHANIEL JOHNSON, Regis-
ter.

Book R, p. 141   CHARLES KING, planter, to JOHN BERESFORD, ESQ.
20 & 21 Nov. 1734   for Ł 2100 currency, 600 a. (except 200 a.
L & R   sold to JOHN DANIEL) & 100 a. Whereas RICHARD
                        BERESFORD, planter, of Berkeley Co., by will
dated May 1715 bequeathed to his nephew CHARLES KING, on coming of age,
600 a. (lately purchased from the Lords Proprs.) on Cooper River, in
Berkeley Co., between the lands of THOMAS BURTON & RICHARD CODNER, upon
the condition that CHARLES KING pay his sister, MARY KING, when 18 or on
the day of her marriage, Ł 150 currency; & whereas KING has paid his sister the money; & whereas KING has sold to JOHN DANIEL, planter 200 a. out
of the 600 a.; & whereas the Hon. ROBERT GIBBES & Lords Proprs. on 23
July 1707 granted RICHARD CODNER 100 a., English measure, in Berkeley Co.;
& whereas CHARLES CODNER, son & heir of RICHARD, & ANN his wife, on 16
Nov. 1734 sold to CHARLES KING the 100 a. in St. Thomas Parish, on E side
Cooper River, bounding N on CHARLES KING; E on THOMAS PAGIT; S on EDWARD
BULLARD & JOHN PRIMAT; now CHARLES KING sells 500 a. to BERESFORD. Wit-
nesses: BENJAMIN WHITAKER, WILLIAM GEORGE FREEMAN. NATHANIEL JOHNSON,
Register.

Book R, p. 147   FRANCIS GODDARD, planter, to JOHN BERESFORD,
16 & 17 Feb. 1734   ESQ., both of Berkeley Co., for Ł 1600 SC mon-
L & R   ey, Hearty's Island on Wando River, containing
                        300 a. Witnesses: GEORGE FREEMAN, BENJAMIN
WHITAKER. NATHANIEL JOHNSON, Register.

Book R, p. 151   EDWARD BULLARD, carpenter, & ELIZABETH his
14 & 15 Jan. 1734   wife, to JOHN BERESFORD, ESQ., of St. Thomas
L & R   Parish, Berkeley Co., for Ł 1000 SC money, 300
                        a. in St. Thomas Parish, bounding W on marsh &
a creek; S on JOHN BERESFORD COOKE; NE on THOMAS PAGITT; N on JOHN BERES-
FORD & RICHARD CODNER. Witnesses: WILLIAM FRYER, ROWLAND VAUGHAN. NA-
THANIEL JOHNSON, Register.

Book R, p. 151   EDWARD BULLARD, carpenter, & ELIZABETH his
14 & 15 Jan. 1734   wife, to JOHN BERESFORD, ESQ., of St. Thomas
L & R   Parish, Berkeley Co., for Ł 1000 SC money, 300
                        a. in St. Thomas Parish, bounding W on marsh &
a creek; S on JOHN BERESFORD & BENTLY COOKE; NE on THOMAS PAGITT; N on

JOHN BERESFORD & RICHARD CODNER. Witnesses: WILLIAM FRYER, ROWLAND VAUGHAN. NATHANIEL JOHNSON, Register.

Book R, p. 155 JOHN FILLEBIEN (FIL-BIN) & KATHRIN his wife,
15 Apr. 1710 to MARK SLOWMAN & JOSEPH SPENCER, for ₤ 200
Deed of Sale currency, 2 tracts in Craven Co., purchased
from JACOB LAPOTRE, 500 a. & 200 a. Whereas
JOHN, Lord Granville, Palatine, & the Lords Proprs. on 5 May 1704 granted
DANIEL MACGRIGORY 500 a. in Craven Co., bounding N on Santee River; E on
PATRICK STEWARD; S on vacant land; W on RICHARD CODNER; & whereas MACGRIGORY on 10 Oct. 1704 sold the 500 a. to JOSEPH LAPOTRE, merchant, of
Charleston, & ELIAS HORRY, planter, of Craven Co., & whereas ELIAS HORRY
on 10 Oct. 1708 sold his half to LAPOTRE; & whereas JOHN, Lord Granville,
Palatine, & the Lords Proprs. on 12 Jan. 1705 granted JACOB LAPOTRE 200 a.
English measure in Craven Co., on N side Santee River; bounding E on Santee River & Nahaw Creek; S on the creek & vacant land; & whereas LAPOTRE
conveyed the 2 tracts to JOHN FILLEBIEN; now FILLEBIEN & his wife convey
theres to SLOWMAN & SPENCER. KATHERINE signs voluntarily. Witnesses:
ELIAS HORRY, JONAH COLLINS, ISAAC PORCHER, JONAH BONHOSTE. "Santee Feb.
14th 1720/ I do hereby assign & make over to MR. RALPH INMAN all my right
& title to the within mentioned tract of land as witness our hands this
14th Feb. 1720. Test. ELIAS HORRY, JOHN (his mark) SHAW, SARAH (her mark)
SHACKLEFORD." JONAH COLLINS appeared before HENRY GIBBES, J.P. on 21 Feb.
1736 & testified that notwithstanding the length of time since the above
deed was executed & the names of this deponant & of ELIAS HORRY "were all
wrote with bad ink & so obliterated as scarcely to be read without difficulty yet he well remember the execution of the deeds by the said JOHN
FILBIN & KATHERINE FILBIN." NATHANIEL JOHNSON, Register.

Book R, p. 161 STEPHEN (his mark) MONCK, planter, of Berkeley
8 Feb. 1734 Co., to SAMUEL PRIOLEAU, ESQ., of Charleston,
Mortgage for ₤ 400 currency, 1 Negro woman, all his
neat cattle, 1 riding horse, 1 set copper's
tools, 1 gun, 2 feather beds, his household goods & chattles. Date of
redemption, 1 Mar. next. Witnesses: GEORGE TABART, DELMESTRE. Before
DANIEL GREENE, J.P. NATHANIEL JOHNSON, Register.

Book R, p. 162 GILES COOK, planter, of Craven Co., to MARTHA
4 June 1737 COMBE, widow of PHILIP COMBE, & JOHN COMBE,
Mortgage planter, of Berkeley Co., for ₤ 630 currency,
500 a. in Craven Co., being the same 500 a.
conveyed by MARTHA & JOHN COMBE to GILES COOK on 23 June 1737, bounding
on all sides on vacant land; conditioned for the payment of 2 bonds
amounting to ₤ 630 on the dates mentioned. Witnesses: HENRY VIDEAU, DAVID CORNUT, ANTHONY BONNEAU. Before JOHN HARLESTON, J.P. NATHANIEL JOHNSON, Register.

Book R, p. 164 CHARLES CODNER, planter, to JOHN BERESFORD,
17 & 18 Jan. 1736 ESQ., for ₤ 6000 SC money, 3 tracts, 350 a. on
L & R Ittiwon Island; now called St. Thomas Island,
Berkeley Co., bounding N on Beresford Creek;
NE & SE on Monhoms Creek; S on Wando River; SW on CAPT. THOMAS WALKER
(formerly JOHN MORGAN); NW on CHARLES CODNER (formerly CHRISTOPHER SMITH);
which tract was granted by the Lords Proprs. to PHOEBE CODNER & by various conveyances descended to RICHARD CODNER; then to CHARLES CODNER, his
only son & heir; also 70 a. on St. Thomas's Island, bounding N on marsh;
E & S on the above 350 a.; W on land conveyed by CHARLES CODNER to
CHARLES KING; also 105 a. on St. Thomas's Island, bounding N on creeks &
marshes; S on the above 350 a.; E on above 70 a.; W on CAPT. THOMAS WALKER; which 105 a. was part of 210 a. granted by the Lords Proprs. to ROBERT DANIELL, ESQ. & by him conveyed to RICHARD CODNER, & inherited by
CHARLES CODNER, only son & heir of RICHARD. ANN, wife of CHARLES CODNER,
to renounce her dower within 3 months. Witnesses: JOHN STEWARD, JOHN
COOKE, HERCULES COYTE. NATHANIEL JOHNSON, Register.

Book R, p. 169 NICHOLAS TROTT, ESQ., & SARAH his wife, of St.
7 & 8 May 1736 Philip's Parish, Charleston, to JOHN BERESFORD,
L & R ESQ. of Berkeley Co., for ₤ 925 SC money, on
island of 125 a., English measure, in Berkeley
Co., on Wando River. Witnesses: ELIZABETH BULMER, HESTER JOHNSTON.

NATHANIEL JOHNSON, Register.

Book R, p. 174 JAMES ST. JOHN, Surv. Gen., laid out for MRS.
26 June 1736 ELIZABETH BAMPFIELD, 900 a. Hell Hole Swamp,
Warrant Berkeley Co., bounding N & S on vacant land; W
on JOHN BERESFORD, ESQ.; E on CAPT. ROBERTS.

Book R, p. 174 GEORGE, II, to MRS. ELIZABETH BAMPFIELD, 900 a.
13 Sept. 1736 in Berkeley Co., bounding N & S on vacant land;
Grant W on JOHN BERESFORD, ESQ.; E on CAPT. ROBERTS.
Signed by Lt. Gov. THOMAS BROUGHTON. Witness:
ALEXANDER CRAMAHÉ. Recorded in Secretary's office 21 Mar. 1736 in Bk.
G G, fol. 314 by J. HAMPTON. NATHANIEL JOHNSON, Register.

Book R, p. 176 ELIZABETH BAMPFIELD, widow of St. Philip's Par-
3 & 4 June 1737 ish, Charleston, to JOHN BERESFORD, ESQ., of
L & R Berkeley Co., for ₺ 100 SC money, 900 a. in
Berkeley Co., bounding N & S on vacant land; W
on JOHN BERESFORD; E on CAPT. ROBERTS. Witnesses: MARY SATUR, JOHN COOKE.
NATHANIEL JOHNSON, Register.

Book R, p. 181 ROBERT FLADGER, planter, to JOHN BERESFORD,
12 Mar. 1737 ESQ., for 5 shillings, 300 a. in Christ Church
Lease Parish, Berkeley Co., at head of a branch of
Wando River, bounding S on creek, marsh, &
ROBERT FLADGER (formerly WILLIAM RUBERRY); E on RICHARD CAPUS; N & W on
THOMAS LYNCH & JOHN BERESFORD; also 100 a. bounding N on above land; E on
Wando River; S on DAVID BATCHELLOR; W on JOHN BERESFORD; which 100 a. was
conveyed to FLADGER by CHARLES LEWIS. Witnesses: THOMAS WITTER, JOHN
COOKE, HERCULES COYTE. NATHANIEL JOHNSON, Register.

Book R, p. 182 JOSEPH BUGNION, clerk of Craven Co., to ISAAC
26 & 27 May 1737 MAZYCK, merchant, of Charleston, for ₺ 2900 SC
L & R by Mortgage money, 600 a. in Craven Co., bounding S on DAN-
IEL JAUDON (formerly RALPH IZARD, then of
JAMES ROBERT); NE on JOSEPH BUGNION (formerly BOHANNON'S); N on JOHN DU-
BOSE; SW on Wadbaccan Creek; NW on JAMES ROBERT; also 250 a. in Craven
Co., bounding SW on HENRY DURANT; SE on DANIEL JAUDON; other sides on va-
cant land; which 2 tracts were conveyed to BUGNION on 9 & 10 Feb. 1736 by
HENRY DURANT, planter, of Craven Co. Date of redemption, 1 Jan. next.
Witnesses: WILLIAM HAMILTON, CHILDERMAS CROFT. Before MAURICE LEWIS, J.P.
NATHANIEL JOHNSON, Register.

Book R, p. 188 DAVID MONGIN, watchmaker, to DR. JOHN MARTINI,
29 June 1737 both of Charleston as security for payment of
Mortgage ₺ 588:5 SC money with interest on 1 Jan. next;
2 Negroes. Signed by DAVID MONGIN & PRESILE
MONGIN. Witnesses: JOHN YONG CHURCH, WILLIAM SIMMONS.

Book R, p. 189 THOMAS (his mark) WANNEL, planter, of Gran-
Not dated ville Co., to WILLIAM GRAY, planter, of Colle-
Bill of Sale ton Co., for ₺ 210, 100 a. in the freshes of
Cumbene River, part of 300 a. formerly belong-
ing to his father JOHN WANNEL. Witnesses: ANDREW DEVEAU, JR., WILLIAM
PALMER, JOHN ELLIS. Before STEPHEN BULL, J.P., 23 Sept. 1736. NATHANIEL
JOHNSON, Register. (See p. 319 for Renunciation of Dower).

Book R, p. 189 JOSEPH SHUTE, merchant, & ANNA his wife & ISA-
16 & 17 May 1737 BEL KIMBERLY, widow, to JAMES THOMSON, butcher,
L & R all of Charleston; for ₺ 3000; 6 a. & premises
on Charleston Neck, St. Philip's Parish, Berke-
ley Co., bounding E on the Broad Path leading to Charleston; S on the
Free School road; W on the Free Schools; N on JOSEPH or (& ?) SAMUEL
WRAGG, ESQS. Witnesses: MOSES BENNETT, ROBERT BREWTON, JR. Before HENRY
GIBBES, J.P. NATHANIEL JOHNSON, Register.

Book R, p. 193 JOSEPH DOBSON, planter, of Craven Co., to JO-
20 & 21 June 1737 SEPH WRAGG & RICHARD LAMBTON, merchants, of
L & R by Mortgage Charleston, as security for the repayment of
₺ 1137 SC money on 1 Jan. next; & SW 300 a. in

Craven Co., bounding NW & NE & SW on vacant land; SE on THOMAS HUSK; also 200 a. in Craven Co., bounding NE on JOSEPH DOBSON; other sides on vacant land. Whereas by letters patent dated 4 June 1735, signed by Lt. Gov. THOMAS BROUGHTON, JOSEPH DOBSON was granted 300 a. in Craven Co., & on 30 Sept. last, was granted 200 a. in Craven Co.; & whereas on 3 Nov. last, DOBSON gave bond to WRAGG & LAMBTON in the penal sum of Ł 2274 for payment of Ł 1137 on 1 Jan. 1737/8; now he gives the 2 tracts as security. Witnesses: WILLIAM ROMSAY, THOMAS LEITH. Before WILLIAM WHITESIDE, J.P. NATHANIEL JOHNSON, Register.

Book R, p. 198
21 & 22 June 1737
L & R by Mortgage

JOHN (his mark) HUDDY, of Craven Co., to WILLIAM ROMSEY & CO., merchants, of Charleston, as security on bond of even date in penal sum of Ł 230 currency for payment of Ł 114:19 with interest on 1 Mar. 1738; 300 a. in Craven Co., bounding N on Georgetown Creek & vacant land; E on MR. PORT; S on MR. WILKS; W on MR. SMITH. Witnesses: ALEXANDER HOPE, WILLIAM BROWN. Before WILLIAM WHITESIDE, J.P. NATHANIEL JOHNSON, Register.

Book R, p. 202
13 & 14 June 1737
L & R

WILLIAM LIVINGSTON, ESQ., & MARY his wife, of St. Paul's Parish, Colleton Co., to PETER HORRY, merchant, of Charleston, for Ł 887:8 currency, 1109 a. & an island of 64 a. in Colleton Co., bounding W on vacant land; N on an impassable Bay Swamp; S & SE on Chehaw River & marsh; MARY to renounce her dower within 3 months. Witnesses: JOSEPH BOUREY, WILLIAM HANCOCK. Before MAURICE LEWIS, J.P. NATHANIEL JOHNSON, Register.

Book R, p. 205
29 & 30 June 1737
L & R by Mortgage

ROBERT BROWN, planter, of Prince George Parish, Craven Co., to PETER HORRY, merchant, of Charleston, as security on bond for Ł 700 SC money; 640 a. in Craven Co., bounding E on a salt marsh; W on Waccamaw River; other sides on WILLIAM ALSTON. Should BROWN release HORRY from paying any part of the bond, with interest, on 25 Mar. 1738 to ANTHONY MATHEWS & CO. the Friendly Society, for which bond HORRY became security with BROWN, this deed to be void. Witnesses: SAMUEL WIGFALL, BENJAMIN STEAD, WILLIAM HANCOCK. Before HENRY GIBBES, J.P. NATHANIEL JOHNSON, Register.

Book R, p. 209
18 & 19 Aug. 1736
L & R by Mortgage

DAVID MONGIN, watch-maker, of Charleston, to THOMAS ELLERY, gentleman, of Charleston, for Ł 460 SC money, part of 3 lots in Charleston, #188, #189, & #79; bounding E 30 ft. on the garden fence of THOMAS COOPER; W 360 ft. on the great street leading from Ashley River by the Market Place & Presbyterian Meeting House; S 132 ft. on THOMAS ELLERY; N on lands & burying ground belonging to Presbyterian congregation. Half the sum to be re-paid by MONGIN on 19 Aug. 1737; the other half on 19 Aug. 1738. Witnesses: GEORGE HUNTER, gentleman, LEWIS LORIMER. Before THOMAS DALE, J.P. NATHANIEL JOHNSON, Register.

Book R, p. 213
3 & 4 Nov. 1736
L & R by Mortgage

RICHARD BRICKLES, house carptner, & SARAH his wife, to THOMAS ELLERY, gentleman, all of Charleston, for Ł 900 SC money, part of 3 lots in Charleston, #188, #189, & #79, bounding E 50 ft. on the garden fence of THOMAS COOPER; W 50 ft. on the great street leading from Ashley River to the Market Place & Presbyterian Meeting House; S 130 ft. 9 in. on THOMAS ELLERY; N on DAVID MONGIN; Ł 450 to be re-paid with interest, on 4 May 1737; Ł 450 on 4 Nov. 1734. Witnesses: JOHN COLLETON, ESQ., NICHOLAS MATTEYSON. Before ROBERT AUSTIN, J.P. NATHANIEL JOHNSON, Register.

Book R, p. 218

"Memorandum: That all the principal & interest money due to me on the mortgage recorded from RICHARD BRICKLES & his wife is paid except the sum of 680 pounds 13 shillings & 4 pence & for which sum I have assigned the said mortgage to MR. CHILDERMAS CROFT 4th Mar. 1737. THO. ELLERY. Test: ROBERT AUSTIN." (p. 215). "I do acknowledge satisfaction of the sum for which the within deed was assigned to me as witness my hand the 11th day of June 1743 - CHILDERMAS CROFT."

Book R, p. 219
15 & 16 Feb. 1736
L & R by Mortgage

JOHN ABBOTT, carpenter & planter, of Craven Co., to JOSEPH WRAGG & RICHARD LAMBTON, merchants, of Charleston, for ₤ 144:15 money of Great Britain, 650 a. in Craven Co., bounding on N side of Waccamaw River on Rum Bluff; NE & SE on vacant land; SW on JOHN ABBOTT (formerly JOSIAH SMITH); which tract was granted to ABBOTT on 14 Feb. 1735; also 350 a. in Craven Co., on N side Waccamaw River, bounding NE on above 650 a.; SE & SW on vacant land; which tract was part of 700 a. purchased by ABBOTT from JOSIAH SMITH; also 430 a. purchased by ABBOTT from JONATHON CALKINS, carpenter, being part of 1000 a. in Prince George Parish between the sea & SW branch of Little River, being that part of the 1000 a. which begins at a cedar stake on the bluff, running a SW line 69°. Date of redemption, 16 Nov. next. Witnesses: EDWARD WIGG, WILLIAM WITHERS. Before ROBERT AUSTIN, J.P. NATHANIEL JOHNSON, Register. On 12 Apr. 1778 RICHARD LAMBTON, survivor of WRAGG & LAMBTON, declared he received full satisfaction of 430 a. purchased from JONATHAN CALKINS & sold to JOSEPH ALLSTON by L & R, 4 & 5 Mar. 1758, recorded in Bk. Q. Q. pages 331-336. Witness: WILLIAM HOPTON.

Book R, p. 224
Probate

See Book P. fol. 108. WILLIAM STOBOE, on 15 July 1737 appeared before JACOB MOTTE, J.P. & declared he saw HENRY YOUNGE sign & deliver the instrument of writing & that WALTER WELCH & himself signed as witnesses. NATHANIEL JOHNSON, Register.

Book R, p. 224
5 July 1736
Lease (see p. 60)

RICHARD GODFREY, planter, & JANE his wife, of Colleton Co., to WILLIAM CATTELL, ESQ., of Berkeley Co., for 5 shillings, half of 1100 a. in Colleton Co., bounding N on JOHN SEABROOK; S & W on another tract called HORRY'S & belonging to JOHN SEABROOK; & runs from a stake SE 75 until it intersects the line of JOHN SEABROOK'S land commonly called Seabrooks Island. Witnesses: JAMES SCARLETT, ANDREW LETCH. Before STEPHEN BULL, J.P. NATHANIEL JOHNSON, Register.

Book R, p. 226
13 & 14 June 1737
L & R by Mortgage
Tripartite

JOHN SKENE, ESQ. of 1st part; ALEXANDER SKENE of 2nd part; WILLIAM CATTELL, ESQ. of 3rd part. Whereas ALEXANDER SKENE owned 1300 a., part of 2700 a. in Berkeley Co., bounding SE on SAMUEL WRAGG; NW on WILLIAM WALLACE; SW on PETER CATTELL; NE on Ashley River, & by L & R, 9 & 10 Aug. 1736 conveyed to JOHN SKENE & HANNAH his wife 500 a., part of the 1300 a., bounding SE on other part of 2700 a.; SW on THOMAS GADSDEN; NW on ROBERT WRIGHT, ESQ.; NE on ALEXANDER SKENE, ESQ.; & whereas HANNAH, wife of JOHN SKENE, died, & JOHN became sole owner of the 500 a.; & whereas ALEXANDER SKENE now owns 800 a., the remaining part of the 1300 a.; & whereas JOHN SKENE, this date, gave bond to WILLIAM CATTELL in penal sum of ₤ 3108:12:8 SC money for payment of ₤ 1554:6:4 with interest on 1 Jan. next; now, as security on the bond, JOHN SKENE conveys to CATTELL 500 a., part of 1300 a. in Berkeley Co.; & ALEXANDER SKENE, as further security, conveys to CATTELL, 800 a., the remaining part of the 1300 a.; the lands being free from all mortgages except a mortgage given by ALEXANDER SKENE to WILLIAM TRYON, merchant, of London, dated 23 & 24 Apr. 1722 & L & R dated 30 & 31 Dec. 1735, given with TRYON'S consent, by ALEXANDER SKENE to JOHN CARRUTHERS, master of the ship Malloy galley now residing in SC. Witnesses: GEORGE NICHOLAS, WILLIAM GEORGE FREEMAN. Before JAMES MICHIE, J.P. NATHANIEL JOHNSON, Register. JOHN CATTELL, surviving executor of will of his father WILLIAM CATTELL on 24 Oct. 1770 declared he received from WILLIAM WRAGG, ESQ., full satisfaction of this mortgage.

Book R, p. 232
13 & 14 July 1737
L & R by Mortgage

NATHANIEL PARTRIDGE, planter, to BENJAMIN WHITAKER, ESQ., as security on bond of even date in penal sum of ₤ 126 sterling of Great Britain, for payment of ₤ 62:17:3 on 14 July next; 70 a. in Berkeley Co., on N side Ashley River, bounding N on JOHN PENDARVIS; E on WILLIAM MACLOUGHLING & JAMES PICKENS; SW on SAMUEL WEST; W on marsh & a creek; which land was granted by the Lords Proprs. to MAJOR WILLIAM SMITH, & conveyed by WILLIAM SMITH, son & heir of MAJOR WILLIAM SMITH, to NATHANIEL PARTRIDGE, who, by will bequeathed it to NATHANIEL PARTRIDGE, party hereto. Witnesses: THOMAS WITTER, WILLIAM GEORGE FREEMAN. Before JAMES MICHIC, J.P. NATHANIEL JOHNSON, Register.

BENJAMIN WHITAKER acknowledge receipt of ₤ 41:4:8:1/2, part payment, 26 May 1739. Witness: ROBERT AUSTIN.

Book R, p. 236
18 & 19 July 1737
L & R
JAMES ROULAIN, joiner, & MAGDALAINE (her mark) his wife, to JOHN LAURENS, saddler, of Charleston, as security because LAURENS joined ROULAIN in given a bond this date to CHARLES PINCKNEY, ESQ., in penal sum of ₤ 900 currency for payment of ₤ 450 with interest on 1 Jan. next; part of a moiety or half part of 3 lots near the Market Place in Charleston, #30, #69, #59, fronting S 20 ft. on the Market Place, bounding E 100 ft. on THOMAS ROGER; W on part of the 3 lots; N on part of the 3 lots; also part of lot #98, bounding E 46 ft. on PAUL DE ST. JULIEN; W on part of the above 3 lots; S on ISAAC MAZYCK; N 120 ft. on JANE DUPUY, widow. Witnesses: LAWRENCE COULLIETT, ROBERT BREWTON, JR. Before HENRY GIBBES, J.P. NATHANIEL JOHNSON, Register.

Book R, p. 241
6 & 7 July 1737
L & R
JOHN GOUGH, planter, of St. John's Parish, Berkeley Co., to RICHARD GOUGH, planter, for ₤ 10,000 currency, an inland tract of 2830 a. in Berkeley Co., bounding E on the head of Cooper River; SW on EDWARD HOWARD; NW on vacant land; NE on MICHAEL MAHON; plat certified by THOMAS BROUGHTON, Surv. Gen. Witnesses: FRANCIS ROCHE, JOHN NICHOLSON. Before FRANCIS LEJAU, J.P. NATHANIEL JOHNSON, Register.

Book R, p. 245
28 Feb. & 1 Mar. 1736
L & R by Mortgage
THOMAS (his mark) HUMPRESS, planter, to CHARLES PERONNEAU & CO., both of Colleton Co., for ₤ 279 currency, 140 a. on Wadmalaw Island, bounding E on Bohicket Creek; W on CHARLES JONES; S on land sold by JOHN NEWINTON to WILLIAM TAYLOR but not yet laid out to him; N on a branch of Bohicket Creek. Date of redemption, 1 Mar. 1737. Witnesses: JONATHAN THOMAS, WILLIAM EDDINGS. Before YONGE, J.P. NATHANIEL JOHNSON, Register.

Book R, p. 249
8 & 9 July 1737
L & R by Mortgage
JOHN WATKINS, planter, & MARY (her mark) his wife, of Berkeley Co., to GEORGE LEA, shipwright, of Charleston, as security, for joining WATKINS in giving bond to ANTHONY MATHEWS, CHARLES PINCKNEY, JAMES CROKATT, HENRY PERONNEAU, JR., & JACOB MOTTE, of Charleston; in penal sum of ₤ 1000 currency for payment of ₤ 500 with interest on 25 Mar. next; 175 a. commonly called Hobcaw, in Berkeley Co., bounding NW on WILLIAM WATSON; NE on CARTER COLLIS; other sides on marsh of Cooper River; also 10 Negro slaves. Witnesses: WILLIAM WATSON, ROBERT BREWTON, JR. Before HENRY GIBBES, J.P. NATHANIEL JOHNSON, Register.

Book R, p. 254
16 July 1737
Deed of Sale
TOUNIS VISSIER (THEUNIS VISSER), chandler, of Charleston, to NICHOLAS MATTHISON, blacksmith, for ₤ 700 currency, lot #103 fronting on Queen Street bounding N 100 ft. on MR. BURTALL'S land; E 25 ft. on DR. MARTINI'S land; S 100 ft. on the French Church; all English measure, W 50 ft. on the street leading from MR. BRAND'S to Ashley River. Witnesses: LAWRENCE COULLIETTE, ED. STEPHENS. Before THOMAS DALE, J.P. NATHANIEL JOHNSON, Register.

Book R, p. 255
1 May 1736
(Inaccurate?) Suyt Carolina Dem. Ebaght van MR. WILLEM VISSER E in Stuck grout in Charleston A 50 voet Cnut L 100 Voet (?) lot Noorde o^t MR. PANTAEL lot Oasten of DR. JAN MARTINIES L'SUYDEN of li Laut Van de france Cont^t lot l'Westen Van MR. MANTI JACT EIJ de No. 103 L dat Voor deforn Lan Nigen hondret. Pond. Legge ₤ 900. THUINISS VISSER. Witness: CLASS VISSER. Before HENRY GIBBES, J.P. NATHANIEL JOHNSON, Register.

Book R, p. 256
13 & 14 July 1737
L & R by Mortgage
THOMAS MONCK, ESQ., to JOHN CARRUTHERS, mariner, of London, master of the <u>Molly</u> galley, now living in SC as security on bond of even date in penal sum of ₤ 1000 British for payment of ₤ 500 with interest at City of London on 14 July 1742; the S part of lot #113 fronting 57 ft. 3 in on Church Street; bounding N 113 ft. 4-3/4 in. on other part of said lot; 54 ft. on JOHN BERESFORD; S on NICHOLAS TROTT with that new messuage thereon erected or to be erected; also the lot fronting 57 ft. 8 in. on Church Street, & 49 ft. on Queen Street,

"backwards to Queen Street adjoining to the aforesaid lot" of THOMAS MONCK, & backwards to Church Street from the theatre; also 7-1/2 a. on Charleston Neck, St. Philip's Parish, bounding SE on MRS. DAWES; SW on the high road leading to Charleston; NW on COL. JOSEPH BLAKE; NE on marsh. Witnesses: BENJAMIN WHITAKER, MAURICE LEWIS. Before JOHN HAMMERTON, J.P. NATHANIEL JOHNSON, Register.

Book R, p. 260
1 & 2 July 1737
L & R Quadrupartite

JOSEPH DEWDING, planter, of Craven Co., of 1st part; JOSEPH WRAGG & RICHARD LAMBTON, merchants, of Charleston of 2nd part; EDWARD CROFT, merchant, of Berkeley Co., of 3rd part; PETER HORRY, merchant, of Charleston of 4th part. Whereas JOSEPH DOWDING this date gave a bond to JOSEPH WRAGG & RICHARD LAMBTON in the penal sum of ₺ 5120:15 SC money for payment of ₺ 2560:7:6 on 25 Mar. next; & whereas DOWDING this date gave bond to EDWARD CROFT in the penal sum of ₺ 1035 for payment of ₺ 517:16:11-1/2 on 21 Mar. next; & whereas he also gave bond this date to PETER HORRY in penal sum of ₺ 1470 for payment of ₺ 735 on 25 Mar. next; now, as security on the above bonds, DOWDING conveys to WRAGG, LAMBTON, CROFT & HORRY 500 a. in Berkeley Co., on E side Four Hole Swamp, granted to JOHN MOORE on 17 May 1734 & sold by him to JOSEPH DOWDING. Memo (p. 265). It is agreed that DOWDING shall be obliged to pay only 1/2 the sums on 25 Mar. next & the other half, with interest, on 25 Mar. 1739. Witnesses: WILLIAM WITHERS, THOMAS HEPWORTH. Before ROBERT AUSTIN, J.P. NATHANIEL JOHNSON, Register.

Book R, p. 266
2 Oct. 1735
Deed of Sale

GEORGE BUTTERWORTH, to MOSES MITCHELL, both of Berkeley Co., for ₺ 65 currency, lot #13, part of the undivided land near the town plat of Dorchester, containing 2 a.; sold by THOMAS WARING, attorney for JOSEPH LORD, formerly of SC now of Chatham, New England, on 29 Aug. 1735 to GEORGE BUTTERWORTH. Witnesses: JOHN DORSEY, ROBERT BELL. NATHANIEL JOHNSON, Register.

Book R, p. 267
6 July 1737
L & R by Mortgage

GILES HOLLIDAY, merchant, to JOHN WATSON, merchant, both of Charleston, as security on bond dated 8 June 1737 in penal sum of ₺ 123:7:6 sterling for payment of ₺ 61:13:9 with interest on 1 July next; 500 a. in Williamsburgh Township, Craven Co., bound NW on vacant land; SE on MR. COOKE; NE on Peedee River. Witnesses: JOHN LOUIS, JOHN RATTRAY. Before LEWIS, J.P. NATHANIEL JOHNSON, Register.

Book R, p. 271
19 & 20 July 1737
L & R by Mortgage

JAMES ROBERT, planter, of Craven Co., to RALPH IZARD, ESQ., of Berkeley Co., as security on bond of even date in penal sum of ₺ 976 SC money for payment of ₺ 495:11:6 on 1 Jan. next; 600 a. in Craven Co., through which Peedee River runs; bounding SE on JOHN BROWN; NW on the Rev. MR. SAMUEL HUNTER; SW & NE on vacant land; which 600 a. was granted WILLIAM BROWN on 7 June 1735 who sold the land to ROBERT. Witnesses: ROBERT HALL, THOMAS HEPWORTH. Before ROBERT AUSTIN, J.P. NATHANIEL JOHNSON, Register.

Book R, p. 276
19 & 20 July 1737
L & R

JOHN HAMMERTON, ESQ., & ELIZABETH his wife, of Charleston, to ALEXANDER BENNETT of London, for ₺ 380 sterling of Great Britain, 46 a. in St. Philip's Parish, Charleston, bounding E on JOSEPH BLAKE, ESQ.; S on THOMAS GADSDEN, ESQ.; W & N on RICHARD CARTWRIGHT. Witnesses: MARY HARLEY, JAMES WRIGHT, JAMES MICHIE. Before MAURICE LEWIS, J.P. NICHOLAS JOHNSON, Register.

Book R, p. 280
24 & 25 Mar. 1737
L & R by Mortgage

SAMUEL STOCK, planter, to BENJAMIN WHITAKER, ESQ., both of Berkeley Co., as security on bond of even date in penal sum of ₺ 440 British money for payment of ₺ 220 on 25 Mar. 1738; 210 a. in Berkeley Co. bounding N on WILLIAM BULL, ESQ.; S on MADAM GODFREY & PETER LESADE; E on HENRY SAMWAYS; W on ROBERT WILKINSON; which 210 a. was part of 1080 a. granted by the Lords Proprs. to WILLIAM BULL, ESQ., & sold by him, & MARY his wife, to JOHN GIRARDEAU, & conveyed by him to STOCK. Witnesses: RICHARD MASON, WILLIAM GEORGE FREEMAN. Before MAURICE LEWIS, J.P. NATHANIEL JOHNSON, Register. (See Bk. Y, p. 392 for assignment of mortgage to ROBERT LADSON, executor, of SAMUEL STOCK).

Book R, p. 283   JOHN HAMMERTON, ESQ., of Charleston, to ALEX-
21 & 22 July 1737   ANDER BENNETT, ESQ., of the City of London,
L & R by Mortgage   for ₤ 500 British money, 1000 a. in Granville
                           Co., bounding NW on vacant land; SE on ARTHUR
MIDDLETON, ESQ., also 1000 in Queensborough Township, Craven Co., purchased by HAMMERTON from JAMES WRIGHT, ESQ., bounding NW on GILES HOLLI-
DAY; SE on WILLIAM WALLACE; SW on vacant land; NE on Peedee River; also
800 a. in Williamsburgh Township, Craven Co., purchased by HAMMERTON from
THOMAS LAKE, ESQ., bounding NW on CAPT. ROBERT AUSTIN; NE on Black River;
other sides on vacant land; also lot #13 in Town of Williamsburgh; also
1500 a. in Colleton Co., bounding S on ROBERT WRIGHT, ESQ.; other sides
on vacant land; also 600 a. on S side Black River, in Township of Williamsburgh, Craven Co., purchased by HAMMERTON from MRS. HARGRAVE, bounding
NE on the Rev. MR. JOSEPH BIGNION; other sides on vacant land; also 1 lot
#250 containing half an acre in said town. Date of redemption, 19 July
next. ELIZABETH to renounce her dower within 12 months. Witnesses: THOM-
AS HENNING, MAURICE LEWIS. Before JAMES MICHIE, J.P. NATHANIEL JOHNSON,
Register.

Book R, p. 289   WILLIAM GUY, clerk, of St. Andrews Parish,
21 June 1737   Berkeley Co., to his loving wife REBECCA GUY,
Deed of Gift   for natural love & affection & other consider-
                           ations, lot #16 in St. Andrew's Town near Ash-
ley River Ferry, containing 1/4 a., English measure, bounding SE on
Church Street; SW on Little Street; NE on lot #17; NW on lot #5; also the
brick messuage or tenement on the lot. Witnesses: JANE HILL, JAMES SCAR-
LETT. Before WILLIAM BULL, JR., J.P. NATHANIEL JOHNSON, Register.

Book R, p. 290   WILLIAM GUY, clerk, of St. Andrew's Parish,
21 June 1737   Berkeley Co., to his loving wife REBECCA GUY,
Deed of Gift   for natural love & affection, & other consid-
                           erations, lot #73 in Charleston, fronting 20
ft. on Tradd Street; bounding W on part of same lot allotted to JONATHAN
COLLINGS & SARAH his wife; E on GEORGE DUCAT; S on THOMAS ROSE; also the
tenement on the lot. Witnesses: HENRY CAMPBELL, JAMES SCARLETT. Before
WILLIAM BULL, JR. NATHANIEL JOHNSON, Register.

Book R, p. 290   By warrant signed by Gov. CHARLES CRAVEN, dat-
Warrant   ed 29 Mar. 1715, FRANCIS YONGE, Surv. Gen.,
                           laid out to WILLIAM BROCKINTON 500 a. in
Craven Co., on N side Black River, inland, bounding S on BROCKINTON; E on
SAMUEL COMMANDER; N on SAMUEL COMMANDER & JOSEPH SINGLETARY. Plat certi-
fied & returned 24 Oct. 1717. NATHANIEL JOHNSON, Register.

Book R, p. 291   WILLIAM BROCKINTON, planter, & SARAH his wife,
7 & 8 Feb. 1736   to THOMAS POTTS, planter, both of Craven Co.,
L & R   for ₤ 500 currency, 500 a. in Craven Co.,
                           bounding N on ELISHA SCRIVEN & JEREMIAH ROPER;
E on JOSEPH COMMANDER; S on WILLIAM BROCKINTON; W on JOSEPH ROPER & THOM-
AS POTTS. Whereas on 30 Sept. 1736 Lt. Gov. THOMAS BROUGHTON granted
WILLIAM BROCKINTON 2140 a. in Craven Co., bounding S on Black River; N on
vacant land; E on WILLIAM SWINTON & SAMUEL COMMANDER; W on CAPT. THOMAS
HENNING, JOHN BONNELL, JOSEPH ROPER & ELISHA SCRIVEN; now BROCKINTON
sells 500 a. to POTTS free from SARAH'S claim of dower. Witnesses: HENRY
NEWBERRY, GEORGE WALKER, JOHN SMITH. Before JOHN WALLIS, J.P. NATHANIEL
JOHNSON, Register.

Book R, p. 295   BURTENHEAD BOUTWELL to JOHN COMMANDER, both of
5 & 6 July 1737   Craven Co., for ₤ 200 currency, 200 a. in
L & R   Craven Co., granted 4 Dec. 1735 by Lt. Gov.
                           THOMAS BROUGHTON to BOUTWELL; bounding SW on
THOMAS HURST; NW on JOHN GASQUE; SE & NE on vacant land; free from ELIZA-
BETH'S claim of dower. Witnesses: SAMUEL CLYATT, JOHN SMITH. Before
HENRY GIBBES, J.P. NATHANIEL JOHNSON, Register.

Book R, p. 298   THOMAS LANDEN, carpenter, of Georgetown, Win-
1 Mar. 1736   yaw, Craven Co., to DANIEL LAROCHE & THOMAS
Bond   LAROCHE, merchants, of Georgetown, in penal
                           sum of ₤ 844 SC money for payment of ₤ 422
with interest on 1 Aug. 1737. Witnesses: ISAAC SECARE, JAMES CRADDOCK.

Before WILLIAM WHITESIDE, J.P. NATHANIEL JOHNSON, Register.

Book R, p. 299　　　　　　THOMAS LANDEN, carpenter, to DANIEL LAROCHE &
4 & 5 May 1737　　　　　　THOMAS LAROCHE, merchants, all of Georgetown,
L & R by Mortgage　　　　as security on bond dated 1 Mar. 1736 in penal
　　　　　　　　　　　　　sum of L 844 SC money, for payment of L 422
with interest on 1 Aug. 1737; lot #61 in Georgetown, fronting NE 100 ft.
on Prince Street; NW 217.9 ft. on Broad Street; SW on lots #25 & 26; SE
on lot #62. Witnesses: ISAAC SECARE, JAMES CRADDOCK. Before WILLIAM
WHITESIDE, J.P. NATHANIEL JOHNSON, Register.

Book R, p. 302　　　　　　SAMUEL COMMANDER, planter, to JOHN COMMANDER,
13 Aug. 1737　　　　　　　planter, both of Craven Co., as security on
Mortgage　　　　　　　　　bond dated 6 Aug. 1737, given by SAMUEL & JOHN
　　　　　　　　　　　　　COMMANDER to MRS. ELIZABETH COMMANDER & ELISHA
SCRIVEN, in penal sum of L 2586 SC money for payment of L 1293:5:8 with
interest on 25 Mar. next; the bond being for SAMUEL'S debt; SAMUEL giving
JOHN a bond dated 6 Aug. 1737 in penal sum of L 2586 for payment of
L 1293:5:8 with interest, payable on 25 Mar. next; 265 a. in Craven Co.,
bounding SW on MR. EDWARDS; NW & NE on Black River; SE on MR. DURANT;
which 265 a. was granted 6 Aug. 1735 by Lt. Gov. THOMAS BROUGHTON to SAM-
UEL COMMANDER. Witnesses: JOSEPH DOPSON, JOHN SMITH. Before HENRY GIB-
BES, J.P. NATHANIEL JOHNSON, Register.

Book R, p. 305　　　　　　WILLIAM HENDRICK, planter, of Berkeley Co., to
11 & 12 Aug. 1736　　　　 DOROTHY WEBB, widow, of St. Philip's Parish,
L & R　　　　　　　　　　 Charleston, for L 375 SC money, a part of a
　　　　　　　　　　　　　plantation commonly called Rhettsberry (bury)
Point, in St. Philip's Parish, Charleston, which parcel of land fronts
70 ft. English measure "to the NE & by E on a marsh & going backward of
the same breadth of 75 ft. towards the SW & by W 200 ft."; that is, "from
front line 40 ft. & then leaving 20 ft. for a street or passage & then
going further upon the said line towards the said SW & by W 160 ft. more",
in all 200 ft. which said land fronts "on the said marsh on the SE & by S
on a parcel of land sold by" NICHOLAS TROTT & SARAH his wife to JOHN
SCOTT, shipwright, "on the SW & by W & on the NW & by N on other parts of
the said plantation called Rhettsbury Point." Witnesses: CHRISTOPHER
SMITH, JOHN HAYNES, JAMES FULTON. Before JACOB MOTTE, J.P. NATHANIEL
JOHNSON, Register.

Book R, p. 310　　　　　　WILLIAM BROWN, planter, to JAMES ROBERT, plant-
2 & 3 Feb. 1736　　　　　 er, both of Craven Co., for L 700 currency, &
L & R　　　　　　　　　　 in consideration that WILLIAM BROWN has paid
　　　　　　　　　　　　　all the expenses of surveying, etc., 600 a.
granted as vacant land to WILLIAM BROWN, through the middle which Peedee
River flows, bounding SE on JOHN BROWN; NW on the Rev. MR. SAMUEL HUNTER;
SW & NE on vacant land. Witnesses: SAMUEL HUNTER, ANDREW DELAVILLETTE,
WILLIAM FLEMING. Before ROBERT AUSTIN, J.P. NATHANIEL JOHNSON, Register.

Book R, p. 313　　　　　　JAMES WRIGHT, ESQ. to ROBERT HUME, ESQ., both
24 & 25 Aug. 1737　　　　 of Charleston, for L 125 SC money, 1000 a. on
L & R　　　　　　　　　　 Lynch's Lake within Queensborough Township,
　　　　　　　　　　　　　Craven Co., bounding NE on JOSEPH JOLLEY & vacant land; other sides on vacant land; which 1000 a. were granted by
letters patent dated 13 July last, signed by Lt. Gov. THOMAS BROUGHTON,
to JAMES WRIGHT. Witnesses: JERMYN WRIGHT, THOMAS HEPWORTH. Before ROB-
ERT AUSTIN, J.P. NATHANIEL JOHNSON, Register.

Book R, p. 317　　　　　　MARTHA DANIEL, widow, to SARAH DANIEL, widow,
16 Apr. 1719　　　　　　　both of Charleston, the N part of lot #34,
L & R　　　　　　　　　　 fronting E 100 ft. towards Cooper River; bound-
　　　　　　　　　　　　　ing W on unknown land; N on the wall or fortification of Charleston; S on MARTHA DANIEL; also all the sandy beach,
commonly called the flat directly fronting the 150 ft. down to low water
mark. Whereas SARAH DANIEL owned for the term of her natural life 2 lots
#33 & 34, in Charleston, 600 ft. front, bounding E on Cooper River, W on
unknown land, N on marsh belonging to MARTHA DANIEL; S on part of a lot
belonging to FRANCIS HOLMES; & whereas SARAH on 16 Apr. 1719 surrendered
the 2 lots to MARTHA & her heirs, to whom the inheritance belonged by the
terms of the will of the Hon. COL. ROBERT DANIEL, husband of MARTHA; now

MARTHA conveys part of lot #34 to SARAH. Witnesses: WILLIAM BLAKEWAY, WILLIAM BILLING. NATHANIEL JOHNSON, Register.

Book R, p. 319
12 Aug. 1736
Renunciation of Dower

(See p. 189). ANNA SHUTE, wife of JOSEPH SHUTE, merchant, of St. Philip's Parish, Charleston, appeared before the Hon. ROBERT WRIGHT, C.J., & acknowledged that she freely joined with her husband in conveying to JAMES THOMSON, butcher, of Charleston, their interest in the land owned by JOSEPH & ANNA SHUTE & ISABELA KIMBERLY, being 6 a. in Charleston Neck, bounding E on the Broad Path; S on Free School road; W on Free School land; N on JOSEPH or SAMUEL WRAGG. NATHANIEL JOHNSON, Register.

Book R, p. 321
23 July 1737
Deed of Gift

JAMES WALKER, to JOHN FRASER, both of Charleston, for friendship & affection, 350 a. in Colleton Co., bounding S on DR. ORD; W on WILLIAM HARVEY & JOSEPH FOX, ESQRS.; E on JOHN BAYLY. Witnesses: JORDAN ROCHE, JAMES MATHEWS, JAMES WEDDERBURN. Before THOMAS DALE, J.P. NATHANIEL JOHNSON, Register.

Book R, p. 322
19 & 20 Apr. 1737
L & R

JOSEPH ELLIOTT, planter (son of WILLIAM ELLIOTT) & ELIZABETH his wife, of Berkeley Co., to JOSEPH ELLICOTT, carpenter, of Colleton Co., for ₺ 1000 SC money, 348-1/2 a. in Colleton Co., bounding N & E on THOMAS ELIOTT (son of THOMAS ELLIOTT); W on JAMES SCREVEN; S on JOSEPH ELLIOTT; free from ELIZABETH'S claim of dower. Witnesses: WILLIAM CHAPMAN, DANIEL (his mark) BETHRAY, SUSANNAH (her mark) GORDIN. Before ROBERT AUSTIN, J.P. NATHANIEL JOHNSON, Register.

Book R, p. 326
21 & 22 Apr. 1737
L & R

JOSEPH ELLICOTT, carpenter, of Colleton Co., to JOSEPH ELLIOTT (son of WILLIAM ELLIOTT) of Berkeley Co., for ₺ 1000 SC money, 348-1/2 a. in Colleton Co., bounding N & E on THOMAS ELLIOTT (son of THOMAS ELLIOTT); W on JAMES SCREVEN; S on JOSEPH ELLIOTT. Witnesses: THOMAS SIMMONDS, THOMAS ELLIOTT, THOMAS JONES. Before THOMAS DALE, J.P. NATHANIEL JOHNSON, Register.

Book R, p. 330
15 & 17 Aug. 1737
L & R by Mortgage

GILES HOLLIDAY, merchant, to JOHN WATSON, merchant, both of Charleston, as security on bond dated 8 June 1737 in penal sum of ₺ 123:7:6 sterling for payment of ₺ 61:13:9 with interest on 1 July (Jan?) next; 500 a. in Craven Co., bounding SW on JOHN GOODWYNN & THOMAS CHARMOCK; NW on MAURICE LEWIS, ESQ.; SE on ISAAC AMYAND; NE on vacant land. Witnesses: JOHN RATTRAY, JOHN LOUIS. Before MAURICE LEWIS, J.P. NATHANIEL JOHNSON, Register.

Book R, p. 334
29 & 30 Aug. 1737
L & R

NICHOLAS MATTHISEN, blacksmith, & MARY (her mark) his wife, to ANTHONY PORTALL, all of Charleston, for ₺ 500 currency, part of lot #103 in Charleston which he purchased from THOMAS VISSER; fronting W 50 ft. on King Street which leads by MR. BRAND'S to Ashley River; bounding S 100 ft. on land belonging to the French Church; E on part same lot belonging to DR. JOHN MARTINI; N on part same lot belonging to ANTHONY PORTALL. Witnesses: ROBERT BREWTON, JR., SAMUEL GLESER. Before THOMAS DALE, J.P. NATHANIEL JOHNSON, Register.

Book R, p. 338
13 & 14 Jan. 1735
L & R by Mortgage

WILLIAM LINTHWAITE, brazier, of Charleston, to MARGARET CHILD, widow, of Berkeley Co., as security on bond of even date in penal sum of ₺ 739:6:8 SC money for payment of ₺ 869:13:4 on 14 Jan. 1736, part of lot #105, bounding E 80 ft. on JAMES PAINE; W on part same lot; N on part same lot; S 60 on "the Broad Street wherein the Market is now kept." Witnesses: FRANCIS LEJAU, WILLIAM HAMILTON. Before ANTHONY BONNEAU, J.P. NATHANIEL JOHNSON, Register. This mortgage assigned by FRANCIS LEJAU, Executor of MARGARET CHILD, to WILLIAM HOPTON who paid LEJAU the full amount due, being later repaid by ELEANOR LINTHWAITE, widow & executrix of WILLIAM LINTHWAITE. This mortgage & the original conveyance from JOB ROTHMAHLER to WILLIAM LINTHWAIT were in HOPTON'S (?) possession but were burned "in the dreadful fire in Charleston

18 Nov. 1740."

Book R, p. 342　　　　　　　THOMAS BAKER, blacksmith, to ISAAC HOLMES,
4 & 5 Apr. 1737　　　　　　merchant, both of Charleston, for ₤ 307:5 SC
L & R by Mortgage　　　　　money, 130 a. in Berkeley Co., part Ashley
　　　　　　　　　　　　　　Barony or St. Giles, bounding NW on JOHN STE-
VENS; NE on Ashley River; SE on MICHAEL BACON & JOSIAH OSGOOD; SW on SAM-
UEL CLARKE; which 130 a. were purchased by BAKER from JACOB SATUR. Date
of redemption, 5 Apr. 1738. Witnesses: BENJAMIN GODIN, JR., JOHN MCKEN-
ZIE. Before HENRY GIBBES, J.P. NATHANIEL JOHNSON, Register.

Book R, p. 347　　　　　　　JOHN BRAND, gentleman, to JOHN STEVENSON &
12 Dec. 1729　　　　　　　 MARY his wife, all of Charleston, for ₤ 150
Bill of Sale　　　　　　　 currency, 1/2 of lot #187 in Charleston,
　　　　　　　　　　　　　　fronting E 42 ft. on a little street leading
from Ashley River; W on ELIAS HANCOCK; N 200 ft. on JOHN BRAND; S on
other half of lot belonging to JOHN LEAY & MARY his wife. Witnesses:
JOHN DORSEY, HUMPHREY PEYER, THOMAS BECKETT. BECKETT appeared before
DANIEL GREENE, J.P. in May 1731 & before HENRY GIBBES, J.P. in May 1735.
NATHANIEL JOHNSON, Register.

Book R, p. 349　　　　　　　MARMADUKE DANIELL, gentleman, to (CAPT.) JOHN
22 & 23 Jan. 1723　　　　　HARLESTON, gentleman, both of Berkeley Co.,
L & R　　　　　　　　　　　 for ₤ 800 SC money, the N part of lot #34 in
　　　　　　　　　　　　　　Charleston, near Craven's Bastion, fronting E
100 ft. on Cooper River; W on the Hon. JAMES MOORE, ESQ.; N on a wall or
fortification of the town; S on MARTHA DANIELL, widow, (now MARTHA LOGAN,
widow); also all the sandy beach or "flat" directly fronting the 100 ft.
down to low water mark. Witnesses: NICHOLAS TROTT, PETER TAYLOR, CAPT.
ELIAS BALL, ARTHUR HAMILTON. Before ANTHONY BONNEAU, J.P. NATHANIEL
JOHNSON, Register.

Book R, p. 355　　　　　　　ELIZABETH (her mark) FAIRCHILD, widow & execu-
14 & 15 Feb. 1736　　　　　trix of will of THOMAS FAIRCHILD, butcher of
L & R　　　　　　　　　　　 Charleston, & WILLIAM FAIRCHILD, butcher, (son,
　　　　　　　　　　　　　　devise & executor of said THOMAS FAIRCHILD),
to BENJAMIN MAZYCK, merchant, of Charleston, for ₤ 1400 SC money, 25 a.
on Charleston Neck, St. Philip's Parish, Charleston, bounding E on the
Broad Path; N on WILLIAM ELLIOTT (formerly CAPT. BENJAMIN SCHENGKINGH);
W on a small creek; S on SAMUEL WRAGG. Whereas CATHERINE LA POSTRE, widow, of Charleston, was granted the above mentioned 25 a. by the Lords
Proprs. on 21 Mar. 1715 & be deed of feoffment dated 26 Mar. 1719 conveyed the land to THOMAS FAIRCHILD & RICHARD FAIRCHILD (brothers); & whereas
RICHARD died before the property was divided & the whole became the prop-
erty of THOMAS FAIRCHILD, who, by will dated 26 June 1733, impowered his
executors (ELIZABETH & WILLIAM) to dispose of his real & personal estate
in order to pay any debt incurred by him; now the executors sell to
MAZYCK. Witnesses: JOSEPH FIDLER, ANN GALLWAY, ISAAC MAZYCK. Before
HENRY GIBBES, J.P. NATHANIEL JOHNSON, Register.

Book R, p. 360　　　　　　　HUGH WIRE, store keeper, of Granville Co., to
13 & 14 Sept. 1737　　　　 LEWIS JONES, clerk, of same place, as security
L & R by Mortgage　　　　　on bond dated 8 Sept. 1737 in penal sum of
　　　　　　　　　　　　　　₤ 4000 for payment of ₤ 2000 currency on 1
Jan. 1741; 500 a. on Port Royal Island, bounding E on Dicks Buck Creek; N
on ALEXANDER MACKEY; W on vacant land; S on KNATCHBULL. Witnesses: SAM-
UEL CLEE, ISAAC PARMENTER. Before THOMAS WIGG, J.P. NATHANIEL JOHNSON,
Register.

Book R, p. 364　　　　　　　JOSEPH HARLEY, planter, to JOHN MATHEWES, both
20 & 21 Sept. 1737　　　　 of Colleton Co., as security on bond of even
L & R by Mortgage　　　　　date in penal sum of ₤ 2347:5 SC money for
　　　　　　　　　　　　　　payment of ₤ 1173:12:6 on 21 Sept. 1739; 410 a.
in Colleton Co., bounding W on freshes of Edisto River; E on JOSEPH DID-
COTT; S on JOSEPH ANDREW; W on PAUL HAMILTON. Witnesses: JAMES MATHEWES,
OBADIAH WILKINS. Before JACOB MOTTE, J.P. NATHANIEL JOHNSON, Register.

Book R, p. 369　　　　　　　JAMES LAURENS & JOHN LAURENS, saddlers, of
12 July 1726　　　　　　　 Charleston, as attorneys (by virtue of a let-
Bond　　　　　　　　　　　　ter from their brother CHARLES, dated 25 Jan.

1724/5) for their brother CHARLES LAURENS, cooper, formerly of Charleston but now living in Philadelphia, give bond to NOAH SERRE, planter, of Craven Co., for ₤ 200 currency, as security on release of even date, conveying 250 a. in Craven Co. to SERRE; which land was granted by the Lords Proprs. to PETER PERDRIAU. Witnesses: HENRY GIGNILLIAT, JOHN CROFT. Before WILLIAM RHETT. NATHANIEL JOHNSON, Register.

Book R, p. 370
11 & 12 July 1726
L & R

JAMES LAURENS & JOHN LAURENS, saddlers, of Charleston, as attorneys (by virtue of a letter from their brother CHARLES, dated 25 Jan. 1724/5) for their brother CHARLES LAURENS, cooper, formerly of Charleston but now of Philadelphia; to NOAH SERRE, planter of Craven Co.; for ₤ 40 currency; 250 a. in Craven Co. formerly granted on 6 Sept. 1714 by the Lords Proprs. to PETER PERDRIAU, bounding SW on Santee River; W on PETER ROYER. Witnesses: HENRY GIGNILLIAT, JOHN CROFT. Before WILLIAM RHETT. NATHANIEL JOHNSON, Register.

Book R, p. 373
1 Sept. 1737
Bill of Sale

FRANCIS (FRANCOIS) DEMANE, of Granville Co., to JOHN DE LA BERE of Beaufort, for ₤ 250 currency, 1 Mullatto boy. Date of redemption 1 Jan. 1737. Witnesses: JOHN PRICE, HUGH WIRE. Before RICHARD WOODWARD, J.P. NATHANIEL JOHNSON, Register.

Book R, p. 376
17 Sept. 1737
Release by Mortgage

RICHARD GOUGH, planter, of Berkeley Co., to JOHN HENTIE, surveyor, of St. James Santee, Craven Co., for ₤ 800 SC money, 720 a.; bounding NW on PETER GUERARD; SE on RICHARD GOUGH; SW on ELIAS BALL; NE on DANIEL HUGER; as by plat signed by JOHN GOUGH, JR., Dep. Sur. Whereas RICHARD GOUGH owns about 3500 a. on E branch of Cooper River, which land was conveyed to him by L & R, 7 July 1737 by his father JOHN GOUGH. If RICHARD GOUGH, or his father JOHN, pay HENTIE ₤ 800 on 3 Jan. next (for which payment JOHN GOUGH has given his bond this date) this deed to be void. Witnesses: JOHN GOUGH, JR., EDWARD GOUGH. Before FRANCIS LEJAU, J.P. NATHANIEL JOHNSON, Register.

Book R, p. 377
5 Sept. 1737
Mortgage

EXPERIENCE HOWARD, house carpenter, to JOHN BEE, planter, both of Charleston, as security on bond, of even date in penal sum of ₤ 1000 SC money for payment of ₤ 500 on 28 Mar. next; the house in which he lives & part of a lot, on Rhettsbery Point Town; also 5 Negro men, 4 Negro women. Witnesses: JUSTINUS STOLL, DAUCHTERLONY (D. AUCHTERLONG?). Before JACOB MOTTE, J.P. Possession given by delivery of "earth & twig as use is," also "1 wench." Witnesses: JOHN BEDON, DAUCHTERLONY. NATHANIEL JOHNSON, Register. This mortgage assigned to ELIZABETH JENYS, mother of WILLIAM RAVEN. RAVEN acknowledged to HOPTON receipt of satisfaction 18 Dec. 1762.

Book R, p. 378
12 & 13 Sept. 1737
L & R by Mortgage

WILLIAM BARTON, planter, to ELIZABETH HILL, widow & executrix of will of CHARLES HILL, ESQ., as security on bond of even date in penal sum of ₤ 228:12 British money for payment of ₤ 114:6 on 1 Jan. next; 750 a. in Craven Co., adjoining JOSEPH JOHNSON'S land, bounding S on vacant land; W & N on JOHN VICARIDGE; which tract was granted to HENRY LEWIS & conveyed by him to WILLIAM BARTON. Witnesses: GEORGE FREEMAN, GEORGE NICHOLAS, JR. Before ROBERT AUSTIN, J.Q. NATHANIEL JOHNSON, Register.

Book R, p. 382
11 Oct. 1737
Agreement

THOMAS ELLIOTT, son of THOMAS ELLIOTT, gentleman, of Stono, & SUSANNAH his wife of 1st part; & THOMAS GATES, shop keeper, of Charleston of 2nd part. Whereas Lt. Gov. THOMAS BROUGHTON by warrant dated Jan. 1735, directed to JAMES ST. JOHN, Sur. Gen., directing him to lay out a tract of 5000 a. on Waccamaw Neck, Craven Co., bounding E on JOSEPH PRINCE & ELIAS FOISSIN; SE on JOHN ALSTON; NW on Soccateg Creek; & to return the plat, certified by him, to the Secretary's office in order that a grant might be made; & whereas he had the land surveyed in the name of THOMAS ELLIOTT & a grant dated 5 Aug. last past recorded in Book G. G. fol. 378 by JAMES _____, Dep. Sec., witnesses by Lt. Gov. THOMAS BROUGHTON; .... & whereas the name of THOMAS ELLIOTT was used only in trust for THOMAS GATES (GATES having paid expenses); now THOMAS & SUSANNAH ELLIOTT agree to protect GATES & suffer him to hold the land. Witnesses: RICHARD GODFREY, MARY LEECH. Before HENRY GIBBES, J.P. NATHANIEL JOHNSON, Register.

Book R, p. 384 By order of Gov. ROBERT JOHNSON, dated 15 June
Warrant 1732, JAMES ST. JOHN, Sur. Gen., had 180 a. in
St. John's Parish, Berkeley Co., surveyed for GEORGE COLLETON; bounding E & N on the estate of MAJOR CHARLES COLLETON; S on JOHN COLLETON, ESQ.; NW on RENE MERCHANT. NATHANIEL JOHNSON, Register.

Book R, p. 384 GEORGE II to GEORGE COLLETON, 180 a., in Berke-
Sept. 1736 ley Co., bounding E & N on the estate of MAJOR
Grant CHARLES COLLETON; S on JOHN COLLETON; NW on
RENE MERCHANT; with the usual provisoes. Signed by Lt. Gov. THOMAS BROUGHTON & ALEXANDER CRAMAHE. NATHANIEL JOHNSON, Register.

Book R, p. 386 JAMES ST. JOHN, Sur. Gen., by order of Gov.
6 Oct. 1735 ROBERT JOHNSON, caused 105 a. in Berkeley Co.,
Warrant to be surveyed for GEORGE COLLETON, ESQ.;
bounding S on said COLLETON & MRS. RUSSELL; N on JAMES RIPALT; E on MRS. ANN COLLETON. NATHANIEL JOHNSON, Register.

Book R, p. 386 GEORGE II to GEORGE COLLETON, ESQ., 105 a. in
12 Dec. 1735 (?) Berkeley Co., bounding S on JOHN COLLETON; W
Grant on said COLLETON & MRS. RUSSELL; N on JAMES
RIPALT; E on ANN COLLETON; with the usual provisoes. Signed by Lt. Gov. THOMAS BROUGHTON & ALEXANDER CRAMAHE. NATHANIEL JOHNSON, Register.

Book R, p. 387 GEORGE COLLETON, ESQ., & ELIZABETH his wife,
11 & 12 Mar. 1736 to THOMAS MONCK, ESQ.; all of Berkeley Co.;
L & R for ₤ 570 currency, 2 tracts, total 285 a.;
105 a., English measure, bounding S on JOHN COLLETON, ESQ.; W on GEORGE COLLETON & MRS. RUSSELL; N on JAMES RIPAULT; E on heirs of MRS. ANNE COLLETON; & 180 a. bounding E & N on estate of MAJOR CHARLES COLLETON; S on JOHN COLLETON; N on RENE MERCHAND. ELIZABETH renounces her claim of dower. Witnesses: J. BADENHOP, MAURICE LEWIS. NATHANIEL JOHNSON, Register.

Book R, p. 392 ELIZABETH COLLETON, wife of GEORGE COLLETON,
15 Mar. 1736 ESQ., of St. John's Parish, Berkeley Co., ap-
Renunciation of Dower peared before the Hon. ROBERT WRIGHT, C.J. &
voluntarily renounced her title of dower to the 2 tracts conveyed to THOMAS MONCK (p. 387). NATHANIEL JOHNSON, Register.

Book R, p. 393 BENJAMIN WHITAKER, ESQ., of Charleston, to
8 & 9 June 1737 THOMAS MONCK, ESQ., for ₤ 1100, a lot in
L & R Charleston, fronting 57 ft. 8 in. on Church
Street; 49 ft. on Queen Street; adjoining lot of THOMAS MONCK & backward to Church Street from the theatre. Witnesses: MAURICE LEWIS, GILES HOLLIDAY. NATHANIEL JOHNSON, Register.

Book R, p. 396 ANNE HEPWORTH, widow of THOMAS HEPWORTH, to
16 & 17 Dec. 1736 JOHN BARKSDALE, gentleman. Whereas THOMAS
L & R HEPWORTH, ESQ., by will dated 11 Sept. 1727
devised to his loving wife, ANNE, for the term of her natural life, the new messuage or tenement adjoining his dwelling house, being part of a lot, he bought from MR. DISTON; & after ANNE'S death, to his daughter, ANNE HEPWORTH; & whereas daughter ANNE (with her mother's consent) married JOHN BARKSDALE; now for natural love & affection & other considerations, ANNE, the mother, conveys to JOHN BARKSDALE the house mentioned above. Witnesses: C. SACKVILLE, MRS. SARAH BARKSDALE. Before HENRY GIBBES, J.P. NATHANIEL JOHNSON, Register.

Book R, p. 400 PAUL HAMILTON, to JOSEPH GIBBON, planter, both
29 & 30 Mar. 1737 of Colleton Co., for ₤ 2650 SC money, 1060 a.
L & R in Colleton Co., granted to HAMILTON by

letters patent, dated 12 Oct. 1736 & signed by Lt. Gov. THOMAS BROUGHTON; bounding N on THOMAS WINBORN & Leadenway Creek; E on MR. JARVIS & CHARLES JONES; W on a branch of Bohicket Creek, JOHN HEXT THOMAS WINBORN & Leadenway Creek; S on Bohicket Creek. Witnesses: WILLIAM PETER, THOMAS SACKVILLE, WILLIAM BURD. Before JACOB MOTTE, J.P. NATHANIEL JOHNSON, Register.

Book R, p. 404
24 & 25 Feb. 1736
L & R

SAMUEL JONES, ESQ., & MARY his wife, of St. Philip's Parish, Charleston, to JOHN BULL, planter, of Colleton Co., for L 100 currency; 120 a. between PonPon & Ashepoo Rivers, Colleton Co., bounding SW on a creek of Ahsepoo River & HENRY YONGE; NW on WILLIAM OSWELL & ISRAEL ANDREWS; NE on CAPT. ANTHONY MATHEWS; SE on HENRY LIVINGSTON & PAUL HAMILTON. Witnesses: CHARLES PINCKNEY, ROBERT BREWTON, JR. Before HENRY GIBBES, J.P. NATHANIEL JOHNSON, Register.

Book R, p. 408
21 & 22 Oct. 1737
L & R by Mortgage

JOSEPH BUGNION, clerk, of St. James Santee, to WILLIAM CATTELL, JR. & GEORGE AUSTIN, merchants, of Charleston, as security on bond of even date in penal sum of L 7000 SC money for payment of L 3516 on 1 Jan. 1738; 600 a. in Craven Co., bounding SE on JAMES ROBERT (formerly RALPH IZARD); NE partly on BOHANNON'S; N on JOHN DUBOSE; SW on Wadbaccan Creek; NW on JAMES ROBERT; also 250 a. in Craven Co., bounding SW on MR. DURANT; SE on DANIEL JAUDON; other sides on vacant land; ELIZABETH, wife of JOSEPH BUGNION, to renounce her dower within 12 months. Witnesses: JACOB PICHARD, JOHN RATTRAY. Before MAURICE LEWIS, J.P. NATHANIEL JOHNSON, Register.

Book R, p. 412
9 Mar. 1736
Mortgage

JOHN DOMINIQUE AUDET (ODDET), smith, to JOSEPH BARRAGUY, laborer, both of Granville Co., for L 115:13:9 currency, 1/5 oa an acre (7/8 of a lot) with house with 2 rooms, oven, chimney & a smith shop in the town of Purysburgh & a pendulum clock an assignment on the estate of the late COL. PURY # L 52-1/2 currency. Date of redemption, Mar. 1737. House with 2 rooms & chimney, & smith's shop valued at L 60; a pendulum clock valued at L 15; an assignment on CHARLES PURY, being the debt of the late COL. PURY, L 525:1-1/2 total L 127:5:1-1/2. Witnesses: PIERE ST. BLANQUART, ANDREW VERDIER. Before PETER LAFITTE, J.P. NATHANIEL JOHNSON, Register. (See 414 on page 24).

Book R, p. 414
Certificate

At the request of WILLIAM JONES on ___ Sept. 1734, GOUGH, Dep. Sur., surveyed 30 a., part of grant to STEPHEN WILLIAMS; bounding W on RICHARD CAPERS; SW on part said land; NE on CAPT. GEORGE BENESON. NATHANIEL JOHNSON, Register.

Book R, p. 414
27 July 1734
Bond

WILLIAM (his mark) JONES, planter, to JOHN EVANS, shipwright, in penal sum of L 300 currency for payment of L 300 currency for payment of L 150 on 1 Jan. 1735. Witnesses: THOMAS KER, CHARLES FOGG. NATHANIEL JOHNSON, Register.

Book R, p. 415
27 July 1734
L & R

JOHN EVANS, shipwright, & ANNE his wife, to WILLIAM JONES, planter, all of Christ Church Parish, Berkeley Co., for L 300 SC money, 30 a. English measure, part of 50 a., on NW end of the NE part of the 50 a., on NW side of "She-A-Wee" Sound on a place called Boo Wat breach; bounding SW on JOHN & ANNE EVANS; NE on GEORGE BENTLEY & vacant land. Witnesses: THOMAS KER, CHARLES FOGGE, ANDREW L____. NATHANIEL JOHNSON, Register.

Book R, p. 419
29 Sept. 1737
Deed of Sale

RICHARD ALLEIN, gentleman, & ESTER his wife, of St. James Santee, Craven Co., to ROBERT AUSTIN, merchant, of Charleston, for L 800; 400 a. part of 550 a. belonging to RICHARD ALLEIN, lying partly in St. James Santee, that is, the part adjoining the land which ALLEIN sold recently to EDWARD THOMAS; the 400 a. lying in a long square from the swamp on parallel lines with THOMAS'S land, & bounding N on Santee River Swamp; E on THOMAS; W on remainder of the 550 a.; S on vacant land; "with the benefit of running the swamp land fronting the same to Santee River." Witnesses: JOB ROTHMAHLER, JOHN COACHMAN, SAMUEL THOMAS. Before MAURICE LEWIS, J.P. NATHANIEL JOHNSON, Register.

Book R, p. 421 ROBERT WRIGHT, the elder, ESQ., to JOSEPH
24 & 25 Sept. 1737 WRAGG, ESQ., both of Berkeley Co., as security
L & R by Mortgage for payment of Ł 9780:13:6 & interest, &
Ł 612:17:2 on 20 Nov. next; several tracts total 9000 a.; 1000 a. in Colleton Co., on E branch of Saltcatcher River Swamp; bounding S on JOHN ROBERT'S Barony; other sides on vacant land; also 2000 a. in Craven Co., on NE side of Peedee River in Queensborough Township, bounding NW on JOHN HAMMERTON, ESQ. & vacant land; NE on vacant land; SE on JOSEPH WRAGG, ESQ. & vacant land; SW on ____; also 2000 a. in Granville Co., rounding NW on surveyed land; SE on WILLIAM FISHBURN; also 2000 a. in Craven Co., Queensborough Township, bounding NW & SE on vacant land; NE on HENRY MICHAEL COOK; SW on LYNCHES; also 2000 a. in Amelia Township on SW side Santee River, Berkeley Co., bounding NE on lands within said township part belonging to ROBERT WRIGHT & part not laid out; all other sides on land in the township not yet laid out; also lot #73 in Amelia Township containing 1/2 a., bounding NE on the front street; SE on lot #72 not laid out; SW on #75 not laid out; NW on #74 belonging to JOHN BERESFORD, ESQ. Whereas on 6 Feb. 1735 ROBERT WRIGHT was granted 1000 a. in Colleton Co.; & on 25 June 1736 he was granted 2000 a. in Craven Co.; & on 30 Sept. 1736, 2000 a. in Granville Co.; & on 12 Nov. 1736, 2000 a. in Craven Co., Queensborough Township; & on 12 Nov. 1736, 2000 a. in Amelia Township, Berkeley Co.; also lot #73 (1/2 a.) in Amelia Township; & whereas ROBERT WRIGHT the elder & ROBERT WRIGHT, the younger, his son, gave bond dated May 1730 to JOSEPH WRAGG for payment of a total of Ł 789:13:6 still unpaid on date specified, to be secured by the various lands granted (above); & whereas ROBERT WRIGHT the elder, gave JOSEPH WRAGG another bond, of even date, in penal sum of Ł 3225 for payment of Ł 1612:17:2 SC money on 20 Nov. next; now WRIGHT conveys the 9000 a. to WRAGG as security on the 2 bonds. Witnesses: EDWARD WIGG, WILLIAM WITHERS. Before ROBERT AUSTIN, J.P. NATHANIEL JOHNSON, Register.

Book R, p. 428 JOHN SPENCER, planter, & DOROTHY his wife, of
16 & 18 July 1737 Craven Co., to ANTHONY BONNEAU, JR., planter,
L & R of Berkeley Co., for Ł 1200 SC money, 3 tracts
of land, total 600 a. in Craven Co.; 2 of them containing 250 a. each, adjoining, bounding N on Santee River; E on RALPH JERMAN; S on vacant lands; W on DANIEL HORRY; also 100 a., the middle part of an island in Santee River, bounding E on RALPH JERMAN; W on DANIEL HORRY; N & S on Santee River. Whereas JOHN, Lord Granville, Palatine, & the Lords Proprs. on 5 May 1704 granted DANIEL MCGRIGORY 500 a. in Craven Co., bounding N on Santee River; E on PATRICK ____ (now ISAAC MA Y MAZYCK); S on vacant land; W on RICHARD CODNER (now JOHN SPENCER); & whereas MCGREGORY by deed of feoffment on 10 Oct. 1704 conveyed the 500 a. to JACOB LAPOTRE, merchant, of Charleston & ELIAS HORRY, planter, of Craven Co.; & whereas ELIAS HORRY by deed of feoffment dated 10 Oct. 1708, conveyed his half of the land to JACOB LAPOTRE, who now became sole owner; & whereas JOHN, Lord Granville & the Lords Proprs. on 12 Jan. 1705 granted JACOB LAPOTRE 200 a., English measure, part of an island in Santee River in Craven Co. opposite the 500 a.; bounding N on Santee River; E on Santee River & Wahaw Creek; S on said creek; W on lands not laid out (now DANIEL HORRY); & whereas JACOB LAPOTRE by deed of feoffment dated 12 Nov. 1709 conveyed the 500 a. & 200 a. to JOHN FILLEBIEN, planter, of Berkeley Co.; & he, with KATHERINE his wife, by deed of feoffment conveyed the 2 tracts to MARK SLOWMAN & JOSEPH SPENCER, planter, of Craven Co.; & whereas they, in SPENCER'S lifetime, did not divide the land but agreed that SPENCER should have the W half of both tracts & SLOWMAN the E half; & whereas the Lords Proprs. on 23 July 1711 granted RICHARD CODNER, planter, of Berkeley Co., 250 a. in Craven Co., bounding N on Santee River; E on JOHN SPENCER (formerly DANIEL MCCRIGORY); S on vacant land; W on vacant land (now DANIEL HORRY); & whereas RICHARD CODNER & SABINA his wife, by deed of feoffment dated 11 Sept. 1814 (/) conveyed the 250 a. to JOSEPH SPENCER, planter, of Craven Co. (father of JOHN SPENCER) who, by will dated 30 Nov. 1729 conveyed the 3 tracts to his son JOHN; & whereas MARK SLOWMAN & JOHN SLOWMAN (MARK'S eldest son & heir) by deed of feoffment dated 1 Mar. 1736 conveyed to JOHN SPENCER all the W half of the 500 a. & of the 200 a. (part of the island); now JOHN SPENCER sells to ANTHONY BONNEAU. Witnesses: RALPH JERMAN, FRANCIS DESCHAMPS, AUGUSTUS

LAURENS.   Before ANTHONY BONNEAU, ESQ., J.P.   NATHANIEL JOHNSON, Register.

Book R, p. 435 WILLIAM GREENALND, planter, & MARTHA his wife,
28 & 29 Oct. 1737 of Berkeley Co., to CAPT. JOSEPH CANTEY, of
L & R Craven Co., for L 30 currency, 300 a. in Craven Co., granted GREENLAND by Lt. Gov. THOMAS
BROUGHTON 16 Dec. 1736; bounding W on EDWARD THOMAS; E on CAPT. JOSEPH
CANTEY; other sides on vacant land. Witnesses: JAMES MCDONALD, MARTHA
WARD, JOHN COOK. Before THOMAS FERGUSON, J.P. NATHANIEL JOHNSON, Register.

Book R, p. 438 JOSEPH PENDARVIS, planter, son & heir of JOHN
6 & 7 Sept. 1731 PENDARVIS, of Berkeley Co., to ELISHA CARLILE,
L & R planter, of Colleton Co., for L 80 currency,
100 a., part of 500 a. in Colleton Co., granted by the Rt. Hon. CHARLES CRAVEN & the Lords Proprs. on 25 Feb. 1714 to
JOHN PENDARVIS; the 100 a. bounding N on ELISHA CARLILE; E on MRS. ANN
DRAYTON; W on JOHN CATTELL; S on JOSEPH PENDARVIS. Witnesses: JOHN BARTON, WILLIAM SMITH. Before THOMAS DALE, J.P.

Book R, p. 441 JOSEPH HASFORT, planter, & HANNAH his wife, of
22 June 1733 Berkeley Co., to ELISHA CARLILE, carpenter,
Lease for 5 shillings currency, 100 a. in St. Paul's
Parish, Colleton Co., bounding according to
plat attached to grant. Witnesses: WALTER GOREING, SAMUEL ELMES. Delivery of possession, livery & seizin witnessed. Before THOMAS LAMBOLL, J.P.
NATHANIEL JOHNSON, Register.

Book R, p. 443 ELISHA CARLILE, planter, with the consent of
22 & 23 Sept. 1737 ELIZABETH (her mark) his wife, to CHARLES FIL-
L & R BIN (FILLEBIEN?), both of Berkeley Co., of 100
a. each. Whereas Gov. CHARLES CRAVEN & the
Lords Proprs. on 25 Feb. 1714 granted JOHN PENDARVIS 500 a. in Colleton;
& whereas, after his death his son & heir, JOSEPH PENDARVIS, by L & R dated 6 & 7 Sept. 1731 sold 100 a. (a part of the 500) to ELISHA CARLILE,
bounding N on CARLILE; E on DRAYTON; W on CATTELL; S on other part of
500 a.; & whereas by letters patent signed by Lt. Gov. THOMAS BROUGHTON,
dated 4 Sept. 1735, JOSEPH HASFORT was granted 132 a. in Colleton Co.,
bounding on BOBS SAVANNAH; S on JOSEPH PENDARVIS; W on JOHN CATTELL & HENRY NICHOLS; NE on DRAYTON; but whereas a mistake was made & a more accurate survey showed the grant measured 100 a. & not 132 a.; & whereas JOSEPH HASFORT & HANNAH his wife on 22 June 1733 conveyed to ELISHA CARLILE
the 100 a.; now CARLILE conveys the 2 tracts to FILBIN. Witnesses: BENJAMIN CHILD, CHARLES BARKER, WILLIAM COCKFIELD. Before THOMAS LAMBOLL,
J.P.

Book R, p. 452 JOHN BROWN, planter, of Berkeley Co., to his
17 Aug. 1736 beloved son JOHN, planter, for love & affec-
Deed of Gift tion & other considerations, 100 a., part of
253 a. in Berkeley Co., bounding N & E on WILLIAM BULL, ESQ.; S on STEPHEN BULL, ESQ.; W on SILAS WELLS & JOHN CHAMPNEYS. One crown bill delivered. Witnesses: JOHN COOK, CHRISTIANA BROWN.
Before THOMAS FERGUSON, J.P.

Book R, p. 454 THOMAS JENKINS, planter, to STEPHEN BEAUCHAMP
16 ....1736 & CO., merchants, for L 512:10:6, 400 a. in
Mortgage Township of Kingston, also, 1 Negro woman; to
be redeemed 4 months after date. Witnesses:
JAMES CRICHLOW, JOHN ALEXANDER "in said Township", JOHN BARNS "in said
Township".

Book R, p. 455 JOSEPH HURST to CHARLES FILBIN, as security to
23 .... 1737 FILBIN for joining HURST in a bond dated 22
Mortgage Sept. 1737, payable to Landgrave THOMAS SMITH,
in sum of L 2000 currency; 575 a. on Cooper
River, bounding on JAMES STREETER & MRS. SARAH SUMMER; also 294 a., purchased from Landgrave THOMAS SMITH, bounding on JAMES STREETER & RALPH
IZARD, ESQ.; the bond being payable, with interest before 1744. Witnesses: WILLIAM COCKFIELD, JAMES ELDERTON. Before THOMAS LAMBOLL, J.P.

Book R, p. 457 WILLIAM HOLMAN, planter, of Colleton Co., to
11 & 12 Nov. 1737 CHRISTOPHER SMITH, shopkeeper, of Charleston,
for L 700 currency, 650 a. in Colleton Co., granted to HOLMAN on 11 July 1733, at the head of Cuckells Creek. Witnesses: GEORGE HESKIT, JOHN WALTON. Before HENRY GIBBES, J.P.

Book R, p. 461 THOMAS CONN, tailor, to PETER HORRY, JAMES
29 & 30 Apr. 1736 CROKATT, JOHN DART, & JAMES OSMOND, merchants,
L & R by Mortgage of Charleston, 500 a. in Craven Co., bounding
NE on JOHN CONN; NW on Peedee River; SW on vacant land. Whereas THOMAS CONN & PETER HUNTER, of Charleston, for payment of their debt to HORRY, CROKATT, DART & OSMOND, & other creditors of HUNTER & CONN by the first schedule attached to the deed, on 28 Apr. 1736 assigned to HORRY, CROKATT, DART & OSMOND all money then due HUNTER & CONN by virtue of the 2nd schedule also attached to the deed; & appointed HORRY, CROKATT, DART, & OSMOND their attorneys, to receive & recover the money due them; & delivered to the attorneys the goods & merchandise listed in the inventory (or 3rd schedule); & whereas a considerable balance is still due their creditors; now, as further security, CONN conveys to the creditors 500 a. of land. Date of redemption, 30 Apr. 1739. Witnesses: THOMAS DALE, GEORGE LIVINGSTON. Before THOMAS DALE, J.P.

Book R, p. 466 DAVID FERGUSON, planter, of Colleton Co., to
12 Oct. 1728 WILLIAM NASH, planter, in sum of L 3600 SC
Bond money, conditioned for keeping terms of following bill of sale. Witnesses: SAMUEL JONES, SAMUEL SHADDOCK, THOMAS WENBORN. Before DANIEL GREENE, J.P. (See Bk. S p. 142).

Book R, p. 467 DAVID FERGUSON, planter, & MARTHA (her mark)
12 Oct. 1728 his wife, to WILLIAM NASH, planter, all of
Bill of Sale Colleton Co., for L 1800 currency, 500 a. on
an island, bounding E & SE on Bohicket Creek; S & W on WILLIAM WELLS; N on JOHN JEAN'S (?) & JAMES RAMSAY; NE on ROGER NEWINGTON; also all cattle, hogs, horses & periauger. Witnesses: SAMUEL JONES, SAMUEL SHADDOCK, THOMAS WENBORN. Before DANIEL GREENE, J.P. (See Bk. S. p. 141).

Book R, p. 469 ALEXANDER TRENCH, merchant, of Charleston, as
15 & 16 Jan. 1727 attorney for JOHN BAYLY, of Ballinaclough, Co.
L & R of Tipperary, Ireland, to JOHN HINES (HINDES),
cooper, of Colleton Co., for L 25 SC money, 100 a. Colleton Co., bounding S & W on COL. ARTHUR HALL; N & E on THOMAS FARR, SR. & THOMAS FARR, JR. Whereas the Rt. Hon. JOHN, Earl of Bath, & the Lords Proprs. by letters patent dated 16 Aug. 1698 created JOHN BAYLY (the father) a Landgrave & Cassick of SC, granting him 48,000 a.; & whereas JOHN BAYLY (son & heir) on 9 Nov. 1722 appointed ALEXANDER TRENCH, merchant, of Charleston, his attorney, with authority to set aside 8000 a. for BAYLY'S use & dispose of the rest; now TRENCH sells 100 a. to HINES. Witnesses: BENJAMIN DE LA CONSEILLERE, JOHN CROFT. Before ROBERT AUSTIN, J.P.

Book R, p. 473 JOHN HICKS, planter, to WILLIAM NASH, planter,
14 June 1731 in sum of L 600 currency, conditioned for
Bond keeping agreements in following bill of sale
of 150 a. Witnesses: THOMAS WENBORN, MARY WENBORN, EDMOND JERVICE (JARVIS). Before DANIEL GREENE, J.P. (See Bk. S. p. 139).

Book R, p. 473 JOHN HICKS, planter, to WILLIAM NASH, planter,
14 June 1731 both of Colleton Co., for L 300 SC money; 150
Bill of Sale a. in Colleton Co., on S side Littenwaw Creek,
bounding S & W on JOHN HICKS. Witnesses: THOMAS WENBORN, MARY WENBORN, EDMOND JERVICE (JARVIS). Before DANIEL GREENE, J.P. (See Bk. S. fol. 137).

Book R, p. 475 ARTHUR BULL, to WILLIAM NASH, planter, in sum
19 July 1734 of L 360 currency, conditioned for keeping the
Bond agreements in the following bill of sale for
80 a. Signed by ARTHUR BULL & SARAH BULL (his

wife). Witnesses: JONATHAN THOMAS, EDMOND JARVIS. Before ROBERT YONGE, J.P. (See Bk. S. p. 140).

Book R, p. 476 ARTHUR BULL & SARAH his wife, to WILLIAM NASH,
19 July 1734   planter, of Colleton Co., for L 180 SC money,
Bill of Sale   80 a. on S side Littenwaw Creek, Colleton Co.,
a tract included in a plat of the land of JOHN HICKS & separated from it by a ____ run from the head of the fishing creek to a bluff called Bow Bluff; bounding E on WILLIAM NASH; S & W by Fishing Creek. Witnesses: JONATHAN THOMAS, EDMOND (his mark) JARVIS. Before ROBERT YONGE, J.P. (See Bk. S. p. 139).

Book R, p. 478   (See Bk. S. p. 216). THOMAS BROUGHTON & AR-
Date ?   THUR MIDDLETON, advising & counseling RALPH
Confirmation of Sale IZARD & DOROTHY his wife, confirm their grant
                      to RALPH IZARD, JR. Whereas RALPH IZARD, gen-
tleman, of Berkeley Co., & DOROTHY his wife (late widow & executrix of CHRISTOPHER SMITH, gentleman), convinced the General Assembly that for the payment of the just debts of CHRISTOPHER SMITH, it was necessary that his real estate be sold & they obtained an Act (1709) allowing them, with the advice & consent of BROUGHTON & MIDDLETON, to sell the real estate; now they sell to RALPH IZARD, JR., for a certain consideration, 600 a., English measure in Berkeley Co., bounding N on WILLIAM STEPHENS, MR. LIVING, & CAPT. HOWITT; E on MR. ODENSEL & THOMAS PERONNEAU; S on Ashley River; W on ?; also 1000 a., English measure in Berkeley Co., commonly called Upper Stock, bounding NE on Landgrave THOMAS SMITH; E & SE on EDWARD ? & WILLIAM DRY; S & SW on MR. WILLIAMS & THOMAS PINCKNEY; N & W on vacant land. Witnesses: The Hon. SIR NATHANIEL JOHNSON, Knight; JAMES INGERSON; ISAAC PORCHER. Before H. BUTLER, J.P.

Book R, p. 480   JOHN FRASER, merchant, & JUDITH his wife, to
31 July & 1 Aug. 1735 GEORGE HAIG & FREDERICK MEYER, gentlemen, all
L & R   of Charleston, for L 500 SC money, 950 a. in
                       Colleton Co., bounding W on THOMAS FORD; NW on
THOMAS ELLIOTT; other sides on vacant land; which tract was granted to JOHN FRASER by letters patent dated Apr. 1733, signed by Gov. ROBERT JOHNSON. Witnesses: JOHN COWARD, WILLIAM STAPLES (gentleman). Before THOMAS LAMBOLL, J.P. (See Bk. S. p. 151).

Book R, p. 484   By order of Gov. ROBERT JOHNSON, dated __ 1731,
Warrant   JAMES ST. JOHN, Sur. Gen. surveyed for JOHN
                  FRASER 950 a. in Colleton Co., bounding W on
THOMAS FORD; NW on THOMAS ELLIOTT; other sides on vacant land. Certified 2 June 1732. (See Bk. S. p. 156).

Book R, p. 484   GEORGE II to JOHN FRASER, 950 a. in Colleton
6 Apr. 1733   Co., bounding W on THOMAS FORD; NW on THOMAS
Grant   ELLIOTT; other sides on vacant land. Signed
                 by ROBERT JOHNSON & BADENHOP (Clerk of the
Council). See Bk. S. p. 156.

Book R, p. 486   FREDERICK MEYER, Indian trader, to RIPTON HUT-
30 & 31 Aug. 1736   CHINSON & FREDERICK GRIMKE, merchants, all of
L & R by Mortgage   Charleston, as security on bond of even date
                      in penal sum of L 396 SC money, for payment of
L 198:2:3 on last day of Nov. next. half the tract of 950 a. in Colleton Co., bounding SE on THOMAS FORD; W on THOMAS ELLIOTT. Witnesses: CHARLES CORDES, ALEXANDER LIVIE (LEVIE). (See Bk. S. p. 154).

Book R, p. 488   JOHN SOMERVILLE, gentleman, late of North Bri-
2 Dec. 1734   tain, brother & heir at law of TWEEDIE SOMER-
Agreement   VILLE, ESQ., of SC of 1st part; SARAH SOMER-
                 VILLE, widow & executrix of TWEEDIE SOMERVILLE,
of 2nd part. Whereas TWEEDIE SOMERVILLE owned, various lands, goods & chattles in SC & elsewhere, & by will dated 25 Dec. 1733, bequeathed to his wife SARAH 350 a., all the stock, & all "other utensils belonging thereto"; also the plantation on Port Royal commonly called Salt Water Bridge, with all the stock & utensils thereon; also all his Negores & household goods, etc.; & all the rest of his land, etc., to be equally divided between his brother JOHN & his wife SARAH; & whereas SARAH, in

consideration of her love & affection for her brother-in-law & of the
covenants mentioned herein, renounced her right & title under the will to
the estate of TWEEDIE SOMERVILLE over & above what JOHN was entitled to
under the will; & whereas JOHN, for the love & affection he bore his sister-in-law SARAH, in consideration of the covenants to be kept, & in consideration of her renouncing her title to the estate above what he was
entitled to, & to settle any disputes that may arise between JOHN & SARAH
& their heirs; they agree: 1st; JOHN promises that SARAH shall have 1/2
(the whole to be divided & allotted) of TWEEDIE SOMMERVILLE'S real estate;
& 2nd; that, until the estate shall be divided between them, JOHN shall
have half the real estate; as tenants in common; all receipts to be
equally divided; all debts (funeral expenses, etc.) to be paid by SARAH
within 6 months out of his personal estate, if sufficient; otherwise, the
expenses to be borne equally. Witnesses: WILLIAM CATTELL, ANTHONY MATH-
EWS, ALEXANDER NISBETT. Before JACOB MOTTE, J.P.

Book R, p. 492　　　　　　NICHOLAS HARLESTON, planter, & SARAH his wife,
2 & 3 Aug. 1736　　　　　 to RENÉ RAVENEL, all of Berkeley Co., for an
L & R　　　　　　　　　　　unnamed sum; 100 a. in Berkeley Co., granted
　　　　　　　　　　　　　　by the Lords Proprs. to JAMES CHILD; bounding
NE on WILLIAM BALL; SE & SW on RENÉ RAVENEL; W on PETER DE ST. JULIEN.
Witnesses: JAMES STEWART, RENÉ RICHEBOURG, DAVID LASONS (?). Before
JAMES LEBAS, J.P.

Book R, p. 496　　　　　　JOHN CATTELL, planter, & SARAH his wife, of
30 & 31 May 1735　　　　 Berkeley Co., to JOHN FILBIN, planter, of Col-
L & R　　　　　　　　　　　leton Co., for L 1500 (?) currency, 509 a. in
　　　　　　　　　　　　　　Colleton Co., 509 a. granted JOHN CATTELL 28
May 1734; bounding E on JOSEPH PENDARVIS & ELISHA CARLILE; S on MR.
BUTOLPH; W on SILAS WELLS; N on HENRY NICHOL. Witnesses: CHARLES BARKER,
ROBERT LADSON, JR., WILLIAM CATTELL, JR. (See Bk. S. p. 168).

Book R, p. 500　　　　　　DANIEL LAROCHE & THOMAS LAROCHE, merchants, of
25 Nov. 1737　　　　　　　Georgetown, to RICHARD MALONE, planter, of
Release　　　　　　　　　　Craven Co., for L 400 SC money, 300 a., part
　　　　　　　　　　　　　　of 918 a. in Prince George Parish, granted by
Lt. Gov. THOMAS BROUGHTON on 8 May 1736 to MRS. MARY SMITH; bounding NE
on ANTHONY WHITE, CAPT. SOUTHERLAND, & JOHN SAMS; N on MR. MALONE & WIL-
LIAM SHACKELFORD; SW on JOSEPH PORT, THOMAS BONNY, & CAPT. GRICHLOW; SE
on a creek; which land she quit claimed to DANIEL & THOMAS LAROCHE; the
300 a. tract bounding E on JOHN LANE; N on MR. MALONE & WILLIAM SHACKEL-
FORD; W on SHACKELFORD & JOSEPH PORT; S on the half part of the 918 a.
laid out to MARY SMITH. Witnesses: SAMUEL JENNINGS, JAMES CRADDOCK. Before WILLIAM WHITESIDE, J.P. (See Bk. S. p. 221).

Book R, p. 502　　　　　　ALCIMUS GAILLARD, planter, & SARAH his wife,
30 Dec. 1737　　　　　　　to RICHARD MALONE, gentleman, all of Craven
Release　　　　　　　　　　Co., for L 850 currency, 300 a. formerly be-
　　　　　　　　　　　　　　longing to FREDERICK GAILLARD; on Santee River,
bounding SE on CAPT. BARTHOLOMEW GAILLARD; other sides on vacant land.
Witnesses: WILLIAM SHACKELFORD, ESTHER SHACKELFORD, THOMAS WISE. Before
WILLIAM WHITESIDE, J.P. (See Bk. S. p. 223).

Book R, p. 504　　　　　　ALCIMUS GAILLARD, planter, & SARAH his wife,
30 Dec. 1737　　　　　　　to RICHARD MALONE, gentleman, all of Craven
Mortgage　　　　　　　　　Co., as security on 2 bonds of even date in
　　　　　　　　　　　　　　total penal sum of L 7028 for payment of
L 3514:10 SC money; 1 for payment of L 1372:10 on 1 Dec. 1738; the other
for payment of L 2140 (L 2144) on 1 Dec. 1739; 500 a. on which he lives,
bounding W on WILLIAM SHACKELFORD; E & N on THEODORE GAILLARD; also 300
a. in Craven Co., on S side Winyaw River, bounding S on Masketer Side; SW
& NW on vacant land; also 21 Negro slaves; also all sorts of stock; & all
his goods & chattles. Witnesses: WILLIAM SHACKELFORD, ESTHER SHACKELFORD,
THOMAS WISE. Before WILLIAM WHITESIDE, J.P. (See Bk. S. p. 246).

DEEDS BOOK "S"
1737 - 1739

Book S, p. 1
7 Oct. 1737
Mortgage (L. p. 211)

JOHN THOMSON, JR., planter, of Winyaw, to DANIEL LAROCHE & THOMAS LAROCHE, merchant, of Georgetown, as security on various bonds, 4 tracts of land; 200 a. in Craven Co., where he now lives, on N branch of Black River; bounding all sides on JOHN THOMSON, JR.; also 1500 a. in Craven Co., part of 2000 a. granted COL. WILLIAM RHETT by the Lords Proprs., purchased by ROGER MOORE, on Black River, bounding SW on SAMUEL HUNTER; N on ANTHONY WHITE; N on JOHN THOMSON, JR., also 250 a. on N branch of Black River, bounding NW on JOHN THOMSON, JR.; SE on WILLIAM SWINTON; also 975 a. in Craven Co., on S side of N branch of Black River, bounding NW on WILLIAM THOMSON, JR.; SE on JOHN THOMSON, JR. Whereas JOHN THOMSON & WILLIAM THOMSON, JR., gave 2 bonds to the LAROCHES, 1 dated 1 May 1737 in penal sum of L 4419 for payment of L 2209:16:7 with interest on 1 Jan. next; the other dated 20 July 1737 in penal sum of L 4060 for payment of L 4029:13:4-1/2 on 1 Sept. next; & whereas THOMAS LAROCHE & WILLIAM THOMPSON, JR., gave a bond on 11 May 1737 to JOSEPH WRAGG & RICHARD LAMBTON, merchants, of Charleston, in the penal sum of L 1633 for payment of L 831:10 with interest on 1 Mar. next; & another bond to DANIEL CRAWFORD, merchant, of Charleston, on 15 May 1737, in penal sum of L 436:14 for payment of L 218:7 & interest on 1 Mar. next; & another bond to JAMES CROKATT, merchant, of Charleston, on 10 May 1737, in penal sum of L 530 for payment of L 265 & interest on 1 Mar. next; & another bond on 10 May 1737 to JAMES CROKATT in penal sum of L 529:8 for payment of L 264:14 interest on 1 Mar. 1738; & another bond to RICHARD WRIGHT, ESQ., on 11 May 1737, in penal sum of L 240 for payment of L 120 & interest on 1 Mar. next; & another bond to MAURICE LEWIS, ESQ., on 23 Sept. 1737, in penal sum of L 268 for payment of L 134 on 1 Mar. next; & whereas THOMAS LAROCHE & JOHN THOMSON, gave bond to ANTHONY MATHEWS, CHARLES PINCKNEY, JAMES CROKATT, HENRY PERONNEAU & JACOB MOTTE, merchant, of Charleston, on 7 Oct. 1737, in penal sum of L 1400 for payment of L 700 & interest on 1 Mar. next; & whereas DANIEL LAROCHE & WILLIAM THOMSON, on 7 Oct. 1737, gave bond to ANTHONY MATHEWS, CHARLES PINCKNEY, JAMES CROKATT, HENRY PERONNEAU & JACOB MOTTE in penal sum of L 1400 for payment of L 700 & interest on 1 Mar. next; all bonds given on account of debts of JOHN THOMSON, JR.; now JOHN THOMSON conveys 4 tracts, total 2925 a., as security. Witnesses: JAMES CRADDOCK, ISAAC SECARE. Before WILLIAM WHITESIDE, J.P. ROBERT AUSTIN, Register.

Book S, p. 7
21 & 22 Nov. 1737
L & R by Mortgage

DEBORAH DAVIS, widow, to DANIEL LAROCHE & THOMAS LAROCHE, merchant, of Georgetown, as security on bond dated 20 Nov. 1737 given by DEBORAH DAVIS & JOSEPH CHAMBERLIN to DANIEL & THOMAS LAROCHE in penal sum of L 1724:6:6 for payment of L 862:3:3 SC money with interest on 1 Mar. next; 460 a. in Craven Co., bounding NE on Black River; NW on PETER JOHNSON; SE on ISAAC DAVIS. Witnesses: STEPHEN BEAUCHAMP, JOHN OULDFIELD, JR. Before WILLIAM WHITESIDE, J.P. ROBERT AUSTIN, Register.

Book S, p. 10
22 & 23 Sept. 1737
L & R

JOHN (his mark) ARTHUR, vintner, & CATHERINE (her mark) his wife, to ISAAC SECARE, gentleman, all of Georgetown, for L 75 SC money, 500 a. in Queensborough Township, Craven Co., granted by letters patent signed by Lt. Gov. THOMAS BROUGHTON on 13 July 1737 to JOHN ARTHUR, bounding W on ROBERT FLADGER; S on MAURICE LEWIS; SE on JOHN JOULLY (?); NE on Little Peedee or Cypress Creek. Witnesses: JAMES GORDON, THOMAS LAROCHE. ROBERT AUSTIN, Register.

Book S, p. 13
14 & 15 Dec. 1737
L & R

ISAAC AMYAND, ESQ., of Charleston, to PETER SECARE, bricklayer, of Craven Co., for L 50 SC money, 500 a. in Craven Co., in Queensborough Township, granted ISAAC AMYAND by letters patent dated 13 July 1737 & signed by Lt. Gov. THOMAS BROUGHTON; bounding SE on ALEXANDER TALLY; SW on THOMAS CHARNOCK; NW on GILES HOLLIDAY; NE on vacant land. Witnesses: JAMES SMALLWOOD, GILES HOLLIDAY. Before WILLIAM WHITESIDE, J.P. ROBERT Austin, Register.

Book S, p. 16 14 Oct. 1737 L & R		MARY SMITH, widow, of Winyaw, to DANIEL LA- ROCHE & THOMAS LAROCHE, merchant, of Winyaw, Craven Co., as tenants in common & not as joint tenants for ₤ 92 SC money; 918 a. in

Prince George Parish, granted 8 May 1736 by Lt. Gov. THOMAS BROUGHTON to MARY SMITH; bounding NE on CAPT. ANTHONY WHITE & CAPT. SOUTHERLAND & JOHN LANE; N on RICHARD MELONE & WILLIAM SHACKELFORD; SW on JOSEPH PORT & THOMAS BONNY & CAPT. JAMES CRICHLOW; SE on a creek. Witnesses: AMOS MICHELL, THOMAS LAINI. ROBERT AUSTIN, Register.

Book S, p. 19
6 & 7 July 1737
L & R.

WILLIAM DRAKE, ESQ., of St. James Santee, to THOMAS LAROCHE, Merchant, of Prince George Parish, Winyaw, for ₤ 5300 SC money, 3 tracts of 500 a. each. Whereas Gov. ROBERT JOHNSON, by letters patent dated 17 Jan. 1732 granted WILLIAM DRAKE, 2 adjoining tracts of 500 a. each, making 1 tract of 1000 a., bounding S on JAMES GORDON (formerly WILLIAM WATIES); W on DANIEL & THOMAS LAROCHE (formerly vacant); E on Peedee River; NW on JOHN OULDFIELD, JR. (formerly GEORGE PAWLEY); & whereas Gov. ROBERT JOHNSON by letters patent dated 16 Mar. 1732 granted WILLIAM DRAKE 500 a. in Craven Co., bounding NW on Waccamaw River; NE now on JAMES STEWART (laterly SAMUEL MASTERS, formerly CHARLES HART, ESQ.); SW & SE on vacant land. Witnesses: RICHARD ALLEIN, CAPT. JONATHAN SKRINE, ARTHUR CROUCH. Before WILLIAM WHITESIDE, J.P. ROBERT AUSTIN, Register.

Book S, p. 22
7 July 1737
Bond & Mortgage

WILLIAM DRAKE, ESQ., of St. James Santee, to THOMAS LAROCHE, of Prince GEORGE WINYAW, a bond for ₤ 4600 SC money given as security on the above release of 1500 a. Witnesses: RICHARD ALLEIN, JONATHAN SKRINE, ARTHUR CROUCH. ROBERT AUSTIN, Register.

Book S, p. 23
19 Jan. 1715
Deed of Sale

JOHN PALMER, planter, of Granville Co., & ELIZABETH, his wife, & with her free consent, to RICHARD WOODWARD, planter, of Colleton Co., for ₤ 100 SC money, 540 a. granted by Gov. NATHANIEL JOHNSON & the Lords Proprs. on 15 Sept. 1705 to JOHN PALMER; bounding S on Combahee River; E on RICHARD WOODWARD; N on sedge marsh & deep ponds; W on land run out by PRICE (?) HUGHES, ESQ. Witnesses: WILLIAM CHAPMAN, JOHN PRICHARD, D. SHUTE. ROBERT AUSTIN, Register.

Book S, p. 24
24 Nov. 1710
Bill of Sale

JOHN (his mark) PALMER, planter, of Chiha, Colleton Co., in consideration of 320 a. of purchased land (200 of which is platted granted, the rest run out by CAPT. THOMAS NAIRN), with all hogs, messuages & tenements, delivered to him by JAMES ATKINS, planter, of Combehe, Granville Co., delivers to ATKINS 382 a., platted, 1 old sawpit formerly belonging to THOMAS AYRES, 1 tract west of this running N according to plat, a mare, & ₤ 26 currency. Witnesses: ELIAS FISHER, ROBERT ANDERSON.

Book S, p. 24
4 Mar. 1712/13
Bill of Sale

JAMES ATKINS, planter, of Colleton Co., for ₤ 40 currency, makes over to RICHARD WOODWARD, planter, all his right & title to above bill of sale. Signed: JOHN (his mark) ATKINS Witnesses: ROWLAND EVANS, CHRISTOPHER SMITH, JOHN WILLIAMS.

Book S, p. 24
19 Jan. 1715
Bond

JOHN PALMER, of Granville Co., to RICHARD WOODWARD, of Colleton Co., in sum of ₤ 1000 currency, to keep agreements in bill of sale of even date covering 540 a. Witnesses: WILLIAM CHAPMAN, JOHN PRICHARD, D. SHUTE. ROBERT AUSTIN, Register.

Book S, p. 25
30 Dec. 1714/15
Quitclaim

JOHN PALMER, planter, of Granville Co., releases RICHARD WOODWARD, planter, of Colleton Co., from all debts, etc. Witnesses: D. SHUTE, JOHN WILLIAMS, JOHN PRICHARD.

Book S, p. 25
2 Mar. 1714/15
Receipt

JAMES ATTKINS acknowledges receipt from RICHARD WOODWARD of ₤ 40 currency (viz. in cattle ₤ 20; 1 mare ₤ 10; cash paid to CAPT. JOHN

WOODWARD Ł 10) in full for a tract of land bought from JOHN PALMER, SR., & resigns his title to the land. Witnesses: JOHN WHITEHEAD, JOHN WILLIAMS. ROBERT AUSTIN, Register.

Book S, p. 25
29 July 1734
Deed of Gift

ROBERT COLE, SR., of Wadwadmelaw Island, St. John's Parish, Colleton Co., to his beloved son JOHN COLE, for natural affection & other considerations, his dwelling house & 610 a. & improvements adjacent to Wadwadmelaw Bridge "as also the seaside & Long Island & other small island adjoining"; a Negro man; a Negro woman & her child; 2 Negro boys; 2 mares; a young horse; & such cattle as are branded with a heart & an I in the middle of the heart; all cattle with crop in right ear & 2 slits & 2 halfpennies in left ear. Should JOHN die without heirs or before coming of age then ROBERT'S "niest" male heirs to inherit. Witnesses: THOMAS UPHAM, WILLIAM FLECKNOWE. Before ROBERT YOUNG, J.P. ROBERT AUSTIN, Register.

Book S, p. 26
26 July 1737
Confirmation of Deed
of Conveyance

GEORGE MOORE, gentleman, of Cape Fear, NC, to ALEXANDER HEXT, ESQ., of Colleton Co. Whereas MARY MOORE (born MARY RAYNOR) owned several tracts of land in SC & several lots in Charleston & married ROGER MOORE, ESQ., formerly of Berkeley Co., now of Cape Fear; & whereas she died & left said GEORGE MOORE her only child & heir at law; but ROGER MOORE, the father, entered upon the same as life tenant by courtesy of England & by deed dated 2 Nov. 1020 conveyed to ALEXANDER HEXT 1020 a., English measure in Colleton Co.; & whereas ROGER MOORE did not have the power to sell the land but GEORGE MOORE acknowledged that he received from his father the full value & more than the value for his right in the land sold to HEXT; now GEORGE MOORE confirms the conveyance & renounces all claim. Witnesses: THOMAS AKIN, REBECCA COKE, SARAH SMITH. Before WILLIAM TREWIN. ROBERT AUSTIN, Register.

Book S, p. 29
25 & 26 Sept. 1737
L & R

WILLIAM SNOW, planter, & MARY his wife, to JOHN SUMMERS, planter, all of St. John's Parish, Berkeley Co., for Ł 300 currency, 300 a. in Craven Co., bounding NE & SW on NATHANIEL SNOW; other sides on vacant land. Witnesses: SAMUEL GANDY, JOHN ROBINSON, THOMAS (his mark) HALL. Before JOHN WALLIS, J.P. ROBERT AUSTIN, Register.

Book S, p. 32
25 & 26 Aug. 1737
L & R

ANDREW COLLINS, & SARAH his wife, to JOHN PYATT, planter, for Ł 500 SC money, 400 a. in Craven Co., on S side Peedee River, bounding S on vacant land; E on ANTHONY ATKINSON; W on JOHN CONN; grant dated 17 Feb. 1736/7. Witnesses: FRANCIS AVANT, ANTHONY ATKINSON, ELIZABETH ATKINSON. Before WILLIAM WHITESIDE, J.P. ROBERT AUSTIN, Register.

Book S, p. 34
9 & 10 Aug. 1736
L & R by Mortgage

PETER VILLEPONTOUX, planter, & FRANCES his wife, of James Island, to DANIEL GREEN, merchant, of Charleston, as security on 2 bonds; both dated 8 Aug. 1736; both in penal sum of Ł 1600 for payment of Ł 800 SC money, with interest; 1 payable 8 Aug. 1737, the other 8 Aug. 1738; 200 a., English measure, on E side Ashley River, bounding SE on GEORGE HADDERELL (formerly FLORENCE O'SULLIVANE & formerly of JOSEPH BARKER, merchant); NW on NEAL WALKER (sold by FLORENCE O'SULLIVANE to MAJOR ROBERT DANIEL); NE on JOHN BARKSDALE, ESQ., (formerly FLORENCE O'SULLIVANE); also 200 a. in Berkeley Co., on NE side Ashley River, adjoining JOHN BARKSDALE & bounding N on DANIEL GREENE (formerly STEPHEN GIBBS); the 2 tracts forming 1 of 400 a., bounding SE on GEORGE HADDERELL; NW on ELIAS HANCOCK (formerly JOHN BARKSDALE); NE on JOHN BARKSDALE; also 7 Negro slaves. Witnesses: RICHARD ALLEIN, JOHN GREEN, D. AUCHTERLONY. Before JACOB MOTTE, J.P. ROBERT AUSTIN, Register. Mortgage satisfied by several payments to JACOB MOTTE as executor of estate of ELIZABETH GREENE, widow of DANIEL GREENE. Witnesse: JOHN BEALE.

Book S, p. 38
13 & 14 Oct. 1736
L & R

JOHN ABBOTT, merchant, & ELIZABETH his wife, to WILLIAM BROCKINTON, planter, all of Georgetown, Winyaw, Craven Co., for Ł 700 currency, free from ELIZABETH'S 2 tracts of 250 a. each, on S side Black River, in Craven Co., both tracts granted 6 Aug. 1735 by Lt. Gov. THOMAS BROUGHTON, to JOHN ABBOTT; 1 bounding E on JOSEPH JOHNSON & JOHN ABBOTT, other sides on vacant land; the other bounding S on ABBOTT, other sides on vacant land. Witnesses: GEORGE DICK, SARAH JOHNSON. Before DANIEL LAROCHE, J.P. ROBERT AUSTIN, Register.

Book S, p. 40
24 & 25 Aug. 1737
L & R

GILES (his mark) BOWER, planter, & MARTHA his wife, to WILLIAM BROCKINTON, planter, all of Craven Co., for L 500 currency, free from MARTHA'S claim of dower, 350 a. in Craven Co., granted 3 Dec. 1732 by Lt. Gov. THOMAS BROUGHTON to GILES BOWER, bounding NW on WILLIAM BROCKINTON, other sides on vacant land. Witnesses: WILLIAM SNOW, SAMUEL GANDY, THOMAS WRIGHT. Before JOHN WALLIS, J.P. ROBERT AUSTIN, Register.

Book S, p. 42
25 Oct. 1737
Release in Trust

MARY (her mark) STEVENSON, widow of JOHN STEVENSON, glazier, to RICHARD MARTIN, painter, & EXPERIENCE HOWARD, carpenter, all of Charleston, in trust for herself & her children, JOHN, JAMES, MARY & ANN STEVENSON. Whereas JOHN STEVENSON, by will dated 28 Mar. 1735 bequeathed all his real & personal estate to his wife & children, the executors to divide the personal estate into 5 equal parts but the land to be divided into 2 parts for 2 of the children they to pay so much money out of their shares as will make the value of their dividend no more than that of any of the other children or that of the wife; & whereas MARY (widow) intends to marry JAMES HILLIARD, watchmaker, of Charleston, she, with HILLIARD'S consent, assigns to MARTIN & HOWARD, in trust for herself & children, all real estate in St. Philip's Parish, Charleston, all Negro slaves & all goods & chattles listed in inventory attached. Witnesses: SUSANN STEVENSON, JOHN RATTRAY. Inventory of real & personal estate of JOHN STEVENSON: 1 feather bed, 3 blankets, 2 pillows, 1 pair sheets & bedsteads fitted a table desk a box & dressing glass, 2 trading guns, a parcel of old books, a hand brush, 7 chairs, a cradle, 2 feather beds, 2 bolsters, 3 pillows, 3 blankets, 1 quilt, 2 pair sheets, 2 bedsteads, "1 sute of curtains & rods", 1 pair dog irons, 1 suit of clothes, 3 old coats, 1 pair britches, 1 morning gown, 1 old trunk, 1 old cloak, 1 old cedar table, 15 chairs, a couch, 1 square table & 1 oval, 1 coffee mill, some "Crackry ware", 4 iron pots, 6 jugs, 39 lb. (?) pewter, 4 brass candlesticks, 1 iron mill, 1 load iron (?) & moulds, old scales & weights, parcel of paint brushes, 4 oil jars, 3 dwelling houses & kitchen & the land 42 ft. front (?) feet rear, 2 pews in St. Philip's Church, 6 teaspoons, 1 dozen silver soup spoons, 1 chest drawers, 1 large glass, 2 Negro men, 2 Negro girls, 7 gold rings, & "at my death all my wearing apparel for my 2 daughters".

Book S, p. 43
25 Oct. 1737
Renunciation of Title

JAMES HILLIARD, watchmaker, of Charleston, acknowledges that the above deed in trust was executed with his full knowledge & consent & promises to execute a legal conveyance within 1 month after his intended marriage of all his title to JOHN STEVENSON'S estate. Witnesses: SUSANN STEVENSON, JOHN RATTRAY. Before ROBERT AUSTIN, J.P. & Pub. Reg.

Book S, p. 44
11 Jan. 1737
Mortgage

JAMES POLLARD, gentleman, of Charleston, to JOHN DALRYMPLE, merchant, as security on bond of even date in penal sum of L 200 for payment of L 100 SC money on 11 July next; 350 a. & 1 lot in Williamsburgh. Witnesses: WILLIAM SMITH, SARAH TURME. "Charlestown printed & sold by LEWIS TIMOTH." (?). Before ROBERT AUSTIN, J.P. & Pub. Reg.

Book S, p. 45
20 & 21 Jan. 1737
L & R

JOHN GOUGH, SR., gentleman, JOHN GOUGH, JR. (his eldest son), & RICHARD GOUGH (another son), planters, to DANIEL HUGHES, (probate gives HUGER) ESQ., all of Berkeley Co., for L 2720 currency, 320 a., (part of 2830 a.), at head of E branch of the T of Cooper River, in St. John's Parish, bounding E on DANIEL HUGHES (HUGER); other sides on JOHN GOUGH, SR., JOHN GOUGH, JR., & RICHARD GOUGH; as surveyed by JOHN HORRY, Dep. Sur., of JAMES ST. JOHN, Sur. Gen., on 19 of this Jan. Whereas the Hon. SIR NATHANIEL JOHNSON, Knight, & the Lords Proprs., on 12 Oct. 1709 granted JOHN GOUGH, SR. (then merchant of Island of Barbados) 3500 a., part of the Barony heretofore belonging to THOMAS COLLETON, ESQ.; & whereas by L & R dated 6 & 7 July 1737 JOHN GOUGH, for Ł 10,000 currency, sold to his son RICHARD, planter, of St. John's Parish, 2830 a. (part of the 3500 a.), bounding E on head of Cooper River; SW on EDWARD HOWARD; NW on vacant land; NE on MICHAEL MALION (?). Witnesses: THOMAS CORDES, JAMES BOISSEAU, FRANCIS ROCHE. Before FRANCIS LEJAU, J.P. Note: Probate states "& further they did take notice that the name HUGER is wrong spelt throughout the within instrument"; also a "Memorandum that before the signing & sealing the within release notice was taken by us the evidences that the name of HUGER is wrong spelt throughout the said instrument." Plat & certificate on page 49. ROBERT AUSTIN, Register.

Book S, p. 49
7 Mar. 1734
Mortgage

ILLIAM JONES (his mark), planter to JOHN EVANS, shipwright, as security on 2 bonds, both dated 27 July 1734, each in penal sum of Ł 300 for payment of Ł 150 currency; 1st payment 1 Jan. 1735; 2nd on 1 Jan. 1736; 30 a., English measure, in Berkeley Co., on NW side of She-A-Wee Sound on a place called Boo-Watt Breach; bounding SW on JOHN EVANS & ANN his wife; NE on GEORGE BENTLEY & vacant land; NW on vacant land. Witnesses: THOMAS KER, CHARLES FOGGO, ANDREW LOROMOND, STEPHEN HARTLEY, JOHN EVANS. Before HENRY GIBBES, J.P. ROBERT AUSTIN, Register.

Book S, p. 50
24 & 25 Mar. 1737
L & R by Mortgage

NATHANIEL SNOW, planter, to ELIZABETH HILL, widow & executrix of will of CHARLES HILL, as security on bond of even date in penal sum of Ł 147 for payment of Ł 73:10 sterling British money, on 25 Mar. next; 313 a. on Forster's Creek, Berkeley Co., which on resurvey was found to be 408 a., bounding S & E on NATHANIEL SNOW; also 650 a., English measure, in Berkeley Co., bounding N on Foster's Creek, NATHANIEL SNOW & PETER LAMB; E on CAPT. GILL; S on JOB HOW, NATHANIEL SNOW, SR., & JOHN EMPEROUR; which 2 tracts in Goose Creek Parish were granted by the Lords Proprs. to SNOW, the elder, father of above named NATHANIEL SNOW. Witnesses: WILLIAM GEORGE FREEMAN, GEORGE NICHOLAS, JR. Before ROBERT AUSTIN, J.Q. & Pub. Reg.

Book S, p. 52
13 Feb. 1734
Renunciation of Title

THOMAS DRAYTON, planter, eldest son of THOMAS DRAYTON, planter, of Berkeley Co., to his mother, ANNE DRAYTON, & to his brother, JOHN DRAYTON, all title to the real estate given her by the will of his brother, STEPHEN FOX DRAYTON. Whereas THOMAS DRAYTON, the father, by will dated 12 June 1714 gave his son, STEPHEN FOX DRAYTON, his plantation at Stono, formerly ANTHONY BEAUVAIS'S (?) Quarter (?) 360 a.; also half the residue of his Stono lands & all the lands at his Cowpen viz. Abrams Savanna; & should either of his sons (THOMAS & STEPHEN FOX) die without heirs, or before reaching 21, the land to fall to the survivors heirs; & whereas the father made a codicil to his will on 5 June 1716 stating that on 12 June 1714 he published his last will bequeathing son STEPHEN FOX DRAYTON 1/2 the residue of his Stono lands & all the lands at his Cowpen, Abrams Savanna, & since then he had another son born, named JOHN, for whom he must also provide, & he therefore revoked that part giving half the residue of his lands at Stono & Abrams Savanna to STEPHEN FOX & gave those lands to JOHN & STEPHEN FOX, to be equally divided; & whereas STEPHEN FOX DRAYTON by will dated 2 Feb. 1732 devised to his mother, ANNE DRAYTON, all his lands on the N branch of Stono River, being 4 adjoining tracts, & his house, & after her death to his brother JOHN, & bequeathed the rest of his estate (real & personal) to JOHN; but inasmuch as doubts have been raised as to the validity of the will because STEPHEN FOX DRAYTON was not 21 years old at the time of his death; & whereas THOMAS DRAYTON (party hereto) believing his father desired to leave the land to JOHN & STEPHEN FOX DRAYTON & the heirs of the survivor, believing that STEPHEN FOX DRAYTON was of sound & disposing mind, & being willing to conform to his brother's will & waive his advantages as the elder brother; now THOMAS quitclaims to his mother & brother. Witnesses: NICHOLAS TROTT, MADAM SARAH TROTT, SAMUEL BROWNE. Before HENRY GIBBES, J.P. ROBERT AUSTIN, Register.

Book S, p. 55   JOHN MULLRYNE, ESQ., to THOMAS HENNING,

9 & 10 Jan. 1737   merchant, of Charleston, as security on bond
L & R by mortgage   of even date in penal sum of ₤ 4006:19:8 for
                        payment of ₤ 2003:9:10 currency with interest
on 1 May next; the undivided half part of 2052 a., bounding N on Cumbahee
River; S on ROBERT STEEL & the Hon. WILLIAM BULL & THOMAS LOWNDES; 550 a.
of which were granted on 12 Jan. 1705 to JOSEPH BRYAN, & 1497 a. granted
to COL. JOSEPH BLAKE on 22 Sept. 1733. Witnesses: JOHN RATTRAY, JOHN
JOHNSON, JR. Before MAURICE LEWIS, J.P. ROBERT AUSTIN, Register.

Book S, p. 57   JOHN BERESFORD, ESQ., of the Parish of St.
13 & 14 Apr. 1737   Thomas & St. Dennis, Berkeley Co., to JOHN BEE,
L & R   carpenter, of Charleston, for ₤ 1125 SC money,
                        the W part of lot #90 in Charleston, fronting
32 ft. 6 in. on S side of Queen Street, & running S the whole depth of
the lot; also lot #70 lying S of the above lot, the 2 parts of lots making 1 long square 32 ft. 6 in. side & from Queen Street running S to lot
of MRS. DUPUY; bounding E on JOHN BERESFORD; W on JOHN BEE. Witnesses:
ROBERT BREWTON, JR., CHARLES PINCKNEY. Before HENRY GIBBS, J.P. ROBERT
AUSTIN, Register.

Book S, p. 60   THOMAS TATTNELL & ELIZABETH his wife, & MICH-
19 & 20 Jan. 1735   EAL BERISFORD, planters, of St. Paul's Parish,
L & R   to GILSON CLAPP, merchant, of Charleston, for
                        ₤ 950 SC money, 1 of the lots in Charleston
devised by MARY MULLINS to THOMAS TATTNELL & MICHAEL BERISFORD, bounding
N on RICHARD BREWER; S on CHARLES BURNHAM; S on a street leading from
Oyster Point by the Market Place; W on MRS. SARAH POWIS. Whereas MARY
MULLINS, widow, owned 2 lots in Charleston, granted by the Lords Proprs.
to MRS. SARAH POWIS, & by will dated 21 Nov. 1730 devised to her 2 nephews, THOMAS TATNELL & MICHAEL BERISFORD, the 2 lots, to be equally divided by a line running "between street & street on which the said lots do
front." Witnesses: JOHN MOULTRIE, WILLIAM LINTHWAITE, THOMAS SIMMONDS,
JR. Before ROBERT AUSTIN, J.P. & Register.

Book S, p. 63   HUGH BRYAN, gentleman, to The Society for the
3 & 4 Feb. 1737   Propagation of the Gospel in Foreign Parts, as
L & R by Mortgage   security on bond of even date in penal sum of
                        ₤ 220 for payment of ₤ 110 sterling, British
money, with interest, on 4 Feb. 1738; 300 a. in Granville Co., on E side
Coosaw River (should be Pocotaligo River), lately granted by the Society
to BRYAN; bounding E on CAPT. JOHN CROFT; N on JOSEPH BRYAN; W on GEORGE
PAWLEY. Witnesses: BENJAMIN WHITAKER, GEORGE NICHOLAS. Before ROBERT
AUSTIN, J.P.

Book S, p. 66   PHILIP GIVENS, planter, to the Society for the
23 & 24 Mar. 1736   Propagation of the Gospel in Foreign Parts by
L & R by Mortgage   their attorneys, the Rev. MR. ALEXANDER GARDEN
                        & WILLIAM GUY, clerks; as security on bond of
even date in penal sum of ₤ 68:13 for payment of ₤ 34:6:6 British money,
with interest, on 24 Mar. next; 229 a., part of 343 a., on Port Royal Island, Granville Co., bounding E on Stewart's River; S on WILLIAM LESLY; W
on WILLIAM BULL; N on DANIEL DICK; which 229 a. was purchased from the
Society by GIVENS. Witnesses: EDWARD BOXLEY, WILLIAM GEORGE FREEMAN.
Before ROBERT AUSTIN, J.P. & Pub. Reg.

Book S, p. 68   JOHN HUTCHINSON, gentleman, of Charleston, to
6 & 7 Feb. 1737   DANIEL LAROCHE & THOMAS LAROCHE, merchants of
L & R   Georgetown, Craven Co., ELIAS FOISSIN, JR.,
                        gentleman, of Berkeley Co., & MARY CHARDON,
widow, of Berkeley Co., for ₤ 168 currency, 2100 a. in Craven Co., bounding NW on Landgrave THOMAS SMITH; W on COL. THOMAS LYNCH; S on MESSRS.
CHARDON, LAROCHE & FOISSIN; E on a great marsh: NE on Winyaw Bay; which
2100 a. were granted by letter patent, dated 12 Aug. 1737, signed by Lt.
Gov. THOMAS BROUGHTON to JOHN HUTCHINSON. Witnesses: ISAAC AMYAND, GILES
HOLLIDAY. Before ROBERT AUSTIN, J.P., Pub. Reg.

Book S, p. 71   THOMAS SISSON (SOISSON), joiner, & MARY his
7 & 8 July 1735   wife, of St. Andrews Parish, Berkeley Co., to
                        BENJAMIN STILES, ZEBULON GUY & JEREMIAH STORY,
planters, of James Island, for ₤ 600 currency, 2 adjoining & united

tracts of land, 24 a. & 20 a., total 44., on James Island; the 24 a. bounding S on Newton Creek; E on JOHN STARLING; N & W on WILLIAM WILKINS; which 24 a. was purchased from the Lords Proprs. by JOSEPH NEWS on 11 May 1699, the boundings given in the grant being, lying on N side Newton's Creek & marsh, N on land formerly of ROBERT GIBBS, W on land granted JAMES DEGUE, which said NEWS & DOROTHY his wife sold to ZACHARIAH ARES; the 20 a. sold by CAPT. DAVID DAVIS to ZACHARIAH ARES, DAVIS & ARES agreeing to have the land run out according to plat signed & certified by ARTHUR MIDDLETON, Dep. Sur., 12 Dec. 1704. Whereas ARES left only 1 daughter & sole heiress, ELIZABETH, who married THOMAS ELLIS, died, & left 2 daughters, ELIZABETH & MARY, co-heiresses; & whereas ELIZABETH died, under age & unmarried; & MARY who had married ZACHARIAH STORY, carpenter, of James Island, & after his death married THOMAS SOISSIONS, party hereto, became sole heiress to the 2 tracts; now MARY & THOMAS SISSONS agree with STILES, GUY & STORY as follows: that whereas ZACHARIAH STORY willed to his son ZACHARIAH STORY the 2 tracts althought the right of inheritance lay only in his then wife MARY (now MARY SISSON), & whereas STILES, GUY & STORY were appointed executors of the will, the remaining money after discharging all debts being L 600; the executors agree to let the SISSONS have the use of the land until ZACHARIAH STORY (son) reaches 14 yrs. of age in consideration of bringing up & furnishing ZACHARIAH & ELIZABETH, his sister, with clothing, "meat, drink, washing, & lodging, wholesome & sufficient, answering at least to such interest money might arise from the same with schooling reasonably deemed", then, at proper time, the SISSONS shall pay the executors L 600. Witnesses: WILLIAM ALLIN, NICHOLAS SMITH. Before HENRY GIBBS, J.P. ROBERT AUSTIN, Register.

Book S, p. 75
30 Apr. 1737
Bond

FREDERICK MEYER, Indian trader, to CHARLES WATKINS, gentleman, of Berkeley Co., in penal sum of L 320 for payment of L 162 currency with interest on 1 Nov. next. Witnesses: WILLIAM MARTIN, JOHN (his mark) WILLIAMS. Before PETER DE ST. JULIEN, J.P. ROBERT AUSTIN, Register.

Book S, p. 75
29 & 30 Apr. 1737
L & R by Mortgage

FREDERICK MEYER, Indian trader, to CHARLES WATKINS, gentleman, of Berkeley Co., as security on above bond (p. 75); half of 500 a. (250) on Dawfuskee Island, Granville Co., bounding N on JAMES ST. JOHN (formerly JAMES COCHRAN); E on FREDERICK MEYER; S on ANDREW ALLEN; W on West River, marsh & New River. Witnesses: WILLIAM MARTIN, JOHN (his mark) WILLIAMS. Before PETER DE ST. JULIEN, J.P. ROBERT AUSTIN, Register.

Book S, p. 76
26 & 27 Dec. 1737
L & R

JOSEPH BOWREY, gentleman, to JAMES BROZET, ESQ., late of Island of St. Christopher, now of SC. Whereas by L & R dated 22 & 23 Sept. 1735, WILLIAM LIVINGSTON, ESQ. & MARY his wife, of St. Paul's Parish, Colleton Co., sold to JOSEPH BOWREY, gentleman, of Charleston, for L 3000 SC money, 1109 a., also an island of 64 a., in Colleton Co., bounding W on vacant land; N on an impassable Bay Swamp; S & SE on Chehow River & marsh; now JOSEPH BOWREY declares that his name was used by the "special nomination" of JAMES BROZET & in trust for him, that the land was purchased with BROZET'S money, & therefore BOWREY released the land to BROZET. Deed signed by: JOSEPH BOWREY, ELIZABETH BOWREY (his wife). Witnesses: WILLIAM BUCHANAN, WILLIAM HOLMAN. Before JOB ROTHMAHLER, J.P. ROBERT AUSTIN, Register.

Book S, p. 79
28 & 29 Dec. 1737
L & R by Mortgage

JAMES BROZET, ESQ., late of Island of St. Christopher now of SC, to JOHN WILLETT, ESQ., of Island of St. Christopher, as security on bond of even date in penal sum of L 1268:5:10 for payment of L 634:2:11 sterling, British money, with interest on 29 Dec. 1739; the plantation formerly belonging to WILLIAM LEVINGSTON & MARY his wife, & lately conveyed to JOSEPH BOWREY in trust for the use of JAMES BROZET, containing 1109 a., also an island of 64 a., in Colleton Co., bounding W on vacant land; N on an impassable Bay Swamp; S & SE on Chehow River & marsh. Signed by JAMES BROZET & ANN BROZET (his wife). Witnesses: WILLIAM BUCHANAN, WILLIAM HOLMAN. Before JOB ROTHMAHLER, J.P. ROBERT AUSTIN, Register.

Book S, p. 81   JAMES BROZET, ESQ., formerly of St. Christo-
29 Dec. 1737   pher's Island, now of SC to JOHN WILLETT, of
Bond   St. Christopher's Island, in penal sum of
                       ₺ 1268:5:10 for payment of ₺ 634:2:11 sterling,
British money, with interest, on 29 Dec. 1739. Witnesses: WILLIAM BUCHAN-
AN, WILLIAM HOLMAN. Before JOB ROTHMAHLER, J.P. ROBERT AUSTIN, Register.

Book S, p. 81   ANTHONY BONNEAU, JR., planter, & MARGARET HEN-
23 & 24 Sept. 1737   RIETTE, his wife, to COL. THOMAS LYNCH, plant-
L & R   er, all of Berkeley Co., for ₺ 1533 currency,
                       part of 340 a. in Berkeley Co., bounding W on
ANTHONY PORTWINE; S on THOMAS LYNCH; E on GEORGE BENISON (formerly DANIEL
MCGRIGORY); N on MAYRANTS MINOR (formerly PETER PORTWINE & part of the
340 a.). Whereas the Hon. ROBERT GIBBS & the Lords Proprs. on 28 June
1711 granted ANTHONY BONNEAU (father of above named ANTHONY) 340 a. in
Berkeley Co., bounding W on SOLOMON BRIMAR (now to ANTHONY PORTWIN); S on
THOMAS LYNCH; E on DANIEL MCGRIGORY; & N on ANTHONY BONNEAU, & whereas
JANE ELIZABETH his wife, by deed of gift & feoffment, dated 9 Nov. 1732
conveyed the 340 a. to their eldest son, ANTHONY; now he sells to LYNCH.
Witnesses: JOSEPH JULLY (?), JOHN FOGARTIE, ANTHONY POITWINE. Before
JACOB MOTTE, J.P. (plat).

Book S, p. 84   ABRAHAM WARNOCK, planter, of Prince George Par-
28 Feb. & 1 Mar. 1736 ish, Craven Co., to JAMES FISHER, merchant, of
L & R   Charleston, for ₺ 1050 currency, 500 a. in
                       Berkeley Co., on N side Wando River, bounding
W on JOSEPH MARBEAUF & RICHARD BERESFORD; N on JOHN RUSS; E on JOSEPH WAR-
NOCK; which 500 a. is half of 1000 granted by the Lords Proprs. to ABRAM
WARNOCK (father of above ABRAHAM) & by him on 20 Oct. 1719, conveyed in
fee to the son. Witnesses: WILLIAM SCOTT, JR., STEPHEN HAVEN, ISAAC SYM.
Before JACOB MOTTE, J.P.

Book S, p. 86   JOHN, Lord Carteret, Palatine; the Most Noble
25 Oct. 1726   HENRY, Duke of Beaufort; the Rt. Hon. WILLIAM,
Grant   Lord Craven; the Hon. JAMES BERTIE; HENRY BER-
                       TIE, his brother; SIR JOHN COLLETON, Baronet;
& SIR JOHN TYRRELL, Baronet; 7 of the Lords Proprs. of Carolina; to
CHARLES EDWARDS; 1 Barony, or tract of 12,000 a.; paying the Lords Proprs.
1 penny sterling yearly at the Royal Exchange of London on the Feast of
St. Michael the Archangel; & the Lords Proprs. authorize the Surveyor
General, within 20 days after notice of this grant to allot & set out the
Barony in any place in SC. Whereas THOMAS LOWNDES has surrendered a
grant for 4 Baronies in Carolina, containing 48,000 a., together with the
title, dignity & honour of Landgrave, heretofore granted to JOHN PRICE,
gentlemen, the Lords Proprs. agree to grant CHARLES LOWNDES on Barony of
12,000 a., another Barony to ISAAC LOWNDES, another Barony to JOHN BERES-
FORD, gentleman, & another Barony to THOMAS LOWNDES; total 48,000 a. On
July 5, 1727, CHARLES EDWARD, gentleman, of St. Paul's Covent Garden, declared that his name was used in trust for THOMAS LOWNDES, of St. Margaret's, Westminster, & that he had no claim. Witnesses: ESTER JOHNSON.
Memo: On 8 Sept. 1732 THOMAS LOWNDES declared that 1/2 of this Barony be-
longed to the Hon. WILLIAM BULL, ESQ., & the other half to himself.
"Memorandum: 1 moiety of this within granted Barony belongs to my father
WILLIAM BULL & the other to MR. THOMAS LOWNDES. Sept. 8, 1732. WILLIAM
BULL." A true copy from the inrollments in the Auditors Office in SC old
grant Book S. fol. 456, 457, dated 11 July 1733. JAMES ST. JOHN, Dep.
Aud. ROBERT AUSTIN, Register.

Book S, p. 87   THOMAS LOWNDES, gentleman, of St. Margaret's,
8 July 1727   Westminster, to WILLIAM BULL, ESQ., of SC, 1/2
Deed of Sale   of the Barony above granted, for ₺ 200 sterl-
                       ing; BULL to plan & lay out the Barony within
10 months & transmit to the Carolina Coffee House in London a plan showing 2 equitable half parts so that LOWNDES may choose his half & leave
the other to BULL. Witnesses: CHARLES EDWARDS, ESTER JOHNSON. Memo: the
land was not taken up by the time limited but THOMAS LOWNDES chose B & D
in the survey. ESTER JOHNSON, widow, of St. Anne's Parish, Westminster,
Co. of Middlesex, appeared on 15 Sept. 1732, in the Kings Majestys Court,
Chamber of Guild Hall, London, & declared she saw CHARLES EDWARD sign the
endorsement on a deed dated 25 Oct. 1726 (a grant from the Lords Proprs.),

stating his name was used in trust for THOMAS LOWNDES & that she also saw THOMAS LOWNDES sign the deed dated 8 July 1727 conveying 1/2 to WILLIAM BULL. JAMES ALLEN, gentleman, of London, appeared at same time to identify the papers as true copies. FRANCIS CHILD, ESQ., mayor of London, affixed his seal 15 Sept. 1732. Signed: JACKSON. A true copy from the inrollment in the Auditor's office in SC. Old grant Book S. fol. 458, 459, 460. JAMES ST. JOHN, Dep. Aud. ROBERT AUSTIN, Register.

Book S, p. 88
1 & 2 Nov. 1737
L & R

JOHN JACKSON, planter, to JOHN SPLATT, planter, both of Colleton Co., for L 885 SC money; 236 a. in Colleton Co., bounding E on Ponpon River; S on JOHN PETER; W on JOHN JACKSON; N on JOHN SPLATT. Witnesses: ISAAC HAYNE, JOHN ANDREW, THOMAS ANDREW. Before ROBERT YONGE, J.P. ROBERT AUSTIN, Register.

Book S, p. 89
2 Nov. 1737
Bond

JOHN JACKSON, planter, to JOHN SPLATT, planter, both of Colleton Co., in penal sum of L 3540 currency, to keep the conditions of the above sale. Witnesses: ISAAC HAYNES, JOHN ANDREW, THOMAS ANDREW. Before ROBERT YONGE, J.P. ROBERT AUSTIN, Register.

Book S, p. 90
16 & 17 Feb. 1737
L & R

JOHN SMITH, mariner, & LEIZABETH (her mark) his wife, late of Island of Bermuda, now of Charleston, SC, to JOHN ATKINS & EDMUND ATKINS, merchants, of Charleston, for L 345 SC money, the tract in Hamilton Tribe, Bermuda, 34 ft. N & S, bounding E on a new storehouse lately built by CAPT. GEORGE BALL; W & S on part of same land; NE on the channel of the Flats; it being part of 2 a. of common land purchased by RICHARD JENNINGS from CHARLES MOLAGAN, mariner, of Bermuda. Witnesses: WILLIAM SMITH, ROBERT BREWTON, JR. Before ROBERT AUSTIN, J.P. & Pub. Reg.

Book S, p. 92
13 & 14 Feb. 1737
L & R

ABIAH (her mark) SMALL, widow of SAMUEL SMALL, planter, to RICHARD THOMPSON, planter, & ELEANOR his wife (only surviving daughter of SAMUEL SMALL) all of Berkeley Co., to GEORGE HOGG, planter, of Granville Co., for L 1600 currency, 800 a. in Granville Co., granted by letters patent dated 4 June 1734 (?) to SAMUEL SMALL; bounding E on marsh of Port Royall River; S & N on branches of said river; W on estate of COL. ARTHUR HALL; which lands are now legally vested in ABIAH SMALL, RICHARD THOMPSON & ELEANOR his wife. Witnesses: WILLIAM BRUCE, GEORGE LOGAN (gentleman). Before WILLIAM TREWIN, J.P. ROBERT AUSTIN, Register.

Book S, p. 94
4 Aug. 1736
Bill of Sale

WILLIAM FLAVELL (FLAVEL), of Cape Fear, NC, to REBEKAH FLAVELL, widow, for L 181 currency, 1 black horse with a star & snip & branded on the mounting shoulder with   , with saddle & bridle; 1 mare & colt branded   bought from DANIEL DONOVAN; lot #65 at Beaufort; all his books, cahs, & everything he owned on Cape Fear; also 4 debts due him there; 1 due from HUDSON for about L 30; 1 from JOHN ANDERSON for about L 22; 1 from estate of CAPT. JAMES SMITH for about L 53; 1 from HENRY SIMMS for about L 15; also 1 from MR. HAWKINS for L 12:10. Witnesses: ELIZABETH PETERSON, ELIZABETH COLLETON. Before HENRY GIBBS, J.P. ROBERT AUSTIN, Register.

Book S, p. 95
14 Nov. 1737
Mortgage

FIELD COSSETT (CROSSET), mariner, & LOIS, his wife, of Colleton Co., to EDWARD NORTH, planter of St. Paul's Parish, for L 141 currency, 20 a. which DAVID GALLIWAY bought from JOHN BIDDLE, being part of a tract belonging to THOMAS ELMS, & adjoining ELMS; on E side Ashley River, about 5 miles above the ferry; also a gray horse branded   , a sorrel mare with same brand. Date of redemption: 1 Nov. 1738. Witnesses: THOMAS BOTELER, THOMAS GRAHAM MARY (her mark) LAFONTAINE. Before ROBERT AUSTIN, J.P. & Pub. Reg.

Book S, p. 96
17 & 18 Sept. 1736
L & R by Mortgage

FREDRICK (his mark) MEYER, Indian trader, to JOHN CROKATT & GEORGE SEAMAN, merchants, all of Charleston, as security on bond of even date in penal sum of L 1084 for payment of

Ł 542:11:7 SC money on 1 May next; 400 a. (half of 800 a.) on Dawflaskee Island, Granville Co., bounding N on JOHN ALLEN & FREDERICK MEYER; S on the Sound; E by JAMES ST. JOHN; W by JOHN WRIGHT. Witnesses: THOMAS BARKER, MOSES AUDEBORT. Before ROBERT AUSTIN, J.P. & Pub. Reg.

Book S, p. 97   JOHN LAURENS, saddler, & ESTER his wife, of
31 Mar. & 1 Apr. 1736 St. Philip's Parish, Charleston, to AUGUSTUS
L & R   LAURENS, planter, of Santee, Craven Co., for
                      Ł 100 SC money, 770 a. on Wambaw, Craven Co.,
bounding NE on PAUL MAZYCK; NW & SW on JOHN LAURENS; SE on vacant land; also 186-1/2 a. on Wambaw, bounding SE on the 770 a., other sides on vacant land; also 93-1/2 a. on Wambaw, adjoining 1 of the above tracts, other sides on vacant land. Witnesses: ABRAHAM SATUR, BENJAMIN ADDISON (saddler, of St. Philip's Parish). Before HENRY GIBBS, J.P. ROBERT AUSTIN, Register.

Book S, p. 100   DANIEL CRAWFORD, merchant, & SARAH his wife,
20 & 21 Feb. 1735   of Charleston, to WILLIAM SWINTON, ESQ., of
L & R   Craven Co., for Ł 15 SC money, 160 a. in Craven Co., bounding SE on Peedee River; NW & SW on vacant land; NE on AMOS HARTLEY. Witnesses: JOHN LINING, JOHN JOHNSON. Before HENRY GIBBS, J.P. ROBERT AUSTIN, Register.

Book S, p. 101   PAUL BRUNEAU, planter, & ELIZABETH his wife,
20 & 21 Aug. 1736   of St. James Santee, to WILLIAM BORCKINTON,
L & R   planter, of Winyaw, Craven Co., for Ł 50 currency, free from ELIZABETH'S claim of dower, 400 a. in Craven Co., on head of N branch of Black River, bounding N on MR. HUNTER; S on GEORGE CHICKEN; E on vacant land; which 400 a. was granted to PAUL BRUNEAU by Lt. Gov. THOMAS BROUGHTON on 4 June 1735. Witnesses: AUGUSTUS LAURENS, SUSANNEE SNOW, ANN FRANCIS LEGRAND. Before HENRY GIBBS, J.P. ROBERT AUSTIN, Register.

Book S, p. 104   BENJAMIN GODFREY, butcher, & MARTHA (her mark)
23 July 1737   his wife, to WILLIAM FULLER, planter, of Berke-
L & R by Mortgage   ley Co., with MARTHA'S consent 64 a. in St. Andrew's Parish, Berkeley Co., bounding SW on COL. WILLIAM BULL; NW on JOHN BROWN; N on MR. CERARDEAU; SE & S on RICHARD GODFREY; which 64 a. is part of 672 a. in 3 lots formerly belonging to CAPT. RICHARD GODFREY, afterwards to SAMUEL JONES, & lately sold to BENJAMIN GODFREY by ISAAC WEIGHT & DOROTHY JONES. Whereas WILLIAM FULLER, at GODFREY'S request, endorsed GODFREY'S bond dated 21 July (inst.) given to ANTHONY MATHEWS, CHARLES PINCKNEY, JAMES CROKATT, HENRY PERONNEAU, JR., & JACOB MOTTE, in penal sum of Ł 1000 for payment of Ł 500 currency & interest on 25 Mar. 1738; & whereas GODFREY & SAMUEL STOCKS, butcher, of Berkeley Co., gave FULLER a bond, this date, in penal sum of Ł 2000 to insure GODFREY'S payment of above Ł 500; now GODFREY secures FULLER from loss. Witnesses: EDWARD ORD, JAMES SCARLITT, SAMUEL ELMES. Before WILLIAM BULL, JR. This mortgage was assigned to BENJAMIN WHITAKER who, on 20 Feb. 1744, acknowledged satisfaction.

Book S, p. 106   HUGH BUTLER, ESQ., & ANN his wife, of Exeter,
12 & 13 May 1737   SC (?) to MARY BETTESON, spinster, of SC, as
L & R by Mortgage   security on bond dated 7 May 1735 in penal sum
                      of Ł 2000 for payment of Ł 1000 & interest on
7 Jan. 1735; 500 a. in Berkeley Co., (grant dated 8 Aug. 1716), bounding N & S on HUGH BUTLER; E on CAPT. LEBAIS; W on vacant land. Witnesses: ANTHONY HUGGETT, GEORGE CHICKEN. Before JOB ROTHMAHLER, J.P. for Colleton Co. ROBERT AUSTIN, Register.

Book S, p. 109   EDWARD (his mark) ORAM, butcher, of Berkeley
24 Feb. 1737/8   Co., to his loving friend, ELIZABETH DAVIS,
Deed of Gift   for love & affection, 200 a. about 16 miles
                     from Charleston, bounding on BENJAMIN HOOD &
THOMAS MILLS, adjoining the widow BOSWOOD; 1 Negro man; 1 Negro girl; all his horses, mares, cattle & sheep, & his debts. Witnesses: JAMES (his mark) SMITH, MARMADUKE ASH, WILLIAM FRANCKLYN. Before ROBERT AUSTIN, J.P. & Pub. Reg.

Book S, p. 109   JOHN BOSWOOD, planter, & ANNE ("NANSEY") his

31 Mar. & 1 Apr. 1737   wife, to EDWARD ORAM, butcher, all of Berkeley
L & R   Co., for ₤ 400 SC money, 200 a. on N side Ash-
                        ley River, bounding E on BENJAMIN WOOD, S on
THOMAS DRAYTON; W on WILLIAM BOSWOOD & JOSIAH CANTEY; N on CANTEY. Wit-
nesses: ROBERT WRIGHT, JAMES WRIGHT. Before ROBERT AUSTIN, J.P. & Pub.
Reg.

Book S, p. 111   JOHN GUERRY, planter, of Craven Co., & MARGA-
24 & 25 Nov. 1737   RET GUERRY, widow, acting & only surviving ex-
L & R   ecutors of will of PETER GUERRY, planter, to
                        THOMAS BOONE, planter, of Christ Church Parish,
Berkeley Co., for ₤ 1200 SC money, 4 tracts of 250, 150, 50, & 50 a., as
follows: (#1) 250 a. in Craven Co., bounding SW on Wadbaccan Creek; SE on
PETER GUERRY; NE on JAMES ROBERT; NW on ISAAC DUBOSE & JONATHAN WHILDEN;
also 150 a., (#2) bounding NW on above tract; SW on Wadbaccan Creek; SE
on PETER GUERRY & JOHN DUBOSE; NE on JAMES ROBERT; also (#3) 1/3 of 150 a.
(50 a.) bounding NW on last named tract; SW on Wadbaccan Creek; SE & NE
on JAMES ROBERT; the 50 a. to be taken joining the middle tract from the
creek, the whole length of the tract & 6-1/2 chains being the front of
the middle tract 26 chains front, 25 chains being the front of the 250 a.
purchased by ISAAC DUBOSE, planter, & makes altogether 51 chains in front
on Wadbaccan Creek, the depth to be according to plat; (the 3 tracts making 450 a.); also 50 a. (#4) part of a tract purchased by JAMES ROBERT
(grant signed by Lt. Gov. THOMAS BROUGHTON 7 Aug. 1735) the 50 a. to be
taken out of the tract adjoining the 250 a. purchased by ISAAC DUBOSE,
i.e., on SE side & to join the head of the tract adjoining the aforesaid
tract, the head line 78 chains from Wadbaccan Creek (purchased by JOHN
DUBOSE) & the 50 a. so joining the SE line of the old tract, & the head
of the new tract shall be 26 chains long from said line of old tract to
run SE & 19 chains 25 links from head line of new purchased tract which
makes that just complement of land & makes it to bound as follows: NW &
SW on PETER GUERRY; all other sides on JAMES ROBERT; the original tract
granted to JAMES ROBERT containing 1050 a., out of which the 50 a. are to
be taken as specified. Whereas by L & R, 15 & 16 Nov. 1735, JOHN BARNETT,
planter, & JUDITH his wife, of Craven Co., sold PETER GUERRY, planter,
250 a. (#1); also 150 a. (#2); also 1/3 of 150 a. or 50 a. (#3); also
(#4) 50 a.; & whereas PETER GUERRY by will dated 1 Mar. 1736 appointed
his beloved wife MARGARET GUERRY, JOHN BARNETT, & JOHN GUERRY, his executors, & willed that his land on N side Santee River be sold; now they
sell 500 a. to THOMAS BOONE; also 1 ferry boat & 2 canoes. Witnesses:
GEORGE OLIVER, RICHARD CAPERS, JOHN HOLMES. Before JACOB MOTTE, J.P.

Book S, p. 115   WILLIAM WILKINS, planter, of Berkeley Co., to
27 Dec. 1737   his well beloved son WILLIAM WILKINS, JR., for
Deed of Gift   love & affection, 500 a. on John's Island, Col-
                        leton Co., 150 a. being part of a tract grant-
ed by the Lords Proprs. to RICHARD WILLSON, bounding S on WILLIAM SHIPPEY;
W on 350 a. laid out to MADAM ELIZABETH GODFREY, which 350 a. is the remaining part of said 500 a., bounding N on Abpoolaw Creek out of Stono
River; W on land purchased by ELIZABETH GODFREY, now owned by WILKINS;
also 5 Negro men & 1 Negro woman; reserving certain priviledges for himself. Witnesses: ARCHIBALD WILKINS, JOHN PURKIS. Before JACOB MOTTE,
J.P. ROBERT AUSTIN, Register.

Book S, p. 116   JOHN BONHOSTE, planter, & MARIAN his wife, to
21 & 22 Nov. 1737   ELIAS FOISSIN, planter, all of Christ Church
L & R   Parish, Berkeley Co., for ₤ 350 SC money, 350
                        a. in Craven Co., near Peedee, bounding NE on
WILLIAM BUCHANAN; NW on FRANCIS BRITTON; other sides on vacant land;
which 350 a. was granted by Lt. Gov. THOMAS BROUGHTON on 14 Feb. 1735 to
JOHN BONHOSTE; MARIAN to renounce her dower when requested before ROBERT
WRIGHT, C.J. Witnesses: BENTLEY COOK (COKE), ALEXANDER FRISELL. Before
WILLIAM WHITESIDE. ROBERT AUSTIN, Register.

Book S, p. 118   THOMAS (his mark) BLYTHE, Dep. Sur., & JANE
21 & 22 Jan. 1735   his wife, of Georgetown, to JOHN HENTIE, Dep.
L & R   Sur., of Charleston, for ₤ 40 SC money, 300 a.
                        on NW side Bever Creek, bounding all sides on
vacant land; granted by Lt. Gov. THOMAS BROUGHTON to THOMAS BLYTHE on 12
May 1735; plat certified by JAMES ST. JOHN, Sur. Gen. Witnesses: WILLIAM

GRIPPS, THOMAS TODD. Before DANIEL LAROCHE, J.P. ROBERT Austin, Register.

Book S, p. 120
22 & 23 Dec. 1726
L & R
DAVID BATCHELER, planter, & SARAH his wife, of Berkeley Co., to ELIAS FOISSIN of Charleston, for ₤ 600, 200 a., English measure, on N side of E branch of Wando River, part of 260 a. laid out to BATCHELER, bounding according to plat. Witnesses: BENJAMIN WHITAKER, WILLIAM MORALL. Before DANIEL GREENE, J.P. ROBERT AUSTIN, Pub. Reg. Plat in book as resurveyed & certified 23 Dec. 1726 by WILLIAM WINDRA, D.S.

Book S, p. 122
9 & 10 Feb. 1737
L & R
ALCIMUS GILLARD, planter, of Winyaw, Craven Co., (1 of the sons & devise of BARTHOLOMEW GAILLARD), to JOSEPH WRAGG, merchant, of Charleston for ₤ 600 SC money, 10 a. in Berkeley Co., bounding S on Charleston; W on the parsonage land; N on THOMAS KIMBERLY; E on the Broad Path. Witnesses: WILLIAM SHACKELFORD, MARY ATHARTON, ESTER SHACKELFORD. Before WILLIAM SHITESIDE, J.P.

Book S, p. 124
25 & 26 Jan. 1737
L & R by Mortgage
JOSEPH SINGLETARY, planter, of Berkeley Co., to HENRY PERONNEAU, JR. & ALEXANDER PERONNEAU, merchants, of Charleston, as security on bond of even date in penal sum of ₤ 2208 for payment of ₤ 1104 currency, with interest, on 1 Feb. 1738; 505 a. in Berkeley Co., bounding SW on JOHN DUNHAM & on vacant lands as by plat attached to grant dated 1 June 1709 from Lords Proprs. to JOSEPH SINGLETARY. Witnesses: ALEXANDER STEWART (STUART), BENJAMIN STEAD. Before HENRY GIBBS, J.P. ROBERT AUSTIN, Register. Mortgage declared satisfied 22 Apr. 1752. Witness: WILLIAM HOPTON.

Book S, p. 126
30 & 31 May 1735
L & R Tripartite
JOHN FILBIN, planter, of 1st part; WILLIAM CATTELL, ESQ., of 2nd part; BENJAMIN CATTELL, an infant under 21 years, of 3rd part. JOHN FILBEN, for ₤ 480, conveyed to WILLIAM CATTELL, on behalf of BENJAMIN CATTELL, 40 a., English measure, on N side Ashley River, St. Andrews Parish, Berkeley Co., part of 500 a. formerly belonging to THOMAS ROSE but now to WILLIAM CATTELL & RALPH IZARD, which 40 a. was sold by ROSE to THOMAS DALTON; bounding SW, NW, & NE on THOMAS ROSE; SE on JOSEPH FITCH (formerly CHARLES FIELD). Witnesses: WILLIAM LADSON, CHARLES BARKER, WILLIAM CATTELL, JR. Before JACOB MOTTE, J.P. ROBERT AUSTIN, Register.

Book S, p. 128
20 & 21 Feb. 1737
L & R by Mortgage
RICHARD HALL, gentleman, of Williamsburgh, to WILLIAM CATTELL & GEORGE AUSTIN, merchants, of Charleston, for ₤ 5000 SC money, 550 a. in Williamsburgh Township, Craven Co., bounding SW on Black River; SE on JOHN ANDERSON; NE on JOHN PORTER; NW on RICHARD HALL; also 500 a. in said Township bounding S on Black River; E on vacant land; N on WILLIAM MORGAN & MR. BORLAND; W on WILLIAM HAMILTON; also 500 a. set apart for the Township of Williamsburgh, bounding SW on Black River; SE on THOMAS HALL; NE on vacant land; NW on JOHN BASSNETT; also a 1/2 a. lot #3 in Williamsburgh, bounding SW on the Bay of the town; SE on THOMAS HALL; NE on vacant land; NW on WILLIAM MORGAN. Date of redemption: 1 June next. Witnesses: MAURICE LEWIS, JOHN RATTRAY. Before ROBERT AUSTIN, Ass't. J. of Ct. of C.P. & Pub. Reg.

Book S, p. 130
30 & 31 July 1736
L & R
WILLIAM HAMILTON, vintner, & ISABELLA his wife, of Berkeley Co., to DAVID ALLAN, planter, of Craven Co., for ₤ 100 SC money, 200 a. in Williamsburgh Township, Craven Co., bounding N & E on RICHARD HALL; S on Black River; W on JOHN BAXTER; also half a lot in the Township, bounding SW on the Bay; SE on JOHN BASSNETT; NW on other half belonging to WILLIAM HAMILTON. Witnesses: JOB ROTHMAHLER, ALEXANDER THOMPSON. Before HENRY GIBBS, J.P. ROBERT AUSTIN, Register.

Book S, p. 132
10 & 11 Feb. 1737
L & R
WILLIAM MCPHERSON, & ANNE (her mark) his wife, of Colleton Co., to WILLIAM BUCHANAN, of Granville Co., granted by Lt. Gov. THOMAS BROUGHTON to WILLIAM MCPHERSON on 26 June 1737,

bounding E on Saltketcher River; N on MR. HARTGROVE; S on JAMES BURR; other sides on vacant land. Witnesses: JAMES SKIRVING, JOHN LOVEKIN, JOSEPH BEVERLY. Before STEPHEN BULL, J.P.

Book S, p. 134　　　　　　JOHN (his mark) READ, JR., planter, & MARY
24 & 25 Jan. 1737　　　　(her mark) his wife, to JOHN RYAN, merchant,
L & R　　　　　　　　　　of Charleston, for Ł 150 SC money, 676 a. in
　　　　　　　　　　　　　Craven Co., granted to him on 12 Aug. 1737, on W side Winyaw River, bounding SE on Landgrave SMITH; NE on MR. BRETON (BRITON); NW & SW on vacant land; the land to be free from MARY'S claim of dower. Witnesses: JEREMIAH BANKS, ROBERT (his mark) REED, MILLAR ST. JOHN. Before JAMES BULLOCK, J.P. ROBERT AUSTIN, Register.

Book S, p. 136　　　　　　THOMAS BROWN, buther, & ESTER (her mark) his
27 & 28 Feb. 1737　　　　wife, to JOHN RYAN, merchant, all of Charles-
L & R　　　　　　　　　　ton, for Ł 55 SC money, 550 a. in Williams-
　　　　　　　　　　　　　burgh Township, Craven Co., granted to him 3 Feb. 1737, bounding NW on the Township line; other sides on vacant land; also lot #136 (1/2 a.). Witnesses: ANTHONY WILLIAMS, ROWLAND SERJEANT, WILLIAM SMITH. Before THOMAS DALE, J.P. ROBERT AUSTIN, Register.

Book S, p. 137　　　　　　JOHN HICKS, planter, to WILLIAM NASH, planter,
14 June 1731　　　　　　　both of Colleton Co., for Ł 300 SC money, 150
Deed of Sale　　　　　　　a. in Colleton Co., on S side Littenwaw Creek,
　　　　　　　　　　　　　bounding E on THOMAS WENNBONN (WINBORN); S & W on JOHN HICKS. Witnesses: THOMAS WENBORN, MARY WENBORN, EDMOND JERVICE. Before DANIEL GREEN, J.P. A memorial entered in Auditor's office 16 May 1733. Recorded in office of Pub. Reg. in Book R. fol. 473 & 475, 23 Nov. 1737 by NATHANIEL JOHNSON, Pub. Reg., per JOHN PENNYMAN. "The above is a copy of what is written in Book R but not of record but is now recorded in book S, Folio 137 & 138 this 9th day of March 1737 per ROBERT AUSTIN, Pub. Reg."

Book S, p. 139　　　　　　JOHN HICKS, planter, to WILLIAM NASH, planter,
14 June 1731　　　　　　　in penal sum of Ł 600 currency, to keep agree-
Bond　　　　　　　　　　　ments in above bill of sale. Witnesses: MARY
　　　　　　　　　　　　　WINBORN, EDMUND JERVIS, THOMAS WINBORN. Before DANIEL GREEN, J.P. Recorded in Pub. Reg. office in Book R. fol. 473 on 23 Nov. 1737 by NATHANIEL JOHNSON, Pub. Reg. per JOHN PENNYMAN, but not attested by JOHNSON. Now recorded by ROBERT AUSTIN, Pub. Reg.

Book S, p. 139　　　　　　ARTHUR BULL, planter, & SARAH his wife, to
19 July 1734　　　　　　　WILLIAM NASH, planter, all of Colleton Co.,
Deed of Sale　　　　　　　for Ł 180 SC money, a tract of 80 a. included
　　　　　　　　　　　　　in a plat of JOHN HICK'S land & separated therefrom by a line run from the head of Fishing Creek to Bow Bluff; on S side Littinwaw Creek, bounding E on WILLIAM NASH; S & W on Fishing Creek. Witnesses: JONATHAN THOMAS, EDMUND (his mark) JARVIS (JERVOISE). Before ROBERT YONGE, J.P. Recorded in Pub. Reg. office in Book R. fol. 476 & 477 on 23 Nov. 1737 by NATHANIEL JOHNSON, Pub. Reg. per JOHN PENNYMAN, but not attested by JOHNSON therefore now registered by ROBERT AUSTIN, Pub. Reg.

Book S, p. 140　　　　　　ARTHUR BULL to WILLIAM NASH, planter, in penal
19 July 1734　　　　　　　sum of Ł 360 for keeping agreements in above
Bond　　　　　　　　　　　bill of sale. Witnesses: JONATHAN THOMAS, ED-
　　　　　　　　　　　　　MOND (his mark) JARVIS. Before ROBERT YONGE, J.P. Recorded in Pub. Reg. office in Bk. R. fol 475 & 476 on 23 Nov. 1737 by NATHANIEL JOHNSON, Pub. Reg., per JOHN PENNYMAN, but not attested by JOHNSON, therefore registered now by ROBERT AUSTIN, Register.

Book S, p. 141　　　　　　DAVID FERGUSON & MARTHA (her mark) his wife,
12 Oct. 1728　　　　　　　to WILLIAM NASH, planter, for Ł 1800 currency,
Deed of Sale　　　　　　　500 a. on Wadmahlah Island, Colleton Co. as
　　　　　　　　　　　　　laid out by Lords Proprs., bounding E & SE on Bohickett Creek; S & W on WILLIAM WELLS; N on JOHN JERVIS & JAMES (?) RAMSEY; NE on ROGER NEWINGTON; all their stock of cattle, hogs, horses, & periauger. Witnesses: SAMUEL SHADDOCK, THOMAS WENBORN. Before DANIEL GREENE, J.P. Recorded in Pub. Reg. office in Bk. R. fol. 467 & 469 on 28 Nov. 1737 by NATHANIEL JOHNSON, Pub. Reg., per JOHN PENNYMAN, but not

attested by JOHNSON, therefore registered now by ROBERT AUSTIN, Register.

Book S, p. 142　　　　　　　DAVIS FERGUSON, planter, to WILLIAM NASH,
12 Oct. 1728　　　　　　　　planter, both of Colleton Co., in penal sum of
Bond　　　　　　　　　　　　Ł 3600 currency, to keep all agreements in
　　　　　　　　　　　　　　above bill of sale. Witnesses: SAMUEL JONES,
SAMUEL SHADDOCK, THOMAS WENBORN. Before DANIEL GREENE, J.P. Recorded in
Pub. Reg. office in Bk. R. fol 466 & 467 on 21 Nov. 1737 by NATHANIEL
JOHNSON, Register, per JOHN PENNYMAN, but not attested by JOHNSON, therefore registered now by ROBERT AUSTIN, Register.

Book S, p. 142　　　　　　　SAMUEL SLEIGH, planter, & MARY his wife, to
5 & 6 Apr. 1737　　　　　　 JAMES SKIRVIN & MOSES MARTIN, all of Colleton
L & R　　　　　　　　　　　 Co., for Ł 50 currency, 397 a. in Colleton Co.,
　　　　　　　　　　　　　　bounding SW on MADAM BOONE; NW on JAMES KELLEY;
N on JOHN MUSGROVE; NE on PAUL JENYS; E on PAUL JENYS & MOSES MAORTIN; SE
on SAMUEL SLEIGH. Delivered with plot & grant. Witnesses: LAURENCE
SAUNDERS, JAMES SAUNDERS, ISAAC MARTIN. Before MALACHI GLAZE, J.P. ROBERT AUSTIN, Register.

Book S, p. 144　　　　　　　PATRICK MARTIN, merchant, of Berkeley Co., to
6 Apr. 1709　　　　　　　　 MATHEW BEE, planter, of Colleton Co., for Ł 12
Deed of Sale　　　　　　　　currency, 200 a. on E side Bee's Creek, Colleton Co., granted by JOHN, Earl of Bath, Palatine, & the Lords Proprs., signed by Gov. JAMES MOORE, on 5 Nov. 1701 to
PATRICK MARTIN; bounding N on JONATHAN HARRIS & vacant land; E on vacant
land; S on JAMES ROGERS. Witnesses: GEORGE DUCATT, JOSEPH THORNTON, THOMAS (his mark) BEE. Memorial entered in Auditor's office 16 May 1733. Before THOMAS DALE, J.P. ROBERT AUSTIN, Register.

Book S, p. 145　　　　　　　HENRY LIVINGSTON, planter, & ANNE his wife,
31 Mar. 1737　　　　　　　　with her free consent, to THOMAS SACHEVERELL,
L & R　　　　　　　　　　　 planter, all of Colleton Co., for Ł 1600 currency, 562-1/2 a., part of 4000 a. granted Gov.
ROBERT GIBBS & the Lords Proprs. to Landgrave ROBERT DANIEL in part of
his patent for 48,000 a., on 27 June 1711; the 562-1/2 a. being the NW
part of the N end of the 4000 a., in Colleton Co., on E side PonPon River,
bounding SE on WILLIAM SINGLETON; NW on RICHARD GIRARDEAU; NE on Coosaw
Indian lands. Whereas JOHN, Earl of Bath, Palatine, & the Lords Proprs.
by letters patent dated 12 Aug. 1698 created ROBERT DANIEL, ESQ., a Landgrave, granting him 48,000 a. of land; & whereas Gov. ROBERT GIBBS & the
Lords Proprs. on 27 June 1711 granted Landgrave ROBERT DANIEL 4000 a.
(part of the 48,000 above mentioned), in Colleton Co., & whereas ROBERT
DANIEL by deed poll dated 28 June 1711, conveyed to WILLIAM LIVINGSTON,
clerk (father of HENRY), the 4000 a.; & whereas WILLIAM LIVINGSTON some
time after 17 July 1723, (having first sold part of the 4000 a.) made his
will & bequeathed all that unsold part of the 4000 a. to his first wife
(making together with his part of what he sold her (?)) 2250 a., to be
equally divided between his wife HANNAH (now wife of JOHN DART) & his
sons (WILLIAM & said HENRY) & his daughter MARGARET, (but son WILLIAM
might have the part the Bluff should fall upon if he pleased); & whereas,
after his death, WILLIAM & HENRY LIVINGSTON (sons), JOHN DART (in behalf
of his wife HANNAH), & said JOHN DART (in right of wife HANNAH as guardian of MARGARET, a minor, & on behalf of MARGARET) with the consent of
JOSEPH MOODY, MARGARET'S surviving guardian appointed in the will, caused
an equal division of the 2250 a. to be made & the allotment to HENRY was
562-1/2 a., being the NW part of N end of the 4000 a., on E side PonPon
River, bounding SE on the part now owned by JOHN DART; SW on WILLIAM LIVINGSTON; NW on RICHARD GIRARDEAU; NE on the Cusoe Indians land; now HENRY
sells to SACHEVEREL. Witnesses: JOHN COOK, JOHN LEARY. Before JAMES
BULLOCK, J.P. Memo. Entered in Auditor's office 7 Mar. 1737 by JAMES
ST. JOHN, D.A. ROBERT AUSTIN, Register. Plat in Book.

Book S, p. 149　　　　　　　DAVID CHRISTINAZ, carpenter, of Charleston, to
5 & 6 Mar. 1737　　　　　　 JACOB JENNERET, planter, of St. James, Santee,
L & R　　　　　　　　　　　 for Ł 1000 currency, part of lot #105, in
　　　　　　　　　　　　　　Charleston, bounding N on JOB ROTHMAHLER; S on
REBECCA FLAVEL; E 13-1/2 ft. on JAMES PAIN; W 13-1/2 ft. on a street leading from White Point to Quakers Meeting house; the depth being the depth
of the lot. Witnesses: JOHN LAURENS, DAVID DELESCURE. Before HENRY

GIBBS, J.P. ROBERT AUSTIN, Register.

Book S, p. 151   DAVID CHRISTINAZ, carpenter, of St. Philip's
6 Mar. 1737   Parish, Charleston, to JACOB JEANNERETTE,
Bond   planter, of St. James, Santee, in penal sum of
                        ₤ 2000 currency, for keeping agreements in
above deed. Witnesses: JOHN LAURENS, DAVID DELESCURE. Before HENRY
GIBBS, J.P. ROBERT AUSTIN, Register.

Book S, p. 151   JOHN FRASER, merchant, & JUDITH his wife, to
31 July & 1 Aug. 1735   GEORGE HAIG & FRED MEYER, gentlemen, all of
L & R   Charleston, for ₤ 500 currency, 950 a. in Col-
                        leton Co., bounding SE on THOMAS FORD; W on
THOMAS ELLIOT; other sides on vacant land; which 950 a. was granted to
FRASER by letters patent dated 6 Apr. 1733, signed by Gov. ROBERT JOHNSON.
Witnesses: JOHN COWAND, WILLIAM STAPLES (gentleman). Before THOMAS LAM-
BOLL, J.P. Recorded in Bk. R. fol. 481-484 by NATHANIEL JOHNSON, Pub.
Reg., per JOHN PENNYMAN, but not attested, therefore, registered now by
ROBERT AUSTIN, Register.

Book S, p. 154   FREDERICK MEYER, Indian trader, to RIPTON HUT-
30 & 31 Aug. 1736   CHINSON & FREDERICK GRIMKE, merchants, all of
L & R by Mortgage   Charleston, as security on bond of even date
                        in penal sum of ₤ 396 SC money, for payment of
₤ 198:2:3 on last day of Nov. next; half the tract of 950 a. in Colleton
Co., bounding SE on THOMAS FORD; W on THOMAS ELLIOTT; other sides on vacant land. Witnesses: CHARLES CORDES, ALEXANDER LEVIE. Recorded in Bk.
R. fol. 486-487 by NATHANIEL JOHNSON, per JOHN PENNYMAN, but not attested
by JOHNSON, therefore, recorded now by ROBERT AUSTIN, Register.

Book S, p. 156   ROBERT JOHNSON, Gov., to JOHN FRASER, 950 a.
6 Apr. 1733   in Colleton Co., bounding W on THOMAS FORD; NW
Grant   on THOMAS ELLIOTT; other sides on vacant land.
                        J. BADENHOP, clerk, Con. Recorded in Secre-
tary's office 25 Apr. 1733 in Grant Book AA fol. 85. J. HAMMERTON, Sec.
Plat in book S. By warrant dated 27 Nov. 1731, signed by Gov. ROBERT
JOHNSON, the 950 a. were surveyed by JAMES ST. JOHN, Sur. Gen. Recorded
in Bk. R. fol. 484-486 by NATHANIEL JOHNSON, Register, per. JOHN PANNYMAN,
but not attested by JOHNSON, therefore, recorded now by ROBERT AUSTIN,
Register.

Book S, p. 157   SAMUEL MILLER, planter, & REBECCA his wife, to
3 & 4 Mar. 1737/8   CORNELIUS DUPRE, planter, all of Berkeley Co.,
L & R   for natural love & affection & ₤ 200 currency,
                        400 a., English measure, in Berkeley Co., on a
place commonly called Indian Field Swamp, bounding NW on BENJAMIN COACH-
MAN, other sides on vacant land. REBECCA renounced her dower. Witnesses: A (?) DUPONT, GID. DUPONT, JAMES SINGLETON. Before ROBERT AUSTIN,
J.P. & Pub. Reg.

Book S, p. 159   CAPT. SAMUEL MORRIS, of Berkeley Co., to WIL-
30 July 1734   LIAM WATIES, ESQ., of Craven Co., as security
Mortgage   on 5 bonds dated 29 July last, for ₤ 1400 cur-
                        rency with interest, payable in various sums
on various dated; 700 a. on N side Goose Creek, formerly belonging to
JOHN & JAMES GRAING, lately to WILLIAM WATIES then purchased by SAMUEL
MORRIS; bounding E on ROBERT HUME, ESQ., W on HUGH GRAING & JOHN LARENCE.
Witnesses: MOSES WILSON, MATHEW DRAKE. Before DANIEL WELSHUYSEN, J.P.
ROBERT AUSTIN, Register.

Book S, p. 160   WILLIAM SWINTON, gentleman, & HANNAH his wife,
9 & 10 Mar. 1737   of Craven Co., to THOMAS LAROCHE, merchant, of
L & R   Georgetown, for ₤ 1000 SC money, 300 a. on
                        Peedee River, granted to SWINTON 7 June 1735
by Lt. Gov. THOMAS BROUGHTON; bounding E on WILLIAM ALSTON; S on JAMES
GORDON, ESQ.; N on a thoroughfare from Waccamaw River. Witnesses: JOHN
OULDFIELD, JR., THOMAS LEITH. Before MAURICE LEWIS, J.P. ROBERT AUSTIN,
Register.

Book S, p. 162   WILLIAM SWINTON, gentleman, to THOMAS LAROCHE,

10 Mar. 1737   merchant, of Georgetown, in penal sum of
Bond   ₤ 2000 SC money, for keeping agreements of
                                above sale. Witnesses: JOHN OULDFIELD, JR.,
THOMAS LEITH. Before MAURICE LEWIS, J.P. ROBERT AUSTIN, Register.

Book S, p. 163   JOHN ABBOTT, merchant, & ELIZABETH his wife of
16 & 17 Feb. 1735   Georgetown, Winyaw, to HENRY JAMES DAUBAWZ,
L & R   mariner, of London, England, for ₤ 750 SC cur-
                                rency, 500 a. in Craven Co., part of 1000 a.
sold by Landgrave THOMAS SMITH & MARY his wife to JOHN RIDLEY; bounding S
on Sampit River; E on the Rev. MR. THOMAS MORRETT; W on CAPT. GEORGE
SMITH; N on JOSHUA WILKS. Witnesses: THOMAS LAROCHE, THOMAS RYAN. Before ROBERT AUSTIN, J.P. & Pub. Reg.

Book S, p. 165   MAURICE LEWIS, ESQ., of Charleston, to JOHN
15 & 16 Mar. 1737   OULDFIELD, gentleman, for ₤ 500, that undivid-
L & R   ed half part of 500 a. in Queensborough Town-
                                ship, Craven Co., bounding NE on MAURICE LEWIS;
SE on GILES HOLLIDAY & JOHN GOODWYN; SW on land laid out; NW on vacant
land; also the undivided half of that other tract of 1000 a. in Queensborough Township, bounding NE on head lines of land laid out to GEORGE
LEA, WILLIAM BORLAND, & ROBERT FLEDGER; other sides on vacant land. Wit-
nesses: JAMES VARNOR, THOMAS LAROCHE. Before ROBERT AUSTIN, J.P. & Pub.
Reg.

Book S, p. 166   GEORGE PAWLEY, planter, & MARY his wife, of
5 & 6 Sept. 1737   Prince George Parish, to JOHN OULDFIELD, JR.,
L & R   planter, of Craven Co., for ₤ 1690 SC money,
                                556 a. in Craven Co., on Peedee River, bound-
ing N on JOSEPH LABRUCE; S on THOMAS LAROCHE (formerly WILLIAM DRAKE); W
on DANIEL & THOMAS LAROCHE; also 176 a. on E side Peedee River, bounding
S on Squirrel Creek; E on a large creek; N on JOSEPH LABRUCE. Whereas
Lt. Gov. THOMAS BROUGHTON on 12 Aug. 1737 granted GEORGE PAWLEY 556 a. in
Craven Co., & on 4 Dec. 1735 granted him 176 a. in Craven Co., now PAWLEY
sells both tracts to OULDFIELD. Witnesses: WILLIAM WHITESIDE, DANIEL LA-
ROCHE, THOMAS LAROCHE. Before MAURICE LEWIS, J.P. ROBERT AUSTIN, Regis-
ter.

Book S, p. 168   JOHN CATTELL, planter, & SARAH his wife, of
30 & 31 May 1735   Berkeley Co., to JOHN FILBIN, planter, of Col-
L & R   leton Co., for ₤ 1527 currency, 509 a. in Col-
                                leton Co., bounding E on JOSEPH PENDARVIS &
ELISHA CARLISLE; S on MR. BUTOLPH; W on SILAS WELLS; N on HENRY NICHOLS
(NICHOLAS). Whereas on 20 May 1734 JOHN CATTELL was granted 514 a. which
when resurveyed was found to be 509 a., now he sells to FILBIN. Witnesses: CHARLES BARKER, ROBERT LADSON, JR., WILLIAM CATTELL, JR. Before
THOMAS LAMBOLL, J.P. Memorial entered in Auditor's office, 29 July 1736
by JAMES ST. JOHN, D.A. Recorded in Book R. fol. 497-500 by NATHANIEL
JOHNSON, Pub. Reg., per JOHN PENNYMAN, but not attested by JOHNSON,
therefore recorded now by ROBERT AUSTIN, Register.

Book S, p. 171   RICHARD ALLEIN, gentleman, of St. James, San-
7 & 8 Nov. 1737   tee, Craven Co., to BENJAMIN GODIN, merchant,
L & R by Mortgage   of Charleston, as security on bond dated 9
                                Oct. 1737 in penal sum of ₤ 1300 for payment
of ₤ 1300 for payment of ₤ 650 SC money, with interest on 9 Nov. next;
500 a. in St. James, Santee known as "Peachtree", on which he lives &
which he purchased from WILLIAM DRAKE, bounding NW on JOHN BUDDEN, other
sides on RICHARD ALLEIN; also 150 a. adjoining, being part of 1200 a.
purchased from WILLIAM WATIES, known as Yaughaun, bounding NW on above
500 a.; SE on 400 a. lately sold by ALLEIN to CAPT. ROBERT AUSTIN; NE on
Santee River Swamp. Witnesses: ZENOBIA BILLING, GIDEON BILLING, B. GODIN,
JR. Before ROBERT AUSTIN, J.P. & Pub. Reg.

Book S, p. 172   WILLIAM SPENCER, planter, & SARAH his wife,
9 & 10 Feb. 1736   Of James Island, St. Andrews Parish, Berkeley
L & R   Co., to JAMES MURDOCK, chapman, of Johns Is-
                                land, Colleton Co., for ₤ 300 currency, 200 a.
in Colleton Co., bounding SE on WILLIAM SPENCER; S on COL. HALL (formerly
EDWARD & HUGH HEXT); W on DR. KILPATRICK (formerly AMIES HEXT); N on

CALEB KNIGHT (formerly ALEXANDER HEXT); the 200 a. being part of 400 a. granted 29 May 1702 by the Lords Proprs. to COL. ROBERT GIBBES (plat dated 20 Dec. 1691) in Colleton Co., at head of Wadwadmalaw River, bounding N on the river & vacant land; W on ABRAHAM WEIGHT & vacant land. GIBBES bequeathed the land to his son JOHN, who, on 17 July 1718, for ₤ 400 sold to THOMAS SEABROOK. SEABROOK made an agreement with ALEXANDER HEXT that HEXT should pay various debts of SEABROOK'S & for 20 shillings paid to them, THOMAS SEABROOK & MARY his wife, conveyed the 400 a. to HEXT on 27 Aug. 1719. On 10 June 1720, ALEXANDER HEXT sold to HUGH HEXT & he, on 8 July 1728 sold to HENRY NICKOLLS 1/2 or 200 a. He bequeathed the 200 a. to his son ISAAC, who on 6 Aug. 1733 sold to WILLIAM SPENCER, who now sells to MURDOCK. Witnesses: ALEXANDER SPENCER, NICHOLAS SMITH. Before HENRY GIBBES, J.P. ROBERT AUSTIN, Register.

Book S, p. 175
3 Jan. (?) & 14 Aug. 1733
Deed of Gift

COL. THOMAS LYNCH, gentleman, of Christ Church Parish, Berkeley Co., to JAMES BELLING, JR., & SARAH his wife, & ALLARD BILLING & JAMES BILLING, JR. (sons of JAMES & SARAH), for love & affection, 1000 a. on Santee River, in Prince George Parish, bounding N on Landgrave THOMAS SMITH'S Barony; S on COL. THOMAS LYNCH; W on FENEAS SPRY. Witnesses: FRANCIS BRITTEN, WILLIAM REED, WILLIAM REED (2 cousins of same name). Before ELIAS HORRY, J.P. ROBERT AUSTIN, Register.

Book S, p. 177
15 & 16 Mar. 1737
L & R

JAMES MURDOCK, merchant, to WILLIAM CHAMBERS, planter, both of Colleton Co., for ₤ 550 currency, 200 a. part of 400 a., purchased from WILLIAM SPENCER & SARAH his wife, of James Island; bounding SE on WILLIAM SPENCER; S on COL. HALL; W on DR. KILPATRICK; N on CALEB KNIGHT. Witnesses: JAMES MCKEE, JAMES FISHER. Before ROBERT AUSTIN, J.P. & Register.

Book S, p. 178
17 & 18 May 1734
L & R by Mortgage

JAMES WATHEN, merchant, of Charleston, to JAMES HASELL, merchant, of St. James, Goose Creek, for ₤ 2000 currency, 700 a. in St. James, Goose Creek, bounding E on Back River (also Medway River); W on BENJAMIN WARING & THOMAS TAYLOR; N on Landgrave THOMAS SMITH; S on a creek & SAMUEL PRIOLEAU. Date of redemption, 15 Sept. next. Witnesses: SARAH BAKER, JOHN BAKER. Memo: There remains unpaid ₤ 750 currency to ABRAHAM SATUR on JAMES HASELL'S mortgage to said SATUR, due next Nov. which HASELL promises to pay out of the ₤ 2000. On 13 Feb. 1734/5 PAUL JENYS acknowledges receipt of ₤ 821:3:6 from CAPT. JAMES WATHEN on account of HASELL. PER J. HASELL mortgage to SATUR, taken up per CAPT. WATHEN, ₤ 750; by CATTELL & AUSTIN, ₤ 71:3:6; ₤ 821:3:6. CHARLES SMITH identified hand writing of SARAH BAKER & JOHN BAKER before THOMAS DALE, J.P. ROBERT AUSTIN, Register. Mortgage declared satisfied 20 Apr. 1770 by E. VANDERHORST, administrator to WILLIAM RAVEN, who was executor to ELIZABETH GIBBES, executrix to PAUL JENNYS to whom mortgage was assigned. (See p. 181).

Book S, p. 181
16 Sept. 1734
Assignment of Mortgage

JAMES HASELL, merchant, of St. James, Goose Creek, to PAUL JENYS (JENNYS) & JOHN BAKER, merchants, of Charleston, for ₤ 2000, the 700 a. contained in mortgage from JAMES WATHEN, (see p. 178). Witnesses: THOMAS DALE, GOERGE HUNTER. Before THOMAS DALE, J.P. ROBERT AUSTIN, Register.

Book S, p. 182
22 & 23 Feb. 1737
L & R by Mortgage

RICHARD HALL, gentleman, of Williamsburgh, SC, to ELIZABETH JENYS & THOMAS JENYS, executors, of will of PAUL JENYS, merchant, of Charleston, as security on certain debts, 800 a. on N side Black River, Craven Co., in Williamsburgh Township; also 200 a. in same township on N side Black River; which 2 tracts were granted to RICHARD HALL by 2 grants on 13 July 1737 signed by Lt. Gov. THOMAS BROUGHTON. Whereas RICHARD HALL on 23 Feb. 1737 owed ELIZABETH JENYS & THOMAS JENYS ₤ 688 currency, & by his bond dated 17 this Feb. also became indebted to WILLIAM HOPTON of Charleston for ₤ 67:5:6, which bond has since been assigned by HOPTON to ELIZABETH & THOMAS JENYS; now HALL secures payment of debts. Witnesses: CHARLES SMITH, JOHN BASSNETT. Before THOMAS DALE, J.P. ROBERT AUSTIN, Register.

Book S, p. 183　　　　　　　WILLIAM DONNING, gentleman, eldest son & heir-
31 Jan. & 1 Feb. 1737　　　at-law of THOMAS DONNING, gentleman, (who was
L & R by Mortgage　　　　　eldest son, heir-at-law, & device of WILLIAM
　　　　　　　　　　　　　　DONNING, gentleman, formerly of Parish of St.
Clements Danes, Co. of Middlesex, Great Britain, but late of SC) & FRAN-
CES his wife, to JOHN CARRUTHERS, mariner, (attorney to MAGDALENE COLE of
Stradey, Co. Caermarthen, Wales, widow & executrix of will of LAWFORD
COLE, of SC & administrator of COLE'S goods, chattels, debts, etc., dur-
ing the absence of said executrix). Whereas WILLIAM DONNING gave bond
dated 1 Feb. 1737 to JOHN CARRUTHERS (as attorney for MAGDALENE COLE) for
L 1507:14:6 sterling, of Great Britain, with condition that whereas WIL-
LIAM DONNING, deceased of Parish of St. Clements Danes, gave bond dated
19 Oct. 1728 to LAWFORD COLE in penal sum of L 800 sterling, for payment
of L 468:10:4 British money, with interest, on 19 Oct. 1729; & whereas on
9 Aug. last L 717:19:3-1/2 was due; & whereas on 9 Aug. after the 1st recited obligation there will be due, for interest, an additional
L 35:17:11-1/2 sterling, the condition of the obligation was that DONNING
should on 9 Aug. then next, transmit to CARRUTHERS bills of exchange for
L 753:17:3 sterling drawn by some able person in SC, payable to & endorsed by WILLIAM DONNING or some person in SC; now DONNING conveys to CAR-
RUTHERS, as security, 1238 a., English measure, according to recent survey, on N side Ashley River, in St. George's Parish, Berkeley Co., formerly called PAUL PARKER'S Plantation, later called PERCIVAL'S Lower Plantation, & lately called MR. DONNING'S Lower Plantation, bounding NE on
GEORGE NICHOLAS; SE on THOMAS DISTANT (formerly FRANCIS TURGIS); NW on
land formerly belonging to GEORGE BARNETT, ANDREW PERCIVAL & MR. VIRENE
but now to WILLIAM DONNING; RICHARD EAGLE & MALACHI GLAZE. Witnesses:
GEORGE DONNING, GEORGE NICHOLAS. Before ROBERT AUSTIN, J.P. & Pub. Reg.

Book S, p. 186　　　　　　　THOMAS GOBLE, planter, of Colleton Co., to
15 & 16 Mar. 1738　　　　　JAMES BEATTY, Indian trader, of Granville Co.,
L & R　　　　　　　　　　　for L 75 SC money, 600 a. in Craven Co., bound-
　　　　　　　　　　　　　　ing NW on MOSES WILSON; SW on Peedee River;
other sides on vacant land. Witnesses: LAWRENCE COULLIETTE, JAMES FULTON.
Before JACOB MOTTE, J.P. ROBERT AUSTIN, Register.

Book S, p. 188　　　　　　　MARK (his mark) SLOWMAN, planter & JOHN SLOW-
1 Mar. 1736　　　　　　　　MAN, planter, (eldest son & heir of MARK), of
Confirmation of Sale　　　 Craven Co., confirm JOHN SPENCER, planter,
　　　　　　　　　　　　　　(son & devise of JOSEPH SPENCER), also of Craven Co., for L 10 currency, in his title to the W half of 500 a. (the E
half being in possession of RALPH GERMAN), bounding N on Santee River; W
on JOHN SPENCER (formerly RICHARD CODNER); S on vacant land; also 200 a.,
the middle part of an island in Santee River, lying opposite the W part
of said 500 a.; bounding E on RALPH GERMAN; W on DANIEL HORRY. Whereas
JOHN, Lord Granville, Palatine, & the Lords Proprs., on 5 May 1704 granted DANIEL MCGRIGORY 500 a. in Craven Co., bounding N on Santee River; E
on JOSEPH SPENCER, 1 of the sons of said JOSEPH SPENCER (then PATRICT
STEWART); S on vacant land; W on JOHN SPENCER (then RICHARD CODNER); &
whereas MCGRIGORY on 10 Oct. 1704 conveyed the 500 a. to JACOB LAPOTRE,
merchant, of Charleston, & ELIAS HORRY, planter, of Craven Co., & whereas
HORRY on 10 Oct. sold his share to LAPOTRE, who became sole owner; &
whereas JOHN, Lord Granville, Palatine, & the Lords Proprs. on 12 Jan.
1705 granted JACOB LAPOTRE 200 a., English measure, in Craven Co., bounding N on Santee River; E on Santee River & Watiaw Creek; S on the creek;
W on vacant land (now DANIEL HORRY); 200 a. is part of an island opposite
said 500 a.; & whereas LAPOTRE on 12 Nov. 1709 sold the 2 tracts to JOHN
FILLEBIEN, planter, of Berkeley Co., & whereas JOHN FILLEBIEN & KATHERINE
on 15 Apr. 1710 sold the 2 tracts to MARK SLOWMAN & JOSEPH SPENCER, planters of Craven Co.; & whereas in SPENCER'S lifetime they divided the 2
tracts & agreed that SPENCER should have the W half & SLOWMAN the E half;
& whereas JOSEPH SPENCER by will dated 30 Nov. 1729 devised his share to
JOHN SPENCER (MARK SLOWMAN having sold his half to FRANCIS SHACKLEFORD);
now the SLOWMANS give JOHN SPENCER clear title. Witnesses: JONAH COLLINS,
RALPH JERMAN. Before JACOB MOTTE, J.P. ROBERT AUSTIN, Register.

Book S, p. 190　　　　　　　JAMES COACHMAN, planter, of Berkeley Co., to
27 & 28 Mar. 1738　　　　　GABRIEL MANIGAULT, ESQ., Public Treasurer of
L & R in Trust　　　　　　　SC, in trust for the Notchee & Peedee Indians
　　　　　　　　　　　　　　who had made application to the government for

a small piece of land to be given them to live on & the General Assembly
having agreed to this purchase; for ₤ 100 currency; 100 a. in Berkeley
Co., bounding N on the widow ELIZABETH MOORE & vacant land; NE on land
laid out; other sides on JAMES COACHMAN; which 100 a. is part of 710 a.
granted 13 July 1737 to CAPT. WILLIAM SAUNDERS, SR., & by L & R dated 21
& 22 Dec. 1737 conveyed by SAUNDERS to JAMES COACHMAN. Witnesses: ALEX-
ANDER CRAMAHE, CHILDERMAS CROFT. Before ROBERT AUSTIN, J.P. & Register.
Plat in book.

Book S, p. 192 JOHN MARTINI, surgeon, & THUNIS FISHER (THEU-
17 & 18 July 1734 NIEL VISSER) soapboiler, & BILETYE his wife,
L & R to JOHN VAUGHAN, bricklayer, of Charleston,
for ₤ 625 currency, lot #121 fronting N 25 ft.
on Broad Street, bounding E 104 ft. on RALPH RODDA; S on an alley through
the lot; W on a street leading from the Broad Path by the Quaker's Meeting House. Witnesses: RALPH RODDA, ROBERT BREWTON, JR., CHARLES PINCKNEY.
Before ROBERT AUSTIN, J.P. & Register.

Book S, p. 194 JAMES MCKAIE (KAYE), planter, & ELIZABETH (her
23 & 24 Mar. 1738 mark) his wife, to ABRAHAM MICHAU, planter,
L & R all of Craven Co., for ₤ 350 SC money, 262 a.
on N side Santee River, Craven Co., bounding E
on vacant land; N on ABRAHAM MICHAU & Radkoon Creek; S & W on Wita Creek.
Witness: ALRAN PETER LIEUBREY (LEWBRA). Before JAMES GREENE, J.P. ROB-
ERT AUSTIN, Register.

Book S, p. 196 THOMAS LYNCH, ESQ., to JOHN ATCHISON, planter.
11 & 12 Apr. 1735 & MARY his wife (adughter of THOMAS LYNCH),
all of Berkeley Co., for natural love & affec-
tion, 500 a. on Wando River, Christ Church Parish, commonly called Croskeys, bounding N on White's Creek, W on land called Wilson's Neck; S on
vacant land; E on MR. WHITE. Witnesses: JOHN LINNING, JOSEPH COOK. Before THOMAS DALE, J.P. ROBERT AUSTIN, Register.

Book S, p. 198 WILLIAM WHITE, carpenter, & SUSANNA (her mark)
27 Jan. 1709/10 his wife, to NATHANIEL LOTEN (LOOTEN) (LLOUGH-
Deed of Feoffment TON) carpenter, all of Berkeley Co., for ₤ 20
SC money, 100 a., English measure, in Berkeley
Co., bounding W on ROGER PLAYER; S on WILLIAM WHITE; E on WILLIAM WHITE'S
Creek; N on Wando River. Witnesses: THOMAS LEVEY (?), SAMUEL TORSHALL.
Before HENRY WIGINGTON, J.P. ROBERT AUSTIN, Register.

Book S, p. 200 SARAH LOUGHTON, widow of NATHANIEL LOUGHTON,
20 Oct. 1713 joiner, of Berkeley Co., to SOLOMON LEGARE,
Deed of Feoffment goldsmith, of Charleston, for ₤ 40 currency,
100 a., English measure, in Berkeley Co., con-
veyed by WILLIAM WHITE, carpenter, & SUSANNA his wife, to NATHANIEL LOUGH-
TON, 27 Jan. 1709/10; bounding W on ROGER PLAYER; S on WILLIAM WHITE; E
on WILLIAM WHITE'S Creek; N on Wando River; which 100 a. was part of a
greater tract granted WILLIAM WHITE, father of WILLIAM, & devised by him
to WILLIAM the younger. NATHANIEL LOUGHTON, by will dated 11 July 1713,
bequeathed 100 a. lying between ROGER PLAYER & WILLIAM WHITE to his beloved wife SARAH LOUGHTON; now she sells to LEGARE. Witnesses: WILLIAM
WHITE, Dec. 24; HUGH GREAR, Jan. 13. Before WIGINGTON. ROBERT AUSTIN,
Register.

Book S, p. 201 SOLOMON LEGARE, silversmith, of Charleston, to
22 & 23 Aug. 1737 his son DANIEL LEGARE, planter, of Christ
Deed of Gift Church Parish, for natural love & affection,
100 a. in Christ Church Parish, Berkeley Co.,
bounding W on ROGER PLAYER; S on WILLIAM WHITE; E on White's Creek; N on
Wando River; also 125 a. on S side Wando River, Christ Church Parish,
bounding W on CAPT. JOHN BENSTONE; E on above 100 a.; S on ROGER (or THOM-
AS) PLAYER. Witnesses: JOHN HODSDEN, ROBERT BREWTON, JR. Before HENRY
GIBBES, J.P. ROBERT AUSTIN, Register.

Book S, p. 203 ROGER PLAYER, planter, of Christ Church Parish,
28 & 29 Apr. 1729 to SOLOMON LEGARE, SR., goldsmith, of Charles-
L & R ton, for ₤ 250 currency, 125 a. on S side Wando River, being 1/4 the tract granted by Gov.

NATHANIEL JOHNSON & the Lords Proprs. to ROGER PLAYER & bequeathed by him
to his son ROGER PLAYER, JR.; bounding W on CAPT. JOHN BENSTONE; E on
SOLOMON LEGARE; S on part of the 500 now owned by THOMAS PLAYER. Witnesses: THOMAS BARKSDALE, ELIAS HANCOCK, JOHN LAURENS. Before DANIEL GREEN,
J.P. ROBERT AUSTIN, Register.

Book S, p. 205   JOHN BENSTONE, planter, of Berkeley Co., to
11 & 12 Jan. 1733   DANIEL LEGARE, planter, for L 500 SC money,
L & R   100 a. in Berkeley Co., part of 500 a. which
                      BENSTONE purchased from WILLIAM HARVEY & PAUL
CHARRON; bounding NW on Wando River; SW on a creek; E on SOLOMON LEGARE;
S on JOHN BENSTONE. Witnesses: WILLIAM WHITE, JOHN WHITE. Before ANDREW
RUTLEDGE. ROBERT AUSTIN, Register.

Book S, p. 207   WILLIAM WATIES, ESQ., of Craven Co., to SAMUEL
20 July 1734   MORRIS, of Berkeley Co., for L 1400 currency,
Deed of Sale   500 a. formerly belonging to JOHN GRANGE, gentleman; also 200 a. formerly belonging to JAMES GRANGE, gentleman; which 2 tracts are in St. James, Goose Creek, bounding on N side of Goose Creek on ROBERT HUME, ESQ.; E on JOHN LAWRENCE (?)
& HUGH GRANGE. Witnesses: MOSES WILSON, MATHEW DRAKE, GEORGE STRINGER.
Before THOMAS DALE, J.P.

Book S, p. 209   ICHABOD WINBORN, planter, of Edisto Island,
16 Nov. 1736   Colleton Co., to WILLIAM JENKINS, planter, of
Bond   same island, in penal sum of L 2800 to keep
                      agreements in sale, this date, of 200 a.

Book S, p. 209   ICHABOD WINBORN, to WILLIAM JENKINS, planter,
15 & 16 Nov. 1736   both of Edisto Island, Colleton Co., for
L & R   L 1400 currency, 200 a. on Edisto Island granted WINBORN by Gov. NATHANIEL JOHNSON in 1709,
bounding NE on ICHABOD WINBORN; SE on WINBORN & JAMES MITCHELL; SW on
EPHRAIM MIKELL & JAMES CLARK; NW on FRAMPTON. Signed by ICHABOD WINBORN
& MARY WINBORN, his wife. Witnesses: JAMES LANNING, JOHN JENKINS, JR.,
JOSHUA GRIMBALL, JAMES CLARK. Before ROBERT YONGE, J.P.

Book S, p. 211   JOHN THOMPSON, JR., planter, of Winyaw, to DAN-
-- 1737   IEL LAROCHE & THOMAS LAROCHE, merchants, of
Lease (R on p. 1)   Georgetown, for 5 shillings, 200 a. in Craven
                      Co., where THOMPSON lives; bounding on N
branch of Black River; other sides of JOHN THOMPSON, JR., also 1500 a. in
Craven Co., bounding on Black River; SW on SAMUEL HUNTER; N on ANTHONY
WHITE; N on JOHN THOMPSON, JR.; also 550 a. on N side of N branch of
Black River, bounding W on JOHN THOMPSON, SR., SE on WILLIAM SWINTON;
also 975 a. on S side of N branch of Black River. Witnesses: ISAAC SECARE, JAMES CRADDOCK. Before MAURICE LEWIS, J.P. ROBERT AUSTIN, Register.

Book S, p. 212   JONATHAN FITCH, planter, of Colleton Co., to
3 & 4 Apr. 1738   BENJAMIN WHITAKER, ESQ., of Charleston, as se-
L & R by Mortgage   curity on bond of even date in penal sum of
                      L 71 for payment of L 35:10:3 sterling of
Great Britain on 4 Apr. 1730; 844 a. in Colleton Co., granted FITCH 13
July 1737, bounding SW on WILLIAM FAIRCHILD, FRANCIS SAREAU, & vacant
land; NE on ROGER SAUNDERS; NW on vacant land. Witnesses: THOMAS SELLIVANT (SILLAVANT), GEORGE NICHOLAS. Before ROBERT AUSTIN, J.P. & Pub. Reg.

Book S, p. 214   RICHARD DAWSON, planter, JOHN (his mark) MACEY
1 & 2 Feb. 1736   planter, & MARGARET (her mark) his wife, to
L & R   THOMAS SNIPES, planter, & ELIZABETH his wife,
                      all of Colleton Co., for L 500 currency, 200 a.
in Colleton Co., granted to HENRY MESHEW; on W side Pon Pon River, bounding E on JOHN MACOY; other sides on ELIZABETH SNIPES (lately called ELIZABETH MESHEW (MECHEW), widow). Witnesses: THOMAS CLIFFORD, JOHN VORCKLES
(?). Before CULCH GOLIGHTLY, J.P. ROBERT AUSTIN, Register.

Book S, p. 216   Whereas RALPH IZARD, gentleman, of Berkeley
-- 1709   Co., & DOROTHY his wife (late wife & executrix
Confirmation of Sale of CHRISTOPHER SMITH, gentleman), convinced

the General Assembly that it was necessary to sell SMITH'S real estate to
pay his debts & obtained an Act (7 May 1709) permitting them to sell,
with the advice & consent of THOMAS BROUGHTON & ARTHUR MIDDLETON, ESQRS.,
& on this date sold to RALPH IZARD, JR. 600 a., English measure, commonly
called Stock Prior, in Berkeley Co., bounding N on WILLIAM STEPHENS, JOHN
PILKINGTON & CAPT. HEWITT; E on MR. ODENSALS & THOMAS PERONNEAU; S on
Ashley River; W on WILLIAM ELLIOTT; also 1000 a., English measure, commonly called Upper Stock in Berkeley Co., bounding NE on Landgrave THOMAS
SMITH; E & SE on EDWARD WEEKLY & WILLIAM DRY; S & SW on WILLIAM WILLIAMS
& THOMAS PINCKNEY; N & W on vacant land; now BROUGHTON & MIDDLETON gave
their consent to the sale. Witnesses: The Hon. SIR NATHANIEL JOHNSON,
Knight, JAMES INGERSON, ISAAC PORCHER. Before HUGH BUTLER, J.P. Recorded in Bk. R. fol. 477-480 by NATHANIEL JOHNSON, Pub. Reg. but not attested by him, therefore recorded here by ROBERT AUSTIN, Register.

Book S, p. 217   EDWARD RAWLINGS to ROBERT NEWMAN (NUMAN), for
13 Feb. 1737/8   ₤ 150 SC money, 450 a. in Craven Co., bounding
Bill of Sale   NW on RICHARD ALLEIN; NE on vacant land; SE on
                 WILLIAM NUMAN; SW on Santee River Swamp. Wit-
nesses: JOHN WELSTAD (WENSTAED, WELLSTEED); SAMUEL NEWMAN. Before DANIEL
WELSHUYSEN, J.P. ROBERT AUSTIN, Register.

Book S, p. 218   CAPT. GEORGE HEARNE, to THEODORE VERDITY (VAR-
22 Nov. 1712   DITY), planter, both of Berkeley Co., for
Bill of Sale   ₤ 100 currency, 560 a., commonly called White
                 Hall, purchased from the Lords Proprs. in 2
tracts of 500 & 60 a. Witnesses: JOEL POINSETT, JOHN CROFT. Before JA-
COB MOTTE, J.P. ROBERT AUSTIN, Register.

Book S, p. 219   JAMES FULTON, of Charleston to GEORGE MITCHELL,
13 & 14 June 1737 surgeon, of Ponpond, for ₤ 1200 SC money, 250
L & R   a. in Colleton Co., purchased from the Lords
                 Proprs. 25 Feb. 1714 by JAMES FULTON "old fa-
ther" of JAMES, party hereto, bounding according to plat. Witnesses: DR.
JOHN LINNING, EDWARD BULLARD, JOHN ATCHISON. Before MAURICE LEWIS, J.P.
ROBERT AUSTIN, Register.

Book S, p. 221   CHARLES CRAVEN & CHARLES HART, RALPH IZARD,
25 Feb. 1714/5   SAMUEL EVELEIGH, NICHOLAS TROTT, & ROBERT DAN-
Grant   IELL, Lords Proprs. for ₤ 7:10 grant JAMES FUL-
                 TON 250 a. in Colleton Co. Memorial entered
in Auditor's office 22 May 1733. THOMAS BROUGHTON, Sur. Gen., by warrant
dated 19 Feb. 1707/8 laid out to JAMES FULTON 250 a. in Colleton Co., E
of the freshes of Edisto River, bounding on all sides on vacant land.
Plat certified 17 Nov. 1709.

Book S, p. 221   DANIEL LAROCHE & THOMAS LAROCHE, merchants, of
25 Nov. 1737   Georgetown, to RICHARD MALONE, planter, of
Release   Craven Co., for ₤ 400 SC money, 300 a. in
                 Prince George Parish, bounding E on JOHN LANE;
N on MR. MALONE & WILLIAM SHACKELFORD; W on SHACKELFORD & JOSEPH PORT; S
on other part of 918 a. laid out to MARY SMITH. Whereas Lt. Gov. THOMAS
BROUGHTON on 8 May 1736 granted MRS. MARY SMITH 918 a., bounding (broken)
SW on JOSEPH PORTE, THOMAS BONY; & CAPT. CRUCHLOW; SE on a creek; & she
on 14 & 15 Oct. 1737 conveyed the land to DANIEL & THOMAS LAROCHE; now
they sell part to RICHARD MALONE. Witnesses: SAMUEL JENNINGS, JAMES CRAD-
DOCK. Before WILLIAM WHITESIDE, J.P. Recorded in Bk. R. fol. 500-502 by
NATHANIEL JOHNSON, Pub. Register, per JOHN PENNYMAN but not attested by
him, therefore recorded here by ROBERT AUSTIN, Register.

Book S, p. 223   ALCIMUS GAILLARD, planter, & SARAH his wife,
30 Dec. 1737   to RICHARD MALONE, gentleman, all of Craven
Release   Co., for ₤ 850 currency, 300 a. in Craven Co.,
                 on Santee River, formerly belonging to FRED-
ERICK GAILLARD, bounding SE on CAPT. BARTHOLOMEW GAILLARD; other sides on
vacant land. Witnesses: WILLIAM SHACKELFORD, ESTER SHACKELFORD, THOMAS
WISE. Before WILLIAM WHITESIDE, J.P. Recorded in Bk. R. fol. 502-504 by
NATHANIEL JOHNSON, Pub. Register, per JOHN PENNYMAN, but not attested by
JOHNSON, therefore recorded now by ROBERT AUSTIN, Register.

Book S, p. 224   WILLIAM FLAVELL, merchant, to REBECCA FLAVELL,
19 & 20 Mar. 1727   widow, both of Charleston, for L 1400 SC money,
L & R   a brick messuage or tenement or part of lot
                         #38 in Charleston, fronting S 16-1/2 ft. on
Broad Street, being the middlemost of 3 brick tenements which JOHN FLA-
VELL (WILLIAM'S father) built; bounding E on REBECCA FLAVELL'S brick tenement; W on ARTHUR MIDDLETON'S brick tenement (formerly ROBERT FLAVELL'S,
afterwards SAMUEL FLAVELL'S). Witnesses: THOMAS CAPERS, JOHN BEE. Before WILLIAM RHETT, J.P. ROBERT AUSTIN, Register.

Book S, p. 226   ALCIMUS GAILLARD, planter, & SARAH his wife,
30 Dec. 1737   to RICHARD MALONE, gentleman, all of Craven
Mortgage   Co., as security on 2 bonds of even date in
                         total penal sum of L 7028 for payment of
L 3514:10 SC money, 1 for payment of L 1372:10 on 1 Dec. 1738; the other
for payment of L 2144 on 1 Dec. 1739; 500 a. on which he lives, bounding
W on WILLIAM SHACKELFORD; E & N on THEODORE GAILLARD; also 300 a. on S
side Winyaw River, Craven Co., bounding S on Masketer Side; SW & NW on
vacant land; also 21 Negro slaves; also all sort of stocks; & all his
goods & chattels. Witnesses: WILLIAM SHACKELFORD, ESTER SHACKELFORD,
THOMAS WISE. Before WILLIAM WHITESIDE, J.P. Recorded in Bk. R. fol.
504-506 by NATHANIEL JOHNSON, Pub. Reg., per JOHN PENNYMAN, but not
attested by JOHNSON, therefore recorded here by ROBERT AUSTIN, Register.
CHARLES BENOIST, as executor to RICHARD MALONE, acknowledged satisfaction
of mortgage 11 Aug. 1740. ROBERT AUSTIN, Register.

Book S, p. 227   ROBERT BROWN, surgeon, of St. James, Goose
3 & 4 Mar. 1736   Creek, Berkeley Co., to THOMAS WRIGHT, mer-
L & R   chant, of Charleston, for L 5320 currency,
                         1330 a. in St. Thomas Parish, Berkeley Co.,
bounding NW on ROBERT QUASH & FRANCIS ROCHE; SE on JOHN HARLESTON, JR.; S
on Gov. ROBERT JOHNSON; NE on ROBERT TALLIN (?). Witnesses: RICHARD
WRIGHT, CHARLES PINCKNEY, ROBERT BREWTON, JR. Before ROBERT AUSTIN, J.P.
& Pub. Reg.

Book S, p. 229   JAMES WATHEN, gentleman, of SC to WILLIAM ROP-
17 & 18 Apr. 1738   ER, merchant, of Charleston, as security on
L & R by Mortgage   bond of even date in penal sum of L 1300 for
                         payment of L 650:18:9 SC money, with interest,
on 18 May next; & also as security on bond to BENJAMIN SAVAGE, merchant,
of Charleston, signed by ROPER & WATHEN for WATHEN'S debt, dated 27 Oct.
1737, in panel sum of L 420 payment of L 210 SC money on 1 Jan. next;
700 a. in St. James, Goose Creek, bounding E on Back River (alias Medway
River); W on BENJAMIN WARING & THOMAS TAYLOR; N on Landgrave THOMAS SMITH;
S on a creek & SAMUEL PRIOLEAU; which plantation was conveyed by Landgrave THOMAS SMITH & MARY his wife to ABRAHAM SATUR, who conveyed to JAM-
ES HASELL, who conveyed to JAMES WATHEN. Witnesses: THOMAS WRIGHT, ROB-
ERT MARSHALL. Before ROBERT AUSTIN, J.P. & Pub. Reg.

Book S, p. 232   JOHN COCFIELD (CORFIELD) the elder, planter, &
17 & 18 Apr. 1738   RACHEL his wife; & JOHN COCFIELD, the younger,
L & R   planter, of Berkeley Co., to BENJAMIN WHITAKER,
                         ESQ., & SARAH his wife, of Charleston, for
L 800 currency paid & secured to be paid 101 a. 3 rods (part of 500 a. in
St. Andrews Parish granted to CAPT. BARNABY BULL) bounding E on BENJAMIN
WHITAKER, ESQ., & WILLIAM ELLIOTT; S on marsh; SW by part of 500 a. & JO-
SEPH BUTLER; N by the Hon. WILLIAM BULL, ESQ., & BENJAMIN WHITAKER, ESQ.
RACHEL to renounce her dower on 10 May next. Witnesses: WILLIAM ELLIOTT,
JR., WILLIAM GEORGE FREEMAN. Before ROBERT AUSTIN, J.P. & Pub. Reg.
Plat certified 25 Mar. 1738 by GEORGE HUNTER.

Book S, p. 234   JOHN PALMER, planter, of Colleton Co., only
10 June 1714   son & heir of JOHN PALMER, to CHARLES REED,
Deed of Feoffment   merchant, of Limington, in Hampshire, Great
                         Britain, for L 450 currency paid by MRS. ELIZ-
ABETH REED on account of her father CHARLES REED, 3 tracts, total 1074 a.,
in Colleton Co. Whereas the Gov. NATHANIEL JOHNSON & the Lords Proprs.
on 14 May 1707 granted JOHN PALMER, the elder, 412 a. on Cumbee Neck,
bounding NE on Chehaw River; SE on said PALMER & THOMAS TOWNSEND; SW on
JOHN WARNEL; NW on SAMUEL TURNER; & whereas on same date they granted

JOHN PALMER, another tract of 350 a., English measure, on Cumbee Neck, bounding NE on Chehaw River; SE on JOSEPH PAGE; SW on THOMAS TOWNSEND; NW on JOHN PALMER: & whereas on 9 June 1714, Gov. CHARLES CRAVEN & the Lords Proprs. granted JOHN PALMER 312 a. on Chehaw River, lying the 2 tracts mentioned above, 1 being to the N, the other to the S, now his son JOHN sells the 3 tracts to REED. Witnesses: WILLIAM FULER, GEORGE RODD, BENJAMIN DELA CONSEILLER, EDWARD BELLINGER. Witnesses to possession & seizin: JOHN RUSSELL, EBENEZER MOODY, BURNABY BULL. "In the great Record book 350 a. folio 245/412 a. folio 246 in Book # 312 a. folio 442." Memorial entered in Auditor's office 24 May 1733 by JAMES ST. JOHN, D. AUD. BENJAMIN DELA CONSEILLERE appeared before MAURICE LEWIS, J.P. 5 Jan. 1737. Recorded at request of WILLIAM HARVEY of Charleston 26 Apr. 1738 by ROBERT AUSTIN, Register.

Book S, p. 237
18 & 19 Dec. 1733
L & R

JOHN ATCHISON, planter, of St. Paul's Parish, Colleton Co., to GILSON CLAPP, merchant, of Charleston, for ₤ 25 currency, 650 a. being 1/2 an island of 1300 a., known as Middle Ground, between N & S branches of Santee River; in Craven Co., the 650 a. bounding E on JOHN ATCHISON; N & W on Six Mile Creek. Witnesses: THOMAS LYNCH, STEPHEN BEDON, JR., EDMOND COPENS. Before ROBERT AUSTIN, J.P. & Pub. Reg.

Book S, p. 238
17 Jan. 1735
Deed of Gift

JOHN JENKINS, SR., planter, of St. Johns Parish, Colleton Co., after his death, to his son JOHN JENKINS, planter, of same place, for ₤ 500; 200 a., bounding W on JOSEPH RUSSELL; E on his son WILLIAM JENKINS; 50 a. of the 200 to be for the use of his wife ELIZABETH JENKINS during her widowhood; after her death the 50 a. to return to the 200 a. to his son JOHN, he paying to the children of his father, as they come of age, their share of the ₤ 500 with interest; the names of the children being JOSEPH CHRISTOPHER, THOMAS, ELIZABETH, BENJAMIN & CHARLES. Witnesses: WILLIAM JENKINS, SAMUEL VARIN. Before ROBERT YONGE, J.P.

Book S, p. 239
3 Sept. 1735
Grant

GEORGE II to PETER BELTON, with the usual provisoes 1155 a. in Colleton Co., bounding NE on ISAAC STEWART & HENRY WILDBORES land; S & SW on marshes of Combe River; NW on CAPT. JOHN TUCKER. Signed by Lt. Gov. THOMAS BROUGHTON (?) & BADENHOP, C.C. Plat in book.

Book S, p. 240
29 Mar. 1738
Quit Claim

JOHN GODWIN, planter, of Colleton Co., & MARGARET (her mark) his wife (formerly the widow of PETER BELTON), being heirs by will of PETER BELTON to all his real & personal estate, convey to JOB RATHMAHLER, ESQ., of Berkeley Co., for ₤ 100 currency, all their title to the above mentioned 1155 a. (p. 240). Delivery by turf & twig. Witnesses: FRANCIS KIRK, BENJAMIN (his mark) NEEDHAM. Before STEPHEN BULL, J.P. ROBERT AUSTIN, Register.

Book S, p. 240
26 Mar. 1724
Deed of Sale

AARON WAY, SR., & WILLIAM WAY, SR., to ALEXANDER GARDEN, all of Berkeley Co., for ₤ 15 currency, lot #56 containing 1/4 a., in Dorchester Town. Witnesses: THOMAS WARING, JOSEPH SMITH, AARON WAY, JR. Before ALEXANDER SKENE, J.P. ROBERT AUSTIN, Register.

Book S, p. 241
5 Nov. 1730
Release Quadripartite

ANDREW ALLEN, merchant, of Charleston, & ROBERT TRADD, gentleman, executors of will of MATHEW PORTER, sawyer, of Charleston, of 1st part; MILES BREWTON, gentleman, of Charleston, & SUSANNAH (her mark) his wife (late SUSANNAH PORTER, widow & executrix of will of MATHEW PORTER), of 2nd part; the Rev. MR. ALEXANDER GARDEN, rector of St. Philip's Parish, Charleston, JOHN FENWICKE, ESQ., & ELEAZAR ALLEN, ESQ., of Charleston (3 of the commissioners for finishing the new brick church in Charleston) of the 3rd part; ROBERT BREWTON & JACOB MOTTE, merchants, churchwardens for the time being of St. Philip's Parish, of the 4th part. Whereas by L & R dated 7 & 8 Mar. 1717 JOHN MILNER, mariner, of Charleston, & ELIZABETH his wife, for ₤ 54 currency, conveyed to

ANDREW ALLEN & ROBERT TRADD the tenement occupied by the widow SUSANNAH PORTER, also part of lot #66 bounding W 200 ft. on a street leading to the new brick church; S on the French church, being 60 ft. on the street on which said church stands; N on the new church; E on part of same lot owned by MRS. MARY MULLINS; & whereas MATHEW PORTER by will dated 15 Nov. 1717 bequeathed all his real estate to his loving wife SUSANNAH during her life, & appointed SUSANNAH & ANDREW ALLEN & ROBERT TRADD his executrix & executors; & whereas MATHEW MILNER in his lifetime had agreed to purchase the premises from JOHN MILNER for ₤ 54 SC money & had paid JOHN MILNER ₤ 20 & before the conveyance could be executed PORTER died; & whereas by deed poll dated 8 Oct. 1717 (& recorded Book E p. 35), ALLEN & TRADD, as executors, declared that the ₤ 54 belonged to PORTER'S estate & that their ALLEN & TRADD'S) names were used only in trust & that they would permit SUSANNAH to occupy the house & lot during her lifetime; & whereas an Act of Assembly ratified 17 Apr. 1725 authorized the commissioners of the new brick church to purchase at reasonable prices lots for a church yard needed as a burying ground, there being no adjoining land appropriated for that purpose; & whereas ALEXANDER GARDEN, JOHN FENWICKE & ELEAZAR ALLEN deisred to purchase from MILES BREWTON & SUSANNAH his wife, their interest in the part of the lot behing said tenement, now enclosed for a churchyard & appointed WILLIAM YEOMANS, BENJAMIN D'HARRIETTE & GABRIEL MANIGAULT, freeholders, their representatives, & MILES & SUSANNAH BREWTON appointed ANDREW ALLEN, ROBERT TRADD, & THOMAS LAMBOLL, gentleman, their representatives, & they appraised the land at ₤ 4 currency per foot from S to N; Now, for ₤ 337:6:8 SC money, the BREWTONS convey to the church commissioners (BREWTON & MOTTE) (broken see Bk. E) the land bounding S on the BREWTONS; E on MRS. MARY MULLINS; W on the street leading from Ashley River to the new brick church. Witnesses: ROBERT HUME, STEPHEN DRAYTON. Before JOSEPH WRAGG, J.P. ROBERT AUSTIN, Register.

Book S, p. 245
10 & 11 Dec. 1732
L & R
WILLIAM MCCLUER, planter, of Johns Island Stono, to ROBERT STEEL, tanner, of Charleston, for ₤ 100 SCmoney, 200 a. in Colleton Co., bounding S on Cumbee River; W on Cuccold Creek; N on COL. WILLIAM BULL; E on a cypress swamp. Witnesses: ANN STEEL, FREDERICK MEYER. Before HENRY GIBBES, J.P. ROBERT AUSTIN, Register.

Book S, p. 247
20 & 21 Apr. 1738
L & R
ROBERT STEEL, tanner, of Charleston, to ROYAL SPRY, planter, of Ponpon, Colleton Co., for ₤ 500 currency, 200 a. in Colleton Co., bounding S on Cumbee River; W on Cuccold Creek; N on COL. WILLIAM BULL; E on a cypress swamp. Witnesses: EBENEZER SIMMONS, CHRISTOPHER SMITH. Before HENRY GIBBES, J.P. ROBERT AUSTIN, Register.

Book S, p. 248
20 Apr. 1738
Mortgage
SAMUEL MASTERS, of Prince George Parish, Craven Co., to WILLIAM WATIES, as security on his bond for ₤ 1200, now due, & as security on debt of ₤ 400 which WATIES advanced for him to MATHEW DRAKE & others; all his stock of cattle & horses. Witnesses: JOHN KEEN, BENJAMIN COACHMAN. Before WILLIAM WHITESIDE, J.P. ROBERT AUSTIN, Pub. Reg. "I found my mistake in registering the above deed & desired COL. WATIES to have it recorded in the Secretarys Office. R.A."

Book S, p. 249
26 & 27 Jan. 1737
L & R
WILLIAM MORRALL, planter, to WILLIAM BRUCE, chirurgeon, both of Berkeley Co., for ₤ 500 SC money, 800 a. in Craven Co., granted by letters patent dated 12 Aug. last, signed by Lt. Gov. THOMAS BROUGHTON, to WILLIAM MORRALL, & bounding on all sides on vacant land. Witnesses: THOMAS DEARINGTON, HENRY BONNEAU. Before ANTHONY BONNEAU, J.P. ROBERT AUSTIN, Register.

Book S, p. 251
8 & 9 May 1738
L & R
DANIEL CARTWRIGHT, planter, & SARAH his wife, to JOHN BRAITHWAITE, ESQ., for ₤ 6000 currency, 2 tracts of 74 a. & 153 a. 2 roods, (227 a. 2 roods) in St. Philip's Parish, bounding E on OTHNIEL BEALE, merchant, & the Broad Road leading from Charleston; W on Ashley River & marshes; N on estate of ROBERT HUME, ESQ., & on 29 a. belonging to HUGH CARTWRIGHT & marshes of a small creek; S on marsh & JOSEPH BLAKE, ESQ., & JOHN HAMMERTON, ESQ. Whereas RICHARD CARTWRIGHT,

father of DANIEL, owned several plantations in St. Philip's Parish, Charleston, (broken page) bounding ----- Road & lands heretofore of DANIEL GALE; W on Ashley River & marsh; N on estate of ROBERT HUME (formerly COL. GEORGE LOGAN); S on marsh & WILLIAM SMITH, planter, (formerly WILLIAM SMITH, merchant); & whereas RICHARD CARTWRIGHT bequeathed to his son HUGH, when 21 years old, that part of 1 plantation bounding E on the Broad Path; W on a creek of Ashley River; N on COL. GEORGE LOGAN & said creek; S on a dividing line to be run separating HUGH'S land from that part intended to be given to his son DANIEL; & willed that HUGH'S part should contain 6 chains to the Broad Path & run in a direct course to the pond dug to water his cattle; & HUGH at same time to receive his share of his (RICHARD'S) personal estate, equal to that of son RICHARD'S; & bequeathed to son DANIEL the remainder of the land formerly belonging to GEORGE BEDON; bounding E on Broad Path; W on Ashley River; N on lines to be run; S on lands formerly belonging to JOHN WALKER & DOVE WILLIAMSON; PATRICK SCOTT to hold DANIEL'S portion until he comes of age; & bequeathed to son RICHARD, when 21, a tract fronting the Broad Path 8 chains to S upon & through the middle of the swamp that formerly divided the lands of PATRICK SCOTT & DOVE WILLIAMSON; N on son DANIEL; W on Ashley River; E on Broad Path & gave the remainder of his land, not already given away, to son ROBERT, when 21; & whereas a division was made, according to the will, & RICHARD became owner of 74 a., part of the several tracts, bounding E on JOSEPH BLAKE, ESQ.; W on marshes of Ashley River; N on DANIEL CARTWRIGHT; S on 46 a. owned by JOHN HAMMERTON, ESQ.; & whereas DANIEL received 153 a. 2 roods bounding E on OTHNIEL BEALE, merchant, & on the Broad Road leading from Charleston; W on Ashley River & marsh; N on estate of ROBERT HUME, ESQ., & 29 a. belonging to HUGH CARTWRIGHT; S on 74 a. belonging to the son RICHARD CARTWRIGHT; & whereas RICHARD CARTWRIGHT, the son, by L & R dated 6 & 7 Apr. 1736, for ₤ 1480 currency, sold to DANIEL CARTWRIGHT the 74 a. in St. Philip's Parish, Berkeley Co., bounding E on JOSEPH BLAKE; W on marsh; N on DANIEL CARTWRIGHT; S on JOHN HAMMERTON; now DANIEL CARTWRIGHT sells to BRAITHWAITE 2 tracts. Witnesses: EDWARD SCULL, GEORGE NICHOLAS. Before ROBERT AUSTIN, J.P. & Pub. Reg.

Book S, p. 254
4 & 5 Oct. 1737
L & R by Mortgage

JAMES TAYLOR, to THOMAS HALL & RICHARD HALL, all of Williamsburgh Township, for ₤ 261 SC money, 300 a. on S side Black River, Williamsburgh Township, Craven Co., bounding on all sides on vacant land. Date of redemption, 5 Jan. next. Witnesses: MAURICE LEWIS, JOHN RATTRAY, JAMES VARNON.

Book S, p. 256
19 & 20 May 1736
L & R

MATHEW (his mark) NELSON, planter, of Santee, Berkeley Co., to JOHN COLLETON, ESQ., of Fairlawn Barony, St. John's Parish, Berkeley Co., for ₤ 450 currency, 75 a. in Berkeley Co., bounding NW on MRS. BRUNSTON; SE on MATHEW NELSON; SW on vacant land; NE on Santee River; also 200 a. in Berkeley Co., bounding N & W on Santee River; other sides on vacant land. Whereas by letters patent dated 4 Dec. 1735 Lt. Gov. THOMAS BROUGHTON granted MATHEW NELSON 75 a., as above & on 9 Apr. 1736 granted him 200 a., as above; now NELSON sells both tracts to COLLETON. Witnesses: S. COLLETON, ELIZABETH (her mark) WILLIAMS. Before JOHN HARLESTON, J.P. ROBERT AUSTIN, Register.

Book S, p. 259
29 Apr. 1738
Mortgage

HUGH BUTLER, ESQ., of Exeter, Berkeley Co., to JOHN COLLETON, ESQ., of Fairlawn Barony, in trust for SIR JOHN COLLETON, Baronet, as security on various debts, 1500 a. with houses & improvements. Whereas BUTLER gave COLLETON a bond dated 1 Jan. 1735 in penal sum of ₤ 142:18 sterling, in trust for SIR JOHN COLLETON, Baronet, of Exmough, Great Britain, for payment of ₤ 71:9 sterling with interest on days mentioned; & whereas BUTLER by mortgage dated 1 Jan. 1735 for ₤ 1917:18:9 sterling British, delivered to JOHN COLLETON, in trust of SIR JOHN COLLETON, 54 Negro slaves; & whereas BUTLER gave bond of this date to COLLETON in trust for SIR JOHN, in penal sum of ₤ 509:15 British for payment of ₤ 254:15 & interest on certain days; & whereas SIR JOHN COLLETON & JOHN COLLETON, his eldest son & heir, by lease dated 1 Oct. 1726 farm let to BUTLER for 4 score & 19 years if HUGH BUTLER, JOHN BUTLER, & GEORGE BUTLER, sons of HUGH BUTLER, party hereto, live so long, 1500 a. on which BUTLER has built several houses & improvements; now BUTLER conveys the 1500 a. to secure payment. Witnesses: ANTHONY HUGGETT, WILLIAM

MEAN. Before J. SKENE, J.P., 300 a. of the 1500 a. next the Barony line, joining the Broad Path W & S on Mulberry Plantation were by mistake inserted in mortgage & were agreed by all parties to be excepted from the mortgage, 29 Apr. 1738. Signed J. COLLETON. Witnesses: JAMES GREEME, JAMES DRUMMOND. ROBERT AUSTIN, Register.

Book S, p. 261
5 June 1738
L & R

The Hon. JOHN BRATHWAITE, ESQ., of Berkeley Co., to DANIEL PEPPER, commander of Fort Moore, Granville Co., for Ł 100 currency 1000 a. in Granville Co., granted 10 Apr. 1738 by the Hon. WILLIAM BULL, President, to JOHN BRATHWAITE, bounding SW on Savanna River; NE on vacant land; NW & SE on JOHN BRATHWAITE. Witnesses: MICHAEL MILLURE, WILLIAM LEA. Before ROBERT AUSTIN, J.P. & Pub. Reg.

Book S, p. 263
29 & 30 May 1738
L & R by Mortgage

WILLIAM WHITESIDE, ESQ., of Prince George Parish, Craven Co., to ROBERT AUSTIN, ESQ., of Charleston, for Ł 230:6 sterling British, 585 a. in Craven Co., bounding, at time of original grant, N on HENRY LEWIN; S & W on vacant land; E on DOMINIQ ROCHE. Date of redemption, 1 Jan. next. Witnesses: MAURICE LEWIS, JOHN RATTRAY. WHITESIDE promises AUSTIN that ELIZABETH (wife of WILLIAM WHITESIDE) shall remounce her dower within 6 months. Before JACOB MOTTE. ROBERT AUSTIN, Register.

Book S, p. 266
1 & 2 Apr. 1737
L & R

WILLIAM CARWITHEN, cabinet maker, & MARY his wife, & with her free consent, of Berkeley Co., to SAMUEL FLEY, carpenter, of Charleston, for Ł 450 currency, 450 a. in Colleton Co., granted by letters patent dated 7 Aug. 1735, signed by Lt. Gov. THOMAS BROUGHTON, to CARWITHEN, bounding SW on ALEXANDER MCELROY; N on WILLIAM PERRIMAN; E on Edisto River. Witnesses: RICHARD DRAYCOTT, JAMES BURNLEY. Before THOMAS LAMBOLL, J.P. ROBERT AUSTIN, Register.

Book S, p. 268
19 & 20 July 1731
L & R

ROBERT AUSTIN, merchant, & MARY his wife, of Charleston, to GEORGE CHICKEN, planter, of St. James, Goose Creek, Berkeley Co., for Ł 1700 SC money, 500 a. in Berkeley Co., bounding S & E on Landgrave THOMAS SMITH; N on RICHARD BAKER; W on BARNABY REALLY. MARY to renounce her dower within 3 months. Witnesses: JOHN KING, CHARLES BURLEY. Before MAURICE LEWIS, J.P. ROBERT AUSTIN, Register.

Book S, p. 270
1 Feb. 1737
Farm Lease

HUGH BUTLER, ESQ., merchant, of Exeter, Berkeley Co., farm lets to THOMAS ELLERY, gentleman, of Moore Park, Berkeley Co., for Ł 1200 SC money, 300 a., English measure, part of 1500 a. ("farm let" to BUTLER by SIR JOHN COLLETON, Baronet, of Exmouth, Devon Co., Great Britain, & JOHN COLLETON, his eldest son & heir, 1 Oct. 1726 (broken page) for 4 score & 19 years if HUGH BUTLER, JOHN BUTLER & GEORGE BUTLER, sons of HUGH BUTLER, party hereto, should live so long); the 300 a. extending from a white oak 3 X corner along the Barony old line of SIR JOHN COLLETON, an E course & distance 84 chains 20 links to a red oak 3 X corner; from thence a N course bounding E on Mulberry Plantation of NATHANIEL BROUGHTON, ESQ., distance 35 chains 62 links near to a white oak station in said line; from thence a W course distance 84 chains 20 links to intersect the W line; from thence along said line a S course distance 35 chains 62 links to white oak 3 X first mentioned; the 300 a. bounding E on Mulberry Plantation; S by Seaton Plantation of ANDREW BROUGHTON, ESQ., N & W by residue of 1500 a. & Broad Path; also all timber, etc., particularly a cartway & passages to landing places called Wassumsaw Landing & Little Landing, thence to any part of the 300 a. Witnesses: ANTHONY HUGGETT, JAMES SHERINGHAM. Witness to receipt: GEORGE NICHOLAS. Before ROBERT AUSTIN, J.P. & Register. (See p. 280).

Book S, p. 272
14 & 15 July 1738
L & R

WILLIAM FAIRCHILD, of Charleston, surviving executor, of will of THOMAS FAIRCHILD, his father, to ELISHA PRIOLEAU, gentleman, of Charleston, for Ł 1160 due & owing PRIOLEAU for principal & interest on a bond, & for Ł 50 cash, (Ł 1210), part of lot #191 in Charleston. Whereas on 15 June 1736 ELIZABETH FAIRCHILD & WILLIAM FAIRCHILD, executors of will of THOMAS FAIRCHILD, conveyed to

ELISHA PRIOLEAU (as security on bond dated 15 June 1736, in penal sum of
₤ 1920 for payment of ₤ 960 currency with interest on a day "long since
past") part of lot #191, fronting 90 ft. on Friend Street, running back
130 ft., which lot as resurveyed measures 94 ft. front with 86 ft. at
lower end, & 140 ft. from E to W; now FAIRCHILD gives PRIOLEAU possession.
Witnesses: COL. SAMUEL PRIOLEAU, CLEMENT SACKVILLE, WILLIAM SMITH. Before HENRY GIBBES, J.P. ROBERT AUSTIN, Register.

Book S, p. 274　　　　　　THOMAS BARTON, WILLIAM BARTON, & JOHN BARTON,
23 & 24 May 1738　　　　 planters, JOHN SEVERANCE & ANNE his wife (late-
L & R　　　　　　　　　　ly ANNE BARTON), all of SC; to SAMUEL WRAGG,
　　　　　　　　　　　　　merchant, of London, for ₤ 800 British, all
those messuages or tenements & gardens in Moor Mead, Parish of St. Leonard Shoreditch, Co. of Middlesex, also 2 a. of garden ground in Parish of
Stepney (alias Stebunheath), Co. of Middlesex. Whereas on 13 May 1737
REBECCA BARTON, widow of the Parish of St. Mary Islington, Co. of Middlesex, & SAMUEL HARTOPP, ESQ., of Little Dalby, Leicester Co., in obedience
to 2 orders of High Court of Chancery conveyed to THOMAS BARTON, WILLIAM
BARTON, JOHN BARTON, & ANNE BARTON (now wife of JOHN SEVERANCE) as tenants in common & not as joint tenants several messuages or tenements &
gardens in Moor Mead occupied severally by KATHERINE BROWN, HENRY VICKERS,
WILLIAM CLENCH, ROBERT BURGESS, SAMUEL CRABTREE, GEORGE JENKINS, WILLIAM
LAW, & WILLIAM JAMES; also 2 a. in Stepney, occupied by SAMUEL HARLEY,
later by KATHERINE HARLEY, widow; also those messuages, cottages, shops &
sheds built upon the garden ground occupied by KATHERINE HARLEY; now the
BARTONS sell to WRAGG. Witnesses: EDWARD BOND, EDMOND HAWKINS. Before
THOMAS LAROCHE, J.P. ROBERT AUSTIN, Register. The Hon. WILLIAM BULL,
ESQ., Pres. & Commander in Chief in SC certifies (per JAMES MICHIE, Dep.
Sec.) that THOMAS LAROCHE is J.P. in good standing & that EDWARD BOND is
worthy of credit. Great seal affixed 19 July 1738. ROBERT AUSTIN, Reg-
ister.

Book S, p. 277　　　　　　JOSEPH FIDLER, upholsterer, to JOSEPH MOODY,
1 & 2 Mar. 1737　　　　 both of Charleston, for ₤ 350 SC money, 350 a.
L & R　　　　　　　　　　in Berkeley Co., bounding on E side of a great
　　　　　　　　　　　　　cypress swamp called Four Hole Swamp, made by
a branch of Edisto River. Witnesses: JOHN SAVAGE, TIMOTHY PHILLIPS, WIL-
LIAM WRIGHT. Before THOMAS DALE, J.P. ROBERT AUSTIN, Register.

Book S, p. 279　　　　　　ELIZABETH STANLEY, of St. James Santee, Berke-
3 Aug. 1738　　　　　　　 ley Co., to JOHN OULDFIELD, SR., of St. James,
Mortgage　　　　　　　　 Goose Creek, for ₤ 1284 currency, 500 a. where
　　　　　　　　　　　　　she dwells, bounding N on WILLIAM WRIGHT.
Whereas JOHN OULDFIELD, at the request of ELIZABETH STANLEY, & for her
debts by 2 bonds, 1 to OULDFIELD in penal sum of ₤ 834 for payment of
₤ 417 on 1 Mar. 1738, the other in penal sum of ₤ 450 for payment of
₤ 225 on 20 June 1738, OULDFIELD being jointly bound with PETER STANLEY
to JAMES KINLOCH, therefore, if ELIZABETH should pay OULDFIELD or KINLOCH
the several sums this mortgage shall be void. Witnesses: EDWARD KEATING,
MARY KEATING. Before JOB MOTHMAHLER, J.P. ROBERT AUSTIN, Register.

Book S, p. 280　　　　　　(See p. 270). Whereas on 1 Feb. 1737 HUGH
25 Apr. 1738　　　　　　 BUTLER, ESQ., of Berkeley Co., farm let to
Agreement　　　　　　　　 THOMAS ELLERY, gentleman, of Moore Park, Berke-
　　　　　　　　　　　　　ley Co., for ₤ 1200, 300 a., English measure,
granted BUTLER by SIR JOHN COLLETON & his son JOHN COLLETON for 4 score &
19 years should the said (?) HUGH BUTLER & JOHN BUTLER & GEORGE BUTLER,
his sons, should live so long. Whereas the conveyance was made to ELLERY
to secure him against several obligations ELLERY had entered into, for
BUTLER'S debts, to CAPT. OTHNIEL BEALE & BENJAMIN WHITAKER; now ELLERY &
BUTLER agree that should BUTLER fail to pay the debts by 1 Mar. next then
ELLERY may sell the property at public sale. Witnesses: ANTHONY HUGGETT,
G. COLLETON. Before ROBERT AUSTIN, J.P. & Pub. Reg.

Book S, p. 281　　　　　　JOSEPH (his mark) SPENCER, planter, & MARY his
5 & 6 July 1737　　　　 wife; & JOHN SPENCER, planter, & DOROTHY his
L & R　　　　　　　　　　wife; all of St. James Santee; to ISAAC MAZYCK,
　　　　　　　　　　　　　ESQ., of Charleston; for ₤ 1200 currency; 500
a., English measure, in Craven Co. Whereas the Lords Proprs. on 5 May
1703 granted PATRICK STEWART 500 a. on S side Santee River, bounding E on

a creek & swamp; W on DANIEL MCGREGORY; & whereas by will dated 29 June 1797 STEWART bequeathed to his sons, JOHN, JAMES, ROBERT, & CHARLES, all his real & personal estate; & whereas CHARLES died a minor, & JOHN, JAMES & ROBERT on 15 Dec. 1730 sold the 500 a. to JOSEPH SPENCER & JOHN SPENCER; now they sell to MAZYCK. Witnesses: RALPH JERMAN, ROBERT BREWTON, JR., EBENEZER FOORD, JOHN GENDRON. Before HENRY GIBBES, J.P. ROBERT AUSTIN, Register.

Book S, p. 284
5 & 6 June 1738
L & R

GEORGE LIVINGSTON, planter, to EPHRAIM MIKELL, planter, both of Granville Co., for Ł 3060 currency, 765 a., being 1/2 of 4 tracts containing 1530 a. on Port Royal Island left him by his father to be equally divided according to agreement dated 29 Oct. 1737. Witnesses: RICHARD WIGG, KENNITH MACKENZIE. Before THOMAS WIGG, J.P.

Book S, p. 286
15 Feb. 1737/8
Mortgage

HUGH BUTLER, ESQ., of Exter, Berkeley Co., to OTHNIEL BEALE & THOMAS COOPER, merchants, of Charleston, for Ł 500 currency, 500 a. in Berkeley Co., bounding N & S on HUGH BUTLER; E on the Hon. THOMAS BROUGHTON, ESQ., W on land not laid out in 1716. Date of redemption of this mortgage & 1 bond of even date for Ł 500 & interest, 1 Jan. 1738. Witnesses: PHILIP PRIOLEAU, JOHN STONE. Before ROBERT AUSTIN, J.P. & Register.

Book S, p. 288
21 Nov. 1724
Deed of Sale

THOMAS ELLIOTT, SR., & ANNE (her mark) his wife, to JOSEPH LAW, planter, both of Berkeley Co., for Ł 400 SC money, 200 a. in Berkeley Co., on S side Wackindaw Creek, bounding E on JOSEPH LAW; S on Shimhe Creek; W on COL. ALEXANDER PARRIS. Witnesses: RICHARD MASON, JOHN GODFREY. Before JOHN BARKSDALE, J.P. ROBERT AUSTIN, Register.

Book S, p. 289
7 & 8 Mar. 1736
L & R

BENJAMIN LAW, planter, & SARAH his wife, of Christ Church Parish, Berkeley Co., to JOHN ATKIN & EDMOND ATKIN, merchants, of Charleston, for Ł 832 SC money, 208 a. on S side Wackindaw Creek, now called Quelches Creek, in Christ Church Parish, bounding NE on BENJAMIN LAW; SW on Shimhe Creek, now called Parris's Creek; SW on JOHN PARRIS (formerly COL. ALEXANDER PARRIS). Witnesses to BENJAMIN'S signature: RICHARD ALLEIN, WILLIAM BROWNE. Witnesses to SARAH'S signature: ROBERT WRIGHT, JAMES PAINE. Memo: Agreed that LAW shall have free ingress, egress, & regress into & out of the premises to bury their dead in the ancient & usual place of burial on a certain plot of land which his ancestors have used as a burying place in times past. Recorded by ROBERT AUSTIN, Register, 9 Sept. 1738. Probate recorded by AUSTIN 4 Dec. 1738. "The reason the deed could not be proved before was, 1 of the witnesses: vizt. WM. BROWNE, is gone off the Province & RICH'D. ALLEIN is in the countrey at a great distance & the principall could not come to town sooner to acknowledge it at the time it was registered because of the small pox was not clear of the town & he never had it. Test. R. AUSTIN." PAINE appeared before AUSTIN 16 Feb. 1738.

Book S, p. 292
10 Apr. 1714
Bill of Sale

WILLIAM WILKINS, planter, & ELIZABETH his wife, heirs of WILLIAM DAVIS (their father) to CHARLES ARMSTRONG, planter, for Ł 100 currency, 600 a., English measure, in Colleton Co., on 10 Apr. 1703 granted by Gov. NATHANIEL JOHNSON, NICHOLAS TROTT & the Lords Proprs. to WILLIAM DAVIS; bounding NW on Bohicket Creek; SW on other lands of DAVIS, other sides on vacant land. Witnesses: ROWLAND STORY, WILLIAM CHAPMAN, ROBERT (his mark) GUY. "MR. MIKILL RAYNALS. I desire you wood doe me that kindnes as to give MR. ARMSTRONG possession of that land of mine next to you in my behalf in which you will much oblidge your assured frind to command WM. WILKINS." Enrolled in Auditor's office 23 July 1732 in Old Grant Book fol. 202 by DANIEL GIBSON for JAMES ST. JOHN, Auditor. Before WILLIAM BULL, JR., J.P. ROBERT AUSTIN, Register.

Book S, p. 293
12 Sept. 1738

STEPHEN LEAYCROFT, mariner, of Charleston, to NATHANIEL FORD, shipwright, of Berkeley Co.,

Mortgage   as security on bond dated 10 July 1737 in pe-
                                  nal sum of ₤ 560 for payment of ₤ 280 currency,
with interest, on 14 July 1738; part of lot #204 in Charleston, with the
dwelling house & buildings thereon, bounding E on Cooper River; W on the
Hon. JOHN FENWICKE, ESQ. Witnesses: ALEXANDER SANDS, SEYMOUR MALLORY
(MALLOY). Before ROBERT AUSTIN, J.P. & Pub. Reg.

Book S, p. 294   JOHN ASH, ESQ., of Colleton Co., & ANN his
25 Apr. 1711   wife, (formerly ANN BOLTON, only surviving
Bill of Sale   daughter & heir of THOMAS BOLTON), with her
                                  free consent to SHEM BUTLER, planter, of Berke-
ley Co., for ₤ 60 currency; part of a quarter part of lot #26 in Charleston, formerly the property of THOMAS BOLTON, merchant, father of ANN, now
vested in ANN; bounding S 43 ft. on a neighborhood alley running from the
street next Cooper River to a back street running parallel with the river;
N 88 ft. (10 ft. being ASH'S part of the street) on ISAAC PORCHER (formerly TERTE LASALL ?); E on ELISHA PRIOLEAU (formerly JACOB VARNE); W on
SHEM BUTLER. ANNE renounces all her claim. Witnesses: PETER SLANN, JOHN
CROFT. Witnesses to ANN'S signature: JAMES THOMAS, DEBORAH (her mark)
WOODMAN, MRS. ESTER ELLIOTT. Before ROBERT WRIGHT, J.P. Witness: THOMAS
LIVINGSTON. ROBERT AUSTIN, Register.

Book S, p. 295   THOMAS BUTLER, planter, & ELIZABETH his wife,
26 June 1733   to EDWARD SIMPSON, gentleman; all of Berkeley
Bill of Sale   Co., for ₤ 950 SC money, part of lot #26 on
                                  Elliott (or Pointsett) St., Charleston, now
occupied by THOMAS BUTLER; bounding S 27 ft. on Elliott or Poinsett St.
or Alley; W 88 ft. on ARTHUR HALL; E on JOEL POINSETT; N on ELISHA PRIO-
LEAU. Witnesses: JOSEPH SHUTE (Quaker), WILLIAM DANDRIDGE. Before ROB-
ERT AUSTIN, J.P. & Pub. Reg.

Book S, p. 296   EDWARD SIMPSON, gentleman, & SARAH his wife,
20 & 21 Aug. 1733   of Berkeley Co., to JOHN ATKIN & EDMUND ATKIN,
L & R   merchants, of Charleston, as tenants in common
                                  & not as joint tenants; for ₤ 1100 SC money,
half of lot #26 in Charleston occupied by EDWARD SIMPSON; bounding 27 ft.
on Elliott or Poinsett St.; W 88 ft. on ARTHUR HALL; E on JOEL POINSETT;
N on ELISHA PRIOLEAU, which property was lately purchased by EDWARD SIMP-
SON from THOMAS BUTLER, planter, of St. Andrews Parish, Berkeley Co.,
also the other half of lot #26. SARAH to renounce her dower when requested. Witnesses: JAMES SMALLWOOD; STEPHEN BEDON, JR. Before ROBERT AUSTIN,
J.P. & Pub. Reg.

Book S, p. 299   GEORGE LIVINGSTON, gentleman, of Charleston,
5 Sept. 1737   brother & heir-at-law of THOMAS LIVINGSTON,
Confirmation of Title   gentleman, of same place (who was eldest son &
                                  heir of ANNE LIVINGSTON formerly called ANNE
ASH, wife of JOHN ASH, ESQ., of Colleton Co., & 1 of the daughters & co-
heiresses & devisees of THOMAS BOLTON, merchant of Charleston), to JOHN
ATKINS & EDMOND ATKINS, merchants, of Charleston. Whereas ANNE BOLTON
(otherwise ANNE ASH, otherwise ANNE LIVINGSTON) owned a part of a quarter
part of lot #26 in Charleston fronting S 43 ft. on Elliott St. (that
leads from the Bay to the street now called Church Street); N on PETER
LESALL (formerly ISAAC PORCHER); E 88 ft. on ELISHA PRIOLEAU or JOEL POIN-
SETT (formerly JACOB VARINE); W on SHEM BUTLER; & whereas that part of
the lot is supposed to be vested in JOHN ATKIN & EDMOND ATKIN, having
been in their possession four 4 years; but several doubts having arisen
regarding the conveyance of the property from ANNE BOLTON to SHEM BUTLER,
planter, of Berkeley Co., under whom JOHN & EDMOND ATKINS held the same
(the title, if any remaining in ANNE LIVINGSTON & at her death descending
to THOMAS LIVINGSTON as her eldest son & heir, on his death descending to
GEORGE LIVINGSTON as "only brother of the whole blood" of THOMAS LIVING-
STON); now, to remove all doubt & establishing the title of JOHN ATKIN &
EDMOND ATKIN in the property, & for ₤ 50 currency, GEORGE LIVINGSTON re-
nounces all his claim & confirms JOHN & EDMOND ATKIN in their possession.
Witnesses: STEPHEN BEDON, JR., ROBERT BREWTON, JR., CHARLES PINCKNEY.
Before ROBERT AUSTIN, J.P. & Pub. Reg.

Book S, p. 300   ROBERT HUME, gentleman, to STEPHEN BEDON, join-
16 & 17 Nov. 1724   er, both of Charleston, for ₤ 80 SC money, the

L & R   SE quarter part of lot #311 in Charleston,
                             part of that square of land formerly taken up
by JOHN ARCHDALE & known as #97 which bounding SW on WILLIAM SADLER, being part of the square; N on a street leading from Cooper River by the
lots formerly owned by MAYBANK & PENDARVIS; E on the Broad Street; S on
THOMAS CARY'S lot, part of said square, the said quarter part of the lot
bounds S on THOMAS CARY; E on the street leading from the Market Place
toward the Presbyterian Meeting House; N & W on other parts of the lot.
Witnesses: MRS. MARY BLAMYER (a Quaker); JOSEPH JONES; WILLIAM HOLMES.
Before ROBERT AUSTIN, J.P & Pub. Reg.

Book S, p. 302   STEPHEN BEDON, carpenter, to JOHN ATKIN & ED-
19 & 20 Apr. 1736   MUND ATKIN, merchants, all of Charleston; for
L & R   ₤ 1000 SC money, the SE quarter part of lot
                             #311 in Charleston, part of the square of land
formerly taken up by JOHN ARCHDALE & known as #97 bounding W on WILLIAM
SADLER, a part of said square; N on a street leading from Cooper River by
the lots formerly belonging to MAYBANK & PENDARVIS; E on the Broad Street;
S on THOMAS CARY, a part of said square; which quarter part bounds S on
THOMAS CARY; E on the street leading from the Market Place toward the
Presbyterian Meeting House; N & W on other parts; being 50 ft. front &
124 ft. deep. Witnesses: RICHARD ALLEIN, WILLIAM BRONWE. Before ROBERT
AUSTIN, J.P. & Pub. Reg.

Book S, p. 304   STEPHEN BEDON, carpenter, to JOHN ATKIN & ED-
15 & 16 Apr. 1736   MUND ATKIN, merchants, all of Charleston, for
L & R   ₤ 3500 SC money, lot #36 in BEDON'S alley,
                             Charleston, bounding E 51 ft. on lots formerly
belonging to ANDREW PERCIVAL, ESQ., & ROBERT GIBBS & now on BEDON's Alley;
W heretofore on a street running almost parallel with Cooper River & now
of MRS. SMITH'S; S on MR. SMITH (formerly of MR. SWEETING); N 110 ft. on
DANIEL FIDLING (formerly MRS. SARAH ERPE). Witnesses: RICHARD ALLEIN,
WILLIAM BROWNE. Before ROBERT AUSTIN, J.P. & Pub. Reg.

Book S, p. 307   MARY SMITH, widow, of Craven Co., to THOMAS
31 May & 1 June 1737   BLYTHE, cabinet-maker, of Craven Co., for ₤ 20
L & R   SC money, 232 a., granted by letters patent
                             dated 30 Sept. 1736, signed by Lt. Gov. THOMAS
BROUGHTON to MARY SMITH, bounding N on a branch of Little River; SW & SE
on SAMUEL MASTERS; NE on JUDITH LEWIS. Witnesses: DANIEL LAROCHE, JAMES
CRADDOCK. Before WILLIAM WHITESIDE, J.P. ROBERT AUSTIN, Register.

Book S, p. 309   JUDITH LEWIS, widow, to THOMAS BLYTHE, cabinet
1 & 2 June 1737   maker, both of Craven Co., for ₤ 40 SC money,
L & R   400 a., granted to JUDITH LEWIS by letters
                             dated 30 Sept. 1736, signed by Lt. Gov. THOMAS
BROUGHTON; bounding SE on the Sound; NW on Little River; NE on THOMAS
BLYTHE; SW on "Barons Land" & "Mastars Land". Witnesses: THOMAS LAROCHE,
JAMES CRADDOCK. Before WILLIAM WHITESIDE, J.P. ROBERT AUSTIN, Register.

Book S, p. 311   THOMAS BLYTHE, cabinet maker, to DANIEL LA-
13 & 14 June 1738   ROCHE & THOMAS LAROCHE, merchants, all of Cra-
L & R by Mortgage   ven Co., as security on bond of even date in
                             penal sum of ₤ 1184:13 for payment of
₤ 592:6:9 currency on 16 Dec. 1738; 250 a. in Craven Co., bounding E on
SIMON DAVID STEDD & JAMES AKIN; NW on vacant land; SW on WILLIAM SIMSON;
SE on Waccamaw River; also 232 a. in Craven Co., bounding NW on a branch
of Little River; SW & SE on a SAMUEL MASTARS; NE on MRS. JUDITH LEWIS;
also 400 a. in Craven Co., bounding SE on salt water marsh; NE on JOHN
MORRELL; NW on Little River; SW on MARY SMITH. Witnesses: THOMAS MOSES,
JAMES CRADDOCK, Before WILLIAM WHITESIDE, J.P. ROBERT AUSTIN, Register.

Book S, p. 313   WILLIAM SIMSON, planter, of Craven Co., to DAN-
10 June 1738   IEL LAROCHE & THOMAS LAROCHE, merchants, of
Bond   Georgetown, in penal sum of ₤ 1368:2:6 for pay-
                             ment of ₤ 684:1:3 currency on 1 Dec. 1738.
Witnesses: THOMAS MADDOCK, JAMES CRADDOCK. Before WILLIAM WHITESIDE, J.P.
ROBERT AUSTIN, Register.

Book S, p. 314   WILLIAM SIMSON, planter, of Craven Co., to

9 & 10 June 1738   DANIEL LAROCHE & THOMAS LAROCHE, merchants, of
L & R by Mortgage   Georgetown, as security on bond of even date
                          in penal sum of ℒ 1368:2:6 for payment of
ℒ 684:1:3 currency on 1 Dec. 1738; 500 a. in Craven Co., Winyaw, bounding
S on vacant land; E & N on JAMES STEWART; W on ISAAC CHARDON. Witnesses:
THOMAS MADDOCK, JAMES CRADDOCK. Before WILLIAM WHITESIDE, J.P. ROBERT
AUSTIN, Register.

Book S, p. 316   NATHANIEL SNOW & FRANCES his wife, of Parish
9 Sept. 1738   of St. James, Goose Creek, to their loving
Deed of Gift   friends EDWARD SHREWSBURY & MARY his wife, for
                          natural love & affection & other good causes,
during their natural lives, the cleared land belonging to SNOW adjacent
to the "Cutt" of Cooper River; also the use of all the woodland in partnership with SNOW in making bricks; & SHREWSBURY may clear & plant land &
take what wood he pleases for the use of the Island Plantation, paying
SNOW 5 shillings sterling per annum; SNOW to pay tax & quit rent. Witnesses: RICHARD BODDICOTT, ANN (her mark) BODDICOTT. Before ROBERT AUS-
TIN, J.P. & Pub. Reg.

Book S, p. 316   OWIN SULLIVEN, planter, of Craven Co., to WIL-
20 Sept. 1738   LIAM FLEMING, merchant, of Craven Co., as se-
Bond & Mortgage   curity on bond for ℒ 142:5 SC money to be paid
                          on 1 Mar. next, conveys 25 branded head of
eat cattle. (Incomplete. No signatures).

Book S, p. 316   SIR JOHN BARNARD, Knight, Lord Mayor of the
London, 18 Aug. 1738   City of London, in pursuance of the Act for
Affidavit   the Recovery of Debts in the Plantations of
                          America certified that JOHN CARRUTHERS, gentle-
man, of the Parish of Bromley, Co. of Middlesex, & WILLIAM VAUGHAN,
scrivener, of London, appeared before him & declared the affidvait annexed to be true. Signed: BAYNBRIDGE. JOHN CARRUTHERS & WILLIAM VAUGHN
stated that JOHN HAMMERTON, ESQ., of SC, stands indebted to CARRUTHERS by
Mortgage, bonds deed poll & indorsement, in several sums & that CARRUTH-
ERS has not received payment of the ℒ 400 & ℒ 200 or any part of them.
VAUGHN declared he saw JOHN HAMMERTON, ESQ., of SC (then in London) sign
various papers & that he & JOSIAH SHAW subscribed their names to the various papers as witnesses. (Copies below).

Book S, p. 317   JOHN HAMMERTON, ESQ., of SC now in London, to
13 May 1738   JOHN CARRUTHERS, gentleman, of the Parish of
Mortgage   Bromley, Co. of Middlesex. Whereas GEORGE II
                          by letters patent under the Great Seal of
Great Britain, dated Westminster 11 Feb. (1729?) granted EDWARD BERTIE,
ESQ., & JOHN HAMMERTON the Officers of Secretary & Register of SC to hold
during their lives; & whereas BERTIE died & HAMMERTON is sole possessor
of the offices for his lifetime; & whereas HAMMERTON owns several parcels
of land in SC by several grants; & also owns several Negroes; now for
ℒ 400 British he conveys to CARRUTHERS the said letters patent & the said
offices of Secretary & Register of SC; also those several parcels of land
called Salt Catchers in Colleton Co., on N Edisto River, containing 1500
a.; also those known as Ashepoo in same Co., on same river, containing
1000 a.; also those in Craven Co., near Winyaw, containing 1000 a.; also
those on Santee River, Craven Co., containing 1300 a.; also those at Lower Santee, Craven Co., near MR. HORRY, containing 750 a.; also those in
Williamsburgh, Craven Co., containing 1000 a.; also those in Queensburgh,
Craven Co., containing 3000 a.; also those in Berkeley Co., containing
1500 a.; (total approximately 11,050 a. granted to HAMMERTON); also 5
Negro slaves now residing on a plantation next to CAPT. GADSDEN, near
Charleston; should HAMMERTON pay CARRUTHERS ℒ 400 sterling at the courthouse in Charleston on 1 Feb. next, with interest, this mortgage to be
void. Witnesses: WILLIAM VAUGHAN, JOSIAH SHAW.

Book S, p. 319   JOHN HAMMERTON, ESQ., of SC, now in London, to
13 May 1738   JOHN CARRUTHERS, gentleman, of Parish of Brom-
Bond   ley, Co. of Middlesex, in penal sum of ℒ 800
                          British conditioned for keeping all agreements
in above mortgage. Witnesses: WILLIAM VAUGHAN, JOSIAH SHAW.

Book S, p. 319　　　　　　　　JOHN HAMMERTON, ESQ., OF SC, now in London, to
1 Aug. 1738　　　　　　　　　JOHN CARRUTHERS, gentleman, of Parish of Brom-
Bond　　　　　　　　　　　　ley, Co. of Middlesex, in penal sum of L 400
　　　　　　　　　　　　　　British for payment of L 200 sterling at the
Courthouse in Charleston on 1 Feb. next, with interest. Witnesses: WIL-
LIAM VAUGHN; JOHN ELLIS, scrivener.

Book S, p. 319　　　　　　　　Whereas JOHN HAMMERTON gave JOHN CARRUTHERS a
18 Aug. 1738　　　　　　　　 bond of even date in penal sum of L 400 Brit-
Mortgage　　　　　　　　　　 ish for payment of L 200 sterling at the Court-
　　　　　　　　　　　　　　house in Charleston, SC, on 1 Feb. next, with
interest; now HAMMERTON charges & makes liable all the within mortgaged
premises to the payment of the further sum of L 200 & interest in discharge of same bond; the mortgaged premises to stand as security. Witnesses: WILLIAM VAUGHAN; JOHN ELLIS, scrivener. ROBERT AUSTIN, Register.

Book S, p. 320　　　　　　　　WILLIAM MELVIN, to his loving friend HUGH
22 Sept. 1735　　　　　　　　CAMPBELL, of St. Bartholomew's Parish, for
Deed of Gift　　　　　　　　 love & affection; 400 a. in Colleton Co., on E
　　　　　　　　　　　　　　branch of Saltcatcher River, bounding on all
sides on land not laid out. Witnesses: JOHN ANDREW, MOSES MARTIN, WIL-
LIAM WESTBURY. Before JAMES BULLOCK, J.P. ROBERT AUSTIN, Register.

Book S, p. 320　　　　　　　　GEORGE II to all people. Know ye that amongst
21 June 1738　　　　　　　　 the pleas inrolled at Westminster in 8 days of
Judgment　　　　　　　　　　 St. Hillary & in 15 days of St. Hillary, be-
　　　　　　　　　　　　　　fore ALEXANDER DENTON, ESQ., SIR JOHN FORTES-
CUE ALAND, Knight; & THOMAS REEVE, ESQ.; & on the morrow of the Purification of the blessed Virgin Mary, & in 8 days of the Purification of the
blessed Virgin Mary, before SIR THOMAS REEVE, Knight, & his brethren
Justices of the Court of Common Bench of the Term of St. Hillary, in the
9th year of our reign, in the 1310th roll it is thus contained; Middlesex, to wit: SAMUEL HORSEY, ESQ., late of Westminster, in the Co. of Middlesex, otherwise called SAMUEL HORSEY, ESQ., of Whitehall, in the Co. of
Middlesex, was summoned to answer JAMES GASCOIGNE'S plea that he render
to him L 311:17 which he owes to & unjustly detains from him & whereupon
the said JAMES, by RICHARD BANKS, his attorney, complains that whereas
SAMUEL HORSEY on 16 Mar. 1735 at Westminster gave JAMES GASCOIGNE a bond
for L 311:17 payable on demand which he failed to pay after several re-
quests, to the damage of said JAMES L 20 & he brings suit. SAMUEL by his
attorney, WILLIAM MIDFORD defends, but MILFORD as not instructed by HOR-
SEY to give answer. It is adjudged that JAMES recover from SAMUEL. Witness: SIR JOHN WILLIS, Knight. Signed: MAIDSTONE. ROBERT AUSTIN, Register.

Book S, p. 321　　　　　　　　JAMES SMALLWOOD, merchant, of Charleston, to
28 June 1737　　　　　　　　 MARGARET GODFREY, widow, of Wando, Christ
Bond & Mortgage　　　　　　　Church Parish, as security on bond in penal
　　　　　　　　　　　　　　sum of L 3000 for payment of L 1500 currency
within 2 months after grants are passed for said tracts; 600 a. in Kingstown Township, on Waccamaw River, bounding on upper line of Township & on
MR. NISBETT; also 1400 a. laid out for NATHANIEL WICKHAM & assigned to
SMALLWOOD, bounding on upper line of Kingstown Township. Witnesses:
LOUISE FOISSIN, ELIAS FOISSIN, JR. ROBERT AUSTIN, J.P. & Register.

Book S, p. 321　　　　　　　　Landgrave THOMAS SMITH, & MARY his wife, to
22 Sept. 1737　　　　　　　　JOSEPH HURST, both of Berkeley Co., for L 2352
Bill of Sale　　　　　　　　 currency, 293-3/4 a., according to plat. Wit-
　　　　　　　　　　　　　　nesses: ARCHER SMITH, RICHARD CARTWRIGHT,
JAMES ELDERTON. Before THOMAS LAMBOLL, J.P. Plat of 293-3/4 a., part of
3 tracts belonging to Landgrave THOMAS SMITH, ESQ., at head of Beaker's
Creek, out of Cooper River, in Berkeley Co., bounding NW on Landgrave
THOMAS SMITH; NE on JAMES STRAYTOR & CHARLES FILBIN; E on MRS. SARAH
SUMMERVILLE & JAMES STRAYTOR; S on STRATOR & CAPT. DRY; W on the road
leading from Goose Creek to Charleston & on MR. IZARD. Certified 15
Sept. 1737 by THOMAS WITTER, Dep. Sur. ROBERT AUSTIN, Register.

Book S, p. 323　　　　　　　　THOMAS LOWNDES, gentleman, of St. Margarets,
18 Nov. 1734　　　　　　　　 Westminster, to ROBERT THORPE, merchant, of
Deed of Sale　　　　　　　　 Thames Street, London, in performance of an

agreement dated 20 Sept. last, & for ₤ 1050 British, 2 tracts, total 6000 a., English measure, being part of a Barony of 12,000 a. in Granville Co., SC, on S side Cumbee River, which Barony was laid out to THOMAS LOWNDES & WILLIAM BULL, of St. Andrews, SC, (a purchaser from & under LOWNDES) on 2 Nov. 1728 by grant from Lords Proprs. dated 25 Oct. 1726; 1 of which tracts, marked with B on plan, containing 5000 a. & bounding NW on COL. WILLIAM BULL; NE on COL. JOHN PALMER & JOSEPH BRYAN; SE on FRANCIS YONGE & HUGH BRYAN; SW on CAPT. THOMAS INNS; the other tract, marked D, containing 1000 a., bounding NW on HUGH BRYAN; NE on Cumbee River marsh; SW on COL. WIBLIAM BULL. Witnesses: ROBERT HUME, NATHANIEL NEAL. Acknowledged by LOWNDES 18 Nov. 1734 before M (?) THURSTON, master of High Court of Chan. Exam. by JOHN DERT (?) BIRKHEAD. ROBERT AUSTIN, Register. This is final agreement made in Court of Westminster before ROBERT EYRE, ALEXANDER DENTON, JOHN FORTESCUE ALAND, & THOMAS REEVE, justices, & afterwards allowed & recorded before same justice & others; ROBERT THORPE, merchant, planter, & THOMAS LOWNDES, gentleman, aft., of 6000 a. of furze & heath in SC; LOWNDES quitclaims to THORPE; THORPE pays LOWNDES ₤ 600 sterling. Delivered by proclamation. ROBERT AUSTIN, Register.

Book S, p. 325
27 Nov. 1738
Bill of Sale

DANIEL CARTWRIGHT, planter, in St. Andrews Parish, to JOHN STEELE, vintner, of Charleston, for 5 shillings, a lot of land "bluff" to Ashley River, bounding on Broad Street, opposite MR. BOWMAN, & known as #90. Witnesses: WILLIAM GUY, JR., EDWARD NORRIS, ADAM SALE. Before HENRY GIBBES, J.P. ROBERT AUSTIN, Register. Full satisfaction received 26 Feb. 1739 by JOHN STEELE, the "original also cancelled". Witness: ROBERT AUSTIN.

Book S, p. 325
11 & 12 Nov. 1737
L & R

EMANUEL SMITH, tailor, & MARY his wife, of Charleston, to CHRISTOPHER LINKLY, planter, of Berkeley Co., for ₤ 929:10 SC money, 286 a. in Colleton Co., on SW side Chehaw, within land, bounding according to plat, & being part of 550 a. granted to EMANUEL SMITH on 23 May 1734 by Gov. ROBERT JOHNSON. Witnesses: THOMAS STOCK, JOHN CROFT, WILLIAM SMITH. Before HENRY GIBBES, J.P. ROBERT AUSTIN, Register.

Book S, p. 328
10 June 1736
L & R

JOHN (his mark) FABIAN, & MARY (her mark) his wife, to JAMES BERRIE, planter, for ₤ 600 SC money, 200 a., part of Bare Island, St. Paul's Parish, Colleton Co., on E side Ashepoo River, bounding W on vacant land; N on marsh land; E on Musketer Creek; S on marsh & Bare Island Creek. Witnesses: JOHN FABIAN, JR., THOMAS CONDON, WILLIAM FABIAN. Before JOSEPH BLAKE, J.P. ROBERT AUSTIN, Register.

Book S, p. 330
30 Dec. 1737
Bill of Sale

THOMAS HEPWORTH, gentleman, of Chaarleston, to WILLIAM STONE, merchant, for ₤ 170 SC money, pew #15 on N aisle of St. Philip's Church. Witnesses: MAURICE LEWIS, JOHN RATTRAY. Witnesses to possession & seizin: LAWRENCE WITHERS, PETER DALLAS. Before ROBERT AUSTIN, J.P. & Register.

Book S, p. 331
1 Nov. 1735
Mortgage

Whereas JOHN HAMMERTON, ESQ., of Charleston, SC, by letters patent dated at Westminster 11 Feb. 1730 (?) was appointed, with EDWARD BERTIE, since deceased, to be secretary & register of SC for life; & whereas HAMMERTON is indebted to ALEXANDER BENNETT, ESQ., of London, in the sum of ₤ 700 sterling of England by bond of even date, made payable, with interest, to THOMAS HENNING, merchant, of Charleston (BENNETT'S attorney & trustee); now, as security, HAMMERTON conveys to HENNING, in trust for BENNETT, the rights, priviledges, fees, etc., of the offices of secretary & register of SC during HAMMERTON'S natural life. HAMMERTON appoints THOMAS HENNING (in trust for BENNETT) his attorney to recover from JAMES MICHIE, gentleman, his present Dep. Sec., such sums of money due him towards paying this debt. Witnesses: JAMES MICHIE, THOMAS ELLERY. Before ROBERT AUSTIN, J.P.

Book S, p. 332
6 Oct. 1738
Agreement

Whereas by letters patent, GEORGE II granted EDWARD BERTIE, ESQ., & JOHN HAMMERTON, ESQ., the offices of secretary & register of SC for life; & whereas BERTIE died & HAMMERTON became sole possessor; & whereas on 13 May last JOHN HAMMERTON conveyed the letters patent & offices to JOHN CARRUTHERS, gentleman, of the Parish of Bromley, Co. of Middlesex for the term of HAMMERTON'S life subject to the payment of ₺ 400 sterling at the court house in Charleston on 1 Feb. next, with interest; & whereas by deed poll dated 18 Aug. last, HAMMERTON endorsed on the indenture a bond to CARRUTHERS for payment of ₺ 200 sterling on 1 Feb. with interest, & agreed that the mortgaged premises should stand as security for both sums; & whereas HAMMERTON intends to go to SC shortly; & whereas HAMMERTON had appointed JAMES MICHIE his Dpeuty to execute the offices; now HAMMERTON declares that in case he shall not arrive at Charleston by 1 Feb. next; or shall not within 30 days after that date pay CARRUTHERS the ₺ 400 & ₺ 200, then MICHIE may pay CARRUTHERS such sums received by him out of the profits, & remaining in his hands on 1 Feb. over & above the ₺ 500 currency a year salary allowed him by HAMMERTON, also such other sums received until the whole debt be paid. Witnesses: JOHN JOHNSTON, THOMAS WHYTE, JR. Before ROBERT AUSTIN, J.P. & Register.

Book S, p. 334
11 & 12 Mar. 1733
L & R in Trust

SUSANNAH DUBOSE, widow, of Berkeley Co., of 1st part; JOHN LAURENS, saddler, of Charleston, of 2nd part; BENTLEY COOKE, of 3rd part.
Whereas a marriage is intended between BENTLEY COOKE & SUSANNAH DUBOSE, & it is agreed that SUSANNAH shall dispose of all real estate, slaves, cattle, sheep & horses to which she is entitled in her own right or as executrix to her late husband ISAAC DUBOSE; now, for ₺ 20 currency, she conveys to LAURENS, 500 a. in Berkeley Co., formerly belonging to HENRY LEWIS, bounding E on FRANCIS BRITTON; N on ELIAS FOISSIN; NW & SW on MR. CAPERS & CHARLES LEWIS; NE on JONAS BONHOSTE; also 2 other tracts formerly belonging to FRANCIS COURAGE (?), 1 of 150 a. bounding N on Santee River; the other of 200 a. bounding S on the river; also 500 a. in Berkeley Co., commonly called Atthoe, formerly belonging to CATHERINE LAPOSTRE; also 200 a. in Craven Co., formerly belonging to PETER COUILLANDAUX, bounding N on Santee River; all upon trust for SUSANNAH'S use; & whereas SUSANNAH owns 8 slaves, 100 head of cattle, 10 sheep, & 9 horses & mares, she conveys them to LAURENS to be disposed of for her; or, in case of her death for her children. Witnesses: PHANUEL COOKE, CHARLES CAVANAGH, RICHARD BODDICOTT. Before ROBERT AUSTIN, J.P. & Register.

Book S, p. 337
17 Aug. 1724
Grant of a Pew

Whereas by Act of General Assembly for carrying on the building & for completing the brick church in Charleston & for declaring it to be the Parish Church of St. Philip's, Charleston, passed 9 Dec. 1720, the Act since being received & confirmed, it was enacted that the pews should be built by the direction of the commissioners named, with the consent of the vestry; now the vestry & church commissioners, in consideration "of the generous benefaction" of THOMAS FAIRCHILD to the church, & his paying ₺ 70, grant FAIRCHILD, forever, Pew #21 in the middle aisle of the church; FAIRCHILD, however, shall not alter the uniformity by raising or lowering the pew, taking down the partition, etc., nor dispose of the pew to any one not actually a resident or inhabitant of the Parish. Signed: FRANCIS NICHOLSON, A. GARDEN, WILLIAM GIBBON, ALEXANDER PARRIS, JOSEPH WRAGG, WILLIAM BLAKEWEY, ELISHA PRIOLEAU, J. HUTCHINSON, THOMAS HEPWORTH. WILLIAM FAIRCHILD, executor of will of THOMAS FAIRCHILD, for ₺ 200 currency, conveyed to JOHN LAURENS, saddler, of Charleston, Pew #21 in the New Brick Church in Charleston on 22 Nov. 1738. Witnesses: BENJAMIN ADDISON, DANIEL WOOD, JOHN CARION. Before HENRY GIBBES, J.P. Recorded in Secretary's office 30 Nov. 1738 in Book N. N. fol. 54 by JAMES MICHIE, Dep. Sec., now recorded by ROBERT AUSTIN, Register.

Book S, p. 337
1 Apr. 1738
Bill of Sale

WILLIAM WATIES, & DOROTHY his wife, of Craven Co., to JOHN ALLSTON, of Winyaw, for ₺ 50 currency, 246 a. in Craven Co., Prince George Parish, on an island between Peedee & Waccamaw Rivers, bounding E & NE on WILLIAM WATIES; NW on JOHN ALLSTON. Witnesses: WILLIAM ALLSTON, STEPHEN PEAK. Before THOMAS LAROCHE, J.P. ROBERT AUSTIN, Register.

Book S, p. 338   WILLIAM WATIES, & DOROTHY his wife, of Craven

1 Apr. 1738   Co., to JOHN ALLSTON, of Winyaw, for L 75 cur-
Bill of Sale   rency, 428 a., part of 578 a., in Craven Co.,
                         fronting on Wando Passo granted WATIES on 2
Aug. 1733, according to plat. Witnesses: WILLIAM ALSTON, STEPHEN PEAK.
Before THOMAS LAROCHE, J.P. The plat represents 428 a., the N part of
578 a. granted WATIES 12 May 1735 & conveyed to JOHN ALLSTON, bounding N
& S on WATIES; W on the thoroughfare called Wando Passo thoroughfare into
Waccamaw River. ROBERT AUSTIN, Register.

Book S, p. 339   PETER ALLSTON, planter, of Winneau, Craven Co.,
1 & 2 Aug. 1737   to JOHN ALLSTON, planter, of same place, for
L & R   L 100 currency, 300 a. in Craven Co., bounding
                         N on COL. WATIES; E on Peedee River; S on JOHN
ALLSTON; W on vacant land. Witnesses: GEORGE PAWLEY, JOSEPH HUGGINS,
RICHARD HAYES. Before WILLIAM WHITESIDE, J.P. ROBERT AUSTIN, Register.

Book S, p. 341   JOSEPH PRINCE, planter, to JOHN ALLSTON, plant-
11 & 12 Sept. 1738   er, both of Craven Co., for L 440 currency,
L & R   551 a. in Craven Co., on S side Waccamaw River,
                         bounding SE & SW on impassable lands; other
sides on vacant land, according to plat dated 3 Sept. 1735; which tract
was granted to PRINCE by Gov. THOMAS BROUGHTON, ELIZABETH MARY PRINCE,
wife of JOSEPH PRINCE, renounced her title. Witnesses: THOMAS MACKCLEL-
LAN, BENJAMIN WEBB, HENRY WARNER. Before THOMAS LAROCHE, J.P. ROBERT
AUSTIN, Register.

Book S, p. 344   JOSEPH PRINCE, planter, to JOHN ALLSTON, plant-
11 & 12 Sept. 1738   er, both of Craven Co., for L 359 currency,
L & R   449 a. in Craven Co., on S side Waccamaw River,
                         bounding SW on Sacausey Creek; SE on GEORGE
PAWLEY; NE & NW on vacant land, according to plat dated 3 Sept. 1735,
which tract was granted to PRINCE by Gov. THOMAS BROUGHTON. ELIZABETH
MARY PRINCE, wife of JOSEPH, assigned all her title. Witnesses: THOMAS
MACKCLELLAN, BENJAMIN WEBB, HENRY WARNER. Before THOMAS LAROCHE, J.P.
ROBERT AUSTIN, Register.

Book S, p. 347   ABRAHAM WARNOCK, planter, to JOHN ALLSTON,
1 & 2 Aug. 1737   planter, both of Winneau, Craven Co., for
L & R   L 100 SC money, 150 a. in Craven Co., bounding
                         N on JOHN ALLSTON; E near the Waccamaw lands;
S on JOHN ALLSTON; W on Peedee River. Witnesses: GEORGE PAWLEY, RICHARD
HAYES, PETER ALLSTON. Before WILLIAM WHITESIDE, J.P. ROBERT AUSTIN,
Register.

Book S, p. 349   JOSEPH ALLEN, planter, & SUSANNAH his wife, to
11 & 12 Mar. 1736/7   JOHN ALLSTON, planter, all of Winneau, Craven
L & R   Co., for L 600 SC money, 490 a. in Craven Co.,
                         part of 1490 a. known as "Unnisaw", now in
possession of WILLIAM ALLSTON, bounding according to plat. Witnesses:
JOSEPH LABRUCE, PETER ALLSTON, THOMAS EDINFIELD. Before GEORGE PAWLEY,
J.P. ROBERT AUSTIN, Register.

Book S, p. 351   ARTHUR FOSTER, planter, & MARY, his wife, of
7 & 8 Dec. 1738   Prince George Parish, Craven Co., to STEPHEN
L & R   BEAUCHAMP, merchant, of Georgetown, for
                         L 286:4 SC money, 108 a., in Craven Co., part
of 500 a. purchased by FOSTER from BENJAMIN LAW; bounding SE on ARTHUR
FOSTER; SW on JOHN WHITE; N on ARTHUR FOSTER & the Broad Path; NW on JOHN
DEXTER. Whereas by letters patent dated 22 Sept. 1733, signed by Gov.
ROBERT JOHNSON, BENJAMIN LAW was granted 1150 a. in Craven Co., bounding
N on BENJAMIN LAW; S on JOHN PETER SUMMERHOOFT; E on MR. FURBUSH; & where-
as BENJAMIN LAW yb L & R, 13 & 14 Dec. 1733 sold to ARTHUR FOSTER 500 a.
(part of the 1150 a.), bounding N on BENJAMIN LAW; S on JOHN PETER SUMMER-
HOOFT; E on MR. FURBUSH; W on JOHN WHITE; now FOSTER sells 108 a. to
BEAUCHAMP, free from MARY'S claim of dower. Witnesses: JOSEPH SHUTE (a
Quaker), JAMES CRADDOCK. Before ROBERT AUSTIN, J.P. Plat given. ROBERT
AUSTIN, Register.

Book S, p. 353   ARTHUR FOSTER, planter, of Prince George Par-
8 Dec. 1738   ish, Craven Co., to STEPHEN BEAUCHAMP,

Mortgage   merchant, of Georgetown, as security on bond
                                      in penal sum of ₤ 500 for procuring MARY'S
(wife of ARTHUR FOSTER'S) renunciation of dower before 8 Dec. 1739, to
the 108 a. in Craven Co., sold by FOSTER & his wife; by L & R dated 7 & 8
Dec. 1738, to BEAUCHAMP; bounding SE on ARTHUR FOSTERS; SW on JOHN WHITE;
N on ARTHUR FOSTER & the Broad Path; NW on JOHN DEXTER. Witnesses: JO-
SEPH SHUTE (a Quaker), JAMES CRADDOCK. Before ROBERT AUSTIN, J.P. & Pub.
Reg.

Book S, p. 354   WILLIAM CATTELL, ESQ., of Berkely Co., to
5 & 6 Apr. 1738   GEORGE AUSTIN, merchant, of Charleston, for
L & R   ₤ 904:10 SC money, the N half (the whole divid-
                            ed into 2 equal parts) of 1100 a. in Colleton
Co., bounding N on JOHN SEABROOK; NE on a creek of Ashepoo River; which
tract of 1100 a. was granted to RICHARD GODFREY, planter, of Colleton Co.,
& the above-mentioned half conveyed by GODFREY to CATTELL. Witnesses:
THOMAS NICHOLAS, WILLIAM CATTELL, JR. Before ROBERT AUSTIN, J.P. & Pub.
Reg.

Book S, p. 356   JOHN ALLEN, merchant, to JAMES ST. JOHN, ESQ.,
18 & 19 Sept. 1735   both of Charleston, for ₤ 550 currency, 1 full
L & R   10th part of a square in Charleston formerly
                            known as Hawetts Square, since called Gibbon &
Allens Square, numbered 271; bounding S 92 ft. on Broad St.; E & N on
lots #270 & 273 belonging to JOHN ALLEN; W 240½ ft. on lot #274 belonging
to DAVID HEXT, butcher, of Charleston; which Square, called Gibbon &
Allens Square, was granted by the Lords Proprs. to WILLIAM HAWETT, ESQ.,
& several conveyances became vested in ANDREW ALLEN, merchant, who bequeathed it to his son JOHN ALLEN, party hereto. MARY, the wife of JOHN
ALLEN, being under 21 years of age, shall renounce her title upon coming
of age. Witnesses: JAMES PAINE, JAMES PAINE, JAMES GREEME. Before BEN-
JAMINE WHITAKER, J.P. ROBERT AUSTIN, Register.

Book S, p. 359   WILLIAM HINKLEY, mariner, of Craven Co., to
22 & 23 Aug. 1738   DANIEL LAROCHE & THOMAS LAROCHE, merchants, of
L & R   Georgetown, for ₤ 900 currency, 500 a. in Cra-
                            ven Co., granted HINKLEY by Gov. ROBERT JOHN-
SON, on 22 Sept. 1733; bounding NE on Black River; SW on Green's Creek &
land granted to PHILIP CHANDLER but now belonging to WILLIAM CRIPPS; W &
NW on JOHN WHITE. Witnesses: THOMAS JEWNING, JAMES CRADDOCK. Before WIL-
LIAM WHITESIDE, J.P. ROBERT AUSTIN, Register.

Book S, p. 361   WILLIAM HINKLEY, mariner, of Craven Co., to
23 Aug. 1738   DANIEL LAROCHE & THOMAS LAROCHE, merchants, of
Bond   Georgetown, in penal sum of ₤ 200 for payment
                            of ₤ 100 SC money, with interest, on 1 Mar.
1738. Witnesses: THOMAS JEWING, JAMES CRADDOCK. Before WILLIAM WHITE-
SIDE, J.P. ROBERT AUSTIN, Register.

Book S, p. 362   ALEXANDER VANDERDUSSEN, ESQ., to JOSEPH EDWARD
25 & 26 Jan. 1738   FLOWER, merchant, for ₤ 2756 currency, 689 a.
L & R   in 2 tracts, 1 of 500 a. on Wambe Island,
                            Granville Co., granted by the Lords Proprs. to
WILLIAM LESLEY & after his death descended to his only daughter & heir-
at-law, KATHRINE DUVALL, who by deed poll conveyed to EDWARD SCOTT; & conveyed by EDWARD SCOTT & MARY his wife, to ALEXANDER VANDERDUSSEN; bounding W on WILLIAM BULL; N on WILLIAM LESSLEY; S on Bull's Creek; E on
marsh & small creeks out of Little Port Royall River; also 189 a. within
the boundaries of the above 500 a., & granted to VANDERDUSSEN on 18 Jan.
1738. Witnesses: MAURICE LEWIS, JOHN RATTRAY. Before ROBERT AUSTIN,
J.P. & Pub. Reg.

Book S, p. 363   GEORGE OLIVER, gentleman, of Christ Church
26 & 27 Oct. 1737   Pairsh, & MARY his wife (1 of the daughters &
L & R   co-heiresses of JOHN SIMES, gentleman, of
                            Berkeley Co.), to JAMES WHITE, surgeon, of
Christ Church Parish, for ₤ 380 currency & other considerations, half of
100 a. of land. Whereas JOHN SIMES owned 100 a. in Christ Church Parish,
conveyed to him by ANN BEAVILL, widow of TIMOTHY BEAVILLE on 1 June 1706,
bounding NE & NW on RICHARD BUTLER; SE & SW on FRANCIS JONES; part of a

larger tract laid out to FRANCIS JONES; & whereas at the death of JOHN SIMES the 100 a. were divded between his 2 daughters MARY & SARAH in 2 equal parts; 1/2 to MARY (now wife of GEORGE OLIVER, party hereto) the other half to SARAH (now wife of JAMES WHITE, party hereto); now MARY; with her husband's consent, willingly sells her half to JAMES & SARAH WHITE. Witnesses: JOSEPH MILNER, ANTHONY DEANE. Before ANDREW RUTLEDGE, J.P. ROBERT AUSTIN, Register.

Book S, p. 365
1 Mar. 1737
Confirmation Tripartite

THOMAS BOONE, ESQ., of Christ Church Parish, & MARY his wife (formerly MARY SIMES, widow of JOHN SIMES, gentleman, of Berkely Co.), of 1st part; GEORGE OLIVER, gentleman, of Christ Church Paris, & MARY his wife (daughter & co-heir of JOHN SIMES) of 2nd part; JAMES WHITE, Doctor of Physick, of same Parish, & SARAH his wife (the other daughter & co-heir of JOHN SIMESO of 3rd part. Whereas JOHN SIMES owned divers houses, lands, lots & tenements & by will dated 25 Aug. 1716 bequeathed to his eldest daughter MARY (now wife of GEORGE OLIVER) 200 a. formerly belonging to BENJAMIN QUELCH, ESQ., lying between lands of JAMES EDEN & JOHN HENRICK; & also gave her a house in Charleston on Church Street, in which JOSEPH MASSEY then lived, but that the profits should enure to his loving wife MARY, (now wife of THOMAS BOONE) during her life; & bequeathed to daughter (SARAH (now wife of JAMES WHITE) 2 tracts at a place called Lebanan in Christ Church Parish; & also devised to his wife MARY 460 a. in Christ Church Parish, said to be between the lands of JOTHAN GIBBONS, CHARLES HILL, ESQ., & SOLOMON LEGARE; & whereas MARY SIMES (widow of JOHN) became owner of the 400 a. & also of the house & lot in Church Street; & whereas MARY, eldest daughter of JOHN SIMES (now wife of GEORGE OLIVER) in conformity to the will of her father & with the consent of THOMAS & MARY BOONE (her mother) & of JAMES & SARAH WHITE (her sister) has taken the 200 a. (between the lands of EDEN & HENRICK); & whereas SARAH, daughter of JOHN SIMES, with the consent of the others, has taken the 2 tracts at Lebanon; & whereas the will of JOHN SIMES has never been proved or established (because of the absence or death of the witnesses) & disputes may arise; now it is agreed that MARY BOONE is to have the house & lot on Church Street, during her lifetime also the 460 a.; MARY OLIVER to inherit the house & lot after the death of MARY BOONE, & the 200 a. whereon GEORGE & MARY OLIVER now live; SARAH WHITE to have the 2 tracts at Lebanon. Witnesses: RICHARD CAPERS, JACOB (his mark) BURDELL, ROBERT SMALL. Before ANDREW RUTLEDGE, J.P. ROBERT AUSTIN, Register.

Book S, p. 368
22 & 23 Jan. 1738
L & R by Mortgage

DAVID ARNETT, planter, of Christ Church Parish, to THOMAS BOLTON, merchant, of Charleston, for ₤ 585:15 SC money, 400 a. on the beach, in Christ Church Parish, part of 1055 a. granted NATHANIEL LAW; bounding E on BENJAMIN LAW (part of the 1055 a.); SE on the seacoast; S on THOMAS BARKSDALE; W on RICHARD FOWLER; the 400 a. having been lately surveyed by THOMAS WHITER & granted by BENJAMIN LAW to DAVID ARNETT. Date of redemption; 22 July 1739. Witnesses: HENRY GIBBES, WILLIAM SMITH. Before ROBERT AUSTIN, J.P. & Pub. Reg.

Book S, p. 370
13 Feb. 1711/12
Bill of Sale

WILLIAM FORD, of Port Royall Island, Granville Co., to THOMAS SIMONS, planter, for ₤ 55 currency, 250 a. on Port Royall Island, conveyed to FORD by WILLIAM FORD on 13 Feb. 1711/12; bounding NE on MARK MATHEWS; NW on THOMAS HYOTT; S on a creek; SE on PETER PALMETER. Signed: WILLIAM (his mark) BRAY. Before THOMAS DALE, J.P. ROBERT AUSTIN, Register.

Book S, p. 371
27 & 28 Nov. 1738
L & R

RICHARD GOUGH, planter of St. John's Parish, Berkeley Co., to JOHN GOUGH, planter of same place, for ₤ 10,000 currency, 2830 a., inland, bounding E on head of Cooper River; SW on EDWARD HOWARD; NW on vacant land; NE on MICHAEL MAHONE. Witnesses: FRANCIS ROCHE, MATTHEW ROCHE, DANIEL HANLEY (HENDLEY). Before FRANCIS LEJAU, J.P. ROBERT AUSTIN, Register.

Book S, p. 373
10 Sept. 1731
Release & Confirmation

ISAAC LOWNDES, apothecary, of St. James Parish, Westminster, of 1st part; THOMAS LOWNDES, gentleman, of the Parish of St. John the

Evangelist, City of Westminster, of 2nd part; ROBERT THORPE, merchant, of Thames Street, London, of 3rd part. Whereas ISAAC LOWNDES is entitled to the inheritance of the Barony in SC containing 12,000 a. which he holds by grant from the Rt. Hon. JOHN, Lord Carteret; the most Noble HENRY, Duke of Beaufort; & other Lords Proprs. of SC in trust for THOMAS LOWNDES & his heirs; & whereas THORPE has agreed to pay ₤ 450 for 9000 a. (part of the Barony); now, for that sum, THOMAS & ISAAC LOWNDES, convey to THORPE the same 9000 a. mentioned in L & R of even date. Witnesses: JOHN THORPE, JONAH ENGLAND, SAMUEL POWELL. Endorsed (?) by STEPHEN DOWNES, Extur. Before J. TOTHILL. ROBERT AUSTIN, Register.

Book S, p. 374
2 Nov. 1736
Release

JAMES ST. JOHN, ESQ., to ROBERT THORPE, gentleman, both of Charleston, for ₤ 1360 SC money & other considerations, lot #271 in Charleston, fronting S 92 ft. on Broad Street; N on lot # belonging to JOHN ALLEN, merchant; E on WILLIAM PINCKNEY & part of lot #220 belonging to JAMES JOHN; W on lot #274 belonging to DAVID HEXT, butcher; also another piece of ground 3 ft. x 144 ft. bounding N on JAMES ST. JOHN; E on Allen Street; S on WILLIAM PINCKNEY, JOHN ALLEN & HENRY CRISTIE; W on above lot. Witnesses: WILLIAM SMITH, WILLIAM IRVIN. Before JAMES GREEME, J.P. ROBERT AUSTIN, Register.

Book S, p. 376
17 & 18 Jan. 1737/8
L & R

THOMAS LYNCH, ESQ., to JOHN BAXTER, clerk, & SARAH his wife, daughter of THOMAS LYNCH, all of Berkeley Co., for natural love & affection & 15 shillings, 166-2/3 a. on Wando River, in Christ Church Parish, commonly called Will's Neck, bounding N on the River; S on THOMAS LYNCH; W on CAPT. JOHN VANDERHORST. Witnesses: JOHN ATCHINSON, ALEXANDER AGNEW. Before ROBERT AUSTIN, J.P. & Reg. Plat given.

Book S, p. 378
19 & 20 July 1737
L & R

CHARLES CODNER, planter, & ANN his wife; & SABINA ROUS (ROWES), widow, all of Berkeley Co., to THOMAS BOLTON, merchant, of Charleston, for ₤ 3000 currency, part of lot #17 fronting E 24-1/2 ft. on the Bay of Charleston, belonging to CHARLES, ANN & SABINA, now in the possession of JAMES WITHERS, bricklayer, bounding S 24-1/2 ft. on BENJAMIN D'HARRIETTE, merchant; N on EDWARD HEXT, merchant; W on Union Street; also the low water lands before lot #17 lying E from the front wall to low water mark. Witnesses: BENJAMIN BURNHAM, FRANCIS MERRETT, JOHN (his mark) ST. MARTIN. Before HENRY GIBBES, J.P. ROBERT AUSTIN, Register.

Book S, p. 381
25 Sept. 1738
Agreement

WILLIAM (his mark) KEMP, planter, of Williamsburgh Township, Craven Co., in consideration of 2 Negro men slaves already delivered to him by GODDARD & of 1 other Negro man slave to be delivered, promises FRANCIS GODDARD, gentleman, of St. James Goose Creek Parish, that on 5 Nov. next he will deliver to GODDARD 2 tracts of land; 1 of 300 a. now in possession of WILLIAM KEMP & lately surveyed; the other of 150 a. lately surveyed & granted to FRANCIS TURBURVILLE; both tracts being within Williamsburgh Township. GODDARD promises to buy for & deliver to KEMP 1 choice new Negro man out of the first "Gineau" (Guinea?) ship that shall arrive after 1 Feb. next, provided a good title shall have been made of the 2 tracts to GODDARD. Whereas WILLIAM KEMP this day executed a warrant of attorney to confess judgment to GODDARD in the sum of ₤ 600 & costs of suit, they agree that the judgment be taken as security for performance of agreement. Witnesses: WILLIAM TREWIN, SAMUEL FLEY. Before ROBERT AUSTIN, J.P. & Pub. Reg.

Book S, p. 381
4 & 5 Dec. 1738
L & R by Mortgage

JOHN GODWIN (GOODWIN) of Craven Co., & MARTHA (her mark) his wife, to DANIEL LAROCHE & THOMAS LAROCHE, merchants, of Georgetown, for ₤ 1200 SC money, 700 a. in Craven Co., bounding NW on JOHN WALLES, ESQ.; SE on WILLIAM SWINTON, ESQ.; NE partly on vacant land; SW on N branch of Black River. Date of redemption: 1 Mar. next. Witnesses: PAUL TRAPIER, WILLIAM WHITESIDE, JR. Before WILLIAM WHITESIDE, J.P. ROBERT AUSTIN, Register. THOMAS LAROCHE acknowledged satisfaction of mortgage on 30 May 1739. Witness: ROBERT AUSTIN, Register.

Book S, p. 383   WILSON WILSON, tailor, of Georgetown, Winyaw,
13 & 14 Feb. 1738   to MAURICE LEWIS, ESQ., of Charleston, as se-
L & R by Mortgage   curity on bond dated 5 June 1737 (?) in penal
                         sum of ₤ 8000 for payment of ₤ 6000 SC money,
with interest, on 5 Sept. next; 1350 a. in Queensborough Township, on NE
side of Peedee River, bounding NE on vacant land; SE on vacant land &
ROBERT WRIGHT, ESQ.; NW on THOMAS MONK, ESQ.; MARY, wife of WILSON WILSON,
to renounce her dower within 6 months. Witnesses: JOHN OULDFIELD, JR.,
JAMES CRADDOCK. Before THOMAS LAROCHE, J.P. ROBERT AUSTIN, Register.

Book S, p. 385   JAMES KINLOCH, ESQ., of Berkeley Co., to
7 July 1738   GEORGE HUNTER, gentleman, of Charleston, for
Release   ₤ 325 SC money, 3249 a. in Craven Co., granted
                         by letters patent, dated 5 July 1737 by Lt.
Gov. THOMAS BROUGHTON to JAMES KINLOCH; bounding E on CAPT. WILLIAM BROCK-
INGTON; N on ANTHONY WHITE & JOHN LANE; W N & S on land surveyed by pat-
ent for heirs of ROBERT YEAMANS, ESQ., & part S on vacant land. ALEXAN-
DER ROBERTSON made oath that he saw the words "JAMES KINLOCH" interlined
twice in this deed. Witnesses: JOHN CROKATT, JR., ALEXANDER ROBERTSON.
Before JACOB MOTTE, J.P. ROBERT AUSTIN, Register.

Book S, p. 386   JAMES MACKCOY, tailor, of Craven Co., to WIL-
14 Feb. 1736/7   LIAM NEWMAN, planter, of Craven Co., as securi-
Mortgage   ty on bond of even date in penal sum of
                         ₤ 1354:10 currency, for payment of ₤ 676:5 cur-
rency on 20 Mar. ensuring, all his lands, tenements, & 8 slaves. Witnesses: JOHN BROWN, JOHN JUNE. Before WILLIAM DRAKE, J.P. Recorded in
Secretary's office in Bk. K.K. fol. 164-167 by JAMES MICHIE, Dep. Sec.
ROBERT AUSTIN, Register.

Book S, p. 387   JAMES COFING, planter, to JAMES BOSWOOD, plant-
16 Jan. 1738/9   er, both of St. Andrews Parish, Berkeley Co.,
Mortgage   for ₤ 275; 100 a. in St. Andrews Parish, bound-
                         ing E on JAMES BOSWOOD; W on HANNAH BURNLEY; N
on JOSIAH CANTEY; S on HUGH FORGISON. Date of redemption: 2 Jan. next.
Witnesses: JAMES ROULAIN, THOMAS MELL. Before RALPH IZARD, J.P. ROBERT
AUSTIN, Register. JAMES BOSWOOD declared mortgage satisfied 17 May 1742.
ROBERT AUSTIN, Register.

Book S, p. 388   JOSEPH SHUTE, merchant, to THOMAS HENNING,
2 & 3 Mar. 1738   merchant, both of Charleston, for ₤ 4000 SC
L & R in Trust   money, 430 a. in Craven Co., on S side of Lit-
                         tle River, bounding E on the sea; W on NICHO-
LAS TRUCK; also all cattle marked A lately the property of JOHN ABBOT,
also that lot in Georgetown, Winyaw, on the corner of Scriven Street &
all buildings thereon; also that lot in Georgetown on Broad Street, with
the buildings thereon; in trust for THOMAS HENNING & JOSEPH SHUTE in co-
partnership; subject to the payment of the debts due to HENNING & SHUTE
"in Company", & to JOSEPH SHUTE from JOHN ABBOT, late proprietor of the
premises. Witnesses: JOHN RATTRAY, JAMES VARNER. Before MAURICE LEWIS,
J.P. ROBERT AUSTIN, Register.

Book S, p. 390   ISAAC COSTE, shoemaker, & MAGDELENA, his wife,
25 & 26 Nov. 1738   to PETER DELMESTRE, doctor, of Charleston, for
L & R   ₤ 52:10 currency, 150 a. in Purysburgh Town-
                         ship, Granville Co., bounding N on SAMUEL ANGS-
BOURGER; E on Day's Creek (called New River) at Rogersons Bluff; S on
MATHEW MOORE; W on vacant land; which tract was granted to COSTE by Lt.
Gov. WILLIAM BULL on 16 Sept. 1738. Witnesses: DAVID VILLARET, JOHN
SASOUBRE, DAVID PIERRE HUMBERT. Before ROBERT AUSTIN, J.P. & Pub. Reg.

Book S, p. 392   JOHN HICKS, planter, of Colleton Co., to
31 Jan. & 1 Feb. 1738   CHARLES PERONNEAU & Co., merchants, of Colle-
L & R by Mortgage   ton Co., for ₤ 200 currency, 197 a. on Wadma-
                         law Island, Colleton Co., bounding N on heirs
of WILLIAM NASH; S on a branch of Bohicket Creek; E on JOSEPH GIBBONS &
THOMAS WANBORN; W on a marsh. Date of redemption: 1 Feb. 1739. Witnesses: ISAAC WEATHERLEY, GEORGE HOLMES. Before ROBERT YONGE, J.P. ROBERT
AUSTIN, Pub. Reg.

Book S, p. 394　　　　　　JOHN SKENE, ESQ., of Berkeley Co., to ROBERT
1 & 2 Jan. 1738　　　　　AUSTIN, ESQ., of Charleston, for ℔ 500 SC mon-
L & R by Mortgage　　　 ey, 500 a. on N side Steeds Creek, bounding on
　　　　　　　　　　　　all sides on vacant land. Date of redemption:
5 Jan. 1739. Witnesses: PHILIP AYTON, JAMES COLSON. Before RICHARD WAL-
TERS, J.P. ROBERT AUSTIN, J.P.

Book S, p. 396　　　　　　CHARLES CODNER, planter, of St. Thomas Parish,
13 & 14 Aug. 1736　　　　Berkeley Co., to the Rev. MR. THOMAS HASELL,
L & R by Mortgage　　　 JOHN BERESFORD, JAMES AKIN, ISAAC LESESNE, JR.,
　　　　　　　　　　　　JOHN DANIEL, WILLIAM TREWIN & THOMAS WALKER, 7
of the vestrymen of St. Thomas Parish, as security on bond of even date
in penal sum of ℔ 1000 for payment of ℔ 500, with interest, on 25 Mar.
1737 (being the "proper money" belonging to the pious & charitable dona-
tion of RICHARD BERESFORD, ESQ.); 170 a., on an island formerly called
Ettiwan (alias Ittiwan) now known as Daniels Island in St. Thomas Parish,
a point of land bounding N on Itchecaw Creek; S on Landgrave ROBERT DAN-
IEL (formerly WILLIAM JACKSON); W on Cooper River; E on JOHN DANIEL, ESQ.,
(formerly TIMOTHY RUSSELL); also the land lying between the line of the
above tract & MR. NORTON'S line toward the W & E & bounding S on land
formerly belonging to WILLIAM JACKSON; N on a marsh in Itchecaw Creek.
Witnesses: WILLIAM (his mark) STANDFAST, ROBERT HOW. Before ROBERT AUS-
TIN, J.P. & Pub. Reg.

Book S, p. 399　　　　　　THOMAS LYNCH, ESQ., of Berkeley Co., & ROBERT
17 July 1738　　　　　　 FLADGER, planter, of Craven Co., 2 of the ex-
L & R　　　　　　　　　　ecutors of will of JAMES ARMSTRONG, of Christ
　　　　　　　　　　　　Church Parish to JOHN MCEVER, planter, of
Berkeley Co., for ℔ 1875 SC money, 300 a., English measure, in St. Thomas
Parish, Berkeley Co., bounding NE on LEWIS DUTARQUE; NW on ROBERT HUME;
NW on STEPHEN FOGARTIE; S on JAMES ARMSTRONG; also 75 a., English measure,
in same Parish, bounding NE on LEWIS DUTARQUE; SE on above 300 a.; SW on
STEPHEN FOGARTIE, according to plat dated 7 Aug. 1735 attached to grant.
Whereas Gov. EDWARD TYNTE & the Lords Proprs. on 14 Apr. 1708 granted
JOHN FOGARTIE 640 a., English measure, according to plat; & whereas FO-
GARTIE afterwards sold 200 a. (on NE part of the 640) to LEWIS DUTARQUE &
gave 140 a. (the SW part) to his son STEPHEN FOGARTIE, & by bill of sale
dated 4 June 1728 sold the remainder of the 640 a. (or 300 a.) to JOHN
COLWELL, butcher, of Berkeley Co.; & whereas JOHN COLWELL bequeathed to
JUDITH SIMMONS (now JUDITH SIMMONS (now JUDITH SWINTON), after other leg-
acies, the remainder of his real & personal estate; & whereas HUGH SWIN-
TON & JUDITH his wife, by L & R dated 8 & 9 Mar. 1732 sold the 300 a. to
JAMES ARMSTRONG, planter, of Christ Church Parish; & he by will dated 29
Jan. 1734, after other things, ordered the remainder of his real & per-
sonal estate sold by his executors for the benefit of his children; now
the executors sell the 300 a. & a tract of 75 a. to MCEVER. Witnesses:
JOHN THOMSON, SR., ELIZABETH FLADGER. Before JOHN WALLIS, J.P. ROBERT
AUSTIN, Register.

Book S, p. 402　　　　　　JOSEPH ELLIOTT, planter, of Berkeley Co., to
27 June 1737　　　　　　 THOMAS GOODMAN, watchmaker, of Charleston,
Bond　　　　　　　　　　 bond in penal sum of ℔ 1000 British, with the
　　　　　　　　　　　　condition that ELLIOTT shall convey to GOODMAN,
as soon as a grant may be obtained, a good title to such lands as may be
run out on a certain warrant of survey dated 24 May 1737 granted ELLIOTT
by Lt. Gov. THOMAS BROUGHTON, for laying out 2500 a. Witnesses: WILLIAM
SMITH, MARGARET (her mark) DUCATT. Before THOMAS DALE, J.P. ROBERT AUS-
TIN, Register.

Book S, p. 403　　　　　　The Hon. GEORGE LUCAS, ESQ., to the Hon.
5 July 1738　　　　　　　CHARLES DUNBAR, ESQ., both of the Island of
Mortgage　　　　　　　　 Antigua, for ℔ 350 sterling British, 600 a. on
　　　　　　　　　　　　Wappoo Creek, near Charleston, SC, lately owned by JOHN LUCAS, ESQ., of Antigua father of GEORGE LUCAS; bounding E on
MR. WOODWARD & other lands (formerly BENJAMIN GODFREY); N & SW on MRS.
HILL, a widow; & the buildings; also 12 Negro men, 8 Negro women, & all
cattle & horses & all utensils on the plantation. Date of redemption:
6 July 1740. Witnesses: DELACOURT WALSH, GEORGE STARRATT. On 5 July
1738 GEORGE LUCAS, of Antigua, appointed EDWARD WHITAKER, ESQ., & ALEXAN-
DER SKENE, ESQ., of SC, his attorneys to acknowledge this deed. Same

witnesses. STARRAT appeared before THOMAS LAROCHE, J.P. ROBERT AUSTIN, Pub. Reg.

Book S, p. 404
12 & 13 June 1738
L & R by Mortgage

WILLIAM COLT, planter, & REBECCA ANNE his wife, of Prince George Parish, Winyaw, Craven Co., to JOHN CLELAND & WILLIAM WALLACE, merchants, of Charleston. Whereas COLT gave CLELAND & WALLACE a bond dated 2 Jan. 1737 in penal sum of ₤ 3900 for payment of ₤ 1950 SC money, with interest, on 1 Jan. 1738; & whereas COLT on 2 Jan. 1737 to secure payment, delivered to them 11 Negro men & 5 Negro women; now for further security they mortgage 500 a. on Waccamaw Swamp in Craven Co. bounding NW & SW on the swamp; NE & SE on lands not laid out; also 2 lots in Georgetown #211 & #212. REBECCA ANNE to renounce her dower before ROBERT WRIGHT, C.J. Witnesses: WILLIAM WHITESIDE, CHARLES HOPE. Before THOMAS LAROCHE, J.P. ROBERT AUSTIN, Register.

Book S, p. 408
3 May 1737
Letter of Attorney

FREDERICK GAILLARD, planter, of Craven Co., appointed his friends ANDREW DE LAVILLETTE, planter, ISAAC LEGRAND DONEVILLE, planter, & CAPT. JONATHAN SKRINE, planter, all of Craven Co., attornies to act for himself & his wife ELIZABETH, for the benefit of GAILLARD'S creditors; giving his attornies power to sell his 2 tracts of land; total 900 a.; 1 of 500 a. in St. James Santee, bounding E on COL. GENDRON, fronting on Savannah or Wetee Creek; the other of 400 a. bounding W on ANDREW LAVILLETTE; E on ALCIMUS GAILLARD; also 11 slaves, horses, mares & neat cattle. Whereas GAILLARD has already mortgaged some of the slaves to PAUL JENYS, merchant, of Charleston, & 2 to JONAH COLLINS, as security on several debts, GAILLARD instructs his attorneys to pay JENYS & COLLINS first, then to pay the costs & charges of several court actions; then to pay his creditors; & whereas the sale of the land & slaves may not bring in sufficient money, GAILLARD promises that, in such case, he will transfer his title to a legacy or estate devised to his wife ELIZABETH by will of her grandfather, ANDREW REMBERT. Witnesses: JAMES FREEMAN, THOMAS GALLWAY, DAVID DALBIAC (?) (DALBINE?). Before PETER DE ST. JULIEN, J.P. Creditors: PAUL JENYS, ANDREW DELAVILLETTE, ISAAC MAZYCK, JOHN LAURENS, JONAH COLLINS, STEPHEN MILLER, MRS. ELIZABETH LEJANDRA, JONATHAN SKRINE, LEGRAND DONERVILLE. ROBERT AUSTIN, Pub. Reg.

Book S, p. 409
22 & 23 Feb. 1738
L & R

JOHN MCKAY, merchant, to GABRIEL GUIGNARD, cooper, both of Charleston, for ₤ 1400 currency, part of lot #13 in Charleston, bounding E on part of same lot; W 77 ft. on ISAAC MAZYCK; N 15-1/2 ft. on Broad Street; S on ISAAC MAZYCK; with privilege of using 5 ft. path at W side. Witnesses: JOEL POINSET, LAWRENCE COULLIETTE. Before ROBERT AUSTIN, J.P. & Pub. Reg.

Book S, p. 411
3 Nov. 1738
Deed of Gift

WILLIAM SAMS, planter, of Wadmalaw Island, St. John's Parish, Colleton Co., to his beloved son WILLIAM SAMS, for love & affection, 200 a. on Edisto Island, bounding E on land formerly belonging to THOMAS GRIMBALL; S on a marsh & Governours Creek. Witnesses: ROBERT SAMS, JOHN HOGG, THOMAS STANYARNE. Before JACOB MOTTE, J.P. ROBERT AUSTIN, Register.

Book S, p. 412
3 Nov. 1738
Deed of Gift

WILLIAM SAMS, planter, of Wadmalaw Island, St. John's Parish, Colleton Co., to his beloved son JOSEPH SAMS, for love & affection, 250 a. bounding E on THOMAS STANYARNE, according to plat. Witnesses: ROBERT SAMS, JOHN HOGG, THOMAS STANYARNE. Before JACOB MOTTE, J.P. ROBERT AUSTIN, Register.

Book S, p. 412
28 & 29 Mar. 1739
L & R

WILLIAM HENDRICK, planter, of Berkeley Co., to EPHRIAM MIKELL, planter, of Granville Co., for ₤ 774 currency, 387 a. in Granville Co., known as Hog Island, bounding N on marsh of Port Royall River; other sides on branches of Port Royall River; according to plat attached to original grant dated 23 July 1711 from the Lords Proprs. to his father JOHN HENDRICK, who by will bequeathed the island to his son WILLIAM. Witnesses: BENJAMIN SMITH, ROBERT CLELAND, WILLIAM SMITH. Before ROBERT AUSTIN, J.P. & Pub. Reg.

Book S, p. 414 20 & 21 Mar. 1738 L & R	THOMAS BOLTON, merchant, & ELIZABETH his wife, to COL. MILES BREWTON, all of Charleston, for ₤ 500 currency, 70 a. in Christ Church Parish, Berkeley Co., bounding N & E on JOSHUA WILKS;

W on CAPT. EDMUND ROBINSON & WILLIAM VISSER; S on GARRAT FITZGARLD; as by plat attached to original grant; which land formerly belonged to JOHN FITZGARLD & by several conveyances became vested in JOHN HALE & ELIZABETH his wife & ANDREW QUELCH & ELIZABETH his wife; all of Berkeley Co., & from whom it was lately purchased. Witnesses: EDWARD HEXT, ARD YOUNG, WILLIAM SMITH. Before ROBERT AUSTIN, J.P. & Pub. Reg.

Book S, p. 416 17 & 18 July 1738 L & R by Mortgage	JAMES CRICHLOW, planter, & MARY (her mark) his wife, of Prince George Parish, Winyaw, to JOHN CLELAND & WILLIAM WALLACE, merchants, of Charleston, as security on a bond & mortgage;

300 a. on Sampit Creek, Craven Co., bounding SW on JOHN OLDFIELD; N & NE on DANIEL BRITTON; SE on Three-mile Creek. MARY CRICHLOW to renounce her dower before ROBERT WRIGHT, C.J., when requested. Whereas CHRICHLOW gave CLELAND & WALLACE a bond dated 2 Jan. 1737 in penal sum of ₤ 990 for payment of ₤ 495 currency with interest on 1 Jan. 1738 & on 2 Jan. 1737, as security, conveyed to them 3 Negro slaves; now as further security, they convey 300 a. Witnesses: WILLIAM COLLINS, CHARLES HOPE. Before THOMAS LAROCHE, J.P. ROBERT AUSTIN, Register.

Book S, p. 419 30 & 31 May 1737 L & R	HENRY (his mark) MEWS & ANN (her mark) his wife, of Berkeley Co., to NICHOLAS MATTHISON, of Charleston, for ₤ 15 currency, half of 2 tracts on Lynches Creek in Craven Co., contain-

ing 250 a.; 1 tract bounding NE on DR. BRUCE; other sides on lands not laid out; the other bounding SE & NW on lands not laid out; NE on NICHOLAS MATHISON & HENRY MEWS; SW on MR. DE LESSENNE. Witnesses: JOHN YERWORTH, EDWARD BULLARD. Before HENRY GIBBES, J.P. ROBERT AUSTIN, Register.

Book S, p. 421 18 Oct. 1737 Bill of Sale	JOHN (his mark) MACOY, planter, of Colleton Co., to RICHARD DAWSON, planter, of Colleton Co., for ₤ 200 currency, 200 a. near Horse Shoe Savanna, bounding N on WILLIAM EBBERSON;

SW on JOHN COOK; SE on MR. BETTISON; other sides on vacant land. Witnesses: THOMAS SNIPES, THOMAS JENNINGS, JOHN SALSBERRY (SELSBE) BARTON. Before CULCHETH GOLIGHTLY, J.P. ROBERT AUSTIN, Pub. Reg.

Book S, p. 422 11 & 12 Apr. 1739 L & R Tripartite	JOHN CARRUTHERS, gentleman, of London, of 1st part; NATHANIEL BROUGHTON & ANDREW BROUGHTON, ESQ., of St. John's Parish, of 2nd part; THOMAS MONCK, ESQ., of 3rd part. Whereas by L & R

dated 13 & 14 July 1737 MONCK conveyed to CARRUTHERS the S part of lot #113 in Charleston, fronting 57 ft. 3 in. on Church Street; bounding N 113 ft. 4-3/4 in.; breadth (N to S) adjoining JOHN BERESFORD, ESQ., 54 ft.; S on NICHOLAS TROTT; also the new messuage thereon; also part of a lot fronting 57 ft. 8 in. on Church Street; 49 ft. on Queen Street; backwards to Queen Street, adjoining said lot of THOMAS MONCK; backwards to Church Street from the theatre; & all houses thereon; also 7-1/2 a. on Charleston Neck, bounding SE on MRS. DAW; SW on high road leading to Charleston; NW on COL. JOSEPH BLAKE; NE on marsh; MONCK to pay CARRUTHERS ₤ 500 sterling British, with interest, in London on 14 July 1742; & whereas NATHANIEL & ANDREW BROUGHTON went on MONCK'S bond to CARRUTHERS dated 14 Mar. 1738 in penal sum of ₤ 1069:3:4 for payment of ₤ 534:11:8 sterling British, with interest, at the Royal Exchange, London, on 14 Mar. 1739; now CARRUTHERS, in consideration of the bond, conveys to the BROUGHTONS the 2 lots in Charleston & the 7-1/2 a., subject to redemption. Witnesses: MAURICE LEWIS, JOHN RATTRAY. Before ROBERT AUSTIN, J.P. & Pub. Reg.

Book S, p. 424 3 & 4 Apr. 1739 L & R by Mortgage	JAMES GORDON, planter, of Winyaw, to JOHN CLELAND & WILLIAM WALLACE, merchants, of Charleston, as security on bond of even date in penal sum of ₤ 606:14:8 for payment of

₤ 303:7:4 British, with interest, on 9 Apr. next; 1050 a. in Craven Co., bounding S on PETER SMITH; E on WILLIAM WHITESIDE; W & N on vacant land;

NE on EDWARD BULLARD; also 650 a. in Craven Co., on Peedee River, granted to WILLIAM CHICKEN & by several conveyances became vested in JAMES GORDON; also 300 a. granted to PETER BONHOIST & conveyed to JAMES GORDON; bounding N on Swintons Creek; NE on Peedee River & Gordon's thoroughfare; S on Glen's Thoroughfare; SE on GEORGE PAWLEY; also 100 a. (part of 200 a. granted to BONHOIST & conveyed to GORDON) bounding E on WILLIAM ALSTON & Pawley's Creek; N on WILLIAM SWINTON; SW on Peedee River & Gordon's Thoroughfare; also 1550 a. on Sampit Creek, Winyaw, lately granted to PETER SMITH, bounding N on said 1050 a. granted to GORDON; also 500 a. in Queensborough Township, bounding NE on Peedee River; SE on JAMES GORDON; SW on vacant land; NW on SOLOMON HUGHS; also 300 a. bounding NW on MRS. MOORE; NE on Peedee River; SW on Lynches Creek; also 400 a. in Queensborough Township, bounding NE on Peedee River; SE on JAMES ABERCROMBY; SW on vacant land; NE on MR. CLARK; also 500 a. in Queensborough, bounding SW on vacant land; SE on MRS. MOORE; NE on Peedee River; NW on JAMES GORDON; also 250 a. bounding SW on Peedee River; SE on SAMUEL BAKER; NE on vacant land; NW on HUGH DAY. Witnesses: MAURICE LEWIS, JOHN MCKENSIE. Before ROBERT AUSTIN, J.P. & Pub. Reg.

Book S, p. 426 ROGER MOORE, ESQ., of NC, & CATHARINE his wife,
26 & 27 Jan. 1735 to WILLIAM MIDDLETON, ESQ., of SC, for Ł 162
L & R SC money, 324 a. on NE side Ashley River,
Goose Creek Parish, Berkeley Co., SC bounding S on GIDEON FAUCHERAUD; E on MATHEW BAIRD; N on COL. THOMAS SMITH; W on ABRAHAM BRUNSON; which 324 a. were granted by the Lords Proprs. to THOMAS GRAVES, planter, of Colleton Co., who conveyed to MOORE. Signed at Cape Fear, NC & witnessed by EDWARD MOSELY, & WILL DRY. DRY appeared before JOHN HAMMERTON, J.Q. of SC. Memorial entered 11 Apr. 1739 by JAMES ST. JOHN, Dep. Aud. ROBERT AUSTIN, Pub. Reg.

Book S, p. 428 JOSEPH WRAGG, merchant, & JUDITH his wife, of
1 & 2 June 1734 Charleston, to WILLIAM MIDDLETON, ESQ., of St.
L & R James, Goose Creek, for Ł 800 currency, 500 a.
in Berkeley Co., bounding N on ARTHUR MIDDLETON; E on JOHN JONES. Whereas on 14 July 1726 SAMUEL RUSCO gave JOSEPH WRAGG a bond in penal sum of Ł 2000 for payment of Ł 1000 SC money on 1 Jan. 1726 & for security conveyed to WRAGG, 500 a. in Berkeley Co., bounding as above; & whereas WRAGG agreed to purchase the land & RUSCO conveyed it to him on 1 Feb. 1733; now WRAGG sells the land to MIDDLETON. Witnesses: RICHARD LAMBTON, EDWARD WIGG. Before ROBERT AUSTIN, J.P. & Pub. Reg.

Book S, p. 431 ISAAC PERONNEAU, planter, & MARY his wife,
20 & 21 Nov. 1738 (lately MARY FITCH sole daughter & heir-at-law
L & R of TOBIAS FITCH & MARION his wife, & great
grand-daughter of ABRAHAM FLOREY DELAPLANE, planter), to WILLIAM MIDDLETON, ESQ., all of Berkeley Co., for Ł 840 SC money, 186 a., part of 500 a. granted said DELAPLANE, according to plat attached. Witnesses: CHARLES PERONNEAU, JOHN WEAVER, GASPER (his mark) MORGANTAL. Before RALPH IZARD, J.P. A memorial entered in Auditors office 11 Apr. 1739 by JAMES ST. JOHN, Dep. Aud. Plat certified 2 June 1737 by JOHN DORSEY, Dep. Sur. showing 186 a., butting on lands of IZARD, GARIN, PERONNEAU, WILLIAM MIDDLETON, ROBERT AUSTIN, Register.

Book S, p. 433 ARTHUR MIDDLETON, ESQ., to WILLIAM MIDDLETON,
17 & 18 Aug. 1736 ESQ., both of St. James, Goose Creek, for love
Deed of Gift & affection, 950 a. (half of 1900 a.) at Wampee, Berkeley Co., bounding N & W on ARTHUR MIDDLETON; S on WILLIAM MIDDLETON; E on THOMAS FERGUSON; also part of lot #199 in Charleston, bounding E 175-2/3 ft. on lot #79 belonging to RICHARD SPLATT (formerly THOMAS AMORY, JR.); S 120 ft. on Queen St.; W 178-1/3 ft. on JOHN MILLER (formerly TWEEDIE SOMERVILLE); N 120 ft. on part belonging to ARTHUR MIDDLETON. Witnesses: I. MILLECHAMP, ELIZABETH CHAMBERLAIN, SAMUEL MORRIS. ROBERT AUSTIN, J.P. & Pub. Reg.

Book S, p. 435 WILLIAM WILKINS, planter, & SARAH his wife, of
10 & 11 Apr. 1739 Berkeley Co., to EDWARD HEXT, gentleman, of
L & R by Mortgage Charleston (with SARAH'S consent) for Ł 4400
currency, 617 a. on James Island, Berkeley Co., bounding N on Wappoo Creek & marsh of Ashley River; S on New Town Creek &

MR. SESSION (formerly RICHARD SIMPSON); W on BELTESHAZZER LAMBRIGHT (formerly ROBERT GIBBES, then SHABISHARD?); E on marsh of New Town Creek & Ashley River; according to plat certified 15 May 1701 by JAMES WITTER & annexed to original grant to DAVID DAVIS dated 18 Sept. 1703 from Gov. NATHANIEL JOHNSON & the Lords Proprs. Witnesses: JOHN MATHEWS, WILLIAM BOWER, JAMES LARDANT, CHARLES LANE. Before THOMAS LAMBOLL, J.P. ROBERR AUSTIN, Pub. Reg. On 26 Mar. 1740 EDWARD HEXT declared mortgage satisfied. Witness: ROBERT AUSTIN, Register.

Book S, p. 437
24 & 25 Mar. 1738
L & R by Mortgage

BENJAMIN DIDCOTT, planter, to CHARLES PERONNEAU & Co., merchants, all of Colleton Co., for L 380:12:3 currency, 332 a. at head of Tooboodoo Creek, Colleton Co., bounding E on marsh & JOHN FABIAN (formerly WILLIAM DERHAM) & SAMUEL DAVIS; S on CAPT. WILLIAM EDINGS; W on JAMES COCHRAN; N on heirs of JOSEPH DIDCOTT. Should DIDCOTT pay PERONNEAU & Co. L 192:16:3 SC money, with interest, on 1 Mar. 1739 the mortgage to be void. Witnesses: ISAAC SMALLWOOD, HENRY (his mark) BEACH. Before HENRY GIBBES, J.P. ROBERT AUSTIN, Pub. Reg.

Book S, p. 440
15 Mar. 1738/9
Mortgage

BENJAMIN LAW, planter, of Berkeley Co., to WILLIAM EDINGS, planter, & THEODORIA, his wife, of Edisto Island for L 500 currency, all that plantation on Wando, known as Ushasau, formerly belonging to JOSEPH LAW, being part of a plantation formerly belonging to FRANCIS JONES. Witnesses: THOMAS ROBINSON, WILLIAM RUSSELL, ALGERNOON ASH. Before JAMES BULLOCK, J.P. ROBERT AUSTIN, Register.

Book S, p. 440
16 & 17 Mar. 1738
L & R

SAMUEL BOWMAN, planter, & SARAH his wife, of Beach Hill, SC, to JOSEPH ROBINSON, cordwinder, of Berkeley Co., for L 1000 SC money, 675 a. in Craven Co., bounding N on SAMUEL BOWMAN, S on JOSEPH ROBINSON; E on Little Peedee River; being the S half of 1350 a. granted SAMUEL BOWMAN on 23 Feb. last by the Hon. WILLIAM BULL. Witnesses: JOHN BILLIALD, ROBERT BOWMAN. Before ROBERT AUSTIN, J.P. & Pub. Reg.

Book S, p. 442
24 & 25 Apr. 1739
L & R

WILLIAM BULL, ESQ., of Charleston, to JAMES OGLETHORPE, ESQ., late of Great Britain, now residing in America, for L 636 currency, 5365 a. in Granville Co., bounding W on Savannah River; E on THOMAS OWEN & JOSEPH WRAGG; N on ROBERT WRIGHT, MR. DUBOURDIEU, & JAMES KINLOCH; S on Township of Purysburgh; which tract Lt. Gov. THOMAS BROUGHTON, by letters patent dated 12 Aug. 1737 granted to COL. WILLIAM BULL, with the usual provisoes. Witnesses: ALEXANDER CRAMAHE, WILLIAM HAMILTON. Before THOMAS LAMBOLL, J.P. Memorial entered in Auditor's office 25 Apr. 1739 by JAMES ST. JOHN, Dep. Aud. ROBERT AUSTIN, Pub. Reg.

Book S, p. 444
27 July 1738
Letter of Attorney

ROBERT KNIGHT, peruke maker, of Distaff Lane, London, & MARY his wife (lately widow of MARMADUKE DANIEL, gentleman, of Charleston, SC) to JONATHAN SCOTT, merchant, of Charleston. Whereas ROBERT KNIGHT, & MARY his wife, by assignment dated 30 June last surrendered to JONATHAN SCOTT, merchant, of Charleston, all dower rights & interest in lots #33 & 34 fronting 150 ft. on the Bay of Charleston, leading down to low water mark, lately owned by MARMADUKE DANIEL, now by JONATHAN SCOTT; & whereas it is necessary to register the deed in Charleston; now ROBERT & MARY appoint SCOTT their attorney for that purpose. Witnesses: JAMES COPPELL (clerk to MR. ALEXANDER, attorney, Threadneedle Street, London), JONATHAN BURNYEAT, of Charleston (a Quaker). BURNYEAT appeared before ROBERT AUSTIN, J.P. & Pub. Reg. in Charleston. On 16 Aug. 1738 SIR JOHN BARNARD, Knight, mayor of London, certified that JAMES COPPELL, gentleman, of Threadneedle Street, London, testified that ROBERT & MARY KNIGHT delivered a parchment dated 30 June last purporting to be an assignment of MARY'S dower in said lots & a letter of attorney dated 27 July folloiwng, enabling JONATHAN SCOTT to register the assignment in Charleston, SC.

Book S, p. 445
30 June 1738
Assignment of Dower

ROBERT KNIGHT, peruke-maker, of Distaff Lane, London, & MARY his wife, (lately widow of MARMADUKE DANIEL, gentleman, of Charleston, SC;

to JONATHAN SCOTT, merchant, of Charleston, for ₤ 2:2 British money, surrendered all dower & interest in lots #33 & #34 leading down to low water mark, fronting 100 ft. on the Bay, which lots were formerly owned by MARMADUKE DANIEL but now by JONATHAN SCOTT. Witnesses: JAMES COPPELL (clerk to MR. ALEXANDER, attorney, Threadneedle Street, London) & JONATHAN BURNYEAT (a Quaker), of Charleston. BURNYEAT appeared before ROBERT AUSTIN, J.P. & Pub. Reg.

Book S, p. 446
21 & 22 Apr. 1739
L & R

JOHN GODWIN, cordwainer, & MARTHA (her mark) his wife, to ELISHA SCREVEN, planter, all of Berkeley Co., for ₤ 1600 SC money, 700 a. in Craven Co., bounding NW on JOHN WALLIS, ESQ., SE on WILLIAM SWINTON, ESQ., NE on vacant land; SW on N branch Black River; which land the Hon. WILLIAM BULL, by letters patent dated 19 July 1738, had granted MARTHA GODWIN (wife of JOHN GODWIN, lately called MARTHA BULL). Witnesses: WILLIAM FLEMING, HENRY GODWIN, MATTHEW CREED. Before THOMAS LAROCHE, J.P.

Book S, p. 448
28 & 29 Mar. 1735
L & R

FRANCIS MURRIL, planter, & ELIZABETH his wife, to MOSES BENNET, planter, all of Berkeley Co., for ₤ 650 SC money, 500 a. in Berkeley Co., bounding S on PETER MAY; W on PETER HERMAN; N on RENE RICHEBOURG; E on EDWARD THOMAS. Witnesses: RENE RICHEBOURG, WILLIAM MARTIN, MARY (her mark) MARTIN (wife of WILLIAM). Before PETER DE ST. JULIEN, J.P. ROBERT AUSTIN, Pub. Reg.

Book S, p. 450
12 & 13 Nov. 1736
L & R

JAMES CROKATT, merchant, of Charleston, & ESTHER his wife (with ESTERS free consent), to ELIZABETH MAYRANT, spinstress, of Santee Parish, for love & affection & 20 shillings, the 500 a. in Craven Co., granted by Lt. Gov. THOMAS BROUGHTON on 26 Feb. 1735 to JAMES CROKATT; on Little Peedee River, bounding SW on MR. PIERCE?; other sides on the river & on vacant land. Witnesses: BENJAMIN SMITH (merchant), JOHN LLOYD. Before MAURICE LEWIS, J.P. ROBERT AUSTIN, Pub. Reg.

Book S, p. 452
17 & 18 Mar. 1736
L & R

JAMES (his mark) DALTON, planter, of St. George's Parish, to WILLIAM ROMSEY, storekeeper, of Georgetown, Winyaw, for ₤ 30 SC money, the 300 a. in Winyaw, Craven Co., granted JAMES DALTON by Lt. Gov. THOMAS BROUGHTON on 13 Sept. 1736; bounding N on WILLIAM ROMSEY; S on land laid out; W & E on vacant land. Witnesses: JOHN RIGG, BENJAMIN STEAD, WILLIAM HANCOCK. Before ROBERT AUSTIN, J.P. & Pub. Reg.

Book S, p. 454
20 & 21 Feb. 1738
L & R

JOSEPH SPENCER, planter, to THOMAS DIXON, planter, both of Berkeley Co., for ₤ 36 currency, 3 a. on James Island, Berkeley Co., inherited by JOSEPH SPENCER from his father ALEXANDER SPENCER; bounding N on THOMAS DIXON; E on JOSEPH SPENCER & THOMAS DIXON; W on JOHN CROSKEYS; S on THOMAS DIXON. Witnesses: JOHN BONNETHEAU, ABRAHAM CROFT. Before THOMAS DALE, J.P. ROBERT AUSTIN, Pub. Reg.

Book S, p. 455
22 & 23 Jan. 1738/9
L & R

JOHN MCKAY, merchant, & MARY his wife, to THOMAS DIXON, bricklayer, all of St. Philip's Parish, Charleston, Berkeley Co., for ₤ 270 SC money, 18 a., English measure, on James Island, St. Andrews Parish, Berkeley Co., part of 230 a.; bounding NW on part of same tract belonging to JOSEPH DILL; SE on ALEXANDER SPENCER; NE on JOHN CROSKEYS; SW on THOMAS DIXON; according to plat attached to deed of sale dated 15 Nov. 1726 from JOHN CROSKEYS (son of JOHN CROSKEYS & ELIZABETH his wife) to JOHN MACKAY, party hereto. Witnesses: GEORGE (his mark) HAMBLETON, ABRAHAM CROFT. Before THOMAS DALE, J.P. ROBERT AUSTIN, Pub. Reg.

Book S, p. 457
2 & 3 Feb. 1738
L & R

JOHN MCKAY, merchant, & MARY his wife, of Charleston, to THOMAS DIXON, planter, of Berkeley Co., for ₤ 600 SC money, 50 a. on James Island (free from MARY'S claim of dower); bounding N on WILLIAM STOBO (formerly AMBROSE DENNISON); E on JOHN MCKAY;

W & S on JOSEPH SPENCER; being part of 400 a. originally granted to EDWARD WESTBURY & JOAN PULFORD & afterwards vested in THOMAS WESTBURY (son of EDWARD) & by several mesne conveyances in JOHN MCKAY. Witnesses: ABRAHAM CROFT, EDWARD WIGG, GEORGE (his mark) HAMBLETON. Before THOMAS DALE, J.P. ROBERT AUSTIN, Pub. Reg.

Book S, p. 458
2 & 3 May 1739
L & R by Mortgage

WILLIAM COLT, planter, of Prince Frederick Parish, to JOHN JOHNSTON & WILLIAM FLEMING & Co., merchants, of said Parish, as security on bond of even date in penal sum of L 1163:16 conditioned for the payment of L 581:18 SC money on 1 Mar. 1739/40; 200 a. in Craven Co., bounding E on JAMES WITHERS; S on Sampit Creek; W on WILLIAM WHITESIDE; N on land unknown. Witnesses: THOMAS LEITH, JAMES CRADDOCK. Before THOMAS LAROCHE, J.P. ROBERT AUSTIN, Pub. Reg.

Book S, p. 460
29 & 30 June 1732
L & R

NICHOLAS TROTT, ESQ., & SARAH his wife, of St. Philip's Parish, Charleston, to WILLIAM HENDRICK, planter, of Berkeley Co., for L 375 SC money, part of a plantation called Rhutsbury Point, in St. Philip's Parish, Charleston, fronting NE by E 75 ft., English measure, on a marsh & going backward the same breadth of 75 ft. toward SW by W 200 ft.; that is, from the front line 40 ft. & then leaving 20 ft. for a street & then going further on same line toward the SSW & by W 160 ft. more; in all 200 ft. fronting SE & S on the marsh & bounding SW & W on a piece of land sold by NICHOLAS & SARAH TROTT to JOHN SCOTT, shipwright, of Charleston; NW & N on other part said plantation. Witnesses: SAMUEL PARSONS, JOHN ARNOLD. Before GABRIEL MANIGAULT, J.P. ROBERT AUSTIN, Pub. Reg.

Book S, p. 462
6 Aug. 1737
Bond

NATHANIEL PARTRIDGE, planter, of Berkeley Co., to BENJAMIN WHITAKER, ESQ., in penal sum of L 57:3 British money, conditioned for the payment of L 31:3:4 British on 14 July 1738. PARTRIDGE & WHITAKER agree that 77 a. already mortgaged to WHITAKER by PARTRIDGE on another bond shall stand as security on this bond also. Witnesses: WILLIAM GEORGE FREEMAN. The first mortgage is recorded in Book R fol. 232-236. ROBERT AUSTIN, Pub. Reg. WHITAKER acknowledge receipt of full satisfaction 26 May 1739. ROBERT AUSTIN, Register.

Book S, p. 463
3 Oct. 1738
Bill of Sale

GILES COOKE, surgeon, of Prince Frederick Parish, Craven Co., to ELIANER (ELIZABETH?) MORTIMER, widow, of Christ Church Parish, Berkeley Co., for L 350 currency, the 500 a. granted to GILES COOKE, by the Hon. WILLIAM BULL on 10 Nov. 1737/8; bounding NE on Black River, NW on JONATHAN CHRISTMASS (CHRISTMAS?); other sides on vacant land. Witnesses: GILES HICKS, JOHN DUCKER, MARY HICKS. Before JOHN EDWARDS, J.P. ROBERT AUSTIN, Pub. Reg.

Book S, p. 464
26 Aug. 1731
Deed of Gift

JONATHAN RUSS, carpenter, son & heir of JONATHAN RUSS, planter, of Berkeley Co., to his loving brother, ABIJAH RUSS, planter, of same place, for brotherly love & affection & other considerations; the 240 a. in the Parish of St. Thomas & St. Dennis; bequeathed to ABIJAH by will of their father JONATHAN; bounding on RICHARD BERESFORD & on MR. MARTIN. Witnesses: ANN BERCHES, CHARLES PINCKNEY. Before ROBERT AUSTIN, J.P. & Pub. Reg.

DEEDS BOOK "T"
1739 - 1740

Book T, p. 1
30 & 31 Mar. 1739
L & R by Mortgage

LAWRENCE WITHERS, peruke-maker, & ELIZABETH his wife, to JOHN LINING, physician, all of Charleston. Whereas WITHERS this date gave LINING a bond in the penal sum of L 504:10 currency, conditioned for the payment of L 252:5, with interest at 10% on 3 Apr. 1739. Now WITHERS, to secure payment, conveys to LINING part of lot #49 in Charleston on which 2 tenements are built, 1 occupied by JOHN GARNET, the other occupied by RICHARD BAILLIES, carpenter; fronting W on New

Church Street & running E backwards to the fence of the lot occupied by
THOMAS CLARK; bounding N on PAUL DOUXSAINT; S on an alley leading from
Church Street to Union Street. Witnesses: DAVID MCCLELLAN, JAMES DRUM-
MOND. Before ROBERT AUSTIN, J.P. & Register.

Book T, p. 5　　　　　　　　WILLIAM LIVINGSTON, planter, & MARY his wife,
20 & 21 Feb. 1737　　　　　& with her unconstrained consent, to THOMAS
L & R　　　　　　　　　　　　SACHEVERELL, planter, all of Colleton Co., for
　　　　　　　　　　L 1200 currency, 562-1/2 a. in Colleton Co.
Whereas the Hon. ROBERT GIBBS, ESQ., Gov. & the Lords Proprs. granted
Landgrave ROBERT DANIEL 4000 a. in Colleton Co., part of his patent for
48,000 a.; & whereas Landgrave ROBERT DANIEL sold the 4000 a. to WILLIAM
LIVINGSTON, clerk, father of said WILLIAM; & whereas WILLIAM LIVINGSTON,
after selling part of the 4000 a., bequeathed the unsold portion, 2250 a.,
to be equally divided between his wife HANNAH (later wife of JOHN DART),
his osns WILLIAM & HENRY, & his daughter MARGARET; & whereas WILLIAM &
HENRY LIVINGSTON, JOHN DART (by right of his wife HANNAH) as guardians of
MARGARET, a minor, with the consent of JOSEPH MOODY, surviving guardian
by will made an equal division of the 2250 a. & allotted to WILLIAM LIV-
INGSTON as his share 562-1/2 a. on the E side of Pon Pon River, in Colle-
ton Co., bounding S on MARGARET LIVINGSTON'S tract; N on HENRY LIVINGSTON
& JOHN DART; W on Swamps lands adjoining Pon Pon River. Witnesses: ALGER-
NOON ASH, ANTHONY LAMBRIGHT. Before JAMES BULLOCK, J.P. ROBERT AUSTIN,
Register.

Book T, p. 10　　　　　　　 SILVINUS (his mark) RICH, planter, & MARY, his
25 & 26 Jan. 1738/9　　　　wife with MARY'S free consent, to THOMAS SACH-
L & R　　　　　　　　　　　　EVERELL, planter, all of Pon Pon, Colleton Co.,
　　　　　　　　　　for L 100 currency, 34 a., part of 225 a., NE
side Pon Pon River, Colleton Co., bounding N on MR. SPRY; E on part of
the 225 a.; S on MR. MORTON; beginning at a stake in the westermost corner of the tract, running due E 33 chains 50 links to a 3 notched stake,
then due S 11 chains 50 links to a 3 notched stake, then SW 12 deg. 30
min. 8 chains across the 225 a. to a gum, then NW 49 deg. 37 chains 20
links to 1st stake; which 225 a. were granted by letters patent on 24 May
1734 under the hand of his excellency ROBERT JOHNSON, ESQ., Gov. to SIL-
VINUS RICH with the usual conditions. Witnesses: JOHN BEE, JR., WILLIAM
EDINGS. Before ROBERT AUSTIN, J.P. & Register.

Book T, p. 15　　　　　　　 JAMES WRIXHAM, planter, of Colleton Co., "farm
12 Jan. 1736　　　　　　　　lets" to JAMES BERRIE, planter, for 7 years
Lease　　　　　　　　　　　　payable yearly for 3 years in full of the
　　　　　　　　　　whole term; at the rent of L 1 currency for
every a. cleared & used during the 7 years, 150 a., on the E part of his
500 a. on Pon Pon River; bounding E on THOMAS ELLIOTT; W on JACOB BRAD-
WELL. Witnesses: GEORGE (his mark) DOUGLASS, DENIS DOYLE, DAVID JOHNSTON.
Before JAMES BULLOCH, J.P. ROBERT AUSTIN, Register.

Book T, p. 16　　　　　　　 MOSES MARTIN, planter, of Colleton Co., to his
6 Sept. 1737　　　　　　　　loving brother JOHN MARTIN, for love & affec-
Deed of Gift　　　　　　　　tion & a hearty desire for his welfare & com-
　　　　　　　　　　fortable dwelling, 215 a. in Colleton Co.
Witnesses: JAMES SKIRVING, JAMES SANDERS, JOHN MCCOLLUM. Before MALCOLM
GLAZE, J.P. ROBERT AUSTIN, Register. Plat made by JOHN ANDREW.

Book T, p. 17　　　　　　　 MOSES MARTIN, planter, of Colleton Co., to his
6 Sept. 1737　　　　　　　　loving brother ISAAC MARTIN, for love & affec-
Deed of Gift　　　　　　　　tion & hearty desire for his welfare & comfort-
　　　　　　　　　　able dwelling, 215 a. in Colleton Co. Witnesses: JAMES SKIRVING, JAMES SANDERS, JOHN MCCOLLUM. Before MALCOLM GLAZE,
ROBERT AUSTIN, Register. Plat made by JOHN ANDREW.

Book T, p. 19　　　　　　　 WILLIAM ELLIOTT, bricklayer, & PATIENCE, his
4 & 5 Aug. 1737　　　　　　wife, of Craven Co., to FRANCIS VARAMBAUT,
L & R　　　　　　　　　　　　planter, of Berkeley Co., for L 575 currency,
　　　　　　　　　　500 a. in Craven Co., bounding SW on PETER
STANLEY (formerly EDWARD STANLEY); NW on WILLIAM WATIES; NE & SE on vacant land. Witnesses: GUILLAUME GALLATIN, JEAN BONNOIT, PETER PAGETT.
Before ROBERT AUSTIN, J.P. & Register.

Book T, p. 22   WILLIAM ELLIOTT, bricklayer, of Craven Co., to
5 Aug. 1737   FRANCIS VARAMBAUT, planter, of Berkeley Co.,
Bond   in penal sum of ₺ 1150 SC money, as security
                           in the above conveyance (p.-19). Witnesses:
JEAN BONNIOT, PETER PAGETT.   Before ROBERT AUSTIN, J.P. & Register.

Book T, p. 23   (See page 77) MARGARET RAMSAY (alias NICOL),
2 Mar. 1736   of Edenburgh sidow of JOHN RAMSAY, shop keeper
Assignment   of Charleston, SC, (son of DAVID RAMSAY & HEL-
                           EN SEEMYSS, his wife, of the Parish of Lew-
chars, Shire of Fife, North Brittain States that whereas it is reported
that JOHN RAMSAY, her husband, had by will bequeathed to THOMAS, JEAN, &
MARGARET RAMSAY (his brother & sisters) ₺ 300 sterling to be equally divided amongst them, & gave the remainder of his personal estate & all his
real estate to MARGARET RAMSAY (only daughter of JOHN & MARGARET) to be
paid her on demand within 7 years; but in case no demand were made the
real & personal estate to be divided amongst his brother & sisters; & appointed WILLIAM SCOTT, THOMAS FLEMING & THOMAS LAMBOLL, merchants, of
Charleston, his executors, to handle his real estate; & whereas MARGARET
RAMSAY (JOHN'S widow) claims title to 1 equal third share of his estate &
has reason to think that if her husband did make such a will he did it believing her to be dead at the time; & whereas WILLIAM NICHOL, merchant,
in Edinburgh had advanced to her several sums of money; therefore for
love & favour & other considerations MARGARET, widow of JOHN RAMSAY, assigns to WILLIAM NICOL her third share of JOHN'S estate; with power to
hold MARGARET RAMSAY, (her daughter) & JOHN CROKATT her husband, or any
inter meddlers liable; & have the will declared null & void; & in all
ways to act as her attorney. This instrument written by THOMAS SINCLAIR
in Edinburgh, signed by MARGARET RAMSAY in Edinburgh & witnessed by DAVID
LIVERIGHT of Miggatland, THOMAS YOUNG, City Treasurer of Edinburgh, JOHN
SCOTT, merchant, in Edinburgh, LUDOVICH BRODIE, writer to The Signet, &
THOMAS SINCLAIR. ROBERT AUSTIN, Register.

Book T, p. 26   WILLIAM NICOLL, merchant, of Edinburgh, North
21 Sept. 1736   Brittain, appoints WILLIAM SCOTT, merchant, of
Letter of Attorney   Charleston, SC his attorney, to demand a legal
                           share in the estate of JOHN RAMSAY from the
executors & from MARGARET RAMSAY, his daughter (wife of JOHN CROCKATT &
if necessary have the will annulled. Whereas JOHN RAMSAY, shopkeeper, of
Charleston, SC (son of DAVID RAMSAY & HELEN WEEMYSS, his wife, inhabitants of the Parish of Leuchars, Co. of Fife, North Brittain), by will
dated 15 July 1734 bequeathed THOMAS, JEAN & MARGARET RAMSAY, his brother
& sisters, ₺ 300 sterling, giving the rest of his real & personal estate
to his daughter, MARGARET, & appointed THOMAS FLEMING, WILLIAM SCOTT &
THOMAS LAMBOLL, merchants, of Charleston his executors; & whereas MARGA-
RET RAMSAY (alias NICOLL), widow of JOHN RAMSAY, on 2 Mar. 1736, claimed
a right to a third share of her husband's estate & conveyed her share to
WILLIAM NICHOLL, appointing him her attorney; & whereas it is necessary
for him to appoint some proper person his attorney; now he appoints WIL-
LIAM SCOTT. Witnesses: WILLIAM NICHOLSON, merchant, of Edinburgh; ROBERT
SIMPSON, writer hereof. Before the following Magistrates of Edinburgh,
Scotland. THOMAS CROKATT, JAMES CALHOUN, GAVIN HAMILTON BAILLIE, J.P.'S
& GEORGE HUME of Kello, City Clerk. ROBERT AUSTIN, Register.

Book T, p. 30   JORDAN ROCHE, gentleman, & REBECCA his wife,
18 & 19 Nov. 1737   of St. Philip's Parish, Charleston, to ROBERT
L & R   LADSON, JR., planter, of St. Andrews Parish,
                           for ₺ 4000 SC money, 400 a. on S side Ashley
River, bounding E on JOHN GREENE; N on BENJAMIN STANCARD; S on THOMAS
DRAYTON. Whereas the Lords Proprs. on 2 Apr. 1718 granted ALEXANDER
SKENE, 750 a. in Berkeley Co., on S side of Ashley River, bounding NW on
THOMAS DRAYTON & SAMUEL PAGE; SW on SAMUEL PAGE; SE on JAMES STANYARN; NE
on JOHN GREEN; & whereas ALEXANDER & JEMIMA SKENE on 17 June 1718 sold
the 750 a. to FRANCIS YONGE; & whereas FRANCIS YONGE & LYDIA his wife on
27 Mar. 1733 sold 400 a. (part of 750 a.) to JORDAN ROCHE; now ROCHE
sells to LADSON. Witnesses: SAMUEL STOCK, MATTHEW ROCHE. Before ROBERT
AUSTIN, J.P. & Pub. Reg.

Book T, p. 34   JAMES BERRIE, planter, & PURCHASE, his wife,
28 & 29 May 1739   of Colleton Co., to WILLIAM ELLIOTT, planter,

L & R   of St. Andrews Parish, for ₤ 2000 currency,
                            200 a. in Colleton Co., on E side Ashepoo River, formerly belonging to JOHN TOBEY, bounding W on vacant land; N on marsh lands; E on Musketa Creek; S on marsh & Beer (Bare) Island Creek; also 800 a. of marsh in Colleton Co., bounding NE on JOHN TOBEY & vacant marsh; S & SW on JOHN TOBEY & WILLIAM ELLIOTT, JR., E on JOHN MARSHALL; W & NW on vacant marsh. Witnesses: WILLIAM HENDRICK, ROBERT BREWTON, JR. Before HENRY GIBBS, (GIBBES), J.P. ROBERT AUSTIN, Pub. Reg.

Book T, p. 38   JOHN OWEN, tailor, of Charleston, to ELISHA
25 & 26 Oct. 1738   SCRIVEN, planter, of Craven Co., for ₤ 400
L & R   currency, 900 a. in Craven Co., on W side Little Peedee River, bounding NE on ELISHA SCRIVEN & on all other sides on vacant land. Whereas his majesty King GEORGE the Second by letters patent on 10 Apr. 1738 under the hand of the Hon. WILLIAM BULL, ESQ., Lt. Gov. & Commander in Chief, granted JOHN OWEN 900 a. in Craven Co., with the usual conditions, now OWEN sells to SCRIVEN. Witnesses: HENRY PERONNEAU, JR., ALEXANDER PERONNEAU. Before HENRY GIBBES, J.P. ROBERT AUSTIN, Pub. Reg.

Book T, p. 42   EDWARD HEXT, merchant, of Charleston, to ELI-
10 & 11 Aug. 1738   SHA SCRIVEN, planter, of Craven Co., for ₤ 120
L & R   currency, 1250 a. in Craven Co. on W side N
                            branch of Little Peedee River in 2 tracts.
Whereas his majesty King GEORGE the Second by his letters patent on 10 Apr. 1738 under the hand of the Hon. WILLIAM BULL, ESQ., Lt. Gov. & Commander in Chief, granted EDWARD HEXT 1250 a. in Craven Co. on W side of N branch of Little Peedee River in 2 tracts, 1 tract of 1000 a. bounding SW on DANIEL BRITON & all other sides on vacant land; the 250 a. bounding NW on EDWARD HEXT & all other sides on vacant land; with the usual provisoes; now HEXT sells the 2 tracts to SCRIVEN. Witnesses: HENRY PERONNEAU, ALEXANDER PERONNEAU. Before HENRY GIBBES, J.P. ROBERT AUSTIN, Pub. Reg.

Book T, p. 46   THOMAS MADDOCKS, mariner, to SAMUEL JENNINGS,
14 & 15 May 1739   mariner, both of Craven Co., for ₤ 400 SC mon-
L & R   ey, 400 a. in Kingston Township, on Waccamaw,
                            Craven Co. Whereas his majesty by his letters
patent on 3 Feb. 1737 under the hand of the Hon. WILLIAM BULL, ESQ., Pres., Gov. of SC, granted THOMAS MADDOCKS 400 a. in Kingston Township, on Waccamaw, Craven Co., bounding W on JOSEPH HOLDER; S & N on vacant land; E on SAMUEL JENNINGS; now MADDOCKS sells the 400 a. to JENNINGS. Witnesses: THOMAS JENNINGS, JAMES CRADDOCK. Before THOMAS LAROCHE, J.P. ROBERT AUSTIN, Pub. Reg.

Book T, p. 49   JOSEPH HOLDER (HOULDER), planter, to SAMUEL
1 & 2 May 1739   JENNINGS, mariner, both of Craven Co., for
L & R by Mortgage   ₤ 116:15:10 currency, 150 a. in Kingston Township, Craven Co., bounding on all sides on vacant land; also 1 lot in Kingston. Whereas JOSEPH HOLDER gave bond this date to SAMUEL JENNINGS in the penal sum of ₤ 233:11:8 conditioned for the payment of ₤ 116:15:10 with interest on 1 Mary next, now, for security, HOLDER conveys to JENNINGS the above lot in Kingston & 150 a. Witnesses: THOMAS JENNINGS, JAMES CRADDOCK. Before THOMAS LAROCHE, J.P. ROBERT AUSTIN, Pub. Reg.

Book T, p. 52   JOSEPH HOLDER (HOULDER), planter, to SAMUEL
2 May 1739   JENNINGS, mariner, both of Craven Co., in the
Bond   penal sum of ₤ 233:11:8 SC money, conditioned
                            for the payment of ₤ 116:15:10 with interest
on 1 May 1740. Witnesses: THOMAS JENNINGS, JAMES CRADDOCK. ROBERT AUSTIN, Pub. Reg.

Book T, p. 53   FREDERICK GAILLARD, planter, & ELIZABETH his
14 & 15 Feb. 1736/7   wife, to JAMES BOISSEAU, planter, all of Cra-
L & R   ven Co., for ₤ 200 currency, 500 a. in Craven
                            Co., commonly called Savannah Creek, bounding
S on DANIEL HUGER; W on JOHN GENDRON; N on BARTHOLOMEW GAILLARD. Witnesses: ISAAC LEGRAND, JOHN BARNET, PAUL BRUNEAU. Before FRANCIS LEJAU, J.P. ROBERT AUSTIN, Pub. Reg.

Book T, p. 56   FRANCIS ROCHE, planter, of the Parish of St.
29 & 30 May 1739   Thomas & St. Dennis, Berkeley Co., to DANIEL
L & R   HUGER, ESQ., of St. John's Parish, Berkeley
                       Co., for ₤ 1796 currency, 794 a. in 3 tracts;
whereas the Lords Proprs. on 12 Oct. 1709 under the hands of SIR NATHAN-
IEL JOHNSON, Knight, Gov.; HENRY NOVLE, ROBERT GIGGS, & others, granted
MICHAEL MAHON, planter, of Berkeley Co., 3500 a. at the head of the E
branch of Cooper River; & whereas MICHAEL MAHON on 30 Feb. 1709/10, for
5 shillings currency, sold to DOMINICK ARTHUR, planter, of Berkeley Co.,
95 a. (part of 3500) bounding N S & W on the tract of 3500 a., as recorded 10 May 1710 by ISAAC PORCHER, Dep. Reg.; & whereas the Lords Proprs.
on 12 Oct. 1709 under the hands of SIR NATHANIEL JOHNSON, Knight, Gov.;
HENRY NOBLE, ROBERT GIBBES, & others, granted DOMINICK ARTHUR 5000 a. adjacent to Cooper River, bounding E on vacant land; S on the head of the E
Branch of Cooper River; W on MICHAEL MAHON; N on vacant land; & whereas
CHRISTOPHER ARTHUR, planter, nephew & heir of DOMINICK inherited the
5000 a. & by will dated 24 Oct. 1724 devised 1/2 his real & personal es-
tate to his beloved kinsman PATRICK ROCHE, merchant, of the City of Lim-
erick, son of CHRISTOPHER'S uncle FRANCIS ROCHE & ANSTACE ROCHE (alias
ARTHUR) his wife; & ordered that 150 a. then cleared & settled should, in
the division of the land, fall to PATRICK ROCHE, & therefore PATRICK RO-
CHE received that half part which crosses the Broad Path leading from
Strawberry to Santee; & whereas PATRICK ROCHE died intestate & FRANCIS
ROCHE, his eldest son & heir became owner of the 95 a. & also of his fa-
ther's half of the 5000 a.; now FRANCIS ROCHE sells to DANIEL HUGER 794 a.
in 3 tracts, partly in Berkeley Co. & partly in Craven Co., bounding in
the whole, N on lands unknown; S on the Rev. MR. THOMAS HASELL & FRANCIS
ROCHE; E on JOHN NICHOLSON; W on DANIEL HUGER, according to plat dated 20
May 1739 & signed by JOHN HORRY & JOHN HENTIE, surveyors. Witnesses:
JOHN GARNETT, JOHN HENTIE. Before FRANCIS LEJAU, J.P. ROBERT AUSTIN,
Pub. Reg.

Book T, p. 63   ALEXANDER ROBERTSON, planter, to JOHN JOHNSTON
2 June 1739   & WILLIAM FLEMING, merchants, all of Craven
L & R   Co., for ₤ 1000 currency, 300 a. in Craven Co.,
                       Queensburgh Township, on Peedee River, bound-
ing SE on ALEXANDER SKENE, ESQ., SW on CAPT. JOHN CLELAND; NW on Lynch's
Creek; NE on vacant land. Witnesses: THOMAS LEITH, JOHN KEEN. Before
WILLIAM WHITESIDE, J.P. ROBERT AUSTIN, Pub. Reg.

Book T, p. 66   SARAH (her mark) HOOKER, widow, of Seawee,
22 Mar. 1735   Christ Church Parish, Berkeley Co., to WILLIAM
Deed of Sale   PORTER, noncomformist pastor & teacher in the
                       Parish, for ₤ 30 currency, 350 a. Witnesses:
ROBERT JEFFRIES, ALEXANDER FRISSOL, JOHN MERRIL. ROBERT AUSTIN, Pub. Reg.

Book T, p. 66   MRS. SARAH (her mark) HOOKER, widow, of Seawee,
15 & 16 Apr. 1736   Christ Church Parish, Berkeley Co., to WILLIAM
L & R   PORTER, noncomformist pastor & teacher in the
                       Parish, for ₤ 2 & for ₤ 30 currency, 350 a. in
Craven Co., bounding SW on Waccamaw Township & on all other sides on vacant land. Witnesses: ROBERT JEFFRYS, JOHN (his mark) MURRELL, SARAH
(her mark) MURRELL. Before HENRY GIBBES, J.P. ROBERT AUSTIN, Pub. Reg.

Book T, p. 68   ISAAC DAVIS (DAVIDS) DAVID) planter, & DEB-
8 & 9 Sept. 1735   ORAH, his wife, to JOHN BARTON, planter, all
L & R   of Prince Frederick Parish, Craven Co., for
                       ₤ 350 currency, the 350 a., tranted under the
hand of the Hon. THOMAS BROUGHTON to ISAAC DAVIS, bounding SE on JOSEPH
JOHNSON; NW on HENRY DURANT; & on all other sides on vacant land (except
fruit trees, white pines & other trees excepted by the King's grant).
Signed: ISAAC DAVIS, DEBORAH DVAIS. Witnesses: SAMUEL GANDY, WILLIAM
BARTON, PETER JOHNSON. Before ANDREW RUTLEDGE, J.P. ROBERT AUSTIN, Pub.
Reg.

Book T, p. 73   JOSEPH WHITE, planter, of Dorchester, Berkeley
12 & 13 June 1739   Co., to JOSEPH WRAGG & RICHARD LAMBTON, mer-
L & R by Mortgage   chants, of Charleston, for ₤ 410:14:8-1/2 cur-
                       rency, with interest at 10%, payable 1 Jan.
1740, 200 a. where JOSEPH WHITE lives & another tract of 33 a. Whereas

JOSEPH WHITE this dategave bond to WRAGG & LAMBTON in the penal sum of
Ŀ 820 currency, conditioned for the payment of Ŀ 410:14:6-1/2 with interest at 10% on 1 Jan. next, & by deed poll this date conveyed to them 1
Negro man & 1 Negro boy, now to secure payment of the bond, & for Ŀ 20
WHITE conveys to WRAGG & LAMBTON 200 in Berkeley Co., bounding N & W on
COL. JOSEPH BLAKE; S on DANIEL STEWART; also 33 a. bounding W on COL. JOSEPH BLAKE; E on GITSON CLAPP. Witnesses: JOHN WALTER, JAMES WRIGHT.
Before ROBERT WRIGHT, J.P. ROBERT AUSTIN, Pub. Reg.

Book T, p. 77　　　　　MARGARET RAMSAY (alias NICOLL) widow of JOHN
14 June 1739　　　　　RAMSAY (see p. 23), shopkeeper of Charleston,
L & R　　　　　　　　　son of DAVID RAMSAY & HELEN WEEMYSS (alias
　　　　　　　　　　　　RAMSAY) his wife, heretofore of the Parish of
Lewchars, Fife Co., North Britain, of the 1st part; WILLIAM NICHOL, merchant, of Edinburgh, North Britain, assignee & attorney of MARGARET RAMSAY, of the 2nd part; WILLIAM SCOTT, merchant of Charleston, substitute &
attorney for WILLIAM NICOL (NICHOL), of the 3rd part; & JOHN CROKATT,
late of Dundee, Great Britain, now merchant in Charleston, SC, of the 4th
part. Whereas JOHN RAMSAY owned part of a lot in Charleston fronting 26-1/2 ft. on the N side of Broad Street, bounding W 102 ft. on MR. DUGUE; E
on TIMOTHY BELLAMY; N on MRS. BRUTELL; also the lot on the N side of
Tradd Street on which a stable is erected, bounding E on RICHARD MASON &
JAMES MCKEWN; NW on a lot fronting N on Broad Street; also 180 a. of unimproved land in Colleton Co., called Bohicket, part of 500 a. granted by
the Lords Proprs. to WILLIAM GREENE; & whereas being so seized RAMSAY by
will dated 15 July 1734 bequeathed all his real estate, with certain conditions, to his daughter MARGARET RAMSAY, then living in North Britain; &
whereas MARGARET RAMSAY (alias NICOL) on the death of her husband became
legally entitled to dower; & whereas JOHN CROKATT on 17 Feb. 1734 married
MARGARET RAMSAY (daughter & devisee of JOHN) & they have a daughter MARGARET, living at Beanston, North Britain, & therefore JOHN CROKATT became
possessed of the land & premises on the death of his wife MARGARET as
tenant for life by courtesy of England; & whereas MARGARET RAMSAY (alias
NICOL), being entitled to dower, on 2 Mar. 1736, at Edinburgh, assigned
to WILLIAM NICOL all her interest in JOHN'S real estate, with power to
recover; & whereas WILLIAM NICOL at Edinburgh on 1 Sept. 1736 appointed
WILLIAM SCOTT his attorney to recover & sell MARGARET'S dower; & whereas
after various conferences with WILLIAM SCOTT has agreed to purchase MARGARET RAMSAY'S share at its estimated value; now MARGARET RAMSAY & WILLIAM NICOL, by their substitute attorney WILLIAM SCOTT, convey to JOHN
CROKATT, for Ŀ 500 SC money, all their claim to JOHN RAMSAY'S estate.
Witnesses: JAMES CROKATT, CHARLES PINCKNEY, ROBERT BREWTON, JR. Before
ROBERT AUSTIN, J.P. & Pub. Reg.

Book T, p. 80　　　　　JOHN STEELE, of Dorchester, Berkeley Co., to
18 & 19 May 1739　　　JOHN HOUGHTON & WILLIAM WEBB, merchants, & co-
L & R　　　　　　　　 partners, of Charleston, for Ŀ 1220 SC money,
　　　　　　　　　　　lot #15 in Dorchester, containing 1/4 a.
Whereas AARON WAY, SR. by deed poll dated 22 Mar. 1725 conveyed to THOMAS
BARNS of Berkeley Co., lot #15 in Dorchester, containing 1/4 a., with a
memorandum stating that on 22 Mar. 1725 AARON WAY delivered the lot &
premises; whereas by indentures of bargain & sale & release dated 20 & 21
Oct. 1737 THOMAS BARNS conveyed to JOHN STEELE lot #15, bounding E on
High Street; S on DR. WILLIAM WHITE; W on undivided land; N on MRS. BOONE,
now STEELE sells the lot & the dwelling house on it to HOUGHTON & WEBB.
Witnesses: JOHN RATTRAY, JOHN JOHNSON, JR. Before MAURICE LEWIS, J.P.
ROBERT AUSTIN, Pub. Reg.

Book T, p. 85　　　　　JAMES BOISSEAU, planter & JANE his wife, of
2 & 3 May 1738　　　　Craven Co., to DANIEL HUGER, planter of Berke-
L & R　　　　　　　　 ley Co., for Ŀ 200 currency, 500 a. in Craven
　　　　　　　　　　　Co., bounding N on BARTHOLOMEW GAILLARD; S on
DANIEL HUGER; W on JOHN GENDRON; E on vacant land. Whereas the Rt. Hon.
ROBERT GIBBES & the Lords Proprs. on 28 June 1711 granted BARTHOLOMEW
GAILLARD 500 a., which he bequeathed to his eldest son FREDERICK; & whereas FREDERICK GAILLARD & ELIZABETH, his wife, on 15 Feb. 1736/7 sold to
JAMES BOISSEAU, for Ŀ 200 currency, the 500 a., known as Savana Creek;
now BOISSEAU sells to HUGER. Witnesses: PAUL BRUNEAU, JEREMIAH CUTTINO,
JOHN DELPON. Before FRANCIS LEJAU, J.P. ROBERT AUSTIN, Pub. Reg.

Book T, p. 89　　　　　　　JOHN ABBOTT, planter, formerly of SC, for val-
20 Mar. 1737/8　　　　　 uable considerations appoints DANIEL LAROCHE &
Letter of Attorney　　　THOMAS LAROCHE, merchants of Georgetown, his
　　　　　　　　　　　　　　attorneys to dispose of his property in SC,
including his Negroes, servants, cattle, horses, goods, etc.; most of
which property has been mortgaged. Witnesses: MARGARET SCHENCKINGH, MARY
PORTER, JOHN PORTER. Before ELEAZER ALLEN, J.P. of New Haven precinct,
NC; certified by GAB. JOHNSTON, 13 July 1738. ROBERT AUSTIN, Pub. Reg.

Book T, p. 91　　　　　　　WILLIAM (his mark) THOMAS, planter, of Winyaw,
25 & 26 Sept. 1738　　　 Craven Co., to CHARLES WATKINS, gentleman, of
L & R by Mortgage　　　　Berkeley Co., for ℔ 632 currency, 600 a., 3
　　　　　　　　　　　　　　Negro men, 4 saddle horses, & 34 black cattle.
Whereas WILLIAM THOMAS on 23 Sept. 1738 gave bond to CHARLES WATKINS in
the penal sum of ℔ 1264 SC money conditioned for the payment of ℔ 632 on
23 Sept. 1739, now, for security, THOMAS conveys to WATKINS the 600 a. on
which he lives, at Winyaw, Craven Co., bounding E on WILLIAM BROCKINGTON
& RICHARD HUTCHINSON; on all other sides on vacant land; which 600 a.
were granted to THOMAS in 2 tracts of 300 a. each; also the Negroes, horses & cattle mentioned above. Witnesses: RICHARD ALLEIN, MARY ALLEIN,
JOHN WILLIAMS. Before PETER DE ST. JULIEN, J.P. ROBERT AUSTIN, Pub. Reg.

Book T, p. 95　　　　　　　WILLIAM (his mark) THOMAS, planter, of Winyaw,
23 Sept. 1738　　　　　　 Craven Co., to CHARLES WATKINS, gentleman, of
Bond　　　　　　　　　　　 Berkeley Co., in penal sum of ℔ 1264 SC money,
　　　　　　　　　　　　　　conditioned for the payment of ℔ 632 currency
on 23 Sept. 1739. Witnesses: RICHARD ALLEIN, MARY ALLEIN, JOHN WILLIAMS.
Before PETER DE ST. JULIEN, J.P. ROBERT AUSTIN, Pub. Reg.

Book T, p. 96　　　　　　　ISAAC PERONNEAU, of St. James, Goose Creek,
2 Aug. 1738　　　　　　　　Berkeley Co., to PETER MARION, of the same
Release　　　　　　　　　　place, for ℔ 278 currency, 140 a. in St. James,
　　　　　　　　　　　　　　Goose Creek, part of 330 a. granted on 15 Sept.
1705 to ABRAHAM DELAPLANE & bequeathed by him on 2 Aug. 1721 to ISAAC
FLORE for his natural life & afterwards to ABRAHAM'S granddaughter MARIAN,
wife of TOBIAS FITCH, & after her death to his great grandson STEPHEN
FITCH, & by default, to great grand daughter MARY FITCH (wife of ISAAC
PERONNEAU). ISAAC & MARY PERONNEAU now being lawful owners: MARY to re-
lease her dower upon request. Witnesses: DANIEL GALIOT, CHARLES PERON-
NEAU, Before ROBERT AUSTIN, J.P. & Pub. Reg. Plat of 140 a. in St. James,
Goose Creek bounding SE on JOHN BULLEN; SW on I. DEFRANCE; NW partly on
main road from Dorchester to Goose Creek; NE on ISAAC PERONNEAU, surveyed
1 July 1738 by NATHANIEL DEAN, Dep. Sur.

Book T, p. 99　　　　　　　DANIEL HUGER, ESQ., of St. John's Parish,
1 & 2 June 1739　　　　　 Berkeley Co. & DANIEL HORRY, planter, of St.
L & R　　　　　　　　　　　James Santee, Craven Co., as executers of will
　　　　　　　　　　　　　　of ELIAS HORRY, SR. to ELIAS HORRY, ESQ., of
Prince George Parish, Craven Co., son of ELIAS HORRY, SR., for ℔ 1750 SC
money, 500 a. on N side Santee River, Craven Co., bounding NE on ELIAS
HORRY; SE on JOHN HORRY; SW on Wadbaccon Creek; W & NW on TACITUS GAIL-
LARD. Whereas ELIAS HORRY, SR. by will dated 19 Sept. 1736 gave all his
real estate, except 750 a., to his executors to be sold by them to such
of his children as should be highest bidders & to no one else, now they
sell 500 a. to son ELIAS HORRY. Witnesses: EDWARD GOUGH, NEALE GOUGH.
Before FRANCIS LEJAU, J.P. ROBERT AUSTIN, Pub. Reg.

Book T, p. 103　　　　　　 DANIEL HUGER, ESQ., of St. John's Parish,
1 & 2 June 1739　　　　　 Berkeley Co., DANIEL HORRY, planter, & ELIAS
L & R　　　　　　　　　　　HORRY, planter, of Prince George Parish, Cra-
　　　　　　　　　　　　　　ven Co., as executors of the will of ELIAS
HORRY, SR., to JOHN HORRY, planter, of Prince George Parish, son of ELIAS
HORRY, SR., for ℔ 1375 SC money, 500 a., part of ELIAS HORRY, SR.'s estate, on N side Santee River, in Craven Co., bounding S on Wadbaccon
Creek & Santee River; E on MR. SUMMERFIELD (SUMMERVILLE); W on ELIAS
HORRY. Whereas ELIAS HORRY, SR., by will dated 19 Sept. 1736, gave to
his executors DANIEL HUGER, DANIEL HORRY & ELIAS HORRY, his 2 sons, all
his real estate, except 750 a., to be sold to such of his children should
be the highest bidders & to no one else, now they sell 500 a. to son JOHN
HORRY. Witnesses: EDWARD GOUGH, NEALE GOUGH. Before FRANCIS LEJAU, J.P.

ROBERT AUSTIN, Pub. Reg.

Book T, p. 107
5 & 6 Dec. 1737
L & R

Between DANIEL HORRY, planter, of St. James Parish, Craven Co., & ELIAS HORRY, ESQ., of Prince George Parish, trustees of the will of their father ELIAS HORRY, SR., to JOHN HORRY, planter, of Prince George Parish, for Ł 360 currency, 750 a. in Prince George Parish, Craven Co., granted ELIAS HORRY 17 May 1734 bounding NW on WILLIAM LEWIS; NE on JOHN DELIESSLINE; SW on the MESSRS. GAILLARD & ELIAS HORRY. Whereas ELIAS HORRY, of Prince George Parish, by will proved 29 Sept. 1736 gave to his executors, DANIEL & ELIAS HORRY, in trust, 750 a. to be sold to the highest bidder & the money used toward erecting & endowing a Charity School for the sole benefit of the natives of the Parish, & appointed DANIEL & ELIAS HORRY, trustees of the Charity. Witnesses: JOHN GOUGH, JR., RICHARD GOUGH. Before FRANCIS LEJAU, J.P. ROBERT AUSTIN, Pub. Reg.

Book T, p. 110
1 & 2 June 1739
L & R

ROBERT WRIGHT, the elder, ESQ., of Berkeley Co., to JAMES CROKATT, merchant, of Charleston, for Ł 1200 SC money, 1400 a. in Granville Co. Whereas KING GEORGE the Second on 9 Apr. 1736 under the hand of THOMAS BROUGHTON, Lt. Gov., granted ROBERT WRIGHT 1400 a. in Granville Co., bounding N on JAMES KINLOCH; S on land set apart for the Township of Purysburgh; E & W on vacant land, now WRIGHT sells to CROKATT. Witnesses: THOMAS LLOYD, JR., JAMES WRIGHT. Before MAURICE LEWIS, J.P. ROBERT AUSTIN, Pub. Reg.

Book T, p. 113
1 & 2 June 1739
L & R by Mortgage

WILLIAM WILKINS, planter, & SARAH his wife, of James Island, St. Andrews Parish, to JAMES CROKATT, merchant, of Charleston, for Ł 763:5 money of Great Britain, 640 a. on SW side Stono River, in Colleton Co., bounding N on JOHN PRESCOTT & ROBERT COLE; E on JOHN PRESCOTT & ELIZABETH GODFREY; S on JOHN GODFREY & PAUL TORQUET; W on PAUL TORQUET; also 140 a. (part of 228 a.) on S side James Island, St. Andrews Parish, Berkeley Co., bounding W on BENJAMIN STILES; S on marsh of the Sound & BENJAMIN STILES; E on marsh & a creek; N on a creek, marsh land called The Savannah, conditioned for the payment of Ł 763:5 money of Great Britain by WILKINS to CROKATT, on 1 Jan. 1740. Witnesses: THOMAS LLOYD, JR., ROBERT BREWTON, JR. Before MAURICE LEWIS, J.P. BENJAMIN SMITH, as attorney for JAMES CROKATT, on 23 July 1747 declared this mortgage satisfied. Witness: JOHN BEALE. ROBERT AUSTIN, Pub. Reg.

Book T, p. 117
20 June (?) 1739
Mortgage

DANIEL CRAWFORD, planter, of Christ Church Parish, Berkeley Co., to JAMES CROKATT, merchant, of Charleston, for Ł 409 sterling, 200 a. in Christ Church Parish where CRAWFORD lives, bounding S on MR. STOCK; E on THOMAS PLAYER; N on DANIEL LEGARE; W on CAPT. JOHN VANDERHORST & ANDREW RUTLEDGE; conditioned for the payment by CRAWFORD of Ł 409 money of Great Britain with interest to CROKATT on 1 Mar. 1740. Witnesses: THOMAS LLOYD, JR., THOMAS BOTELER. Before MAURICE LEWIS, J.P. BENJAMIN SMITH, as attorney for JAMES CROKATT on 18 May 1742 declared this mortgage satisfied. ROBERT AUSTIN, Pub. Reg.

Book T, p. 119
28 & 29 June 1739
L & R

ALEXANDER SKENE, ESQ., to JAMES CROKATT, ESQ., for Ł 480 currency, 1000 a., part of the land set apart for the Township of Queensborough, in Craven Co., on S side Peedee River, bounding NE on ALEXANDER SKENE; SW on vacant land; NW on ALEXANDER ROBERTSON. JEMIMA, wife of ALEXANDER SKENE, to renounce her dower within 3 months. Witnesses: JOHN RATTRAY, JOHN JOHNSTON, JR. Before ROBERT AUSTIN, J.P. & Pub. Reg.

Book T, p. 123
30 June & 2 July 1739
L & R by Mortgage

PETER (his mark) CUTTINO, SR., planter, of Craven Co., to ELIZABETH & THOMAS JENYS, executrix & executor of will of PAUL JENYS, merchant, of Charleston. Whereas PETER CUTTINO, SR. on 2 June 1736 gave bond to PAUL JENYS & JOHN BAKER, partners, in the penal sum of Ł 264:4:2 SC money, conditioned for the payment of Ł 132:2:1 on 1 Jan. 1740; & whereas PETER CUTTINO, SR. & PETER CUTTINO, JR., his son, on 30 June 1736 gave bond to JENYS & BAKER in the penal sum of

L 1350 SC money, conditioned for the payment of L 675 like money on 1 Jan. 1737; & whereas the 2 CUTTINOS on 30 June 1736 gave JENYS & BAKER another bond in the penal sum of L 1350 SC money conditioned for the payment of L 675 on 1 Apr. 1737; & whereas JOHN BAKER died & the right to settle the accounts became vested in PAUL JENYS; & whereas PAUL JENYS died, having appointed ELIZABETH JENYS & THOMAS JENYS executrix & executor of his will; & whereas PETER CUTTINO, SR. is indebted to ELIZABETH JENYS & THOMAS JENYS for another sum of L 10 SC money; now, to secure payment of the various bonds & debts with interest CUTTINO conveys to them 400 a. in Craven Co., granted to JOHN HOLLYBUSH on 12 Jan. 1705 by the Lords Proprs. through SIR NATHANIEL JOHNSON, JAMES MOORE & NICHOLAS TROTT, & sold by HOLLYBUSH to JOHN COLLINS; by him conveyed to ARTHUR HALL; by him sold to JOHN BASKERFIELD; & by JOHN BASKERFIELD & ANN his wife sold to PETER CUTTION, SR.; also 500 a. in Craven Co., bounding NE on Peedee River; also 450 a. in Craven Co., bounding NE on Peedee River, which 2 tracts were granted to PETER CUTTINO on 16 Dec. 1736 by 2 grants signed by the Hon. THOMAS BROUGHTON, Lt. Gov. & Commander in Chief, also 9 Negro slaves. Witnesses: PETER CUTTINO, JR., GEORGE WARING, WILLIAM HOPTON. Before ROBERT AUSTIN, J.P. & Pub. Reg.

Book T, p. 128
22 Dec. 1733
Deed of Gift

HENRY JACKSON, planter, of Colleton Co., at the request of his beloved sons SAMUEL & WILLIAM JACKSON that he give them during his lifetime such part of his estate as he desires them to have, & for other considerations (hereby utterly depriving sons SAMUEL & WILLIAM from claiming any other part of the estate except that bequeathed to them), grants sons SAMUEL & WILLIAM 376 a., English measure, in St. Bartholomew's Parish on SW side of S Edisto River, bounding N on JOHN WHITMARSH; W on Horse Shoe Creek; E on MR. OSWELL; S on Pocotaligo Swamp; which 376 a. HENRY JACKSON purchased from JOHN COX (heir of ROBERT COX) on 12 Jan. 1730; also 6 Negro slaves. Witnesses: JOHN ANDREWS, JR., THOMAS MALLDEN. Before WILLIAM LIVINGSTON, J.P. ROBERT AUSTIN, Pub. Reg.

Book T, p. 129
22 Oct. 1735
Deed of Gift

HENRY JACKSON, planter, of Colleton Co., to beloved son WILLIAM, for love & good will & a desire for his future welfare, 55 a. granted HENRY JACKSON, through purchase, on 7 Aug. 1735, witnessed by THOMAS BROUGHTON, Lt. Gov. & recorded in Bk. C.C. folio 701; which 55 a. lies on a branch of Ashepoo River commonly called Horse Show Creek, bounding E on JOSEPH ELLIOTT; S on ROBERT COX; N on vacant land. Witnesses: JAMES MARTIN, JOHN MITCHELL, JOSEPH MITCHELL. Before CULCHETH GOLIGHTLY, J.P. ROBERT AUSTIN, Pub. Reg.

Book T, p. 130
24 Jan. 1735
Mortgage

WILLIAM SIMSON, of Prince George Parish, Craven Co., to secure payment of 3 bonds given by SIMSON to WILLIAM WATIES this date in the total sum of L 1039:13:4 SC money, conveys to WATIES 500 a. in Prince George Parish, commonly called Witecaw, fronting on Waccamaw River. Witnesses: EBENEZER (his mark) SHINGLETON, WILLIAM CRIPPS, PAUL TRAPIER. Before THOMAS LAROCHE, J.P. ROBERT AUSTIN, Pub. Reg.

Book T, p. 131
4 July 1739
Release

CAPT. JOHN ALLEN, gentleman, of Berkeley Co., to GEORGE HUNTER, surveyor, of Charleston, for L 100 sterling of Great Britain, 800 a. Whereas King GEORGE the Second by his letters patent on 30 Sept. 1736 under the hand of THOMAS BROUGHTON, Lt. Gov. & Commander in Chief, granted JOHN ALLEN 800 a. in Craven Co., bounding NW on CAPT. WILLIAM DRY & on all others sides on vacant land; now ALLEN sells to HUNTER. Witnesses: JOHN BURFORD, ALEXANDER RIGG. Before ROBERT AUSTIN, J.P. & Register.

Book T, p. 133
18 & 19 July 1739
L & R

RICHARD CAPERS, SR., planter, of Colleton Co., to JOSEPH STANYARNE, planter, of Colleton Co., for L 3000 SC money, 500 a. at head of W branch of Stono River bounding E on marsh & swamp; N on JOSEPH ELLICOTT & vacant land; W & S on vacant land. Whereas the Lords Proprs. on 29 May 1704 granted ROBERT GIBBS, ESQ., 500 a., English measure, in Colleton Co.; which ROBERT GIBBS on 4 Oct. 1710 gave to his son JOHN GIBBS; which JOHN GIBBS on 24 Feb. 1718 sold to RICHARD

CAPERS sells to STANYARNE. Witnesses: KENNETH MICHIE, ARTHUR STRAHAN, GEORGE NICHOLAS. Before ROBERT AUSTIN, J.P. & Pub. Reg.

Book T, p. 136　　　　　　　　HENRY DURANT, of Craven Co., to WILLIAM ROMSEY
23 June 1739　　　　　　　　 & PAUL TRAPIER, merchants, of Georgetown, as
L & R by Mortgage　　　　　　security for the payment of a bond of this
　　　　　　　　　　　　　　　date, in the penal sum of L 655:5 currency,
conditioned for the payment of L 327:12:6 with interest on 1 Mar. 1739/40; 300 a., bounding S on THOMAS BOSHER; N on JOHN READ; W on WILLIAM WHITESIDE; E on WILLIAM SHACKELFORD. Witnesses: HANNAH DURANT, WILLIAM CROOK. Before THOMAS LAROCHE, J.P. ROBERT AUSTIN, Pub. Reg.

Book T, p. 139　　　　　　　　THOMAS PAGETT, of Craven Co., to WILLIAM ROM-
3 & 4 May 1739　　　　　　　 SEY & PAUL TRAPIER, merchants, of Georgetown,
L & R by Mortgage　　　　　　as security for the payment of a bond of this
　　　　　　　　　　　　　　　date, in the penal sum of L 2525:7:0 SC money,
conditioned for the payment of L 1262:13:10-1/2, with interest, on 1 Jan. next; 600 a. in Craven Co., bounding S on PERCIVAL PAWLEY; W on Waccamaw River & vacant land. Witnesses: WILLIAM GRIPSS, GEORGE THREADCRAFT. Before THOMAS LAROCHE, J.P. ROBERT AUSTIN, Pub. Reg.

Book T, p. 142　　　　　　　　JAMES FISHER, merchant, MICHAEL JEANS, glazier,
17 & 18 Feb. 1737　　　　　　 both of Charleston, & JOHN MCTEER, planter, of
L & R　　　　　　　　　　　　Colleton Co., as executors, & MARY CARMICHAEL,
　　　　　　　　　　　　　　　widow, as executrix, of the will of JOHN CAR-
MICHAEL dated 11 Dec. 1735, to ALEXANDER MOON, planter, of Colleton Co., for L 505 SC money, 875 a. in Granville Co., bounding NE on Combahee (Cumbee) River; SE on JOHN MCTIER; SW on JOHN LLOYD; & NW on vacant land, as by plat dated 27 Nov. 1731 & grant dated 16 Mar. 1732. Witnesses: THOMAS ARLEY, THOMAS HAMILTON SCOTT, BARNABY RAILY. Before JAMES BULLOCK, J.P. ROBERT AUSTIN, Pub. Reg.

Book T, p. 145　　　　　　　　ALEXANDER MOON, planter, & SARAH his wife, to
3 & 4 July 1739　　　　　　　 JOHN MACTEER, planter, all of Colleton Co.,
L & R　　　　　　　　　　　　for 505 SC money, 875 a. in Granville Co.,
　　　　　　　　　　　　　　　bounding NE on Combahee River; SE on JOHN MAC-
TEER; SW on vacant land; which tract formerly belonged to JOHN CARMICHAEL, plat dated 27 Nov. 1731, grant dated 16 Mar. 1732. Witnesses: EDWARD BROUGHTON, JOHN STEWART, BENJAMIN FLETCHER, BARNABY REILY. Before JAMES BULLOCK, J.P. ROBERT AUSTIN, Pub. Reg.

Book T, p. 149　　　　　　　　MATTHEW BEARD, planter, of Berkeley Co., to
5 & 6 Sept. 1733　　　　　　　JOHN MACTEER, planter, of Colleton Co., for
L & R　　　　　　　　　　　　L 300 currency, 300 a. in Colleton Co., bound-
　　　　　　　　　　　　　　　ing S on JAMES FERGUSON; E on THOMAS JONES; N
& W on MR. SANDERS. Witnesses: JOHN SALTER, RICHARD GOUGH, LAWRENCE COULLIETTE. Before HENRY GIBBES, J.P. ROBERT AUSTIN, Pub. Reg.

Book T, p. 151　　　　　　　　JOHN BENSTON, planter, to JONATHAN STOCKS,
16 & 17 Oct. 1734　　　　　　 both of Berkeley Co., for L 1200 currency, 200
L & R　　　　　　　　　　　　a. in Christ Church Parish, Berkeley Co., part
　　　　　　　　　　　　　　　of 500 a. which BENSTON purchased 26 Mar. 1729
from WILLIAM HARVEY & PAUL CHARSON, executors of the will of JOHN BASSET, of Charleston, bounding S on JOHN HENDRICKS (formerly ARCHIBALD COCHRAN); W on JOHN SEVERSANCE; E on CHARVEL WINGOOD (formerly JOHN SAUSSANS); N on JOHN BENSTON. The 500 a. were originally granted by the Lords Proprs. to WILLIAM LOUGHTON & by sundry conveyances became vested in JOHN BENSTON in fee simple. Witnesses: JOHN HENDRICK, JOHN EVANS, STEPHEN HARTLEY. Before J. HAMMERTON. ROBERT AUSTIN, Pub. Reg.

Book T, p. 155　　　　　　　　JAMES MCKAYE, tailor, & ELIZABETH (her mark)
9 & 10 July 1739　　　　　　　his wife, to PETER LIEUBREY, vintner, all of
L & R　　　　　　　　　　　　Craven Co., for L 220 SC money, 438 a. in
　　　　　　　　　　　　　　　Prince Frederick Parish, Winyaw, bounding N on
MR. KNIGHT; E & SE on CAPT. ABRA MICHAUX; S & SE on WILLIAM NEWMAN & MR. MARION; W on vacant land; which 438 a. were granted under the hand of the Hon. WILLIAM BULL, ESQ., Pres., etc., on 12 Jan. 1737 to JAMES MCKAYE. Witnesses: ABRAHAM JEANNERET, GEORGE (his mark) JUNE, JAMES ROBERTS. Before WILLIAM WHITESIDE, J.P. ROBERT AUSTIN, Pub. Reg.

Book T, p. 158　　　　　　WILLIAM TREWIN, ESQ., & HELEN his wife, to
31 July & 1 Aug. 1739　　ISAAC MAZYCK of Charleston & THOMAS LAROCHE,
L & R by Mortgage　　　　of Georgetown, merchants, as security for the
　　　　　　　　　　　　　payment of a bond given this date by TREWIN to
MAZYCK & LAROCHE, in the penal sum of ₤ 2112 SC money, conditioned for
the payment of ₤ 1056 with interest, on 25 Mar. next; 100 a., English measure, in Parish of St. Thomas, Berkeley Co., bounding NW on the Parish
Glebe lands; NE & SE on JONATHAN RUSS (formerly COL. ROBERT DANIEL) &
JOHN BERESFORD; which 100 a. was purchased by HERCULES COITE from DAVID
HARTY, who had purchased it from JAMES FUGART, gentleman; also 300 a.,
part of 500 a. purchased from the Lords Proprs. by ROBERT DANIEL, JR. &
by him conveyed to JONATHAN RUSS; which 300 a. is in St. Thomas Parish,
Berkeley Co., bounding NW on ABIJAH RUSS; NE on land formerly belonging
to CHARLES KING but now to ROBERT HEW CAINHOY Meeting House & JAMES TAGGART; SW & W on JOHN BERESFORD & JAMES TAGGART; (NE on POITEVING & POLLOCK). Witnesses: JOHN JOHNSON, JR., JOHN RATTRAY. Before MAURICE LEWIS,
J.P. ROBERT AUSTIN, Pub. Reg.

Book T, p. 163　　　　　　ARTHUR HALL, planter, to ROBERT H. COLE, plant-
17 Nov. 1720　　　　　　　er, for ₤ 200 currency, 100 a. on Wadmalaw Is-
Deed of Sale　　　　　　　land, Colleton Co., bounding SE on WILLIAM WIL-
　　　　　　　　　　　　　LIAMS; N on part of same tract; SW on JOHN
JAMES. MARTHA, wife of ARTHUR HALL, freely surrenders her dower. Witnesses: SAMUEL JONES, ROBERT (his mark) DAUSE.

Book T, p. 164　　　　　　ROBERT COLE, planter, of Colleton Co., to his
30 Apr. 1733　　　　　　　son MICAJAH COLE, for love & affection, 100 a.
Deed of Gift　　　　　　　(see p. 163). Signed by ROBERT COLE, MARY
　　　　　　　　　　　　　(her mark) COLE, his wife. Witnesses: WILLIAM
FLECKNOW, ELIZABETH FREEMAN. Before ROBERT YONGE, J.P. ROBERT AUSTIN,
Pub. Reg.

Book T, p. 165　　　　　　HENRY SNELL, planter, of Berkeley Co., to his
24 July 1739　　　　　　　beloved daughter MARGARET MENSON, for love &
Deed of Gift　　　　　　　affection & other considerations, 1/2 of a
　　　　　　　　　　　　　tract of 350 a. or 175 a. in Orangeburg Township, Berkeley Co., bounding NE on PETER FONT & HENRY GALLO; NW on PETER
FONT; SW on HENRY BUHMAN & PETER WERN; SE on vacant land. Witnesses:
WILL IRWIN, EDWARD KNIGHT, JOHN MIENSON. Before HENRY GIBBES, J.P. ROBERT AUSTIN, Pub. Reg.

Book T, p. 166　　　　　　ANTHONY WHITE, planter, & MARY his wife, to
30 & 31 July 1739　　　　 WILLIAM FLEMING, merchant, all of Colleton Co.,
L & R　　　　　　　　　　 for ₤ 2000 currency, 500 a. in Craven Co.,
　　　　　　　　　　　　　free from MARY'S claim of dower; bounding S on
Black River; E on the N branch of Black River; W & N on JOHN THOMPSON,
JR. Witnesses: WILLIAM SWINTON, JOHN WHITE, ALEXANDER ROBERTSON. Before
JOHN WALLIS, J.P. ROBERT AUSTIN, Pub. Reg.

Book T, p. 169　　　　　　ANTHONY WHITE, planter, of Craven Co., to MAU-
8 & 9 Aug. 1739　　　　　 RICE LEWIS, ESQ., of Charleston, for ₤ 1793 SC
L & R by Mortgage　　　　money, 2 tracts; 1 of 500 a.; purchased by
　　　　　　　　　　　　　ANTHONY WHITE from ALEXANDER TRENCH (as attorney for JOHN BAYLY, son & heir of JOHN BAYLY of the Co. of Tipperary, Ireland), bounding NW, SW & SE on ANTHONY WHITE; the other of 1150 a., part
of 1400 a. purchased by ANTHONY WHITE from MRS. ALICE GIBBS, widow, of
Berkeley Co., bounding NW on JOHN THOMSON, SR. & WILLIAM BROCKINGTON; N
on land granted to THOMAS WRIGHT & agreed to be conveyed to JASPER KING;
S on ANTHONY WHITE. Should ANTHONY WHITE pay MAURICE LEWIS ₤ 1793:18:6
SC money, with interest, on 1 Jan. 1740 the bond & this mortgage to be
void. MARY, the wife of ANTHONY WHITE to renounce her dower in case of
nonpayment. Witnesses: CHARLES SHEPHEARD, JOHN RATTRAY. Before ROBERT
AUSTIN, J.P. & Pub. Reg. JACOB MOTTE, executor of will of MORRIS (MAURICE) LEWIS declared the mortgage paid. Witness: RICHARD HARRISON.

Book T, p. 172　　　　　　ISAAC NICHOLAS, planter, to ISAAC HAYNES,
1 & 2 Mar. 1738/9　　　　planter, both of Colleton Co., for ₤ 900 SC
L & R　　　　　　　　　　money, 2 tracts; 1 of 246 a. in Colleton Co.,
　　　　　　　　　　　　　bounding S on THOMAS FORD; W on THOMAS FORD &
HUGH CAMPBELL; N on ISAAC HAYNES; E on ISAAC HAYNES & JOHN JACKSON; which

246 a. were granted by the Hon. THOMAS BROUGHTON, Lt. Gov., to ISAAC NICH-
OLAS on 12 Aug. 1737; the other of 150 a. in Colleton Co., bounding W on
Pon Pon River; N on MR. FORD; E on JOHN JACKSON; W on vacant land; which
150 a. were granted by the Hon. THOMAS BROUGHTON, Lt. Gov., to JOHN GOD-
FREY on 4 Dec. 1735, & on 25 Jan. 1737/8 sold by GODFREY to ISAAC NICHO-
LAS. Witnesses: EZEKIEL BRANFORD, JOHN SPLATT, JAMES CLEMENT. Before
JAMES BULLOCK, J.P. ROBERT AUSTIN, Pub. Reg.

Book T, p. 176　　　　ISAAC NICHOLAS, planter, to ISAAC HAYNES, both
2 Mar. 1738/9　　　　 of Colleton Co., in the penal sum of ₺ 1800 SC
Bond　　　　　　　　 money, conditioned for keeping the agreements
　　　　　　　　　　 in the above transaction. Witnesses: EZEKIEL
BRANFORD, JOHN SPLATT. Before JAMES BULLOCK, J.P. ROBERT AUSTIN, Pub.
Reg.

Book T, p. 177　　　　JOHN HAYNES & MATHEW HAYNES, planters, of Col-
5 Nov. 1736　　　　　 leton Co., to their youngest brother, ISAAC
Quit Claim　　　　　 HAYNES. Whereas JOHN HAYNES, their father, by
　　　　　　　　　　 will dated 20 Dec. 1717 bequeathed all his
lands, to his sons, to be equally divided amongst them; & whereas their
mother, MARY, widow of JOHN, in her widowhood purchased 4 tracts in Colleton Co. containing 856 a. in all & afterwards married JOHN LONG, of
Colleton Co., & JOHN & MARY LONG on 16 June 1724 conveyed to JOHN HAYNES
(eldest son of JOHN HAYNES, & eldest brother of JOHN & MATHEW), & to JOHN
WILLIAMSON & TIMOTHY HENDRICKS the 4 tracts; that is, (1) 250 a. bounding
N on MATHEW BEE & JOHN PEACON; (2) 286 a.; (3) 200 a.; (4) 120 a.; all on
the E side of Edisto River; with 4 separate plats & 4 separate grants;
the conveyance being in trust equally for the use of JOHN, EDWARD, JOSEPH,
HANNAH HAYNES, (children of JOHN & MARY) & MATHEW SUSANNA, & ISAAC HAYNES,
minors, children of JOHN, JR.; & whereas the youngest brother, ISAAC, accepted 1 tract of 514 a. in Colleton Co., bounding N on Boons Barony; E &
S on EDWARD FLEHARTY; W on JOHN ANDREWS, which tract was part of the land
owned by their father JOHN; now JOHN & MATHEW declare themselves satisfied to let ISAAC accept the 514 a. as his share & renounce any claim they
may have. Witnesses: EZEKIEL BRANFORD, JOSEPH BRANFORD. Before JAMES
BULLOCK, J.P. ROBERT AUSTIN, Pub. Reg.

Book T, p. 180　　　　ISAAC DUMONS, planter, of Craven Co., to CAPT.
31 Nov. 1738　　　　　PETER ROBERT, planter, for 10 shillings cur-
Lease　　　　　　　　 rency, 2 tracts; 1 of 30 a. the other of 120 a.
　　　　　　　　　　 making 150 a., at head of Itchaw Creek, adjoining the land of PETER ROBERT & lately purchased by DUMONS from ROBERT.
Witnesses: CAPT. ABRAHAM SATUR, PETER SCHULT, WILLIAM MCALLA. Before
JAMES KINLOCH, J.P. ROBERT AUSTIN, Pub. Reg.

Book T, p. 181　　　　HUGH (his mark) CAMPBELL, planter, & ANN his
16 & 17 Aug. 1738　　 wife, to JAMES SKIRVING, surgeon, all of Col-
L & R　　　　　　　　 leton Co., for ₺ 574 SC money, 164 a. in Col-
　　　　　　　　　　 leton Co., (136 a. of which had been purchased
on 2 Sept. 1726 from ALEXANDER TRENCH by GEORGE BADGER, & sold by BADGER
to CAMPBELL on 12 Jan. 1730; the other 28 a. being part of 31 a. granted
to CAMPBELL by COL. BROUGHTON on 25 June 1736); bounding S on LAWRENCE
WOOLFORDSON & JOSEPH BARKER; E on ISAAC HAYNES; N on ISAAC HAYNES & JOHN
ANDREWS; W on CHRISTOPHER SMITH. Witnesses: JOHN ANDREW, ALEXANDER
SPROULL. Before JAMES BULLOCK, J.P. ROBERT AUSTIN, Pub. Reg.

Book T, p. 184　　　　JAMES ATKINS, planter, of Winyaw, to JOHN DAN-
16 & 17 July 1739　　 IEL, merchant, of Charleston, for ₺ 400 SC mon-
L & R by Mortgage　　 ey, 110 a. on Black River, Craven Co., bound-
　　　　　　　　　　 ing S on GEORGE HADRELL; N on JOHN BOGS; conditioned for the payment of ₺ 400 with interest on 1 Jan. 1741. Witnesses: ABRAHAM CROFT, MATHEW ROCHE. Before HENRY GIBBES, J.P. ROBERT AUS-
TIN, Pub. Reg.

Book T, p. 187　　　　JOHN BARKSDALE, gentleman, of Charleston, to
1 Oct. 1738　　　　　 PETER HUME, gentleman, of St. James Goose
Deed of Sale　　　　　Creek, Berkeley Co., for ₺ 200, part of lot
　　　　　　　　　　 #26 in Charleston with the new tenement on it,
for the term of ANNE HEPWORTH'S life. Whereas THOMAS HEPWORTH, of
Charleston, by will dated 11 Sept. 1727 devised to his wife ANNE for life

the new tenement adjoining his dwelling house in Charleston, being part of lot #26 purchased by him from MR. DISTON, & after her death to daughter ANNE; & whereas by L & R, 16 & 17 Dec. 1736 ANNE HEPWORTH, widow of THOMAS, conveyed to JOHN BARKSDALE (who had married ANNE the daughter) for love & affection for daughter ANNE & other considerations, the new tenement; now BARKSDALE conveys to HUME. Witnesses: THOMAS HUTCHINSON, BENJAMIN WHITAKER. Witness to livery & seizin: LEWIS LORMIER, SIXTUS STEIGER. Before ROBERT AUSTIN, J.P. & Pub. Reg.

Book T, p. 190　　　　JOHN CHAPMAN, of Colleton Co., to THOMAS ELL-
20 July 1733　　　　　IOTT, son of THOMAS ELLIOT, for L 136, 13-3/4
Deed of Sale　　　　　a. in Colleton Co., part of a larger tract,
　　　　　　　　　　　bounding S & W on JOHN CHAPMAN; N on JOSEPH
ELLIOT & ELIZABETH ELLIOT. WILLIAM WILLIAMSON, JOSEPH ELLIOT, JR., BENJAMIN WILLIAMSON. Before R. WRIGHT. ROBERT AUSTIN, Pub. Reg.

Book T, p. 191　　　　JOSEPH ELLIOT, & ELIZABETH his wife, of Berke-
24 July 1733　　　　　ley Co., to THOMAS ELLIOT, son of THOMAS ELL-
Deed of Sale　　　　　IOT of Colleton Co., for L 510, 51-1/2 a. in
　　　　　　　　　　　Colleton Co., a neck of land between JOSEPH
ELLIOT & JOHN CHAPMAN; bounding N & E on THOMAS ELLIOT; S on JOHN CHAPMAN; W on JOSEPH ELLIOT; being part of 400 a. granted JOHN CHAPMAN, their father. Witnesses: WILLIAM WILLIAMSON, BENJAMIN WILLIAMSON, JOHN CHAPMAN. Before ROBERT YONGE, J.P. ROBERT AUSTIN, Pub. Reg.

Book T, p. 193　　　　The Hon. JAMES KINLOCH, ESQ., to GEORGE HUNTER,
10 May 1733　　　　　 gentleman, both of Berkeley Co., for L 15 SC
Release　　　　　　　 money, an island containing 153 a. in Gran-
　　　　　　　　　　　ville Co., bounded E by Charleton Island; W by
Hilton Head Sount; S by May River; N by DAWFUSKIE; which island was granted to KINLOCH on 6 Apr. 1733 under the hand of His Excellency ROBERT JOHNSON, ESQ., Gov. Witnesses: JAMES CROKATT, JOHN LLOYD. Before THEOPHILUS GREGORY, J.P. ROBERT AUSTIN, Pub. Reg.

Book T, p. 195　　　　DAVID MALLACE, butcher, of Berkeley Co., to
10 & 11 Mar. 1737　　 JOHN HEARN, planter, of Orangeburg Township,
L & R　　　　　　　　 Berkeley Co., for L 50 currency, 350 a. on E
　　　　　　　　　　　side Pon Pon River, Berkeley Co., bounding E &
W on vacant land; N on JOSEPH HORSFORD; S on JOHN HEARN; which 35 a. were granted by King GEORGE the Second by letters patent on 12 Jan. 1737, witnessed by the Hon. WILLIAM BULL, ESQ., Pres., to DAVID MALLACE. Witnesses: WILLIAM STERLAND, JOHN NEILSON, DAVID ALEXANDER. Before HENRY GIBBES, J.P. ROBERT AUSTIN, Pub. Reg.

Book T, p. 198　　　　JOHN LANE, of Prince Frederick Parish, to son
20 May 1738　　　　　 PETER LANE, for love & affection, 1 large
Deed of Gift　　　　　house & 2 lots #9 & #10 in Georgetown, front-
　　　　　　　　　　　ing the Bay. Witnesses: JOHN ADDERLEY, WIL-
LIAM SMITH, EDWARD (his mark) HISTED. Before ROBERT AUSTIN, J.P. & Pub. Reg.

Book T, p. 199　　　　PETER LANE, planter, of Craven Co., to JOHN
4 & 5 Sept. 1739　　　STEEL, of Charleston, for L 300 SC money a
L & R　　　　　　　　 dwelling house & 2 lots, #9 & #10, in George-
　　　　　　　　　　　town, Craven Co., fronting the Bay. Witness-
es: JOHN LAURENS, HENRY POWELL, WILLIAM SMITH. Before HENRY GIBBES, J.P. ROBERT AUSTIN, Pub. Reg.

Book T, p. 203　　　　JOHN ABRAHAM KORTEN, merchant, of London, for
24 Apr. 1738　　　　　himself & as surviving partner & executor of
Letter of Attorney　 the will of his borther PETER KORTEN, appoint-
　　　　　　　　　　　ed ROBERT THORPE, now in London but soon to
set out for a voyage to SC, his attorney to receive from THOMAS HENNING & JOSEPH SHUTE, merchants, of Charleston, lately partners under the name of HENNING & SHUTE, such money or goods due from them & in general to act for him. Before BENJAMIN BONNET of London, Notary & Tabellion Royal & Publick. Witnesses: JACOB AYERS, HUGH PERCY. CAPT. HUGH PERCY appeared before ROBERT AUSTIN, J.P. & Pub. Reg.

Book T, p. 204　　　　JOHN VAUGHAN, bricklayer, to GABRIEL MANIGAULT,

7 & 8 June 1739   ESQ., both of Charleston, for ₤ 1100 currency,
L & R   part of lot #121 in Charleston, fronting N 25
                        ft. on Broad Street, bounding E 104 ft. on the
part belonging to RALPH RODDA; S on an alley through the lot; W on a
street leading from the Broad Path by the Quakers Meeting House, now called Kings Street. Witnesses: ELIJAH BREBANT, JOHN ROYER. Before ROBERT
AUSTIN, J.P. & Pub. Reg.

Book T, p. 208   JOHN LANE, planter, of Craven Co., to JOHN
18 & 19 May 1738   LAURENS, saddler, of Charleston, for ₤ 20 SC
L & R   money, lot #60 in Georgetown, fronting NE 100
                        ft. on Prince Street; 217.9 ft. deep, bounding
SE on Broad Street, SW on lots #23 & #24; NW on lot #59. SARAH, wife of
JOHN LANE, to renounce her dower within 3 months. Witnesses: JAMES LANE,
EDWARD HISTED. Before THOMAS LAROCHE, J.P. ROBERT AUSTIN, Pub. Reg.

Book T, p. 211   WILLIAM SMITH, planter, & MARY his wife, to
2 Nov. 1737   GIDEON DUPONT, planter, all of Berkeley Co.,
Deed of Sale   with MARY'S free consent, for ₤ 500 SC money,
                        500 a., English measure, in Berkeley Co., on
Four Hole Swamp, bounding SE on TOBIAS FITCH; N on CAPT. GOODBEY; NW & N
on GIDEON DUPONT; & on other sides on vacant land. Witnesses: FRANCIS
CORBIN, WILLIAM PARTRIDGE. Before ISAAC PORCHER, J.P. ROBERT AUSTIN,
Pub. Reg.

Book T, p. 214   DAVID ALEXANDER, planter, to SAMUEL IRVINE,
21 & 22 Feb. 1737   planter, both of Granville Co., for ₤ 100 SC
L & R   money, 100 a., part of 300 a., called Trench's
                        Island, on Hilton Head, bounding N on DAVID
ALEXANDER; S on ALEXANDER TRENCH; W on Scull Creek. Witnesses: BENJAMIN
LLOYD, ROBERT GRISBANE, HILL WIGG. Before RICHARD WOODWARD, J.P. ROBERT
AUSTIN, Pub. Reg.

Book T, p. 217   PATRICK MACKAY, of Granville Co., to SAMUEL
8 Sept. 1739   MONTAIGNT (?) & CHARLES PURRY, to secure pay-
Mortgage   ment of bond of this date in penal sum of
                        ₤ 2547:8 SC money, conditioned for the payment
of ₤ 1273:14 on 15 Jan. 1739, 2 adjoining tracts on N branch of Savannah
River, called Back River, Granville Co., 1 of 800 a., the other 360 a.;
also the crop on the land. Witnesses: GEORGE BUNCH & ADRIAN MAYER. Before BERENGER DE BEAUFAIN, J.P. at Purisburgh, Granville Co. ROBERT AUS-
TIN, Pub. Reg.

Book T, p. 218   JAMES MACGIRT, & PRISCILLA (her mark) his wife,
3 & 4 Feb. 1737   to JOHN NIELSON, all of Craven Co., for ₤ 150
L & R   SC money, 150 a. on Cadoes Lake, Craven Co.,
                        bounding S on the lake; E N & W on vacant land;
which 150 a. was granted on 8 Oct. 1737 by his Majesty to JAMES MACGIRT.
Witnesses: JAMES FRANCIS, PETER TURNER, HENRY FOX, JR., JOHN ADDERLY. Before H. FOX, J.P. ROBERT AUSTIN, Pub. Reg.

Book T, p. 223   WILLIAM HAMILTON, carpenter, to HENRY WILLIAMS,
26 & 27 June 1738   vintner, both of Charleston, for ₤ 100 SC mon-
L & R   ey, 200 a. in the township of Williamsburgh,
                        Craven Co., granted to WILLIAM HAMILTON by
letters patent on 12 Jan. 1737, & witnessed by the Hon. WILLIAM BULL,
ESQ., Pres., Gov., etc.; bounding NE on Black River; SE on CRAFTON KERWON
& an impassable swamp; on all other sides on vacant land; also 1 1/2 a.
town lot #319 in Williamsburg. Witnesses: GEORGE TABART, JOHN PENNYMAN.
Before ROBERT AUSTIN, J.P. & Pub. Reg.

Book T, p. 228   JAMES GORDON, planter, of Craven Co., to JOHN
15 & 16 Mar. 1738   FRASER, merchant, of Charleston, to secure pay-
L & R by Mortgage   ment of bond of this date in penal sum of
                        ₤ 1619:13 SC money, conditioned for the pay-
ment of ₤ 809:16:6 with interest on 16 Mar. 1741; 500 a. in Queensborough
Township, Craven Co., bounding NW on town land & vacant land; SW on vacant land; NW on Peedee River; SE on JAMES GORDON; which tract was granted to JAMES GORDON on 16 Feb. 1735; also 250 a. in same township, bounding NW on JAMES GORDON; SW on vacant land; NE on Peedee River; SE on

SAMUEL BAKER; granted GORDON on 16 Feb. 1735; also 400 a. in same township, bounding NW on JAMES GORDON; SW on vacant land; NE on Peedee River; SE on JAMES GORDON; granted to GORDON on 8 Apr. 1735. Witnesses: ARTHUR STRAHAN, GEORGE NICHOLAS. Before ROBERT AUSTIN, J.P. & Pub. Reg.

Book T, p. 232
2 & 3 Sept. 1734
L & R Tripartite

ANDREW ALLEN, merchant, of Charleston, of 1st part; JAMES PAYNE & JOHN FRAZIER, merchants, of Charleston, of 2nd part.; ROBERT PRINGLE, merchant, & JANE his wife, daughter of ANDREW ALLEN, of Charleston, of 3rd part. In consideration of the marriage between ROBERT PRINGLE & JANE ALLEN, daughter of ANDREW ALLEN, & for JANE'S security, & for natural love & affection for daughter JANE, & to secure disposition of certain property, ANDREW ALLEN conveys to JAMES PAYNE & JOHN FRAZIER, in trust, part of lots #87 & 88 in Charleston, bounding E 195 ft. on part of lots 87 & 88 now in possession of ANDREW ALLEN; W on part of same lots in possession of JAMES MATHEWS; N on part of lot #88 in possession of DANIEL BOURGET; S 73 ft., English measure, on Tradd Street, to the use of ROBERT PRINGLE during his lifetime, then to JANE during her lifetime, then to the heirs. Witnesses: BENJAMIN WHITAKER, WILLIAM G. FREEMAN. Before ROBERT AUSTIN, J.P. & Pub. Reg.

Book T, p. 236
23 & 24 Apr. 1739
L & R

NATHANIEL BROUGHTON, ANDREW BROUGHTON, & GABRIEL MANIGAULT, executors & trustees of will of Gov. ROBERT JOHNSON, to ROBERT JOHNSON, (see p. 248), eldest son, now of Silkhope plantation. Gov. ROBERT JOHNSON owned much real & personal estate, including plantations, slaves, horses, cattle, tools, & also a pew in a church in Charleston, & by will dated 21 Dec. 1734 appointed, as trustees to manage & apportion his estate, his brother-in-law COL. THOMAS BROUGHTON, his nephews NATHANIEL & ANDREW BROUGHTON (sons of ANDREW BROUGHTON), & his kinsman GABRIEL MANIGAULT; & by will bequeathed certain property to each of his sons, ROBERT, NATHANIEL & THOMAS; ROBERT to receive 1/2 of all the estate not otherwise devised; the other half to be divided equally between NATHANIEL & THOMAS. COL. THOMAS BROUGHTON, trustee, died before the execution of the will. NATHANIEL died before reaching the age of 21, therefore his portion was divided equally between ROBERT & THOMAS. The trustees, having divided such property, real & personal, not otherwise devised, & having divided NATHANIEL'S portion into 2 parts; they now set over to ROBERT as his inheritance: 6855 a., part of the Barony, near Seawee: (see Plat A); 750 a., or 1/2 of 1500 a. purchased from his overseer DYER, Plat B; 650 a., or 1/2 of 1130 a. called Mt. Pleasant, Plat C; 250 a., or 1/2 of 500 a. purchased from EDWARD CRISPE, Plat D; 100 a., or 1/2 of 200 a. called Tryall, Plat E; & the northern half of a town lot on the Bay of Charleston purchased from JAMES CROKATT, & bounding N on another lot owned by ROBERT JOHNSON; S on the half of the lot owned by THOMAS JOHNSON; also the Negroes, horses, cattle, etc., named in Schedule F. The plows, carts, carriages, tools, etc., on Silk Hope Plantation were allotted to ROBERT; those on Salt Ponds were allotted to THOMAS. Witnesses: THOMAS BROUGHTON, JOHN CORSS, ELIJAH BREBANT. Stock of horses, etc., on Silkhope & Seawee Plantations divided by FRANCIS LEJAU & SAMUEL WIGFALL. Before HENRY GIBBES, J.P. ROBERT AUSTIN, Pub. Reg.

Book T, p. 248
7 & 8 May 1739
L & R

ROBERT JOHNSON, of Silkhope Plantation, Berkeley Co., eldest son of Gov. ROBERT JOHNSON, to GABRIEL MANIGAULT, of Charleston, for ₺ 7000 money of Great Britain; Silk Hope Plantation & New Keblesworth, making 5518 a. near the head of the E branch of Cooper River; also 300 a. in Berkeley Co., purchased from MR. SIMONDS & bounding part on Silkhope & part on JOHN ASHBY; 146 a. on Charleston Neck called The Point; a lot on the Bay in Charleston, purchased from SAMUEL WRAGG of London, bounding E on Cooper River, S on the lot purchased from JAMES CROKATT, W on MATHEW PORTER'S lot; also the N half of a lot on the Bay in Charleston, purchased from JAMES CROKATT, bounding E on Cooper River, S on THOMAS JOHNSON, W on MATTHEW PORTER, N on lot bought from SAMUEL WRAGG; also the low water land E of the 2 parts of said lots; also 4000 a. in Granville Co., being the NE half of 8000 a. surveyed by HUGH BRYAN, a Dep. Sur., the whole bounding NE & SE on branches of Port Royall River, SW on COL. RAYCROFT, NW on the Hon. COL. THOMAS BROUGHTON; also the several tracts of 6855 a., 750 a., 650 a., 250., & 100 a. described in Plats A, B, C, D, & E; also, all the other lands, plantations, etc., in SC in which

359

ROBERT has an interest (except the pew in a church in Charleston); also
106 Negroes & slaves, 46 cows, etc., etc., listed in Schedule F. Whereas
Gov. ROBERT JOHNSON owned several baronies, plantations, etc., also Negroes, slaves, cattle, horses, personal estate, etc., and by will dated
21 Dec. 1734 devised to his eldest son ROBERT the tract called Silkhope,
which with the new tract called New Keblesworth contained 5518 a.; also
300 a. near Silkhope purchased from MR. SIMONDS; also 146 a. on Charleston Neck called The Point; also a lot on the Bay in Charleston purchased
from SAMUEL WRAGG of London; also 1/3 of a tract of 8000 a. in Granville
Co., all household goods, plate, pictures, furniture, books, coach,
chaise, coach horses, etc.; & whereas he appointed his brother-in-law COL.
THOMAS BROUGHTON & his nephews NATHANIEL BROUGHTON & ANDREW BROUGHTON
(sons of THOMAS BROUGHTON), & his kinsman GABRIEL MANIGAULT trustees of
his estate consisting of 1700 a. called Saltpond; 200 a. called Tryall;
1500 a. bought from his overseer DYER; 12,000 a. called The Barony, near
Seawee; 500 a. bought from EDWARD CRISPE; 1130 a. called Mt. Pleasant,
bought from his brother-in-law THOMAS BROUGHTON; a lot in Charleston
bought from JAMES CROKATT; Negroes, slaves, etc., etc., with instructions
that they convey to ROBERT 4570 a., part of the Barony; 1/2 the Negroes,
etc. (except as devised to daughters); & his half share of the profits,
ect.; to convey to NATHANIEL, when 21, 4570 a. of the Barony; 200 a.
called Tryall; 1500 a. called Dyers; 500 a.called Crispes; 1130 a. called
Mt. Pleasant; the lot in Charleston bought from CROKATT; 1/2 the Negroes,
cattle, utensils on the plantations not before conveyed to ROBERT; to
convey to THOMAS, when 21, 2860 a. of The Barony; 1700 a. called Saltponds with Negroes, etc. (except as deivsed to daughters); but should
either NATHANIEL or THOMAS die before 21, his portion to be divided equally between ROBERT & the survivor; & whereas COL. BROUGHTON & NATHANIEL
JOHNSON died before the execution of the will, the surviving trustees allotted to ROBERT & THOMAS according to Schedules A, B, C, D, E, & F, the
plantation tools on Silkhope to ROBERT, those on Saltponds to THOMAS: &
whereas Gov. ROBERT JOHNSON devised to his trustees all his ready money,
debts, rice & personal estate in SC not before devised; & whereas he
appointed his brother-in-law ARCHIBALD HUTCHINSON, kinsman JOHN SCHULTZ,
kinsman JOHN COOKE, sister-in-law PHEBE BONNER his trustees to handle his
debts, money, securities & estate in Great Britain & Ireland in trust for
his daughters MARGARET & MARY; & whereas ROBERT JOHNSON (the son) has
agreed to convey to GABRIEL MANIGAULT all his property in SC, & GABRIEL
MANIGAULT has agreed to pay ROBERT JOHNSON ₺ 7000 money of Great Britain
as follows: ₺ 3000 sterling on 25 Apr. 1740, ₺ 1500 sterling to MARGARET
JOHNSON when she marries or reaches 21; ₺ 1500 sterling to MARY JOHNSON
when she marries or reaches 21; ₺ 1000 sterling to THOMAS when ROBERT directs; now ROBERT JOHNSON, the son, conveys to GABRIEL MANIGAULT as stated. Witnesses: CHARLES PINCKNEY, ROBERT BREWTON, JR., NATHANIEL BURNHAM.
Before HENRY GIBBES, J.P. ROBERT AUSTIN, Pub. Reg.

Book T, p. 261
18 & 19 May 1739
L & R in Trust

ANDREW DEVEAUX, planter of St. Andrews Parish,
& MAGDELENE, his wife, lately MAGDELENE JUNEAU,
widow, of Charleston, to ISAAC MAZYCK, merchant, of Charleston, in trust. Whereas it
was agreed between ANDREW DEVEAUX & MRS. MAGDELENE JUNEAU, before their
marriage, that the several parcels of real estate mentioned herein should
be conveyed in trust for certain uses, now they convey to ISAAC MAZYCK,
as trustee, part of lot #163 in Charleston fronting S 48 ft. on Broad
Street, bounding W on JAMES GREEME (formerly GIBBON & ALLEN); E on JOHN
LEWIS; N on SAMUEL SMITH, butcher; also part of lot #11 fronting S 27 ft.
on Broad Street, & 90 ft. deep, occupied by ABRAHAM SKINNER, shopkeeper;
also 1 Negro man; also that silver dish & silver bowl marked I^m B; the
rents from the real estate to go to ANDREW DEVEAUX during MAGDELENE'S
life; the lot #163, after MAGDELENE'S death, to go to ISAAC MAZYCK until
he raises the sum of ₺ 500 out of the rents or until STEPHEN BEAUCHAMP,
the son of MAGDALENE DEVEAUX, shall pay MAZYCK ₺ 500, when the lot shall
go to STEPHEN. Lot #11 after the death of MAGDELENE to be conveyed to
JOHN METHRINGHAM, son of MAGDELENE, the silver dish & silver bowl, after
MAGDELENE'S death to be conveyed to her son STEPHEN BEAUCHAMP; the Negro
man, after MAGDELENE'S death, to be conveyed to NATHANIEL WITHERS; grandson of MAGDELENE, & son of ELIZABETH & LAWRENCE WITHERS, but in case of
his death before 21 to ANDREW DEVEAUX. The ₺ 500 to be obtained from
rents to go to ELIZABETH WITHERS. In consideration of his receiving the
rents during MAGDELENE'S lifetime, ANDREW DEVEAUX agrees to give MAZYCK,

within 6 months after MAGDELENE'S death, Ł 500 for the use of NATHANIEL WITHERS. Witnesses: PAUL DE ST. JULIEN, ROBERT BREWTON, JR. ROBERT AUSTIN, J.P. & Pub. Reg.

Book T, p. 269
20 & 21 Apr. 1739
Deed of Gift

NOAH SERRÉ, ESQ., of St. James Santee, Craven Co., to JOHN SHACKLEFORD, his nephew & Godson, for love & affection, 1047 a. between the N & S branches of Little Peedee River bounding SW on DANIEL HORRY; NE on MR. LEJEAU; other sides on vacant land. Witnesses: ANDREW DELAULETTE, JOHN HENTIE. Before THOMAS LAROCHE, J.P. ROBERT AUSTIN, Pub. Reg.

Book T, p. 271
10 & 11 Aug. 1739
L & R

THOMAS BUTLER, JR., planter & CONSTANT his wife, to WILLIAM GUY, JR., all of Colleton Co., for 10 shillings, 508 a. in Colleton Co., bounding SE on SAMUEL SLEIGH; SW on MRS. BOONE; NE on JOHN POSTELL; NW on land laid out. Witnesses: WILLIAM SMYES, ROWLAND PRICKETT, JOHN (his mark) REED. Before ROBERT AUSTIN, J.P. & Pub. Reg.

Book T, p. 275
17 & 18 May 1739
L & R

JOHN HALE, planter, & ELIZABETH (her mark) his wife, of St. James Santee, to THOMAS BOLTON, shopkeeper, of Charleston, for Ł 607 SC money, 500 a. Whereas JOHN HALE, gentleman, of Christ Church Parish, owned 500 a. in Craven Co., bounding S on the creeks & marshes of Seawee Bay; NE on Tibwin Creek & CAPT. JOHN COLLINS; W on MARK SLOMAN, NW on vacant land; & by will dated 25 May 1727 bequeathed the 500 a. to his son JOHN; now JOHN, JR. sells to BOLTON. Witnesses: RICHARD BODDICOTE, ROBERT BREWTON, JR., VINCENT GUERIN, JOHN BISHOP. JAMES ST. JOHN, Dep. Aud. Before ROBERT AUSTIN, J.P. & Pub. Reg.

Book T, p. 280
1 & 2 May 1739
L & R by Mortgage

NATHANIEL PARTRIDGE, planter, of Berkeley Co., to ISAAC AMY, gentleman, of Charleston, for Ł 150 money of Great Britain, 81 a. on Charleston Neck, Berkeley Co., bounding N on JOHN PENDARVIS; S on SAMUEL WEST; E on JAMES MCCLOULIN; W on marsh; conditioned for the payment of Ł 150 with interest by PARTRIDGE to AMY on 2 May 1740. Witnesses: ALEXANDER CRAMAHE, GEORGE WALSH, CHILDERMAS CROFT. Before ROBERT AUSTIN, J.P. & Pub. Reg.

Book T, p. 285
21 & 22 July 1737
L & R

JOHN HALE, planter, & ELIZABETH (her mark) his wife, of St. James Santee, & ANDREW QUELCH, planter, & ELIZABETH his wife, of Christ Church Parish, Berkeley Co., to THOMAS BOLTON, merchant, of Charleston, for Ł 350 currency, 70 a. in Christ Church Parish, formerly belonging to JOHN FITZGARLD & by several mesne conveyances descended to JOHN HALE, gentleman, of Hobcaw, who bequesthed the land to his son JOHN & daughter ELIZABETH (now wife of ANDREW QUELCH); which 70 a. is bounding N & E on JOSHUA WILKS; W on CAPT. EDMUND ROBINSON & WILLIAM VISSER; S on GUARRATT FITZGARLD. Witnesses: FOWLER (his mark) PEIRCEY, WILLIAM (his mark) BOLLOUGH, WILLIAM MORRALL. Witnesses to receipt: WILLIAM ROPER, WILLIAM POWELL, WILLIAM SAXBY, WILLIAM SMITH. Before ROBERT AUSTIN, J.P. & Pub. Reg.

Book T, p. 290
13 Aug. 1739
Confirmation & Release
of Equity of Redemption

HUGH BUTLER, (his mark), ESQ., of Exeter, to JOHN COLLETON, ESQ., of Fairlawn Barony, both of Berkeley Co., SC. Whereas HUGH BUTLER on 1 Jan. 1735 gave bond to JOHN COLLETON, in the penal sum of Ł 142:18 sterling to be paid COLLETON in trust for the Hon. SIR JOHN COLLETON, baronet, of Exmouth, Great Britain, conditioned for the payment of Ł 71:9 sterling with interest either in currency or bills of exchange; & whereas HUGH BUTLER, by mortgage dated 1 Jan. 1735 for Ł 1917:18:9 sterling money of Great Britain delivered to SIR JOHN COLLETON, baronet, 54 Negro slaves, & whereas HUGH BUTLER on 29 Apr. 1738 gave bond to JOHN COLLETON, ESQ., in the penal sum of Ł 509:15 sterling of Great Britain conditioned for the payment of Ł 254:15 sterling with interest; & whereas SIR JOHN COLLETON, baronet, & the said JOHN COLLETON, his eldest son & heir, "farm let" to HUGH BUTLER 1500 a. in SC for 99 years, & fully to be completed if HUGH BUTLER, JOHN BUTLER, & GEORGE BUTLER, sons of HUGH BUTLER live so long; & whereas HUGH

BUTLER built sundry houses on the land & made various improvements; & whereas by certain indentures dated 29 Apr. 1738 HUGH BUTLER as security for the payment of his debts with interest to JOHN COLLETON, ESQ., in trust for SIR JOHN COLLETON, conveys to JOHN COLLETON, ESQ., the 1500 a.; & whereas there is now due ₤ 2477:11:2 now BUTLER conveys to JOHN COLLETON, ESQ., in trust for SIR JOHN COLLETON, the 44 slaves & 1500 a. Witnesses: PETER COLLETON, HUGH BUTLER, JR. Memo: It is agreed that 300 a. is to be excepted. On 5 Nov. 1739 PETER COLLETON, ESQ. appeared before JOHN BRAITHWAITE, ESQ. ROBERT AUSTIN, Pub. Reg.

Book T, p. 297
3 Aug. 1739
Affidavit

MACAJAH PERRY, ESQ., Lord Mayor of City of London, certifies that THOMAS FODEN, gentleman, of Lincoln's Inn, Co. of Middlesex, testified to the truth of the matters contained in the affidavit annexed. FODEN deposes he saw JOHN HAMMERTON of SC, now in London, sign, seal & deliver the original indenture, of which the annexed is a copy, & that JOHN SWALE, the other witness, subscribed his name on the back.

Book T, p. 297
1 Aug. 1739
Agreement

JOHN HAMMERTON, ESQ., of SC now in London, & JOHN CARRUTHERS, gentleman, of Bromley Parish, Co. of Middlesex, Great Britain, make the following agreement: Whereas King GEORGE II by letters patent under the Great Seal of Great Britain bearing date Westminster 11 Feb. in 4th year of his reign granted EDWARD BERTIE, ESQ., & JOHN HAMMERTON the Office of Secretary & Register of his Province of SC to hold during their lives; & whereas BERTIE died & HAMMERTON became holder of the office for live; & whereas JOHN HAMMERTON owned by grants several parcels of land in SC & several Negroes, on 13 May 1738 for ₤ 400 money of Great Britain he conveyed to JOHN CARRUTHERS the letters patent & the offices of Secretary & Register of SC, for the term of HAMMERTON'S life, also several parcels of land & several Negroes, subject to the payment of ₤ 400 sterling with interest at the Courthouse in Charleston on 1 Feb. last past; & whereas on 18 Aug. 1738 JOHN HAMMERTON gave JOHN CARRUTHERS a bond in the penal sum of ₤ 400 money of Great Britain conditioned for the payment of ₤ 200 with interest on 1 Feb. & agreed that the mortgaged property should stand as security for the payment; & whereas on 10 Oct. 1738 HAMMERTON gave CARRUTHERS another bond of ₤ 50 sterling with interest on 1 Feb. & agreed that the mortgaged property should stand as security; & whereas HAMMERTON has paid CARRUTHERS all the interest on the various sums to date but the principal sums remain due; & whereas HAMMERTON & CARRUTHERS have agreed that HAMMERTON shall go to SC & execute the offices & out of the profits pay CARRUTHERS the yearly sum of ₤ 200 until the ₤ 655 with interest, & all sums expended by CARRUTHERS for insurance, etc., are repaid; now HAMMERTON agrees with CARRUTHERS that the foregoing agreements shall stand; & that should HAMMERTON fail to make his payments he will appoint such fit person to be his Dep. as CARRUTHERS shall nominate; & whereas HAMMERTON has authorized certain attorneys to confess a judgment for ₤ 1000 debt; now CARRUTHERS agrees not to sue HAMMERTON & when all the money is paid him he will acknowledge satisfaction on the record of judgment. Should HAMMERTON not sail for SC he shall appoint CARRUTHERS his deputy to execute the offices & remove JAMES MICHIE as deputy. Witnesses: JOHN SWALE, THOMAS FODEN. ROBERT AUSTIN, Pub. Reg.

Book T, p. 302
4 Aug. 1739
Mortgage

GEORGE CHICKEN to ALEXANDER NISBET, for ₤ 108 sterling of Great Britain, 94 a. in St. John's Parish, part of Colt Baw, conveyed by NISBET on 2 Aug. 1739, bounding of GEORGE CHICKEN, MR. CHEILDS, & ALEXANDER NISBETT. Witnesses: THOMAS AKIN, JONATHAN DRAKE. Before ANTHONY BONNEAU, J.P. ROBERT AUSTIN, Pub. Reg.

Book T, p. 304
15 & 16 Nov. 1739
L & R

THOMAS BOLTON, shopkeeper, & ELIZABETH his wife, of Charleston, to SAMUEL SMITH, butcher, of Charleston, for ₤ 800 currency, 500 a. purchased on 18 May last by BOLTON from JOHN HALE planter, of St. James Santee & ELIZABETH his wife, in Craven Co., bounding S on the creeks & marshes of Seawee Bay; NE on Tibwin Creek & CAPT. JOHN COLLINS; W on MARK SLOWMAN; NW on vacant land. Witnesses: WILLIAM SAXBY, ROBERT RAPER. Before ROBERT AUSTIN, J.P. & Pub. Reg.

Book T, p. 308　　　　　　　JOHN BASSNETT, planter, of Williamsburgh, SC
16 Nov. 1739　　　　　　　　this date gave bond to ROBERT PRINGLE, mer-
Bond & Mortgage　　　　　　chant, of Charleston, in the penal sum of
　　　　　　　　　　　　　　Ł 8000 SC money conditioned for payment of
Ł 4000 & interest on 1 Mar. next & for security conveys 400 a. in Wil-
liamsburgh Township, Craven Co., bounding SW on Black River; SE on RICH-
ARD HALL; NE & NW on vacant land. Witnesses: WILLIAM SMITH, WILLIAM
ALLEN. Before ROBERT AUSTIN, J.P. & Pub. Reg.

Book T, p. 309　　　　　　　ANTHONY BONNEAU, SR., planter, & JANE ELIZA-
13 Aug. 1739　　　　　　　　BETH, his wife, of Berkeley Co., to PETER BON-
Deed of Gift　　　　　　　　NEAU their son, for love & affection, 3 tracts
　　　　　　　　　　　　　　of land, or 1100 a. on SE side E branch of T
of Cooper River, bounding NW on said branch; SW on Lynch's Creek; NE on
JOHN CUMING (formerly JOHN BLAKE); SE on ABEL BOCHET & PHILIP COMBE, be-
ing the 1100 a. purchased from PETER ROBERT & MARY his wife; SUSANNAH
MARGARET LYNCH, widow: &, MARGARET LYNCH on 17 & 18 Dec. 1734. Witnesses:
SAMUEL WELLS, FLORIDE BONNEAU. Before FRANCIS LEJAU, J.P. ROBERT AUSTIN,
Pub. Reg.

Book T, p. 310　　　　　　　EZEKIEL COX, planter, of Amelia Township,
8 & 9 June 1738　　　　　　 Berkeley Co., to ALEXANDER TATE, victualer,
L & R　　　　　　　　　　　 for Ł 50 currency, 200 a. in Berkeley Co., on
　　　　　　　　　　　　　　Great Poplar Branch, on SE side Amelia Town-
ship, bounding on all sides on vacant land, granted by King GEORGE II on
12 Jan. 1737 by letters patent under the hand of the Hon. WILLIAM BULL to
EZEKIEL COX. Witnesses: JEROME LEBEUFF, WILLIAM BODDINGTON (shoemaker).
Before GEORGE HAIG, J.P. ROBERT AUSTIN, J.P.

Book T, p. 313　　　　　　　DAVID ALEXANDER, planter, to PATRICK POOR,
15 & 16 Aug. 1738　　　　　 planter, both of Granville Co., for Ł 400 cur-
L & R　　　　　　　　　　　 rency, 200 a. in Hilton Head, Granville Co.,
　　　　　　　　　　　　　　bounding N on COL. BARNWELL; W on Sculls Creek;
E & S on ALEXANDER TRENCH. Whereas his Excellency, JOHN, Earl of Bath, &
the Lords Proprs. on 16 Aug. 1698 by letters patent created JOHN BAYLY of
Ballinaclough, Co. of Tipperary, Ireland, a Landgrave, granting him
48,000 a. in SC, & whereas JOHN BAYLY, son & heir, on 9 Nov. 1722 appointed ALEXANDER TRENCH his attorney with authority to set aside 8000 a. for
the use of JOHN BAYLY & dispose of the rest; & whereas ALEXANDER TRENCH,
as attorney, on 5 Jan. 1725 sold a portion of the land to DAVID ALEXANDER;
now ALEXANDER sells 200 a. (part of a tract of 300 a.) to PATRICK POOR.
Witnesses: BENJAMIN CALIS, HILLDERSON WIGG, ROBERT BRISBANE. Before RICH-
ARD WOODWARD, J.P. ROBERT AUSTIN, Pub. Reg.

Book T, p. 318　　　　　　　JOHN JENKINS, SR., planter, of St. John's Par-
17 Jan. 1735　　　　　　　　ish, Colleton Co., to his son WILLIAM JENKINS,
Deed of Sale　　　　　　　　planter, of same Parish, for Ł 500, 200 a.
　　　　　　　　　　　　　　(bounding E on JOHN FRAINTON, planter), after
his death; 50 a. of said land, together with the dwelling house, gardens,
orchards, etc., for the use of his beloved wife ELIZABETH JENKINS during
her widowhood, & after her death to son WILLIAM, he paying the other
children, JOSEPH, CHRISTOPHER, RICHARD, THOMAS, ELIZABETH, BENJAMIN, &
CHARLES JENKINS, as they come of age, their equal parts of the Ł 500 with
interest. Should any die before reaching 21, their share to be equally
divided. Witnesses: JOHN JENKINS, JR., JAMES CLARK. Before ROBERT YONGE,
J.P. ROBERT AUSTIN, Pub. Reg.

Book T, p. 318　　　　　　　ISAAC DUMONS, planter, to CAPT. PETER ROBERT,
1 Dec. 1738　　　　　　　　 planter, both of Craven Co., for Ł 400 SC mon-
Mortgage　　　　　　　　　　ey, 2 tracts of 150 a., being 30 a. & 120 a.;
　　　　　　　　　　　　　　at head of Itchaw Creek, Craven Co., purchased
from PETER ROBERT, as security for the payment of bond dated 12 Nov. 1737
for Ł 400. Witnesses: ABRAHAM SATUR, PETER SCHULT, WILLIAM MCALLA. Before JAMES KINLOCK, J.P. ROBERT AUSTIN, Pub. Reg.

Book T, p. 320　　　　　　　PAUL BRUNEAU, with the consent of his wife
4 Sept. 1736　　　　　　　　ELIZABETH, to ANDREW REMBERT, all of St. James
Deed of Sale　　　　　　　　Santee, Craven Co., for Ł 900 SC money, 486 a.,
　　　　　　　　　　　　　　English measure, bounding SE on Wambaw Creek;
E on PETER DE ST. JULIEN; N on ABRAHAM PERDRIAU; W & S on PAUL BRUNEAU;

being part of 900 a. granted 27 Nov. 1735 & bounding SE on Wambaw Creek; E on PETER DE ST. JULIEN; N on ABRAHAM PERDRIAU; S on PAUL MAZYCK; W on vacant land. Witnesses: ISAAC LEGRAND, PETER SCHULT, ALEXANDER CHOVEN, DAVID COULET. Before HENRY GIBBES, J.P. ROBERT AUSTIN, Pub. Reg.

Book T, p. 323
11 Oct. 1735
Deed of Sale

THOMAS CHARNOCK, shopkeeper, to GEORGE HUNTER, surveyor, both of Charleston, for ₤ 200 SC money, 450 a. on SW side Peedee River, Craven Co., purchased from WILLIAM LEANDER, peruke maker, bounding N on ABRAHAM STAPLES, planter; E on THOMAS MORRETT, clerk. Witnesses: WILLIAM MCKENSIE, PETER LANE. Before WILLIAM TREWIN, J.P. ROBERT AUSTIN, Pub. Reg.

Book T, p. 324
26 Mar. 1739
Deed of Sale

JOSEPH HOLDER, yeoman, to JOHN ESHFIELD, yeoman, both of Kingstown, SC, for ₤ 15 SC money, the house & lot #134 in Kingstown. Witnesses: HUGH CAMPBELL, NATHANIEL FORD. Before HENRY GIBBES, J.P. ROBERT AUSTIN, Pub. Reg.

Book T, p. 325
14 & 15 Nov. 1739
L & R by Mortgage

JAMES STEWART of Craven Co., to WILLIAM ROMSEY & PAUL TRAPIER, merchants, of Georgetown, as security for the payment of a bond this date in penal sum of ₤ 2150:10:2-1/2 SC money conditioned for the payment of ₤ 1079:15:1 forthing: on 1 Jan. 1739; 800 a. in Craven Co., bounding N on JAMES STEWART; W on JOHN MUSGROVE; S on Georgetown River; E on Turkey Creek. Witnesses: JOHN SKRINE, PETER DUBOURDIEU. Before WILLIAM WHITESIDE, J.P. ROBERT AUSTIN, Pub. Reg.

Book T, p. 328
24 & 25 July 1738
L & R

PHILIP (his mark) CHANDLER, cooper, & SARAH (her mark) his wife, of Craven Co., to WILLIAM CRIPPS, surgeon, of Georgetown, for ₤ 500 SC money, 250 a. in Craven Co., granted to CHANDLER on 13 July, 1733, witnessed by the Hon. THOMAS BROUGHTON, Lt. Gov. bounding S on Greens Creek; E & N on Black River; W & S on WILLIAM HINKLEY. Before JAMES CRADDOCK, JOHN WHETFELD. Before THOMAS LAROCHE, J.P. ROBERT AUSTIN, Pub. Reg.

Book T, p. 331
1 & 2 Jan. 1738
L & R

THOMAS LAROCHE, ESQ., to JOHN OULDFIELD, gentleman, both of Prince George Parish, Craven Co., for ₤ 5 SC money, 79 a., part of 1000 a. purchased from WILLIAM DRAKE, bounding E on Peedee River; N on JOHN OULDFIELD; S on THOMAS LAROCHE; also 28 a., part of 300 a. purchased from WILLIAM SWINTON; bounding W on Peedee River; S on THOMAS ROCHE; N & E on Squirrel Creek. Witnesses: DANIEL LAROCHE, JUDITH LEWIS. Before WILLIAM WHITESIDE, J.P. ROBERT AUSTIN, Pub. Reg.

Book T, p. 334
16 & 17 Aug. 1738
L & R

JOHN BULL & MARY his wife, of St. Pauls Parish, to STEPHEN BULL, son of BARNABY BULL, planter, of Granville Co., for ₤ 1000 SC money, 500 a. in Granville Co., bounding N on BARNABY BULL; E on Pocotaligo River; S on ARTHUR MIDDLETON; W on JAMES ST. JOHN. Witnesses: ROBERT COOPER, JAMES FREEMAN. Before ROBERT YONGE, J.P. ROBERT AUSTIN, Pub. Reg.

Book T, p. 337
16 & 17 Aug. 1738
L & R

JOHN BULL & MARY his wife, of St. Pauls Parish, to STEPHEN BULL, son of BARNABY BULL, planter, of Granville Co., for ₤ 1000 SC money, 500 a. in Granville Co., bounding N on JOHN BULL; E on Pocotaligo River; S on CAPT. ANTHONY MATHEWS; W on JAMES ST. JOHN. Witnesses: ROBERT COOPER, JAMES FREEMAN. Before ROBERT YONGE, J.P. ROBERT AUSTIN, Pub. Reg.

Book T, p. 340
22 & 23 Dec. 1738
L & R

WILLIAM ANDREE, planter, of Craven Co., to DANIEL LAROCHE & THOMAS LAROCHE, merchants, of Georgetown, for ₤ 250 SC money, 500 a. in Queensborough Township, Craven Co., bounding NW on ALEXANDER STEWART; SE on DAVID MCCLELLAN; SW on vacant land; NE on Peedee River. Whereas by letters patent dated at Charleston 12 Nov. 1736 & attested by the Hon. THOMAS BROUGHTON, Lt. Gov. his Majesty granted GEORGE ANDREE 500 a.; & whereas ANDREE died intestate & his eldest son

WILLIAM became heir, now WILLIAM sells to the LAROCHES. Witnesses: JOHN OULDFIELD, JOHN OULDFIELD, JR. Before WILLIAM WHITESIDE, J.P. ROBERT AUSTIN, Pub. Reg.

Book T, p. 344
29 & 30 June 1739
L & R by Mortgage

JACOB BUCKHOLTS, planter, to DANIEL LAROCHE & THOMAS LAROCHE, merchants, of Craven Co., as security on bond of this date in penal sum of L 1044 SC money, conditioned for the payment of L 522 with interest on 1 Jan. 1739, 250 a. in Queensborough Township, Craven Co., bounding NE on Peedee River; NW & SW on vacant land; SE on JACOB BUCKHOLTS; also 300 a. in same Township, bounding NE on Peedee River; NW on JACOB BUCKHOLTS; SW on vacant land; SE on SAMUEL BROWN. Witnesses: JOHN OULDFIELD, JR., JAMES CRADDOCK. Before WILLIAM WHITESIDE, J.P. ROBERT AUSTIN, Pub. Reg.

Book T, p. 348
19 & 20 July 1739
L & R by Mortgage

EBENEZER (his mark) SINGLETON, planter, of Craven Co., to DANIEL LAROCHE & THOMAS LAROCHE, merchants, of Georgetown, as security on bond dated 1 Dec. 1734 in penal sum of L 1256:4 SC money, conditioned for the payment of L 628:2 on 1 Dec. 1735; & on another bond dated 1 Feb. 1738 in penal sum of L 173:18 conditioned for the payment of L 86:19 on 1 Mar. 1738 with interest; 375 a. in Craven Co., bounding on S side of Waccamaw River; E on EBENEZER SINGLETON; N on said River; W on vacant land; also 375 a. in Craven Co., bounding on S side Waccamaw River; E on WILLIAM CRIPPS; N on the River; W on EBENEZER SINGLETON. Witnesses: PAUL LEPAIR, JAMES CRADDOCK. Before WILLIAM WHITESIDE, J.P. ROBERT AUSTIN, Pub. Reg.

Book T, p. 352
25 & 26 Nov. 1739
L & R by Mortgage

JOHN GODWIN, cordwainer, & MARTHA (her mark), his wife, to DANIEL LAROCHE & THOMAS LAROCHE, merchants, all of Craven Co., as security for payment of L 1302:10 SC money with interest on 1 Mar. 1739; 500 a. in Queensborough Township, Craven Co., bounding SE on JAMES GORDON; SW on vacant land; NW on DANIEL & THOMAS LAROCHE; NE on Peedee River. Witnesses: JAMES (his mark) KENNIGAIN, MARY ALLEIN. Before JOHN WALLIS, J.P. ROBERT AUSTIN, Pub. Reg.

Book T, p. 356
27 Mar. 1738
Confirmation of Title

RICHARD CAPERS, gentleman, to JAMES WHITE & SARAH his wife who was daughter & co-heir of JOHN SIMES, all of Christ Church Parish. Whereas WILLIAM CAPERS, father of RICHARD CAPERS, owned 1700 a. at the head of Wando River at a place called Lebanon & agreed to sell part, or 500 a., to JOHN SIMES, & JOHN SIMES paid WILLIAM CAPERS a valuable consideration & the 500 a. was surveyed & SIME'S right to the land was never contradicted by WILLIAM CAPERS; whereas the 500 a. has been held by SARAH, daughter of JOHN SIMES & WIFE of JAMES WHITE, but no conveyance or record of conveyance can be found; & whereas RICHARD CAPERS, uncle of SARAH WHITE, wished to remove all doubt of her title now, for natural love & affection & other causes, he releases 500 a. to SARAH WHITE according to plat drawn by WILLIAM WINDERAP, surveyor, 31 Mar. 1725. Witnesses: GEORGE OLIVER, MARY BOONE. Before ANDREW RUTLEDGE, J.P. ROBERT AUSTIN, Pub. Reg.

Book T, p. 358
18 & 19 Dec. 1739
L & R

BENJAMIN ROBERTS, cordwinder, & MARY his wife, to SAMUEL SMITH, carpenter, all of Charleston, for L 550 currency, part of lot #222 in Charleston, on Charleston Green, fronting E 35 ft. on King Street; S 140 ft. on BENJAMIN ROBERTS (formerly WILLIAM DEXTER); W on WIDOW HOLME'S garden; N on JOHN DANIEL; with the dwelling house & buildings. Witnesses: DAVID BURNEY, ANNA MIDDLETON, ANN DEXTER, WILLIAM SMITH. Before ROBERT AUSTIN, J.P. & Pub. Reg.

Book T, p. 361
27 & 28 June 1739
L & R

DAVID FAUCCUNET, planter, & JUDITH (her mark) his wife, to HUGH ROSE, dep. surveyor, all of Purysburgh, Granville Co., for L 96 SC money, 250 a. in Purysburgh, by letters patent signed by the Hon. WILLIAM BULL, Lt. Gov. granted on 11 May 1739 to DAVID FAUCOUNET & recorded in Secretary's Book DD p. 337 bounding N & E on DANIEL VERNEROBRE; S on vacant land; W on the back river of Savannah River. Witnesses: PETER EMERY, THOMAS GANTLETT. Before JAMES MICHIE, J.P. ROBERT

AUSTIN, Pub. Reg.

Book T, p. 366 THOMAS WARING, SR., to his son THOMAS WARING,
2 May 1739 planter, of St. George Parish, Berkeley Co.,
Deed of Gift for love & affection, 12 slaves & 1/4 a. lot
#6 in Dorchester Town. Witnesses: RICHARD
WARING, ANDREW SLANN, JOSIAH WARING. Before MAL. GLAZE, J.P. ROBERT
AUSTIN, Pub. Reg.

Book T, p. 366 HERMAN CHRISTIAN DETRING (DUTERING), planter,
9 Apr. 1739 & ANNA MARIA his wife, to HERMAN GEEGER, plant-
Deed of Sale er all of Saxegotha Township, for L 50 currency, 50 a. in Berkeley Co., bounding N on DUT-
RING; NE on Santee River; S on JACOB HAGENBUCH. Witnesses: CONRAD (his
mark) KUNSTER, DOROTHEA (her mark) KUNSTER. Before CHRISTIAN MOTTE, J.P.
ROBERT AUSTIN, Pub. Reg.

Book T, p. 368 PETER LANE, planter, only son & heir of JOHN
16 & 17 Jan. 1739 LANE, planter, of Craven Co., to THOMAS HEN-
L & R NING, merchant, of Charleston, for L 500 SC
money, 570 a. in Craven Co., bounding on N
side, Sampit Creek; S on MR. BRETTON & MR. RAY; N on MR. GOFFE; E on AN-
THONY WHITE; W on MR. LAROCHE; which land was granted under the hand of
the Hon. ROBERT JOHNSON on 23 May 1734 to JOHN LANE & inherited by PETER
LANE, only son & heir of JOHN. SARAH LANE, wife of PETER, to renounce
her dower within 6 months. Witnesses: SARAH JEANES, JOHN BARKSDALE. Before ROBERT AUSTIN, J.P. & Pub. Reg.

Book T, p. 372 WILLIAM WHITESIDE, gentleman, to JOHN BROWN,
4 & 5 May 1736 planter, both of Craven Co., for L 28 SC money,
L & R 500 a. in Craven Co., granted by the Hon. THOM-
AS BROUGHTON, Lt. Gov., on 4 Dec. 1735, to
WILLIAM WHITESIDE, bounding on N side of N branch of Black River; NW & E
on vacant land; S on WILLIAM SWINTON. Witnesses: WILLIAM COLT, THOMAS
LEITH. Before THOMAS LAROCHE, J.P. ROBERT AUSTIN, Pub. Reg.

Book T, p. 375 ALEXANDER TRENCH, merchant, of Charleston, as
5 & 6 Nov. 1731 attorney for JOHN BAYLY, to JOHN BROWN, eldest
L & R son of JAMES BROWN, of Prince George Parish,
Craven Co., planter, for L 162:10 SC money,
650 a. in Prince George Parish, bounding N on RALPH JERMAN; S on N branch
of Black River; S S E on MARY KELLY. Whereas the Rt. Hon. JOHN, Earl of
Bath, & the Lords Proprs. by letters patent on 16 Aug. 1698, created JOHN
BAYLY of Balliaclough, Co. of Tipperary, Ireland, a Landgrave & Cassique,
granting him 48,000 a. in SC; & whereas JOHN BAYLY, son & heir of JOHN
BAYLY, on 19 Nov. 1722, appointed ALEXANDER TRENCH of Charleston his attorney with authority to reserve 8000 a. for the use of JOHN BAYLY & dispose of the rest; now TRENCH sells 650 a. to BROWN. Witnesses: WILLIAM
YEOMANS, WILLIAM SMITH. Before ROBERT AUSTIN, J.P. & Pub. Reg. Plat
dated 20 Nov. 1731 surveyed by WILLIAM SWINTON, D.S.

Book T, p. 380 JOHN SAMMS, planter, to son JAMES MITCHELL, &
21 Apr. 1734 MARTHA his wife, of Edisto Island, for natural
Deed of Gift affection, fatherly love & other causes, 100 a.
on Edisto Island, bounding N & W on ICHABOD
WYNBOURN; E on PAUL GRIMBALL; S on JOHN SAMMS. Signed by JOHN, SAM &
HANNAH (her mark) SAMMS, CHARLES ODINGSELLS, ARCHIBALD CALDER, PAUL GRIM-
BALL, RICHARD COLWALL. Before ROBERT AUSTIN, J.P. & Pub. Reg.

Book T, p. 381 DAVID CRAWFORD, merchant, of SC, second son of
? 1737 WILLIAM CRAWFORD of Scotland, to DANIEL CRAW-
Deed of Sale FORD, for L 66:13:4 sterling 1200 Scots marks
to be paid out of the tenement, close & waste
ground. Whereas WILLIAM CRAWFORD by a deed subscribed at Glasgow, by
CHARLES HOLMES, writer, on 25 Mar. 1734 before ROBERT LOGAN, merchant, in
Glasgow & CHARLES HOLMES, as witnesses, & signed WILLIAM CRAWFORD, SR.;
ROBERT LOGAN, witness, CHARLES HOLMES, witness; for the provision & advancement of children, & other considerations, & in payment of 1200 marks
Scots money due to DANIEL CRAWFORD to make his share equal the shares of
the other children, & L 100 sterling more than any of them according to

the terms of a contract of marriage; & in payment of 1200 marks Scots yet due DAVID CRAWFORD, his 2nd son, to make his share equal to the provisions made to JOHN, MARY, CHRISTIAN & HELEN CRAWFORD, & in order that the remainder of the price of the lands should they be sold, might be equally divided amongst DANIEL, DAVID, MARY, CHRISTIAN, & HELEN CRAWFORD, his children, & JOHN BUCHANAN & LAWRENCE DUNWOODIE (husbands of MARY & CHRISTIAN) for their respective interests. (DANIEL CRAWFORD drawing & receiving L 100 sterling more than the others); WILLIAM CRAWFORD gave to DANIEL, DAVID, JOHN, MARY, CHRISTIAN, & HELEN CRAWFORD, & to JOHN BUCHANAN & LAWRENCE DUNWOODIE, equally, all his land with the waste ground at the back, lying in the Burgh of Glasgow, on E side of High Street leading from the "Marcait Cross" to the High Church; bounded N on JOHN FALCONER; E on RICHARD ALLEN; S on the Black Fryar Wind; W by the High Street. Witnesses: JOHN RATTRAY, JAMES VARNOR. Before JACOB MOTTE, J.P. ROBERT AUSTIN, Pub. Reg.

Book T, p. 383
2 & 3 Aug. 1739
L & R

LAURENCE NEILL, clerk, of the Parish of St. Mary Rotherhithe, Surrey Co., England (devisee of ANN GIBSON, widow of DANIEL GIBSON, surgeon, of SC by ANDREW RUTLEDGE, gentleman, attorney duly appointed by LAURENCE NEILL; to THOMAS HENNING, ESQ., of Charleston; for L 300 SC money, 13 a. lately belonging to ANN GIBSON, being the residue of 18 a. formerly belonging to DANIEL GIBSON, surgeon; part of which now belongs to THOMAS MONCK, ESQ., near the Broad Path, about a mile or more from Charleston. Whereas DANIEL GIBSON, husband of ANN, owned 18 a. partly on the E side & partly on the W side of the Broad Path, about a mile from Charleston, & for natural love & affection for his wife, by L & R, 5 & 6 May 1735 conveyed the 18 a. to THOMAS BOLTON, merchant, of Charleston, in trust for ANN for her lifetime, then to her heirs; & whereas ANN, with the consent of DANIEL & of THOMAS BOLTON, conveyed 5 a. to THOMAS MONCK (being the part on the E side of the Broad Path); & whereas ANN survived her husband, & by will at London bequeathed her plantation in SC to the Rev. MR. LAURENCE NEILL; now NEILL sells 13 a. to HENNING. Witnesses: ADAM MCDONALD, WILLIAM HARVEY. Before ROBERT AUSTIN, J.P. & Pub. Reg.

Book T, p. 388
8 & 9 May 1739
L & R

DANIEL HUGER, ESQ., of Berkeley Co., DANIEL HORRY & ELIAS HORRY of Craven Co., executors of will of ELIAS HORRY, SR., to ANTHONY BONNEAU, JR., planter, of Berkeley Co., for L 500 SC money, 500 a. in Craven Co., bounding N & W on DANIEL HORRY; S on ELIAS HORRY & vacant land; E on CAPT. JOHN VANDERHORST & vacant land. Whereas the Rt. Hon. SIR NATHANIEL JOHNSON, Gov., on 1 June 1709 for L 10 granted ELIAS HORRY, SR. 500 a. in Craven Co. (recorded in Secretary's Book F page 201); & whereas by will dated 19 Sept. 1736 HORRY devised all his real estate (except 750 a.) to his executors (DANIEL HUGHER, & his 2 sons DANIEL HORRY & ELIAS HORRY) in trust, to sell the land to such of his children as should be the highest bidders & to no one else, & to divide the money equally amongst his children (DANIEL, ELIAS, JOHN, PETER, MARGUERITE HENRIETTE, & MAGDELIN); & whereas ANTHONY BONNEAU married MARGUERITE-HENRIETTE; now the executors sell BONNEAU 500 a. of the estate. Witnesses: JOHN GENDRON, JOHN HENTIE, FRANCIS ROCHE. Before FRANCIS LEJAU, J.P. ROBERT AUSTIN, Pub. Reg.

Book T, p. 393
26 Jan. 1739
Mortgage

SARAH GLASER, widow, of Charleston, to JOHN BRAND, gentleman, as security on bond this date in penal sum of L 600 currency conditioned for payment of L 300 with interest on 26 Jan. 1742, conveys part of lot #121 in Charleston fronting N 25 ft. on Broad Street, & bounding E 104 ft. on JOHN MARTINS; S on an alley. Witnesses: JAMES DRUMMOND, JAMES LOURY. Before ROBERT AUSTIN, J.P. & Pub. Reg.

Book T, p. 394
16 & 17 Mar. 1737
L & R

THOMAS HEPWORTH, gentleman, to WILLIAM ALSTON, gentleman, for L 1840 currency, 420 a. on the seaside near Winyaw River, Craven Co., bounding on 28 June 1711 (date of original grant) E on the sea shore; S on DR. JOHN HUTCHINSON; N on CAPT. CROFT; also 500 a. on Winyaw River bounding (28 June 1711) E on the sea; N on CAPT. CROFT; W on Waccamaw Branch. Witnesses: W. POOLE, PAUL TRAPIER, MAURICE

LEWIS, JOHN RATTRAY. Before ROBERT AUSTIN, J.P. & Pub. Reg. On 31 Dec. 1753 FRANCIS MCCASTEN, partner with MARTIN CAMPBELL, executors of JOHN LYCOTT who married the daughter of JOHN BRAND, & 1 of his executors, declared this mortgage satisfied by SARAH JOHNSTON, widow of JOHN JOHNSTON, formerly SARAH GLASER the mortgagor. Witness: PETER MONCLAR.

Book T, p. 399
20 Dec. 1722
Deed of Sale

JOSEPH WRIGHT & MARY (her mark) his wife, of Colleton Co., to ELIZABETH IRELAND, for ₤ 55 currency, 50 a. on Wadmalaw Island, bounding S & W on Fishing Creek; a branch of Bohicket Creek; N on back part of creek; E & NE on JOHN HICKS. Witnesses: EDMOND JERVIS, MARY JERVIS, THOMAS WENBORN, MARY WENBORN. MARY JERVIS, wife of EDMOND JERVIS later married a HUTCHINSON. Before THEOPHILUS GREGORY, J.P. ROBERT AUSTIN, Pub. Reg.

Book T, p. 401
29 & 30 Mar. 1737
L & R

REBECCA (her mark) BROUMHEAD, widow of & attorney for ROBERT BROUMHEAD, cabinet maker, to JOSEPH CHAMLETT, mariner, both of Charleston, for ₤ 150 SC money, 50 a. on Wadmalaw Island, Colleton Co., bounding S on Fishing Creek, a branch of Bohicket Creek; N on back part said creek; NE E & SE on JOHN HICK. Witnesses: MARY ELLIS, WILLIAM SMITH. Before ROBERT AUSTIN, J.P. & Pub. Reg.

Book T, p. 404
1 & 2 Jan. 1733
L & R

JOSEPH BACON, planter, to JERMYN WRIGHT, gentleman, both of Berkeley Co., for ₤ 500 SC money, 80 a., part of Ashley Barony or St. Giles, bounding NW on Ashley River & THOMAS BAKER; SW on JOSIAH OSGOOD; SE on ROBERT WRIGHT & Ashley River. Witnesses: SUSANNA WRIGHT, JAMES WRIGHT. Before ROBERT WRIGHT, J.P. ROBERT AUSTIN, Pub. Reg.

Book T, p. 407
23 & 24 Dec. 1736
L & R

ANNE HARGRAVE, widow, of Charleston, to JERMYN WRIGHT, gentleman, of Berkeley Co., for ₤ 350 SC money, 500 a. in Granville Co., bounding NW on public land; NE on Combahee River; SE on WILLIAM MCPHERSON; SW on vacant land; which 500 a. were granted to ANNE HARGRAVE by Gov. ROBERT JOHNSON on 8 Apr. 1733. Witnesses: GEORGE HUNTER, WILLIAM GUY, JR. Before I. HAMMERTON, J.P. ROBERT AUSTIN, Pub. Reg.

Book T, p. 411
2 & 3 July 1739
L & R

HUGH SWINTON, planter, to JOHN JOHNSTON & WILLIAM FLEMING, merchants, all of Craven Co., for ₤ 500 currency, 306 a. in Craven Co., bounding SW on Peedee River; NW on HUGH SWINTON; SE on JOHN SNOW. Witnesses: WILLIAM LAING, JOHN MCMECHAN. Before THOMAS LAROCHE, J.P. ROBERT AUSTIN, Pub. Reg.

Book T, p. 414
5 July 1739
L & R by Mortgage

ROBERT BROWN, to WILLIAM POOLE, planter, both of Craven Co., as security for payment of bond of this date in the penal sum of ₤ 6400 currency conditioned for the payment of ₤ 3200 with interest on 1 Feb. 1739, 640 a. in Craven Co., bounding E on saltwater marsh; W on Waccamaw River; S on WILLIAM ALLSTON; N on WILLIAM ALLSTON & COL. WILLIAM WATIES. Witnesses: PAUL TRAPIER, THOMAS THREADCRAFT. Before WILLIAM WHITESIDE, J.P. ROBERT AUSTIN, Pub. Reg.

Book T, p. 417
15 & 16 June 1739
L & R by Mortgage

JOHN GUERY (GUERRY), planter, to ABRAHAM SATUR, ESQ., both of St. James Santee, Craven Co., for ₤ 900 SC money, (payable with interest as follows: ₤ 300 on 1 Mar. 1739 without interest; ₤ 300 on 1 Mar. 1740 with interest for 1 yr.; ₤ 300 with interest for 2 yrs. on 1 Mar. 1741) 460 a., on Itchaw Swamp, Craven Co., bounding NE & SE on ABRAHAM SATUR; NW on ISAAC LEGRAND; SW on PETER ROBERT. Whereas Gob. ROBERT JOHNSON granted PETER ROBERT, ESQ., 1070 a. on Itchaw Swamp, Craven Co., & whereas PETER ROBERT & MARY his wife on 9 & 10 Nov. 1736 sold 460 a., part of the 1070 a. to ABRAHAM SATUR; & whereas ABRAHAM SATUR & JANE his wife on 13 & 14 June 1739 sold the 460 a. to JOHN GUERY; now GUERY gives SATUR a mortgage & a bond in the penal sum of ₤ 1800. Witnesses: WILLIAM THOMAS, ISAAC LEGRAND. Before JOHN GENDRON, J.P. ROBERT AUSTIN, Pub. Reg.

Book T, p. 421
8 June 1739
L & R
JOSEPH (his mark) BIRMONT, planter, & SUSANNAH (her mark), his wife, to JOHN THOMSON, planter, all of Craven Co., for Ł 350 SC money, 250 a. in Craven Co., bounding SE on land laid out; W on MR. LEGARE; NW on DR. ROBERT BROWN; NE on DANEIL HORRY. Witnesses: RALPH JERMAN, JOHN FITCH, MOSES SCUDDER. Before NOAH SERRÉ, J.P., of St. James Santee. ROBERT AUSTIN, Pub. Reg.

Book T, p. 425
18 & 19 July 1739
L & R by Mortgage
WILLIAM LEWIS, planter, to JAMES LESESNE, planter, both of Craven Co., as security on bond of this date in penal sum of Ł 800 conditioned for the payment of Ł 400 currency on 1 Jan. 1740, 500 a. in Craven Co., bounding S on RICHARD SMITH; N on ROBERT DANIEL; E & W on vacant land; also 200 a. bounding N & S on vacant land; W on ISAAC LESESNE; E on land laid out. Witnesses: JOHN DUNNAM, JEREMIAH CUTTINO, JAMES CRADDOCK. Before THOMAS LAROCHE, J.P. ROBERT AUSTIN, Pub. Reg.

Book T, p. 428
22 & 23 Aug. 1739
L & R
PETER LANE, & SARAH his wife, to PETER JOHNSON, all of Prince Frederick Parish, Craven Co., for Ł 350 currency, 520 a. in Craven Co., bounding NE on JAMES JOHNSON; NW on JOHN ABBOTT; S on HENRY LEWIS; W & E on vacant land. Witnesses: WILLIAM BARTON, JOHN BARTON, JAMES LANE. Before JACOB BOND, J.P. ROBERT AUSTIN, Pub. Reg.

Book T, P. 433
22 & 23 Jan. 1739
L & R
JAMES MOORE, JOHN MOORE, & JEHU MOORE, of St. James Goose Creek (sons & devisees of the Hon. COL. JAMES MOORE, ESQ.), & ELIZABETH MOORE (widow & devisee of JAMES MOORE the elder) to SARAH MIDDLETON, widow of the Hon. ARTHUR MIDDLETON, for Ł 4300 SC money, 900 a. Whereas JAMES MOORE, the father, owned 900 a. in St. James Goose Creek, bounding SE on BENJAMIN SMITH; SW on WILLIAM MCKENZIE; W on JOHN LOYD, ESQ.; & NW on ROBERT HUME, ESQ. & by will dated 16 Apr. 1722 gave his son JAMES 300 a. on which JAMES lived & to son JOHN 300 a. on which JOHN lived, & to son JEHU the 300 a. on which he lived, & bequeathed to his wife ELIZABETH for the term of her life 1 room in the dwelling house in which he lived on the 900 a.; now the sons & widow sell the 900 a. to SARAH MIDDLETON. Witnesses: BENJAMIN GODIN, JAMES GORDON, THOMAS MIDDLETON. Before RALPH IZARD, J.P. At request of CAPT. JAMES MOORE on 21 Feb. 1737 NATHANIEL DEAN, Dep. Sur., measured the land & found it to be 927 a. ROBERT AUSTIN, Pub. Reg.

Book T, p. 438
14 & 15 Jan. 1739
L & R
RICHARD LAKE, ESQ., of Lake Farm, St. Andrews Parish, Berkeley Co., & WILLIAM HARE, merchant, of Charleston, as attornies for THOMAS CHEESMAN, ESQ., formerly of St. James Goose Creek but now of the Island of Barbadoes, to THOMAS MIDDLETON, gentleman, of St. James Goose Creek, for Ł 2500 SC money, 340 a. called How Hall, & 305 a. called Pine Lane, in St. James Goosecreek, free of the dower of ELIZABETH, wife of THOMAS CHEESMAN. Whereas THOMAS CHEESMAN on 15 Feb. 1738, & also on this date, owned 340 a. in St. James Goose Creek called How Hall, bounding N on ARTHUR MIDDLETON (formerly Boochaw); NE on PAUL MAZYCK; E on Fosters Creek; S on CHARLES PINCKNEY & ARTHUR MIDDLETON; W on ARTHUR MIDDLETON; also 305 a. in St. James Goose Creek, called Pine Land, bounding S & SW on PAUL MAZYCK; SE on COL. ALEXANDER PARRIS, & on all other sides on SABINA SMITH & THOMAS TAYLOR; & whereas on 15 Feb. 1738 THOMAS CHEESEMAN appointed RICHARD LAKE & WILLIAM HARE his attorneys with authority to sell all CHEESMAN'S lands, goods, & chattles; now LAKE & HARE sell the 2 tracts to THOMAS MIDDLETON. Witnesses: TIMOTHY MILLECHAMP, JAMES GORDON, MRS. JANE MILLECHAMP. Before RALPH IZARD, J.P. ROBERT AUSTIN, Pub. Reg.

Book T, p. 443
15 Feb. 1738
Letter of Attorney
THOMAS CHEESMAN, ESQ., of St. James Goose Creek appointed his brother-in-law RICHARD LAKE & his nephew WILLIAM HARE his attorneys to handle his estate. Witnesses: GABRIEL ESCOTT, WILLIAM TREWIN. Before THOMAS LAMBOLL, J.P. Recorded 4 Jan. 1739 in Secretary's book O.O. page 164 by JAMES MICHIE. ROBERT AUSTIN, Pub. Reg.

Book T, p. 444　　　　　　　JOHN GREENE, planter, & PHEBE his wife, to
1 & 2 Mar. 1738　　　　　　JOHN DRAYTON, planter, all of St. Andrews Par-
L & R　　　　　　　　　　　ish, for L 3500 SC money, 350 a., bounding NE
　　　　　　　　　　　　　　on Ashley River; NW on THOMAS DRAYTON; SW on
ROBERT LADSON; SE on JAMES STANYARN. Whereas the Lords Proprs. on 2 Apr. 1718 granted ALEXANDER SKENE 750 a. on S side Ashley River, bounding NW on THOMAS DRAYTON & SAMUEL PAGE; SE on JAMES STANYARN; & whereas ALEXANDER SKENE & JEMIMA his wife on 17 June 1718 sold (part of ?) the land to FRANCIS YONGE; & whereas FRANCIS YONGE & LYDIA his wife, through their attorney, on 9 Oct. 1734 sold 350 a. to JORDAN ROCHE; & whereas JORDAN ROCHE & REBECCA his wife on 19 Oct. 1737 sold the 350 a. to JOHN GREENE; now GREENE sells to DRAYTON. Witnesses: JOHN DRAYTON, SR., MARY (her mark) DRISDROW. Before ROBERT AUSTIN, J.P. & Pub. Reg.

Book T, p. 448　　　　　　　VINCENT GUERIN, planter, of Berkeley Co., to
1 May 1736　　　　　　　　　son JOHN GUERIN, for love & affection, 400 a.
Deed of Gift　　　　　　　　in Berkeley Co., the northern part of 1050 a.
　　　　　　　　　　　　　　called Bull Head, adjoining the land of CAPT.
MICHAEL DARBY. Witnesses: ROBERT HOW, ELIZABETH HOW. Possession & delivery of a silver spoon. Before PETER PAGETT, J.P. ROBERT AUSTIN, Pub. Reg.

Book T, p. 449　　　　　　　THOMAS HENNING, merchant, of Charleston, to
19 & 20 June 1739　　　　　ROBERT THORPE, ESQ., of Granville Co., for
L & R　　　　　　　　　　　L 2003:9:10 SC money, 1/2 of 2052 a. (1026 a.)
　　　　　　　　　　　　　　bounding N on Combahee River; S on ROBERT
STEELE, the Hon. WILLIAM BULL & THOMAS LOWNDES. Part of the 2052 a. (i.e. 550 a.) was granted to JOSEPH BRYAN on 12 Jan. 1705. The other part (1497 a.) was granted to COL. JOSEPH BLAKE on 22 Sept. 1733. Whereas on 10 Jan. 1737 JOHN MULRYNE mortgaged 1/2 the above 2052 a. to THOMAS HENNING for the above amount, payable with interest on 1 May 1737, now HENNING conveys the half part to THORPE subject to the above mortgage. Witnesses: JOHN JOHNSON, JR., JOHN RATTRAY. Before ROBERT AUSTIN, J.P. & Pub. Reg.

Book T, p. 453　　　　　　　ESTHER ELLIOTT, widow of WILLIAM ELLIOTT, SR.,
12 July 1732　　　　　　　　of Charleston, to her son-in-law DANIEL CART-
Deed of Sale　　　　　　　　WRIGHT, planter, of Berkeley Co., for L 60 SC
　　　　　　　　　　　　　　money, 12 town lots at Ashley River Ferry, Nos.
68, 69, 70, 71, 72, 76, 77, 78, 79, 80, 81, & 82, being part of ESTHER'S legacy by will of her husband SHEM BUTLER, ESQ. Witnesses: PETER GIRARDEAU, REBECKAH BUTTLER. Before ROBERT AUSTIN, J.P. & Pub. Reg.

Book T, p. 456　　　　　　　THOMAS MONCK, ESQ., of Mitton Plantation, to
22 & 23 Mar. 1738　　　　　NATHANIEL BROUGHTON, ESQ., of Mulberry & AN-
Deed in Trust　　　　　　　DREW BROUGHTON, ESQ. of Seaton, all of Berke-
　　　　　　　　　　　　　　ley Co., for certain considerations, 600 a.,
in trust. Whereas an agreement dated 6 Jan. 1731 between the Hon. THOMAS BROUGHTON, NATHANIEL BROUGHTON, & ANDREW BROUGHTON of the 1 part & THOMAS MONCK of the other part recited that a marriage was intended between THOMAS MONCK & JOANA, daughter ot THOMAS BROUGHTON & that THOMAS BROUGHTON, wishing to increase MONCK'S riches agreed that within 40 days after JOANNA'S marriage to MONCK on 6 Jan. next, he would give MONCK the necessary papers for conveying to MONCK certain slaves, & that on 6 Mar. next he would pay MONCK such a sum as, plus the value of the slaves, would amount to L 3000 currency; & whereas MONCK promised to give the 3 BROUGHTONS 2 bonds for the payment of such a sum as, plus the value of the Negroes, should amount to L 3000 currency & for the sum of L 500 sterling of England, to be paid by his heirs for JOANNA'S support; & whereas MONCK gave bond dated 6 Mar. 1731 for L 1000 sterling to secure payment of L 500 sterling to the 3 BROUGHTONS for the support of JOANNA; & gave another bond of same date for L 1800 SC currency for same purpose; now MONCK conveys to NATHANIEL & ANDREW BROUGHTON, trustees, 600 a., the southern part of 1000. in St. John Parish, Berkeley Co., on W side Biggin Creek, bounding E on JOHN COLLETON (of London), JAMES LEBASS, & PETER COLLETON; S on JOHN COLLETON; W on JOHN COLLETON & MR. REYNE, merchant; N on MAJ. HUGH BUTLER; according to plat to a release dated 2 Apr. 1735 from JAMES LEBAS to THOMAS MONCK; the 600 a. to be divided from the remaining 400 a. by a due E & W line. Witnesses: MARY SUREAU, MAURICE LEWIS. Before ALEXANDER SKENE, J.P. ROBERT AUSTIN, Pub. Reg.

Book T, p. 462　　　　　　　JOHN (his mark) HUGGINS, planter, of Christ
29 Mar. 1738　　　　　　　 Church Parish, Berkeley Co., to his daughter
Deed of Gift　　　　　　　 MARY SPRY, of Prince George Parish, for love &
　　　　　　　　　　　　　　affection, 600 a., 1/2 of a tract of 1200 a.
on Black River, according to plat owned by DAVID ALLEN, the plat of 1200
a. to be divided by a black line drawn through the middle by JOHN HUGGINS.
Witnesses: JOSEPH HUGGINS, NATHANIEL ARTHUR, PRISCILLA ARTHER. Before
WILLIAM WHITESIDE, J.P. ROBERT AUSTIN, Pub. Reg.

Book T, p. 462　　　　　　　WILLIAM COLT, planter, of Craven Co., to JOHN
20 & 21 Feb. 1739　　　　　 CLELAND & WILLIAM WALLACE, merchants, of
L & R by Mortgage　　　　　 Charleston, as security for payment of bond of
　　　　　　　　　　　　　　this date in penal sum of ₤ 431:7:4 money of
Great Britain conditioned for the payment of ₤ 215:13:8 with interest on
1 Jan. 1740, conveys 900 a. in Craven Co., bounding S on Black River; N
on THOMAS MORRITT & the river; E on JOHN WHITE; S on CALEB AVANT & Green
Creek; which land was granted by Gov. ROBERT JOHNSON on 24 May 1734 to
WILLIAM COLT & recorded 8 July 1734. Witnesses: MARTHA MICHIE, JAMES
MICHIE. Memo. At the time of delivery of this mortgage ₤ 121:14:3 sterling
of Great Britain is due from WILLIAM COLT to THOMAS JENYS & ELIZA-
BETH JENYS for which JOHN CLELAND & WILLIAM WALLACE are jointly bound
with WILLIAM COLT unto THOMAS JENYS & ELIZABETH JENYS, executor & executrix of will of PAUL JENYS; in case COLTS pays THOMAS & ELIZABETH JENYS
₤ 60:17:1:1/2 sterling on 1 Jan. 1740 & a like sum on 1 Jan. 1741 with
interest, then the mortgage to be chargeable for only the balance of
₤ 215:13:8 sterling with interest. Before ROBERT AUSTIN, J.P. & Pub.
Reg.

Book T, p. 467　　　　　　　JOSEPH ELLIOTT, ESQ., of St. Andrews Parish,
27 Mar. 1739　　　　　　　 Berkeley Co., "farm lets" to JOSHUA MORGAN &
Lease　　　　　　　　　　　ANN his wife, daughter of RICHARD CAPERS, of
　　　　　　　　　　　　　　St. Helena, for 20 years at 5 shillings a year,
100 a., taken from the S part of 950 a., on St. Helena Island, bounding S
on COL. BULL; W on Doatee Creek; N & E on JOSEPH ELLIOTT; should MORGAN
sublet any of the acreage he shall pay ELLIOTT ₤ 200 currency yearly for
every a. sublet. Witnesses: FRANCIS THOMPSON, RICHARD CAPERS, JOSEPH
ELLICOTT. Before THOMAS WIGG, J.P. ROBERT AUSTIN, Pub. Reg.

Book T, p. 469　　　　　　　SUSANNA NASH, widow, to ROYALL SPRY, planter,
14 & 15 Mar. 1739　　　　　 of St. Pauls Parish, Colleton Co., for ₤ 300
L & R　　　　　　　　　　　currency, 120 a. in St. Pauls Parish, bounding
　　　　　　　　　　　　　　S & E on ROYALL SPRY; W on JAMES BULLOCK; N on
ROYALL SPRY & JAMES BULLOCK. Witnesses: PHINEAS SPRY, GEORGE JACKSON,
ABRAHAM CAIN. Before JACOB MOTTE, J.P. ROBERT AUSTIN, Pub. Reg.

Book T, p. 472　　　　　　　JONATHAN DRAKE & MARY his wife, of St. John's
8 Apr. 1737　　　　　　　　Parish, Berkeley Co., to JOHN DUBOIS, of St.
Deed of Sale　　　　　　　 James Santee, Craven Co., for ₤ 700 currency,
　　　　　　　　　　　　　　2 tracts; 1 of 550 a., the other of 400 a.,
making 950 a., in St. James Santee, on Mattases Creek & Santee River,
bounding E on JOHN DRAKE; W on ABRAHAM CHROUCH; the 400 a. to be held by
him under the same conditions expressed in the fourth grant. MARY to renounce her dower when required. Witnesses: JOHN COACHMAN, ABRAHAM CROUCH.
Before ROBERT AUSTIN, J.P. & Pub. Reg.

Book T, p. 473　　　　　　　JAMES MITCHELL & MARTHA MITCHELL, of Edisto
20 Apr. 1734　　　　　　　 Island, release to JOHN SAMS all land which
Quit Claim　　　　　　　　now or may belong to JOHN SAMS, except 100 a.
　　　　　　　　　　　　　　which JOHN SAMS has given to JAMES & MARTHA
MITCHELL should SAMS die without heirs. Witnesses: CHARLES ODINGSELLS,
ARCHIBALD CALDER, PAUL GRIMBALL, RICHARD COLLWALL. Before ROBERT AUSTIN,
J.P. & Pub. Reg.

Book T, p. 474　　　　　　　SAMUEL BAKER, planter, of Queensborough Town-
11 & 12 May 1736　　　　　 ship, Craven Co., to DANIEL LAROCHE & THOMAS
L & R　　　　　　　　　　　LAROCHE, merchants, of Georgetown, for ₤ 400
　　　　　　　　　　　　　　currency, 500 a. in 2 tracts of 250 a. each,
granted SAMUEL BAKER by 2 grants dated 9 Apr. 1736 & signed by THOMAS
BROUGHTON, Lt. Gov.: 1 tract bounding NW & SW on vacant land, SE on SOLO-
MAN HUGHES; the other bounding NW on JAMES GORDON; SW on Peedee River;

other sides on vacant land. Witnesses: THOMAS JEWNING, PETER SECARE. Before WILLIAM WHITESIDE. ROBERT AUSTIN, Pub. Reg.

Book T, p. 478
4 Mar. 1740
Mortgage

JOSEPH CRELL, of Saxegotha Township, to MRS. ELIZABETH TIMOTHY, widow & executrix of LEWIS TIMOTHY, as security on bond given LEWIS TIMOTHY dated 5 Oct. 1738 in penal sum of ₤ 440 currency conditioned for the payment of ₤ 220 with interest on 5 Oct. 1740, 500 a. in 2 tracts in Saxegotha Township, the Congarees, Berkeley Co., bounding NE on Santee River; S on HANNAH MARIA STOLER; SW on vacant land; NW on STEPHEN CRELL. Witnesses: JOHANNA CRELL, STEPHEN CRELL. Before GEORGE HAIG, J.P. Mortgage satisfied 25 Jan. 1745 by PHILIP PUHL paying full amount to ELIZABETH TIMOTHY. Witness: J. A. HOME. ROBERT AUSTIN, Pub. Reg.

Book T, p. 480
26 & 27 Jan. 1736
L & R

JOSEPH JONES, planter, of Colleton Co., & MARY his wife (daughter & heir-at-law of THOMAS TUCKER, planter) to WILLIAM PINCKNEY, vintner, of Charleston, for ₤ 440 SC money, 200 a. Whereas the Lords Proprs. on 23 July 1711 granted THOMAS TUCKER 200 a. within land, in Colleton Co., bounding W on WILLIAM REEP; N on HENRY JACKSON; N & W on OWEN BAGEN; S on vacant land; & whereas TUCKER died intestate & the land descended to his daughter MARY; now MARY & her husband JOSEPH JONES sell the land to PINCKNEY. Witnesses: THOMAS ROBERTS, STEPHEN RUSSELL, JAMES LANNING. Before ROBERT AUSTIN, J.P. & Pub. Reg.

Book T, p. 484
25 & 26 Mar. 1740
L & R

WILLIAM PINCKNEY, gentleman, & RUTH, his wife, of Berkeley Co., to JOHN PEACOMB, planter, of St. Bartholomews Parish, for ₤ 1035:17:6 SC money, 295-1/4 a. in Colleton Co., bounding N on HENRY JACKSON & JOHN PEACOMB; S on WILLIAM PINCKNEY & EDWARD NORTH; W on MR. EBERSON & WILLIAM PINCKNEY; E on EDWARD NORTH & HENRY JACKSON. Witnesses: ROBERT BREWTON, JR., WILLIAM COE, SARAH NUBOLL. Before ROBERT AUSTIN, J.P. & Pub. Reg.

Book T, p. 489
8 & 9 July 1736
L & R

JAMES PAINE, merchant, & MARY his wife, to HUGH STUART, minister of the Gospel, all of Charleston, for ₤ 50 SC money, 500 a. in Craven Co., free from claim of MARY'S dower, bounding SE on JAMES PAINE; all other sides on vacant land; which 500 a. was granted to PAINE on 14 Feb. 1735 by the Hon. THOMAS BROUGHTON, Lt. Gov. Witnesses: WILLIAM BUCHANAN, JOHN KEATING, THOMAS SMITH. Before HENRY GIBBES, J.P. ROBERT AUSTIN, Pub. Reg.

Book T, p. 492
22 & 23 Feb. 1739
L & R

BENJAMIN WRIGHT, carpenter, & ANNE (her mark) his wife, of Granville Co., to ARTHUR JOHNSTONE, victualer, of Beaufort, for ₤ 80 SC money, lot #70 in Beaufort, on Port Royall Island, bounding S on lot #71; W by West Street; N by lot #69; E by lot #79; which lot #70 was granted by the Hon. ROBERT DANIELL, Dep. Gov., on 2 July 1717. Certificate signed by FRANCIS YONGE, Surv. Gen., 14 Aug. 1718. Witnesses: WILLIAM MARTIN, WILLIAM GOUGH. Before ROBERT AUSTIN, J.P. & Pub. Reg.

Book T, p. 495
17 & 18 Dec. 1734
L & R

THOMAS FERGUSON, planter, & ANN his wife, to JOHN COOK, planter, all of Berkeley Co., for ₤ 2000 SC money, 407 a. in Berkeley Co., within land, on a swamp made by W branch of Cooper River; bounding S on SAMPSON BALL (formerly WILLIAM BALL); W on ARTHUR MIDDLETON; N on WILLIAM MOORE (formerly JOSEPH GOODBYEE); E on JOSEPH ST. JULIEN. Witnesses: VICTOR FERGUSON, SAMPSON BALL, NICHOLAS (MAHAM). Before DANIEL WELSHHUYSEN, J.P. Before ROBERT AUSTIN, Pub. Reg.

Book T, p. 499
19 & 20 Dec.
L & R

JOHN COOK, planter, to THOMAS FURGUSON, planter, both of Berkeley Co., for ₤ 2000 SC money, 407 a. in Berkeley Co., within land, on a swamp made by W branch of Cooper River, bounding S on SAMPSON BALL (formerly WILLIAM BALL); E on ARTHUR MIDDLETON; N on WILLIAM MOORE (formerly JOSEPH GOODBEE); E on JOSEPH ST. JULIEN. Witnesses: SAMPSON BALL, NICHOLAS MAHAM, VICTOR FERGUSON. Before DANIEL

WELSHHUYSEN, J.P. ROBERT AUSTIN, Pub. Reg.

Book T, p. 502　　　　　　　JOHN SPLATT, planter, to WILLIAM BRANFORD,
17 May 1733　　　　　　　　planter, both of Colleton Co., for Ł 5 curren-
Deed of Sale　　　　　　　cy, 205 a. on W side Pon Pon River, Colleton
　　　　　　　　　　　　　Co., bounding E on the river; N on BOONE'S
Barony; W on THOMAS BUER; S on JOHN SPLATT. Witnesses: JOHN (his mark)
PEACOM, THOMAS MELVIN, JOHN BEE, JR. Before WILLIAM LIVINGSTON, J.P.
ROBERT AUSTIN, Pub. Reg.

Book T, p. 504　　　　　　　THOMAS INNS, planter, of Granville Co., to
15 & 16 July 1736　　　　　JOHN BULL, planter, of Colleton Co., for Ł 700
L & R by Mortgage　　　　　currency, 300 a. in Granville Co., bounding S
　　　　　　　　　　　　　on marsh; all other sides on GARRET VANVELSIN;
conditioned for the payment of the above amount with interest, on 16 July
1737. Witnesses: WILLIAM SCOTT, THOMAS (his mark) WENNELL (WANNEL). Before STEPHEN BULL, J.P. ROBERT AUSTIN, Pub. Reg.

Book T, p. 507　　　　　　　WILLIAM TREWIN, ESQ., & HELEN his wife, of
15 & 16 Aug. 1739　　　　　Charleston, to JONATHAN BRYAN, planter, of
L & R　　　　　　　　　　　Granville Co., for Ł 500 SC money, 230 a.
　　　　　　　　　　　　　Whereas King GEORGE II by his letters patent
on 22 Sept. 1733 granted WILLIAM TREWIN & JAMES KILPATRICK, physician,
230 a. in Granville Co., & whereas KILPATRICK conveyed his interest to
TREWIN; now TREWIN sells to BRYAN; HELEN to renounce her dower. Witnesses: WILLIAM FREEMAN, RICHARD TIDDEMAN. Before ROBERT AUSTIN, J.P. & Pub.
Reg.

Book T, p. 512　　　　　　　GEORGE STARRAT, planter, of Craven Co., to
10 & 11 Aug. 1739　　　　　GEORGE LUCAS, ESQ., of the Island of Antigua,
L & R　　　　　　　　　　　West Indies, for Ł 1725:10 SC money, 1150 a.
　　　　　　　　　　　　　in Craven Co., bounding NW on Waccamaw River;
SE on ADAM STEWART; other sides by vacant land. Witnesses: WILLIAM HOP-
TON, MANOEL TAUERES. Before OTHNIEL BEALE, J.P. ROBERT AUSTIN, Pub.
Reg.

Book T, p. 515　　　　　　　RALPH BAILEY, planter, of South Edisto, Colle-
16 Feb. 1738　　　　　　　　ton Co., to JOHN EVANS & WILLIAM EVANS, plant-
L & R　　　　　　　　　　　ers, of St. Helena Parish, Granville Co., for
　　　　　　　　　　　　　Ł 600 SC money 175 a. in Granville Co., granted to RALPH BAILEY on 13 July 1737, bounding NE on ARCHIBALD CALDER; SE
on Raynolds Creek; SW & NW on RALPH BAILEY. Signed by RALPH BAILEY &
MARY (her mark) BAYLY. Witnesses: WILLIAM BOWER, EDWARD PENDERGAST. Before ROBERT AUSTIN, J.P. & Pub. Reg.

Book T, p. 518　　　　　　　RALPH BAILEY & HENRY BAILEY, planters, of
16 Feb. 1738　　　　　　　　South Edisto, Colleton Co., to JOHN EVANS &
L & R　　　　　　　　　　　WILLIAM EVANS, planters, of St. Helena Parish,
　　　　　　　　　　　　　Granville Co., for Ł 860 SC money, 480 a.
Whereas JOHN, Earl of Bath, Palatine; GEORGE, Lord Carteret; SIR JOHN
COLLETON, Baronet; THOMAS AMY & WILLIAM THORNBURGH, Lords Proprs. on 3
Feb. 1702 granted WALTER MELVIN 480 a. in Colleton Co., bounding N on
Wambee Creek; E & SE on MR. NAIRN; S & SW on vacant land; grant enrolled
in Auditor's office 6 Apr. 1733; & whereas JOHN MELVIN, son & heir of
WALTER MELVIN conveyed the land to RALPH & HENRY BAILEY; deed enrolled in
Auditor's office 6 Apr. 1733; now the 2 BAILEYS convey to the 2 EVANSES,
the deed being signed not only by RALPH & HENRY but also by the marks of
2 women of the same name, that is MARY (her mark) BAYLEY. Witnesses:
WILLIAM BOWER, EDWARD PENDERGAST. Before ROBERT AUSTIN, J.P. & Pub. Reg.

Book T, p. 522　　　　　　　JONATHAN NORTON, planter, & MARYAN his wife;
12 Jan. 1735/6　　　　　　　RANDOLPH (his mark) EVANS, planter, & SARAH
Deed of Sale　　　　　　　 EVANS (alias NORTON) (her mark) his wife, of
　　　　　　　　　　　　　Granville Co., to GEORGE NORTON, planter, of
Colleton Co., for good causes & Ł 30 SC money, relinquish their full por-
tion, 192 a., on St. Helena Island, Granville Co. Whereas Gov. JAMES
MOORE, JOSEPH NORTON, ESQ., & EDMUND BELLINGER, ESQ. & the Lords Proprs.
for Ł 19:4 on 28 Aug. 1701 granted JOHN NORTON 960 a. in Granville Co., &
whereas JOHN NORTON by will dated 30 Sept. 1705 bequeathed to his wife
SARAH 1/3 of his real & personal estate, the other 2/3 to be divided

equally among all his children, by which JONATHAN NORTON & MARYAN NORTON, his wife, & RANDOLPH EVANS & SARAH EVANS, his wife, became entitled to 192 a.; now they convey their portion to GEORGE NORTON. Witnesses: RALPH BAILEY, JOSEPH WILLCOCKS, LEONARD DOBBINS. Before ROBERT AUSTIN, J.P. & Pub. Reg.

Book T, p. 524　　　　　JOHN NORTON, cooper, of Granville Co., to his
18 June 1724　　　　　 brother GEORGE NORTON, cordwainer, of Colleton
Deed of Sale　　　　　 Co., for good causes & L 100 SC money, 280 a.,
　　　　　　　　　　　 being 1/2 of 560 a., on an island known by its
Indian name Washua, Granville Co., divided on the S by a creek from JOHN COWEN & JOHN NORTON; divided on the E by a creek from Data Island; N by a river between Cambhee Island & St. Helena; also 200 a. on St. Helena Island, Granville Co., bounding W on JOHN COWEN; N divided by a creek from Washua Island; E on THOMAS STANYARNE. Whereas Gov. JAMES MOORE, JOSEPH MORTON & EDMUND BELLINGER, Lords Proprs., on 28 Aug. 1701 for L 19:4 granted JOHN NORTON, the father, 960 a. in Granville Co., & by will dated 30 Sept. 1705, NORTON devised to his wife SARAH 1/3 of all his real & personal estate, the other 2/3 to be divided equally amongst his children; & whereas SARAH, widow of JOHN, died intestate, & son WILLIAM (brother of JOHN, party hereto) died before reaching 21, & JOHN became heir to 480 a.; now he conveys to his brother GEORGE 280 a. on Washua Island & 200 a. on St. Helena's Island. Witnesses: WILLIAM MAGGOTT, DANIEL MCFARLAND. JONATHAN NORTON, brother of JOHN NORTON, party hereto appeared before ROBERT AUSTIN on 12 Apr. 1740, declared all witnesses dead, & swore to his brother's handwriting. ROBERT AUSTIN, Pub. Reg.

Book T, p. 527　　　　　JOHN COWEN, cordwainer, of Granville Co., to
7 July 1724　　　　　　 GEORGE NORTON, cordwainer, of Colleton Co.,
Deed of Sale　　　　　 for good causes & L 30 SC money, his full 7th
　　　　　　　　　　　 part of 960 a., or 96 a., on St. Helena Island, Granville Co. Whereas Gov. JAMES MOORE, JOSEPH MORTON & EDMUND BELLINGER, Lords Proprs., for L 14:4 on 28 Aug. 1701 granted JOHN NORTON, the father, 960 a.; & whereas JOHN NORTON by will dated 30 Sept. 1705 bequeathed to his wife SARAH 1/3 of all his real & personal estate, the other 2/3 to be divided equally amongst his children, by which JOHN COWAN, having married DOROTHY NORTON (daughter of JOHN & SARAH), became heir to 1/7, or 96 a.; now COWEN sells his share to GEORGE NORTON. Witnesses: RALPH BAILEY, HENRY BAILEY, DANIEL MCFARLAND. Before ROBERT AUSTIN, J.P. & Pub. Reg.

Book T, p. 529　　　　　GEORGE NORTON, cordwainer, of Granville Co.,
... Jan. 1736　　　　　 to JONATHAN NORTON, carpenter, of Granville
Deed of Sale　　　　　 Co., for good causes & L 30 currency, 96 a. on
　　　　　　　　　　　 St. Helena Island from the Pine Station tree upon the E line over to the W line to a live oak by the marsh. Whereas the Lords Proprs. (see pages 522, 524, 527) granted JOHN NORTON 960 a., 1/3 of which he devised to his wife, SARAH, the other 2/3 to his children in equal shares, & GEORGE NORTON became entitled to the above 96 a.; now he sells to JONATHAN. Witnesses: RALPH BAILEY, JOSEPH WILLCOCKS, LEONARD DOBBIN. ELIZABETH NORTON confirms the sale & renounces her dower, under date of 12 Jan. 1735. Before ROBERT AUSTIN, J.P. & Pub. Reg.

Book T, p. 532　　　　　THOMAS GOREING, planter, & JANE his wife, of
30 Jan. 1735　　　　　　Berkeley Co., to GEORGE NORTON, planter, of
Deed of Sale　　　　　 Colleton Co., for good causes & L 100 SC money,
　　　　　　　　　　　 their share of 960 a., or 96 a. on St. Helena Island, Granville Co. Whereas the Lords Proprs. (see p. 522, etc.) granted JOHN NORTON 960 a. in Granville Co., & he devised 1/3 of all his real & personal estate to his wife SARAH, the other 2/3 to his children in equal shares, whereby THOMAS GOREING & JANE his wife became entitled to 96 a.; now they convey their share to GEORGE NORTON. Witnesses: THOMAS BLONDELL, JAMES CRADDOCK. Before THOMAS DRAYTON, J.P. ROBERT AUSTIN, Pub. Reg.

Book T, p. 534　　　　　JOHN BAYLY, son & heir of JOHN BAYLY, of Bal-
9 & 10 Aug. 1729　　　 linaclough, Co. of Tipperary, Ireland, by his
L & R　　　　　　　　　attorney, ALEXANDER TRENCH, merchant, of
　　　　　　　　　　　 Charleston, to JOHN BAYLY, gentleman, of Goose Creek, for L 100 SC money, 407 a.; on W side Pon Pon River, St.

Bartholomews Parish, Colleton Co., bounding N on JOHN BAYLY of Goose Creek; E on COL. CHARLESWORTH GLOVER; S & W on BRYAN KELLY & vacant land. Whereas the Rt. Hon. JOHN, Earl of Bath, & the Lords Proprs. on 16 Aug. 1698 created JOHN BAYLY, the father, Landgrave & Cassique, granting him 48,000 a. in SC; & whereas JOHN BAYLY, the son & heir on 9 Nov. 1722, appointed ALEXANDER TRENCH, merchant, of Charleston, his attorney, with authority to set aside 8,000 a. for JOHN BAYLY & sell the rest; now TRENCH conveys 407 a. in St. Bartholomews Parish to JOHN BAYLY of Goose Creek. Witnesses: JOHN HUTCHINSON, JONATHAN MAIN, THOMAS ELLERY. Before THEOPHILUS GREGORY, J.P. Survey & plat by FRANCIS YONGE, Surv. Gen. ROBERT AUSTIN, Pub. Reg.

Book T, p. 539
20 Oct. 1731
L & R

JOHN BAYLY, gentleman, of Goose Creek, to WILLIAM TENANT & JOHN MCGILLIVRAY, Indian traders, of SC, for L 407 SC money, 407 a. (purchased from JOHN BAYLY, see p. 534) on W side Pon Pon River, St. Bartholomews Parish, Colleton Co., bounding N on JOHN BAYLY of Goose Creek; E on COL. CHARLESWORTH GLOVER; S & W on BRYAN KELLY & vacant land. Witnesses: JOHN FRASER, HENRY HARGRAVE. Before ROBERT AUSTIN, J.P. & Pub. Reg.

Book T, p. 544
11 Jan. 1739
Agreement

(See page 297). JOHN CARRUTHERS, gentleman, Bromley Parish, Middlesex Co., England, agreed to advance to JOHN HAMMERTON of SC now in London, for the support of himself & his wife, L 200 beyond the L 650 mentioned within. JOHN HAMMERTON agrees that the premises mentioned within shall stand as security for the L 200 & the L 53:16:3 sterling paid by CARRUTHERS last August as premium for insuring L 650, part of sum of L 650 within mentioned, on the life of JOHN HAMMERTON for 1 year, & such further sums as CARRUTHERS shall spend on like insurance from year to year until the insurance is fully paid. Whereas HAMMERTON intends to go to SC to take charge of the offices of Secretary & Register of SC himself but has appointed CARRUTHERS his deputy to execute the offices & receive the profits but should CARRUTHERS not be minded to go to SC HAMMERTON has appointed CHILDERMAS CROFT, gentleman, & WILLIAM FREEMAN, gentleman, both of Charleston, his deputies; & has appointed CARRUTHERS, FREEMAN, & BENJAMIN WHITAKER of Charleston, his attorneys to settle accounts with JAMES MICHIE touching such moneys received by him; now in consideration of the loan of L 200 HAMMERTON consents to continuation of all agreements & agrees as long as CARRUTHERS executes the offices he may retain 1/2 the yearly profits & perquisites of office, after all incidental office expenses are paid; & that the deputies retain for their trouble in executing the offices not more than L 150 sterling yearly; the residue of the profits & perquisites to be used to satisfy the several loans by CARRUTHERS, with interest. Witnesses: GEORGE MORLEY, THOMAS FODEN. THOMAS FODEN, gentleman, of Lincoln's Inn, Co. of Middlesex, testified before SIR JOHN SALTER, Knight, Lord Mayor of London 18 Jan. 1739. Signed BAYNBRIDGE. FODEN also testified to HAMMERTON'S signature to original indenture dated 1 Aug. 1739 & to his & JOHN SWALE'S signatures as witnesses. FODEN also testified to signatures of HAMMERTON & CARRUTHERS on original deed dated 11 Jan. 1739 & to signatures of himself, GEORGE MORLEY as witness; also to HAMMERTON'S signature to receipt for L 200, & his & GEORGE MORLEY'S as witnesses: also to HAMMERTON'S signature to deed poll dated 11 Jan. 1739, & to his & GEORGE MORLEY'S signatures as witnesses. ROBERT AUSTIN, Pub. Reg.

Book T, p. 549
28 July 1739
Mortgage

ROBERT BROWN, physician, to ALEXANDER NISBETT, for L 300 sterling of Great Britain, 2 tracts; 1 of 932 a. in Craven Co., bounding on Wambaw Creek & ELIAS HORRY, purchased 8 Apr. 1735 from JOHN GENDRON; the other of 290 a. in Craven Co., on Wambaw Creek & MR. DE RICHBOUGH, granted 3 Feb. 1737 to JOHN GENDRON & sold by him to ROBERT BROWN on 10 July 1739. Witnesses: CHARLES LYON, WILLIAM (his mark) BROAD. Before FRANCIS LEJAU, J.P. ROBERT AUSTIN, Pub. Reg.

Book T, p. 551
17 & 18 Nov. 1736
L & R

JOHN SOMERVILLE, brother & heir-at-law of TWEEDIE SOMERVILLE, & SARAH SOMERVILLE, widow of TWEEDIE SOMERVILLE, to JAMES KINLOCH, ESQ., of Berkeley Co., for L 950 currency, their half part of 3 lots in Charleston, Nos. 66, 67, & 217, bounding S on Dock

Street, now called Queen Street; E on ARTHUR MIDDLETON; W on the other half of the 3 lots; N on lot #218; which 3 lots were originally granted to JOSEPH PENDARVIS who conveyed the E half of the 3 lots to WILLIAM HAWETT of the Island of Jamaica, who conveyed to WILLIAM GIBBON & ANDREW ALLEN the half which descended to ELIZABETH SOMERVILLE (formerly CAWOODO as heiress-at-law to WILLIAM GIBBON. She conveyed the half part to TWEEDIE SOMERVILLE who bequeathed it to JOHN SOMERVILLE & SARAH SOMERVILLE. Witnesses: HENRY FLETCHER, CHILDERMAS CROFT. Before ROBERT AUSTIN, J.P. & Pub. Reg.

Book T, p. 554
7 & 8 Apr. 1740
L & R

GEORGE HUNTER, surveyor, of St. Philip's Parish, Berkeley Co., to JOHN BAXTER, clerk, of Christ Church Parish, for Ł 2158 currency, 1500 a. at head of Black Mingo Creek, Craven Co., being the SE part of 3249 a. granted the Hon. JAMES KINLOCH by the Hon. THOMAS BROUGHTON, Lt. Gov., on 5 July 1737 & conveyed by KINLOCH to HUNTER on 7 July 1738 (see p. 385); bounding SE on CAPT. WILLIAM BROCKINGTON; NE on JOHN MCIVER & GEORGE HUNTER; NW on GEORGE HUNTER; running from a small pine 3 x near Coldwater Run, NE 25° 7350 links to tupelo 3 thence NW 55° 8.10 links to gum 3 x thence NW 45° 105 chains to a corner not yet made which is to extend 1105 links beyond a gum 3 on the NE side of a lake & from said corner SW 87° 62 chains thence SW 25° 81 chains thence SE 65° 160 chains to the small pine 3 x aforesaid near Coldwater Run "as is nearly represented by the annexed plat wherein that part to the SE of scrubby oak 3 & gum 3 pr lake has lately been resurveyed & new marked". Witnesses: RICHARD SHUBRICK, HENRY PERONNEAU, JR. Before ROBERT AUSTIN, J.P. & Pub. Reg.

Book T, p. 559
1 & 2 Apr. 1740
L & R

STEPHEN BEDON, shopkeeper, of Charleston, to RICHARD ASH & SAMUEL PERONNEAU, as executors of JAMES COCHRAN, for Ł 550 SC money, 1100 a. in Craven Co., bounding SW on Peedee River; NW on SAMUEL BULLOCK; NE on land laid out; SE on MR. LEJAU. Signatures: STEPHEN BEDON, MARY BEDON. Witnesses: WILLIAM COE, SARAH BEDON. Before ROBERT AUSTIN, J.P. & Pub. Reg.

Book T, p. 563
29 Feb. & 1 Mar. 1739
L & R by Mortgage

GEORGE LIVINGSTON, planter, of Port Royal Island, Granville Co., to JORDAN ROCHE, gentleman, of Charleston, as security on bond this date in penal sum of Ł 10,000 currency conditioned for the payment of Ł 5000:13:10 on 1 Mar. 1740, 770 a. on Port Royall Island bounding W on Port Royall River; N on lands sold by LIVINGSTON to EPHRAIM MICHAEL; E on NICHOLAS HATCHER; S on JOHN HENDRICK; which 770 a. is 1/2 of several tracts devised to GEORGE LIVINGSTON by his father the Rev. MR. WILLIAM LIVINGSTON. Witnesses: GEORGE HUNTER, STEPHEN BEDON. Before ROBERT AUSTIN, J.P. & Pub. Reg.

Book T, p. 568
7 Mar. 1739/40
Power of Attorney

CORNELIUS HINSON, ESQ., son & heir of EDWARD HINSON, mariner, appointed BENJAMIN TUCKER, gentleman, all of Bermuda, (or Somers Island) his attorney to handle his property in Charleston, SC. Before ALURED POPPLE, Gov. of Bermuda. ROBERT AUSTIN, Pub. Reg.

Book T, p. 569
12 & 13 May 1729
L & R

STEPHEN (his mark) MONK, ESQ., of Goose Creek, son & heir of JOHN MONK, Gassique, to JAMES BASFORD, planter, of Colleton Co., for Ł 50 SC money, 165 a. in Colleton Co., part of 24,000 a. granted 22 Feb. 1682 by the Lords Proprs. to JOHN MONK; bounding N on SAMUEL FARLEY; E on MR. JACKSON; S on vacant land; W on Whitmarsh Neck. Witnesses: GEORGE SMITH, BENJAMIN WARING, JOHN BAYLY. Before OTHNIEL BEALE, J.P. Plat certified 6 May 1729 by JOSHUA SANDERS, JR. ROBERT AUSTIN, Pub. Reg.

Book T, p. 574
19 & 20 Oct. 1739
L & R

THOMAS WRIGHT, ESQ., to ROBERT QUASH, both of Berkeley Co., for Ł 884:12:6 SC money, 337 a. partly in Berkeley, partly in Craven Co., bounding NE on THOMAS AIKEN; NW on FRANCIS ROCHE; SW on ROBERT QUAST; SE on THOMAS WRIGHT. Witnesses: FRANCIS ROCHE, CHARLES LYON, MATTHEW QUASH. Before FRANCIS LEJAU, J.P. ROBERT AUSTIN, Pub. Reg.

Book T, p. 577 JOSIAH BAKER, planter, & REBECCA his wife to
1 & 2 Feb. 1738 WILLIAM MILES, planter, all of St. Andrews Par-
L & R ish, Berkeley Co., for Ł 2500 SC money, 313 a.
on S side Ashley River, devised to REBECCA by
will of her father SHEM BUTLER dated 19 Oct. 1718, which land was measured & allotted 10 Mar. 1735 by RICHARD BUTLER & EDMUND BELLINGER, executors of will of SHEM BUTLER; bounding NE on THOMAS BUTLER & DANIEL CART-
WRIGHT; SE on CAPT. EDMUND BELLINGER by the Ferry path; SW on MRS. HESTER
ELLIOTT & MRS. ABIGAIL BUTLER (later the wife of JOHN WATSON, merchant);
NW on WIDOW MONGER. Witnesses: THOMAS GOERING, BENJAMIN STANYARN, JAMES
SCARLETT. Before WILLIAM BULL, JR., J.P. ROBERT AUSTIN, Pub. Reg.

Book T, p. 581 JOHN ALLEN, merchant, to JAMES ST. JOHN, ESQ.,
29 & 30 Apr. 1736 both of Charleston, for Ł 1200 currency, "near
L & R 1/10 part" of HAWETT'S Swuare, later known as
Gibbon & Allen's Square, being part of 2 lots
#269 & 272, bounding N 144 ft. on Queen Street; E 141 ft. on Allen's
Street; S & W on JOHN ALLEN in the Square; which Square was granted by
the Lords Proprs. to WILLIAM HAWETT & after several conveyances descended
to ANDREW ALLEN, merchant, & bequeathed by him to his son JOHN. MARY,
wife of JOHN ALLEN, now udner age, to renounce her dower after reaching
21. Witnesses: WILLIAM SMITH, WILLIAM IRWIN. Before BENJAMIN WHITAKER,
J.P. ROBERT AUSTIN, Pub. Reg.

Book T, p. 586 JOHN ALLEN, merchant, to JAMES ST. JOHN, ESQ.,
18 & 19 Oct. 1736 both of Charleston, for Ł 1500 currency, "near
L & R 1/8 part" of HAWETT'S Square, later known as
Gibbons & Allen Square, being part of 4 lots,
#268, #269, #270, & #272, bounding N 144 ft. on lots 269 & 272 belonging
to JAMES ST. JOHN; fronting E 200 ft. on JOHN ALLEN'S Street; S on lots
268 & 270 now belonging to WILLIAM PINCKNEY, JOHN ALLEN, & HENRY GRISTIE;
W on part of lot #271 belonging to JAMES ST. JOHN & on part of lot 273
belonging to JOHN ALLEN in the Square; which Square was granted to WIL-
LIAM HAWETT & by various conveyances descended to ANDREW ALLEN & bequeathed by him to his son JOHN ALLEN. MARY, wife of JOHN ALLEN, now udner age,
to renounce her dower after reaching 21. Witnesses: WILLIAM IRWIN, WIL-
LIAM SMITH. Before BENJAMIN WHITAKER, J.P. ROBERT AUSTIN, Pub. Reg.

Book T, p. 590 JOHN POSTELL, ESQ., of Berkeley Co., to MELLER
26 & 27 Mar. 1740 ST. JOHN, gentleman, of St. Bartholomews Par-
L & R ish, Colleton Co., for Ł 200 currency, 490 a.
in Colleton Co., granted by the Hon. WILLIAM
BULL, Lt. Gov., on 3 Feb. 1737 bounding SE on JOHN LAX; NE & SW on vacant
land; NW on JOHN CARMICHAEL. Witnesses: JONATHAN THOMPSON, NATHANIEL
DEAN. Before JAMES ABERCROMBY, J.P. ROBERT AUSTIN, Pub. Reg.

Book T, p. 593 ELIAS HORRY, gentleman, to JOSEPH DELPH, coop-
8 & 9 Feb. 1739 er, both of Craven Co., Winyaw, for Ł 150 SC
L & R money, 454 a. in St. James Santee, Craven Co.,
granted ELIAS HORRY on 4 Sept. 1735, by the
Hon. THOMAS BROUGHTON, Lt. Gov., bounding SE on ANTHONY BONNEAU, JR.; NW
on DANIEL HORRY; NE on ELIAS HORRY; SW on MR. STOUTOMBORA. Witnesses:
DAVID BALDY, DANIEL JANDON, RALPH BUGNION. Before NOAH SERRÉ, J.P.
ROBERT AUSTIN, Pub. Reg.

Book T, p. 596 PETER VILLEPONTEAUX, gentleman, to EBENEZER
7 & 8 Feb. 1738 SIMMONS & ISAAC MAZYCK, merchants, all of
L & R by Mortgage Berkeley Co., as indemnity for EBENEZER SIM-
MONS, ISAAC MAZYCK, & JOHN ALLEN; part of lot
314 in Charleston, fronting W 30 ft. on a little street running from
White Point by the Quakers Meeting House to the high road that goes into
the country, called King Street; N on the Quakers Meeting House; S on lot
#314; also a neck of land on James Island, occupied by JOSEPH RIVERS,
planter, of Berkeley Co., containing 17 a., English measure; bounding N &
E on Kiskewa Creek; W on GABRIEL MANIGAULT; S on a great marsh; & for
further indemnity, VILLEPONTEAUX delivers to them 19 Negro slaves. Whereas EBENEZER SIMMONS, ISAAC MAZYCK & JOHN ALLEN at the request of PETER
VILLEPONTEAUX & for his debt on 30 Jan. 1738 gave a bond to BENJAMIN SAV-
AGE & THOMAS LAMBOLL (administrators of the estate of GEORGE SMITH, ESQ.)
in the penal sum of Ł 3960 SC money conditioned for the payment of Ł 1980

on 30 Jan. 1739, now as security, VILLEPONTEAUX conveys to them part of lot #314 in Charleston, 17 a. on James Island; & 19 Negroes. Witnesses: JAMES PAINE, JOHN HOUGHTON. Before ROBERT AUSTIN, J.P. & Pub. Reg.

Book T, p. 602
3 May 1740
Deed of Sale

WILLIAM MATTHEWS & MARY his wife, & BENJAMIN SMITH & ANN his wife, to JOHN DANIEL, ship carpenter, of Charleston, with the full consent of MARY & ANN, for Ł 2800 SC money, the corner part of lot #14 where JOHN DANIEL lives, fronting S 19 ft. 3 in. on Broad Street; bounding W 110 ft. on Union Street; E on part same lot occupied by JOHN BESWICK, merchant; N on EDWARD CROFT. MARY & ANN appoint their husbands their attorneys. Whereas JOHN, Lord Berkeley, Palatine, & the Lords Proprs. on 1 Feb. 1678 granted JOHN BULLEN lot #14 in Charleston; who sold it on 1 Jan. 1678 to LAURENCE READ, merchant; who sold it on 6 Feb. 1679 for Ł 3 sterling to EDWARD MIDDLETON, gentleman, who, at the time of his death owned 1/2 the lot #14 in his own right which was inherited by his eldest son HENRY MIDDLETON, oilman, of London; who on 10 Oct. 1696 sold it for Ł 140 currency to JOSEPH CROSSKEYS; who on 11 Dec. 1698 sold for Ł 120 currency to EDWARD LOUGHTON that part of the half lot bounding S 40 ft. 7 in. on Broad Street; N 42 ft. on WILLIAM DRY (formerly PETER HEARN); W on a street or lane left by consent of JOSEPH CROSSKEYS & EDWARD LOUGHTON between the half lot & part of a lot owned by heirs of GEORGE PAWLEY; E on the other part of the half lot owned by JOSEPH CROSSKEYS; & whereas EDWARD LOUGHTON by will dated 24 Dec. 1707 bequeathed to his son DAVID LOUGHTON all his houses & buildings in the alley that ran by his corner house from the corner house to the garden, also the storehouse to be built at the corner of the garden; also his dwelling house in the corner after the death of his wife; & whereas DAVID LOUGHTON by will dated 3 Nov. 1713 bequeathed all his real & personal estate to his wife ANN, who afterwards married GEORGE BARNET, & afterwards married DAVID HEXT, gentleman, of Charleston, in whom the property became invested, & joined him on 17 Sept. 1717 in conveying to JOHN BEE, merchant, of Charleston for Ł 550 SC money, the part of the town lot; who by will dated 14 Jan. 1724 bequeathed his real & personal estate to his wife MARY BEE; who, by will dated 24 Oct. 1730 left all her property to her 2 grand daughters MARY LOUGHTON & ANN LOUGHTON, wives of WILLIAM MATHEWS & BENJAMIN SMITH; now they convey to JOHN DANIEL as above. Witnesses: JOHN RATTRAY, JOHN JOHNSON. Witnesses to possession & seizen: RICHARD SHUBRICK, WILLIAM FRANKLIN, JOHN RATTRAY. Before ROBERT AUSTIN, J.P. & Pub. Reg.

Book T, p. 609
2 & 3 Nov. 1739
L & R by Mortgage

GEORGE LUCAS, ESQ., formerly of Island of Antigua, now of SC, to RICHARD BODDICOTT, merchant of London, as security on bond of even date in penal sum of Ł 512:10 of Great Britain conditioned for payment of Ł 256:5 like money with interest at 5% on 21 Feb. 1739, 500 a. in Kingstown Township, on Waccamaw River, Craven Co., bounding SE on JAMES SMITH; NE, NW & SW on vacant land; also 1150 a. in Craven Co., bounding NW on Waccamaw River; SE on ADAM STUART; other sides on vacant land; & delivers 30 Negro slaves. Witnesses: FRANCES FAIRWEATHER, THOMAS NICHOLAS, GEORGE NICHOLAS. Before ROBERT AUSTIN, J.P. & Pub. Reg.

Book T, p. 614
3 Nov. 1739
Bond

GEORGE LUCAS, ESQ., formerly of Island of Antigua, now of SC, to RICHARD BODDICOTT, merchant, of London, in penal sum of Ł 512:10 money of Great Britain, conditioned for payment of Ł 256:5 of Great Britain with interest at 5% on 21 Feb. 1739. Witnesses: FRANCES FAIRWEATHER, THOMAS NICHOLAS, GEORGE NICHOLAS. ROBERT AUSTIN, Pub. Reg.

Book T, p. 614
2 & 3 May 1740
L & R

JOHN FRASER, merchant, of Charleston, executor of will of JOHN MCKAY, planter, of Berkeley Co., to PETER DELMERTRE, gentleman, of Charleston, for Ł 800 currency, part of lot #13 in Charleston, purchased by JOHN MCKAY from ISAAC MAZYCK, bounding E 77 ft. on DAVID GUERARD; W on GABRIEL GUIGNARD; N 15-1/2 ft. on Broad Street; S on ISAAC MAZYCK. Witnesses: JAMES ABERCROMBY, WILLIAM MACKEY. Before ROBERT AUSTIN, J.P. & Pub. Reg.

Book T, p. 618
16 & 17 May 1740
L & R by Mortgage

PETER DELMESTRE, gentleman, & MARY (MARIE) his wife, to DANIEL BOURGETT, baker, all of Charleston, part of lot #13 on S side Broad Street, bounding E 77 ft. on DAVID GUERARD; W on GABRIEL GUIGNARD; N 15-1/2 ft. on Broad Street; S on ISAAC MAZYCK; conditioned for the payment of ₤ 500 currency with interest at 10% on 19 May 1741. Witnesses: CHARLES PINCKNEY, ROBERT BREWTON, JR. Before ROBERT AUSTIN, J.P. & Pub. Reg. Mortgage satisfied 18 May 1756. Witness: WILLIAM HOPTON.

Book T, p. 622
2 & 3 Apr. 1730
L & R

PERCIVAL PAWLEY, gunsmith, to WILLIAM ALLSTON, planter, both of Prince George Parish, Craven Co., for ₤ 1250 SC money, 1000 a. on E side Waccamaw River, inherited from his father, PERCIVAL PAWLEY, (will dated 5 June 1722) who had purchased 1490 a. from Landgrave THOMAS SMITH on 20 Sept. 1711; which 1000 a. bounded E on the sea; S on JOHN ALLSTON; W on Waccamaw River; N on JOHN LLOYD. Witnesses: GEORGE PAWLEY, JOSEPH LABRUCE. Before THOMAS LAROCHE, J.P. ROBERT AUSTIN, Pub. Reg.

Book T, p. 627
11 & 12 Apr. 1740
L & R

WILLIAM WILKINS, planter, & SARAH his wife, of Berkeley Co., to LOIS MATHEWS, widow, & BENJAMIN MATHEWS, of Charleston, (with SARAH'S consent), for ₤ 4800 currency, 617 a. on James Island, Berkeley Co., bounding N on Wappoo Creek & marsh; S on New Town Creek & GREGORY SOISON (formerly RICHARD SIMPSON); W on BELSHAZZAR LAMBRIGHT (formerly ROBERT GIBBES, & Later to MR. SHABISHERE); plat certified 15 May 1701 by JAMES WITTER & annexed to grant to DAVID DAVIS dated 18 Sept. 1703, under the Hon. SIR NATHANIEL JOHNSON, Gov. of NC & SC. Witnesses: HANNAH SIMMONDS, GEORGE MATHEWS, BENJAMIN MATHEWS. Before ROBERT AUSTIN, J. P. & Pub. Reg.

Book T, p. 632
24 Apr. 1729
Deed of Sale

JAMES BASFORD, planter to ROYALL SPRY, planter, both of Colleton Co., for ₤ 1000 SC money, 595 a. bounding on THOMAS SACHEVERILL & ROYALL SPRY. Witnesses: JOSHUA SANDERS, THOMAS SACHEVERILL, JOHN (his mark) PAYCOM (PEACOM). SACHEVERIL testified according to his profession. Before CHARLES PINCKNEY, J.P. ROBERT AUSTIN, Pub. Reg.

Book T, p. 633
24 Apr. 1729
Bond

JAMES BASHFORD, planter, to ROYALL SPRY, planter, both of St. Paul's Parish, Colleton Co., in penal sum of ₤ 2000 as security on above sale. Witnesses: JOSHUA SANDERS, THOMAS SACHEVERILL (according to his profession), JOHN (his mark) PEACOM. ROBERT AUSTIN, Pub. Reg.

Book T, p. 634
15 Apr. 1731
Deed of Sale

JOSEPH HAYNES, planter, to ROYAL SPRY, cooper, both of Colleton Co., for ₤ 400 SC money, 80 a. part of a tract purchased from WILLIAM MCPHERSON by MARY HAYNES, widow of JOHN HAYNES, for the use of her 7 children, in Colleton Co., bounding W on JAMES BULLOCK; N on WILLIAM NASH; E & S on ROYALL SPRY. Witnesses: THOMAS SACHEVERELL (according to his profession), MARY SACHEVERELL, GEORGE BARNETT. Before CHARLES PINCKNEY, J.P. ROBERT AUSTIN, Pub. Reg.

Book T, p. 636
19 Nov. 1737
Lease

JUDITH BARNETT, widow of JOHN BARNETT, of Craven Co., to MOSES DUTART, tanner, of same place, during his lifetime, for 5 shillings, 2 a. in St. James Santee, bounding W on JACOB BOND; E on said JUDEA BARNETT. Signed: JUDE BARNET. Witnesses: ISAAC DUBOSE, WILLIAM THOMAS. Before JAMES KINLOCK, J.P. ROBERT AUSTIN, Pub. Reg.

Book T, p. 637
22 & 23 Aug. 1739
L & R

DANIEL HUGER, ESQ., of St. John's Parish, Berkeley Co., to BENJAMIN PERDRIAU, planter, of St. James Santee, Craven Co., for ₤ 5 SC money, 200 a. in Craven Co., bounding SE on BENJAMIN PERDRIAU; SW on JAMES SAVENEAU; other sides on vacant land; which 200 a. is part of 289 a. granted 2 June 1739 by the Hon. WILLIAM

BULL, ESQ., Lt. Gov., to DANIEL HUGER as recorded in Secretary's office in Book K K folio 362. Witnesses: JAMES BOISSEAU, ROBERT QUASH. Before ANTHONY BONNEAU, J.P. ROBERT AUSTIN, Pub. Reg.

Book T, p. 640
16 & 17 May 1740
L & R by Mortgage

RICHARD FREEMAN, planter, to CHARLES PERONNEAU & Company, merchants, all of Colleton Co., for Ł 1000 currency, 300 a. (part of which was conveyed to RICHARD FREEMAN by SAMUEL SMITH & MARY his wife & HENRY FENDIN & SARAH his wife on 21 July 1732, & the other part conveyed to FREEMAN by ROBERT SAMS & BRIDGET his wife, & ELIZABETH BURTT on 25 Mar. 1734), on Wadmalaw Island, bounding S on part of same tract sold by FREEMAN to JOHN HOGG; N on Wadmalaw River; E on SAMUEL UNDERWOOD; W on JOHN SAMS; conditioned for the payment of Ł 1000 on 1 Jan. 1740. Witnesses: JOSEPH GIBBONS, SR., JOSEPH GIBBONS, JR. Before ROBERT AUSTIN, J.P. & Pub. Reg.

Book T, p. 644
23 Mar. 1738
Deed of Sale

ABRAHAM (his mark) BRUNSON & MARY (her mark) BRUNSON, of Berkeley Co., to JONATHAN WOOD, for Ł 183:15 currency, 147 a. in Berkeley Co., according to plat in WOOD'S possession. Witnesses: PETER FAURE, JACOB (his mark) BRUNSON, JOHN PEARSON. Before CHRISTIAN MOTE, J.P. ROBERT AUSTIN, Pub. Reg.

Book T, p. 646
22 & 23 Mar. 1738
L & R

THOMAS WAY, SR., to GEORGE SOMMERS, both of Dorchester, Berkeley Co., for Ł 700 currency, 50 a. in Dorchester, purchased 24 Feb. 1715 from SAMUEL WAY, SR., bounding E on HENRY WAY; S on Ashley River; W on PETER SAVOY; N on THOMAS OSGOOD & WILLIAM PRATT. ELIZABETH, wife of THOMAS WAY, to renounce her dower when required. Witnesses: JOHN STEELE, JOHN DORSEY. Before ALEXANDER SKENE, J.P. ROBERT AUSTIN, Pub. Reg.

Book T, p. 650
10 & 11 June 1740
L & R

SAMUEL JONES, merchant, of Charleston, to PAUL GRIMBALL, planter, of Colleton Co., for Ł 4000 SC money, 2 plantations; 1 of 802 a. on an Island on W side of Edisto Island, formerly called Schinking"s now called Linkly's, granted CHRISTOPHER LINKLY on 14 Mar. 1694; the other an island of 40 a., commonly called Rippon's Island, bounding E, S, W, & N by a creek from S Edisto River & marsh of Linkly's Island. Witnesses: JAMES GRAME (GREENE), JAMES DRUMMOND. Before ROBERT AUSTIN, Pub. Reg.

Book T, p. 655
3 June 1740
Deed of Sale

ISRAEL ANDREW, planter, to ISAAC GRIMBALL, planter, both of Colleton Co., for 5 shillings, 550 a. in Colleton Co., (390 a. having been purchased from the King), bounding W on ISRAEL ANDREW; N on WILLIAM CROCKRAM; S on JOHN PAGE; E on the dividing branch of Bryan's & Wannel's Neck laid out to JANE MUNGER, also 155 a. (part of 300 a. belonging to JOHN WANNELL) bounding W on Wannell's Creek; N on JOHN PAGE. Witnesses: ALEXANDER SPROULL, JOHN MITCHELL, SARAH MITCHELL. Before JAMES SKIRVING, J.P. ROBERT AUSTIN, Pub. Reg.

Book T, p. 657
13 & 14 June 1740
L & R

JOHN CARRUTHERS, gentleman, of Bromley, Middlesex Co., Great Britain, now residing in SC, to WILLIAM CATTELL, ESQ., Ł 377:10:11:1/2 of Great Britain 2700 a. in Berkeley Co., (except as excepted below); 20 slaves; also 10 other Negro men & 12 Negro women, etc. (see below). Whereas ALEXANDER SKENE & JEMIMA his wife delivered to WILLIAM TRYON, merchant, of London, indentures of L & R dated 23 & 24 Apr. 1722 in which skene acknowledged that on 24 Apr. 1722 he gave 2 bonds to WILLIAM TRYON 1 in penal sum of Ł 970 sterling of Great Britain, conditioned for payment of Ł 485:9:9 with interest at 5% on 27 Apr. 1725; the other for Ł 485 payable 27 Apr. 1727; & for security on the 2 bonds conveyed to TRYON 2700 a. in Berkeley Co., bounding SE on SAMUEL WRAGG: NW on WILLIAM WALLACE; SW on PETER CATTELL; NE on Ashley River; also 20 slaves; & whereas TRYON, on 9 Nov. 1727, by the name of WILLIAM TRYON, merchant, of London, sole executor of will of ROLAND TRYON of London, appointed BENJAMIN GODIN, merchant, of SC his attorney to recover from SKENE; & whereas, by L & R Tripartite on 30 & 31 Dec. 1735, between WILLIAM TRYON by his attorney, BENJAMIN GODIN, of the 1st part; ALEXANDER

SKENE of the 2nd part; & JOHN CARRUTHERS, master of the ship Molly, galley, of the 3rd part; reciting that the 2 sums of L 485:9:9 & L 485 & interest had not been wholly paid & there remained L 622:12:4 money of Great Britain due TRYON which JOHN CARRUTHERS (at SKENE'S request) had paid GODIN as attorney for TRYON; & whereas CARRUTHERS had also paid SKENE L 77:7:8 money of Great Britain; & whereas SKENE had given CARRUTHERS, as security, a bond in the penal sum of L 1400 of Great Britain conditioned for the payment of L 700 with interest at 10% & with the consent of TRYON (by GODIN) conveyed to CARRUTHERS 2700 a. in Berkeley Co., except 1000 a. conveyed by SKENE to CAPT. WILLIAM DOUGLAS & then in possession of JOHN WALTER; also except 300 a. conveyed by SKENE to THOMAS GADSDEN; also the 20 slaves; upon the condition that SKENE pay CARRUTHERS L 700 with interest on 31 Dec. 1736; whereas SKENE by deed poll on 31 Dec. 1735, reciting the above obligations, delivered to CARRUTHERS 10 Negro men, 12 Negro women; & whereas the L 700 & interest had not been paid CARRUTHERS; now CARRUTHERS conveys to CATTELL the 2700 a. (except as excepted; the 20 slaves; the other 10 Negro men & 12 Negro women; & all the above mentioned papers); & appoints CATTELL his attorney. Witnesses: GEORGE NICHOLAS, WILLIAM FREEMAN. Before ALEXANDER CRAMAHE, J.P. ROBERT AUSTIN, Pub. Reg.

Book T, p. 669
23 May 1739
Deed of Gift

SAMUEL (his mark) KING, SR., & ELIZABETH, his wife, to THOMAS VALLEY & ELIZABETH, his wife, daughter of SAMUEL & ELIZABETH KING, for love & affection, 100 a. in Berkeley Co., on E side Cooper River, on Ashby's Swamp, being part of 180 a. on which SAMUEL KING lives; which 180 a. was granted to KING by the Hon. SIR. NATHANIEL JOHNSON, Gov. on 12 June 1709; & a part of a tract of 324 a. granted to KING by the Hon. ROBERT DANIELL, Dep. Gov., on 24 Jan. 1716/7; which 100 a. bounds SE on PETER SIMONS & on all other sides on SAMUEL KING. Witnesses: PETER SIMONS, PETER SALLENS. SAMUEL SIMONS. Before ANTHONY BONNEAU, J.P. ROBERT AUSTIN, Pub. Reg.

Book T, p. 672
1 & 2 May 1740
L & R

HUGH CARTWRIGHT, bricklayer, of Charleston, to JAMES STREETOR, butcher, of Berkeley Co., for L 815:10 SC money, 32 a. 2 roods 26-1/2 perches of land & marsh & the messuage thereon erected, in St. Philip's Parish, Charleston, bounding N on marsh & ROBERT HUME; E on the Broad Road; S & W on DANIEL CARTWRIGHT. Whereas the Lords Proprs. on 17 Aug. 1676 granted HUGH CARTWRIGHT (grand-father of the above) 117 a. in St. Philips Parish, Charleston, (recorded at Sur. Gen. office 23 May 1733; & whereas he died intestate & his son & heir, RICHARD CARTWRIGHT became the owner & by will dated 5 Mar. 1715/6 bequeathed to his son HUGH (party hereto) part of 1 of his plantations butting E on the Broad Path; W on a creek running into Ashley River; N on COL. GEORGE LOGAN & the Creek; S on a dividing line to be run to make a partition between that part & the part to be given son DANIEL CARTWRIGHT; the part given HUGH to contain 6 chains fronting the Broad Path & run in a direct course to the pond dug for watering the cattle. Witnesses: RICE PRICE, HENRY FLETCHER, JOHN REMINGTON. Before ROBERT AUSTIN, J.P. & Pub. Reg.

Book T, p. 675
21 & 22 Feb. 1739
L & R

WILLIAM BROCKINTON, gentleman, & SARAH his wife, to JOHN MCCANTS, planter, all of Winyaw, Craven Co., for L 884:10 shillings currency, 488 a. (of which 288 a. is part of 400 a. granted PAUL BERNEAU on 4 June 1735, the other 200 a. having been granted to BROCKINTON); in Craven Co., bounding NW on MR. HUNTER; NE on JOHN THOMSON; SE on CAPT. BROCKINTON; SW on JAMES CAMBELL. Witnesses: RICHARD (his mark) WALKER, THOMAS POTTS, JAMES LANE. Before JOHN WALLIS, J.P. ROBERT AUSTIN, Pub. Reg.

Book T, p. 679
9 & 10 June 1738
L & R by Mortgage

WILLIAM SIMPSON, planter, to DANIEL LAROCHE & THOMAS LAROCHE, merchants, all of Craven Co., as security on bond of even date in penal sum of L 1368:2:6 SC money, conditioned for the payment of L 684:1:3 on 1 Dec. 1738, 500 a. on which SIMPSON lives, in Craven Co., bounding SE on Waccamaw River; NE on THOMAS BLYTHE; SW on WILLIAM PINKNEY. Witnesses: THOMAS LEITH, JAMES CRADDOCK. Before THOMAS HENNING, J.P. ROBERT AUSTIN, Pub. Reg.

Book T, p. 685   WILLIAM HENDRICK, planter, to WILLIAM PORTER,
6 & 7 June 1740   nonconformist pastor & teacher, both of Christ
L & R   Church Parish, Berkeley Co., for L 32 SC money,
400 a. in Prince George Parish, Craven Co.,
bounding NW on the Rev. MR. PORTER'S land; all other sides on vacant land.
Witnesses: ROBERT LEWIS, JAMES (his mark) DUFF, MARY & ELIZABETH (her
mark) DUFF. Witnesses to receipt: MARTHA BEE, TABITHA PETER. Before DANIEL CRAWFORD, J.P. ROBERT AUSTIN, Pub. Reg.

Book T, p. 688   WILLIAM GUY, JR., gentleman, of Colleton Co.,
22 & 23 July 1740   to JAMES ST. JOHN, ESQ., of Charleston, for
L & R   L 762 SC money, 508 a. in Colleton Co., purchased by WILLIAM GUY from THOMAS BUTLER, JR.
& CONSTANT his wife on 11 Aug. 1739, bounding SE on SAMUEL SLEIGH; SW on
MRS. BOONE; NE on JOHN POSTELL; NW on land laid out. Witnesses: JONATHAN
THOMPSON, WILLIAM IRWIN. Before JAMES ABERCROMBY, J.P. ROBERT AUSTIN,
Pub. Reg.

Book T, p. 694   GEORGE CHICKEN (son & heir of GEORGE CHICKEN,
8 & 9 June 1731   ESQ.) & LYDIA, his wife, to CATHERINE CHICKEN,
L & R   widow of GEORGE CHICKEN the father, for L 1300
currency, all that 1/4 part of 1/2 lot #41 in
Charleston, now occupied by CATHERINE BETTISON fronting 29 ft. N on a
street leading W from Cooper River, & bounding E 99 ft. on THOMAS ELLIOTT;
W on ROBERT TRADD; also lot # ( ) being the northernmost lot of Schenckingh's Square occupied by DR. DANIEL GIBSON. Witnesses: NOAH SERRÉ,
JEAN MCCLELAN. Before NOAH SERRÉ, J.P. ROBERT AUSTIN, Pub. Reg.

Book T, p. 699   CATHARINE CHICKEN, widow, of St. James Goose
17 & 18 June 1740   Creek, Berkeley Co., to NOAH SERRÉ, ESQ. of St.
L & R   James Santee, Craven Co., for L 800 SC money,
1/4 of the 1/2 of lot #41 in Charleston (i.e.
the westernmost half quarter part), fronting N 29 ft. on a street (now
called Tradd Street) leading from Cooper River W towards Ashley River;
bounding E 99 ft. on THOMAS ELLIOTT; S on COL. BREWINGTON; W on COL.
HICKS. Whereas WILLIAM, Earl of Craven, Palatine, & the Lords Proprs. on
5 Oct. 1681 granted CAPT. THOMAS CLOWTER lot #41 in Charleston; & whereas
the westernmost half quarter part has by several conveyances become the
property of CATHERINE CHICKEN; now she conveys to SERRÉ. Witnesses:
GEORGE CHICKEN, THOMAS CHICKEN. Before ISAAC MAZYCK, J.P. ROBERT AUSTIN,
Pub. Reg.

Book T, p. 702   ARTHUR FOSTER, planter, of Craven Co., to JOHN
21 & 22 July 1740   CROKATT, merchant, of Charleston, as security
L & R by Mortgage   on 2 debts of L 381:13:11 & L 108:7 SC money,
3 tracts; 1 of 107 a. in Prince George Parish,
Winyaw, near Georgetown, bounding E on JOHN FURBISH; S on JOHN WHITE; N
on CAPT. STEPHEN BEAUCHAMP; also, 800 a. in Craven Co., bounding S on
BENJAMIN AVANT; & on all other sides on vacant land; also, 200 a. in Craven Co., bounding NW on MR. FOSTER; NE on the MESSRS. LAROCHE; SW on EDWARD BULLARD; SE on MRS. SARAH JOHNSON. Whereas ARTHUR FOSTER & ANTHONY
WHITE, planter, of Craven Co., gave bond dated 19 Dec. 1735 (for the proper debt of FOSTER) to THOMAS FLEMING, WILLIAM SCOTT, & THOMAS LAMBOLL,
executors of will of JOHN RAMSAY, in penal sum of L 763:7:10 currency
conditioned for payment of L 381:13:11 on 19 June 1736 with interest; &
whereas soon after the death of JOHN RAMSAY the said JOHN CROKATT married
MARGARET (daughter, devise & residuary legatee of JOHN RAMSAY) by whom he
had children, so that the residue of RAMSEY'S real estate became vested
in JOHN & MARGARET CROKATT in her lifetime; & whereas, after her death,
he sued out letters of administration of her personal estate from the
Prerogative Court of Conterbury, & after his arrival in SC became legally
entitled to receive the rents, issues & profits of JOHN RAMSAY'S real estate, & exhibited his bill of complaint to the Court of Chancery of SC
against FLEMING, SCOTT, & LAMBOLL, stating that RAMSAY died possessed of
much real estate & personal property of great value & that soon after RAMSAY'S death his executors took possession of everything; & whereas the
court on 22 Feb. 1738 decreed that the executors should deliver all RAMSAY'S estate to CROKATT as set forth in the schedules & accounts annexed
to their answer; & whereas the interest money on L 381:13:11 is paid, &
ARTHUR FOSTER & ANTHONY WHITE acquitted; & whereas FOSTER stands bound to

CROKATT for the 2nd bond; now FOSTER gives CROKATT as security, the 3 tracts of land, also 1 Negro man, 1 perriagua with her mast, rigging & furniture. Witnesses: JOHN LINING, JAMES MICHIE. Before ROBERT AUSTIN, J.P. & Pub. Reg.

LANGLEY ABSTRACTS VO. I.
INDEX

Prepared by
Barbara Dickey & Kit McFarland
Arlington, Texas

ABBOTT, Elizabeth 302,303, 315
  John 228,243,302,303, 315,338,351,369
ABERCROMBY, James 166,168, 201,206,209,228,231, 233,238,265,342,377, 378,382
ACKENE, James 154
ADAMS, David 24
  Elizabeth 24,74
  James 233,280,281
  Mary 228
  Nathaniel 24
  William 120,145,181
ADDERL(E)Y, John 357,358
ADDISON, Benjamin 152,157, 163,221,246,259,309, 333
AGNEW, Alexander 337
AIGVINTS, John 5
AIKIN, James 140
  Thomas (Aiken) 125,140, 376
AKERS, Edmond 137
AKINS, ___ 34
  Eliz. (Akin) 140,141
  James (Akin) 98,141,144, 194,233,234,252,329,339
  John (Akin) 18,141,327, 328
  Margaret (Akin) 147,170
  T. (Akin) 70,73,80
  Thomas (Akin) 60,141, 147,170,302,362
ALAND, John Fortescue 331, 332
ALDERMANBARY, Maria 13
ALDRICHE, William 5
ALEXANDER, ___ 14
  David 357,358,363
  John 120,296
  Mr. 343,344
ALIEN, Joseph 181
ALLAN, David 311
ALLEIN, David 208 (Allien)
  Esther 294
  Mary 351,365
  Richard 5,20,23,40,59, 65,67,73,74,76,84,86, 93-95,111,116,117,119, 173,189,190,191,204,212, 222,231,241,247-249,254, 262,278,279,294,301,302, 315,320,327,329,350
ALLEIR, Richard 58
ALLEN, ___ 27,28
  Andrew 1,13,17,27,30, 56,64,68,71-74,81-84, 99-101,107,108,110,111, 149,153,155,156,159,167, 182,195,196,198,204,208, 220,228,233,239,279,306, 322,323,335,359,376,377
  Bridget 152
  David 62,148,171,371
  Eleazer 17,29,33,35,42, 58,59,74,76,84,125,143-145,156,174,322,323,351
  James 173,308
  Jane 359
  John 239,266,309,335, 337,353,377
  Joseph 334
  Mary 335,377
  Obadiah 152,162

ALLEN, cont'd:
  Richard 57,82,144,367
  Sarah 74
  Susannah 323,334
  Thomas 35,212,280
  William 69,128,217,237, 363
ALLIN, William/Wm. 144,306
AL(L)STON, Deborah 261
  John 87,88,102,148,184, 261,292,333,334,379
  Joseph 285
  Peter 334
  Stephen 148
  William 252,261,274,275, 284,314,333,334,342,367, 368,379
ALRAN, John 273
ALURENS, John 163
AMANT, Mary 277
AMBROSE, John 253
AMORY, Jonathan 10,11,74, 82,85,140,141,144,256
  Jonathan, Sr. 52,60,67
  Martha 10,256
  Mr. 84
  Rebecca/Rebekah 42,43, 125
  Robert 10,256
  Sarah 10,256
  Thomas 10,42,52,60,125, 256,342
AMY, ___ 361
  Thomas 8,90,187,236
AMYAND, Isaac 172,277,290, 300,305
ANDERSON, David 106,175
  John 308,311
  Robert 301
  William 262
ANDRAS, ___ 216
ANDREE, George 364
  William 364
ANDREW(S), Israel 152,294, 380
  John 54,57,180,308,331, 346,353,356
  John, Jr. 216
  Joseph 216,291
  Thomas 308
ANGSDOURGER, Samuel 338
ANN, Mad'm Hall 3
ANNANT, John 111,175
  Mary 111,175
ANSON, George 90,186,226, 229
ANTEL, Rebecca 141
ANTHONY, Lord Ashley, Earl of Shaftsburg 8,11,22, 37,45,68,69,90,132,146, 187
  Samuel 117
APPELBY, Benjamine 212
ARBURY, Henry 30
ARCHBALD, Thomas 209
ARCHDALE, John 13,26,38,74, 90,114,135,186,236,245, 329
  Thomas 8,90,187
ARDEN, Edward 18,36
  John 18
  Margaret 51,65
ARES, Elizabeth 306
  Zachariah 306
ARLEY, Thomas 354
ARMSTRONG, Charles 225,327

ARMSTRONG, cont'd:
  James 339
ARNETT, David 224,336
  John 162
ARNOLD, Capt. 145
  Ephraim 6
  George 30
  John 97,173,192,193, 259,345
  Martha 97,192,193
  Mary 173
  William 95,191
ARNOLL, John 97,113,130
  Martha 97
ARNOLT, John 151
ARNOTT, David 251
  John 96
  Martha 96
ARTHUR, Bartholomew 235, 241,247
  Catherine 300
  Christopher 48,60,61, 78,121,157,241,349
  Dominick 48,121,349
  John 300
  Nathaniel 371
  Pricilla 371
ASH, Algerno(o)n 88,184, 199,217,232,343,346
  Ann 328
  Isabella 184
  John 12,36,88,133,184, 242,328
  John Baptista 12
  John Richard 88
  Marmaduke 309
  Richard 92,184,188,376
  Samuel 88,184,229
ASHBY, Constantia 82
  Elizabeth 120,268
  Jemima 120
  John (also Ashbey) 42, 61,80,82,86,108-111, 120,121,126,140,142, 160,174,211,268,359
  Mary 121
  Theodesia 120
  Thomas 98,121,127,172, 194,233,234
ASHLEY, Anthony 132
  John 48,61
  Maurice 22,35,37,45,61, 63,68,69,132,146,211
  Samuel 146
ASHTON, Jacob 27,43
ASHWORTH, Hawett 17
  Jasper 16,17
  Susanna 16,17
ASKINS, John 276
ASPENELL, John 164
ASSHETON, Ralph 258
ATCHINSON, John 145,337
ATCHISON, David 88,184,185
  George (Acheson) 88, 184,185
  John 166,318,320,322
  Mary 318
ATHARTON, Mary 311
ATKIN(S), Anthony 136
  Edmond/Edmund 308,327, 328,329
  James 301,356
  John(also Attkin) 18, 172,212,213,301,308,329
ATKINSON, Anthony 44,84, 136,273,302

ATKINSON, cont'd:
    Elizabeth 302
    John 165
    Thomas 172
ATTWOOD, Martha 28
ATWELL, Benjamin 130,213
    Jifford 3
    Joseph 130,213
ATTWELL(ATWELL), Tifford 7,22
    Joseph 44
AUCHTERLONY, D. 302
AUDEBORT, Moses 309
AUDET, John Dominique 294
AUGUSTINE, Wm. 125
AUNAN, Pierre 120
AURANT, Mary 277
AUSTIN, Benjamin 59,83,147
    George 200,294,311,335
    Mary 325
    Robert 109,130,156,172,
      202,205,224,248,253,254,
      263,265,268,271,273,275,
      277,279,280,284-290,292,
      295,297,300-341,343-
      353,355-366,368-383
AVANT, Benjamin 382
    Caleb 371
    Francis 44,302
    Mary 44
AVERY, Waitstill 264
AVILLE, William 149
AXALL, Humphrey 74
AXSON, Mary 172
    Jacob 266
    Samuel 98,194
    Wm. 98,172,194
AXTELL, Lady Rebecca/Re-
    bekah 52,77,82,175,183
AYERS, Jacob 357
AYRES, Thomas 240,301
AYTON, Philip 201,222,230,339

BACON, Joseph 135,368
    Michael 22,37,174,179,
      197,213,291
    Thomas 135
BACOT, Mary 95,191
    Peter 95,191
BADENHOP, ____ 298
    C. C. 210
    J. 148,293,314
BADGER, George 356
BADSDEN, Charles 5
BAFFORD, ____ 263
BAGEN, John 182
    Owen 182,372
BAGGS, ____ 3
BAILEY, Ann 234
    Brian 274
    Henry 373,374
    Joseph 234
    Ralph 373,374
    William 27
BAILIE, Richard 17
BAILLIE, Gavin Hamilton 347
    R. 9
BAILLIES, Richard 345
BAILY, John 87
BAIN, James 154
BAIRD, Mathew 81,342
BAKER, Elizabeth 21,22,70,178
    Francis 255,265
    James 42
    Johanna 21
    John 2,121,135,158,178,
      200,220,225,228,310,352,353
    Joseph 42,114
    Josiah 377
    Mary 172

BAKER, cont'd:
    Philip 264
    Rebecca 377
    Richard 12,21,37,42,63,
      65,70,77,88,135,146,
      155,170,173,177,178,
      184,213,230,245,246,
      248,325
    Samuel 342,359,371
    Sarah 121,124,316
    Susannah 114
    Thomas 22,37,60,76,135,
      239,242,247,291,368
    Widow 22
    William 63
BALDOCK, William 224
BALDWIN, Samuel 247
BALDY, David 151,270-273,277,377
BALIR, James 202
BALL, David 201
    Elias 89,185,270,291,292
    George 308
    John 169
    John Coming 270
    Papillion 171
    Richard 21
    Sampson 372
    William 90,91,165,186,187,299,372
BALANTINE, David 115
BALLANTINE, James 196,263,266
    John 182,206,266
BALLAUGH, William 49,72,102,187
BALLANTINE(BALLINTINE),
    James 100,137
    John 37,137
    Simon 138
BALLOUGH, Elizabeth 110
    John 110
    Martha 110
    Wm. 110
BALNEAVIS, James 22,58,59
BAMBURG, James 82,84
BAMFIELD, Elizabeth 265
BAMPFIELD, Elizabeth 265,283
    George 103,109,144,145,238
BANBURY, James 9
    Judith 82
BANKS, Jeremiah 312
    Mary 129
    Richard 331
BANOE, John 234
BARBER, John 205
BARBOT, Francis 254
BARBOUR, Edward 128
BARGER, John 205
BARKER, Charles 87,112,183,
      270,279,296,299,311,315
    John 112,244
    Joseph 302,356
    Rebeckah 37
    Sarah 112
    Thomas 91,187,225,309
    Thomas, Jr. 118
    Thomas, Sr. 118,124
BARKERSFIELD, Sarah 255
BARKFIELD, Thomas 128
BARKSDALE, Anne 357
    John 9,14,15,16,19,22,
      24-27,30,35,36,38,40,
      42-44,48,49,54,60,62,
      64-66,68-70,77-81,89,
      91-94,96,97,158,162,
      183,185,188-190,192,
      193,201,221,293,302,
      327,356,357,366
    Sarah 201,271,293

BARKSDALE, cont'd:
    Thomas 77,83,118,201,
      224,319,336
BARLYCORN, Anne 150
    Nicholas 150
    Richard 150
BARNARD, John 330,343
BARNES, Thomas 95,191,251
BARNET(T), Ann 378
    George 249,256,257,
      317,378,379
    Hannah 268
    John 258,310,348,379
    Jude(a) 379
    Judith 310,379
    William 45
BARNS, John 296
BARNWELL, Col. 363
    John 1,29,65,98,102,
      194,272
    Nathaniel 111
BARONS, Samuel 52
BARRIE, James 223
    Purchase 223
BARRY, Edward 244
    Joseph 265
    Victor 107
BARSKERFIELD, Thomas 255
BARTON, Anne 219,326
    Henry 71
    John 2,93,103,129,189,
      219,220,268,270,296,
      326,349,369
    Mary 112
    Rebecca 219,326
    Thomas 12,15,35,71,106,
      129,142,146,151,155,
      161,163,166,219,252,
      253,263,273,326
    William/Wm. 219,292,
      326,349,369
BARTRAM, Thomas 89,175,200
BARTRAU, Thomas 185
BASDEN, Charles 5,45,46,
      55,100,112,137,160,
      169,196
    Mary 5,27,38,39,45,46,
      54,55,67,72,79,112,133,
      137,163,166
    Rebecca 5,45,46
    Sarah 5,45,46,160
BASFORD, James 35,96,192,
      201,376,379
BASKERFIELD, Ann 353
    Jasper 124
    John 353
    Thomas 200,255
BASNETT, Mary 158,159,160
BASSETT, Elias 171
    George 20,21
BASSETT(BISSETT), Jane
    (alias Packquenett)
      171,172
    John 94,190,354
    Mary 200
    Nathan 120,206
BASSNELL, John 228
BASSNETT, John 248,311,316,363
BARWICK, George 9
BATCHELLER(BATCHELLOR,
BATCHELOR,BATCHELER),
    David 64,174
    Sarah 311
BATEMAN, Robert 66
BATH, Hon. John 55
BATOON, ____ 38
    Cornelius 8,42,68,84
BAUGH, Edmund 2
BAXTER, John 311,337,376
    Sarah 337
BAYLEY, Barnaby 21

BAYLEY, Hannah 181
  Honey 216
BAYLEY(BAILEY,BAYLY), John
  32,37,39,47,55,79,86,
  87,90-93,98,100,102-
  107,114,115,122,124,
  126,130-132,134,142,
  143,152,156,165,166,
  168,181,183,184,186-
  189,194,196,240,261,
  290,297,355,363,366,
  374,375,376
  Martha 21
  Mary 373
  William 38,67,79,163,
  166,181
BAYNARD(BANARD), William
  63
BAYN(E)BRIDGE, ____ 330,
  375
BEACH, Henry 343
BEADEN, Elizabeth 205,206
BEADEN(BEDON), George 206
BEADON, Richard 49
BEALE, John 28,302,352
  Othniel(e) 12,53,138,
  147,167,168,170,171,172,
  223,226,228,230,231,235,
  264,279,323,324,326,327,
  373,376
BEAMOR, Florence 45
BEAMOR(BEAMER), Jacob 29,
  68,119,165,187
  James 91,93,94,102,104,
  119,120,123,165,187,189
  Johanna 29,68
  John 23,24,29,45,68,101,
  119,197
  Margaret 68,119
  Sarah 15,44,49,91,93,
  102-104,119,120,123,
  129,138,150,187,189,
  190
BEAMOUR, Jacob 15,140
  James 15
  John 15,20
  Margaret 15
  Sarah 14,15
BEAN, Ester 7
  John 7
BEARD, Mathew 104,105,131,
  132,235,354
BEATTY, James 317
BEAUCHAMP, Adam 6,158,168
  Stephen 208,234,296,300,
  334,335,360,382
BEAUVAIS, Anthony 304
BEAVILL, Ann 335
  Timothy 335
BECKHAM, Ebenezer 47
BECKER, Edward 119
BECKETT, Thomas 265,291
BECKITT, John 101,196
BECKETT, Thomas 170
BEDON, ____ 10,12
  Henry 116,122,142,266,
  267
  John 292
  Mary 376
  Richard 9,10,12,14,18,
  64,84,172
  Sarah 376
  Stephen 171,172,218,322,
  329,376
  Thomas 129,152
BEE, Charles 131
  Dorothy 97,192
  John 1,54,82,147,151,
  157,158,171,207,241,
  267,271,278,292,305,
  346,373,378
  Joseph 95,97,192,193
  Martha 95,97,192,193,
  241,382

BEE, cont'd:
  Mary 95,192,378
  Matthew 95-98,133,134,
  147,171,192,193,313,
  356
  Sarah 95
  Sawah 191
  Thomas 313,321
BEECH, Christinia 146
  Christoper 125,126,146,
  150,153,234,268
  Christopher, Sr. 125
  Grace 146
  John 126,153
  Joseph 125,126,146,152,
  153
  Mary 146
  Richard 125,126,146,
  153
BELCHER, Elizabeth 223
  Gill 47,223
  Joseph 223
BELIN, Allard 267
  James 267
BELL, Ann 58
  Daniel(Daniel) 36,58,
  69,167
  Elias 148
  Jacob 17,43,66
  John 1,58,61,66,85,90,
  95,187,191
  John, Jr. 66
  John, Sr. 51,61,99,195
  Mathew 199
  Priscilla 51,99,195
  Robert 287
  Thomas 104
BELLAMY, Edward 265
  Timothy 5,350
BELLING, James 316
  William 47
BELLINGER, ____ 240
  Edmd./Edmund 6,23,26,
  55,63,73,88,107,134,
  147,184,210,221,232,
  233,236,244,252,271,
  373,374,377
  Edward 322
  Elizabeth 56,147,210
  William 15,102,119,120,
  189,190
BELTON, Margaret 322
  Peter 322
BENATONE, John 277
  BENESON, George 294
BENHOSTE, ____ 201
BENHOST, Jonas 200
BEN(N)ISON, George 71,83,
  166,307
BENNET(T), Alexander 268,
  287,288,332
  Edward 3
  Elisha 70
  Henry 155
  John 6,83,166,225
  Mary 117
  Moses 84,169,283
  Nicholas 82,106,117
  Samuel 19,51,62,162
  Sarah 117
  Thomas 129,149,166
BENNOIT, Jean 346,347
BENOIST, Charles 321
  James 168
  Peter 168,260,261,274,
  275
  Susanna 243
BENSON, Geo. 222
BENSTON(E), John 90,106,
  110,111,186,217,318,
  319,354
BENTLY(Bennett?), ____ 83
BENTLEY, Ellener 50
  George 71,294,304

BERCHES, Ann(e) 168,345
BERE, Per. 5
BERESFORD, ____ 198
  John 98,127,144,224,
  226,227,233,236,241,
  249,251,281-283,286,
  295,305,339,341,355
  Richard 19,27,40,45,
  46,61,98,105,107-111,
  127,144,150,156,176,
  194,200,233,234,258,
  281,307,339,345
BERGERON, James 7
BERISFORD, Michael 305
BERNCHETT, Nicholas 6
BERNEAU, Paul 381
BERRIE, James 143,153,332,
  346,347
  Purchase 347
BERRINGER, John 191
BERRY, Benjamin 88,184
  Edward 84
  Elizabeth 17
  Isabella (Ash) 88,184
  James 17
  John 255
  Julian (female) 84
BERTIE, Edward 330,332,
  333,362
  Henry 307
  James 307
BERTINSHAW, Thomas 102
BESHER, Thomas 251
BESKETT, Nicholas 125
BEST, Wm. 168
BESWICK(E), Charles 182
  John 200,378
BETHRAY, Daniel 290
BETSON, Mary 64,82-84,99,
  168,194
BETTSON(BETSON), William
  18,21,46
BETTESON(BETTISON), Cath-
  erine 129,166,172,382
  Hester 182
  Jonathan 182
  John 166
  Mary 166,309
  Mr. 164
  Wm. 166
BETTERSON, John 254
BEVERLY, Joseph 312
BICARIDGE, ____ 73
BIDDLE, John 308
BIDEAU, Henry 142
BIGGS, Stephen 167,168
BIGNION, Joseph 288
BILLIALD, John 343
BILLING, Allard 316
  Gideon 315
  James 316
  Sarah 316
  W. 10
  William 3,7,12,16,19,
  20,22,25,28,49,54,57,
  62,65,70,71,76,83,84,
  94,96,115,128,190,192,
  230,290
  Zenobia 315
BINDORD, Thomas 161
BINFORD, Thomas 54,228
BIRD, John 91,123,138,165,
  187
BIRGIS, John 243
BIRK, John 166
BIRMONT, Joseph 369
  Susannah 369
BISCOE, Joseph 119
BISHOP, Mary 79
  John 361
  Robert 79
BLACHARD, Francis 177
BLACKWELL, Michael 147,150
BLAIR, James 148

BLAKE, ____ 88,102,185
    Elizabeth 53,84,121,220
    John 74,152,160,363
    Joseph 15,20,25,26,33,
       38,49,55,63-65,85,88,
       96,121,134,140,141,152,
       166,170,172,174,183,184,
       192,204,205,214,220,221,
       225,227,232,236,254,259,
       262,268,287,305,323,324,
       332,341,350,370
    Josiah 114,115
    Richard 153
    Sarah 254
BLAKEWAY, Sarah 232
    William 22,24,186,187,
       290
BLAKEWEY, William 2,3,8,10,
    13,16,17,19,40,41,52,
    53,64,68,82,90,91,108,
    126,135,333
BLAMYER, John 153,253,254
    Mary 39,44,72,78,92,101,
       114,131,133,163,166,188,
       202,329
BLANSHAW(E), Francis 55,122
BLANTON, Thomas 58
BLONDELL, Thomas 374
BLUNDELL, Anne 164
    Easter 164
    John 164
    Samuel 164,234
BLY, Harral 38,72
BLYDESTEYN, John 270
BLYTHE, Jane 310
    Thomas 310,329,381
    Samuel 66,94,95,191
BLYTHE/BLYTH, Thomas 207
BOAN(BOEN), John 39
BOCHET, Abel 363
    Mary 154
    Nicholas 113,139,140,
       150,151
BOCKING, Thomas 16,147
BOCKINGTON, William 270
BODDICOTE, Richard 361
BODDICOTT, Ann 330
    Richard 227,330,333,378
BODDINGTON, William 363
BOGAR, Mathurine 36
BOGARD, Mathurin 205,231
    Susannah 231
BOGGS, James 141
BOGS, John 356
BOHANAN, Robert 66
    William 51,270
BOHUN, Nicholas 12
BOIGARD, Mathurine 103,215
BOISIER, Thomas 128
BOISSEAU, James 304,348,350,
    380
    Jane 350
    John 170,175
BOISSO, James 146
BOLL, John 276
BOLLARD, ____ 5
BOLLOUGH, William 91,170,
    361
BOLTON, Ann(e) 65,328
    Elizabeth 340,362
    Rebecca 65
    Thomas 65,220,227,272,
       328,336,337,341,361,
       362,367
BONALLE, Daniel 137
BOND, Edward 326
    J. 160
    Jacob 69,124,127,131,
       142,145,252,221,222,
       369,379
BONEE, John 74,81
BONERS, John 216
BONHOIST, Peter 342
BONHOSTE, Elizabeth 222

BONHOSTE, John 71,127,208,
    222,310
BONHOSTE(BONHAST), Jonas
    51,62,71,124,208,222,
    282,333
    Marianne/Mareann/Mar-
       ian 71,127,310
BONNEAU, Anne 164
    Anthony 6,23,71,87,113,
       125-127,137,140,141,
       146,147,150,152,153,
       168,184,208,220,222,
       224,229,234,237,238,
       240,248,259,261,262,
       268,282,290,291,295,
       296,307,323,362,363,
       367,377,380,381
    Anthony, Jr. 50
    Anthony, Sr. 119,120
    Floride 363
    Henry 323
    Jacob 103,126,139,263
       268
    Jane(Jeanne) Elizabeth
       237,307,363
    John Henry 125,126,164
    Margaret Henriette 307
    Mary 137
    Peter 363
BONNELL, John 270,288
BONNER, Phebe 360
BONNET, Benjamin 357
BONNETHEAU, J. 41,123
    John 344
BONNIN, John 43,131,230,
    253
BONNY, Thomas 144,150,232,
    233,234,244,299,301
BONOIST, Abigail 249
    Peter 249
BONY, Thomas 320
BOONE, Ann 84
    John 50,70,142,158
    Joseph 76,129,130,136,
       143,158,216,220,225,
       233,252
    Madam 313
    Mary 336,365
    Mr. 87,183
    Mrs. 350,361
    Thomas 50,71,85,112,
       129,130,140,141,143,
       164,166,310,336
BORDEAUX, Andrew 128
    Anthony 193
BORGARD, Mathurin 34
BORLAND, Mr. 311
    William 315
BORROSE, John 46
BOSHER, Thomas 203,224,225,
    354
BOSIER, Thomas 237
BOSCOE, Mr. 179
BOSSARD, Henry 123,167,176
BOSWICK, Thomas 222
BOSWOOD, ____ 309
    Anne 309
    Elizabeth 146
    Ja. 124
    James 76,146,338
    John 309
    Sindinah 146
    William 310
BOTELER, Thomas 308,352
BOUDON(BEDON), Peter 50
BOULEE, C. 163
BOULT, Henry 247
BOULTON, Thomas 242
BOUNETHEAU, John 208
BOURAN, Anthony 33
BOURDEAUX, Anthony 96,249
    James 139
    Mariane 266
BOUREY, Joseph 284

BOURGAINE(BURGAINE), Allen
    61
BOURGET(T), Daniel 158,159,
    263,359,379
BOURY, Joseph 276
BOUTWELL, Burtonhead 270,
    288
BOWDON, Peter 71
    Tannah 71
BOWEN, John 51,255
BOWER, Ann 199
    Giles 303
    Martha 303
    Sarah 278,279
    Thomas 199,200
    William 92,188,199,
       268,278,279,343,373
BOWLIN, Susannah 126
    Thomas 120
BOWLING, Thomas 135
BOWMAN, Arthur Lone 147
    Mr. 332
    Robert 343
    Samuel 35,343
    Sarah 343
BOWNE, William 247
BOWREY, Elizabeth 306
    Joseph 238,306
BOXLEY, Edward 305
BOYD, James 269
    John 269
BOYDEN, John 50,103
BOYNTON, Peter 3,46,56,258
BOZIER, Thomas 128
BRADLEY, Robert 31
BRADLY, Wm. 152,172
BRADSHAW, John 7
BRADWELL, Jacob 346
BRADY, Thomas 7
BRAGGAINS, Rachel 106
    Wm. 106
BRAILSFORD, Bridget 45
    Edward 35,36,104,106
    John 206,209
BRAITHWAITE, John 323,325,
    362
BRAMHAM, Francis 129
BRAND, ____ 64
    Elizabeth 62,230
    John 61,62,102,105,
       114,115,170,200,230,
       265,291,367,368
    Mary 200
    Mr. 286,290
BRANDFORD, John 225,230
    William 251
BRANFORD, Barnsby 170
    Ezekiel 356
    Joseph 356
    Mary 114
    Thomas 117,118
    William 114,178,180,
       224,373
    Zekiel 223
BRAY, William 336
BREAMER, James 139
    Peter 139
BREBANT, Daniel 142,237
    Elijah 358,359
    Magdalene 142
BREBRANT, Daniel 139
BREMAR(BREMER), James 139,
    237,251
    Margaret 29
    Martha 139
    Peter 139
    Solomon 139,200,236,
       237,266
BRENANT, Dr. 19
BRETON(BRETTON), John 23,
    76,77,91,113,187,208,
    247,268
    Magdalen June 268
    Michael 44

BRETON, Mr. 312
BREWER, Richard 305
BREWTON, Jehoida 163
  M. 161
  Mary 225
  Melicent 137
  Michael 32,71
  Miles 40,44,63,71,142,
    155,163,164,166,214,
    215,225,229,269,322,
    323,341
  Rebecca 225
  Robert 23,138,143,155,
    251,252,262,265,266,
    273,283,286,290,294,
    305,318,321,322,348,
    350,352,360,361,372,
    379
  Robert, Jr. 214,219,225,
    227,228,232,235,239,246
  Susannah 322,323
BRIAN, Ken. 179
BRICKLES, Richard 242,275,
  284
  Sarah 275,284
BRICKLOS, Richard 279
BRIGGS, John 250
BRIMAR, Solomon 307
BRISBANE, Robert 363
  William 166,265
BRITON, Daniel 348
  John 260
BRITTEN, Francis 99,195,
  316
  John 5,6
BRITTIAN, Daniel 244,250
BRITTON, Daniel 251,341
  Francis 85,124,310,333
BROAD, William 375
BROCK, Peter 126
  Sarah 213
  William 213
BROCKHAS, William 66
BROCKINGTON, Sarah 381
  William 101,117,196,
    276,338,351,355,376,
    381
BROCKINTON, Sarah 288
  Wm. 288,302,303,309
BRODIE, Ludovich 347
BROOK, Anna 153
  Catherine 153
  Robert 153
BROUGHTON, Andrew 38,81,
    119,123,227,230,341,
    359,360,370
  Ann(e) 35,41,123,172
  Charlotta Henrietta 264
  Daniel 173
  Edward 354
  Hannah 119
  Joana 370
  John 350
  Margaret 360
  Mary 360
  Nathaniel 62,81,119,
    123,155,164,227,264,
    341,359,360,370
  Peter 359
  Robert 359
  Thomas 3,10,21,46,48,
    49,55,61,63,68,69,81,
    82,89,98,108-111,119,
    123,127,140,142,144,
    147,150,164,169,172,
    174,176,185,194,211,
    228,231,233,234,237,
    238,240,241,244,246,
    247,249,251,253-255,
    257-259,262,270,271,
    276-281,283,284,286,
    288,289,292-294,296,
    298-301,303,305,309-
    311,314-316,320,322-

BROUGHTON, Thomas cont'd:
    -325,327,329,334,338,
    339,343,344,349,352,
    353,356,359,360,364,
    366,370-372,376,377
BROUMHEAD, Rebecca 368
  Robert 368
BROUNSON, Ann 113
  Joseph 113
BROWN, Andrew 236
  Catherine 219
  Christiana 296
  Clement 84
  Edward 28
  Ester 312
  Francis 114,178
  George 125
  Hannah 51
  James (also Browne)
    15,16,17,51,52,55,70,
    87,183,366
  John 6,24,28,36,43,57,
    114,131,132,137,143,
    149,158,168,178,180,
    201,229,245,249,287,
    296,309,338,366
  Katherine 326
  Lucy 6
  Peter 69,237
  Robert 235,236,247,252,
    280,284,321,368,369,
    375
  Samuel 365
  Sarah 252
  Thomas 147,249,257,312
BROWNE, Samuel 211,304
BROWN(BROWNE), William 226,
    249,268,284,287,289,
    327,329
BROWNING, John 155
BROWNSON, Joseph 175
BROZET, Ann 306,307
  James 306,307
BRUCE, James 145
  John 117,242
  Thomas 143,154
  William 198,308,323
BRUFFEAU, Paul 269
BRUINGTON, Michael 181
BRUM(M)ER, Solomon 23,236
BRUNEAU, Elizabeth 309,363
  Henry 81,93,189
  Mary Anne 93,189
  Paul 276,309,348,350,
    363
BRUNSON, Abraham 342,380
  Ann 96,192,268
  Isaac 52
  Jacob 380
  John 199,268
  Joseph 64,179,182,183
  Joseph, Sr. 113,114
  Mary 380
BRUNSTON, Mrs. 324
BRUTELL, Madam ___ 65
  Mrs. 350
  Peter 5
BRYAN(alias BARNABY RILEY)
  246
  Catherine 272
  Hugh 107,118,152,232,
    272,305,332
  John 137
  Jonathan 272,373
  Joseph 103,204,254,272,
    305,332,370
BUCHANAN, John 153,367
  William 306,307,310,
    311,372
BUCKALL, Jane 30
BUCKHOLTS, Jacob 365
BUCKLAND, John 264,265
  Sarah 264,265

BUCKLEY, ___ 38
  Grace 69,78,83,109
  Henry 55
  John 14,120,160
  Philip 137
BUCKNALL(BUCKNELL), John
  48,58
BUDDEN, John 315
BUER, Thomas 373
BUGG(S), John 76,77
BUGNION, Elizabeth 294
  Joseph 280,281,283,294
  Ralph 377
BUHMAN, Henry 355
BULL, Arthur 200,297,298,
  312
  Barnaby 244,252,322,
    364
  Farmer 80,120
  John 118,152,232,294,
    364,373
  Martha 343
  Mary 94,165,190,191,
    287,364
  Sarah 297,298,312
  Stephen 20,83,94,141,
    190,191,222,283,285,
    296,312,364,373
  William 12,26,36,37,
    47,52,65,70,74,84,91,
    93,94,98,114,115,119,
    129,135,137,148,149,
    165,167,183,187,189,
    190,194,197,204,222,
    232,240,241,252,254,
    277,280,287,288,296,
    305,307-309,321-323,
    325-328,332,335,338,
    343-345,348,354,357,
    358,363,365,370,377,
    380
  William Tredwell 59,
    104,132,159
BULLARD, Edward 256,261,
    274,275,281,320,341,
    342,382
  Elizabeth 275,281
  Hopkin 8
  Richard 8
BULLEN, John 351,378
BULLENE, Thomas 226
BULLINE, Thomas 112
BULLING, Thomas 30
BULLOCK, ___ 134
  Daniel 253
  Eliza 219
  Elizabeth 111
  James 74,75,97,133,
    145,171,193,232,245,
    276,312,313,331,343,
    346,354,356,377,379
  Jane 133,171
  John 165
  Mary 138
  Samuel 111,212,219,
    253,271,280,376
  Stephen 3,280
BULMER, Elizabeth 282
BUMARD, Martha 125
  Solomon 125
BUNCH, George 358
BURCHAM, Samuel 120
BURD, John 199
  William 294
BURDELL, Jacob 164,336
BURENS, John 132,133,137,
  138
BURETELL, Elizabeth 27
BURFORD, John 353
BURGES, Vickers 156
BURGESS, Robert 219,326
  Thomas 243
BURHAM, Charles 189

BURKE, John 51,70,121,131
BURKLEY, John 137
BURLEY, Charles 59,120,155,
    161,325
BURN, Walter 134
BURNET, Edward 215
BURNETT, George 28,112
    Job 5
    Mary 28
BURNEY, David 365
BURNHAM, Benjamin 337
    Charles 42,49,54,61,93,
    123,129,135,150,260,305
    Dr. 82
    Judith 135
    Mary 123
    Nathaniel 360
    Nicholas 209
BURNLEY, Abraham 105
    Hannah 338
    James 325
    Thomas 214
    William 112,197,272,
    274,279
BURNYEAT, Jonathan 343,344
BURR, James 312
BURRAGUY, Joseph 294
BURRELL, Thomas 259
BURRIDGE, Joseph 78
BURROWS, John 34
    Jroff 21
    Seamore 79
BURT, Absalom 153
    Nathaniel 235
BURTALL, Mr. 286
BURTELL, Elizabeth 50,264
    Peter 264
BURTON, Thomas 108,126,281
BURTT, Elizabeth 380
BUTLER, Abigail 377
    Ann(e) 34,62,309
    Constance 361,382
    Daniel 258
    Elisha 240
    Elizabeth 328
    Esther 48,73,244
    George 324,325,326,361
    H. 164,298
    Hugh 62,96,110,192,227,
    309,320,324,325,327,361,
    362,370
    John 21,34,35,325,**326**,
    361
    Joseph 167,168,208,252,
    321
    Mary 18,167,168,208,209
    Rebecca 252
    Richard 29,30,48,178,
    210,225,234,240,252,
    335,377
    Sarah 242
    Shem 73,156,244,252,
    263,328,370,377
    Thom 242,252
    Thomas 38,179,210,232,
    328,361,377,382
BUTOLPH, _____ 222,299,315
BUTTER, Elisha 210
BUTTERWORTH, George 160,287
    Lawrence 129,160
BUTTLER, Rebeckah 370
BYNON, Lewis 258

CAHUSAC, John 200
CAIN, Abraham 371
CAINHOY, Robert How 355
CALDER, _____ 245
    Archibald 148,366,371,
    373
CALHOUN, James 347
CALIS, Benjamin 363
CALKINS, Jonathan 285
CALLENDER, James 212,213

CALLENDER, Anna 213
CALVERT, William 45
CAMBELL, James 381
CAMPBELL, Ann 356
    Duncan 203
    Henry 288
    Hugh 86,94,97,98,101,
    114,120,122,190,193,
    194,196,232,239,244,
    277,331,355,356,364
    Martin 368
CAMPLIN, Richard 74
CAMPNEY(CHAMPNEY), John 38
CANTY, Elizabeth 51,64
CANTY(CANTEY), George 51,
    64,124
    James 51,64,87
    Joseph 217,296
    Josiah 124,217,310,338
    Wm. 124,217
CAPERS, Mary 15
    Mr. 124
    Richard 15,24,74,87,
    100,137,196,206,245,
    270,294,310,336,353,
    354,365,371
    Thomas 15,25,32,87,321
    William 48,137,365
CAPUS, Richard 283
CAREER, John 117
CARIEN(CARION), John 152,
    163,246,271,272,333
    Moses 269
CARLILE, Ann 212,256
    Elisha 66,266,299
    Elizabeth 66,296
    William 212,256
    Zekriah 66
CARLISLE, Elisha 315
CARLOW, Sarah 205,207
CARMICHAEL, John 54,56,86,
    93,175,190,240,262,
    274,354,377
    Mary 354
CARNICHAEL, John 54
CARPENTER, Benjamin 6
    Edward 276
    Oliver 6
CARRIER, John 100,196
CARROLL, Ann 5
    Anne 4
    Benjamin 4,5
    Bryan 4
    John 4,5
    Mary 18
    William 4,5
CARRON, Hugh 138
CAR(R)UTHERS, John 205,215,
    243,285,286,317,330,
    331,333,341,362,375,
    380,381
CART, South 60
CARTER, Mrs. 135
    Thomas 129
    Zebulon 135
CARTICE, Daniel 192
CARTOR, John 139
CARTWRIGHT, _____ 42,191
    Daniel 134,174,178,205,
    210,213,224,241,242,
    252,253,259,272,323,
    324,332,370,377,381
    David 252
    Hugh 323,324,381
    Joseph 174
    Mary 131
    Richard 95,191,205,262,
    268,287,323,324,331,
    381
    Robert 134,174
    Sarah 174,178,205,210,
    212,241,242,252,323
CARWITHEN, Mary 171,172,325

CARWITHEN, Wm. 171,172,
    325
CAREY(CARY), Thomas 13,26,
    33,114,140,154,172,329
CASHWELL, Jane 239
CASWELL, John 95-97,191,
    193
    Martha 95,191
    Sarah 96,97,192
CATER(S), Thomas 54,78
CATESBY, Mark 46
CATTELL, _____ 101
    Ann 199
    Benjamin (Cattle) 1,
    214,311
    Jane 199
    John (Cattle) 133,146,
    148,182,199,212,217,
    296,299,315
    Peter (Cattle) 28,33,
    78,122,243,285,380
    Sarah 133,299,315
    William 35,94,110,133,
    135,154,167,168,190,
    199,209,210,215,232,
    233,242,250,257,258,
    271,278,279,285,294,
    299,311,315,335,380
    William, Jr. 85,152,
    224
CAUTEY, Ann 112
CAVANAGH, Charles 333
CAVANAH, Dr. James 6
CAWOOD(CAYWOOD), Eliza-
    beth 65,88,184,376
    Gibbon 108
    John 11,12,48,51,55,
    56,65,67,72,108,157,
    204
CEELY, Peter 33,46,55,69,
    73
CERADEAU, _____ 309
CHABAR, Bierre 124
    Pierre 127
CHAMBERLAIN, Elizabeth 342
CHAMBERLINE(CHAMBERLAIN),
    Job 49,65,76
    Joseph 300
CHAMBERS, Thomas 104
    William 316
CHAMLETT, Joseph 368
CHAMPIGNON, Charles 93,189
CHAMPNEYS, John 1,29,122,
    148,182,239,296
CHANDLER, Philip 335,364
    Sarah 364
    Stephen 153
CHAPLIN, John 144
    Phoebe 144
    William 245
CHAPMAN, John 157,207,357
    Mr. 84,99,212
    William 39,72,96,100,
    102,137,160,167,192,
    196,248,290,301,327
CHARDON, Isaac 86,89,169,
    185,202,203,207,214,
    261,262,330
    Mary 305
CHARLES, Hon. _____ 28
CHARMOCK, Thomas 290
CHARNACK, Thomas 247
CHARNOCK, Thomas 243,246,
    247,300,364
CHARRON, Paul 88,103,184,
    319
CHARSON, Paul 354
CHASTAIGNE(R), Alexander
    264
    Daniel 197
    Henry Augustus 269
CHATAIGNER, Theodore 211
CHEESMAN, Elizabeth 369

CHEESMAN, Thomas 253,369
CHEEVERS, Ann 233
    Philip 7
CHEILDS, Mr. 362
CHERNLEY(CHEARNLEY), Edward 60
CHESSMAN, Thomas 216
CHESTER, Edward, Sr. 35
    John 92,99,188
    Jon. 195
CHEZALIER, Peter 78
CHICKEN, Catherine 130,231,
        382
    Francis 37
    George 2,17,21,44,55,
        58,59,86,99,115,130,
        150,155,161,175,178,
        195,215,231,269,271,
        277,309,325,361,382
    Lydia 269,382
    Thomas 382
    William 342
CHIDLEY, Anne 151
    Henry 151,208
CHILD(S), Benjamin 87,169,
        183,296
    Edward Keeting 150
    Francis 173,179,308
    Hester 239
    Isaac 125,253
    James 125,164,239,299
    Joseph 87,183,217
    Margaret 290
CHINNERS, Elizabeth 127
    Mr. 123
    Thomas 127
CHISWELL, Charles 6
CHOVEN(CHOVIN), Alexander
        269,276,364
    Isaac 269
CHRICKTEN, George 175,205,
        240
CHRISTINAZ, David 259,273,
        313,314
    Francoise 273
CHRISTMAS, Jonathan 202,345
CHRISTOPHER, Duke of Albemarle 8
CHURCH, John Yong 283
CITTENS, ____ 220
CLAGUE, Samuel 280
CLAPP, Elizabeth 95,191
    Gillson/Gilson 92,95,
        108,121,188,191,218,
        232,305,322
    Gitson 350
    John 25,38,39,72,176
    Margaret 95,191
CLARE, Joseph 14,56,244
CLARIDGE, George 36
CLARK, Edward 106
CLARK(E), James 54,319,363
    Jeremiah 63,133
    Jonathan 115,178,198
    George 48,64
    Robert 79
    Samuel 11,12,46,55,115,
        178,198,248,291
    Thomas 114,178,346
CLAY, Richard 210
    William 209,218,223,
        228,233,263
CLAYPOOLE, George 116,160
    Joseph 116
    Rebecca 116
CLAYTON, Seth 2
    Thomas 2
CLEE, Samuel 291
CLEIFT, Edward 98,194
CLEILAND, William 244
CLELAND, John 270,271,340,
        341,349,371
    Robert 340
CLEMENTS, Edward 7,221

CLEMENT(CLEMENTS), cont'd:
    James 356
CLEMMONS, Robert 269
CLEMONS, John 75,80
CLEMONS(CLEMMENTS), Robert 166
CLENCH, Alexander 49,83
    William 219,326
CLERK, Samuel 22,204
CLEWER, Elizabeth 85
CLIFFORD, ____ 78
    Benjamin 223,228
    Elias 118
    Mary 178,216,217
    Sarah 83,118,223,228
    Stephen 29,242
    T. 115
    Thomas 80,81,86,118,
        174,178,182,216,232,
        250,275,319
CLIFT, Edward 87,183
    Jeane 83
CLINCH, Michael 51,55,118,
        152
CLIPPERTON, John 36
CLOP, John 134
CLOWTER, Thomas 382
CLYATT, Hannah 18
    Robert 17,18,139,140,
        143,147,152,233,255
    Samuel 288
COACHMAN, Benjamin 214,314,
        323
    James 254,317,318
    John 264,295,371
COBB, Joseph 114,131
COBLEY, Jemmot 240
COBUS, Job 87
COCFIELD(CORFIELD), John
        321
    Rachel 321
COCHRAN(COCKRAN), Archibald
        33,354
    Hugh 168,217
    James 89,107,129,147,
        159,166,168,169,174,
        185,186,204,220,234,
        242,306,343,376
    John 14,232
    Mary 168
    Robert 33,121
COCKFIELD, ____ 95,191
    John 101,168,196,242,
        244,252
    Moses 244,245
    Rachel 244
    William 296
CODFREY, John 132
CODNER(GODNER), ____ 82
    Ann(e) 168,229,272,281,
        282,337
    Charles 167,168,229,
        272,281,282,337,339
    John 16
    Phebe/Phoeby 229,282
    Richard 42,84,108,127,
        135,144,168,172,174,
        202,229,234,255,281,
        282,295,317
    Sabina 135,295
COE, William 372,376
COFFARD, Henry 143
COFING, James 338
COGNER, Richard 172
COGSWELL, Mary 61,62
COIT(E), Hercules 355
    John 235,271
COKE, Bently 251
    Joseph 251
    Rebecca 302
COKER, James 2
COLCOCK, John 86,152,258
COLE, Joanna 25
    John 302

COLE, cont'd:
    Lawford 317
    Magdalene 317
    Mary 355
    Micajah 355
    Michael 99,195
    Robert 25,179,221,302,
        352
    Robert H. 355
    Thomas 31,47
COLKINS, Jonathan 264,275
COLLENS, Jonah 216
COLLES, Robert 222
COLLETON, ____ 177
    Ann 293
    Charles 21,243,254,293
    Elizabeth 293,308
    George 276,293
    J. 259,275
    James 16,40,110
    John 32,35,63,123,169,
        175,176,211,227,236,
        246,248,279,284,293,
        307,324-326,361,362,
        370,373
    Judith 16
    Peter 8,78,90,121,142,
        157,187,227,253,362,
        370
    Susannah 250
    Thomas 48,140
COLLIER, Joseph 4,200
    Rebecca 200
    Thomas 200
COLLINGS, Jona./Jonathan
        66,89,149,185,263,288
    Sarah 263,288
COLLINS, Alexander 35,77
    Andrew 44,51,302
    Ebwer 248
    Elizabeth 40
    Hannah 266
    Jonah 56,77,266,282,
        317,340
    Jonathan 38,39,55,72,
        79,95,112,191
    John 35,40,147,148,353,
        361,362
    Mary 44
    Sarah 35,38,39,55,72,
        112,302
    William 49,341
COLLIS, Carter 263,286
COLLWALL, Richard 151,371
COLLWEL(L), John 107
COLSON, James 339
    Thomas 220
COLT, Rebecca Anne 340
    William 207,251,340,
        345,366,371
COLWALL, Richard 366
COLWELL, John 339
COMBES, Elizabeth 35
    John 2,24,35,238,282
    Martha 282
    Philip 113,168,282,363
COMING, Affra 64,116
    John 10,11
COMMANDER, Abigail 258
    Dorothy 258
    Elisha 289
    Elizabeth 258,289
    Frances 258
    John 258,288,289
    Joseph 258
    Rachel 258
    Samuel 19,45,46,108,
        258,288,289
    Spriggs 54
CONANT, Richard 78,85,140,
        141
CONDON, Thomas 332
CONIERS, Thomas 19,118
CONLIES, Peter 117

CONN, John 22,297,302
    Thomas 297
CONYBEAR, Thomas 87,183
CONYERS, Esther 32
CON(N)YERS, John 108,134
CONYERS, Thomas 4,8
COOK(E), Ann 53,117
    Bently 10,11,164,234,
        281,310,333
    Giles 104,109,113,131,
        219,252,253,280,282,345
    Henry Michael 295
    John 208,217,282,283,
        296,313,341,360,372
    John Beresford 281
    Joseph 318
    Mr. 287
    Phanuell 219,220,333
    Rebecca 164
    Thomas 4,5,39
    William 278,279
COOKFIELD, John 167
COONE, Angelle 87
COOPER, Bernard Christian
        1,126
    Christian 72
    Dr. 38,39,40
    Edward 61
    Eleana 81,84,144
    Joseph 230
    Margaret Magdalene 113,
        148,198,255,256
    Robert 240,364
    Thomas 32,41,81,84,96,
        101,113,123,135,144,
        148,149,163,166,172,
        182,192,198,205,218,
        223,228,229,235,255,
        256,270,275,279,284,
        327
    William Allen 50
COPEN, Henry 175
COPENS, Edmond 322
COPPELL, James 343,344
CORANT, Edward 8
CORBEN, Rebecca 24
CORBETT, John 132
    Thomas 157
CORBIN, Francis 358
    James 77
    Rebecca 83
CORD, Isaac 84
CORDES, Catherine 261
    Charles 298,314
    Francis 120,253
    Thomas 95,123,191,261,
        268,304
CORNUT, David 282
CORREAR, John 244
CORUNT, Edward 179
COSENS, John 76
COSSENS, Nicholas 265
COSSETT, Field 308
    Lois 308
COSSINS, Edmond 229
COSTE, Isaac 338
    Magdalena 338
COSWELL, John 192
COTTINGHAM, John 45,264
COTTON, John 226
COUGH, John, Jr. 249
COUILLANDAU(X), Peter 184,
        261,333
COUILLANDANDAU, Peter 87
COUK, Wm. 112
COULET, David 364
COULIANDAU, Peter 269
COULLIETTE, Lawrence 46,71,
        76,80,95,105,108,191,
        218,231,238,286,317,
        340,354
COURAGE, Francis 157,333
    Manasseh 157

COUSIERAT, Isaac 154
COWEN, Benjamin 245
COWAN, Dorothy 37
COWAN(COWEN), John 37,245,
        374
COWAND, John 314
COWARD, John 298
COWEN, Marian 245
    Sarah 245
COWLES, James 121
COX, Ezekiel 363
    John 353
    Robert 353
    Walter 102,149,150,201
COYTE, Hercules 233,282,
        283
CRABTREE, Samuel 219,326
CRADDOCK, James 202,203,
        216,262,288,289,299,
        300,319,329,330,334,
        335,338,345,348,364,
        365,369,374,381
CRAFORD, Samuel 34
CRAIGIE, Charles 148
    James 257
CRAMA(C)HE, Alexander 264,
        283,293,318,343,361,
        381
CRAMAKE, Alexander 205,206
CRAVEN, Charles 12,13,35,
        61,65,70,117,121,125,
        130,150,163,172,225,
        226,247,268,288,296,
        320,322
CRAWFORD, Christian 367
    Daniel 300,309,352,366,
        367,382
    David 366,367
    Helen 367
    John 367
    Mary 367
    Robert 75
    Sarah 309
    William 366,367
CRAWLEY, Percival 70
CREAFORD, Samuel 27
CREAST, Nathew 100
CREED, Matthew 343
CRELL, Johanna 372
    Joseph 372
    Stephen 372
CRICHLOW, James 341
    Mary 341
CRICKLOW, James 244,251,
        296,301
CRICHTON, George 12,118
    James 31
CRIMSTON,   62
CRIPPS, William 335,353,
        364,365
CRISPE, Edward 359,360
CRISTIE, Henry 337
CRO(C)KATT (CROCKETT),
    Esther 165,174,215,344
    James 165,171,174,176,
        179,199,202,214,215,
        261,262,275,280,286,
        297,300,309,344,352,
        357,359,360
CROCKET, James 248
CROCKRAM, William 380
CROFT, Abraham 95,191,228,
        344,345,356
    Childermus 27,34,35,38,
        40,41,51,67,68,72,77,
        78,79,85,95,120,123,
        124,133,150,166,178,
        191,202,204,274,283,
        318,361,375,376
    Edward 9,26,38,39,41,
        45,60,79,89,128,167,
        185,221,222,266,267,
        287,378

CROFT, cont'd:
    Hilderson/Hill 4,31,
        79,145,198,199,272
    John 4-13,26,30-35,
        38,41,43-46,48,52,54,
        55,58-60,72,77,79,81,
        82,86,89,96,97,99,100,
        102,104,107,108,115,
        116,123,124,126,128,
        131,132,135,137,147,
        148,160,161,164,165,
        178,180,181,185,192,
        193,195-197,201,202,
        230,231,248,256,292,
        297,305,320,332
    Mr. 145
    Rebecca 83
    William 267
CROGAN, Thomas 30
CROHATT, David 145
    James 145
CROKATT, John 308,338,350,
        382,383
    Margaret 382
    Thomas 347
CROLL, Thomas 232
CRONY, Mary 11
CROOK(E), Martha 69,72,73,
        204
    William 19,39,63,64,
        83,204,354
    Sarah 11
CROSS(E), John 359
    Mary 27,38,67,72,79,
        114,133,137,163,166
    Mr. 91,187
CROS(S)KEYS, Elizabeth 4,
        75,96,105,192,248,344
    John 4,52,53,74,75,105,
        116,162,225,248,344
    Joseph 5,67,74,75,77,
        105,170,198,378
    Margaret 5
    Thomas 75,96,192
CROUCH(CHROUCH), Abraham
        263,264,371
    Arthur 301
CROWLEY, John 39
CRUBIN, Charles 167,168,
        210,214
CRUCHLOW, ___ 320
CRUGER, John, Jr. 172
CRUSTOE, Mary 112
CUMING(COMINGS), Alexan-
        der 145
    Grace 146
    Hugh 5
CUMING(S), John 5,20,125,
        126,146,152,153,224,
        229,234,244,277,363
CUMPPUS, Patience 266
CUMYNG, Jo. 197
CUNE, ___ 220
CURBISH, Elizabeth 225
CURRENT, Edward 29,56
CURSIN, Alexander 117,118
CURSON, Alexander 180
CURTIS, Daniel 20
    Edward 2
    Elizabeth 20
    Robert 4
CUTFIELD, Richard 177
CUTFIELD(CUTTFIELD),
    Thomas 42,77,86,114
CUTLER, Thomas 4
CUTTINO, Jeremiah 350,369
    Peter 352,353
CUTTION, Peter 353

DALBIAC, David 261
DALE, Thomas 207,209,211-
    213,216,217,219-223,
    225,227-229,232,234,

DALE, Thomas cont'd:
    238-241,244,246,247,
    249,253,257,260,263,
    265,266,269,270,273,
    286,290,296,297,312,
    313,316,318,319,326,
    336,339,344,345
DALLAS, Peter 332
    Walter 120,237
DALLEY, Charles 35
DALRYMPLE, John 303
DALTON, Catherine 171
    Jane 171
    James 171,273,344
    Thomas 311
    William 244
DANBRIDGE, George 41
DANDFORD, Joseph 82
DANDRIDGE, Francis 234
    Martha 123,154
    Mary 154
    William 165,328
DANERLY, Edward 139
DANFORD, Joseph 130,161
    Margaret 130
    Wm. 200
DANFORTH, Mary 30
    Wm. 128
DANIEL(L), Ann 13,98,194
    Col. 91,111
    Catherine 145
    Hellen 42,167,191
    Ja. 8
    John 13,58,108,127,128,
    144,150,163,167,173,
    176,200,232,243,281,
    339,356,365,378
    Jonathan 59
    Marmaduke 16,42,108,
    127,291,343,344
    Martha 10,16,41,67,98,
    108,116,117,135,194,
    198,289,291
    Martha, Sr. 13
    Mary 343
    Robert 10,13,16,23,31,
    35,41,42,55,58,59,60,
    63,65,67,77,80,84,88,
    95,98,105,106,108-111,
    116,117,123,127,135,
    137,140,141,149,150,
    154,156,162,164,165,
    167,172,176,184,191,
    194,198,203,206,226,
    229,230,236,263,282,
    289,302,313,320,339,
    346,355,369,372,381
    Robert (Jr.) 16
    Sarah 10,16,289
    Wm. 145
DANZEY, Sarah 264
DARB(E)Y, Michael 96,105,
    128,170,180,193,200,
    222,233,234,255,263,
    370
DARESLY, George 67
DARGON, Cornelius 199
DARNY, Richard 110
DART, Hannah 313,346
    John 49,106,146,155,
    221,222,247,313,346
DASHWOOD, Ann 50
    John 50
DAUBAWZ, Henry James 315
DAUCHTERLONY, 292
DAUSE, Robert 355
DAVENPORT, John 239
DAVIDSON, Robert 115
DAVIS, Ann(e) 82,106,216
    David 216,306,343,379
    Debora(h) 300,349
    Elizabeth 309
    Isaac 236,300,349

DAVIS, cont'd:
    James 43
    John 36,82,92,106,115,
    143,188,201,223
    Margaret 43
    Mary 221
    Mrs. 27
    Owen 236
    Samuel 54,126,343
    Samuel, Jr. 54
    William 180,221,327
DAWES, 227
    Anne 265,270
    Mrs. 287
    Philip 265,270
    Thomas 26
DAWFUSKIE, 357
DAWKINS, Richard 159
DAWS, Philip 225
DAWSON, John 205,319
    Macey 319
    Margaret 319
    Richard 249,250,319,
    341
DAY, Hugh 342
    James/Jas. 30
D'BORDEAUX, Anthony 142
    James 142
    Judith 142
DEAN(E), Anthony 336
    Daniel 21,211,254
    Mary 67
    Nathaniel 120,351,369,
    377
    Samuel 1,2,6,29,67,69,
    233
DEAR (DARE), John 21
DEAR, John, Jr. 21,69
    John, Sr. 69
DEARINGTON, Prudence 229
    Thomas 323
DEARSLEY, Edward 27
    George 27,72
    John 49
DEAS, John 252
DE BEAUFAIN, Berenger 358
DEBOURDEAUX, Anthony 34
    James 34
    Marian 34
DECHAMP, Francis 39,263,
    269
DEDCOTT, Abraham 232
    John 232
    Joseph 225
    Rebecca 232
DEDMIER, Albert 247
DEGUE, James 306
DEHEE, John Christofell
    164
DELABASTIE, A. 146
    Augustus 89,185
DELABERE(DELEBERE), John
    3,29,31,56,101,102,
    112,119,123,149,153,
    197,292
DELACONSEILLERE, 110
DE LA CONSEILLERS, Benja-
    min 12,24,42,65,79,91,
    94,111,115,116,126,
    154,155,162,187,190,
    215,218,219,243,250,
    252,254,255,297,322
DELA CONSEILLERE, Mr. 111
DELAMERE, Hallan 265
DELAMOTTE, Alexander 237
DELA PLAIN(E), 191
DELAPLAINE (DELAPLANE),
    Abraham 81,351
DELAPLAN(DELAPLAINE), Mr.
    95
DELAPLANE, Abraham Florey
    342
DELAULETTE, Andrew 361

DELAVELLETTE, John 271,272
DELAVILLETTE, Andrew 249,
    258,289,340
DELBIAC, David 340
DELEAUHE, John 50
DELESCURE, David 313,314
DE LESSENNE, Mr. 341
DE LETTERS, Andrew 276
DELIESSLIN(N)E, John 93,
    189,271,352
    Magdelane 93,189
DELMERTRE, Peter 378,379
DELMESTRE, 282
    Mary (Marie) 379
    Peter 338
DELONGUEMARE, Alexander
    137
    Nicholas 120
DELPH, Joseph 377
DELPON, John 350
DEMANE, Francis 292
DEMINE, Aeills 174
DENHAMP, William 240
DENISE, John 3
DENISON(DENNISON), Ambrose
    86,344
    George 83
DENNIS, 134
    Benjamin 1,36,93,126,
    129,149,158,189,198,
    201,223
    Capt. 176
    Lawrence 25,90,91,104,
    109,187,247
    Providence 91,187
DENNISTON, George 272
DENTON, Alexander 331,332
DERHAM, William 343
DE RICHBOUGH, Mr. 375
DERT, John 332
DESCHAMPS, Francis 113,
    168,202,295
DE ST. JULIAN, Demaris 62
    Elizabeth Demaris 212,
    280
    Henry 184
    James 88,90,91,184,186,
    187,279
    Joseph 54,87,91,165,
    184,187
    Paul 91,187,286
    Peter 37,49,62,86,87,
    88,90,91,103,127,145,
    164,182,184,186,187,
    212,265,270,280,299,
    306,340,344,351,361,
    363,364
DETMAR, Albert 82,209
DETMAR(DETMER), Christian
    209
DETRING, Anna Maria 366
DETRING(DUTERING), Herman
    Christian 365
DEVEAUX, A. 85
DEAVEAU(X), Andrew 6,38,
    122,131,132,152,178,
    224,237,251,283,360
    Anne 122,132
    Israel 256
    James 152
    Magdelene 360
DEVON, Charles 153
    John 153
    Richard 42,65,70,153
DEWDING, Joseph 287
DEXTER, Ann 365
    John 334,335
    William 365
DEYS, Joseph 156
D'HARRIETTE, Ann(e) 90,91,
    187
    Benjamin 36,163,164,
    256,323,337

D'HARRIETTE, cont'd:
    Benjamin Jr. 90,91,187
    Jamin 156
DICK(S), Arthur 103,111
    Daniel 22,305
    Ebenezer 102,103,111
    Edward 244
    Ellinor 219
    George 234,244,255,303
    Providence 22,47
DICKINSON, John 7
DICKSON, James 130,167
DIDCOTT, Benjamin 343
    Joseph 136,159,180,291,
       343
DIDLEY, Thomas 69
DILL, Elizabeth 4,75
    Joseph 4,60,75,105,344
DILLON, James Cornelius 43
DIMES, Thomas 3
DINGLE(E), John 86,95,191
    Mary 95,191
DISTANCE, Charles 132
DISTANT, Thomas 317
DISTON, Anne 293
    Charles 64,113
    Elizabeth 12
    Mr. 293
    Sarah 273
    Thomas 12,36,61,149,175,
       273,279
DIVEAU, Henry 237
DIXCE(Y), William 43,128
DIXON, Charles 126
    Mary 89,103,126,128,
       164,185
    Thomas 38,40,42,89,101,
       103,128,151,163,164,
       185,196,344
DOBBIN(S), Leonard 49,374
DOBSON, Joseph 283,284
DODSWORTH, Anthony 6,200
DONERVILLE, Legrand 340
DONEVILLE, Isaac Legrand
    340
DONNING, Frances 317
    Thomas 317
    William 174,237,248,
       279,317
DONNIS(DENIS), Benjamin 43
DONOMAN, ___ 34
DONOVAN, Anne 165
DONOVAN(E), Daniel 85,91,
    103,165,187,308
DOPSON, Thomas 289
DORROM, Jacob 151
DORSEY, John 107,273,287,
    291,342,380
DOSSEY, John 21
DOUGHLASS, William 122
DOUGLASS, George 346
DOUGLAS, William 243,381
DOUGLASS, John 45,46
    Sarah 5,45,46
DOUXSAINT, Paul 49,65,76,
    86,91,182,187,345
DOW, John 198
DOWDING, Joseph 287
DOWNES, Elizabeth 241
    Jeremiah 277
    Sarah 241
    Stephen 337
    William 241
DOWNS, Christopher 4
    Wm. 151
DOWSE, Abigail 63,178
    Stephen 63,197,198
DOYELL, Edward 208
DOYLE, Denis 346
D'PETERSEN, Jacob 172
DRACHE, Elizabeth 6
DRAKE, Edward 25,44,134,
    176
    John 371

DRAKE, cont'd:
    Jonathan 44,57,74,81,
       104,134,167,176,179,
       201,263,277,362,371
    Mary 44,74,134,167,176,
       201,213,371
    Mathew 179,314,319,323
    Samuel 44,57,134,176,
       213,248
    William 84,134,264,301,
       315,338,364
    William, Jr. 44
DRAYCOTT, Richard 325
DRAYTON, Ann(e) 14,29,34,
    35,73,74,147,230,296,
    304
    Elizabeth 222
    John 304,370
    Mrs. 115
    Stephen 138,148,150,
       163,210,323
    Stephen Fox 304
    Thomas 73,205,210,217,
       222,233,234,241,251,
       269,304,310,347,370,
       374
DREPER, Edward 21
D'RICHBOURG, Anna 176
    Claudius 176
    Elizabeth 176
    James 176
DRISDROW, Mary 370
DRIVER, John 164
DRUMMOND, James 325,346,
    367,380
DRY, Capt. 331
    Will 342
    William 2,21,63,73,77,
       80,88,115,116,118,157,
       184,244,270,298,320,
       353,378
DUBOIS, ___ 71
    Jasper 276
    John 371
DUBONDIEU, Judith 76
    Samuel 76
DUBORDEAUX, Mr. 259
DUBOSE, Isaac 249,310,333,
    379
    James 76
    John 139,249,270,280,
       281,283,294
    Mary 76
    Susannah 124,139,222,
       333
DUBOURDEAUX, James 50
DUBOURDIEU(DEBORDIEU),
    James 78
    Judith 16
    Judith (Jr.) 16
    Mr. 164,166
    Peter 364
    Samuel 16,164
DUBRUIL, John 78
DUCALL, George 167
DUCATT, George 156,157,288,
    313
    Margaret 339
DUCKER, John 345
DUCKETT, George 220
    Margaret 220
DUFF, Elizabeth 382
    James 382
    Mary 382
DUGEE, Mr. 89
DUGUE, Elizabeth 50
    Isaac 50
    James 62
    James, Jr. 75,76
    James, Sr. 50,75,76
    Judith 50
    Mariane 50,76
    Mary 50
    Mr. 185,350

DUGUE, cont'd:
    Peter 6,50,76
DUMAY, Etienne 93,189
    Peter 281
DUMONS, Isaac 160,224,356,
    363
DUMONT, Isaac 280
DUNBAR, Charles 339
DUNCAN, John 135
DUNDON, Edmund 245
DUNFORD, James 7
DUNHAM, Hannah 122
    John 122,127,234,311
DUNLAP, James 174
DUNLEP, James 197
DUNLOP, James 101
DUNNAM, John 369
DUNNIDGE, Ja.(bus) 21
    Jacobus 30
    James 4,5,15,16
DUNNING, Mr. 115
DUNSCOMB, Wm. 161
DUNSTON, John 23
    John (Sr.) 23
    Wilson 23
DUNWOODIE, Lawrence 367
DUNWOODS, James 243
DUPEY(DUPUY), Andrew 150,
    185
    James 161
    Jane 160
DUPOIDSDOR, James Mazyck
    8
    Mary Magdalen 131
DUPONT, A. 314
    Abraham 178,211,254
    Gid. 314
    Gideon 358
DUPRE, Ann 241
    Cornelius 120,121,314
    Jane 120,121
    Josias 18,203
    Josias Gar 241,261
    Josias, Jr. 121
    Josias, Sr. 120,121
    Martha 120
    Samuel 202,261
DUPUE(DUPEY), Andrew 76,89
DUPUY, Jane 150,263,286
    Mrs. 305
DURANT, Ann 281
    Hannah 354
    Henry 53,180,276,280,
       281,283,349,354
    James 281
    John 262
    Mr. 289
DURHAM, David 59,130
    John 172
    Lydia 142,163
DUROUZEAU, Michael 6
DUTARAUE, Lewis 125
DUTARQUE, John 105,200,269
    Lewis 200,263,339
DUTART(E), Lewis/Louis 40,
    107,124
    Moses 379
    Peter 113
DUTARTRE, Daniel 258
    Peter 147
DUVALL, Catherine 123,149
    Etienne 171,172
    Katherine 335
DWIGHT, Daniel 229
DYER, Joan 241
    Stephen 251
DYMES, Thomas 3,4,5,21,30,
    32,43,73,74,101,233
DYNES, ___ 10
    Thomas 9
DYPRY, Samuel 200

E__VE, Elizabeth 78

EAGLE(S), Richard 167,230, 317
EARLE, John 117
EARLESTON, Nicholas 253
EASON, William 43
EAVER, Zachariah 96
EAVES, Zachariah 192
EBBERSON, William 341
EBETTS, Oliver 240
EDDINGS, William 199,286
EDDLESTON, ___ 247
EDEN, James 112,164,336
EDGAR, Samuel 270
EDGELL, Rachel 112
  Richard 3,25,58,116, 118,162,163
  Robert 210
EDGHILL, Richard 51
EDINFIELD, Thomas 334
EDINGS, Theodoria 343
  William 343,346
EDMONDS, John 241
EDWARDS, Christopher 44,49, 150
  Charles 307
  Edward 19,78,99,100,109, 157,195,196
  John 25,345
  Mary 78,99,100,157,195, 196
  Mr. 289
  Rebecca 134
  Uriah 134,179,197,198
  Wm. 165,217
EGLEN, John 212
EHNDRICK, William 269
ELDER(S), John 74,106,117, 141,161,168
  Mary 74
  Sarah 117
ELDERTON, James 296,331
ELEAZER, Sarah 174
ELKYNS, Wm. 181
ELLERY, Anna 198
  Ann(e) 88,110,148,149, 167,182,184,223,228, 255,275,279
  Thomas 17,18,21,25,29, 32,47,57,59,63,66,69, 73,77,85,88,91,93,94, 96,102,103,108-111,117, 122,127,128,142,144,148- 150,167,177,182,184,187, 189,190,198,199,201,218, 239,246,255,259,275,276, 279,280,284,325,326,332, 375
ELLICOTT, Elizabeth 12
  Joseph 12,220,290,371
  Wm. 169,171
ELLIOT(T), Ann(e) 123,154, 327
  Bernard 234
  Catherine 24,162
  Champernoon/Champernown 67,122
  Charles 100,196
  Edith 208
  Elizabeth 29,290,357
  Esther/Ester 48,328,370
  Hester 377
  John 135
  Joseph 29,122,154,207, 208,234,240,266,267, 290,339,353,357
  Patience 346
  Robert 35,252
  Samuel 153
  Susanna(h) 228,280,292, 293
  Thomas 19,20,24,33,42, 52,54,103,136,144,148, 154,162,207,215,218,223, 225,226,228,233,235,239,

ELLIOTT, Thomas cont'd: 280,292,293,298,314, 346,357,382
  Thomas John 36
  Thomas, Jr. 165,233
  Thomas, Sr. 29,123,142, 233
  William 7,24,41,48,101, 121,122,135,144,162, 171,196,207,209,222, 234,244,246,263,270, 290,291,320,321,346, 347,348,370
  Wm., Jr. 154,242
ELLIS, Edmond 85,102
  Edward 123
  Elizabeth 96,164,192, 306
  James 164
  John 23,24,25,26,81, 96,134,176,179,283,331
  Juliana 25
  Mary 96,192,306,368
  Morgan 102
  Thomas 25,96,192,306
  Wm. 103
ELMES, Ralph 217
  Samuel 217,296,309
  Thomas 217,308
ELMS (see Elmes above)
ELSINOR, James 244
ELTON, Abra 2
ELY, John 55,63,88,184,236
EMANUEL, Isaac 36
  Wm. (Isaac) 173
EMERSON, Wm. 249
EMERY, Peter 365
EMMA, Ralph 132
EMMENES, John 37
EMMET, Ralph 280
EMMS, Hezekiah 148
  Ralph 103,144,148
  Ralph, Sr. 140
EMONS, Ralph 233,280
EMPEROR, Amerante 124
EMPEROR(EMPEROUR), John 137, 220,250,304
ENDENBOROUGH, Mr. 168
ENGLAND, Jonah 337
ENGLISH, Henroyda/Hinroydah 204,211,212
  John 25
ERPE, Sarah 329
ESCOTT, Gabriel 156,369
ESHFIELD, John 364
EVANS, Ann(e) 294,304
  Daniel 19
  Eleanor 220
  Elizabeth 82
  George 85,135,170
  Hugh 220,247
  John 7,181,234,253,294, 304,354,373
  Jonathan 19,82
  Mary 24,63,64
  Moreah(negro) 19
  Penelope 7
  Peter 258
  Randolph 373,374
  Rowland 37,216,301
  Sarah 373,374
  William 373
EVE, Abraham 20,36,50,215, 231
  Hannah 50
  John 50
  William 50
EVELEIGH, Elizabeth 203,204
  Samuel 1,4,6,8,11-14, 16,21,22,26,39,44,45, 48,52,59,60,61,71-74, 93,136,149,150,159,163, 170,189,203,204,226, 320

EVERARD, Archibald 78
  Richard 104
EYCOTT, Mary 265
EYRE, Robert 332
EYSAM, Tobias 280
EZARD, Walter 261

FABIAN, John 332,343
  Mary 332
  William 332
FAIRAND, Isaac 96,193
FAIRCHILD, Elizabeth 245, 254,256,266,267,291, 325
  John 243,245,253-255
  Martha 233
  Richard 236,245,267, 291
  Rachel 253,254
  Thomas 57,62,79,120, 138,161,168,169,172, 245,254,256,267,291, 325,333
  William 56,79,228,233, 236,245,256,267,291, 319,325,333
FAIRLASS, Thomas 149,162
FAIRWEATHER, Francis 378
FALCONER, John 367
FARLEY, Elizabeth 236
  George 232,236
  Joseph 87,183,216
  Samuel 236,376
FARMER, Wm. 203
FARR, Amarintia 220
  Elizabeth 220
  John 68
  Mr. 103
  Nathaniel 86
  Thomas 29,50,68,118, 220,297
  Thomas, Jr. 98,102,194
  Thomas, Sr. 102
  Wm. 203
FARRILL, Michael 17
FARWELL, Henry 42
  Thomas 148
FAUCCUNET, David 365
  Judith 365
FAUCHERAUD, Gideon 211,342
  Mary 211
FAUCHRAUD, Gendeon 33
FAUCOUNET, David 365
FAURE, Peter 380
FELL, John 175
FELTON, James 259
FENDIN(FENDEN), Henry 240, 380
  John 173
  Sarah 380
FENWICK(E), John 1,5,6,29, 33,34,47,68,69,83,87, 94,99,102,104,128,138, 143,147,156,177,184, 190,194,195,226,231, 245,279,322,328
  Robert 20,52,55,67,142, 170
  Sarah 142,170
FERGUSON, Ann 230,260,372
  David 52,297,312,313
  J. 136,156
  James 112,212,230,231, 268,354
  John 63
  Martha 297,312
  Thomas 8,230,250,251, 260,267,296,342,372
  Victor 372
  William 133
FERRELL, Samuel 28
FERRON, Catherine 150
  Gabriel 150

FERRON, cont'd:
  Gideon 150
FIDLER, Joseph 182,218,238,
  252,291,326
  Thomas Gallway 252
FIDLING, Daniel 78,79,126,
  171
  Francis 232
  John 180,257
  Mary 232
  Paul 78
FIELD, Charles 197,311
  John 101,145
FILBIN, Charles 296,331
  John 124,299,311,315,
  317
FILLEBIEN(FIL-BIN), John
  282,295,317
  Kathrine/Kathryn 282,
  295,317
FILLEUX(FILLEAUX), Peter
  171,253
FILLIEW, Peter 7
FINLEY, John 54
FIRTH, Samuel 162
FISHBURN, William 29,141,
  162,198,216,295
FISHER, Elias 179,301
  Hugh 197
  James 69,103,142,170,
  179,199,307,316,354
  John 180
  Hugh 156
  Samuel 240
  Thunis 318
  Viletye 318
  William 80,212,280
FITCH, Anne (Annette) 25,
  32
  Capt. 145
  Constant 25,212
  Constantine 101
  John 269,369
  Jonathan 14,25,33,45,
  46,52,112,124,132,204,
  208,211,212,319
  Jonathan, Sr. 52
  Joseph 25,32,43,54,101,
  112,212,311
  Marian(a) 24,351
  Marianne 2,75,76
  Marion 342
  Mary 211,342,351
  Peter (Livingston) 1
  (negro)
  Rachel 52
  Sarah 52
  Stephen 112,351
  Susannah 2,24,25,32,34,
  43,112,208,212
  Tobias 1,2,17,24,25,27,
  43,75,76,85,112,146,
  163,211,226,342,351,
  358
  Thomas 112,212
FITZGARLD, Garrard 85
  John 85,361
  Garrat 341
FITZGERALD, Gerard 239
  James 27,75,80
  John 239,341
  Martha 239
  Thomas 3,35,75,82,85,
  212,239,280
FLACK, Ann 213
FLADGER, Elizabeth 339
  Robert 94,107,190,227,
  228,265,269,283,300,339
  John 78
FLAREL(L), Rebecca 78,101,
  102
  Samuel 101,102
  Wm. 102

FLAVEL, ___ 126
  Elizabeth 19
FLAVELL, John 19,56,135,
  169,321
  Rebecca/Rebekah 44,56,
  134,135,148,169,170,
  179,180,260,273,308,
  313,321
  Robert 169,321
  Samuel 56,135,169,170,
  321
  William 43,44,56,135,
  145,308,321
FLAY, Elizabeth 148
FLECKNOW(E), Mary 128,179
  William 36,128,179,302,
  355
FLEDGER, Robert 315
FLEET, ___, Sr. 154
FLEHARTY, Edward 356
FLEMEN, ___ 248
FLEMIN, Thomas 66,72,150,
  160
FLEMING, Thomas 24,113,165,
  181,213,256,347,382
  William 255,289,330,
  344,345,349,355,368
FLETCHER, Benjamin 354
  Henry 376,381
FLEY, Samuel 171,206,260,
  325,337
FLING, Hugh 140,141
FLOOD, George 12,42,65,70
  Thomas 257
  William 234
FLORE, Isaac 351
FLOWERS, James 102,110
  Jeffry 269
  Joseph Edward 232,254,
  335
  Peter 232
FLOYD, Jemima 95,191,235
  Joseph 235
  Richard 6,12,95,191,231
  Richard, Jr. 6
  Richard, Sr. 235
FODEN, Thomas 362,375
FOGARTIE, James 200
FOGARTIE(FOGARTY), John 34,
  40,105,107,117,124,125,
  152,263,307,339
  Stephen/Steven 40,105,
  107,200,339
FOGG, Charles 294
FOGGO, Charles 304
FOIGIN, Elias 124
FOISSEN, Elias 51,207,208,
  220,222,224,246,251,252,
  277,292,305,310,311,331,
  333
  Mary 251,252
FOLKEN, James 259
FONT, Peter 355
FOOKES, George 2
FORBES, John 5
FORD, Ebenezer 19,80,93,189
  George 19,103
  Jane 163
  Joseph 18
  Mary 163,241
FORD(FOARD), Nathaniel 22,
  55,136,156,223,234,235,
  327,364
  Patience 224
  Stephen 181,233
  Stephen, Jr. 66,163,212
  Stephen, Sr. 66,103,163,
  212
  Thomas 66,224,225,236,
  298,314,355,356
  William 336
FORGISON, Hugh 338
FORREST, Edward Horn 252

FORSTER, Andrew 195
  Arthur 195,276
  John 195
  R. 104
FOSTER(FORSTER), ___ 15,67
  Andrew 99
  Arthur 44,49,60,99,
  150,229,255,334,335,
  382,383
  Francis 121
  John 99
  Mary 44,49,129,150,334,
  335
  Peter 174,234
  Richard 45
  William 22
FOUCHARD, Mary Madelaine
  65
FOUNTAINEA, Mr. 115
FOURE, Peter 120
FOWLER, Edward 240
  James 138,139,234,246
  John 43,215
  Martha 138,139
  Peircey 361
  Richard 224,269,336
FOX, Henry 358
  John 199
  Joseph 44,181-183,197
  -206,290
  Stephen 33,133,217
  William 16
FOYE, Joseph 22
FRAINTON, John 363
FRAMPTON, ___ 319
  John 239
FRANCHOME(FRANCHOMME),
  Charles 40,41,131
FRANCIS, James 358
FRANCKLYN, George 43
  William 309
FRANKLIN, John 2,206
  William 378
FRASER, John 314,358,375,
  378
  Judith 298,314
FRASER(FRASIER,FRAZIER),
  John 20,37,137,138,173,
  246,290,298
FRAZER, Wm. 166
FRAZIER, John 359
FREEMAN, Elizabeth 355
  George 281,292
  James 340,364
  John 47,110,111
  Joseph 149
  Richard 150,235,240,
  380
  William 54,117,118,180,
  249,250,253,259,264,
  373,375,381
  William G. 359
  William George 209,213,
  215,234,242,243,248,
  252,274,275,281,285,
  287,304,305,321,345
FREER, John 69
FRENCH, Richard 31
FRENCHAM, Henry 159
FRENCHOMME, Charles 160
FRIP, John 261
FRISELL, Alexander 310
FRISSOL, Alexander 349
FRITCH, Samuel 86
FRIZEDON, Daniel 139
FROST, George 163,164
  John 163
FROWMAN, John 37,102
FRY, Elizabeth 2
FRY(E), Ichabod 100,268
  Peter 138
  Thomas 2
FRYER, William 200,281,282

FUGART, James 355
FULER, William 322
FULLER, Ann Booth 74
  Elizabeth 98,193
  Joseph 148
  Mary 73,74
  Richard 14,73,74,85
  William 78,98,102,106,
    133,193,209,309
  William, Sr. 94,190
FULTON, David 245
  James 89,138,147,151,
    169,174,180,182,186,
    234,266,289,317,320
FURBISH, John 382
FURBUSH, ___ 229
  Mr. 334
FUTHEY, James 245

GABLE, Thomas 128
GADSDEN, Mr. 145
  Thomas 35,43,89,90,122,
    134,145,146,155,160,
    185-187,243,262,268,
    381
GADSEN, Capt. 330
  Thomas 174,211,287
GAILLARD, Alcimus 258,267,
    270,299,311,320,321,
    340
  Bartholomew 61,86,182,
    258,267,271,276,277,
    299,311,320,348,350
  Capt. 51
  Elizabeth 258,267,276,
    340,348,350
  Erick 320
  Fred(e)rick 258,266,267,
    271,276,299,340,348,350
  John 269
  Sarah 320,321
  Tacitus 276,351
  Thoedore 269,271,299,
    321
  Sarah 299
GALE, Daniel 54,169,218,
    324
  Hannah 228,243
  John 74
  Sarah 74
GALIOT, Daniel 351
GALLATIN, Guillaume 238
  Guillaume 346
GALLIWAY, David 308
GALLO, Henry 355
GALLWAY, Ann 291
  Thomas 235,340
GANDY, Samuel 302,303,349
GANGUME, Abraham 141
GANTLETT, Elizabeth 26
  Marian 26
  Thomas 365
GANTLITT, Mrs. 144
GARCIA, Francis 86
GARDEN, A. 53,333
  Alexander 64,104,119,
    143,144,159,305,322
  Alexander, Jr. 110,150,
    156
  Martha 119
GARDENER, Bononi 117
GARDNER, John 251
GARNER, John 79
GARNETT, John 349
GARNIER, John (Jean) 85,91,
    124,131,132,161,187
  Magdalen 85
GARON, Peter 112
GARRAN, Alexander 138
GARTICE, Daniel 96
GARY, Thomas 141
GASCOIGNE, James 331
  John 124,125,147,148,
    173,205,210,211

GASCOIGNE, William 277
GASDEN, Elizabeth 145
GASQUE, Elizabeth 288
  John 269,288
GATES, Thomas 292
GAY, James 145
GEBSON, Ann 265
GEEGER, Herman 366
GENDRON, ___ 340
  John 7,40,41,89,178,
    185,348,350,367,368,
    375
  Philip 86,271,276
GENES, Peter 179
GENRON, Peter 183
GENT, Jacob 29,224
GEORGE, Lord Carteret 8,
    63,90,187,236,373
GERARD, Christopher 100,196
GERARDEAU, Anne 122
  John 122
  Peter 114
GERMAN, Ralph 317
GEVINS, John 142
GIBENS, Jotham 50
GIBB(E)S, Alice 68,69,355
  Ann(e) 41,81,95,191
  Benjamin 21,80,81,118
  Dennis 159
  Elias 228
  Elizabeth 152,316
  Henry 102,114,180,214,
    215,218,222,224,225,
    227,228,232,233,235,
    237,239,244,247-249,
    251-253,255,256,258,
    260,263,266,267,269,
    272-277,280,282,283,
    286,288,289,291,293,
    294,296,304-306,308,
    309,311,314,316,318,
    323,326,332,333,336,
    337,341,343,348-350,
    354-357,359,360,364,
    372
  John 15,21,41,65,79,81,
    95,119,123,191,261,316,
    353
  Philip 246
  Robert 12,15,22,47,48,
    55,61,63,65,70,77,88,
    89,93,94,135,140,150,
    152,159,164,174,179,
    184,185,189,190,211,
    213,222,229,242,257,
    258,279,281,306,307,
    313,316,329,343,346,
    349,353,379
  Stephen 80,93,189,302
  W. 58
  William 29,68,69,187
  Willougby/Willeby 91,
    220,221
GIBBON(S), ___ 27,28
  Daniel 31
  Elizabeth 107
  John 3,4
  Jotham 1,66,85
  Jothan 336
  Joseph 240,268,293,338,
    380
  William 17,26,27,30,34,
    40,41,46,47,49,53,56,
    64,65,68,83,91,107,111,
    121,122,124,147,187,
    208,333,376
GIBINS, Joseph 181
GIBSON, Ann(e) 215,227,231,
    367
  Daniel 205,215,225,227,
    228,231,232,270,327,
    367,382
  Dr. 239

GIGMILLIAT, Henry 76,79,
    84,91,100
GIGNILLIATT, Henry 124,131,
    145,148,161,165,169,
    187,196,212,229,250,
    280,292
  Hester 212,280
GILBERT, Barnabas 149
  Ephraim 7
GILBERTSON (alias Atchi-
    son), James 50,88,184
GILCHRIST, Archibald 270
GILCREST, Robert 96,192
GILES, Richard 89,165,185
GILL, Capt. 304
  Henry 163
  John 250
GILLESPIE, J. 243
GIRARD, Judith 62
GIRARD(GIRRARD), Peter 62,
    70,260
GIRARDEAU, Ann 177
  Peter 370
  Richard 313
GIRRARDEAU(GIRARDEAU),
  John 132,177,178,287
GITTENS, Nathaniel 218,220
GIUCHARD, Levi 106
GIVEN(S), John 118,137,138,
    149,166
  Mary 149
  Philip 1,305
GIVV(E)S, Robert 140,142
GLASER, Sarah 367,368
GLAZE, Malachi 76,178,217,
    224,249,251,253,254,
    277,279,313,317,365
  Malcolm 346
GLAZE(GLASE), William 114,
    115
GLENN, John 246
GLESER, Samuel 290
GLOVER, Charlesworth 115,
    126,129,130,375
  John 178
GOALE, Anna 24,41
GOBLE, Mr. 177,178
  Thomas 96,193,240
GODBOLD, John 269
GODDARD, Francis 98,105,
    108-111,149,194,281,
    337
  Mary 217
GODDING(GODDEN), Benjamin
    23,24
GODFREY, ___ 200
  Benjamin 28,31,32,42,
    57,65,151,152,242,309,
    339
  Elizabeth 65,221,310,
    352
  Jane 277,285
  John 28,47,55,56,65,
    87,93,103,132,133,151,
    152,177,183,189,224,
    242,327,352,356,365
  Madam 287
  Margaret 152,242,331
  Martha 309
  Mary 87,132,133,183
  Richard 25,28,42,47,
    56,87,122,132,148,183,
    271,277,278,285,293,
    309,335
  Sarah 28
  Susanna 25
GODIN(G), Benjamin 11,47,
    65,77,78,91,115,116,
    118,119,163,170,171,
    181,182,187,217,227,
    232,243,250,254,255,
    291,315,369,380
  David 254

GODIN(G), cont'd:
  Maryanne 227
GODWIN, Henry 344
  John 322,337,343,365
  Margaret 322
  Martha 337,343,365
GOEMENS, Wm. 156
GOFF, Deborah 161
  Katherine 158
GOFFE, Mr. 366
GOFF, Robert 25
  Roger 161
GOLDING(GOULDING), Peter 12,22
GOLIGHTLY, Culch 69,319
  Clucheth 341,353
GONTELETT, Marian 144
GOODBE(E), Alexander 163,232,233,243
  Anne 232
  Elizabeth 53
  James 53,227,232
  John (also Goodby) 53,216,232
  John, Jr. 53
  John, Sr. 53,163
  Joseph (also Goodbey) 165
  Rebekah 180
GOODBYEE, Joseph 372
GOODILL, Wm. 176
GOODMAN, Thomas 339
GOODWIN, Robert 17
GOODWINN, John 315
GOODWYNN, John 290
GOOL, Anne 162,163
GORDEN, Alexander 59
GORDIN, Susannah 290
GORDON, James 249,260,261,274,275,277,300,301,314,341,342,358,359,365,369,371
GOREING, Jane 374
  Thomas 142,210,374,377
  Walter 296
GORING, ____ 200
GORTON, John 134,174,197,198
GOUDET(T), Peter 14,200
GOUGH, ____ 294
  Edward 292,351
  John 142,157,249,253,286,292,303,304,336,352
  Mary 142,249,253
  Neale 351
  Richard 249,253,286,292,303,304,336,352,354
  William 372
GOULD, Thomas 244
GOULDING(GOLDING), Peter 37,42,64
GOULLIETTE, Lawrence 170
GRACIA, Francis 60,171,172,253
GRADY, Charles 129
GRAEME, James 265,268,275
GRAHAM, Abraham 174
  Thomas 308
GRAING, Hugh 314
  James 314
  John 314
GRAME, James 145,277,380
GRANGE, Col. 187
  Hugh 124,246,319
  James 250,319
  John 319
  Thomas 124
GRANT, Capt. 146
  Lud. 107
  Ludwick 258
  Margaret 145

GRANVILLE, John 120,121,140,176
GRANY, (Col.) 90
GRASSETT, Samuel 79
GRAVES, Martha 64,114
  Moses 64,263,272,274
  Thomas 64,113,263,342
GRAY, Elizabeth 217,242
  Hannah 216
  James 145,217
  Margaret 82
  William 82,216,239
GREAR, Hugh 318
GRECIA, Francis 164
GREEME, Ja. 49
  James 149,155,156,158,165,249,264,325,335,337,360
GREEN(E), Arthur 213
  Catherine 4,5
  Elizabeth 302
  Daniel 3,16,30,35,49,52,57,58,59,66,67,69,71,75,77,83,85,89-96,98,100-113,117,120-124,127-131,134-137,140,144-146,148-150,152,154,156,157,160-163,165,167-169,171-173,175,176,178-180,182,183,185-191,193-201,216,221,228,247,251,258,261,262,268,282,291,297,302,311-313,319
  Elizabeth 30,57,162
  Francis 16,57,58
  James 179,181,240,245,246,255,318
  John 106,112,148,162,167,179,200,262,302,347,370
  Joseph 231
  Joshua 47,162,230,233
  Katherine 4
  Phebe 370
  Samuel 28
  Susannah 162,179,181
  Thomas 30
  William 4,5,158,179,223,350
GREENLAND, John 32,35,61,62,107
  Martha 267,296
  William 110,129,165,267,296
GREGORY, John 43
  Theodore 165
  Theophilus 170,173-176,181,205-207,209-214,357,368,375
GREY, Mary 78,80
  Samuel 125,152
GRICE, Elizabeth (Lea) 14
  John 14
GRICHLOW, Campt. 299
GRIFFIN, Elin 97
  Helen 244
  Joseph 87,168,183
  Joyce 87,183
  Richard 87,193,244
GRIFFIS, Mary 28
GRIMBALL, Isaac 380
  John 40
  Joshua 207,319
  Paul 85,100,102,103,140,141,189,196,207,239,366,371,380
  Thomas 100,196,340
GRIMBOLD(GRIMBALL), Paul 93
GRIMKE, Fredrick 298,314
GRIMSTON, ____ 230

GRIMSTON, Elenor/Ellinor 161,185
  Richard 89,160,185
GRIPPS, William 311
GRIPSS, William 354
GRISBANE, Robert 358
GRISTIE, Henry 377
GROOME, James 229
GUARDIN, Lewis(Louis) 123
GUARRATT, Fitzgarld 361
GUERARD, Benjamin 118
  David 118,119,378
  Hannah 119
  Jacob 6
  John 11,91,118,119,171,175,180,187,227,237
  Js. 6
  Judith 91
  Martha 118,119
  Peter 13,41,48,54,91,187,188,292
  Peter Jacob 119
GUERIN, Francis 95,191
  Isaac 96,193,266
  John 370
  Judith 255
  Mary 163
  Mathew 182
  Mathurin 157,163
  Peter 248
  Vincent 96,105,193,200,255,361,370
  Vinson 255
GUERING, Francis 95
GUERING(GURRIN), Judith 127
  Vincent 127
GUERON, Peter 87
GUERRIN, Isaac 128
  Thomas 169
  Vincent 128
GUER(R)Y, John 310,368
  Margaret 310
  Peter 269,310
GUICHARD, Levy 117
GUIGNARD, Gabriel 340,378,379
GUMBERS, Solomon 135
GUN, Mr. 125
GUNN, Rebecca 8
  Thomas 8
GUNSTON, John 31
GUPPEL(L), John 42,82,148,174
GUY, Rebecca 5,38,39,54,55,72,112,159,160,250,288
  Robert 327
  William 1,5,38,39,40,54,55,67,72,94,104,112,159,190,250,288,305,332,361,368,382
  Zebalon/Zebulon 144,237,305
GWIN(GWYN), John 216,225

HADDERELL, George 302
HADDOCK(HAYDOCK), William 7
HADDRELL(HADRELL), George 156,221,356
  Mary 221
  Susannah 156,157
HADWEN, Robert 32
HAGENBUCH, Jacob 366
HAIGE, Eliner 168
HAIG(E),George 220,223,298,314,363,372
HAINES, Greg. 92,188
HALBEATH, Joseph 46
HALE, Elizabeth 85,130,341,361

HALE, cont'd:
  John 75,85,181,266,269,
    341,361,362
  John, Jr. 130
  John, Sr. 130
HALEBURTON, Robert 74,75
HALES, Wm. 105
HALL, Arthur 29,35,57,75,
    107,116,133,146-148,
    150,235,297,308,328,
    353,355
  Elizabeth 213
  Fayr. 38
  George 223
  John 17,27
  Martha 355
  Mary 107
  Richard 154,248,311,
    316,324,363
  Richard, Jr. 232
  Robert 217,235,277,287
  Sarah 209,213
  Thomas 302,311,324
HALLAWAY, Wm. 153
HAMBLETON, George 344,345
HAMERTON, William 54,160,
    167,170
HAMILTON, Archibald 120,140,
    141,147,170,249,271-
    273,277
  Arthur 247,291,293,294
  David 160
  Gen. 33
  Isabella 311
  John 56,82,182,234
  Magdalen 271
  Margaret 140
  Mr. 160
  Paul 291,294
  Thomas 209
  William 283,290,311,
    343,358
HAMLIN, Anne 170
  George 25,118,166,170,
    223
  Thomas, Jr. 166
  Thomas, Sr. 166
HAMMERTON, Elizabeth 198,
    247,287
  I. 368
  J. 247,314,354
  John 175,198,221,238,
    242,243,246,249,259,
    261,262,268,287,288,
    295,323,324,330,331,
    332,333,342,362,375
  Richard J. 247
  William 13,33,182,198
HAMPTON, J. 283
HANBURY, John 121
HANCOCK, ____ 244
  Elias 3,5,17,73,84,85,
    89,90,111,160,170,185,
    186,200,201,230,266,
    267,291,302,319
  Mary 161
  William 284,344
HANLEY, Daniel 152,336
HARBERT, John 220,221
HARDEN, William 19,232
HARDY, Dr. John 74
HARE, William 369
HARELING, Richard 67
HARGRAVE, Anne 368
  Henry 55,63,65,81,82,
    91,95,104,106,115,131,
    132,137,138,157,174,
    187,191,221,375
  Mrs. 288
HARLESTON, ____ 82
  John 13,32,64,125,265,
    282,291,321,324
  John, Jr. 236

HARLESTON, cont'd:
  Nicholas 253,299
  Sarah 299
HARLEY, Joseph 180,291
  Katherine 326
  Mary 287
  Samuel 326
HARMAN, Peter 86
HARRIS, Francis 89,185
  Henry 109
  John 217
  Jonathan 313
  Richard 13,54,80,98,99,
    101,108-111,127,144,
    172,175,194,195
  Sarah 89,185
HARRISON, Richard 34,231,
    266,355
HARSDWOOD, Edward 161
HART, Charles 13,46,50,55,
    56,58,59,60,61,64,81,
    95,101,103,104,106,108,
    129,150,191,218,222,
    225,226,243,263,301,
    320
  Robert 43
  William 2,270
HARTGROVE, ____ 312
HARTLEY, Amos 309
  John 33
  Stephen 269,304,354
HARTMAN, ____ 48
  Elizabeth 43
  Hannah 43
  John 43,93,189
  Mary 43,93,189
  Warren 43
  William 43
HARTOP, ____ 219
  Samuel 326
HARTY, David 355
HARVEY, Elizabeth 84
  Maurice 11,51,54,58,66,
    71,77,79,80,239,269
  Robert 37,84
  Sarah 115
  William 14,69,76,105,
    152,207,242,245,253,
    254,266,290,319,322,
    354,367
  Wm., Jr. 115
HARWOOD, John 179
HASCOTT, George 174
HASELL, Elizabeth 268
  James 181,316
  Robert 321
  Susannah 181
  Thomas 98,108-111,120,
    121,127,144,150,194,
    233,234,268,339,349
HASELWOOD, Elizabeth 237
HASFORT, Hannah 296
  Joseph 296
HASKINES, Potter 153
HASTINGS, Jane 32,38
  Theophilus 32,38
HASWELL, Thomas 172
HATCHER, Nicholas 376
HATCHMAN, Joseph 280
HATFIELD, Joseph 58
HATTON, Margaret 86
  William 86,120,218
HAVEN, Stephen 307
HAWCKES, John 228
HAWETT, Mary 17
  William 17,20,33,140,
    141,161,165,239,335,
    376,377
HAWKINS, Edmond 326
  Ester 85
HAWKS, Gersham 52
  Gershom 175
HAWKS(HAWKES), John 113,..

HAWKS, John cont'd:
  114,170,175,178,179,
    197,198
HAY, John 171
  Thomas 47
HAYDON, John 232
HAYES, Charles 19,58,59,
    142,180
  Delia 59
  Dennis 100,125,142
  George 180
  Joanna 58,59
  John 107,147,180
  Richard 334
HAYNES, Edward 356
  Hannah 356
HAYNE(S), Isaac 308,355,
    356
  John 289,356,379
  Jonathan 193
  Joseph 180,356,379
  Martha 128
  Mary 356,379
  Mathew 356
  Nicholas 103,128,201,
    247,258
  Susanna 356
  Thomas 31
  William 112,149
HAYNS, Jonathan 97
HAYWOOD, Powell 43
HAZARD, George 117
  Richard 22,149
HAZELWOOD, Edward 237
HAZZARD, W7. 103,123
  Wm., Sr. 222
HEADINGTON, Thomas 16
HEALY, Thomas 106
HEAPE, Benjamin 233
  Joseph 33,87,183
HEARD, Ester 269
HEARN(E), George 320
  James 226
  John 6,57,130,167,176,
    221,247,357
  Peter 57,134,176,247,
    378
HEARTY, David 154
HEATL(E)Y, Richard 153,244
HEIDLERBERG, Isabell 227,
    228
HEIRN, John 112
HEIVSON, John 209
HELLEWARD, John 175
HENDERSON, Samuel 106,107
HENDRICK(S), Daniel 90,96,
    97,186,192
  John 112,163,354,376
  Purchas 223
  Timothy 63,89,129,133,
    185,186,216,259,356
  William 5,25,118,222,
    223,289,340,345,348,
    382
HENLY, Bryan 121
HENNEWAY, John 152
HENNING, Thomas 261,270,
    288,304,332,338,357,
    366,367,370,381
HENRICK, John 336,340
HENRY, Duke of Beaufort
    307,337
HENRY, Duke of Portland 43
HENRY, John 247
  (Dame) Marian 75
HENTIE, John 178,201,241,
    292,310,349,361,367
HEPWORTH, Ann(e) 39,87,91,
    92,114,123,131,138,165,
    183,187,188,293,356,
    357
  S. 46
  T. 1

HEPWORTH, cont'd:
  Thomas 1,2,3,4,5,6,7,8,
    9,13,14,23,28,30,32-34,
    36,39-41,43-45,47,49-
    59,63,65,66,67,69,70,
    71,73,74,76-79,81,84-
    87,89,91-95,102,114,123,
    124,131,138,139,153,156,
    158,160,165,183,185,187-
    189,191,202,249,250,253-
    255,260,265,270,273,279,
    280,287,289,293,332,333,
    356,357,367
HERBERT(T), John 21,22,37,
    46,47,51,91,120,157,163,
    168,187,227,250
  William 277
  Major 12
  Mary 69
  Sarah 91,187
  Thomas 69
  Willoughby 250
HERMAN, Peter 48,50,110,344
HERNE, James 228
HERON, John 30
HERRING,   134
  John 132,133,145
HESCOT(T), George 6,42
HESKET(T), George 92,173,
    188
HESKIT, George 297
HEWITT, Capt. 320
HEWS, Solomon 203
HEWSON, John 209,254
HEXT, Alexander 302,316
  Amies 315
  Ann 378
  Daniel 239
  David 335,337,341,342,
    378
  Edward 54,159,315,343,
    348
  Francis 128
  George 128
  Hugh 36,59,103,128,156,
    315,316
  John 5,294
  Sarah 156
HEYWARD, Margaret 116
  Thomas 116
HEYWORTH, T. 7,12
HICKS, Giles 345
  John 181,297,298,312,
    338,368
  Mary 345
HIETT, Robert 143
HIGGINSON, Richard 36
HILDERLY, Capt. 9
HILDERSLEY, Rowland 22
HILL, Ambrose 95,191,231
  Charles 1,14,19,23,24,
    28,32,38,40,41,43,45-
    48,50-56,58,60,62-67,
    69,71,77,78,81-85,94,
    96,98,105,107,108,113,
    115,120,122,126,130-132,
    137-139,142,151,152,154,
    158,159,169,175,180,181,
    184,191,192,194,199,214,
    234,242,248,250,252,292,
    304,332
  Elizabeth 47,48,65,85,
    115,138,164,234,242,248,
    250,252,292,304
  James 45
  Jane 288
  John 51,64,65,77,89,96,
    102,160,164,185,192,201,
    208
  Mary 96,192
  Mrs. 240,339
  Richard 1,55,169,204,
    215,249,264,267
  Thomas 106
HILLES, Samuel 10

HILLIARD, James 303
HINES, John 297
HINKLEY, William 335,364
HINSON, Cornelius 376
  Edward 376
HISTED, Edward 357,358
HITCHING, John 2
HOB, Thomas 121
HODGES, Joseph 137
HODGKIN(S), Henry 146,240,
    245
  Tho. 21,30
HODGKINSON, Wm. 144
HODGSON, John 39,106,161
  William 277
HODSDEN, John 318
HODSON, William 227
HOGG, George 308
  John 47,101,279,340,
    380
HOKE, George 76
HOLBEATH(HOLDBEALETT),
    Joseph 45,52
HOLDER, Joseph 348,364
HOLDRIDGE, Joseph 124
HOLLAND, Edmond 266
HOLLIDAY, Giles 262,277,
    287,288,290,293,300,
    305,315
HOLLINS, Thomas 267
HOLLYBUSH(HOLIBUSH), John
    51,114,131,172,219,280,
    352
  Judah (Holybush) 91,123,
    138,165,187
HOLMAN, Burt 168
  Rachel 266
  Thomas 14,168,209
  Walter 214
  William 114,179,214,
    215,266,297,306,307
HOLMES, Charles 366
  Ebenezer 125
  Elizabeth 240
  Francis 10,34,42,52,54,
    77,78,125,138,139,198,
    201,214,248,289
  Francis, Jr. 12,23,24
  Francis, Sr. 23,24,49,
    52,60
  George 338
  Isaac 42,79,81,113,125,
    172,174,201,260,262,
    267,291
  Joel 87
  John 310
  Mark 239
  Richard 128
  Samuel 240
  Widow 365
  William 19,121,168,329
HOLT, Martin 230,241
HOLTON, Anne Catherine 161
  Thomas 7,40,82,103,128,
    130,145,161,173,201,240
HOLY(HALFY), Joseph 159
HOME, J. A. 372
HONAHAN, Thomas 144
HOOD, Benjamin 309
HOOGLANT, Dyreck 40
HOOK, Abraham 2
  John 239
HOOKER, Sarah 349
HOOPER, Elizabeth 221
  John 93
HOOVER, John 189
HOPE, Alexander 284
  Charles 340,341
HOPKINS, James 257
  Mary 29
  Thomas 43
HOPTON, William 72,110,144,
    150,228,248,275,285,290,
    311,316,353,373,379

HORN, William 252
HORNBY, William 215
HORRY, Daniel 55,152,266,
    267,295,317,351,352,
    361,367,369,377
  Elias 51,55,60,61,80,
    118,152,233,249,258,
    266,269,282,295,316,
    317,351,352,367,375,
    377
  John 152,303,349,351,
    352,367
  Magdelin 367
  Martha 266
  Marguerite Henriette
    367
  Peter 126,143,157,277,
    284,287,297,367
HORSEY, Samuel 331
HORSFORD, Joseph 357
HOSE(HOW), George 24
HOSIER, Philemon 76
HOUGHTON, John 255,378
HOUSER, H. 41
  Henry 6,47,65,81
HOWARD, Ann 235
  Edward 48,120,121,270,
    286,304,336
  Experience 235,292,303
  Mary 215
  Mr. 143
  Susanna 235
  Thomas 41,105,131,157
  Tody 61
  William 235
HOWITT, Capt. 298
HOW(E), Edward 138
  Elizabeth 149,370
  Gresham 77
  Job 10,80,81,115,140,
    141,304
  Mary 80
  Peter 233
  R. 34
  Robert 6,8,14,15,32,
    60,80,81,96,109,124,
    127,128,139,149,154,
    162,163,176,190,193,
    194,200,234,237,339,
    370
  Job 11,13,35,52,63,
    121,169,211,214,216,
    217,232,241,250,254,
    257
  John 22
  Martha 216,217
  Robert 94,216,217,250
  Sarah 250
HOWSIN, Thomas 197
HOY, Alice 42
HUBBARD, Thomas 148
HUDDY, John 284
HUDSON, Robert 219
HUFFEY, Edward 209
HUGER, Daniel 10-13,41,42,
    48,56,59,60,61,88,89,
    106,107,116,120,121,
    123,124,131,138,142,
    143,146,147,152,170,
    185,197,236,237,241,
    261,266,292,303,304,
    348,349,350,351,367,
    380
  Daniel, Jr. 13
  Daniel, Sr. 61
  Elizabeth 123,152,261
HUGGETT, Anthony 132,240,
    309,324,325,326
HUGGINS, John 87,94,95,155,
    184,191,208,261,371
  Joseph 269,334,371
HUGHES, Daniel 303
  Henry 64
  (cont'd. next page)

HUGHES, cont'd:
  Meredith 44,51,93,136,
    144,152,189,272
  Price 301
  Solomon 342,371
HUGO, Bastian 174
HUGYAN, John 222
HULBERT, James 268
HULIEN, Elias 1
HULL, Humphrey 3
HUMBERT, David Pierre 338
HUME, George 347
  Peter 356
  Robert 1-9,12-15,18,21,
    22-24,26-28,30,32,34,
    35,39,40,44,47,49,51,
    52,57,64,66-73,75,76-
    79,81,82,85,88,90-92,
    95,98,99,101-108,111,
    112,115,116,119,123,
    124,131,133,138,148,
    150,151,153,157,159,
    160,163,170,172,185,
    187,188,191,193-195,
    202,218,233,240,243,
    246,249,250,253,254,
    263,270,273,277,279,
    289,314,319,323,324,
    328,339,369,381
  Sophia 39,72,157,270
HUMPRESS, Thomas 286
HUNT, Brian 36
  Daniel 130,145
  Edward 142
  Joseph 63,236
  Martha 129
HUNTER, ___ 309
  G. 243,246
  George 227,231,265,284,
    316,321,338,353,357,
    368,376
  Peter 297
  Samuel 287,289,300,319
HURLEY, Catherine 219
HURST, Joseph 88,184,296,
    331
  Thomas 288
HUSK, Thomas 284
HUTCHINSON, Anne 14,76,158
  Archibald 360
  Charlotte 158
  Edward 30
  J. 9,53,333
  James 236,305
  John 4,5,14,21,30,67,
    68,70,76,78,90,125,138,
    156,158,186,259,367,375
  Mary 368
  Richard 351
  Ripton 298,314
  Thomas 76,357
HYDE, Elizabeth Wigfall 67
  William 67,78
HYOTT, Thomas 336
HYRNE, Barbara 37
  Burrell Massingbird
    88,99,185,190
  Edward 37,99,128,169,
    195
  Elizabeth 88,184
  Henry 88,184,185

IEBOTT, ___ 256
INGERSON, James 126,298,320
  Margaret 67,179
INGLIS, John 36
INMAN, Ralph 282
INNES, Robert 202
INNS, Thomas/Thos. 37,102,
    112,180,332,373
IOOR(E), Catherine 142,169
  John 260
IRELAND, Elizabeth 368
IRISH, Richard 175

IRVIN(E), Samuel 358
  William 337
IRVING, Alexander 145
IRWIN, Will 355
  William 377
IZARD, ___ 15
  Benjamin 175
  Dorothy 298,319
  Elizabeth 276
  George 52
  Magdalaine Elizabeth
    264
IZARD(ISARD), Ralph 10,13,
    44,49,52,64,76,80,93,
    94,100,101,102,104,117,
    118,146,150,153,169,
    183,189,196,204,208,
    211,212,214,225,230,
    257,258,264,270,276,
    280,281,283,287,294,
    296,298,311,319,320,
    338,342,369
  Walter 121,270,273

JACKSON, ___ 27,205,308
  George 371
  Henry 175,208,353,372
  John 25,96-98,159,174,
    192,194,206,225,246,
    308,355,356
  Joseph 208
  Mr. 133
  Samuel 208,353
  William 208,339,353
JAMES, Jonathan 199
  John 303,355
  Robert 188
  William 219,326
JANDON, Daniel 377
JARRARD(HANARD), Christo-
    pher 137,256
JARVIS, ___ 294
  Edmond 298,312
  John 126
JASPER, Edward 147,173
JAUDON, Daniel 151,201,255,
    276,280,281,283,294
JAY, Augustus 36
JEAN, John 297
JEANE, Michael 239
JEAN(E)S, Michael 50,92,
    170,175,188,274,354
  Sarah 366
JEANNFRET, Abraham 354
JEANNERETT(E), Jacob 93,
    189,314
JEFFERS, John 196
JEFFINS(JEFFEINS), John 1,
    66
JEFFORDS(JEFFERDS), John
    39,42,92,188
JEFFREY, Rachel 232
JEFFREYS, Robert 266
JEFFRIES, Robert 349
JENEAN(JUNEAU), Magdalene
    113
JENKINS, Benjamin 322,363
  Charles 322,363
  Christopher 363
  Elizabeth 322,363
  George 219,326
  John 319,322,363
  Joseph 363
  Joseph Christopher 322
  Richard 363
  Thomas 203,296,322,363
  William 319,322,363
JENNER, James 60
JENNERET, Jacob 313
JENNINGS, Richard 308
  Samuel 234,299,320,348
  Thomas 348
JENNYS(JENYS, Paul 76,84,
    129,138,147,200,217,

JENNYS, Paul cont'd:
    226,228,264,279,313,
    316,340,352,353,371
JENYS, Elizabeth 292,316,
    352,353,371
  Thomas 316,352,353,371
JERMAN, Margaret 180
  Ralph 180,295,317,366,
    369
JERVICE, Edmond 297,312
JERVIS(JERVES), Edmond/
  Edmund 44,200,312,368
  John 312
  Mary 368
JESSINS(GEVINS), John 85
JEWNING, Thomas 335,341,
    372
JODFREY, John 130
JOHN, Earl of Bath 23,52,
    55,63,77,87,88,91,92,
    98,100,102,103,105,
    106,122,123,124,126,
    131,134,142,150,183,
    184,206,221,224,232,
    236,244,261,297,313,
    363,366,373,375
JOHN, James 337
JOHN, Lord Berkeley 77,378
JOHN, Lord Carteret 35,61,
    63,141,173,205,211,307,
    337
JOHN, Lord Granville 23,
    35,61,63,77,88,93,103,
    125,126,139-141,158,
    184,185,189,211,212,
    237,282,295,317 (see
    John Granville)
JOHN, Lewis 52
  Sir Nathaniel 35
JOHNS, Dorothy 94
  Samuel 94
JOHNSON, Deborah 97,193,
    244
  Edward 25
  Ester 307
  Humphrey 157
  James 99,195,369
  John 305,309,350,355,
    370,378
  Joseph 292,303,349
  Margaret 360
  Mary 360
  N. 56,60
  Nathaniel 13,23,44,47,
    48,61,63,77,87,88,90,
    94,95,104,105,121,125,
    128,140-142,147,149,
    156,158-160,163,168,
    176,177,180,181,183-
    186,190,191,201,206-
    213,215-245,247-255,
    257,259,261-263,
    265-291,293-296,298,
    301,304,312-315,319-
    321,327,332,349,353,
    360,367,379,381
  Peter 139,147,151,244,
    300,349,369
  Peter, Jr. 97,117,193,
    239
  Peter, Sr. 150,151
  Robert (alias BLACK
    ROBIN) 9,11,18,21,42,
    46,55,56,95,102,111,
    116,135,160,165,174,
    181,199,200,201,204,
    206,208,209,214,215,
    217-220,222,225,226,
    236,238,245,248,254,
    261,266,269,270,276,
    280,293,298,301,314,
    321,332,334,335,343,
    346,357,359,360,366,
    368,371

JOHNSON, cont'd:
    Sarah 303,382
    Thomas 166,172,236,359
    William 2
JOHNSTON, Gov. 139
    David 346
    Francis 33
    Gabriel 351
    Hester 282
    John 102,103,333,345,
        349,352,367,368
    Robert 22,34
    Sarah 368
JOHNSTONE, Arthur 372
JOLL(E)Y, Joseph 112,289
JOMER, David Laughton 120
JONATHAN, Ann 181
JONES, ___ 62,170,177
    Anne 44
    Charles 210,286,294
    Dorothy 190,263,309
    Edward 31
    Elizabeth 136
    Francis 335,336,343
    George 5
    Gilbert 1,29,54,160
    John 33,54,77,86,91,92,
        136,143,161,188,235,342
    Joseph 156,329,372
    J. Q. 148
    Lewis 104,119,253,254,
        291
    Margaret 253,254
    Martha 161
    Mary 220,294,372
    Mr. 102,110,111,170
    Philip 43,138
    Samuel 128,177,190,209,
        235,239,263,294,297,
        309,313,355,380
    Thomas 3,44,130,136,
        155,199,220,230,231,
        235,251,269,277,290,
        354
    William 294,304
JORDAN, Daniel 270
    John 234
JOULLY, John 300
JOY, William 269
JOYCE, Lewes 31
JOYES, Mary 265
    Peter 265
JULLY, Joseph 164
JULY, Joseph 307
JUNE, Ann 138
    George 147,168,354
    John 152,338
    Josias 143
    Solomon 252
JUNEAU, Magdelene 360,361
JURETINE, John 231

KANE, Joseph 5
KARWON, Crafton 213
    Cranston 255
KEATING, Edward 32,73,150,
    246,249,254,326
KEATING(S), George 110,111
    John 372
    Mary 150,326
KEELING, George 89,102,185,
    267
KEEN, John 323,349
KELLEY, James 313
KELLY, Bryan 130,257,375
    James 251,257
    Joan(Jeane) 251,257
    Mary 366
KEMBERLY(KIMBERLY), Thomas
    42,112,116
KEMP, Aaron 119
    William 337
KEN(N)EWAY, John 159,180
KENNIGAIN, James 365

KER, Thomas 294,304
KERR, James 236,266,267
KERWON, Crafton 358
KETTELL, Richard 45
KEY, Joseph 122
KEYNARD(KINARD), John 40
KILPATRICK, Alexander 257
    Dr. 315,316
    James 50,123,130,145,
        156,165,188,270,373
KIMBERLY, Isaac 283
    Isabel 24,41,162
    Isabela 290
    Thomas 24,41,66,77,86,
        160,162,166,311
KINARD(KINNAIRD), John 1,66
    Tony (negro) 1
KINDALL, Elizabeth 96,192
KING, Ann 280
    Charles 162,281,355
    Elizabeth 381
    Hester 104
    Jasper 355
    John 2,25,26,91,123,
        138,155,160,165,187,
        206,325
    Mary 156,281
    Robert 20
    Samuel 211,381
    Violetta 25
    Walter 2
KINLOCK(KINLOCH), Alexan-
    der 26,74,120,129
    James 23,74,75,93,130,
        174,178,179,181,188,
        189,231,272,273,277,
        326,338,343,352,356,
        357,363,375,376,379
KIPPIN, Joseph 2
KIRK, Francis 322
KITCHEN, Elizabeth 131
    Hugh 275
KITCHEN(KITCHIN), John 64,
    96,113,114,131,179,192
    William 164,261,274
KNATCHBULL, George 242
KNIGHT, Caleb 316
    Edward 355
    Mary 343
    Mr. 354
    Robert 343
    William 122
KNOTT, Jeremiah 258
KORTEN, John Abraham 357
    Peter 357
KUNSTER, Conrad 366
    Dorothea 366
KURFORD, Susanna 27
KYNASTON, A. 45

L___, Andrew 294
LABRUCE, Joseph 315,334,379
LACEY, Daniel 278,279
LADSON, Abraham 35
    Francis 74,133,153,210,
        217
    Jacob 35
    John 45,50,60
    Judith 50
    Robert 74,135,153,287,
        299,315,347,370
    Samuel 35
    Sarah 128
    Thomas 128,175,179
    William 35,311
LAFITTE, Peter 294
LA FONTAINE, Louis 181,214
LAFONTAINE, Mary 308
LAFORS, David 267
LAGRAND(E), Ann(e) Francis
    81,309
LAING, William 368
LAINI, Thomas 301
LAKE, Richard 209,247,253,

LAKE, Thomas cont'd: 369
    Thomas 111,242,288
LALO, Samson 198
LAMB, Peter 267,304
LAMBALL, Benjamin 278,279
LAMBELL(LAMBOLL), Thomas
    4,14,32-34,58,59,67,
    88,108,138,147,150,
    153,155,166,181,184,
    220,226,231,236,239,
    248,273-275,279,288,
    289,296,298,314,315,
    323,325,331,343,347,
    369,377,382
LAMBRIGHT, Anthony 167,238,
    276,346
    Belshazzar 379
    Belteshazzar 343
    Richard 68,72,86,99,
    117,151,179,195,218,
    226,255,258,260,275,
    280,283,285,287,300,
    342,349
LANCASTER, Joshua 202
    Mary 17
LANDEN, Thomas 288,289
LANE, Charles 343
    James 358,369,381
LANE(LANCE), John 130,249,
    299,301,320,338,357,
    358,366
LANE, Peter 264,357,364,
    365,369
    Sarah 358,366,369
    William 219
LANG, John 22
LANGHORNE, Arthur 111,116
LANGLOIS, Nicholas 93,143,
    189
LANNING, James 319,372
LAPIER, John 147,150
LAPIERE, Susannah 150
LAPIERRE, John 48,98,120,
    194
LAPORTE, Jacob 127
    John 127
    Thomas 127
LAPOSTRE, Catherine 51,291,
    333
LAPOTRE, Jacob 71,282,295,
    317
LARDA(I)N(LARDANT), James
    60,76,343
LARENCE, John 314
LAROACH(ES), Daniel 90
    John 62,90
    Mary 62,89,90
LAROCHE(S), Dan 225
    Daniel 142,169,202,203,
    207,222,225,244,251,
    252,255,261,277,288,
    289,299-301,303,305,
    311,315,319,320,329,
    330,335,337,350,364,
    365,371,381
    James 208
    John 125,169,186,230
    Mary 169,186,208,230,
    251
    Thomas 85,126,132,138,
    142,180,202,203,207,
    216,225,244,251,255,
    261,277,299-301,305,
    314,315,319,320,326,
    329,330,333-335,337,
    338,340,341,344,345,
    348,350,353-355,358,
    361,364-366,368,369,
    371,379,381
LARUSH(LAROCHE), ___ 54
LASALL, Peter 137
    Terte 328
LASCELL, George 121
LASONS, David 299

LATOUCHE, David 5
LATOUR, Charlotte 172
LATSON, ―― 248
LAUGHARNS, Arthur 198
LAUGHTON, Mary 79
　Mr. 92
　William 54,79
LAURAN, Andrew 7
　Jane 7
　John Samuel 7
LAURANCE, Augustus 51
　John 5,23
LAURENCE, Charles 268
　Thomas 116,258
LAURENS, Andrew 247
　Augustus 118,295,296,
　　309
　Charles 291,292
　Ester 70,103,172,263,
　　309
　Hannah 273
　Hester 246
　James 131,291,292
　John 8,43,62,67-70,103,
　　118,124,137,152,157,163,
　　172,220,235,246,259,260,
　　263,273,286,291,292,309,
　　313,314,319,333,340,357,
　　358
LAUSAE(LAUSAC), Lewis 138,
　　139
LAVILLETT, Andrew 340
LAVIS, John 257
LAWRENCE, John 319
　Mary Ann 268
　Thomas 116
LAW(S), Anne 154,173
　Benjamin 154,224,229,
　　327,334,336,343
　Bula 154
　Hepziba 154
　Joseph 88,122,154,184,
　　327,343
　Nathaniel 154,224,336
　Peter 264
　Sarah 224,327
　Theadore (Ash) 88,184
　Thomas 173
　William 326
LAX, John 377
LAYCROFT, Stephen 110
LEA, Catherine 99,100,196
　Elizabeth 14
　George 82,92,142,174,
　　188,286,315
　Isabel 137
　Johanne/Johnnis 13
　John 14,15,200,239
　Joseph 82,92,99,100,
　　137,188,195,196
　Lydia 92,188,252
　Robert Syer 99,100
　William 222,233,250,325
LEANDER, William 167,220,
　　364
LEARY, John 313
LEAY, John 230,260,273,291
　Mary 230,260,291
LEAYCROFT, Stephen 327
LEBAS, James 119,166,175,
　　227,276,299,370
　Paul Peter 16,227
LEBEUFF, Jerome 363
LEBRASSEUR, Catherine 145
　Francis 5,67,78,89,90,
　　124,145,160,185,186
LEE, Edward 173,200
　George 42
　Lydia 277
　Stephen 123,140
　William 277
LEECH, Mary 293
LE ESCOT(T), Paul 7,22
LEGARE, ―― 7

LEGARE, Anne 44
　Daniel 318,319,352
　Mr. 217
　Solomon 10,40,44,91,92,
　　187,188,208,214,240,
　　263,318,319,336
　Solomon, Jr. 118
LEGER, Andrew 27
　Mary 93,189
　Peter 93,189
LEGRAND(E), Isaac 80,81,
　　84,86,91,93,187,189,
　　236,249,269,271,348,
　　364,368
LEITH, Thomas 284,314,315,
　　345,349,366,381
LEJANDRA, Elizabeth 340
LEJAU, Francis 35,241,280,
　　286,290,292,304,336,
　　348-352,359,361,363,
　　367,375,376
　Mr. 268
LEMONIER, James 139
LEMUD, Nicholas 84
LENOIR, John 52,53,70,113,
　　131
　Martha 113
　Robert 113
LENUD, Albert 157
　Magdeline/Magdalen 157,
　　271,272,273
　Nicholas 157,271,272,
　　273
　Nicholas, Jr. 157
　Rene 157
LENTHWAITE, William 273
LEPAIR, Paul 365
LEPPOR, John 199
LEROCHE, John 12
　James, Jr. 158
　James, Sr. 158
LESADE, Ann(e) 58,122,259,
　　260
　Ann Gabriel 177
　Elizabeth 177
　James 38,132,177
　Peter 38,58,122,132,
　　177,178,224,251,287
LESCOTT, Francis (also
　　Francoise L'Escott) 22
L'ESCOT(T), Paul 49,65
LESESENE, Elizabeth 135
LESESNE, Isaac 42,108,123,
　　127,135,167,172,176,
　　234,339,369
　Isaac, Jr. 233
　Isaac, Sr. 206
　James 152,268,369
LESEUR(LESIR), Joseph 38
LES(SEUR (LE SUEUR), Abra-
　　ham 7,57,78
LESLIE, Charles 146
LESL(E)Y, William 305,335
LESOEUR(LESSUR), Abraham
　　171
LESSLEY, Catherine Duvall
　　119
　Wm. 119,149
LESUR, James 278,279
LETCH, Andrew 278,285
LETCHY, Andrew 245
LETON, John 211
LETTUD, Nicholas 269
LEURN, Henry 228
LEVEY, Thomas 318
LEVIE, Alexander 314
LEVINGSTON, Wm. 222
LEWIN, Henry 325
LEWIS, Charles 124,283,333
　Francis 277,287
　Gideon 169
　Henry 124,127,202,268,
　　292,333,369
LEWIS(LUIS), Isaac 109,169,

LEWIS(LUIS), Isaac cont'd:
　　228,247
LEWIS, John 92,98,110,125,
　　145,163,169-171,175,
　　181,188,194,199,205,
　　208,268,279,360
　Judith 329,364
　Maurice 232,242,244,
　　268,276,277,283,284,
　　287,288,290,293-295,
　　300,305,311,314,315,
　　319,320,322,324,325,
　　332,335,338,341,342,
　　344,350,352,355,368,
　　370
　Morris 355
　Robert 69,128,382
　Sarah 109
　Sedgwick 228
　William 27,258,352,369
LEYCROFT, Stephen 145
LEYDELL, James 30
LIEUBREY, Alran Peter 318
　Peter 354
LIGHTWOOD, Edward 167,170
LINING, John 214,215,244,
　　309,345,383
LINKLY, Christopher 332,
　　380
LINNING, John 318,320
LINTHWAITE, Eleanor 290
　William 259,263,290,
　　305
LISTON, Robert 235
LITTEN(S), Martha 50,92,
　　188
LIVERIGHT, David 347
LIVIE, Alexander 298
LIVING, Mr. 298
LIVINGSTON, Ann(e) 49,65,
　　115,242,313,328
　George 297,327,328,376
　Hannah 25,44,49,313,
　　346
　Henry 51,52,70,159,229,
　　294,313,346
　Margaret 313,346
　Mary 78,88,184,217,230,
　　237,284,306,346
　Thomas 238,242,276,328
　William 1,7,9,25,44,
　　49,65,78,88,115,134,
　　146,150,159,166,168,
　　177,180,184,199,206,
　　208,217,230,232,237,
　　238,242,276,284,306,
　　313,346,353,373,376
LLOYD, Benjamin 358
　Elizabeth 272
　James 209
LLOYD(LOYD), John 4,20,53,
　　70,73,99,100,141,195,
　　196,203,204,207,214,
　　215,262,275,344,354,
　　357,379
　Mr. 145
　Philemon 28
　Sarah 141
　Thomas 84,99,150,194,
　　195,272,352
LOCKWOOD, Jos'a 262
　Sarah 262
LOCKYE(A)R, Thomas 83,
　　102,114
LODGE, Richard 74
LOGAN, George 13,20,42,66,
　　80,95,96,108,163,191,
　　193,270,308,324,330
　George, Sr. 13
　John 232
　Martha 13,24,66,67,
　　108,206,291
　Robert 366
LONDON, John 8

LONG, George 3
    John 3,4,356
    Joyce 153
    Mary 356
LONGHAIR(LONGHARE), Cor-
    nelius 55,86
LORD, Joseph 45,114,170,
    175,178,179,182,183,
    197,287
    Thomas 45
LOREY, Thomas 50,253
LORIMER, Lewis 284,357
LOROMOND, Andrew 304
LOTEN, Nathaniel 318
LOUGHTON, Ann 378
    David 378
    Edward 6,135,378
    Mary 33,378
    Mr. 82,188
    Nathaniel 318
    Sarah 318
    William 30,57,93,189,
    267,354
LOUIS, John 287,290
LOURY, James 367
LOVEKIN, John 312
LOWELL, Samuel 174
LOWLE, Morgery 89
    Samuel 89
LOWNDES, ___ 177
    Charles 170,176,246,
    248,307
    Isaac 307,336,337
LOWNDES(LOUNDES), Thomas
    173,226,227,232,254,
    305,307,308,331,332,
    336,337,370
LOYADELL, James 167
LOYD, John 369
    Thomas 110
LOYDELL, James 4,5,197
LOYELL, Samuel 234
LUCAS, ___ 33
    George 235,339,373,378
    John 22,339
LUCE, Jacob 7,47
LUCUSS, James 68
LUDLAM, Ann 129
LUDLOW, Lamber 153
LUPTON, John 162,196
LYCOTT, John 368
LYDELL, James 21,101
LYDON, Robert 114,131
LYNCH, John 42,51,101,126,
    170
    Johnson/Jonson 113,
    150-152,168,176,236,
    237
    Madam 237
    Major 125
    Margaret 152
    Nicholas 250
    Sabina 199
    Susannah Margaret 363
    Thomas 139,176,199,200,
    220,231,232,262,263,
    269,270,283,305,307,
    316,318,322,337,339
LYNDE, Benjamin 248
    Samuel 45
    Thomas 277
LYNE, Thomas 140
LYON, Charles 375,376
    Ebenezer 160
LYONS, Joseph 250

MC ALLA, William 356,363
MC BRIDE, Alexander 145
MC CALL, James 159
    Sarah 159,160
MC CANTS, John 258,381
MC CASTEN, Francis 367
MC CLELAN(D), Jean 269,382

MC CLELLAN, David 346,364
    James 271
MC CLEUR, William 174
MC CLOULIN, James 361
MC CLUFR, William 323
MC COLLUM, John 346
MC COON, James 5
MC COY, John 278
MC DANIEL, Daniel 147,170
    Timothy 219
MC DONALD, Adam 367
    James 296
MC ECHEM, William 92
MC ECHEN, William 166,180,
    188
MC ELROY, Alexander 325
MC EUEN, Daniel 171
MC EVER, John 339
MC FARLAND, Daniel 177,374
MC GILLEVERY, Alexander 257
    Elizabeth 257
    Mary 257
    Robert 257
    William 257
MC GILLIVRAY, Archibald
    271
    John 375
    William 182
MC GILLVARY, Wm. 179
MC GINNE, Daniel 136
MC GREGOR, Martha 141
MC GREGORY(MC GREIGORY),
    Daniel 51,71,127,327
    Duncan/Dunkin 138,140
    John 138
    June 138
    Mary 138
    Sarah 71,127
MC GRIGOR, Daniel 137
MC GRIGORY, Daniel 295,307,
    317
MC IVER, John 376
MC KAIE, Elizabeth 318
    James 318
MC KAY(MC KOY), Alexander
    153
MC KAY, John 86,96,180,192,
    340,344,345,378
    Mary 344
MC KAYE, Elizabeth 354
    James 354
MC KEE, James 316
MC KEGGAN, Dugald 183
    Dugee 87
MC KELLVEY(MC KELVEY),
    Daniel 93,189
MC KELVEY, James 234
MC KELVIN, Robert 129
MC KENZIE, ___ 116
    John 291,342
    W. 118
MC KENZIE(MC KENSIE), Wil-
    liam 160,163,364,369
MC KEWN, James 350
MC KOY, Alexander 171
MC KYE, James 249
MC LOUGHLIN, James 83,129
MC MECHAN, John 368
MC MORTHY, Madame 96
MC MORTR(A)Y, Madame 128,
    193
MC MURTRY, John 53
MC NABNY, James 122,167
MC NAIRE, John 117
MC PHERSON, Anne 311
MC PHERSON(MACKPHERSON),
    William 18,151,241,311,
    368,379
MC PHERSIN, Wm. 117,118
MC QUEEN, David 114
    Dunken 269
MC TIER, John 354

MACAGOINE(MACKAGOINE),
    James 218
MACALPIN, James 136
MACARTHY, Daniel 173
MAC COY, John 249
MACDOWELL, Archibald 142
MACGIRT, Pricilla 358
    James 358
MAC GRIGORY, Daniel 282
MACHELL, Jean 43
MAC HEYSON, N. 260
MACKALL, James 5
    Sarah 5
MACKAY(MC KEY), Alexander
    47
    Helena 47
MAC KAY, Patrick 358
MACKCLELLAN, Thomas 334
MACKCOY, James 338
MAC KENZIE, George 260
    Kennith 327
MACKEWN, James 29,30,172
    Mary 267
MACKEY, Alexander 22,219,
    238,253,291
    Catherine 225
MAC KEY, Ellinor 219
MACKEY, Joseph 136,145,216,
    225
    William 139,378
MAC LOUGHLING, William 285
MAC MARVILL, Mary 250
MAC NEMARA Michael 125
MACOY, John 319,341
MAC QUEEN, David 58
MACRENZIE, George 274,275
MAC TEER, ___ 200
    John 21,136,354
MADDOCK(S), Thomas 329,
    330,348
MADINA, Moses 21
MAETLEYSENE, Nichilas 208
MAGGETT, William 63
MAGGOTT, John 145
    William (also Magott)
    133,374
MAGILLIVRAY, Elizabeth 237
    William 237
MAHAM, Nicholas 372
MAHON(E), Michael 286,336,
    349
MAHUM, Nicholas 216
MAIDSTONE, ___ 331
MAIN, Jonathan 375
MAKEKEN, Dugat 102
MALION, Michael 304
MALLACE, David 357
MALLDEN, Thomas 182,353
MAL(L)ERY, Ebenezer 44,142
MALLETT, James 94,164,190
    Mary 94,190
MALLORY, Seymour 328
MALONE, Richard 249,299,
    320,321
MAN, John 214
MANGAULT, Gabriel 377
MANIGAULT, Anne 67
    Gabriel 56,110,156,157,
    164,165,167,169,180,
    211,233,247,253,264,
    265,317,323,345,357,
    359,360
    Mrs. 133
MANIGAULT(MENIGAULT),
    Peter 7,22,27,67,163
    Pierre 112
MANNING, Thomas 181
    Wm. 159
MAORTIN, Moses 313
MARBEUF(MARBEAUF), Joseph
    150,307
MARCHAND, Rene 129
MARDEN, Nicholas 68

MARENSY, Julien 233
MARETT, Philip 30
MARION, Benjamin 81,86,95,
  191
  Gabriel 261
  Henry 131
  John 86
  Joseph 248
  Peter 264,351
MARINEUR(E), Josue 38,72
MARONEY, Julian 228
MARQUEZ(MARQUIS), Elizabeth 163,164
  Emanuel 163,164
MARR, William 47
MARRANT, Mr. 119
MARRIOTT, Joseph 4,5
  Mehitable 4,5
MARSCHALCK, Andrew 79
MARSDEN, Richard 4
  Rid/Ridley 4,15
  Thomas 4,15
MARSEAU, Francis 26
MARSH, James 247
MARSHALL, Beulah 220
  Charles 220
  John 9,74,180,348
  Margaret 220
  Robert 321
  Wm. 137
MARTEN, John 6
MARTIN, Findla 102,220
  Finley 85
  Grace 180
  Henry 252
  Isaac 277,313,346
  Jacob 231
  James 136,171,216,353
  John 143,236,346
  Mary 344
  Mr. 345
  Moses 29,77,84,89,129,
   130,174,180,186,206,
   277,313,331,346
  Moses, Jr. 234
  Patrick 176,313
  Richard 303
MARTIN(MARTYN), Samuel 9,
  252
  William 143,306,344,372
MARTINI, Dr. 286
  John 206,283,290,318
MARTINS, John 367
MASON, Abraham 255
  Christian 209
  John 73,160,199,208,209
  Richard 172,236,245,267,
   287,327,350
  Susannah 236
MASSY, Benjamin 12,159
MASSEY, James 157
  Joseph 3,159,201,336
  Mr. 145
MASTERS, Anna 148
  John 17
  Samuel 148,202,264,301,
   323,329
MATHEWS, Anthony, Jr. 69,
   119,168
  Anthoney, Sr. 95,191,
   231
  Benjamin 379
  George 379
  James 130,136,159,165,
   290,291,359
  John 165,231,291,343,
   379
  Lois 165,379
  Maurice 70,93,103,120,
   189
  Thomas 78
MATTEYSON, Nicholas 252,284
MAT(T)HEWS, Anthony 12,62,
MAT(T)HEWS, Anthony cont'd
   64,82,83,84,90,111,129,
   157,165,168,180,186,
   230,231,235,284,286,
   294,299,300,309,364
  Mark 149,336
  Mary 378
  William 378
MATTHEYSON, N. 275
MATTHISEN, Mary 290
  Nicholas 258,286,290,
   341
MAURICE, Lord Ashley, Earl
  of Shaftebury 11
MAVERICK, John 124
MAXWELL, James 80,98,121,
   150,194,273
  Mary 121
MAY, Christopher 268
  Henry 128
  Peter 344
  Susannah 184
  Wm. 117
MAYBANK, ___ 26
  David 63,67,77,78,184
  Susannah 63,88
MAYER, Adrian 358
MAYRANT, Elizabeth 344
  James 98
  James Nicholas 12,51,
   60,88,89,185
  John Nicholas 131
  Mr. 125
  Nicholas 89,131,263
  Paul 12,89,185
  Susannah(Susanne) 88,
   185
MAYS, Edward 45
MAZYCK, Benjamin 291
  Catharina 264
  Isaac 10,11,12,37,42,
   43,47,54,65,70,76,78,
   82,90,106,116,135,150,
   182,186,187,196,232,
   239,280,283,287,291,
   326,327,340,355,360,
   377-379,382
  Isaac, Jr. 88,163,184,
   197,224,225
  Isaac Many 295
  Isaac, Sr. 212,249
  James 9
  Marian(n)a/Marian 70,
   78,90,186
  Marianne 47
  Mr. 117
  Paul 54,89,115,185,216,
   264,309,364,369
  Rebecca 116
  Thomas 80
MEAD(E), Joseph 28,30,61
  Mary 30
MEAN, William 324,325
MEBSHOE, ___ 22
MEDLICOAT, Edmond 54
MEDLICOTT, Edward 247
MEECHEN, ___ 134
MEFFANT(MIFFANT), James 119
MEGET, James 261
MEGGETT, William 25
MELL, John 101,105,196,197
MELL(S), Margaret 101,196
  Mary 146
  Thomas 146,175,338
MELLENS, John 103
MELLICHAMP, Timothy 264
  William 239
MELONE, Richard 301
MELVEN, Alexander 180
  Thomas 180
  Wm. 151
MELVIN, John 373
  Thomas 373
MELVIN, cont'd:
  Walter 159,373
MENOSHAM, ___ 219
MENSON, Margaret 355
MENZIES, James 97,160,193
MERCHAND, Rene 293
MERCHANT, Rene 293
MEREDITH, Edward 106
MEREWETHER, John 21,30
MERRETT, Francis 337
MERRIL, John 349
MERRILL, Samuel 28
MERRITT, Thomas 136,189
MERRYES, ___ 15
MESHEW, Abraham 249
  Elizabeth 319
  Henry 249,319
MESMITH, John 114
METHERINGHAM, John 23,113,
   141,360
METHRINGHAM, Mary 141
MEWS, Ann 341
  Henry 341
MEYER, Fred. 314
  Fredrick 204,208,220,
   231,241,248,251,298,
   305,308,309,314,323
MEYRICK, Wm. 209
MICHAEL, Ephraim 376
MICHAU(MICHAW), Abraham
   157,268,271,272,273,
   318
MICHAUS, Henry 33
MICHAUX, Abra 354
MICHELL, Amos 301
  Jane 43
  Nicholas 43
MICHIE, James 172,224,238,
   249,262,263,265,279,
   280,285,287,288,326,
   332,333,338,362,365,
   369,371,375,383
  Kenneth 353
  Martha 371
MICKALLS, Michael 172
MICKIE, James 204
MIDDLETON, ___ 271
  Anna 266,365
  Arthur 3,35,36,47,49,
   50,52,59-61,64,76,80-
   82,86,93,95,96,101,103,
   106,115,118,124,125,
   163,178,189,191,192,
   216,227,230-232,250,
   268,288,298,306,320,
   321,342,364,369,372,
   376
  Edward 21,216,378
  George 145
  Henry 378
  Sarah 216,230,231,369
  Solomon 14,130,210,211,
   266
  Thomas 369
  William 264,342
MIDFORD, William 331
MIDWELL, Nevil 29
MIENSON, John 355
MIKELL, Benjamine 207
  Ephraim 182,207,319,
   327,340
  Ephraim, Jr. 100,196
  John 207
  Joseph 207
  Mary 100,196
  Mikell 207
MILES, Jeremiah 114
  John 155
  Richard 94,115,155,
   162,190
  Thomas 114
  William 34,94,190,214,
   377

MILL, Richard 9
MILL(S), Thomas 217,309
MILLECHAMP, I. 342
　　Jane 230,231,369
MILLECHAMP(P), Timothy 230,
　　231,369
MILLER, Agnes 8
　　Alice 8
　　Andrew 212
　　Henry 4,8
　　John 342
　　Magdalene 269
　　Moses 255,269
　　Mr. 87,183
　　Peter 8
　　Rebecca 314
　　Richard 101,197
　　Robert 174,175,178,179,
　　182,183
　　Robert, Jr. 113
　　Robert, Sr. 52,64
　　Samuel 250,263,269,314
　　Stephen 68,103,128,137,
　　172,201,202,255,340
　　Thomas 265
MILLES, John 129
MILLEX, John 66
MILLINS, Mary 156
MILLMAN, John 18
MILLNER, John 100,196
MILLS, John 252
MILNIAN, John 233
MILLURE, Michael 126,200,
　　222,325
MILNER, Elizabeth 71,322
　　Jeremiah 67
　　Jonathan 3
　　John 71,157,207,322,323
　　Joseph 67,336
　　Mary 3
MINOR, Mayrants 307
MITCHELL, George 320
　　James 319,366,371
　　John 45,216,232,353,380
　　Joseph 276,353
　　Martha 366,371
　　Moses 287
　　Sarah 380
　　William 102,111
MOLAGAN, Charles 308
MOLLETION, Mr. 143
MOLLOCH, Robert 21
MOLLOY, Charles 111
MON, Stephen 136
MONCLAR, Peter 368
　　Peter John 119
MONEIR, Stephen 131
MONFIN, David 275
MONGIN, David 283,284
　　Presile 283
MONIER, Moses 113,168
　　Peter 113
MONK(MONCK), John 47,115,
　　168,376
　　Stephen 47,115,168,282,
　　376
　　Thomas 110,211,225,227,
　　228,241,286,293,338,341,
　　367,370
MONGE, Jane 250
MONGER, Ger'd/Gerrard/Geo.
　　1,22
　　Jane 22,242
　　Margaret 242
MONTAIGNT, Samuel 358
MONTGOMERY, Ann 221
　　Elizabeth 26
MONTJOY, Thomas 85
MOODY, Ebenezer 1,44,322
　　Joseph 170,263,313,326,
　　346
MOON, Alexander 354
　　John 6
　　Sarah 354

MOOR, Michael 239
MOORE, Catherine 99,174,
　　195,342
　　Elizabeth 318,369
　　George 4,21,302
　　James 11,12,13,20,23,
　　26,33,34,35,49,52,55,
　　56,60,63,65,70,73,77,
　　82,88,91,99,118,134,
　　137,140-142,149,150,
　　161,176,184,187,195,
　　211,221,222,232,236,
　　237,240,241,254,263,
　　291,313,353,369,373,
　　374
　　Jehu 369
　　John 19,37,38,42-44,
　　48,57,60,65,66,70,73,
　　79,81,84,85,92,96,98,
　　108-111,131,132,137,
　　144,148,150,156,188,
　　192,194,214,230,239,
　　242,369
　　Margaret 48
　　Martha 48
　　Mary 302
　　Mathew 338
　　Maurice 36
　　Nathaniel 37,76,82,92,
　　188
　　Rachel 73,148
　　Roger 22,32,40,66,73,
　　76,80,86,99,100,106,
　　124,161,164,195,196,
　　221,241,265,300,302,
　　342
　　Sarah 76,82,92,188
　　Thomas 21,50,81
　　William 148,372
MOORE(MORE), Rebecca 118
MOORS, George 276
MORAINE, Dennis 112
　　Edmund 112
　　John 112
MORALL(MORILL), William
　　27,311,323
MORAN, Robert 238,268
MORANEY, Mary 18
MORELAND, George 173,181
MORGAN, Ann(e) 135,371
　　John 2,22,50,167,229,
　　282
　　Joshua 220,371
　　Lewis 236
　　William 240,311
MORGANTAL, Gasper 342
MORINA(MORRINA), Francis
　　139,176
MORLEY, George 375
MORPHY, Dominick 277
MORRAIN, Dennis 164
　　Edmund 163,164
　　Elizabeth 164
　　John 164
MORRALL(MURRILL), John 165
　　Wm. 361
MORRELL, John 329
　　Thomas 251
MORRETT, Thomas 315,364
MORRICE, James 31
MORRIS, George 153
　　Mathew 147
　　Samuel 92,95,144,188,
　　191,314,319,342
　　William 5
MORRITT, Thomas 93,136,228,
　　371
MORTIMER, Elianer 345
MORTIMORE, Benjamin 125,
　　126
　　Maryann 125
MORTIMER, Mr. 145
　　Richard 223
MORTON, ___ 69

MORTON, cont'd:
　　John 33
　　Joseph 12,13,20,23,26,
　　33,36,45,55,63,65,88,
　　89,93,103,134,140,141,
　　182,184,186,189,236,
　　374
　　Sarah 36,45
MOSELY, Edward 342
MOSER, John 156
MOSES, Thomas 329
MOTTE, Christian 366,380
　　Elizabeth 85
　　Ellioner 89
　　Isaac 33,48
　　Jacob 3,4,14,38-44,46,
　　47,49-56,58-181,183-
　　197,204,278,279,285,
　　286,289,291,294,299,
　　300,302,307,309-311,
　　317,320,322,325,338,
　　340,355,367,371
　　John 40
　　John Abraham 33,48,71
MOULES, William 35
MOULTRIE, John 144,305
MOUNTJOY, Thomas 21,116
MOUSON, Lewis 87,184,261
MOUZON, Louis(Lewis) 237,
　　255
MULCASTER, John 14,16
MULLER, Albert 69,70,81
MULLINS, Mary 71,305,323
MUL(L)RYNE, John 254,304,
　　370
MUNGER, Jane 380
MURDOCK, James 315,316
MURFEE, Morris 106,107
MURPHEY, Richard 232
MURRELL, John 349
　　Sarah 349
MURRIL(L), Elizabeth 344
　　Francis 110,344
MURPHY, Richard 171
MURRAY, Martha 214
MURREL, John 208
MURRILL, Jonathan 222
　　William 56
MURRILLE, James 155
　　Jonathan 155
MURRY, Susanna 13
　　William 13
MURSEE, Morris 51
MUSGROVE, John 91,313,364
　　Jon. 187
MYRANT, James 194

NAIRN, Thomas 301
NARY, Mary 38,39,45,46,67,
　　92,131,188
　　Nicholas 38,39,79,115
NASH, John 182
　　Prudence 69
　　Susanna(h) 182,371
　　Thomas 7
　　William 69,297,298,312,
　　313,338,379
　　Wm., Sr. 182
NATHAN, Mordecai 106
NEAL(E), Abraham 114
　　Daniel 177
　　Edward 179
　　Jacob 114
　　James 134,142
　　Mary 177
　　Nathaniel 332
　　Peter 177
　　Susannah 177
NEEDHAM, Benjamin 322
NEILL, James 168
　　Lawrence 225,227,367
NEILSON, George 267
　　John 357,358
NELSON, Mathew 324

NERBOROUGH, M. 80
NESBITT, Mary 156
NESMITH, John 144
NESS, John 77,80
NEUFVILLE, John 254,260, 273
NEUISON, Mathew 212
NEVES, Joseph 269
NEWBERRY, Henry 288
NEWBOROUGH, M. 42
   Mathew 92-94,188-190
   Nathaniel 201
NEWFULLE, John 147
NEWINGTON, Hester 181
   John 286
   Roger 44,96,193,297, 312
NEWLIN, Nicholas 60
NEWMAN, Edward 32
NEWMAN(NUMAN), Robert 320
   Samuel 320
   William 268,338,354
NEWMITH, John 87
NEWS, Dorothy 306
   Joseph 306
NEWTON, John 143,165,212, 236
   Robert, Jr. 241
NEVEAU, Francis 143
NICHIE, James 236
NICHOL, William 347,350
NICHOLAS, ___ 219
   Elizabeth 248,279
   George 174,247,248,249, 279,292,304,305,317, 319,324,325,354,359, 378,381
   Henry 212
   Isaac 355,356
   Joan 245
   Mathew 239
   Nathaniel 245
   Samuel 245
   Thomas 335,378
   William 245
   William J. 212
NICHOL(E), Wm. 126,146
NICHOLS, Henry 68,233,296, 299,315
   John 81
NICHOL(L)S, Nathaniel 98, 164,194,245
   Samuel 98,194,223
   Sarah 164
NICHOLSON, FFR. 53
   Francis 64,333
   John 48,61,80,121,140, 286,349
   William 347
NICKOLLS, Henry 316
NINIAN(NINEAN), John 252
   Robert 252
NISBETT, Alexander 31,74, 75,85,86,94,97,100,101, 106,112,120,122,179, 190,193,196,197,239, 240,241,244,250,252, 261,271,274,277,299, 362,375
   Mr. 331
   Robert 57,75,87,156,183
   Walter 86,97,101,122, 179,193,196,240
NISMITH, John 183
NOBLE, Catherine 161
   George 228
   Henry 48,61,140,147, 169,211,255,279,349
NOBEL, Thomas 137
NORELAND, George 199
NORMAN, Barak 110,198
   Isaac 150
   Joseph 32

NORMAN, cont'd:
   Moses 49,63,76,198
   Rebekah 49
NORMAND, Peter (Pierre) 143
NORRIS, Edward 332
   Patrick 257
NORTH, Edward 156,308,372
   William 34,127,128,255
NORTON, Dorothy 374
   Elizabeth 374
   George 245,373,374
   John 52,167,373,374
   Jonathan 101,197,373, 374
   Joseph 373
   Maryan 373,374
   Mr. 339
   Sarah 52,374
   William 374
NOWELL, William 83,84,158
NUBOLL, Sarah 372
NUMAN, William 320
NUTKINS, John 95,191
NUTTALL, Jos. 5
NUTTING, Jonas 26

OARD, Edward 163
ODENSALS, ___ 320
ODENSEL, ___ 298
ODINGFELLS, Charles 126, 207,366,371
ODINGSELLS, Charles 104, 109
OESSER, Wm. 169
OGLETHROPE, James 343
OLDFIELD, John 109,169,341
OLE(COLE?), Robert 69
OLIVER, George 270,310,335, 336,365
   Isabell 227
   Mark(e) 49,62,72,85, 92,100,114,137,188,195, 196,227
   Mary 227,335,336
OLLIER, Jane 205
OMER, James 129,157
ORAM, Edward 309,310
ORD, Edward 309
ORGILL, S. 17
ORWILL, Wm. 152
OSBORNE, Alexander 251
   Eleanor (Helenah) 219, 238,251
   William 219,238,251
OSGOOD, Jacob 291
   Josiah 12,22,33,37,76, 108,114,115,170,174, 198,368
   Thomas 37,113,115,174, 197,198,209,272,380
   Thomas, Jr. 29,37,179, 197,198
   Thomas, Sr. 49,183
OSMOND, James 228,279,297
O'SULLIVAN, Florentia 201
O'SULLIVANE, Florence 302
OSWELL, Mr. 352
   Robert 199
   William 294
OSWILL, William 171,208
OTTERSON, John 257
OULDFIELD, David 130
   James 192
   Job 364,365
   John 32,96,192,227,244, 252,254,300,301,314, 315,338
OWEN(S), Frances 255
   Jerimiah 255
   John 348
   Nathaniel 255
   Thomas 201,255,259,343

OWENS, cont'd:
   William 78
OXFORD, Nicholas 266

PACE, Joseph, Jr. 155
PACKER, John 238,276
PADGETT(PAGITT), Ann(e) 94,190
   Francis 201
PADGETT(PACET,PAGITT),
   Thomas 7,94,98,109, 110,127,144,190
PADGITT, Francis, Jr. 80
PAGE, John 56,199,380
   Joseph 322
   Samuel 347,370
   William 223
PAGETT(PAGITT,PAGET),
   Francis 14,18,19,139, 142,259
   Peter 237,266,346,347, 370
   Thomas 172,194,354
PAGISS, Thomas 150
PAGITT, John 109,110
PAGITT, Francis 151,244
   Thomas 164,233,234,281
PAICE, Joseph, Jr. 162
PAIGE, Robert 2
PAIN(E), James 74-76,89, 98,145,146,154,185, 193,200,214,226,231, 259,290,313,327,335, 372,378
   Mary 200,372
   William 16
PAINTER, John 224,229,238
   Naomi 229
PALMARIN, Mary 277
PALMARIN, Lewis 277
PALMAVIN, Louis 139
PALMENTER, Joseph 207
PALMETER, Peter 336
PALMER, Elizabeth 301
   Hannah 136
   Henry 31
   Isabel 136
   Jonathan 73
   John 63,133,136,138, 144,179,181,204,263, 301,302,321,322,332
   Joseph 136
   Lewis 277
   Mr. 148
   Robert 136
   Thomas 48,87,184
   William 283
PALMERIN, ___ 249
PAMOR, John 145
PANTAEL, Mr. 286
PANTON, John 238
PARETREE(PEARTRA), James 47
PARHAM, Mary 267
PARIS, Peter 41
   Pierre 41
PARKER, Benjamin 28,30
   Elizabeth 8
   John 5,28,30,112,169, 270
   Joseph 28,30
   Martha 28,30
   Mary 27,28,30
   Mr. 268
   Paul 317
   Sarah 28,30
PARMENTER, Isaac 291
   James 207,216
PARMENTER(PARMETER), Joseph 22,37,112
   Peter 149
   Thomas 22,112,245
   Thomas, Jr. 149

PARMETER, Philymon 237
PARRIS, Alexander 4,6,16,
    27,29,31,35,36,45-48,
    52,53,56-59,64,75,76,
    85,92-95,97,100,101,
    104,115,117,120-124,
    126-128,133,142-144,
    147,149,150,161,167,
    169,176,182,188-191,
    193,196,198-200,202,204,
    206,208,210,212,213,
    215,216,218,221,223,
    228,230,231,239,240,
    246,327,333,369
  Alexander, Jr. 5,6,56,
    101,197
  John 56,327
  Mary 56,57,147,148,210
PARROT(T), Anne 40,214
  William 40,53,75,107,
    214
PARRY, Richard 214
PARTRIDGE, Mrs. 129
  Nathaniel/Nath. 6.7.24.
    46,83,160,285,345,361
  Rebecca 228
  William 243,358
PARSONS, Samuel 345
PASQUEREAU, Lewis 237,250
PATEY, Edward 158
  Theophilus 142,158
PATTERSON, John 145
PATTERY, Edward 278
PATTEY, Edward 279
  Martha 278,279
PAULLING, Robert 272
PAVIT, William 238
PAWLEY, Ann 77
  Anthony 200
  George 7,77,148,249,
    252,261,274,275,301,
    305,315,334,342,378,
    379
  Joseph 181
  Mary 315
  Percival/Percivel 16,
    48,53,70,125,164,203,
    204,252,354,379
PAYCOM(B), John 182,379
PAYNE, Ephraim 242
  James 359
  John 219
PEACOCK, Gabriel 198
PEACOM(B) (PEACUM) (PECUM),
  John 97,133,171,193,
    372,373
PEACON, John 356
PEAK, Stephen 333,334
PEARCE, Mary 11
PEARSON, John 380
  Thomas, Jr. 111
PEARTREE, James 33
PECKHAM, Ebenezer 239
  Joseph 100
  Lydia 239
PEEKHAM, Joseph 196
PELE, Ester (widow) 7
PELLET, Jane 96,192
PELLET(T), Felix 117
PELOQUIN, John 36
PEMBERTON, Elizabeth 144
PENDARVIS,   26
  John 83,285,296,361
  Joseph 95,167,191,256,
    296,299,315,376
  Mary 256
PENHALLOW, Samuel 69
PENNY, John 174
  Robert 175
PENDERGAST, Edward 373
PENNYMAN, John 156,235,258,
    266,312-315,320,321,358
PEPPER, Daniel 214,325
  Mary 214

PERCIVAL(L), Andrew 10,45,
    93,103,122,172,189,249,
    317,329
PERCY, Hugh 200,357
PERDRIAN, Abraham 363,364
PERDRIAU, Benjamin 379
  Peter 123,292
PERIET, Francis 273
PERNELL, Mary 220
PERONNEAU, Alexander 106,
    276,311,348
PERONNEAU(PERANNEAU),
    Charles 137,240,268,
    286,338,342,343,380
  Henry 3,39,51,81,106,
    137,276,286,300,309,
    311,348,376
  H., Jr. 86
  Henry, Jr. 81,235,243
  Henry, Sr. 108
  Isaac 342,351
  Mary 342
  Samuel 376
  Thomas 298,320
PEROT, Daniel 5,8
PERRIE, Anne 35,43
  Dorothy 35,43
  Elizabeth 35,43
  Edward 35,43
  John 35,43
  Mary 35,43
PERRIMAN, Benjamin 129
  John 93,129,189
  Mary 189
  Thomas 165
  William 143,325
PERRIMAY, Mary 93
PERRY, Benjamin 135,229
  Edward 35,114,135,244
  John 71
  Macajah 362
  Peter 135
PERRYMAN, Benjamin 1,8
  John 93
PETER(S), Christopher 180
  John 90,180,186,199,
    206,242,308
  Hannah 174,175
  John, Jr. 117,118
  Phebe 87
  Tabitha 206,382
  Thomas 92,188
  William 118,175,199,
    206,234,294
PETERSON, Abigail 179
  Elizabeth 19,145,170,
    308
  George 19,47,145
  John 104,109,221,222
  Mary 221
  Richard 104
  Richard, Jr. 221,222
PETRE(PETER), Phebe 92,188
PET(T)INEAU, John (Jean)
    13,125,126
PETTY, Thomas 31
PEYER, Humphrey 291
PEYRE, Catherine 113
PHELPS, John 241
PHENIX, Alexander 36
PHIPPS, Benjamin 4,5,21,30
  Joseph 263
PICHARD, Jacob 294
PICK, John 35
PICKENS, James 285
PICKERING, Samuel 2,9,56,
    98,194
PICOT, Peter 263
PIERCE, Mr. 344,351
PIGHT, John 1
PILKINGTON, John 320
PINCKNEY, Charles 64,82,83,
    84,99,106,113,117,124,
    126,159,163,167,168,

PINCKNEY, Charles cont'd:
    171,172,174,180,194,
    195,200,204,206,209,
    211,214-216,219,221,
    222,225,227,228,231,
    232,235,236,238,239,
    241,242,246,251-253,
    262-266,276,286,294,
    300,305,309,318,321,
    328,345,350,360,369,
    379
  E. 117
  Mary 64
  Ruth 111
  Thomas 60,63,64,82-84,
    99,101,111,143,194,
    205,298,320
  Thomas (Sr.) 64
  Ruth 372
  William 64,82,83,99,
    111,143,145,194,230,
    337,372,377,381
PINGREE(PINGREY), Moses
    96,192,242
PINNEY, Hannah 234
PINN(E)Y, John 34,234
PLATT, William 21
PLAYER, Roger 253,318,319
  Susannah 253
  Thomas 217,318,319,352
PLOMER, E. 229
PLUMBE, Boyfield 26
  Mary 26
PLUMMER, Jane 7
PLUM(M)ER, Moses 7,82
POINSETT(POINTSETT), Eli-
    sha 257-260
  Jamoin Joel 176
  Jane 7
  Joel 7,66,68,79,87,98,
    101,106,183,194,197,
    259,260,269,320,328,
    340
  Peter 7
  Susannah 7,259,260
POINTEVANT, Peter 23
  Susanna 23
POINTEVIN(T)(E), Anthony
    23,85,86,125,263,266,
    269
  Jonathan 23
  Margaret 142
  Mary 263
  Peter 125,139,142,177
  Peter, Sr. 147
  Susannah 125
POLLARD, James 303
POLLIXSON, Robert 219
POLLOCK, John 78
  Mary 162
PONNEYMEAN, William 213
POOL(E), William 18,19,110,
    127,172,233,274,275,
    367,368
POOR, Patrick 363
POPELL(POPPELL), William
    60,137
POPPLE, Alured 376
PORCHER, Elizabeth Mari-
    anne 243
  Isaac 10,40,52,61,120,
    165,169,211,243,250,
    251,253,254,257,282,
    298,320,328,349,358
  Isaac, Jr. 179,197
  Isaac, Sr. 7,176
  Marianne 120
  Peter 120,243,253,254
  Rachel 243,253,254
PORT, Joseph 299,301,320
PORTALL, Anthony 290
PORTER, Edmond/Edmund 31,
    32,36,54,104,109,221,
    222

PORTER, cont'd:
　Elizabeth 104,109,221,
　　222
　Hannah 71,119
　James 71,119
　John 119,311,351
　Mary 71,119,351
　Matthew 46,52,67,70,71,
　　76,119,214,215,322,323,
　　359
　Susanna(h) (Mrs.) 67,
　　71,119,322,323
　William 208,349,382
PORTOVINE(PORTEVINE,POITE-
　VIN), Anthony 91,187
PORTWINE, Anthony 307
　Peter 307
POSTEL(L), James 49,76
　John 41,232,361,377,
　　382
　John, Jr. 85
　Margaret 85,199
　Mary Ester 41
POSTON, William 280
POTTS, Thomas 288,381
POUND, Ann 116
POWELL, Henry 357
　Isaac 28
　Martha 28
　Robert 22
　Samuel 337
　William 198,361
POWIS, Sarah 305
POYST, John 95
PRANPAIN, Cornelius 23
PRATT, William 169,183,209,
　380
PRENTICE, Thomas 177
PRESCOTT, John 191,352
PRESTON, Thomas 45
PRICE, Ann 264
　John 292,307
　Rice 381
　William 164,264
PRICEHARD, John 301
PRICKETT, Rowland 361
PRIMAT(E), John 164,281
PRINCE, Elizabeth Mary 334
　Joseph 292,334
PRINGLE, Jane 359
　Robert 223,227,248,359,
　　363
PRIOLEAU, Camuel 77
　Elisha 14,40,53,116,
　　158,161,169,256,258,
　　260,325,326,328,333
　Elisha, Jr. 77
　Magdaline 169
　Mary Magdeline 20,27,
　　131
　Peter 262
　Philip 223,228,255,327,
　　328
　Samuel 8,20,27,41,72,
　　76,77,86,93,131,161,
　　169,181,182,189,259,
　　266,267,282,316,326
　Samuel, Jr. 229
　Susannah 260
PRITCHARD, John 199,245
　Thomas 6
PROCTOR, Hannah 274
　Stephen 200,219,249,
　　274
PROSS, Mary 202
PROST, Richard 55
PUCKLE, Wm. 74
PUGSON, Samuel 126
PUHL, Philip 372
PULFORD, Joan 86,345
PULMAN, Nathaniel 269
PUNNETT, John 136
PURCELL, Richard 235,243
PURKIS, John 310

PUR(R)Y, Charles 294,358
PUTLAND, Thomas 5
PYATT, John 302

QUARRYON, Robert 161
QUARTERMAN, Robert 148
QUASH, Matthew 98,121,136,
　140,194,241,376
　Robert 241,321,376,380
QUAST, Robert 376
QUEENS, Thomas 166
QUELCH, Andrew 130,228,341,
　361
　Benjamin 28,67,94,163,
　　164,336
　Benjamin, Jr. 46,163
　Elizabeth 28,94,122,
　　190,341,361
　William 28
QUICK, Richard 31
QUIN, Thomas 5
QUINTARD, Daniel 26

RABENEL, Daniel 90
RAILEY, Barnaby 354
　Brian 273
　Martha 274
RAINER, George 54
RAKE, Thomas 207
RALEY, Bryan 8
RAMBERT, Piere 281
RAMSAY, David 215,347,350
　James 297
　Jean 347
　John 347,350,382
　Margaret (Nicol) 347,
　　350
　Thomas 347
RAMSEY, Benjamin, Jr. 32
　James 312
RAMACK, Isaac 8,29
　Mary 29
RANDALL, Hannah 209
　Richard 209
　Robert 89,102,185
　William 238
RAPER, Catherine 95,144,
　　191
　John 144,145,174,190
　Joseph 159
　Robert 165,168,362
RASBERRY, Thomas 205
RATHMAHLER, Job 5
RATTELL, John 8
RATTRAY, John 268,273,276,
　　277,287,290,294,303,
　　305,311,324,325,332,
　　335,338,341,350,352,
　　355,367,368,370,378
RAVEN, Elizabeth 206
　John 47,68,116,153,206,
　　260
　John, Jr. 128
　William 292,316
RAVENEL, Daniel 127,186
　Paul 127
　Rene 164,299
RAWLINGS, Edward 13,26,27,
　　34,114,133,138,163,166,
　　202,320
　James 22
　Mary 27,34
　Susanna(h) 27,38,67,
　　72,133,163
RAWLY, Major Percival 32
RAYCROFT, Col. 359
RAYLES, Barnaby 86
RAYLY, Byran 175
RAYNALS, Mikill 327
RAYNER, Ann(e) 4,5
　Catherine 4,5
RAYNER(RAYNOR), George 54,
　　55
　Mehitabel 4.5

RAYNER, cont'd:
　Robt. 5
RAYNOR, Mary 302
READ, John 5,312,354
　Laurence 378
　Mary 312
READING, Roger 170
REALLY, Barnaby 37,155,
　　170,177,248,325
REALY(RELEY,RELY), Bryan
　　56,100,196,223
REAPING, Edward 216
REED, Charles 321,322
　Elizabeth 321
　John 269,361
　Robert 312
　William 316
REEP, William 372
REEVES, Ambrose 222,253,
　　254
　Charles 222
REEVE(S), Thomas 322,331
REILY, Philip 118
REMBERT, Andrew 236,249,
　　258,340,363
　Andrew, Jr.237
　Jean 237
　Judith 237
REMINGTON, John 381
RENDELL, William 14
RENIERE, John 213
RENOLDS, Joseph 117
　Michael 12,191,231,235
RESCOE, Samuel 85
REYNOLDS, James 261
　John 148,170,211
　Michael 95
　Richard 261
　Robert 117
REYNOR, George 221,222
RHETT, Capt. 38
　Benjamin 58
　Sarah 8,10,11,84,89,
　　90,143,145,185,187,
　　256
　William 4,5,8,11,13,
　　24,30,33,35,38,39,43,
　　79,84,102,109,116,137,
　　143,291,300,321
　William, Jr. 6,8,13,20,
　　24,54,76
　Wm., Sr. 6,8,14,20,54
RIBELLEAU, Gabriel 57
RICH, Mary 346
　Sylvanus/Silvanus 271,
　　346
RICHARD, James 169
RICHARDSON, Bartholomew 10
　Thomas 72,73
　William 31
RICHBELL, Mr. 162
RICHBOURG, Claudius 253
RICHEBOURG, Charles 127
　Elizabeth 250
　James 253
　Rene 299,344
RIDER, Richard 155
　William 54
RIDLEY, John 228,276,315
　Unity 276
RIDNEY, John 136
　Unity 136
RIGBY, Anne 35,43
　Richard 35,43
RIGG(S), Alexander 353
　Alice 165
　John 148,171,204,214,
　　215,244,344
　Samuel 257
RILEY, Barnaby 86,246
RIMBERLY, Isabell 160
　Thomas 160
RIPAULT(RIPALT), James
　　145,293

RIPPEN(RIPIN), Edward 136,
  216,225
RISBEE, James 70,158
  Jane 70,71,157
RISBEY,William 218
RISCO, Nathaniel 12
RIVERS, Elizabeth 26
  George 167,176
  Jeremiah 26
  John 206,215,218,223,
    263,271
  Joseph 25,96,192,214,
    377
  Miles 271
  Morris 42
  Robert 26
  Robert, Jr. 214
  Sarah 26
  Samuel 75
  Thomas 209,210,215,218,
    271
  William 181,278,279
RIXAM(BIXHAM), James 88,
  184
ROACHE, ___ 236
  Francis 236
ROATHE, Robert 3
ROBBERY(ROOBERY), John 128
ROBERT, Abigail 268
  Benjamin 268
  James 139,157,270-273,
    276,277,280,281,283,
    287,289,294,310
  John 295
  Judith 178
  Mary 363,365,368
  Peter 84,157,178,258,
    267,356,363,368
  P., Jr. 126
  Samuel 281
  Sarah 280,281
ROBERTOWN, John 8
ROBERTS, Benjamin 365
  Bishop 242
  George 283
  James 354
  John 173,205
  Peter 269,271,276
  Sara 270
  Thomas 371
ROBERTSON, Alexander 261,
  275,338,349,352,355
  Rachel 249
  William 32
ROBESON, John 232
  Martha 232
ROBINSON, Anne 34,35
  David 62
  Edmund 34,35,44,57,58,
    85,341,361
  John 302
  Joseph 343
  Thomas 343
  William 32
ROCHE, Anstace 349
  Dominick/Doniniq 142,
    169,325
  Francis 241,249,286,
    304,321,336,349,367,
    376
  Jordon 205,290,347,370,
    376
  Matthew 336,347,356
  Patrick 349
  Rebecca 347,370
RODD, George 322
RODDA, Ralph 318,357
RODOTA, Ralph 265
ROE, Thomas 257
ROGER, Ann 268
  Peter 268
  Thomas 286
ROGERS, James 97,193,313
  Phineas 110,234

ROGERS, cont'd:
  Woodes 14,16
ROKEBY(TOKEBY), William
  35,36
ROLFE, George 165,168
ROLLINGS(ROLINGS), Edward
  68,212
ROMSEY, Benjamin 2,72,204
  Benjamin, Jr. 1
  Benj'a., Sr. 1
  Martha 204
  William 143,157,212,
    284,344,354,364
ROOBERRY, John 255
ROOE, John 74
ROPER, Jeremiah 288
  John 94,128,229
  Joseph 105,152
  William 154,321,361
ROSCO, Samuel 91
ROSE, Aquila 167,197
  Elizabeth 135
  Henrietta 247
  Huge 365
  Pricillah 256
  Thomas 89,130,160,165,
    178,185,197,224,232,
    247,251,288,311
ROSELATE, Thomas 206
ROSS, Aquilla 101
  John 258
ROTHMAHLER, ___ 10,32
  Ann 259
  Job 4,9,10,15,16,21,
    30,31,86,90,116,150,
    162,166,186,198,249,
    259,273,295,306,307,
    309,311,313,322,326
ROUCH, Nicholas 238
ROULAIN, Abraham 263
  James (Jacque) 68,286,
    338
  Magdalen/Magdalaine
    68,286
  Margaret 68
ROULIN, James 263
ROUS(ROWES), Sabina 337
ROUSE, Humphrey 64,116
  James 185
ROUSHAM, James 199
ROW, Rachel 268
  William 268
ROWAN, Andrew 3
  Dr. Andrew 14
  Ann 255
  Martha (Moore) 48
  Richard 13,19,24,33,
    40,42,48,65,66,70,73,
    109,111,132,143,145
ROWES, S. D. 229
ROWLAIN, James 103
ROWLAND(ROWLINE), James 19
ROWS(E), James 89,95,191
  Sabina(h) 168,206
ROYER, ___ 137
  Hannah 68
  John 76,265,358
  Noah 76(see Royes)
  Noah, Jr. 91,187
  Noah, Sr. 60,91,187
  Peter 292
ROYES, Noah 6
RUBERY(RUBERRY), William
  94,190,283
RUBERRY, John 200,266
RUBURRY, Mr. 165
RUCK, John 162
RUDDOCK, Noblest 30
  Robert 21
RUMSEY, Benjamin 83
RUSCO, Arthur 165
  Samuel 188,342
RUSS, Abijah 105,117,154,
  345,355

RUSS, cont'd:
  Andrew 212
  Catherine 271
  David 85,86,122,176
  Hezekiah 100,101,117,
    196,240,271
  John 122,179,307
  Jonathan 7,23,42,105,
    174,176,345,355
  Joseph 122,179
  Thomas 176,248
RUSSAT, George 247
RUSSELL, Abigail 130
  Charles 201,249,257,
    262,272
  Elizabeth 141
  George 6,53
  Henry 110,129
  Jean 53
  Jeremiah 18,19,141,147
  John 322
  Joseph 20,141,322
  Mary 70,141
  Mrs. 293
  Stephen 6,40,50,53,
    214,371
  Timothy 339
  William 6,53,130,278,
    343
RUTLEDGE, Andrew 205,207,
  217,220,235,247,250,
  269,270,272,319,336,
  349,352,365,367
RYAN, John 312
  Thomas 315

SABB, Thomas 227
SACHEVERILL(E),(SACHEVE-
  RELL), Mary 90,95,96,97,
    186,191-193,379
  Thomas 90,95,96,97,
    129,182,186,191-193,
    259,313,345,379
SACKVILLE, C. 275,293
  Clement 326
  Thomas 294
SADLER, Elliner/Ellinor
  92,188
  James 82,92,188
  Mr. 26
  William 329
ST. BLANQUART, Piere 294
ST. JOHN, James 210,225,
  232,238,243,248-250,
  255,259,280,283,292,
  293,298,313,314,315,
  322,327,335,337,342,
  343,361,364,377,382
  Millar (Meller) 312,
    377
ST. JULIEN, James 27,37,76,
  82,86
  Mr. 65
  Joseph 372
  Henry 87 (see De St.
    Julien)
ST. MARTIN, John 117,135,
  176,337
SALE, Adam 332
SALLENS, Peter 381
SALLEY, Robert 236
SALSBERRY, John 341
SALTER, John 354,375
SALTON, John 48
SALTUS, Anne 161
  Bartholemew 161
  Henry 117,120
  John 117,120
  Mary 161
  Martha 161
  Providence 117,120
SAM, John 181
SAMS, Bonum 240
  Bridget 380

SAMS, cont'd:
    John 299,371,380
    Joseph 340
    Robert 380
SAMMS, Hannah 360
    John 366
    Robert 149,201,223,257,
        340
    Sam 366
    William 149,340
SAMWAYS, Henry 213,287
    James 114
    Henry 165,177
SANDERS, Abraham 59,110,
        127,165,270
    Anna 52
    Elizabeth Clark 223
    James 346
    Joshua 136,156,171,175,
        216,223,233,267,376,
        379
    Lambert 87,184
    Laurence 258,277
    Lawrens 175
    Margaret 52,165,175
    Mr. 123
    Peter 44
    William 3,52,136,145,
        153,156,168,175,229
    William (Sr.) 52
    Willison 268
    Wilson 129,136,168
SANDFORD, Abraham 40
SANDIFORD, John 6,25,26,
        53,130,176,247
SANDS, Alexander 328
SANEO, John 66
SANSON, John 95,191
SARAZEN, Stephen 71
SAREAU, Francis 319
SARRAZIN, Moseau 228
    Stephen 239
SASOUBRE, John 338
SATUR, Abraham 77,78,92,
        93,106,107,168,181,188,
        189,205,309,316,321,
        356,363,368
    Jacob 3,9,11,20,22,23,
        29,37,43,45,76,78,122,
        142,160,168,291
    Jane 368
    Mary 11,283
    Thomas 22,33,37,76,77,
        113,182,209
SAUNDERS, Ester 3
    James 313
    John 21
    Laurence 313
    Peter 144
    Roger 3,70,101,105,112,
        197,208,226,247,252,
        319
    William 70,318
    Wilson 145,258
SAUREAU, Mary 177
SAUSSANS, John 354
SAVAGE, Benjamin 226,321,
        377
    Jamin 226
    John 326
SAVENEAU, James 379
SAVERANCE, John 220
    Joseph 220
SAVEY, Peter 209
SAVOY, Peter 380
SAVINEAU, James 123
SAVY, John 3
SAXBURY, John 113
SAXBY, Anthony 90
    William 90,187,361,362
    Wm., Jr. 210,214
SCANNELL, David 57
SCARLETT(SCARLITT), James
        233,242,278,285,288,

SCARLETT, James cont'd:
        309,377
SCHENCKINGH,   220
    Barnard 76,112
    Benjamin 19,36,37,40,
        64,94,115,118,145,155,
        160,162,190,215,261,
        291
    Elizabeth 242,265
    Margaret 19,94,115,
        155,160,190,216,351
SCHENKING, Mr. 218
SCHERKING, Bernard 55
SCHULTZ, George 265
    John 360
    Peter (Schult) 356,
        363,364
SCOTT, Edward 111,119,123,
        149,335
    George 280
    Jonathan 244,343,344
    John 289,345,347
    Mary 119,149,335
    Patrick 94,134,176,
        190,234,324
    Sarah 176
    Susanah 143,144,154
    Thomas Hamilton 277,
        354
    William 17,23,24,27,
        34,51,52,101,142-144,
        154,168,197,230,307,
        347,350,373,382
SCREVEN, Elisha 251,258,
        343
    James 130,290
    Samuel 44,132,133
    William 164,278
SCRIVEN, Elisha 288,348
SCRIZEN, Samuel 74
SCUDDER, Moses 369
SCULL, Edward 40,324
SEABROOK, John 240,278,
        285,335
    Mary 316
    Robert 107
    Thomas 107,133,316
SEALE, Mr. 85
SEALS,   27
SEAMAN, George 308
SEARES, Anne 78
    Anthony 59
    Mary 78
    Robert 78
SEARLES, Christina 210
SEARL(E)S, James 149,210
SEARON(SERON), James 50,93
SEASEAU, John 164
SEAVEY, Stephen 35
SECAR, Mr. 176
SECARE, Isaac 202,203,207,
        216,251,288,289,300,
        319
    Peter 251,252,300,372
SEEMYSS, Helen 347
SELLERY, John 200,203
SELLIVANT, Thomas 319
SEREVEN, Robert 55
    William 213
SERGEANT, Rowland 312
SERON, James 189
SERRE, Elizabeth 225
    Noah 60,131,163,178,
        210,258,267,268,269,
        271,273,276,280,281,
        292,361,369,377,382
SERURIER(SERRURIER), alias
SMITH   7,9,65
SESSION, Mr. 343
SETHELL, Seth 8
SEVERANCE, Anne 326
    John 326
SEVERSANCE, John 354
SHABISHERE, Mr. 379

SHACKELFORD, Esther/Ester
        225,299,311,321
    Francis 317
    John 249,361
SHACKLEFORD, Sarah 282
    William 224,225,281,
        299,301,311,320,321,
        354
SHADDOCK, Samuel 297,312,
        313
SHAFFTSBURY, Lord 153
SHAND,   248
SHAPLEY, Andrew 163
SHARPE, Thomas 153
SHARTOCK, Samuel 158
SHAW, John 5,282
    Josiah 330
    Peter 254
    Robert 215,218
    Samuel 2
SHEIFFIELD, Samuel 117
SHELTON, Richard 205
SHEPHEARD, Charles 246,
        253,273,355
SHEPPARD, John 64,84,106,
        172,217,264,265
SHEPHERD, Peter 169
SHEPPARD, Samuel 179
SHERIFF(E), Henry 158,264
    Martha 158
SHERINGHAM, James 325
SHERRIFF, Isabel 62
    William 62
SHINGLETON, Ebenezer 353
SHIPPER, William 64
SHIPPEY, John 264,265
    Mary 264,265
    William 310
SHODDOCK, Samuel 181
SHOREY, Anthony 77,78,120
    Anthony, Jr. 77
    Mary 77
SHREW(S)BURY, Edward 225,
        330
    Mary 330
SHUBRICK, Jane 84
    Richard 14,84,175,222,
        376,378
    Richard, Jr. 159,162
SHUTE, Anna 160,283,290
    D. 301
    John 162
    Joseph 160,166,243,
        283,290,328,334,335,
        338,357
SIBLEY,   48
    Samuel 208
SIMCOS, Richard 121
SIMES, John 163,335,336,
        365
    Mary 336
    Sarah 336
SIMONA, George 179
SIMONDS, Henry 62,143,170
    Judith 62
SIMMONDS, Hannah 379
    Thomas 290,305
SIM(M)ONS,   60,270
    Ann 150,160
    Benjamin 150,268,277
    Ebenezer 377
    Francis 122,150,160
    George 237
    Henry 16,47,62,85,86,
        91,95,97,103,110,160,
        164,187,188,191,193,
        239,276
    John 1,3,49,54,76,125,
        156,198,229,230
    Judith 91,97,103,164,
        187,193,339
    Madam 60
    Mary 43
    Mr. 82

SIM(M)ONS, Peter 121,381
    Samuel 35,95,122,127,
        172,194,233,234,381
    Thomas 336
    William 97,193,283
SIMMS(SIMONS), John 66,85
    Jotham 66
SIMPSON, Alexander 16
    Edward 261,270,328
    Richard 343,379
    Robert 347
    Sarah 328
    William 381
SIMSON, Thomas 52
    William 329,353
SINCKLARE, Robert 144
SINCLAIR, George 68
    Thomas 347
SINDRY, Elizabeth 95,191
SINGLETARY, Jonathan 42,
    141,193,233
    Joseph 96,128,288,311
    Richard 135
SINGLETON,   17
    Ebenezer 365
    James 3,250,251,314
    Richard 251
    William 18,269,313
SINGELLTON, Sarah 269
SISON, Gregory 149
SISSON, Thomas 305,306
SISSONS, Mary 300,305
SKELTON, Robert 6,74
SKENE, A. 59,64,113-115,
    134,141
    Alexander 11,12,20,22,
        28,46,49,55,68,69,80,
        86,108,122,131,132,136,
        145,146,155,160,174,179,
        182,197,198,243,248,285,
        322,339,347,349,352,370,
        380,381
    Hannah 155
    J. 325
    Jamimah/Jemima 28,29,
        46,55,122,131,155,243,
        347,352,370,380
    John 20,50,122,136,155,
        251,256,285,339
SKERRETT, Dominick 54
SKINNER, Abraham 360
    Ann(e) 150,261
    David 246
    John 239
    Joseph 102
    Mary 241
    Mr. 162
    William 150,176,239
SKIPPER, Anne 26
    William 26,44,49,150
SKIRVIN(G), James 251,312,
    313,346,356,380
SKRINE, Elizabeth 7,9,21
    J. 22
    John 364
    Jonathan 7,9,18,21,32,
        47,86,157,277,301,340
SLANN, Andrew 366
    Peter 328
SLEIGH, Mary 313
    Samuel 21,277,313,361,
        382
SLO(W)MAN, John 137,210,
    295,317
    Mark 35,137,281,295,
        317,361,362
SLUDDER, William 258
SMALL, Abiah 308
    Eleanor 308
    Robert 336
    Samuel 217,308
SMALLWOOD, Isaac 240,343
    James 242,277,300,328,
        331

SMALLWOOD, cont'd:
    Mathew 96,192,250
SMELIE, James 133
    John 25,133,245
SMILEY, John 63
SMILIE, Elizabeth 88,184
    John 96,97,159,184,192
SMITER, John 28
SMITH, Alexander 236
    Alice 170,200
    Ann(e) 21,207,378
    Archer 331
    Benjamin 174,214,340,
        344,352,369,378
    Catherine 266,267
    Charles 272,316
    Christopher 96,97,117,
        118,165,167,180,193,
        199,211,229,259,282,
        289,297,298,301,319,
        356
    Col. 115
    Dorothy 70,71,158,206
    Edward 31,81
    Elizabeth 226,308
    Emanuel 236,332
    George 24,25,27,29,30,
        33,39,44,48,49,53,69-
        72,74,76,80,83-85,121,
        128,140,158,164,206,
        226,228,315,376,377
    James 14,133,308,309,
        378
    John 79,128,131,164,
        288,289,308
    Joseph 34,49,175,182,
        272,322
    Josiah 258,262,285
    Mary 37,53,80,84,124,
        207,228,264,299,301,
        315,320,321,329,331,
        332,358,380
    Nicholas 133,229,247,
        306,316
    Peter 261,274,275,341,
        342
    Richard 7,66,77,80,123,
        207,208,244,277,369
    Sabina 162,181,369
    Samuel 30,42,82,96,97,
        135,151,192,193,247,
        268,360,362,365,380
    Sarah 78,80,302
    Susannah 118,175
    Thomas 22,23,27,32-34,
        37,39,47,53,59,63,67,
        70-72,76-78,80,84,85,
        88,90,92,106,111,120,
        124,128,129,136,140-
        142,149,155,158,163-
        165,170,177,181,184,
        187,188,203,204,206-
        208,214,216,228-230,
        246,248,256,262,264,
        296,298,305,312,315,
        316,320,321,325,331,
        342,372,379
    Thomas, Jr. 25,34,53,
        88,105,128,184
    W. 195,196
    William 6,20,39,41,45,
        48,69,83,93,94,100,106,
        122,134,152,189,190,
        220,225,227,238,245,
        265,270,272,285,296,
        303,308,312,314,326,
        332,336,337,339,340,
        341,357,358,361,363,
        365,366,368,377
SMYES, William 361
SMYTER, John 14,69
    Edmond 162
SMYTH, James 89,154,168,
    185,186

SMYTH, cont'd:
    Mary 168
SNARD,   175
SNEED, Nicholas 81
SNELL, Henry 355
SNIPES, Elizabeth 319
    Thomas 319,341
SNOW, Ann 74
    Hannah 134,198
    John 120,202,271,368
    Mary 302
    Nathaniel 112,120,237,
        250,302,304,330
    Nathaniel, Sr. 74
    Susannee 309
    Thomas 33,75,112,134,
        174,198,213
    Susannah 271
    William 112,120,240,
        302,303
SNOWDEN, Elizabeth 258
    Joshua 258
SOISON, Gregory 379
SOISSIONS, Mary 306
    Thomas 306
SOLOMON, Searah 210
SOMERHOEFF, John Peter
    80
SOMERHOOSE, John Peter
    229
SOMERVILLE, Elizabeth 107,
    121,159,376
    John 298,299,375,376
    Sarah 298,299,375,376
    Tweedie 107-111,117,
        119,121,123,125,128-
        130,133,138,139,143,
        144,148,149,151,154-
        157,159,167,170,171,
        200,206,298,299,342,
        375,376
SOMMERS, George 273,380
SOMMERVILLE, John 279
    Sarah 279
SONCLIES, John 107
SORTIN, Charlotte 40
SOUTHACK, G. 186
SOUTHECK, Charles 90
SOUTHELL, Seth 90,187
SOUTHERLAND, Capt. 299,301
SPARKES, Thomas 3,30
SPENCER, Alexander 50,86,
    168,214,316,344
    Anthony 55,56
    Dorothy 295
    John 51,231,232,251,
        295,326,327
    John Joseph 317
    Joseph 231,232,282,
        295,326,327,344,345
    Joseph, Jr. 51
    Mary 180
    Nicholas 248
    Oliver 67,160
    Sarah 315,316
    William 53,144,315,316
SPLATT, Anne 160
    John 118,180,308,356,
        373
    Richard 1,2,7,8,22,39,
        40,52,56,83,144,160,
        202,263,342
SPROULL, Alexander 356,380
SPRY, Feneas 316
    Mary 371
    Phineas 371
    Purchas 263
    Royall 87,90,180,186,
        371,379
SPUT, Robert 223
STAMMERS, Richard 161
STANBROUGH, Fleet 274
    Jonah 274

STANCARD, Benjamin 347
STANDFAST, William 339
STANDLEY, Peter 48
STANLEY, Amey/Amy 140,147,
  170
  Edward 48,61,121,140,
    346
  Elizabeth 320
  Peter 61,140,346
  Susanna 121
STANWAY, James 163
STANYARD, Joseph 38
  Josiah 171
  Rivers 38
STANYARN(E), Anne 85
  Benjamin 205,377
  Dorothy 149
  James 23,35,52,347,370
  Jane 23
  Jehu 175
  John 85,104,128,180,
    181,221,222,235,240,
    245
  Joseph 69,82,180,181,
    278,279,353,354
  Magdalen 180,181
  Rachel 52
  Rivers 180,278,279
  Thomas 65,69,85,132,
    133,149,218,340,374
  William 85,181,245,278,
    279
STAPLES, Abraham 364
  William 298,314
STARKEY, John 224
STARLING, George 201
  John 201,306
STARNE(S), Charles 160,198
STARRAT(T), George 235,339,
  340,373
STEAD(S), Benjamin 284,311,
  344
  Mr. 129
  Edwin 157
  William 1,144
STEDD, Simon David 329
STEED, William 175
STEEL(E), Ann 323
  John 332,350,357,380
  Robert 108,204,208,209,
    254,305,323,370
STEER(S), Thomas 172,230,
  231
STEIGER, Sixtus 357
STENT, Daniel 279
  Samuel 278,279
STEPHENS, Edward 286
  Elizabeth 64
  Francis 2
  John 33,64
STEPHENS (ETIENNE) TAWRON
  (RAUVERON) 161
  William 298,320
STEPHENSON, Mr. 160
STERLAND, William 357
STERLING, Hannah 201
  Wm. 201 (also Starland)
STEVENS, 201
  Elizabeth 34,157,222
  John 33,34,96,113,134,
    141,169,174,179,182,
    183,192,197,214,222,
    263,291
  Nicholas 165
  Robert 99,161,195,212
  Roger 73
  Samuel 135
  Wm. 135
STEVENSON, Anniball 95,96,
  97,192
  Dorothy (Bee) 95,97,192
  John 27,75,85,261,291,
    303
  Joseph 248

STEVENSON, cont'd:
  Mary 291,303
  Susann 303
  William 95,97,192
STEWARD, Frances 111,175
STEWARD (STEWART), James
  175
  John 108-111,175,282
  Patrick 110,111,175,
    282
  Robert 127,172,175
STEWART, Adam 235,373
  Alexander 137,145,274,
    311,364
  Benjamin 135
  Charles 135,231,327
  Daniel 76,134,350
  Isaac 322
  James 176,231,240,270,
    299,301,327,330,364
  John 108,123,165,221,
    229,231,327,354
  Mary 270
  Patrick 102,231,317,
    326,327
  Robert 127,144,150,231,
    327 ·
  Sarah 103
  Wm. 135
STICKLEN, Richard 168
STILES, Benjamin 19,144,
  305,352
  Samuel 272,274
STILL, Charles 120
STOBO, Archibald 17,50,68,
  166,175
  Elizabeth 68,166
  James 69,166,245
  William 166,245,344
STOBOE, William 285
STOCK(S), Ellinor 83
  Elizabeth 266
  John 2,24,25,146
  Jonathan 83,177,181,
    354
  Mr. 217,352
  Samuel 178,266,287,309,
    347
  Thomas 215,233,263,332
  William 101,196
STOLER, Hannah Maria 372
STOLL, Justinus 292
STOLLARD, John 43,221
STONE, Benjamin 18
  Deborah 18
  Elias 24
  Hannah 18
  John 7,18,112,233,327
  John, Jr. 17,18
  John, Sr. 19
  Joseph 17,18,233
  Susanna 18
  Thomas 22,102,112
  William 332
STOODLEY, Christopher 35
STORY, Elizabeth 12,29,157
  Jeremiah 305
  John 30,118
  Mary 306
  Rowland 12,29,40,157,
    167,327
  Thomas 80
  Zachariah 306
STOUPAN, Pierre 237
STOUTENBURG(H), Luke 212,
  248
STRACHAN, Elizabeth 156
STRACHAN(Y), John 146,224,
  229,238
  Naomi/Noami 224,229,
    238
STRAHAM, John 153
STRAHAN, Arthur 354,359
STRA(Y)HAN, Elizabeth 121

STRA(Y)HAN, cont'd:
  John 121,125,126
STRAYTOR, James 331
STREET, Elizabeth 8,73
  William 8,35,36,73
STREETER(STREETOR), James
  296,380
STRINGER, George 319
STROUDS, ___ 170,177
STUART, Adam 378
  Hugh 372
  Isaac 94,190
  John 103,261
  Thomas 256,257
SULLAVANT, Thomas 251
SULLIVAN, John 101,196
SULLIVANT, Martha 269
SULLIVANT(SILLAVANT,SULL-
  AVANT), Thomas 269
SULLIVEN, Owin 330
SUMMER, Sarah 296
SUMMERFIELD, Mr. 351
SUMMERHOOFT, John Peter
  334
SUMMERS, Alexander 2
  George 247
  Henrietta 247
  John 82,92,165,188,
    270,302
  Mr. 123
  Roger 49,225
  Samuel 49
  Susannah 82,92
  Thomas 135,164,165
SUMMERVILLE, Sarah 331
SUMNER, Benjamin 37,63,76,
  174,274
  David 274
  Daniel 272,274
  Elizabeth 272,274
  Increase 63,110,183,
    230
  John 272,274
  Joseph 37,110,197,272,
    274
  Nathaniel 62,63,110,
    182,183,197,209
  Persis 37
  Roger 63,76,169,174,
    183,212,213
  Samuel 110,114,165,178,
    197,272,274
  Samuel, Sr. 169
  Sarah 178
  Susannah 188
  Thomas 272
  William 62,63
  Wm. Way 110
SUMNERS (see above)
SUREAU(SURREAU), Francis
  131,161
  Mary 370
SUSSEX, Hannah 200
  Wm. 200
SUTHERS, James 72
SUTHESS, James 39
SUTTON, Walter 9
SWAIN, F. 111
  John 28
SWALE, John 362,375
SWEENY, Miles 228
SWEETING, ___ 329
  Henry 45,46,52
SWEETMAN(SWETMAN,SWETTMAN),
  Margaret 19,45,46,105,
    126
  Robert 19,45,46,105,
    126,258
SWINFEN(SWINSEN), Edward 6
SWINHOE, James 200
SWINSEN, Edward 73
SWINTON, Catherine 145
  Hannah 314
  Helen 145

SWINTON, Hugh 202,261,271,
  273,368
  Judith 339
  William 99,106,180,195,
  199,200,208,241,245,
  246,249,260,261,275,
  288,300,309,314,319,
  337,339,342,344,355,
  364,365
SYER, Ann 83
  Catherine 99,100,195,
  196
  Joseph 195,196
  Mary 99,100
  Rober 83
  Robert 195,196
SYM, Isaac 307
SYMONDS, Henry 45
SYMONS, Samuell 1

TABART, George 282,358
TAGGART, James 154,162,355
TALLIN, Robert 321
TALLY, Alexander 300
TAMKERD, Elizabeth 248
TAMPLETT, Christinia 146
TAMPLET(T), Peter 125,126,
  270
TANKERD, ____ 33
TANNER, James 214
TATE, Alexander 363
TATNELL, Joseph 279
  Martha 279
TATTNELL, Elizabeth 305
  Thomas 146,305
TAUERES, Manoel 373
TAURON, Catherine 160
TAUVRON, Stephen 208
TAVERCON, Stephen 115
TAVERON, Stephen 251
TAVERSON, Stephen 61,62
TAYLOR, Ann(e) 4,5
  Benjamin 4
  Ebenezer 4,5,212
  George 137
  Hezekiah 266
  Isaac 128,138
  James 324
  Jacob 128
  John 28
  Mehitabel 4,5
  Mercy 266
  Peter 4,48,60,65,70,71,
  74,76,132,205,216,222,
  265,291
  Robert 5,62,91,92,127,
  129,145,166,188,279
  Sabina 216
  Samuel 4
  Shubael 266
  Thomas 216,316,321,369
  William 69,286
TELLERS, James 129
TENANT, William 375
TENDEN(TENDIN), John 146,
  180
TENNATT(TANNATT), Robert
  50,51
TENNANT, Wm. 154
THATCHER, Peter 266
THOMAS, Abraham 139
  Edward 42,96,142,148,
  163,192,294,296,344
  Henry 25
  James 328
  John 14,156,160,250,257
  Jonathan 69,178,182,
  237,257,286,298,312
  Rachel 236,247,252
  Richard 30
  Samuel 295
  Walter 214
  William 214,351,368,379
THOMASON, Robert 146,153

THOMPSON, Alexander 311
  Doctrina 224
  Eleanor 308
  Francis 371
  George 9
THOM(P)SON, James 283,290
  John 79,180,246,319
  John, Sr. 241
  Jonathan 377,382
  Richard 225,308
  Thomas 238
THOMSON, John 300,339,355,
  369,381
  William 300
THORNBURG, Amy 373
THORNBURGH, Thomas 373
  William 236,373
THORNTON, Joseph 313
THOROWGOOD, William 73
THORPE, John 280,337
  Robert 280,331,332,337,
  357,370
THREADCRAFT(THREADCROFT),
  George 244,354
THR(E)ADCRAFT(THRIDCROFT),
  Thomas 205,220,244,368
THREDCRAFT, Geo. 141
THRIFT, Samuel 81,82
TIDDEMAN, Richard 373
TILBURN, William 31
TILLY, James 145
  William 101,268
TILSON, James 79
TIMOTH, Lewis 303
TIMOTHY, Elizabeth 372
  Lewis 234,372
TINTE, Edward 186
TIPPER(TIPOR), John 162,
  238
  Mary 238
TIREER, John 271
TITTMARSH, Giles 256
  Mary 256
TIVETOR, Thomas 28
TOBEY(TOBYE), John 223,347
TODD, Thomas 311
TODMARSH, Richard 230
TOMAN, Dr. 109,228
TOMKINS, John 265
TOMPLETT, Peter 239
TOMSON, Robert 152
TOOKERMAN, Katherine 2
  Richard 2
TOOMER, Caleb 140,246
  Elizabeth 84,246
  John 84,85,245,246
  Joshua 210,217
  Tucker 246
TOPAR(TOPER), John 37,42,
  84
TORQUETT, Jane 125,126
TORQUET(T), Paul 125,126,
  140,141,352
TORSHALL, Samuel 318
TOSHELL, Samuel 166
TOTHILL, J. 337
  Master 219
TOWLE, Margery 185,186
TOWLE(LOWLE), Samuel 185,
  186
TOWNSEND, Daniel 5,19,24,
  42,98,155,167,194
  James 218,220
  Joseph 49
  Mary 49
  Nicholas 6,60
  Palmer 321
  Thomas 19,103,163,164,
  175,321,322
  Wm. 175
TOZER, Solomon 55,111,201,
  203
TRADD, Richard 40,89,160,
  185

TRADD, cont'd:
  Robert 9,40,71,85,155,
  156,158,167,176,322,
  323,382
TRAMPLETT, Peter 146
TRAPIER, Elizabeth 50
  Paul 16,50,86,164,202,
  279,337,353,354,364,
  367
TREADWELL(TREDWELL),
  Charles 115,174
TREBELL, John 4
TREDWELL, Charles 64
TRENCH, Alexander 55,87,
  90-93,98-100,102,103,
  105-107,114,122,124,
  126,130,131,134,142,
  143,145,151,152,156,
  165,171,183,184,186-
  189,194-196,261,297,
  355,356,358,363,366,
  374,375
  Joseph 121
TRESBANT, Theodore 125
TRESEVANT, D. 139,140
TRESEVANT(TREZVANT,TREZE-
  VANT), Isaac 139,140,151
TREWIN, Helen 355,373
  William 216,217,218,
  302,308,337,339,355,
  364,369,373
TREZEVANT, Daniel 23
  Susanna 23
  Theodore 151
TREZVANT, Isaac 266
  Susannah 266
TRICKER, John 173
TROTT, Nicholas 8,13,19,
  23,35,43,48,56,60,61,
  63,67,71,76,85,91,120,
  140,141,143,147,149,
  150,187,211,222,226,
  241,255,265,279,282,
  286,287,289,291,304,
  320,327,341,345,353
  Sarah 143,283,289,304,
  345
TROZELL, Alexander 222
TRUCK, Nicholas 243,338
TRUCKET, Mare 179
TRUEHART, Aaron Bartholo-
  mew 258
TRYON, Ro(w)land 20,380
  William 28,29,143,285,
  380
  William, Sr. 19
TUBB, ____ 55
  Jonathan 42,112,167,
  239,240
TUCKER, Benjamin 376
  George 236
  John 102,103,246,322
  Mr. 268
  Thomas 372
TULLADA, Mathew 98,194
TUNL(E)Y, Wm. 98,103,194
TURBERVILLE, Fortesque 70
TURBEVILLE, Thomas 142
TURBURVILLE, Francis 337
TURGIS, Francis 249,317
TURME, Sarah 303
TURNER, Benjamin 179,266
  Henry 145,234
  John 168,172
  Peter 358
  Samuel 114,321
  Sarah 66
  Thomas 66
TURQUE, Humphrey 110
TURQUET (TORQUET), Paul
  140
TUTWELL, Joseph 277
  Martha 278
TWINE, Samuel 103

TYDMARSH, Gyles 256
TYLER, Samuel 45
TYNTE, Edward 50,61,70,90,
  339
TYRELL, John 307

UNDERWOOD, Richard 107
  Samuel 107,128,240,380
UPHAM, Thomas 179,302
UPTON, Arthur 113

VAL(L)ENTINE, Simon 91,
  123,165,187
VALLEY, Elizabeth 381
  Thomas 135,140,206,381
VANDERDUSSEN, Alexander
  149,154-156,250,262,
  335
VANDERHORST, Capt. 217
  E. 316
  John 47,142,242,266,
  337,352,367
VANDERPOOLE, John 137
VANVELSEN, Guer. 142
VANVELSIN, Catherine 255
  Edward 255
VANVELSIN(VANVELSEN), Gar-
  rat 12,25,29,32,159,
  160,373
VANVELSIN, Gerrard 32
VANVELZIN, Edward 173
  Garet 181
VARAMBAUT, Francis 346,347
VAREEN, Jeremiah 117
VARIN, James 259,260
  Samuel 322
  Susannah 259,260
VARNE, Jacob 328
VARNOD, Francis 253
VARNON, James 315,324
VARNOR, James 367
VARNS(VARNER), Henry 41
VAUGHAN(VAUGHN), John 239,
  265,269,318,357
  Robert 218
  Rowland 144,154,168,
  173,212,219,223,224,
  226,229,240,243,250,
  251,281,282
  William 330,331
VERDIER, Andrew 294
VEREDITTY, Elizabeth 254
VEREDITTY(VERDITY,VARDITY),
  Theodore 52,320
VERDITY, Mary 129
VEREEN, Elizabeth 233
  Jeremiah 233
  William 233
VERNER, James 338
VERNEROBRE, Daniel 365
VERNOD, J. 222
VIART, Paul 18,146
VICARIDGE, Anne 270
  Elizabeth 109,270
VICARIDGE(VICCARDIGE),
  John 22,35,37,59,73,
  160,175,270,279,280,
  292
VICKARIDGE, John 110
VICKERS, Henry 219,326
VIDEAU, Henry 150,282
  Henry Joseph 237
  Peter 139,236
  Pierre 237
VILLARET, David 338
VILLEPONTEAUX, Peter 377,
  378
VILLEPONTOUX, Frances 81,
  302
  Peter 27,42,65,73,81,
  106,302
  Zachariah 117
VINSON, George 29
VIPER, William 35,103

VIRENE, Mr. 317
VISHER, Wm. 85
VISSIER, Tounis 286
VISSER, Theuniel 318
  Thomas 290
  William 70,75,88,181,
  184,239,269,286,341,
  361
VORCKLES, John 319

WADLAND, Amos 22
WAGNER, William 14
WAIES, Thomas 96
WAIGHT, Abraham 68
  Abraham, Jr. 128
  Isaac 146,173,263
  Mr. 85
WAITES, William 216,261,
  262
WAITIES, Dorothy 275
  Wm. 106,274,275
WALBANK, John 244
WALCOAT(WALCOTE), Ebene-
  zer 97,98,193
WALCOOT, Ebenezer 171
WALCUT, Ebenezer 133,137,
  174
WALCUT(T), Elizabeth 174
WALES, Dorothy 264
  William 264
WALKER, Alexander 63,100,
  196
  Anna 212
  Catherine 73
  Charles 212,213
  Daniel 4
  George 288
  Henry 128,177,178,240
  Sir Hovenden 6,28,170,
  175
  James 290
  John 172,206,210,211,
  234,324
  Joseph 5
  Mary 28,134
  Neal 302
  Ovenden 28
  Richard 73,99,195,276,
  381
  Thomas 8,172,212,234,
  282,339
  William 24,169
WALKERLY, Anna Mehitabel
  126
WALLACE, Elizabeth 33,34
  Thomas 246
  William 11,12,22,28,
  29,33,34,37,46,51,55,
  64,108,178,243,248,256,
  259,285,288,340,341,
  371,380
WALLCOT, Ebenezer 234
  Elizabeth 234
WALLES, John 337
WALLIS, Elizabeth 1
  John 1,19,27,28,81,94,
  95,114,144,148,190,191,
  203,216,245,258,288,
  302,303,339,344,355,
  365,381
  Josiah 125
WALSBE, William 180
WALSH, Delacourt 339
  George 361
WALTER, Dallas 86
  John 199,243,350,381
  William 256,259
WALTERS, Richard 339
WALTON, John 297
WANBORN, Thomas 338
WANNEL, John 283
  Thomas 283
WARD, John 3,170,177,221,
  248

WARD, cont'd:
  Martha 296
WARDEN, William 148,149,
  167,179,255
WARE, John 22
  Lydia 265
WARHAM, Charles 263
WARING, Alexander 321
  Ann 162
  B. 183
  Benjamin 12,49,74,80,
  86,128,162,181,316,
  376
  George 353
  Josiah 64,366
  Richard 110,178,197,
  263,366
WARING(WARRING), Thomas
  22,34,37,42,45,49,51,
  63,64,65,96,114,156,
  170,178,182,192,197,
  198,213,214,266,287,
  322,366
WARMINGHAM, John 100,195,
  196
  Joseph 81
WARNEL, John 321
WARNER, Henry 334
  John 21
WARNOCK, Abraham 20,156,
  176,307,334
  Abraham (Jr.) 20
  Abram 307
  Ebzr. 20
  Joseph 180,248,307
  Judith 20
  Mary 124,128,200,255
  Samuel 248
WARREN, Henry 113
  Robert 113
WARRINGTON, Richard 17
WARWICK, George 4
WASTCOAT, John 200
WATERS(WHETTERS), Joseph
  47,55
WATHEN, James 316,321
WATIES, Catherine 74
  Dorothy 264,333
  William 74,84,89,90,
  96,110,185,186,188,
  192,264,301,314,319,
  323,333,334,346,353,
  368
WATKINS, ____ 42
  Charles 306,351
  John 6,50,59,82,103,
  108,191,263,286,287
  Mary 263,286
WATKINSON, John 12,22,23,
  82,92,95,188
WATLINGTON, Samuel 119
WATS, John 78
WATSON, John 130,290,377
  Mary 173,178
  William 12,60,69,82,
  173,230,235,260,263,
  286
WATTS, George 31
  James 75
  Mary Penelope 173
  Samuel 112,148
WATTSON, Samuel 112
WAY, Aaron 209,263,322,
  350
  Aaron, Jr. 63,151,169,
  182
  Aaron, Sr. 62,63,77,
  151,169
  Ebenezer 37,113,197
  Elizabeth 380
  Henry 197,209,380
  Moses 110,113,178,179,
  183
  Nathaniel 183

WAY, Rachel 209
  Samuel 114,175,198,380
  Samuel, Jr. 77,182
  Samuel, Sr. 178,179,192,
    209,214
  Sarah 113
  Thankfull 113
  Thomas 63,76,77,114,
    209,213,380
  William 114.322
  Wm., Jr. 76,113,183
  William, Sr. 62,96,183
WEATHERLEY, Isaac 338
WEATHERLY, Thomas, Jr. 7
WEAVER, Mr. 145
  John 342
  Lucy 268
  Sarah 268
  Thomas 238,239,241
WEBB, Benjamin 224,334
  Dorothy 289
  Edward 207
  Joseph 224
  Sarah 224
  Thomas 224
  William 263,350
WEBSTER, David 99,161,195
  Thomas 5
  Wm. 114
WEDDERBURN(E), James 201,
  209,223,224,226,240,
  252,271,277,290
WEEKL(E)Y, Edward 2,26,51,
  53,63,77,78,88,95,134,
  175,178,184,191,239,
  240,262,268,320
  Elizabeth 37,53,63,88,
    184
  Martha 262
  Thomas 34.46,239,262
  William 2,23,79,81,106,
    134,176,262
WEEKLY, Rebecca 116
  Richard 116
WEEMYSS, Helen 350
WEIGHT, Abraham 245,316
  Isaac 245,309
  Jacob 245
WELCH, George 31
  Walter 285
  William 241
WELDON, John 208
WELLIS, John 202,207
WELLS, Edgar 37,105,121
  Mr. 124
  John 15,154
  Samuel 269,363
  Silas 215,222,260,263,
    296,299,315
  William 44,141,198,297,
    312
WELS, Walter 245
WELSH, Mungo 145
WELSH(H)UYSEN, Daniel 155,
  314,320,372,373
WELSTAD(WENSTEAD,WELLSTEED)
  John 320
WENBORN, Mary 297,312,368
  Thomas 297,312,313,368
WENNBORN(WINBORN), Thomas
  312
WENNELL, Thomas 373
WENTWORTH, Hugh 128
WERN, Peter 355
WESBORY(WESBURY), Thomas
  44,74,86,134
WEST, Charles 210
  Joseph 78,227,264
  Samuel 59,82,210,217,
    252,285,361
  Sarah 217
  William 181
  Willoby 210

WESTBERRY, Edward 50
WESTBERY, Joan 277
  William 277,278
WESTBURY, Edward 86,345
WESTBURY(WESTBURRY), Thom-
    as 176,345
  William 165,331
WESTCOAT, John 127,255
WES(T)LYD, Thomas 91,187
WESTON, Mary 253
WETHERLY, Thomas, Sr. 7
WETHERSPOON, Ruth 271
WEVERLY, Thomas 173
WHALEY, Thomas 244
WHELDON, Ann 210
  Samuel 210
  Sarah 210
WHETFELD, John 364
WHETHERICK, Elizabeth 123
WHIGG, Richard 33
WHILDEN, Jonathan 55,124,
  127,310
WHIPPY, Joseph 129
  Robert 129
  William 63,89,129,185,
    186
WHITAKER, ___ 77
  Benjamin 2,7,14,16,18,
    19,23,27-32,35,36,38,
    39,43,46,48,49,51,52,
    54,57,58,65,66,67,68,
    70,73,80,88,99,105,108,
    132,135,136,144-146,
    151,152,158,178,184,
    194.195,213,215,227,
    231,234.241-243,248-
    251,253,259,264,268,
    271-275,281,285-287,
    293,305,309,311,319,
    321,326,335,345,357,
    359,375,377
  Edward 339
  Sarah 28,241,321
WHITE, Anthony 51,52,75,
  80,106.107,130,163,200,
  229,299,300,301,319,
  338,355,366,382
  Eleanor 109,221,222
  Jacob 175
  James 335,336,365
  John 57,67,75,80,145,
    182,200,202,270,319,
    334,335,355,371,382
  Joseph 64,349,350
  Mary 355
  Nathan 141
  Sarah 336,365
  Susanna 318
  Thomas 217
  William 51,70,114,131,
    161,253,270,318,319,
    350
WHITEHEAD, John 302
WHITER, Thomas 336
WHITESIDE, William/Wm. 202,
  203,207,244,250,251,
  261,274,277,284,289,
  299-302,310,311,315,
  320,321,323,325,329,
  330,334,335,337,340,
  341,345,349,354,364-
  366,368,371,372
WHITFIELD, John 213,215,
  218,223,224,225,230,
  243,251
WHITMARSH, John 171,353
  John, Sr. 1
WHITTER, Thomas 224
WHITTIER(WHITTA), John 57,
  166,168
WHITTON, Thomas 48
WHYTE, Thomas 333
WICKHAM, Mary 248

WICKHAM, Nathaniel 230,
  248,331
WIGFALL, Samuel 87,184,
  222,261,284,359
WIGG, Edward 159,202,223,
  277,280,285,295,342,
  345
  Hill 358
  Hillderson 363
  Richard 126,152,165
  Thomas 119,222,254,
    261,272,291,327,371
WIGHT, William 173
WIGINGTON, H. 74,78,125
  Henry 78,117,120,126,
    164,220,318
  R. 124
  Susannah 38,39,67,114.
    133,163,166,202
WILDBORES, Henry 322
WILKES, Joshua 250
WILKINS, ___ 66,248
  Archibald 310
  Elizabeth 213,221,327
  James 175
  John 167,213
  Obadiah 291
  Richard 168
  Sarah 144,342,352,379
  William 95,144,167,
    180,191,218,221,306,
    310,327,342,352,379
WILKINSON(WILKENSON), ___
  103
  Christopher 20,29,50,
    68,69,88-90,102,118,
    133,184-186
  Clement 250
  Elizabeth 66
  H. 45
  Robert 26,287
  Sarah 66
  Thomas 2,21
WILKS, ___ 284
  Joshua 67,85,315,341,
    361
WILLARD, J. 42
  Josiah 43
  Thomas 92,188
WILLCOCKS, Joseph 374
WILLEY, Joseph 53
WILLIAM (Lord Craven),
  Earl of Craven 8,20,
  22,35,45,48,52,60,61,
  63,67,70,74,80,84,86,
  90,112,114,137,140,
  141,147,158,160,165,
  187,210,211,222,237,
  255,256,307,382
WILLIAMS, Anthony 312
  Daniel 103
  Elizabeth 82,324
  Francis 48,61,121,140
  Mrs. Francis 48
  Henry 275,358
  James 99,161,195
  John 97,193,267,271,
    301,302,306,351
  Joseph 209
  Martha 48,138
  Morrice 212
  Mr. 298
  Nathaniel (alias Black
    Nat) 69,83,99,109,195
  Stephen 89,185,294
  Thomas 121,252
  William 8,83,84,92,
    104,179,211,212,320,
    355
WILLIAMSON, Benjamin 357
  Dove 324
  John 15,20,29,33,68,
    86,87,92,119,140,188,
    228,356

WILLIAMSON, cont'd:
  Manly 37,38,52,98,101,
    105,132,194
  Margaret 92,188
  Martha 280
  Mary 92,188
  Nathaniel 135
  Samuel 117
  Stanley 245
  William 100,101,188,
    196,233,280,357
WILLIMOTT, Robert 153
WILLIS, Elizabeth 8
  George 28
  John 331
  Mrs. 23
WIL(L)SON, James 1
  John 79,163,164,181,
    235,243
  Margaret 230
  Mary 338
  Moses 51,67,78,79,126,
    138,139,156,223,230,
    314,317,319
  Richard 310
  Robert 12,29,76
  Wilson 338
WILLETT, John 306,307
WILMOTT, Richard 35,36
WILSON, Samuel 8
WINBORN, Ichabod 319
  Mary 312,319
  Thomas 294,312
WINBOURN, Ichabod 207
WINCHESTER, Amaviah 223
WINDERAP, William 365
WINDERAS, William 96,193
WINDERS, William 177
WINDRA, William 311
WINGOOD, Charvel 354
  Ephraim 83
WINN, Robert 76,182
WINSLOW, John 266
WINTER, Margaret 267
  William 237
WIRE, Hugh 291,292
WISE, Richard 23
  Thomas 213,281,299,320
WITAKER, Benjamin 78
WITE, John 71
WITHERS, Elizabeth 247,345,
    360
  James 242,244,250,272,
    337,345
  Lawrence 247,332,345,
    360
  Mr. 170
  Nathaniel 360,361
  William 223,277,285,
    287,295
WITHERSPOON, John 171
WITTEN, Thomas 138
WITTER, James 6,130,142,
    176,247,343,379
  John 26,57,75,96,130,
    134,176,192,213,221,
    247,248
  Mary 75
  Samuel 6,26
  Thomas 283,285,331
WOLFORD, James 271
WOMSLY, James 56
WONSLOW, William 232
WOOD, Abraham 114
  Benjamin 210
  Daniel 333
  Henry 2,24,172
  Hezekiah 114
  James 280
  John 213,216,241,276
  Jonathan 380
  Robert 172
  Sarah 241
  Thomas 161

WOOD, cont'd:
  Wm. 122
WOODEN, Samuel 247
WOODIN, Ishamar 83
  Ithamar 142
WOODING, John 66
  Mr. 71
WOODMAN, Catherine 172
  Deborah 328
  Richard 31
WOODSON, John 162
  Phillis 162
WOODWARD, Elizabeth 218,
    238,261
  Isaac 208
  John 28,35,36,55,65,
    87,122,151,152,183,
    222,230,238,242,301,
    302
  Mary 218
  Mr. 339
  Richard 122,218,254,
    292,301,358,363
  Sarah 132,133,218
WOOLFORD, Elizabeth 172
  Jab. 9
  Jacob 18,21,98,108-
    111,127,128,148,172,
    175,194,233
  James 81
WOOLFORDSON, Lawrence 356
WORSLEY, Henry 113,114
WOTT, ──── 29
WRAGG, ──── 10,32
  Jacob 95
  Joseph 2,4,5,6,8,9,10,
    15,16,21,30,38-40,47,
    49,53,62,64,69,72,79,
    86,94,95,99,101,102,
    104,111,112,116,126,
    137,138,145,147-151,
    157,166,179,190,191,
    195,198,199,206,208,
    212,214,219,226,233,
    240,246,249,253-255,
    259,260,263,274,275,
    277,279,280,283,285,
    287,290,295,300,311,
    323,333,342,343,349
  Joseph, Jr. 151
  Joseph, Sr. 151,163
  Judith 72,342
  Robert 259
  Samuel 5,6,11,22,28,
    30,37,45,67,68,69,101,
    111,116,117,122,131,
    132,136,155,170,179,
    198,206,215,243,285,
    290,291,326,359,360,
    380
WRATH, Hannah 13
WRIGHT, Anne 372
  Benjamin 372
  Eleanor 23
  Elizabeth 132,218
  Jacob 29,59,123
  James 246,274,287,288,
    289,310,350,352,368
  Jermin/Jermyn 155,275,
    289,368
  John 85,101-103,106-
    108,110,111,115-117,
    122-124,131-133,143,
    148,160,162,170,220,
    309
  Joseph 158,261,368
  Mary 368
  Mr. 145
  Richard 218,244,256,
    300,321
  Robert 107,108,110,125,
    146,149,155,156,165,
    174,178,179,198,224,
    226,227,230,231,238,

WRIGHT, Robert cont'd:
    241,246,249,251,258,
    259,262,270,273,275,
    277,280,281,285,288,
    290,293,295,310,327,
    328,338,340,341,343,
    350,352,368
  Susanna 368
  Thomas 303,321,355,
    376
  William 61,121,326
WRITTER, James 25,26
WRITTER(WITTER), John
    25,26
  Samuel 25
WRIXHAM, James 20,25,117,
    118,346
  Jane 21
WYATT, Ebenezer 244
  Joseph 145
WYCH, Thomas 135
WYE, William 36
WYNBOURN, Ichabod 366

YANAM, Francis 221
YEAMANS, Robert 338
YEATS, Elizabeth 247
YEOMANS, J. 7
YERWORTH, John 341
YOEMANS(YEOMAN), William
    56,98,145,156,157,171,
    172,194,208,323,366
YONGE, Archibald 110,150
  Francis 8,14,22,69,
    102,133,135,150,159,
    160,179,204,205,207,
    288,332,347,370,372,
    375
  Henry 179,245,294
  James 128
  Lydia 207,347,370
  R. 14
  Robert 14-38,166,168,
    180-182,199,200,207,
    212,216,217,221,241,
    245,286,298,308,312,
    319,322,338,355,357,
    363,364
YORK, William 249
YOUNG, Ann 177
  Archibald 107,176
  Ard. 341
  Francis 55,58,59,63
  Hannah 50
  James 177,240
  John 71,83
  Robert 50,68,302
  Thomas 347
YOUNGE, Henry 285

ZACHARIAN, Carlile 180
ZILSER, John 1

SHIP NAMES INDEX:

The Alborough (HMS) 124, 205
Bonetta (sloop) 9
Cambridge (galley) 2
Dove 121
Dolphin (sloop) 6
Duck (sloop) 3
Elizabeth (sloop) 48
Flamborough (HMS) 9
Garland (HMS) 226
Greyhound (HMS) 31
The Happy (HMS) 122,209
Hawk 30
John Adventure (snow) 1
Louisa (sloop) 56
Malloy (galley) 285
Mary 36
Molly (galley) 205,243,286, 381
Pearl (galley) 50
Pheasant 22
Pink Elizabeth 3
Pink Sea Nymph 54
Quadrumity (sloop) 14
Raymond (galley) 4,5,21,30
Scarborough (HMS) 90,186
Sea Nymph (sloop) 14
Squirrel (HMS) 226
True Love 129

PLACE NAME INDEX:

Abonages Plantation 272
Abrams Savanna (Cow Pen) 304
Africa 1
Alatamaha River 264
Albermarle co., N. C. 104
Ambrose Hill 12
Amelia township 363
Andrews Plantation 112
Annapolis 28
Antiqua (Island of) 22,33, 35,43,57,121,235,252, 339,373,378
Appeboo creek 74
Archers Island 29,31,56, 247
Archwood (Colleton co.)166
Arteburry, Oxfordshire, England 160
Ashby's creek 109
Ashepoo creek/river 21,208, 238,294,330,332,335, 348,353
Ashley Ferry 51,64,167 210
Ashley River (through out the entire text)
Atthoe Plantation 333
Avalon 28
Back River 74,358
Bahamas 14
Baho 88
Ballinaclough, County Tipperary, Ireland 55,87, 91,92,98,100,102,103, 105,106,107,122,124, 126,142,143,152,156, 165,183,184,187,188, 189,194,196,261,297, 355,363,366,374
Baltimore, Maryland 28
Barbadoes/Barbados (Island of) 1,32,33,52,53,70, 95,121,191,209,216,242, 253,369
Bath county, N. C. 12,36
Bay street 19,122

Beach Hill, S. C. 49,113, 162,178,343
Beaufort 29,31,58,59,79, 101,102,106,119,143, 149,201,218,222,277, 372
Beaufort River 26
Bennson's Landing 40
Benson's Point 78,230
Berkeley county, S. C. (through out text)
Bermuda 7,70,158,161,308, 376
Bermudoes Town 80,106,212, 280
Black River (through out text)
Boascoo 175
Bohera Creek 44
Bohicket 62,177
Boston (Massachusetts/New England) 6,17,42,43, 45,52,60,125,223
Brady's Island 135
Bristol(Bristoll), England 1,2
Bullhead 96,128,139,193, 370
Burks County (Great Britain) 28
Burmada Town (Berkeley County) 35
Butters(Butlers) Town 73, 210
Cadoes Lake 358
Cane Acres (Colleton Co.) 222
Canehoy Plantation 262
Caintin Plantation 162
Callibeufs Lane 24,41,54
Camba(c)hee River 106,254, 370
Cambhee Island 374
Canterbury, England) 14, 35,43
Cape Fear River, N. C. 138, 157,216,250,302,308, 342
Cawcaw Swamp 98,194
Caywah Island 104
Cedar Swamp 63,110
Charing Cross, London 16
Charles City 26,30,32,33, 34,38,47,48,50,51,52
Charleston Bay 3,37,44,49, 59,72,73,83,90,93,99, 156,160,210,360
Charleston Island 357
Charleston Neck 10,11,50, 59,64,83,91,93,94,95, 102,103,104,108,123, 165,187,191,287,359, 360,361
Charleston, S. C. (through out text)
Charles Town 15,179
Chatham, Barnstable County, Massachusetts 45,182
Chehaw Island 218
Chehaw River 179,217,238, 266,306,321
Chesapeake Bay 28
Childbury Town 239
Christ Church Parish, S.C. (through out text)
Clarendon County 34
Clouters(Clowters) Creek 99,109
Coatbow/Colt Baw) 74,362
Colleton Co., S. C. (Thruout text)
Colleton River 96,97,98

Combahee River 98,240,301, 354,368
Combe Island 121,175
Combee/Combey River 218, 223,322
Concord, Co. Middlesex, Province of Mass. Bay 128
Cooper River (through out text)
Coosa(Coosow) River 79, 121,169,272,305,313
Coppehee(Copahee,Copshee) Sound 85,166
Cornbow Creek 80
Cornwall Co., England 24
County of Shallop, Great Britain 54
Courtbaw 75
Cow Savanna 46,55,156,248
Craven Co., S. C. (through out text)
Cumbahee River 240,305
Cumbee Neck 321,322,323
Cumberhees Parish, Stewarty of Anadate, No. Britain 184
Curacoa Island, West Indies 172
Cusahatchee River (Granville Co.) 151
Data Island 374
Dawfuskie River 124
Defaskee Island (Dawfuskee), Granville Co. 220,306
Deleware River 56
Dorchester, New England 62,63,110
Dorchester, S. C. 29,37, 49,51,52,62,64,76,77, 96,110,113,122,134, 141,151,160,162,169, 175,178,183,209,222, 243,263,264,265,349, 350,366,380
Dover County, Kent, Great Britain 7,22
Drumboon/Drumgoon County, (Fermanah) 99,195
Drumhall 25
Dublin, Ireland 4,5
Edenton, N. C. 104
Edisto Island 100,129,196, 199,207,319,340,343, 366,380
Edisto River 87,88,89,90, 96,100,107,117,118,129, 130,136,143,154,159, 183,184,186,200,217, 225,230,232,239,242, 245,268,273,325,330, 353,356,371
Etiwan/Etewan River 44,49
Exeter, S. C. 309,361
Fairlawn 127,361
Fair Spring 62
Falmouth, England 24
Ferry Town 73,213
Fisherman's Strand 24
Forsters Creek 82,106
Forsters River 74
Fort Moore, S. C. 172,235
French Church 71,76,286
French Santee, Craven Co. 93
Georgetown 207,243,244, 277,299,300,302,305, 310,314,315,319,320, 329,330,334,335,337, 338,340,344,350,354, 355,357,358,364,365, 371,382

Georgetown, Prince George Parish 216,264,275,289
Georgetown River 364
Gibbons Bluff 44,49,150
Glasgow, Scotland 366
Goose Creek 1,8,17,22,37, 47,56,73,81,91,94,95, 109,115,124,141,148, 157,187,190,227,314, 331,337,374,375,376
Goose Creek Parish, S. C. 6,112,169,304,342
Granville County, S. C. (throughout text)
Great Britain 3,4,21,88,89, 90,184,205,247,343
Great Marlow 28
Great Swamp (Tupelow Swamp) 106,214
Greensted, Essex Co. 104, 159
Hagar Creek 8
Hartyes(Hearty's) Island 105,109,281
Harlowing(Horlowing) Place 98,194
Hilton Head 363
Hobcaw Neck 80,286
Hobcow, N. C. 228,361
Hog/Hogg Island 56,147,201, 210,238,340
Horse Shoe Savannah 182, 228,341
Honduras (Bay of) 244
Indian Field Swamp 314
Iniskellen Fermanah 99
Ireland 5,90,98,100,102,114, 130,131,134
Island of Jamaica 2,4,6,8, 17,35
Island of Madeira(Maderas) 54,94
Island of Providence 14
Islington(Island) Plantation 122
Ittewan(Itawan) Creek 99, 109
Ittawan Island 167,229,282, 339
Jamaica 74,109,117,120,126, 158,212,221,376
James Island 6,25,26,29,38, 44,50,53,57,74,81,82, 86,89,96,104,109,133, 134,144,162,167,176, 180,185,192,214,218, 247,248,258,278,279, 302,305,306,315,316, 342,344,352,377,378, 379
James Town Creek 44
Johns Island 95,104,163,164, 191,192,213,245,248, 256,310,315
Jupiters Plantation 271
Kingston, Jamaica 8,43,126
Lebanan, S. C. 336,365
Little Mount 99,195
Little River 243,264,338
London, England (throughout text)
Long Island Plantation 7
Long Point, Berkely Co. 154
Lookout Island 219
Lynch's Creek 113,143,150, 151,363
Lynch Grove Plantation 15, 16,17,51,52,70,131
Mackey Island 219
Madera/Maderas Island 155, 190
Maggotts Island 218

Maryland 28
Maverick's (land) 124
May River 357
Medeira 162
Medway River 27,74,168,316
Middlesex Co., England 7, 317
Milton, Suffolk Co., Mass. 223
Mitton Plantation 370
Misley Hall, Essex Co., Great Britain 35
Mount Hope 107
Mount Pleasant 62,164
Molschi Glaze 115
Mulberry Plantation 325, 370
Nassau, New Providence 104
Newbury, Essex Co., Mass. 30
New Church 12
New England 7,17
Newington (Hill G.) 84
New London, S. C. 25,143, 217
New Providence 3,167
New River 124,338
New York 36
New York City 7
North Kingstown 117
Old Town Plantation 122, 177,224,251
Orangeburg Township 355, 357
Pyster Point 78,91,187,305
Peach Tree Plantation 315
Peedee River (throughout text)
Pigeon Swamp 62,63
Philadelphia 116
Pinckley Line 72,73
Pocotaligo River 272,305
Pocotaligo Swamp 353
Poitiers, Province of Poiton, France 62
Pompion Hill 121
Ponds Plantation 247,248
Ponpon, Colleton Co. 89, 90,117,118,128,171, 184,242,268,373
Ponpon River 29,54,63,88, 97,98,133,134,136,159, 174,180,186,193,206, 217,219,222,223,236, 259,294,308,313,319, 346,357,374,375
Ponts Berry (Pontsbury), Co. of Shallop, Shropshire, Gr. Britain 54,57
Port Royall Parish, Island of Jamaica 8,17
Port Royal Island, S. C. 22,74,123,336,372,376
Port Royal, Granville Co. 119,149,169,201,253, 261,264,265,291,305
Port Royall River 31,34, 56,102,103,111,112, 121,149,238,251,308, 335,340,359,376
Prince Frederick Parish 345,349,354,357,369
Prince George Parish, Craven Co. 93,99,106,107, 130,136,157,178,195, 200,203,228,229,233, 258,264,275,284,285,299, 301,307,315,316,320, 323,333,334,340,351, 353,364,366,379,382
Providence. Bahamas 169, 170

Province of Poiton, France 62
Puragety Swamp 63
Purisburg/Purysburgh 294, 338,343,352,358,365
Queenby Hall 280
Queensborough Township 289,330,338,342,349, 352,358,364,365,371
Quaker Meetinghouse 61, 62,279,358,377
Rat Trap Plantation 59,81, 263
Reading, Burke Co. 119
Red Bank Plantation 112
Rhettsberry Plantation 289
Rhutsburg Point Plantation 345
Rhode Island 117
Round Savanna 100
St. Andrews Parish, Jamaica 8
St. Andrews Parish 6,17,35, 36,38,39,42,54,72,87, 94,96,114,177,178,183, 190,192,207,209,239, 241,247,250,288,305, 309,311,328,332,338, 344,347,352,360,369, 370,377
St. Anne's Parish (Goose Creek) 80
St. Augustine 9
St. Bartholomews Parish, Colleton Co. 233,236, 244,266,331,353,372, 375,377
St. Christopher Island 306,307
St. Dennis Parish, Berkeley Co. S. C. 105,127, 128,147,170,200,237, 244,305,345,349
St. George's Parish, S.C. 18,52,64,87,112,115, 122,129,130,135,160, 174,183,189,214,222, 230,246,317,344,366
St. George's Parish, Island of Jamaica 17, 175
St. Giles 11,37,45,368
St. Helena's Island 111, 261,374
St. Helena's Parish 219, 232,245,261,272,371, 373
St. Jagoes Island 135
St. James Goosecreek 21, 32,37,73,76,81,82,86, 92,96,99,117,118,142, 188,192,195,216,217, 218,220,221,227,228, 230-232,246,250,252, 253,259,264,316,319, 321,325,326,330,342, 351,356,369,382
St. James Parish 17,37,56, 81,84,109,118,152,163, 172,179,263,264,266, 270,275,294,301,309, 313,314,315,336,337, 340,352,361,362,368, 369,371,377,379
St. James Parish, Westminster, Middlesex Co. 35,43
St. John's Island 6,35,47
St. John's Parish, Barbados 32
St. John's Parish, S. C. 36,48,59,81,85,96,99, 109,110,119,127,131,

St. John's Parish cont'd:
142,145,152,163,164,
166,175,192,224,229,
234,238,239,247,249,
263,264,274,276,286,
293,302-304,322,336,
340,341,349,351,362,
363,370,371,379
St. Joseph's Parish 79
St. Leonard, Shorditch, Co.
  of Middlesex 219
St. Martin's Lane, London
  4,15
St. Mary Magdelin, Bermondsey, Surrey Co., Eng.
  153
St. Michael Parish, Corn-
  hill, London 43
St. Michaels, Barbadoes 53,
  60,113,131
St. Pauls Parish, Colleton
  Co., S. C. (throughout
  text)
St. Paul's Churchyard, Lon-
  don 32
St. Phillips Parish, S. C.
  (throughout text)
St. Thomas Island 16,127
St. Thomas Parish
  (Throughout text)
Saltketcher(Salt-Catcher
  Cowpen) 218,258,295,
  312,330,331
Sampit Creek/River 99,136,
  195,228,262,275,315,
  341,342,345,366
Santee Parish 344,361,362,
  368
Santee River (throughout
  text)
Saw Pitt 52
Savannah River 358,365
Saxegotha Township 366,372
Seaton 370
Seawee/Sewee Bay 47,48,349,
  359,362
Shropshire, Gr. Britain 54
Simmons Creek 19,45,46,108
Silkhope Plantation 359,
  360
Sociable Hill 86
Somers Island 161
Somersetshire Co., England
  7
South Edisto, Colleton Co.
  River 25
Spoon Savanna Cowpen 74,98,
  112,194
Staten Island 7
Stephney, Co. Middlesex 119
Stevens Bridge 12
Stewart River 305
Stoney River 53
Stono River 15,28,29,47,85,
  86,87,92,104,119,154,
  188,197,221,245,246,
  280,304,310,352,353
Sweatman's Bridge 98,194
Tebwin, Craven Co. 35
Thomas's Island 108,127,
  135,172
Thorowgoods Plantation 17,
  99,195
Tooboodoo/Toogoodoo Creek
  20,50,199,343
Topsham/Topsam, Gr. Brit.
  46,55
Tower Hill, London 23
Tradd Street 12,84
Tugedoo/Tupedoo Creek 88
Unnisaw 334
Ushasau Plantation 343
Uxbridge 50

Wacamaw/Waccamaw River 39,
  72,106,203,204,230,
  235,247,249,252,261,
  284,285,301,314,329,
  331,333,334,340,348,
  353,364,365,367,373,
  378,379,381
Wadlemaw River 20
Wadmalaw/Wadmelah River
  and Island 96,107,128,
  149,181,182,235,240,
  257,312,338,340,355,
  368,380
Wadwadmelaw/Wadmalaw Is-
  land and River 177,179,
  192,201,237,302,316
Walnut Bluff 26
Wambaw Creek/Swamp 86,91,
  187,271,309,363,364
Wambee Island Granville
  Co. 119,149,222,335
Wampee 62,270,342
Wampee Savanah Plantation
  122,146
Wando Neck 17,51,70,131,
  239,269,270,331
Wando River 3,7,16,23,27,
  35,49,51,72,94,105,
  108,109,111,127,128,
  162,167,172,175,190,
  200,212,234,250,253,
  255,280,281,282,283,
  307,311,318,319,334,
  337,343,365
Wappo/Wappoo 87,183,218,
  339,342,379
Wapta 193
Wasensaw Swamp 120,325
Washua Island, Granville
  Co. 374
Waste Savannah 12
Watboo Barony 47,175
Watch Island 239
Weekley's Plantation 63
Westminster, Gr. Britain
  11,62
Westminster, S. C. 36,111,
  336,337
Westmoreland Parish, Island
  of Jamaica 8
Westpenny Creek 122,132,
  177
Westpenny (land) 122
West Smithfield, London 9
Westow Armes 75
White Hall 129,320
White Haven Co., Cumberland
  160
White Point 33,47,163,223,
  259,260,266,313
Wilkinsons Swamp 211
Williamsburg, Craven Co.
  248,287,288,330,337,
  363
Williamsburg, Va. 6
Williamsburgh, S. C. 311,
  312,316,324,358
Willtown 89,118,159,168,
  171,185,186,199,217,
  245
Wimbee Island 26
Winchester St., London 57
Winners Plantation 144
Winneau 334
Winyah/Winyaw River
  (throughout text)
Witecaw Plantation 353
Yaughaun Plantation 315
Yought Hall 71

OCCUPATION INDEX:

Apothecary 14,135,158,336

Baker 379
Barber 85,132
Blacksmith 47,50,67,134,
  168,169,179,238,252,
  258,264,266,286,291,
  294
Block maker 7
Boatswain 28
Bookkeeper 248
Brewer 158
Bricklayer 7,38,40,42,58,
  89,101,103,128,151,
  155,185,196,239,240,
  246,250,265,269,272,
  300,318,337,344,346,
  347,357,381
Butcher 14,57,78,84,89,
  107,115,156,172,185,
  243,253,254,266,268,
  283,290,309,310,311,
  335,339,357,360,362,
  381
Cabinet Maker 171,325,329,
  368
Carpenter 3,6,34,49,51,54,
  58,61,64,74-76,82,83,
  92,105,110,117,151,
  176,178,188,198,199,
  216,224,225,228,230,
  234,238,239,247,259,
  260,265,266,269,273,
  275,276,277,281,290,
  292,296,303,305,306,
  313,314,318,329,345,
  358,365,372,378
Carpenter (ships) 28,173,
  276,288
Chairmaker/Chairmaster 7,
  24,41,116,162
Chamois Dresser 171
Chandler 286
Church Warden 64
Cleric 38
Clothier 5
Cooper 6,8,14,19,21,25,48,
  49,57,75,81,89,125,
  137,148,158,179,180,
  186,202,213,217,249,
  251,254,260,273,297,
  340,364,377,379
Clerk 1,4,5,7,22,25,39,44,
  45,49,54,59,72,88,104,
  184,185,294,305,337,
  376
Cordwainer/Cordwinder 6,
  12,18,25,38,44,50,53,
  54,57,67,79,83,90,95,
  101-105,126,140,146,
  154,165,167,181,186,
  191,196,199,201,231,
  232,255,268,269,343,
  344,365,374
Cutler 208
Draper 28
Feltmaker 9,44,130
Fisherman 82
Flax dresser 119
Gardener 36
Glazier 175,274,303,354
Glover 43
Goldsmith 5,159,208,263,
  318
Gunsmith 33,161,379
Hatmaker 6,25,116,221,247
House carpenter 25
Housewright 228
Indian Trader 47,86,104,
  119,129,145,169,219,
  247,257,298,306,308,
  314,317,375
Innholder 97,170
Innkeeper 209
Iron Monger 168

Jeweler 20,169
Joiner 12,27,34,54,56,60,
    75,78,80,85,102,103,
    110,116,124,141,163,
    168,192,207,230,242,
    245,256,260,263,305
Leather gilder 32
Linen draper 119
Mariner (throughout text)
Marshall 6
Master (ship) 1,9,14,36,
    54
Mate (ship) 28,74,129
Mayor 2
Mechanic 125
Merchant tailor 62,137,138
Minister of the Gospel 78,
    120,121,170,372
Missionary 36
Notary and Tabellion Pub-
    lic 4-6,9,23,45,79
Oilman 378
Painter 303
Peruke maker 343,345,364
Pilot 128
Rope maker 153
Saddler 67,68,70,103,124,
    152,157,163,172,220,
    221,246,263,286,291,
    309,333,358
Sail maker 238
Sailor 28
Sawyer 42,71,119
School master 98,108,158
Seaman 31
Sheriff 2
Shipwright 29,35,47,50,74,
    88,92,100,121,125,126,
    136,137,142,153,181,
    184,188,195,196,220,
    235,289,294,304,345
Shoe maker 2,6,18,98,115,
    159,194,236,237,256,
    338
Shop keeper 37,103,159,
    171,173,201,220,259,
    263,272,297,344,347,
    360,361,362,364,376
Showmaker 236
Silver smith 248,318
Soap boiler 318
Sole trader 126
Sugar baker 2
Surgeon/Chirurgeon 1,31,
    99,161,162,168,172,
    195,205,222,225,227,
    231,247,253,264,265,
    274,318,335,345,356,
    367
Surveyor 12,26,35,47,58,
    61,364,365,376
Tailor 8,22,29,73,141,162,
    220,236,297,338,348,
    354
Tanner 7,15,17,39,72,198,
    204,212,236,250,255,
    379
Tobacconist 28
Vestryman 98,108-111
Victualer 22,49,61,67,68,
    72,73,84,92,119,169,
    188,201,210,363,372
Vintner 6,43,67,72,89,122,
    128,138,144,161,163,
    171,185,200,201,212,
    215,232,235,247,251,
    260,262,280,300,311,
    354,358,372
Watch maker 283,303,339
Weaver 4,103,141,169,259
Wheelwright 126,146,160,
    169,198
Yeoman 57,86,128,239,266,
    270,364

www.ingramcontent.com/pod-product-compliance
Lightning Source LLC
Chambersburg PA
CBHW031401290426
44110CB00011B/226